Quilter's 1,000 BLOCKS

A Collection of Quilt Blocks From Today's Top Designers

Previously published as *Quiltmaker's 1,000 Blocks*

Krause Craft

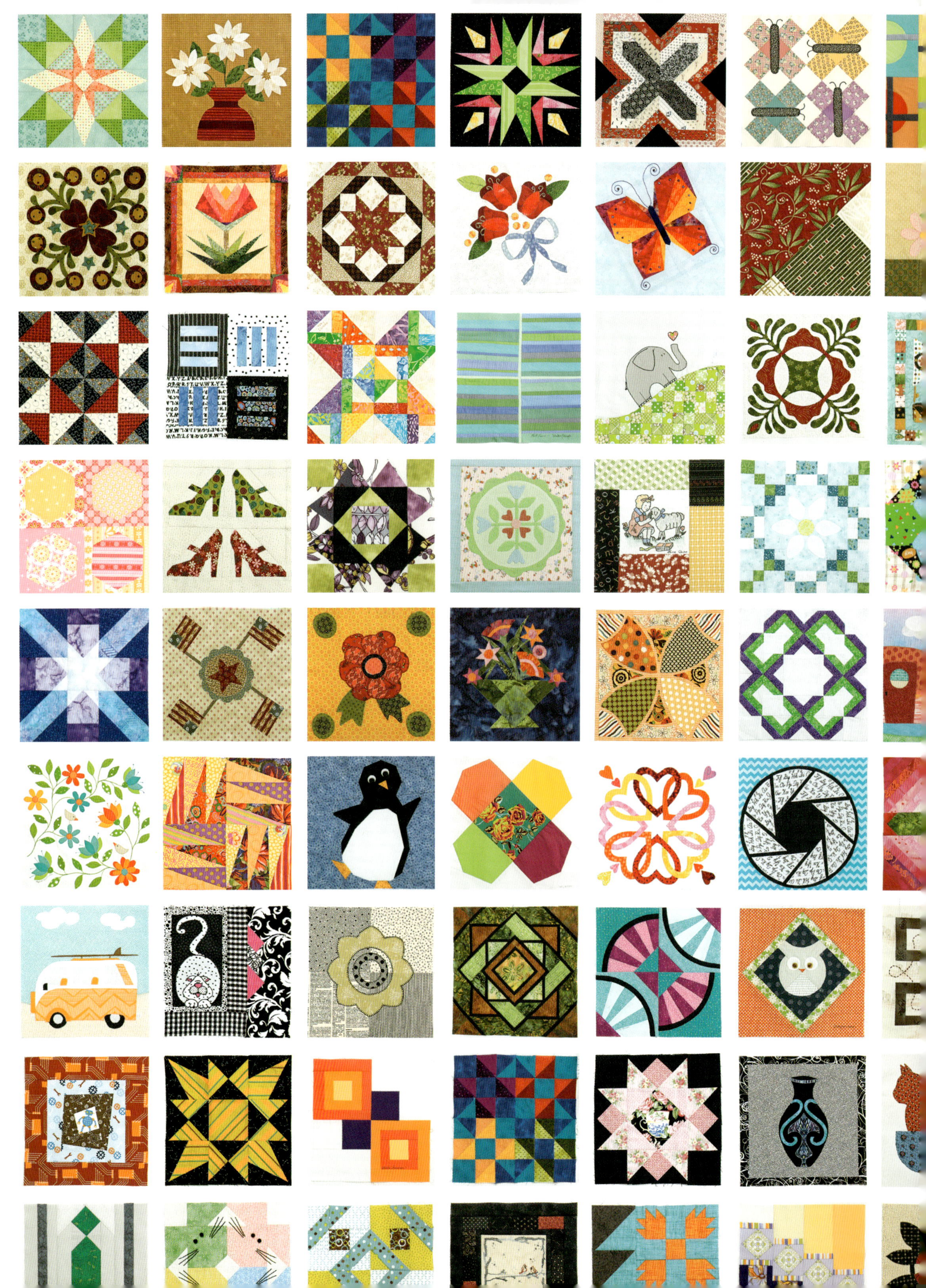

Quilter's 1,000 BLOCKS

A Collection of Quilt Blocks From Today's Top Designers

Edited by Carolyn Beam, Paula Stoddard, Diane Volk Harris, Denise Starck & Amy Rullkoetter

TABLE OF CONTENTS

INTRODUCTION

In this impressive collection, you'll find a stunning array of blocks in a variety of styles—pieced, appliquéd, foundation-pieced and mixed techniques—from some of the most talented designers in the industry. Styles range from traditional to modern, whimsical to funky, simple to complex and so much more!

Templates, foundations, appliqué patterns, embroidery designs and techniques information can be found as a PDF download at:

https://sites.prh.com/kcbonus

Each of these blocks finishes at 12" (12½" unfinished) and will work in many different quilt settings. You can find a variety of quilt settings starting on page 508, along with general yardage information for different quilt sizes. Try one of these for your next quilt or use your own favorite setting.

I hope you'll find this collection to be as inspirational as I have. I'm sure you'll find blocks that are just calling your name!

Carolyn Beam

THE BLOCKS

block no. 1

Lillebet's Bouquet

by Beth Ferrier • Applewood Farm Publications
applewoodfarmquilts.com

Wash-Away Appliqué Sheets from C&T Publishing, ctpub.com.

Beth is the author of *More! Hand Appliqué by Machine* for C&T Publishing, ctpub.com.

See page 32 on the PDF for pattern

Off-White Tone-on-Tone
1 square (A) 13½" × 13½" (trim to 12½" × 12½" after appliqué)
Assorted Green Tone-on-Tones
3 pattern B
Assorted Red Tone-on-Tones
3 *each* patterns C, D and E
Gold Tone-on-Tone
7 pattern F
Assorted Blue Tone-on-Tones (Beth used the wrong side of 1 fabric for shading on her ribbon)
2 *each* patterns G, Gr and H
1 *each* patterns I, Ir, J, Jr, K, L
Yellow embroidery floss

Fold A in half both ways and lightly crease the folds. Prepare the patches for turned-edge appliqué.

Use the creases and the appliqué placement diagram as a guide to arrange the patches on A. The stitch diagrams are in the Techniques file on the PDF.

Appliqué the patches in place in alphabetical order using monofilament thread and a machine zigzag stitch. Use a variegated thread to add a straight stitch just inside the edges of the bow patches and veins to the leaves. Add detail to the flowers, as shown below, using a backstitch and 2–3 strands of yellow embroidery floss.

Center the appliqué and trim A to 12½" × 12½". ■

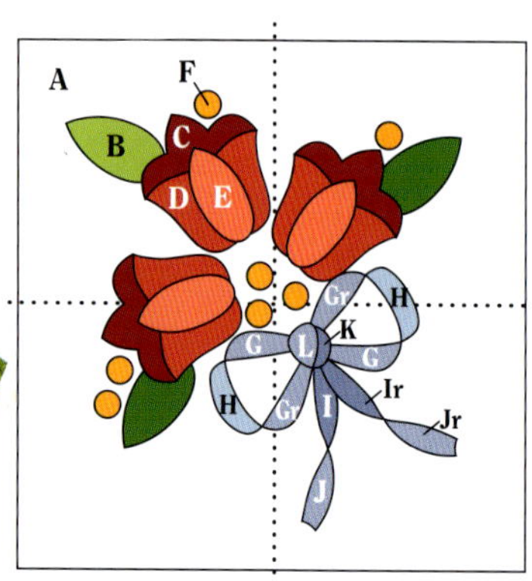

Applique Placement

block no. 2

Uncle Sam's Hat

by Laurie Simpson • Minick and Simpson
minickandsimpson.com

Fabric: Minick and Simpson for Moda Fabrics, unitednotions.com.

See page 20 on the PDF for pattern

Cream Stripe
1 square (A) 13½" × 13½" (trim to 12½" × 12½" after appliqué)
Green Tone-on-Tone
1 bias strip 1" × 11" for stems
Assorted Red, Cream and Blue Prints and Tone-on-Tones
1 *each* patterns B–Cr, H–M
3 *each* patterns D, E and G
2 pattern F
Brown Tone-on-Tone
1 bias strip 1" × 6½" for flag pole

Fold A in half diagonally both ways and lightly crease the folds. Prepare B–M for turned-edge appliqué.

To make the bias stems, refer to "Bias Strips" in the Techniques file on the PDF. Cut the green bias strip into smaller strips as shown on page 20 of the PDF.

Use the creases and appliqué placement diagram as a guide to arrange the patches and bias strips on A. Use matching thread and a blind stitch to appliqué the patches in place as shown. Center the appliqué and trim A to 12½" × 12½". ■

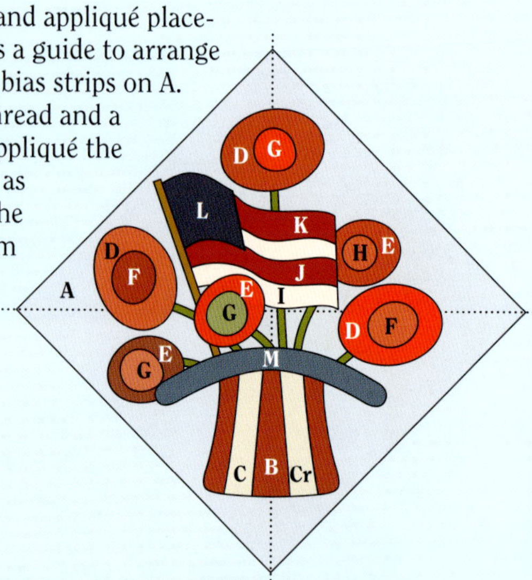

Applique Placement

block no. 3

Winding New Ways

by Bobbi Finley and Carol Gilham Jones

Bobbi and Carol are the authors of *Tile Quilt Revival: Reinventing a Forgotten Form* for C&T Publishing, ctpub.com.

See page 28 on the PDF for pattern

Orange Check
1 square (A) 13½" × 13½" (trim to 12½" × 12½" after appliqué)

4 Assorted Dot Prints
from *each*
1 pattern B

Multicolor Stripe
4 pattern C

Cream Print
4 pattern D

Gold Print
4 pattern E

Fold A in half both ways and lightly crease the folds. Prepare patches B–E for turned-edge appliqué.

Use the creases and the appliqué placement diagram as a guide to arrange the patches on A.

The stitch diagrams can be found in the Techniques file on the PDF. Using a blind stitch, sew the patches in place. Center the appliqué and trim A to 12½" × 12½".

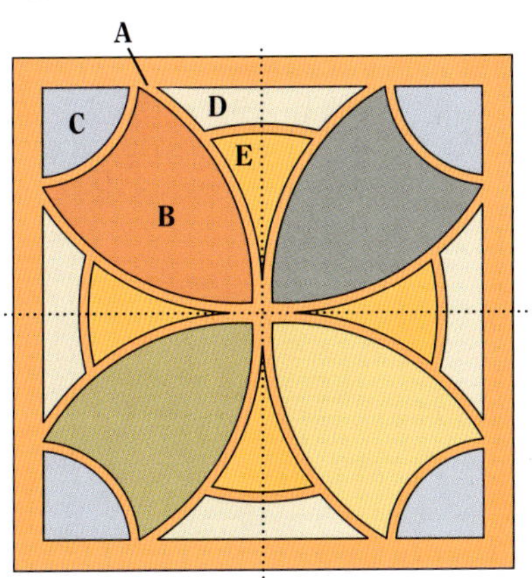

Applique Placement

block no. 4

How About a Kiss?

by Heidi Pridemore • The Whimsical Workshop
thewhimsicalworkshop.com

Fabric: Blank Quilting, blankquilting.com.

See page 24 on the PDF for pattern

Blue Tone-on-Tone
1 square (A) 13½" × 13½" (trim to 12½" × 12½" after appliqué)

Assorted Tone-on-Tones
1 *each* patterns B–J and N–T (add ½" to all outside edges of T)

White Solid
2 pattern L

Black Solid
1 pattern K
2 pattern M

Fusible web

Fold A in half both ways and lightly crease the folds. Prepare patches B–S for fusible appliqué. Prepare patch T for turned-edge appliqué.

Use the creases and the appliqué placement diagram as a guide to arrange patches B–S on A. Fuse the patches to A in alphabetical order. Use black thread and a blanket stitch to sew around all of the patches.

Appliqué T to A using a blind stitch and matching or invisible thread.

Center the appliqué and trim A to 12½" × 12½".

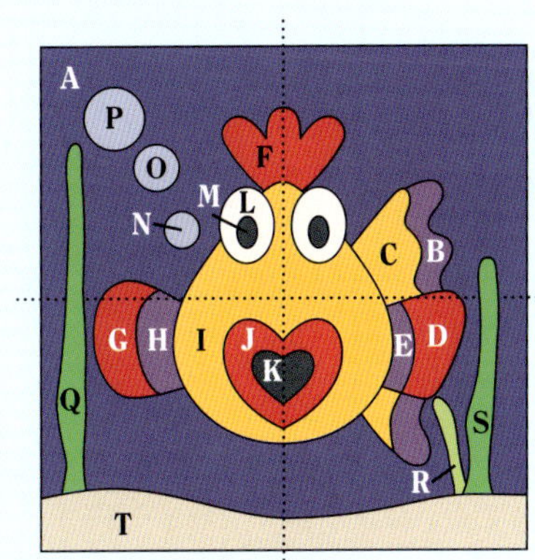

Applique Placement

block no. 5

Midnight Sun Garden

by Jane Quinn • Quilting in the Country
quiltinginthecountry.com

Jane is the author of *Quilting in the Country* for Martingale & Company, martingale-pub.com.

See page 25 on the PDF for pattern

Green Tone-on-Tone
- 1 square (A) 13½" × 13½" (trim to 12½" × 12½" after appliqué)

Purple Print
- 4 pattern B

Yellow Print
- 4 pattern B

Green Print
- 8 pattern C

Red Print
- 4 pattern D

Fusible web

Green embroidery floss

Fold A in half horizontally, vertically and diagonally and lightly crease the folds. Prepare the patches for fusible appliqué.

Use the creases and the appliqué placement diagram as a guide to arrange the patches on A; fuse in alphabetical order. Use the green floss and a blanket stitch to sew around all of the patches. Center the appliqué and trim A to 12½" × 12½".

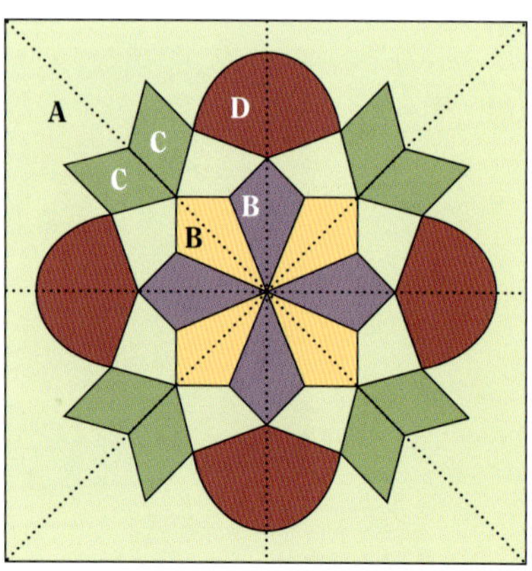

Applique Placement

block no. 6

Rising Star

by Toni Kay Steere and Jenny Foltz • Wing and a Prayer Design, wingandaprayerdesign.com

Fabric: Pinwheel Stars designed by Wing and a Prayer Design for Timeless Treasures, ttfabrics.com.

See page 27 on the PDF for pattern

Beige Tone-on-Tone
- 1 square (A) 13½" × 13½" (trim to 12½" × 12½" after appliqué and embellishment)

Assorted Tone-on-Tones
- 1 *each* patterns B–H

Fusible web

Beads and buttons as desired

Embroidery floss

Fold A in half both ways and lightly crease the folds. Prepare the patches for fusible appliqué.

Use the creases and the appliqué placement diagram as a guide to arrange the patches on A; fuse in place.

Using thread to match each patch, machine blanket stitch around the patches. Use a stem stitch to embroider the curved lines. Referring to the detail photo, add beads as desired and stack several buttons at the center of the small star; sew in place.

Center the appliqué and trim A to 12½" × 12½".

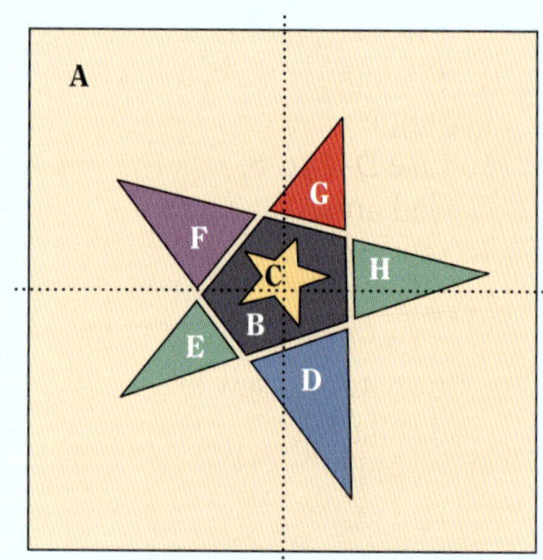

Applique Placement

block no. 7

Wish You Were Here

by Joni Pike • Sew Special Designs
sewspecialdesigns.com

Button: Just Another Button Company. Beads: Hillcreek Designs. Thread: Wonderfil.

Joni is the author of *Cute as a Button Quilts* for C&T Publishing, ctpub.com.

See page 22 on the PDF for pattern

Aqua Tone-on-Tone
1 rectangle (B) 6½″ × 9½″ (trim to 6″ x 9″ after appliqué)

Off-White Tone-on-Tone
1 pattern C (add ½″ to the outside edges)

Assorted Prints and Solids
1 *each* patterns D, E, G, H and I
2 pattern F

Olive Green Print
1 square (A) 12½″ × 12½″

Fusible web

¾″ button and beads for embellishment

Black Pigma Micron pen

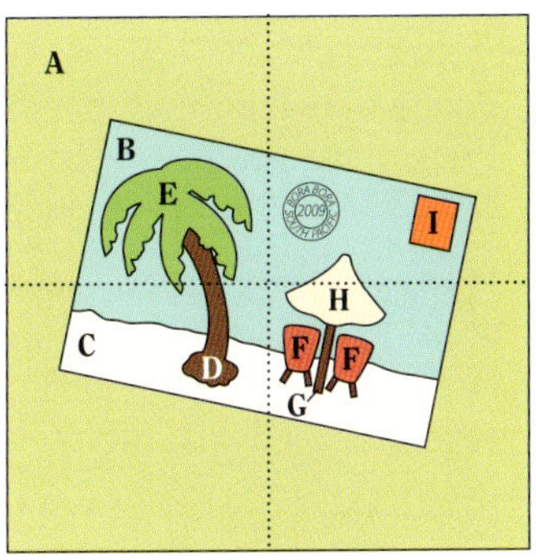

Applique Placement

Use a satin stitch to sew C to B. Prepare patches D–I for fusible appliqué. Refer to the appliqué placement diagram to fuse D–I to B. Use brown thread and a blanket stitch to sew around the tree (D and E), chairs (F) and umbrella (H). Use brown thread and a satin stitch to sew around the umbrella pole (G) and stamp (I). Add legs to the chairs with a satin stitch.

Iron fusible web to the wrong side of B. Center the design and trim B to 6"× 9". Fuse the postcard to A as shown. Use orange thread and a satin stitch to sew around the edges. Add a button to the stamp and beads to the umbrella as shown. Use the pen to add a "postmark" to the postcard.

block no. 8

Watering Can

by Kay Mackenzie • Quilt Puppy Publications & Designs
quiltpuppy.com; allaboutappliqué.net

Kay is the author of *Easy Appliqué Blocks, 50 Designs in 5 Sizes* for Martingale & Company, martingale-pub.com.

See page 35 on the PDF for pattern

Off-White Tone-on-Tone
1 square (A) 13½″ × 13½″ (trim to 12½″ × 12½″ after appliqué)

Blue print
1 *each* patterns B, C and E

Blue Check
1 pattern D

Green Tone-on-Tone
2 pattern F
1 *each* patterns H–Ir

Red Print
1 *each* patterns G and K

Gold Print
1 pattern J

Fold A in half both ways and lightly crease the folds. Prepare the patches for turned-edge appliqué.

Use the creases and the appliqué placement diagram as a guide to arrange the patches on A. The stitch diagrams can be found in the Techniques file on the PDF Use matching thread and a blind stitch to appliqué the patches in place.

Center the appliqué and trim A to 12½"× 12½".

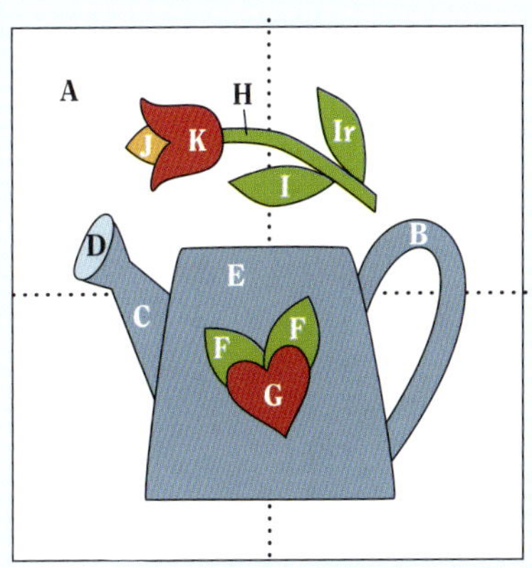

Applique Placement

block no. 9

One Happy Family

by Kathy Patterson • Senior Editor, *McCall's Quilting*
mccallsquilting.com

Cream Toile
1 square (A) 13½″ × 13½″ (trim to 12½″ × 12½″ after appliqué)
Purple Tone-on-Tone
3 pattern B
Pink Tone-on-Tone
1 pattern B
Assorted Green Prints
20 pattern C
Gold Tone-on-Tone
4 pattern D
Fusible web
Gold metallic thread

Template for One Happy Family block on page 12 of the PDF Templates file.

Prepare the patches for fusible appliqué. Arrange the patches as shown on A and fuse in place. Using gold metallic thread, machine blanket stitch around the patches. Center the appliqué and trim A to 12½" × 12½".

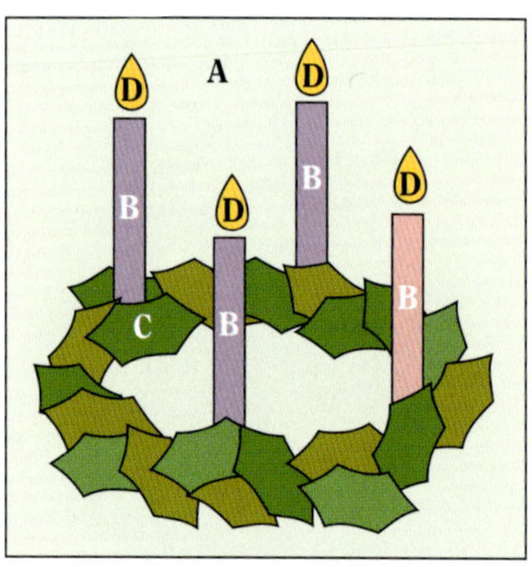

Block

block no. 10

Spring Snowflake

by Kathy K. Wylie
kathykwylie.com

See page 7 on the PDF for pattern

White-on-White Print
1 square (A) 13½″ × 13½″ (trim to 12½″ × 12½″ after appliqué)
Green Tone-on-Tone
1 pattern B
Pink Tone-on-Tone
6 pattern C

Fold A in half both ways and lightly crease the folds. Prepare the patches for turned-edge appliqué (B will need to be flipped 3 times to trace the whole pattern).

Use the creases and the appliqué placement diagram as a guide to arrange the patches on A. The stitch diagrams can be found in the Techniques file on the PDF. Use matching thread and a blind stitch to appliqué the patches.

Center the appliqué and trim A to 12½" × 2½".

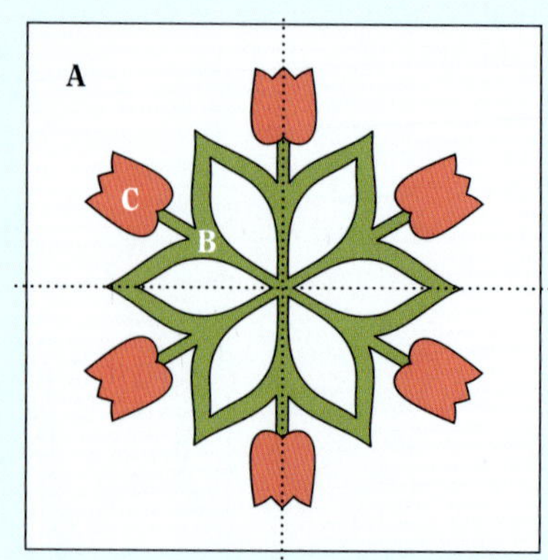

Applique Placement

block no. 11

My Peony

by Diana McClun • From Me to You
dianaandlaura.com

Diana McClun is co-author of the classic *Quilts! Quilts!! Quilts!!! The Complete Guide to Quiltmaking* (Second Edition) for the NTC Division of McGraw-Hill, as well as several other quilt-related titles for C&T Publishing, ctpub.com.

See page 26 on the PDF for pattern

Cream Tone-on-Tone
- 1 square (A) 13½″ × 13½″ (trim to 12½″ × 12½″ after appliqué)

Assorted Green Prints
- 1 bias strip (B) 1″ × 11″ for stem
- 1 *each* patterns L–R

Assorted Blue/Purple Prints
- 1 *each* patterns C–K

Fusible web

Fold A in half both ways and lightly crease the folds. Refer to "Bias Strips" in the Techniques file on the PDF. Prepare the bias strip for turned-edge appliqué. Prepare the remaining patches for fusible appliqué.

Use the creases and the appliqué placement diagram as a guide to arrange the patches on A.

Curving it casually, appliqué the bias strip B (stem) to A with a blind stitch. Fuse the remaining patches in alphabetical order as shown. Sew around the patches with a machine blanket stitch. Center the appliqué and trim A to 12½″ × 12½″.

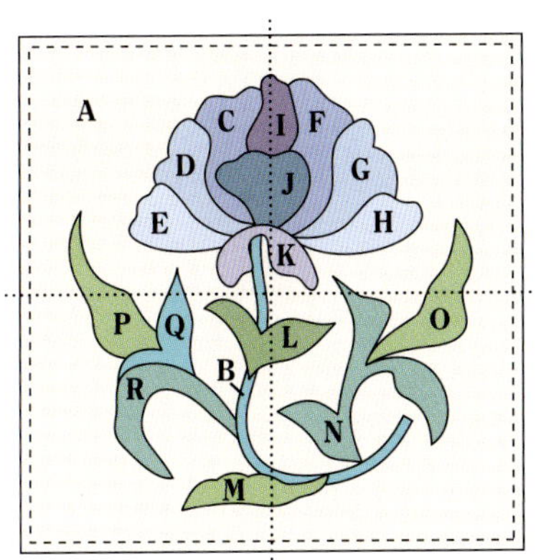

Applique Placement

block no. 12

Asian Grapes

by Laura Nownes • From Me to You
dianaandlaura.com

Laura Nownes is co-author of the classic *Quilts! Quilts!! Quilts!!! The Complete Guide to Quiltmaking* (Second Edition) for the NTC Division of McGraw-Hill, as well as several other quilt-related titles for C&T Publishing, ctpub.com.

See page 21 on the PDF for pattern

Cream Tone-on-Tone
- 1 square (A) 13½″ × 13½″ (trim to 12½″ × 12½″ after appliqué)

Assorted Green Prints
- 1 bias strip 1½″ × 32″ for circle (B)
- 1 *each* patterns C–H and Q–X
- 1 bias strip 1″ × 8″ for stems (see below to cut I, J and K)

Assorted Purple Prints
- 1 *each* patterns L and O
- 2 *each* patterns M and P
- 3 pattern N

Fold A in half both ways and lightly crease the folds. Refer to "Bias Strips" in the Techniques file on the PDF. Prepare the patches and bias strips for turned-edge appliqué. Refer to page 21 on the PDF Templates file to cut the narrow bias strip into shorter lengths to make patches I, J and K.

Use the creases and the appliqué placement diagram as a guide to arrange the patches on A.

Placing the ends so they will be covered by G/H, center B and appliqué its *outside* perimeter to A using a blind stitch. In alphabetical order, appliqué the remaining patches and bias strips to A; notice that several patches are tucked underneath the inside perimeter of B. When all of the patches have been added, appliqué the inside perimeter of B.

Center the appliqué and trim A to 12½″ × 12½″.

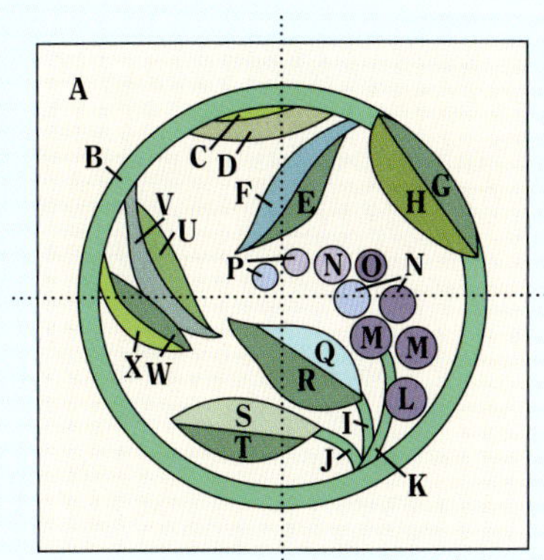

Applique Placement

block no. 13

Isabelle

by Lynda Howell • The Stitch Connection
stitchconnection.com

See page 32 on the PDF for pattern

Blue Tone-on-Tone
1 square (A) 11½″ × 11½″ (trim to 10½″ × 10½″ after appliqué)

Gray Tone-on-Tone
1 pattern B (add ½″ to all outside edges)

Assorted Prints and Tone-on-Tones
1 *each* patterns C, F, H–N and P–W
2 pattern D

White Felt
1 *each* patterns E and O
2 pattern G

Red Tone-on-Tone
1 rectangle (X) 1½″ × 10½″
1 rectangle (Y) 1½″ × 11½″

Green Check
1 rectangle (Y) 1½″ × 11½″
1 rectangle (Z) 1½″ × 12½″

Black and blue embroidery floss

Fusible web

Acrylic paint or powder blush for cheeks

Applique Placement & Block Piecing

Prepare patches B–W for fusible appliqué. Refer to the appliqué placement diagram and arrange the patches in alphabetical order on A. Before fusing, tuck pieces of blue floss under the ends of the scarf (L and M) to create fringe. Fuse the patches in place. Use matching thread and a machine blanket stitch to sew around all of the patches. Lynda used a variety of machine stitches along with the blanket stitch.

Use a satin stitch for the eyes and a backstitch for the mouth. Add color to the cheeks using the acrylic paint and a dry brush or powder blush. Center the appliqué and trim A to 10½″ × 10½″. Add patches X–Z as shown to complete the block.

block no. 14

Love Bird

by Marian Mapes

Fabric: Bali Batiks and Handpaints for Hoffman California Fabrics, hoffmanfabrics.com.

See page 17 on the PDF for pattern

Pale Gold Batik
1 square (A) 13½″ × 13½″ (trim to 12½″ × 12½″ after appliqué)

Brown Batik
1 pattern B (see instructions below)

Assorted Green Batiks
2 pattern C
6 pattern Cr

Assorted Blue Batiks
1 *each* patterns D–F

Black Batik
1 pattern G

Fusible web

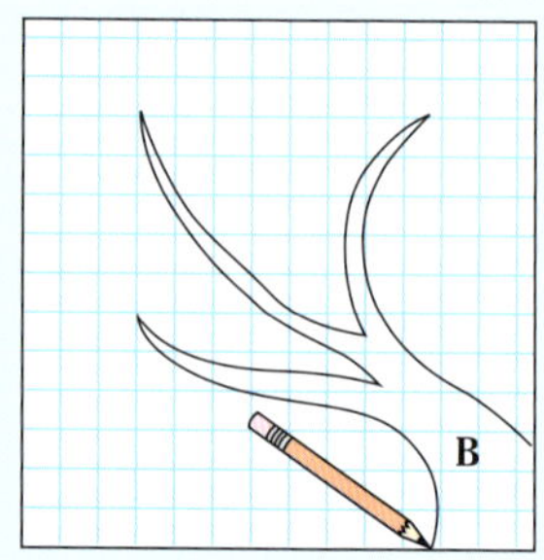

Each square = 1″

Create a template for B by drawing a freeform branch on a 13½″ × 13½″ piece of graph paper, using the illustration to the right as a guide.

Fold A in half both ways and gently crease the folds. Prepare the patches for fusible appliqué.

Applique Placement

Use the creases and the appliqué placement diagram as a guide to arrange the patches on A; fuse in alphabetical order. Using matching thread and a straight stitch, sew close to the edges of each patch. Center the appliqué and trim A to 12½″ × 12½″.

block no. 15

Homestead Hearts

by Martha Walker • Wagons West Designs
wagonswestdesigns.com

Martha is the author of *Vintage Christmas* for Wagons West Designs.

See page 16 on the PDF for pattern

Cream Print
- 1 square (A) 11½" × 11½" (trim to 10½" × 10½" after appliqué)

Assorted Green Prints
- 4 pattern B
- 48 pattern E

Burgundy Print
- 1 pattern C
- 8 rectangles (F) 1½" × 3"
- 2 squares (G) 1½" × 1½"

4 Assorted Medium Purple Prints

from *1*
- 1 pattern D
- 8 rectangles (F) 1½" × 3"
- 2 squares (G) 1½" × 1½"

from *3*
- 1 pattern D

Fold A in half diagonally both ways and lightly crease the folds. Prepare B–E for turned-edge appliqué.

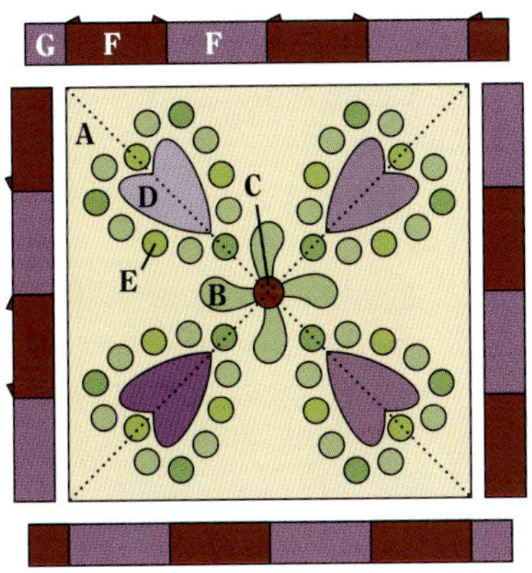

Applique Placement & Block Piecing

Use the creases and the appliqué placement diagram as a guide to arrange the patches on A. Use a blind stitch to sew the patches in place. Center the appliqué and trim A to 10½" × 10½".

Sew the F's and G's to A as shown to complete the block.

block no. 16

Summer Pop

by Pat Sloan • Pat Sloan & Co.
patsloan.com

Fabric: Arabella by Pat Sloan for P&B Textiles, pbtex.com.

See page 19 on the PDF for pattern

Gold Print
- 1 square (A) 13½" × 13½" (trim to 12½" × 12½" after appliqué)

2 Green Prints

from *1*
- 1 pattern B
- 4 pattern F

from *1*
- 1 pattern C
- 4 pattern G

Red Print
- 1 pattern D

Pink Print
- 3 pattern E

Black Print
- 1 pattern F

Pink Tone-on-Tone
- 1 pattern G

Fusible web

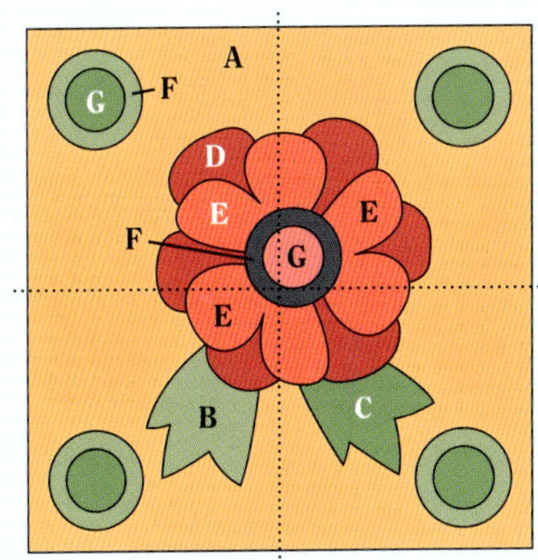

Applique Placement

Fold A in half both ways and lightly crease the folds. Prepare patches B–G for fusible appliqué.

Use the creases and the appliqué placement diagram as a guide to arrange the patches on A; fuse in alphabetical order. The stitch diagrams can be found in the Techniques file on the PDF. Use matching thread and a machine blanket stitch to sew around the patches.

Center the appliqué and trim A to 12½" × 12½".

block no. 17

Birds and Blooms

by Pearl P. Pereira • P3 Designs
p3designs.com

Fabric: Robert's Country Garden by Robert Callaham for Red Rooster Fabrics, redroosterfabrics.com.

See page 12 on the PDF for pattern

Beige Tone-on-Tone
1 square (A) 13½″ × 13½″ (trim to 12½″ × 12½″ after appliqué)
Assorted Tone-on-Tones
1″ wide bias strips for curved stems
appliqué patches
Gold and black embroidery floss

Refer to "Bias Strips" in the Techniques file on the PDF to make the stems. Use the appliqué placement diagram on page 12 of the PDF Templates file to cut the appliqué patches and bias stems. For the patches shown in gray, cut a reverse patch also. Prepare the patches for turned-edge appliqué.

Fold A in half diagonally both ways and gently crease the folds. Use the creases, the appliqué placement guide and the photographed block to arrange the patches on A. To help with patch placement, you may wish to trace the appliqué placement onto A.

Use matching thread and a blind stitch to appliqué the patches to A, starting with patches that lie underneath other patches. Use a backstitch to add antennae to the bumblebees and a French knot for the birds' eyes. Refer to the detail photo below to add embroidery to the flowers.

Center the appliqué and trim A to 12½″ × 12½″.

Applique Placement

block no. 18

Southern Blooms

by Pat Wys • Silver Thimble Quilt Co.
silverthimblequilt.com

See page 27 on the PDF for pattern

Assorted Cream Prints
4 squares (A) 7½″ × 7½″
(trim to 6½″ × 6½″ after appliqué)
Assorted Green Prints
8 bias strips ⅞″ × 5″ for stems
16 pattern B
Assorted Red Prints
8 pattern C
Assorted Gold Prints
8 pattern D
8 small brown buttons

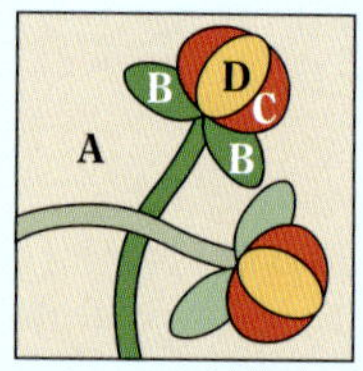

Unit Applique

Each block is made from 4 units. The appliqué placement is casual; each unit is different. When placing the appliqué, keep in mind where the seam allowance will be once the unit is trimmed, leaving space between the flower and the seam allowance.

Block Piecing

Prepare the bias strips and patches B–D for turned-edge appliqué. Using a hand or machine blanket stitch, appliqué 2 bias strips (stems) to an A, followed by the patches B–D in alphabetical order as shown. Sew a button to each flower.

You may want to wait to add the buttons after your project is quilted.

Repeat for each section. Center the appliqué and trim each section to 6½″ × 6½″. Join 4 sections as shown to make the block.

block no. 19

Patriotic Pinwheel

by Susan McDermott
windhamfabrics.com

Fabric: Valley Forge by Nancy Gere; Clara Barton 1821–1912, both for Windham Fabrics, windhamfabrics.com.

See page 18 on PDF for pattern

Tan Print
- 1 square (A) 13½" × 13½" (trim to 12½" × 12½" after appliqué)

Brown Print
- 4 pattern B

Red Stripe
- 4 pattern C

Blue Print #1
- 4 pattern D

Blue Print #2
- 1 pattern E

Dark Tan Print
- 1 pattern F

Red Print
- 1 pattern G

Fusible web

Fold A in half diagonally both ways and lightly crease the folds. Prepare the patches for fusible appliqué.

Use the creases and the appliqué placement diagram as a guide to arrange the patches on A; fuse in place. Use monofilament and a tiny zigzag stitch to sew around all the patches.

Center the appliqué and trim A to 12½" × 12½".

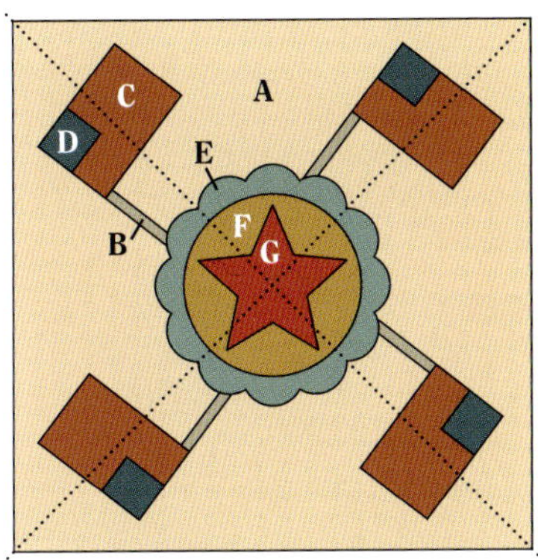

Applique Placement

block no. 20

Hungry

by Terry Clothier Thompson • Peace Creek Book and Pattern Company • terrythompson.com

Fabric: Moda Fabrics, unitednotions.com; thread, DMC.

Terry Clothier Thompson teaches a popular "FabriCamp" and designs fabric for Moda Fabrics. She is the author of numerous quilt-related titles for Kansas City Star Quilts, pickledishstore.com.

See page 29 on PDF for pattern

Cream Print
- 1 square (A) 13½" × 13½" (trim to 12½" × 12½" after appliqué)

Assorted Green Prints
- 1 *each* patterns B and H
- 2 pattern D
- 3 pattern F

Large-Scale Multiprint
- 1 pattern C

Black Print
- 1 pattern E

Yellow Print
- 6 pattern F
- 1 pattern I

Red Tone-on-Tone
- 1 pattern G

Fold A in half both ways and lightly crease the folds. Prepare the patches B–H for turned-edge appliqué (patches C, G, H and I will need to be flipped to trace the second half).

Use the creases and the appliqué placement diagram as a guide to arrange the patches on A. Use a tiny machine zigzag stitch to appliqué the patches in alphabetical order to A.

Terry recommends DMC machine embroidery thread for the appliqué.

Center the design and trim A to 12½" × 12½".

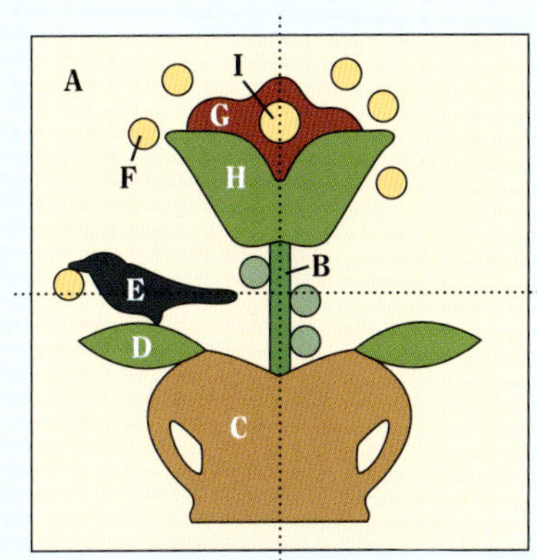

Applique Placement

block no. 21

Rosie's Posie

by Cara Bonner • Quilt Nook Gal Designs
thequiltnook.com

Fabric: Maison de Garace designed by French General for Moda Fabrics, unitednotions.com.

Cream Print
1 square (A) 13½"x 13½" (trim to 12½"x 12½" after appliqué)
Green Print
3 bias strips 1¼"x 8¼" for stems
Assorted Prints
3 circles 5" diameter for large yo-yos
11 circles 4" diameter for medium yo-yos
8 circles 2¾" diameter for small yo-yos
Rickrack 21"
Light green embroidery floss
Clover small, large and extra-large yo-yo makers (optional)

Fold A in half both ways and lightly crease the folds. Refer to "Bias Strips" in the Techniques file on the PDF to make stems from the green print. Make yo-yos using the assorted prints.

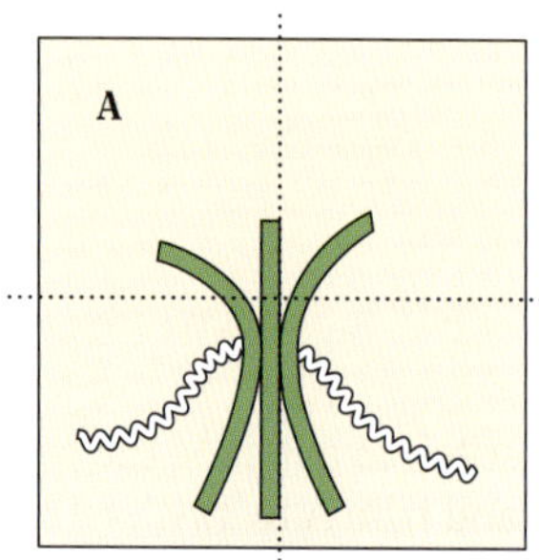

Rickrack Placement

Use the creases and the appliqué placement diagram as a guide to arrange the stems on A. Tuck the white rickrack under the stems. Using a contrasting thread and a machine blanket stitch, sew around the stems. Referring to the placement diagram, arrange the large yo-yos on A; tack them in place. Repeat with the medium yo-yos, followed by the small yo-yos.

Embroider tendrils and small stems using a stem stitch as shown. Stitch French knots randomly. Tie the rickrack in a bow around the stems to complete the bouquet. Center and trim the block to 12½"× 12½".

Applique and Embroidery Placement

block no. 22

Norse Bloom

by Karen Comstock • Quiltricks
quiltricks.com

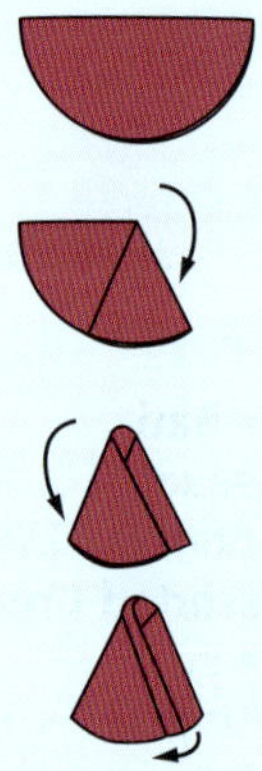

Rosebud Folding

See page 28 on the PDF for pattern

Cream Tone-on-Tone
1 square (A) 13½"x 13½" (trim to 12½"x 12½" after appliqué)
Green Tone-on-Tone
1 bias strip 1"x 20" for stems leaves
Dark Pink Tone-on-Tone
3 circles 2" diameter
Medium Pink Tone-on-Tone
1 *each* pattern B, C, D and E
Fusible web
Brown, green and dark pink embroidery floss

Fold A in half both ways and lightly crease the folds. Refer to "Bias Strips" in the PDF Techniques file. Cut one stem 12¼" long and 1 stem 7¾" long. Prepare the leaves and flower petals (B–E) for fusible appliqué.

Use the creases and the appliqué placement diagram to arrange the stems on A. Use matching thread and a blind stitch to appliqué the stems in place. Arrange and fuse B to A. Use matching thread and a machine blanket stitch to sew around the patches.

To make a folded rosebud, refer to the diagrams above to fold a dark pink circle in half, wrong sides together, and then fold the sides as shown. Make 3 folded rosebuds. Use a running stitch along the bottom of each one to secure to A as shown at the end of the stems and on the B patch. Fuse patches C–E and leaves as shown above.

Use a backstitch, lazy daisy stitch and French knots to add details as shown. Center the appliqué and trim A to 12½"x 12½".

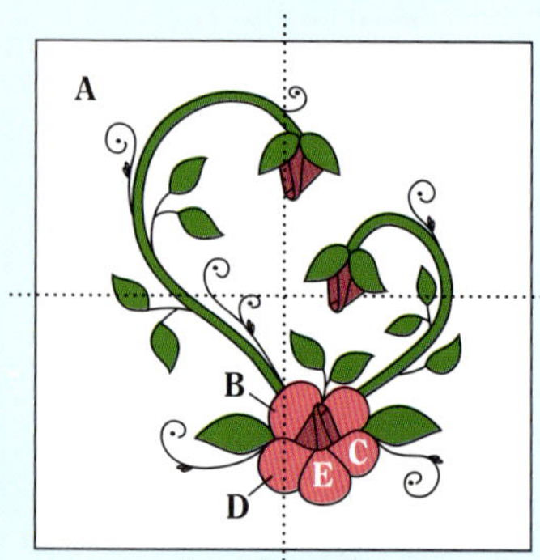

Applique Placement

block no. 23

Snowman Farm

by June Dudley • Editor-in-Chief, *Quiltmaker*
quiltmaker.com

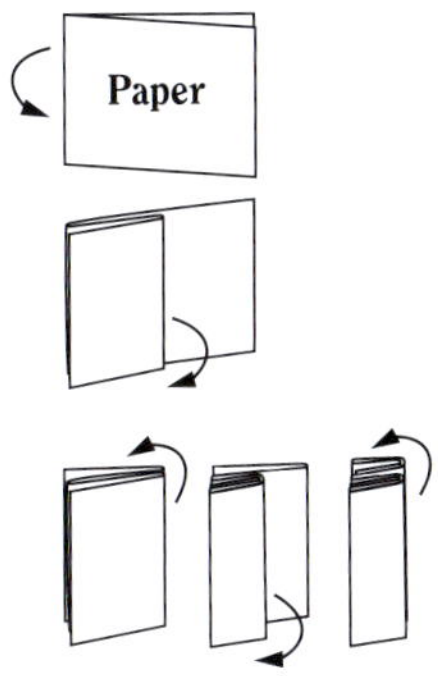

See page 75 on the PDF for pattern

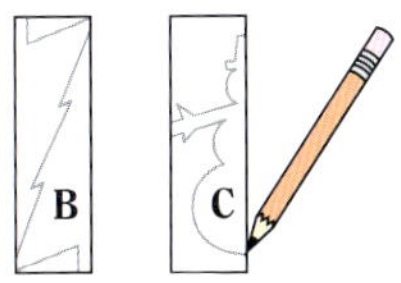

Blue Batik
1 square (A) 13″x 13″
(trim to 12½″x 12½″ after appliqué)
3 Assorted Green Batiks from *each*
1 strip 5½″x 13″
1 White on White Print
1 strip 5½″x 13″
Legal size paper 2 sheets
Fusible web
Removable marker

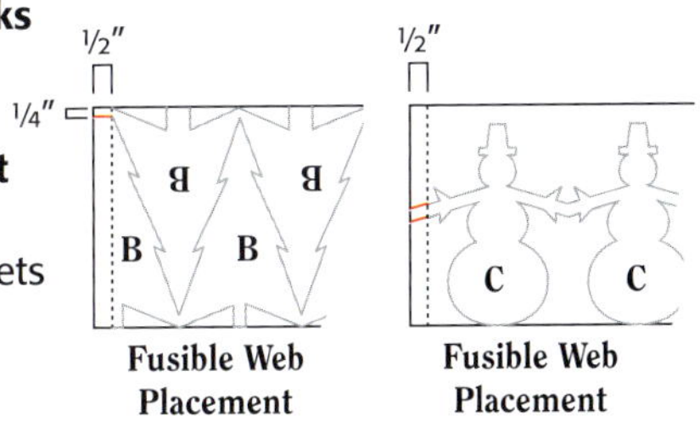

The trees and snowmen are cut from patterns that you make paperdoll-style. An extra row of trees will be made from each green batik.

Fold a 5½"× 12" strip of paper as shown above. Trace the trees (B), including both trunks, onto the top panel of the folded paper. Cut on the traced lines through all layers. Repeat to make the snowmen (C).

Unfold the patterns. Center and trace both tree rows onto a 5½"× 13" strip of fusible web as shown, adding the line shown in red to each end. Repeat to trace 3 sets of trees and 1 row of snowmen. Fuse a set of trees to *each* green strip. Fuse the snowmen to the white strip. Carefully cut on the drawn lines.

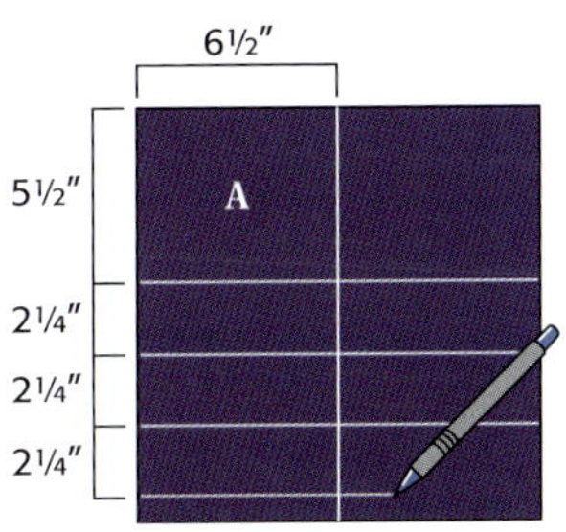

Mark A as shown. Center the first row on the top line; fuse in place. Use a matching thread and sew close to the patch edges. Repeat for the remaining rows, offsetting them as shown. Center and trim the block to 12½"× 12½".

Trim to 12½″x 12½″ after applique.

block no. 24

Hearts Bejeweled

by Susan Guzman • SuzGuz Designs
suzguzdesigns.com

White Dot
1 square (A) 13½″x 13½″ (trim to 12½″x 12½″ after appliqué
Brown Dot
1 square (B) 1¼″ x 1¼″
12 pattern G
Yellow Print
4 squares (C) 2″x 2″
Green Solid
4 rectangles (D) 1″x 3½″
Pink Tone-on-Tone
4 pattern E
Blue Print
4 pattern F

Template for Hearts Bejeweled block on page 39 of the PDF Templates file.

Fold A in half both ways and lightly crease the folds. Prepare patches B–G for turned-edge appliqué. Use the creases and the appliqué placement diagram as a guide to arrange the patches on A. Use matching thread and a blind stitch to appliqué the patches in place. Center the appliqué and trim A to 12½"× 12½".

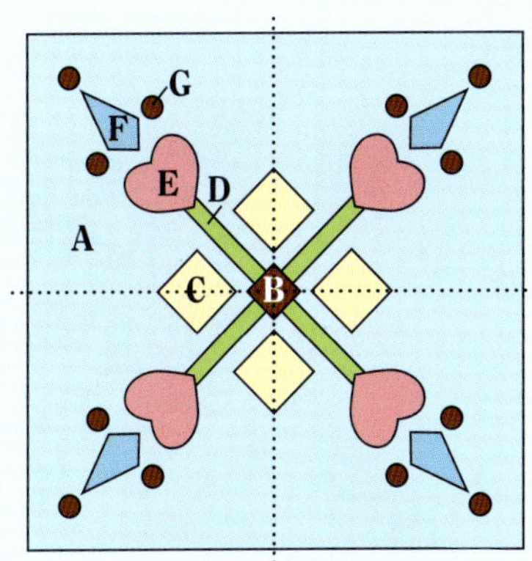

Applique Placement

block no. 25

Hope Blooms

by Nancy Halvorsen • Art to Heart
arttoheart.com

Fabric: Tidings designed by Nancy Halvorsen for Benartex, benartex.com.

Nancy Halvorsen is the author of numerous books and patterns for her company, Art to Heart. She designs fabric for Benartex.

See page 64 on the PDF for pattern

Cream Tone-on-Tone
 1 square (A) 12½"x 12½"
Green Tone-on-Tone
 4 squares (B) 4½"x 4½"
Assorted Prints
 1 set of appliqué patches
Fusible web
Embroidery floss

Refer to "Stitch-and-Flip" in the Techniques file on the PDF; add the B patches to the corners of A. Prepare the remaining patches for fusible appliqué. Fold A in half both ways and lightly crease the folds. Use the creases and the appliqué placement diagram as a guide to arrange the patches on A. Mark the placement of the embroidered words. Set the flower and leaf patches aside; fuse the heart/stem patches in place.

Use matching thread and a machine blanket stitch to sew around the heart/stem patches. Repeat the process for the flower and leaf patches. Use 3 strands of embroidery floss and a backstitch to complete the hand embroidery of the words.

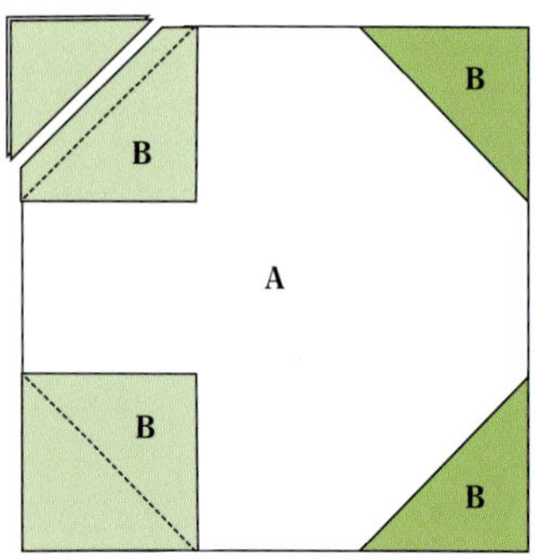

Block Piecing

Applique/Embroidery Placement

block no. 26

Rising Star

by Reeze L. Hanson • Morning Glory Designs
morningglorydesigns.net

See page 71 on the PDF for pattern

Purple Mottled Batik
 1 square (A) 12½"x 12½"
Lime Green Batik
 1 pattern B
Gold Dot Batik
 4 *each* patterns C, D, E and G
Blue Print Batik
 4 *each* patterns C, D and F
Dark Green Tone-on-Tone
 4 *each* patterns C, D and E
Fusible web
Tear-away stabilizer

Fold A in half both ways and lightly crease the folds. Prepare patches B–G for fusible appliqué. Use the creases and the appliqué placement diagram as a guide to arrange the patches on A, beginning with the outside patches and working toward the center of the block. Fuse the patches to A.

Using tear-away stabilizer on the back, sew around the patches with gold thread and a machine blanket stitch. Remove the excess stabilizer.

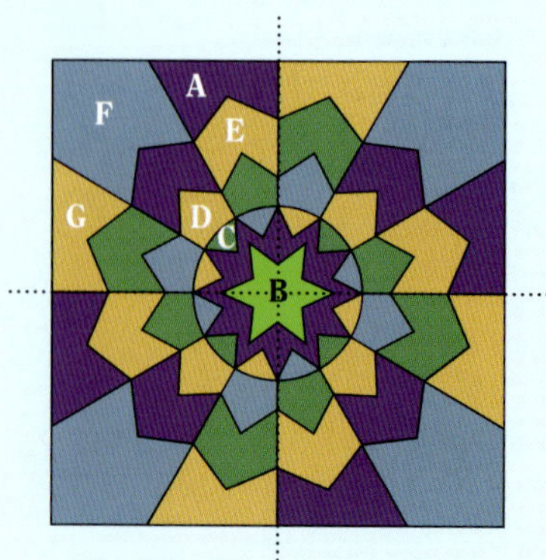

Applique Placement

block no. 27

Paisley Punch

by Diane Harris • Associate Editor, *Quiltmaker*
quiltmaker.com

See 46–47 on the PDF for pattern

Aqua Print

1 square (A) 13½″x 13½″ (trim to 12½″x 12½″ after appliqué)

Assorted Prints and Batiks

1 *each* patterns B, D, Dr and E
2 *each* patterns C and F

Fold A in half both ways and lightly crease the folds. Prepare the patches for turned-edge appliqué.

Use the creases and the appliqué placement diagram as a guide to arrange the patches on A. Use matching thread and a blind stitch to appliqué the patches in place.

Center the appliqué and trim A to 12½" × 12½".

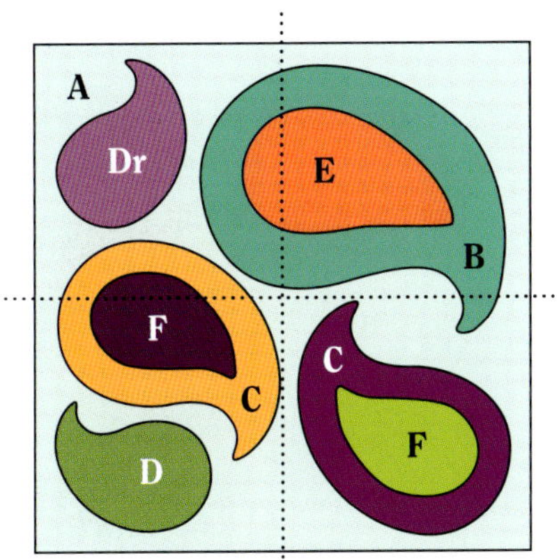

Applique Placement

block no. 28

Bird's Eye View

by Dawn Heese
dawnheesequilts.blogspot.com

Fabric: Kansas Troubles for Moda Fabrics, unitednotions.com.

Dawn Heese is the author of *Geese in the Rose Garden* for Kansas City Star Quilts, pickledish.com.

See page 38 on the PDF for pattern

Tan Dot

1 square (A) 13½″x 13½″ (trim to 12½″x 12½″ after appliqué)

Black Print

1 pattern B

2 Red Prints

from *1*
1 pattern C
from *1*
5 pattern D

Green Plaid

bias strip 1″x 13″ for stem
1 *each* patterns D and Dr

2 Gold Prints

from *1*
1 pattern D
from *1*
1 pattern E

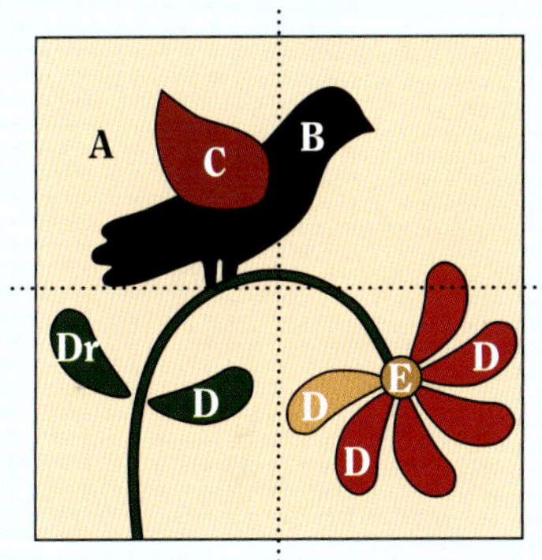

Applique Placement

Fold A in half both ways and lightly crease the folds. Prepare patches B–E for turned-edge appliqué. To make the bias stem, refer to "Bias Strips" in the Techniques file on the PDF.

Use the creases and the appliqué placement diagram as a guide to arrange the stem and patches on A. Use matching thread and a blind stitch to appliqué the patches in place.

Center the appliqué and trim A to 12½" × 12½".

block no. 29

Simply Sweet

by Barbara Jones • QuiltSoup
quiltsoup.com

Fabric: Simply Sweet designed by Barbara Jones for Henry Glass Fabrics, henryglassfabrics.com.

Barbara Jones is the author of *Cradle to Cradle* for Kansas City Star Quilts, pickledish.com.

See page 75 on the PDF for pattern

White Dot
1 square (A) 13½" x 13½" (trim to 12½" x 12½" after appliqué)

2 Green Prints
from *1*
1 *each* patterns B and C
from *1*
1 pattern B

Red Print
1 pattern D

Blue Print
1 pattern E

White Print
1 pattern F

Buttons 1 flower at 1⅛", 1 at ½"

Fold A in half both ways and lightly crease the folds. Prepare patches B–F for turned-edge appliqué. Use the creases and the appliqué placement diagram as a guide to arrange the patches on A. Use matching thread and a blind stitch to appliqué the patches in place. Center the appliqué and trim A to 12½"× 12½". Add the ½" button for the bird's eye and the flower button at the top of the flower as shown.

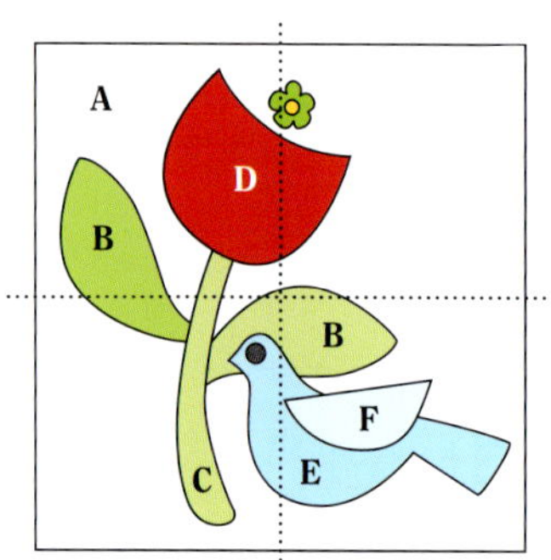

Applique Placement

block no. 30

Delectable Grapes

by Marian Mapes

Fabric: Batiks and Handpaints by Hoffman California Fabrics, hoffmanfabrics.com.

See page 69 on the PDF for pattern

Light Gold Batik
1 square (A) 13½" x 13½" (trim to 12½" x 12½" after appliqué)

Assorted Purple Batiks
34 pattern B
6 pattern C

Dark Green Batik #1
1 pattern D

Dark Green Batik #2
1 pattern E

Medium Green Batik
1 pattern F

Light Green Batik #1
1 pattern G

Light Green Batik #2
1 pattern H

Fusible web

Templates for Delectable Grapes block on page 69 of the PDF Templates file.

Fold A in half both ways and lightly crease the folds. Prepare the patches for fusible appliqué. Use the creases and appliqué placement diagram to arrange the patches on A; fuse in alphabetical order. Using matching thread and a straight stitch, sew close to the edges of each patch.

Center the appliqué and trim A to 12½"× 12½".

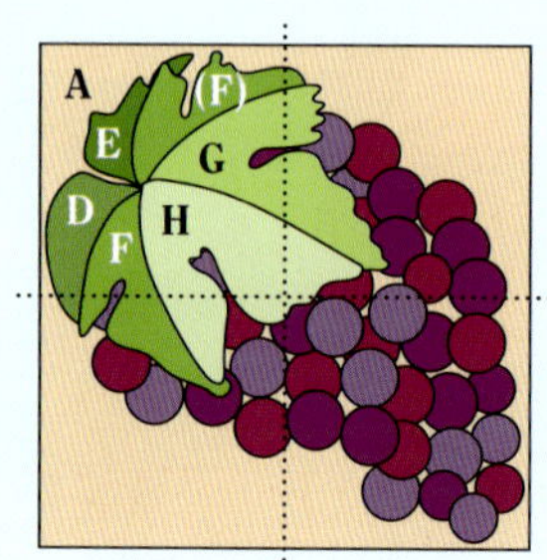

Applique Placement

block no. 31

Spring Flowers

by Lynda Milligan and Nancy Smith • Possibilities
possibilitiesquilt.com

Nancy Smith and Lynda Milligan are co-owners of Great American Quilt Factory in Denver, Colorado. They currently design fabric for Quilting Treasures and QT Express, quiltingtreasures.com, and publish books and patterns through their company, Possibilities, possibilitiesquilt.com.

See page 48 on the PDF for pattern

Dark Blue Batik

1 square (A) 13½"x 13½" (trim to 12½"x 12½" after appliqué)

Assorted Green Batiks

1 *each* patterns B–D, I, J, M, N, P, Pr and Q
2 pattern O

Assorted Pink and Orange Batiks

1 *each* pattern E, G, H, K and L
3 pattern F
2 *each* patterns R–T

Fusible web

Nonstick pressing sheet

Fold A in half both ways and lightly crease the folds. Prepare patches B–T for fusible appliqué.

Lay the nonstick pressing sheet on a hard ironing surface. Using the diagram below as a guide, lightly fuse the appliqué patches B–T in alphabetical order to the pressing sheet. Let the patches cool, peel off and position to the background as shown. Fuse in place.

Use matching thread and a machine blanket stitch to sew around all of the patches.

Center the appliqué and trim A to 12½"× 12½".

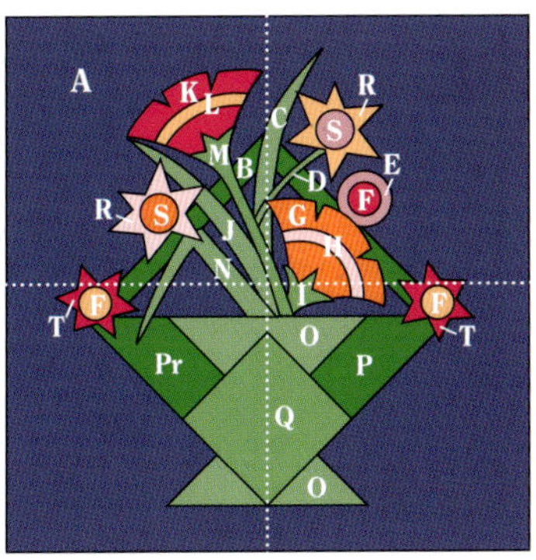

Applique Placement

block no. 32

Love Apple

by Jo Morton • Jo Morton Quilts
jomortonquilts.com

Fabric: Various lines designed by Jo Morton for Andover Fabrics, andoverfabrics.com.

Jo Morton is the author of many self-published books including Vintage Journey, Timeless and Remembrances.

See page 41 on the PDF for pattern

Tan Print

1 square (A) 13½"x 13½" (trim to 12½"x 12½" after appliqué)

Assorted Green Prints

2 pattern B
4 pattern D
8 pattern F

Assorted Red Prints

4 each patterns C and G

Assorted Gold Prints

4 pattern E

Fold A in half both ways and lightly crease the folds. Prepare patches B–G for turned-edge appliqué. Use the creases and the appliqué placement diagram as a guide to arrange the patches on A. Use matching thread and a blind stitch to appliqué the patches to A.

Center the appliqué and trim A to 12½"× 12½".

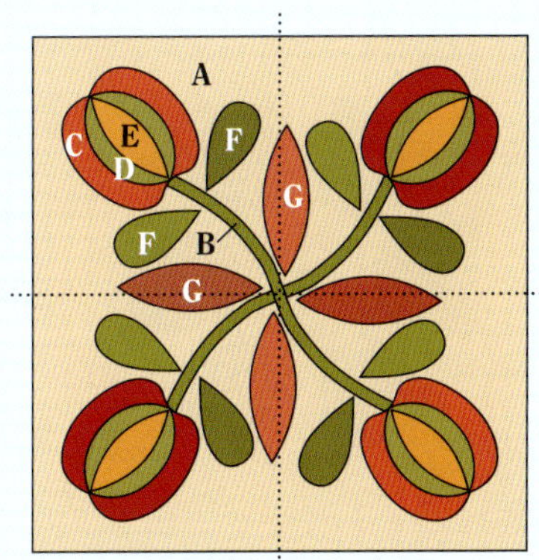

Applique Placement

block no. 33

Merry Little Flower

by Kari Ramsay • Fresh Cut Quilts Pattern Co.
freshcutquilts.com

Kari Ramsay is the author of *Tidbits From Triangles for Fresh Cut Quilts* Pattern Co., freshcutquilts.com.

See page 67 on the PDF for pattern

White Tone-on-Tone
1 square (A) 13½″ x 13½″ (trim to 12½″ x 12½″ after appliqué)
Light Green Print
1 *each* patterns B and E
Red Print
1 pattern C
Black Print
6 pattern D
Yellow Print
1 circle 4″ diameter for yo-yo

Fold A in half both ways and lightly crease the folds. Prepare the patches B–E for turned-edge appliqué. Use the creases and the appliqué placement diagram as a guide to arrange the patches on A.

Use matching thread and a blind stitch to appliqué the patches in place. Use the yellow print to make a yo-yo. Tack the yo-yo in place at the flower's center.

Center the appliqué and trim A to 12½" × 12½".

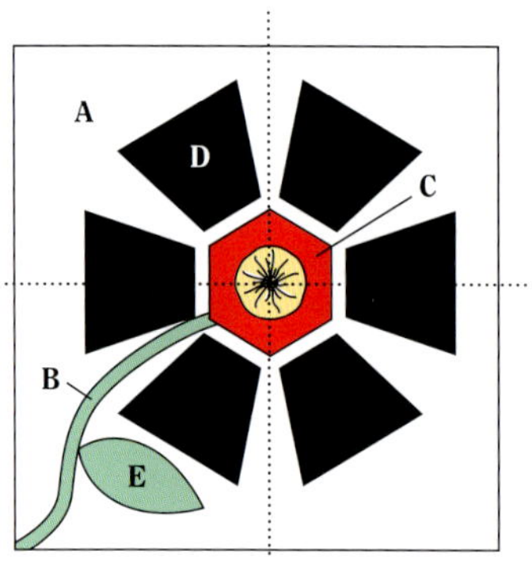

Applique Placement

block no. 34

Nucleus

by Scarlett Rose • Scarlett Rose's Celtic & More
scarlettrose.com

Scarlett used a fusible bias tape maker and fusible web to prepare her bias strips. If you prefer this method, follow the manufacturer's instructions for cutting the bias strips.

See page 46 on the PDF for pattern

Medium Teal Batik
1 square (A) 13½″ x 13½″ (trim to 12½″ x 12½″ after appliqué)
Pale Yellow Batik
1 pattern B
Light Blue Tone-on-Tone
1 pattern C
Dark Teal Tone-on-Tone
bias strip 1¼″ x 82″ (see note above)
Mauve Tone-on-Tone
bias strip 1¼″ x 31½″ (see note above)
Clover fusible bias tape maker ⅜″ (optional)
Clover 5mm fusible web (optional)

Fold A in half both ways and lightly crease the folds. Use the creases and the appliqué placement diagram as a guide to center B on A. Baste B in place around the outer edges and cut away the excess A under the appliqué. Repeat to add C and cut away the excess B.

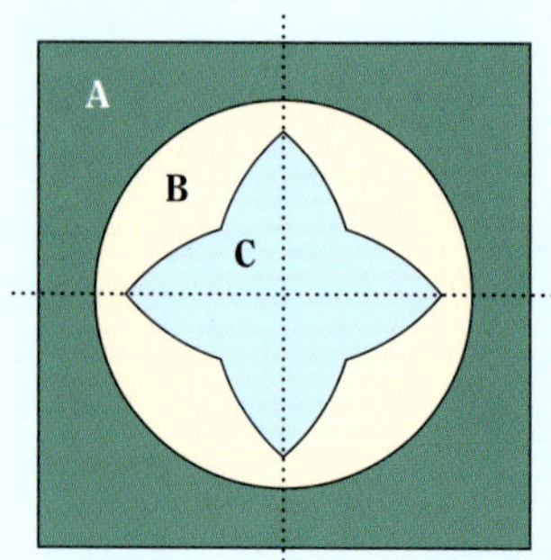

Applique Placement

Refer to "Bias Strips" in the Techniques file on the PDF to prepare the bias strips. Refer to the diagram to arrange the bias strips on A covering the raw edges of B and C, noting that some strips overlap others and some underlap. Fold the strips at the corners. Use matching thread and a machine blind stitch to sew the strips in place. Center the appliqué and trim A to 12½" × 12½".

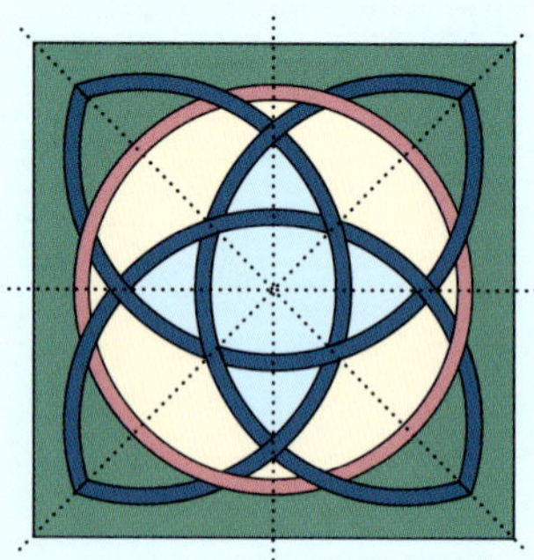

Bias Strip Placement

block no. 35

Snow Happy Home

by Monica Solorio-Snow • Happy Zombie
thehappyzombie.com

Fabric: Holiday Happy by Monica Solorio-Snow and Color Basics, all from Lecien, lecien.co.jp/en/hobby.

See page 68 on the PDF for pattern

Yellow Dot
- 1 square (A) 13½" x 13½" (trim to 12½" x 12½" after appliqué)

Assorted Prints
- 1 set appliqué patches

Buttons
- 1 at ⅝", 1 at ½" for doorknob

Fold A in half both ways and lightly crease the folds. Prepare the patches for turned-edge appliqué. Use the creases and the appliqué placement diagram as a guide to arrange the patches on A.

Use matching thread and a blind stitch to appliqué the patches in place. Center the appliqué and trim A to 12½" × 12½". Stack the small button on top of the larger button as shown in the photograph and sew them to the block for a doorknob.

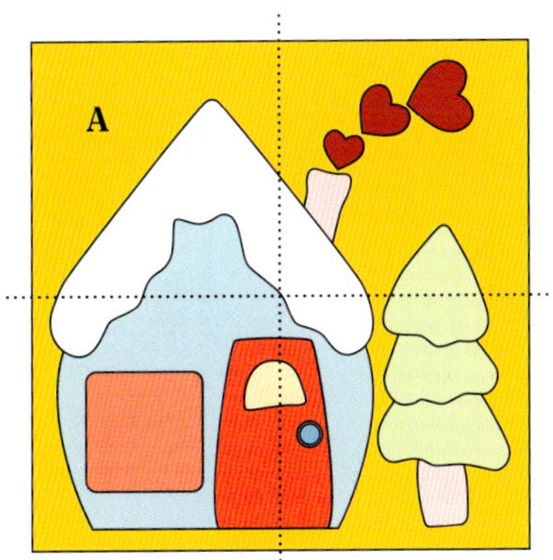

Applique Placement

block no. 36

Faire la Bise

by Helen Stubbings • Hugs 'N Kisses
hugsnkisses.net, hugsnkisses.typepad.com

Fabric: Rural Jardin designed by French General for Moda Fabrics, unitednotions.com.

Helen Stubbings is the author of *Faux Appliqué* for American Quilter's Society, americanquilter.com.

See page 40 on the PDF for pattern

Tan Solid
- 1 square (A) 13½" x 13½" (trim to 12½" x 12½" after appliqué)

Blue Print #1
- 4 pattern B

Red Print #1
- 4 pattern C

Blue Print #2
- 5 pattern D
- 4 pattern E

Red Print #2
- 4 pattern F

Red and medium blue embroidery floss

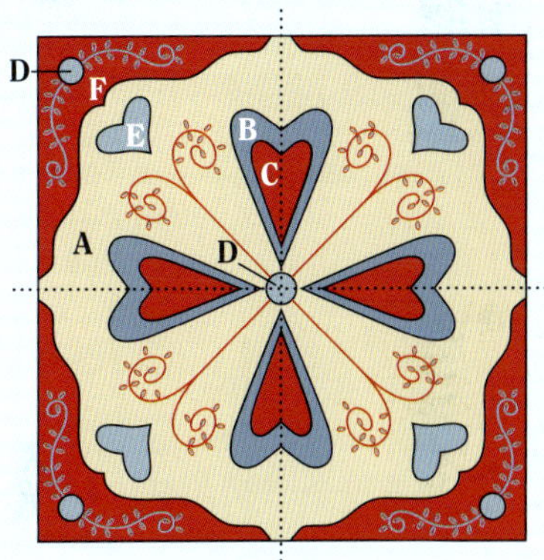

Applique Placement

Fold A in half both ways and lightly crease the folds. Prepare patches B–E for turned-edge appliqué. Use the creases and the appliqué placement diagram as a guide to arrange the B's, C's, 1 D and the E's on A.

Use matching thread and a blind stitch to appliqué *only* these patches in place. Center the appliqué and trim A to 12½" × 12½".

Prepare the curved edges of the F's for turned-edge appliqué. Use matching thread and a blind stitch to appliqué an F and D to each corner of the block.

Use a stem stitch and lazy daisy stitch to add the embroidery. Notice that each lazy daisy on F is doubled, and the red lazy daisy stitches encircle a blue straight stitch.

Embroidery Detail

block no. 37

Hummingbird Haven

by Cathy Van Bruggen • Cathy Van Bruggen Designs
cathyvb.com

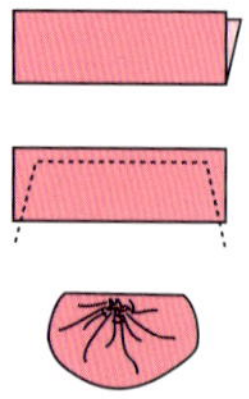

Flower Blossom
Make 2

See page 66 on the PDF for pattern

Light Green Tone-on-Tone
1 square (A) 13½"x 13½" (trim to 12½"x 12½" after appliqué)

Brown Tone-on-Tone
1 bias strip ¾"x 13" for stem

Assorted Prints and Tone-on-Tones
1 set of leaf patches (notice that Cathy fussy cut some of the leaves from a leaf print)
1 *each* patterns B–R
2 bias strips 2"x 3" for flower blossoms

Embroidery floss

12 pink seed beads

Brown Micron Pigma pen

Fold A in half both ways and lightly crease the folds. Refer to "Tiny Bias Stems" in the Techniques file on the PDF. Prepare the brown bias strip and appliqué patches for turned-edge appliqué. Use the creases and appliqué diagram to arrange the stem on A. Use a stem stitch to embroider the end of the bias strip, the small stem and the "ground" line as shown.

Arrange the leaves and patches B–D, G–I and L–R on A. Use a blind stitch and matching thread to sew around the leaves and patches in alphabetical order. To create each flower blossom, fold a bias strip in half lengthwise, wrong sides together. Sew a small running stitch ⅛" from the edge. Pull the stitches to gather. Baste the blossoms to B and G as shown. Add patches E, F, J and K.

Beading diagrams can be found in the Techniques file on the PDF. Use beads and embroidery floss in a combination of satin, outline, couching and stem stitches to add the details and the spider web. Draw the hummingbird's feet and underbelly using the brown pen. Center the appliqué and trim A to 12½"× 12½".

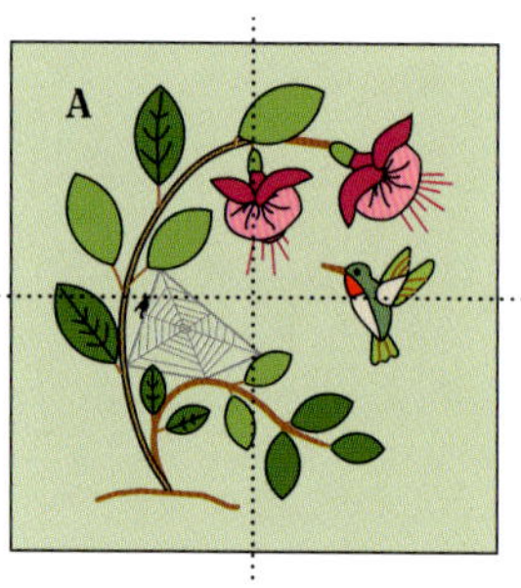

Applique & Embroidery Placement

block no. 38

Button Basket

by Ann Weber • Gingham Girls LLC
ginghamgirls.biz

Fabric: Meadow Sweet designed by Sandi Henderson for Michael Miller Fabrics, michaelmillerfabrics.com.

See page 50 on the PDF for pattern

Light Yellow Tone-on-Tone
1 square (A) 13½"x 13½" (trim to 12½"x 12½" after appliqué)

Large-scale Plaid
1 pattern B

Light Green Print
1 bias strip 1¾"x 14½" for handle

Light Green Check
1 bias strip 1½"x 11" for basket trim

Buttons 4 at ⅝", 1 at ⅞"

Fold A in half both ways and lightly crease the folds. Refer to "Bias Strips" in the Techniques file on the PDF. Prepare the bias strips and B for turned-edge appliqué. Use the creases and the appliqué placement diagram as a guide to arrange the basket followed by the handle and basket trim on A.

Use matching thread and a blind or straight stitch to appliqué the patches in place. Sew the buttons on the basket as shown. Center the appliqué and trim A to 12½"× 12½".

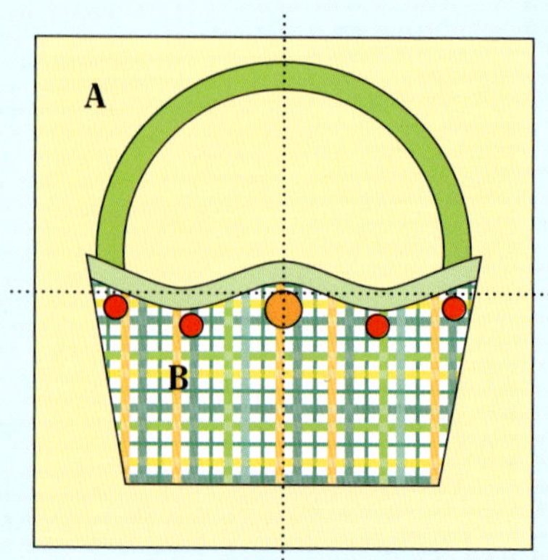

Applique Placement

block no. 39

Seven Eighths

by Vicki Willems

Fabric: Rose of Sharon for Island Batik, Inc., islandbatik.com.

Vicki's design was a finalist in the Rose of Sharon Block Challenge and is included in *The Rose of Sharon Block Book* by Sharon Pederson for Martingale & Co., martingale-pub.com.

Cream Batik

1 square (A) 13½" x 13½" (trim to 12½" x 12½" after appliqué)

Assorted Red, Orange and Gold Batiks

1 *each* patterns B and D

7 *each* patterns H, I and J

Blue Batik

1 pattern C

Assorted Green Batiks

7 *each* patterns E, F and G

Fusible web

Template for Seven Eighths block on page 38 of the PDF Templates file.

Fold A in half both ways and lightly crease the folds. Prepare patches B–J for fusible appliqué.

Use the creases and the appliqué placment diagram as a guide to arrange the patches on A. Fuse the patches to A in alphabetical order. Use invisible thread and a machine zigzag stitch to sew around the patches.

Center the appliqué and trim A to 12½" × 12½".

Applique Placement

block no. 40

Flower Box

by Kathy York
aquamoonartquilts.blogspot.com

Fabric: Urban Landscapes designed by Kathy York for Clothworks, clothworks.com.

See page 53 on the PDF for pattern

Blue Solid

1 square (A) 13½" x 13½" (trim to 12½" x 12½" after appliqué)

Assorted Prints and Solids

4 pattern B
4 pattern C
4 *each* patterns D and Dr
4 pattern E
4 pattern F
4 pattern G
1 pattern H

Fusible web

Kathy fussy cut patches from her Urban Landscapes prints.

Fold A in half both ways and lightly crease the folds. Prepare patches B–H for fusible appliqué.

Use the creases and the appliqué placement diagram as a guide to arrange the patches on A. Fuse the patches to A in alphabetical order. Use matching thread and a machine satin stitch to sew around all patches.

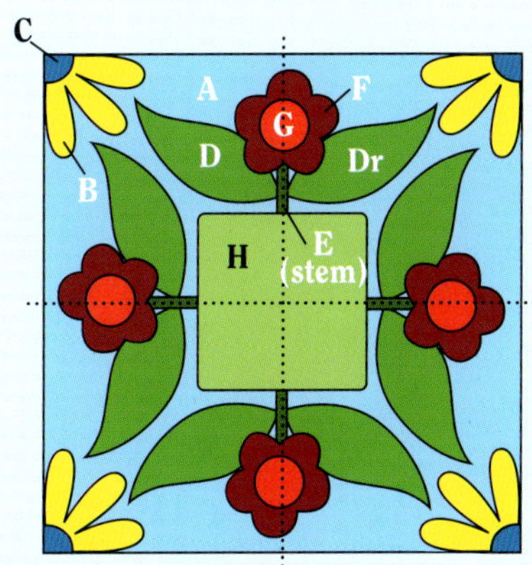

Applique Placement

block no. 41

Holiday Season

by Cynthia Foster • Carter Creek Quilts
etsy.com/people/cartercreekquilts

See page 102 on the PDF for pattern

Cream Tone-on-Tone
1 square (A) 13½" x 13½" (trim to 12½" x 12½" after appliqué)

Dark Green Tone-on-Tone
6 *each* patterns B and Br

Gold Tone-on-Tone
6 *each* patterns C and Cr
3 pattern G

Red Tone-on-Tone
6 *each* patterns D and F

Light Green Tone-on-Tone
12 pattern E

Fusible web

Template for Holiday Season block on page 102 of the PDF Templates file.

Fold A in half both ways and lightly crease the folds. Prepare patches B–G for fusible appliqué.

Use the creases and appliqué placement diagram as guides to arrange the patches on A. Fuse the patches to A in alphabetical order. Use matching thread and a machine blanket stitch to sew around the patches. Center the appliqué and trim A to 12½" × 12½".

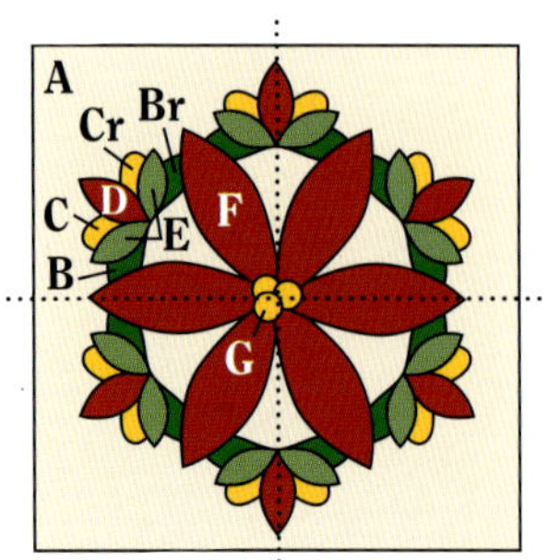

Applique Placement

block no. 42

Love of Country

by Dianne Gardner

See page 84 on the PDF for pattern

Cream Tone-on-Tone
1 square (A) 13½" x 13½" (trim to 12½" x 12½" after appliqué)

Red Print
1 pattern B

Blue Print
1 pattern C

Fold A in half both ways and lightly crease the folds. Prepare patches B and C for turned-edge appliqué.

Use the creases and appliqué placement diagram as guides to arrange the patches on A. Use matching thread and a blind stitch to appliqué the patches in place. Center the appliqué and trim A to 12½" × 12½".

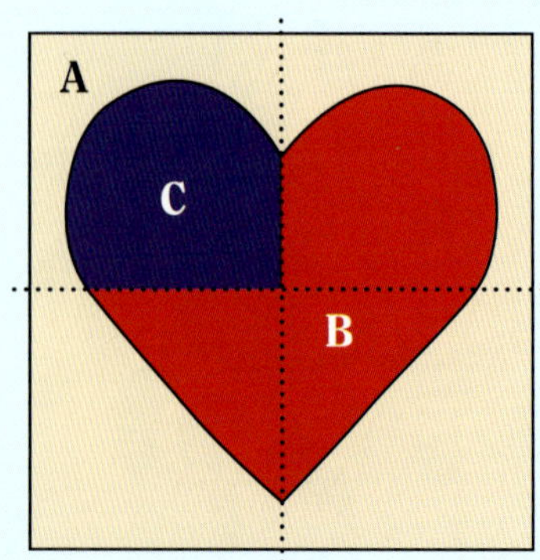

Applique Placement

block no. 43

Bertrand's Arrows

by Susan Guzman • SuzGuz Designs
suzguzdesigns.com

See page 110 on the PDF for pattern

Cream Tone-on-Tone
1 square (A) 13½"x 13½" (trim to 12½"x 12½" after appliqué)

Assorted Prints and Tone-on-Tones
1 *each* patterns B, C and D
4 *each* patterns E, F, G, H and J
8 pattern I

Fold A in half both ways and lightly crease the folds. Prepare patches B–J for turned-edge appliqué.

Use the creases and appliqué placement diagram as guides to arrange the patches on A. Use matching thread and a blind stitch to appliqué the patches in place. Center the appliqué and trim A to 12½" × 12½".

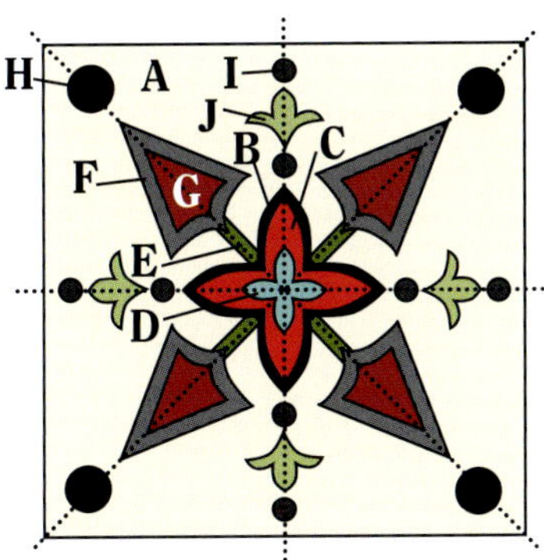

Applique Placement

block no. 44

Floral Wreath

by Cheryl Haynes • Prairie Grove Peddler
prairiegrovepeddler.com

See page 84 on the PDF for pattern

Cream Tone-on-Tone
1 square (A) 12½"x 12½"

Dark Purple Tone-on-Tone #1
4 squares (B) 4"x 4"
4 *each* patterns G and Gr

Green Tone-on-Tone #1
4 *each* patterns C and D

Green Tone-on-Tone #2
4 pattern E

Dark Purple Tone-on-Tone #2
4 pattern F

Medium Purple Tone-on-Tone
4 pattern H

Fusible web

Gold embroidery floss

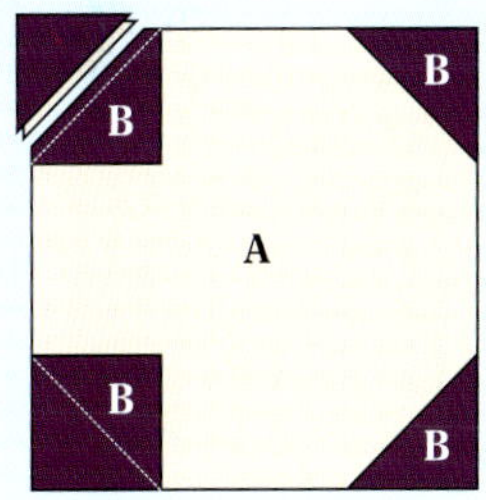

Stitch & Flip

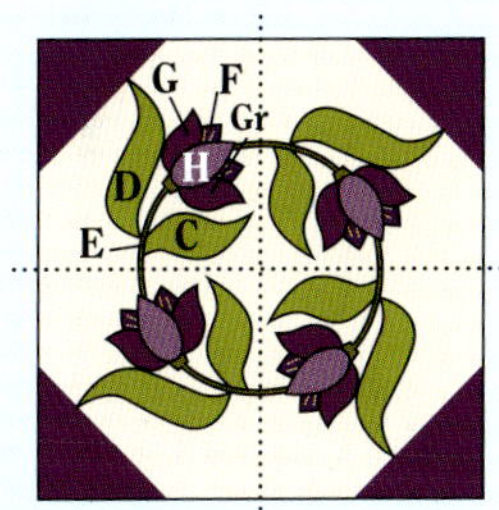

Applique Placement

Refer to "Stitch-and-Flip" in the Techniques file on the PDF. Use the cream A and dark purple B's to make the block.

Fold the block in half both ways and lightly crease the folds. Prepare patches C–H for fusible appliqué. Use the creases and appliqué placement diagram as guides to arrange the patches on the block. Fuse the patches to the block in alphabetical order. Use matching thread and a straight stitch and sew close to the patch edges.

Use a stem stitch and French knots to embroider the details on the flowers.

block no. 45

Camelia's Basket

by Dawn Heese • Linen Closet Designs
dawnheesequilts.blogspot.com

Dawn Heese is the author of *Cottage Charm* and *Geese in the Rose Garden* for Kansas City Star Quilts, pickledish.com.

See page 81 on the PDF for pattern

Beige Tone-on-Tone
1 square (A) 13½″ x 13½″ (trim to 12½″ x 12½″ after appliqué)
Blue Print
1 bias strip 1″ x 18″
1 pattern B
Mauve Print
2 pattern C
1 pattern F
Light Pink Print
2 pattern D
1 pattern E
2 Green Prints
from *1*
2 pattern G
from *1*
2 pattern H

Fold A in half diagonally both ways and lightly crease the folds. Refer to "Bias Strips" in the Techniques file on the PDF to make the basket handle. Prepare patches B–H for turned-edge appliqué.

Use the creases and appliqué placement diagram as guides to arrange the handle and patches on A. The stitch diagrams are on the PDF in the Techniques file. Use matching thread and a blind stitch to appliqué the patches in place. Center the appliqué and trim A to 12½" × 12½".

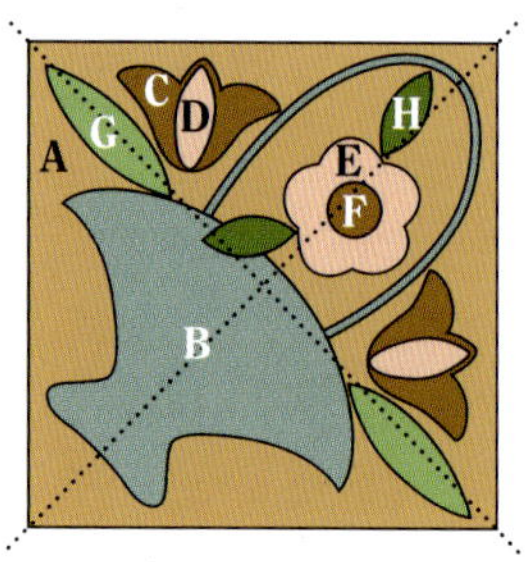

Applique Placement

block no. 46

Party Frock

by Kay Mackenzie
kaymackenzie.com, allaboutappliqué.net

Kay Mackenzie is the author of several books, including the new *Inspired by Tradition: 50 Appliqué Blocks in 5 Sizes* for Martingale & Co., martingale-pub.com.

See page 104 on the PDF for pattern

Cream Tone-on-Tone
1 square (A) 13½″ x 13½″ (trim to 12½″ x 12½″ after appliqué)
Brown Tone-on-Tone
1 *each* patterns B and C
Yellow Print
1 *each* patterns D and F
Red Print
1 pattern E
Green Tone-on-Tone
1 pattern G
Fusible web

Template for Party Frock block on page 104 of the PDF Templates file.

Fold A in half both ways and lightly crease the folds. Prepare patches B–G for fusible appliqué.

Use the creases and appliqué placement diagram as guides to arrange the patches on A. Fuse the patches to A in alphabetical order. Use matching thread and a small blanket stitch to sew around the patches. Center the appliqué and trim A to 12½" × 12½".

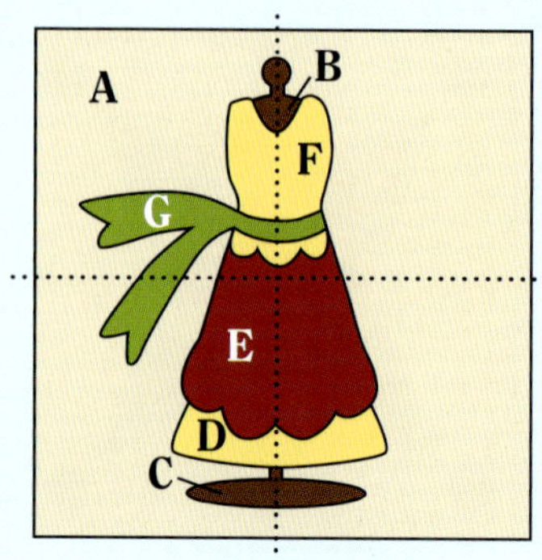

Applique Placement

block no. 47

Pretty Bird

by Marian Mapes

Fabric: Batiks and Handpaints by Hoffman California Fabrics, hoffmanfabrics.com.

See page 94 on the PDF for pattern

Dark Green Batik
1 square (A) 13½"x 13½" (trim to 12½"x 12½" after appliqué)

Assorted Gold, Orange, and Purple Batiks
1 *each* patterns B–J

2 Green Batiks
from *1*
1 pattern K
from *1*
1 pattern L

Fusible web

Fold A in half both ways and lightly crease the folds. Prepare patches B–L for fusible appliqué.

Use the creases and appliqué placement diagram as guides to arrange the patches on A. Fuse the patches to A in alphabetical order. Use matching thread and a machine straight stitch to sew close to the edges of all of the patches. Center the appliqué and trim A to 12½"× 12½".

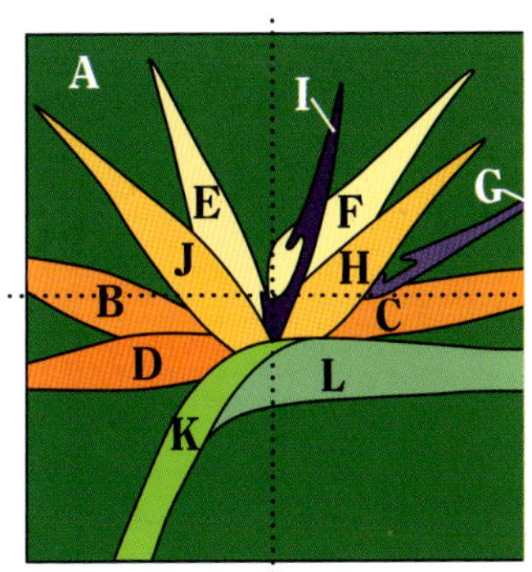

Applique Placement

block no. 48

Freedom

by Susan Marth • Suzn Quilts
suznquilts.com

See page 101 on the PDF for pattern

Tan Print
1 square (A) 13½"x 13½" (trim to 12½"x 12½" after appliqué)

Blue Print
1 *each* patterns B, C, E–H
2 pattern D

Black Tone-on-Tone
1 pattern I

Assorted Red Prints
2 pattern J
3 pattern K

Fusible web

Tan embroidery floss

Template for Freedom block on page 101 of the PDF Templates file.

Fold A in half both ways and lightly crease the folds. Prepare patches B–K for fusible appliqué.

Use the creases and appliqué placement diagram as guides to arrange the patches on A. Fuse the patches to A. Use tan thread and a blanket stitch to sew around the patches. Center the appliqué and trim to 12½" × 12½".

Applique Placement

block no. 49

Mediterranean Tile

by Lynda Milligan and Nancy Smith • Possibilities
possibilitiesquilt.com

Lynda Milligan and Nancy Smith design fabric for Quilting Treasures, quiltingtreasures.com, and publish books and patterns through their company, Possibilities, possibilitiesquilt.com.

See page 85 on the PDF for pattern

Tan Batik
1 square (A) 13½″ x 13½″ (trim to 12½″ x 12½″ after appliqué)
Light Green Batik
4 *each* patterns B, C and Cr
Medium Green Batik
4 *each* patterns C and Cr
Purple Batik
4 pattern D
1 pattern F
Orange Batik
4 pattern E
Gold Batik
4 pattern F
Fusible web

Template for Mediterranean Tile block on page 85 of the PDF Templates file.

Fold A in half both ways and lightly crease the folds. Prepare patches B–F for fusible appliqué.

Use the creases and appliqué placement diagram as guides to arrange the patches on A. Fuse the patches to A in alphabetical order. Use matching thread and a machine blanket stitch to sew around the patches. Center the appliqué and trim to 12½" × 12½".

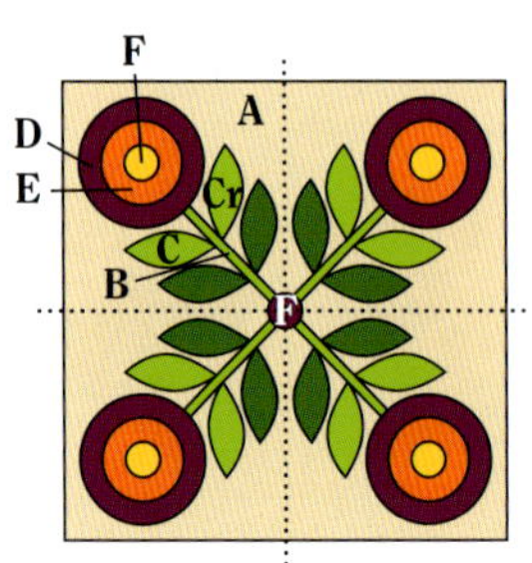

Applique Placement

block no. 50

Sharon's Roses

by Sharon Pederson • Nine Patch Media
ninepatchmedia.com

Sharon Pederson is the author of *Reversible Quilts, More Reversible Quilts, Sensational Sashiko, Color for the Terrified Quilter, Machine Appliqué for the Terrified Quilter,* and *The Rose of Shron Block Book* for Martingale & Co., martingale-pub.com.

See page 84 on the PDF for pattern

Light Peach Batik
1 square (A) 13½″ × 13½″ (trim to 12½″ × 12½″ after appliqué)
Assorted Purple Batiks
2 *each* patterns B and F
1 pattern I
Assorted Peach Batiks
2 pattern G
Assorted Green Batiks
1 bias strip 1″ x 20″ for stems
4 pattern C
2 *each* patterns D and H
10 pattern E
1 pattern I
Fusible web

Fold A in half both ways and lightly crease the folds. Refer to "Bias Strips" in the Techniques file on the PDF to make the stems. Cut 2 stems 7" and 2 stems 1½". Prepare patches B–I for fusible appliqué. Use the creases and appliqué placement diagram as guides to arrange the stems and patches on A. Fuse the patches to A in alphabetical order. Use invisible thread and a machine blind stitch to sew around the patches. Center the appliqué and trim A to 12½" × 12½".

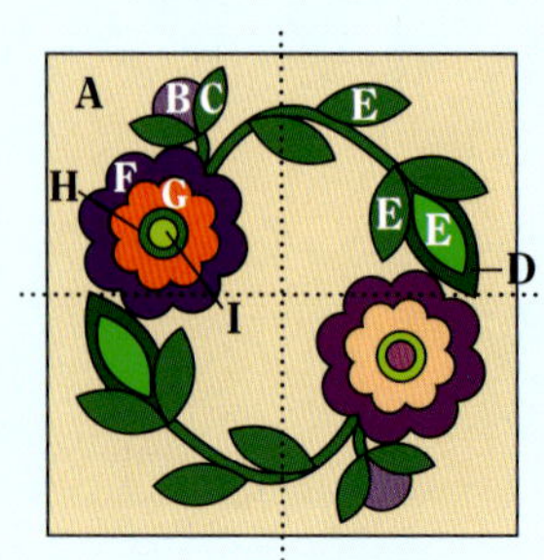

Applique Placement

block no. 51

Night Lights

by Gina Reddin • Splinters and Threads
splintersandthreads.com

"Night Lights" is also digitized for use on an embroidery machine at splintersandthreads.com.

See page 104 on the PDF for pattern

Black Tone-on-Tone
1 square (A) 13½″ × 13½″ (trim to 12½″ × 12½″ after appliqué)

Lime Green Batik
4 pattern B

Orange Batik
4 pattern Br

Dark Blue Batik
4 pattern C

Light Blue Batik
4 pattern D

Fusible web

Tear-away stabilizer

Fold A in half both ways and lightly crease the folds. Prepare patches B–D for fusible appliqué.

Use the creases and appliqué placement diagram as guides to arrange the patches on A. Fuse the patches to A. Using tear-away stabilizer on the back and matching thread, satin stitch the 2 long sides of the Br and C patches and around all 4 sides of the B and D patches.

Remove the excess stabilizer. Center the appliqué and trim A to 12½″ × 12½″.

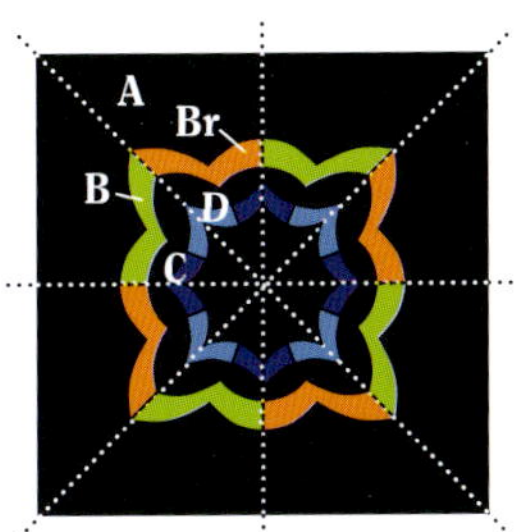

Applique Placement

block no. 52

Spring Trumpets

by Pat Sloan • Pat Sloan & Co.
patsloan.com

Fabric: Red Rose Farm by Elizabeth Scott for P&B Textiles, pbtex.com.

Pat Sloan is the author of *Fast Forward Quilts* for Leisure Arts, Inc., leisurearts.com.

See page 95 on the PDF for pattern

White Tone-on-Tone
1 square (A) 13½″ × 13½″ (trim to 12½″ × 12½″ after appliqué)

Pink Print
4 pattern B

Pink Stripe
4 pattern C

Green Dot
4 pattern D
1 pattern G

Light Blue Dot
12 pattern E
1 pattern F

Fusible web

Fold A in half both ways and lightly crease the folds. Prepare patches B–G for fusible appliqué.

Use the creases and appliqué placement diagram as guides to arrange the patches on A. Fuse the patches to A in alphabetical order. Use matching thread and a machine blanket stitch to sew around the patches. Center the appliqué and trim A to 12½″ × 12½″.

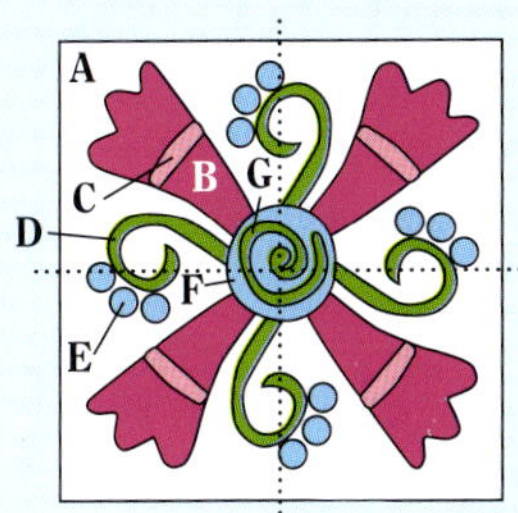

Applique Placement

block no. 53

Blooming Trumpets

by Martha Walker • Wagons West Designs
wagonswestdesigns.com

See page 74 on the PDF for pattern

Cream Print
1 square (A) 13½" × 13½" (trim to 12½" × 12½" after appliqué)

Green Tone-on-Tone
4 *each* patterns B, Br and C

Red Print
1 pattern D

Gold Tone-on-Tone
1 pattern E

Teal Print
1 pattern F
4 pattern G

Red Tone-on-Tone
16 pattern H

Fold A in half both ways and lightly crease the folds. Prepare patches B–H for turned-edge appliqué.

Use the creases and appliqué placement diagram as guides to arrange the patches on A. Use matching thread and a blind stitch to appliqué the patches in place. Center the appliqué and trim A to 12½" × 12½".

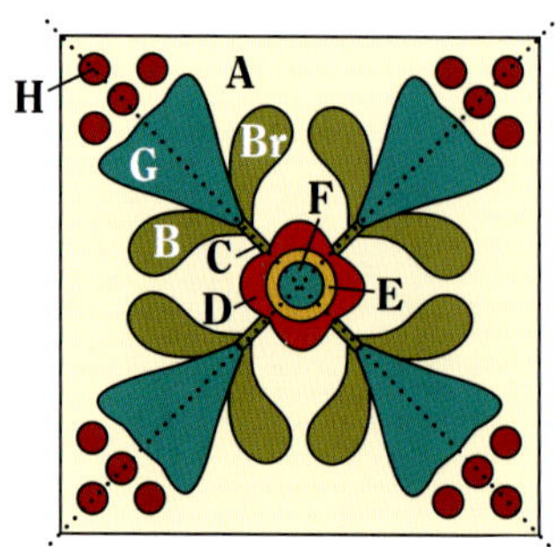

Applique Placement

block no. 54

Spring's Best

by Ann Weber • Gingham Girls
ginghamgirls.biz

Fabric: Bliss by Bonnie and Camille and Origins by Basic Gray, both for Moda Fabrics, unitednotions.com.

See page 84 on the PDF for pattern

Aqua Print
1 square (A) 13½" × 13½" (trim to 12½" × 12½" after appliqué)

Green Print
bias strip 1½" x 12"

Brown Tone-on-Tone
2 pattern B
1 pattern Br

Green Tone-on-Tone
2 pattern C
1 pattern Cr

Red Tone-on-Tone
12 pattern D

Pink Tone-on-Tone and Pink Print
from *each*
6 pattern D

Gold Print
1 pattern E

Red Check
1 pattern F

Fusible web

Fold A in half both ways and lightly crease the folds. Prepare patches B–F for fusible appliqué. Refer to "Bias Strips" in the Techniques file on the PDF to make the stem.

Use the creases and appliqué placement diagram as guides to arrange the stem and patches on A. Fuse the patches to A in alphabetical order. Use matching thread and a straight stitch to sew around the stem. Use matching thread and a machine blanket stitch to sew around the patches. Center the appliqué and trim A to 12½" × 12½".

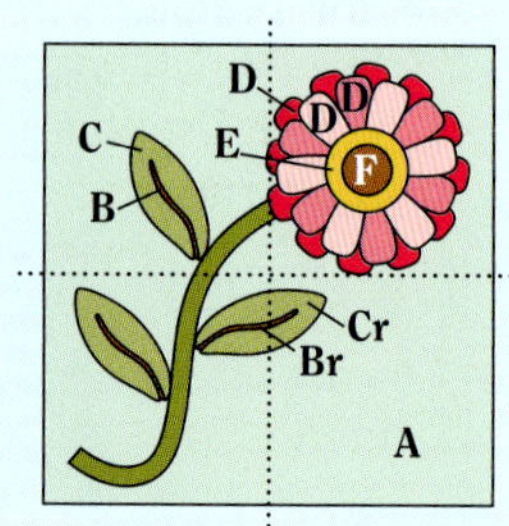

Applique Placement

block no. 55
Winter Friends

by Lynette Anderson • Lynette Anderson Designs
lynetteandersondesigns.com.au

See page 126 on the PDF for pattern

Light Blue Print
1 square (A) 13½" × 13½"
(trim to 12½" × 12½" after appliqué)
Assorted White Prints
1 *each* patterns B and D
Light Blue Tone-on-Tone
1 pattern C
Brown Tone-on-Tone
1 *each* patterns E and F
White Wool
7 pattern G
Red Wool
1 *each* patterns H and I
Dark Blue Wool
1 *each* patterns J and K
Fusible web
Embroidery floss

Fold A in half both ways and lightly crease the folds. Prepare patches B–F for turned-edge appliqué. Use the creases and appliqué placement diagram as guides to arrange the patches on A. Use matching thread and a blind stitch to appliqué the patches in place.

Prepare patches G–K for fusible appliqué; fuse in place. Use matching thread and a long single stitch to make snowflakes over the G's. Use matching thread and a blanket stitch to sew around the remaining patches. Refer to page 126 in the Templates file on the PDF for embroidery placement. Use French knots to make the gold star. Use a backstitch, satin stitch, running stitch, long single stitch and French knots to add the other embroidery details as shown. Center the appliqué and trim A to 12½" × 12½".

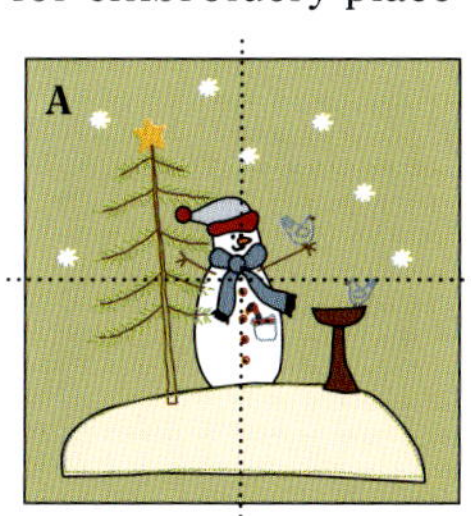

Applique Placement

block no. 56
Basket Full of Posies

by Jina Barney • Jina Barney Designz
jinabarneydesignz.com

Fabric: Happier designed by Deena Rutter for Riley Blake Designs, rileyblakedesigns.com.

See page 126 on the PDF for pattern

White Solid
1 square (A) 13½" x 13½"
(trim to 12½" x 12½" after appliqué)
Green Print #1
1 bias strip 1" x 25" for stems and basket trim
5 pattern B
2 pattern C
Green Print #2
8 pattern B
Assorted Prints
3 pattern D
2 pattern E
7 circles 2½" diameter for small yo-yos
3 circles 3" diameter for large yo-yos
Orange Stripe
1 pattern F

Refer to "Bias Strips" in the Techniques file on the PDF to make the stems and basket trim. Cut 3 stems 4" long and 2 stems 1½" long. Cut the basket trim 8½" long. Make 10 yo-yos for the flower centers and basket trim.

Fold A in half both ways and lightly crease the folds. Prepare patches B–F for turned-edge appliqué. Use the creases and appliqué placement diagram as guides to arrange the patches, stems and basket trim on A. Tuck the ends of the basket trim behind the basket (F).

Use matching thread and a blind stitch to appliqué the patches in place. Tack the yo-yos to the flower centers and basket trim as shown. Center the appliqué and trim A to 12½" x 12½".

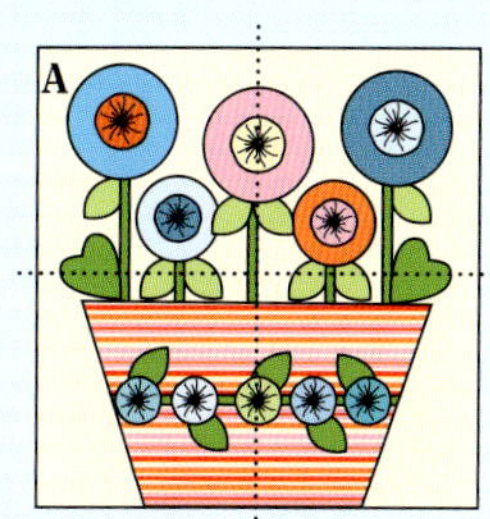

Applique Placement

block no. 57

Cogwheel Daisy

by Debbie Beaves • Violet Patch Quilts
violetpatch.com

Fabric: Simple Pleasures designed by Debbie Beaves for RJR Fabrics, rjrfabrics.com.

See page 119 on the PDF for pattern

Light Blue Print
1 square (A) 13½" × 13½" (trim to 12½" × 12½" after appliqué)

Gold Print
1 circle (B) 12" diameter
6 pattern G

Green Print
6 pattern C

Orange Print #1
1 circle (D) 8" diameter

2 Medium Blue Prints
from *each*
3 pattern E

Orange Print #2
1 circle (F) 4" diameter

Debbie used complete circles rather than individual appliqué patches for the gold B and orange D rings and the orange circle F. To reduce bulk, trim away the excess background fabric behind each layer after it's added.

Fold A in half both ways and lightly crease the folds. Prepare patches B–G for turned-edge appliqué. Use the creases and appliqué placement diagram as guides to arrange the patches on A.

Use matching thread and a blind stitch to appliqué the patches in place. Center the appliqué and trim to 12½"× 12½".

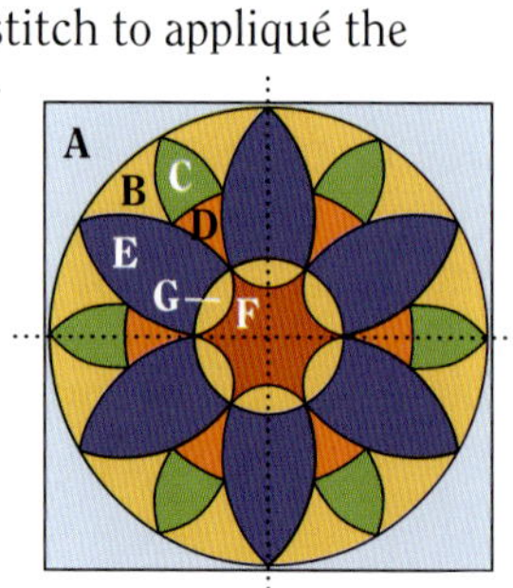

Applique Placement

block no. 58

Welcome Home

by Jenifer Dick • 42 Quilts
milo-designs.blogspot.com

Jenifer Dick is the author of *The Circuit Rider's Quilt* and *Grapefruit Juice and Sugar* for Kansas City Star Quilts, pickledish.com.

See page 140 on the PDF for pattern

Light Gold Tone-on-Tone
1 square (A) 13½"× 13½" (trim to 12½"× 12½" after appliqué)

Black Tone-on-Tone and Tan Check
from *each*
4 squares (B) 1½"× 1½"

Red Tone-on-Tone
1 square (B) 1½"× 1½"

Medium Green Tone-on-Tone
4 *each* patterns C, Cr and D

Dark Gold Print
4 pattern E

Dark Green Tone-on-Tone
4 *each* patterns F and Fr

Nine Patch

Fold A in half both ways and lightly crease the folds. Sew the 9 B's together as shown to make the Nine Patch. Prepare the Nine Patch and patches C–Fr for turned-edge appliqué. Use the creases and appliqué placement diagram as guides to arrange the Nine Patch in place, followed by the patches (note that patches F and Fr slightly overlap the Nine Patch).

Use monofilament thread and a blind stitch to appliqué the patches in place. Center the appliqué and trim A to 12½"× 12½".

Applique Placement

block no. 59

Floral Medallion

by Monique Dillard • Open Gate
opengatequilts.com

Monique Dillard is the author of *Fat Quarter Winners* for C&T Publishing, ctpub.com.

See page 143 on the PDF for pattern

Tan Tone-on-Tone
1 square (A) 13½" × 13½"
(trim to 12½" × 12½" after appliqué)

Green Tone-on-Tone
4 *each* patterns B and E

Red Print #1
4 pattern C
1 pattern H

Red Print #2
4 pattern D
1 pattern F

Pink Tone-on-Tone
1 pattern G

Pink Print
1 pattern I

Fold A in half both ways and lightly crease the folds. Prepare patches B–I for turned-edge appliqué. Use the creases and appliqué placement diagram as guides to arrange the patches on A.

Use matching thread and a blind stitch to appliqué the patches in place. Center the appliqué and trim A to 12½" × 12½".

Applique Placement

block no. 60

In My Garden

by Jennifer Schifano Eutsler • Curlicue Creations
curlicuecreations.etsy.com

See page 144 on the PDF for pattern

Cream Tone-on-Tone
1 square (A) 13½" × 13½"
(trim to 12½" × 12½" after appliqué)

Dark Green Tone-on-Tone #1
1 pattern B
2 *each* patterns F, Fr and G
1 pattern Gr

Gold Tone-on-Tone
1 pattern C

Red Tone-on-Tone
1 pattern D

Brown Print
1 pattern E
1 *each* patterns N–P

Light Green Print
3 pattern G
2 pattern Gr

Purple Print
1 pattern H

Blue Print
1 *each* patterns I–L

Dark Green Tone-on-Tone #2
1 pattern M

Fusible web

Applique Placement

Fold A in half both ways and lightly crease the folds. Prepare patches B–P for fusible appliqué. Use the creases, appliqué placement diagram and template on page 144 of the PDF Template file as guides to arrange the patches on A. Fuse the patches to A in alphabetical order.

Use matching thread and a zigzag stitch to sew around the patches. Center the appliqué and trim A to 12½" × 12½".

block no. 61

Christmas Partridge

by Beth Ferrier • Applewood Farm
applewoodfarmquilts.com

Beth Ferrier is the author of *More! Hand Appliqué by Machine* for Applewood Farm Publications, applewoodfarmquilts.com.

See page 141 on the PDF for pattern

Cream Tone-on-Tone
1 square (A) 13½"x 13½"
(trim to 12½"x 12½" after appliqué)
Light Gold Tone-on-Tone
bias strip 1"x 30" for circle
Brown Tone-on-Tone
bias strip 1"x 9" for branch
Assorted Batiks
1 set of appliqué patches
Bead 1 at ¼"
Embroidery floss
Tear-away stabilizer

Fold A in half both ways and lightly crease the folds. Refer to "Bias Strips" in the Techniques file on the PDF to make the gold circle and the branch. Prepare patches B–M for turned-edge appliqué. Use the creases, appliqué placement diagram and pattern sheet as guides to arrange the bias strips and patches in alphabetical order on A.

Using tear-away stabilizer on the back, appliqué the patches in place with monofilament thread and a machine zigzag stitch. Embroider veins on the leaves and details for the wing and eye using embroidery floss and an outline stitch. Use a backstitch to add the beak, tail and neck detail. Sew the bead in place for the eye.

Center the appliqué and trim A to 12½"× 12½".

Applique Placement

block no. 62

Rose Bud Reel

by Susan Garman
suegarmanblogspot.com

See page 147 on the PDF for pattern

Cream Tone-on-Tone
1 square (A) 13½"x 13½" (trim to 12½"x 12½" after appliqué)
Red Tone-on-Tone
4 pattern B
1 pattern D
Green Print
1 pattern C

Fold A in half both ways and lightly crease the folds. Prepare patches C and D for turned-edge appliqué. Refer to "Reverse Appliqué" in the Techniques file on the PDF. The dashed lines on C indicate the placement of B for reverse appliqué. Use the creases and appliqué placement diagram as guides to arrange the patches on A.

Use matching thread and a blind stitch to appliqué the patches in place. Center the appliqué and trim A to 12½"× 12½".

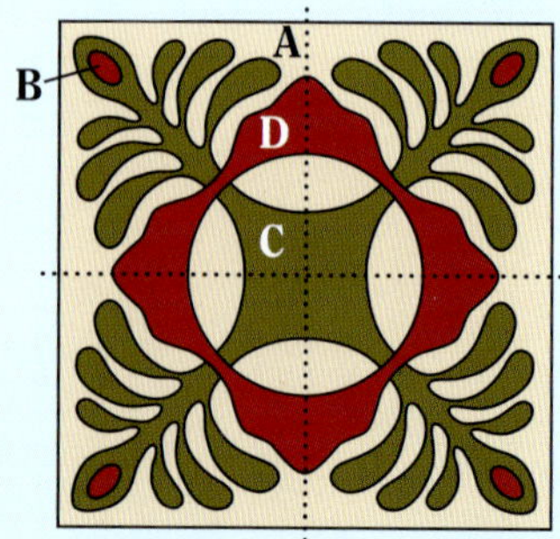

Applique Placement

block no. 63

Winter Blooms

by Cheryl Haynes • Prairie Grove Peddler
prairiegrovepeddler.com

See page 122 on the PDF for pattern

Tan Tone-on-Tone
1 square (A) 13½"x 13½" (trim to 12½"x 12½" after appliqué)
Red Stripe
1 pattern B
Red Dot
1 *each* patterns C and D
Green Tone-on-Tone
6 pattern E
Cream Prints
30 pattern F
Embroidery floss
Fusible web

Fold A in half both ways and lightly crease the folds. Prepare patches B–F for fusible appliqué. Use the creases, appliqué placement diagram and pattern sheet as guides to arrange the patches on A. Fuse the patches to A in alphabetical order.

Use matching thread and a machine blind stitch to sew around the patches. Use green embroidery floss and a chain stitch to make the stems. Use gold embroidery floss to make French knots at the center of each flower as shown. Center the appliqué and trim A to 12½"× 12½".

Applique Placement

block no. 64

Tulip Time

by Linda Jenkins • Piece O' Cake Designs
pieceocake.com

Linda Jenkins and her partner, Rebecca Goldsmith of Piece O' Cake Designs are the authors of numerous titles including *Fresh Picked Posies* for C&T Publishing, ctpub.com.

See page 160 on the PDF for pattern

Light Gray Print
1 square (A) 13½"x 13½" (trim to 12½"x 12½" after appliqué)
Aqua Print
4 pattern B
Green Solid
4 pattern C
Red Print
4 pattern D
Black Print
4 pattern E
1 pattern G
Light Green Print
4 pattern F

Fold A in half both ways and lightly crease the folds. Prepare patches B–F for turned-edge appliqué. Use the creases and appliqué placement diagram as guides to arrange the patches on A.

Use matching thread and a blind stitch to appliqué the patches in place. Center the appliqué and trim to 12½"× 12½".

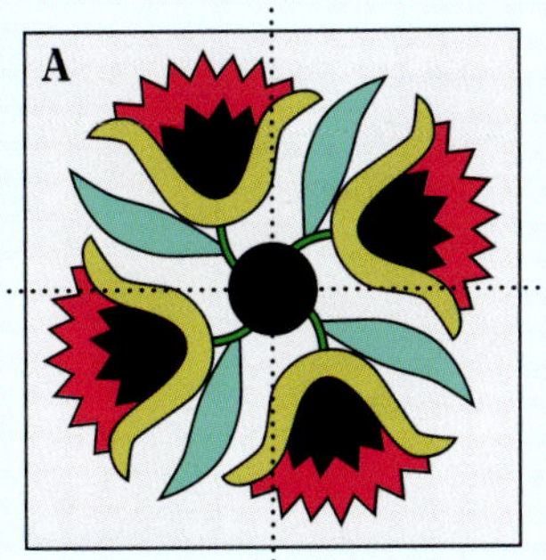

Applique Placement

block no. 65

Watermelon

by Weeks Ringle and Bill Kerr • Fun Quilts
funquilts.com

Weeks Ringle and Bill Kerr are the authors of *Quilts Made Modern* for C&T Publishing, ctpub.com.

See page 131 on the PDF for pattern

Gold Plaid
 1 square (A) 12½"x 12½"
Medium Green Print
 1 pattern B
Light Green Tone-on-Tone
 1 pattern C
Pink Print
 1 pattern D
Black Solid
 9 pattern E
Freezer paper (optional)

Template for Watermelon block on page 131 of the PDF Templates file.

Fold A in half both ways and lightly crease the folds. Prepare the curved edges of patches B–E for turned-edge appliqué.

Optionally, make a freezer-paper pattern for patches B–D. Pin the patterns shiny side up on the wrong side of the fabric. Fold the seam allowance over the freezer paper and press, making sure to not touch the paper with the iron. When positioning a patch, lightly press. The coating on the freezer paper will hold it in place.

Use the creases and appliqué placement diagram as guides to arrange B on A. Use matching thread and a blind stitch to appliqué around the patch. Trim away the excess background fabric. Repeat with patches C and D, trimming the bottom fabric layer after each patch addition. Appliqué the seeds in place with a zigzag stitch.

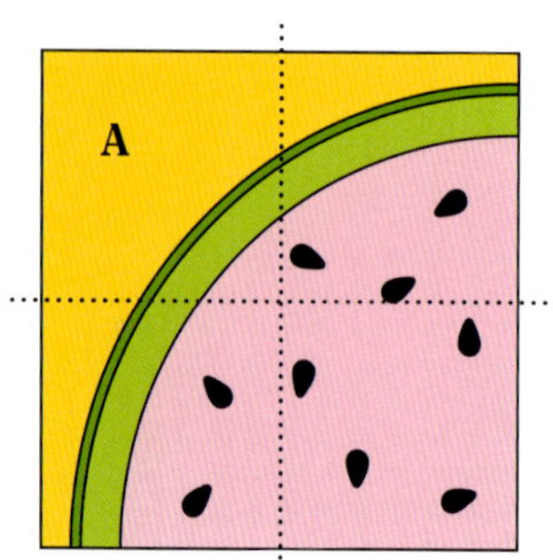

Applique Placement

block no. 66

Heartlets

by Kay Mackenzie • By Kay Mackenzie
kaymackenzie.com

Kay Mackenzie is the author of several books, including *Inspired by Tradition: 50 Appliqué Blocks in 5 Sizes* for Martingale & Co., martingale-pub.com.

See page 121 on the PDF for pattern

White Print
 1 square (A) 13½"x 13½"
 (trim to 12½"x 12½" after appliqué)
Medium Green Tone-on-Tone
 bias strip 1¼"x 30"
Light Green Tone-on-Tone
 5 pattern B
Pink Plaid
 3 pattern C
Pink Tone-on-Tone
 4 pattern D

Refer to "Bias Strips" in the Techniques file on the PDF to make stems from the medium green print. Cut 1 stem 18½" long and 1 stem 11½" long.

Fold A in half both ways and lightly crease the folds. Prepare patches B–D for turned-edge appliqué. Use the creases and appliqué placement diagram as guides to arrange the patches on A. The stitch diagrams are in the Techniques file. Use matching thread and blind stitch to appliqué the patches in place. Center the appliqué and trim A to 12½"× 12½".

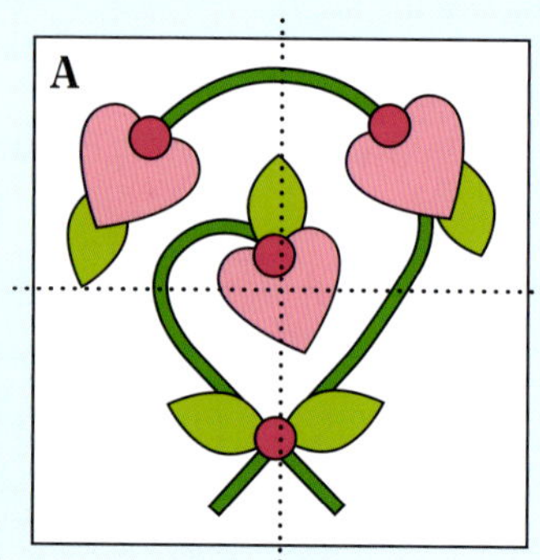

Applique Placement

block no. 67

Olde St. Nick

by Susan Marth • Suzn Quilts
suznquilts.com

See page 131 on the PDF for pattern

Green Dot
1 square (A) 13½″ x 13½″
(trim to 12½″ x 12½″ after appliqué)

White Tone-on-Tone
1 *each* patterns B and D

Light Peach Tone-on-Tone
1 pattern C

Red Print
1 pattern E

White Print
1 *each* patterns F and G

Fusible web

Fold A in half both ways and lightly crease the folds. Prepare patches B–G for fusible appliqué. Use the creases, appliqué placement diagram and pattern sheet as guides to arrange the patches on A. Fuse the patches to A in alphabetical order.

Use black thread and a blanket stitch to sew around the patches. Use a satin stitch to add the eyes. Center the appliqué and trim to 12½" × 12½".

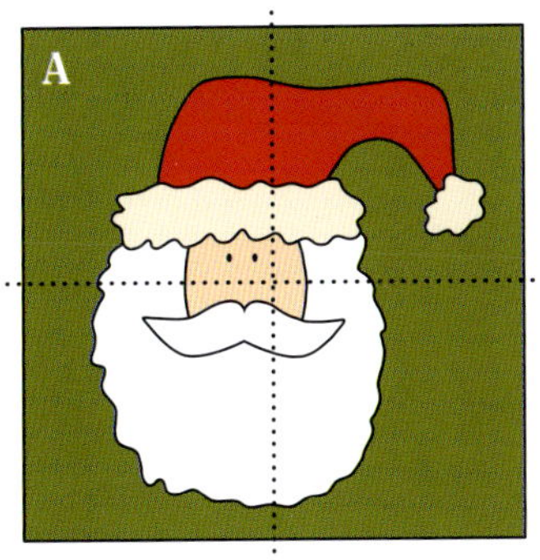

Applique Placement

block no. 68

Please Don't Eat the Daisies

by Janet Maurer • For You Too! Pattern Company
foryoutoopatterns.com

See page 122 on the PDF for pattern

Lime Green Tone-on-Tone
1 square (A) 13½″ x 13½″ (trim to 12½″ x 12½″ after appliqué)

Assorted Prints
1 set of appliqué patches

Button
1 at ½″

Appliqué pressing sheet (optional)

Blue and green embroidery floss

Fusible web

Fold A in half both ways and lightly crease the folds. Prepare the appliqué patches for fusible appliqué. Use the creases, appliqué placement diagram and pattern sheet as guides to arrange the patches on A. Fuse the patches to A in alphabetical order.

Applique Placement

To use the appliqué pressing sheet, arrange the bunny, daisy, stem and leaves as shown and lightly fuse to the pressing sheet. Let the patches cool; peel off and use the creases and assembly diagram as guides to position the patches on A. Fuse the 2 remaining petals in place as shown.

Use matching thread and a machine satin stitch to sew around the patches and add the detail to the bunny. Use embroidery floss and a backstitch to add detail to the petals and leaves. Add the button for the bunny's eye. Center the appliqué and trim A to 12½" × 12½".

block no. 69

Prickly Pear Cactus

by Cleo Mounday • Cleo's Designs
cleodesigns.com

See page 124 on the PDF for pattern

Cream Batik
1 square (A) 13½" x 13½"
(trim to 12½" x 12½" after appliqué)

Assorted Orange Batiks
1 *each* patterns B—G, Br—Gr and V

Assorted Green Batiks
1 *each* patterns H, Hr, I, Ir, L, M, S, Q and X

Assorted Gold Batiks
1 *each* patterns J, K, N, O, P, R, T, U and W

Brown Batik
cactus spine patterns

Fusible web

Fold A in half both ways and lightly crease the folds. Prepare patches B–X and the cactus spines for fusible appliqué. Use the creases, appliqué placement diagram and pattern sheet as guides to arrange the patches on A. Fuse the patches to A in alphabetical order; fuse the spines in place.

Cleo used a variegated thread to machine blanket stitch around the petals.

Use matching thread and a machine blanket stitch to sew around the patches. To add the stamens with dark yellow thread, first attach the darning foot on your sewing machine and lower the feed dogs. Then using a straight stitch, freehand the stamens at the center of the flower. Center the appliqué and trim A to 12½" × 12½".

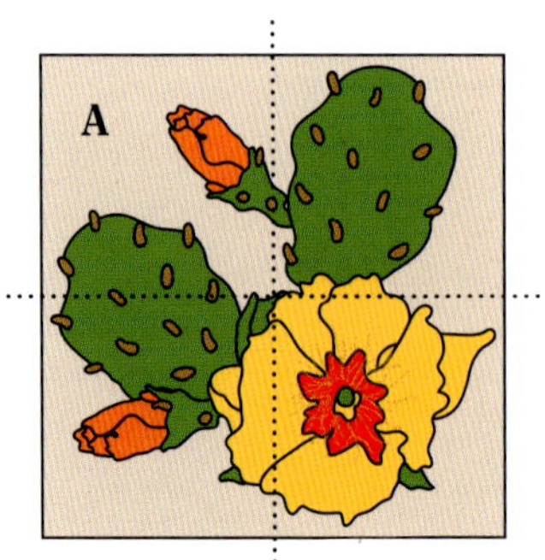

Applique Placement

block no. 70

The Balancing Act

by Denise Russart
justquiltin.wordpress.com

See page 125 on the PDF for pattern

Cream Tone-on-Tone
1 square (A) 13½" x 13½"
(trim to 12½" x 12½" after appliqué)

Assorted Prints and Tone-on-Tones
1 set of appliqué patches

Embroidery floss

Fold A in half both ways and lightly crease the folds. Prepare patches B–L for turned-edge appliqué. Use the creases and appliqué placement diagram as guides to arrange the patches on A.

Use matching thread and a blind stitch to appliqué the patches in place. Use a stem stitch to add the butterfly detail. Center the appliqué and trim A to 12½" × 12½".

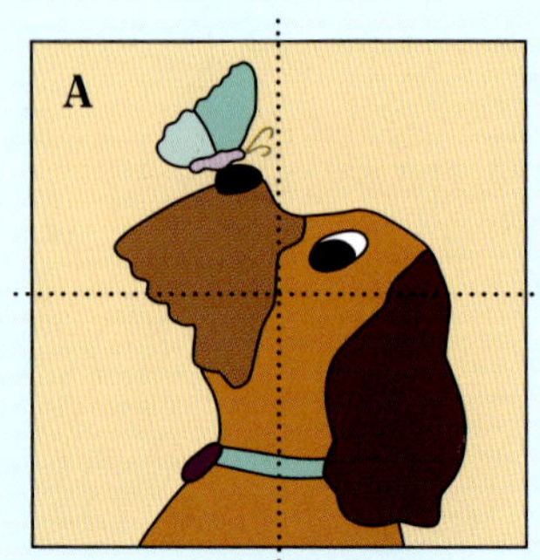

Applique Placement

block no. 71

Posie Pathway

by Erin Russek • One Piece at a Time Quilts
erinrussek.typepad.com

See page 123 on the PDF for pattern

White Solid
1 square (A) 13½″x 13½″ (trim to 12½″x 12½″ after appliqué)

Medium Green Tone-on-Tone #1
4 pattern B
4 *each* patterns D and Dr

Dark Pink Tone-on-Tone
4 pattern C
8 pattern H

Medium Green Tone-on-Tone #2 and Dark Green Tone-on-Tone
from *each*
4 *each* patterns D and Dr

Light Pink Check
5 pattern E

Light Green Print
1 pattern F

Yellow Dot
1 pattern G
1 pattern I

Fold A in half both ways and lightly crease the folds. Prepare patches B–I for turned-edge appliqué. Use the creases and appliqué placement diagram as guides to arrange the patches on A. Note that the leaves (D and Dr) are arranged from lightest to darkest.

Use matching thread and a blind stitch to sew around the patches. Center the appliqué and trim A to 12½"× 12½".

Applique Placement

block no. 72

Bee Inspired

by Maribeth Schmit • Materialgirl
wiquiltjudge.com

See page 133 on the PDF for pattern

Tan Tone-on-Tone
1 square (A) 13½″x 13½″
(trim to 12½″x 12½″ after appliqué)

Assorted Prints and Tone-on-Tones
1 set of appliqué patches

Black and brown fabric markers

Black embroidery thread

Fusible web

Fold A in half both ways and lightly crease the folds. Prepare patches B–AA for fusible appliqué. Use the creases and appliqué placement diagram as guides to arrange the patches on A. Fuse the patches to A in alphabetical order.

Use dark thread and a machine blanket stitch to sew around the stems, leaves, flowers and hive. Use embroidery thread and a running stitch for the bee's path and a stem stitch around the bee body and wings. Add detail to the bee body and wings with fabric markers. Center the appliqué and trim A to 12½"× 12½".

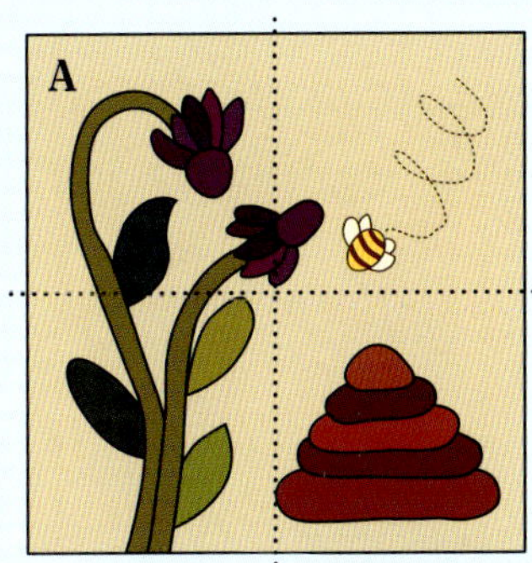

Applique Placement

block no. 73

Buckle Up

by Ann Weber • Gingham Girls LLC
ginghamgirls.biz

See page 140 on the PDF for pattern

White Tone-on-Tone
1 square (A) 13½"x 13½"
(trim to 12½"x 12½" after appliqué)

Light Green Print
1 pattern B

Yellow Check
1 pattern C

Brown Tone-on-Tone
1 pattern D

Gold Print
3 pattern E

Assorted Pink Prints
18 pattern F

Assorted Green Tone-on-Tones
6 pattern G

Fold A in half both ways and lightly crease the folds. Prepare patches B–G for turned-edge appliqué. Use the creases and appliqué placement diagram as guides to arrange the patches on A.

Use matching thread and a blind stitch to appliqué the patches in place. Center the appliqué and trim A to 12½"× 12½".

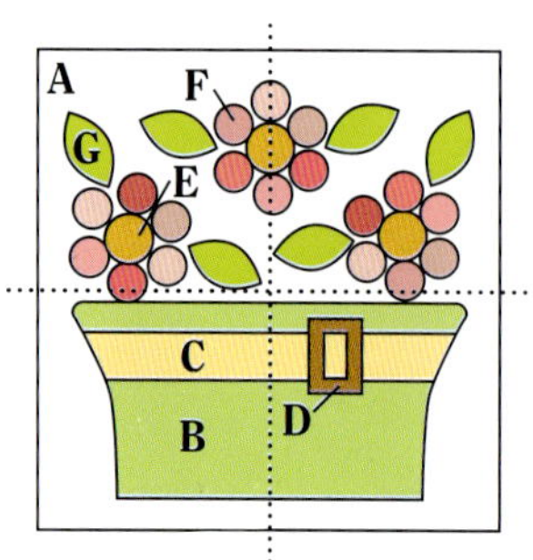

Applique Placement

block no. 74

Petite Garden

by Kellie Wulfsohn • Don't Look Now!
dontlooknow.typepad.com

See page 426 on the PDF for pattern

White Tone-on-Tone
1 square (A) 13½"x 13½"
(trim to 12½"x 12½" after appliqué)

Assorted Prints and Solids
1 set of appliqué patches

Fusible web

Tear-away stabilizer

Thin wool batting (optional)

Basting spray (optional)

Kellie used basting spray to layer a piece of wool batting to A. She used a straight stitch to sew just inside the raw edges of the patches and add the stem, leaf and bird detail. After the appliqué was complete, she cut away the batting outside each of the appliqué patches to create a trapunto effect when the background is quilted. If you prefer not to use batting, pin or baste tear-away stabilizer to the back of A.

Fold A in half both ways and lightly crease the folds. Prepare patches B–K for fusible appliqué. Use the creases and appliqué placement diagram as guides to arrange the patches on A (single flowers are C.) Fuse the patches to A in alphabetical order.

Pin or baste the batting or tear-away stabilizer to A. Use matching thread and a straight stitch to sew just inside the patches and add the stem, flower and bird detail. Use French knots for the eyes and flower detail. Remove the excess stabilizer. Center the appliqué and trim A to 12½"× 12½".

Applique Placement

block no. 75

Abloom

by Barbara Cherniwchan • Coach House Designs
coachhousedesigns.com

Fabric: Full Circle and Towne Square Quilts, both designed by Kathy Schmitz for Moda Fabrics, unitednotions.com.

See page 166 on the PDF for pattern

Beige Print
1 square (A) 13½"x 13½" (trim to 12½"x 12½" after appliqué)

Black Tone-on-Tone
4 pattern B

Black Print
4 pattern C

Red Print
4 pattern D

Fold A in half both ways and lightly crease the folds. Prepare patches B–D for turned-edge appliqué. Use the creases and appliqué placement diagram as guides to arrange the patches on A.

Use matching thread and a blind stitch to appliqué the patches in place. Center the appliqué and trim A to 12½" × 12½".

Applique Placement

block no. 76

Lyric

by Karen Comstock • Quiltricks
quiltricks.com

Fabric: Fusions for Robert Kaufman Fabrics, robertkaufman.com.

See page 103 on the PDF for pattern

Cream Tone-on-Tone
1 square (A) 13½"x 13½" (trim to 12½"x 12½" after appliqué)

Dark Brown Tone-on-Tone
bias strip ⅜"x 11"

Green Tone-on-Tone
1 *each* patterns B, G, J and Jr
3 pattern N

Dark Blue Tone-on-Tone
1 *each* patterns C and D
3 *each* patterns K and Kr

Red Tone-on-Tone
1 *each* patterns E and F
3 pattern L

Yellow Tone-on-Tone
1 pattern H
6 pattern M

Orange Tone-on-Tone
4 pattern I

Fusible web

Embroidery floss

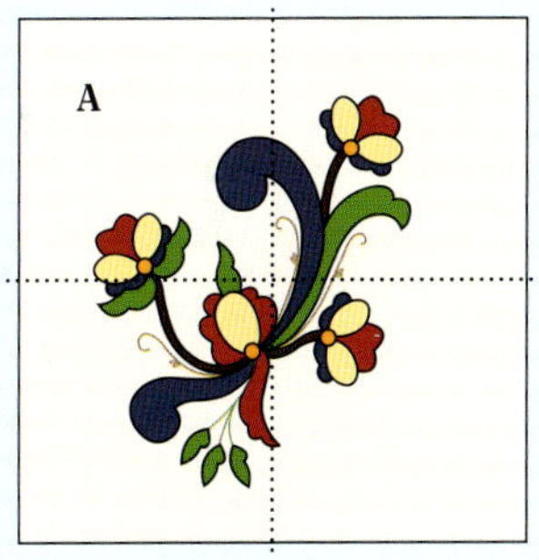

Applique Placement

Refer to "Tiny Bias Stems" in the Techniques file on the PDF. Use the brown bias strip to make the stems. Prepare patches B–N for fusible appliqué. Fold A in half both ways and lightly crease the folds. Use the creases and appliqué placement diagram as guides to arrange the patches on A. Fuse the patches to A in alphabetical order. Use matching thread and a machine blanket stitch to sew around the patches.

Use a lazy daisy stitch and backstitch with 2 strands of floss to add the embroidery detail. Center the appliqué and trim to 12½" × 12½".

block no. 77

Bluebirds and Happiness

by Sarah Fielke • The Last Piece
sarahfielke.com

Sarah Fielke is the author of *Quilting from Little Things* for Krause Publications, krausebooks.com

See page 168 on the PDF for pattern

Light Gold Dot
1 square (A) 13½"x 13½" (trim to 12½"x 12½" after appliqué)
Purple Tone-on-Tone
1 pattern B
Cream Print
1 pattern C
Pink Stripe
4 pattern D
2 Teal Prints
from *each*
2 pattern E

Fold A in half both ways and diagonally and lightly crease the folds. Prepare patches B–E for turned-edge appliqué. Use the creases and appliqué placement diagram as guides to arrange the patches on A. Use matching thread and a blind stitch to appliqué the patches in place.

Center the appliqué and trim to 12½" × 12½".

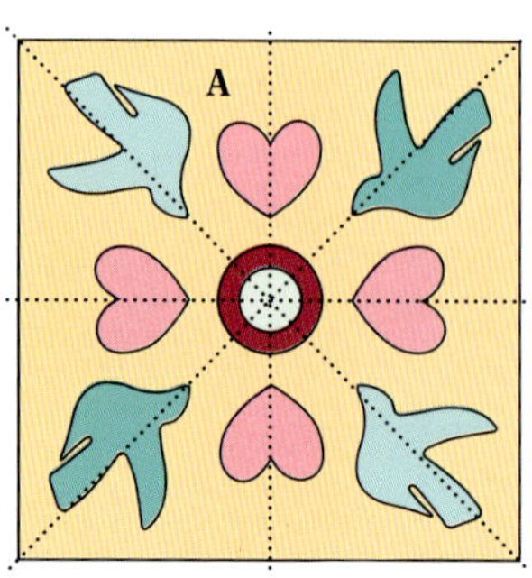

Applique Placement

block no. 78

Afternoon Frolic

by Cynthia Foster • Carter Creek Quilts
etsy.com/shop/cartercreekquilts

See page 167 on the PDF for pattern

Cream Tone-on-Tone
1 square (A) 13½"x 13½" (trim to 12½"x 12½" after appliqué)
Green Tone-on-Tone
1 pattern B
Blue Print
1 pattern C
Dark Blue Tone-on-Tone
1 pattern D
Pink Tone-on-Tone
1 pattern E
Purple Tone-on-Tone
1 pattern F
Brown Tone-on-Tone
1 pattern G
Fusible web
Tear-away stabilizer (optional)
Embroidery thread
Pink beads 14 at ⅛"
Green seed beads 77

Fold A in half both ways and lightly crease the folds. Prepare patches B–G for fusible appliqué. Use the creases and appliqué placement diagram as guides to arrange and fuse the patches on A. Sew around the patches using matching thread and a machine blanket stitch. Embroider the butterfly's antennae using a straight stitch. Center the appliqué and trim to 12½" × 12½". Refer to the beading diagrams in the Techniques file. Tack the beads in place.

Cynthia placed tear-away stabilizer on the back of her block before sewing around the appliqué.

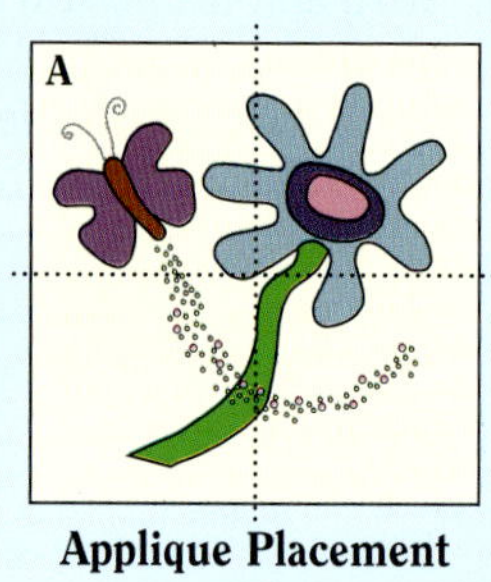

Applique Placement

block no. 79

Bird in the Boughs

by Connie Sue Haidle • Apple Blossom Quilts
appleblossomquilts.com

See page 187 on the PDF for pattern

Light Blue Batik
1 square (A) 13½" x 13½" (trim to 12½" x 12½" after appliqué)
Dark Brown Batik
1 pattern B
Gold Batik
1 pattern C
Medium Blue Batik
1 pattern D
Dark Purple Batik
1 pattern E
Medium Purple Batik
1 pattern F
Assorted Green Batiks
15 pattern G
5 pattern Gr
Red Batik
3 pattern H
Green and gold embroidery floss
Button 1 at ⅜"

Fold A in half both ways and lightly crease the folds. Prepare patches B–H for turned-edge appliqué. Use the creases and appliqué placement diagram as guides to arrange the patches on A. Use matching thread and a blind stitch to appliqué the patches in place.

Add the leaf detail and bird's feet with an outline stitch. Center the appliqué and trim to 12½" × 12½". Tack the button in place for the eye to complete the block.

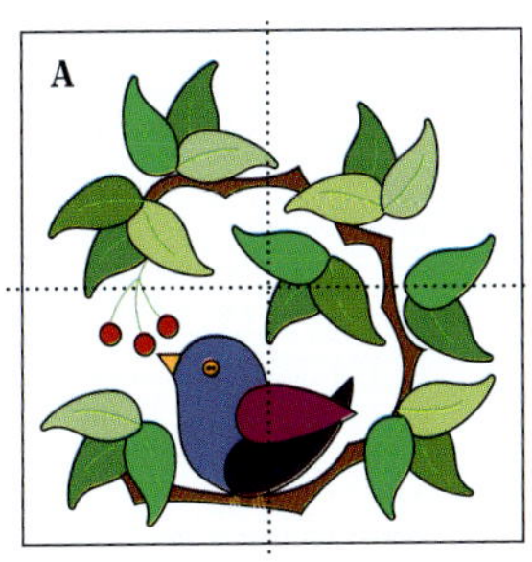

Applique Placement

block no. 80

Fresh Flowers

by Cheryl Haynes • Prairie Grove Peddler
prairiegrovepeddler.com

Fabric: Wintersong designed by Cheryl Haynes for Benartex, benartex.com.

See page 169 on the PDF for pattern

Cream Tone-on-Tone
1 square (A) 13½" x 13½" (trim to 12½" x 12½" after appliqué)
Green Tone-on-Tone
1 each patterns B, E and F
Brown Tone-on-Tone
1 pattern C
Gold Tone-on-Tone
1 pattern D
3 pattern H
Red Tone-on-Tone
3 pattern G
Fusible web
Embroidery floss
Small butterfly button

Fold A in half both ways and lightly crease the folds. Prepare patches B–H for fusible appliqué. Use the creases and appliqué placement diagram as guides to arrange the patches on A. Fuse the patches to A in alphabetical order. Use matching thread and a machine blind stitch to sew around the patches.

Using 3 strands of embroidery floss, add French knots to the flowers. Center the appliqué and trim to 12½" × 12½". Attach the small butterfly button to complete the block.

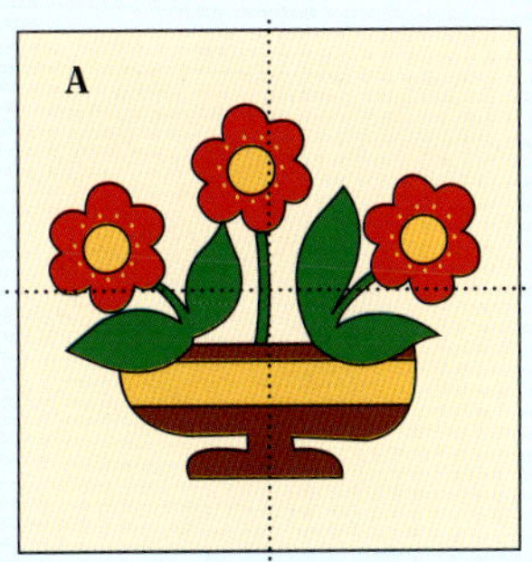

Applique Placement

block no. 81

Ray of Sunshine

by Mary Andra Holmes • Sisters' Quilting Trunk
sistersquiltingtrunk.com

Fabric: Sunkissed designed by Sweetwater for Moda Fabrics, unitednotions.com.

See page 181 on the PDF for pattern

Cream Print
1 square (A) 13½″x 13½″ (trim to 12½″x 12½″ after appliqué)

Green Print
8 pattern B

Pink Print
12 pattern C

Fold A in half horizontally, vertically and diagonally and lightly crease the folds. Prepare B's and C's for turned-edge appliqué. Use the creases and appliqué placement diagram as guides to arrange the patches on the block.

Use matching thread and a blind stitch to appliqué the patches in place.

Center the appliqué and trim A to 12½"× 12½".

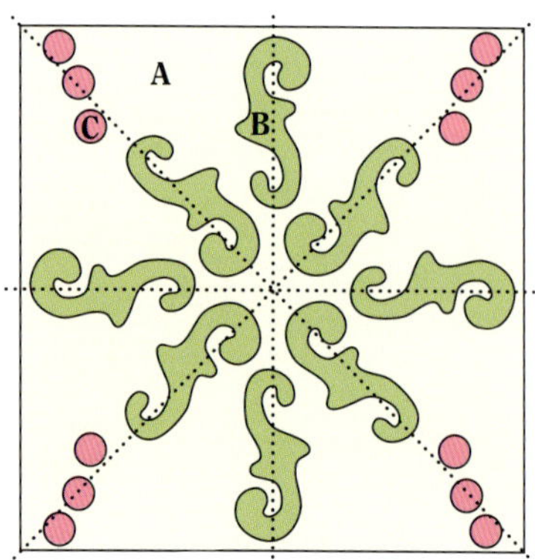

Applique Placement

block no. 82

A Riot of Bloom

by Lynda Howell • The Stitch Connection
stitchconnection.com

Lynda used decorative machine stitches to embellish her appliqué.

See page 186 on the PDF for pattern

Cream Dot
1 square (A) 13½″x 13½″ (trim to 12½″x 12½″ after appliqué)

Assorted Blue Tone-on-Tones
1 pattern B
1 pattern C

Red Print #1 and #2
from each
1 pattern D

Assorted Green Prints and Tone-on-Tones
2 pattern E and 1 pattern Er
4 pattern G
bias strip 1½″x 7″

Red Print #3
4 pattern F

Fusible web

Green rickrack 28″

Red mini rickrack 6″

Buttons 2 at ⅝″

Embroidery floss

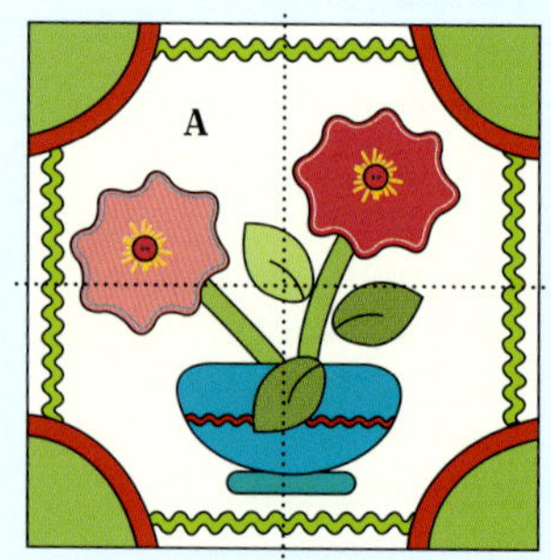

Applique Placement

Fold A in half both ways and lightly crease the folds. Refer to "Bias Strips" in the Techniques file on the PDF for the stems. Prepare B–G's for fusible appliqué. Use the creases and appliqué placement diagram as guides to arrange the green rickrack and stems on A; pin in place. Zigzag the rickrack in place with matching thread. Fuse B–G's in place. Use matching thread and a machine blanket stitch to sew around the stems and patches B–E and a blind stitch to sew around F's and G's curves. Zigzag the red rickrack in place with matching thread.

Add veins to the leaves with a machine zigzag stitch. Using 3 strands of floss, backstitch close to the edge of each flower. To make each flower center, cut 14 lengths of floss 2"-long; tie around the center of the floss bundle. Tack the floss on the flower and fluff the ends. Center the appliqué and trim to 12½"× 12½". Attach the buttons to the flowers to complete the block.

block no. 83

Lazy Daisies

by Meagan Taylor and Kristi Jones • Meags & Me
meagsandme.blogspot.com

Fabric: Shades by Kinkame for Clothworks, clothworks.com.

See page 163 on the PDF for pattern

Cream Solid
1 square (A) 13½"x 13½" (trim to 12½"x 12½" after appliqué)
Light Orange Solid and Pink Solid
from *each*
9 pattern B
Red Solid
9 pattern B
6 pattern E
4 pattern K
Yellow Solid
2 pattern C
1 pattern D
Medium Orange Solid
1 pattern C
1 pattern J
Blue Solid
1 pattern F
3 pattern G
3 pattern H
1 pattern I
Fusible web
Green embroidery floss

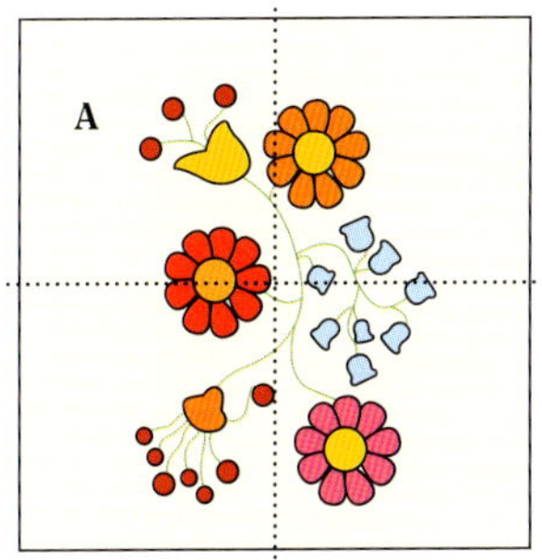

Applique Placement

Fold A in half both ways and lightly crease the folds. Prepare patches B–K for fusible appliqué. Use the creases and appliqué placement diagram as guides to arrange the patches. Fuse the patches to A in alphabetical order. Use matching thread and a machine blanket stitch to sew around the patches.

Backstitch the stem detail with 2 strands of embroidery floss. Center the appliqué and trim to 12½"× 12½".

block no. 84

Sitting Pretty

by Kay Mackenzie • By Kay Mackenzie
kaymackenzie.com

Kay Mackenzie is the author of several books including *Inspired by Tradition: 50 Appliqué Blocks in 5 Sizes* for Martingale & Co., martingale-pub.com.

See page 200 on the PDF for pattern

Cream Tone-on-Tone
1 square (A) 13½"x 13½" (trim to 12½"x 12½" after appliqué)
Red Print
1 *each* patterns B–D
Blue Print
1 *each* patterns E–F
Black Print
1 pattern G

Fold A in half both ways and lightly crease the folds. Prepare patches B–G for turned-edge appliqué. Use the creases and appliqué placement diagram as guides to arrange the patches on A.

Use matching thread and a blind stitch to appliqué around the patches. Center the appliqué and trim to 12½"× 12½".

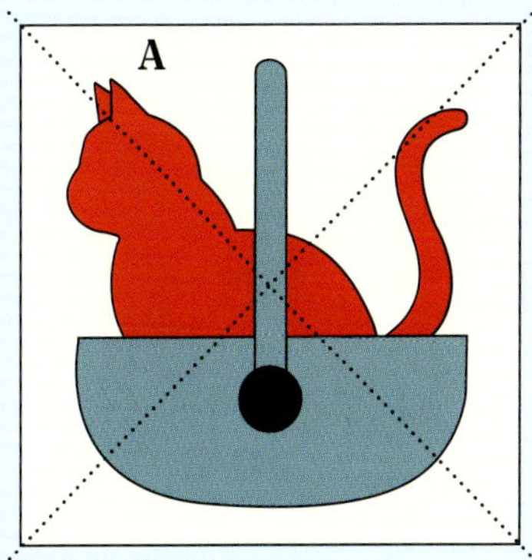

Applique Placement

block no. 85

Spring Love

by Susan Marth • Suzn Quilts
suznquilts.com

See page 182 on the PDF for pattern

Tan Dot
1 square (A) 13½″x 13½″ (trim to 12½″x 12½″ after appliqué)

Purple Print
bias strip 1½″x 26″

Pink Tone-on-Tone
4 pattern B

Yellow Tone-on-Tone
2 pattern B

Green Tone-on-Tone
6 pattern C

Fusible web

Fold A in half both ways and lightly crease the folds. Refer to "Bias Strips" in the Techniques file on the PDF to make the heart. Use the creases and appliqué placement diagram as guides to arrange the bias strip in a heart shape on A. Use matching thread and a blind stitch to appliqué the bias strip in place.

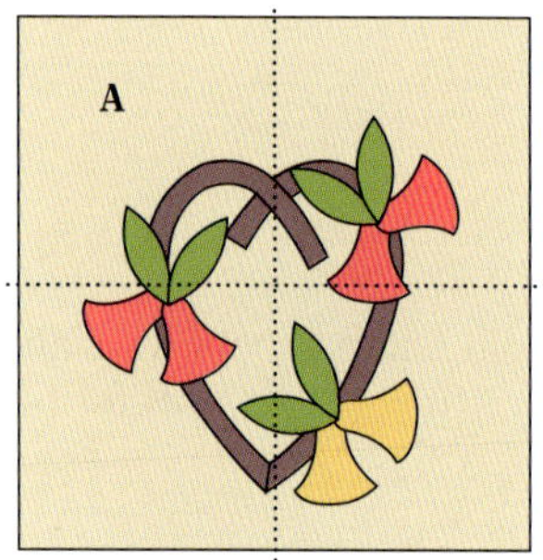

Applique Placement

Prepare patches B–C for fusible appliqué. Position the patches on the heart, then fuse in alphabetical order. Use black thread and a machine blanket stitch to sew around the patches. Center the appliqué and trim to 12½"× 12½" to complete the block.

block no. 86

Blooming Hearts

by Renelda Peldunas-Harter
Outside the Box Quilt Designs

See page 189 on the PDF for pattern

Light Blue Batik
1 square (A) 13½″x 13½″ (trim to 12½″x 12½″ after appliqué)

Dark Green Batik
2 pattern B

Medium Green Batik
2 pattern C

Assorted Red, Pink and Purple Batiks
14 pattern D

Embroidery floss

10 seed beads

Fold A in half both ways and lightly crease the folds. Prepare patches B–D for turned-edge appliqué. Use the creases and appliqué placement diagram as guides to arrange the patches on A. Use matching thread and a blind stitch to appliqué the patches in place. Using 2 strands of matching floss and an outline stitch, embroider along the edges of all patches.

Applique Placement

Center the appliqué and trim to 12½"× 12½". Refer to the beading diagram in the Techniques file. Tack 5 seed beads at the center of each flower to complete the block.

block no. 87

Dresden Love

by Helen Stubbings • Hugs 'n Kisses
hugsnkisses.net

Fabric: Beach House designed by Robyn Pandolph for RJR Fabrics, rjrfabrics.com.

Helen Stubbings is the author of *Faux Appliqué* for American Quilter's Society, americanquilter.com.

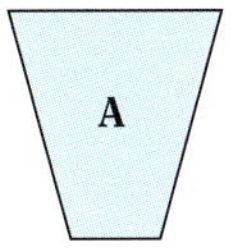

See page 176 on the PDF for pattern

Assorted Prints and Tone-on-Tones
16 template A
Tan Solid
1 square (B) 13½"x 13½"(trim to 12½"x 12½" after appliqué)
7"x 7" square for embroidered center
Pale Pink Tone-on-Tone
1 pattern D
Perle cotton

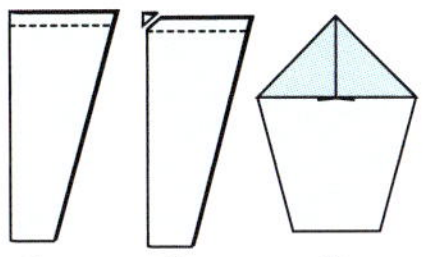

1 2 3

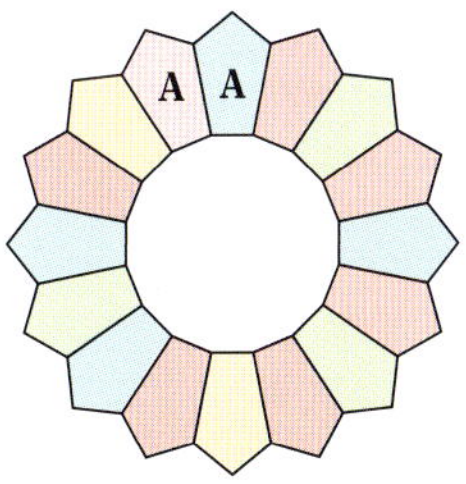

Dresden Plate

Following the diagrams, fold an A in half with right sides together and sew across the end with a ¼" seam allowance (1). Trim a tiny triangle off the folded corner as shown (2). Turn right side out, gently pushing out the point; press the seam open (3). Repeat with all A patches. Sew the A's together as shown to make the Dresden Plate.

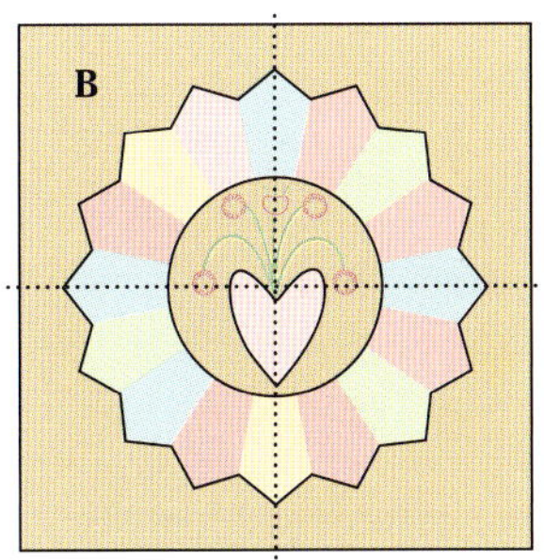

Applique Placement

Trace the circle (C) and the embroidery design onto the 7" × 7" tan square. Use pink perle cotton and a blanket stitch and a stem stitch for the flowers. Use light green perle cotton to chain stitch the stems and a long stitch to add detail to the flower. Prepare D for turned-edge appliqué. Use matching thread and a blind stitch to appliqué D in place.

Fold B in half both ways and lightly crease the folds. Cut out the embroidered C and prepare for turned-edge appliqué. Use the creases and appliqué placement diagram as guides to arrange the Dresden Plate and the C on B. Use matching thread and a blind stitch to appliqué them in place. Use a light pink perle cotton to chain stitch around C. Center the appliqué and trim to 12½" × 12½".

block no. 88

Bittersweet Basket

by Martha Walker • Wagons West Designs
wagonswestdesigns.com

Martha Walker is the author of *Be Merry: Quilts and Projects for Your Holiday Home* for Kansas City Star Quilts, pickledish.com.

See page 188 on the PDF for pattern

Cream Print
1 square (A) 13½"x 13½" (trim to 12½"x 12½" after appliqué)
Green Tone-on-Tone #1
2 bias strips 1½"x 11"
Assorted Gold Prints
8 pattern B
Red Print
8 pattern C
Green Tone-on-Tone #2
1 *each* patterns D and Dr
4 pattern E
2 pattern F
Purple Print #1
1 *each* patterns G, Gr, H and Hr
Purple Print #2
1 *each* patterns I and J
Yellow Print
5 pattern K

Fold A in half both ways and lightly crease the folds. Prepare patches B–K for turned-edge appliqué. Refer to "Bias Strips" in the Techniques file on the PDF to make the stems. Use the creases and appliqué placement diagram as guides to arrange the patches on A.

Use matching thread and a blind stitch to appliqué the stems and patches in place. Center the appliqué and trim to 12½" × 12½".

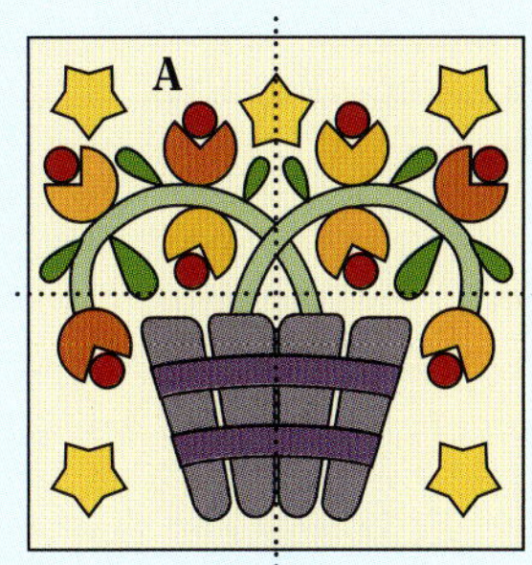

Applique Placement

block no. 89

Black-Eyed Blooms

by Barb Cherniwchan • Coach House Designs
coachhousedesigns.com

Fabric: Town Square Quilts and Crackle designed by Kathy Schmitz for Moda Fabrics, unitednotions.com.

Barb Cherniwchan is the author of *Room by Room Quilts* for Leisure Arts, Inc., leisurearts.com.

See pages 219–220 on the PDF for pattern

Tan Print
1 square (A) 13½"x 13½" (trim to 12½"x 12½" after appliqué)
Green Tone-on-Tone
1 pattern B
Tan Dot
1 pattern C
Red Tone-on-Tone
4 pattern D
Black Tone-on-Tone
4 pattern E
Freezer paper

Trace full-size B and C patterns on the paper side of the freezer paper; cut out the patterns. Pin each freezer-paper pattern with the paper side down to the wrong side of the appropriate fabric; cut out each fabric with a 3⁄16" turn-under allowance. Carefully press the turn-under allowances on the outside curves to the shiny side of the freezer paper.

Fold A in half both ways diagonally and lightly crease the folds. Use the creases and appliqué placement diagram as guides. Center the B on A; pin in place. Using matching thread and a blind stitch, appliqué along the outside curved edge of the B. Repeat to appliqué the C. Carefully cut away A behind the B and C patches to remove the freezer paper.

Prepare the D's and E's for turned-edge appliqué. Use matching thread and a blind stitch to appliqué the patches in place. Center the appliqué and trim to 12½" × 12½".

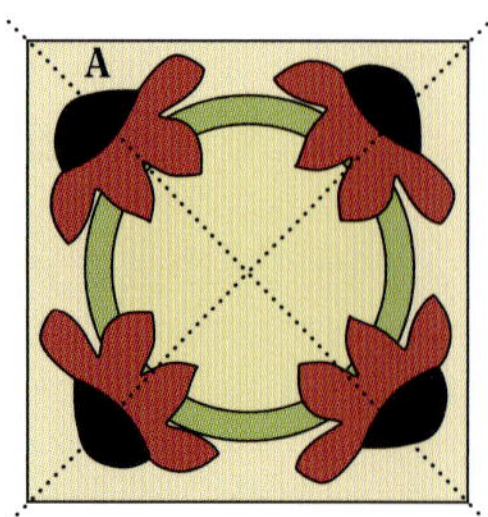

Applique Placement

block no. 90

Little Red Posies

by Beth Ferrier • Applewood Farm
applewoodfarmquilts.com

Beth Ferrier is the author of *More! Hand Appliqué by Machine* for C&T Publishing, ctpub.com.

See page 207 on the PDF for pattern

Red Tone-on-Tone
3 *each* patterns A and C
Red Dot
3 pattern B
Cream Dot
3 pattern D
7 pattern G
Cream Tone-on-Tone
1 square (E) 13½"x 13½" (trim to 12½"x 12½" after appliqué)
Dark Green Tone-on-Tone
bias strip 20"x 1¼"
3 pattern F
Light Green Tone-on-Tone
3 pattern F
Embroidery floss

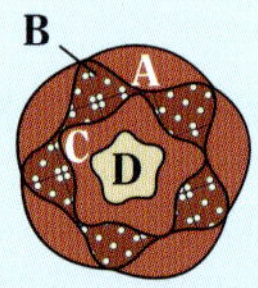

Unit
Make 3

Prepare patches A–G for turned-edge appliqué. Use matching thread and a blind stitch to appliqué B–D on each A to make 3 units as shown.

Refer to "Bias Strips" in the Techniques file on the PDF to make the stems. Fold E in half both ways and lightly crease the folds. Use the creases and appliqué placement diagram as guides to arrange the units, stems, and patches on E. Use matching thread and a blind stitch to appliqué the patches in place.

Backstitch around the B's and C's using 2 strands of matching floss. Use a chain stitch and gold floss around the D's and embellish each D with French knots. Center the appliqué and trim to 12½" × 12½".

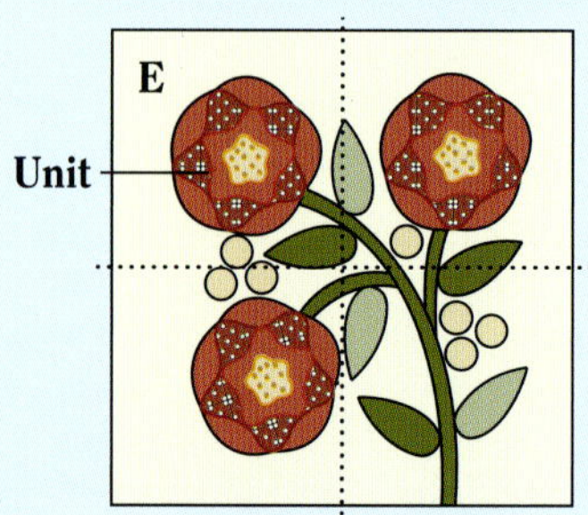

Applique Placement

block no. 91

Bird of Happiness

by Gretchen Gibbons • Celebration of Life Designs
gretchengibbons.com

Gretchen Gibbons is the author of *Pennies from Heaven: Celebrated Quilt and Companion Projects* for Martingale & Co., shopmartingale.com.

See page 202 on the PDF for pattern

Beige Tone-on-Tone
1 square (A) 13½″ x 13½″ (trim to 12½″ x 12½″ after appliqué)
Teal Dupioni Silk
1 *each* patterns B–D
Teal Wool
1 pattern E
Green Wool #1
1 pattern F
Pink Print
2 pattern G and 1 pattern Gr
Assorted Green Tone-on-Tones
3 *each* patterns H and Hr
7 pattern I
Peach Wool and Dark Pink Wool
from *each*
3 pattern J
Fusible web
Embroidery floss
6 glass seed beads

Gretchen used wool, cotton and silk for the leaves (H–I).

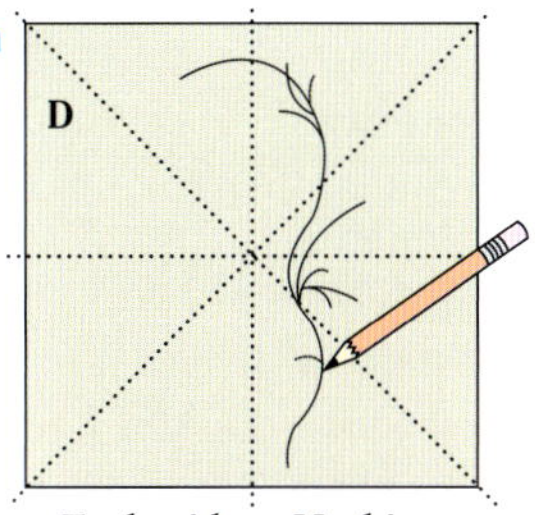

Embroidery Marking

Applique Placement

Embroidery Placement

Fold A in half both ways and diagonally and lightly crease the folds. Using the creases and embroidery marking diagram as guides, draw the stems. Prepare patches B–J for fusible appliqué. Refer to the appliqué placement diagram to arrange the patches on A. Fuse the patches in alphabetical order.

Use matching thread and a machine zigzag to appliqué the silk and cotton patches. Use 2 strands of matching floss and a hand blanket stitch for wool patches. Use a stem stitch for the stems and the flower (G and Gr) details; add French knots to the end of the flower stitches and for the bird's eye. Use a star stitch in the center of the wool buds (J). Center the appliqué and trim to 12½" × 12½". Tack a seed bead to the center of each J.

block no. 92

Love of Tulips

by Lucy Kramer-van der Sluis
Quilting with the Past • lucyquilting.blogspot.com

See page 242 on the PDF for pattern

Unbleached Muslin
1 square (A) 13½″ x 13½″ (trim to 12½″ x 12½″ after appliqué)
Dark Teal Print
bias strip 1½″ x 17″ for stems
2 pattern B
3 Assorted Red Prints
from *each*
1 pattern C
Dark Brown Print
1 square (D) 5″ x 5″

Refer to "Bias Strips" on page 82 to make stems from the dark teal print. Cut 1 stem 8" long and 2 stems 4" long.

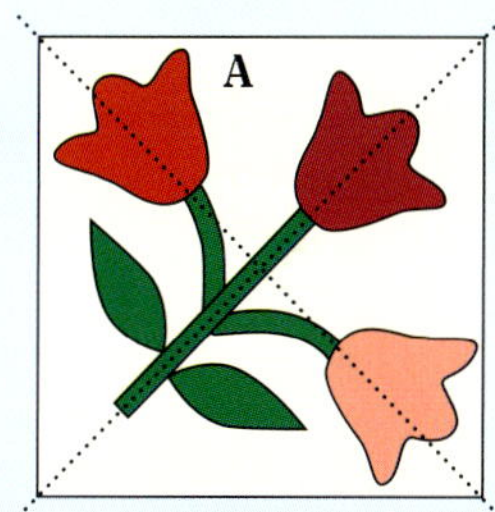

Applique Placement

Fold A in half diagonally both ways and lightly crease the folds. Prepare patches B–C for turned-edge appliqué. Use the creases and appliqué placement diagram as guides to arrange the patches on A. Use matching thread and a blind stitch to appliqué the patches in place. Center the appliqué and trim to 12½" × 12½".

Stitch & Flip

Refer to "Stitch-and-Flip" in the Techniques file on the PDF. Add the dark brown D as shown to complete the block.

block no. 93

Florida Rose

by Nancy Mahoney
nancymahoney.com

Fabric: Tonga batiks from Timeless Treasures, ttfabrics.com.

Nancy Mahoney is the author of *Fast, Fusible Flower Quilts* for Martingale & Co., shopmartingale.com.

See page 241 on the PDF for pattern

Light Gold Batik
1 square (A) 13½"x 13½" (trim to 12½"x 12½" after appliqué)
Turquoise Batik
4 *each* patterns B, C and I
12 pattern D
Red Batik
4 *each* patterns E and J
Black Batik
4 *each* patterns F and H
1 pattern K
Gold Batik
4 pattern G
1 pattern L
Fusible web

Fold A in half diagonally both ways and lightly crease the folds. Prepare patches B–L for fusible appliqué. Use the creases and appliqué placement diagram as guides to arrange the patches on A. Fuse the patches to A in alphabetical order.

Use matching thread and a machine blanket stitch to sew around the patches. Center the appliqué and trim to 12½" × 12½".

Applique Placement

block no. 94

Stars of Glory

by Jo Morton • Jo Morton Quilts
jomortonquilts.com

Fabric: Various lines designed by Jo Morton for Andover Fabrics, andoverfabrics.com.

Jo Morton is the author of many self-published books including *Vintage Journey, Banner Day* and *Prairie Flowers Encore*.

See page 243 on the PDF for pattern

Tan Print
1 square (A) 13½"x 13½" (trim to 12½"x 12½" after appliqué)
Red Print #1
1 pattern B
Red Stripe #1 and Red Print #2
from *each*
4 pattern C
Red Stripe #2
4 pattern D

Fold A in half diagonally both ways and lightly crease the folds. Prepare patches B–D for turned-edge appliqué. Use the creases and appliqué placement diagram as guides to arrange the patches on A.

Use matching thread and a blind stitch to appliqué the patches in place. Center the appliqué and trim to 12½" × 12½".

Applique Placement

block no. 95

Christmas Dove

by Susan Taylor Propst
susantaylorpropst.com

Susan Taylor Propst is the author of *Nature's Beauty in Appliqué—Pretty and Practical Projects* for Martingale & Co., shopmartingale.com.

See page 236 on the PDF for pattern

Dark Green Print
1 square (A) 13½" x 13½" (trim to 12½" x 12½" after appliqué)

Cream Tone-on-Tone
1 *each* patterns B–E

Gold Tone-on-Tone
bias strip 1" x 63" *total* (see note below)

Fusible web

Clover fusible bias-tape maker ¼" (optional)

Clover 5mm fusible web (optional)

Clover Quick Bias Tape ¼" gold lame (optional)

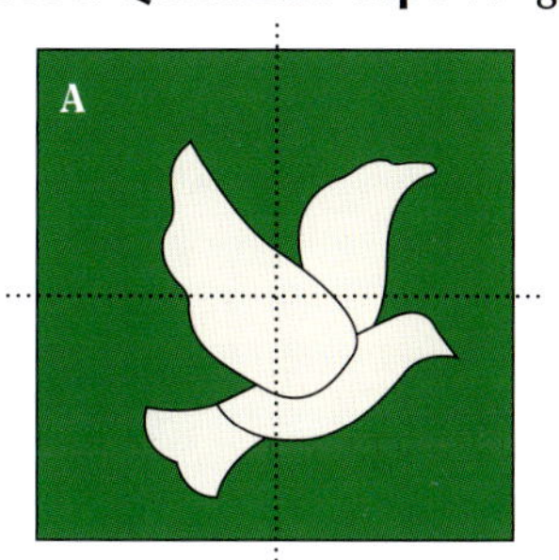

Applique Placement

Bias Strip Placement

Susan used Clover gold lame Quick Bias Tape. Optionally, you can make your own bias tape using a fusible bias tape maker and fusible web. If you prefer this method, follow the manufacturer's instructions.

Fold A in half both ways and lightly crease the folds. Prepare patches B–E for fusible appliqué. Use the creases and appliqué placement diagram as guides to arrange the patches on A. Fuse the patches in alphabetical order.

Refer to "Bias Strips" in the Techniques file on the PDF to prepare the bias strips. Refer to the diagram to arrange the bias strips on A, covering the raw edges of the appliqué patches and tucking the ends of the bias strips under other strips. Use matching thread and a blind stitch to sew the strips in place. Center the appliqué and trim to 12½" × 12½".

block no. 96

Merlin's Keystone

by Scarlett Rose • Scarlett Rose's Celtic & More
scarlettrose.com

See page 208 on the PDF for pattern

Green Solid
1 square (A) 13½" x 13½" (trim to 12½" x 12½" after appliqué)

2 Purple Batiks
from *each*
2 pattern B

On the front side of *1* B patch, mark the cutting lines. Note that the pattern is rotated to mark cutting lines on the second half of the B.

Fold A in half diagonally both ways and lightly crease the folds. Prepare both B's for turned-edge appliqué.

Using the creases and appliqué placement diagram as guides, arrange the B's on A as shown with the marked B on top. Cut the marked lines. Tuck the cut ends under the bottom B as shown to give a woven effect. Pin the patches in place.

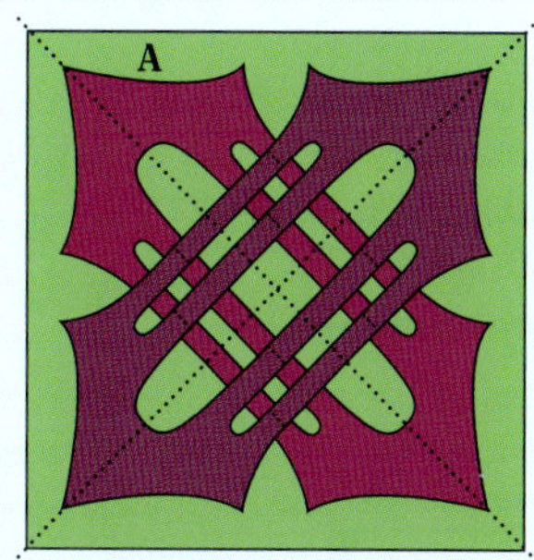

Applique Placement

The stitch diagrams are in the Techniques file on the PDF. Use matching thread and a blind stitch to appliqué the patches in place. Center the appliqué and trim to 12½" × 12½".

block no. 97
Snow Day

by Denise Russart
justquiltin.wordpress.com

Fabric: Bliss Blenders from Hoffman California Fabrics, hoffmanfabrics.com.

See page 244 on the PDF for pattern

Light Blue Tone-on-Tone
1 square (A) 13½"x 13½" (trim to 12½"x 12½" after appliqué)
Dark Cream Tone-on-Tone
1 pattern B
2 *each* patterns K and Kr
Light Cream Tone-on-Tone
1 pattern C
Green Tone-on-Tone #1
1 pattern D
Green Tone-on-Tone #2
1 pattern E
Light Purple Tone-on-Tone
1 *each* patterns F and G
Purple Tone-on-Tone
1 pattern H
Black Tone-on-Tone
1 pattern I
Gray Tone-on-Tone
1 pattern J
Embroidery floss

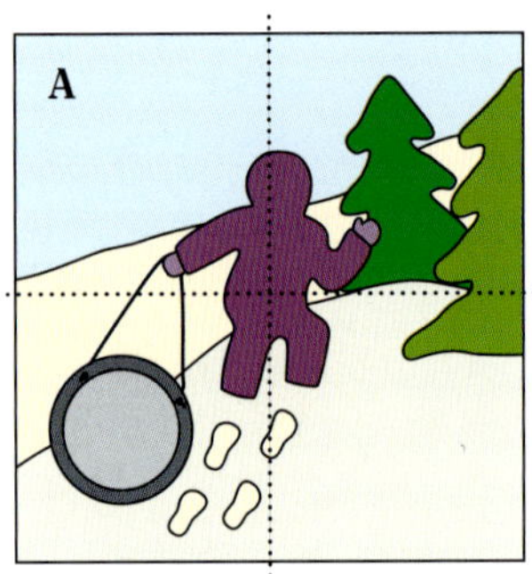

Applique Placement

Fold A in half both ways and lightly crease the folds. Prepare patches B–J for turned-edge appliqué.

Use the creases and appliqué placement diagram as guides to arrange B and C on A. Use matching thread and a blind stitch to appliqué the patches in place. Carefully trim away A behind B and C. Arrange the remaining patches on the block and appliqué in the same way. Use French knots and a backstitch for the sled rope.

Center the appliqué and trim to 12½"× 12½".

block no. 98
Heart Blossom

by Cindy Simms • Kats Design Studio
cindysimms.net

Beige Tone-on-Tone
1 square (A) 13½"x 13½" (trim to 12½"x 12½" after appliqué)
Dark Green Tone-on-Tone
bias strip 1"x 25½"
Light Green Tone-on-Tone
7 pattern B
Purple Batik
bias strip 1⅝"x 17"
Pink Tone-on-Tone
bias strip 1⅝"x 22"

Template for Heart Blossom block on page 217 of the PDF Templates file.

Applique Placement

Fold A in half horizontally, vertically and diagonally and lightly crease the folds.

Refer to "Bias Strips" in the Techniques file on the PDF to make the stems and heart. Cut the purple strip into one 7" and one 10" length. Cut the pink strip into one 7½" and one 14½" length. Prepare the leaves for turned-edge appliqué. Use the creases, appliqué placement diagram and heart outline on this page as guides to arrange the stems, leaves and heart on A.

Use matching thread and a blind stitch to appliqué the patches in place. Center the appliqué and trim to 12½"× 12½".

block no. 99

Happy Puppy

by Rob Stanphill • Willow Bay Designs
willowbaydesigns.com

See page 239 on the PDF for pattern

Blue Tone-on-Tone
1 square (A) 13½"x 13½" (trim to 12½"x 12½" after appliqué)
Light Tan Solid
1 *each* patterns B, E and L
Tan Solid
1 *each* patterns C, D and M
Red Print
1 pattern F
Gold Solid
1 pattern G
Pink Solid
1 *each* patterns H, I and Q
Brown Tone-on-Tone
1 *each* patterns J and K
Black Solid
1 pattern N
White Solid
1 pattern O
Dark Red Solid
1 pattern P
Fusible web
Black and Brown permanent fabric markers

Fold A in half both ways and lightly crease the folds. Prepare patches B–Q for fusible appliqué. Use the creases and appliqué placement diagram as guides to arrange the patches on A. Fuse the patches in alphabetical order.

Use matching thread and a straight stitch to sew close to the edges of each patch. Use the black fabric marker to add the eyes and eyebrows, and the brown fabric marker to add the muzzle and body detail as shown to complete the block. Center the appliqué and trim to 12½"× 12½".

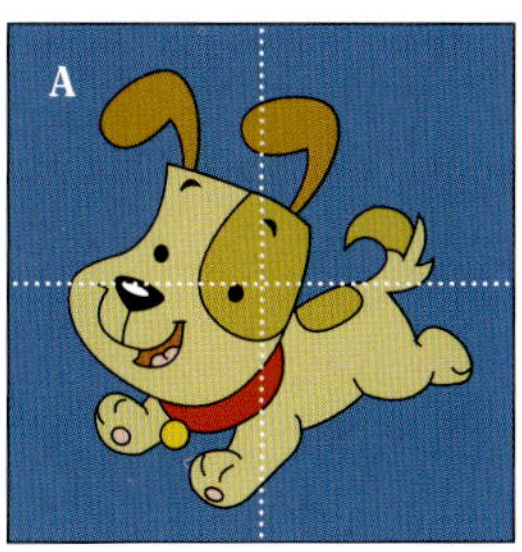

Applique Placement

block no. 100

Spring Bouquet

by Cheryl Almgren Taylor
atimetosewquilts.com

Cheryl Almgren Taylor is the author of *Inspirational Appliqué: Reflections of Faith, Hope and Love* and *Deck the Halls: Quilts to Celebrate Christmas*, for Martingale & Co., shopmartingale.com.

See page 214 on the PDF for pattern

White Tone-on-Tone
1 square (A) 13½"x 13½" (trim to 12½"x 12½" after appliqué)
Green Batik
4 pattern B
8 pattern C
20 pattern D
Light Purple Batik
16 pattern E
Yellow Batik
8 pattern F
1 pattern H
Dark Purple Batik
4 pattern G
Fusible web

Fold A in half horizontally, vertically and diagonally and lightly crease the folds. Prepare patches B–H for fusible appliqué. Use the creases and appliqué placement diagram as guides to arrange the patches on A. Fuse the patches to A in alphabetical order.

The stitch diagrams are in the Techniques file on the PDF. Use matching thread and a machine blanket stitch to sew around the patches. Center the appliqué and trim to 12½"× 12½".

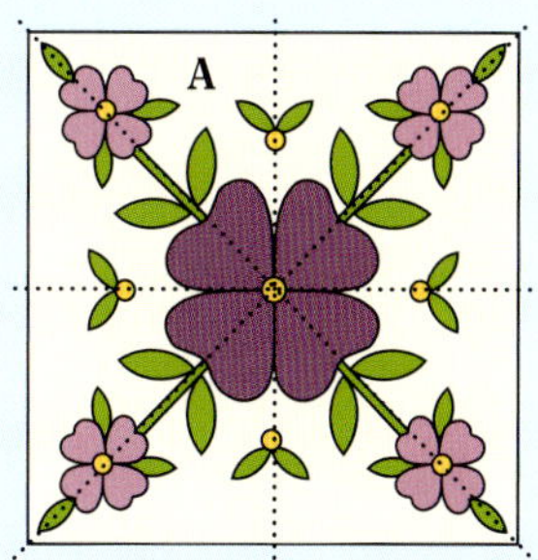

Applique Placement

block no. 101

Tango

by Jennifer Schifano Thomas • Curlicue Creations
curlicuecreations.com

See page 217 on the PDF for pattern

Teal Batik
1 square (A) 13½"x 13½" (trim to 12½"x 12½" after appliqué)
4 pattern D
28 pattern E

Black Tone-on-Tone
4 pattern B

White Solid
4 pattern C

Fusible web

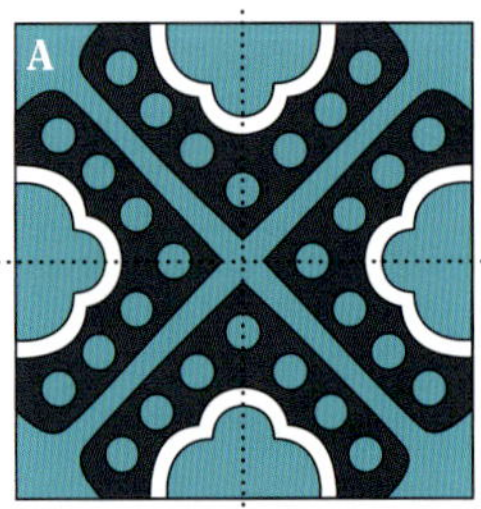

Applique Placement

Fold A in half both ways and lightly crease the folds. Prepare patches B–E for fusible appliqué. Use the creases and appliqué placement diagram as guides to arrange the patches on A. Fuse the patches to A in alphabetical order.

The stitch diagrams are in the Techniques file on the PDF. Use matching thread and a zigzag stitch to sew around the patches. Center the appliqué and trim to 12½"× 12½".

block no. 102

Fall Frolic

by Margie Ullery • Ribbon Candy Quilt Co.
ribboncandyquilts.blogspot.com

See page 205 on the PDF for pattern

Cream Tone-on-Tone
1 square (A) 13½"x 13½" (trim to 12½"x 12½" after appliqué)

Green Tone-on-Tone
4 *each* patterns B and E

Dark Orange Tone-on-Tone
1 pattern C
4 pattern D

Fusible web

Fold A in half both ways and lightly crease the folds. Prepare patches B–E for fusible appliqué. Use the creases and appliqué placement diagram as guides to arrange the patches on A. Fuse the patches to A in alphabetical order.

The stitch diagrams are in the Techniques file on the PDF. Use matching thread and a machine blanket stitch to sew around the patches. Center the appliqué and trim to 12½"× 12½".

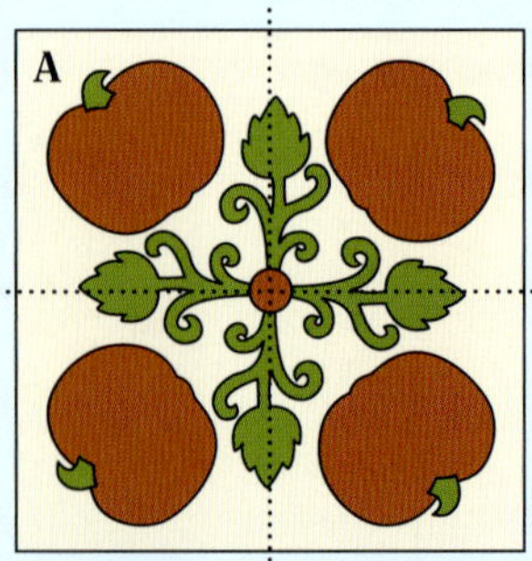

Applique Placement

block no. 103

Holiday Sue

by Mary Ellen Von Holt • Little Quilts
littlequilts.com

Mary Ellen Von Holt is a co-author of *Little Quilts All Through the House* for Martingale & Co., shopmartingale.com.

See page 206 on the PDF for pattern

Tan Check
 1 square (A) 13½"x 13½" (trim to 12½"x 12½" after appliqué)
Black Wool
 1 pattern B
Red Solid Wool
 1 *each* patterns C and F
Red Check Wool
 1 pattern D
Cream Wool
 1 *each* patterns E and H
Gold Wool
 1 pattern G
Fusible web
Embroidery floss
Buttons
 1 at 7/8"
 10 at 5/16"
 1 star at 3/4"

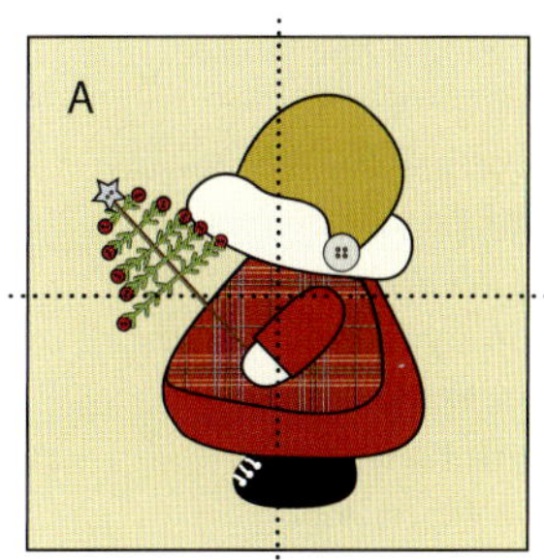

Applique Placement

Fold A in half both ways and lightly crease the folds. Prepare patches B–H for fusible appliqué. Use the creases and appliqué placement diagram as guides to arrange the patches on A. Fuse the patches to A in alphabetical order. Note that the back of the hat (G) overlaps the hat cuff (H). The stitch diagrams are in the Technique file on the PDF. Use 2 strands of matching floss and a blanket stitch to sew around the patches.

Mary Ellen used variegated floss to embroider the tree.

Use a long stitch and French knots for the shoe details. Use a stem stitch for the tree trunk and a long stitch for the branches. Tack the small buttons in place at the ends of the branches and the star button to the treetop as shown. Sew the large button to the hat as shown. Center the appliqué and trim to 12½" × 12½".

block no. 104

Dancing Leaves

by Ann Weber • Gingham Girls
ginghamgirls.biz

See page 204 on the PDF for pattern

Cream Print
 1 square (A) 13½"x 13½" (trim to 12½"x 12½" after appliqué)
3 Assorted Gold Prints
from *each*
 1 pattern B
4 Assorted Red Prints and Tone-on-Tones
from *3*
 1 pattern B
from *1*
 6 pattern C
Fusible web

Fold A in half horizontally, vertically and diagonally and lightly crease the folds. Prepare patches B–C for fusible appliqué. Use the creases and appliqué placement diagram as guides to arrange the patches on A, overlapping the leaves counterclockwise as shown. Fuse the patches to A in alphabetical order.

The stitch diagrams are in the Techniques file on the PDF. Use matching thread and a machine blanket stitch to sew around the patches. Center the appliqué and trim to 12½" × 12½".

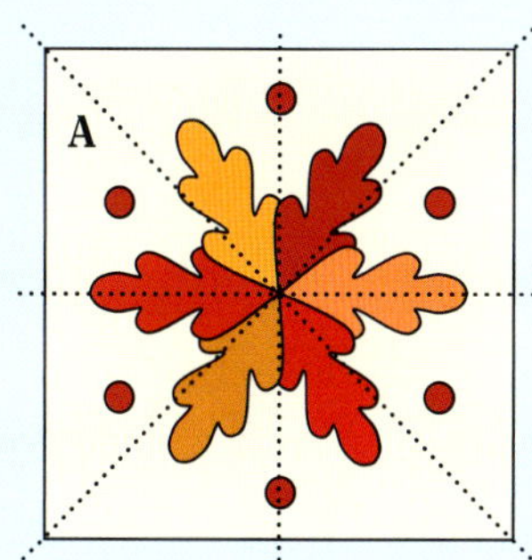

Applique Placement

block no. 105

Patches

by Barbara Bieraugel • Barbara Bieraugel Designs
barbarabieraugeldesigns.com

See page 256 on the PDF for pattern

Cream Tone-on-Tone
1 square (A) 13½" x 13½" (trim to 12½" x 12½" after appliqué)

Assorted Prints and Tone-on-Tones
1 set of appliqué patches B–DD

White and dark blue embroidery floss

Fold A half in horizontally, vertically and diagonally and lightly crease the folds. Prepare patches B–DD for turned-edge appliqué.

Use the creases and appliqué placement diagram as guides to arrange the patches on A.

To help with patch placement, you may wish to lightly trace the appliqué pattern onto A.

The stitch diagrams are in the Techniques file on the PDF. Use matching thread or a monofilament thread and a small zigzag stitch to appliqué the patches in place.

Use 2 strands of blue floss and a chain stitch for the mouth. Use 2 strands of white floss and a satin stitch for the eye detail. Center the appliqué and trim to 12½" × 12½".

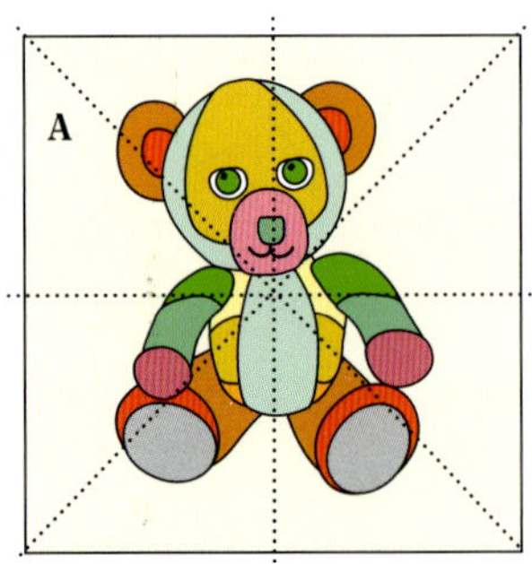

Applique Placement

block no. 106

My Retro Chair

by Cherry Guidry • Cherry Blossoms Quilting Studio
cherryblossomsquilting.com

Fabric: Hello Luscious designed by Basic Gray for Moda Fabrics, unitednotions.com.

See page 263 on the PDF for pattern

Cream Solid
1 square (A) 13½" x 13½" (trim to 12½" x 12½" after appliqué)
1 pattern Q

Green Solid
12 pattern B

Pale Turquoise Solid
1 pattern C
1 *each* patterns F and Fr

Cream Tone-on-Tone
1 pattern D
1 *each* patterns E and Er

Green Print #1
1 pattern G

Green Print #2
1 pattern H

Dark Brown Solid
1 *each* patterns I–M and O
2 pattern N

Pink Print
1 pattern P

Fusible web

Crystals 12 at ⅛" diameter

Applique Placement

Fold A in half diagonally both ways and lightly crease the folds. Prepare patches B–Q for fusible appliqué. Use the creases and appliqué placement diagram as guides to arrange the patches on A. Fuse the patches to A in alphabetical order.

The stitch diagrams are in the Techniques file on the PDF. Use matching thread and a small machine blanket stitch to sew around the patches. Use a straight stitch for the clock hands. Center the appliqué and trim to 12½" × 12½".

Affix the crystals at the clock center and spoke ends as shown to complete the block.

block no. 107

Norwegian Rosemaling

by Marcia Harmening • Happy Stash Quilts
happystashquilts.com

See page 255 on the PDF for pattern

Beige Batik
1 square (A) 13½" x 13½" (trim to 12½" x 12½" after appliqué)

Assorted Batiks
1 set of appliqué patches

Fusible web

Green embroidery floss

Fold A in half both ways and diagonally and lightly crease the folds. Prepare the appliqué patches for fusible appliqué. Use the creases and appliqué placement diagram as guides to arrange the patches on A. Fuse the patches to A in alphabetical order.

The stitch diagrams are in the Techniques file on the PDF. Use matching or monofilament thread and a straight stitch to sew around the patches. Use 2 strands of floss and an outline stitch to embroider the stems.

Center the appliqué and trim to 12½" × 12½".

Applique Placement

block no. 108

Birds of a Feather

by Meagan Taylor and Kristi Jones • Meags & Me
meagsandme.blogspot.com

Fabric: Shades designed by Kinkame for Clothworks, clothworks.com.

See page 275 on the PDF for pattern

Cream Solid
1 square (A) 13½" x 13½" (trim to 12½" x 12½" after appliqué)

White Muslin
1 square (A) 13½" x 13½" (trim to 12½" x 12½" after appliqué

Gold Solid
1 each patterns B and D

Pink Solid
1 pattern B

Yellow Solid
1 pattern Br
1 pattern G

Pale Blue Solid
1 pattern Br

Green Solid
1 each patterns B and C

Dark Pink Solid
1 pattern E

Orange Solid
1 pattern F

Fusible web

Pigma Micron pen (.01 tip)

Embroidery floss

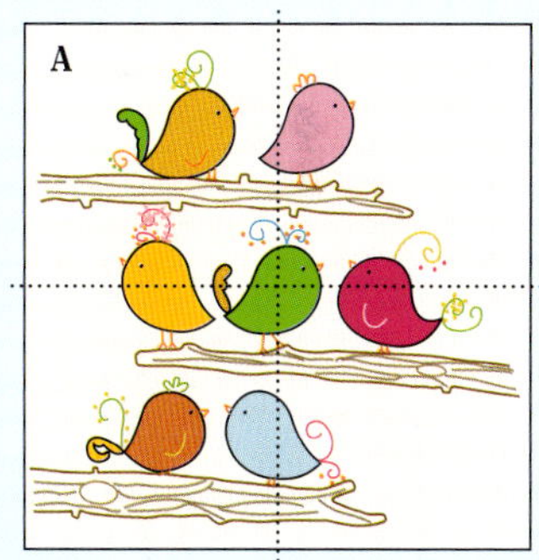

Applique and Embroidery Placement

Fold the cream square in half both ways and lightly crease the folds. Using the creases and placement diagram as guides, trace the embroidery design onto the cream A with the pen. Layer the cream fabric right side up on top of the muslin and baste them together.

Prepare patches B–F for fusible appliqué. Arrange the patches on A and fuse in place. The stitch diagrams are in the Techniques file on the PDF. Use matching thread and a machine blanket stitch to sew around the patches.

Use 2 strands of floss and a combination of backstitch, lazy daisy stitches and French knots to embroider the bird and tree details. Center the design and trim to 12½" × 12½".

block no. 109

Dream Pony

by Kay Mackenzie • By Kay Mackenzie
kaymackenzie.com

Kay Mackenzie is the author of *Scrap-Appliqué Playground* for Martingale & Co., shopmartingale.com.

See page 284 on the PDF for pattern

Medium Blue Print
1 square (A) 13½″ x 13½″ (trim to 12½″ x 12½″ after appliqué)

White Tone-on-Tone
1 *each* patterns B and M

Cream Dot
1 *each* patterns C, D and F

Black Tone-on-Tone
1 *each* patterns E and G–L

Red Tone-on-Tone
3 pattern N
2 pattern O

Pink Tone-on-Tone
3 pattern N
3 pattern O

Purple Tone-on-Tone
2 pattern N
2 pattern O

Yellow Tone-on-Tone
1 pattern N
3 pattern O

Dark Blue Tone-on-Tone
2 pattern N
1 pattern O

Fusible web

Applique Placement

Fold A in half both ways and lightly crease the folds. Prepare patches B–O for fusible appliqué. Use the creases and appliqué placement diagram as guides to arrange the patches on A. Fuse the patches to A in alphabetical order.

The stitch diagrams are in the Techniques file on the PDF. Use matching thread and a machine blanket stitch to sew around the patches.

Center the appliqué and trim to 12½″ × 12½″.

block no. 110

Mr. Snowman

by Sue Marsh • Whistlepig Creek Productions
wpcreek.com

Fabric: Polar Brigade designed by Sue Marsh for RJR Fabrics, rjrfabrics.com.

See page 262 on the PDF for pattern

Dark Blue Print
1 square (A) 13½″ x 13½″ (trim to 12½″ x 12½″ after appliqué)

White Solid
1 *each* patterns B–D and H

Orange Solid
1 pattern E

Black Solid
1 pattern F

Green Tone-on-Tone
1 pattern G

Fusible web

Tear-away stabilizer

Black embroidery floss

Star buttons
3 at ⅜″
2 at ⅝″
1 at ¾″

Applique and Embroidery Placement

Fold A in half both ways and lightly crease the folds. Prepare patches B–H for fusible appliqué. Use the creases and appliqué placement diagram as guides to arrange the patches on A. Fuse the patches to A in alphabetical order.

The stitch diagrams are in the Techniques file on the PDF. Using tear-away stabilizer on the back and matching thread, satin stitch around the patches. Satin stitch the arms with brown thread. Use 2 strands of floss to make French knots for the eyes and a crossstitch for the mouth. Remove the stabilizer.

Center the appliqué and trim to 12½″ × 12½″. Tack the buttons in place on the hat and snowman as shown to complete the block.

block no. 111

Carrot Run

by Michelle May • The Raspberry Rabbits
theraspberryrabbits.com

Fabric: Wool Felt from National Nonwovens, nationalnonwovens.com.

Michelle May is the author of *Briarside Lane* for The Raspberry Rabbits, theraspberryrabbits.com.

See page 260 on the PDF for pattern

Cream Tone-on-Tone
1 square (A) 13½"x 13½" (trim to 12½"x 12½" after appliqué)

Black Wool Felt
2 *each* patterns B and Br

Green Wool Felt
4 pattern C

Orange Wool Felt
4 pattern D

Fusible web

Embroidery floss

Fold A in half both ways and lightly crease the folds. Prepare patches B–D for fusible appliqué. Use the creases and appliqué placement diagram as guides to arrange the patches on A. Fuse the patches to A in alphabetical order.

The stitch diagrams are in the Techniques file on the PDF. Use 3 strands of embroidery floss and a long running stitch to appliqué the patches in place and to add the leaf and carrot details. Use French knots for the rabbit eyes.

Center the appliqué and trim to 12½" × 12½" to complete the block.

Applique Placement

block no. 112

Scooter Girl

by Rob Stanphill • Willow Bay Designs
willowbaydesigns.com

See page 286 on the PDF for pattern

Turquoise Dot
1 square (A) 13½"x 13½" (trim to 12½"x 12½" after appliqué)

Assorted Prints and Tone-on-Tones
1 set of appliqué patches

Fusible web

Nonstick, see-through pressing sheet

Black, brown and red permanent fabric markers

Dark red crayon

Prepare the appliqué patches for fusible appliqué.

A pressing sheet is used to fuse appliqué patches together to create more stable units.

On a hard ironing surface, lay a nonstick, see-through pressing sheet on top of the appliqué pattern. Arrange the girl and scooter appliqué patches over the pattern; lightly fuse the patches to one another on top of the pressing sheet. Allow the patches to cool and gently remove from the pressing sheet.

Fold A in half both ways and lightly crease the folds. Use the appliqué placement diagram and creases as guides to arrange patches on A as shown; fuse in place.

Use matching thread and a straight stitch to sew close to the edges of each patch.

Use the black marker to add the eyes, eyebrows, coat buttons and scooter detail. Use the brown marker for the ear, nose and fingers. Use the crayon for blush. Add the mouth and coat placket with the red marker.

Center the appliqué and trim to 12½" × 12½" to complete the block.

Applique Placement

block no. 113

Summer's End

by Jennifer Schifano Thomas • Curlicue Creations
curlicuecreations.com

Fabric: Wool and Needle Flannels designed by Primitive Gatherings for Moda Fabrics, unitednotions.com.

See pages 248 and 258 on the PDF for pattern

Cream Tone-on-Tone
1 square (A) 13½″x 13½″ (trim to 12½″x 12½″ after appliqué)

Dark Brown Tone-on-Tone #1 Flannel
2 rectangles (B) 3½″x 4¾″

Dark Brown Tone-on-Tone #2 Flannel
1 rectangle (B) 3½″x 4¾″

Green Tone-on-Tone Flannel
1 *each* patterns C, F, Lr, M and N

Cream Plaid Flannel
1 *each* patterns D, J and P

Dark Red Tone-on-Tone Flannel
1 *each* patterns E and Er

Green Plaid Flannel
1 *each* patterns G, K, L and Mr

Assorted Red Plaid Flannels
9 pattern O
1 *each* patterns H, Hr and I

Fusible web

Template plastic

Cut 1

Applique Placement

Fold A in half both ways and lightly crease the folds. Sew the dark brown B's together as shown. Make a full-size plastic template of Q. Trace and cut Q from the joined B's. Prepare patches C–Q for fusible appliqué. Use the creases and appliqué placement diagram as guides to arrange the patches on A. Fuse the patches to A in alphabetical order.

Use matching thread and a small zigzag stitch to sew around the patches. Center the appliqué and trim to 12½" × 12½".

block no. 114

Simple Life

by Martha Walker • Wagons West Designs
wagonswestdesigns.com

Martha Walker is the author of *Annie's Scrapbag* for Wagons West Designs, wagonswestdesigns.com.

See pages 281–282 on the PDF for pattern

Pale Gold Tone-on-Tone
1 square (A) 13½″x 13½″ (trim to 12½″x 12½″ after appliqué)

Blue Tone-on-Tone
1 pattern B

Dark Red Print
1 pattern C

Pink Tone-on-Tone
2 pattern D

Tan Print
1 pattern E

Green Tone-on-Tone
bias strip 1¼″x 31″
6 pattern F

Dark Gold Tone-on-Tone
1 pattern H

Red Print
2 pattern G
4 pattern I

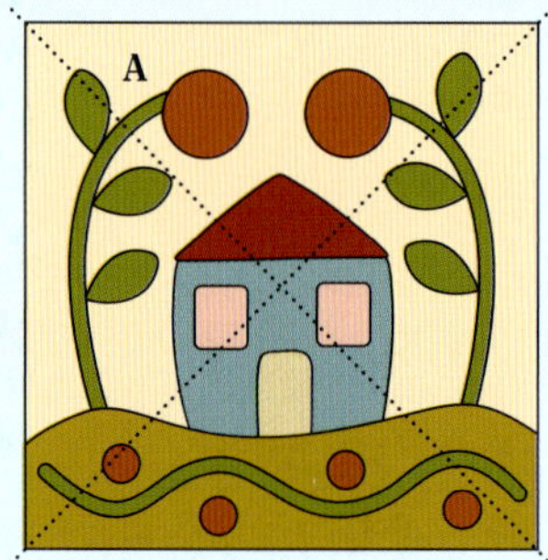

Applique Placement

Fold A in half diagonally both ways and lightly crease the folds. Prepare patches B–I for turned-edge appliqué. Refer to "Bias Strips" in the Techniques file on the PDF for the stems. Cut the bias strip into 2 lengths of 8½" and 1 length of 14". Use the creases and appliqué placement diagram as guides to arrange the patches on A.

Use matching thread and a blind stitch to appliqué the patches in place. Center the appliqué and trim to 12½" × 12½" to complete the block.

block no. 115

Hootie

by Shayla Wolf • Editorial Assistant, *Quiltmaker*
quiltmaker.com

See page 254 on the PDF for pattern

Dark Blue Batik
- 1 square (A) 12¼" x 12¼" (trim to 11¼" x 11¼" after appliqué)

Yellow Batik
- 1 circle (B) 10⅜" diameter

Assorted Prints and Tone-on-Tones
- 1 set of appliqué patches

Dark Brown Tone-on-Tone
- 1 rectangle (O) 1¾" x 11¼"
- 1 rectangle (P) 1¾" x 12½"

Fusible web

Applique Placement

Prepare patches B–N for fusible appliqué. Fold A in half both ways and lightly crease the folds. Use the creases and appliqué placement diagram as guides to arrange the B on A; fuse in place. Arrange patches C–L on A/B; fuse in alphabetical order.

Fold O in half both ways and lightly crease the folds. Use the creases and appliqué placement diagram to arrange M and N on the O; fuse in place.

Trimming Diagram

The stitch diagrams are in the Techniques file on the PDF. Use matching thread and a machine blanket stitch to sew around the patches. Center the design and trim A to 11¼" × 11¼". Join the patches as shown to complete the block.

Block Assembly

block no. 116

Capstone

by Kathy K. Wylie
kathykwylie.com

Kathy K. Wylie is the author of *Sewflakes* for C&T Publishing, ctpub.com.

See page 251 on the PDF for pattern

White Solid
- 1 square (A) 13½" x 13½" (trim to 12½" x 12½" after appliqué)

Dark Blue Tone-on-Tone
- 4 *each* patterns B and Br
- 1 pattern F

Light Gray Tone-on-Tone
- 1 *each* patterns C and G

Dark Gray Tone-on-Tone
- 1 pattern D

2 Red Tone-on-Tones
from *each*
- 1 pattern E

Fold A in half both ways and diagonally and lightly crease the folds.

Using full-size patterns for patches C and D, prepare patches B–G for turned-edge appliqué. Use the creases and appliqué placement diagram as guides to arrange the patches on A.

The stitch diagrams are in the Techniques file on the PDF. Use matching thread and a blind stitch to appliqué the patches in place. Center the appliqué and trim to 12½" × 12½".

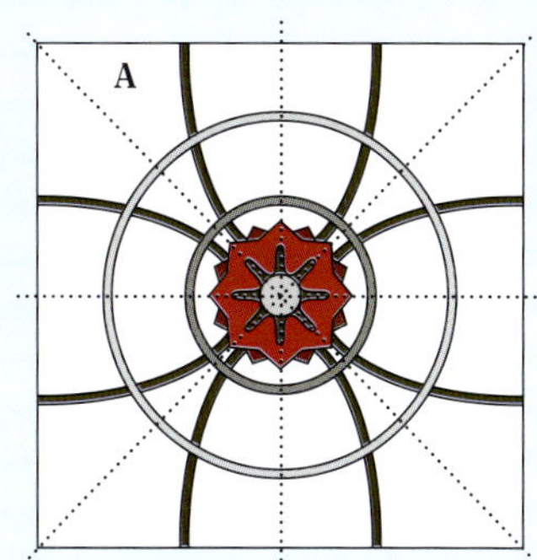

Applique Placement

block no. 117

Ukulele-lei

by Sandi Colwell • Quilt Cabana Patterns
quiltcabanapatterns.com

Sandi Colwell is the author of *Little Quilts for Big Occasions* for Leisure Arts, Inc., leisurearts.com.

See page 297 on the PDF for pattern

Teal Batik
1 square (A) 13½"x 13½" (trim to 12½"x 12½" after appliqué)

Black Tone-on-Tone
1 *each* patterns B, D and E

Dark Pink Tone-on-Tone
1 pattern C

Assorted Gold and Pale Orange Batiks
5 pattern F

Fusible web

Fold A in half both ways and lightly crease the folds. Prepare patches B–F for fusible appliqué. Use the creases and appliqué placement diagram as guides to arrange the patches on A. Fuse the patches in alphabetical order.

The stitch diagrams are in the Techniques file on the PDF. Use pale pink thread and a machine blanket stitch to sew around patches B–E. Use gold thread and a blanket stitch around the flowers and a straight stitch for the flower veins. The ukulele strings are created with a straight stitch.

Sandi used a metallic silver thread for the ukulele strings.

Center the appliqué and trim to 12½" × 12½".

Applique Placement

block no. 118

Grandpa's Gift

by Karen Comstock • Quiltricks
quiltricks.com

See page 329 on the PDF for pattern

Black Tone-on-Tone
1 square (A) 13½"x 13½" (trim to 12½"x 12½" after appliqué)

Assorted Tone-on-Tones
1 complete set of appliqué patches

Fusible web

Use the photographed block and appliqué patterns as guides to selecting fabric colors.

Fold A in half both ways and lightly crease the folds. Prepare the appliqué patches for fusible appliqué. Use the creases and appliqué placement diagram as guides to arrange the patches on A; fuse patches in place.

The stitch diagrams are in the Techniques file on the PDF. Use matching thread and a machine blanket stitch to sew around the patches.

Center the appliqué and trim to 12½" × 12½".

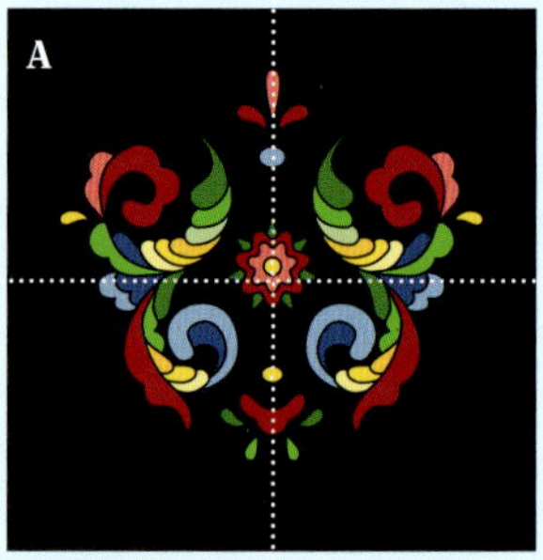

Applique Placement

block no. 119

Blue on Blue

by Beth Ferrier • Applewood Farm
applewoodfarmquilts.com

Beth Ferrier is the author of *Sneaky Piecing* for C&T Publishing, ctpub.com.

See page 299 on the PDF for pattern

White Tone-on-Tone
1 square (A) 13½″ x 13½″ (trim to 12½″ x 12½″ after appliqué)
5 Assorted Dark, Medium and Light Blue Batiks (see below)
1 complete set of appliqué patches
Tear-away stabilizer (optional)

Notice how Beth gradated the blues—from the darkest near the block center to the lightest in the corners.

Fold A in half diagonally both ways and lightly crease the folds. Prepare patches B–I for turned-edge appliqué. Use the creases and appliqué placement diagram as guides to arrange the patches on A.

The stitch diagrams are in the Techniques file on the PDF. Use monofilament thread and a machine zigazag stitch to sew around the patches.

Center the appliqué and trim to 12½″× 12½″.

Applique Placement

block no. 120

Bouclier de la France

by Susan Guzman • SuzGuz Designs
suzguzdesigns.com

See page 331 on the PDF for pattern

Teal Tone-on-Tone
1 square (A) 13½″ x 13½″ (trim to 12½″ x 12½″ after appliqué)
Assorted Prints and Tone-on-Tones
1 complete set of appliqué patches
Fusible web

Fold A in half both ways and lightly crease the folds. Prepare patches B–K for fusible appliqué. Use the creases and appliqué placement diagram as guides to arrange the patches on A. Fuse the patches to A in alphabetical order.

The stitch diagrams are in the Techniques file on the PDF. Use matching thread and a machine blanket stitch to sew around the patches.

Center the appliqué and trim to 12½"× 12½".

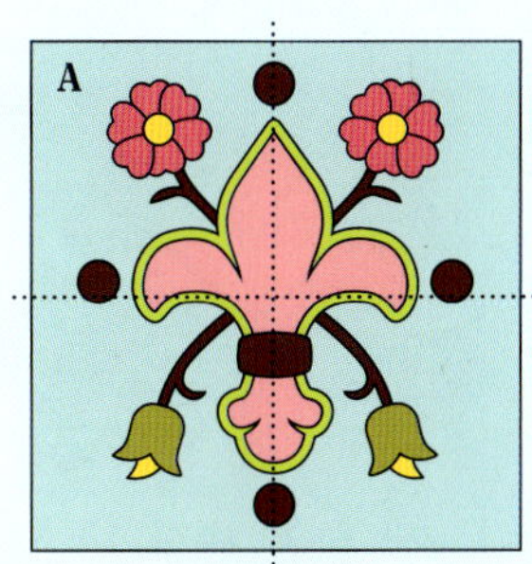

Applique Placement

block no. 121

Tree of Love

by Marcia Harmening • Happy Stash Quilts
happystashquilts.com

Marcia Harmening is the author of *I Love Color!* for Leisure Arts, Inc., leisurearts.com.

See page 307 on the PDF for pattern

White Tone-on-Tone
1 square (A) 13½" x 13½" (trim to 12½" x 12½" after appliqué)

Red Tone-on-Tone
1 *each* patterns B, Br, C, Cr and D

Dark Brown Tone-on-Tone
1 pattern E

Assorted Prints and Tone-on-Tones
13 pattern F
8 pattern G
8 pattern H
16 pattern I
12 pattern J
5 pattern K

Notice that Marcia fussy cut some of her circles to highlight fun designs.

Fold A in half both ways and lightly crease the folds. Prepare patches B–K for turned-edge appliqué. Use the creases and appliqué placement diagram as guides to arrange the patches on A, scattering the dots (F–K) for a pleasing distribution.

Use matching thread and a blind stitch to appliqué the patches in place.

Center the appliqué and trim to 12½" × 12½".

Applique Placement

block no. 122

No Crows

by Mary Andra Holmes • Sisters' Quilting Trunk
sistersquiltingtrunk.com

See page 306 on the PDF for pattern

Cream Tone-on-Tone
1 square (A) 13½" x 13½" (trim to 12½" x 12½" after appliqué)

Dark Green Tone-on-Tone
bias strip 1" x 17"

Assorted Tone-on-Tones
1 complete set of appliqué patches

Fold A in half both ways and lightly crease the folds. Refer to "Bias Strips" in the Techniques file on the PDF to make the stems. Prepare patches B–M for turned-edge appliqué. Use the creases and appliqué placement diagram as guides to arrange the stems and patches on A.

Use matching thread and a blind stitch to appliqué the patches in place.

Center the appliqué and trim to 12½" × 12½".

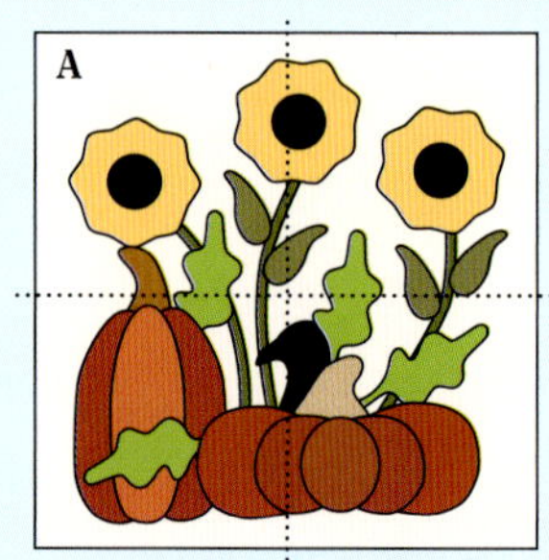

Applique Placement

block no. 123

Rainbow Gum Tree

by Pamela Lincoln
mamaspark.blogspot.com

See page 314 on the PDF for pattern

White Solid

1 square (A) 13½"x 13½" (trim to 12½"x 12½" after appliqué)

Gray Print

1 pattern B

Assorted Prints and Tone-on-Tones

2 pattern C
10 pattern D
17 pattern E

Fusible web

Fold A in half both ways and lightly crease the folds. Prepare patches B–E for fusible appliqué. Use the creases and appliqué placement diagram as guides to arrange the patches on A, scattering the dots (C–E) for a pleasing distribution.

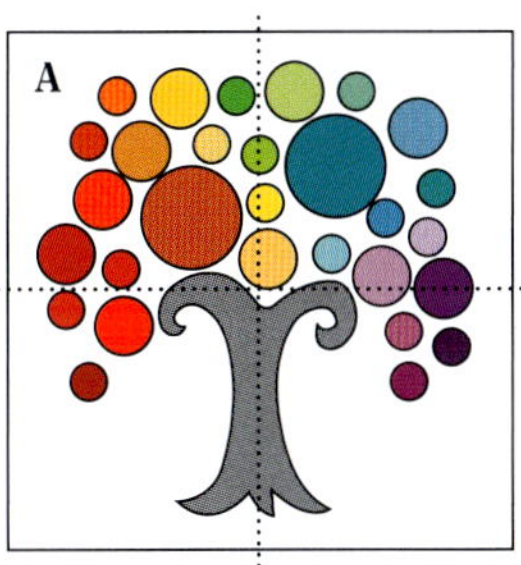

Applique Placement

Use black thread and a straight stitch to sew just inside the edges of the patches. Stitch a second time around the circles. Center the appliqué and trim to 12½"× 12½".

block no. 124

Basket of Oranges

by Kay Mackenzie • By Kay Mackenzie
kaymackenzie.com

Kay Mackenzie is the author of *Scrap-Appliqué Playground* for Martingale & Co., shopmartingale.com.

See page 300 on the PDF for pattern

White Tone-on-Tone

1 square (A) 13½"x 13½" (trim to 12½"x 12½" after appliqué)

Green Tone-on-Tone

1 pattern B

Assorted Orange Tone-on-Tones

5 pattern C

Blue Tone-on-Tone

1 *each* patterns D and E

Red Tone-on-Tone

1 *each* patterns F–H

Fusible web

Fold A in half both ways and lightly crease the folds. Prepare patches B–H for fusible appliqué. Use the creases and appliqué placement diagram as guides to arrange the patches on A. Fuse the patches to A in alphabetical order.

The stitch diagrams are in the Techniques file on the PDF. Use matching thread and a machine blanket stitch to sew around the patches.

Center the appliqué and trim to 12½"× 12½".

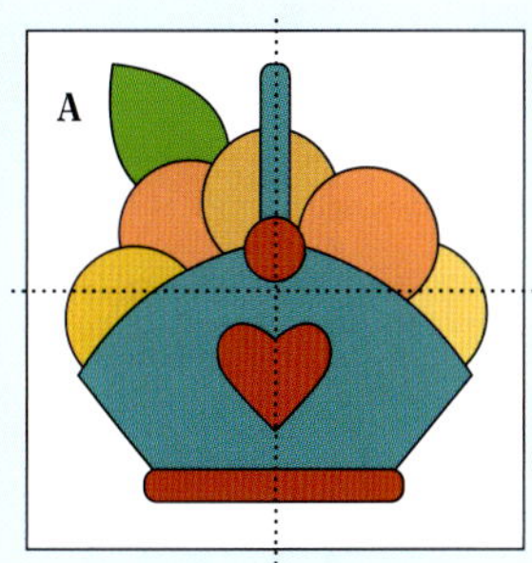

Applique Placement

block no. 125

Dancing Dahlias

by Nancy Mahoney
nancymahoney.com

Fabric: Hello Dahlia! by P & B Textiles, pbtex.com.

Nancy Mahoney is the author of *Kaleidoscope Paper Piecing* and other books for Martingale & Co., shopmartingale.com.

See page 327 on the PDF for pattern

White Print
1 square (A) 13½"x 13½" (trim to 12½"x 12½" after appliqué)
Green Tone-on-Tone
bias strip 1"x 28"
4 *each* patterns B and C
Red with Black Print #1
12 pattern B
Red with White Print #1
8 pattern B
Red with White Print #2 and Red with Black Print #2
from *each* 4 pattern D
Fusible web

Fold A in half both ways and diagonally; lightly crease the folds. With a pencil, draw a centered 12½" square on A. Refer to "Bias Strips" in the Techniques file on the PDF to make the stems. Cut 4 stem pieces 7" long. Prepare patches B–C for fusible appliqué and the D patches for turned-edge appliqué. Use the creases and appliqué placement diagram as guides to arrange the stems and patches B–C on A. Fuse B's–C's in place. Align the D patches on A using the drawn square and placement diagram as a guides; pin in place.

Use matching thread and a machine blanket stitch to sew around the stems and flowers. Blind stitch the D's in place with monofilament thread. Center the appliqué and trim to 12½"× 12½".

Applique Placement

block no. 126

Gertie Goat

by Sue Marsh • Whistlepig Creek Productions
wpcreek.com

Fabric: Handspray and Cotton Supreme Solids by RJR Fabrics, rjrfabrics.com.

See page 311 on the PDF for pattern

Aqua Solid
1 square (A) 13½"x 13½" (trim to 12½"x 12½" after appliqué)
Cream Solid
1 *each* patterns B and F
Dark Brown Tone-on-Tone
1 *each* patterns C and I–K
Pink Tone-on-Tone
1 *each* patterns D and E
Tan Tone-on-Tone
1 pattern G
White Solid
1 *each* patterns H, M and Mr
Light Tan Tone-on-Tone
1 *each* patterns L and Lr
Black Solid
2 pattern N
Fusible web

Fold A in half both ways and lightly crease the folds. Prepare patches B–N for fusible appliqué. Use the creases and appliqué placement diagram as guides to arrange the patches on A. Fuse the patches in alphabetical order.

The stitch diagrams are in the Techniques file on the PDF. Use a machine satin stitch to sew around the patches and add the face detail. Center the appliqué and trim to 12½"× 12½".

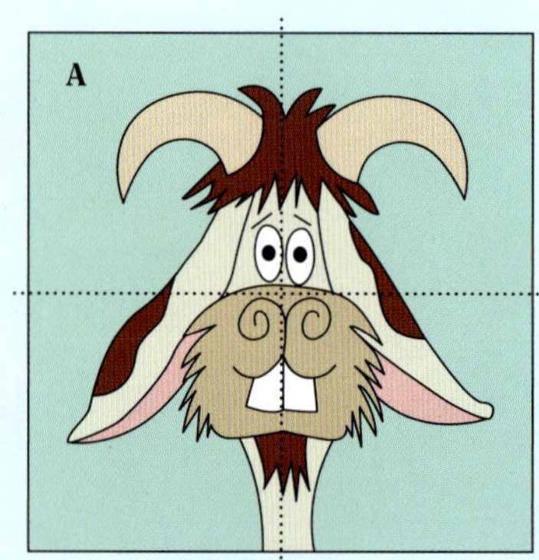

Applique Placement

block no. 127

Flower Power

by Melissa Peda • 100 Billion Stars
100billionstars.com

Fabric: Liberty Art Fabrics designed by Kaffe Fassett for Westminster Fibers, Inc., westminsterfibers.com and Designer Dapples from FreeSpirit Fabrics, freespiritfabrics.com.

See page 290 on the PDF for pattern

White Solid
1 square (A) 13½"x 13½" (trim to 12½"x 12½" after appliqué)
Blue Tone-on-Tone
1 pattern B
7 pattern E
Black Print
1 pattern C
7 pattern D
Fusible web

Fold A in half diagonally both ways and lightly crease the folds. Prepare patches B–E for fusible appliqué. Use the creases and appliqué placement diagram as guides to arrange the patches on A. Fuse the patches to A in alphabetical order.

The stitch diagrams are in the Techniques file on the PDF. Use white thread and a machine zigzag stitch to sew around the patches. Center the appliqué and trim to 12½" × 12½".

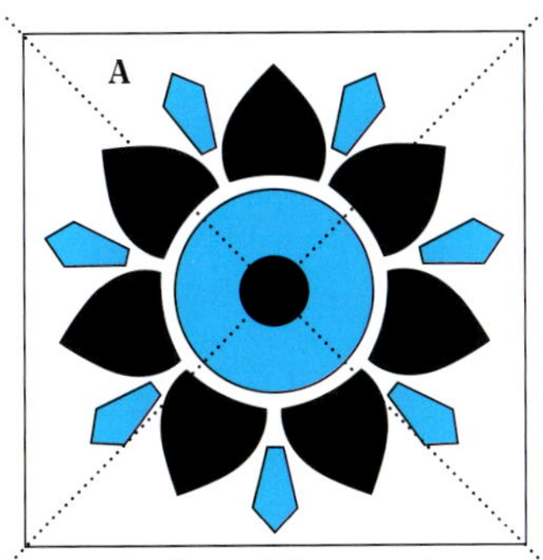

Applique Placement

block no. 128

Stained Glass Flower

by Susan Taylor Propst
susantaylorpropst.com

Susan Taylor Propst is the author of *Nature's Beauty in Appliqué—Pretty and Practical Projects* for Martingale & Co., shopmartingale.com.

See page 295 on the PDF for pattern

Cream Print
1 square (A) 13½"x 13½" (trim to 12½"x 12½" after appliqué)
Assorted Batiks
1 complete set of appliqué patches
Black Solid
bias strip 1"x 118" *total* (see note below)
Fusible web
Clover fusible bias-tape maker ¼" (optional)
Clover 5mm fusible web (optional)
Clover Quick Bias Tape ¼" black (optional)

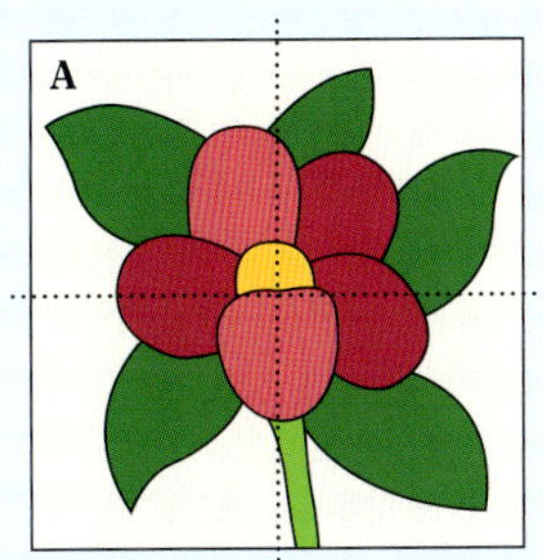

Applique Placement

Bias Strip Placement

Optionally, you can use Clover's Quick Bias Tape or make your own bias tape using Clover's fusible bias-tape maker and fusible web. If you prefer one of these, follow the manufacturer's instructions.

Fold A in half both ways and lightly crease the folds. Prepare patches B–M for fusible appliqué. Use the creases and appliqué placement diagram as guides to arrange the patches on A. Fuse the patches in alphabetical order.

Refer to "Bias Strips" in the Techniques file on the PDF to prepare the bias strips. Refer to the diagram to arrange the bias strips on A, covering the raw edges of the appliqué patches and tucking the ends of the bias strips under other strips. Use black thread and a straight stitch to sew the strips in place. Center the appliqué and trim to 12½"é 12½".

block no. 129

Splash

by Denise Russart
justquiltin.wordpress.com

Fabric: Sand in My Shoes designed by McKenna Ryan for Hoffman California Fabrics, hoffmanfabrics.com.

Cream Tone-on-Tone
1 square (A) 13½"x 13½"
(trim to 12½"x 12½" after appliqué)
Dark Blue Tone-on-Tone
1 pattern B
5 pattern D
Pale Teal Tone-on-Tone
5 pattern C
Medium Teal Tone-on-Tone
5 pattern Cr
Medium Blue Tone-on-Tone
5 pattern C

Denise used a gradated fabric for the appliqué patches.

Fold A in half both ways and diagonally and lightly crease the folds. Prepare patches B–D for turned-edge appliqué. Use the creases and appliqué placement diagram as guides to arrange the patches on A.

The stitch diagrams are in the Techniques file on the PDF. Use matching thread and a blind stitch to appliqué the patches in place. Center the appliqué and trim to 12½" × 12½".

Templates for Splash block on page 301 of the PDF Templates file.

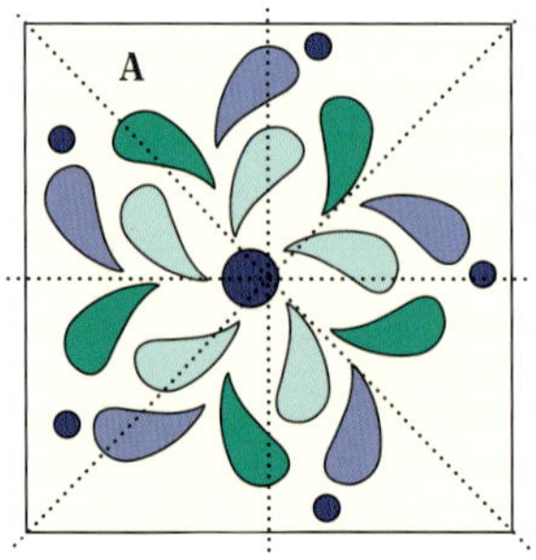

Applique Placement

block no. 130

Shadow Play

by Jennifer Schifano Thomas • Curlicue Creations
curlicuecreations.com

See page 330 on the PDF for pattern

Blue Tone-on-Tone
1 square (A) 13½"x 13½" (trim to 12½"x 12½" after appliqué)
Purple Tone-on-Tone
1 pattern B
4 *each* patterns C, Cr and D
Black Solid
1 pattern E
Fusible web

Fold A in half diagonally both ways and lightly crease the folds. Prepare patches B–E for fusible appliqué. Use the creases and appliqué placement diagram as guides to arrange the patches on A. Fuse the patches to A in alphabetical order.

The stitch diagrams are in the Techniques file on the PDF. Use black thread and a zigzag stitch to sew around E. Center the appliqué and trim to 12½" × 12½".

Applique Placement

block no. 131

Summer Posies

by Pam Vieira-McGinnis
pamkittymorning.blogspot.com

Fabric: Pam Kitty Love designed by Pam Vieira-McGinnis for LakeHouse Dry Goods, lakehousedrygoods.com.

The leaves and flower centers in this block are made 3D by fusing 2 layers of fabric together.

See page 316 on the PDF for pattern

White Print
1 square (A) 13½"x 13½" (trim to 12½"x 12½" after appliqué)

Assorted Red and Pink Tone-on-Tones
from *2*
2 squares 2¾"x 2¾" for the large 3D flower centers (G)
from *1*
2 squares 1¾"x 1¾" for the small 3D flower center (H)
from various (for appliqué)
1 *each* patterns B–D and G
2 pattern F

2 Green Checks
from *each*
3 rectangles 2"x 4" for the 3D leaves (E's)

Fusible web

Red rickrack and pink rickrack 11" length from *each*

Buttons 2 at ⅞", 1 at ½"

Applique Placement

To make the 3-dimensional flower centers, use the red and pink squares. With wrong sides together, fuse matching squares to each other. Trace the flower shapes (G and H) on the fused patches; cut out the shapes. Make the 3D leaves in the same way, using 2 different green rectangles for each leaf (E). Set aside the flowers.

Fold A in half both ways and lightly crease the folds. Prepare patches B–D, F and G for fusible appliqué. Use the creases and appliqué placement diagram as guides to arrange the patches on A. Weave the red and pink rickrack lengths together and pin in place. Tuck the leaves under the flowers as shown; pin the leaves in place. Fuse the patches in place. Use matching thread and a machine blanket stitch to sew around the appliqué. Center the appliqué and trim to 12½"× 12½". Use a straight stitch to tack down the rickrack and stitch a vein down the center of each leaf. Layer the dimensional flowers on top and tack in place with buttons as shown in the photographed block.

block no. 132

Hoot Owls

by Connie Walker • Whistle Stop Designs

See page 304 on the PDF for pattern

Pale Teal Tone-on-Tone
1 square (A) 13½"x 13½" (trim to 12½"x 12½" after appliqué)

Assorted Prints and Tone-on-Tones
1 complete set of appliqué patches

Fusible web

Nonstick pressing sheet

Tear-away stabilizer

Prepare the appliqué patches for fusible appliqué.

Lay the nonstick pressing sheet on a hard ironing surface. Using the appliqué placement diagram as a guide, arrange the owl patches (except for the tails) and lightly fuse to one another on top of the pressing sheet. Allow the patches to cool and gently remove from the pressing sheet.

Applique Placement

Fold A in half both ways and lightly crease the folds. Use the creases and appliqué placement diagram as guides to arrange the tails, branches, owls and leaves on A as shown; fuse in place.

The stitch diagrams are in the Techniques file on the PDF. Using tear-away stabilizer on the back and matching thread, machine blanket stitch around all the patches. Center the appliqué and trim to 12½"× 12½".

block no. 133

Rollin' Along

by Kristy Wolf • Sassafras Lane Designs
sassafras-lane.com

See page 315 on the PDF for pattern

Light Blue Tone-on-Tone
1 square (A) 13½"x 13½" (trim to 12½"x 12½" after appliqué)
Assorted Prints and Tone-on-Tones
1 complete set of appliqué patches
Fusible web
Nonstick pressing sheet
Tear-away stabilizer
Crystal 1 at ⅛" diameter

Prepare the appliqué patches for fusible appliqué.

Lay the nonstick pressing sheet on a hard ironing surface. Using the appliqué placement diagram as a guide, arrange the camper patches and lightly fuse to one another on top of the pressing sheet. Allow the patches to cool and gently remove from the pressing sheet.

Fold A in half both ways and lightly crease the folds. Use the creases and appliqué placement diagram as guides to arrange the camper patches, flag and bird on A as shown; fuse in place. Randomly arrange the cloud patches and fuse in place.

The stitch diagrams are in the Techniques file on the PDF. Using tear-away stabilizer on the back and matching thread, machine blanket stitch around all the patches. Use a straight stitch for the flag pole and blind pull. For the door lock, use a small zigzag around the circle and a satin stitch below it. Use a satin stitch for the bird beak.

Center the appliqué and trim to 12½"× 12½". Affix the crystal for the bird's eye as shown to complete the block.

Applique Placement

block no. 134

Fiddleheads

by Kathy K. Wylie
kathykwylie.com

Kathy K. Wylie is the author of *Sewflakes* for C&T Publishing, ctpub.com.

See page 310 on the PDF for pattern

Tan Tone-on-Tone
1 square (A) 13½"x 13½" (trim to 12½"x 12½" after appliqué)
Medium Brown Print
1 pattern B
2 Red Prints
from *1*
4 pattern C
from *1*
1 pattern D

Fold A in half diagonally both ways and lightly crease the folds. Prepare patches B–D for turned-edge appliqué. Use the creases and appliqué placement diagram as guides to arrange the patches on A.

The stitch diagrams are in the Techniques file on the PDF. Use matching thread and a blind stitch to appliqué the patches in place.

Center the appliqué and trim to 12½"× 12½".

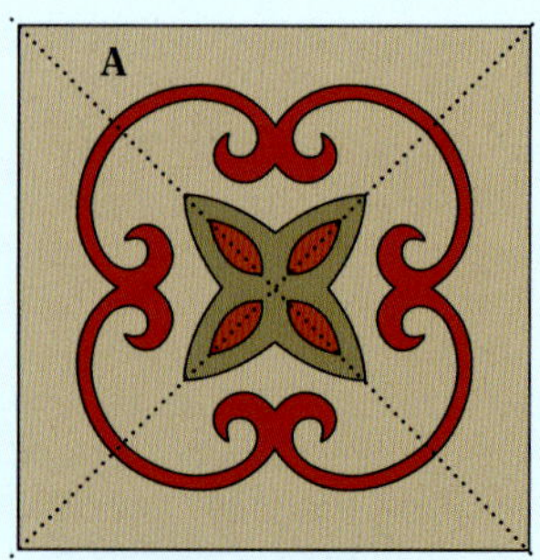

Applique Placement

block no. 135

Folk Art Mexican Rose

by Nancy Allen

Nancy Allen is the author of *Triple-Play Scrap Quilting: Planned, Coordinated, and Make-Do Styles* for Martingale & Co., shopmartingale.com.

See page 349 on the PDF for pattern

Cream Tone-on-Tone
1 square (A) 13½"x 13½" (trim to 12½"x 12½" after appliqué)
Green Print
4 pattern B
Orange Print
4 pattern C
Maroon Tone-on-Tone
4 pattern D
Tan Print
1 pattern D
Fusible web

Fold A in half diagonally both ways and lightly crease the folds. Prepare patches B–D for fusible appliqué. Using the creases and appliqué placement diagram as guides, arrange and fuse the patches in alphabetical order.

The stitch diagrams are in the Techniques file on the PDF. Use monofilament thread and a machine blanket stitch to sew around the patches. Center the appliqué and trim to 12½" × 12½" to complete the block.

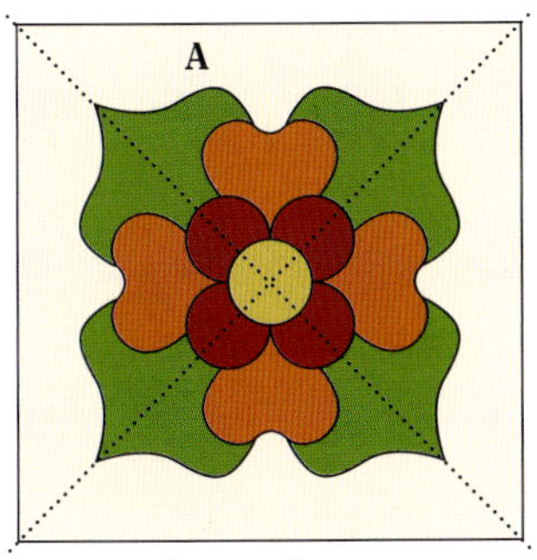

Applique Placement

block no. 136

Quilt Seeds

by Natalia Bonner • Piece N Quilt
piecenquilt.com

Fabric: Bella Solids from Moda Fabrics, unitednotions.com.

Natalia Bonner is the author of *Beginner's Guide to Free Motion Quilting* and *Modern One-Block Quilts* for Stash Books, ctpub.com.

See page 363 on the PDF for pattern

Cream Solid
1 square (A) 12½"x 12½"
Gold Solid
2 pattern B
Dark Purple Solid
1 pattern C
Fusible web

Fold A in half both ways and lightly crease the folds. Prepare patches B and C for fusible appliqué. Using the creases and appliqué placement diagram as guides, arrange and fuse the patches on A.

The stitch diagrams are in the Techniques file on the PDF. To complete the block, use matching thread and a machine blanket stitch to sew around the patches.

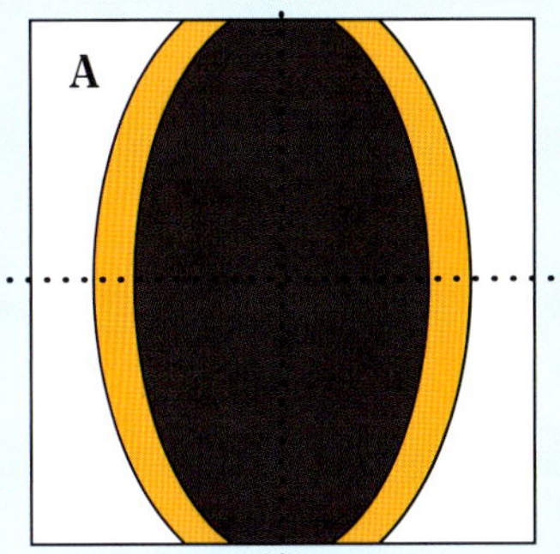

Applique Placement

block no. 137

I "Heart" You

by Kelle Boyd • Ann Kelle
annkelle.com

Fabric: Remix designed by Ann Kelle and Kona Cotton Solids, both from Robert Kaufman, robertkaufman.com.

See page 360 on the PDF for pattern

Yellow Solid, Yellow Dot, Pink Dot, Pink Solid, Blue Stripe, Blue Solid, Red Solid and Red Plaid
from *each*
  1 rectangle 3½" x 6"
White Solid
  1 square (A) 13½" x 13½"
  (trim to 12½" x 12½" after appliqué)
Template plastic
Lightweight tear-away stabilizer

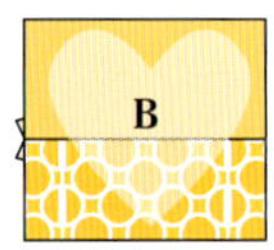

Cut 1

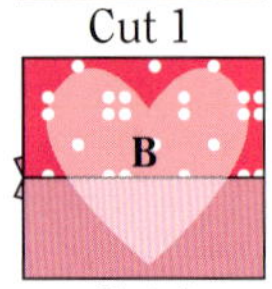

Cut 1

Cut 1

Cut 1

Make a full-size plastic template of B, marking both the dashed line and the dotted center line on the template.

Sew the 2 yellow rectangles together as shown and cut 1 B for raw-edge appliqué, aligning the dashed line with the seam line. Repeat with the 2 pink rectangles. In the same way, join the 2 blue rectangles and 2 red rectangles; aligning the dotted center line with the seam, cut 2 B's as shown.

Applique Placement

Fold A in half both ways and lightly crease the folds. Using the creases and appliqué placement diagram as guides, arrange and pin the B's in place.

With tear-away stabilizer on the back of the A, use white thread and 2 lines of straight stitching around the patches just inside the raw edge. Center the appliqué and trim to 12½" × 12½".

block no. 138

Getting Frondly

by Kelly Eisinger • Editorial Assistant, *Quiltmaker*
quiltmaker.com

Fabric: P&B Textiles, pbtex.com.

See page 376 on the PDF for pattern

Gold Tone-on-Tone
  1 square (A) 15" x 15" (trim to 12½" x 12½" after appliqué)
Assorted Green Tone-on-Tones
  1 complete set of appliqué patches
Fusible web
Pencil

Fold A in half both ways and lightly crease the folds. Prepare the leaves for fusible appliqué.

Kelly used a pencil to draw a casual line for the stem to use as a guide for placement of the leaves. Notice the appliqué is not centered.

Use the creases, appliqué placement diagram and appliqué placement guide on the pattern sheet as guides to arrange the leaves on A; fuse in place.

Applique Placement

The stitch diagrams are in the Techniques file on the PDF. Use green thread and a straight stitch to sew the veins and close to the edges of each leaf. Refer to the stitch placement diagram. Use green thread and a machine satin stitch for the stem (shown in white).

Position a 12½" square ruler on the block and trim to 12½" × 12½", noting that the tips of some leaves will be cut off.

Stitch Placement

block no. 139

Target Practice

by Sue Garman
comequilt.com

See page 341 on the PDF for pattern

Cream Print
1 square (A) 13½"x 13½" (trim to 12½"x 12½" after appliqué)
Red Tone-on-Tone
1 *each* patterns B and D
Medium Green Tone-on-Tone
1 pattern C
Assorted Red Prints and Tone-on-Tones
8 pattern E
Assorted Green Prints and Tone-on-Tones
9 pattern E

Fold A in half both ways and lightly crease the folds. Prepare patches B–E for turned-edge appliqué. Use the creases and appliqué placement diagram as guides to arrange the patches on A.

The stitch diagrams are in the Techniques file on the PDF. Use matching thread and a blind stitch to appliqué the patches in place.

Center the appliqué and trim to 12½" × 12½".

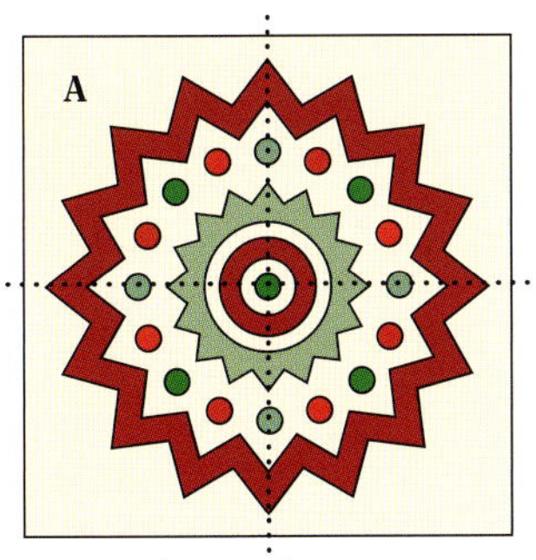

Applique Placement

block no. 140

Circles Around

by Brigitte Heitland • Zen Chic
brigitteheitland.de

Fabric: Bella Solids from Moda Fabrics, unitednotions.com.

See page 369 on the PDF for pattern

Blue Solid
1 square (A) 13½"x 13½" (trim to 12½"x 12½" after appliqué)
Black Solid
1 pattern B
Lime Green Solid
1 pattern C
Fusible web

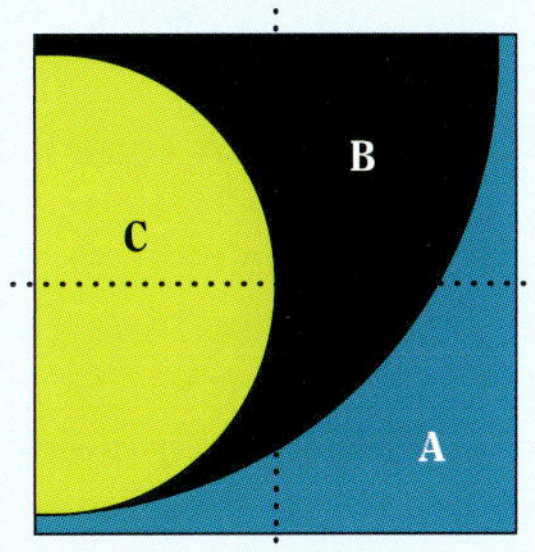

Applique Placement

Fold A in half both ways and lightly crease the folds. Prepare patches B and C for fusible appliqué. Using the creases and appliqué placement diagram as guides, arrange and fuse the patches on A.

The stitch diagrams are in the Techniques file on the PDF. Use matching thread and a machine blanket stitch to sew around the patches.

Center the design and trim A to 12½" × 12½" to complete the block.

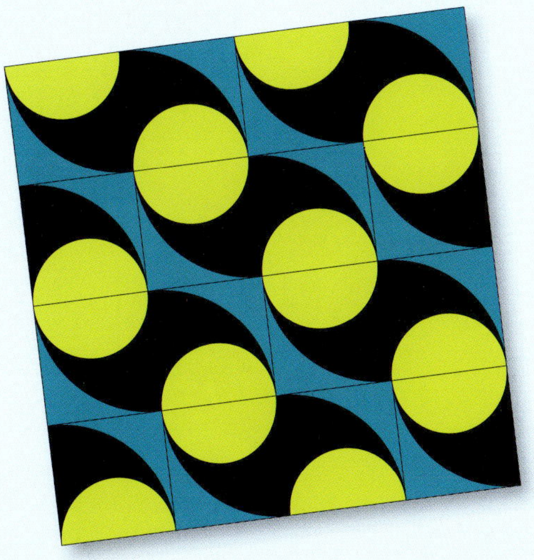

block no. 141

Spring Tulips

by Nancy Mahoney
nancymahoney.com

Fabric: Various collections from P&B Textiles, pbtex.com.

Nancy Mahoney is the author of *Simple Circles and Quick Curves* for Martingale & Co., shopmartingale.com.

See page 366 on the PDF for pattern

White Print
1 square (A) 13½"x 13½" (trim to 12½"x 12½" after appliqué)

Green Tone-on-Tone
bias strip 1¼"x 12"
1 *each* patterns B, Br, C and Cr

Black Tone-on-Tone
1 *each* patterns D, Dr and E

Assorted Pink Tone-on-Tones
4 *each* patterns F and G

Fusible web

Fold A in half both ways and lightly crease the folds. Prepare patches B–G for fusible appliqué. Refer to "Bias Strips" in the Techniques file on the PDF. Cut the bias strip into 2 lengths of 2" and 2 lengths of 4". Using the creases and appliqué placement diagram as guides, arrange the patches in alphabetical order. Arrange the bias stems and tuck the ends under the patches; pin in place. Fuse the patches.

Use matching thread and a machine blanket stitch to sew around the patches. Center the appliqué and trim to 12½" × 12½".

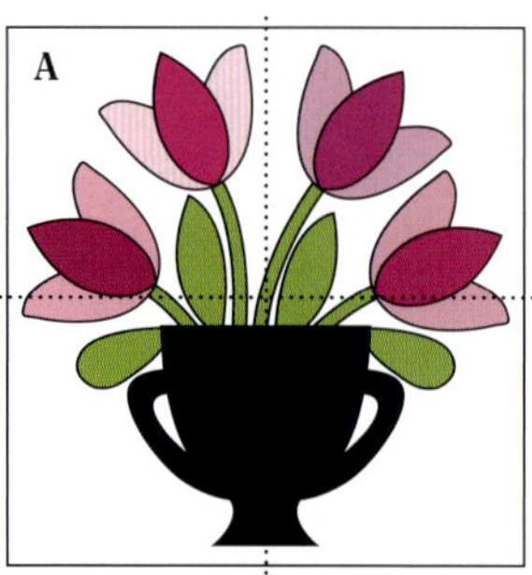

Applique Placement

block no. 142

Greetings Earthling

by Sue Marsh • Whistlepig Creek Productions
wpcreek.com

Fabric: Cotton Supreme Solids by RJR Fabrics, rjrfabrics.com.

See page 338 on the PDF for pattern

Black Print
1 square (A) 13½"x 13½" (trim to 12½"x 12½" after appliqué)

Teal Solid
1 pattern B

Green Solid
1 *each* patterns C and D

White Solid
2 pattern E

Purple Solid
1 *each* patterns F, G and Gr

Orange Solid
1 pattern H

Pink Solid
1 pattern I

Yellow Solid
8 pattern J
1 pattern K
2 pattern L

Fusible web

Black permanent fabric marker

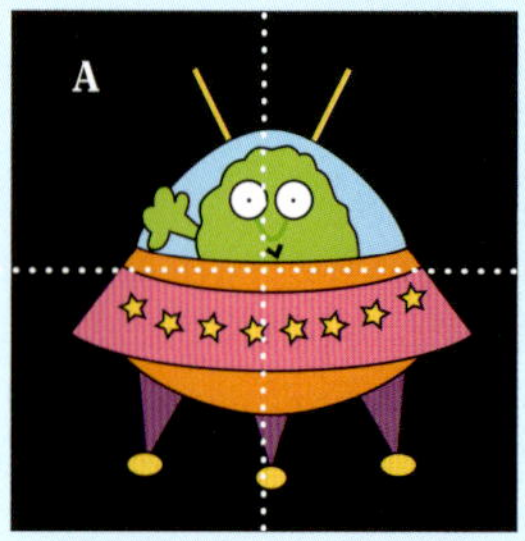

Applique Placement

Fold A in half both ways and lightly crease the folds. Prepare patches B–L for fusible appliqué. Use the creases and appliqué placement diagram as guides to arrange the patches in alphabetical order on A; fuse the patches in place.

The stitch diagrams are in the Techniques file on the PDF. Use matching thread and a machine satin stitch to sew around the patches and add the nose and antennae details. Use black thread to sew around the eyes and add the mouth. Use the black marker to add the eyes. Center the appliqué and trim A to 12½" × 12½".

block no. 143

Hide and Seek

by Janet Maurer • For You Too! Pattern Company
foryoutoopatterns.com

See page 337 on the PDF for pattern

Light Blue Solid
1 square (A) 13½" x 13½" (trim to 12½" x 12½" after appliqué)

Assorted Solids and Tone-on-Tones
1 complete set of appliqué patches

Fusible web

Pink embroidery floss

Buttons
2 black at ½"
1 orange at ¾"

Fold A in half both ways and lightly crease the folds. Prepare patches B–M for fusible appliqué. Using the creases and appliqué placement diagram as guides, arrange and fuse the patches in alphabetical order.

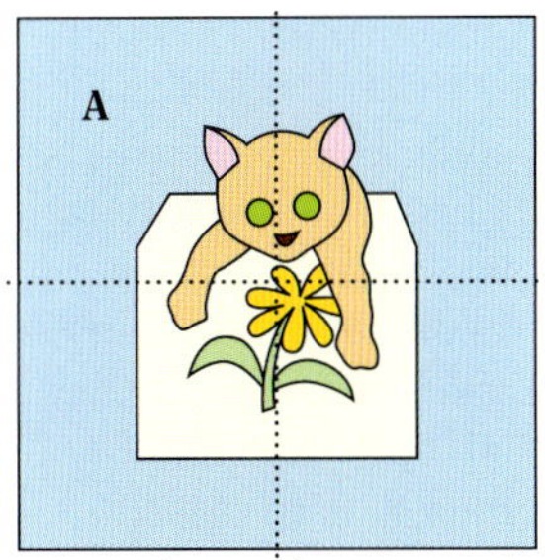

Applique Placement

The stitch diagrams are in the Techniques file on the PDF. Use matching thread and a zigzag stitch to sew around the cat and flower patches. Use tan thread to zigzag around the box and add the box and ear details. Straight stitch the face and paw details with dark brown thread.

Embroidery Placement

Use 3 strands of pink floss and an outline stitch for the letters. Center the appliqué and trim A to 12½" × 12½". Tack the buttons in place as shown to complete the block.

block no. 144

Felicity

by Ellen Murphy • American Homestead
americanhomesteaddesign.com

Fabric: Wool felt from National Nonwovens, nationalnonwovens.com.

Ellen Murphy is the author of *American Homestead Quilts* for C&T Publishing, ctpub.com.

See page 336 on the PDF for pattern

White Solid
1 square (A) 13½" x 13½" (trim to 12½" x 12½" after appliqué)
4 pattern D
1 pattern F
8 pattern G

Green Solid
4 pattern B
1 pattern J

Blue Solid
4 pattern C
8 pattern F
1 pattern G

Red Solid
4 pattern E
1 pattern I

Gold Solid
8 pattern H
1 pattern K

Fusible web

Embroidery Floss

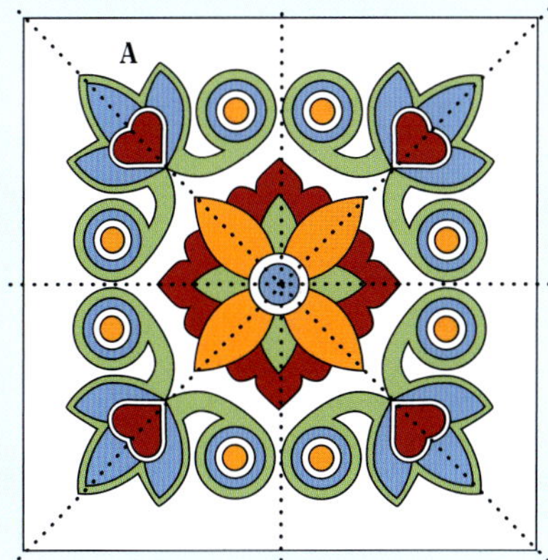

Applique Placement

Ellen used wool felt for her block; cotton can also be used.

Fold A in half both ways and diagonally and lightly crease the folds. Prepare patches B–K for fusible appliqué. Using the creases and appliqué placement diagram as guides, arrange and fuse the patches in alphabetical order.

The stitch diagrams are in the Techniques file on the PDF. Use matching thread and a hand blanket stitch to sew around the patches. Center the appliqué and trim A to 12½" × 12½" to complete the block.

block no. 145

Spring Smile

by Joanne Rowicki • Gingham Girls
ginghamgirls.biz

See page 365 on the PDF for pattern

White Tone-on-Tone
 1 square (A) 13½"x 13½" (trim to 12½"x 12½" after appliqué)
Green Tone-on-Tone #1
 1 pattern B
Green Tone-on-Tone #2
 4 pattern E
Pink Tone-on-Tones #1 and #2
from *each*
 1 pattern C
Pink Tone-on-Tone #3
 1 pattern C
 1 square (F) 4"x 4"
Yellow Tone-on-Tone
 3 pattern D
Fusible web

Applique Placement

Fold the block in half both ways and lightly crease the folds. Prepare patches B–E for fusible appliqué. Using the creases and appliqué placement diagram as guides, arrange and fuse the patches in alphabetical order.

Sew around the patches using matching thread and a machine blanket stitch. Center the appliqué and trim A to 12½"× 12½".

Refer to "Stitch-and-Flip" in the Techniques file on the PDF. Add the pink F to the corner of A as shown to complete the block.

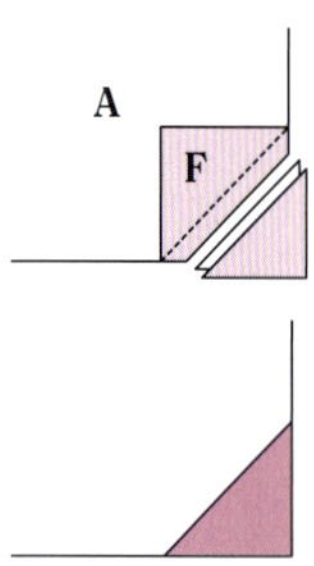

Stitch & Flip

block no. 146

Summer Bouquet

by Pam Vieira-McGinnis
pamkittymorning.blogspot.com

Fabric: Pam Kitty Love by Pam Vieira-McGinnis for Lake House Dry Goods, lakehousedrygoods.com.

See page 372 on the PDF for pattern

Gray Check
 1 square (A) 13½"x 13½" (trim to 12½"x 12½" after appliqué)
Assorted Prints and Tone-on Tones
 1 complete set of flowers, leaves and bowl appliqué patterns
White Tone-on-Tone
 1 pattern M
Fusible web
Yellow buttons 3 at ⅜"
White embroidery floss

Fold A in half both ways and lightly crease the folds. Prepare patches B–M for fusible appliqué. Using the creases and appliqué placement diagram as guides, arrange patches B–L on A in alphabetical order; fuse in place.

Center the appliqué and trim A to 12½"× 12½". Carefully align M on A and fuse in place.

Applique, Button & Embroidery Placement

The stitch diagrams are in the Techniques file on the PDF. Use matching thread and a machine blanket stitch to sew around the patches. Use a lazy daisy stitch to sew 3 flowers as shown. Sew a button to the middle of each daisy to complete the block.

block no. 147
Hearts and Stars

by Martha Walker • Wagons West Designs
wagonswestdesigns.com

Fabric: Elementary by Martha Walker for Studio e Fabrics, studioefabrics.com.

Martha Walker is the author of *Annie's Scrapbag* and *Vintage Christmas* for Wagons West Designs, wagonswestdesigns.com.

See page 335 on the PDF for pattern

Tan Tone-on-Tone
1 square (A) 13½"x 13½" (trim to 12½"x 12½" after appliqué)
Green Print
4 *each* patterns B, Br and C
Red Print
4 pattern D
8 pattern E
Gold Print
12 pattern F
1 pattern J
Green Tone-on-Tone
4 *each* patterns G, Gr, H and Hr
Red Tone-on-Tone
4 pattern I
Blue Print
5 pattern K

Fold A in half diagonally both ways and lightly crease the folds. Prepare patches B–K for turned-edge appliqué. Use the creases and appliqué placement diagram as guides to arrange the patches on A.

Applique Placement

The stitch diagrams are in the Techniques file on the PDF. Use matching thread and a blind stitch to appliqué the patches in place.

Center the appliqué and trim to 12½"× 12½".

block no. 148
Love Buds

by Ann Weber • Gingham Girls
ginghamgirls.biz

Fabric: Happy Go Lucky designed by Bonnie and Camille and other fabrics by Moda Fabrics, unitednotions.com.

Ann Weber is the author of *Season's Best—Celebrate the Seasons with Quilts* for Gingham Girls, ginghamgirls.biz.

See page 339 on the PDF for pattern

White Tone-on-Tone
1 square (A) 13½"x 13½" (trim to 12½"x 12½" after appliqué)
Green Print
bias strip 1¼"x 40"
Red Print
1 pattern B
Yellow Tone-on-Tone
2 pattern C
Aqua Print
2 pattern D
Green Check
4 pattern E
Fusible web
Clover bias-tape maker ⅜"
(optional)

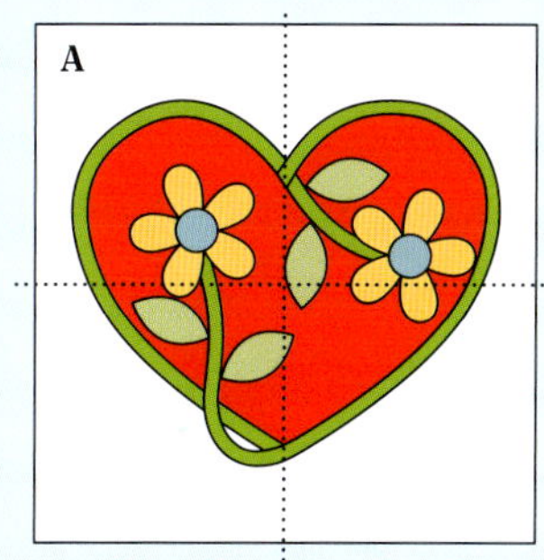

Applique Placement

Follow the manufacturer's instructions if you choose to use Clover's bias-tape maker.

Refer to "Bias Strips" in the Techniques file on the PDF. Cut the bias strip into 1 length of 18" for the left half of the heart outline and 1 length of 22" for the right half.

Fold A in half both ways and lightly crease the folds. Prepare patches B–E for fusible appliqué. Using the creases and appliqué placement diagram as guides, arrange and fuse the heart (B) on A. Arrange the 2 bias strips around the heart tucking 2 of the ends under the strips as shown; pin in place. Use a straight stitch to sew just inside the edges of the bias strips. Arrange the remaining patches in alphabetical order; fuse in place. Use matching thread and a machine blanket stitch to sew around the flowers and leaves.

Center the appliqué and trim to 12½"× 12½" to complete the block.

block no. 149

Surfin'

by Kristy Wolf • Sassafras Lane Designs
sassafras-lane.com

Fabric: Various basics from Timeless Treasures, ttfabrics.com

See page 367 on the PDF for pattern

Aqua Tone-on-Tone
1 square (A) 13½"x 13½" (trim to 12½"x 12½" after appliqué)
Assorted Prints and Tone-on-Tones
1 complete set of appliqué patches
Fusible web
Nonstick pressing sheet
Tear-away stabilizer

Prepare the appliqué patches for fusible appliqué.

Applique Placement

Lay the nonstick pressing sheet on a hard ironing surface. Using the appliqué placement diagram as a guide, arrange the camper and surfboard patches and lightly fuse to one another on top of the pressing sheet. Allow the patches to cool and gently remove from the pressing sheet.

Fold A in half both ways and lightly crease the folds. Using the creases and appliqué placement diagram as guides, fuse the patches to A. Arrange and fuse the clouds in place.

Layer tear-away stabilizer on the back of A. The stitch diagrams are in the Techniques file on the PDF. Use matching thread and a small zigzag stitch to sew around all the patches. Use a zigzag stitch for the lines between the surfboard and camper. Use a straight stitch to add the blind detail. Center the appliqué and trim A to 12½" × 12½".

block no. 150

Shuttered

by Shayla Wolf • Sassafras Lane Designs
sassafras-lane.com

Fabric: Various basics from Timeless Treasures, ttfabrics.com

See page 364 on the PDF for pattern

Teal Tone-on-Tone
1 square (A) 13½"x 13½" (trim to 12½"x 12½" after appliqué)
Black Tone-on-Tone
1 pattern B
White Print
8 pattern C
Fusible web

Fold A in half both ways and lightly crease the folds. Prepare patches B–C for fusible appliqué. Using the creases and appliqué placement diagram as guides, arrange and fuse the patches in alphabetical order. Note that the distance between the curved edges of the B and C's and spaces between the C's is approximately ¼".

The stitch diagrams are in the Techniques file on the PDF. Use matching thread and a zigzag stitch to sew around the patches. Center the appliqué and trim A to 12½" × 12½".

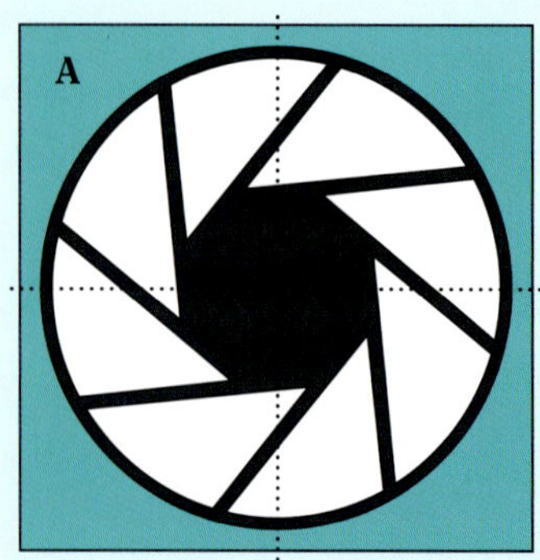

Applique Placement

block no. 151

Le Fleur

by Janice Averill • Iris Quilts
janiceaverill.com

Fabric: Safari from Studio 8 for Quilting Treasures, quiltingtreasures.com.

See page 389 on the PDF for pattern

Black Solid
1 square (A) 13½" x 13½" (trim to 12½" x 12½" after appliqué)
4 *each* patterns F–H
Light Gray Print #1
1 pattern B
4 pattern C
Rust Print
4 pattern D
Light Gray Tone-on-Tone
4 *each* patterns E and Er
Light Gray Print #2
8 *each* patterns F–H
Fusible web

Fold A in half diagonally both ways and lightly crease the folds. Prepare patches B–H for fusible appliqué. Use the creases and appliqué placement diagram as guides to arrange the patches on A. Fuse the patches to A in alphabetical order.

The stitch diagrams are in the Techniques file on the PDF. Use matching thread and a machine zigzag stitch to sew around the patches. Center the appliqué and trim A to 12½" × 12½".

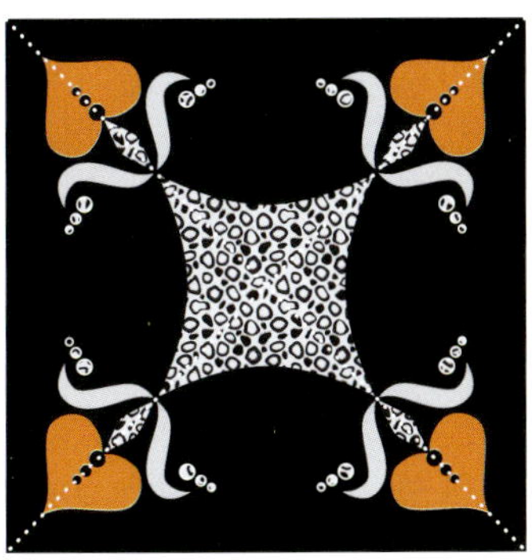

Applique Placement

block no. 152

Hummingbird Haven

by Sandi Colwell • Quilt Cabana Patterns
quiltcabanapatterns.com

Sandi Colwell is the author of *Little Quilts for Big Occasions* for Leisure Arts, Inc., leisurearts.com.

See page 421 on the PDF for pattern

Light Blue Tone-on-Tone
1 square (A) 11½" x 11½" (trim to 10½" x 10½" after appliqué)
Red Tone-on-Tone
1 *each* patterns B, C and Cr
Green Tone-on-Tone
1 *each* patterns D and F
Dark Red Tone-on-Tone
1 pattern E
Black Tone-on-Tone
1 *each* patterns G and Gr
Brown Tone-on-Tone
2 rectangles (H) 1½" x 10½"
2 rectangles (I) 1½" x 12½"
Silver ribbon ⅛" wide x 3"
Fusible web

Fold A in half both ways and lightly crease the folds. Prepare patches B–Gr for fusible appliqué. Using the creases and appliqué placement diagram as guides, arrange the patches in alphabetical order. Tuck the silver ribbon under the top of the feeder and pin in place. Fuse the patches.

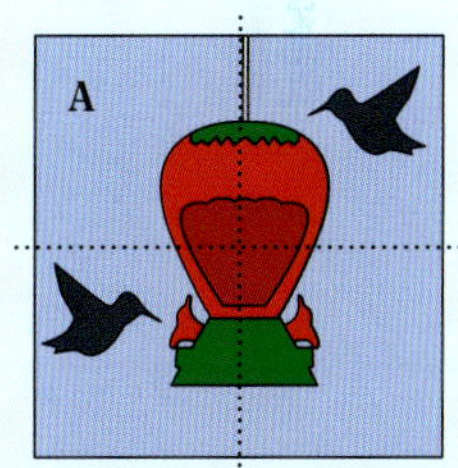

Applique Placement

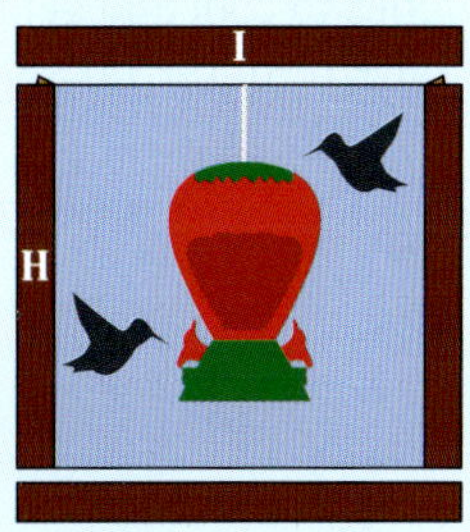

Block Assembly

The stitch diagrams are in the Techniques file on the PDF. With matching thread, straight stitch down the center of the ribbon and just inside the edges of G and Gr. Use a machine blanket stitch to sew around the remaining patches. Center the appliqué and trim A to 10½" × 10½".

Sew the patches together as shown to complete the block.

block no. 153

Half Moon Rising

by Kelly Eisinger • Editorial Assistant, *Quiltmaker*
quiltmaker.com

Fabric: Bali Batiks from Hoffman California Fabrics, hoffmanfabrics.com.

See page 419 on the PDF for pattern

Dark Blue Batik
1 square (A) 13″ x 13″ (trim to 12½″ x 12½″ after appliqué)

Assorted Green Batiks
1 *each* patterns B, C and D

Dark Purple Batik
1 pattern E

Cream Tone-on-Tone
1 pattern F

Fusible web

Tear-away stabilizer

Fold A in half both ways and lightly crease the folds. Prepare patches B–F for fusible appliqué. Use the creases and appliqué placement diagram as guides to arrange the patches on A; fuse in place.

The stitch diagrams are in the Techniques file on the PDF. With tear-away stabilizer on the back of the A, use matching thread and a machine satin stitch to sew around the patches. Center the appliqué and trim A to 12½" × 12½".

Applique Placement

block no. 154

Tulip Flurry

by Pat Harrison • Ocean Waves Quilting Company
oceanwavesqc.com

See page 391 on the PDF for pattern

Aqua Batik
1 square (A) 13½″ x 13½″ (trim to 12½″ x 12½″ after appliqué)

Green Batik #1
8 pattern B

Green Batik #2
8 pattern C

8 Assorted Batiks
from *each*
2 pattern D

Gold Batik
1 pattern E

Fusible web

Fold A in half both ways and lightly crease the folds. Prepare patches B–E for fusible appliqué. Using the creases and appliqué placement diagram as guides, arrange and fuse the patches in alphabetical order.

The stitch diagrams are in the Techniques file on the PDF. Use green thread and a small zigzag stitch to sew around the stems and leaves. Zigzag around the tulips with monofilament thread.

Center the appliqué and trim A to 12½" × 12½" to complete the block.

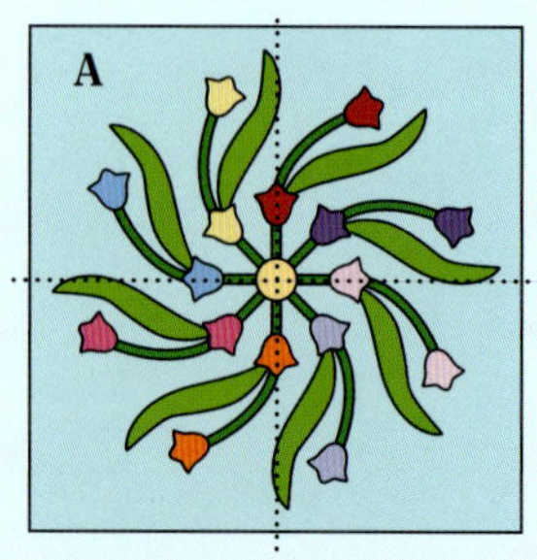

Applique Placement

block no. 155

Cherry Pickin'

by Mary Andra Holmes • Sisters' Quilting Trunk
sistersquiltingtrunk.com

Fabric: Pam Kitty Morning and Pam Kitty Love designed by Pam Vieira-McGinnis for Lakehouse Dry Goods, lakehousedrygoods.com.

See page 407 on the PDF for pattern

White Tone-on-Tone
1 square (A) 13½″ x 13½″ (trim to 12½″ x 12½″ after appliqué)

Black and White Stripe
bias strip 1¼″ x 10¼″

Black Tone-on-Tone
1 *each* patterns B–D

Red Tone-on-Tone
14 pattern E

Black Print
1 pattern F

Green Tone-on-Tone
4 pattern G

Brown and black embroidery floss

Fold A in half both ways and lightly crease the folds. Refer to "Bias Strips" in the Techniques file on the PDF to prepare the basket handle. Prepare patches B–G for turned-edge appliqué. Using the creases and appliqué placement diagram as guides, arrange the handle and patches in alphabetical order.

Use matching thread and a blind stitch to appliqué the patches in place. Use 2 strands of brown floss and an outline stitch to create the cherry stems. Use black floss and a chain stitch for the bird's feet.

Center the appliqué and trim A to 12½″ × 12½″.

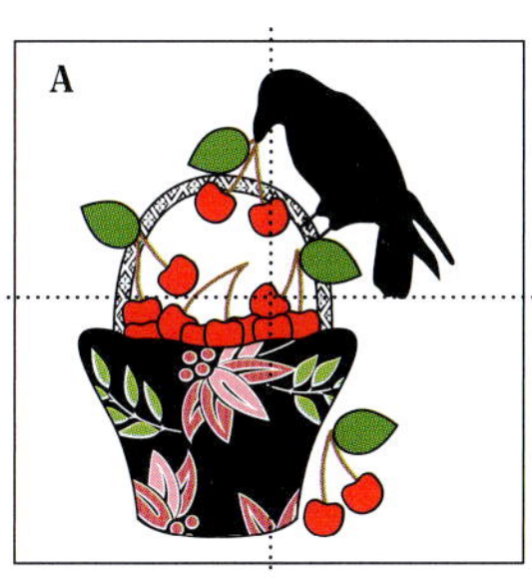

Applique and Embroidery Placement

block no. 156

Ted Turtle

by Sue Marsh • Whistlepig Creek Productions
wpcreek.com

Sue Marsh is the author of *Tablet Covers* for Leisure Arts, Inc., leisurearts.com.

See page 411 on the PDF for pattern

Teal Dot
1 square (A) 13½″ x 13½″ (trim to 12½″ x 12½″ after appliqué)

Green Print
1 pattern B

Green Stripe
1 *each* patterns C, Cr and D

Green Tone-on-Tone
1 pattern E

Purple Tone-on-Tone
1 *each* patterns F and G

Green Dot
1 pattern H

White Solid
1 *each* patterns I and J

Fusible web

Black buttons 2 at ¼″

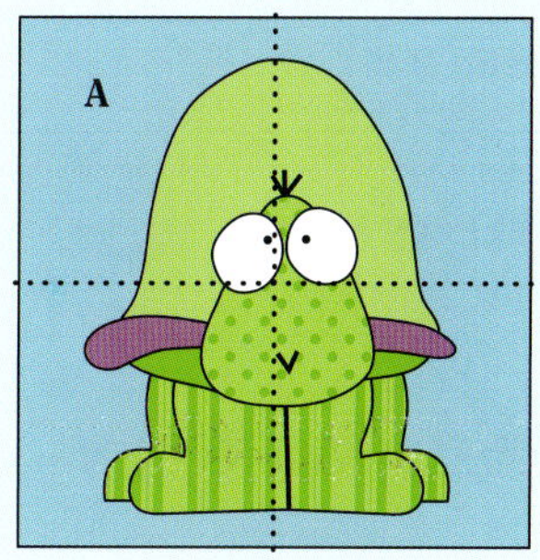

Applique Placement

Fold A in half both ways and lightly crease the folds. Prepare patches B–J for fusible appliqué. Using the creases and appliqué placement diagram as guides, arrange and fuse the patches in alphabetical order.

The stitch diagrams are in the Techniques file on the PDF. Use a machine satin stitch to sew around the patches and add the face and leg detail. Center the appliqué and trim A to 12½″ × 12½″. Tack the buttons in place to complete the block.

block no. 157

The Night Before

by Susan Marth • Suzn Quilts
suznquilts.com

Fabric: Christmas Countdown designed by Deb Strain for Moda Fabrics, unitednotions.com.

Susan Marth is the author of several books including *Vintage Play* and *A Christmas Sampler* for Suzn Quilts, suznquilts.com.

See page 394 on the PDF for pattern

Brown Tone-on-Tone
1 rectangle (A) 2" x 12½"
Cream Dot
1 rectangle (B) 11" x 12½"
Red Print #1
2 *each* patterns C and D
Green Dot
1 *each* patterns C and D
2 pattern E
Red Print #2
1 pattern E

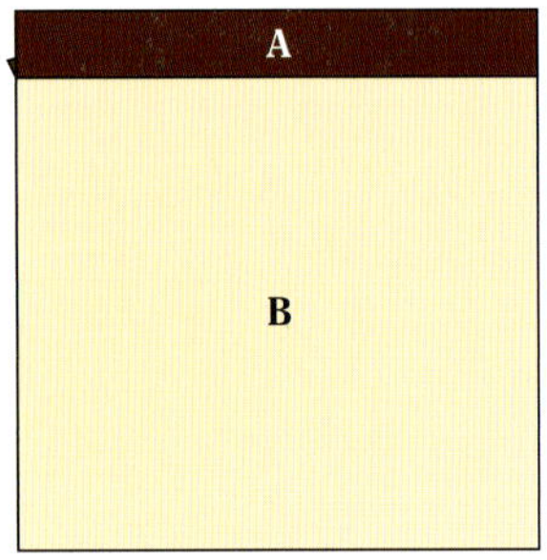

Block Piecing

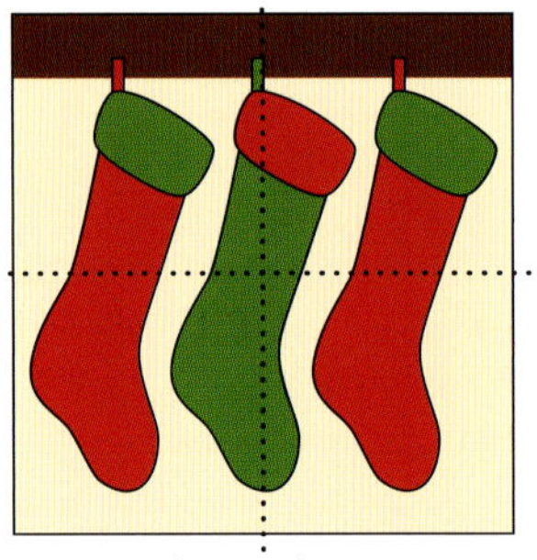

Applique Placement

Sew the brown A and cream B together as shown.

Fold the block in half both ways and lightly crease the folds. Prepare patches C–E for turned-edge appliqué. Use the creases and appliqué placement diagram as guides to arrange the patches.

The stitch diagrams are in the Techniques file on the PDF. Appliqué the patches in place using matching thread and a machine blind stitch to complete the block.

block no. 158

Tweet Tweet

by Rochelle Martin • Cottage Quilt Designs
cottagequiltdesigns.info

Rochelle Martin is the author of *Man Cave Quilts* for Leisure Arts, leisurearts.com.

See page 396 on the PDF for pattern

Yellow Dot
1 square (A) 13½" x 13½" (trim to 12½" x 12½" after appliqué)
Gold Tone-on-Tone
2 pattern B
Aqua Dot
1 *each* patterns C and D
Gold Plaid
1 pattern E
Purple Tone-on-Tone
1 pattern F
Green Print
4 squares (G) 4½" x 4½"
Fusible web
Embroidery floss

Fold A in half both ways and lightly crease the folds. Prepare patches B–F for fusible appliqué. Using the creases and appliqué placement diagram as guides, arrange and fuse the patches in alphabetical order.

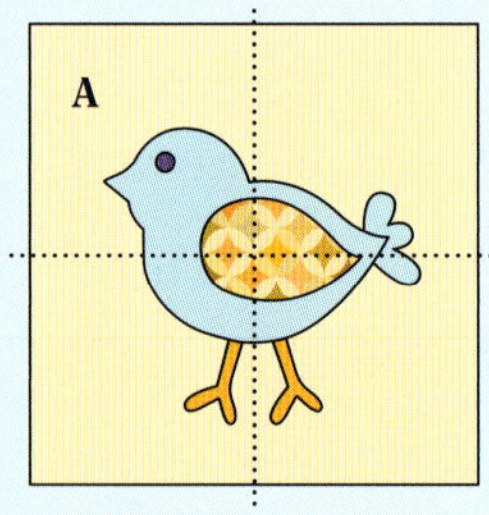

Applique Placement

Use 2 strands of embroidery floss and a hand blanket stitch to sew around the patches. Center the appliqué and trim A to 12½" × 12½".

Refer to "Stitch-and-Flip" in the Techniques file on the PDF. Add the green G's to the corners of A as shown to complete the block.

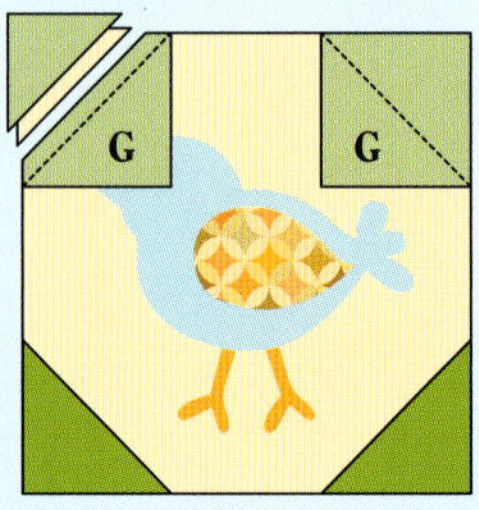

Stitch & Flip

block no. 159

Lazy Days

by Janet Maurer • For You Too! Pattern Company
foryoutoopatterns.com

See page 409 on the PDF for pattern

Light Blue Solid
1 square (A) 10½" x 10½" (trim to 9½" x 9½" after appliqué)
Assorted Tone-on-Tones
1 complete set of appliqué patches
Yellow Print
2 rectangles (K) 2" x 9½"
2 rectangles (L) 2" x 12½"
Black, white and brown embroidery floss
Fusible web
Yellow button 1 at ¾"

Fold A in half both ways and lightly crease the folds. Prepare patches B–J for fusible appliqué. Using the creases and appliqué placement diagram as guides, arrange and fuse the patches to A in alphabetical order.

Applique and Embroidery Placement

The stitch diagrams are on the Techniques file of the PDF. Use matching thread and a machine satin stitch to sew around all the patches. Use 6 strands of black floss and an outline stitch to add the eyelashes and white floss and French knots for the eye highlights. Use brown thread and a machine straight stitch for the face detail; add a French knot at the corner of the mouth. Straight stitch the flower petal detail with light blue thread. Center the appliqué and trim A to 9½" × 9½".

Block Assembly

Sew the yellow print K's and L's to A as shown. Add the button at the center of the flower to complete the block.

block no. 160

Dutch Treat

by Ellen Murphy • American Homestead
amearicanhomesteaddesign.com

Fabric: Wool Felt from National Nonwovens, nationalnonwovens.com.

Ellen Murphy is the author of *American Homestead Quilts* for C&T Publishing, ctpub.com.

See page 385 on the PDF for pattern

Cream Solid
1 square (A) 13½" x 13½" (trim to 12½" x 12½" after appliqué)
Blue Solid
1 pattern B
4 pattern M
Light Green Solid
4 *each* patterns C, F, Fr and K
White Solid
4 *each* patterns D and G
5 pattern I
Dark Pink Solid
4 *each* patterns E, N and Nr
Red Solid
4 *each* patterns G and L
5 pattern H
Dark Green Solid
4 pattern J
Fusible web
Embroidery floss

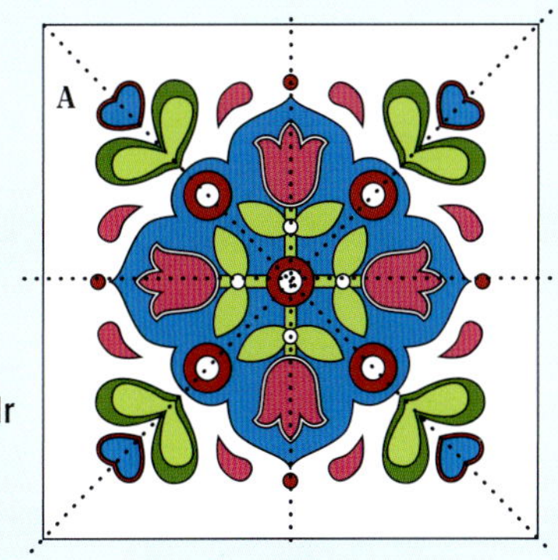

Applique Placement

Ellen used wool felt for her block; cotton can also be used.

Fold A in half both ways and diagonally and lightly crease the folds. Prepare patches B–Nr for fusible appliqué. Using the creases and appliqué placement diagram as guides, arrange and fuse the patches in alphabetical order.

The stitch diagrams are in the Techniques file on the PDF. Use 2 strands of floss and a hand blanket stitch to sew around the patches. Center the appliqué and trim A to 12½" × 12½" to complete the block.

block no. 161

Floppy

by Matthew and Heidi Pridemore • The Whimsical Workshop • thewhimsicalworkshop.com

See page 414 on the PDF for pattern

Light Blue Tone-on-Tone
1 rectangle (A) 4½" x 12½"

Medium Brown Tone-on-Tone
1 rectangle (B) 8½" x 12½"

Assorted Solids and Tone-on-Tones
1 complete set of appliqué patches

Fusible web

Lightweight tear-away stabilizer (optional)

Sew A and B together as shown.

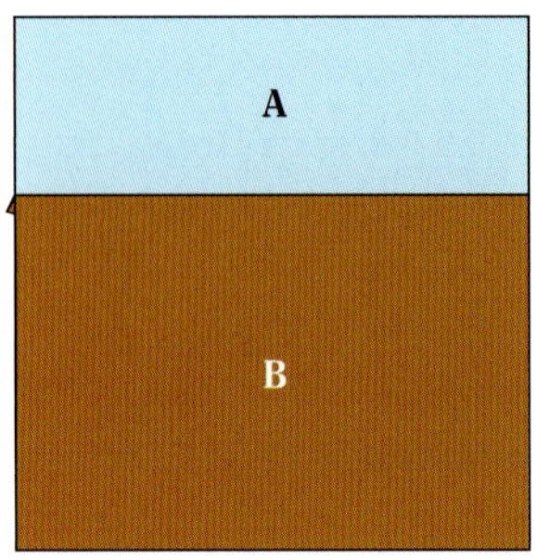

Block Piecing

Fold the block in half both ways and lightly crease the folds. Prepare patches C–Q for fusible appliqué. Using the creases and appliqué placement diagram as guides, arrange and fuse the patches in alphabetical order.

The stitch diagrams are in the Techniques file on the PDF. Use black thread and a machine blanket stitch to sew around the patches. Satin stitch the ground detail to complete the block.

Applique Placement

block no. 162

Tangled Hearts

by Teresa Rawson • Teresa Doodles fabrictherapy.blogspot.com

See page 409 on the PDF for pattern

White Tone-on-Tone
1 square (A) 13½" x 13½" (trim to 12½" x 12½" after appliqué)

Assorted Yellow, Orange, Pink and Red Tone-on-Tones
8 pattern B
4 pattern C
4 pattern D

Fold A in half both ways and diagonally and lightly crease the folds. Prepare patches B–D for turned-edge appliqué. Cut each B at the dotted line where indicated. Use the creases and appliqué placement diagram as guides to arrange the B's on A, weaving the hearts as shown. Position the bottom points of hearts directly opposite each other 1½" apart. Arrange the C's and D's as shown.

The stitch diagrams are in the Techniques file on the PDF. Use matching thread and a blind stitch to appliqué the patches in place. Center the appliqué and trim A to 12½" × 12½".

Placement Detail

Applique Placement

block no. 163

Blessings

by Sindy Rodenmayer • FatCat Patterns
fatcatpatterns.com

See page 380 on the PDF for pattern

Teal Tone-on-Tone
1 square (A) 13½" x 13½" (trim to 12½" x 12½" after appliqué)

Cream Tone-on-Tone #1
1 *each* patterns B and Br

Cream Tone-on-Tone #2
1 *each* patterns C and Cr

Pink Tone-on-Tone #1
1 pattern D

Pink Tone-on-Tone #2
1 pattern E

Cream Batik
1 pattern F

Tan Tone-on-Tone
1 *each* patterns G and H

Fusible web

Fold A in half both ways and lightly crease the folds. Prepare patches B–H for fusible appliqué. Using the creases and appliqué placement diagram as guides, arrange and fuse the patches in alphabetical order.

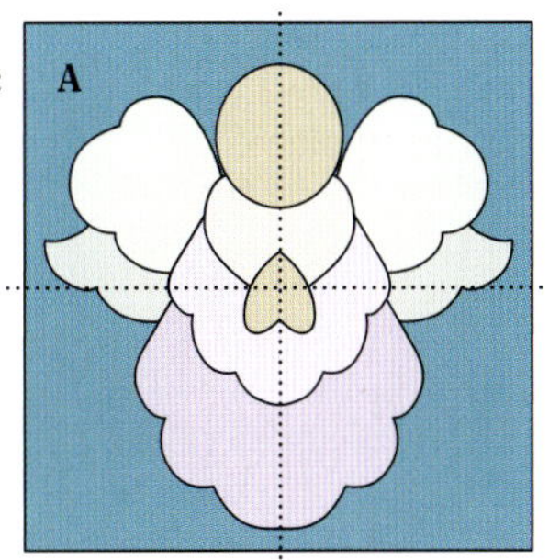

Applique Placement

The stitch diagrams are in the Techniques file on the PDF. Use matching thread and a machine blanket stitch to sew around the patches. Center the appliqué and trim A to 12½" × 12½".

block no. 164

Merry Holidays

by Joanne Rowicki • Gingham Girls
ginghamgirls.biz

See page 390 on the PDF for pattern

White Tone-on-Tone
1 square (A) 13½" x 13½" (trim to 12½" x 12½" after appliqué)

Brown Check
2 pattern B

Green Tone-on-Tone
1 *each* patterns C and Cr

Red Tone-on-Tone
1 pattern D

Fusible web

Fold A in half both ways and lightly crease the folds. Prepare patches B–D for fusible appliqué. Using the creases and appliqué placement diagram as guides, arrange and fuse the patches in alphabetical order.

Applique Placement

The stitch diagrams are in the Techniques file on the PDF. Use matching thread and a machine blanket stitch to sew around the trunks and trees. Use a straight stitch to sew close to the edges of D. Center the appliqué and trim A to 12½" × 12½".

block no. 165

Skating on Thin Ice

by Denise Russart
justquiltin.wordpress.com

See page 423 on the PDF for pattern

Blue Tone-on-Tone
1 square (A) 13½" x 13½" (trim to 12½" x 12½" after appliqué)
Assorted Tone-on-Tones
1 complete set of appliqué patches
Black Perle cotton
Button 1 black at ⅜"

Fold A in half both ways and lightly crease the folds. Prepare patches B–O for turned-edge appliqué. Using the creases and appliqué placement diagram as guides, arrange the patches in alphabetical order.

The stitch diagrams are in the Techniques file on the PDF. Use matching thread and a blind stitch to appliqué the patches in place. Use a long stitch and perle cotton for the skate laces, tying a bow at the tops of the skates as shown.

Center the appliqué and trim to 12½" × 12½". Tack the button in place for the eye to complete the block.

Applique Placement

block no. 166

Floral Garland

by Yoko Saito • Quilt Party
shop.quilt.co.jp/en/

Yoko Saito is the author of *Yoko Saito's Japanese Taupe Color Theory: A Study Guide* for Stitch Publications, stitchpublications.com.

See page 386 on the PDF for pattern

Medium Gray Print
1 square (A) 13½" x 13½" (trim to 12½" x 12½" after appliqué)
Medium Brown Tone-on-Tone
bias strip ⅜" x 48"
Assorted Tone-on-Tones
1 complete set of appliqué patches
Embroidery floss
Black Pigma Micron pen (.01 tip) (optional)

Yoko used Cosmo embroidery floss from Lecien Corporation, lecien.co.jp/en. For more information about Yoko's "Tiny Bias Stems" technique, refer to her book listed above.

Refer to "Tiny Bias Stems" in the Techniques file on the PDF. Use the brown bias strip to make the stems. Prepare patches B–Gr for turned-edge appliqué. Fold A in half diagonally both ways and lightly crease the folds. Use the creases and appliqué placement diagram as guides to arrange the stems and patches on A.

Use matching thread and a blind stitch to appliqué the stems and patches in place. Yoko used the Pigma pen to lightly draw lines down the centers of the white flower petals, leaves and center 2 petals of small flowers.

Refer to the diagram and the pattern sheet for embroidery placement. Use 2 strands of floss and an outline stitch, lazy daisy stitch and French knots for the flower bud detail. Use 1 strand to add the crossstitches around the flower centers. Center the appliqué and trim A to 12½" × 12½".

Applique and Embroidery Placement

block no. 167

Flower Pops

by Pam Vieira-McGinnis
pamkittymorning.blogspot.com

Fabric: Pam Kitty Picnic designed by Pam Vieira-McGinnis for Lake House Dry Goods, lakehousedrygoods.com.

See page 387 on the PDF for pattern

White Print
1 square (A) 13½″x 13½″ (trim to 12½″x 12½″ after appliqué)

Green Plaid
1 pattern B
2 pattern C

Yellow Tone-on-Tone
2 pattern D
1 pattern E

Red Print
3 pattern F

Green Tone-on-Tone
2 pattern G
4 pattern H

Fusible web

Fold A in half both ways and lightly crease the folds. Prepare patches B–H for fusible appliqué. Using the creases and appliqué placement diagram as guides, arrange and fuse the patches in alphabetical order.

The stitch diagrams are in the Techniques file on the PDF. Use matching thread and a machine blanket stitch to sew around the patches. Center the appliqué and trim A to 12½"× 12½".

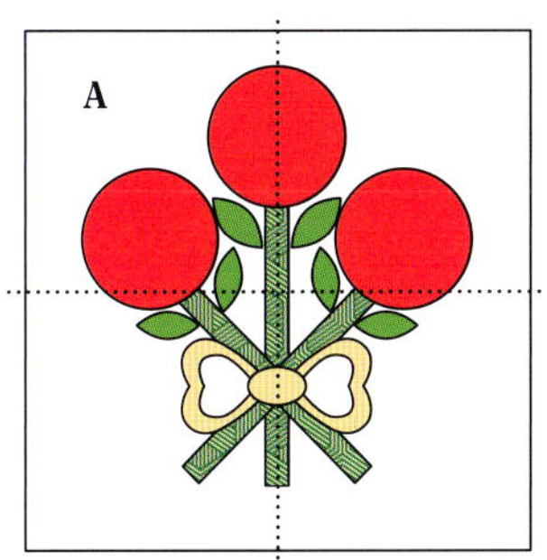

Applique Placement

block no. 168

Believe

by Ann Weber • Gingham Girls
ginghamgirls.biz

Ann Weber is the author of *Season's Best: Celebrate the Seasons with Quilts* for Gingham Girls, ginghamgirls.biz.

See page 418 on the PDF for pattern

Aqua Tone-on-Tone
1 square (A) 13½″x 13½″ (trim to 12½″x 12½″ after appliqué)

Red Check
1 pattern B

White Dot
1 pattern C

White Solid
1 pattern D

Gray Tone-on-Tone
1 pattern E

Fusible web

Ann layered thin white batting beneath the brim and ball patches of the hat for added dimension.

Fold A in half both ways and lightly crease the folds. Prepare patches B–D for turned-edge appliqué. Use the creases and appliqué placement diagram as guides to arrange the patches on A.

The stitch diagrams are in the Techniques file on the PDF. Use matching thread and a blind stitch to appliqué B–D in place. Prepare patch E for fusible appliqué. Arrange and fuse E on B. Use a straight stitch around E. Center the appliqué and trim A to 12½"× 12½".

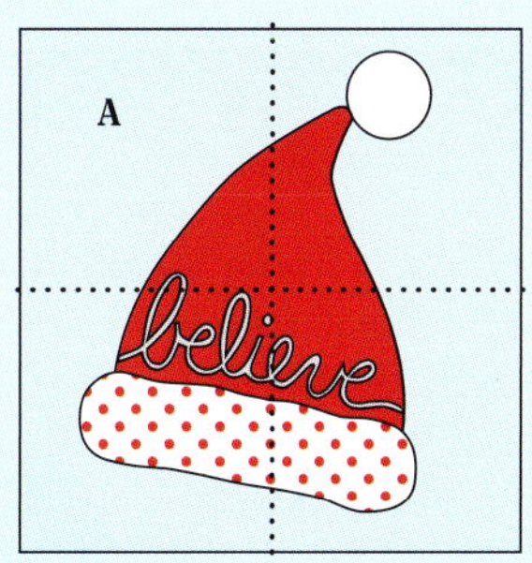

Applique Placement

block no. 169

Travelin' in Style

by Kristy Wolf • Sassafras Lane Designs
sassafras-lane.com

See page 424 on the PDF for pattern

Medium Blue Tone-on-Tone
1 square (A) 13½"x 13½" (trim to 12½"x 12½" after appliqué)
Assorted Prints and Tone-on-Tones
1 complete set of appliqué patches
Fusible web
Nonstick pressing sheet
Tear-away stabilizer

Applique Placement

Prepare the appliqué patches for fusible appliqué.

Lay the nonstick pressing sheet on a hard ironing surface. Using the appliqué placement diagram as a guide, arrange the vehicle and cargo patches and lightly fuse to one another on top of the pressing sheet. Allow the patches to cool and gently remove from the pressing sheet.

Fold A in half both ways and lightly crease the folds. Using the creases and appliqué placement diagram as guides, fuse the road, vehicle/cargo patches to A. Arrange and fuse the clouds in place.

Layer tear-away stabilizer on the back of A. The stitch diagrams are in the Techniques file on the PDF. Use matching thread and a small zigzag stitch to sew around all the patches. Use a zigzag stitch for the lines on the cargo. Center the appliqué and trim to 12½" × 12½".

block no. 170

Finally Spring

by Nancy Zieman • Nancy Zieman Productions
nancyzieman.com

Nancy Zieman is the creator of several sewing and quilting products, including Trace 'N Create Quilt Templates from Clover, clover-usa.com. She is also the author of many sewing and quilting titles including *Quick Column Quilts* for Krause Publications, krausebooks.com.

See page 401 on the PDF for pattern

Medium Gray Batik
1 square (A) 13½"x 13½" (trim to 12½"x 12½" after appliqué)
5–7 Assorted Green Prints and Tone-on-Tones
appliqué patches for ground foliage (see below)
Light Gray Tone-on-Tone
1 *each* patterns B and C
Fabric markers or oil pastels

Nancy created the ground foliage in her landscape block by fussy cutting green fabrics that featured trees.

Fuse a piece of fusible web to the wrong side of each green print and tone-on-tone. Fussy-cut or randomly cut patches to fill up the lower third of A with ground foliage as shown.

Prepare patches B and C for fusible appliqué. Refer to the appliqué placement diagram to arrange the ground foliage and patches on A as shown. Use matching thread and a straight stitch to sew close to the edges of the appliqué patches.

Refer to the pattern page for placement of the branches; use the fabric markers or oil pastels to add branches, leaves and details to the tree trunks to finish the block.

Applique Placement

block no. 171

Jazz Round

by Sunny Steinkuhler
thequiltedcookie.blogspot.com

Sunny Steinkuhler is the author of *Blocks! Borders! Quilts!* for Martingale, shopmartingale.com.

See page 407 on the PDF for pattern

White Tone-on-Tone
8 squares (A) 2½″ x 2½″
1 square (B) 4½″ x 4½″
sections 1 and 2, patches 1, 6 and 7

Green Tone-on-Tone
section 1, patches 2 and 3
section 2, patches 4 and 5

Purple Tone-on-Tone
section 1, patches 4 and 5
section 2, patches 2 and 3

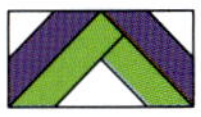

Section 1
Make 8

Section 2
Make 4

Make 12 paper copies *total* of the foundation section. Refer to the foundations for color placement. Colors for section 2 are shown in parentheses. Foundation piece the sections in numerical order, pressing and trimming after each patch addition.

Sew the patches and sections together as shown to complete the block. To reduce bulk, press the seams open.

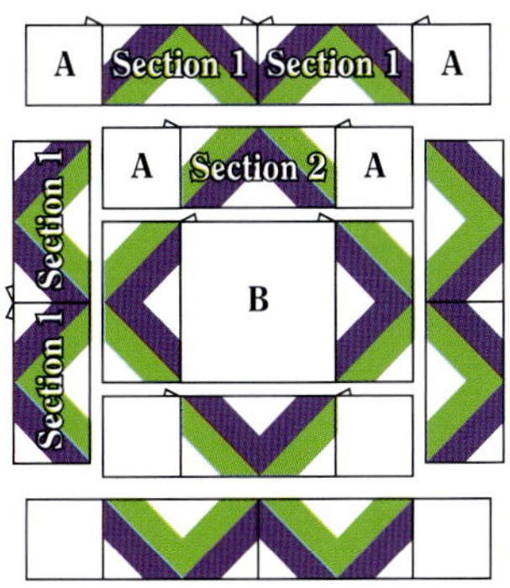

Block Assembly

block no. 172

Wanderlust

by Cindy Wiens
liveacolorfullife.net

Fabric: Dowry designed by Anna Marie Horner for FreeSpirit Fabrics, freespiritfabric.com and Kona Cotton Solids from Robert Kaufman, robertkaufman.com.

See page 413 on the PDF for pattern

Gold Solid
section 1, patch 1

White Solid
sections 1 and 2, patches 2 and 3
sections 3 and 4, patches 2–5

Light Green Solid
section 2, patch 1

Orange Solid
section 3, patch 1

Dark Pink Solid
section 4, patch 1

Teal Print
1 square (A) 5½″ x 5½″

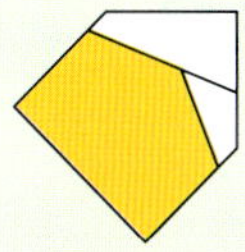

Section 1
Make 1

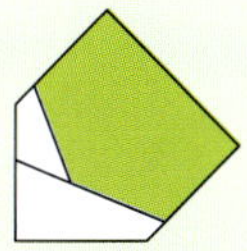

Section 2
Make 1

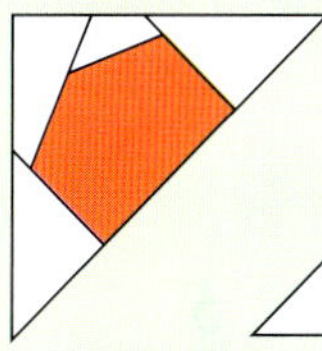

Section 3
Make 1

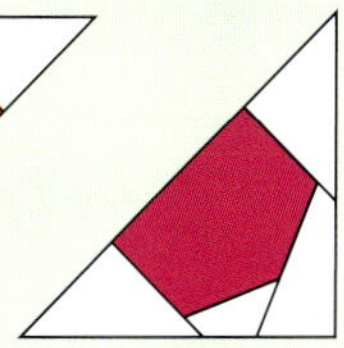

Section 4
Make 1

Make 1 paper copy *each* of foundation sections 1–4. Refer to the foundations and section diagrams for color placement. Colors for sections 2 and 4 are shown in parentheses. Foundation piece the sections in numerical order, pressing and trimming after each patch addition.

Sew the sections and A together as shown to complete the block.

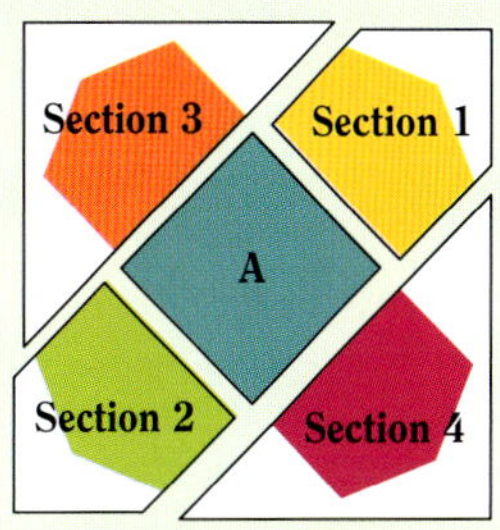

Block Assembly

block no. 173

Midnight Garden

by Carol Doak
caroldoak.com

Carol is the author of a sizeable collection of books on paper-piecing including *Mariner's Compass Stars: 24 Stellar Paper-Pieced Blocks & 9 Easy Quilt Projects* for C&T Publishing, ctpub.com.

See page 6 on the PDF for pattern

Yellow Tone-on-Tone
patch 1
Black Print
patches 2–5, 8–10, 13–15
Light Pink Tone-on-Tone
patch 6
Pink Print
patch 7
Green Print
patch 11
Light Green Tone-on-Tone
patch 12

Each block is made from 4 sections. Make 4 paper copies of the foundation. Foundation piece the sections in numerical order, pressing and trimming after each patch addition. Join the sections as shown to complete the block.

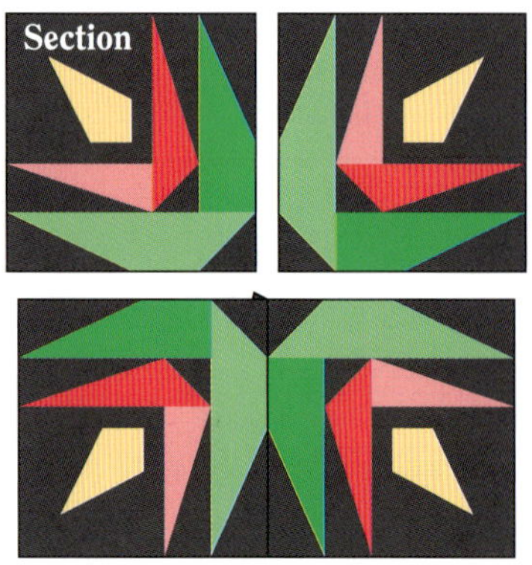

Block Piecing

block no. 174

Stars Upon Stars

by Joen Wolfrom • JWD Publishing
jwdpublishing.com

Joen is the author of *Visual Coloring; Color Play; Patchwork Persuasion*; and the *3-in-1 Color Tool* all for C&T Publishing, ctpub.com.

See page 8 on the PDF for pattern

Rust Tone-on-Tone
patch 1
Beige Tone-on-Tone
patches 2, 4 and 6
Medium Multicolor Print
patch 3
Dark Multicolor Print
patch 5

Each quarter of the block is made from a section and its reverse. Make 4 paper copies of the foundation and 4 paper copies of the reversed foundation. Foundation piece the sections in numerical order, pressing and trimming after each patch addition.

Joen prefers working with a dry iron to prevent stretching the fabrics.

Refer to the block piecing diagram and join a section and a reverse section to make each of the quadrants. Join the quadrants as shown to complete the block.

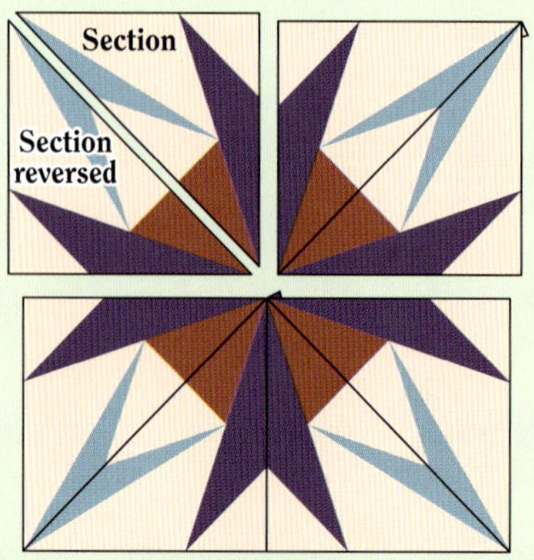

Block Piecing

block no. 175

Hot Fudge Please

by Julie Pieri • Quilted Pleasures
quiltedpleasures.com

See page 5 on the PDF for pattern

◪ = cut in half diagonally

Cream Batik

section 1, patches 1, 3, 5, 7, 9, 11 and 13
5 squares 2⅞" x 2⅞" ◪ (A) (there will be 1 extra patch)

Dark Brown Batik

section 1, patches 2, 4, 6, 8, 10 and 12
4 squares 2⅞" x 2⅞" ◪ (A)

Dark Teal Batik

sections 2 and 2r, patches 1, 3, 5, and 7
1 square 2⅞" x 2⅞" ◪ (A)

Blue Batik

sections 2 and 2r, patches 2, 4, 6, and 8

Red Batik

1 square 2⅞" x 2⅞" ◪ (A) (there will be 1 extra patch)

Light Aqua Batik

1 square 2⅞" x 2⅞" ◪ (A)
2 rectangles (B) 2½" x 8½"
1 square (C) 2½" x 2½"

Make paper copies of the sections 1, 2 and section 2 reversed foundations. Foundation piece the sections in numerical order, pressing and trimming after each patch addition.

Join the sections and the A–C patches as shown in the block piecing diagram.

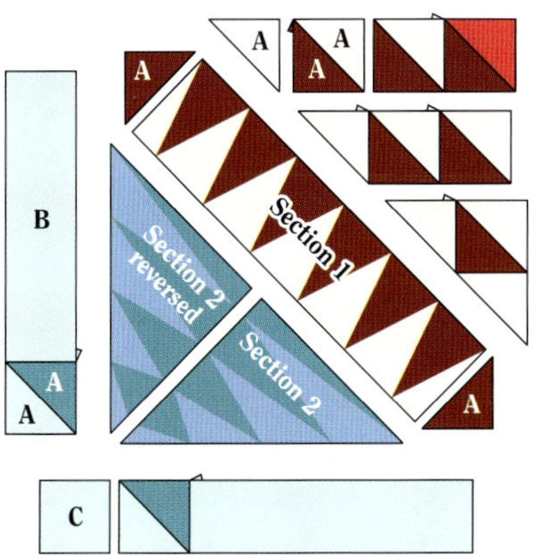

Block Piecing

block no. 176

Timber

by Kay Gentry • Noble Needle Quilting & Sewing
nobleneedle.com

◪ = cut in half diagonally
⊠ = cut in half twice diagonally

Assorted Prints and Tone-on-Tones

strips for foundation piecing (see instructions below)

Muslin

1 panel 13" x 20"

Brown Tone-on-Tone

4 squares 2⅞" x 2⅞" ◪ (B)
1 square 5¼" x 5¼" ⊠ (D)
2 squares 3⅜" x 3⅜" ◪ (F)

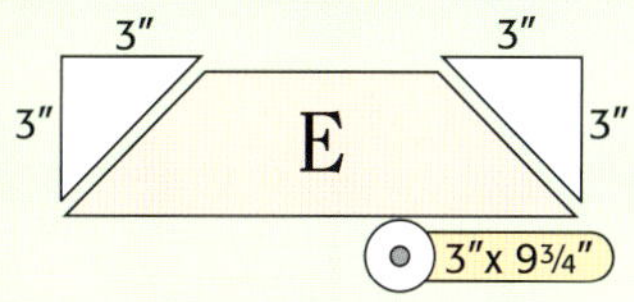

Cutting Diagram

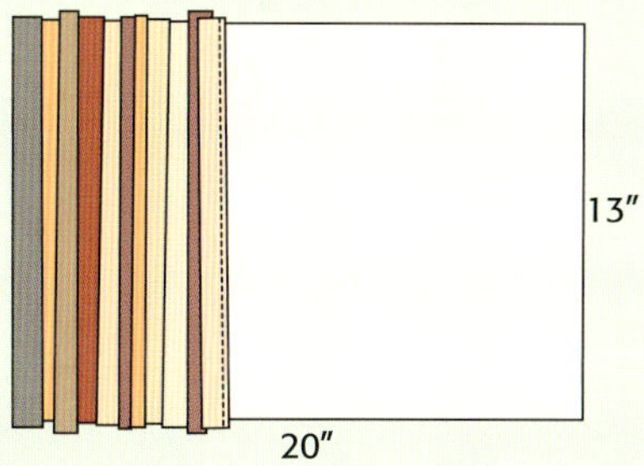

The muslin is used as a foundation. From the assorted prints and tone-on-tones, cut strips that are 14" long and from ½" to 1½" wide, tapering some of the strips slightly. The strips are added in random order. Align the first strip on the left end of the muslin, right side up. Place the second strip on the first strip right sides together, aligning the raw edges. Sew through both strips and the muslin foundation with a ¼" seam allowance. Flip the second strip open and press. Continue to add strips across the muslin as shown, pressing the strips open after each addition. Trim the strips even with the edges of the muslin.

From the strip-pieced foundation, cut 1 lengthwise strip 2½" wide; cut 2 lengthwise strips 3" wide. Cut the 2½" strip into 4 C's at 2½" × 4½". Referring to the cutting diagram above, cut the 3" strips into 4 E's as shown. From the remaining strip-pieced foundation, cut 1 A at 3⅜" × 3⅜".

Assemble the block as shown in the block piecing diagram.

Block Piecing

block no. 177

Swedish Log Cabin

by Lorraine Olsen • Lorraine Olsen Quilts
lorraineolsenquilts.com

Lorraine is the author of *Little Lone Star Quilts* for C&T Publishing, ctpub.com.

See page 9 on the PDF for pattern

Assorted Black Prints
patch 1
Assorted Cream/White Prints
patches 2–5
Assorted Red Prints
patches 6–9
Assorted Pink Prints
patches 10 and 11
Black Solid
patches 12 and 13

Each block is made from 4 sections. Make 4 paper copies of the foundation. Foundation piece the sections in numerical order, pressing and trimming after each patch addition. Join the sections as shown to complete the block.

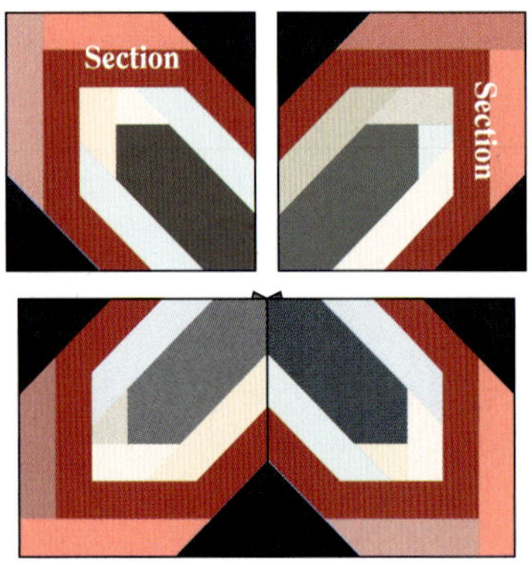

Block Piecing

block no. 178

Twirling Star

by Nancy Mahoney
nancymahoney.com

Fabric: Granny's Treasures designed by Nancy Mahoney for P&B Textiles, pbtex.com.

Nancy is the author of *Quilt Revival* and *Appliqué Quilt Revival* for Martingale & Company, shopmartingale.com.

See page 11 on the PDF for pattern

Assorted Pink Prints
patch 1
Natural Muslin
patches 2 and 4
Assorted Green Prints
patch 3
Yellow Print
1 pattern A

Templates for Twirling Star block on page 11 of the Templates file on the PDF.

Each quarter of this block is made from a section 1 and a section 2. Notice that Nancy used a darker pink and green for section 1; the pink and green in section 2 are lighter values.

Make 4 paper copies of each foundation section. Foundation piece each section in numerical order, pressing and trimming after each patch addition. Join a section 1 to a section 2 to make each of the quadrants. Join the quadrants as shown to make the block.

Prepare A for turned-edge appliqué. Refer to the stitch diagrams in the Techniques file on the PDF. Using a blind stitch, appliqué A at the center of the block as shown.

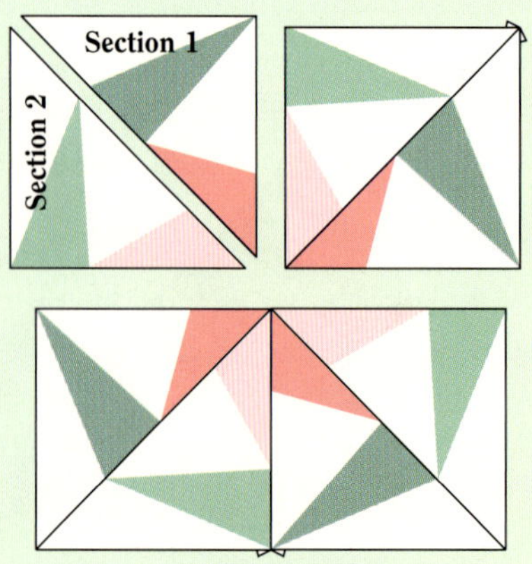

Block Piecing

block no. 179

Art Deco Star

by Susan Cook • Larkspur Lane Designs
larkspurlanedesigns.com

Fabric: Shade Cascade designed by Karen Combs for Blank Quilting, blankquilting.com.

See page 1 on the PDF for pattern

Medium Light Purple Tone-on-Tone
section 1, patch 1
section 2, patch 1

Black Solid
section 1, patches 2, 4 and 5
section 2, patch 2
section 3, patches 2 and 3

Medium Dark Purple Tone-on-Tone
section 1, patch 3
section 3, patch 1

Light Purple Tone-on-Tone
section 2, patch 3

Gold Tone-on-Tone
section 4, patch 1

Dark Purple Tone-on-Tone
section 4, patch 2

Each quarter of the block is made from 4 sections. Make 4 paper copies of *each* of the foundation sections 1–4. Foundation piece the sections in numerical order, pressing and trimming after each patch addition. Refer to the block piecing diagram and join sections 1–4 as shown to make the quadrants. Join the quadrants as shown to complete the block.

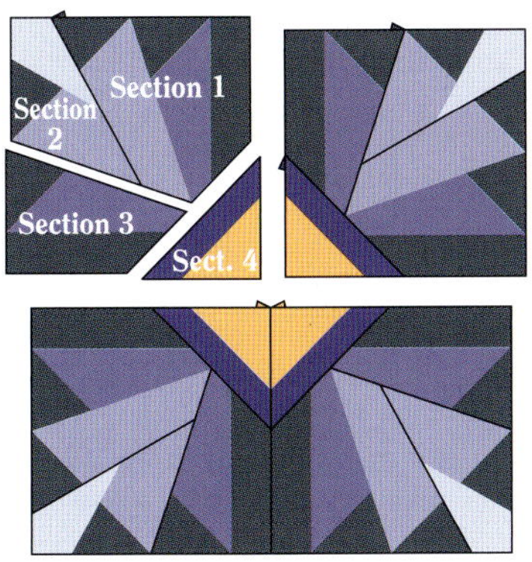

Block Piecing

block no. 180

Happiness in a Block

by Teresa Fields • Quickie Chicks

Teresa is the designer of the Sole Cool Hot Iron Bag pattern published by JWD Publishing, jwdpublishing.com.

See page 4 on the PDF for pattern

Bright Green Tone-on-Tone
patches 1 and 4

Bright Pink Tone-on-Tone
patch 2

Bright Blue Tone-on-Tone
patch 3

Bright Multiprint
patch 5

The block is made from 4 sections. Make 4 paper copies of the foundation. Foundation piece the sections in numerical order, pressing and trimming after each patch addition. Join the sections as shown to complete the block.

Block Piecing

block no. 181
Versailles

by Chloe Anderson and Colleen Reale • Toadusew
toadusew.com

Fabric: La Scala 2 designed by Peggy Toole for Robert Kaufman, robertkaufman.com.

See page 61 on the PDF for pattern

Red Print
section 1, patch 1
1 square (A) 3½″ x 3½″
Dark Green Print
section 1, patches 2 and 3
section 2 and section 2 reversed, patch 1
Gold Tone-on-Tone
section 1, patches 4 and 5
4 squares (B) 2″ x 2″
Cream Print
section 2 and section 2 reversed, patches 2 and 4
Medium Green Print
section 2 and section 2 reversed, patch 3

Unit
Stitch & Flip
Make 1

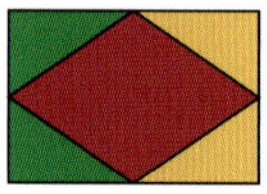

Section 1
Make 4

Refer to "Stitch-and-Flip" in the Techniques file on the PDF. Use the red A and gold B's to make the unit.

Section 2
Make 2

Section 2 Reversed
Make 2

Make 4 paper copies of the section 1 foundation and 2 copies *each* of the section 2 and section 2 reversed foundations. Foundation piece the sections in numerical order, pressing and trimming after each patch addition.

Join the unit and sections as shown to complete the block.

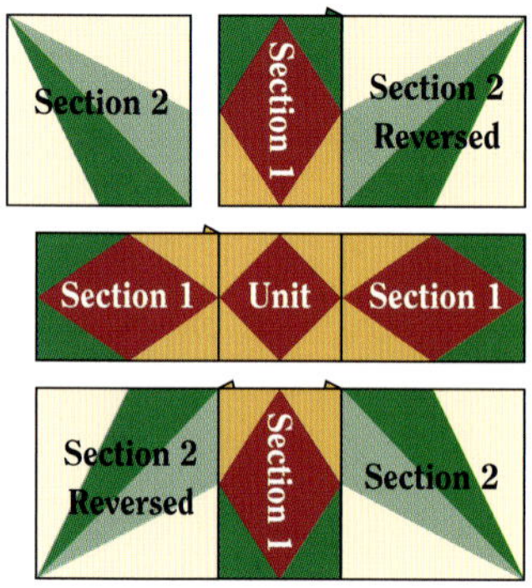

Block Assembly

block no. 182
Ice Crystal

by Eileen Fowler • Associate Editor, *Quiltmaker*
quiltmaker.com

See page 70 on the PDF for pattern

Medium Blue Print #1
sections 1, 2 and 3: patches 1 and 12
Dark Blue Batik #1
sections 1, 2 and 3: patches 2, 3, 5, 7, 13 and 14
Medium Blue Print #2
sections 1, 2 and 3: patches 4 and 8
White Print
sections 1, 2 and 3: patches 6 and 10
Dark Blue Batik #2
sections 1, 2 and 3: patches 9 and 11

Each half of the block is made from 3 sections. Make 2 paper copies *each* of sections 1, 2 and 3.

Foundation piece the sections in numerical order, pressing and trimming after each patch addition.

Refer to the block assembly diagram and join sections 1, 2 and 3 as shown to make *each* block half. To reduce bulk, press the seams open. Join the block halves as shown to complete the block.

Section 1
Make 2

Section 2
Make 2

Section 3
Make 2

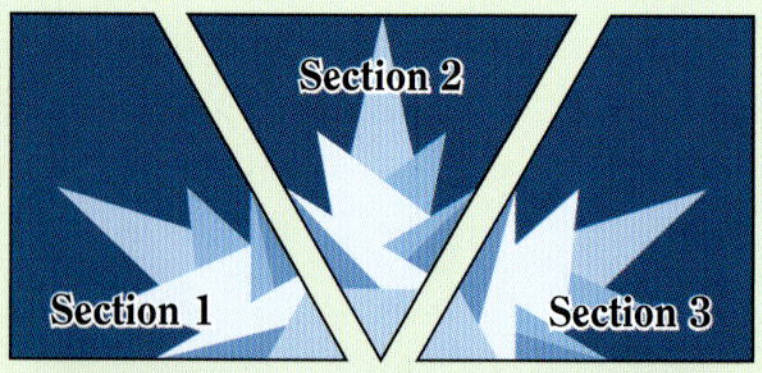

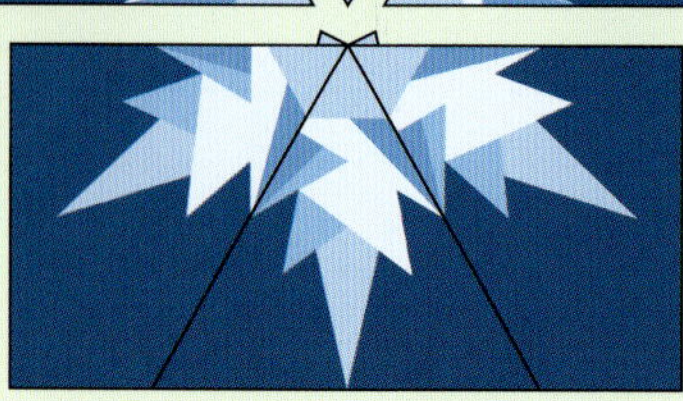

Block Assembly

block no. 183

Pinwheel O'Strings

by Rachel Griffith • P.S. I Quilt
psiquilt.com.com

Fabric: Various Lakehouse collections designed by Holly Holderman for Lakehouse Dry Goods, lakehousedrygoods.com.

Assorted Prints
- 2 strips 2" x 10"
- 1"-wide strips to total 180"

White Tone-on-Tone
- 2 squares (A) 6⅞" x 6⅞"

Foundation paper
- 2 squares 6⅞" x 6⅞"

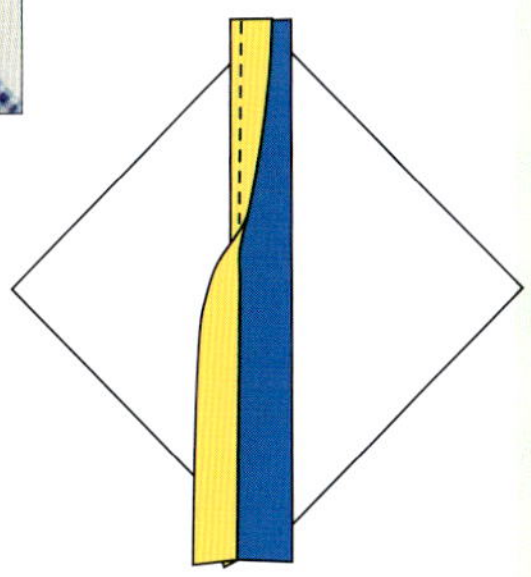

Section Piecing

Position a 2" strip right side up diagonally across the center of the foundation square. Aligning raw edges, lay a 1" strip right side down on the center strip as shown. Join the strips by sewing through all the layers ¼" from the raw edges. Flip the top strip open and press. Continue adding 1" strips from the center outward in both directions until the entire foundation has been covered. Trim the fabric even with the paper. Repeat to make 2 sections.

Section
Make 2

If your machine's feed dogs have trouble feeding the paper, an alternative is a muslin foundation.

Unit
Make 4

Use the "Triangle-Squares" technique found in the Techniques file on the PDF; pair a white A with a section, sewing in the same direction as the strips, to make the unit. Make 4 units.

Join the units as shown to complete the block.

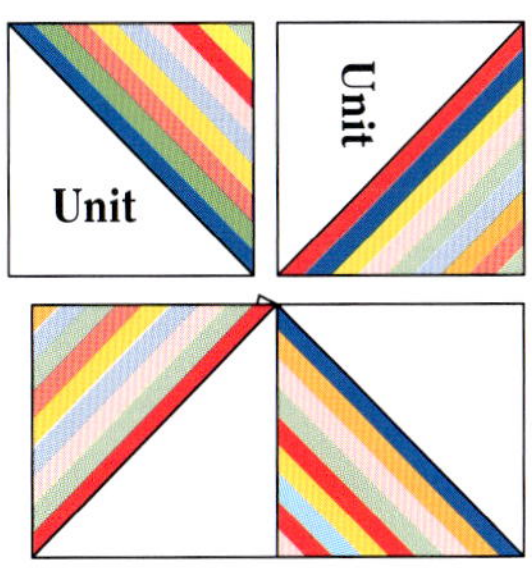

Block Assembly

block no. 184

Nova

by Angie Hodapp • Editor-in-Chief, *Quilters Newsletter*
quiltersnewsletter.com

Fabric: Spirit designed by Lila Tueller for Moda Fabrics, unitednotions.com.

See pages 58–59 on the PDF for pattern

Multiprint
- section 1, patch 1

Brown Tone-on-Tone
- section 1, patches 2–5
- section 2, patch 2

Yellow Tone-on-Tone
- section 2, patches 1 and 3

Green Tone-on-Tone
- section 3, patch 1

Soft Red Tone-on-Tone
- section 3, patch 2
- section 4, patch 4

Dark Teal Tone-on-Tone
- section 4, patch 2
- section 5, patch 1

Medium Teal Tone-on-Tone
- section 4, patch 3
- section 5, patch 2

Brown Print
- section 4, patch 1
- section 5, patch 3

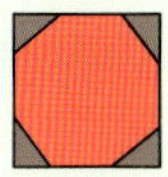

Section 1
Make 1

Section 2
Make 4

Section 3
Make 4

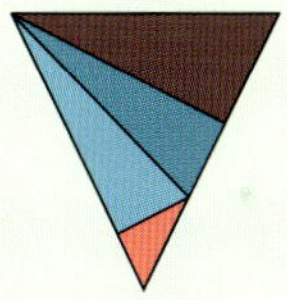

Section 4
Make 4

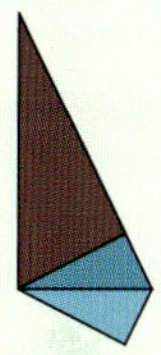

Section 5
Make 4

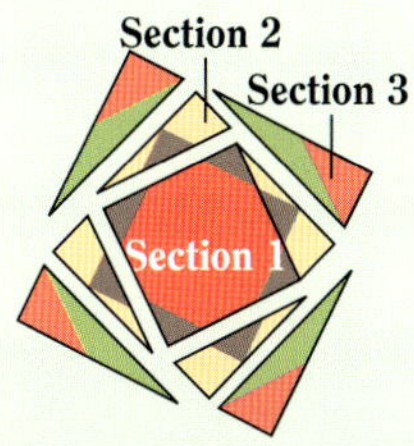

Make 1 paper copy of section 1 and 4 paper copies *each* of sections 2–5. Foundation piece each section in numerical order, pressing and trimming after each patch addition.

To section 1, add the 4 section 2's, pressing after adding each one. Repeat to add the section 3's. Sew each section 4 to a section 5 as shown.

Block Assembly
• = Partial Seam

Add a section 4/5 to the center with a partial seam as shown. Add the remaining section 4/5's, moving counterclockwise. Complete the partial seam.

block no. 185
Spiked Pinwheels

by Robin Koehler • Nestlings by Robin
nestlingsbyrobin.com

See page 76 on the PDF for pattern

Dark Green Batik
patch 1
Orange Batik
patches 2 and 4
Dark Rust Batik
patches 3, 6 and 7
Light Green Batik
patch 5
Brown Tone-on-Tone
patch 8
Tan Batik
patch 9

Section
Make 4

Make 4 paper copies of the foundation section. Foundation piece each section in numerical order, pressing and trimming after each patch addition.

Join the sections as shown to complete the block.

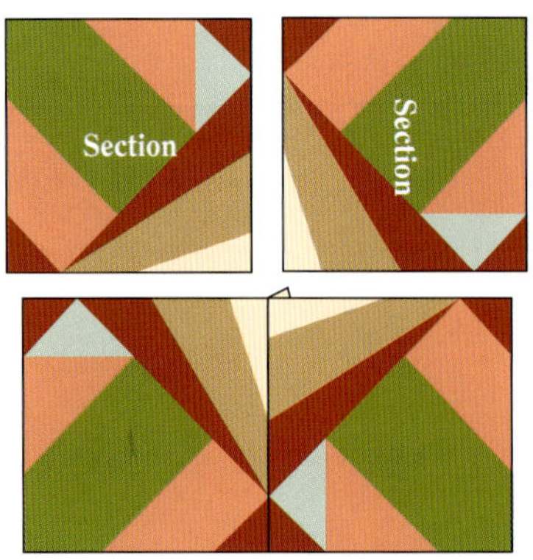

Block Assembly

block no. 186
Midnight Dream

by Carolyn Cullinan McCormick • CM Designs, Inc.addaquarter.com

Carolyn McCormick is the creator of the Add-a-Quarter and Add Enough tools for quilters. She is the author of several books including *Wedding Ring, Pickle Dish & More* and *Quilts for Rosie* for Kansas City Star Quilts, pickledish.com.

See pages 56–57 on the PDF for pattern

Cream Tone-on-Tone
section 1, patches 1 and 7
section 2, patches 4 and 5
section 3, patches 2–5
Light Purple Batik
section 1, patches 2, 3 and 8
section 2, patches 2 and 3
section 3, patch 1
Dark Purple Batik
section 1, patches 4–6
section 2, patch 1

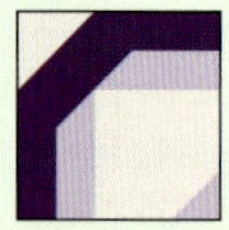

Section 1
Make 4

Section 2
Make 4

Section 3
Make 1

Make 4 paper copies of the section 1 and section 2 foundations and 1 copy of the section 3 foundation. Foundation piece each section in numerical order, pressing and trimming after each patch addition.

Join the sections as shown to complete the block.

Block Assembly

block no. 187

Shoe Boxes

by Denise Starck • Graphic Designer, *Quiltmaker*
quiltmaker.com

Fabric: Garden Whimsy by Kim Schaefer for Andover Fabrics, andoverfabrics.com and Sparkling Paris by Hoodie's Collection for Blank Quilting, blankquilting.com.

See page 74 on the PDF for pattern

Cream Dot
- 2 rectangles (A) 1¼" x 4¾"
- 1 rectangle (B) 1½" x 11¼"
- 2 rectangles (C) 1⅛" x 10"
- 2 rectangles (D) 1¾" x 12½"
- sections 1 and 1 reversed, patches 1, 4 and 5
- sections 2 and 2 reversed, patches 2 and 3
- sections 3 and 3 reversed, patches 1 and 4

Green Print and Red Print
from *each*
- sections 1 and 1 reversed, patches 2 and 3
- sections 2 and 2 reversed, patch 1
- sections 3 and 3 reversed, patches 2 and 3

Each shoe is made from 3 sections. Make 2 paper copies of *each* foundation and reversed foundation section.

Make 1 shoe and 1 reversed shoe from each color. Foundation piece the sections in numerical order, pressing and trimming after each patch addition.

Join the sections to make each shoe. Join the shoes with patches A–D as shown to complete the block.

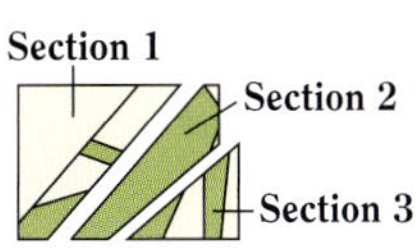

Make 1 and 1 reversed of each color

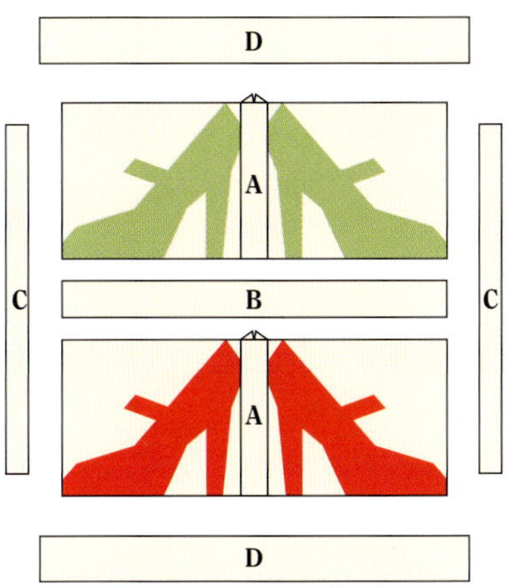

Block Assembly

block no. 188

Isobel's Flight

by Cinzia White
cinziawhite.com

See page 55 on the PDF for pattern

Blue Tone-on-Tone
- section and section reversed, patches 1, 4, 7, 10, 13 and 16
- 2 template B

White Print
- section and section reversed patches 2, 3, 5, 6, 8, 9, 11, 12, 14, 15, 17 and 18
- 1 template A
- 2 template B

Make a paper copy of the section and reversed section foundations. Foundation piece the sections in numerical order, pressing and trimming after each patch addition.

Refer to "Curved Piecing" in the Techniques file on the PDF. Join the sections with patches A–B as shown to complete the block.

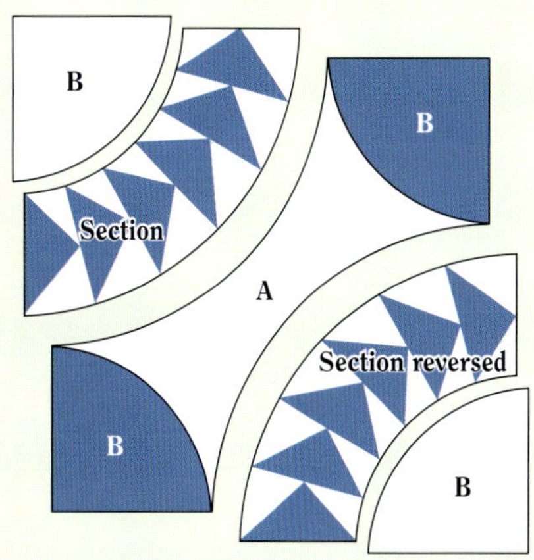

Block Assembly

block no. 189

Cactus Flower

by Sue Beevers • Trillium Ridge Patterns
suebeevers.com

Sue Beevers is the author of *Off the Shelf Fabric Painting* and *Dancing Dragonfly Quilts* for C&T Publishing, ctpub.com.

See page 80 on the PDF for pattern

Blue Batik
patch 1
Cream Tone-on-Tone
patches 2, 4, 6, 8, 9, 11, 13 and 15
Dark Batik #1 (see note below)
patches 3 and 10
Dark Batik #2
patches 5 and 12
Dark Batik #3
patches 7 and 14

The dark batik #1 used in Sue's block is a blend of rusts and greens.

Make 4 paper copies of the foundation section. Foundation piece the sections in numerical order, pressing and trimming after each patch addition. Join the sections as shown to complete the block.

It can be helpful to pin matching points along the seam lines before sewing the sections together.

To reduce bulk, press the seams open.

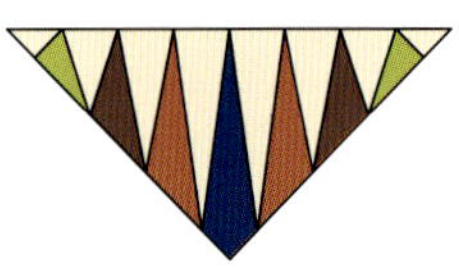

Section
Make 4

Block Assembly

block no. 190

Star Flower

by Barbara Bieraugel • Barbara Bieraugel Designs
barbarabieraugeldesigns.com

See page 87 on the PDF for pattern

Cream Batik
section 1, patch 1
section 2, patch 1
section 3, patches 3 and 4
Brown Batik
section 1, patch 2
section 2, patch 2
Green Batik
section 2, patch 3
section 3, patch 2
Red Batik
section 3, patch 1
Green/Red Batik
1 square (A) 2½" x 2½"

Section 1
Make 4

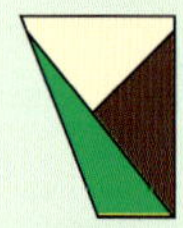

Section 2
Make 4

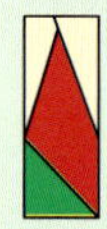

Section 3
Make 4

Barbara fussy cut the green/red batik square (A) to resemble a flower's center.

Make 4 paper copies of sections 1–3. Foundation piece each section in numerical order, pressing and trimming after each patch addition.

Join the sections and A as shown to complete the block.

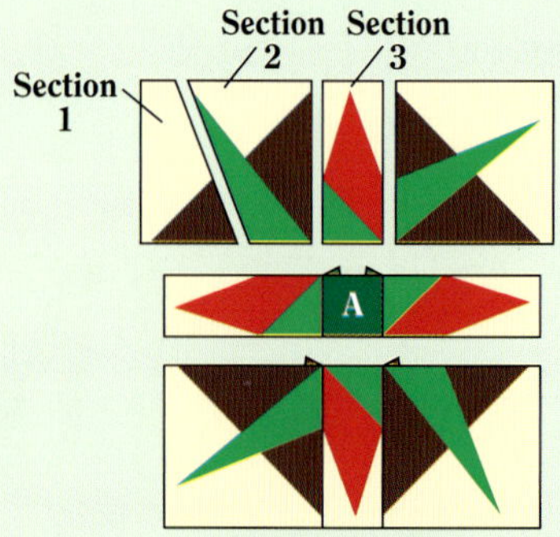

Block Assembly

block no. 191

My Easter Dress

by Sonja Callaghan • Artisania
artisania.wordpress.com

See page 92 on the PDF for pattern

Multiprint
sections 1 and 7, patches 2 and 4
sections 2, 5 and 8, patches 1 and 3
section 3, patch 15

Pink Tone-on-Tone
(Sonja used satin blanket edging)
sections 1 and 7, patch 3
sections 2, 5 and 8, patch 2
section 3, patches 2, 3 and 16
section 4, patches 2 and 3

Purple Solid
sections 1, 6 and 7, patch 1
sections 3 and 4, patches 10–14
sections 5 and 8, patch 4

Pink Solid
sections 3 and 4, patches 5–9

Flesh Tone-on-Tone
sections 3 and 4, patches 1 and 4
section 6, patch 2

Make 1 paper copy of *each* foundation section. Foundation piece the sections in numerical order, pressing and trimming after each patch addition. Join the sections as shown to complete the block.

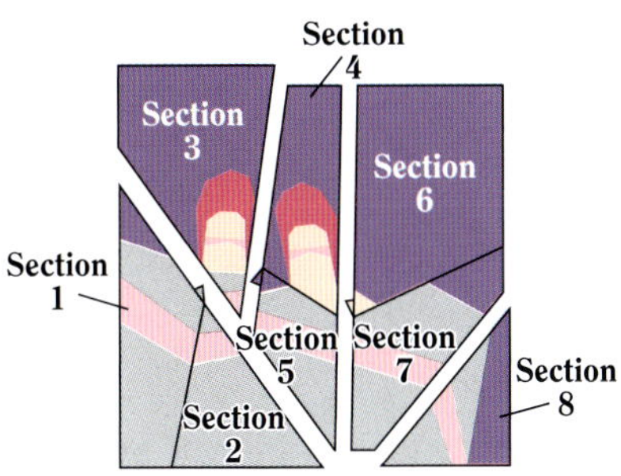

Block Assembly

block no. 192

Star of Glory

by Patty Clayton • Patty Cake Quilt Creations

See page 117 on the PDF for pattern

Red Tone-on-Tone
patches 1, 5, 9 and 13

White Tone-on-Tone
patches 2, 4, 6, 8, 10, 12, 14, 16 and 17

Blue Tone-on-Tone
patches 3, 7, 11, 15 and 19

Navy Tone-on-Tone
patch 18

Section
Make 4

Make 4 paper copies of the foundation section. Foundation piece the sections in numerical order, pressing and trimming after each patch addition. Join the sections as shown to complete the block.

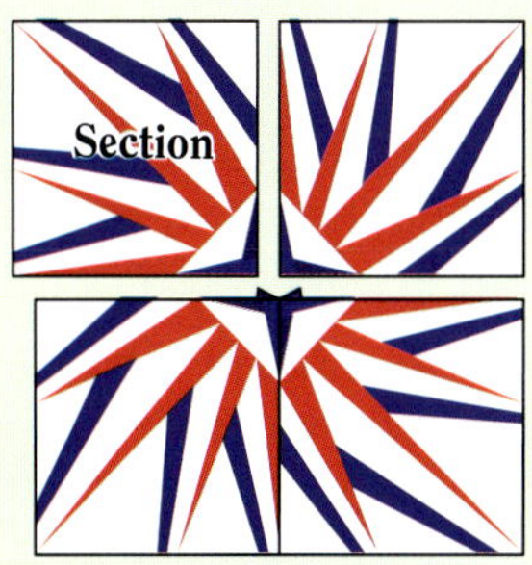

Block Assembly

block no. 193

Clowning Around

by Susan Cook • Larkspur Lane Designs
larkspurlanedesigns.com

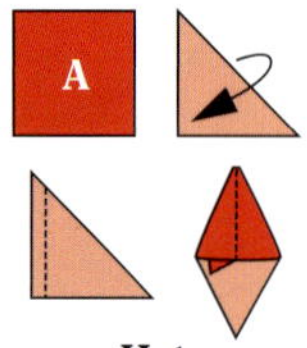

Hat

Hat

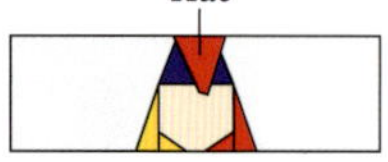

Hat Placement

Section 1
Make 1

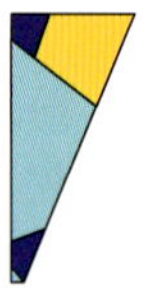

Section 2
Make 1

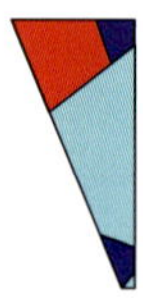

Section 2r
Make 1

Section 3
Make 1

Section 3r
Make 1

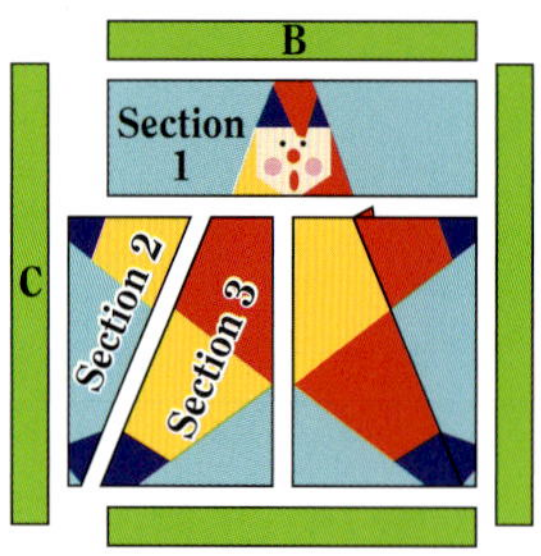

Block Assembly

See pages 112–113 on the PDF for pattern

White Solid
section 1, patch 1

Red Batik
1 square (A) 3″ x 3″
section 1, patches 2 and 5
sections 2r and 3, patch 1
section 3r, patch 2

Yellow Batik
section 1, patches 3 and 6
sections 2 and 3r, patch 1
section 3, patch 2

Dark Blue Batik
section 1, patch 4
section 2 and 2r, patches 2 and 4
section 3 and 3r, patch 3

Aqua Batik
section 1, patches 7 and 8
section 2 and 2r, patches 3 and 5
section 3 and 3r, patch 4

Green Batik
2 rectangles (B) 1½″ x 10½″
2 rectangles (C) 1½″ x 12½″

Susan used QuiltPro to draw her clown's face and printed it on Printed Treasures fabric. An alternative is to hand draw or embroider the face.

To make the hat, fold the red A in half, right sides together, and sew along one side as shown. Turn right side out and press as shown.

Make a paper copy of each foundation section and reversed section. The colors for the reversed sections are shown in parentheses on the foundation. Foundation piece section 1, patches 1–6 in numerical order, pressing and trimming after each patch addition. Pin hat in place on patch 4 as shown, then finish the section. Foundation piece sections 2, 2r, 3 and 3r in numerical order. Join the sections and patches as shown to complete the block.

block no. 194

Nico's Star

by Teresa Fields • Quickie Chicks Design

Fabric: Timeless Treasures, ttfabrics.com.

See page 103 on the PDF for pattern

Dark Blue Print
patch 1

Orange Dot
patch 2

Paisley Print
patches 3 and 5

Pink Print
patch 4

Make 4 paper copies of the foundation section. Foundation piece each section in numerical order, pressing and trimming after each patch addition.

Join the sections as shown to complete the block.

Section
Make 4

Block Assembly

block no. 195

Sunblock

by Eileen Fowler • Associate Editor, *Quiltmaker*
quiltmaker.com

See page 118 on the PDF for pattern

Blue Batik
sections 1 and 3, patches 1 and 3
section 2, patches 2 and 3

Dark Orange Batik
sections 1 and 3, patch 2
section 2, patch 1

Light Orange Batik
sections 1, 2 and 3, patch 4

Yellow Batik #1
sections 1, 2 and 3, patch 5

Yellow Batik #2
sections 1, 2 and 3, patch 6

Yellow Batik #3
sections 1, 2 and 3, patch 7

Light Yellow Batik
sections 1, 2 and 3, patch 8

Section 1
Make 2

Section 2
Make 2

Section 3
Make 2

Each half of the block is made from 3 sections. Make 2 paper copies *each* of sections 1, 2 and 3. Foundation piece the sections in numerical order, pressing and trimming after each patch addition.

Refer to the block assembly diagram. Join sections 1, 2 and 3 as shown to make each block half. To reduce bulk, press the seams open. Join the block halves as shown to complete the block.

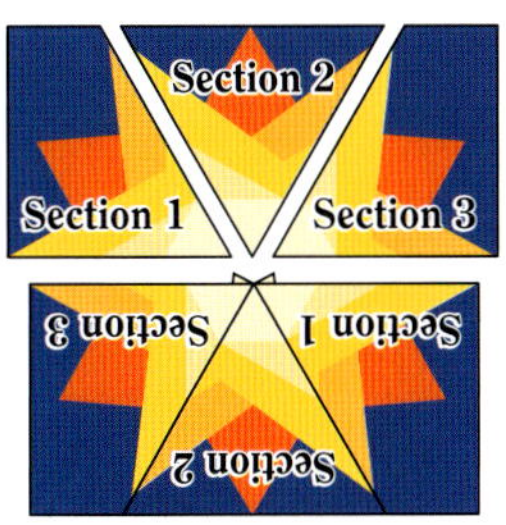

Block Assembly

block no. 196

Rock Stars

by Angie Hodapp

See page 106 on the PDF for pattern

Black Solid
sections 1, 2, 3 and 4, patch 1

Black Print
section 1, patches 2 and 4

White Print
section 2, patches 2 and 4

4 Bright Tone-on-Tones
from *each*
sections 1 and 2, patch 3
section 3, patches 2 and 3
section 4, patch 2

Each quarter of the block is made from 4 sections. Make 4 paper copies of *each* of the foundation sections 1–4.

Note that the black print is used in section 1 and the white print is used in section 2. A different bright tone-on-tone is used in each quarter. Foundation piece the sections in numerical order, pressing and trimming after each patch addition.

Join the sections as shown to complete the block. To reduce bulk, press the seams open.

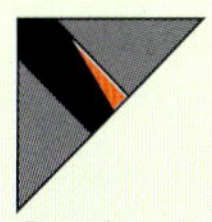

Section 1
Make 4

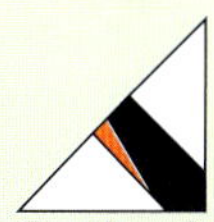

Section 2
Make 4

Section 3
Make 4

Section 4
Make 4

Block Assembly

block no. 197

Point, Counterpoint

by Dana Jones • Managing Editor, *Quilters Newsletter*
quiltersnewsletter.com

Fabric: Stonehenge by Sunshine Cottage for Northcott, northcott.net.

See page 93 on the PDF for pattern

Dark Blue Print #1
section, patches 1 and 8

Dark Gold Print
section, patches 2 and 5

Dark Blue Print #2
section, patches 3, and 7

Dark Green Print
section, patches 4 and 6

Medium Gold Print
section patch 9
section reversed patches 2r and 5r

Medium Blue Print
section reversed, patches 1r, 3r and 7r

Medium Green Print
section reversed, patch 4r

Light Green Print
section reversed, patch 6r

Light Blue Print
section reversed, patch 8r

Light Gold Print
section reversed, patch 9r

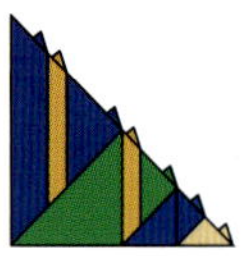

Section
Make 4

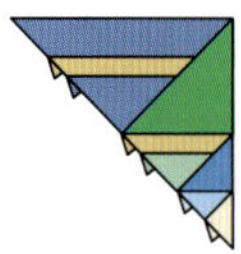

Section Reversed
Make 4

Make 4 paper copies *each* of the section and reversed section foundations. The colors for the reversed sections are shown in parentheses on the foundation. Paying close attention to color placement, foundation piece the sections in numerical order, pressing and trimming after each patch addition.

To complete the block, join the sections as shown, pressing the seams open to reduce bulk.

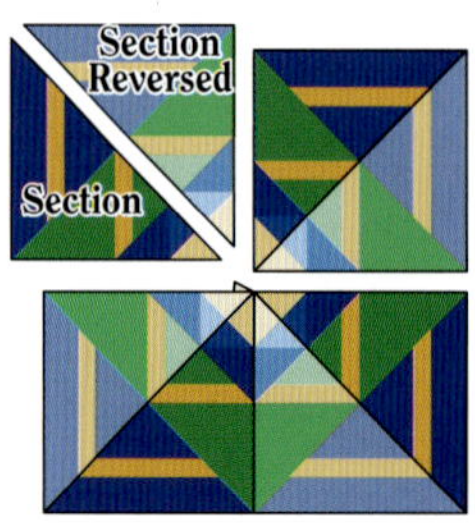

Block Assembly

block no. 198

Searchlight

by Margaret Miller • Miller Quilts, Inc.
millerquilts.com

Margaret Miller is the author of *AnglePlay Blocks* and other titles for C&T Publishing, ctpub.com.

Margaret has also designed a line of AnglePlay Templates to simplify the cutting for these and other similar patches.

See page 104 on the PDF for pattern

⧄ = cut in half diagonally

Green Print
2 rectangles 4¾" x 7" ⧄ (A)
4 squares (B) 2½" x 2½"

Red Batik
2 rectangles 4¾" x 7" ⧄ (A)

Orange Print
section patch 1

Dark Red Tone-on-Tone
section patch 2

Yellow Tone-on-Tone
section patch 3

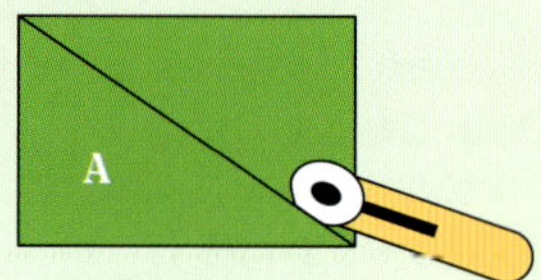

Cutting

Section
Make 4

Make 4 paper copies of the foundation section. Foundation piece each section in numerical order, pressing and trimming after each patch addition.

Join the sections and patches as shown to complete the block.

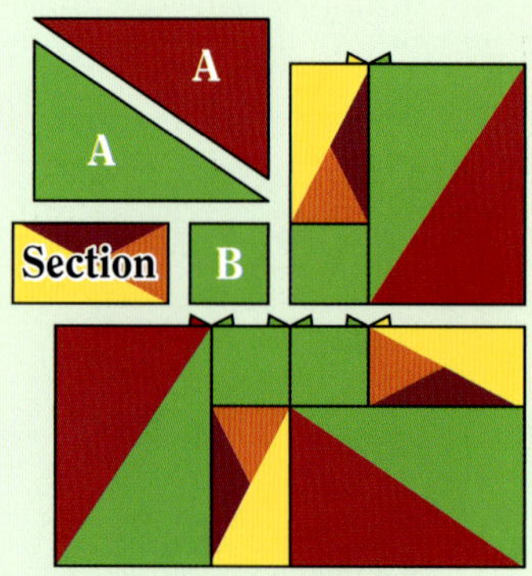

Block Assembly

block no. 199

In the Bag

by Denise Starck • Graphic Designer, *Quiltmaker*
quiltmaker.com

Fabric: Bonnes Amies for Michael Miller Fabrics, michaelmillerfabrics.com.

See page 113 on the PDF for pattern

White Tone-on-Tone
1 rectangle (A) 7¾" x 13"
section patches 5 and 6

Aqua Stripe
section patch 1

Aqua Dot
section patches 2, 3 and 4

10" Rickrack (Denise used Ruffle Rac Pindot from Michael Miller Fabrics.)

Button
1 at 1"

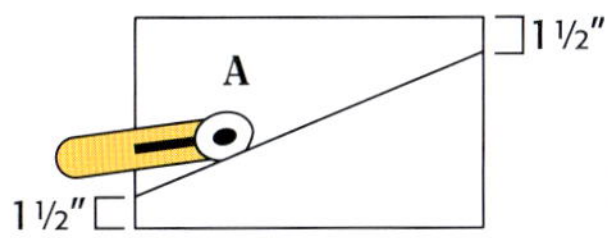

Measure 1½" from the opposite ends of each side of A and cut as shown.

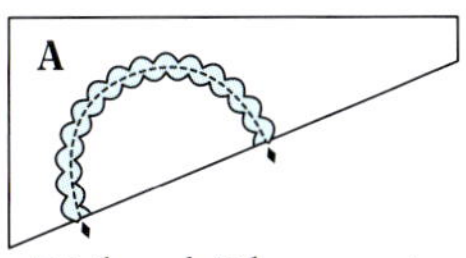

Rickrack Placement

Make 1 paper copy of the foundation section. Aligning the top A portion with the top edge of the foundation, transfer the handle placement marks to the A. Position the rickrack on A as shown and pin in place. Use matching thread to stitch down the handle.

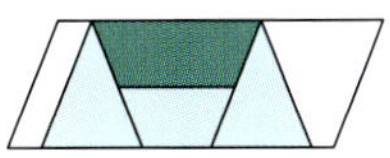

Section
Make 1

Foundation piece the section in numerical order, pressing and trimming after each patch addition. Join the three block sections as shown. Sew the button in place. Trim the block to 12½" × 12½".

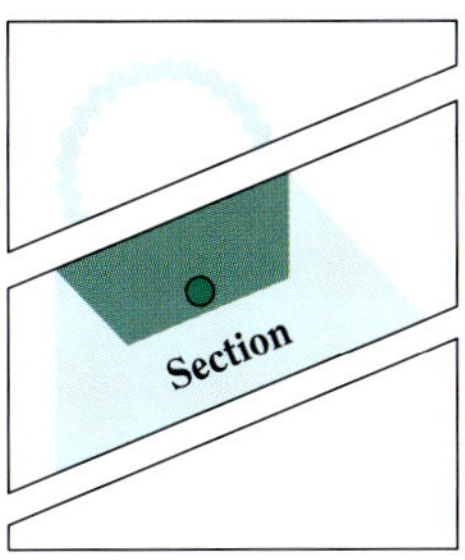

Block Assembly

block no. 200

Radiant Heart

by Faith Wellman • Doodle Time Designs
doodletimedesigns.etsy.com

See pages 96–97 on the PDF for pattern

⍁ = cut in half diagonally

Purple Batik
section 1, patches 1 and 4

Light Blue Batik
section 1, patches 2, 3, 5, 6 and 7

Black Batik
section 2, patches 1 and 4

Medium Green Batik
section 2, patch 2

Blue Batik
section 2, patch 3

Dark Green Batik
2 squares 5⅛" x 5⅛" ⍁ (A)

Make 1 paper copy of the foundation section 1 and 4 copies of section 2. Foundation piece the sections in numerical order, pressing and trimming after each patch addition.

Join the sections and patches as shown to complete the block.

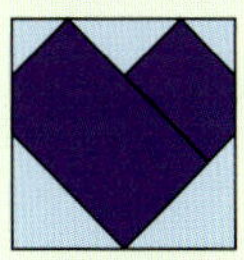

Section 1
Make 1

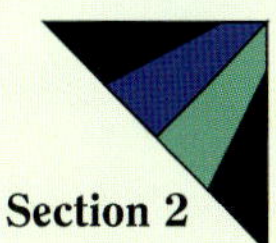

Section 2
Make 4

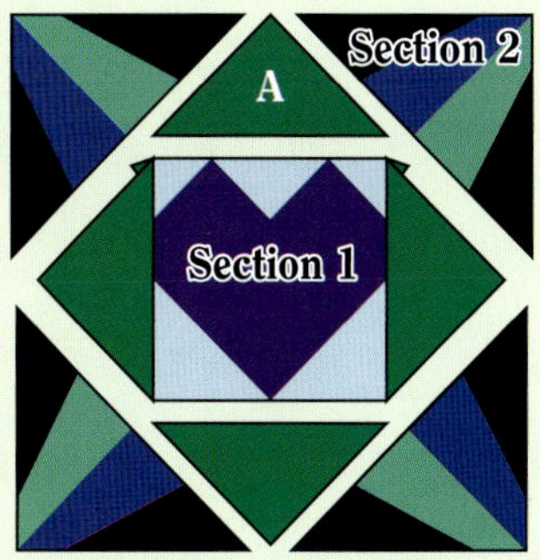

Block Assembly

block no. 201

Flying in Circles

by Donna Benham • DB Designs

See page 148 on the PDF for pattern

Beige Batik
 section patches 1, 3, 4, 6 and 7
Rust Batik
 section patch 2
Black Batik
 section patch 5
Gold Batik
 section patch 8

Section
Make 4

Make 4 paper copies of the foundation section. Foundation piece *each* section in numerical order, pressing and trimming after each patch addition.

Sew the sections together as shown to complete the block.

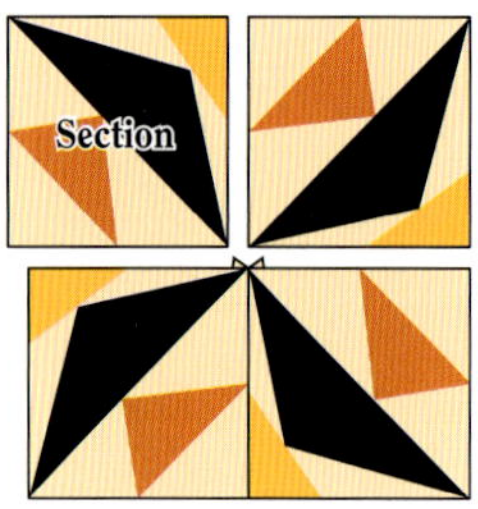

Block Assembly

block no. 202

Lil' Monkey

by Sonja Callaghan • Artisania
artisania.ca

See pages 127–128 on the PDF for patterns

Cream Solid
 sections 1, 2, 4 and 5, patch 1
Dark Brown Solid
 section 1, patches 2, 4 and 5
 section 2, patches 2 and 3
 section 3, patches 2 and 4
Yellow Solid
 section 1, patches 3 and 6
 section 2, patch 4
 section 3, patches 1, 3 and 5
 sections 4 and 5, patches 2–5
 section 6, patches 2 and 3
Blue Solid
 section 6, patch 1
Black Solid
 1 pattern A
Fusible web
Black embroidery floss

Make 1 paper copy of *each* foundation section. Foundation piece each section in numerical order, pressing and trimming after each patch addition. Join the sections as shown.

Prepare the mouth (A) for fusible appliqué. Use the appliqué placement diagram as a guide to arrange the mouth on the face; fuse in place. The stitch diagrams are in the Techniques file on the PDF. Use black embroidery floss and a satin stitch to add the eyes. Backstitch around the mouth and eyes. Backstitch the ears, eyebrow and nose details to complete the block.

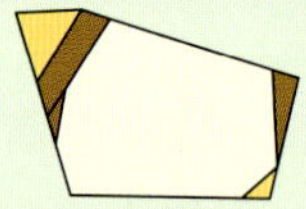

Section 1
Make 1

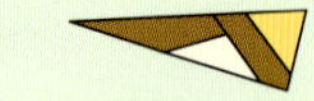

Section 2
Make 1

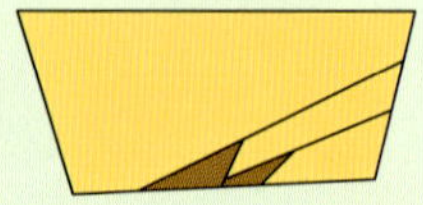

Section 3
Make 1

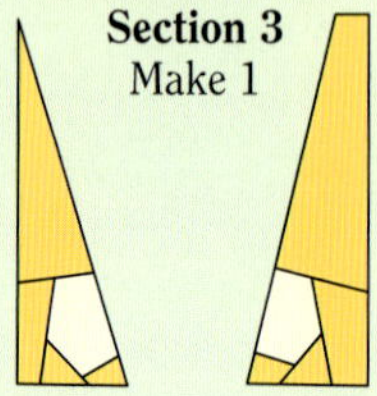

Section 4
Make 1

Section 5
Make 1

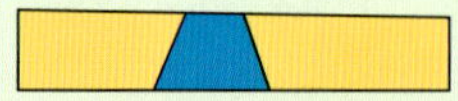

Section 6
Make 1

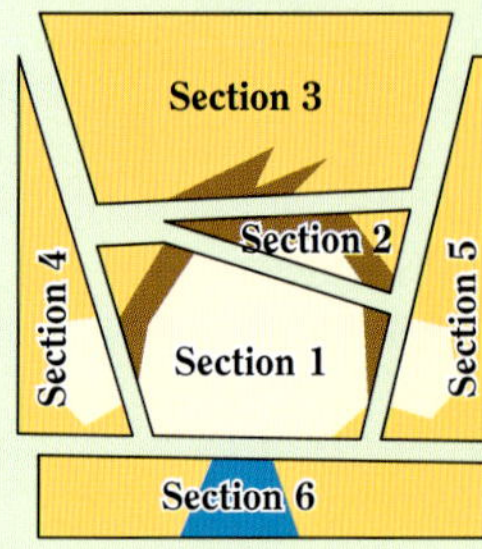

Block Assembly

Applique/Embroidery Placement

Images are presented in reverse for the fusing process.

Templates for Lil' Monkey block on page 127 of the Templates file on the PDF.

block no. 203

Pennants

by Kaffe Fassett and Liza Prior Lucy • Glorious Color
gloriouscolor.com, and kaffefassett.com

Fabric: Kaffe Fassett Collective by Kaffe Fassett, Brandon Mably, and Philip Jacobs for Westminster Fibers Inc., westminsterfibers.com.

Kaffe Fassett and Liza Prior Lucy are the authors of *Simple Shapes Spectacular Quilts* for STC Craft, abramsbooks.com.

See page 138 on the PDF for pattern

Assorted Bright Medium Prints
section patches 1, 3 and 5
Assorted Dark Prints
section patches 2, 4 and 6

Section
Make 4

Make 4 paper copies of the foundation section. Foundation piece *each* section, pressing and trimming after each patch addition.

Sew the sections together as shown to complete the block.

Block Assembly

block no. 204

Re-leaf

by Eileen Fowler • Associate Editor, *Quiltmaker*
quiltmaker.com

Fabric: Shades by Kinkame for Clothworks, clothworkstextiles.com.

See page 146 on the PDF for pattern

Assorted Orange Tone-on-Tones (see below)
sections 1, 1r, 3 and 3r, patches 1–4
sections 2 and 2r, patches 2–4
sections 4 and 4r, patches 2 and 4–6
Blue Solid
sections 1 and 1r, patch 5
sections 2 and 2r, patches 1 and 5
sections 3 and 3r, patches 5 and 6
sections 4 and 4r, patches 1 and 3

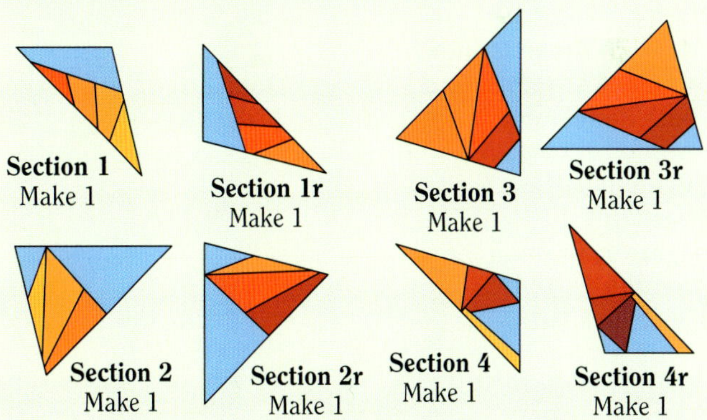

Eileen used 3 different gradated fabrics to get the variety of oranges in the leaf and stem.

Make 1 paper copy of *each* foundation section and reversed section. Foundation piece each section in numerical order, pressing and trimming after each patch addition.

Join the sections as shown to complete the block.

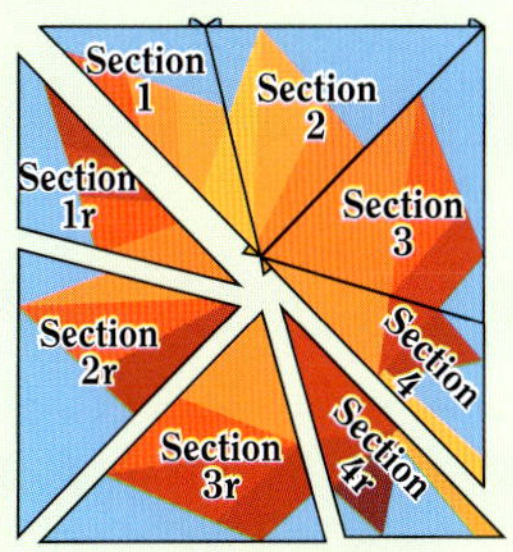

Block Assembly

block no. 205

Sunday Rose

by Chris Hoover • Whirligig Designs
whirligigdesigns.com

See page 158 on the PDF for pattern

Dark Pink Batik
section 1, patch 1
Dark Green Batik
section 1, patch 2
Light Green Batik #1
section 1, patch 3
Cream Batik
section 1, patch 4
section 3, patch 3
Medium Green Batik #1
section 2, patch 1
Medium Green Batik #2
section 2, patch 2
Dark Red Batik
section 2, patch 3
Medium Red Batik
section 3, patch 1
Light Green Batik #2
section 3, patch 2
Light Pink Batik
sections 4 and 5, patch 1
Medium Pink Batik #1
sections 4 and 5, patch 2
Medium Pink Batik #2
sections 4 and 5, patch 3
Yellow Batik #1
section 4, patch 4
Yellow Batik #2
section 5, patch 4

Section 1
Make 4

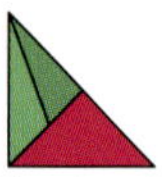

Section 2
Make 4

Section 3
Make 4

Section 4
Make 2

Section 5
Make 2

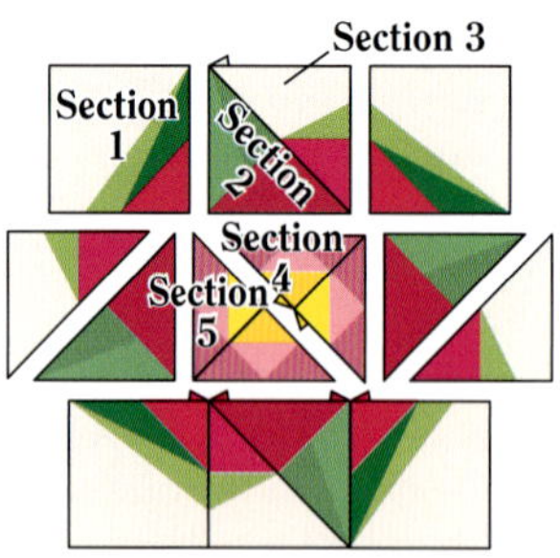

Block Assembly

Make 4 paper copies *each* of foundation sections 1–3 and 2 paper copies *each* of sections 4 and 5. Foundation piece each section in numerical order, pressing and trimming after each patch addition.

Join the sections as shown to complete the block.

block no. 206

Traffic Jam

by Dana Jones • Managing Editor, *Quilters Newsletter* • quiltersnewsletter.com

See page 155 on the PDF for pattern

Dark Blue Solid
Dark Orange Solid
Blue Solid
Orange Solid
Teal Solid
Yellow Solid
Plum Solid #1
Plum Solid #2
Dusty Purple Solid
Dusty Rose Solid

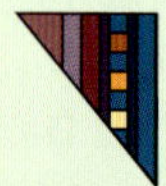

Section 1
Make 4

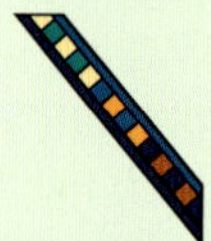

Section 2
Make 4

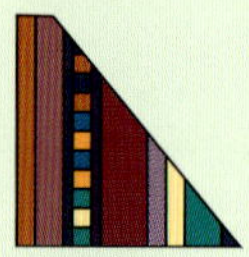

Section 3
Make 4

Make 4 paper copies of *each* foundation section.

Using the colors listed above, refer to the foundations on page 155 of the PDF Templates for color placement. Foundation piece the sections in numerical order, pressing and trimming after each patch addition.

Sew the sections into 4 quadrants. Sew the quadrants together as shown to complete the block.

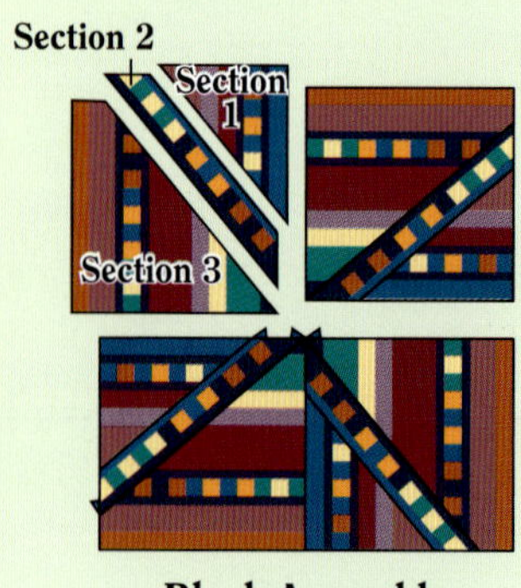

Block Assembly

block no. 207

Star-ring Buttons

by Jan Krentz • Jan P Krentz Designs
jankrentz.com

Fabric: Razzle Dazzle and Dotty from Timeless Treasures, ttfabrics.net.

Jan Krentz is the author of numerous titles including *Quick Star Quilts & Beyond* for C&T Publishing, ctpub.com.

See page 157 on the PDF for pattern

White Tone-on-Tone
sections 1, 3 and 3r, patch 1
Assorted Red, Orange, Yellow, Green, Blue, Teal, Purple, and Pink Tone-on-Tones
section 1, patches 2 and 3
section 2, patches 1–4
sections 3 and 3r, patch 2
Buttons
8 *each* at 1¼″ and ⅞″

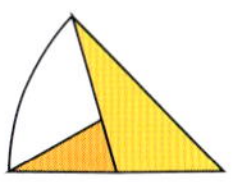

Section 1
Make 8

Section 2
Make 8

Make 8 paper copies *each* of sections 1 and 2. Make 4 paper copies *each* of sections 3 and 3r.

To help with color placement, arrange the paper foundation sections to form the block. Referring to the assembly diagram and photographed block, mark the colors on the foundations.

Section 3
Make 4

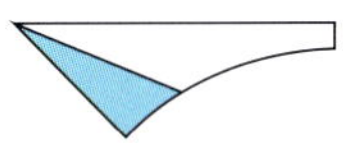

Section 3r
Make 4

Foundation piece the sections in numerical order, pressing and trimming after each patch addition. Refer to "Curved Piecing" in the Templates file on the PDF. Join the sections as shown.

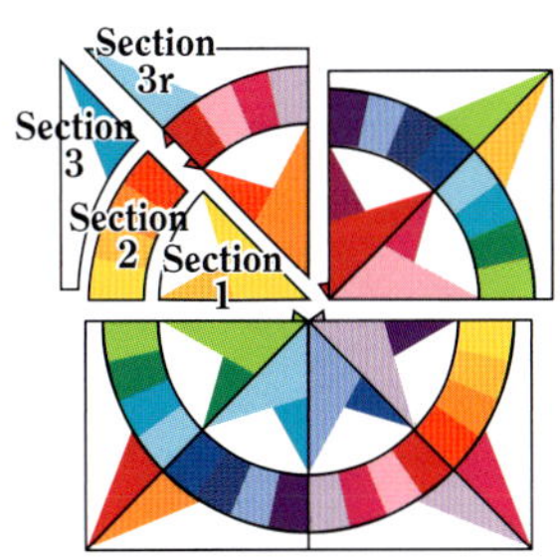

Block Assembly

To ease assembly, carefully remove the foundations before joining the sections.

Pair each large button with a smaller button; refer to the photographed block and sew the buttons in place as shown to complete the block.

block no. 208

Chocolate & Strawberries

by Carolyn Cullinan McCormick • CM Designs
addaquarter.com

Carolyn McCormick is the creator of the Add-a-Quarter and Add Enough tools for quilters. She is the author of several books including *Wedding Ring, Pickle Dish & More* and *Quilts for Rosie* for Kansas City Star Quilts, pickledish.com.

See page 149 on the PDF for pattern

Cream Batik
section 1, patches 1, 4, and 5
section 2, patch 4
section 3, patches 3 and 4
section 4, patches 2 and 3
Red Batik
section 1, patches 2 and 3
section 2, patch 3
sections 3 and 4, patch 1
Dark Brown Batik
section 2, patch 1
section 3, patch 2
Pink Batik
section 2, patches 2 and 5
section 3, patches 5 and 6

Section 1
Make 4

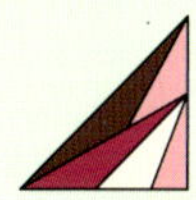

Section 2
Make 4

Section 3
Make 4

Section 4
Make 4

Make 4 paper copies *each* of foundation sections 1–4. Foundation piece each section in numerical order, pressing and trimming after each patch addition.

Join the sections as shown to complete the block.

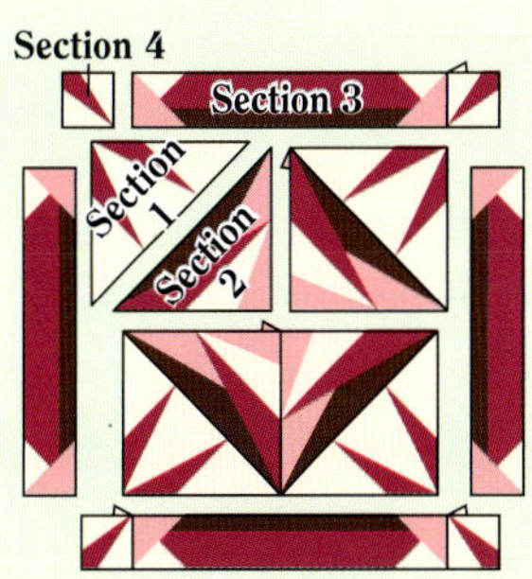

Block Assembly

block no. 209

Stars Over Savannah

by Marti Michell • Michell Marketing
frommarti.com

Fabric: Wild Rose II designed by Marti Michell for Maywood Studio, maywoodstudio.com.

Marti Michell is the author of *Machine Quilting in Sections* and *Log Cabin ABCs* for Michell Marketing, frommarti.com.

See page 139 on the PDF for pattern

◸ = cut in half diagonally

Dark Blue Print #1
sections 1 and 2, patch 1

Gold Tone-on-Tone
4 squares (B) 2″ x 2″
section 1, patch 2

White Print
4 squares 2⅝″ x 2⅝″ ◸ (D)
section 2, patch 2

Dark Blue Print #2
1 square (A) 5½″ x 5½″

Light Blue Check
4 squares (C) 2¼″ x 2¼″

Light Blue Print
2 squares 4⅜″ x 4⅜″ ◸ (E)

Section 1
Make 4

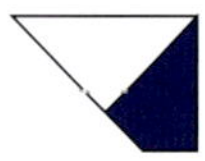

Section 2
Make 4

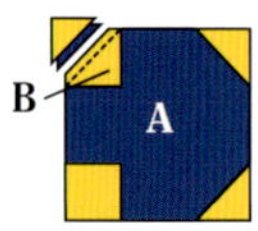

Unit
Stitch & Flip
Make 1

Make 4 paper copies of *each* foundation section. Foundation piece the sections in numerical order, pressing and trimming after each patch addition.

Refer to "Stitch-and-Flip" in the Techniques file on the PDF. Use the dark blue A and gold B's to make the unit.

Sew the patches, sections and unit together as shown to complete the block.

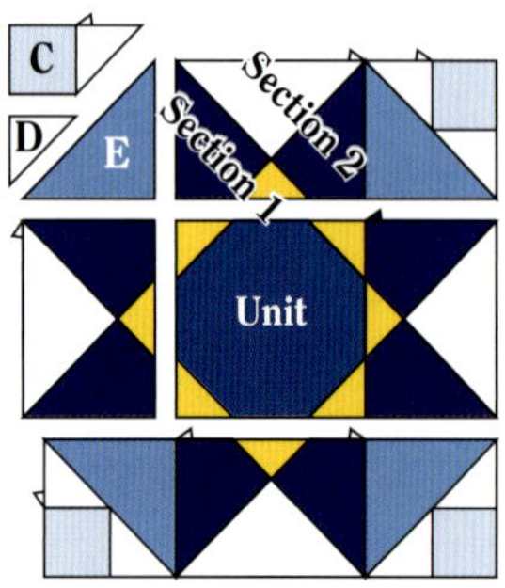

Block Assembly

block no. 210

Quatrefoil

by Scott Murkin • Patchwork Possibilities
patchworkpossibilities.com

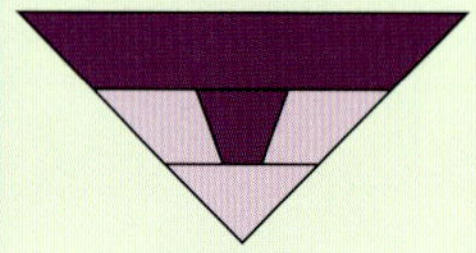

Section 1
Make 2

See page 137 on the PDF for pattern

Multiprint
section 1, patches 1 and 5
section 2, patches 2–4

Light Purple Dot
section 1, patches 2–4
section 2, patches 1 and 5

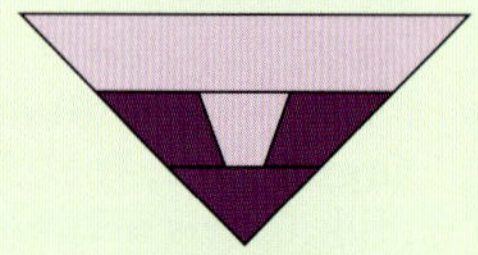

Section 2
Make 2

Make 2 paper copies *each* of the section 1 and section 2 foundations. The colors for section 2 are shown in parentheses on the foundation. Foundation piece each section in numerical order, pressing and trimming after each patch addition.

Sew the sections together as shown to complete the block.

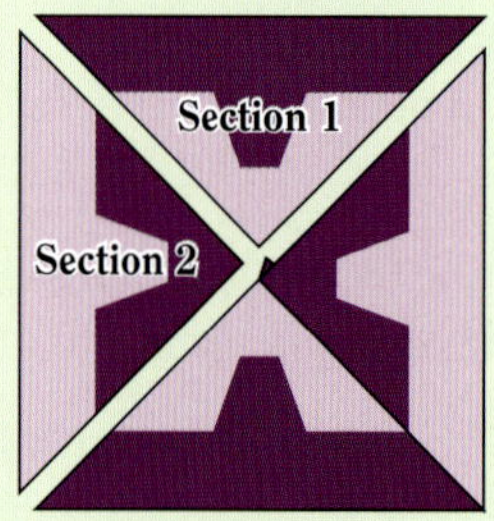

Block Assembly

block no. 211

Happy Blossom

by Nel Whatmore
nelwhatmore.com

Fabric: Happy Go Lucky designed by Nel Whatmore for FreeSpirit Fabrics, freespiritfabric.com.

See page 136 on the PDF for pattern

White Print
section patch 1
Green Print
section patch 2
Multiprint
section patch 3
Blue Print
section patch 4
Transparent template plastic (optional)

Nel fussy cut the multiprint for matching patch 3's and the blue print for matching patch 4's.

To fussy cut the patches, use the transparent plastic to make templates of foundation patches 3 and 4, adding an extra ½" on all sides. Isolate a motif on the print; mark the motif placement on the template as a guide for cutting each patch.

Make 4 paper copies of the foundation section. Foundation piece each section in numerical order, pressing and trimming after each patch addition.

Join the sections as shown to complete the block.

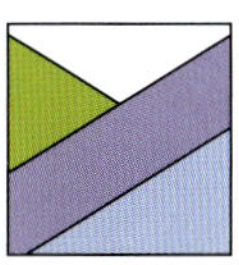

Section
Make 4

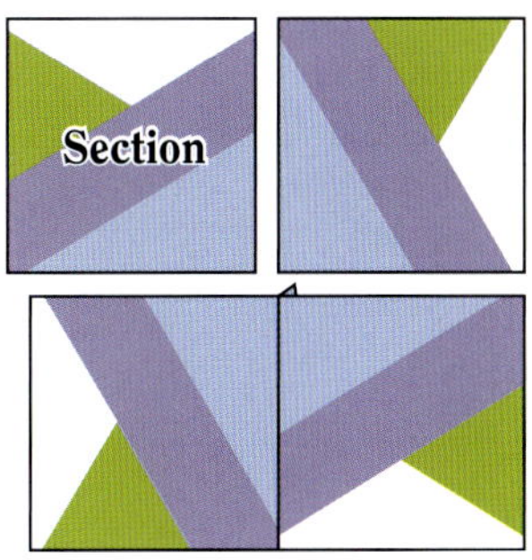

Block Assembly

block no. 212

Yvonne's Mystery

by Cinzia White
cinziawhite.com

See page 146 on the PDF for pattern

White-on-White
section 1, patches 1, 3, 5 and 6
section 2 and 5, patches 1, 3, 5, 7 and 8
section 3, patch 2
section 4, patches 1, 3, 5, 7 and 9
section 6, patch 1
Multiprint
section 1, patches 2 and 4
sections 2 and 5, patches 2, 4 and 6
section 3, patch 1
section 4, patches 2, 4, 6 and 8
section 6, patches 2–5

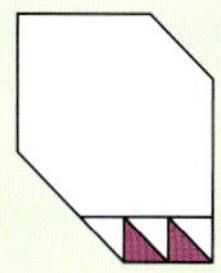

Section 1
Make 4

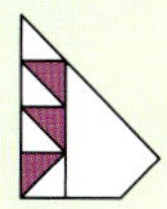

Section 2
Make 4

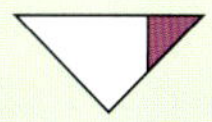

Section 3
Make 4

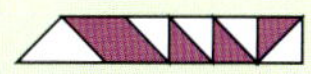

Section 4
Make 4

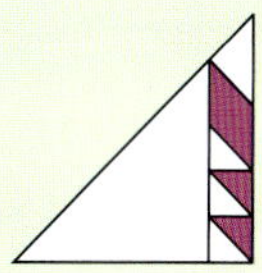

Section 5
Make 4

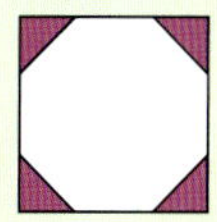

Section 6
Make 1

Make 4 paper copies of the foundation sections 1–5, and 1 copy of section 6. Foundation piece the sections in numerical order, pressing and trimming after each patch addition.

Join the sections as shown to complete the block.

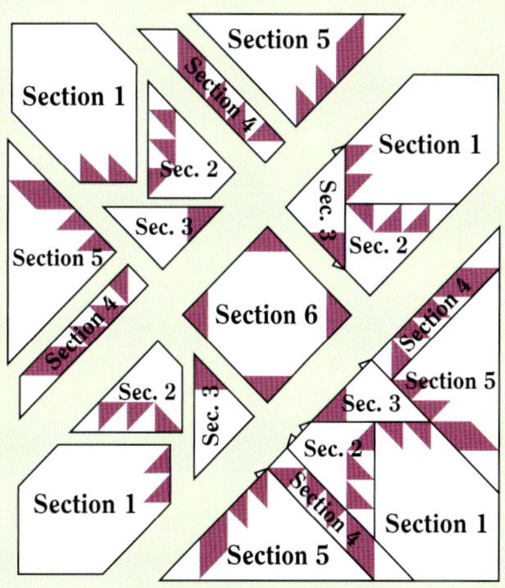

block no. 213
Lil' Matryoshka

by Sonja Callaghan • Artisania
artisania.ca

See page 195 on the PDF for pattern

White Solid
- section 1, patches 1 and 9–14
- sections 2, 4, and 6, patches 3, 4, 7 and 8
- section 3, patches 1 and 10–15
- section 5, patches 1 and 7–10

Black Solid
- sections 1 and 5, patch 2
- section 3, patches 2 and 3

Red Solid
- section 1, patches 3–8
- sections 2, 4, and 6, patches 2, 5 and 6
- section 3, patches 4–9
- section 5, patches 3–6

Cream and Blue Print
- sections 2, 4 and 6, patch 1

Gold Solid
- 1 rectangle (A) 2″ x 12½″

Embroidery floss

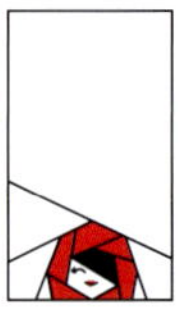

Section 1
Make 1

Section 2
Make 1

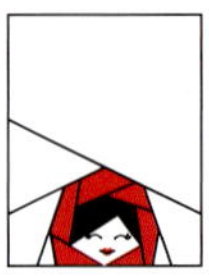

Section 3
Make 1

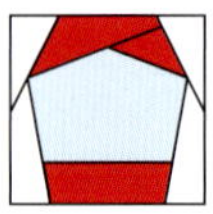

Section 4
Make 1

Section 5
Make 1

Section 6
Make 1

Make 1 paper copy of *each* foundation section. Foundation piece the sections in numerical order, pressing and trimming after each patch addition.

Sew the sections and A together as shown. Carefully remove the foundation papers.

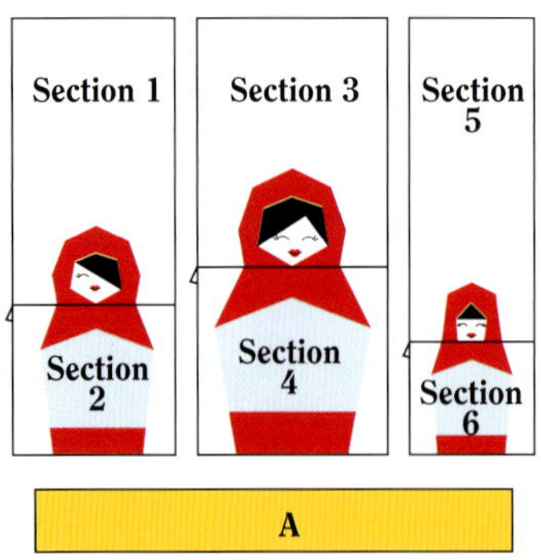

Block Assembly

The stitch diagrams can be found in the Techniques file on the PDF. Using 2 strands of floss, backstitch the eyes; use a satin stitch for the lips and backstitch for the mouth.

block no. 214
Icicle Star

by Sheri Diesburg, Dawn Koltz and Ann Marceca The Quilters Studio • thequiltersstudio.com

See page 180 on the PDF for pattern

Dark Blue Batik #1
- section 1, patch 1

Medium Blue Batik #1
- section 1, patch 2
- section 2, patch 3

Medium Blue Batik #2
- section 1, patch 3

Medium Blue Batik #3
- section 1, patch 4
- section 2, patch 2

Light Blue Batik #1
- section 1, patch 5
- section 2, patch 4

Dark Blue Batik #2
- section 1, patches 6 and 7

Light Blue Batik #2
- section 1, patch 8

White Batik
- section 2, patch 1

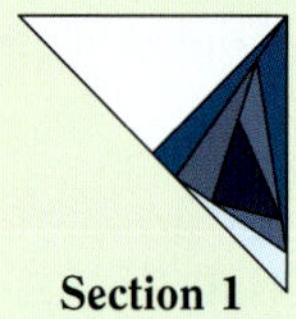

Section 1
Make 4

Section 2
Make 4

Make 4 paper copies of *each* foundation section. Foundation piece the sections in numerical order, pressing and trimming after each patch addition.

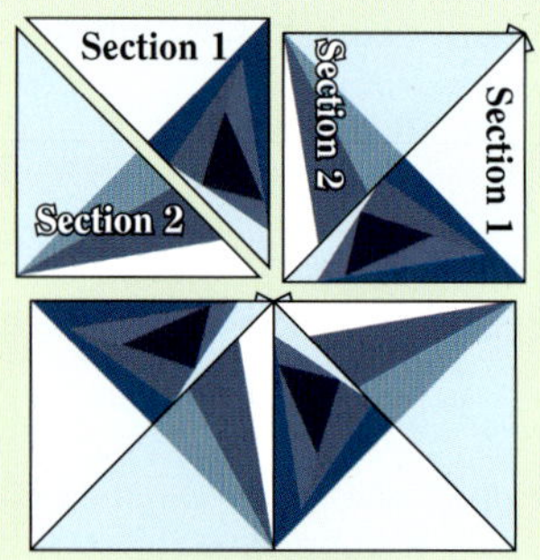

Block Assembly

Sew the sections into 4 quadrants as shown. To reduce bulk, press the seams open. Join the quadrants as shown to complete the block.

block no. 215

Whoopsy Daisy

by Eileen Fowler • Associate Editor, *Quiltmaker*
quiltmaker.com

Fabric: Tonga Batiks from Timeless Treasures, ttfabrics.com.

See page 185 on the PDF for pattern

Pink Batik
section and section reversed, patch 1

Green Batik
section and section reversed, patches 2–6

Orange Batik
section and section reversed, patch 7

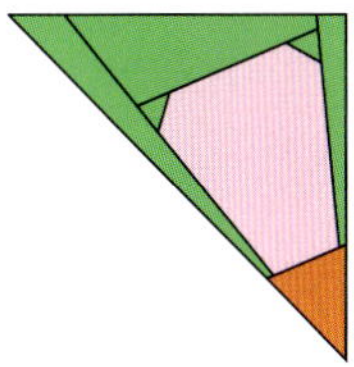

Section
Make 4

Make 4 paper copies *each* of the section and section reversed. Foundation piece the sections in numerical order, pressing and trimming after each patch addition.

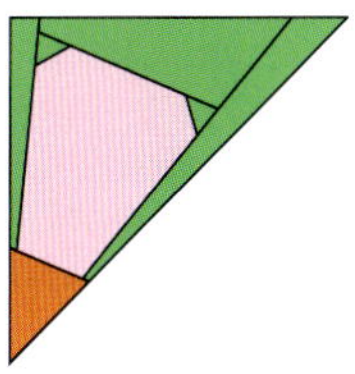

Section Reversed
Make 4

Sew the sections together as shown to complete the block. To reduce bulk, press the seams open.

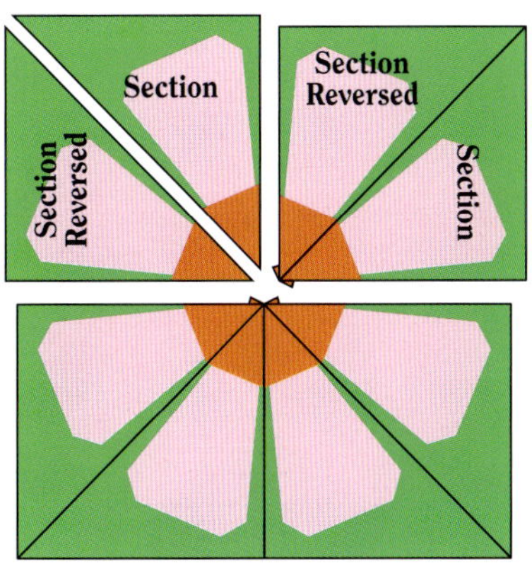

Block Assembly

block no. 216

Luck of the Irish

by Sandi Irish • The Irish Chain
irishchain.com

See pages 197–198 on the PDF for pattern

Medium Green Print
section 1, patch 1

Light Green Print #1
section 1r, patch 1

Cream Print
sections 1 and 1r, patches 2–4
section 2, patches 2 and 3

Light Green Print #2
section 2, patch 1

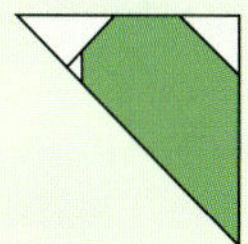

Section 1
Make 3

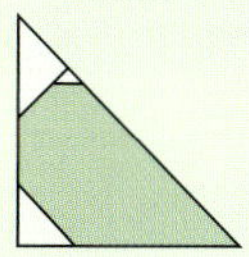

Section 1r
Make 3

Make 3 paper copies *each* of foundation sections 1 and 1r and 1 paper copy of section 2. Foundation piece the sections in numerical order, pressing and trimming after each patch addition.

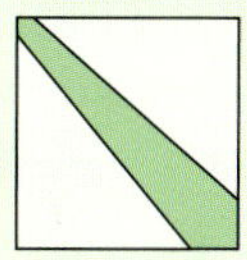

Section 2
Make 1

Sew the sections together as shown to complete the block.

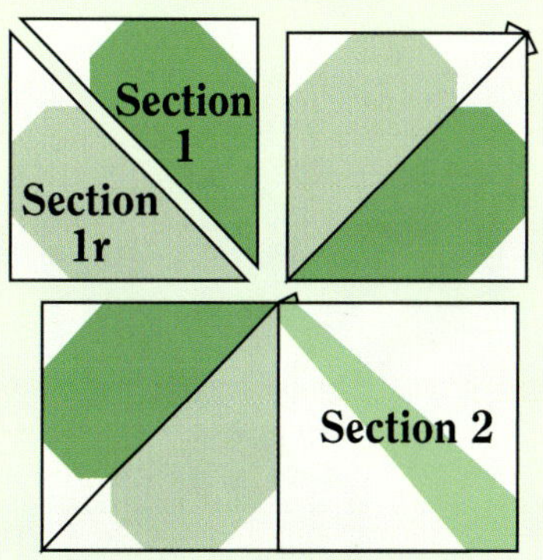

Block Assembly

block no. 217

Pinwheel Salute

by Robin Koehler • Nestlings by Robin
nestlingsbyrobin.com

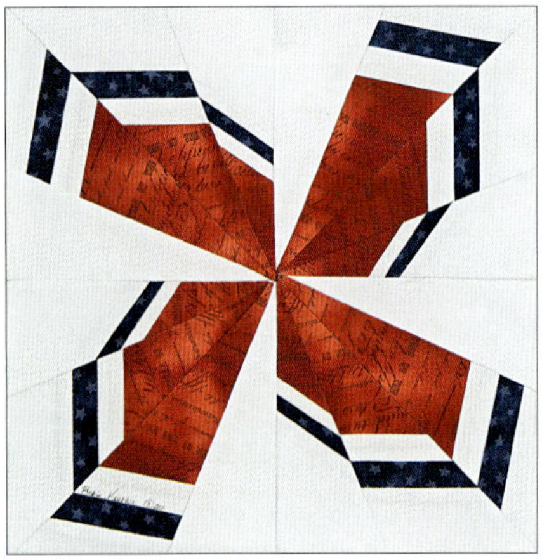

See page 172 on the PDF for pattern

Red Print
sections 1–3, patch 1

White Tone-on-Tone
section 1, patches 2, 4 and 5
sections 2 and 3, patches 2 and 4

Dark Blue Tone-on-Tone
sections 1–3, patch 3

Make 4 paper copies of *each* foundation section. Foundation piece the sections in numerical order, pressing and trimming after each patch addition.

Join the sections as shown. To reduce bulk, press the seams open.

Section 1
Make 4

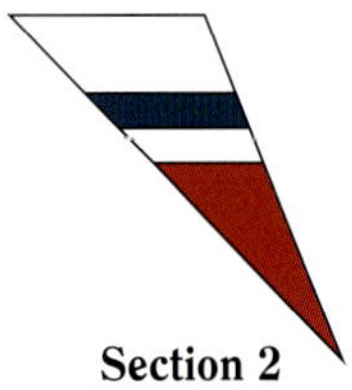

Section 2
Make 4

Section 3
Make 4

Block Assembly

block no. 218

Circle of Friends

by Carolyn Cullinan McCormick • CM Designs
addaquarter.com

Carolyn McCormick is the creator of the Add-a-Quarter and Add Enough tools for quilters. She is the author of several books including *Wedding Ring, Pickle Dish & More* and *Quilts for Rosie* for Kansas City Star Quilts, pickledish.com.

See page 175 on the PDF for pattern

⧄ = cut in half diagonally

Cream Tone-on-Tone
section 1, patch 1
sections 2 and 2r, patches 2 and 3
section 3, patch 1
2 squares $4\frac{7}{8}$" x $4\frac{7}{8}$" ⧄ (A)
2 squares $3\frac{7}{8}$" x $3\frac{7}{8}$" ⧄ (B)

Black Solid
section 1, patches 2 and 3

Assorted Batiks
sections 2 and 2r, patch 1
section 3, patch 2

Make 4 paper copies of *each* foundation section. Foundation piece the sections in numerical order, pressing and trimming after each patch addition.

Sew the sections and patches together as shown to complete the block. To reduce bulk, press the seams open.

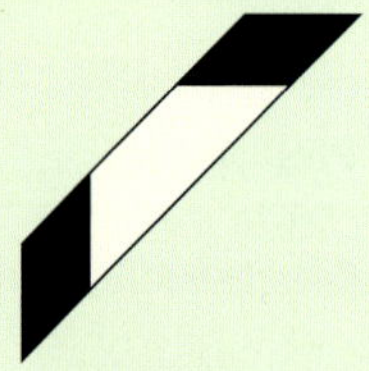

Section 1
Make 4

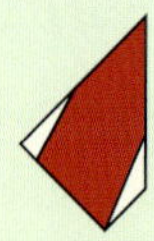

Section 2
Make 4

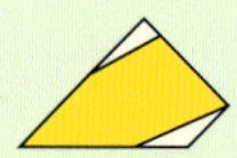

Section 2 Reversed
Make 4

Section 3
Make 4

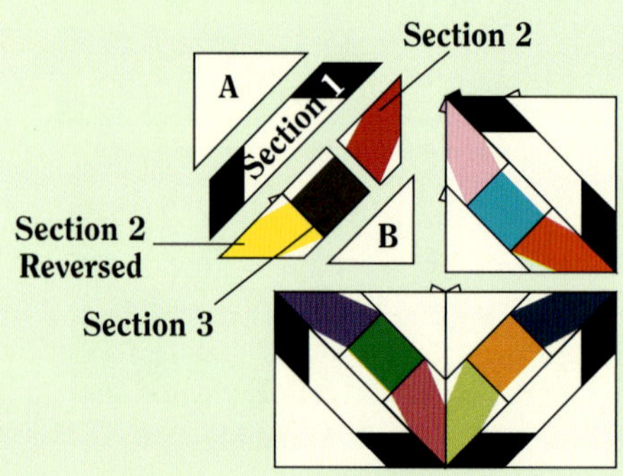

Block Assembly

block no. 219

May Showers

by Jennifer Ofenstein • Sewhooked
sewhooked.com

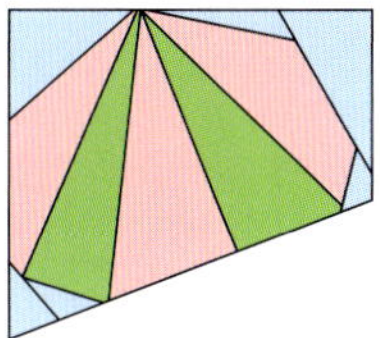

Section 1
Make 1

See page 196 on the PDF for pattern

Pink Tone-on-Tone, Green Dot, Light Yellow Dot, Beige Tone-on-Tone, Yellow Dot, Dark Green Tone-on-Tone and Teal Dot
foundation patches

Light Blue Tone-on-Tone
foundation patches
1 rectangle (A) 2¼″ x 5″
1 rectangle (B) 1¼″ x 5″
1 rectangle (C) 4¼″ x 4½″
1 rectangle (D) 4¾″ x 5″

Section 2
Make 1

Section 3
Make 1

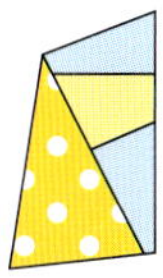

Section 4
Make 1

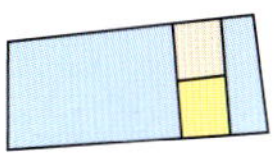

Section 5
Make 1

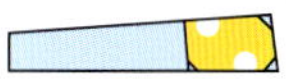

Section 6
Make 1

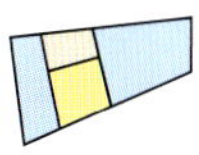

Section 7
Make 1

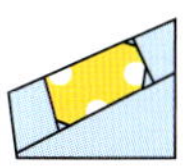

Section 8
Make 1

Section 10
Make 2 and
1 reversed

Section 9
Make 1

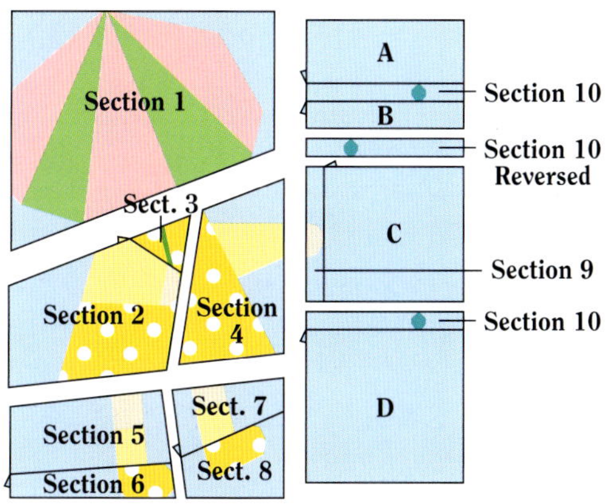

Block Assembly

Make 1 paper copy *each* of foundation sections 1–9 and 10r. Make 2 paper copies of section 10. Referring to the foundations for color placement, foundation piece the sections in numerical order, pressing and trimming after each patch addition.

Join the sections and patches as shown to complete the block.

block no. 220

Jumbo Fun

by Alyssa Thomas • Penguin & Fish
penguinandfish.com

Fabric: Safari Sweet Organic designed by Alyssa Thomas for Clothworks, clothworks.com.

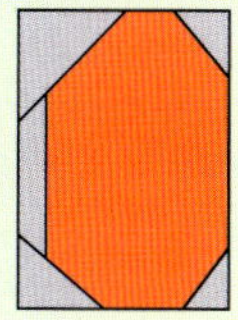

Section 1

See page 192 on the PDF for pattern

Orange Print
sections 1–3, patch 1

Pale Purple Print
section 1, patches 2–6
section 2, patches 3–5
1 rectangle (A) 2″ x 5¼″
1 rectangle (B) 3¾″ x 5¼″
1 rectangle (C) 3¾″ x 11¾″

White Print
section 2, patches 2 and 6–8
section 3, patches 2–5
1 rectangle (D) 1¼″ x 8½″

Black buttons 2 at ⅝″ diameter

Section 2

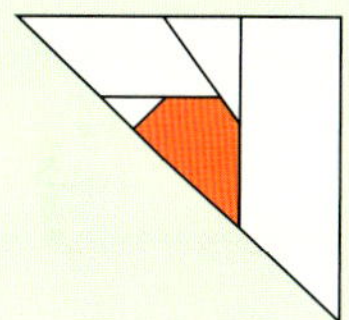

Section 3

Make 1 paper copy of *each* foundation section. Foundation piece the sections in numerical order, pressing and trimming after each patch addition.

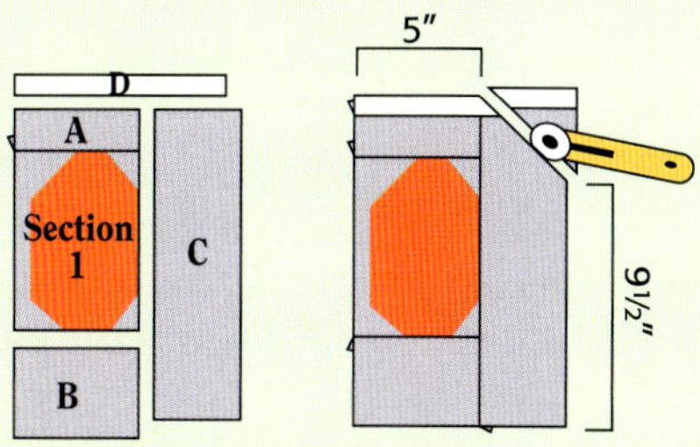

Join patches A–D to the section 1 and trim the corner as shown above. Refer to the block assembly diagram to join the remaining 2 sections.

Sew the buttons for the eyes in place to complete the block.

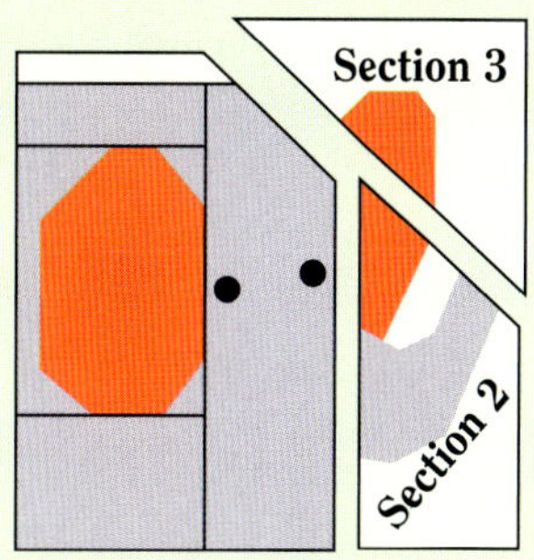

Block Assembly

block no. 221

Crystal Star

by Anelie Belden • Anelie's Quiltworks
dresdenquilt.com

Anelie Belden is the author of *Thoroughly Modern Dresden* for C&T Publishing, ctpub.com.

See page 237 on the PDF for pattern

Pale Multicolor Batik
sections 1–4, patch 1
Medium Blue Tone-on-Tone
section 1, patch 2
Dark Purple Tone-on-Tone
section 1, patch 3
Medium Purple Tone-on-Tone
section 2, patch 2
Dark Green Tone-on-Tone
section 2, patch 3
Medium Green Tone-on-Tone
section 3, patch 2
Dark Red Tone-on-Tone
section 3, patch 3
Medium Red Tone-on-Tone
section 4, patch 2
Dark Blue Tone-on-Tone
section 4, patch 3

Make 2 paper copies *each* of foundation sections 1, 2, 3 and 4. The colors for sections 3 and 4 are shown in parentheses.

Foundation piece the sections in numerical order, pressing and trimming after each patch addition. Sew the sections together as shown to complete the block.

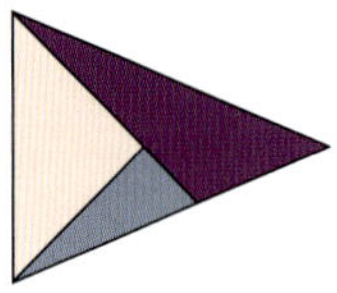

Section 1
Make 2

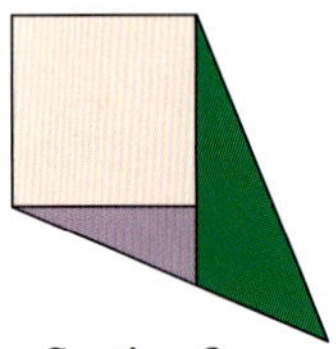

Section 2
Make 2

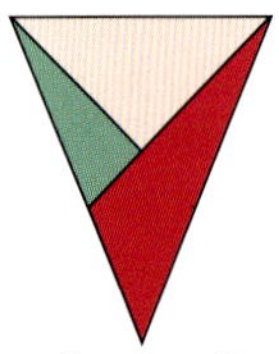

Section 3
Make 2

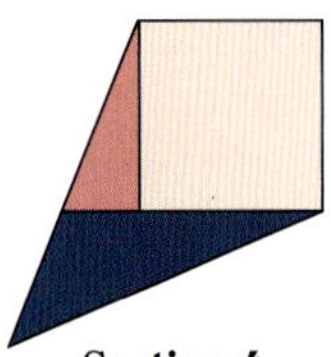

Section 4
Make 2

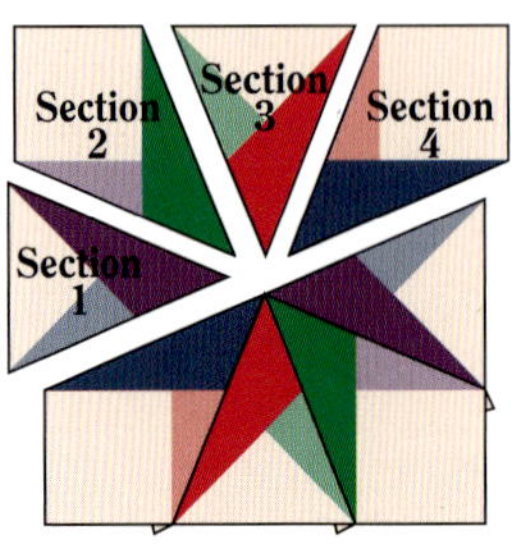

Block Assembly

block no. 222

Something Springy

by Diane Bohn
fromblankpages.blogspot.com

See page 230 on the PDF for pattern

Assorted Gold Prints and Tone-on-Tones
section patches 1–4
Assorted Orange Prints and Tone-on-Tones
section patches 5–6
Assorted Dark Pink Prints and Tone-on-Tones
section patches 7 and 8
White Solid
section patches 9 and 10
Assorted Dark Teal Prints and Tone-on-Tones
section patches 11 and 12
Assorted Medium Teal Prints and Tone-on-Tones
section patches 13–16
Light Teal Print
section patches 17 and 18

Make 4 paper copies of the foundation section. Referring to the foundation for color placement, foundation piece the sections in numerical order, pressing and trimming after each patch addition.

Join the sections as shown to complete the block. To reduce bulk, press the seams open.

Section
Make 4

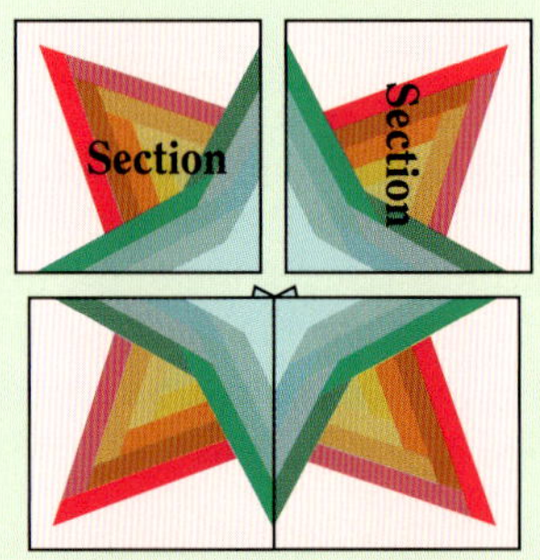

Block Assembly

block no. 223

Swirly Geese

by Cheryl Brown • QuilterChic
quilterchic.com

Cheryl Brown is the author of *Fresh and Fabulous Quilts* for Martingale & Co., shopmartingale.com.

See page 245 on the PDF for pattern

Black Batik
1 square (A) 13½″ x 13½″ (trim to 12½″ x 12½″ after appliqué)
foundation patches
4 Green Batiks
3 Teal Batiks
5 Blue Batiks
8 Purple Batiks
4 Pink Batiks
3 Red Batiks
3 Orange Batiks
4 Yellow Batiks
foundation patches

Section

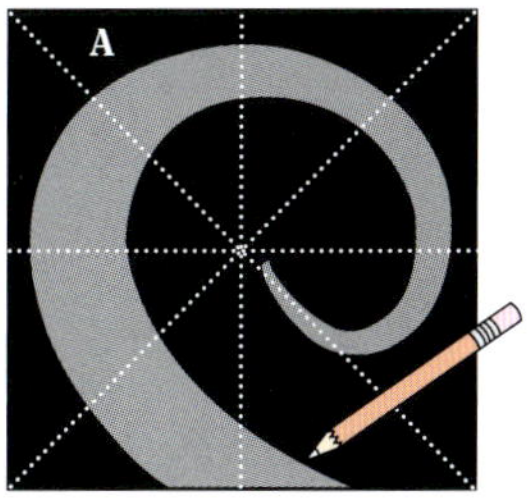

Template Placement

Reverse Applique

Make 2 paper copies of the foundation section. One section will be used as a template to mark A for reverse appliqué.

Refer to the foundation for color placement. Foundation piece the section in numerical order, pressing and trimming after each patch addition. Carefully remove the foundation papers.

Cut out the paper template on the seam line. Fold A in half both ways and lightly crease the folds. Using the creases and appliqué placement diagram as guides, center the template printed side down on the right side of A and trace the design as shown.

Refer to "Reverse Appliqué" in the Techniques file on the PDF. Position the foundation section right side up under the traced design on A; pin in place. Use matching thread and a blind stitch to reverse appliqué the section in place. Center the appliqué and trim to 12½" × 12½".

block no. 224

Arctic Seal

by Sonja Callaghan • Artisania
artisania.ca

See page 235 on the PDF for pattern

White Solid
section 1, patches 1 and 3
section 2, patches 2–5 and 8
section 3, patch 1
section 4, patches 2, 3 and 5
Black Print
section 1, patch 2
section 2, patches 6, 7 and 9–12
section 3, patches 2–5
Aqua Tone-on-Tone
section 1, patch 4
section 4, patches 1, 4 and 6–8
Red Print
section 2, patch 1
Embroidery floss

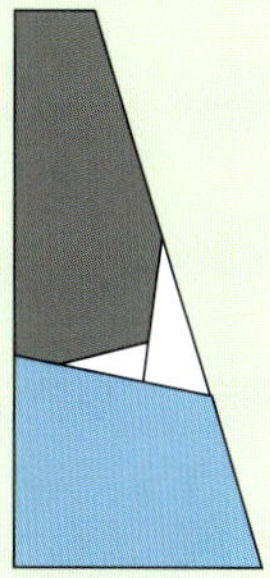

Section 1
Make 1

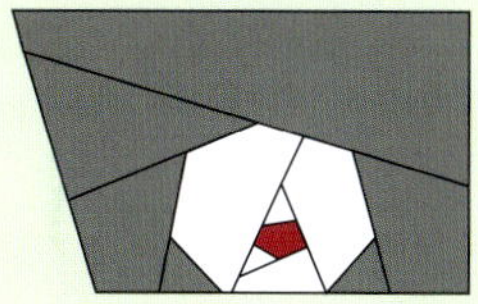

Section 2
Make 1

Section 3
Make 1

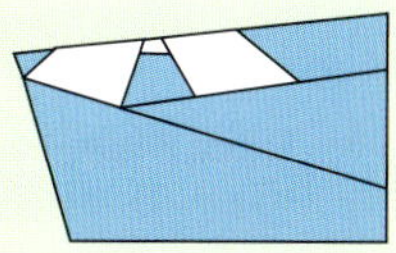

Section 4
Make 1

Make 1 paper copy of *each* foundation section. Foundation piece the sections in numerical order, pressing and trimming after each patch addition.

Sew the sections together as shown. Carefully remove the foundation papers.

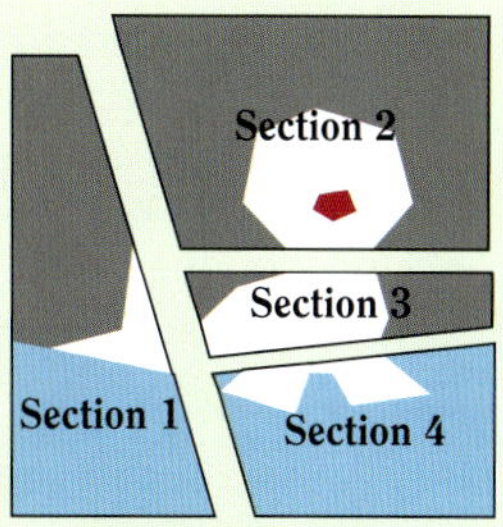

Block Assembly

The stitch diagrams are in the Techniques file on the PDF. Add the eyes using 2 strands of black floss and a satin stitch to complete the block.

Embroidery Placement

block no. 225

Spinstar

by Eileen Fowler • Associate Editor, *Quiltmaker*
quiltmaker.com

Fabric: Legacy from Timeless Treasures, ttfabrics.net.

See page 231 on the PDF for pattern

Cream Print
section patches 1, 5 and 9
Light Blue Print
section patches 2 and 6
Red Print
section patch 3
Dark Red Print
section patch 4
Gold Print
section patches 7 and 11
Multicolor Print
section patch 8
Dark Blue Print
section patch 10

Section
Make 4

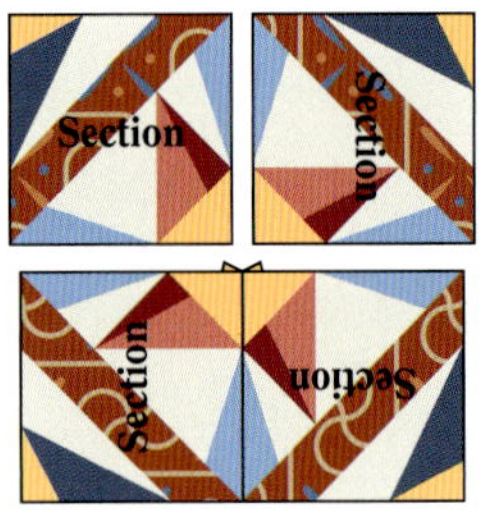

Block Assembly

Make 4 paper copies of the foundation section. Foundation piece the sections in numerical order, pressing and trimming after each patch addition.

Sew the sections together as shown to complete the block. To reduce bulk, press the seams open.

block no. 226

Tropical Flags

by Robin Koehler • Nestlings by Robin
nestlingsbyrobin.com

See page 232 on the PDF for pattern

White Tone-on-Tone
section 1, patch 1
section 2, patch 4
section 3, patch 2
Green Tone-on-Tone
section 1, patch 2
Orange Batik
section 1, patch 3
section 2, patch 2
section 3, patch 1
Medium Teal Print
section 1, patch 4
section 2, patch 1
Dark Teal Batik
section 2, patch 3

Section 1
Make 4

Section 2
Make 4

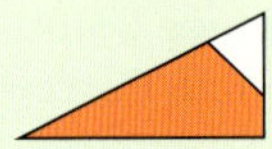

Section 3
Make 4

Make 4 paper copies of *each* foundation section. Foundation piece the sections in numerical order, pressing and trimming after each patch addition.

Sew the sections together as shown to complete the block. To reduce bulk, press seams open.

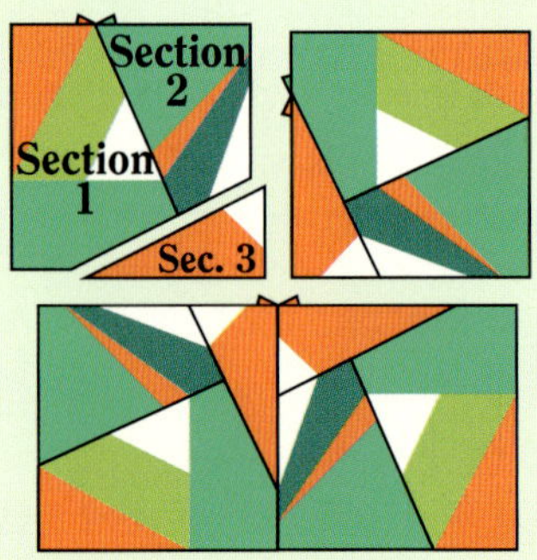

Block Assembly

block no. 227

All Points Bulletin

by Dawn Koltz, Sheri Diesburg and Ann Marceca
The Quilter's Studio • thequiltersstudio.com

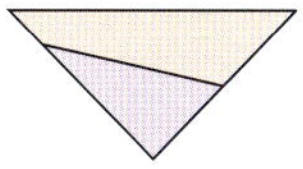

Section 1
Make 4

See page 225 on the PDF for pattern

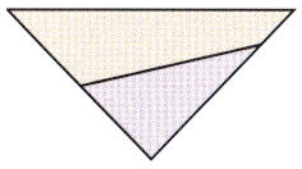

Section 1r
Make 4

Light Purple Batik
sections 1 and 1r, patch 1
Peach Batik
sections 1 and 1r, patch 2
Medium Purple Batik
sections 2 and 3, patch 1
Dark Purple Batik
sections 2 and 3, patch 2
Coral Batik
sections 2 and 3, patch 3
Magenta Batik
sections 2 and 3, patch 4
Yellow Batik
section 3, patch 5

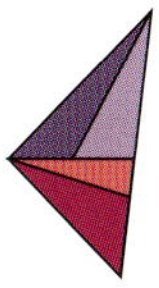

Section 2
Make 4

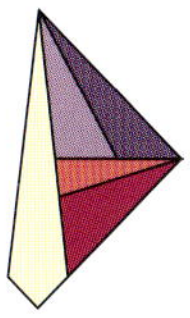

Section 3
Make 4

Make 4 paper copies *each* of sections 1, 1 reversed, 2 and 3. Foundation piece the sections in numerical order, pressing and trimming after each patch addition.

Sew the sections together as shown to complete the block. To reduce bulk, press seams open.

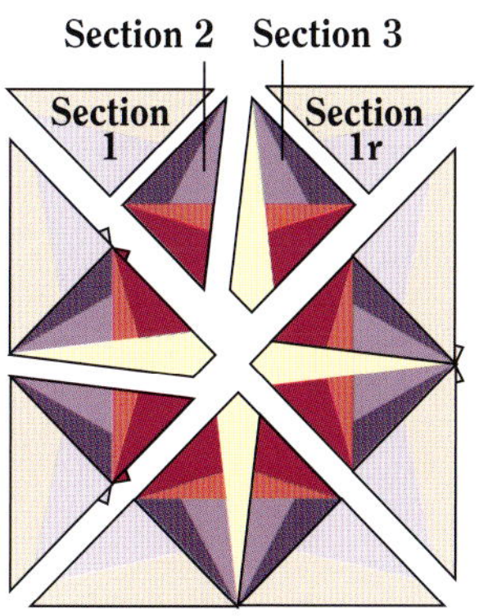

Block Assembly

block no. 228

Divided Diamonds

by Debby Kratovil • Quilter by Design
quilterbydesign.com

Fabric: Normandy Court designed by Michele D'Amore for Benartex, benartex.com.

Debby Kratovil is the author of *Supersize 'Em, 22 Quilts from Oversized Blocks* for Martingale & Co., shopmartingale.com.

See page 238 on the PDF for pattern

Cream Dot
section patches 1 and 3
Brown Tone-on-Tone
section patches 2 and 4
Black Print
4 template A
Black with White Print
1 pattern B

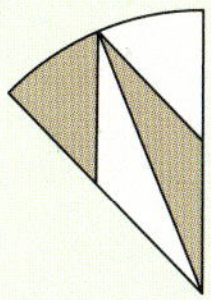

Section
Make 8

Make 8 paper copies of the foundation section. Foundation piece each section in numerical order, pressing and trimming after each patch addition.

Refer to "Curved Piecing" in the Techniques file on the PDF. Join 2 sections and 1 black print A as shown to make 1 quadrant. Repeat with the remaining sections and A's to make 4 quadrants. Sew the quadrants together as shown to make the block. To reduce bulk, press the seams open.

Prepare B for turned-edge appliqué. Center B on the block. Use matching thread and a blind stitch to appliqué around B to complete the block.

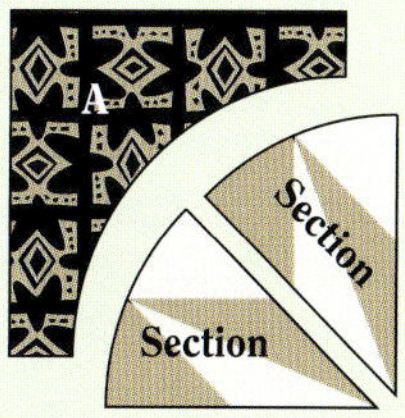

Quadrant Assembly

Block Assembly

Applique Placement

block no. 229

Peaks and Valleys

by Carolyn Cullinan McCormick • CM Designs
addaquarter.com

Carolyn McCormick is the creator of the Add-a-Quarter and Add Enough tools for quilters. She is the author of several books including *Wedding Ring, Pickle Dish & More* and *Quilts for Rosie* for Kansas City Star Quilts, pickledish.com.

See page 223 on the PDF for pattern

Cream Tone-on-Tone
- section 1, patches 1, 4 and 5
- section 2, patches 1, 4 and 7
- 2 rectangles (B) 1¼" x 3"
- 2 rectangles (C) 1¼" x 4½"

Assorted Blue Prints and Brown Prints
- section 1, patches 2, 3 and 6
- section 2, patches 2, 3, 5, 6, 8 and 9
- 1 square (A) 3" x 3"

Section 1
Make 4

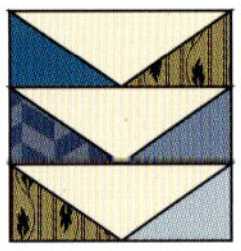

Section 2
Make 4

Make 4 paper copies of *each* foundation section. Foundation piece the sections in numerical order, pressing and trimming after each patch addition.

Sew the sections and patches together as shown to complete the block.

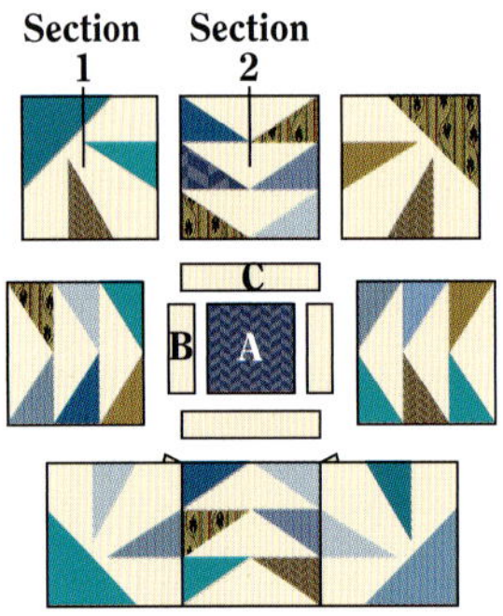

Block Assembly

block no. 230

Scarecrow Surprise

by Jennifer Ofenstein • Sewhooked
sewhooked.com

See page 224 on the PDF for pattern

Pink, Purple, White, Gold, Orange, Beige, Brown, Red, Green and Blue Tone-on-Tones
- foundation patches

Embroidery floss

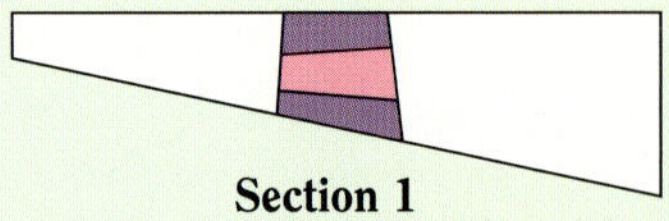

Section 1
Make 1

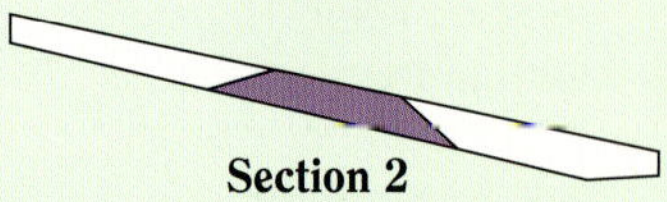

Section 2
Make 1

Make 1 paper copy of *each* foundation section. Refer to the foundations for color placement. Foundation piece the sections in numerical order, pressing and trimming after each patch addition. Sew the sections together as shown.

Section 3
Make 1

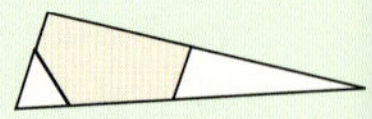

Section 4
Make 1

Section 5
Make 1

Section 6
Make 1

Section 7
Make 1

Use 2 strands of embroidery floss to add a French Knot for the bird's eye, satin stitches for the scarecrow's eyes and long stitches for the remaining embroidery details as shown on the foundation.

Section 8
Make 1

Section 9
Make 1

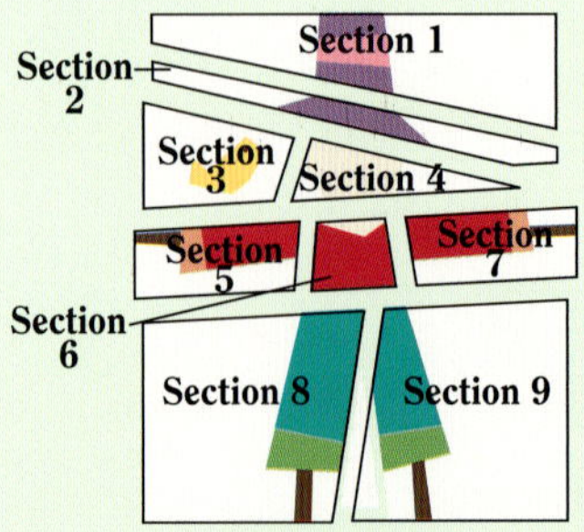

Block Assembly

Embroidery Placement

block no. 231

Two Dresses

by Charise Randell • Charise Creates
charisecreates.blogspot.com

See page 246 on the PDF for pattern

Beige Tone-on-Tone, Yellow Print, Blue Check, Blue Print, Pink Print and Tan Print
foundation patches

Cream Solid
3 rectangles (A) 1″ x 12½″
foundation patches

Make 1 paper copy *each* of foundation sections 1–11 and section 5 reversed. Make 2 paper copies *each* of sections 12–15.

Referring to the foundations for color placement, foundation piece each section in numerical order, pressing and trimming after each patch addition. Sew the sections and A's together as shown to complete the block.

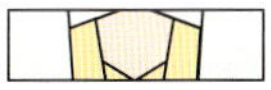

Section 1
Make 1

Section 2
Make 1

Section 3
Make 1

Section 4
Make 1

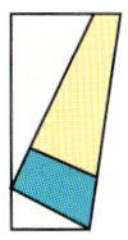

Section 5
Make 1 and 1 reversed

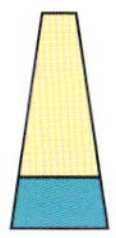

Section 6
Make 1

Section 7
Make 1

Section 8
Make 1

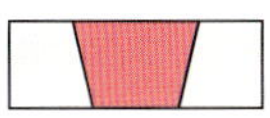

Section 9
Make 1

Section 10
Make 1

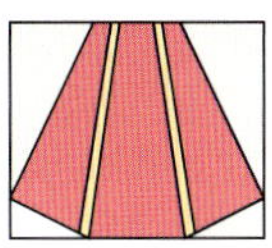

Section 11
Make 1

Section 12
Make 2

Section 13
Make 2

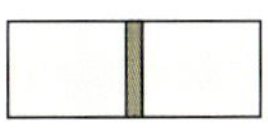

Section 14
Make 2

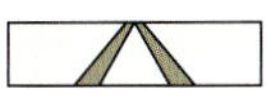

Section 15
Make 2

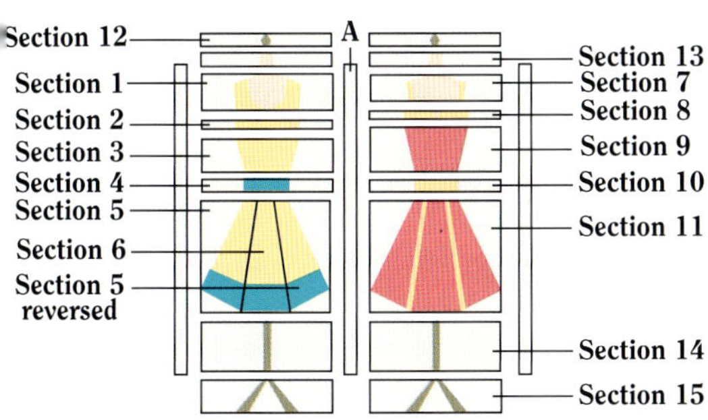

Block Assembly

block no. 232

Kaleidoscope Log Cabin

by Anita Grossman Solomon • Make it Simpler
makeitsimpler.com

Anita Grossman Solomon is the author of *Rotary Cutting Revolution* and *Make It Simpler Paper Piecing*, both for C&T Publishing, ctpub.com.

See page 239 on the PDF for pattern

◸ = cut in half diagonally

18 Assorted Light, Medium and Dark Prints and Tone-on-Tones
from *8*
foundation patches
from *8*
1 rectangle (A) 1⅞″ x 6⅛″
from *2*
1 square 5″ x 5″ ◸ (B) (there will be 2 extra)

Make 2 paper copies of the section foundation. Using light to medium prints in one section and dark prints in the other, foundation piece the sections in numerical order, pressing and trimming after each patch addition.

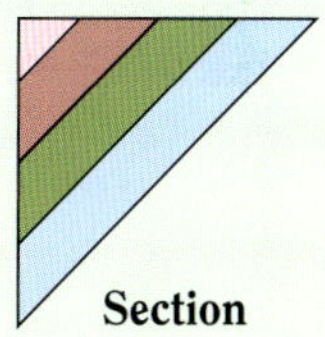

Section
Make 2

Sew the patches and sections together as shown to complete the block.

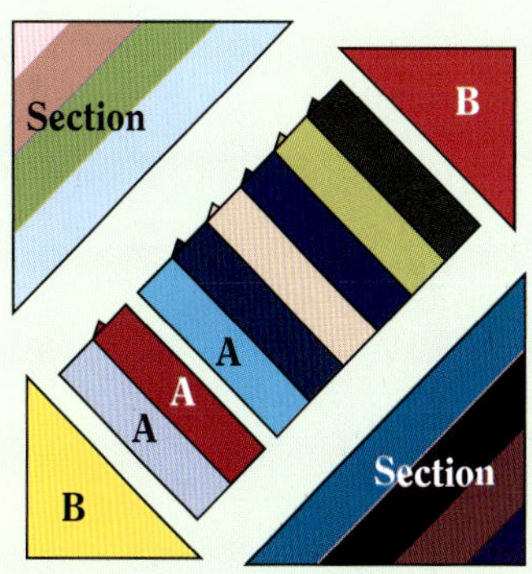

Block Assembly

block no. 233

Boomerang

by Angela Walters • Angela Walters Quilting
quiltingismytherapy.com

Angela Walters is the author of *Free-Motion Quilting with Angela Walters* for C&T Publishing, ctpub.com.

See page 227 on the PDF for pattern

Black Solid
section and section reversed, patches 1 and 6
Gold Solid
section and section reversed, patches 2 and 7
Green Print
section and section reversed, patches 3 and 5
Gray Solid
section and section reversed, patch 4

Make 2 copies *each* of the foundation section and section reversed. Foundation piece each section in numerical order, pressing and trimming after each patch addition.

Sew the sections together as shown to complete the block. To reduce bulk, press seams open.

Section
Make 2

Section reversed
Make 2

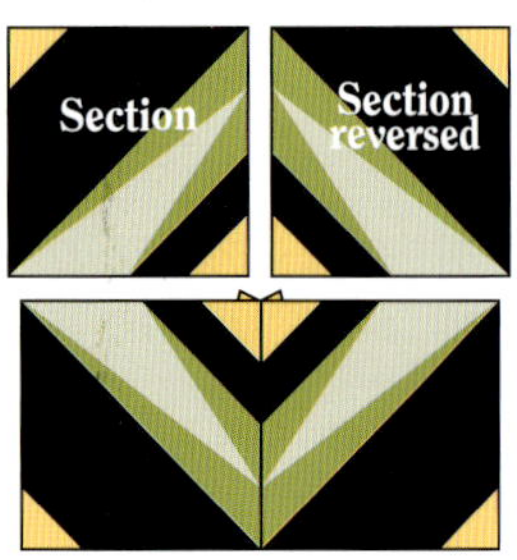

Block Assembly

block no. 234

New Beginnings

by Cinzia White
cinziawhite.com

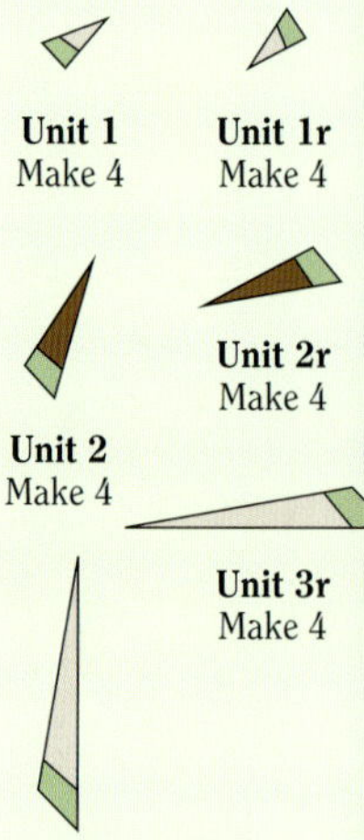

Unit 1 Make 4
Unit 1r Make 4
Unit 2 Make 4
Unit 2r Make 4
Unit 3 Make 4
Unit 3r Make 4

See page 243 on the PDF for pattern

Light Brown Print
units 1, 3, 1r and 3r, patch 1
section and section reversed, patches 2 and 6
Light Green Tone-on-Tone
units 1–3 and units 1r–3r, patch 2
Dark Brown Tone-on-Tone
units 2 and 2r, patch 1
section and section reversed, patch 4
Dark Green Tone-on-Tone
section and section reversed, patch 1

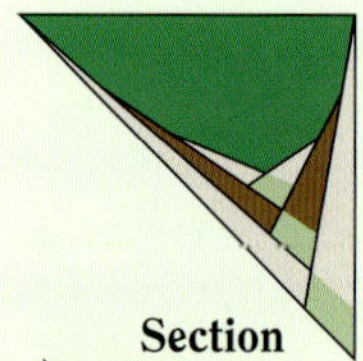

Section
Make 4

Section Reversed
Make 4

The units are foundation-pieced first and then used as patches in the sections. All units are slightly larger than needed to ensure adequate coverage.

Make 4 paper copies of *each* foundation unit and section and each reverse unit and section.

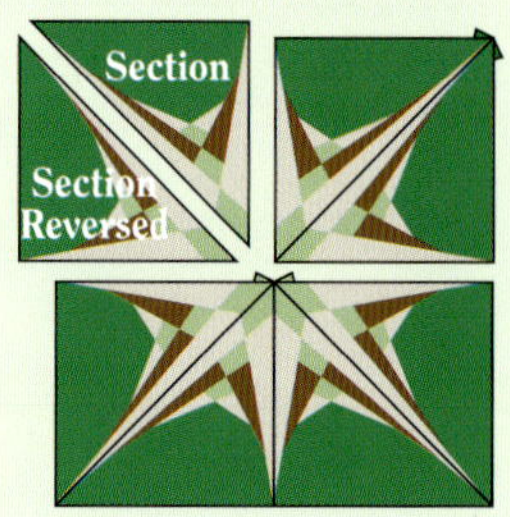

Block Assembly

Foundation piece units 1–3 and 1r–3r; press and trim along the outside unit lines. The dot on each unit is a registration mark used to align the unit on the section. Transfer the dots to the wrong side of the units; carefully remove the foundation papers.

Foundation piece patches 1 and 2 on the section; press and trim. Align unit 1 on patch 3 by matching the dots; secure with pins before stitching in place. Continue foundation piecing the section, aligning units 2 and 3 in the same way as unit 1, and pressing and trimming after each patch addition. Repeat for all sections. For each reversed section, use units 1r–3r.

Join the sections and reverse sections as shown to complete the block. To reduce bulk, press seams open.

block no. 235

Diamond Crossing

by Lisa Bassett • Relatively Creative Patterns
relativelycreativepatterns.com

See page 261 on the PDF for pattern

Orange Tone-on-Tone
sections 1 and 2, patch 1

Teal Tone-on-Tone
section 1, patches 2 and 3

Light Blue Tone-on-Tone
section 2, patches 2 and 3

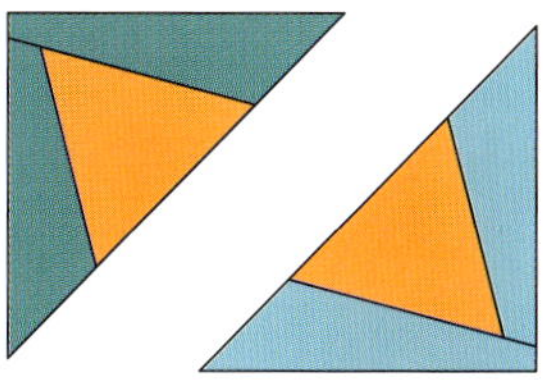

Section 1
Make 4

Section 2
Make 4

Make 8 paper copies of the foundation section. Foundation piece each section in numerical order, pressing and trimming after each patch addition.

Sew the sections together as shown. To reduce bulk, press the seams open.

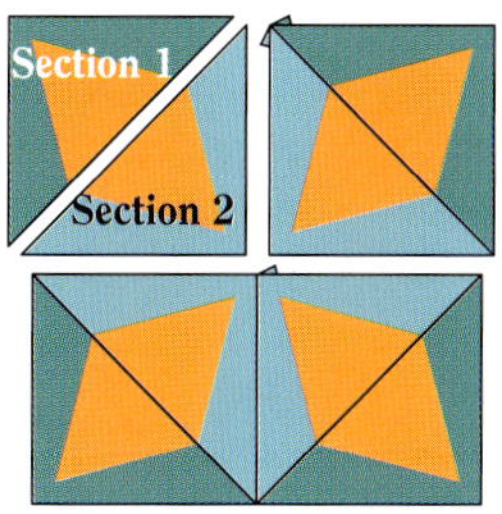

Block Assembly

block no. 236

Russell's Way

by Jennifer Chiaverini
elmcreek.net

Fabric: Elm Creek Quilts: Rosa's Collection designed by Jennifer Chiaverini for Red Rooster Fabrics, redroosterfabrics.com.

Best-selling novelist Jennifer Chiaverini has written several books including *Traditions from Elm Creek Quilts* for C&T Publishing, ctpub.com.

See page 266 on the PDF for pattern

Cream Tone-on-Tone
sections 1 and 1r, patches 1 and 3
sections 2 and 2r, patch 1

Brown Tone-on-Tone
sections 1, 1r, 2 and 2r, patch 2

Green Tone-on-Tone
sections 2 and 2r, patch 3

Make 4 paper copies *each* of foundation sections 1 and 2 and sections 1 and 2 reversed. Foundation piece the sections in numerical order, pressing and trimming after each patch addition.

Sew the sections together as shown. To reduce bulk, press the seams open.

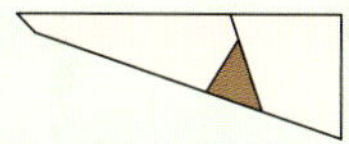

Section 1
Make 4

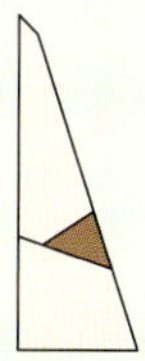

Section 1 Reversed
Make 4

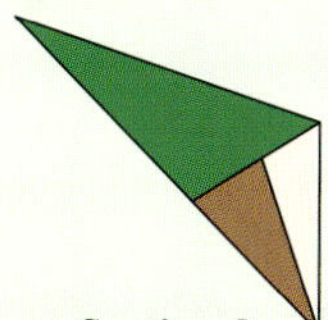

Section 2
Make 4

Section 2 Reversed
Make 4

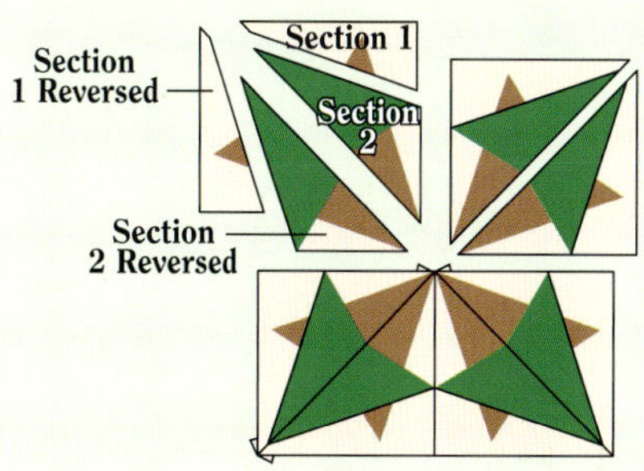

Block Assembly

block no. 237

Santa Fe Star

by Eileen Fowler • Associate Editor, *Quiltmaker*
quiltmaker.com

Fabric: Tonga Batiks from Timeless Treasures, ttfabrics.com.

See page 280 on the PDF for pattern

Cream Batik
section and section reversed, patches 1, 3, 5, 7, 9 and 10
Turquoise Batik
section and section reversed, patches 2, 4, 6 and 8
Brown Batik
section and section reversed, patch 11
Dark Orange Batik
section and section reversed, patches 12 and 13
Light Turquoise Batik
section and section reversed, patch 14

Section
Make 2

Section Reversed
Make 2

Make 2 paper copies *each* of the foundation section and the section reversed. Foundation piece the sections in numerical order, pressing and trimming after each patch addition.

Sew the sections together as shown. To reduce bulk, press the seams open.

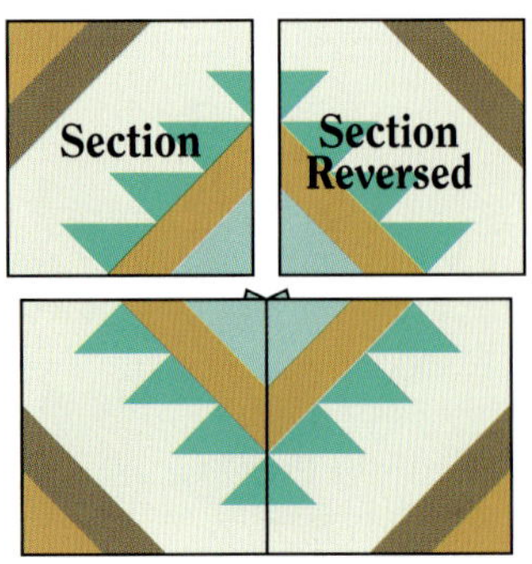

Block Assembly

block no. 238

Pretty Iris

by Yolanda Fundora • Urban Amish
urbanamish.com

Yolanda Fundora is the co-author of *Fuse It and Be Done* for Krause Publications, krausebooks.com.

See page 274 on the PDF for pattern

Orange Tone-on-Tone
sections 1 and 2, patch 1
Medium Purple Tone-on-Tone
section 1, patches 2, 3 and 6
section 2, patches 2 and 3
Light Blue Tone-on-Tone
section 1, patches 4, 5 and 8–10
section 2, patches 4 and 6–8
section 3, patches 1, 3, 5 and 7
Dark Purple Print
section 1, patch 7
Green Tone-on-Tone
section 2, patch 5
section 3, patches 2, 4 and 6

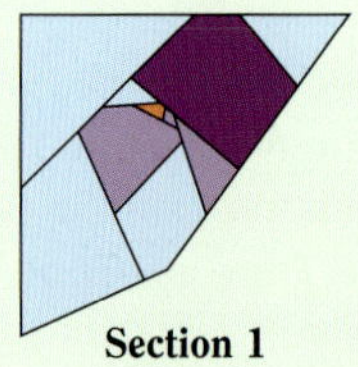

Section 1
Make 1

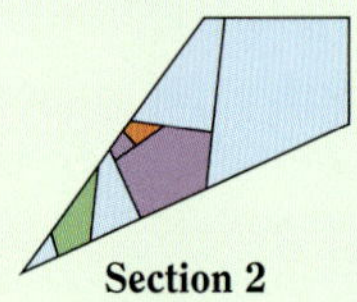

Section 2
Make 1

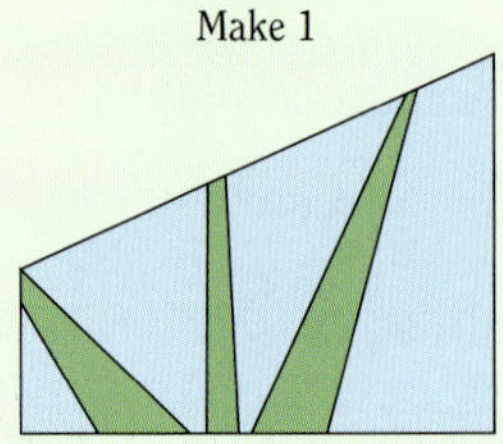

Section 3
Make 1

Make 1 paper copy of *each* foundation section. Foundation piece the sections in numerical order, pressing and trimming after each patch addition.

Sew the sections together as shown to complete the block.

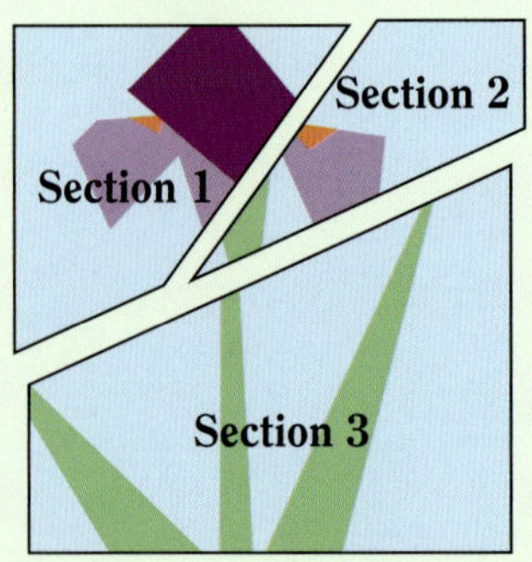

Block Assembly

block no. 239

Spinneret

by Pat Harrison • Ocean Waves Quilting Company
oceanwavesqc.com

Fabric: Sausalito designed by Christine Graf for Quilting Treasures, quiltingtreasures.com.

See page 268 on the PDF for pattern

Section 1
Make 2

Section 2
Make 2

White Print
section 1, patch 1
Blue Tone-on-Tone
section 1, patches 2, 3 and 6
Green Print
section 1, patch 4
section 2, patch 5
Orange Print
section 1, patch 5
section 2, patch 4
Black Print
section 2, patch 1
Red Tone-on-Tone
section 2, patches 2, 3 and 6

Make 4 paper copies of the foundation section. The colors for section 2 are shown in parentheses on the foundation. Foundation piece each section in numerical order, pressing and trimming after each patch addition.

Sew the sections together as shown to complete the block. To reduce bulk, press the seams open.

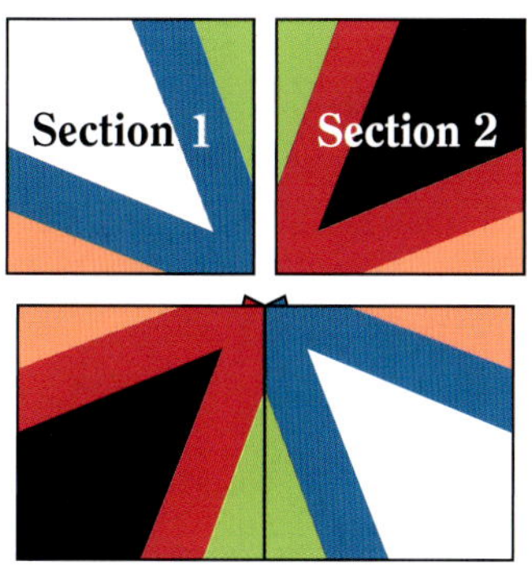

Block Assembly

block no. 240

Sherbet Punch

by Faith Jones • Fresh Lemons Quilts
freshlemonsquilts.com

See 267 on the PDF for pattern

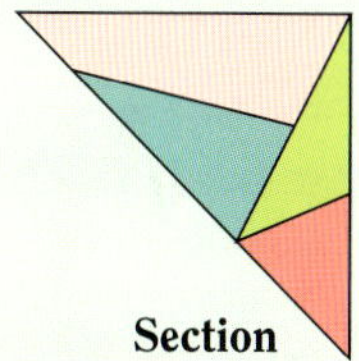

Section
Make 4

Section Reversed
Make 4

Cream and Orange Print
section and section reversed, patch 1
Teal Solid
section and section reversed, patch 2
Light Green Solid
section and section reversed, patch 3
Pink Solid
section and section reversed, patch 4

Make 4 paper copies *each* of the foundation section and the section reversed. Foundation piece each section in numerical order, pressing and trimming after each patch addition.

Sew the sections together as shown to complete the block. To reduce bulk, press the seams open.

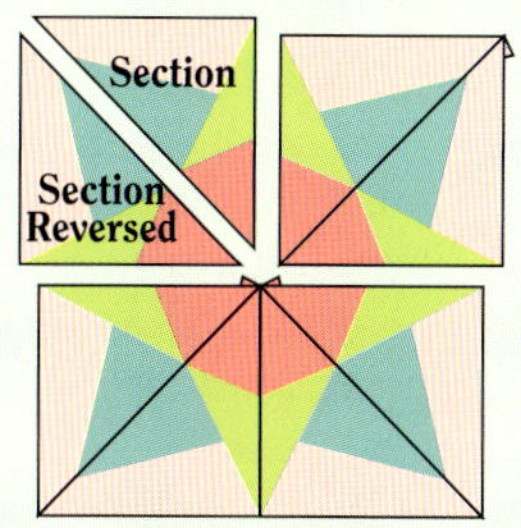

Block Assembly

block no. 241

Penny Penguin

by Beth Maddocks • Piece by Number
piecebynumber.com

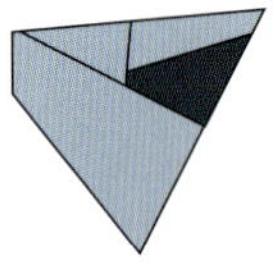

Section 1
Make 1

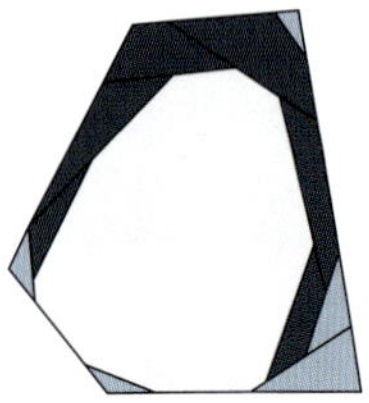

Section 2
Make 1

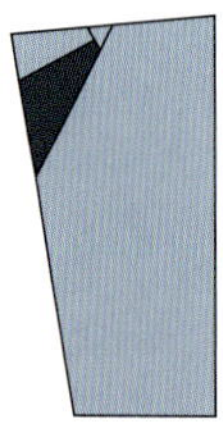

Section 3
Make 1

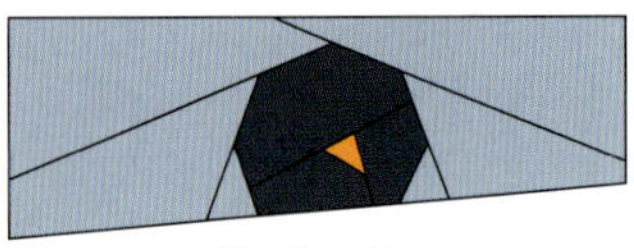

Section 4
Make 1

Section 5
Make 1

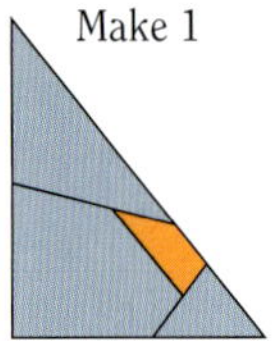

Section 6
Make 1

See page 273 on the PDF for pattern

Medium Blue Tone-on-Tone
sections 1 and 6, patches 1, 3 and 4
section 2, patches 2, 5, 6, 8 and 12
section 3, patches 2–4
section 4, patches 5–10
section 5, patches 1 and 3

Black Tone-on-Tone
section 1, patch 2
section 2, patches 3, 4, 7 and 9–11
section 3, patch 1
section 4, patches 2–4

White Tone-on-Tone
section 2, patch 1
2 pattern B

Orange Tone-on-Tone
section 4, patch 1
sections 5 and 6, patch 2

Light Blue Tone-on-Tone
1 rectangle (A) 1½" x 12½"

Black buttons 2 at ½"

Fusible web

Make 1 paper copy of *each* foundation section. Foundation piece the sections in numerical order, pressing and trimming after each patch addition. Sew the sections and A together as shown. Carefully remove the foundation papers.

Prepare the white B's for fusible appliqué. Refer to the foundation pattern for placement; fuse the B's in place. Use white thread and a short zigzag stitch to sew around the B's. Tack the buttons in place to complete the block.

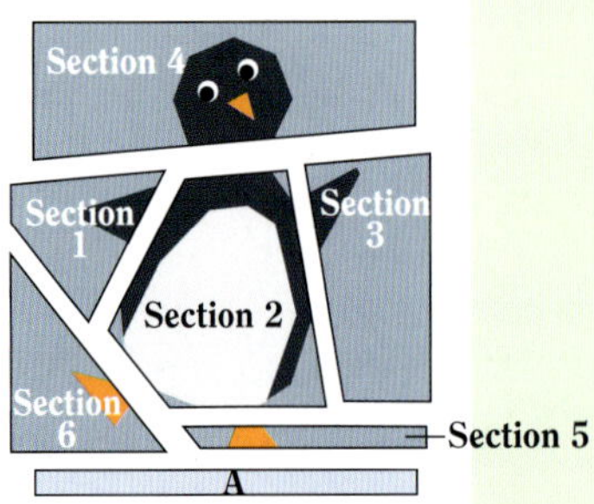

Block Assembly and Applique Placement

block no. 242

Emerald Isles

by Nancy Mahoney
nancymahoney.com

Fabric: Modern Shadows and Basics from P&B Textiles, pbtex.com.

Nancy Mahoney is the author of *Kaleidoscope Paper Piecing: 10 Dynamic Quilt Designs* for Martingale & Co., shopmartingale.com.

See page 270 on the PDF for pattern

Black Tone-on-Tone
section 1, patch 1

Light Green Tone-on-Tone
section 1, patches 2 and 3

Black Print
section 2, patch 1

White Print
section 2, patches 2 and 3

White Tone-on-Tone
section 2, patch 4
section 3, patch 1

Medium Green Print
section 3, patches 2–4

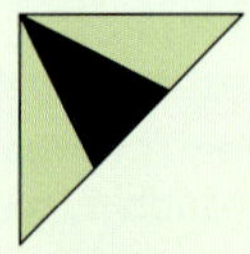

Section 1
Make 4

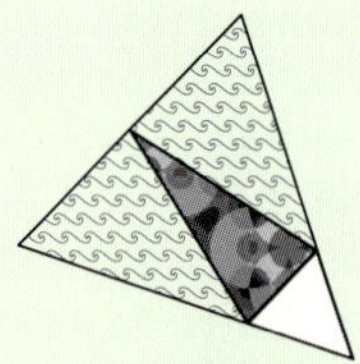

Section 2
Make 4

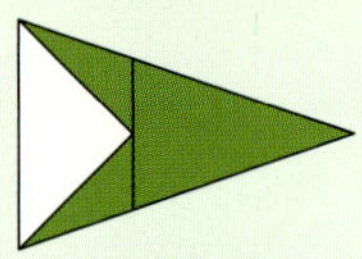

Section 3
Make 4

Make 4 paper copies of *each* foundation section. Foundation piece the sections in numerical order, pressing and trimming after each patch addition.

Sew the sections together as shown to complete the block. To reduce bulk, press the seams open.

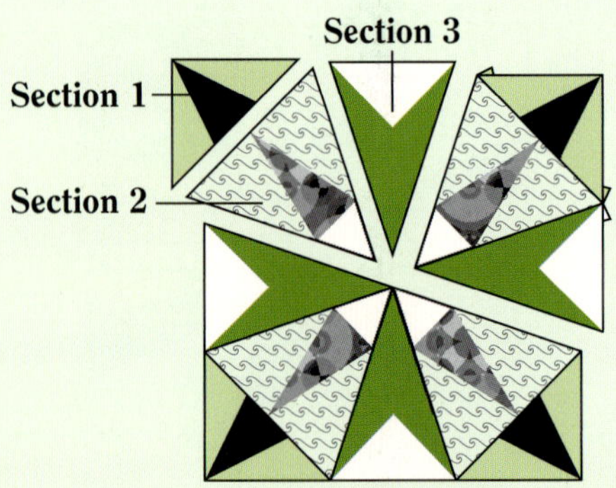

Block Assembly

block no. 243

Point Taken!

by Pam McMahon • Pam's Piece by Piece
piecebypiecequiltdesigns.com

Fabric: Various lines designed by Jo Morton for Andover Fabrics, andoverfabrics.com.

Pam McMahon is the author of *A Passion for Precuts* for Leisure Arts, leisurearts.com.

See page 279 on the PDF for pattern

⧄ = cut in half diagonally

Dark Blue Print
section 1, patch 1

Tan Print
section 1, patches 2 and 3
4 squares 2⅞" x 2⅞" ⧄ (B)

Medium Blue Print
section 2, patch 1
4 squares (A) 2½" x 2½"

Black Tone-on-Tone
section 2, patches 2–5

Brown Print
section 2, patches 6–9
2 squares 4⅞" x 4⅞" ⧄ (C)

Section 1
Make 4

Section 2
Make 1

Make 4 paper copies of foundation section 1 and 1 paper copy of section 2. Foundation piece the sections in numerical order, pressing and trimming after each patch addition.

Sew the sections and patches together as shown to complete the block.

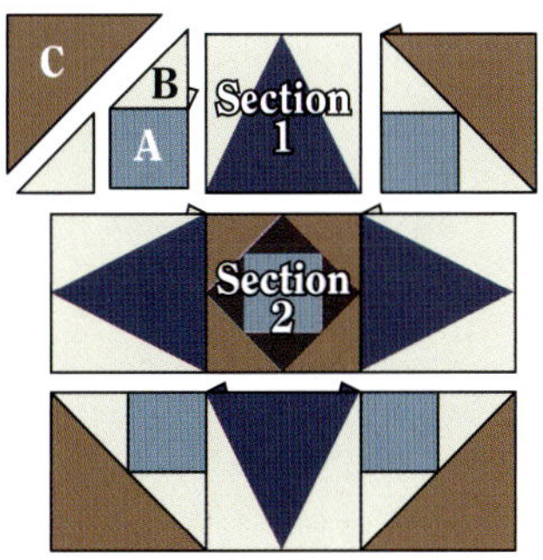

Block Assembly

block no. 244

Barn Swallow

by Nancy McNally
nancysonestitchatatime.blogspot.com

See pages 249–250 on the PDF for pattern

Red Print
section 1, patch 1

White Batik
section 1, patch 2

Black Batik
sections 2–4 and 2–4 reversed, patch 1
2 template A

Gray Batik
sections 2–4 and 2–4 reversed, patch 2

Make 5 paper copies of foundation section 1 and 1 copy *each* of sections 2–4 and 2–4 reversed. Foundation piece the sections in numerical order, pressing and trimming after each patch addition.

Sew the sections and patches together as shown to complete the block.

Section 1
Make 5

Section 2
Make 1

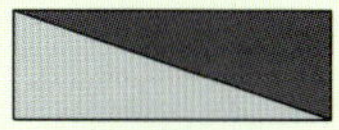

Section 3
Make 1

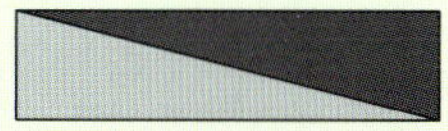

Section 4
Make 1

Section 2 Reversed
Make 1

Section 3 Reversed
Make 1

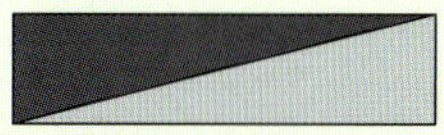

Section 4 Reversed
Make 1

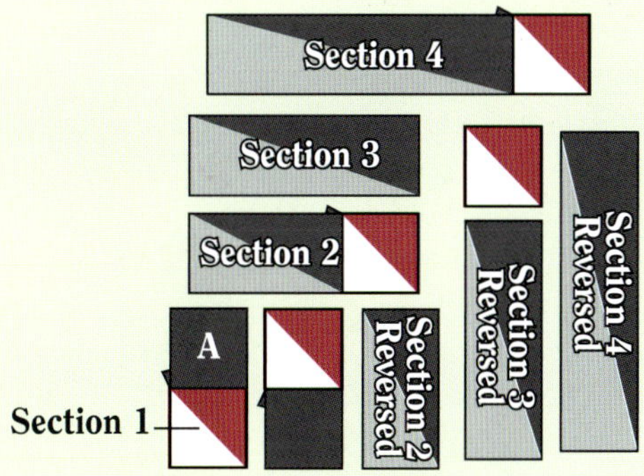

Block Assembly

block no. 245

Lemons into Lemonade

by Jennifer Ofenstein • Sewhooked
sewhooked.com

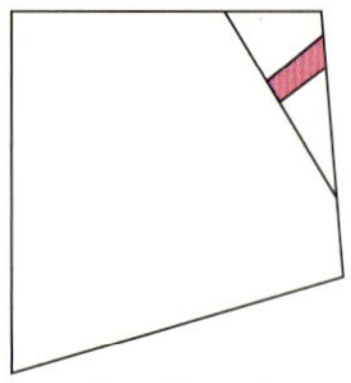

Section 1
Make 1

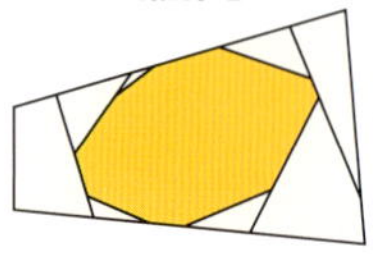

Section 2
Make 1

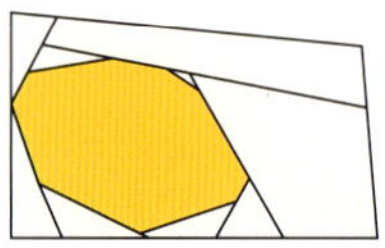

Section 3
Make 1

See pages 277–278 on the PDF for pattern

White Tone-on-Tone
- section 1, patches 1, 3 and 4
- section 2, patches 2–9
- section 3, patches 2–10
- section 4, patches 2–5
- section 5, patches 8–10
- section 6, patches 18–22, 24 and 25

Pink Tone-on-Tone
- section 1, patch 2
- section 6, patch 23

Dark Yellow Solid
- sections 2 and 3, patch 1
- section 5, patches 5–7
- section 6, patches 11–17

Turquoise Dot
- section 4, patch 1

Yellow Stripe
- section 5, patches 1 and 2
- section 6, patches 1–4

Pale Yellow Solid
- section 5, patches 3 and 4
- section 6, patches 5–10

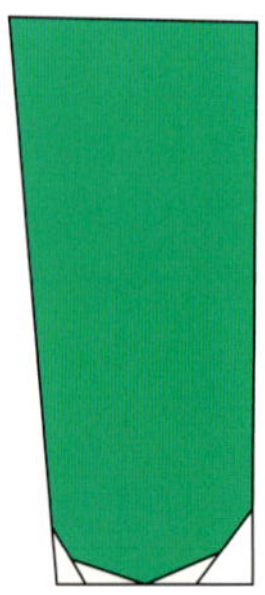

Section 4
Make 1

Section 5
Make 1

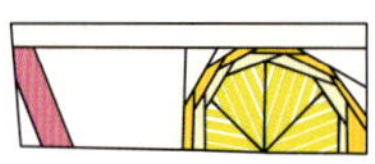

Section 6
Make 1

Make 1 paper copy *each* of foundation sections 1–6. Foundation piece the sections in numerical order, pressing and trimming after each patch addition.

Sew the sections together as shown to complete the block.

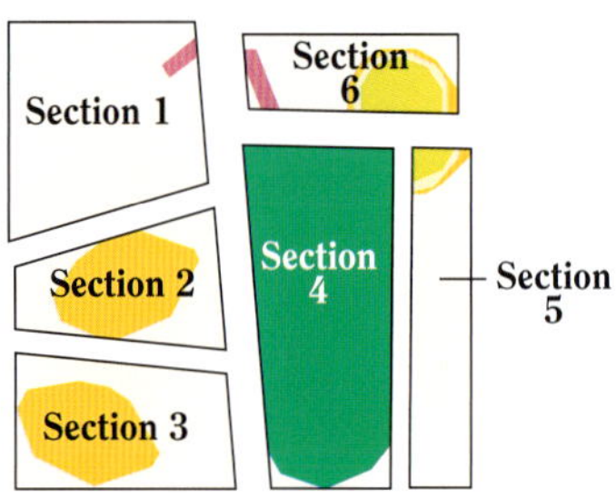

Block Assembly

block no. 246

Little House on the Hill

by Cyrille Zellweger • Bubblestitch
bubblestitchquilts.blogspot.com

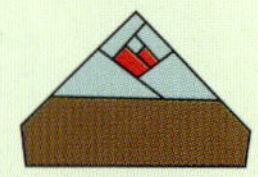

Section 1
Make 1

Section 2
Make 1

Section 3
Make 1

See page 285 on the PDF for pattern

Light Blue Tone-on-Tone
- sections 1 and 7, patches 1 and 4–7

Red Tone-on-Tone
- sections 1 and 7, patches 2 and 3

Brown Print
- section 1, patch 8
- section 2, patches 2, 3, 6 and 7
- section 3, patches 2 and 3

Gold Tone-on-Tone
- sections 2, 3 and 5, patch 1

White Print
- section 2, patches 4 and 5
- 4 rectangles (A) 2½" x 8½"

Tan Print
- section 3, patch 4
- sections 4 and 4r, patch 1

Medium Blue Tone-on-Tone
- sections 4 and 4r, patches 2 and 3
- section 5, patches 2–4 and 6
- section 6, patches 2–4

Black Tone-on-Tone
- section 5, patch 5
- section 6, patch 1

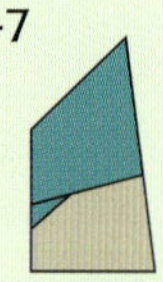

Section 4
Make 1

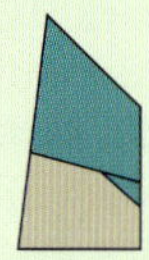

Section 4 Reversed
Make 1

Section 5
Make 1

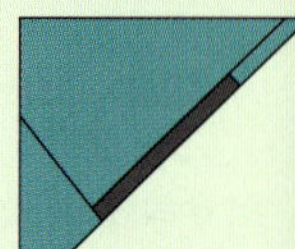

Section 6
Make 1

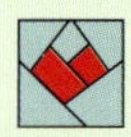

Section 7
Make 4

Make 1 paper copy *each* of foundation sections 1–6 and section 4 reversed. Make 4 paper copies of section 7. Foundation piece the sections in numerical order, pressing and trimming after each patch addition.

Sew the sections and patches together as shown to complete the block.

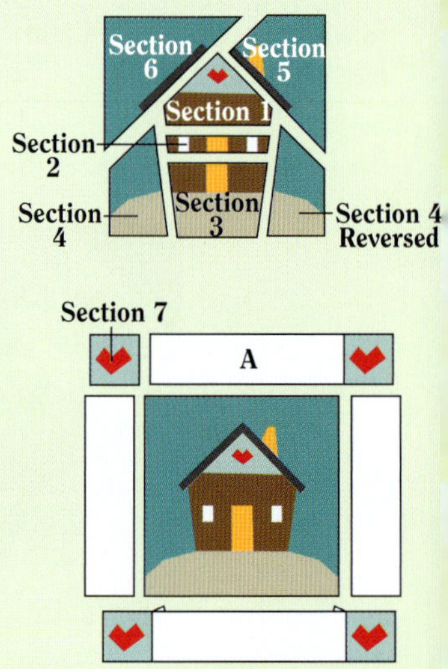

Block Assembly

block no. 247

Arkansas Whirl

by Mickey Depre
mdquilts.com

Mickey Depre is the author of *Pieced Hexies: A New Tradition in English Paper Piecing* and *Ring Around the Hexies—A Collaboration Celebration* with Bonnie Hunter, both for Kansas City Star Quilts, pickledish.com.

See page 287 on the PDF for pattern

Green Tone-on-Tone
section 1, patch 1
Medium Orange Tone-on-Tone
section 1, patch 2
Cream Batik
section 1, patch 3
section 2, patch 1
Yellow Tone-on-Tone
section 2, patch 2
Dark Orange Tone-on-Tone
section 2, patch 3
Red Batik
section 2, patch 4

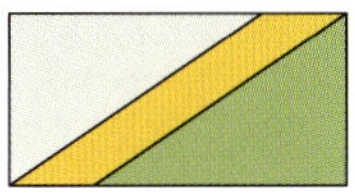

Section 1
Make 4

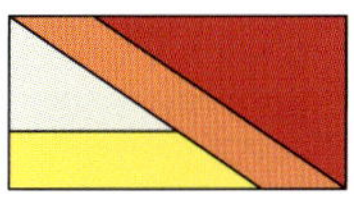

Section 2
Make 4

Make 4 paper copies of *each* foundation section. Foundation piece the sections in numerical order, pressing and trimming after each patch addition.

Sew the sections together as shown to complete the block. To reduce bulk, press the seams open.

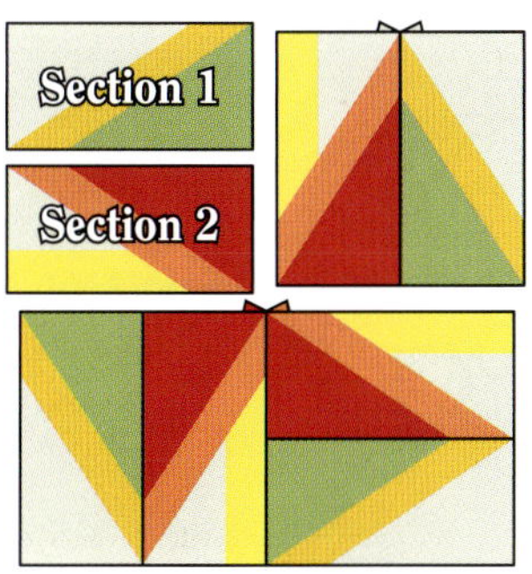

Block Assembly

block no. 248

Polaris

by Sheri Diesburg, Dawn Koltz and Ann Marceca
Studio Designs

See page 321 on the PDF for pattern

Gold Batik #1
section 1, patch 1
Dark Pink Batik
section 1, patch 2
section 3, patch 1
Gold Batik #2
section 2, patch 1
Pale Pink Batik
section 2, patch 2
Pale Green Batik
sections 2 and 3, patch 3
Dark Green Batik
section 3, patch 2

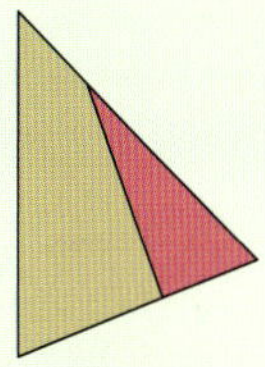

Section 1
Make 4

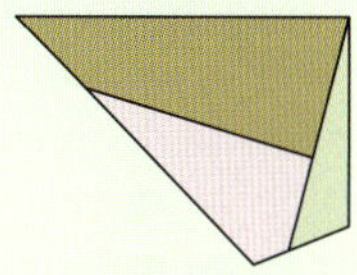

Section 2
Make 4

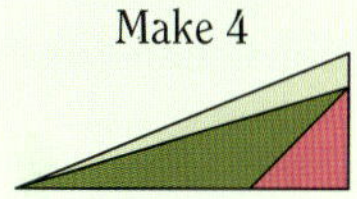

Section 3
Make 4

Make 4 paper copies of *each* foundation section. Foundation piece the sections in numerical order, pressing and trimming after each patch addition.

Sew the sections together as shown to complete the block. To reduce bulk, press the seams open.

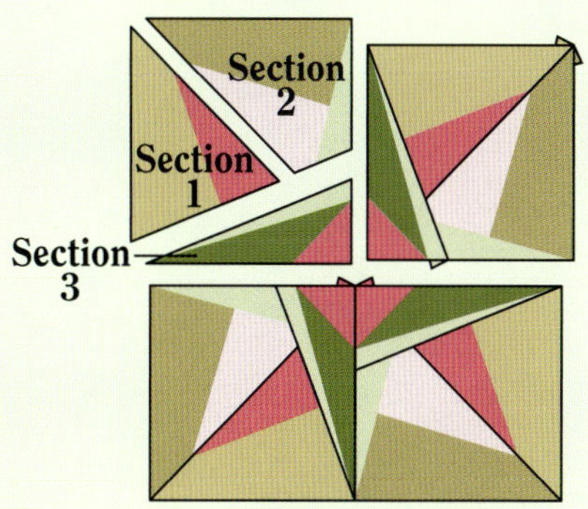

Block Assembly

block no. 249

Pin-whirl

by June Dudley • Editor-in-Chief, *Quiltmaker*
quiltmaker.com

Fabric: Serenity designed by Cheri Strole for Northcott, northcott.com.

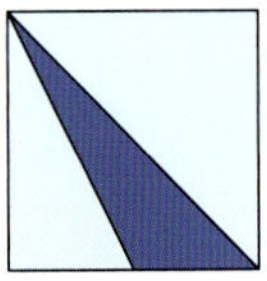

Section 1
Make 4

See page 322 on the PDF for pattern

Blue Tone-on-Tone
section 1, patch 1
Pale Blue Tone-on-Tone
section 1, patches 2 and 3
Medium Teal Tone-on-Tone
section 2, patch 1
Light Teal Print
section 2, patch 2
Light Green Tone-on-Tone
section 3, patch 1
Dark Green Print
section 3, patch 2

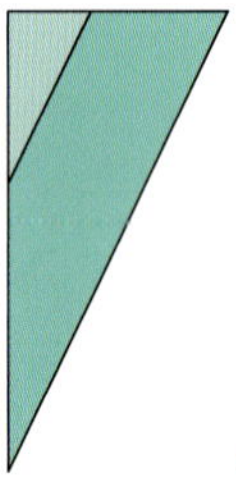

Section 2
Make 2

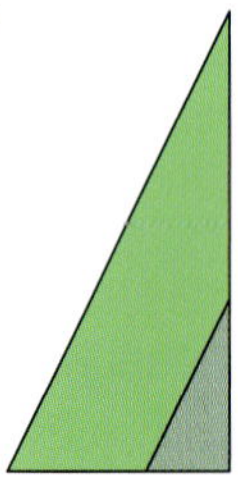

Section 3
Make 2

Make 4 paper copies of foundation section 1 and 2 paper copies *each* of sections 2 and 3. The colors for section 3 are shown in parentheses.

Foundation piece the sections in numerical order, pressing and trimming after each patch addition.

Sew the sections together as shown to complete the block. To reduce bulk, press the seams open.

Block Assembly

block no. 250

Fireworks

by Eileen Fowler • Associate Editor, *Quiltmaker*
quiltmaker.com

Fabric: Bali Handpaints and Hand-dyed Watercolors from Hoffman California Fabrics, hoffmanfabrics.com.

See pages 333–334 on the PDF for pattern

Dark Blue Batik
section 1, section 1 reversed and section 2, patches 1, 3, 5, 6, 8 and 10–12
Pale Pink Batik
section 1, section 1 reversed and section 2, patches 2 and 7
Aqua Batik
section 1, section 1 reversed and section 2, patches 4 and 9

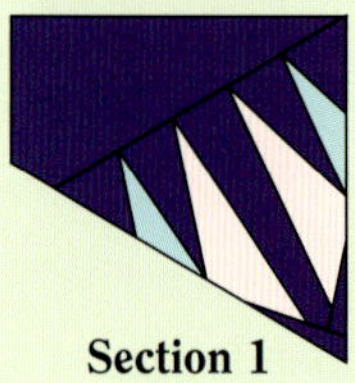

Section 1
Make 2

Section 1 Reversed
Make 2

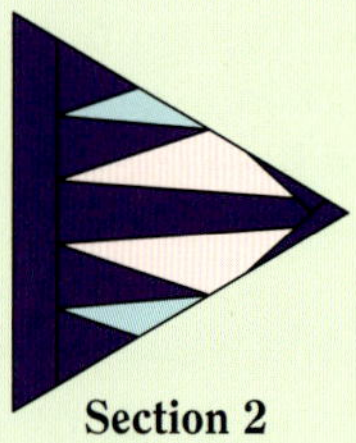

Section 2
Make 2

Make 2 paper copies *each* of the foundation section 1, section 1 reversed and section 2. Foundation piece the sections in numerical order, pressing and trimming after each patch addition.

Sew the sections together as shown. To reduce bulk, press the seams open.

Block Assembly

block no. 251

Supernova

by Diane Harris • Interactive Editor, *Quiltmaker*
quiltmaker.com

Fabric: Close to Home designed by T.S. Post and others, all from P&B Textiles, pbtex.com.

See page 325 on the PDF for pattern

3 Orange Prints, 3 Green Prints and 2 Teal Prints
foundation patches
Black Print
1 rectangle (A) 2″x 11″
1 rectangle (B) 2″x 12½″

Make 1 paper copy *each* of the foundation section and the section reversed. The patch numbers and colors for the reversed section are in italics.

Referring to the foundations for color placement, foundation piece each section in numerical order, pressing and trimming after each patch addition.

Sew the sections and patches together as shown to complete the block.

Section
Make 1

Section Reversed
Make 1

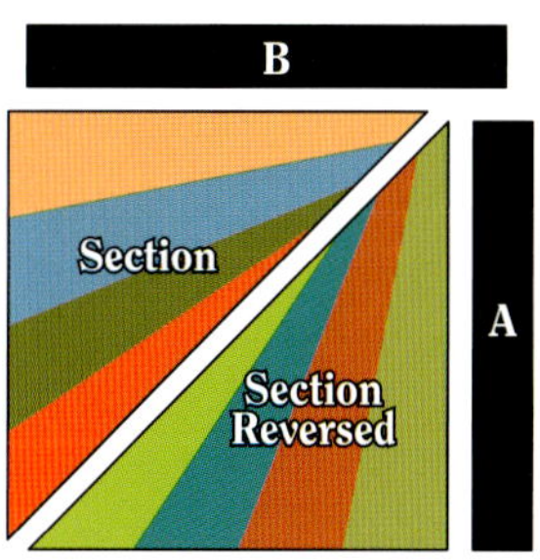

Block Assembly

block no. 252

Snow Star

by Sandy Harris • Sundrop Designs
sundropdesigns.com

See page 324 on the PDF for pattern

Light Blue Tone-on-Tone
section 1, patch 1
section 2, patches 2 and 3
1 square (A) 6½″x 6½″
Medium Blue Tone-on-Tone
section 1, patches 2 and 3
section 2, patch 1
Dark Blue Tone-on-Tone
sections 1 and 2, patches 4 and 5

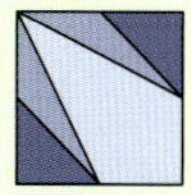

Section 1
Make 4

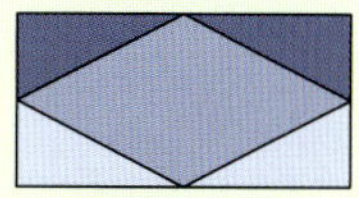

Section 2
Make 4

Make 4 paper copies of *each* foundation section. Foundation piece the sections in numerical order, pressing and trimming after each patch addition.

Sew the sections and light blue A together as shown to complete the block.

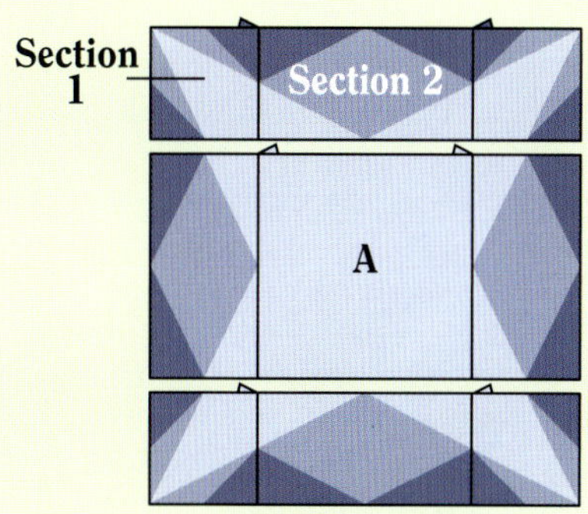

Block Assembly

block no. 253

Starbright

by Kristy Lea • Quiet Play
quietplay.blogspot.com.au

Fabric: Kona Solids by Robert Kaufman, robertkaufman.com.

See page 325 on the PDF for pattern

Gray Solid
section and section reversed, patches 1, 4, 6 and 8
Blue Solid
section and section reversed, patches 2, 7 and 9
Red Solid
section and section reversed, patches 3 and 10
White Solid
section and section reversed, patch 5

Section Make 4 **Section Reversed** Make 4

Make 4 paper copies *each* of the foundation section and the section reversed. Foundation piece the sections in numerical order, pressing and trimming after each patch addition.

Sew the sections together as shown to complete the block. To reduce bulk, press the seams open.

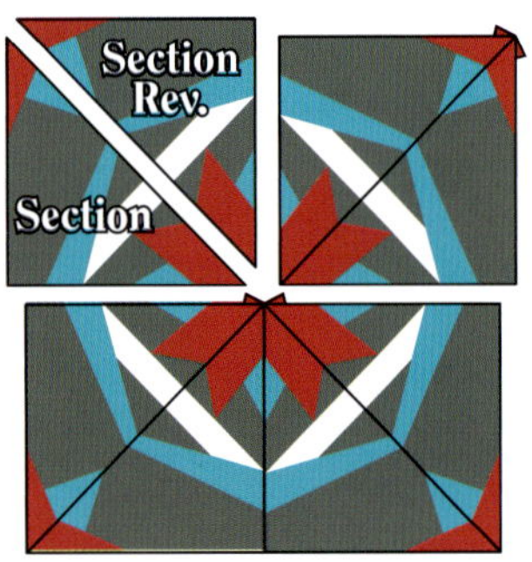

Block Assembly

block no. 254

Dancing Dreidels

by Cheryl Lynch • Oy Vey! Quilt Designs
cheryllynchquilts.com

Cheryl Lynch is the author of *iQuilt Fiesta!* and *Sew Embellished!* for Martingale & Co., shopmartingale.com.

See page 302 on the PDF for pattern

Yellow Tone-on-Tone
section 1, patch 1
section 2, patch 2
Blue Tone-on-Tone
section 1, patches 2–4
section 2, patches 3 and 4
4 rectangles (A) 1″x 6″
4 rectangles (B) 1″x 6½″
Blue Print
section 2, patch 1

Section 1 Make 4

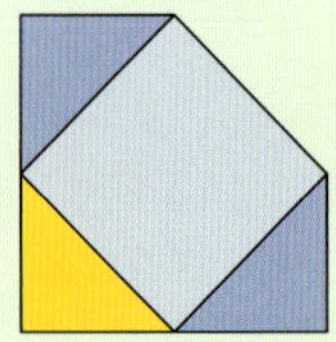

Section 2 Make 4

Make 4 paper copies of *each* foundation section. Foundation piece the sections in numerical order, pressing and trimming after each patch addition.

Sew the sections and patches together as shown to complete the block.

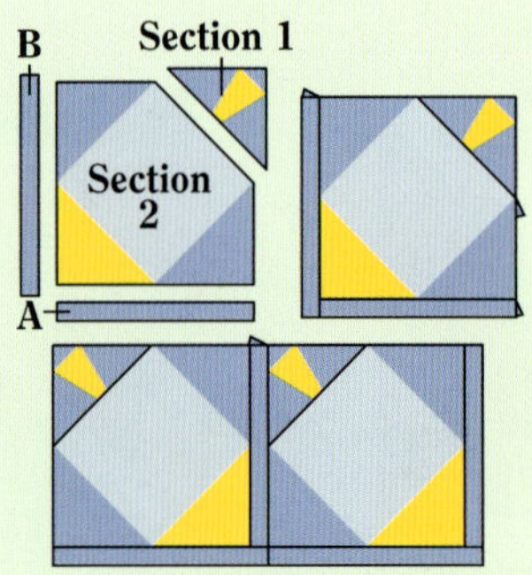

Block Assembly

block no. 255

Circlin' Stars

by Carolyn Cullinan McCormick • CM Designs, Inc.
addaquarter.com

Carolyn McCormick is the creator of the Add-a-Quarter and Add-Enough tools for quilters. She is the author of several books including *A Flock of Feathered Stars* and *Roaring Through the '20s* for Kansas City Star Quilts, pickledish.com.

See page 301 on the PDF for pattern

Tan Tone-on-Tone
section 1, patches 1, 4 and 5
section 2, patches 1, 4, 5, 8 and 9
sections 3 and 4, patches 1, 4, 5, 7 and 8
section 5, patch 1

Red Tone-on-Tone
sections 1 and 2, patches 2, 3, 6 and 7
sections 3 and 4, patches 2, 3 and 6
section 5, patch 2
1 square (A) 4″ x 4″

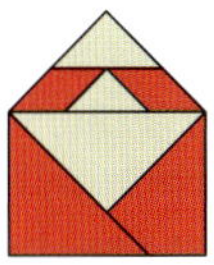

Section 1
Make 2

Section 3
Make 4

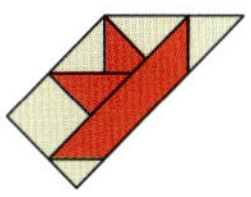

Section 4
Make 4

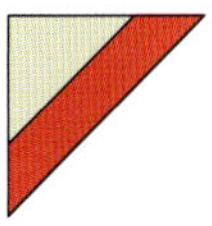

Section 5
Make 4

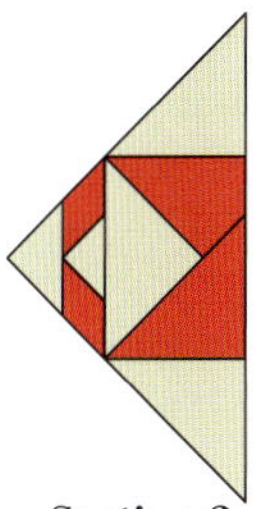

Section 2
Make 2

Make 2 paper copies *each* of sections 1 and 2 and 4 paper copies *each* of sections 3–5. Foundation piece the sections in numerical order, pressing and trimming after each patch addition.

Sew the sections and A together as shown to complete the block.

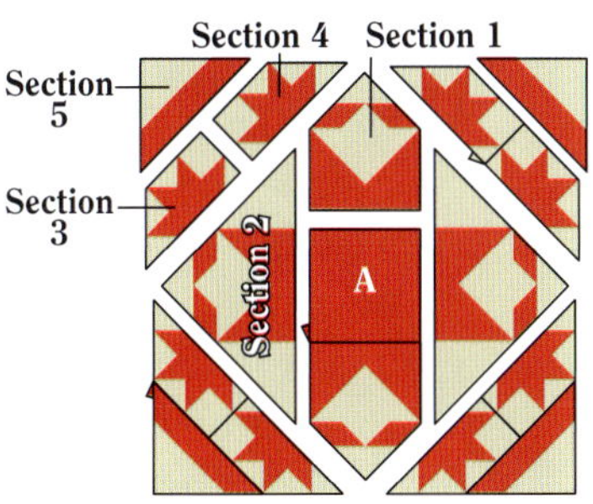

Block Assembly

block no. 256

Red, Black and Celtic

by Moira McSpadden
thequiltedsnail.com

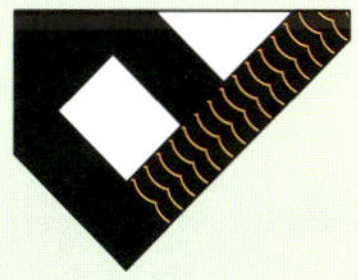

Section 1
Make 2

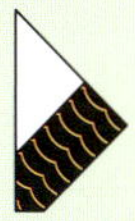

Section 2
Make 4

Section 3
Make 2

Section 4
Make 2

Section 5
Make 2

See page 294 on the PDF for pattern

White Tone-on-Tone
sections 1 and 4, patches 1 and 3
section 2, patch 1
sections 3 and 5, patches 1, 3, 5 and 7

Black Solid
section 1, patches 2, 5 and 6
section 3, patches 2 and 6
section 5, patch 4

Black Stripe
sections 1 and 4, patch 4
section 2, patch 2

Red Tone-on-Tone
section 3, patch 4
section 4, patches 2, 5 and 6
section 5, patches 2 and 6

Make 2 paper copies *each* of foundation sections 1 and 3–5. The colors for sections 4 and 5 are shown in parentheses. Make 4 paper copies of section 2.

Foundation piece the sections in numerical order, pressing and trimming after each patch addition.

Sew the sections together as shown to complete the block. To reduce bulk, press the seams open.

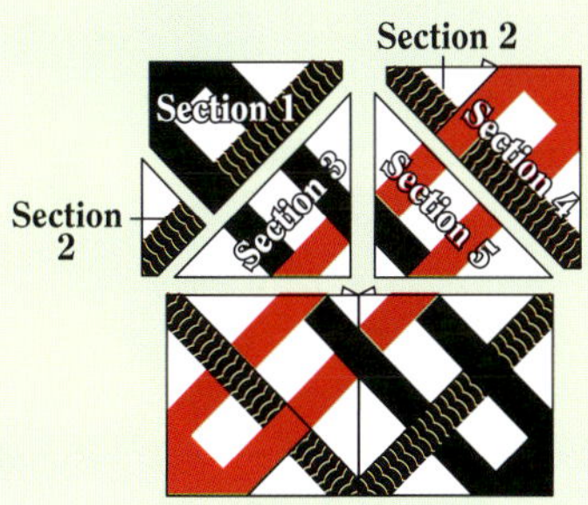

Block Assembly

block no. 257
Spring Action

by Scott Murkin • Patchwork Possibilities
patchworkpossibilities.com

See page 323 on the PDF for pattern

Blue Tone-on-Tone
section patch 1
Yellow Tone-on-Tone
section patches 2–4 and 6
Green Print
section patch 5

Section
Make 4

Make 4 paper copies of the foundation section. Foundation piece the sections in numerical order, pressing and trimming after each patch addition.

Sew the sections together as shown to complete the block.

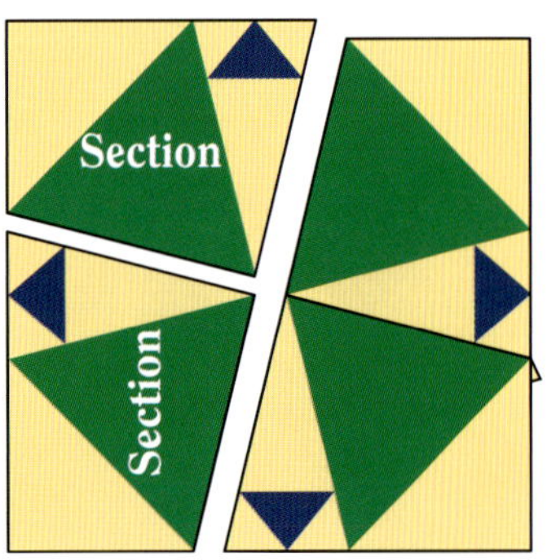

Block Assembly

block no. 258
Diamonds Galore

by Susan Nelson • Prairie Sky Quilting
prairieskyquilting.com

Fabric: Bali Batiks from Hoffman California Fabrics, hoffmanfabrics.com.

See page 303 on the PDF for pattern

Cream Batik
section and section reversed, patches 1 and 6
Teal Batik
section and section reversed, patches 2 and 7
Light Teal Batik
section and section reversed, patches 3 and 8
Rust Batik
section and section reversed, patch 4
Dark Brown Batik
section and section reversed, patch 5

Section
Make 2

Section Reversed
Make 2

Make 2 paper copies *each* of the foundation section and section reversed. Foundation piece each section in numerical order, pressing and trimming after each patch addition.

Sew the sections together as shown to complete the block. To reduce bulk, press the seams open.

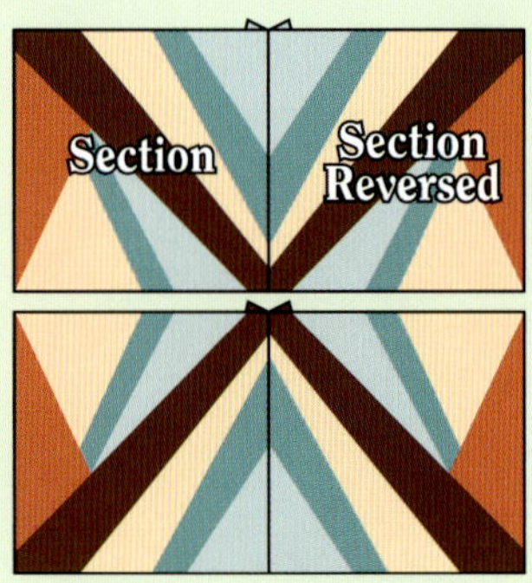

Block Assembly

block no. 259

Circle of Life

by Amy Rullkoetter • Freelance Editor, *Quiltmaker*
quiltmaker.com

Fabric: Safari designed by Studio 8 for Quilting Treasures, quiltingtreasures.com.

See page 288 on the PDF for pattern

Cream Tone-on-Tone
foundation patches
4 Assorted Prints
foundation patches
Green Tone-on-Tone
foundation patches
Blue Tone-on-Tone
foundation patches
Dark Orange Tone-on-Tone
foundation patches
Black Tone-on-Tone
foundation patches

For the 4 assorted prints, Amy selected a snakeskin, tiger, giraffe and leopard print.

Make 4 paper copies of *each* foundation section. Referring to the foundations for color placement, foundation piece the sections in numerical order, pressing and trimming after each patch addition.

Sew the sections together as shown to complete the block. To reduce bulk, press the seams open.

Section 1
Make 4

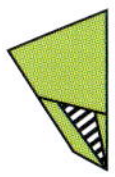

Section 2
Make 4

Section 3
Make 4

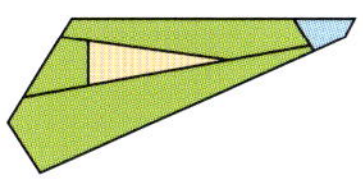

Section 4
Make 4

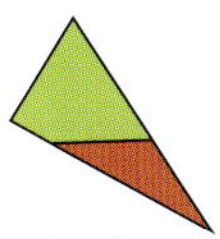

Section 5
Make 4

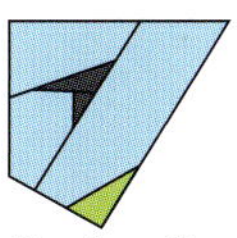

Section 6
Make 4

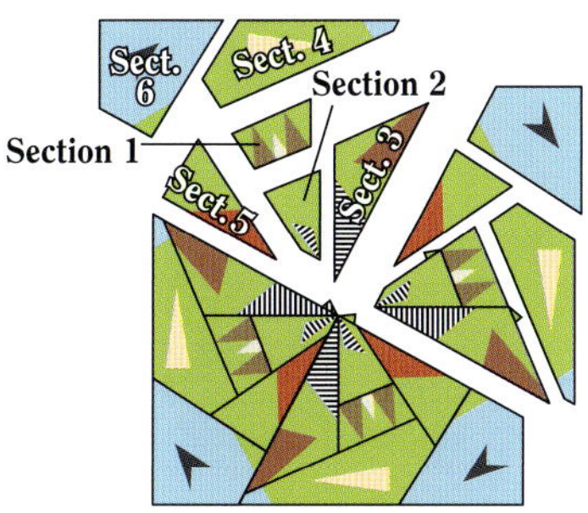

Block Assembly

block no. 260

Patrise

by Cinzia White • Cinzia White Designs
cinziawhite.com

See page 312 on the PDF for pattern

Red Tone-on-Tone
foundation patches
White Print
foundation patches

Make 1 paper copy of the foundation section. Referring to the section for color placement, foundation piece the section in numerical order, pressing and trimming after each patch addition to complete the block.

Section
Make 1

block no. 261

Square Dance

by Sue Beevers • Trillium Ridge Quilt Patterns
suebeevers.com

Fabric: Mulberry Lane designed by Sue Beevers for Northcott, northcott.com.

Sue Beevers is the author of *Dancing Dragonfly Quilts* and *Off-the-Shelf Fabric Painting* for C&T Publishing, ctpub.com.

See page 353 on the PDF for pattern

Cream Tone-on-Tone
section 1, patches 1, 4 and 6

Dark Peach Tone-on-Tone
section 1, patch 2
section 2, patch 5
section 3, patch 4

Brown Tone-on-Tone
section 1, patches 3 and 7
sections 2 and 3, patches 8 and 9

Green Tone-on-Tone
section 1, patch 5
section 2, patches 3 and 4
section 3, patches 2 and 5

Dark Blue Tone-on-Tone
sections 2 and 3, patches 1, 6 and 7

Light Blue Tone-on-Tone
section 2, patch 2
section 3, patch 3

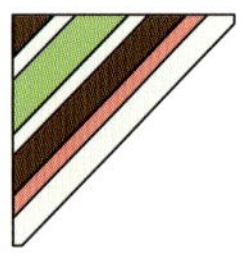

Section 1
Make 4

Section 2
Make 2

Section 3
Make 2

Make 4 paper copies of the foundation section 1 and 2 paper copies *each* of sections 2 and 3. Notice that colors for section 3, patches 2–5 are shown in parentheses on the foundation. Foundation piece the sections in numerical order, pressing and trimming after each patch addition.

Sew the sections together as shown to complete the block. To reduce bulk, press the seams open.

Block Assembly

block no. 262

Triangle Tricks

by Barbara H. Cline • Delightful Piecing
delightfulpiecing.com

Fabric: Stonehenge from Northcott, northcott.com.

Barbara Cline is the author of *Diamond Chain Quilts* for C&T Publishing, ctpub.com.

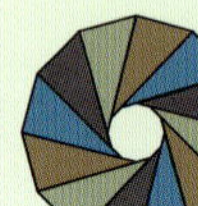

Section 1
Make 1

See page 374 on the PDF for pattern

Cream Tone-on-Tone
sections 1–4, patch 1

Black Tone-on-Tone
section 1, patches 2, 6 and 10
sections 2, 3 and 4, patch 2

Blue Tone-on-Tone
section 1, patches 3, 7 and 11
sections 2, 3 and 4, patch 2

Brown Tone-on-Tone
section 1, patches 4, 8 and 12
sections 2, 3 and 4, patch 2

Green Tone-on-Tone
section 1, patches 5, 9 and 13
sections 2, 3 and 4, patch 2

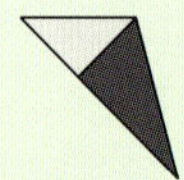

Section 2
Make 1
of each color

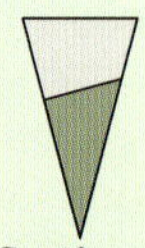

Section 3
Make 1
of each color

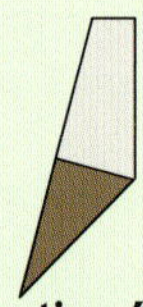

Section 4
Make 1
of each color

Make 1 paper copy of foundation section 1 and 4 paper copies *each* of foundation sections 2–4.

On section 1, foundation piece patch 2 to patch 1 using a short partial seam as shown on the section. Foundation piece the remaining patches in numerical order, pressing and trimming after each patch addition. Use a whip stitch to complete the partial seam after adding patch 13.

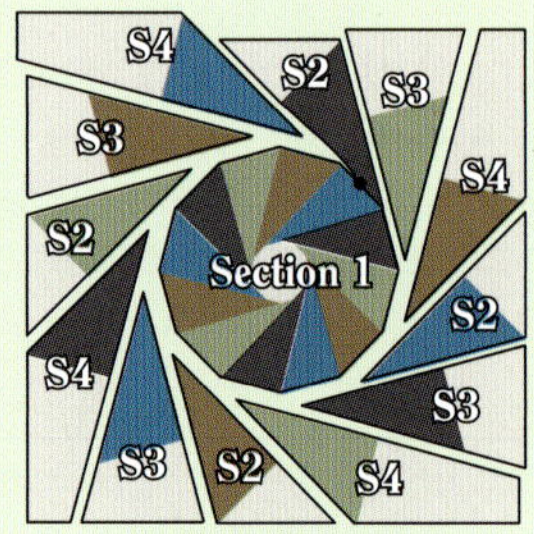

Block Assembly
•= Partial Seam

Making 1 *each* of sections 2–4 in *each* color, foundation piece the remaining sections. Refer to the block assembly diagram for color/section placements. Join section 2 to section 1 with a partial seam as shown. In a clockwise direction, continue joining section 2's–4's as shown. Complete the partial seam to finish the block.

block no. 263

Rubik's Star

by Elizabeth Dackson • Don't Call Me Betsy
dontcallmebetsy.com

Elizabeth Dackson is the author of *Becoming a Confident Quilter* for Martingale & Co., shopmartingale.com.

See page 352 on the PDF for pattern

Dark Gray Tone-on-Tone
sections 1–8, patch 1

Green Tone-on-Tone
sections 1–8, patch 2

Light Purple, Light Yellow, Light Red and Light Blue Tone-on-Tones
sections 1, 3, 5 and 7, patch 3

Medium Purple, Medium Yellow, Medium Red and Medium Blue Tone-on-Tones
sections 1, 3, 5 and 7, patch 4

Dark Purple, Dark Yellow, Dark Red and Dark Blue Tone-on-Tones
sections 2, 4, 6 and 8, patch 3

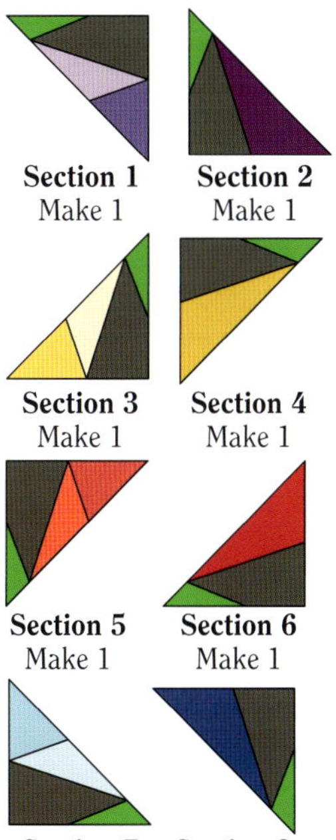

Section 1 Make 1
Section 2 Make 1
Section 3 Make 1
Section 4 Make 1
Section 5 Make 1
Section 6 Make 1
Section 7 Make 1
Section 8 Make 1

Make 4 paper copies of *each* foundation section. Refer to the foundations and section diagrams for color placement. Foundation piece the sections in numerical order, pressing and trimming after each patch addition.

Sew the sections together as shown to complete the block. To reduce bulk, press seams open.

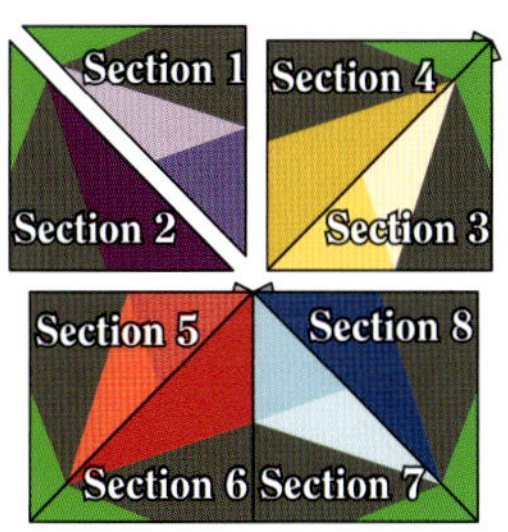

Block Assembly

block no. 264

Butterfly-by

by Eileen Fowler • Associate Editor, *Quiltmaker*
quiltmaker.com

Fabric: Minerals by Fresh Batiks for Clothworks, clothworks.com.

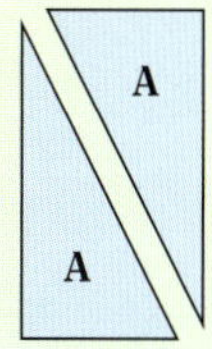

Cutting Diagram

See page 368 on the PDF for pattern

Light Blue Batik
2 rectangles 4¾" x 9¼" for A's foundation patches

Red Batik, Magenta Batik, Multicolor Batik, Orange Batik, Gold Batik and Purple Batik
foundation patches

Embroidery floss

Heat-set crystals assorted sizes

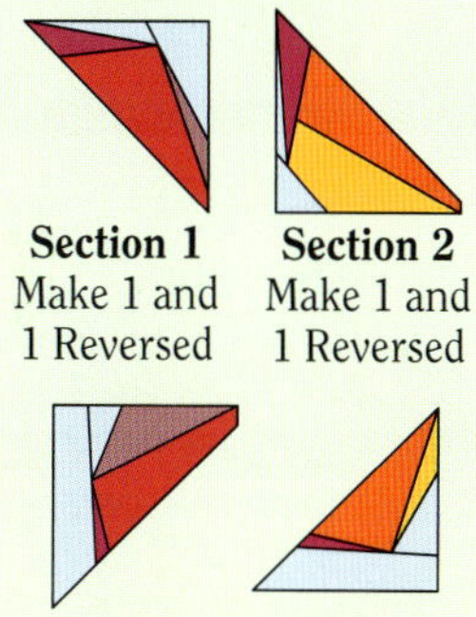

Section 1 Make 1 and 1 Reversed
Section 2 Make 1 and 1 Reversed
Section 3 Make 1 and 1 Reversed
Section 4 Make 1 and 1 Reversed

Refer to the cutting diagram; cut each rectangle diagonally in half as shown to make 4 A's.

Make 1 paper copy of *each* foundation sections 1–5 and sections 1–4 reversed. Referring to the foundations for color placement, foundation piece the sections in numerical order, pressing and trimming after each patch addition. Sew the sections and A's together as shown to make the block. To reduce bulk, press the seams open. Carefully remove the foundation papers.

Section 5
Make 1

Refer to the embroidery and embellishment placement diagram; lightly trace the embroidery lines onto the block. Use 2 strands of embroidery floss and an outline stitch to embroider the butterfly details. Add the crystals to complete the block.

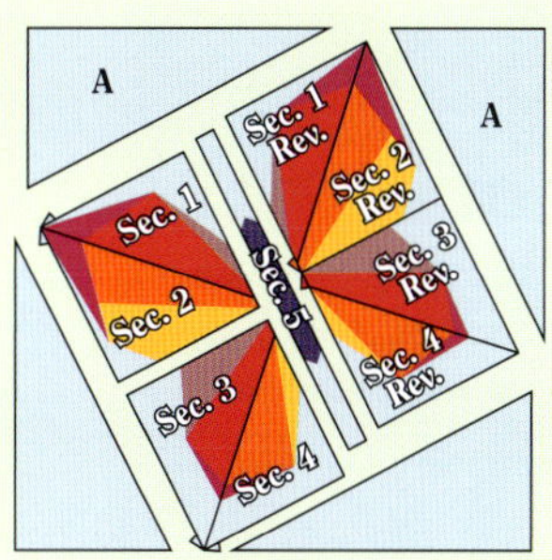

Block Assembly

Embroidery & Embellishment Placement

block no. 265

Red Stapler

by Samarra Khaja
samarrakhaja.com

Fabric: Timeless Treasures, ttfabrics.com.

See page 377 on the PDF for pattern

White Print
sections 1, 3 and 4, patch 1
Red Tone-on-Tone
sections 1 and 4, patches 2–5
section 2, patches 2 and 3
section 5, patch 1
Orange Solid
sections 1 and 4, patch 6
section 2, patch 1
Teal Tone-on-Tone
1 rectangle (A) 4¼" x 12½"
section 1, patches 7–10
section 2, patches 4 and 5
sections 3 and 5, patch 2
section 4, patches 7–9
section 6 patches 2 and 3
Black Print
section 6, patch 1
Silver metallic embroidery thread

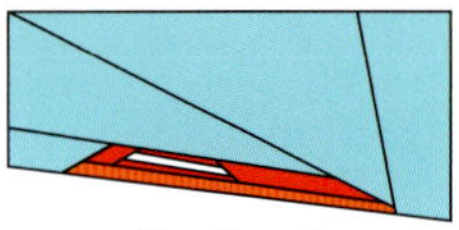

Section 1
Make 1

Section 2
Make 1

Section 3
Make 1

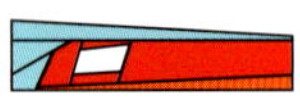

Section 4
Make 1

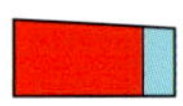

Section 5
Make 1

Section 6
Make 1

Make 1 paper copy of *each* foundation section. Foundation piece the sections in numerical order, pressing and trimming after each patch addition.

Sew the sections and A together as shown. Use the embroidery thread and a satin stitch to add the detail to the stapler.

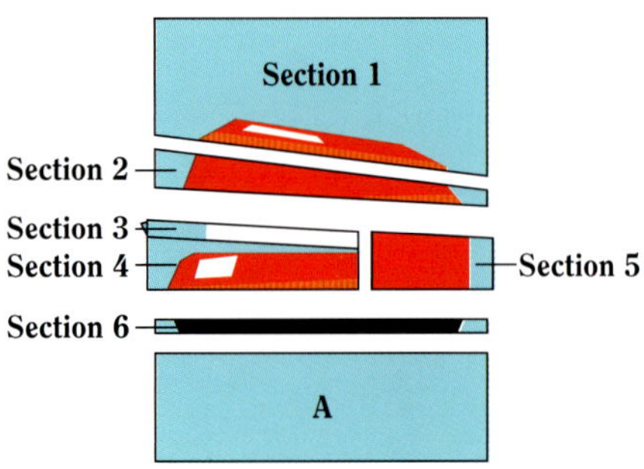

Block Assembly

block no. 266

Tangled

by Kristy Lea • Quiet Play
quietplay.blogspot.com.au

Fabric: Timeless Treasures, ttfabrics.com and P&B Textiles, pbtex.com.

See page 356 on the PDF for pattern

Yellow Tone-on-Tone
sections 1 and 2, patches 1, 5, 8 and 9
Black Tone-on-Tone
section 1, patches 2 and 4
section 2, patch 3
Black and White Print
section 1, patch 3
section 2, patches 2 and 4
White Solid
sections 1 and 2, patches 6 and 10
Black Solid
sections 1 and 2, patches 7 and 11

Section 1
Make 4

Section 2
Make 4

Make 4 paper copies of *each* foundation section. Foundation piece the sections in numerical order, pressing and trimming after each patch addition.

Sew the sections together as shown to complete the block. To reduce bulk, press the seams open.

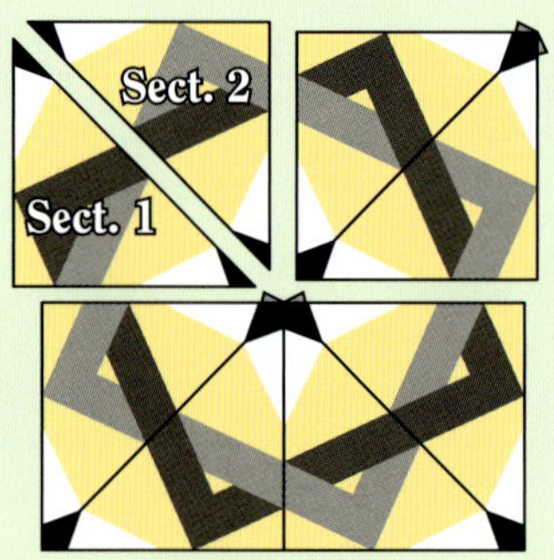

Block Assembly

block no. 267

Abby's Star

by Carolyn Cullinan McCormick • CM Designs, Inc.
addaquarter.com

Fabric: Downton Abbey designed by Kathy Hall for Andover Fabrics, andoverfabrics.com.

Carolyn McCormick is the creator of the Add-a-Quarter and Add-Enough tools for quilters. She is the author of *A Flock of Feathered Friends* for Kansas City Star Quilts, pickledish.com.

See pages 345–346 on the PDF for pattern

⧄ = cut in half diagonally

Cream Print
foundation patches

Purple Tone-on-Tone
foundation patches

Black Tone-on-Tone
foundation patches

Gray Print
2 squares $3\frac{7}{8}$" x $3\frac{7}{8}$" ⧄ (A)
foundation patches

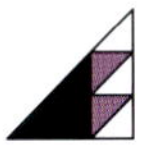

Section 1
Make 4

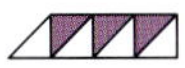

Section 2
Make 4

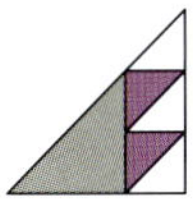

Section 3
Make 4

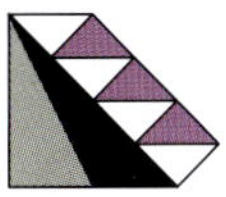

Section 4
Make 4

Section 5
Make 4

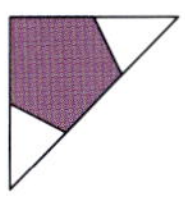

Section 6
Make 4

Make 4 paper copies *each* of foundation sections 1–6 and 1 paper copy of section 7. Foundation piece the sections in numerical order, pressing and trimming after each patch addition.

Sew the sections and A's together as shown to complete the block.

Block Assembly

Section 7
Make 1

block no. 268

Diamond Panes

by Susan Nelson • Prairie Sky Quilting
prairieskyquilting.com

Section
Make 2

Section Reversed
Make 2

See page 347 on the PDF for pattern

Light Teal Batik
section and section reversed, patch 1

Dark Teal Print
section and section reversed, patches 2–5

Tan Batik
section and section reversed, patches 6 and 7

Cream Print
section and section reversed, patch 8

Dark Teal Batik
section and section reversed, patch 9

Gold Batik
section and section reversed, patch 10

Medium Teal Batik
section and section reversed, patch 11

Make 2 paper copies *each* of the foundation section and section reversed. Foundation piece the sections in numerical order, pressing and trimming after each patch addition.

Sew the sections together as shown to complete the block. To reduce bulk, press the seams open.

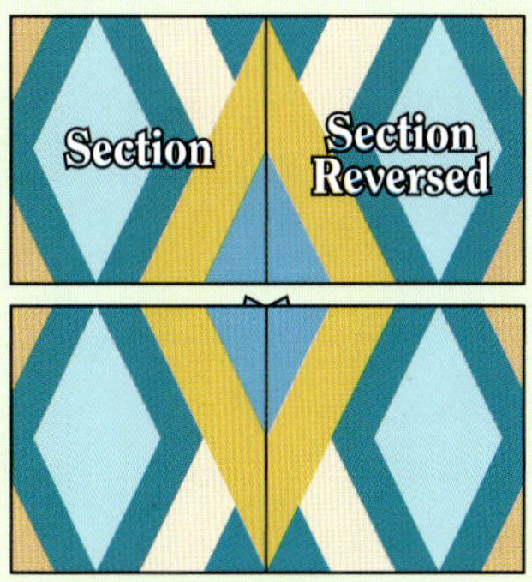

Block Assembly

block no. 269

Starry Path Redux

by Jenny Novinsky • The Electric Quilt Company
electricquilt.com

Section 1
Make 4

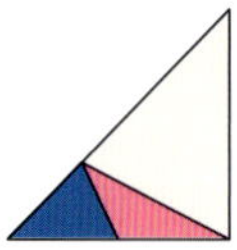

Section 2
Make 4

See page 355 on the PDF for pattern

Light Green Tone-on-Tone
section 1, patch 1
Pink Tone-on-Tone
sections 1 and 2, patch 2
Teal Tone-on-Tone
section 1, patch 3
Cream Solid
section 2, patch 1
Blue Tone-on-Tone
section 2, patch 3

Jenny used Electric Quilt Company software to design her block.

Make 4 paper copies *each* of the foundation sections 1 and 2. Foundation piece the sections in numerical order, pressing and trimming after each patch addition.

Sew the sections together as shown to complete the block.

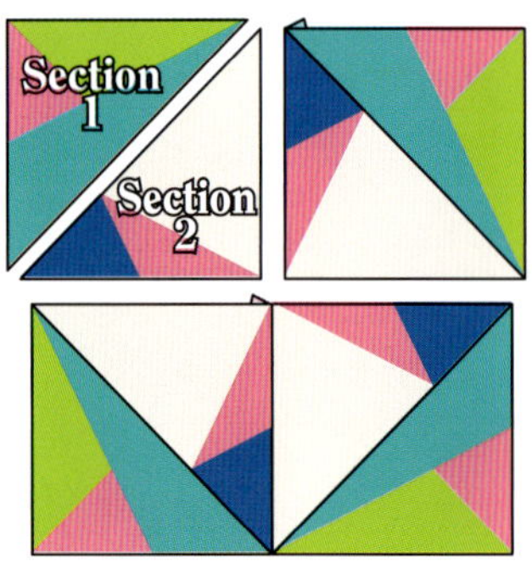

Block Assembly

block no. 270

Yum Yum Strawberry Cake

by Jennifer Ofenstein • Sewhooked
sewhooked.com

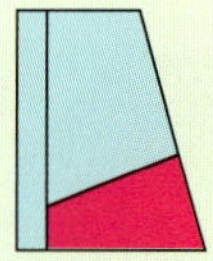

Section 1
Make 1

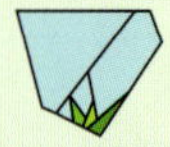

Section 2
Make 1

Section 3
Make 1

Section 4
Make 1

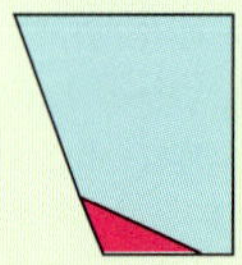

Section 5
Make 1

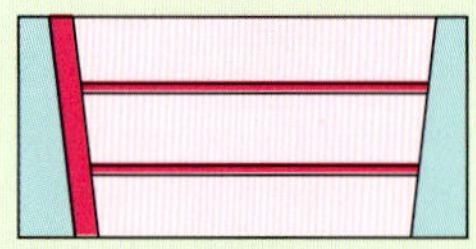

Section 6
Make 1

See page 378 on the PDF for pattern

Dark Pink Tone-on-Tone
foundation patches
Light Teal Tone-on-Tone
foundation patches
Assorted Green Tone-on-Tones
foundation patches
Red Dot
foundation patches
Light Pink Tone-on-Tone
foundation patches
Pigma Micron pen (.01 tip)
Embroidery floss

Make 1 paper copy of *each* foundation section. Referring to the sections for color placement, foundation piece the sections in numerical order, pressing and trimming after each patch addition.

Sew the sections together as shown. To reduce bulk, press the seams open.

Carefully remove the foundation papers. Refer to the embroidery placement diagram and use the pigma pen to trace the words on the block. The stitch diagrams are in the Techniques file on the PDF. Use 2 strands of floss and a backstitch to embroider the words.

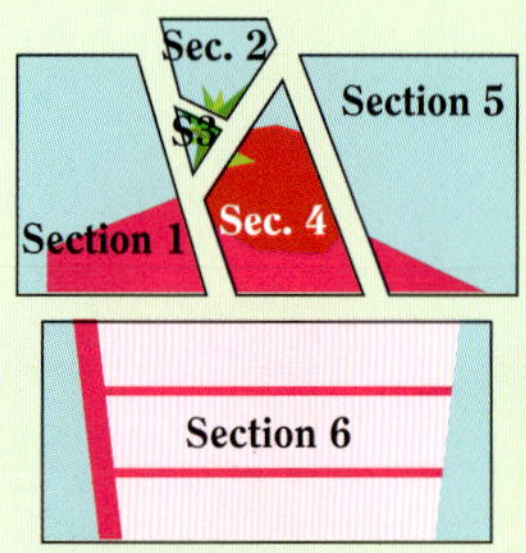

Block Assembly

Embroidery Placement

block no. 271

Flying Dutchman

by Doris Rice • The Quilting Queen
thequiltingqueenonline.blogspot.com

Fabric: Moda Fabrics, unitednotions.com and Andover Fabrics, andoverfabrics.com.

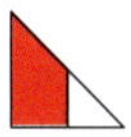

Section 1
Make 8

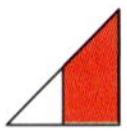

Section 1 Reversed
Make 8

Section 2
Make 8

See page 348 on the PDF for pattern

Red Tone-on-Tone
section 1 and section 1 reversed, patch 1

Cream Tone-on-Tone
section 1 and section 1 reversed, patch 2

Light Blue Print
section 2, patch 1

Dark Blue Tone-on-Tone
section 2, patch 2

Make 8 paper copies *each* of foundation sections 1, 1 reversed and 2. Foundation piece the sections in numerical order, pressing and trimming after each patch addition.

Sew the sections together as shown to complete the block.

Block Assembly

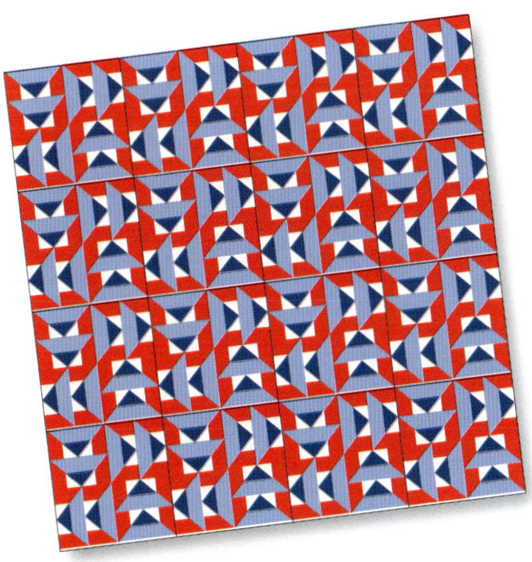

block no. 272

Delta Star

by Sunny Steinkuhler
thequiltedcookie.blogspot.com

Sunny Steinkuhler is the author of *Blocks, Borders, Quilts!* for Martingale & Co., shopmartingale.com.

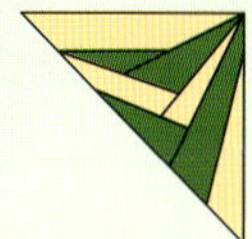

Section
Make 4

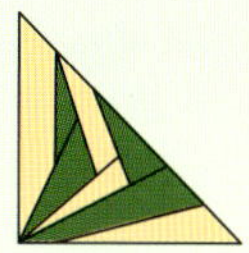

Section Reversed
Make 4

See page 360 on the PDF for pattern

Pale Orange Batik
section and section reversed, patches 1, 4, 5 and 8

Multicolor Batik
section and section reversed, patches 2, 3, 6 and 7

Make 4 paper copies *each* of the foundation section and section reversed. Foundation piece the sections in numerical order, pressing and trimming after each patch addition.

Sew the sections together as shown to complete the block. To reduce bulk, press the seams open.

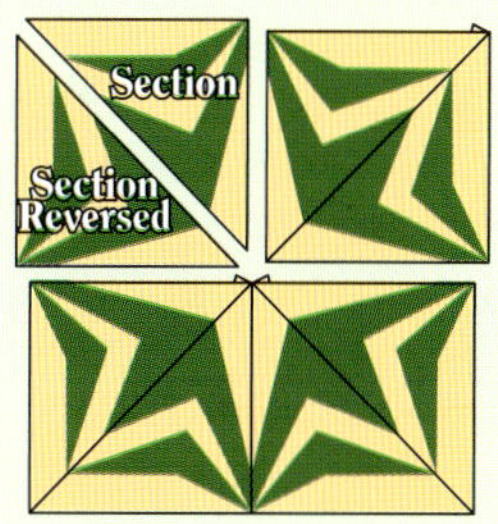

Block Assembly

block no. 273
Whirl Around

by Elizabeth Dackson • Don't Call Me Betsy
dontcallmebetsy.com

Elizabeth Dackson is the author of *Becoming a Confident Quilter* for Martingale, shopmartingale.com.

See page 395 on the PDF for pattern

White Print
sections 1–4, patch 1
Dark Gray Tone-on-Tone
sections 1–4, patch 2
Medium Purple Solid
section 1, patch 3
Light Purple Solid
section 1, patch 4
Dark Purple Solid
section 2, patch 3
Gray Stripe
sections 2 and 4, patch 4
Medium Green Solid
section 3, patch 3
Light Green Solid
section 3, patch 4
Dark Green Solid
section 4, patch 3

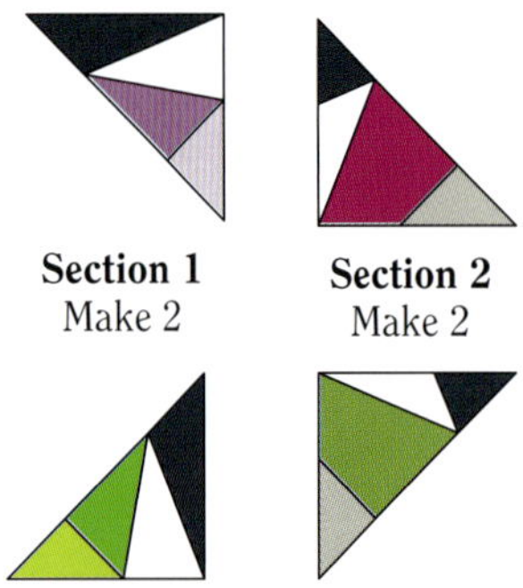

Section 1 Make 2
Section 2 Make 2
Section 3 Make 2
Section 4 Make 2

Make 2 paper copies of *each* foundation section. Refer to the foundations for color placement. The colors for sections 3 and 4 are shown in parentheses.

Foundation piece the sections in numerical order, pressing and trimming after each patch addition.

Sew the sections together as shown to complete the block. To reduce bulk, press the seams open.

Block Assembly

block no. 274
Five and Diamond

by Eileen Fowler • Associate Editor, *Quiltmaker*
quiltmaker.com

Fabric: Bali Batiks from Hoffman California Fabrics, hoffmanfabrics.com.

See page 408 on the PDF for pattern

Multicolor Batik
section and section reversed, patch 1
Purple Batik
section and section reversed, patches 2 and 5
Medium Teal Batik #1
section, patch 3
Light Teal Batik #1
section, patch 4
Medium Teal Batik #2
reverse section, patch 3
Light Teal Batik #2
reverse section, patch 4

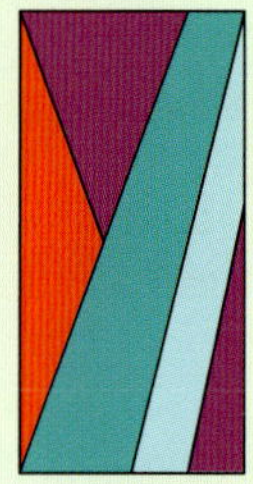

Section Make 1

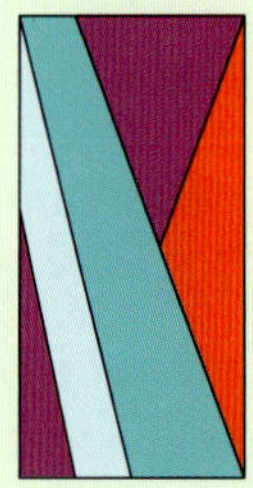

Section Reversed Make 1

Make 1 paper copy *each* of the section and section reversed. Refer to the foundations for color placement. The colors for the reversed section are shown in parentheses.

Foundation piece the sections in numerical order, pressing and trimming after each patch addition.

Sew the sections together as shown to complete the block. To reduce bulk, press the seams open.

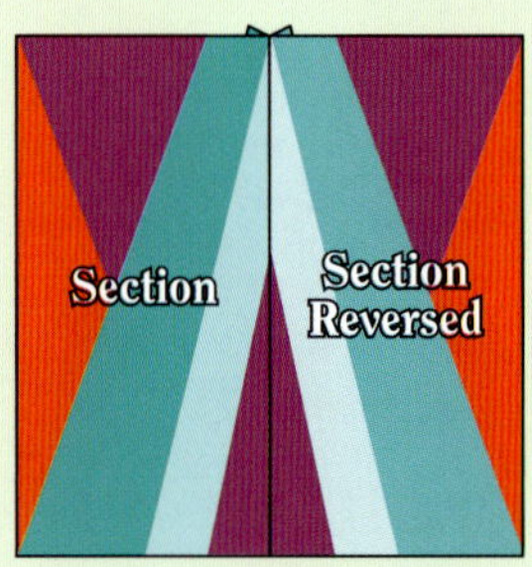

Block Assembly

block no. 275

Little Cottage

by Kristy Lea • Quiet Play
quietplay.blogspot.com.au

Fabric: Sketch from Timeless Treasures, ttfabrics.com, Swirl designed by Bonnie and Camille for Moda Fabrics, unitednotions.com and Kona Cotton Solids from Robert Kaufman, robertkaufman.com.

See page 402 on the PDF for pattern

Cream Print
1 square (A) 2″ x 2″

Red Tone-on-Tone
2 rectangles (B) 1⅛″ x 2″
1 rectangle (F) 2½″ x 3″
foundation patches

White Solid
1 rectangle (C) 1½″ x 2″
1 rectangle (D) 1″ x 2″
1 rectangle (E) 1⅞″ x 4¾″
1 rectangle (G) 1½″ x 6¾″
1 rectangle (H) ¾″ x 5″
foundation patches

Light Blue Solid
2 rectangles (I) 1″ x 5″
1 rectangle (J) 2¾″ x 12½″
foundation patches

Red Print, Green Tone-on-Tone #1 and Brown Solid
foundation patches

Green Tone-on-Tone #2
1 rectangle (K) 3¼″ x 12½″

Section 1
Make 1

Section 2
Make 1

Section 3
Make 1

Section 4
Make 1

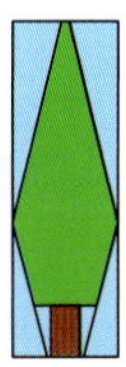

Section 5
Make 2

Kristy fussy cut the cream print A to display a bird in the window.

Make 1 paper copy *each* of foundation sections 1–4 and 2 copies of section 5. Refer to the foundations for color placement. Foundation piece the sections in numerical order, pressing and trimming after each patch addition.

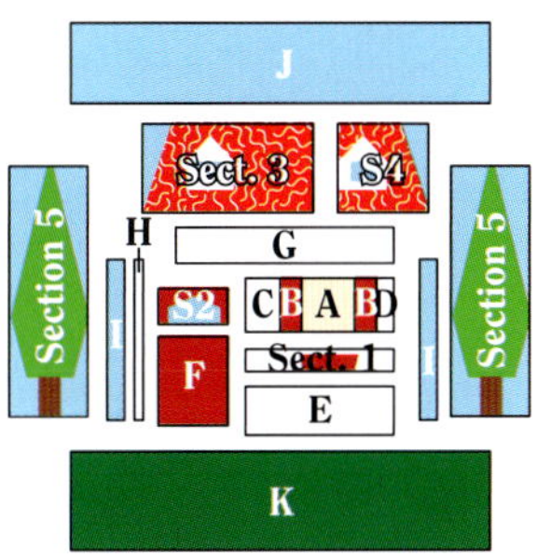

Block Assembly

Sew the sections and patches together as shown to complete the block.

block no. 276

Tranquil

by Carol Le Maitre

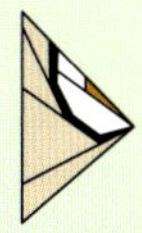

Section 1
Make 4

See page 405 on the PDF for pattern

Gold Batik
sections 1 and 2, patch 1

White Print
sections 1 and 2, patches 2 and 3

Black Solid
sections 1 and 2, patches 4–7
section 3, patches 2–5
section 4, patches 2–5 and 10

Tan Print
sections 1 and 2, patches 8–11
section 3 and 4, patches 6–9

Green Tone-on-Tone
sections 3 and 4, patch 1

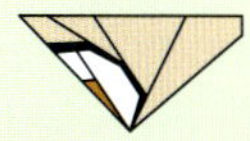

Section 2
Make 4

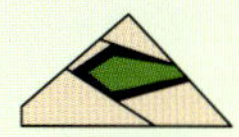

Section 3
Make 4

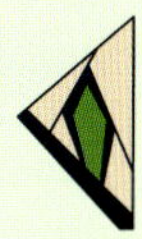

Section 4
Make 4

Make 4 paper copies of *each* foundation section. Foundation piece the sections in numerical order, pressing and trimming after each patch addition.

Sew the sections together as shown to complete the block.

Block Assembly

block no. 277

Roll'n Star

by Carolyn Cullinan McCormick • CM Designs, Inc.
addaquarter.com

Carolyn McCormick is the creator of the Add-a-Quarter and Add-Enough tools for quilters. She is the author of several books including *A Flock of Feathered Stars* for Kansas City Star Quilts, pickledish.com.

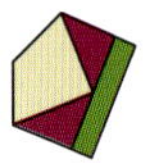

Section 1
Make 2

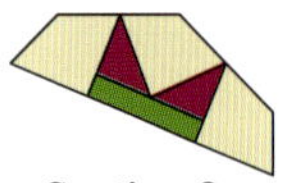

Section 2
Make 2

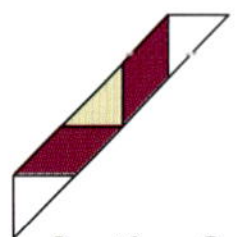

Section 3
Make 4

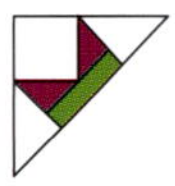

Section 4
Make 4

See page 412 on the PDF for pattern

Cream Print
sections 1 and 3, patch 1
section 2, patches 1, 5 and 6

Dark Red Tone-on-Tone
sections 1–4, patches 2 and 3
1 square (A) 3¾" x 3¾"

Green Tone-on-Tone
sections 1, 2 and 4, patch 4
4 template B

White Print
section 3, patches 4 and 5
section 4, patches 1, 5 and 6

Make 2 paper copies *each* of foundation sections 1 and 2 and 4 paper copies *each* of sections 3 and 4. Foundation piece the sections in numerical order, pressing and trimming after each patch addition.

Sew the sections and patches together as shown to complete the block.

Block Assembly

block no. 278

Diamond Pinwheels

by Susan Nelson • Prairie Sky Quilting
prairieskyquilting.com

Section 1
Make 2

Section 1 Reversed
Make 2

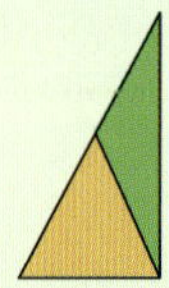

Section 2
Make 2

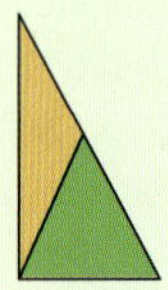

Section 2 Reversed
Make 2

See page 384 on the PDF for pattern

Gold Batik
sections 1 and 2 reversed, patch 1
sections 1 reversed and 2, patch 2

Blue Batik
section 1, patches 2 and 4
section 1 reversed, patches 1 and 4

Green Batik
sections 1 and 1 reversed, patch 3
section 2, patch 1
section 2 reversed, patch 2

Make 2 paper copies *each* of foundation sections 1 and 2 and sections 1 and 2 reversed. Refer to the foundations for color placement. Colors for the reverse sections are shown in parentheses. Foundation piece the sections in numerical order, pressing and trimming after each patch addition.

Sew the sections together as shown to complete the block. To reduce bulk, press the seams open.

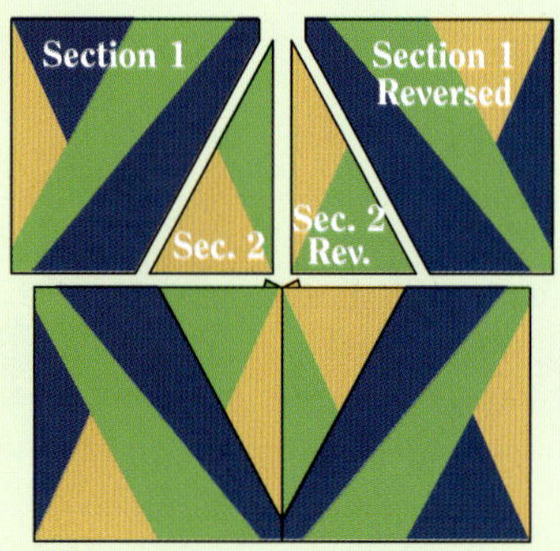

Block Assembly

block no. 279

Spinning Stripes

by Jenny Novinsky • The Electric Quilt Company
electricquilt.com

See page 417 on the PDF for pattern

Teal Print
section patch 1
Medium Purple Tone-on-Tone
section patch 2
Olive Green Tone-on-Tone
section patch 3
Light Teal Tone-on-Tone
section patch 4
Dark Purple Tone-on-Tone
section patch 5
Black Solid
section patches 6 and 7
White Solid
section patches 8 and 9

Section
Make 4

Jenny used Electric Quilt Company software to design her block.

Make 4 paper copies of the foundation section. Foundation piece the sections in numerical order, pressing and trimming after each patch addition.

Sew the sections together as shown to complete the block. To reduce bulk, press the seams open.

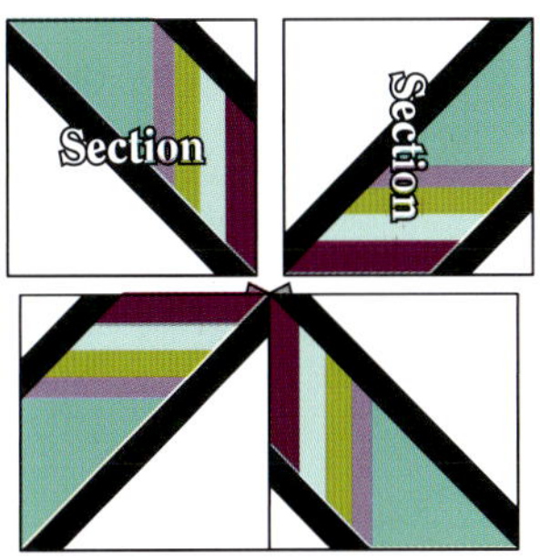

Block Assembly

block no. 280

Jewels of the Wind

by Jennifer Ofenstein • Sewhooked
sewhooked.com

See page 416 on the PDF for pattern

Orange, Purple, Teal, Yellow, Red, Dark Brown, Medium Brown, Green, Dark Pink and Light Brown Tone-on-Tones
foundation patches

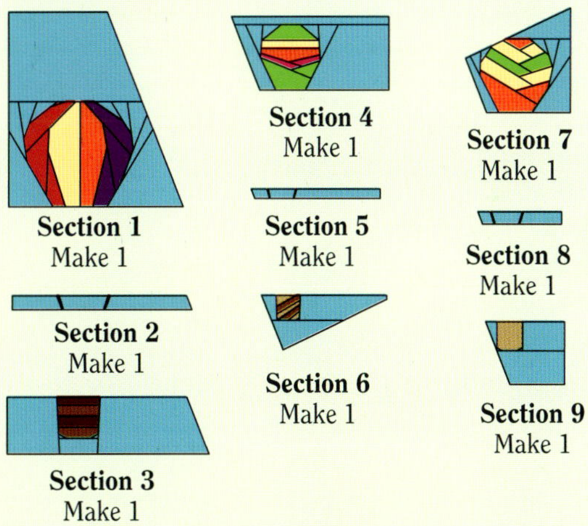

Make 1 paper copy of *each* foundation section. Refer to the foundations for color placement. Foundation piece the sections in numerical order, pressing and trimming after each patch addition.

Sew the sections together as shown to complete the block.

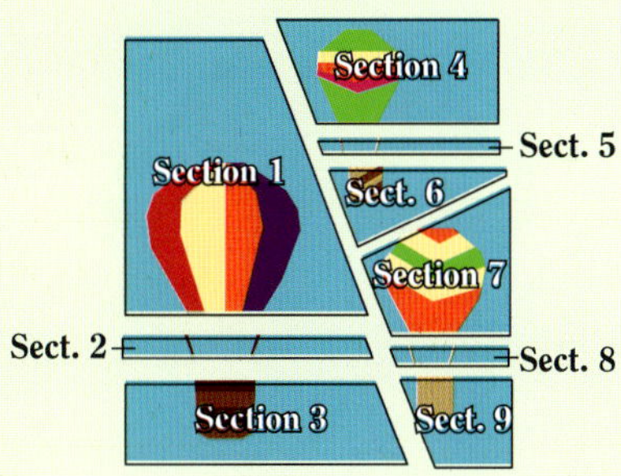

Block Assembly

block no. 281

Bloom Around

by Bonnie Olaveson • Cotton Way
cottonway.com

Fabric: Simple Abundance by Bonnie Olaveson and Camille Roskelley for Moda Fabrics, unitednotions.com.

See page 29 on the PDF for pattern

◪ = cut in half diagonally

Beige Tone-on-Tone
- 1 square (A) 9½″ x 9½″ (trim to 8½″ x 8½″ after appliqué)
- 2 squares 7¼″ x 7¼″ ◪ (E)

Red Tone-on-Tone
- 1 pattern B
- 4 pattern C

Blue Print
- 4 pattern D

Red rickrack
- 4 pieces, *each* 8½″ long

Fusible web

Fold A in half diagonally both ways and gently crease the folds. Prepare B–D for fusible appliqué. Referring to the appliqué placement diagram and using the creases as a guide, position and fuse B–D in alphabetical order to A. Stitches are found on page 10. Use red thread and a blanket stitch to sew around all of the patches. Center the appliqué and trim A to 8½″ × 8½″.

Sew red rickrack to each side of A as shown. Add the E's as shown to complete the block. ▪

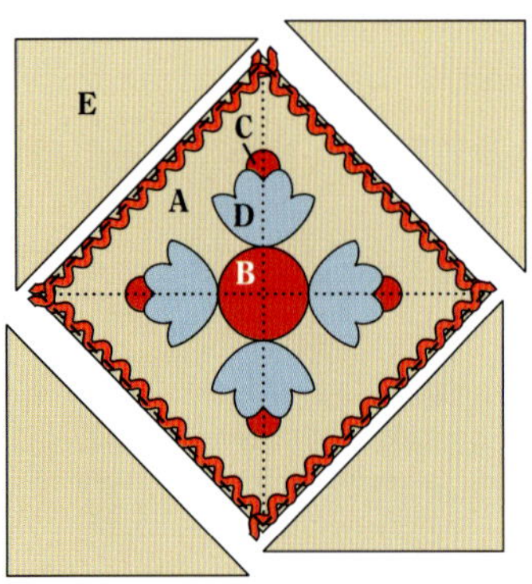

Applique and Block Piecing

block no. 282

Full Bloom

by Bonnie Sullivan • All Through the Night
allthroughthenight.net

Fabric: Woolies (flannel) by Bonnie Sullivan for Maywood Studio, maywoodstudio.com.

See page 15 on the PDF for pattern

Cream Stripe Flannel
- 2 squares (A) 6½″ x 6½″

Black Dot Flannel
- 2 squares (A) 6½″ x 6½″

Medium and Dark Green Wool
from *each*
- 4 pattern B
- 1 pattern C
- 2 pattern F

Light Red Wool
- 4 pattern D

Red Wool
- 4 pattern E

1″ black button

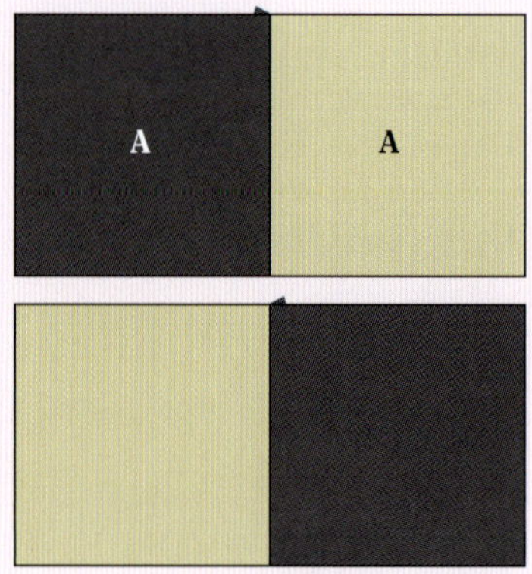

Block Piecing

Sew the A's together as shown.

Refer to the appliqué placement diagram to arrange patches B–F; baste or pin in place. Stitch diagrams can be found in the Techniques file on the PDF. Using matching thread and a whipstitch, sew the patches in place. Sew the button to the center as shown. ▪

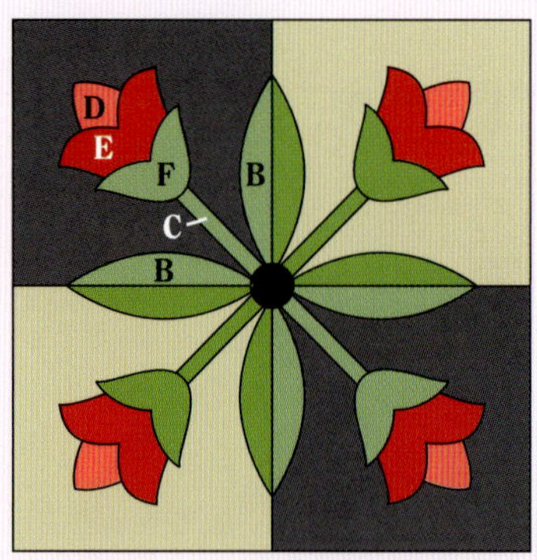

Applique and Button Placement

block no. 283
Flower Frenzy

by Cheryl Brown • Quilter Chic
quilterchic.com

Cheryl is the author of Fresh & Fabulous Quilts for Martingale & Co. shopmartingale.com.

⧄ = cut in half diagonally

Purple Batik and Green Dot Batik
from *each*

- 1 square 9⅞" x 9⅞" ⧄ (A) (there will be one extra A from each fabric)
- 1 pattern B
- 9 squares (C) 2⅞" x 2⅞"
- 1 square (D) 2½" x 2½"

Unit
Make 18

Prepare the B patches for turned-edge appliqué. Mark the center of the A's by folding in half diagonally and creasing. Match the fold lines of the A's and B's as shown. Appliqué the B's in place with a blind stitch. Sew the appliquéd sections together. Center the appliqué and trim A/B to 8½" × 8½".

Template for Flower Frenzy block on page 13 of the Templates file on the PDF.

Pair up C's from each fabric to make 18 units using the "Triangle-Squares" technique found in the Techniques file on the PDF.

Assemble the block as shown.

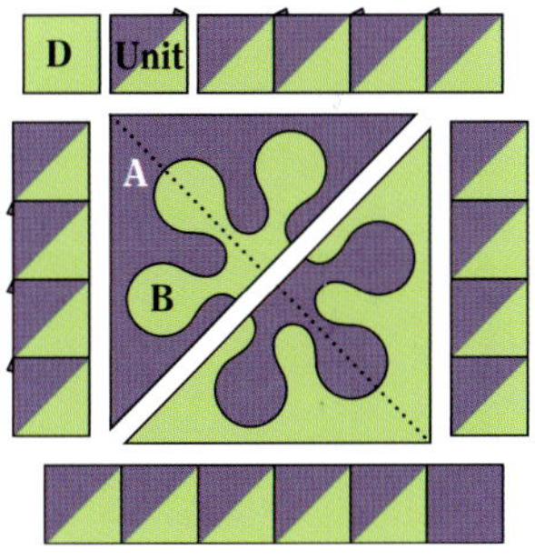

Block Applique and Piecing

block no. 284
Daisez

by Dodi Lee Poulsen • Two Sisters at Squirrel Hollow
twosashquilts.com.

Fabric:
Henry Glass & Co., henryglassfabrics.com.

⧄ = cut in half diagonally
⊠ = cut in half twice diagonally

Light Blue Print

- 1 square (A) 7½" x 7½" (trim to 6½" x 6½" after appliqué)
- 4 squares 3⅞" x 3⅞" ⧄ (E)
- 2 squares (F) 3⅞" x 3⅞"

Red Solid

- 6 pattern B

White and Red Stripe

- 1 pattern C

Blue Dot

- 1 square 7¼" x 7¼" ⊠ (D)
- 2 squares (F) 3⅞" x 3⅞"

Fusible web

Unit
Make 4

Template for Daisez block on page 8 of the Templates file on the PDF.

Prepare the B's and C for fusible appliqué; fuse to A as shown. Using a machine blanket stitch and contrasting thread, stitch around the flower patches. Center the flower and trim A to 6½" × 6½".

Refer to the "Triangle-Squares" technique in the Techniques file on the PDF and use the blue print and blue dot F's to make 4 units.

Sew the patches and units together as shown to make the block.

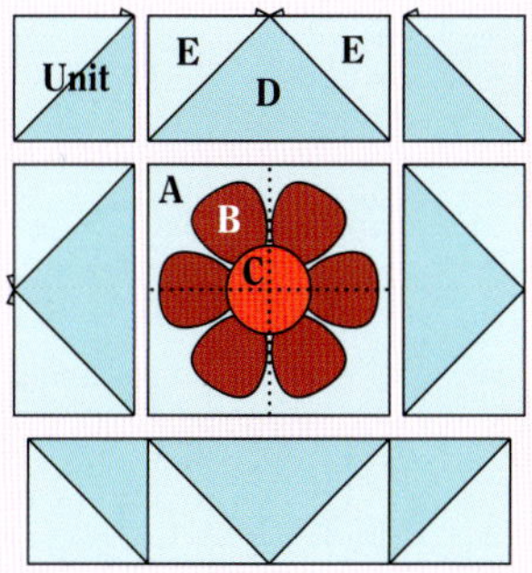

Block Applique and Piecing

block no. 285

Summer's Best

by Ann Weber • Gingham Girls
ginghamgirls.biz

⧄ = cut in half diagonally
⊠ = cut in half twice diagonally

Yellow Tone-on-Tone
4 squares (A) 4¾" x 4¾"

Cream Tone-on-Tone
1 square (A) 4¾" x 4¾"
1 square 7¼" x 7¼" ⊠ (B)
2 squares 3⅞" x 3⅞" ⧄ (C)

Green Print
1 bias strip 1⅜" x 31"

Assorted Prints
11 pattern D
10 pattern E
2 *each* patterns F and G

Fusible web

Template for Summer's Best block on page 14 of the Templates file on the PDF.

Sew the patches together as shown to make the block.

To make the bias stem, refer to "Bias Strips" in the Techniques file on the PDF. Position the bias strip as shown. Use a straight stitch to sew close to both edges of the strip. Prepare patches D–G for fusible appliqué; fuse the flowers and leaves as shown. Use a blanket stitch and matching thread to stitch around all of the appliquéd patches.

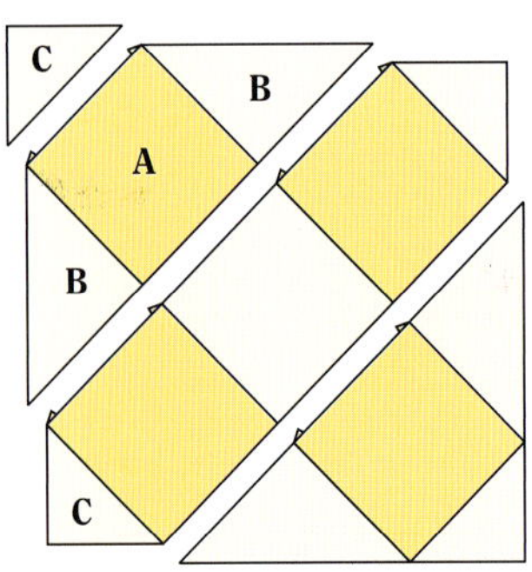

Block Piecing

Applique Placement

block no. 286

Rose Trellis

by Elizabeth Scott • Late Bloomer Quilts
latebloomerquilts.com

Fabric: Mill House Inn designed by Fig Tree Quilts for Moda Fabrics, unitednotions.com.

Elizabeth Scott is the author of The ABC's of Words on Quilts for C&T Publishing, ctpub.com.

Cream and Green Print
2 squares (A) 3⅞" x 3⅞"

Light Green Print #1
2 squares (A) 3⅞" x 3⅞"
4 squares (C) 3½" x 3½"

Cream Dot Print
12 rectangles (B) 2" x 3½"

Light Green Print #2
1 square (C) 3½" x 3½"

Yellow Print
4 squares (D) 2" x 2"

Assorted Green, Red, Peach, and Cream Prints
5 pattern E
3 pattern F
3 pattern G

Fusible web

Template for Rose Trellis block on page 15 of the Templates file on the PDF.

Refer to the "Triangle-Squares" technique found in the Techniques file on the PDF. Pair the cream A's with the green A's to make 4 units. Join the units and patches B–D as shown to make the block.

Prepare patches E–G for fusible appliqué. Refer to the photo for placement and fuse the patches to the block in alphabetical order as shown. Using matching thread, machine blanket stitch around the appliquéd patches.

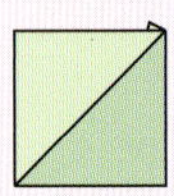

Unit
Make 4

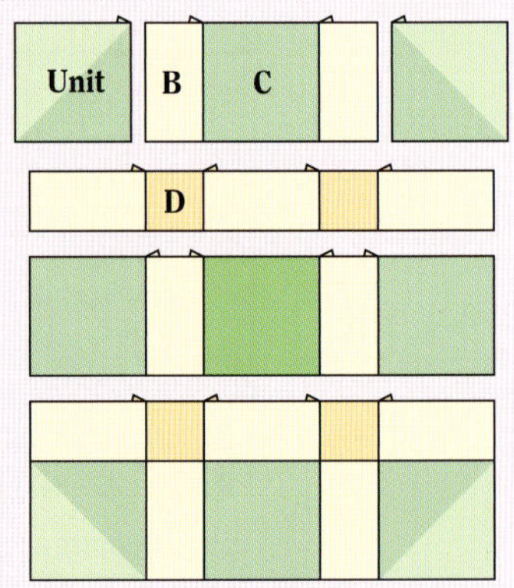

Block Piecing

block no. 287

Eventide Bloom

by Jacquelynne Steves • The Noble Wife
thenoblewife.com

See page 30 on the PDF for pattern

⧄ = cut in half diagonally

Brown Pindot
- 1 square (A) 10″ x 10″ (trim to 9″ x 9″ after appliqué)

Assorted Pastel Prints and Solids
- 1 *each* patterns B–D, F, J and K
- 2 *each* patterns E, G, H and I

Pastel Green Print
- 2 squares 6⅞″ x 6⅞″ ⧄ (L)

Fold A in half diagonally twice and gently crease the folds. Prepare patches B–O for fusible appliqué. Referring to the appliqué placement diagram and using the creased folds, position and fuse the patches to A. Stitch diagrams can be found in the Techniques file on the PDF. Use matching thread and a zigzag stitch to sew the patches in place. Center the appliqué and trim A to 9″ × 9″.

Sew the L's to A as shown to complete the block.

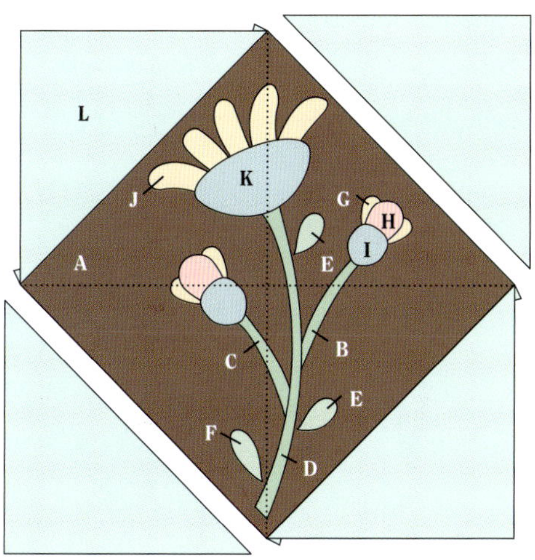

Block Piecing and Applique Placement

block no. 288

Evergreen

by Patty Heath

Fabric: Floragraphix IV by Jason Yenter for In The Beginning Fabrics, inthebeginningfabrics.com.

See page 29 on the PDF for pattern

⧄ = cut in half diagonally

Medium Green Tone-on-Tone
- 2 squares (A) 3⅞″ x 3⅞″
- 1 pattern F

Dark Green Print
- 2 squares (A) 3⅞″ x 3⅞″

Medium Purple Tone-on-Tone
- 6 squares 3″ x 3″ ⧄ (B)

Cream Print
- 2 squares 3″ x 3″ ⧄ (B)

Cream and Green Print
- 4 squares 3⅞″ x 3⅞″ ⧄ (C)

Multiprint
- 1 square (D) 6½″ x 6½″

Black-on-White Print
- 4 pattern E

Light Purple Tone-on-Tone
- 1 pattern G

Fusible web

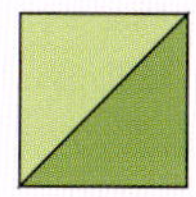

Unit
Make 4

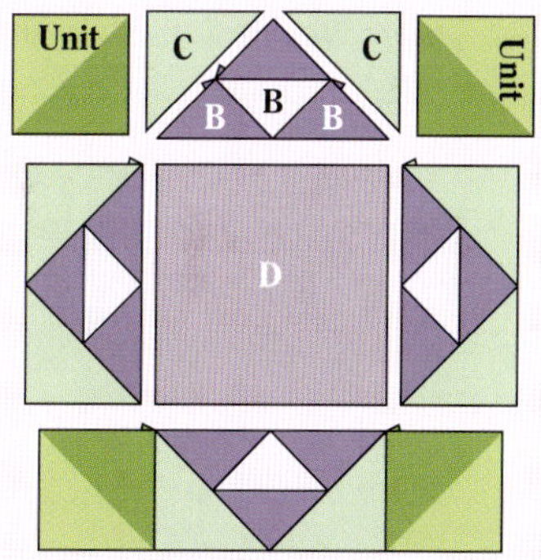

Block Piecing

Use the medium green tone-on-tone and the dark green print A's to make 4 Triangle-Square units. Assemble the units and patches as shown in the block-piecing diagram.

Fold the block in half diagonally twice and gently crease the folds. Prepare the E, F and G patches for fusible appliqué. Note that the circle in the center of the G patch is cut out. Referring to the appliqué placement diagram and using the creased folds as a guide, position and fuse the patches to the block in alphabetical order. Use matching thread and a machine straight stitch to sew around the appliquéd patches.

Applique Placement

block no. 289

Thoughtful Star

by Janet Bate

Fabric: Paisley for Maywood Studio, maywoodstudio.com.

◸ = cut in half diagonally

Cream Solid

1 square 6″ x 6″ (trim to 4½″ x 4½″ after embroidery)

Tan and Cream Multiprint

4 squares (A) 4½″ x 4½″

Black Print

4 squares (B) 3⅜″ x 3⅜″

Cream Dot and Black and Tan Print

from *each*

4 squares 2⅞″ x 2⅞″ ◸ (C)

Fine-point removeable marker

Tan and black embroidery floss

Template for Thoughtful Star block on page 14 of the Templates file on the PDF.

Using the removeable marker, draw a 4″ × 4″ square on the tan fabric. Trace the key and write the following quote within the square as shown in the diagram:

Love is the master key that opens the gates of happiness.
Oliver Wendell Holmes

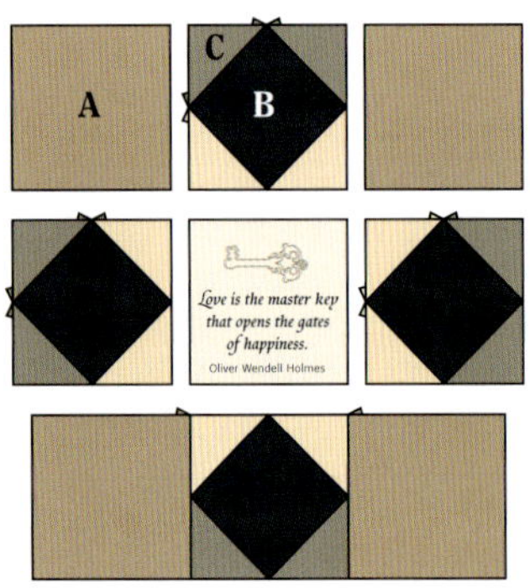

Block Piecing

Ironing freezer paper to the fabric can be useful in stabilizing it for writing.

The stitch diagrams are in the Techniques file on the PDF. Backstitch using 2 strands of tan floss for the key and 1 strand of black floss for the quote. Trim the patch to 4½″ × 4½″.

Sew the patches together as shown to complete the block.

block no. 290

Croaklore

by Karen Brow • Java House Quilts
javahousequilts.com

See page 26 on the PDF for pattern

Gold Batik

1 square (A) 7½″ x 7½″

Dark Green Batik

1 *each* pattern B, D, E and J

Light Green Print

1 pattern C

Medium Green Batik

1 pattern F

Pink Batik

4 rectangles (G) 1″ x 7½″

Multiprint

4 rectangles (H) 2½″ x 7½″

Purple Stripe

4 squares (I) 3″ x 3″

Black Pigma Micron pen

White acrylic paint

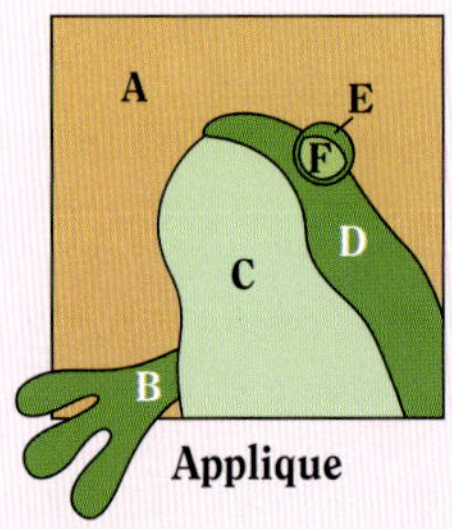

Applique

Prepare patches B–F and J for turned-edge appliqué.

The stitch diagrams are found in the Techniques file on the PDF. Refer to the diagram for appliqué placement. Pin the B in place (it will be finished after the block is pieced) and appliqué patches C–F to A in alphabetical order using a blind stitch.

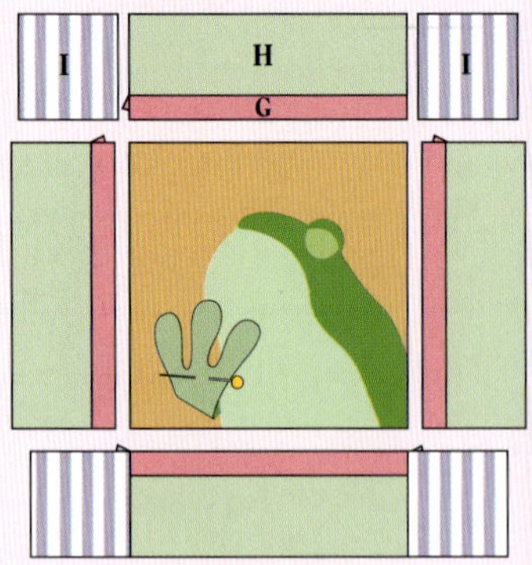

Block Piecing

Pin back the B and assemble the block as shown.

Appliqué the B and J patches in place using a blind stitch.

Use the pen and white paint to add details to the eye as shown.

Applique Finishing

block no. 291

Summer Garden

by Karla Eisenach • Sweetwater
sweetwaterscrapbook.com

Fabric: Authentic by Sweetwater for Moda Fabrics, unitednotions.com.

See page 18 on the PDF for pattern

4 Light Cream and Black Prints
from *each*
  1 square (A) 6½″ x 6½″
Pale Green Print
  1 pattern B
Medium Cream and Black Print
  1 pattern C
Fusible web
Black embroidery floss

Sew the 4 A's together as shown.

Prepare B and C for fusible appliqué. Fold B and C into quarters and gently crease the folds. Align the folds and the seam lines and fuse B and C onto the pieced block.

Refer to the Techniques file on the PDF for the stitch diagrams. Using black floss, blanket stitch all of the B and C patch edges. ■

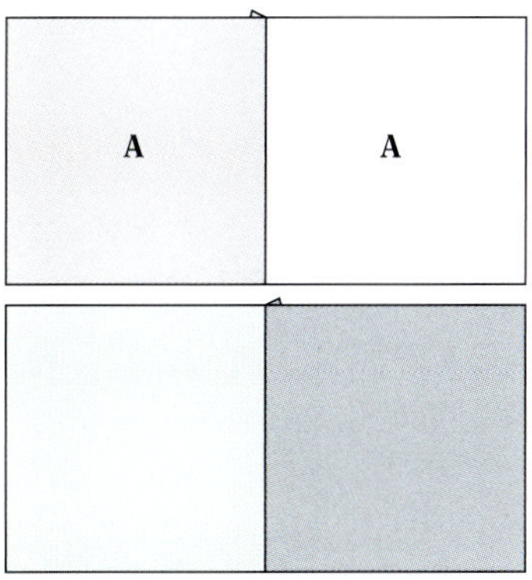

Block Piecing

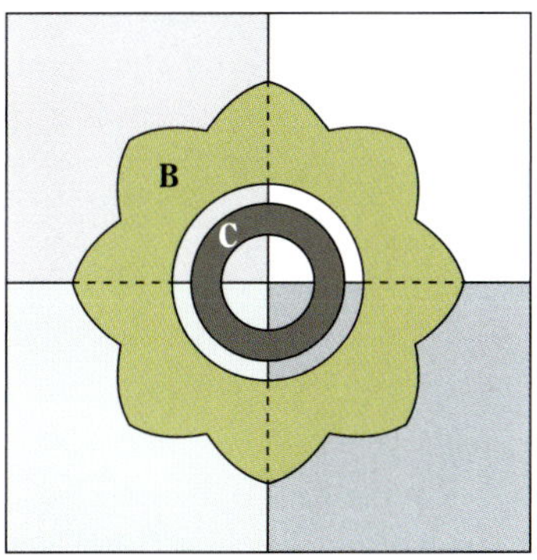

Applique Placement

block no. 292

Garden Flight

by Kathy Schmitz
kathyschmitz.com

Fabric: Kathy Schmitz for Moda Fabrics, unitednotions.com.

⧄ = cut in half diagonally

Green Tone-on-Tone
  2 squares 3½″ x 3½″ ⧄ (A)
  2 rectangles (C) ¾″ x 8″
  2 rectangles (D) ¾″ x 8½″
  4 squares (G) 2½″ x 2½″
Red Tone-on-Tone
  2 squares 3½″ x 3½″ ⧄ (A)
  8 squares (E) 3¼″ x 3¼″
Beige Tone-on-Tone
  2 squares 4⅝″ x 4⅝″ ⧄ (B)
  32 squares (F) 1⅞″ x 1⅞″
Red embroidery floss

Template for Garden Flight block on page 15 of the Templates file on the PDF.

Refer to the "Fast Flying Geese" technique in the Techniques file on the PDF. Use the red E's and beige F's to make 32 Flying Geese.

Sew the patches and Flying Geese together as shown to make the block.

Using a light box, trace the embroidery in the B's, using the seam line as a guide.

Kathy copies her embroidery onto freezer paper. She then irons the shiny side to the back of her fabric and uses a light box to trace the design.

The embroidery stitch diagrams can be found on page 10. Use an outline stitch and 2 strands of floss to embroider each design, filling in the circles with a satin stitch. ■

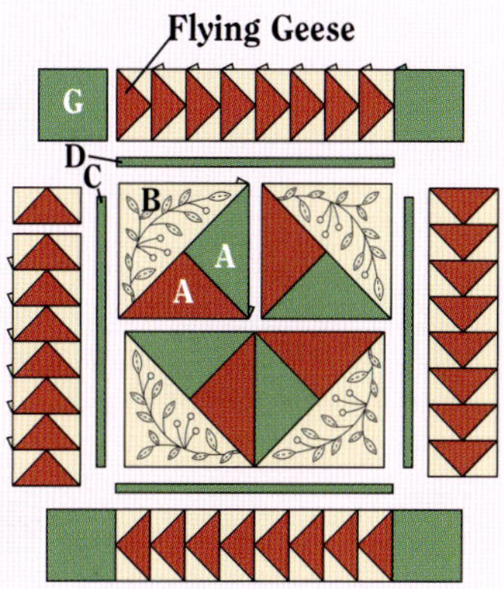

Block Piecing and Embroidery Placement

block no. 293

Pocket Full of Posies

by Laura West Kong
laurawestkong.com

Laura is the author of Fast, Fun & Easy Fabric Cover-Button Jewelry for C&T Publishing, ctpub.com.

See page 7 on the PDF for pattern

Green and Pink Print #1
- foundation section patch 1

Black on White Print
- foundation section patches 2 and 3
- 1 rectangle (A) 7 3/4″ x 12 1/2″
- 2 rectangles (B) 4″ x 5 1/4″

Green and Pink Print #2
- 1 rectangle (C) 1 1/2″ x 5 1/2″

Dark Green Solid
- 1 bias strip 1 1/4″ x 8″ for stems

Pink Solid
- 15 pattern D

Yellow Print
- scraps for covered buttons

Fusible web

Buttons
- 3 at 1 1/4″ for covering
- 1 at 5/8″

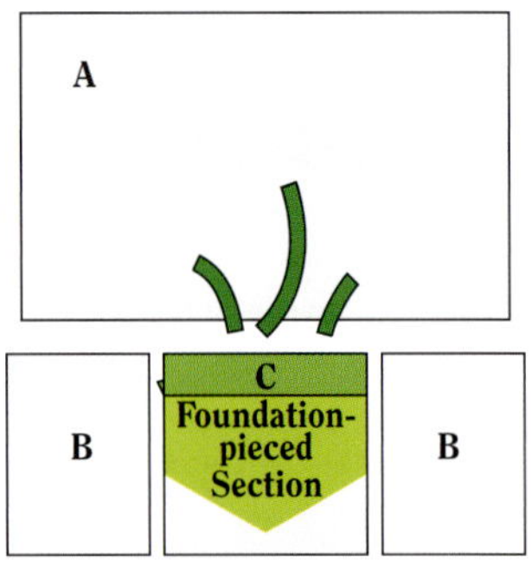

Block Piecing

Foundation piece the center section in numerical order, pressing and trimming after each patch addition.

Refer to "Bias Strips" in the Techniques file on the PDFto make a stem; cut the stem into 3 pieces. Refer to the block piecing diagram and pin the stems to A. Assemble the block as shown.

Prepare the D's for fusible appliqué. Refer to the appliqué diagram and fuse the D's to the block as shown. Using matching thread and a small zigzag stitch, stitch around the flowers and stems.

Follow the manufacturer's instructions to cover the buttons. Sew the covered buttons to the flower centers and the small button to the pocket.

Applique Placement

block no. 294

Born to Fly

by Lori Smith • From My Heart to Your Hands
frommyhearttoyourhands.com

⧄ = cut in half diagonally
⊠ = cut in half twice diagonally

Natural Muslin
- 2 squares 2 3/8″ x 2 3/8″ ⧄ (A)
- 3 squares 4 1/4″ x 4 1/4″ ⊠ (B)
- 5 squares (C) 2 5/8″ x 2 5/8″

Pink, Yellow, Teal and Purple Prints
from *each*
- 4 squares (C) 2 5/8″ x 2 5/8″

Pink, Yellow, Teal and Purple Solids
from *each*
- 1 square (C) 2 5/8″ x 2 5/8″

Black Print
- 4 pattern D

Fusible web

Black embroidery floss

Template for Mediterranean Tile block on page 15 of the PDF Templates file.

Join the patches as shown to make the block. Prepare the D's for fusible appliqué; fuse as shown to make each butterfly.

Use a blanket stitch and the black floss to stitch around each D. Use an outline stitch to embroider the antennae, adding a French knot at each end as shown.

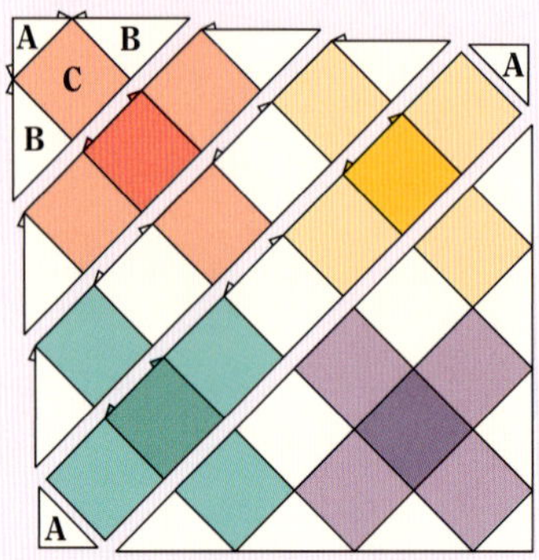

Block Piecing

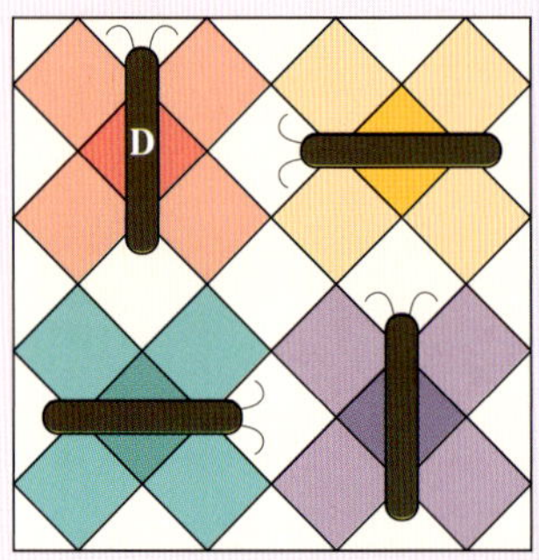

Applique Placement

block no. 295

Friends

by Lynette Anderson-O'Rourke • Lynette Anderson Designs, lynetteandersondesigns.typepad.com

Fabric: Hedgerow by Lynette Anderson Designs for Henry Glass Fabrics, henryglassfabrics.com.

See page 31 on the PDF for pattern

Cream Tone-on-Tone
1 square (A) 8½″ x 8½″
Green Tone-on-Tone
1 pattern B
Brown Tone-on-Tone
1 *each* patterns C–F
Brown Print
1 *each* patterns G and H
Dark Red Print
4 rectangles (I) 2½″ x 8½″
Cream Print
4 squares (J) 2½″ x 2½″
Embroidery floss assorted colors

Prepare patches B–H for turned-edge appliqué. The stitch diagrams can be found in the Techniques file on the PDF. Refer to the appliqué diagram for placement; use matching thread and a blind stitch to appliqué the patches in alphabetical order to A.

Use a lazy daisy stitch and French knots to add sprigs of grass to B. Use a backstitch, satin stitch and French knot to embroider features on the cat and a running stitch to outline B, G and H. Embroider the bird using a backstitch and French knot for the eye.

Join patches I–J to the embroidered patch as shown to complete the block.

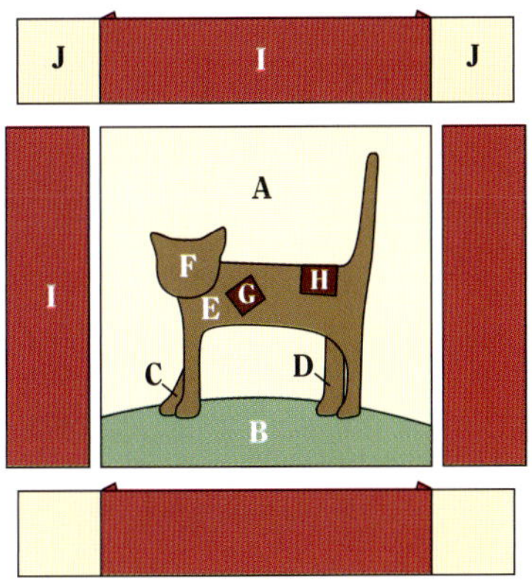

Block Applique and Piecing

block no. 296

The Gilded Age

by Meg Hawkey • Crabapple Hill Studio crabapplehillstudio.com

See page 10 on the PDF for pattern

Cream Tone-on-Tone
1 square (A) 15″ x 15″
Natural Muslin
1 square (A) 15″ x 15″
Brown Pigma Micron pen (.01 tip)
Embroidery floss assorted shades of gold and brown
#7 or #8 embroidery needle

Fold the cream fabric in half both ways and lightly crease the folds. Using the creases as a guide for placement, trace the design onto the cream fabric with the pen. Layer the cream fabric on top of the muslin and baste them together.

Embroider through both layers. Use a buttonhole stitch and various shades of gold and brown for the flowers. Make French knots with dark brown floss for the flower centers. Use a lazy daisy stitch and greenish-gold for the leaves. Crossstitches are made in the urn with gold and in the border with dark brown. Use a backstitch or stem stitch for the remainder of the stitching.

Remove the basting stitches. After the embroidery is complete, center the design and trim A to 12½" × 12½".

Meg cuts a piece of freezer paper 12½"× 12½" to help center the design. Place the freezer paper shiny side down over the top of the completed, pressed stitchery. Center the design and press in place. Reposition if necessary. Use a rotary cutter and ruler to trim around the edges of the freezer paper.

Embroidery Placement

block no. 297

Butterfly Jungle

by Mickey Charleston

Fabric: Bali batiks and hand-dyes by Hoffman California Fabrics, hoffmanfabrics.com.

See pages 2–3 on the PDF for pattern

Orange Batik
- sections 1 and 1r, patch 1
- section 2, patch 1
- section 3, patch 1

Green Batik
- sections 1 and 1r, patch 2

Blue Batik
- sections 1 and 1r, patch 3

Gold Batik
- sections 1 and 1r, patch 4
- section 2, patches 2 and 3
- section 3, patches 2 and 3
- 1 rectangle (B) 1⅝″ x 4″
- 1 rectangle (C) 4″ x 5⅛″

Black Batik
- section 2, patch 4
- 1 square (A) 1⅝″ x 1⅝″

Brown and Black Batik
- 4 rectangles (D) 3¾″ x 10″

Section 1
Make 1 and 1 reversed

Section 2
Make 1

Section 3
Make 1

Make paper copies of the sections 1–3 and reverse section 1 foundations. Foundation piece the sections in numerical order, pressing and trimming after each patch addition.

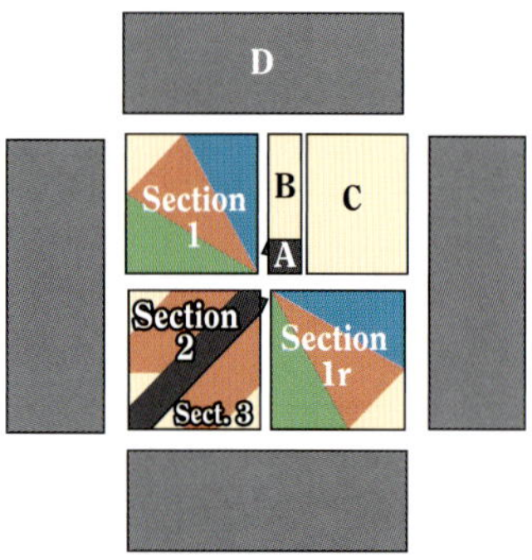

Block Piecing

Join the sections and patches as shown.

Using a 12½" square ruler, trim the block to 12½" × 12½" as shown.

Trim to 12½″ x 12½″.

block no. 298

Flip Side

by Sara Tuttle Khammash • Sew Treasured

Fabric: Berry Delicious from Sew Treasured for Moda Fabrics, unitednotions.com.

See page 14 on the PDF for pattern

Green Tone-on-Tone
- 2 squares (A) 6½″ x 6½″
- 2 squares (B) 3″ x 3″
- 2 *each* patterns Cr and Dr
- 1 pattern E

Yellow Tone-on-Tone
- 2 squares (A) 6½″ x 6½″
- 2 squares (B) 3″ x 3″
- 2 *each* patterns C and D

Fusible web

Using the "Stitch & Flip" technique found in the Techniques file on the PDF, join the A and B patches as shown.

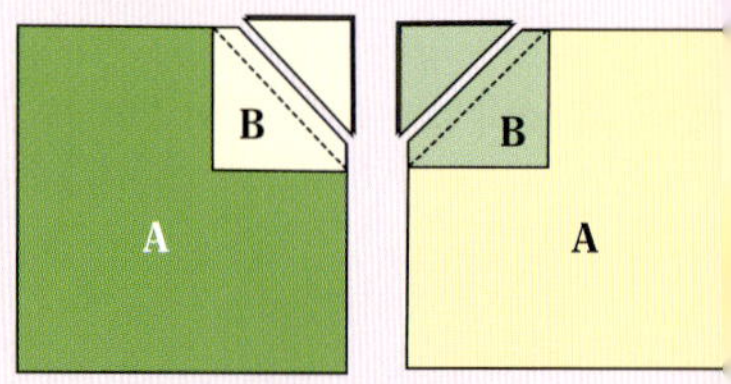

Stitch & Flip
Make 2 of each color

Prepare patches C–E for fusible appliqué. Fuse the C–Dr patches as shown in the appliqué diagram.

With matching thread, blanket stitch the edges of the C–Dr patches.

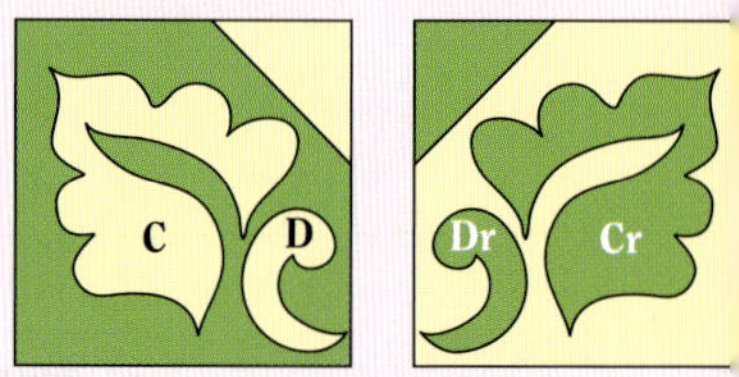

Applique
Make 2 of each color

Join the appliquéd sections as shown. Fuse the E patch to the block center and blanket stitch the edges of E with matching thread.

Block Piecing

block no. 299

Pouncer

by Sue Marsh • Whistlepig Creek Productions
wpcreek.com

See page 34 on the PDF for pattern

Black Tone-on-Tone
- 1 rectangle (A) 5½″ x 9½″

5 Assorted Black-on-White Prints
- from 1
  - 2 rectangles (B) 1″ x 5½″
  - 2 rectangles (C) 1″ x 10½″
- from 1
  - 1 rectangle (D) 2½″ x 10½″
  - 1 rectangle (E) 2½″ x 8½″
- from 1
  - 1 square (F) 4″ x 4″
- from 1
  - 1 *each* patterns H, I K, Kr, L, P, and Pr
- from 1
  - 1 *each* patterns N and Nr

Pink Tone-on-Tone
- 2 squares (F) 4″ x 4″
- 1 *each* patterns J, Jr, M and O

White-on-Black Print
- 1 rectangle (G) 4½″ x 12½″

Fusible web

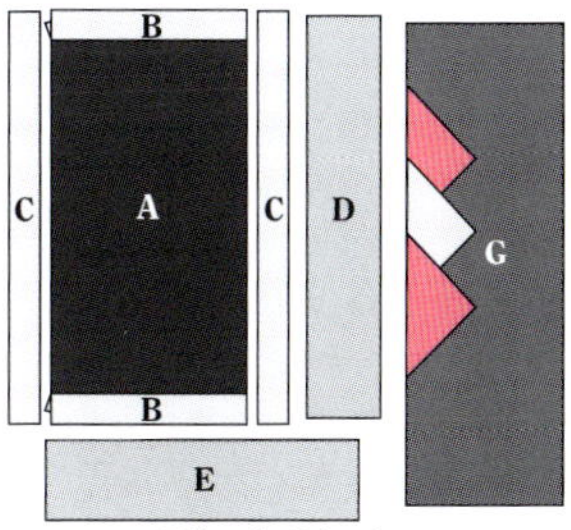

Block Piecing

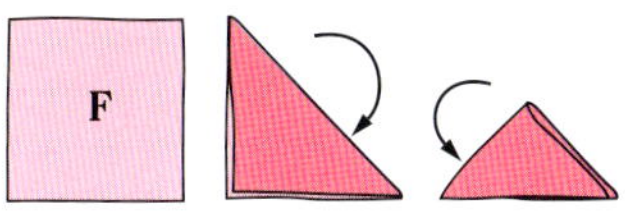

Refer to the diagram above to make Prairie Points from the 3 F's. Pin or baste to the G as shown.

Assemble the block as shown.

Prepare patches H—Pr for fusible appliqué. Fuse the patches to the block in alphabetical order as shown. Satin stitch around the appliqué patches with black thread. Satin stitch the eyebrows and make French knots for the eyes. ■

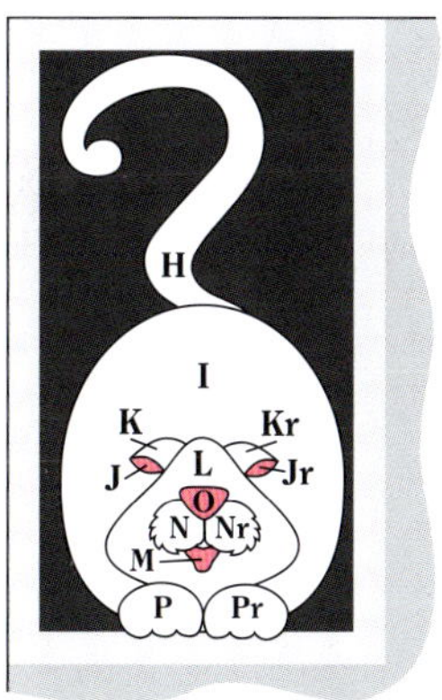

Block Applique

block no. 300

Cinnamon Spice

by Terri Degenkolb • Whimsicals
whimsicalquilts.com

Fabric: Vintage Homestead and Pumpkins & Spice designed by Whimsicals for Red Rooster Fabrics, redroosterfabrics.com.

⧄ = cut in half diagonally
⊠ = cut in half twice diagonally

Beige Print #1
- 1 square (A) 6½″ x 6½″ (trim to 5½″ x 5½″ after appliqué is complete)

Red Tone-on-Tone
- 1 pattern B
- 1 square 3¾″ x 3¾″ ⊠ (D)
- 4 squares 2⅛″ x 2⅛″ ⧄ (E)
- 2 squares 2¾″ x 2¾″ ⧄ (F)

Dark Brown Print
- 7 pattern C
- 1 square 3¾″ x 3¾″ ⊠ (D)
- 2 rectangles (G) 1½″ x 10½″
- 2 rectangles (H) 1½″ x 12½″

Beige Print #2
- 2 squares 3¾″ x 3¾″ ⊠ (D)
- 2 squares 2⅛″ x 2⅛″ ⧄ (E)

Medium Brown Tone-on-Tone
- 2 squares 3¾″ x 3¾″ ⊠ (D)
- 6 squares 2¾″ x 2¾″ ⧄ (F)

Template for Cinnamon Spice block on page 16 of the Templates file on the PDF.

Lightly mark the center of the A. Prepare the B and C's for turned-edge appliqué. Appliqué the B and C's to A as shown using a blind stitch. Center the appliqué and trim A to 5½" × 5½".

Join the patches to complete the block as shown. ■

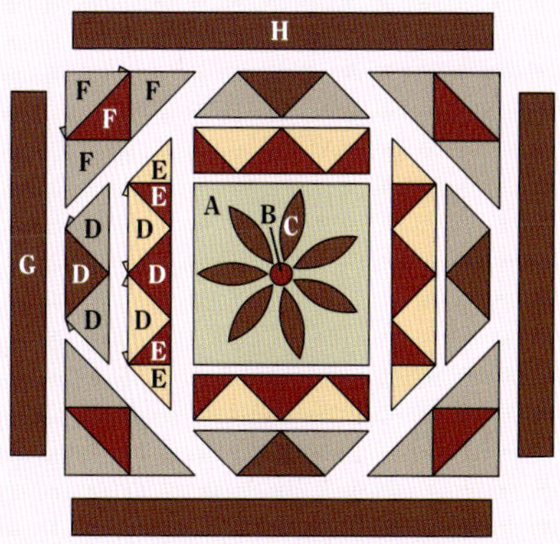

Block Piecing and Applique Placement

block no. 301

Bluebirds Welcome

by Suzanne McNeill • Design Originals
d-originals.com

Suzanne McNeill is the author of numerous titles including *Strip Happy, Honey Buns and Batiks Inspired by Bali*, all for Design Originals, d-originals.com.

See page 13 on the PDF for pattern

Cream Dot Print
- 2 squares (A) 2½" x 2½"
- 1 rectangle (D) 6½" x 8½"
- 2 rectangles (E) 2½" x 12½"

Brown Tone-on-Tone
- 1 rectangle (B) 2½" x 4½"
- 1 rectangle (C) 4½" x 8½"

Assorted Tone-on-Tones
- 1 *each* patterns F–Hr
- 8 pattern I
- 11 pattern J

Fusible web

Perle cotton assorted colors

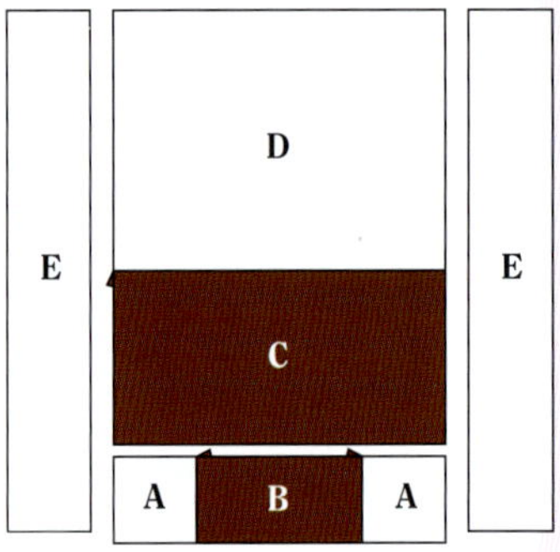

Block Piecing

Join patches A–E as shown to piece the block. Prepare patches F–J for fusible appliqué. Arrange the patches on the block as shown in the appliqué placement diagram and fuse in place.

Using thread to match, machine blanket stitch around the patches. Referring to the detail photo, use perle cotton to add details with a running stitch. Add French knots for the birds' eyes.

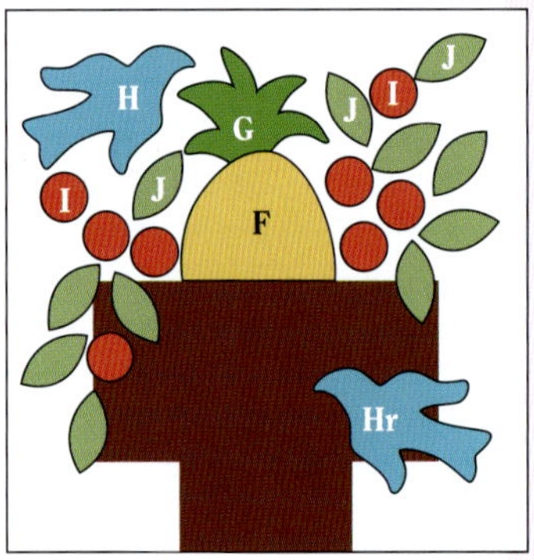

Applique Placement

block no. 302

Queen of Hearts

by Vicki Bellino • Bloom Creek
bloomcreek.com

Fabric: Gallery in Red by Faye Burgos for Marcus Fabrics, marcusfabrics.com.

See page 33 on the PDF for pattern

Assorted White Prints
- 4 squares (A) 5½" x 5½"
- 4 pattern H
- 7 rectangles (J) 1½" x 3"
- 2 rectangles (K) 1½" x 2¾"

Assorted Red Prints
- 4 *each* patterns B, F and G
- 1 *each* patterns C and D
- 2 *each* patterns E and Er
- 12 pattern I
- 7 rectangles (J) 1½" x 3"
- 2 rectangles (K) 1½" x 2¾"

Fusible web

Join the 4 A's as shown.

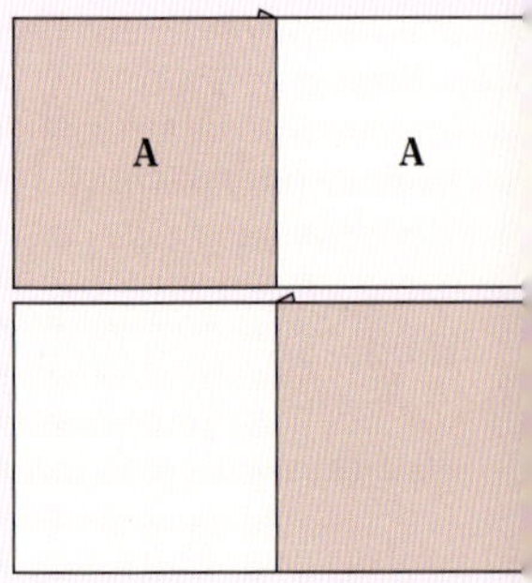

Block Piecing

Prepare patches B–I for fusible appliqué. Referring to the appliqué diagram and using the seams as a guide, position and fuse the patches to the A's in alphabetical order. With matching thread, machine blanket stitch around all of the patches.

Add the J's and K's as shown to complete the block.

Vicki used fabric with 2½"-wide stripes in place of the J's and K's.

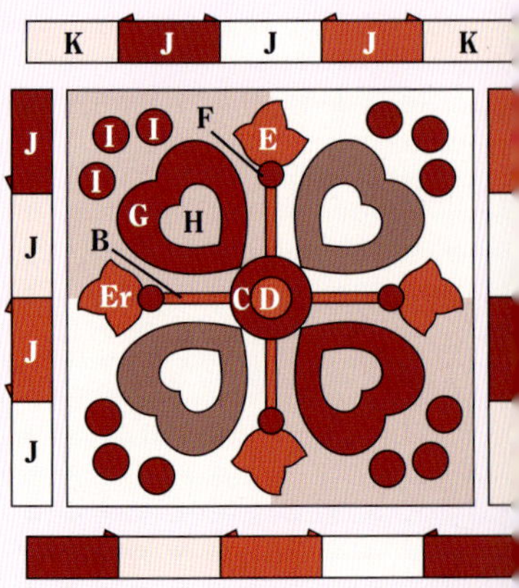

Block Applique and Piecing

block no. 303

Sunny Day

by Vicki Lynn Oehlke • WillowBerry Lane
willowberrylane.com

Fabric: Full Sun II by WillowBerry Lane for Maywood Studio, maywoodstudio.com.

◸ = cut in half diagonally

Off-white Tone-on-Tone
1 square (A) 6″ x 6″

Green Tone-on-Tone
10 pattern B
4 squares (F) 2⅞″ x 2⅞″

Yellow Print
10 pattern C

Blue Print #1
circle 4″ diameter for yo-yo

Blue Print #2
2 rectangles (D) 2″ x 6″
2 rectangles (E) 2″ x 9″

Off-white Print
4 squares (F) 2⅞″ x 2⅞″
6 squares 2⅞″ x 2⅞″ ◸ (H)

Yellow Dot
4 squares (G) 2½″ x 2½″

Button ½″ diameter

Templates for Sunny Day block on page 17 of the Templates file on the PDF.

With right sides together, sew 2 B's together, leaving an opening between the dots and backstitching. Turn the leaf right sides out and press. Make 5 leaves in this way. Use this same method with the C's to make 5 flower petals. Baste across the raw edges of the C's with a long running stitch. Pull the basting thread to gather the edges. Use the blue print #1 circle to make a yo-yo. Vicki used the Clover large Flower Yo-Yo maker for her flower center.

Arrange the leaves, petals and yo-yo on A and tack in place. Add a button to the middle of the yo-yo.

Use the green and the off-white print F's to make 8 Triangle-Square units. Join the patches and units as shown to complete the block. ◼

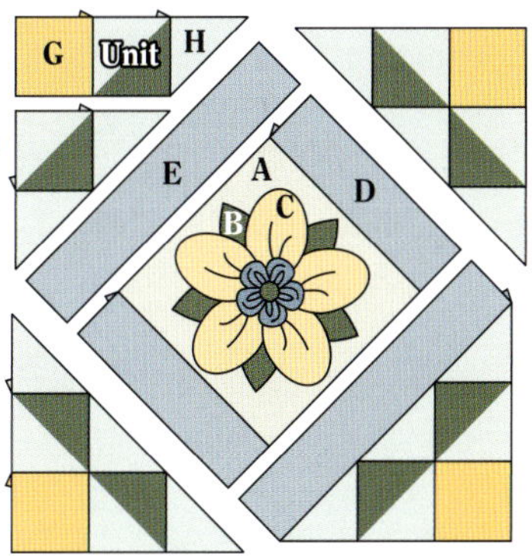

Block Piecing & Applique Placement

block no. 304

Colonial Hospitality

by Wendy Sheppard
wendysheppard.net

See page 23 on the PDF for pattern

◸ = cut in half diagonally

Assorted Beige Prints and Tone-on-Tones
9 squares 4⅞″ x 4⅞″ ◸ (A)

Assorted Gold Prints and Tone-on-Tones
36 squares 1½″ x 1½″

Assorted Green Tone-on-Tones
1 *each* patterns C, D, Dr, E, Er, F, Fr and G

Fusible web

Ramdomly sew the beige A's together in pairs as shown to make the block.

Randomly sew the gold squares together in 6 rows of 6 squares each. Sew the rows together to form a square. Center B over the pieced square and cut out the pineapple.

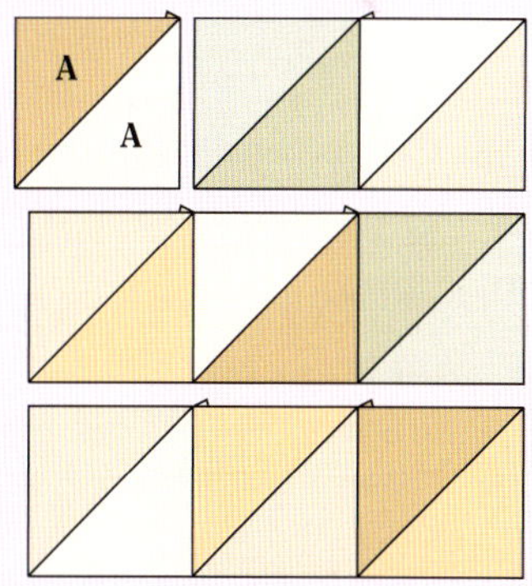

Block Piecing

Fold the block in half both ways and lightly crease the folds. Prepare patches C–G for fusible appliqué. Use the appliqué placement diagram and the creases to position the pineapple (B) and leaves (C–G); fuse the leaves. Use matching thread and a blanket stitch to sew around the patches. Use a decorative machine stitch to sew a grid through the center of the gold squares. ◼

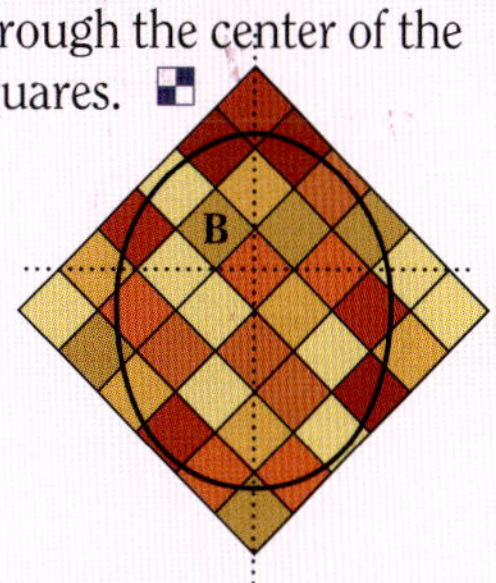

Fig. 1

Applique Placement

block no. 305

Sew Little Time

by Jina Barney • Jina Barney Designz
jinabarneydesignz.com

Fabric: Bloom & Grow designed by My Mind's Eye for Riley Blake Designs, rileyblakedesigns.com.

See page 73 on the PDF for pattern

◪ = cut in half diagonally

Light Teal Tone-on-Tone
- 1 square (A) 10½″ x 10½″ (trim to 9½″ x 9½″ after appliqué)
- 2 rectangles (F) 1″ x 11½″
- 2 rectangles (G) 1″ x 12½″

Assorted Prints and Tone-on-Tones
- 1 square 1⅞″ x 1⅞″ ◪ (B)
- 3 rectangles (C) 1⅛″ x 3¼″
- 1 rectangle (D) 1¼″ x 4″
- 40 squares (E) 1½″ x 1½″
- 1 set of appliqué patches

Buttons 3 at ¼″

Embroidery floss

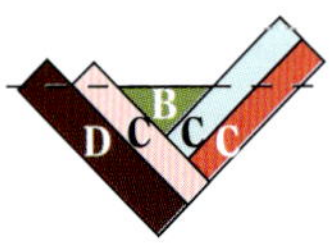

"Quilt Block" Piecing

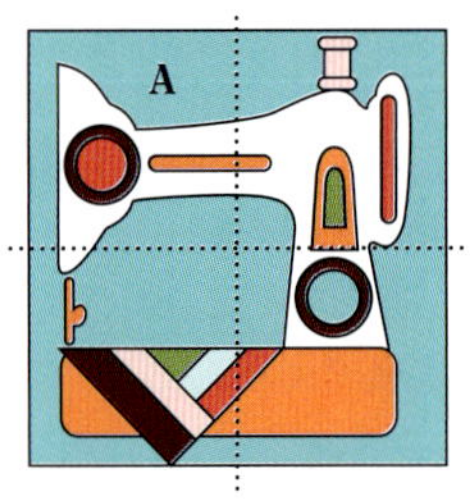

Applique Placement

Fold A in half both ways and lightly crease the folds. Sew patches B–D together as shown to make the "quilt block." Trim the edges even with B as shown. Prepare the patches and the quilt block for turned-edge appliqué.

Use the creases and the appliqué placement diagram as a guide to arrange the patches on A, tucking the long edge of the quilt block under the sewing machine bed patch. Use matching thread and a blind stitch to appliqué the patches in place. Use the floss and a backstitch to stitch the "thread" on the sewing machine as shown. Center the appliqué and trim A to 9½" × 9½".

Randomly sew together 2 sets of 9 E's and sew a set to each side of A as shown. Randomly join 2 sets of 11 E's and sew them to the top and bottom of A. Add the F's and G's as shown. Add buttons to the sewing machine as shown to complete the block.

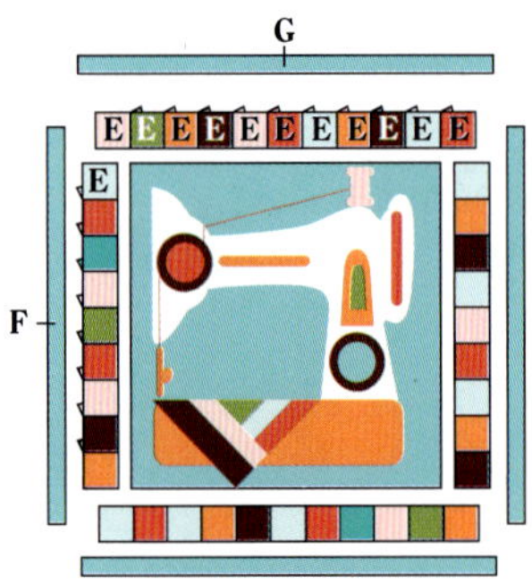

Block Piecing

block no. 306

Spring on the Square

by Cori Blunt • Chitter Chatter Designs
chitterchatterdesigns.com

See page 77 on the PDF for pattern

White Tone-on-Tone
- 1 square (A) 8½″ x 8½″
- 4 pattern C
- 2 rectangles (D) 2½″ x 8½″
- 2 rectangles (E) 2½″ x 12½″

Mottled Green Solid
- 4 pattern B
- 16 pattern G

Blue Tone-on-Tone
- 1 pattern F

Medium Blue Solid
- 4 pattern H

Light Blue Solid
- 4 pattern I

Embroidery floss

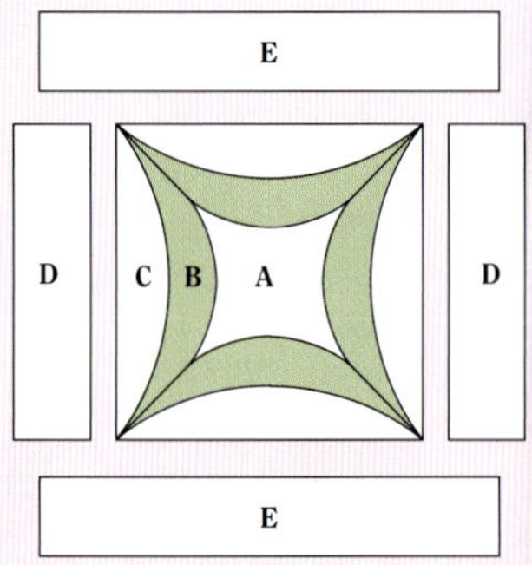

Block Piecing

Prepare the patches for turned-edge appliqué. Fold A in half both ways and lightly crease the folds. Use the creases as a guide to arrange the patches. The stitch diagrams can be found in the Techniques file on the PDF. Use matching thread and a blind stitch to appliqué the B's in place, followed by the C's. Trim away the A fabric from behind the C's, ¼" outside the appliqué seam line.

Join the D's and E's to the block as shown. Appliqué the remaining patches in alphabetical order. Using a stem stitch, embroider the stems as indicated in red.

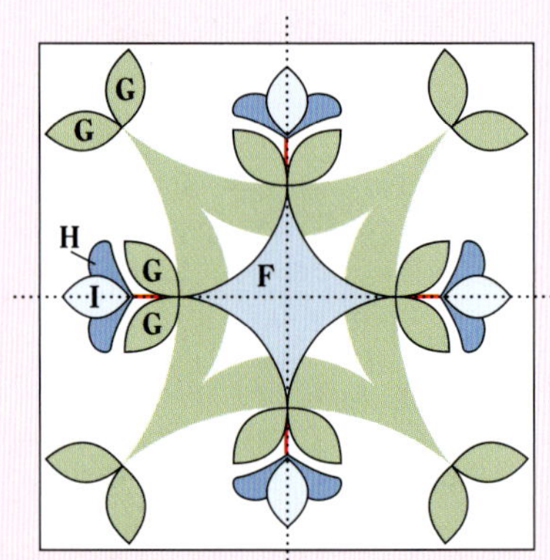

Applique Placement

block no. 307

Sparkles Snow Globe

by Mary Jane Carey • Holly Hill Quilt Designs and The Christmas Shoppe • oldstnick.net

See page 60 on the PDF for pattern

White and Blue Print
1 square (A) 9½″ x 9½″ (trim to 8½″ x 8½″ after appliqué)
Blue Dot
1 pattern B
Brown Tone-on-Tone
1 pattern C
Light Green Tone-on-Tone
1 *each* patterns D–F
10 squares (H) 2½″ x 2½″
Green Print
1 pattern G
White on White Print
10 squares (H) 2½″ x 2½″
Red Tone-on-Tone
4 rectangles (I) 1″ x 8½″
Baby rickrack about 8″
Iron-on crystals about 10

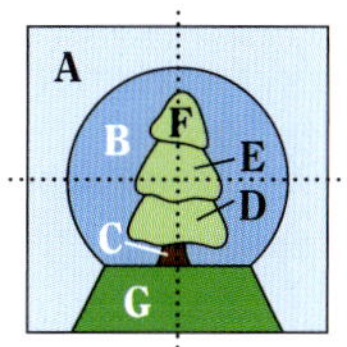

Applique Placement

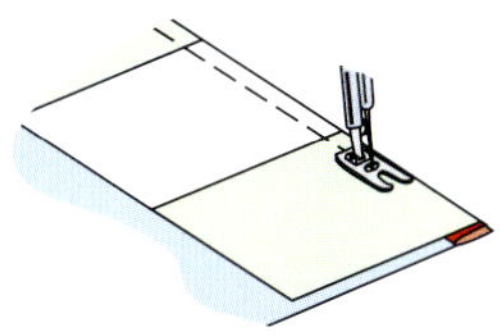

Folded Border

Fold A in half both ways and lightly crease the folds. Prepare patches B–G for turned-edge appliqué.

Use the creases and the appliqué placement diagram as a guide to arrange the patches on A. Add the rickrack to D–F as shown, tucking the ends under the patches. Using a blind stitch and matching thread, sew the patches in place. Center the appliqué and trim A to 8½" × 8½".

Fold the red I's in half lengthwise with the wrong sides together and press. Matching the raw edges, lay an I along one edge of A; machine baste ⅛" from the raw edge. Repeat to add an I to each side. Add H's as shown.

Refer to the block piecing diagram; add crystals to the tree as shown.

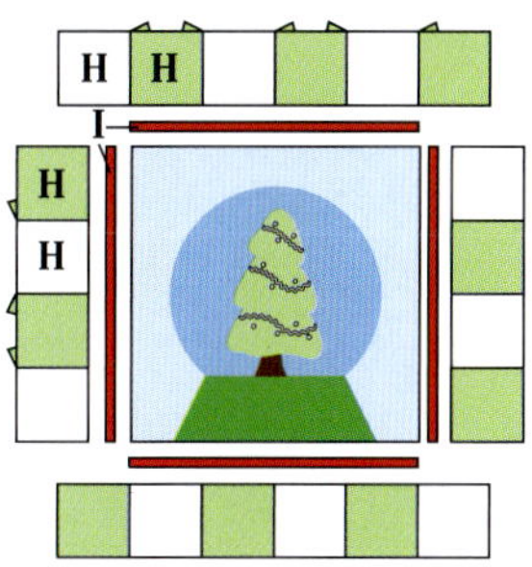

Block Piecing

block no. 308

Sweet Dreams

by Tricia Cribbs • FriendFolks
friendfolks.com

Tricia Cribbs is the author of *Turning Twenty* for FriendFolks, friendfolks.com.

See page 37 on the PDF for pattern

Cream Tone-on-Tone
1 square (A) 9½″ x 9½″ (trim to 8½″ x 8½″ after embroidery)
Natural Muslin
1 square (A) 9½″ x 9½″ (trim to 8½″ x 8½″ after embroidery)
Dark Pink Stripe
4 rectangles (B) 1″ x 8½″
Cream Print
4 rectangles (C) 2″ x 8½″
Pink Print
4 squares (D) 2½″ x 2½″
Brown Pigma Micron pen (.01 tip)
Red embroidery floss

Fold the cream tone-on-tone in half both ways and lightly crease the folds. Using the creases as a guide, trace the design onto the cream fabric with the pen. Layer the cream fabric right side up on top of the muslin and baste them together.

Embroider through both layers using a stem stitch and French knots. Use a satin stitch for the lips and buttons. Remove the basting stitches. After the embroidery is complete, center the design and trim A to 8½" × 8½".

Join the patches B–D to the embroidered A as shown to complete the block.

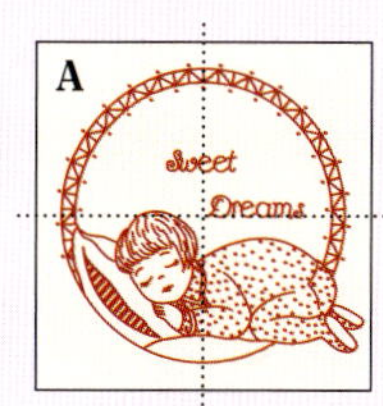

Embroidery Placement

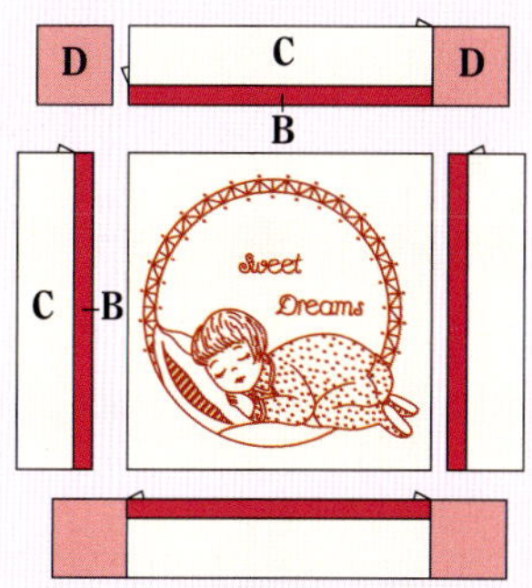

Block Piecing

block no. 309

Allemande

by Sue Daley • Patchwork with Busyfingers
busyfingerspatchwork.com

See page 60 on the PDF for pattern

Yellow Tone-on-Tone and Green Print
from *each*
16 template A
Coral Print
16 template B (see instructions below)
Cream Solid
1 square (C) 13½" x 13½" (trim to 12½" x 12½" after appliqué)
Template plastic
Medium-weight paper (optional)

Sue fussy cut the B's. Notice that 8 matching B's were cut for the center star and 8 matching B's were cut for the outside patches.

The center part of this block was hand sewn using English paper piecing. Purchase 2" pre-cut 45° diamonds and 1" pre-cut squares or create your own from the templates provided. Follow the instructions for English paper piecing in the Techniques file on the PDF; baste the A's and B's to the paper templates and sew them together as shown in the block piecing diagram.

Fold C in half both ways and lightly crease the folds. Use the creases and the appliqué placement diagram to position the pieced design on C. Use matching thread and a hand blind stitch to appliqué the design on C. Center the design and trim C to 12½" × 12½".

Block Piecing

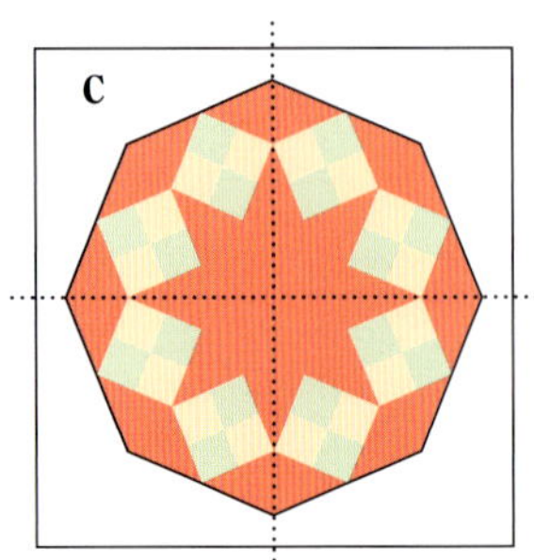

Applique Placement

block no. 310

Egg Plant

by Susan Geddes • Art Director, *Quilters Newsletter*
quiltersnewsletter.com

⧄ = cut in half diagonally
⊠ = cut in half twice diagonally

Gray Print
4 squares (A) 2⅝" x 2⅝"
Purple Tone-on-Tone
2 squares (A) 2⅝" x 2⅝"
1 square 4¼" x 4¼" ⊠ (B)
Tan Print
1 square 6⅞" x 6⅞" ⧄ (C)
1 rectangle (D) 6½" x 12½"
Assorted Prints
14 pattern E
Rickrack 12" total; cut into 3 pieces, 1 at 5" long and 2 at 3½" long for stems
Fusible web
Buttons 3 at 1"

Template for Egg Plant block on page 17 of the Templates file on the PDF.

Join patches A–C as shown to make the bottom section of the block. On D, mark the center as shown by the dotted line; measure 3¾" out on both sides of the center and mark for placement of the side stems.

Using the marks for placement, sew the rickrack stems to the D patch with matching thread and a straight stitch. Prepare the E patches for fusible appliqué. Arrange the E patches on D as shown and fuse in place. Sew this upper section of the block to the lower section, catching the rickrack ends in the seam. Sew a button at the top of each rickrack stem.

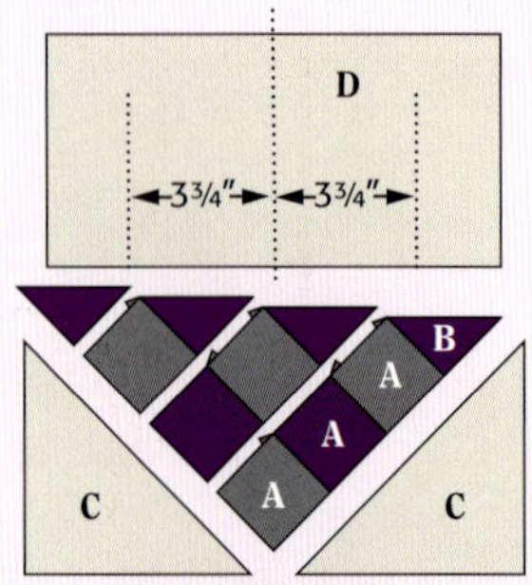

Block Assembly

Applique Placement

block no. 311

Holiday Tea

by Melissa Harris and Arlene Stamper • The Quilt Company, quiltcompany.com

Fabric: Fancy Hill Farm designed by Robyn Pandolph for RJR Fabrics, rjrfabrics.com.

See page 54 on the PDF for pattern

Red Print
1 rectangle (A) 5½" x 6"
1 rectangle (E) 2½" x 4"

Cream Tone-on-Tone
4 squares (B) 1½" x 1½"
2 rectangles (F) 3½" x 4¾"
2 rectangles (G) 3¾" x 4"
1 rectangle (I) 2½" x 12½"

Cream Print
2 squares (C) 2" x 2"
2 rectangles (H) 2" x 3¾"
1 rectangle (I) 2½" x 12½"

Green Tone-on-Tone
1 rectangle (D) 1½" x 4"
1 pattern L

Red Dot 1 *each* patterns J and K

Fusible web

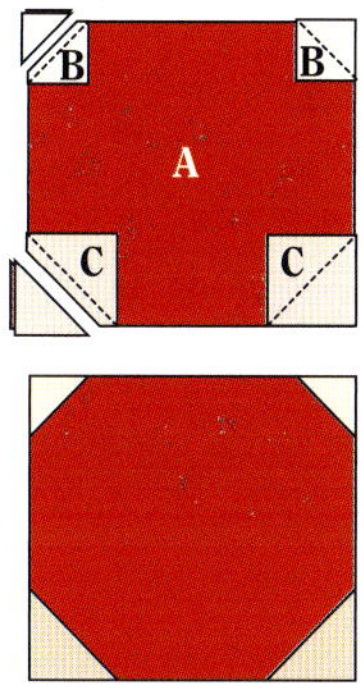

Unit 1
Stitch & Flip
Make 1

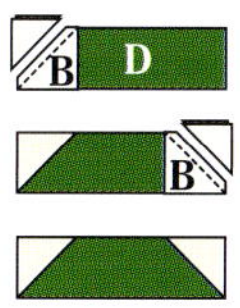

Unit 2
Stitch & Flip
Make 1

Refer to "Stitch-and-Flip" in the Techniques file on the PDF. Noting the orientation of A, use the red print A, the cream B's and the cream print C's to make the unit 1. Use the cream B's and green D to make the unit 2.

Join the patches and units as shown to make the block. Prepare patches J–L for fusible appliqué. Use the appliqué placement diagram as a guide to arrange the patches on the block. Use matching thread and a machine blanket stitch to sew around the patches.

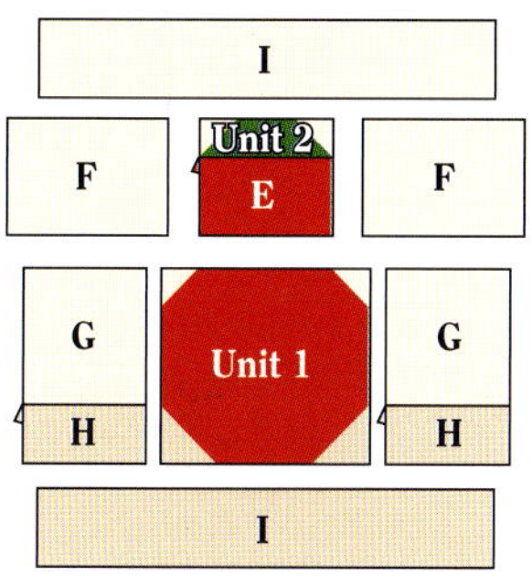

Block Assembly

Applique Placement

block no. 312

Cute as a Button

by Amanda Herring • The Quilted Fish thequiltedfishpatterns.com

Fabric: Sublime by Doohikey Designs for Riley Blake Designs, rileyblakedesigns.com. Buttons: Hillcreek Designs, hillcreekdesigns.com.

See page 52 on the PDF for pattern

Cream Tone-on-Tone
1 square (A) 8½" x 8½"
2 rectangles (C) 2½" x 8½"
2 rectangles (D) 2½" x 12½"

Assorted Prints
32 template B (16 matching sets of 2)
1 *each* patterns E–G
1 circle 4" diameter for yo-yo

Buttons 16 at 5/16", 16 at 9/16"

Fusible web

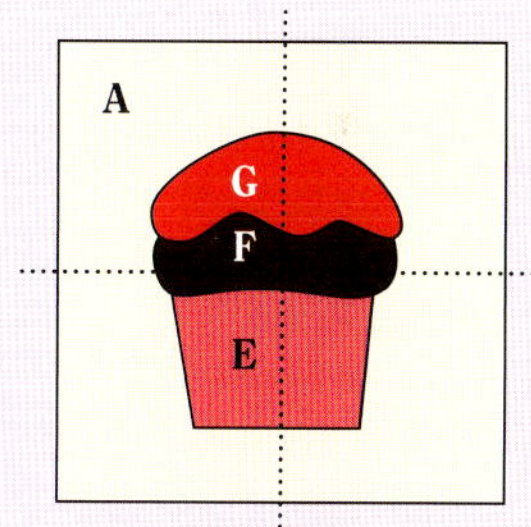

Applique Placement

Fold A in half both ways and lightly crease the folds. Prepare patches E, F and G for fusible appliqué. Use the creases and the appliqué placement diagram as a guide to arrange and fuse the patches on A. Use matching thread and a machine blanket stitch to sew around the patches.

Layer 2 matching B's right sides together. Sew around the curve, leaving the straight edge unsewn. Clip tiny V-shapes in the seam allowance. Turn right sides out and smooth the curve with a pointed tool; press. Repeat with all of the B's to make 16 tabs.

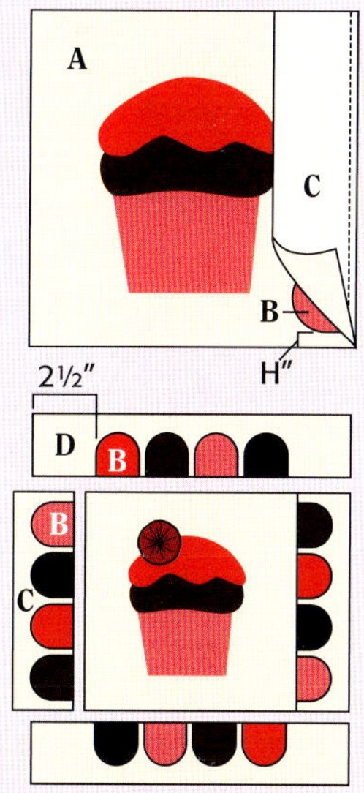

Block Piecing

Referring to the diagram, align raw edges and space 4 tabs evenly along one edge of A; leave ½" at each end as shown. Lay a C patch right side down over the tabs as shown and sew in place. Repeat on the opposite side of A. Press the seam allowances toward A. Repeat the process at the top and bottom of the block with tabs and D patches. Stack 2 buttons and sew to each tab as shown. Make a yo-yo using a 4" circle and sew it to the cupcake as shown.

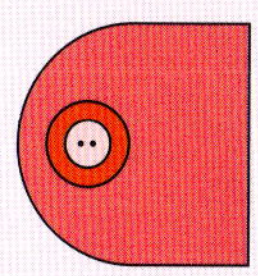

block no. 313

Maywood Blossom

by Deborah Johnson • In the Doghouse Designs
inthedoghousedesigns.com

Fabric: Back to Nature and Fleur, both by Timeless Treasures, ttfabrics.com.

See page 43 on the PDF for pattern

Cream Tone-on-Tone
- 1 square (A) 8½″ x 8½″
- 4 rectangles (B) 1½″ x 8½″

Blue Print
- 4 rectangles (B) 1½″ x 8½″
- 4 squares (C) 2½″ x 2½″

Red Tone-on-Tone
- 2 *each* patterns D and Dr
- 1 pattern E

Green Tone-on-Tone
- 1 *each* patterns F, G, Gr and H

Fusible web

Join patches A–C as shown in the block-piecing diagram. Fold the block in half both ways and lightly crease the folds.

Prepare patches D–H for fusible appliqué. Use the creases and the appliqué placement diagram as a guide to arrange the patches on the block. Fuse the patches in place. The stitch diagrams can be found in the Techniques file on the PDF. Use matching thread and a machine satin stitch to sew around the patches.

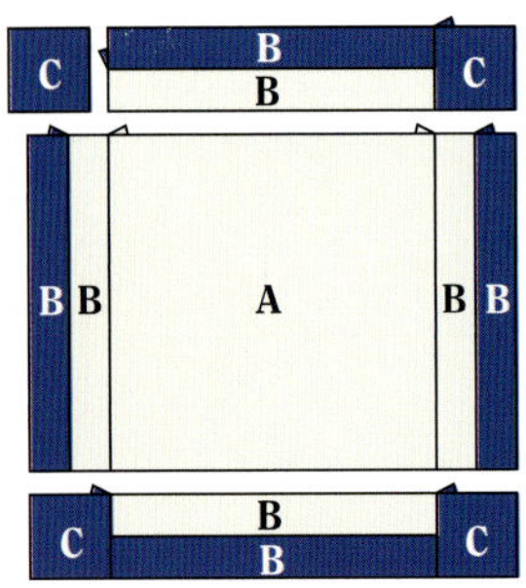

Block Piecing

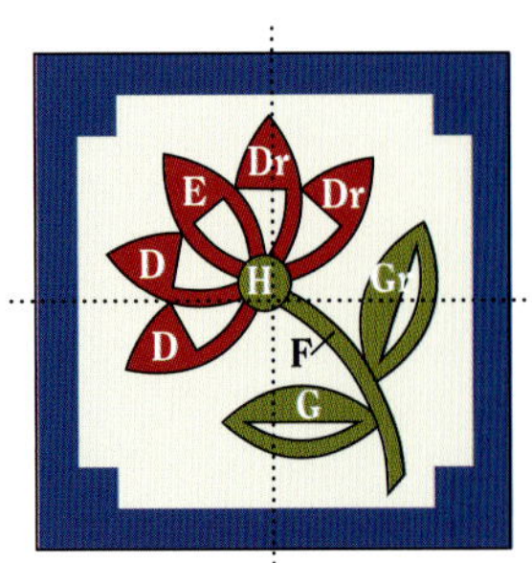

Applique Placement

block no. 314

Cathedral View

by Dana Jones • Contributing Editor, *Quilters Newsletter* • quiltersnewsletter.com

See page 62 on the PDF for pattern

Light Orange Batik
- 1 square (A) 3½″ x 3½″

Black Solid
- 2 rectangles (B) ¾″ x 3½″
- 2 rectangles (C) ¾″ x 4″
- 2 rectangles (F) ¾″ x 5″
- 2 rectangles (G) ¾″ x 5½″
- 2 rectangles (H) ¾″ x 8½″
- 2 rectangles (I) ¾″ x 9″
- section 1, patches 2 and 3
- section 2, patches 2, 3 and 6

Rust Batik #1
- 2 rectangles (D) 1″ x 4″
- 2 rectangles (E) 1″ x 5″
- section 2, patch 1

Light Green Batik #1
- section 1, patch 1

Light Green Batik #2
- section 1, patch 4

Dark Green Batik #1
- section 1, patch 5

Dark Green Batik #2
- section 2, patches 4 and 5

Rust Batik #2
- section 2, patch 7

Section 1
Make 4

Section 2
Make 4

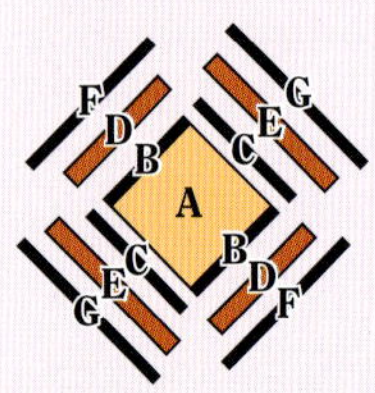

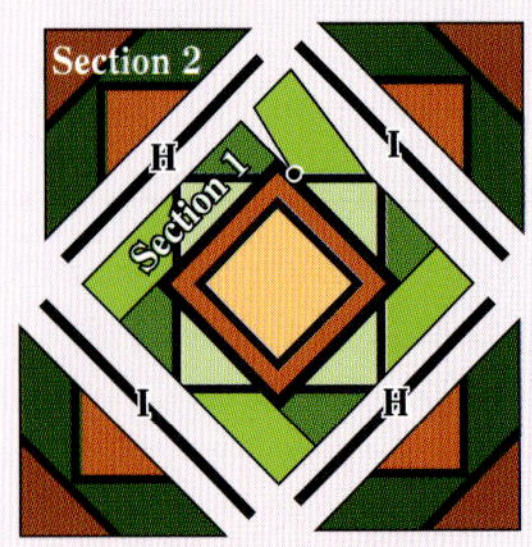

Block Piecing
•= Partial Seam

Join patches A–G to make the block center. Make 4 paper copies of the section 1 foundation and section 2 foundation. Foundation piece the patches in numerical order, pressing and trimming after each patch addition.

Join a section 1 to the block center with a partial seam as shown. Continue adding section 1's clockwise around the center. Complete the partial seam. Add the H's and I's followed by the section 2's as shown to complete the block.

block no. 315

Hugs & Kisses

by Linda Lum DeBono • lindalumdebono.com

Fabric: Hugs & Kisses designed by Linda Lum DeBono for Henry Glass Fabrics, henryglassfabrics.com.

Linda Lum DeBono is the author of several books for Martingale and Co., martingale-pub.com and Leisure Arts, leisurearts.com.

Cream Print #1 and Black Print #1
from *each*
  2 squares (A) 4⅞" x 4⅞"
Pink Print and Green Print
from *each*
  2 squares (B) 4½" x 4½"
Cream Print #2
  1 square (B) 4½" x 4½"
Teal Print
  6 pattern C
Black Print #2
  circle 4½" diameter for yo-yo
Fusible web

Template for Hugs & Kisses block on page 18 of the Templates file on the PDF.

Refer to "Triangle-Squares" in the Techniques file on the PDF and use the cream #1 A's and black #1 A's to make 4 units. Join the units and B's as shown to make the block.

Unit
Make 4

Prepare the C's for fusible appliqué. Arrange the C's on the block as shown in the appliqué placement diagram and fuse in place. Use matching thread and a machine blanket stitch to sew around the patches.

Make a yo-yo from the black print #2 circle. Sew the yo-yo to the center of the block.

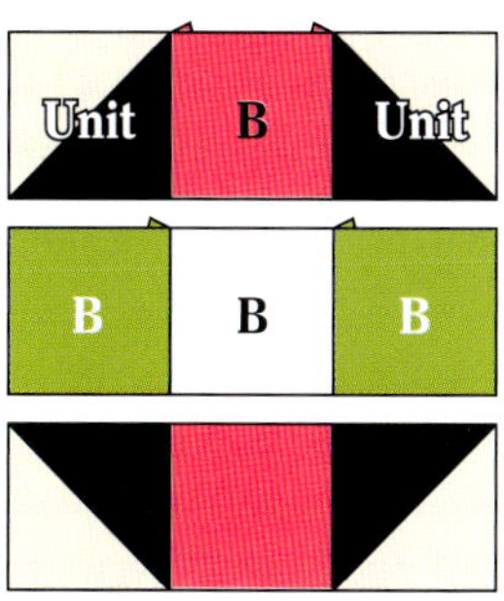

Block Piecing

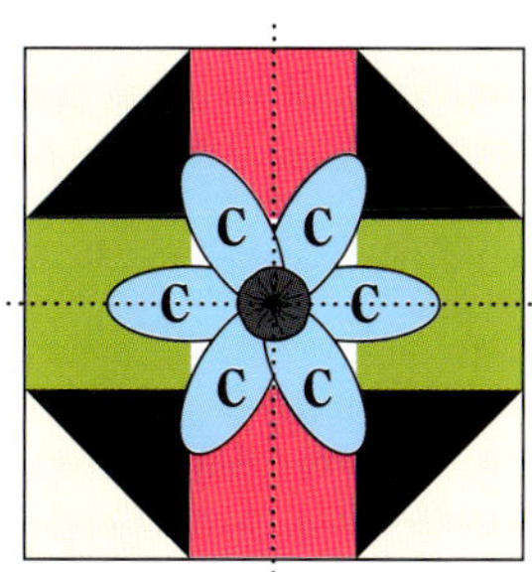

Applique Placement

block no. 316

No Ordinary Flake

by Susan Marth • Suzn Quilts
suznquilts.com

Susan Marth is the author of *Best Friends* for Suzn Quilts, suznquilts.com.

Medium Brown Print and Dark Brown Print
from *each*
  2 squares (A) 6½" x 6½"
Light Pink Print
  6 pattern B
Dark Pink Print
  6 pattern C
  1 pattern D
Fusible web

Template for No Ordinary Flake block on page 21 of the Templates file on the PDF.

Join the 4 A's as shown. Prepare patches B–D for fusible appliqué.

Use the seam lines and the appliqué placement diagram as a guide to arrange the patches on the A's. Fuse in alphabetical order. Using a machine blanket stitch and black thread, sew around all the patches.

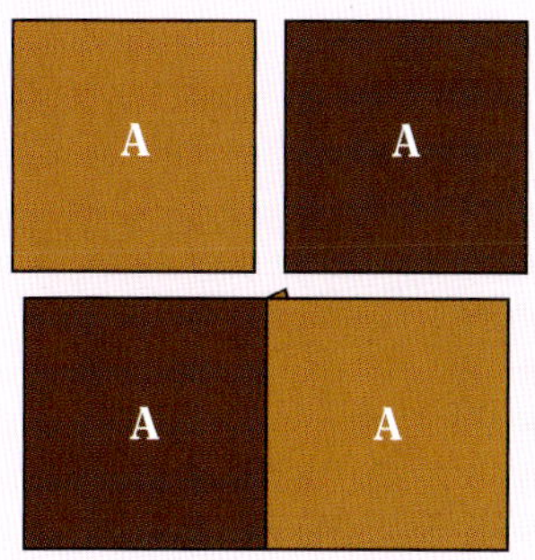

Block Piecing

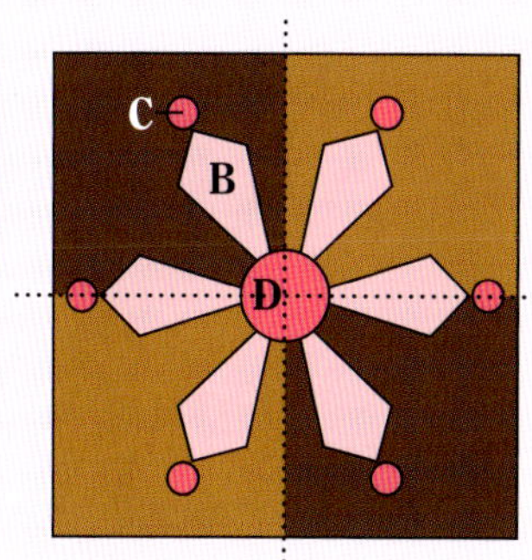

Applique Placement

block no. 317

Companion Star

by Marsha McCloskey • Feathered Star Productions, Inc. • marshamccloskey.com

Fabric: Companions and Staples I designed by Marsha McCloskey for Clothworks, clothworks.com and Toiles designed by Sharon Yenter for In the Beginning Fabrics, inthebeginningfabrics.com.

Marsha McCloskey is the author of *Feathered Star Quilt Blocks II* and other titles for Feathered Star Productions, Inc., marshamccloskey.com. Marsha is the designer of the Feathered Star Ruler.

See page 69 on the PDF for pattern

⧄ = cut in half diagonally

⊠ = cut in half twice diagonally

Cream Toile
- 4 squares (A) 3½″ x 3½″
- 1 square 7¼″ x 7¼″ ⊠ (B)

White Print
- section 1, patch 1
- sections 2 and 3, patches 2 and 6

Black Print
- section 1, patch 2
- sections 2 and 3, patches 1 and 7
- 1 square (A) 3½″ x 3½″

Blue Print
- section 1, patches 3 and 4
- sections 2 and 3, patches 3 and 5

Cream and Blue Print
- sections 2 and 3, patch 4
- 2 squares 3″ x 3″ ⧄ (C)

Section 1
Make 8

Section 2
Make 4

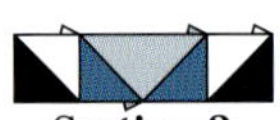

Section 3
Make 4

Make 8 paper copies of the section 1 foundation and 4 paper copies *each* of the section 2 and 3 foundations. Foundation piece the sections in numerical order, pressing and trimming after each patch addition.

Join the sections and patches A–C as shown to complete the block.

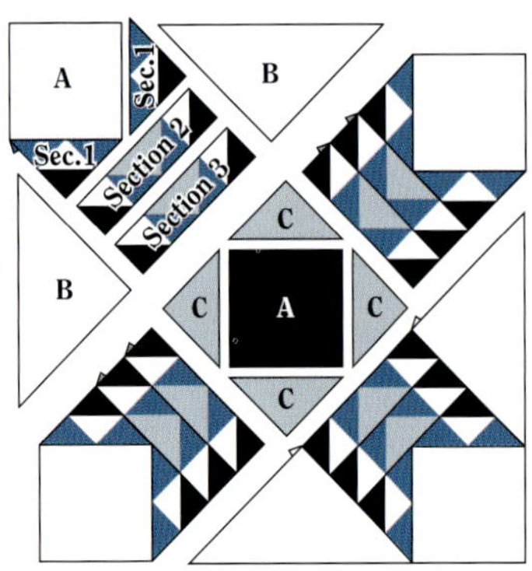

Block Piecing

block no. 318

American Beauty

by Jo Moury • Nain's Hands
nainshands.com

Fabric: Bar Harbor designed by Minick & Simpson for Moda Fabrics, unitednotions.com, plus scraps.

Jo Moury is the winner of the 2009 quilt design contest sponsored by *Quiltmaker* and The Electric Quilt Company.

See page 51 on the PDF for pattern

⧄ = cut in half diagonally

⊠ = cut in half twice diagonally

Blue Plaid and Red Solid
from *each*
- 2 squares (A) 3⅞″ x 3⅞″

Red Print
- 2 squares (B) 3″ x 3″

Dark Blue Tone-on-Tone
- 2 squares (B) 3″ x 3″
- 2 squares 4¼″ x 4¼″ ⊠ (C)

Cream with Red Print
- 4 squares 3⅞″ x 3⅞″ ⧄ (D)

Cream Tone-on-Tone
- 1 square (E) 6½″ x 6½″

Green Tone-on-Tone
- ⅜″-wide bias strips for stems

Assorted Prints
- 1 set of appliqué patches

Red Tone-on-Tone
- 5 circles 1¼″ diameter for stuffed berries

Green embroidery floss

Fiberfill

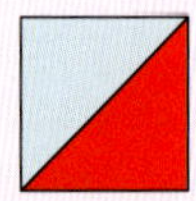

Unit 1
Make 4
using A's

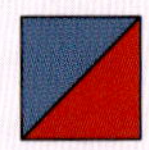

Unit 2
Make 4
using B's

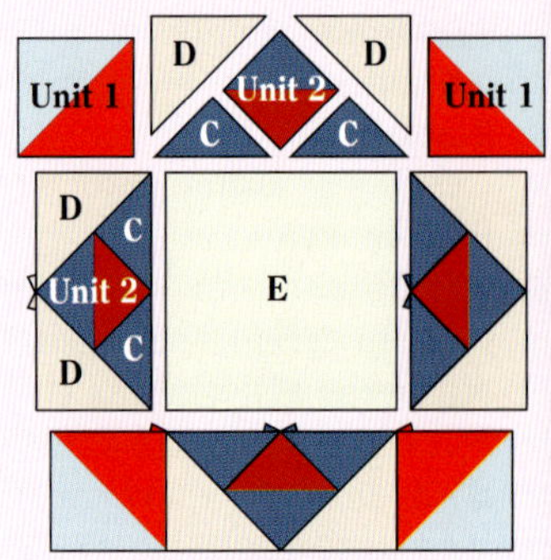

Block Piecing

Refer to "Triangle-Squares" in the Techniques file on the PDF. Use the A's to make the unit 1's and B's to make unit 2's as shown. Join the units and patches as shown to complete the piecing.

Fold the block in half both ways; lightly crease the folds. Refer to "Tiny Bias Stems" in the Techniques file on the PDF. Prepare the appliqué patches for turned-edge appliqué. Use the creases and the dotted lines on the appliqué pattern to arrange the stems and patches. Use matching thread and a blind stitch to appliqué the stems and patches in place.

To make the berries, make a yo-yo, but do not turn under ¼" before basting. Before pulling the threads to gather, insert a small amount of fiberfill into each berry. Tack the berries in place as shown. Use the green floss and a lazy daisy stitch to embroider leaves as shown.

block no. 319

Wool Crazy Crow

by JoAnn Mullaly • JAM
cloft.com

JoAnn Mullaly is the author of *Wool Crazy* for JAM, cloft.com.

See page 49 on the PDF for pattern

Assorted Wool Scraps
  1 *each* patterns A–F and I–P
  5 pattern Q
Green Plaid Wool
  2 rectangles (G) 2½"x 8½"
  2 rectangles (H) 2½"x 12½"
Osnaburg or muslin 8½"x 8½"
Crewel needles #2
Perle cotton #8
Batting 12½"x 12½"

Position patches A–F right sides up on top of the osnaburg or muslin, slightly overlapping the patch edges. Pin in place. Using a ¼" seam allowance, sew a G patch to the top and bottom as shown. Repeat to add an H patch to each side.

Layer the block and batting. Refer to pattern sheet 1 and embroider the patches as shown, stitching through the batting. Using matching thread and a hand blanket stitch, add patches I–P in alphabetical order, sewing around each patch. Add the Q's, embroidering each one with matching thread as shown on the pattern sheet.

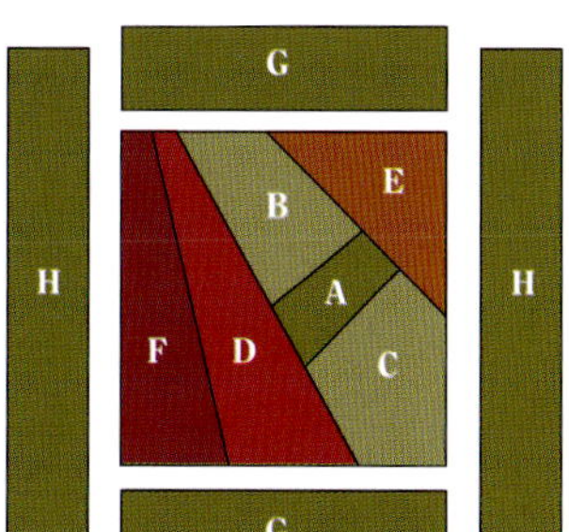

Block Piecing

Applique and Embroidery Placement

block no. 320

How About a Hug?

by Heidi Pridemore • The Whimsical Workshop
thewhimsicalworkshop.com

Fabric: Furry Friends designed by Heidi Pridemore for Blank Quilting, blankquilting.com.

See page 65 on the PDF for pattern

Purple Tone-on-Tone
  1 square (A) 8½"x 8½"
Green Print
  2 rectangles (B) 2½"x 8½"
  2 rectangles (C) 2½"x 12½"
Brown Solid
  1 *each* patterns D, F, I and J
Pink Tone-on-Tone
  1 *each* patterns E and G
Gold Tone-on-Tone
  1 *each* patterns H and M
White Solid
  2 pattern K
Black Solid
  2 pattern L
  1 pattern N
Fusible web
Black embroidery floss

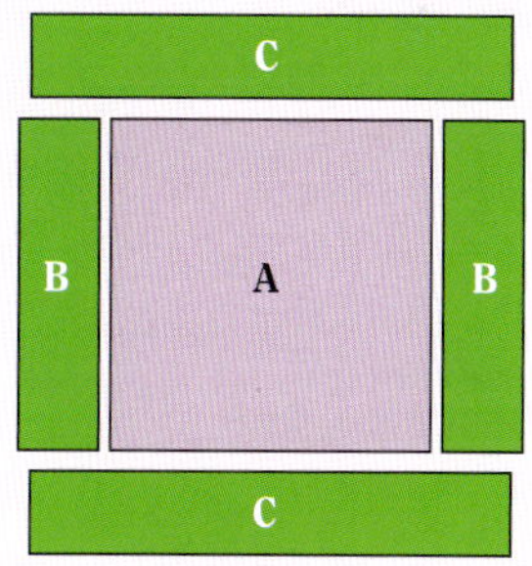

Block Piecing

Join the A–C patches as shown in the block piecing diagram. Fold the block in half both ways and lightly crease the folds. Prepare patches D–N for fusible appliqué.

Use the creases and the appliqué placement diagram as a guide to arrange patches D–N on the block. Fuse the patches in alphabetical order.

Using stabilizer underneath, use brown thread and a machine blanket stitch to sew around all patches except the K's, L's and N. Use white thread to stitch around the K's and black thread to stitch around the L's and N. Use black thread and a backstitch to embroider the mouth.

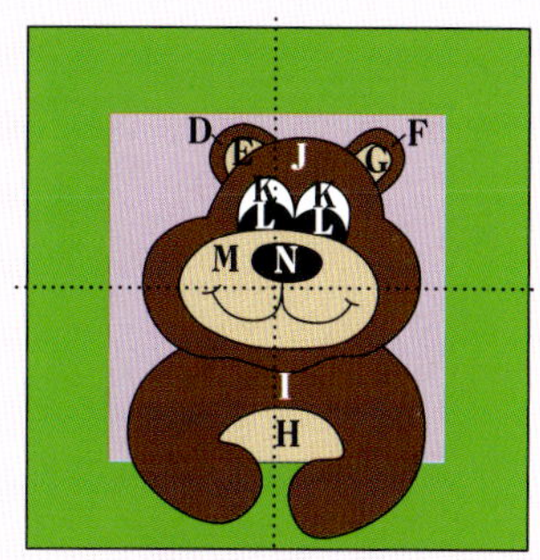

Applique Placement

block no. 321

Sunday Best

by Rosalie Quinlan • Rosalie Quinlan Designs
rosaliequinlandesigns.typepad.com

Fabric: A Day in the Country from Patchways and Lecien, lecien.co/jp/en/hobby.

Rosalie Quinlan is the author of *Gift* and *A Stitch in Time* for Creative Abundance.

See page 67 on the PDF for pattern

Pink Print
- 1 square (A) 11½″ x 11½″ (trim to 10½″ x 10½″ after appliqué)

Medium Green Dot
- 1 pattern B
- 4 pattern D
- 8 pattern G

Pale Green Dot
- 1 pattern C

Pink Dot
- 1 pattern E

Blue Check
- 4 pattern F
- 2 rectangles (I) 1½″ x 10½″
- 2 rectangles (J) 1½″ x 12½″

Red Check
- 4 pattern H

Fold A in half both ways and lightly crease the folds. Prepare patches B–H for turned-edge appliqué. (B and C will need to be flipped 3 times to trace the whole pattern.) Use the creases and the appliqué placement diagram as guides to arrange the patches on A. Use matching thread and a blind stitch to appliqué the patches in place. Center the appliqué and trim A to 10½″ × 10½″.

Add the I's and J's to A as shown to complete the block.

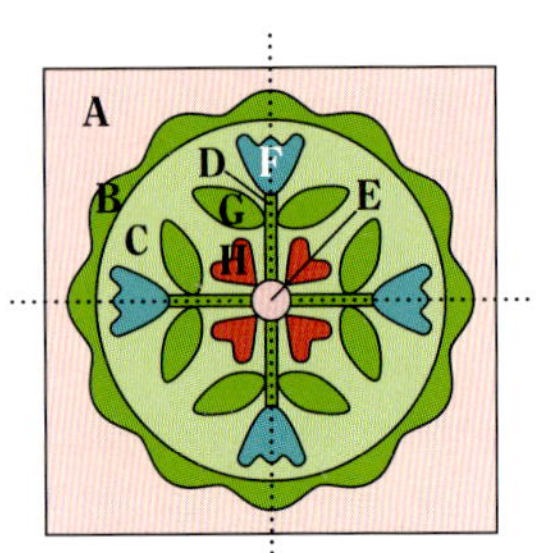

Applique Placement

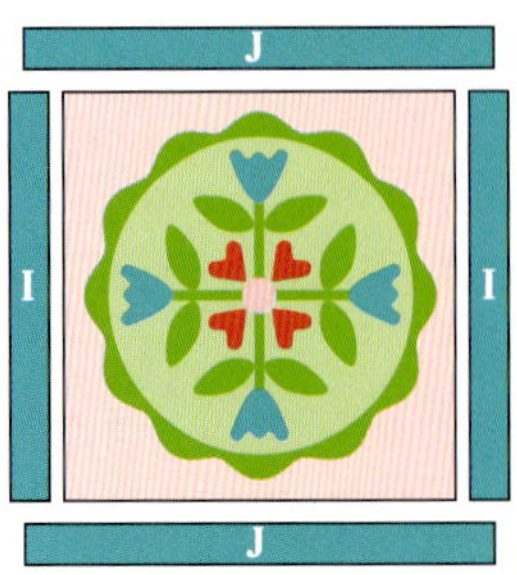

Block Piecing

block no. 322

Blooming Spring

by Carrie Quinn and Katie Reed • Pieceful Gathering Quilt Shop, piecefulgathering.com

See page 39 on the PDF for pattern

⊠ = cut in half twice diagonally

Tan Plaid
- 2 squares 4″ x 4″ ⊠ (A)
- 2 rectangles (D) 3½″ x 6½″
- 2 rectangles (E) 3½″ x 12½″

Green Plaid
- 4 rectangles (B) 1″ x 2⅝″

Red Plaid
- 1 square (C) 4¾″ x 4¾″

Green Wool
- 4 *each* patterns F and Fr

Dark Red Wool
- 4 pattern G

Yellow Wool
- 4 pattern H

Pink Wool
- 4 pattern I

Fusible web

Perle cotton

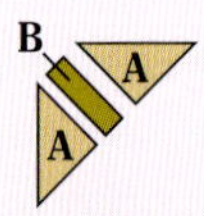

Unit
Make 4

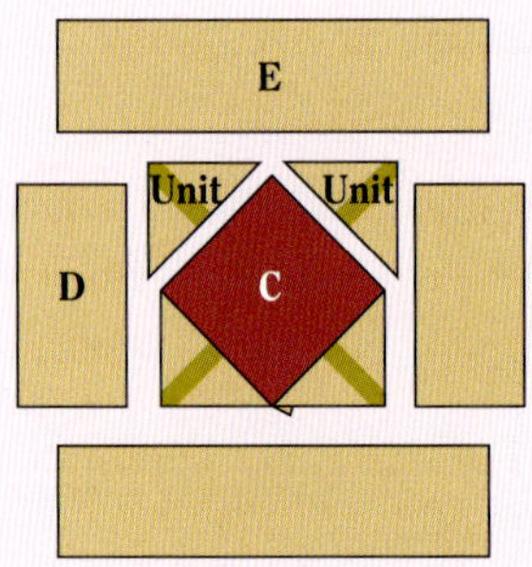

Block Piecing

Use 2 tan A's and a green B to make a unit. Make 4 units. Sew units, C, D's, and E's together as shown to make the block. Prepare patches F–I for fusible appliqué.

Refer to the appliqué placement diagram to arrange patches F–I on the block; fuse to the block in alphabetical order. Use matching thread and a hand blanket stitch to sew around the appliqué patches.

Applique Placement

block no. 323
Dot Goes to School

by Jane Quinn • Quilting in the Country
quiltinginthecountry.com

Fabric: Punctuation by Sandy Klop for American Jane from Moda Fabrics, unitednotions.com.

Jane Quinn is the author of *Quilting in the Country* for Martingale & Company, martingale-pub.com plus three self-published cookbooks.

See page 36 on the PDF for pattern

White Tone-on-Tone
- 2 rectangles (A) 8¼" x 7½" (trim to 7¼" x 6½" after embroidery)

Assorted Prints
- 1 rectangle (B) 3¾" x 7¼"
- 1 rectangle (C) 2½" x 9¾"
- 1 rectangle (D) 3¼" x 9¼"
- 1 rectangle (E) 3¾" x 4½"
- 1 rectangle (F) 3¾" x 8½"

Brown Pigma Micron pen (.01 tip)
Black embroidery floss
Crayons
Paper towel

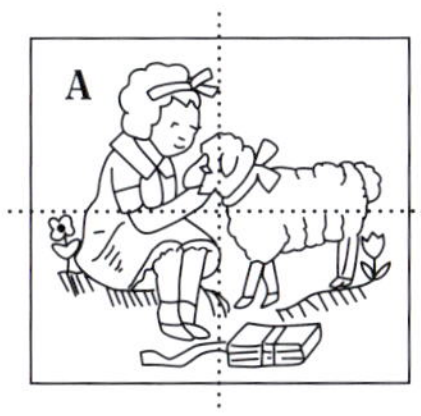

Embroidery Placement

Fold 1 A in half both ways and lightly crease the folds. Using the creases as a guide for placement, trace the design onto the fabric with the pen.

Use the crayons to color in the design. Place a paper towel over the design and set the crayon color with a hot, dry iron.

Layer the 2 A's, one on top of the other with the traced design on top, and baste them together. Use a backstitch to embroider the design through both layers. Use a satin stitch in the flower. Remove the basting stitches. Center the design and trim A to 7¼" × 6½".

Join patches B–F to the embroidered patch as shown to complete the block.

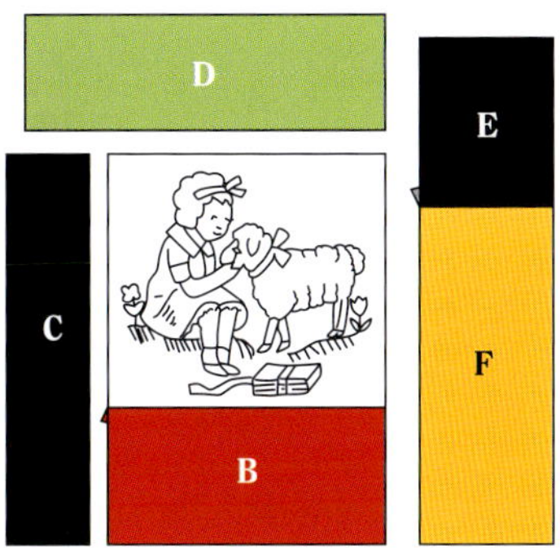

Block Piecing

block no. 324
Simple Celebration

by Anita Grossman Solomon • Make It Simpler
makeitsimpler.com

Fabric: Botanica designed by Lourdes Sanchez and other fabrics all from Timeless Treasures, ttfabrics.com.

Anita Grossman Solomon is the author of *Rotary Cutting Revolution* and *Perfect Blocks in Minutes* for C&T Publishing, ctpub.com.

See page 66 on the PDF for pattern

⧄ = cut in half diagonally

Cream Print
- section patches 1, 4 and 5

Dark Gray Print, Dark Pink Tone-on-Tone, Black Print #1 and Black Print #2
from *each*
- section patches 2 and 3

Gray and Pink Print
- 1 square (A) 4⅛" x 4⅛"

Olive Green Tone-on-Tone
- 2 squares 3½" x 3½" ⧄ (B)
- 4 squares (C) 2⅞" x 2⅞"

Black Tone-on-Tone
- 2 squares 4½" x 4½" ⧄ (D)

Make 4 paper copies of the foundation section.

Notice that the fabric used in patch 3 in one section will be used in patch 2 in the next section.

Foundation piece the sections in numerical order, pressing and trimming after each patch addition.

Join the sections and patches as shown in the block piecing diagram to complete the block.

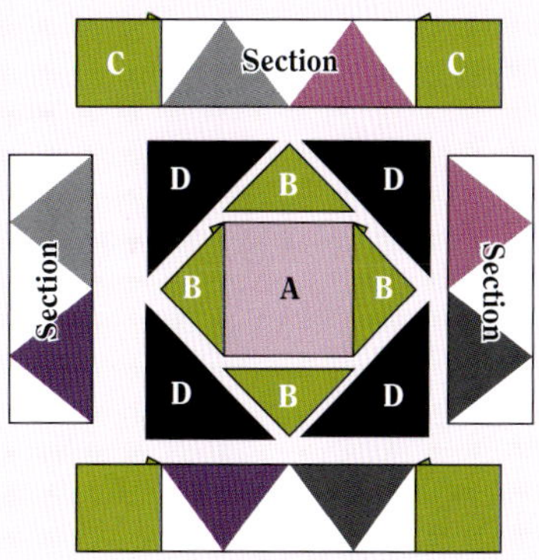

Block Piecing

block no. 325
Irish Spring Surprise

by Peg Spradlin
handicraftsbypeg.com

Green Tone-on-Tone
- 12 squares (A) 1½" x 1½"

Light Aqua Print
- 12 squares (A) 1½" x 1½"
- 8 squares (B) 2½" x 2½"
- 4 rectangles (C) 2½" x 4½"
- 1 square (D) 4½" x 4½"

White Tone-on-Tone
- 16 squares (A) 1½" x 1½"
- 6 pattern F

Medium Teal Print
- 16 squares (A) 1½" x 1½"

Dark Teal Print
- 8 squares (A) 1½" x 1½"

Yellow Tone-on-Tone
- 1 pattern E

Monofilament thread

Templates for Irish Spring Surprise block on page 26 of the Templates file on the PDF

Join patches A–D as shown in the assembly diagram to make the block.

Fold the block in half both ways and lightly crease the folds. Prepare the E and F's for turned-edge appliqué. Use the creases and the appliqué placement diagram as a guide to arrange the patches on the block. Use monofilament thread and a machine blind stitch to appliqué the patches in place.

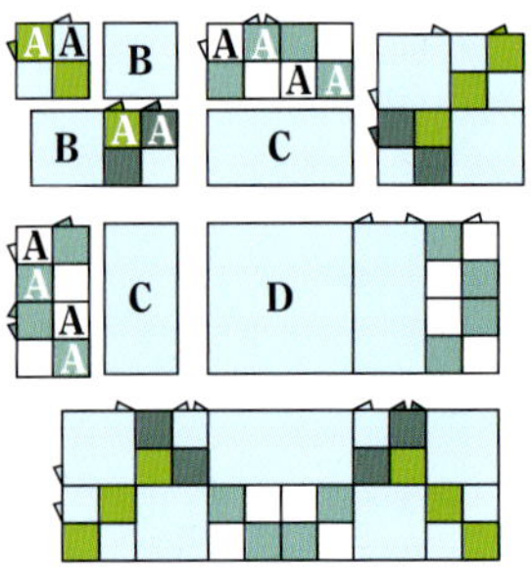

Block Piecing

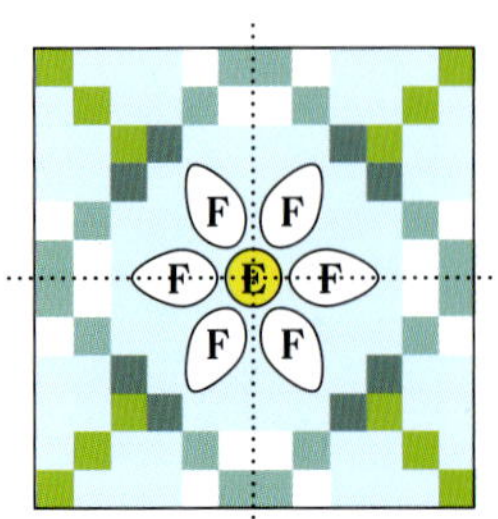

Applique Placement

block no. 326
Flowers for Ewe

by Paula Stoddard • Pacific Patchwork
pacificpatchwork.com

Paula Stoddard is the author of *3 Color Crazy* and other books for Pacific Patchwork, pacificpatchwork.com.

See page 41 on the PDF for pattern

4 Assorted Green Prints
from *each*
- 1 square (A) 3½" x 3½"

Tan Dot
- 1 rectangle (B) 9½" x 12½"

Black Tone-on-Tone
- 4 pattern C
- 1 pattern E
- 3 pattern F

Cream Tone-on-Tone
- 1 pattern D

Purple Tone-on-Tone and Pink Tone-on-Tone
from *each*
- 5 pattern G

Gold Tone-on-Tone
- 2 pattern H

Green Dot
- 4 pattern I

Fusible web

Assorted embroidery floss

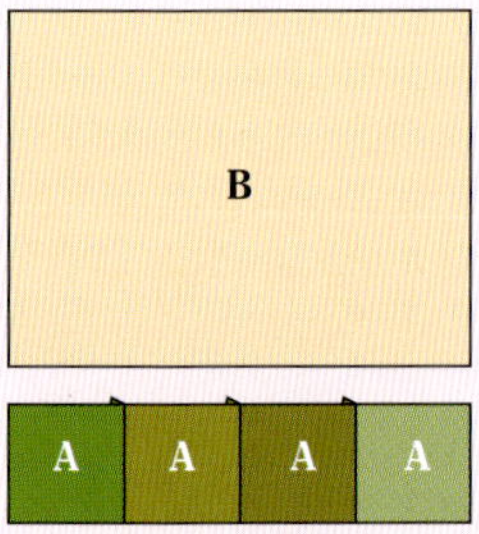

Block Piecing

Applique/Embroidery Placement

Join the A's and B as shown to make the block. Fold the block in half both ways and lightly crease the folds.

Prepare patches C–I for fusible appliqué. Use the creases and the appliqué placement diagram as a guide to arrange the patches on the block; fuse in place. Use matching embroidery floss and a hand blanket stitch to sew around the patches. Use green floss and a chain stitch to embroider the flower stems.

block no. 327

Fantasy Flutterby

by Jo Moury • Nain's Hands

Unit 1
Make 8

Unit 2
Make 4

See page 100 on the PDF for pattern

Light Aqua Solid
1 square (A) $8\frac{1}{2}$″ x $8\frac{1}{2}$″
4 squares (B) $2\frac{7}{8}$″ x $2\frac{7}{8}$″
4 rectangles (C) $2\frac{1}{2}$″ x $4\frac{1}{2}$″

Medium Aqua Batik
4 squares (B) $2\frac{7}{8}$″ x $2\frac{7}{8}$″

Medium Pink Batik
2 squares (B) $2\frac{7}{8}$″ x $2\frac{7}{8}$″
1 *each* patterns E, I, P and R

Light Pink Batik
2 squares (B) $2\frac{7}{8}$″ x $2\frac{7}{8}$″
1 *each* patterns Q and S

Assorted Yellow Batiks
1 *each* patterns D, F–H, J and K

Assorted Light Green Prints and Batiks
bias strip $\frac{3}{8}$″ x 22″
2 pattern L
1 *each* patterns M–O

Green, pink and black embroidery floss

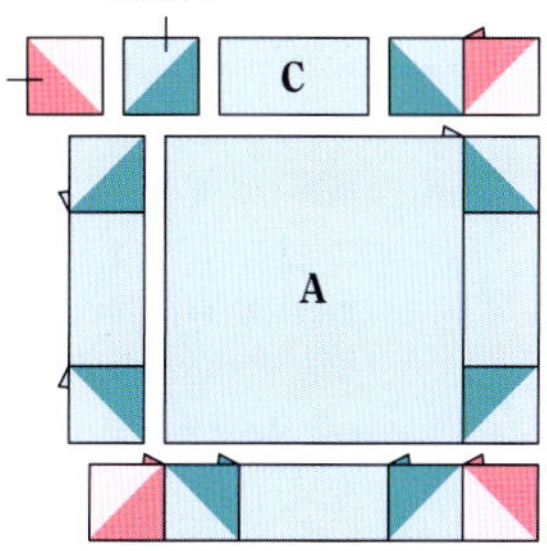

Block Assembly

Applique Placement

Refer to "Triangle-Squares" in the Techniques file on the PDF. Pair the light aqua B's with the medium aqua B's to make 8 unit 1's. Pair the medium pink B's with the light pink B's to make 4 unit 2's. Join the units and patches as shown to make the block.

Refer to "Tiny Bias Stems" in the Techniques file on the PDF. Use the green bias strip to make the stem. Prepare patches D–S for turned-edge appliqué. Fold the block in half both ways and lightly crease the folds. Use the creases and appliqué placement diagram as guides to arrange the patches on the block. Use matching thread and a blind stitch to appliqué the patches in place. Satin stitch the butterfly's body and the flower centers. Use a backstitch, lazy daisy stitch and French knots to add the antennae, flower and stem details.

block no. 328

Swiss Chocolate

by Amanda Murphy • Amanda Murphy Design
amandamurphydesign.com

Fabric: Swiss Chocolate designed by Amanda Murphy for Robert Kaufman, robertkaufman.com.

Tan Tone-on-Tone
4 squares (A) $4\frac{1}{4}$″ x $4\frac{1}{4}$″

Cream Tone-on-Tone
4 rectangles (B) $1\frac{1}{4}$″ x 5″
4 squares (F) 2″ x 2″

Red Print
4 rectangles (C) $\frac{3}{4}$″ x 5″
4 pattern G

Pink Tone-on-Tone
4 rectangles (D) $1\frac{1}{4}$″ x 5″

Brown Stripe
4 rectangles (E) $2\frac{1}{2}$″ x 5″

Brown Print
5 squares (F) 2″ x 2″

Fusible web

Templates for Swiss Chocolate block on page 13 of the Templates file on the PDF

Join the patches as shown to assemble the block. Fold the block in half diagonally both ways and lightly crease the folds. Prepare the G's for fusible appliqué.

Use the creases and appliqué placement diagram as guides to arrange the G's; fuse in place. Use matching thread and a machine blanket stitch to sew around the patches.

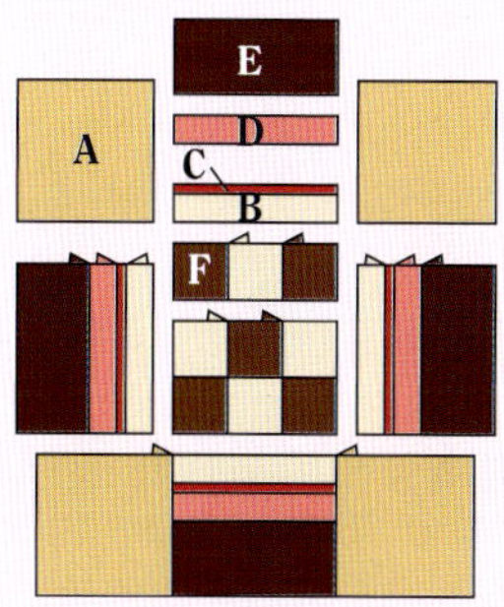

Block Piecing

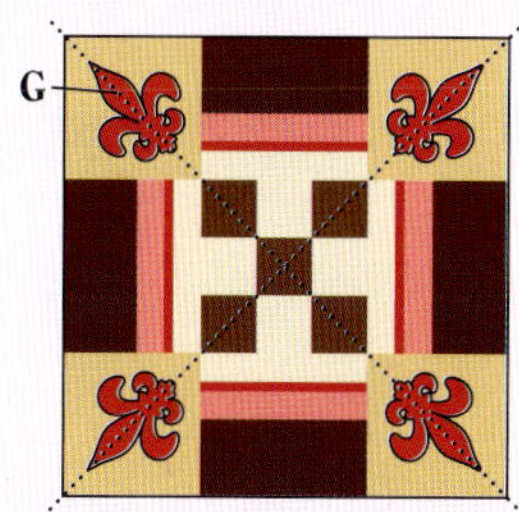

Applique Placement

block no. 329

Say Cheese!

by Joni Pike • Sew Special Designs
sewspecialdesigns.com

Joni Pike is the author of *Cute as a Button Quilts* for C&T Publishing, ctpub.com.

See page 115 on the PDF for pattern

Aqua Dot
1 square (A) 8½″ x 8½″
White Flannel
1 *each* patterns B and C
White Tone-on-Tone
2 rectangles (D) 2½″x 8½″
2 rectangles (E) 2½″x 12½″
Black Solid
4 pattern F
Fusible web
Buttons
5 at ¼″ for mouth, 2 at ½″ for eyes and 1 at 1″ for nose
Black embroidery floss

Fold A in half both ways and lightly crease the folds. Prepare B, C and F patches for fusible appliqué. Use the creases and appliqué placement diagram as guides to arrange B and C on A; fuse in place.

Sew the white D's and E's to A as shown, then fuse the black F's in place.

Use black thread and a machine blanket stitch to sew around the appliqué patches. Use a running stitch and the black embroidery floss to add the smile. Sew on the buttons as shown to complete the block.

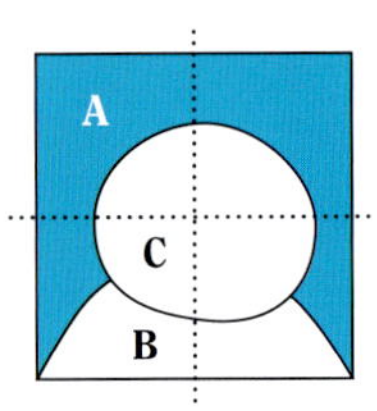

Applique Placement

Block Assembly

block no. 330

Single Beauty

by Dodi Lee Poulsen • Two Sisters at Squirrel Hollow • twosashquilts.com

Fabric: Bliss designed by Bonnie & Camille for Moda Fabrics, unitednotions.com.

Dodi Lee Poulsen is the author of *Fresh Picked* and *Red Hot Redwork* for Two Sisters at Squirrel Hollow, twosashquilts.com.

See pages 13 and 116 on the PDF for pattern

White Tone-on-Tone
section 1, patches 1, 4 and 5
section 2, patches 1 and 10
Red Tone-on-Tone
section 1, patches 2 and 3
2 rectangles (C) 1¼″x 11″
2 rectangles (D) 1¼″x 12½″
Assorted Red Prints
section 2, patches 2–9
Red Print
4 squares (A) 2½″x 2½″
Assorted Blue Prints
8 rectangles (B) 2½″x 3¾″
Assorted Pink Prints
4 *each* patterns E and F
Red button 1 at ½″

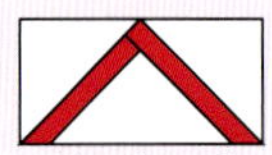

Section 1
Make 1

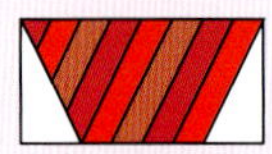

Section 2
Make 1

Make a paper copy of the section 1 and section 2 foundations. Foundation piece each section in numerical order, pressing and trimming after each patch addition. Join the sections and patches as shown.

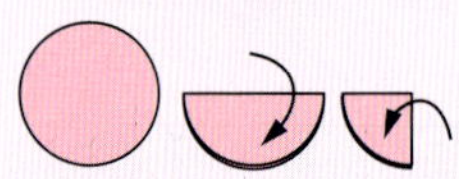

Folded Flower Petals

Using patterns E and F, prepare folded flower petals as shown. Arrange the E petals on the block as shown and tack in place. Arrange the F petals over the E petals and stitch in place. Sew the red button to the center of the F's to complete block.

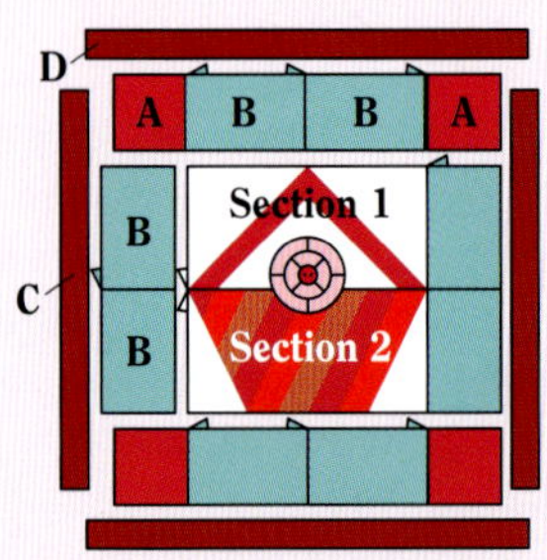

Block Assembly

block no. 331

Spinning Wheels

by Leslee Price • Painted Pony 'n Quilts
ppnq.com

Pink Dot and White Print
from *each*
2 squares (A) 7¼″ x 7¼″
2 circles 5″ diameter
Fusible web

Fold the A's in half both ways and lightly crease the folds. Prepare the circles for fusible appliqué. Use the creases and appliqué placement diagram as guides to arrange the circles on the A's. Pair the pink A's with white circles to make 2 unit 1's as shown. Pair the white A's with pink circles to make 2 unit 2's. Use matching thread and a machine zig-zag stitch to sew around the circles.

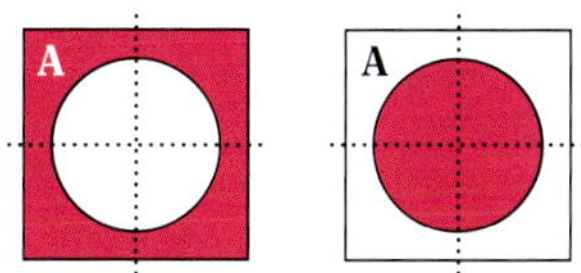

Unit 1 Make 2 **Unit 2** Make 2

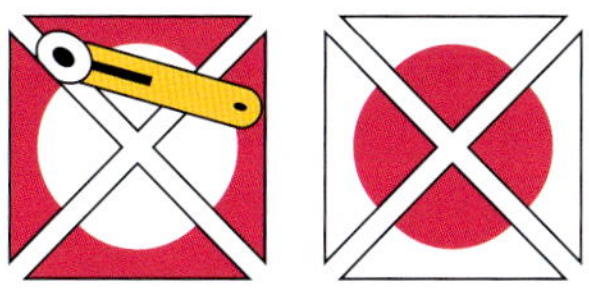

Cut each unit in half twice diagonally as shown; join the triangles as shown to make a section. Make 4 sections. Join the sections as shown to complete the block.

Section Make 4

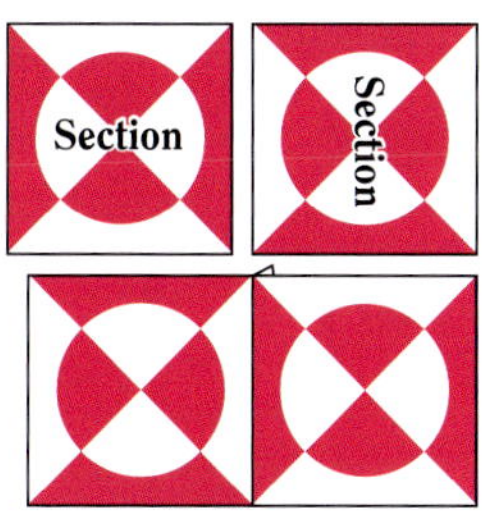

Block Assembly

block no. 332

Rubber Duckie

by Heidi Pridemore • The Whimsical Workshop
thewhimsicalworkshop.com

See page 108 on the PDF for pattern

Light Blue Print
1 square (A) 8½″ x 8½″
Yellow Tone-on-Tone
1 *each* patterns B and F
White Solid
1 pattern C
Black Solid
1 pattern D
Dark Orange Tone-on-Tone
1 pattern E
4 squares (I) 2½″ x 2½″
Dark Blue Print
1 pattern G
Light Orange Tone-on-Tone
4 rectangles (H) 2½″ x 8½″
Fusible web
Black permanent fabric marker

Applique Placement

Fold A in half both ways and lightly crease the folds. Prepare patches B–G for fusible appliqué. Use the creases and appliqué placement diagram as guides to arrange the patches on A. Fuse the patches to A in alphabetical order.

Use black thread and a machine blanket stitch to sew around the appliqué patches. Use a black fabric marker to add the beak detail. Join the patches as shown to complete the block.

Block Assembly

block no. 333

Diamond in the Rough

by Kari Ramsay • Fresh Cut Quilts
freshcutquilts.com

Fabric: Tidbits designed by Kari Ramsay for Henry Glass, henryglass.com.

Kari Ramsay is the author of *Tidbits from Triangles* for Fresh Cut Quilts, freshcutquilts.com.

See page 111 on the PDF for pattern

Light Green Print
patches 1 and 3

Brown Print
patch 2

Brown Tone-on-Tone
patch 4

Pink Print #1
patch 5

Pink Print #2
1 circle 2″ diameter for yo-yo

Make 4 paper copies of the foundation section. Foundation piece each section in numerical order, pressing and trimming after each patch addition.

Section
Make 4

Join the sections as shown to make the block.

Use the pink circle to make a yo-yo. Tack the yo-yo in place at the center to complete the block.

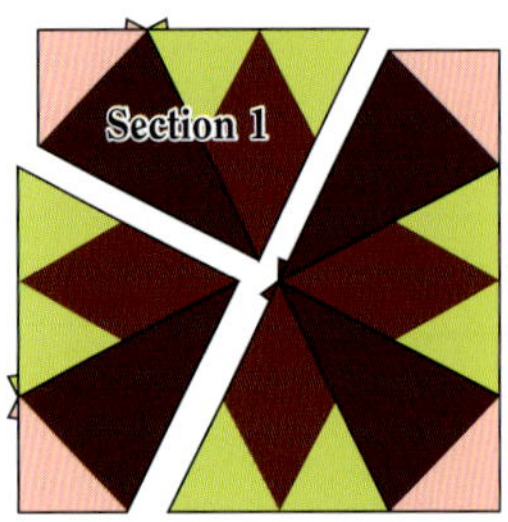

Block Assembly

Yo-yo Placement

block no. 334

Desert Lily

by Caroline Reardon • former *Quiltmaker* Editor

See page 99 on the PDF for pattern

Assorted Gold Prints and Batiks
section 1, patch 1
section 3, patch 1
4 rectangles (A) 1″ x 9½″

Cream Tone-on-Tone
section 1, patches 2, 3, 5, 7, 15, 16, 19 and 20
section 2, patches 2, 3, 6, 7, 10, 11, 14 and 15

Assorted Pink Prints and Batiks
section 1, patches 4, 6 and 8–13
section 3, patches 2–5
4 rectangles (A) 1″ x 9½″

Purple Batik
section 1, patch 14

Assorted Green Batiks
section 1, patches 17 and 18
section 2, patches 4, 5, 8, 9, 12 and 13
section 3, patches 6 and 7

Brown Batik #1
section 2, patch 1

Brown Batik #2
4 rectangles (A) 1″ x 9½″

Section 1
Make 1

Section 2
Make 1

Section 3
Make 4

Make 1 paper copy *each* of foundation sections 1 and 2. Make 4 paper copies of section 3. Notice in the photographed block how the pinks and greens progress from light to dark. Foundation piece each section in numerical order, pressing and trimming after each patch addition.

Join the sections and patches as shown to complete the block.

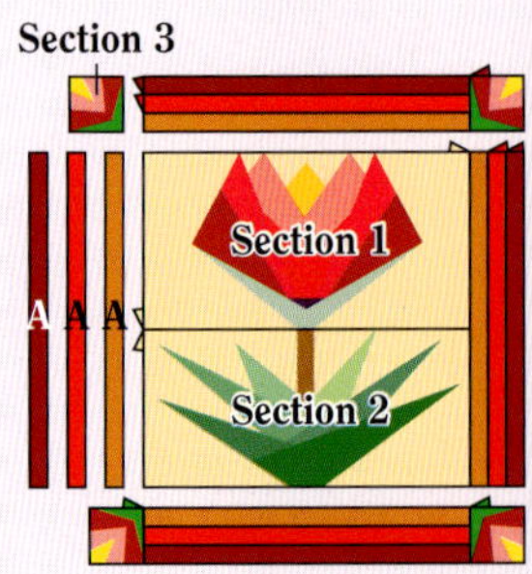

Block Assembly

block no. 335

Patience Puzzle

by Scarlett Rose • Scarlett Rose's Celtic & More
scarlettrose.com

Fabric: Marbled fabrics by Marjorie Bevis for MLB Marbled Fabrics and Accessories, marbledfabrics.com and Color Connectors from FreeSpirit Fabrics, freespiritfabric.com.

Scarlett Rose is the author of both *Celtic Style Floral Appliqué* and *Baskets Celtic Style* for American Quilters Society, americanquilter.com.

Scarlett used a fusible bias-tape maker and fusible web to prepare her bias strips. If you prefer this method, follow the manufacturer's instructions for cutting the bias strips.

Aqua Tone-on-Tone
1 square (A) 8½″ x 8½″
4 Teal Prints
from *each*
1 rectangle (B) 2½″ x 10½″
Gold, Blue, Purple and Pink Tone-on-Tones
from *each*
1 bias strip 1¼″ x 15″
Clover fusible bias tape maker ⅜″ (optional)
Clover 5mm fusible web (optional)

Refer to "Bias Strips" in the Techniques file on the PDF to prepare the bias strips.

Fold A in half horizontally, vertically and diagonally and lightly crease the folds. Refer to the diagram to arrange the bias strips on A, noting that some strips overlap others and some underlap. Pin or baste the strips in place.

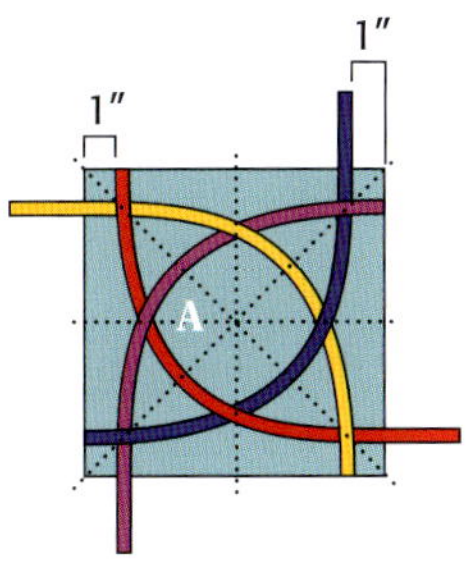

Applique Placement

Pin the extended bias strip edges out of the way; sew a teal B to the right side of A with a partial seam as shown. Sew a B to the bottom, left and top of A. Complete the partial seam. Pin or baste the ends of the bias strips in place.

Using invisible thread, machine blind stitch the strips in place.

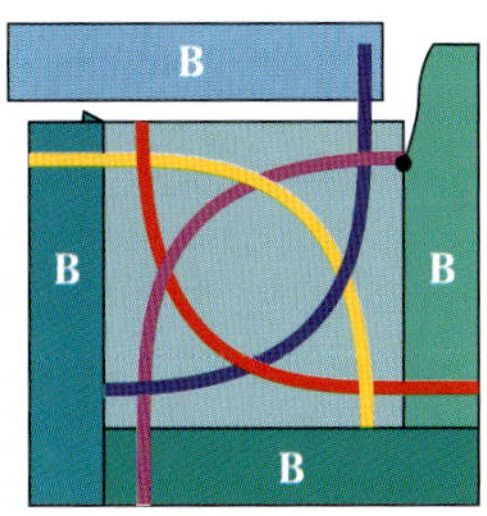

Block Piecing
• = partial seam

block no. 336

Spinner

by Joli Sayasane • Assistant Editor, *Quilters Newsletter*
quiltersnewsletter.com

See page 86 on the PDF for pattern

Dark Purple Tone-on-Tone
section, patch 1
Green Tone-on-Tone
section, patch 2
Pink Tone-on-Tone
section, patch 3
Gold Tone-on-Tone
1 square (A) 13½″ x 13½″
(trim to 12½″ x 12½″ after appliqué)

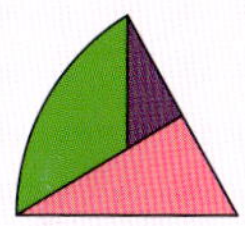
Section
Make 6

Make 6 paper copies of the foundation section. Foundation piece the sections in numerical order, pressing and trimming after each patch addition. Join the sections as shown to make the circle.

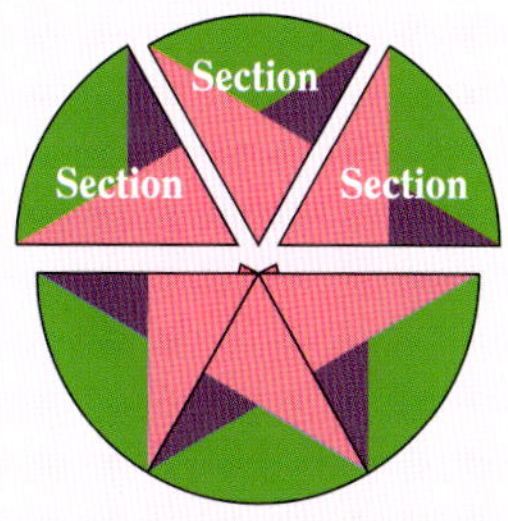

Block Assembly

Fold the circle and the A in half both ways and lightly crease the folds. Prepare the circle for turned-edge appliqué. Use the creases and appliqué placement diagram as guides to arrange the circle on the A. Use matching thread and a blind stitch to appliqué the circle in place. Carefully cut out the background fabric (A) behind the circle. Center the appliqué and trim A to 12½″ × 12½″.

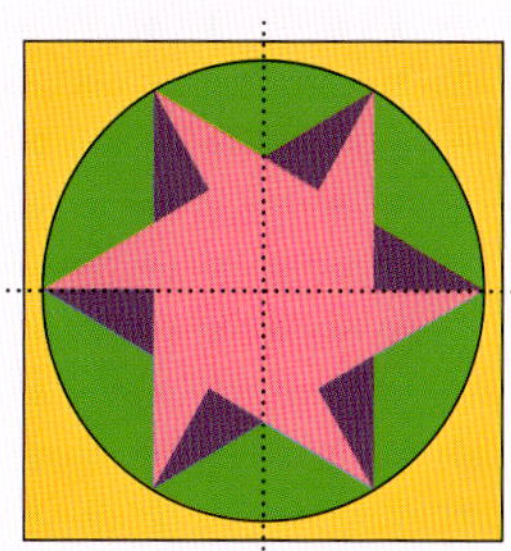
Applique Placement

block no. 337

Pink Lemonade

by Monica Solorio-Snow • Happy Zombie
thehappyzombie.com

Fabric: Sweet Broderie by Rosalie Quinlan for Lecien, lecien.co.jp/en/hobby.

8 Assorted Pink Prints and Yellow Prints
4 squares (A) 7½" x 7½" (trim to 6½" x 6½" after appliqué)
4 pattern B

Fold the A's in half both ways and lightly crease the folds. Prepare the B's for turned-edge appliqué. Use the creases and appliqué placement diagram as guides to arrange one B on each A.

Use matching thread and a blind stitch to appliqué the hexagons in place. Center the appliqués and trim each A to 6½" × 6½". Assemble the patches as shown to complete the block.

Templates for Pink Lemonade block on page 24 of the Templates file on the PDF

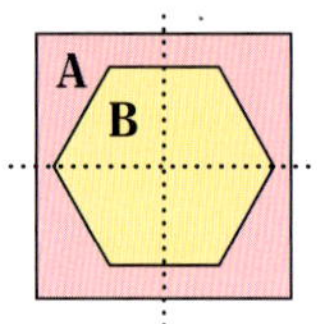

Applique Placement

Block Assembly

block no. 338

Going in Circles

by Paula Stoddard • Associate Editor, *Quiltmaker*
quiltmaker.com

Fabric: Oz designed by Sanae for Moda Fabrics, unitednotions.com.

Paula Stoddard is also the author of several books, including *3 Color Crazy* for Pacific Patchwork, pacificpatchwork.com.

See page 102 on the PDF for pattern

8 Assorted Prints
from *each*
4 squares (A) 3⅞" x 3⅞"

Refer to "Triangle-Squares" in the Techniques file on the PDF. Arrange the fabric into 4 contrasting pairs. From each set of contrasting prints, pair the A's to make 8 units. Make a total of 32 units. Sew 4 matching units together to make a Pinwheel. Make 4 sets of 2 matching Pinwheels.

Make a template of B, adding 3/16" to both sides. Use the template to cut a ring (B) from 1 pinwheel of each set. Prepare the B's for turned-edge appliqué. Use the seam lines as guides to arrange the rings on the matching pinwheels as shown. Use matching thread and a blind stitch to appliqué the rings in place.

Assemble the 4 sections as shown to complete the block.

Unit
Make 32

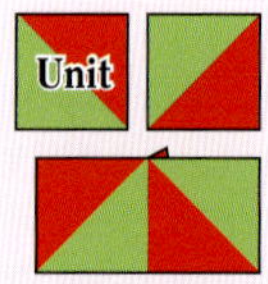

Pinwheel
Make 4 sets of 2 matching

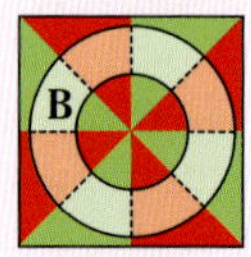

Ring

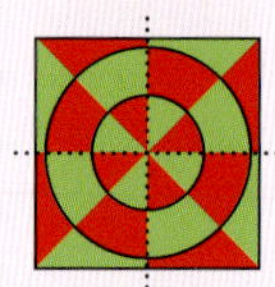

Applique Placement Section
Make 4

Block Assembly

block no. 339

Yo-Yo Glasses

by Debra Taylor • Fat Quarter Shop
fatquartershop.com

Fabric: Sunkissed by Sweetwater for Moda Fabrics, unitednotions.com.

⊠ = cut in half twice diagonally

Pink Stripe
3 squares (A) 4½″ x 4½″

Gray Solid
2 squares (A) 4½″ x 4½″

White Dot, Gray Print, White Print, and Pink Print
from *each*
1 square 5¼″ x 5¼″ ⊠ (B)

5 Assorted White, Gray and Pink Prints
from *each*
1 circle 5″ diameter for yo-yo

Join the B's as shown to make a unit. Make 4 units.

Join the patches and units as shown to make the block.

Make yo-yo's using the circles from the assorted prints. Referring to the placement diagram, center the yo-yo's on the A's and tack in place.

Unit
Make 4

Block Assembly

block no. 340

Joy Framed

by Sarah Vanderburgh
sewjoy.blogspot.com

See page 83 on the PDF for pattern

Green Tone-on-Tone
1 square (A) 6½″ x 6½″
1 square (B) 7¼″ x 7¼″

Yellow Print
4 squares (C) 3⅞″ x 3⅞″

Red Print
4 squares (D) 3½″ x 3½″

White Solid
1 pattern each E–J

Black Tone-on-Tone
1 pattern K

Fusible web

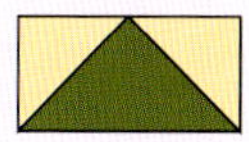

Flying Geese
Make 4

Refer to "Fast Flying Geese" in the Techniques file on the PDF. Use the green B and yellow C's to make 4 Flying Geese. Join the Flying Geese and patches as shown to make the block.

Fold the block in half both ways and lightly crease the folds. Prepare patches E–K for fusible appliqué. Use the creases and appliqué placement diagram as guides to arrange the patches on the block. Fuse the patches to A in alphabetical order. Use matching thread and a blanket stitch to sew around the patches.

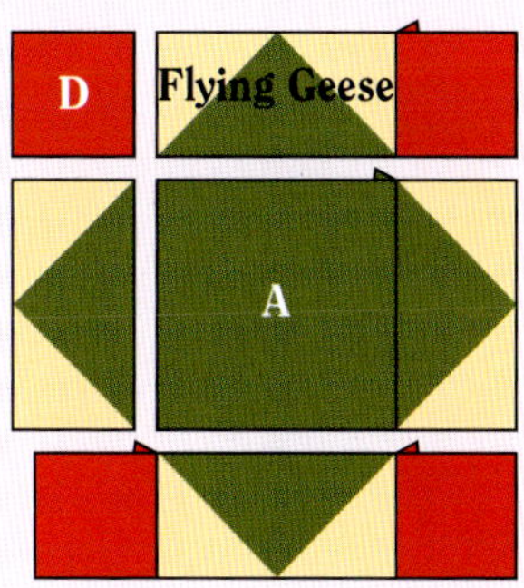

Block Assembly

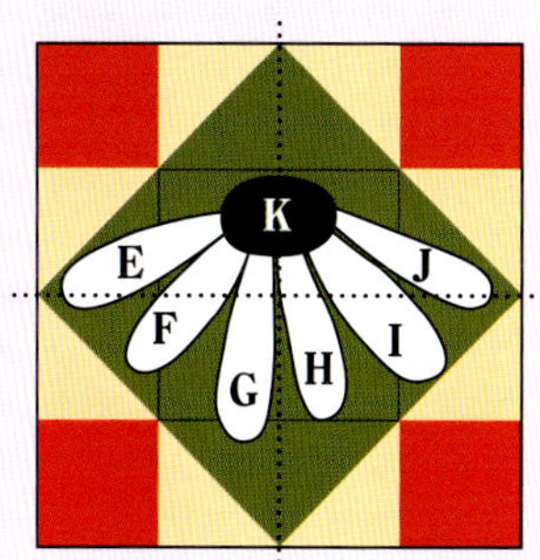

Applique Placement

block no. 341
Horizon

by Vanessa Vargas Wilson • Crafty Gemini
craftygemini.com

See page 90 on the PDF for pattern

White Tone-on-Tone
2 squares (C) 2½″ x 2½″
section patches 1 and 3

Red Solid
section patches 2 and 4

Black Solid
2 rectangles (A) 4½″ x 6½″
2 rectangles (B) 2½″ x 4½″

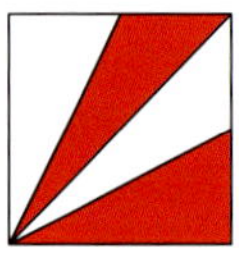

Section
Make 2

Make 2 paper copies of the foundation section. Foundation piece each section in numerical order, pressing and trimming after each patch addition.

Join the sections and patches as shown to complete the block.

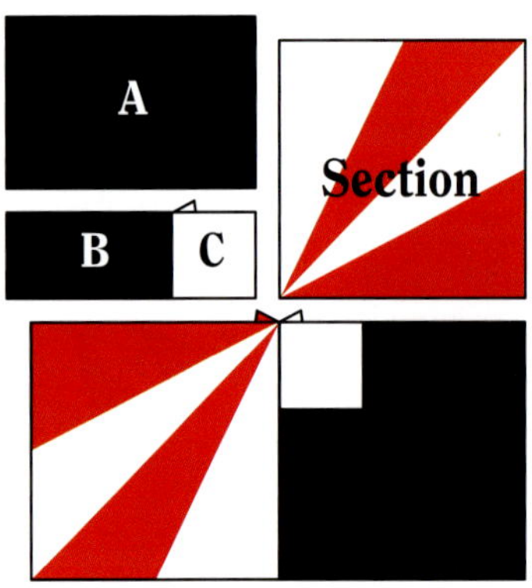

Block Assembly

block no. 342
Privet Patch

by Kathryn Wagar Wright • Senior Designer, *Quilters Newsletter* • quiltersnewsletter.com

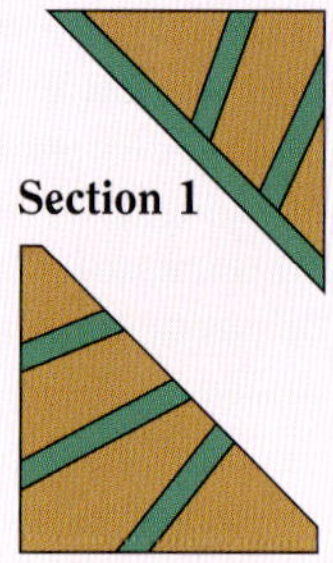

See page 114 on the PDF for pattern

Tan Batik
section 1, patches 1, 3 and 5
section 2, patches 1, 3, 5 and 7

Aqua Batik
sections 1 and 2, patches 2, 4 and 6

Light Green Batik
2 squares (A) 5½″ x 5½″ (trim to 4½″ x 4½″ after appliqué)
1 rectangle 2″ x 15″

Medium Green Batik
1 rectangle 2″ x 15″

Dark Orange Batik
3 squares (A) 5½″ x 5½″ (trim to 4½″ x 4½″ after appliqué)
1 rectangle 2″ x 10″

Light Orange Batik
1 rectangle 2″ x 10″

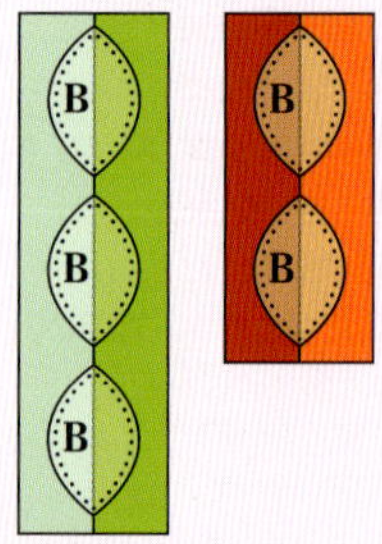

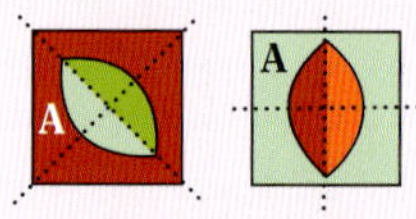

Applique Placement

Make a paper copy of *each* foundation section. Foundation piece the sections in numerical order, pressing and trimming after each patch addition. Join the sections as shown.

Sew the green strips together lengthwise and cut 3 pattern B's as shown. Sew the orange strips together and cut 2 pattern B's as shown. Prepare the leaves for turned-edge appliqué. Fold the A's in half both ways as shown and lightly crease the folds. Use the creases and appliqué placement diagram as guides to arrange the leaves. Use matching thread and a blind stitch to appliqué the leaves in place. Center the appliqués; trim the A's to 4½" × 4½". Join the appliquéd patches to the sections as shown to complete the block.

Block Assembly

block no. 343

How Tweet It Is

by Lynette Anderson • Lynette Anderson Designs
lynetteandersondesigns.com.au

Fabric: Durham Anew by Brenda Riddle for Lecien, lecien.co.jp/en/hobby.

See page 91 on the PDF for pattern

Osnaburg or Tan Tone-on-Tone
1 rectangle (A) 8½″ x 10½″ (trim to 7½″ x 9½″ after appliqué)
Pink Print #1
1 pattern B
Green Print
1 pattern C
2 rectangles (G) 1½″ x 11″
2 rectangles (H) 1¼″ x 10½″
White Print
3 pattern D
Blue Print
2 rectangles (E) 1″ x 9½″
2 rectangles (F) 1¼″ x 8½″
Pink Print #2
2 rectangles (I) 1½″ x 12½″
Assorted Prints
14 circles 1½″ diameter for yo-yos
Brown embroidery thread

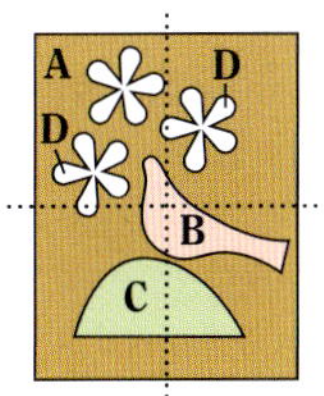

Applique Placement

Fold A in half both ways and lightly crease the folds. Prepare patches B–D for turned-edge appliqué. Use the creases and appliqué placement diagram as guides to arrange the patches on A.

Use matching thread and a blind stitch to appliqué the patches in place. Make 14 yo-yos with assorted prints; tack them in place as shown. Use embroidery thread to add detail to the bird, hill and flowers using a backstitch, satin stitch, crossstitch, running stitches and French knots. Center the appliqué and trim A to 7½" × 9½".

Sew the patches together as shown to complete the block.

Block Assembly

block no. 344

Stepping Stone

by Janice Averill • Iris Quilts and Dyed Fabrics
myspace.com/526795352

Fabric: Mod Floral by Laura Ashley for Quilting Treasures, quiltingtreasures.com.

8 Assorted Prints
from *two*
2 strips (A) 2½″ x 19″
from *two*
2 strips (B) 2½″ x 16″
from *two*
2 strips (C) 2½″ x 11″
from *two*
2 strips (D) 3½″ x 7″
Black Print
1 circle 8¼″ diameter

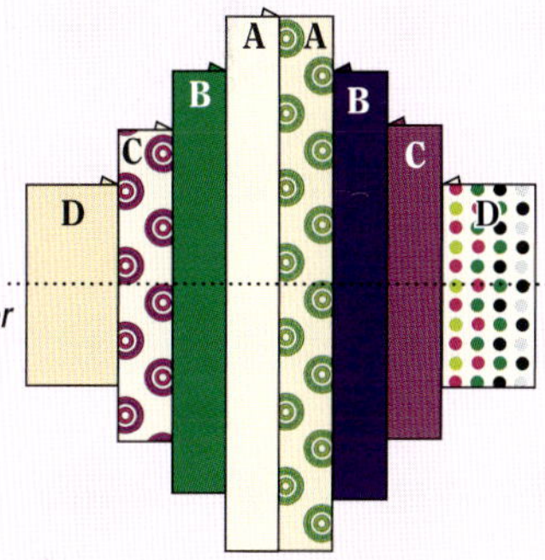

Section Assembly

Matching centers, sew the strips together as shown. Fold the strip section in half both ways and lightly crease the folds. Using the folds as guides, cut a 12½" × 12½" square from the section.

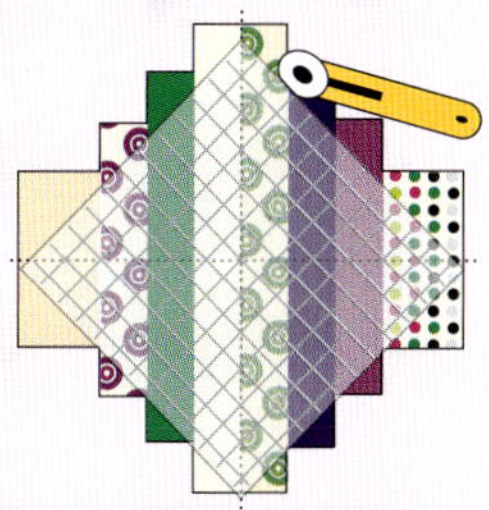

Fold the section in half both ways and lightly crease the folds. Prepare the circle for turned-edge appliqué. Use the creases and appliqué placement diagram as guides to center the circle on the pieced section. Use matching thread and a blanket stitch to appliqué the circle in place. From the wrong side, trim away the excess fabric behind the circle.

Applique Placement

block no. 345

Daisy Maisy

by Cheryl Brown • Quilter Chic
quilterchic.com

Cheryl Brown is the author of *Fresh and Fabulous Quilts* for Martingale & Co., martingale-pub.com.

See page 80 on the PDF for pattern

◸ = cut in half diagonally

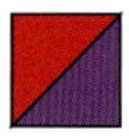

Unit
Make 8

Cream Batik
- 1 square 12⅞" x 12⅞" ◸ (A) (there will be 1 extra)

Red Batik #1
- 1 pattern B
- 6 pattern C
- 4 squares (F) 2⅞" x 2⅞"
- 1 square (I) 2½" x 2½"

Purple Batik
- 1 pattern D
- 4 squares (F) 2⅞" x 2⅞"
- 1 square 2⅞" x 2⅞" ◸ (G)

Red Batik #2
- 1 pattern E

Red Batik #3
- 1 square 8⅞" x 8⅞" ◸ (H) (there will be 1 extra)

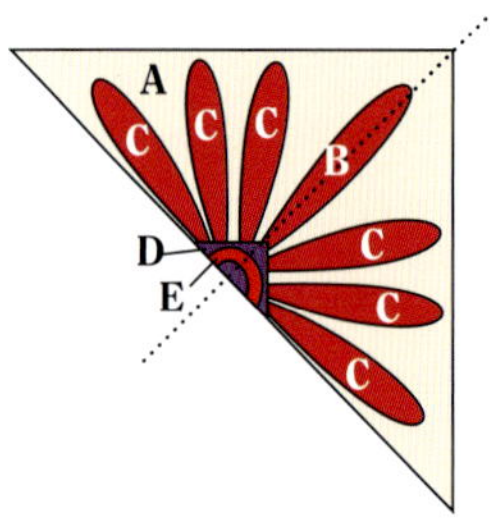

Applique Placement

Fold A in half and lightly crease the fold. Prepare patches B–E for turned-edge appliqué. Use the crease and appliqué placement diagram as guides to arrange the patches on A. Use matching thread and a blind stitch to appliqué the patches in place.

Refer to "Triangle-Squares" in the Techniques file on the PDF. Pair the red and purple F's to make 8 units. Join the units and patches as shown to complete the block.

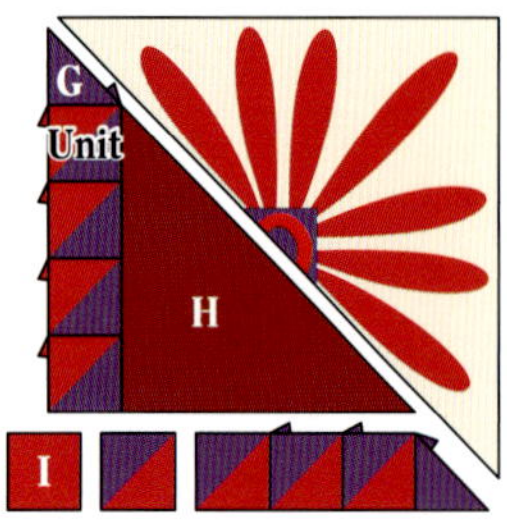

Block Assembly

block no. 346

Golden Gumleaves

by Leesa Chandler • Leesa Chandler Designs
chandlerscottage.com

Fabric: Under the Australian Sun by Leesa Chandler for Robert Kaufman, robertkaufman.com.

See page 102 on the PDF for pattern

Light Gold Tone-on-Tone
- 4 squares (A) 5½" x 5½"

Rust Print
- 2 rectangles (B) 2½" x 5½"
- 1 rectangle (C) 2½" x 12½"
- 8 circles 2¼" diameter for yo-yos

Multiprint
- 8 template (Leesa fussy cut matching D's)

Green Print
- 4 *each* patterns E and Er

Fusible web

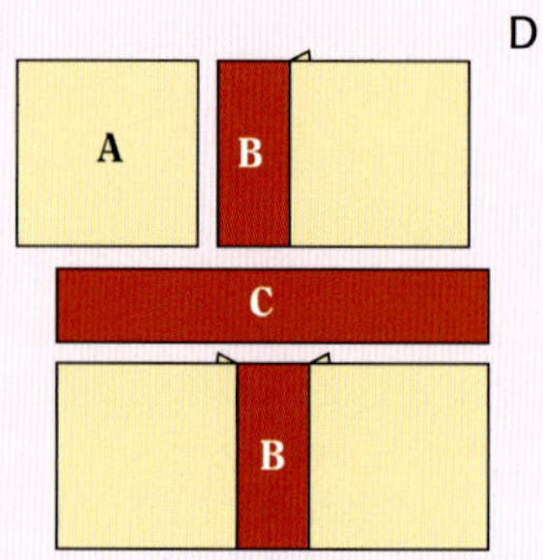

Block Piecing

Join patches A–C to make the block background. Sew the 8 D's together as shown, then prepare the assembled star section for turned-edge appliqué. Fold the background in half both ways and lightly crease the folds. Use the creases and the placement diagram as guides to position the star. Use matching thread and a blind stitch to attach the star to the background.

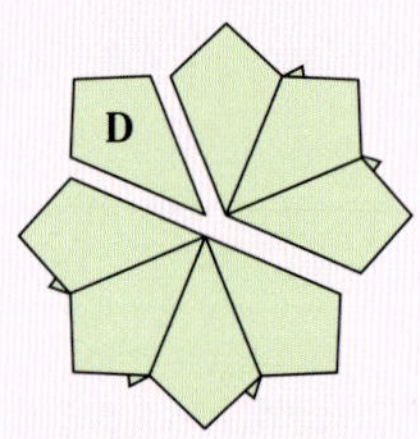

Section Piecing

Prepare patches E and Er for fusible appliqué. Use the placement diagram to arrange the patches. Use matching thread and a small machine blanket stitch to sew around the patches. Make 8 yo-yos from the rust print circles. Tack the yo-yos in place.

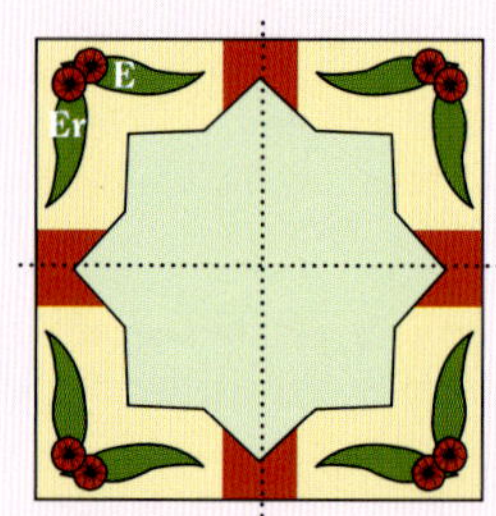

Applique Placement

block no. 347
Annabelle Rae

by Mickey Charleston

Fabric: Annabelle by Hoffman California Fabrics, hoffmanfabrics.com.

Assorted Prints
 14 strips 3″ x 12″
Multiprint
 1 circle (A) 8¼″ diameter
Foundation paper
 1 square 12½″ x 12½″

Mickey fussy cut pattern A from a large-scale floral.

Foundation Paper

To make the foundation section, draw 13 lines on the foundation paper using the illustration to the right as a guide.

Foundation piece the strips to the section starting at the top edge of the section; press and trim after each strip addition.

Section

Prepare pattern A for turned-edge appliqué. Use the assembly diagram to position the patch. Use matching thread and a blind stitch to appliqué the patch in place.

Trim the fabrics to the edge of the foundation paper. Carefully remove the foundation paper.

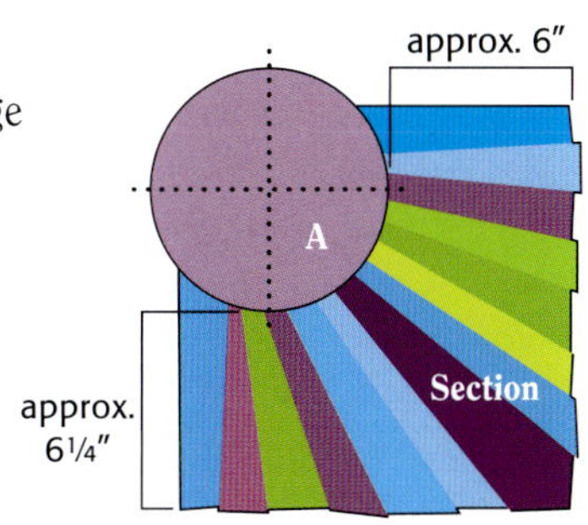

Block Assembly

block no. 348
Zippity Zinnia

by June Dudley • Editor-in-Chief, *Quiltmaker*
quiltmaker.com

Fabric: Artisan Batiks from Lunn Studios for Robert Kaufman, robertkaufman.com, plus scraps.

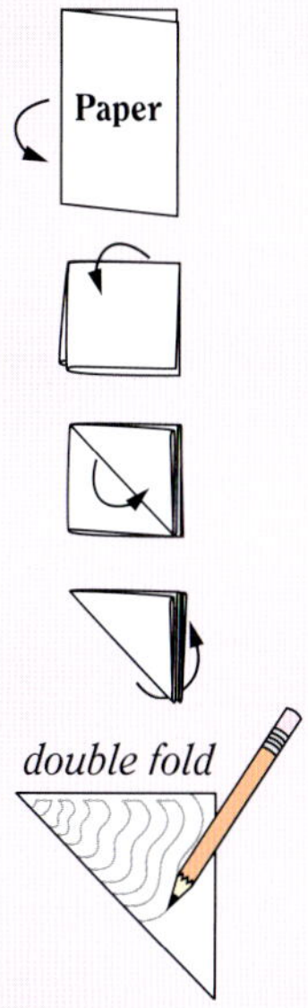

See page 86 on the PDF for pattern

Light Orange Batik
 1 square (A) 11½″ x 11½″ (trim to 10½″ x 10½″ after appliqué)
 4 squares (D) 1½″ x 1½″
Pink Batik
 1 square (B) 10″ x 10″
4 Assorted Green Batiks
from *each*
 1 rectangle (C) 1½″ x 10½″
White Solid and Black Solid
from *each*
 4 squares (D) 1½″ x 1½″
Paper 10″ x 10″
Fusible web

Fold the paper as shown. Trace the flower onto the top panel of the folded paper. Cut on the traced lines through all layers. Unfold the pattern. Trace the flower onto fusible web and fuse to the pink B. Carefully cut on the drawn lines.

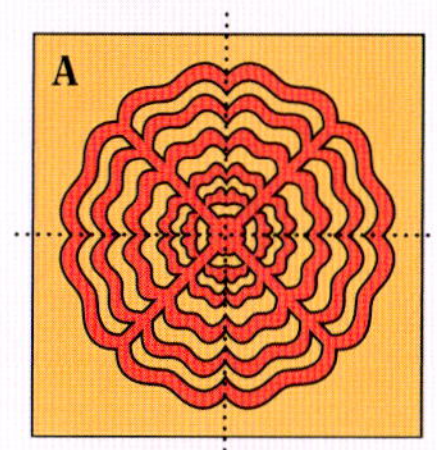

Applique Placement

Fold A in half both ways and lightly crease the folds. Use the folds and the appliqué placement diagram as guides to arrange the flower on A; fuse in place. Use matching thread and a machine blanket stitch to sew around the flower. Center the appliqué and trim A to 10½″ × 10½″.

Stitch & Flip
Unit 1
Make 2

Stitch & Flip
Unit 2
Make 2

Refer to "Stitch-and-Flip" in the Techniques file on the PDF. Use the white and black D's and the green C's to make the unit 1's and 2's as shown. Sew the units and D's to A as shown to complete the block.

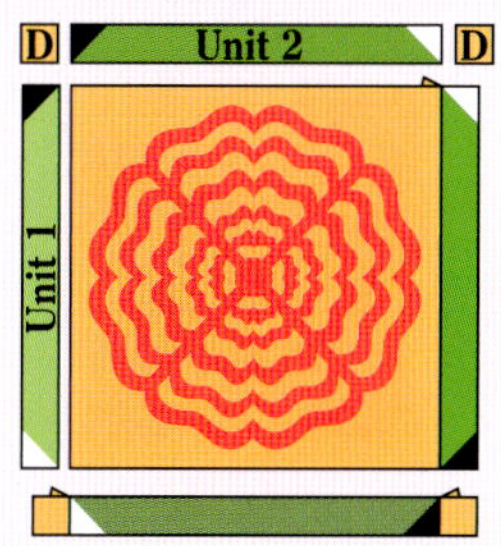

Block Assembly

block no. 349

Pumpkin Patch

by Debbie Field • Granola Girl Designs
granolagirldesigns.com

Fabric: Pheasant and Turkey Season by Debbie Field for Troy Riverwoods Collection, troy-corp.com.

Debbie Field is the author of *Northwoods Flannel Quilts & Projects* for Landauer Corporation, landauercorp.com.

See page 85 on the PDF for pattern

⊠ = cut in half diagonally twice

Cream Print and Tan Print
from *each*
1 square 9¼″ x 9¼″ ⊠ (A) (there will be two extra)

Brown Multiprint
4 rectangles (B) 2½″ x 8½″

Dark Brown Print
4 squares (C) 2½″ x 2½″

Green Tone-on-Tone
1 *each* patterns D, F and G

Orange Tone-on-Tone
1 pattern E

Fusible web

Assemble the patches as shown to make the block. Fold the block in half diagonally both ways and lightly crease the folds.

Prepare patches D–G for fusible appliqué. Use the creases and appliqué placement diagram as guides to arrange the patches on the block. Fuse the patches in alphabetical order.

Use matching thread and a tight machine zigzag stitch to sew around the patches and to add the pumpkin detail to complete the block.

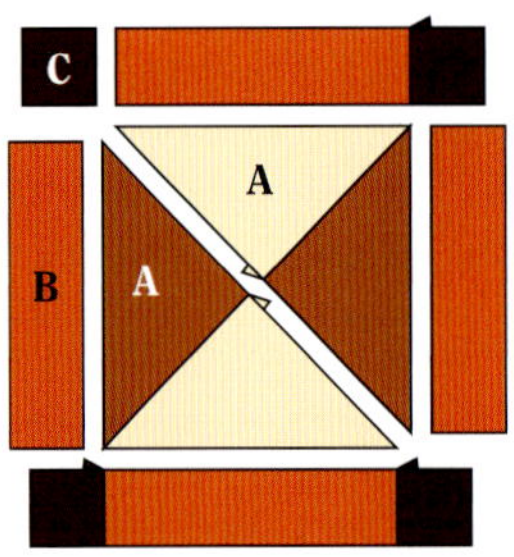

Block Piecing

Applique Placement

block no. 350

Summer Blooms

by Jenny Foltz and Toni Kay Steere • Wing and a Prayer Design • wingandaprayerdesign.com

Fabric: Wildflower Rhapsody designed by Wing and a Prayer Design for Timeless Treasures, ttfabrics.com.

See page 98 on the PDF for pattern

Cream Tone-on-Tone
1 rectangle (A) 8½″ x 10½″
2 rectangles (C) 1½″ x 8½″

Cream Print
12 squares (B) 1½″ x 1½″

Light Green Print #1
8 squares (B) 1½″ x 1½″

Light Green Print #2
4 squares (B) 1½″ x 1½″
4 rectangles (D) 1½″ x 6½″

Assorted Tone-on-Tones
2 *each* patterns E and G
4 pattern F
6 pattern H
3 *each* patterns I, J and K

Fusible web

Buttons 2 at ⅜″, 10 at ¼″

Refer to the block piecing diagrams and join the patches as shown to complete the piecing.

Fold the block in half both ways and lightly crease the folds. Prepare patches E–K for fusible appliqué. Use the creases and the appliqué placement diagram as guides to arrange the patches on A. Fuse the patches to A in alphabetical order. Use matching thread and a machine blanket stitch to sew around the patches. Add the ⅜″ buttons to the large flowers and the ¼″ buttons to the remaining flowers.

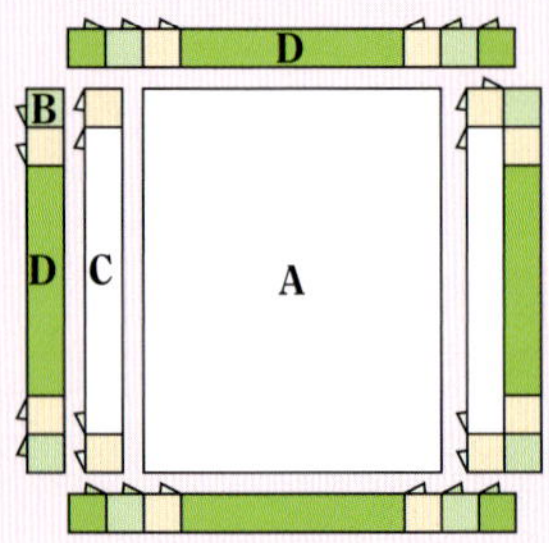

Block Piecing

Applique Placement

block no. 351

Sunnyside Up

by Susan Geddes • Art Director, *Quilters Newsletter*
quiltersnewsletter.com

See page 109 on the PDF for pattern

⊠ = cut in half twice diagonally

Purple Tone-on-Tone
1 rectangle (A) $6\frac{1}{2}$" x $12\frac{1}{2}$"
1 *each* templates J and Jr
Green Tone-on-Tone
1 *each* patterns B, C and D
3 pattern E
Cream Tone-on-Tone
3 pattern F
Gold Batik
3 pattern G
Orange Print
4 squares (H) $2\frac{5}{8}$" x $2\frac{5}{8}$"
Rust Print
2 squares (H) $2\frac{5}{8}$" x $2\frac{5}{8}$"
2 squares $4\frac{1}{4}$" x $4\frac{1}{4}$" ⊠ (I)
(there will be 2 extra)
Fusible web

Applique Placement

Block Piecing

Applique Placement

Fold A in half crosswise and lightly crease the fold. Prepare patches B–G for fusible appliqué. Use the crease and appliqué placement diagram as guides to arrange all of the patches except for the lower flower (F and G) on A as shown. Fuse in place.

Assemble the patches as shown to make the bottom half of the block. Join the 2 block halves; fuse the remaining flower. Using matching thread and a straight stitch, sew close to the edges of each appliqué patch.

block no. 352

Appalachian Spring

by Pamela Griffin

See page 78 on the PDF for pattern

⧄ = cut in half diagonally

Light Blue Batik
1 square (A) 9" x 9"
Green Tone-on-Tone
2 squares $6\frac{7}{8}$" x $6\frac{7}{8}$" ⧄ (B)
4 pattern C
1 *each* patterns D–F
Pink Tone-on-Tone
2 pattern G
1 pattern I
Purple Tone-on-Tone
2 pattern H
1 pattern J
Gray Batik
1 *each* patterns K and L
Black Print
1 pattern M
Fusible web
Embroidery thread

Assemble the patches as shown to make the block. Fold the block in half both ways and lightly crease the folds. Prepare patches C–M for fusible appliqué. Use the creases and appliqué placement diagram as guides to arrange the patches on the block. Fuse the patches to the block in alphabetical order.

Sew around the appliqué patches using matching thread and a machine zigzag stitch. Use embroidery thread and a stem stitch and French knots to add the detail to the leaves and dragonfly.

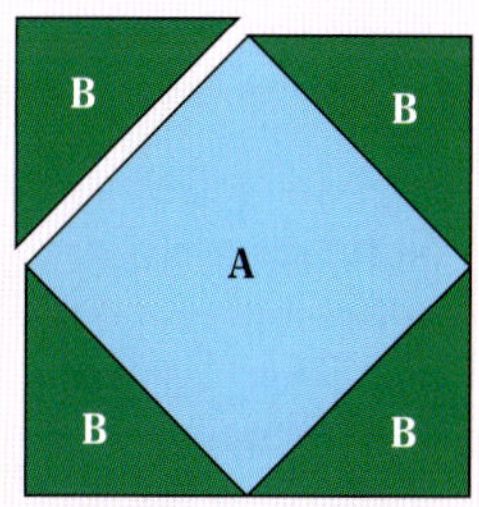

Block Piecing

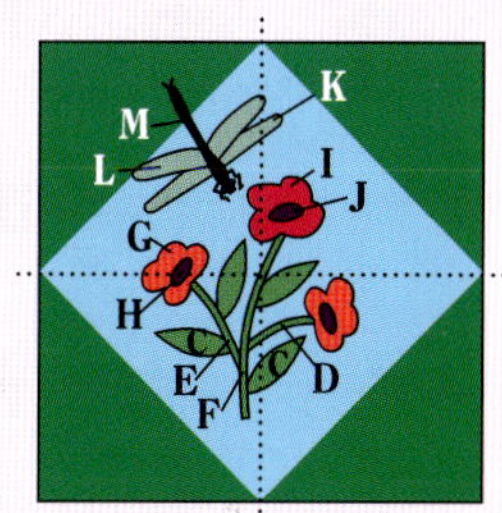

Applique Placement

block no. 353

Wedding Cake

by Melissa Harris and Arlene Stamper
The Quilt Company • quiltcompany.com

Fabric: Scarborough Fair by Robyn Pandolph for RJR Fabrics, rjrfabrics.com.

See pages 24 and 88 on PDF for patterns

Pink Tone-on-Tone
1 rectangle (A) 2¼″ x 4″
1 rectangle (B) 2½″ x 5½″
1 rectangle (C) 5″ x 7″

Cream Dot
4 squares (D) 1″ x 1″
2 squares (E) 1¼″ x 1¼″
1 rectangle (F) 4¼″ x 12½″
2 rectangles (G) 2¼″ x 4¾″
2 rectangles (H) 2½″ x 4″
2 rectangles (I) 3¼″ x 5″

Cream Print
1 *each* patterns J–L

Red Solid
1 pattern M

Aqua Print
1 *each* patterns N and Nr

Perle buttons
9 at 3/16″

Fusible web

Unit 1
Stitch & Flip

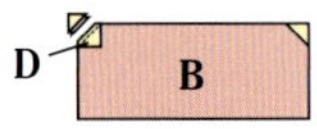

Unit 2
Stitch & Flip

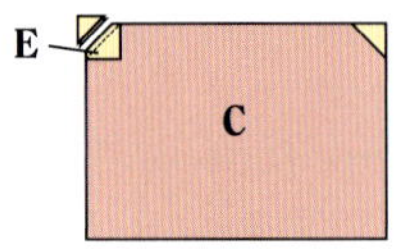

Unit 3
Stitch & Flip

Refer to "Stitch-and-Flip" in the Techniques file on the PDF. Use the pink A and B and the cream dot D's to make units 1 and 2 as shown. Pair the pink C and cream dot E's to make unit 3. Join the units and patches as shown to make the block.

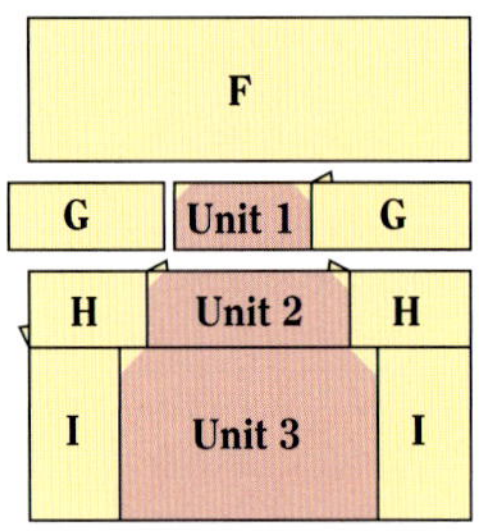

Block Assembly

Prepare patches J–Nr for fusible appliqué. Use the appliqué placement diagram as a guide to arrange the patches on the block. Fuse the patches in alphabetical order. Use matching thread and a machine blanket stitch to sew around the patches. Add the buttons as shown to complete the block.

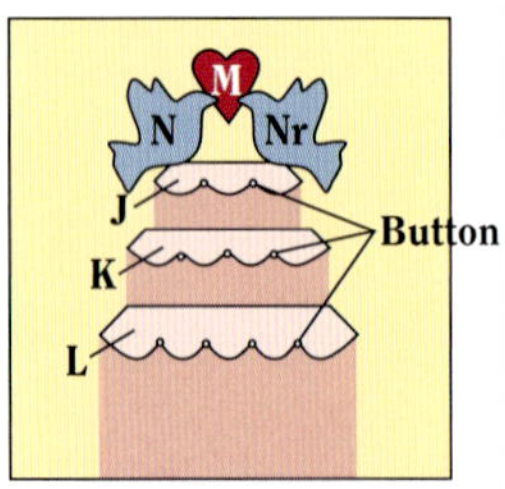

Applique Placement

block no. 354

Blossom Block

by Rebecca LoGiudice • Willow Hill Quilts
willowhillquilts.net

See page 79 on the PDF for pattern

Light Orange Batik
1 square (A) 6½″ x 6½″

Medium Orange Batik
4 squares (B) 2″ x 2″
4 rectangles (E) 2″ x 6½″

Brown Batik
1 pattern C

Dark Brown Print
1 pattern D

Dark Orange Print
8 squares (B) 2″ x 2″
8 squares (F) 3½″ x 3½″

Cream Tone-on-Tone
4 rectangles (E) 2″ x 6½″
4 squares (G) 3½″ x 3½″

Lightweight interfacing

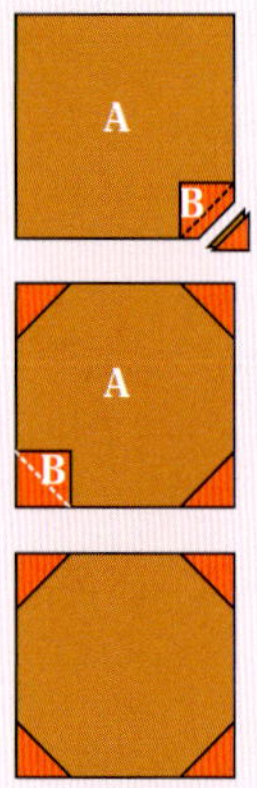

Unit 1
Stitch & Flip
Make 1

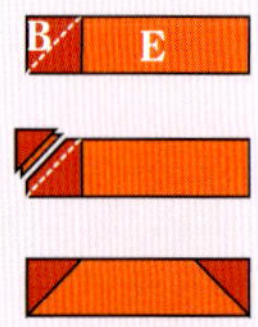

Unit 2
Stitch & Flip
Make 4

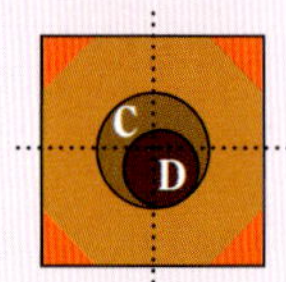

Applique Placement

Refer to the Techniques file on the PDF for all techniques. Use the light orange A and the medium orange B's to make unit 1. Fold unit 1 in half both ways and lightly crease the folds. Refer to "Perfect Appliqué Circles" to prepare patches C and D. Use the appliqué placement diagram to arrange C and D on unit 1. Use matching thread and a machine blind stitch to sew around the edges of C and D. Use the stitch-and-flip method to make 4 unit 2's using the medium orange E's and the dark orange B's.

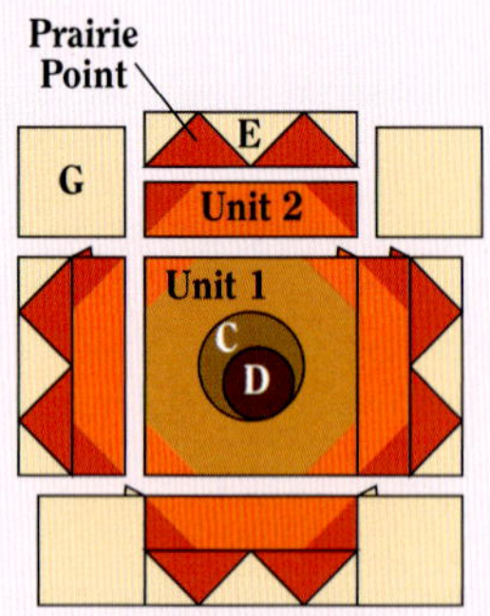

Block Assembly

Refer to the "Prairie Point" technique and use the dark orange F's to make 8 Prairie Points. Arrange the Prairie Points, folded edges down, on the cream tone-on-tone E's and baste using a ⅛" seam allowance.

Join the patches and units as shown to make the block.

mixed technique

block no. 355

Posie Patch

by Nancy Mahoney
nancymahoney.com

Fabric: Nellie's Garden designed by Nancy Mahoney for P&B Textiles, pbtex.com. Thread: Sulky threads, sulky.com.

Nancy Mahoney has authored 10 books for Martingale and Co. Her newest book is *Treasures from the 30's*. Martingale and Co., martingale-pub.com.

Yellow Print
- 2 squares (A) 4⅞" x 4⅞"
- 4 pattern F

Pink Print #1
- 2 squares (A) 4⅞" x 4⅞"

Cream Solid
- 4 squares (B) 5½" x 5½" (trim to 4½" x 4½" after appliqué)

Green Print #1
- 4 pattern C
- 8 Pattern D

Pink Print #2
- 4 pattern E

Green Print #2
- 1 square (G) 4½" x 4½"

Fusible web

Unit
Make 4

Templates for Posie Patch block on page 25 of the Templates file on the PDF

Refer to "Triangle-Squares" in the Techniques file on the PDF. Use the A's to make 4 units.

Fold the cream B's in half both ways; lightly crease the folds. Prepare patches C–F for fusible appliqué. Use the creases and the appliqué placement diagram as guides to arrange the patches on the B's. Fuse the patches in alphabetical order. Use matching thread and a machine blanket stitch to sew around all of the appliqué patches. Center the appliqué and trim the B's to 4½" × 4½". Join the units and patches as shown to complete the block.

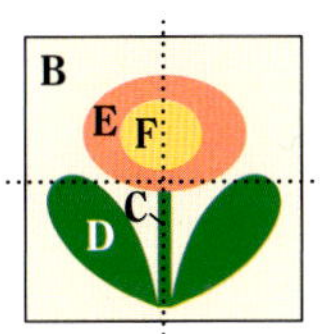

Applique Placement

Block Assembly

block no. 356

Spring Beauties

by Rochelle Martin • Cottage Quilt Designs
cottagequiltdesigns.info

See pages 25 and 86 on the PDF for pattern

Cream Tone-on-Tone
- 5 squares (A) 4½" x 4½"
- 8 squares (B) 2½" x 2½"

Blue Tone-on-Tone
- 4 squares (A) 4½" x 4½"

Pink Tone-on-Tone #1
- 4 *each* patterns C and D

Green Tone-on-Tone
- 8 pattern E

Pink Tone-on-Tone #2
- 4 pattern F

Gold Tone-on-Tone
- 4 circles 2¼" diameter for yo-yos

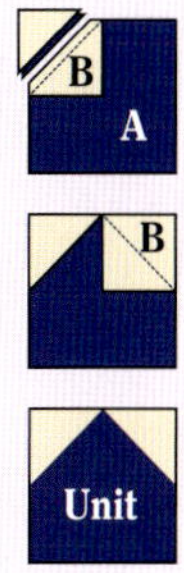

Unit
Stitch & Flip
Make 4

Refer to "Stitch-and-Flip" in the Techniques file on the PDF. Use the blue A's and the cream B's to make 4 units. Assemble the patches and units as shown to make the block.

Fold the block in half horizontally, vertically and diagonally and lightly crease the folds. Prepare patches C–F for turned-edge appliqué.

Use the creases and appliqué placement diagram as guides to arrange the patches on the block. Use matching thread and a blind stitch to appliqué the patches in place. Use the gold circles to make 4 yo-yos. Tack them to the F's as shown to complete the block.

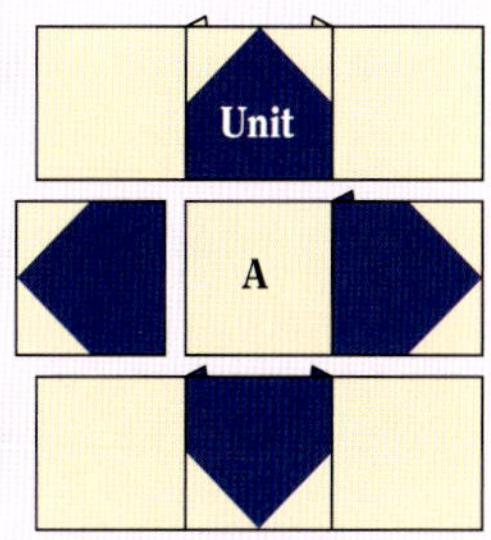

Block Assembly

Applique Placement

block no. 357

A Bird in the Hand

by Cheryl Brown • QuilterChic
quilterchic.com

Cheryl Brown is the author of *Fresh and Fabulous Quilts* for Martingale & Co., martingale-pub.com.

See page 150 on the PDF for pattern

Pale Orange Batik
10 rectangles (A) 2½″ x 4½″
1 square (C) 9½″ x 9½″ (trim to 8½″ x 8½″ after appliqué)
Medium Blue Batik
20 squares (B) 2½″ x 2½″
1 pattern E
Gold Batik
1 *each* patterns D and F
Teal Batik
1 *each* patterns G and K
Light Red Batik
1 *each* patterns H and I
Cream Batik
1 pattern J
Red Batik
1 *each* patterns L and M
Black embroidery floss

Unit
Stitch & Flip
Make 10

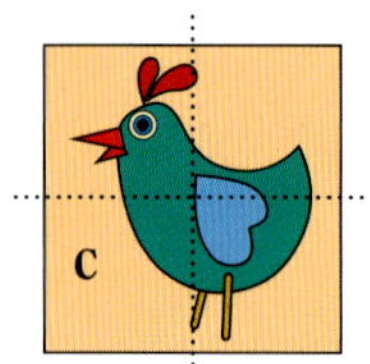

Applique Placement

Refer to "Stitch-and-Flip" in the Techniques file on the PDF. Make 10 units using the pale orange A's and the blue B's.

Fold C in half both ways and lightly crease the folds. Prepare patches D–M for turned-edge appliqué. Use the creases and appliqué placement diagram as guides to arrange the patches on C. Use matching thread and a blind stitch to appliqué the patches in place. Use the embroidery floss and a satin stitch to embroider the eye. Center the appliqué and trim C to 8½" × 8½".

Sew the appliquéd C patch and the units together as shown to complete the block.

Block Assembly

block no. 358

Grandma's Apron

by Lisa Burmann • Burmann Studios
burmannstudios.com

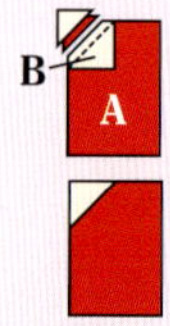

Unit 1
Stitch & Flip
Make 1

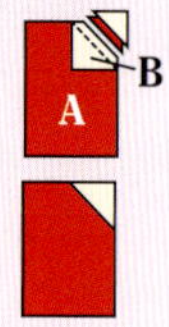

Unit 1r
Stitch & Flip
Make 1

See page 135 on the PDF for pattern

Red Print
2 rectangles (A) 3″ x 4″
2 rectangles (E) 2″ x 3½″
sections 1 and 2, patches 1 and 3
section 3, patches 2 and 4
White Solid
2 squares (B) 1¾″ x 1¾″
2 rectangles (D) 2″ x 3″
2 squares (F) 2″ x 2″
2 rectangles (H) 1½″ x 4½″
section 2, patch 5
section 3, patches 3 and 5
Red and White Print
2 rectangles (C) 1½″ x 3″
sections 1 and 2, patch 4
Yellow Tone-on-Tone
1 rectangle (G) 3½″ x 4½″
section 3, patch 1
Green Stripe
1 rectangle (H) 1½″ x 4½″
sections 1 and 2, patch 2
Lace 18″ long
Buttons 3 at ⅜″

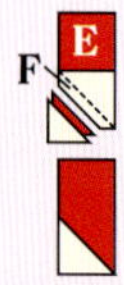

Unit 2
Stitch & Flip
Make 1

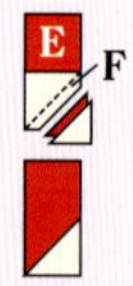

Unit 2r
Stitch & Flip
Make 1

Section 1
Make 1

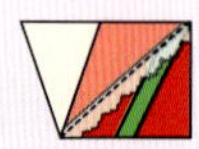

Section 2
Make 1

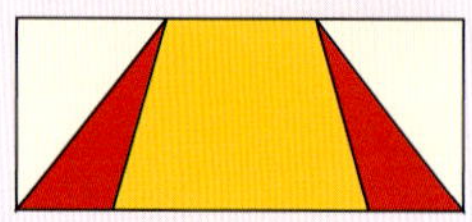

Section 3
Make 1

Refer to "Stitch-and-Flip" in the Techniques file on the PDF. Use the red A's and white B's to make units 1 and 1r. Use the red E's and white F's to make units 2 and 2r.

Make 1 paper copy of each foundation section. Foundation piece each section in numerical order, pressing and trimming after each patch addition.

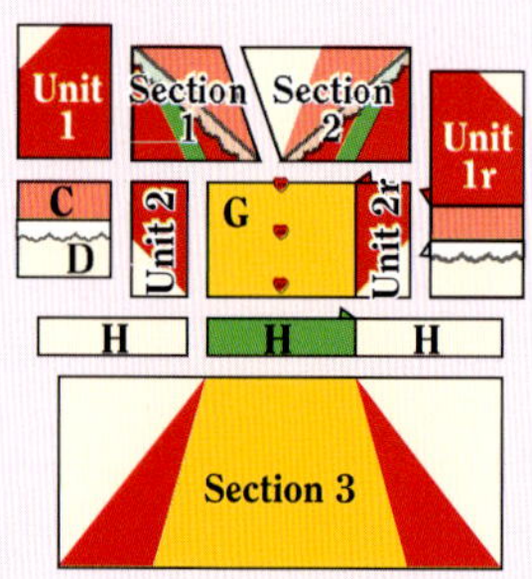

Block Assembly

Use a straight stitch to attach the lace over the seam lines for the collar and sleeves as shown. Sew the sections and units together as shown. Sew the buttons in place to complete the block.

block no. 359

Basket of Love

by Tina Conner

Quick Yo-yo Maker Heart Shaped (small) can be found at clover-usa.com.

See page 152 on the PDF for pattern

White Tone-on-Tone
1 square (A) 13½″ x 13½″
(trim to 12½″ x 12½″ after appliqué)
Brown Print
1 pattern B
Light Green Solid
7 pattern C
Assorted Prints
14 circles 4½″ diameter for yo-yos (see below)
Dark brown jumbo rickrack 20″ long
Perle buttons 14 at ½″
Small Clover Yo-yo Maker Heart Shaped (optional)

Tina made her yo-yos in the shape of hearts using the Clover heart shaped yo-yo maker. Round yo-yos, using the instructions and circle templates on could be used as well.

Follow the manufacturer's instructions to make 14 yo-yo hearts with the assorted prints. Prepare patches B–C for turned-edge appliqué.

Fold A in half both ways and lightly crease the folds. Use the creases and appliqué placement diagram as guides to arrange the rickrack, basket and leaves on A. Use matching thread and a blind stitch to appliqué the rickrack and patches in place. Tack the yo-yos in place as shown. Sew a button to the center of each yo-yo. Center the appliqué and trim A to 12½" × 12½".

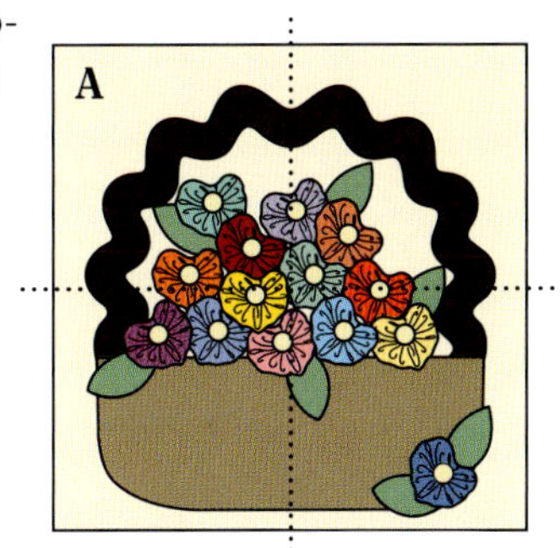

Applique Placement

block no. 360

Fantasy Flower

by Sharyn Craig
sharyncraig.com

Sharyn Craig is a quilt instructor and the designer of the *Cutting Corners Ruler*. She has authored numerous quilting titles including *Layer 'em Up #'s* 1, 2, and 3 for Cozy Quilt Designs, cozyquilt.com.

See page 119 on the PDF for pattern

Light Green Tone-on-Tone
1 square (A) 9¼″ x 9¼″
Cream Print
4 squares (B) 4⅞″ x 4⅞″
1 square (C) 4½″ x 4½″
Dark Green Tone-on-Tone #1
bias strip 1¼″ x 11″
Red Tone-on-Tone
4 pattern D
Gold Print
1 pattern E
Dark Green Tone-on-Tone #2
2 pattern F

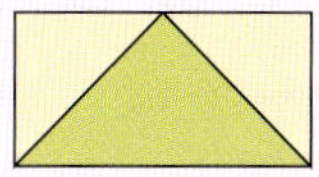

Flying Geese
Make 4

For all techniques, refer to the Techniques file on the PDF. Make 4 Flying Geese using the A and B's. Sew a Flying Geese unit to the right side of C with a partial seam. Sew a Flying Geese unit to the top, left, and bottom as shown. Complete the partial seam to finish the block background.

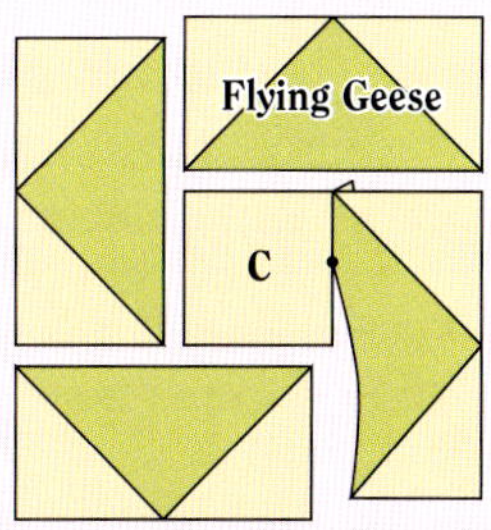

Block Assembly

Fold the block in half both ways and lightly crease the folds. Refer to "Bias Strips" to make the stem. Prepare patches D–F for turned-edge appliqué. Use the creases and appliqué placement diagram as guides to arrange the patches on the block. Use matching thread and a blind stitch to appliqué the patches in place to complete the block.

Applique Placement

block no. 361

Egg-cited

by Susan Geddes • Art Director, *Quilters Newsletter*
quiltersnewsletter.com

See page 153 on the PDF for pattern

⊠ = cut in half twice diagonally

Medium Purple Tone-on-Tone
1 rectangle (A) $6\frac{1}{2}$" x $12\frac{1}{2}$"

Yellow Tone-on-Tone
1 pattern B

Dark Red Print
1 pattern C

Orange Print #1
1 pattern D

5 Assorted Light and Medium Prints
from *each*
1 pattern E

Orange Print #2
4 squares (F) $2\frac{5}{8}$" x $2\frac{5}{8}$"

Brown Print
2 squares (F) $2\frac{5}{8}$" x $2\frac{5}{8}$"
2 squares $4\frac{1}{4}$" x $4\frac{1}{4}$" ⊠ (G) (there will be two extra)

Dark Purple Tone-on-Tone
1 *each* templates H and Hr

Fusible web

Black Micron Pigma pen

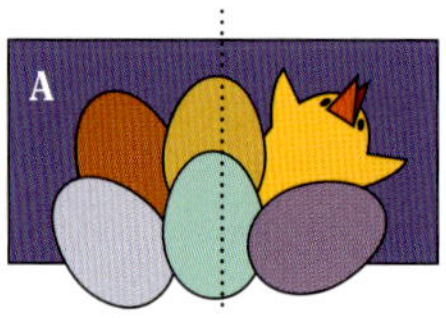

Applique Placement

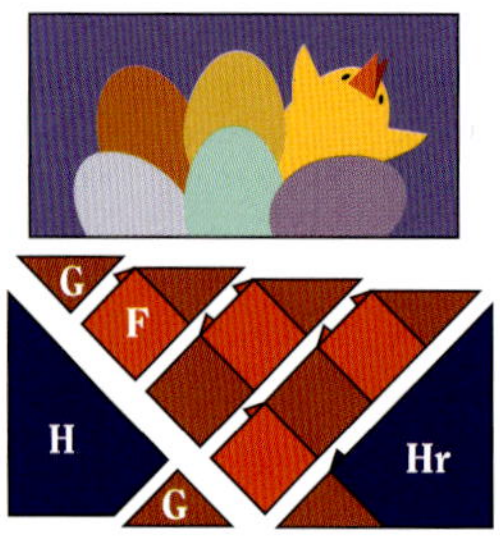

Block Assembly

Fold A in half crosswise and lightly crease the fold. Prepare patches B–E for fusible appliqué. Use the crease and appliqué placement diagram as guides to arrange the patches on A; fuse in place. Using matching thread and a straight stitch, sew close to the edges of each appliqué patch. Draw the chick's eyes with the black pen. Trim the bottom of the E's along the bottom edge of A.

Sew the patches together as shown to make the bottom half of the block. Join the top and bottom halves to complete the block.

block no. 362

Blue Fish

by Bev Getschel • Bev Getschel Designs

Fabric: Night and Day by Skipping Stones Studio and Shades by Kinkame, both for Clothworks, clothworks.com.

See page 132 on the PDF for pattern

Assorted White Prints
5 squares (A) $2\frac{7}{8}$" x $2\frac{7}{8}$"
5 rectangles (C) $2\frac{1}{2}$" x $10\frac{1}{2}$"

Black Print
5 squares (A) $2\frac{7}{8}$" x $2\frac{7}{8}$"
1 square (B) $2\frac{1}{2}$" x $2\frac{1}{2}$"
1 *each* patterns E–H

Blue Print
1 pattern D

Fusible web

Unit
Make 10

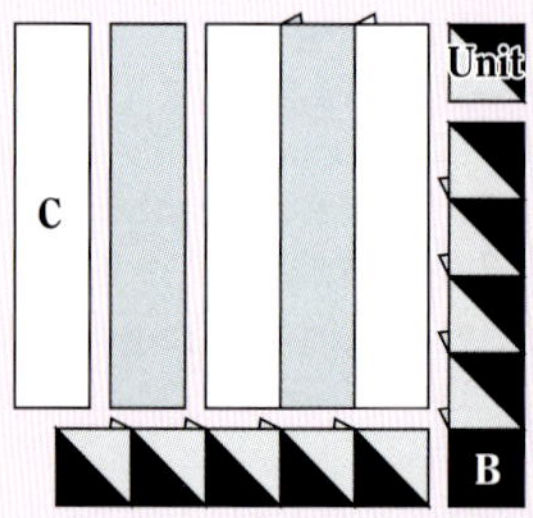

Block Assembly

Refer to "Triangle-Squares" in the Techniques file on the PDF. Make 10 units using the white and black A's. Sew the patches and units together as shown to make the block background.

Fold the block background in half both ways and lightly crease the folds. Prepare D–H for fusible appliqué. Use the creases and appliqué placement diagram as guides to arrange the patches on the background; fuse in place. Use matching thread and a satin stitch to sew around the patches. Use a small satin stitch for the fish details and a straight stitch for the mouth to complete the block.

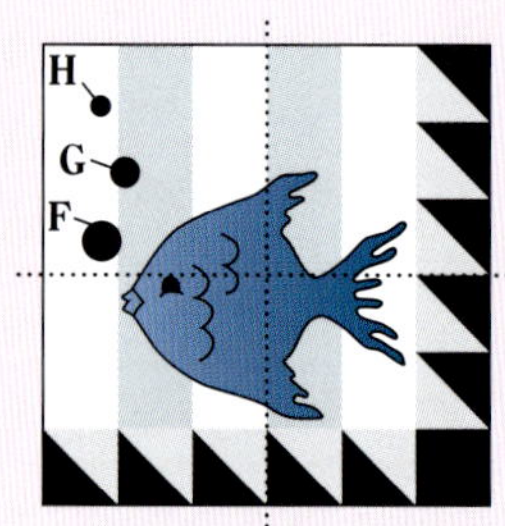

Applique Placement

block no. 363

Safe Harbor

by Pamela Griffin

See page 152 on the PDF for pattern

Light Blue Tone-on-Tone
1 square (A) 6½″ x 6½″
Assorted Prints and Tone-on-Tones
1 set of appliqué patches B–I
White Tone-on-Tone
16 squares (J) 1½″ x 1½″
4 rectangles (K) 1½″ x 6½″
Blue Solid
12 squares (J) 1½″ x 1½″
4 rectangles (K) 1½″ x 6½″
Red Solid
8 squares (J) 1½″ x 1½″
4 rectangles (K) 1½″ x 6½″
Fusible web
Black embroidery thread

Fold A in half both ways and lightly crease the folds. Prepare patches B–I for fusible appliqué.

Use the creases and appliqué placement diagram as guides to arrange the patches on A. Fuse the patches to A in alphabetical order. Use matching thread and a machine zigzag stitch to sew around the patches. Embroider the seagulls with a backstitch.

Join the J's and K's to the appliquéd A as shown to complete the block.

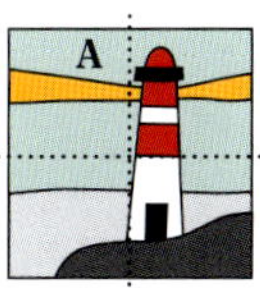

Applique Placement

Block Assembly

block no. 364

Kansas Home

by Lynne Hagmeier • Kansas Troubles Quilters
ktquilts.com

Fabric: Kansas Troubles designed by Lynne Hagmeier for Moda Fabrics, unitednotions.com.

Lynne Hagmeier is the author of *Piecing the Past* for Kansas City Star Quilts, pickledish.com.

Gold Print
2 squares (A) 5¼″ x 5¼″
Cream Print
1 square (A) 5¼″ x 5¼″
1 square (B) 4½″ x 4½″
Tan Print
1 square (A) 5¼″ x 5¼″
4 squares (B) 4½″ x 4½″
Dark Brown Print
4 squares (C) 2¼″ x 2¼″
Maroon Tone-on-Tone
1 square (D) 3″ x 3″

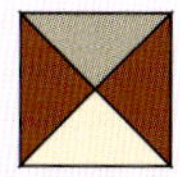

Unit
Make 4

Refer to "Quarter-Square Triangles" in the Techniques file on the PDF. Pair the gold A's with the cream and tan A's to make 4 units as shown.

Align a dark brown C in one corner of each tan B as shown. Using white thread and a machine straight stitch, sew close to the sides of the C's that will not be sewn into the seams. The raw edges of the appliqué will fray. Assemble the units and patches as shown.

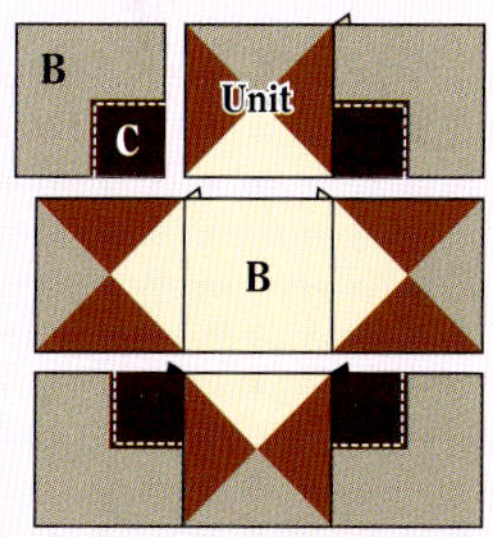

Block Assembly

Fold the block in half both ways and lightly crease the folds. Use the creases and appliqué placement diagram as guides to arrange D on the block; pin in place. Use white thread and a straight stitch to sew close to the edges of D.

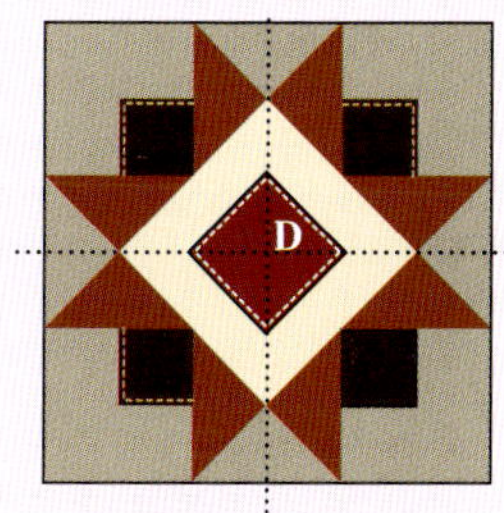

Applique Placement

block no. 365
Merry Merry

by Meg Hawkey • Crabapple Hill Studio
crabapplehillstudio.com

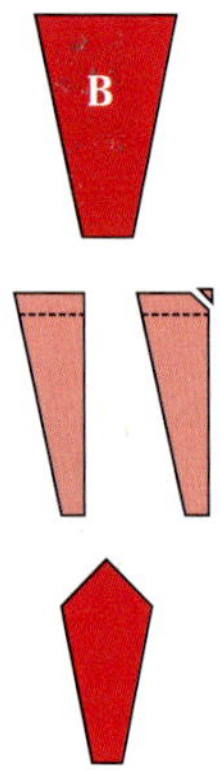

Make 16

See pages 129—130 on the PDF for pattern

White Tone-on-Tone and Natural Muslin
from *each*
1 square (A) 13½" x 13½" (trim to 12½" x 12½" after appliqué)
Assorted Red Prints
16 template B
Green Print
scrap for covering button
Brown Pigma Micron pen (.01 tip)
Crayons
White paper towel
Red and green embroidery floss
Button for covering 1 at 1⅛"

Dresden Plate

Fold the white A in half both ways and lightly crease the folds. Using the creases and placement diagram as guides, trace the design onto the white A with the pen. Use crayons to tint the letters, stick and leaf as shown in the photo. Color all areas that will be tinted with a white crayon first—this layer allows colors to blend better. Use lighter colors first, followed by darker colors to shade. Place a white paper towel over the block and heat set the tinting with a hot, dry iron. Layer the white A on top of the muslin A and baste together.

Embroidery & Applique Placement

Embroider the designs using a backstitch and French knots.

Fold each red B in half with right sides together. Stitch across the top edge as shown. Trim the folded corner; turn right side out and press. Sew the B's together as shown to make the Dresden Plate. Use matching thread and a blind stitch to appliqué it in place. Center the design and trim A to 12½" × 12½". Refer to the manufacturer's instructions to cover the button; tack to the plate as shown to complete the block.

block no. 366
Make A Wish

by Lynda Howell • The Stitch Connection
stitchconnection.com

See page 128 on the PDF for pattern

Medium Blue Tone-on-Tone
1 square (A) 11½" x 11½"
(trim to 10½" x 10½" after appliqué)
Assorted Prints and Tone-on-Tones
1 *each* patterns B, C, E, G–I, K and M–U
White Wool
1 *each* patterns D, F, J and L
Dark Green Tone-on-Tone and Red Tone-on-Tone
from *each*
1 rectangle (V) 1½" x 10½"
1 rectangle (W) 1½" x 12½"
Fusible web
Buttons 5 at ¼"
Black embroidery floss
Pink fabric crayon

Applique Placement

Fold A in half both ways and lightly crease the folds. Prepare patches B–U for fusible appliqué. Use the creases and appliqué placement diagram as guides to arrange the patches on A. Fuse the patches to A in alphabetical order.

Use matching thread and a machine blanket or feather stitch to sew around the patches. Use a satin stitch for the eyes and a backstitch for the mouth. Tack the buttons in place on the tree.

Lynda used a decorative machine stitch to embellish the wings. Use a fabric crayon to make the cheeks rosy.

Center the appliqué and trim A to 10½" × 10½". Sew the patches together as shown to complete the block.

Block Assembly

block no. 367

Fresh Cut

by Sara Tuttle Khammash

Fabric: Lately Arrived from London designed by Barbara Brackman for Moda Fabrics, unitednotions.com.

See page 426 on the PDF for pattern

Cream Print
2 squares (A) 6½″ x 6½″
Tan Print
2 squares (A) 6½″ x 6½″
1 pattern E
Brown Print #1
4 pattern B
Brown Print #2
4 pattern C
Red Tone-on-Tone
1 pattern D
Fusible web

Sew the cream and tan A's together as shown to make the block background.

Fold the block in half diagonally both ways and lightly crease the folds. Prepare patches B–E for fusible appliqué. Use the creases and appliqué placement diagram as guides to arrange the patches on the block. Fuse the patches in alphabetical order.

Use matching thread and a machine blanket stitch to sew around the patches.

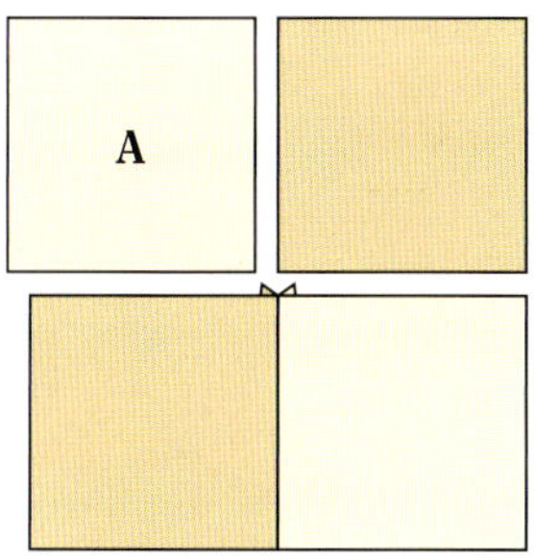

Block Piecing

Applique Placement

block no. 368

EZ Mariner's Compass

by Debby Kratovil • Quilter by Design
quilterbydesign.com

Fabric: Inspiration I, III, IV and Blenders by Blank Quilting, blankquilting.com.

Debby Kratovil is the author of *Supersize 'Em* for Martingale & Co., martingale-pub.com.

See page 120 on the PDF for pattern

Purple Print #1
section patch 1
Light Aqua Print
section patches 2 and 3
Teal Print
section patch 4
Gold Print
section patch 5
Purple Print #2
4 template A
White with Purple Print
1 circle (B) 4¼″ diameter

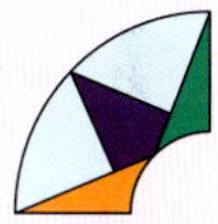

Section
Make 4

Make 4 paper copies of the foundation section. Foundation piece each section in numerical order, pressing and trimming after each patch addition. Refer to "Curved Piecing" in the Techniques file on the PDF. Sew the sections and A's together as shown to make the block background.

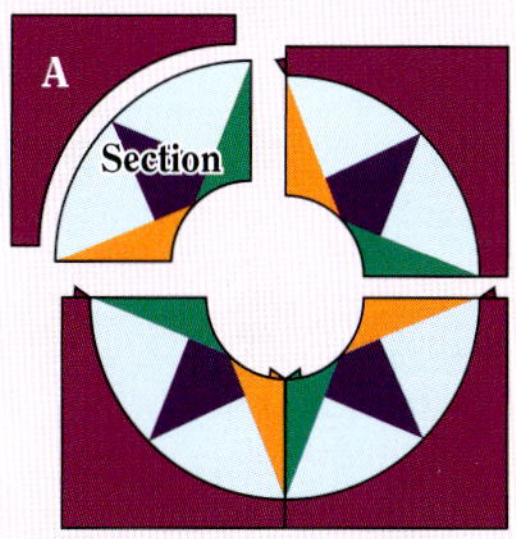

Block Assembly

Fold the block in half both ways and lightly crease the folds. Prepare circle B for turned-edge appliqué. Use the creases and appliqué placement diagram as guides to arrange the circle on the block. Use monofilament thread and a machine zigzag stitch to appliqué the circle in place.

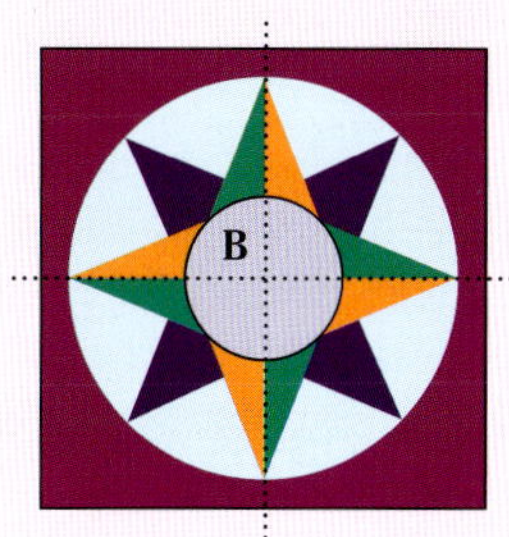

Applique Placement

block no. 369

Sephora

by Becca LoGiudice • Willow Hill Quilts
willowhillquilts.net

See page 154 on the PDF for pattern

White Print
1 square (A) 12½″ x 12½″
(trim to 11½″ x 11½″ after appliqué)
Black Solid
1 pattern B
Purple/Blue Multiprint
1 pattern C
Light Blue Tone-on-Tone
1 *each* patterns D and Dr
Blue Stripe
1 pattern E
Black Print
2 rectangles (F) 1″ x 11½″
2 rectangles (G) 1″ x 12½″
Fusible web

Fold A in half both ways and lightly crease the folds. Prepare patches B–E for fusible appliqué. Use the creases and appliqué placement diagram as guides to arrange the patches on A. Fuse the patches to A in alphabetical order.

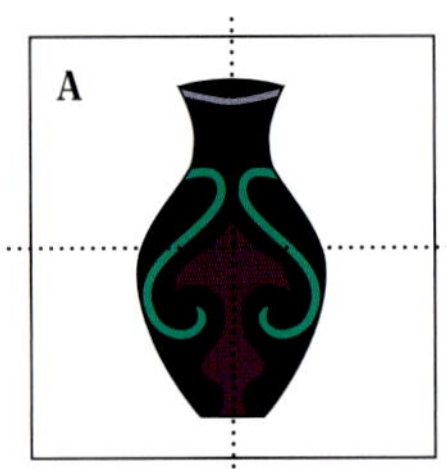

Applique Placement

Use matching thread and a satin stitch to sew around the patches. Center the appliqué and trim to 11½″ × 11½″.

Sew the patches together as shown to complete the block.

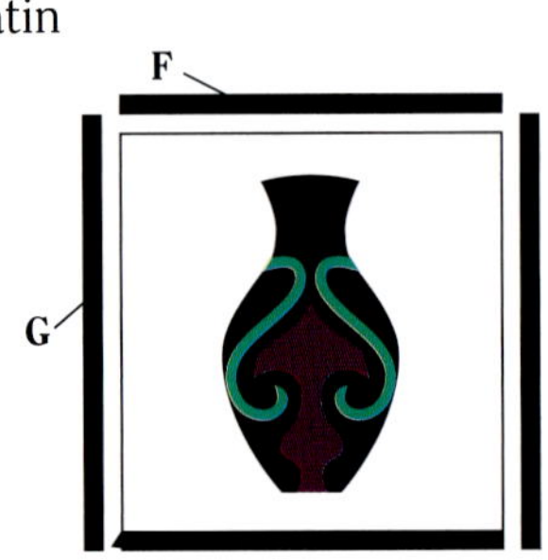

Block Assembly

block no. 370

Rainbow Happy Dance

by Natalie Lymer • Cinderberry Stitches
cinderberrystitches.com

Fabric: Sweet Broderie designed by Rosalie Quinlan Designs for Lecien, lecienusa.com.

See page 425 on the PDF for pattern

White Solid
1 square (A) 9½″ x 9½″
(trim to 8½″ x 8½″ after embroidery)
Natural Muslin
1 square (A) 9½″ x 9½″
(trim to 8½″ x 8½″ after embroidery)
Assorted Prints
80 squares (B) 1½″ x 1½″
Brown Pigma Micron pen (.01 tip)
Embroidery floss

Fold the white square (A) in half both ways and lightly crease the folds. Using the creases as a guide, trace the design onto the white A with the pen. Layer the white fabric right side up on top of the muslin and baste them together.

Embroider the following through both layers using 2 strands of floss: Use a blanket stitch for the hill. Use 2 rows of backstitches for each rainbow color. Use a backstitch for the heads and bodies. Use a satin stitch for the hands, feet, flower centers and circles in the sky.

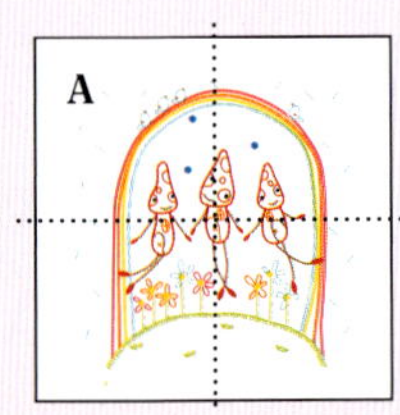

Embroidery Placement

Embroider the following using a single strand of floss: The flowers under the hill are a combination of lazy daisy stitches and French knots. Make French knots for the eyes and beaks on the birds. Use backstitches for the remaining embroidery. Center the design and trim A to 8½″ × 8½″.

Block Assembly

Join the B patches to the embroidered A as shown to complete the block.

block no. 371

Cornflowers

by Nancy Mahoney
nancymahoney.com

Fabric: Flora Bella and Bear Essentials from P & B Textiles, pbtex.com.

Nancy Mahoney has authored numerous books including *Fast, Fusible Flower Quilts* for Martingale & Co., martingale-pub.com.

See page 125 on the PDF for pattern

White Tone-on-Tone
1 square (A) 10½″ x 10½″
(trim to 9½″ x 9½″ after appliqué)

Green Tone-on-Tone
1 *each* patterns B–E
4 pattern F

Dark Blue Print
1 pattern G

Medium Blue Tone-on-Tone
4 circles (H) 3½″ diameter

Light Blue Print
4 rectangles (I) 2″ x 11″

4 buttons ¼″ diameter

4 seed beads

Fusible web

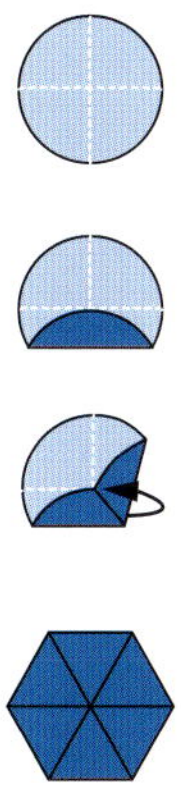

Folded Flower
Make 4

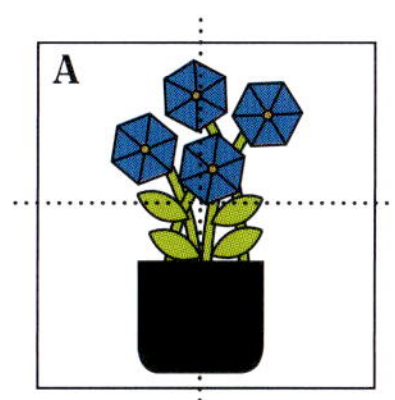

Applique Placement

Fold A in half both ways and lightly crease the folds. Prepare patches B–G for fusible appliqué. Use the creases, appliqué placement diagram and pattern sheet as guides to arrange the patches on A. Fuse the patches to A in alphabetical order. Use matching thread and a machine blanket stitch to sew around the patches.

Block Assembly

Lightly press a circle (H) in half both ways. Fold one edge to the center as shown and press. Bringing one edge of the fold to the center as shown, fold the next edge and press. Continue folding and pressing to make a hexagon flower. Tack down the petals in the flower center. Position a flower on a stem. Sew a button and seed bead to the center of the flower to anchor the flower. Repeat for each flower. Center the appliqué and trim A to 9½″ × 9½″.

Sew a light blue I to the right side of A with a partial seam as shown. Sew an I to the bottom, left and top as shown. Finish the partial seam to complete the block.

block no. 372

Linked

by Moira McSpadden • The Quilted Snail
thequiltedsnail.com

Fabric: Eclipse from Exclusively Quilters for Classic Cottons, classiccottons.com.

See page 121 on the PDF for pattern

Yellow Tone-on-Tone
3 squares (A) 4¼″ x 4¼″
section patches 2 and 3

White Tone-on-Tone
12 squares (B) 2⅜″ x 2⅜″
8 squares (C) 2″ x 2″
4 rectangles (D) 2″ x 3½″
1 square (E) 3½″ x 3½″

Black Print
section patches 1 and 4

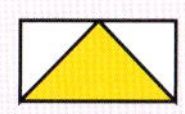

Flying Geese
Make 12

Section
Make 4

Refer to "Fast Flying Geese" in the Techniques file on the PDF. Make 12 Flying Geese with the yellow A's and white B's.

Make 4 paper copies of the foundation section. Foundation piece each section in numerical order, pressing and trimming after each patch addition.

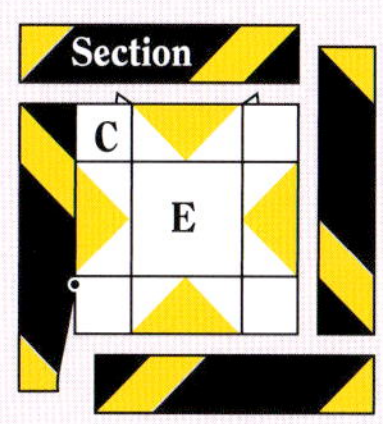

Unit

Join 4 C's and 4 Flying Geese to the E as shown to make the unit center. Sew one foundation-pieced section to the left side of the center with a partial seam as shown. Sew a section to the top, right and bottom, then complete the partial seam.

Sew the unit, remaining Flying Geese and patches together as shown to complete the block.

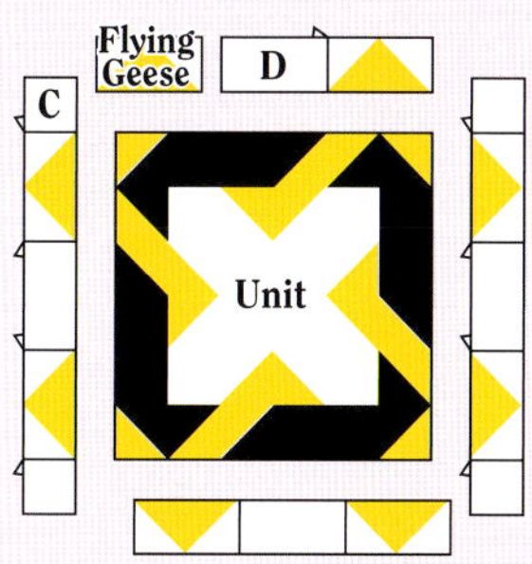

Block Assembly

block no. 373

Patchwork Bouquet

by Amanda Murphy • Amanda Murphy Design
amandamurphydesign.com

Fabric: Veranda designed by Amanda Murphy for Robert Kaufman, robertkaufman.com.

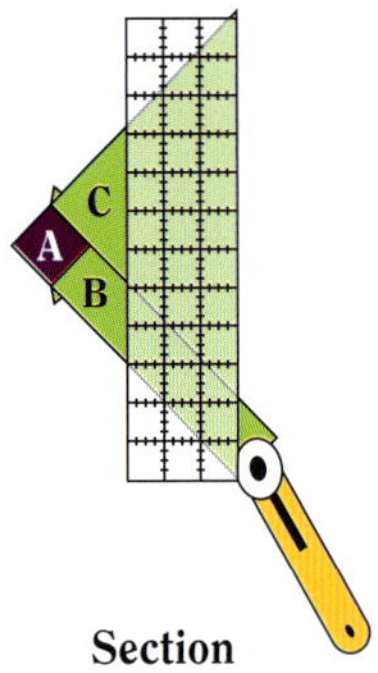

Section
Make 2 Green and Purple
Make 2 White and Yellow

See page 121 on the PDF for pattern

⊠ = cut in half twice diagonally

Dark Purple Print
- 2 squares (A) 2″ x 2″
- 4 pattern K

Green Print
- 2 rectangles (B) 2″ x 7″
- 1 square 10⅛″ x 10⅛″ ⊠ (C) (there will be 2 extra patches)

Yellow Print
- 2 squares (A) 2″ x 2″

White Tone-on-Tone
- 2 rectangles (B) 2″ x 7″
- 1 square 10⅛″ x 10⅛″ ⊠ (C) (there will be 2 extra patches)
- 2 *each* patterns F–I

Multiprint
- 2 rectangles (D) 1″ x 11½″
- 2 rectangles (E) 1″ x 12½″

Light Blue Tone-on-Tone
- 2 *each* patterns F–I

Light Purple Print
- 8 pattern J

Fusible web

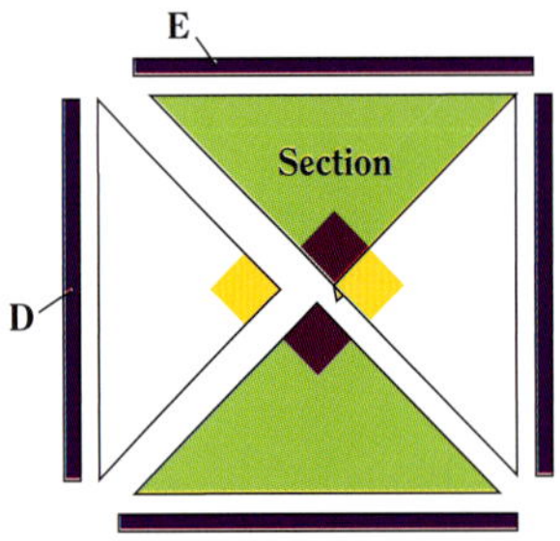

Block Assembly

Applique Placement

Join a dark purple A to one end of each green B. Referring to the section diagram, join each A/B to a green C; trim the B's even with C's long edge as shown. Repeat to make 2 sections using the yellow A's, white B's and white C's. Sew the 4 sections together as shown in the assembly diagram. Add the D's and E's to make the block.

Fold the block in half both ways and lightly crease the folds. Prepare patches F–K for fusible appliqué. Use the creases and appliqué placement diagram as guides to arrange the patches on the block. Fuse the patches in alphabetical order.

Use matching thread and a machine blanket stitch to sew around the patches.

block no. 374

Ocean Life

by Diane Nagle • Peddlecar Quilts
peddlecarquilts.blogspot.com

Fabric: Mermaid Wishes designed by Kim Martin for RJR Fabrics, rjrfabrics.com.

Unit 1 from A's
Make 12

Unit 2 from A's
Make 16

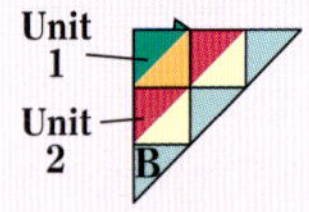

Section
Make 4

See page 157 on the PDF for pattern

⧄ = cut in half diagonally

Dark Teal Tone-on-Tone
- 6 squares (A) 2⅜″ x 2⅜″
- 1 pattern E

Beige Print
- 6 squares (A) 2⅜″ x 2⅜″

Pink Tone-on-Tone
- 8 squares (A) 2⅜″ x 2⅜″

Light Beige Tone-on-Tone
- 8 squares (A) 2⅜″ x 2⅜″
- 2 squares 3⅞″ x 3⅞″ ⧄ (C)
- 1 pattern F

Multicolor Plaid
- 4 squares 2⅜″ x 2⅜″ ⧄ (B)

Light Teal Tone-on-Tone
- 6 squares 2⅜″ x 2⅜″ ⧄ (B)
- 1 pattern G

Light Teal Print
- 1 square (D) 6⅞″ x 6⅞″

Black Solid
- 1 pattern H

Fusible web

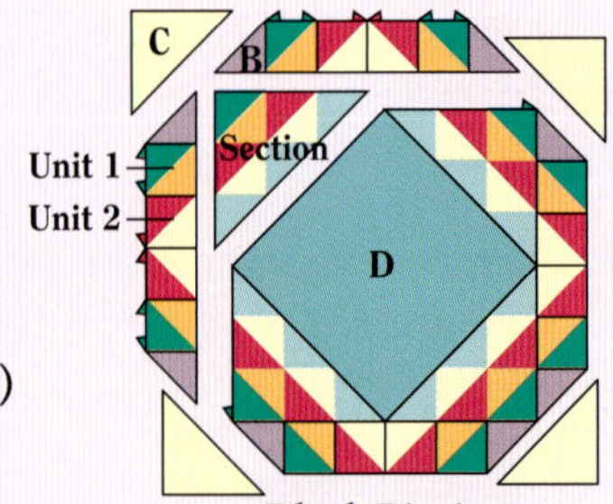

Block Piecing

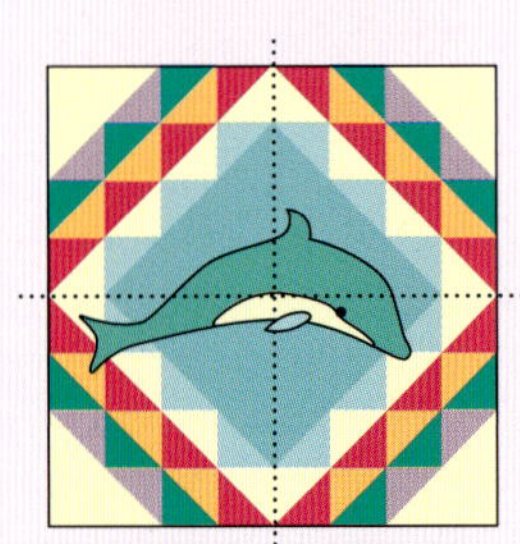

Applique Placement

Refer to "Triangle-Squares" in the Techniques file on the PDF. Pair the dark teal A's with the beige print A's to make 12 unit 1's. Make 16 unit 2's with the pink A's and light beige A's. Sew 1 unit 1, 2 unit 2's and 3 light teal B's together as shown to make 4 sections. Sew the sections, units and patches together as shown to make the block.

Prepare patches E–H for fusible appliqué. Fold the block in half both ways and lightly crease the folds. Use the folds and appliqué placement diagram a guide to arrange the patches on the block; fuse in place. Use black thread and a machine blanket stitch to sew around the patches.

block no. 375

Sweet Romance

by Vicki Oehlke • WillowBerry Lane
willowberry-lane.com

Fabric: Romance designed by Vicki Oehlke for Henry Glass Fabrics, henryglassfabrics.com.

Vicki Oehlke is the author of *Gorgeous Quilts for Gracious Living* for Landauer Corporation, landauercorp.com.

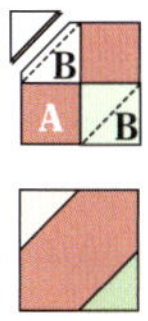

Unit
Stitch & Flip
Make 4

Cream and Red Print
4 squares (A) 2½″ x 2½″

Cream Print #1
4 squares (B) 1½″ x 1½″
4 rectangles (C) 1″ x 2½″
4 rectangles (D) 1″ x 3″
4 rectangles (E) 1½″ x 3″
8 squares (F) 2″ x 2″
4 rectangles (G) 2″ x 3½″

Light Green Tone-on-Tone
4 squares (B) 1½″ x 1½″
1 pattern I

Dark Green Tone-on-Tone
1 square (B) 1½″ x 1½″

Brown Print
8 squares (F) 2″ x 2″
4 rectangles (G) 2″ x 3½″

Tan Floral
4 squares (H) 3½″ x 3½″

Red Tone-on-Tone
4 pattern J
4 pattern K

Fusible web

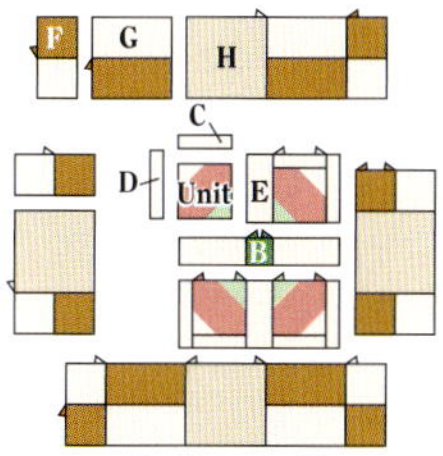

Block Assembly

Templates for Sweet Romance block on page 25 of the Templates file on the PDF

Vicki fussy cut the H's from a large-scale floral print.

Refer to "Stitch-and-Flip" in the Techniques file on the PDF. Use the cream and red A's with the cream #1 B's and the light green B's to make 4 units as shown. Sew the units and patches together as shown to make the block.

Fold the block in half diagonally both ways and lightly crease the folds. Prepare patches I–K for fusible appliqué. Use the creases and appliqué placement diagram as guides to arrange the patches on the block. Use matching thread and a straight stitch to appliqué around the patches.

Applique Placement

block no. 376

Woven Posies

by Leslee Price • Painted Pony 'n Quilts
ppnq.com

See page 148 on the PDF for pattern

White Tone-on-Tone
1 square (A) 5½″ x 5½″
(trim to 4½″ x 4½″ after appliqué
8 rectangles (K) 1¾″ x 2″
16 rectangles (L) 1¾″ x 4½″

Light Green Print #1
2 *each* patterns B and D

Light Green Print #2
2 *each* patterns C and E

Red Print
1 *each* patterns F and H

Pink Solid
1 *each* patterns G and I

Pink Print
1 circle 3″ diameter for yo-yos
1 circle 4″ diameter for yo-yos

Light Green Print #3
4 squares (J) 2″ x 2″
4 rectangles (M) 2″ x 4½″

Fusible web

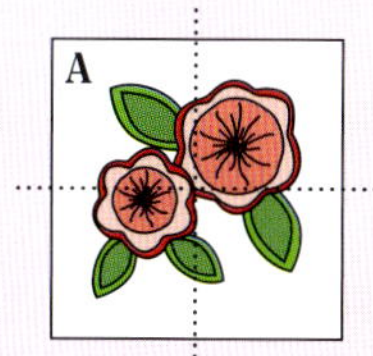

Applique Placement

Fold A in half both ways and lightly crease the folds. Prepare patches B–I for fusible appliqué. Make yo-yos from the pink print circles. Use the creases and appliqué placement diagram as guides to arrange the patches on A. Fuse the patches to A in alphabetical order. Use matching thread and a machine zigzag stitch to sew around the patches. Tack the yo-yos in place. Center the appliqué and trim A to 4½"× 4½".

Sew the patches together as shown to complete the block.

Block Assembly

block no. 377
Brer Bunny

by Marjorie Rhine • Quilt Design NW
quiltdesignnw.com

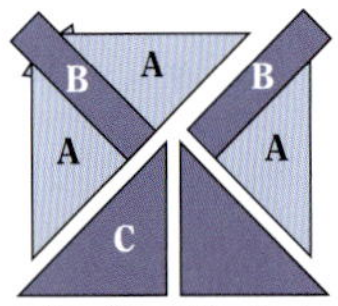

Section Piecing

Trim to 8½" x 9"

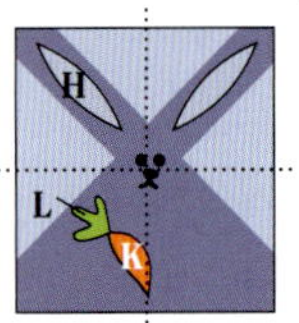

Applique Placement

See page 147 on the PDF for pattern

◪ = cut in half diagonally
⊠ = cut in half twice diagonally

Light Blue Print #1
1 square 7¼"x 7¼" ⊠ (A) (there will be 1 extra)
2 rectangles (D) 2½"x 9"
2 squares (F) 1"x 1"
1 rectangle (G) 2"x 12½"

Medium Blue Tone-on-Tone
2 rectangles (B) 2"x 6"
1 square 6⅜"x 6⅜" ◪ (C)
1 rectangle (E) 1½"x 12½"

Dark Green Print
1 rectangle (E) 1½"x 12½"

Light Blue Print #2
2 pattern H

Black Solid
2 pattern I
1 pattern J

Orange Tone-on-Tone
1 pattern K

Light Green Tone-on-Tone
1 pattern L

Fusible web

Black Micron Pigma pen

Unit
Stitch & Flip
Make 1

Block Assembly

Join the light blue A's to the medium blue B's and C's. Trim the section to 8½" × 9" as shown. Refer to "Stitch-and-Flip" in the Techniques file on the PDF. Use the medium blue E and light blue F's to make the unit. Sew the trimmed section, unit and patches together as shown.

Fold the block in half both ways and lightly crease the folds. Prepare patches H–L for fusible appliqué. Arrange the patches on the block; fuse them in place. Use monofilament thread and a small zigzag stitch to sew around the H's, L and K. Satin stitch around the eyes and nose with black thread. Add the mouth with the black pen to complete the block.

block no. 378
Confetti

by Laura Stone Roberts • Assistant Editor, *McCall's Quilting* • mccallsquilting.com

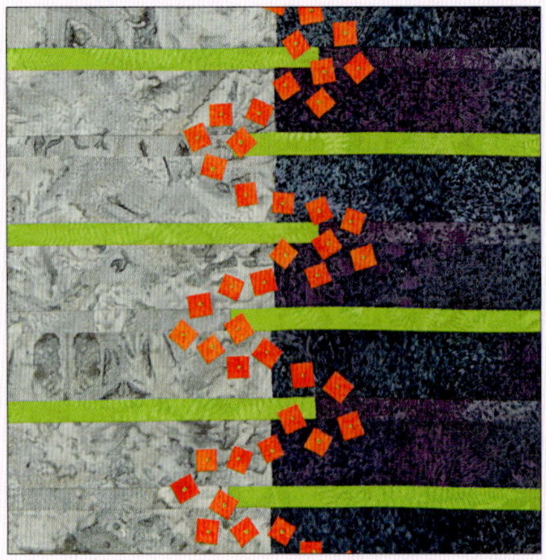

Medium Gray Batik and Dark Blue Print
from each
2 rectangles (A) 1¼"x 6½"
3 rectangles (C) 1"x 5½"
5 rectangles (D) 2"x 6½"

Medium Green Tone-on-Tone
6 rectangles (B) 1"x 7½"

Red Batik
44 squares (E) ½"x ½" (see note before cutting)

Fusible web

Medium green embroidery floss

Cut a piece of fusible web 4"x 4" and fuse to the back of a piece of red batik. Cut the E's from this fabric.

Sew patches A–D together as shown to make the block background.

Prepare the red E squares for fusible appliqué. Using the appliqué placement diagram as a guide, arrange the E's on the block. Fuse in place. Using 2 strands of embroidery floss, make a French knot at the center of each red square. Trim any excess from the E's along the edges of the block to complete the block.

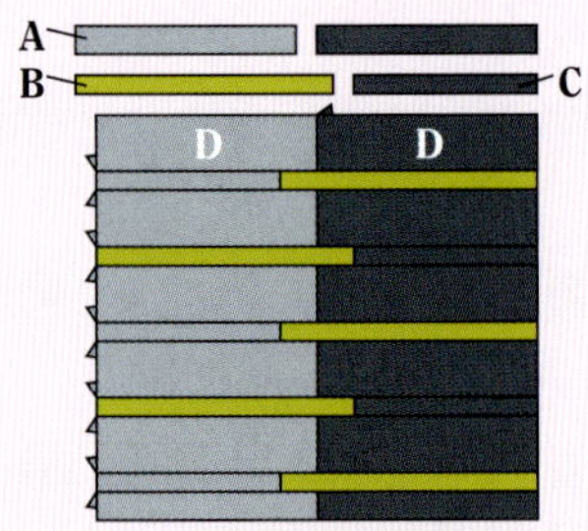

Block Piecing

Project Note: If making multiple blocks, save some E's to sprinkle over seam lines after blocks are sewn together.

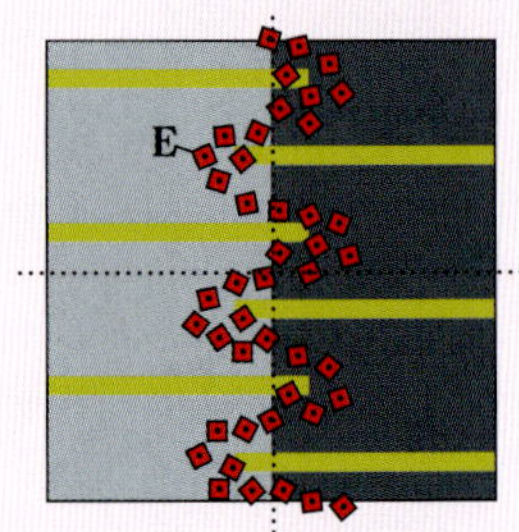

Applique Placement

block no. 379

Crazy Patch Heart

by Benita Skinner • Victoriana Quilt Designs
victorianaquiltdesigns.com

See page 142 on the PDF for pattern

5 Assorted Prints and Tone-on-Tones
section patches 1–5

White Tone-on-Tone
1 square (A) 13½″ x 13½″ (trim to 12½″ x 12½″ after appliqué)

Embroidery Floss

Assorted Embellishments

Make 1 paper copy of the foundation. Foundation piece the section in numerical order, pressing and trimming after each patch addition. Carefully remove the paper.

Embroider the patches as shown on the pattern on page 142 of the PDF.

In addition to embroidery, Benita used lace, braid, rickrack, and other motifs to embellish her heart.

Section
Make 1

Fold A in half both ways and lightly crease the folds. Prepare the heart section for turned-edge appliqué. Use the creases and appliqué placement diagram as guides to arrange the heart on A. Use matching thread and a blind stitch to appliqué the heart in place.

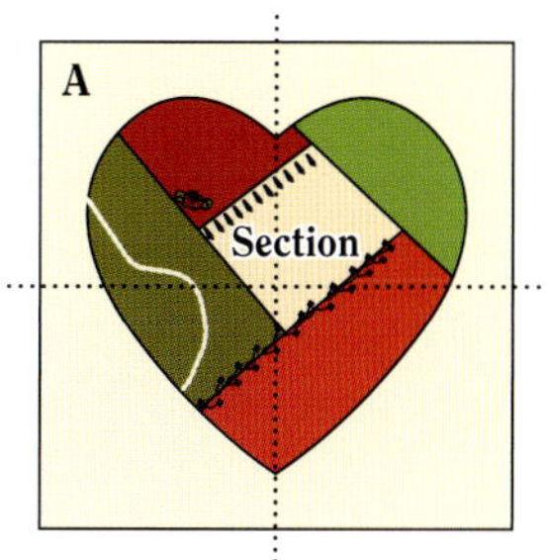

Applique and Embroidery Placement

Center the appliqué and trim to 12½″× 12½″.

block no. 380

Jester

by Anita Grossman Solomon • Make it Simpler
makeitsimpler.com

Anita Grossman Solomon is the author of *Make it Simpler Paper Piecing* and *Rotary Cutting Revolution*, both for C&T Publishing, ctpub.com.

See page 145 on the PDF for pattern

Multicolor Stripe
section patch 1
2 squares (A) 5¼″ x 5¼″
1 square (B) 4½″ x 4½″

Black Print
section patches 2 and 3
2 squares (A) 5¼″ x 5¼″

Section
Make 4

Unit
Make 4

Anita created a lot of movement in her block by placing the stripes in a variety of directions. It's helpful to starch the fabrics if bias edges will be on the outside edges of patches.

Make 4 paper copies of the foundation section. Foundation piece each section in numerical order, pressing and trimming after each patch addition.

Refer to "Quarter-Square Triangles" in the Techniques file on the PDF. Pair the stripe and black A's to make 4 units. Sew the sections, units and B together as shown to complete the block.

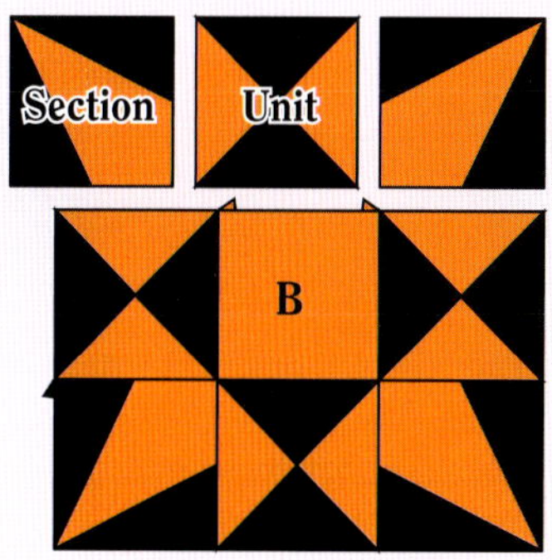

Block Assembly

block no. 381
Kansas Challenge

by Peg Spradlin
handicraftsbypeg.com

Fabric: Perennials and Favorites designed by Kansas Troubles for Moda Fabrics, unitednotions.com.

See page 156 on the PDF for pattern

Rust Print and Gold Print
from *each*
- 2 squares (A) 2⅛" x 2⅛"

Tan Print
- 2 squares (A) 2⅛" x 2⅛"
- section 1, patches 2 and 4

Light Tan Tone-on-Tone
- 2 squares (A) 2⅛" x 2⅛"
- section 1, patches 3 and 5
- section 2, patches 2–5
- 12 squares (B) 2¼" x 2¼"

4 Assorted Dark Prints and Tone-on-Tones
from *each*
- section 1, patch 1
- 1 square (B) 2¼" x 2¼"

Black Multiprint
- section 2, patch 1

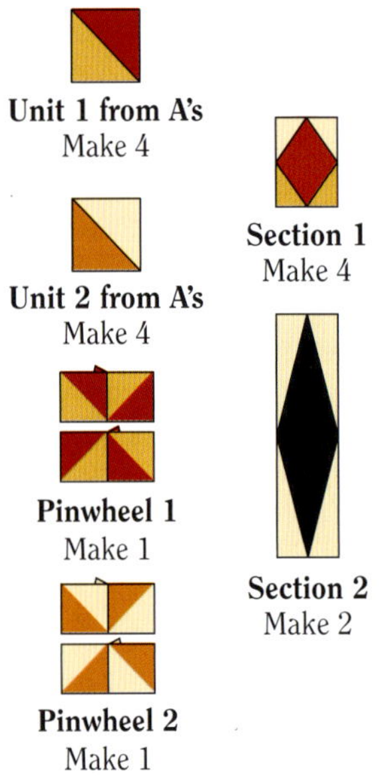

Refer to "Triangle-Squares" in the Techniques file on the PDF. Pair the rust A's with the tan A's to make 4 unit 1's. Pair the gold A's and light tan A's to make 4 unit 2's. Sew the unit 1's together as shown to make a Pinwheel 1. Repeat with the unit 2's to make a Pinwheel 2.

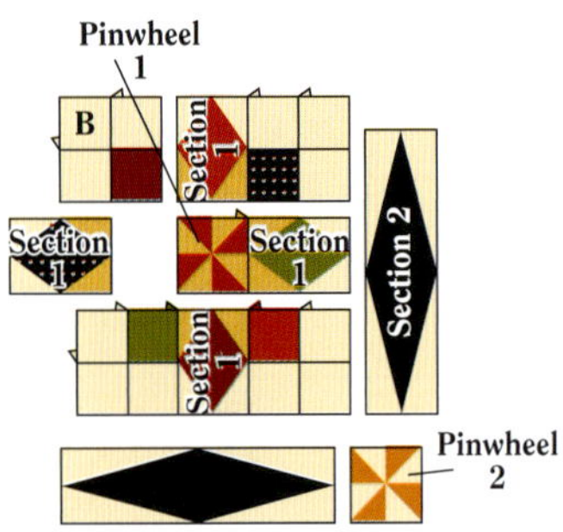

Block Assembly

Make 4 paper copies of the foundation section 1 and 2 paper copies of section 2. Note that a different dark print or tone-on-tone is used in each section 1, patch 1. Foundation piece each section in numerical order, pressing and trimming after each patch addition.

Sew the patches, sections, and pinwheels together as shown to complete the block.

block no. 382
Hat's Off

by Denise Starck • Graphic Designer, *Quiltmaker*
quiltmaker.com

Fabric: Bliss designed by Jane Spolar of Quilt Poetry and Stonehenge Maui by Sunshine Cottage, both for Northcott, northcott.net.

See page 137 on the PDF for pattern

Green Print
- sections 1 and 2, patch 1
- 1 rectangle (A) 3" x 8½"

Medium Blue Print
- 1 rectangle (B) 2" x 8½"
- 1 pattern F

Light Blue Tone-on-Tone
- sections 1 and 2, patches 2 and 3
- 2 rectangles (C) 2½" x 4½"
- 1 rectangle (D) 3¼" x 12½"
- 1 rectangle (E) 3¾" x 12½"

Yellow Tone-on-Tone
- 1 pattern G

Fusible web

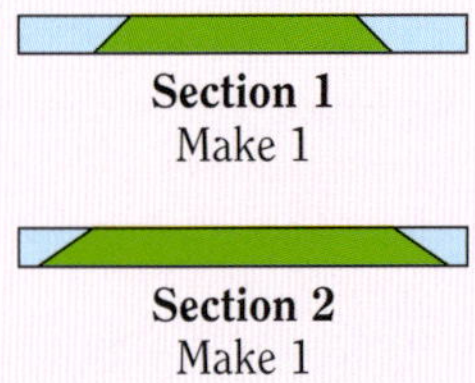

Applique Placement

Make 1 paper copy of each foundation section. Foundation piece the sections in numerical order, pressing and trimming after each patch addition. Sew the sections and patches A–E together as shown to make the block.

Fold the block in half both ways and lightly crease the folds. Prepare patches F and G (flowers) for fusible appliqué. Use the folds and appliqué placement diagram as guides to arrange the flower patches in alphabetical order on the hat; fuse patches in place.

Using matching thread and a straight stitch, sew close to the inside edge of patch G. Blanket stitch around the outside edges of patches F and G.

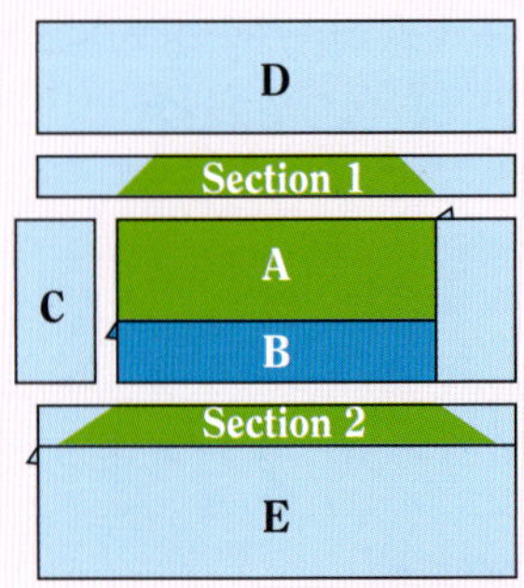

Block Assembly

block no. 383

Jeremy Giraffe

by Debbie Taylor • Fat Quarter Shop
fatquartershop.com

Fabric: Meadow Friends designed by Deb Strain for Moda Fabrics, unitednotions.com.

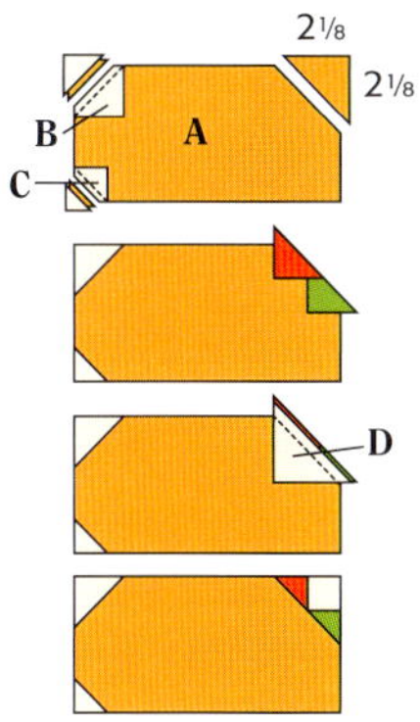

Unit 1
Stitch & Flip
Make 1

⧄ = cut in half diagonally

Yellow Print
- 1 rectangle (A) 4½″ x 8½″
- 1 rectangle (J) 3½″ x 6½″

White Solid
- 1 square (B) 2″ x 2″
- 2 squares (C) 1½″ x 1½″
- 1 square 2⅞″ x 2⅞″ ⧄ (D) (there will be 1 extra triangle)
- 1 square 1⅞″ x 1⅞″ ⧄ (E) (there will be 1 extra triangle)
- 1 rectangle (F) 2½″ x 5½″
- 1 rectangle (G) 2½″ x 4½″
- 1 rectangle (H) 2½″ x 6½″
- 1 rectangle (I) 6½″ x 7½″
- 1 rectangle (K) 2½″ x 10½″

Dark Brown Multiprint
- 1 square 1⅞″ x 1⅞″ ⧄ (E) (there will be 1 extra triangle)

3 Assorted Prints
- 8 squares (B) 2″ x 2″

Buttons 2 at ⅝″ diameter

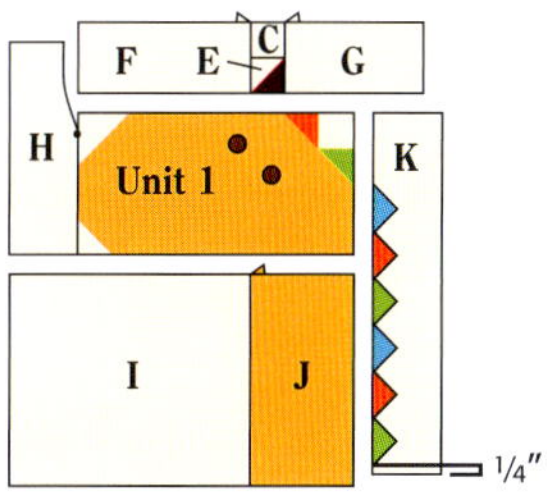

Block Assembly

Refer to "Prairie Points" in the Techniques file on the PDF. Prepare 8 prairie points using the assorted print B's.

Refer to "Stitch-and-Flip" in the Techniques file on the PDF. Sew the white B and C to A as shown. Align 2 prairie points on the trimmed edge of A as shown and pin or baste in place. Add D to complete unit 1.

Sew the C, E's, F and G together as shown to make the top section. Sew the I and J together to make the bottom section. Sew H to the left side of unit 1 with a partial seam as shown. Sew the bottom section below unit 1.

Leaving ¼" at the bottom for seam allowance, pin or baste 6 prairie points to K as shown: sew K to the right side of unit 1. Sew the section to the top, then complete the partial seam.

Sew the buttons for eyes to complete the block.

block no. 384

Patchwork Pansies

by Terry Clothier Thompson • Peace Creek Pattern and Book Company • terrythompson.com

Fabric: Louisa designed by Terry Clothier Thompson for Moda Fabrics, unitednotions.com.

Terry Clothier Thompson is the author of *A Dusty Garden Grows* for Kansas City Star Quilts, pickledish.com.

See page 151 on the PDF for pattern

⧄ = cut in half diagonally
⊠ = cut in half twice diagonally

Red Print
- 4 squares (A) 2¼″ x 2¼″

Tan Print
- 16 rectangles (B) 1⅜″ x 2¼″

Blue Print #1
- 16 squares (C) 1⅜″ x 1⅜″

Beige Tone-on-Tone
- 1 square (D) 4″ x 4″
- 2 squares 3⅜″ x 3⅜″ ⧄ (E)
- 1 square 6¼″ x 6¼″ ⊠ (F)

Blue Print #2
- 2 rectangles (G) 1½″ x 10½″
- 2 rectangles (H) 1½″ x 12½″

Assorted Tone-on-Tones
- 1 set of appliqué patches (I–R)

Embroidery floss

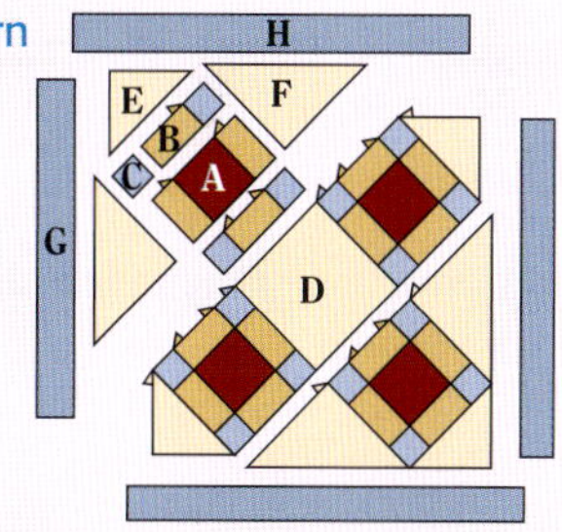

Block Piecing

Sew the patches together as shown to make the block.

Fold the block in half both ways and lightly crease the folds. Prepare patches I–R for turned-edge appliqué. Use the creases and appliqué placement diagram as guides to arrange the patches on the block.

Applique Placement

Using a running stitch, sew close to the edges of the patches, using black thread for the pot and matching thread for the flower patches. Add French knots to the flowers with gold floss as shown in the photographed block. Use black floss and a long stitch to add the remaining flower detail.

block no. 385
USA

by Maria Umhey • Cheerful Quilts

Fabric: Assorted collections from Windham Fabrics, windhamfabrics.com.

See page 160 on the PDF for pattern

Cream Print
- 2 squares (A) 3¼" x 3¼"
- 4 squares (B) 2½" x 2½"
- 1 set of appliqué letters (USA)

Red Print
- 2 squares (A) 3¼" x 3¼"
- 1 square (B) 2½" x 2½"

Assorted Blue Prints
- 18 squares (B) 2½" x 2½"
- 1 square (C) 7½" x 7½" (trim to 6½" x 6½" after appliqué)

Fusible web

Unit
Make 4

Applique Placement

Refer to "Quarter-Square Triangles" in the Techniques file on the PDF. Make 4 units using the cream A's and red A's.

Fold C in half both ways and lightly crease the folds. Prepare the letters for fusible appliqué. Use the creases and appliqué placement diagram as guides to arrange the letters on C; fuse in place. Use matching thread and a machine blanket stitch to sew around the letters. Center the appliqué and trim C to 6½" × 6½".

Sew the patches and units together as shown to complete the block.

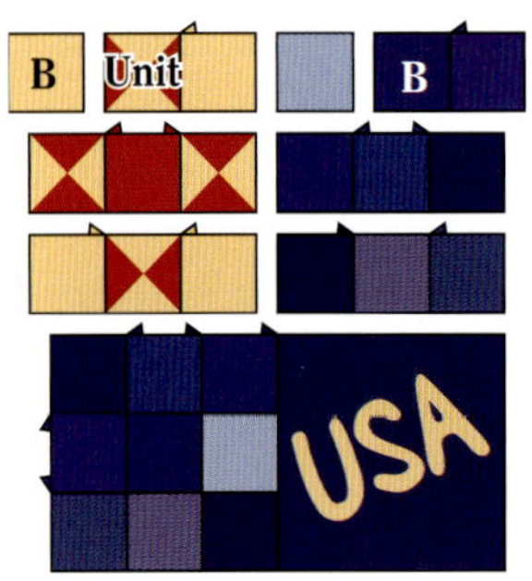

Block Assembly

block no. 386
Jolly Holly

by Sarah Vanderburgh
sewjoycreations.com

See page 145 on the PDF for pattern

White Print
- 1 square (A) 7¼" x 7¼"
- 4 squares (D 3½" x 3½"
- 1 square (E) 6½" x 6½"

Red Solid
- 4 squares (B) 3⅞" x 3⅞"
- 2 rectangles (C) 3½" x 6½"
- 1 pattern G

Green Tone-on-Tone
- 4 pattern F

Fusible web

Buttons 9 at ½"

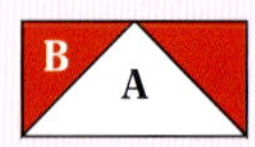

Flying Geese
Make 4

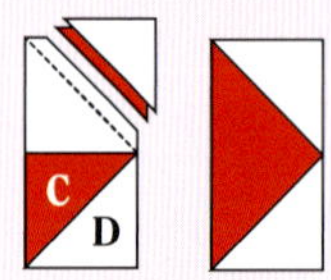

**Unit
Stitch & Flip**
Make 2

Refer to the Techniques file on the PDF for all techniques. Make 4 Flying Geese using the white A and red B's. Use the red C's and white D's to make 2 units. Sew the Flying Geese, units and E together as shown to make the block background.

Block Assembly

Fold the block in half diagonally both ways and lightly crease the folds. Prepare patches F and G for fusible appliqué. Use the creases and appliqué placement diagram as guides to arrange the patches. Fuse the patches in place.

Use matching thread and a blanket stitch to sew around the patches. Tack the buttons in place as shown to complete the block.

Applique Placement

block no. 387
Garden

by Martha Walker • Wagons West Designs
wagonswestdesigns.com

See page 150 on the PDF for pattern

⊠ = cut in half twice diagonally

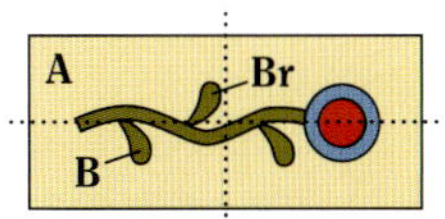

Applique Placement
Make 4

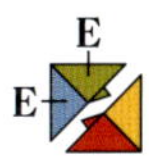

Unit
Make 9

Tan Plaid
4 rectangles (A) 4½″ x 10½″
(trim to 3½″ x 9½″ after appliqué)

Green Tone-on-Tone
4 bias strips 1¼″ x 7½″ for stems
8 pattern B
4 pattern Br

Assorted Red Prints
2 pattern C
2 pattern D

Assorted Blue Prints
2 pattern C
2 pattern D

Assorted Prints
9 squares 3¼″ x 3¼″ ⊠ (E)

Fold the A's in half both ways and lightly crease the folds. Refer to "Bias Strips" in the Techniques file on the PDF to make the stems. Prepare the B's, Br's, C's and D's for turned-edge appliqué. Use the creases and appliqué placement diagram as guides to arrange the stem and patches on each A. Use matching thread and a blind stitch to appliqué the patches in place. Center the appliqué and trim the A's to 3½" × 9½".

Make 9 units using assorted E's, then sew the units together as shown to make the block center. Noting the orientation, sew a tan A to the right side of the center with a partial seam as shown. Sew an A to the top, left, and bottom as shown. Complete the partial seam to finish the block.

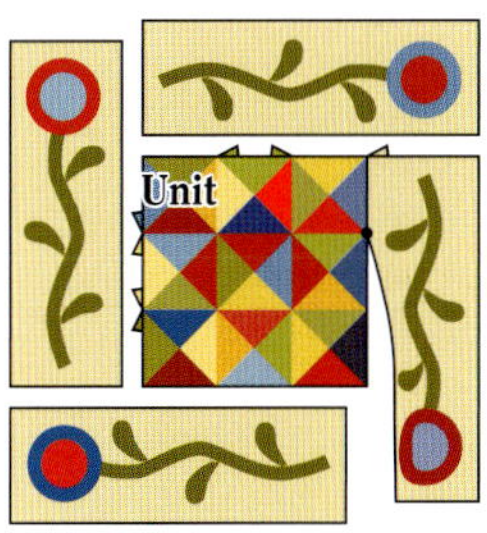

Block Assembly

block no. 388
Little Laundry

by Sandra Workman • Pine Mountain Designs
pinemtndesigns.com

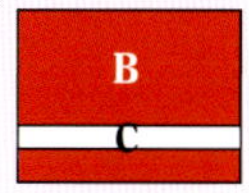

Skirt
Make 1

See page 159 on the PDF for pattern

Unit
Make 12

Blue Dot
1 rectangle (A) 9½″ x 13½″
(trim to 8½″ x 12½″ after appliqué)

Red Print
1 rectangle (B) 4½″ x 6″
1 pattern D

White Solid
1 rectangle (C) ⅝″ x 6″
1 pattern E

Tan Solid
2 pattern F

3 Green Prints
from *each*
2 squares (G) 2⅞″ x 2⅞″

White Print
6 squares (G) 2⅞″ x 2⅞″

Dark brown rickrack

Red embroidery floss

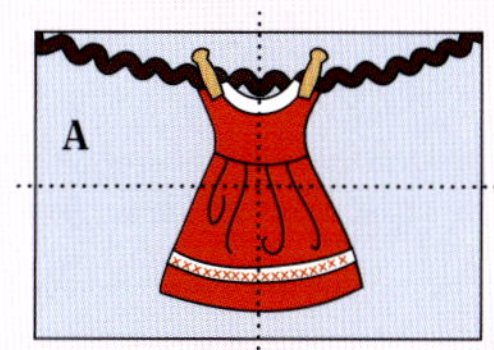

Applique Placement

Block Assembly

Using turned-edge appliqué, stitch the white C to the red B as shown with matching thread and a blind stitch. With the red embroidery floss stitch the X's for the trim detail. Turn the sides of the skirt (B) under a scant ¼". Sew a short basting stitch across the top of B. Pull the thread ends to gather the skirt waist to 2½". Tie off the thread to secure the gather. Hem the bottom of the skirt with a small zigzag stitch.

Fold A in half both ways and lightly crease the folds. Prepare patches D–F for turned-edge appliqué. Use the appliqué placement diagram as a guide to arrange the rickrack, patches and skirt on A. Zigzag the rickrack with matching thread. Tucking the top edge of the skirt under D, appliqué the patches and sides of the skirt in place with a blind stitch and matching thread, leaving the bottom of the skirt loose. Trim A to 8½" × 12½".

Make 12 units with the white print and green G's. Sew the units and A together as shown to complete the block.

block no. 389

Basket DeLight

by Kathleen Brown and DeLoyce Tyler
Mountain Patchwork• mountainpatchwork.com

See page 162 on the PDF for pattern

Assorted Cream Tone-on-Tones
36 squares (A) 2½" x 2½"
Dark Brown Tone-on-Tone
1 pattern B
Green Tone-on-Tone
3 pattern C
Dark Pink Tone-on-Tone
1 circle 6" diameter for yo-yo
Blue Tone-on-Tone
1 circle 5¼" diameter for yo-yo
Light Green Solid, Gold Solid, and Light Purple Print
from *each*
1 circle 3½" diameter for yo-yos
Fusible web
5 Buttons 3 at ⅝", 2 at ½"
Perle cotton

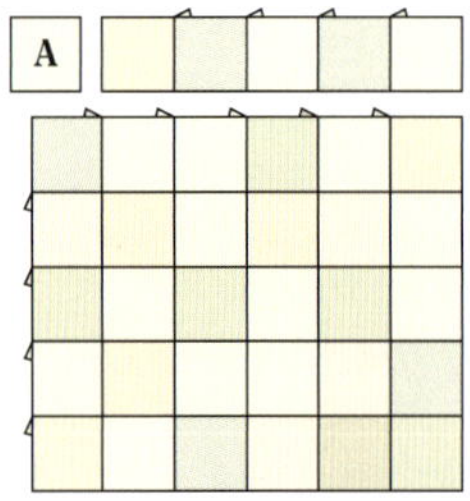

Block Piecing

Sew the cream A's together to make the block background.

Applique Placement

Fold the block in half diagonally both ways and lightly crease the folds. Prepare the basket and leaves for fusible appliqué. Use the creases and appliqué placement diagram as guides to arrange the patches on A. Fuse the basket and leaves in place. Use brown perle cotton and a hand blanket stitch around the basket. Use green perle cotton to blanket stitch the leaves. Add the stem detail with a backstitch and lazy daisy stitch.

Make 5 yo-yos for the flowers. Tack the yo-yo's in place as shown. Sew a button to the center of each yo-yo to complete the block.

block no. 390

Blooming Bias Baskets

by Kari Carr • New Leaf Stitches
newleafstitches.com

Kari Carr is the author of *Just Around the Corner: Quilts with Easy Mitered Borders* for Martingale & Co., martingale-pub.com.

See page 175 on the PDF for pattern

Peach Print
4 squares (A) 4¾" x 4¾"
Black Tone-on-Tone
4 squares (B) 6" x 6"
2 rectangles (C) 1½" x 6"
1 rectangle (D) 1½" x 12½"
Assorted Wool Scraps
4 *each* patterns E, F, H, I and J
8 *each* patterns G, K and L
Fusible web
Fusible stabilizer (optional)
Embroidery floss

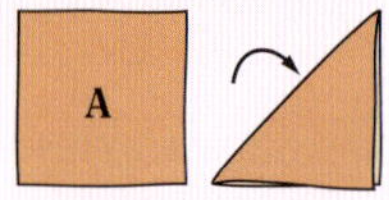

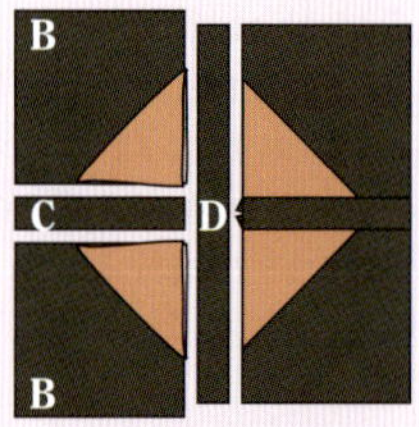

Block Piecing

Fold each A in half diagonally. Align the raw edges of the folded A's with the B's as shown. Sew the patches together to make the block. Turn back the folded edges of the A's to form a gentle curve. Use matching thread and a straight stitch to sew down the folded edges.

Folded Edge

Fold the block in half diagonally both ways and lightly crease the folds. Prepare patches E–L for fusible appliqué. Use the creases and appliqué placement diagram as guides to arrange the patches; fuse in place.

Applique Placement

Kari fused her block to stabilizer before sewing around the appliqué patches.

Sew around the patches with invisible thread and a machine blind stitch. Use 3 strands of floss, French knots and a lazy daisy stitch to embroider the flower detail to complete the block.

block no. 391

Iowa Lily

by Evonne Cook • Clothesline Quilts
clotheslinequilts.com

Fabric: Crimson and Clover designed by Jo Morton for Andover Fabrics, andoverfabrics.com.

⧄ = cut in half diagonally
⊠ = cut in half twice diagonally

Black and Green Print
3 squares (A) 2⅞"x 2⅞"

Cream Tone-on-Tone
3 squares (A) 2⅞"x 2⅞"
2 squares 3¼"x 3¼" ⊠ (B) (there will be 2 extra)
12 squares (D) 2½"x 2½"
1 square (E) 6½"x 6½"

Gold Tone-on-Tone
2 squares 3¼"x 3¼" ⊠ (B) (there will be 2 extra)

Red Print
2 squares 2⅞"x 2⅞" ⧄ (C)
(there will be 1 extra)

Gold and Red Print
5 squares 2⅞"x 2⅞" ⧄ (C)
(there will be 1 extra)

Green Stripe
bias strip 1½"x 51" for stems

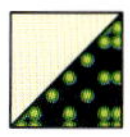

Unit
Make 6

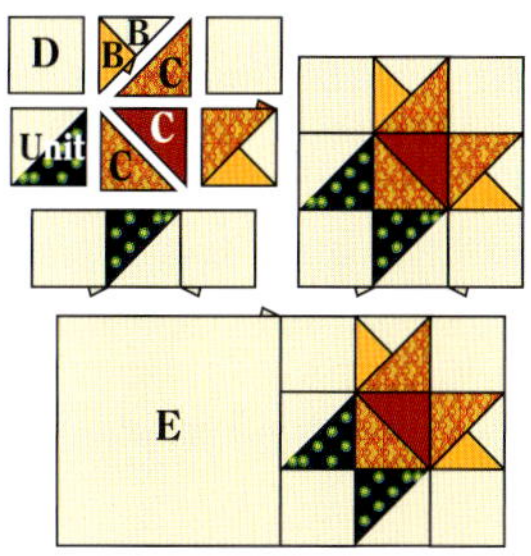

Block Assembly

For all techniques, refer to the Techniques file on the PDF. Pair the black print A's with the cream A's to make 6 unit 1's. Sew the units and patches together as shown to make the block.

Applique Placement

Cut this strip into 2 lengths of 8½" for the outside stems, 2 lengths of 7½" for the stems on both sides of the center, 1 length of 12¼" for the center stem and 1 length of 6" for the shorter stem on the left. Arrange the stems as shown on the block. Use matching thread and a machine blanket stitch to sew around the stems, tucking the top edge of the stems under before stitching.

block no. 392

Parkdale

by Sue Daley • Patchwork with Busyfingers
busyfingerspatchwork.com

Fabric: Patchwork Heritage Classics designed by Judie Rothermel for Marcus Fabrics, marcusfabrics.com.

Sue Daley is the author of *New English Paper Piecing* for C&T Publishing, ctpub.com.

See page 171 on the PDF for pattern

Blue Stripe
6 template A

Red Print #1
1 template A

Red Print #2
6 template B

Tan Solid
1 square (C) 13½"x 13½" (trim to 12½"x 12½" after appliqué)

Template plastic

Medium-weight paper

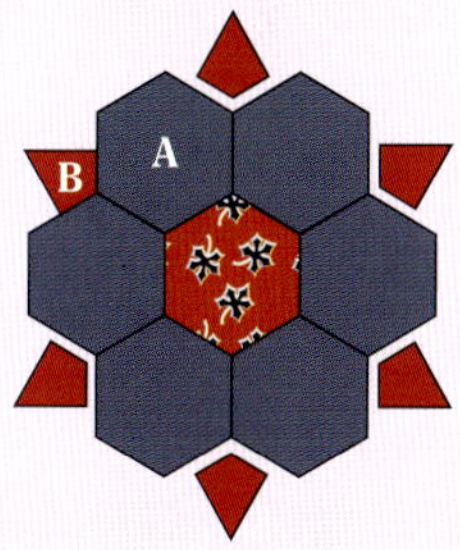

Block Piecing

Sue fussy cut the blue A's so they form a continuous design when sewn together.

The center part of this block was hand sewn using English paper piecing. Follow the instructions for "English Paper Piecing" in the Tecniques file on the PDF; baste the A's and B's to the paper templates and sew them together as shown in the block piecing diagram.

Fold C in half both ways and lightly crease the folds. Use the creases and appliqué placement diagram as guides to position the pieced design on C. Use matching thread and a blind stitch to appliqué the design on C. Center the appliqué and trim to 12½"× 12½".

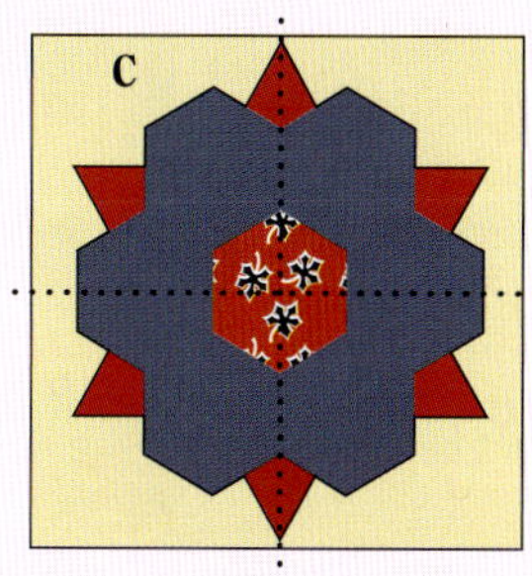

Applique Placement

block no. 393

Daisy Delight

by Terri Degenkolb • Whimsicals
whimsicalquilts.com

Fabric: Heartstrings designed by Terri Degenkolb for Red Rooster Fabrics, redroosterfabrics.com.

Terri Degenkolb is the author of *Buttons and Blooms* for Whimsicals, whimsicalquilts.com.

See page 167 on the PDF for pattern

Brown Print #1
4 squares (A) 2½" x 2½"

Blue Print #1
4 squares (A) 2½" x 2½"
4 rectangles (C) 2½" x 8½"

Dark Teal Tone-on-Tone
12 squares (B) 1½" x 1½"
1 pattern G

Blue Print #2
1 square (D) 8½" x 8½"

Tan Print
1 pattern E

Brown Print #2
6 pattern F

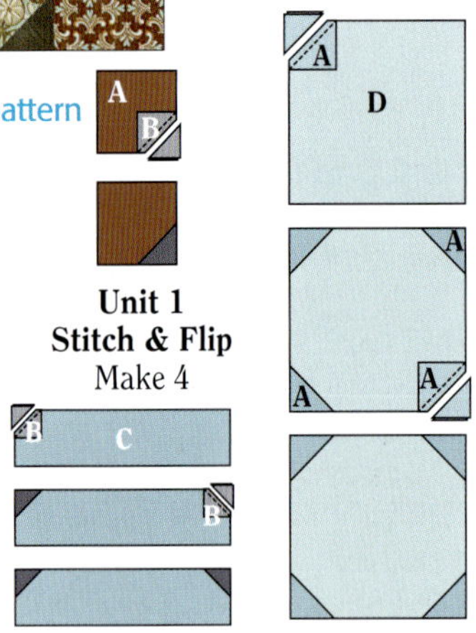

Unit 1 Stitch & Flip Make 4

Unit 2 Stitch & Flip Make 4

Unit 3 Stitch & Flip Make 1

Refer to "Stitch-and-Flip" in the Techniques file on the PDF. Use the brown #1 A's and dark teal B's to make 4 unit 1's. Make 4 unit 2's using the blue #1 C's and dark teal B's. Use the blue #2 D and blue #1 A's to make unit 3. Sew the units together as shown to make the block background.

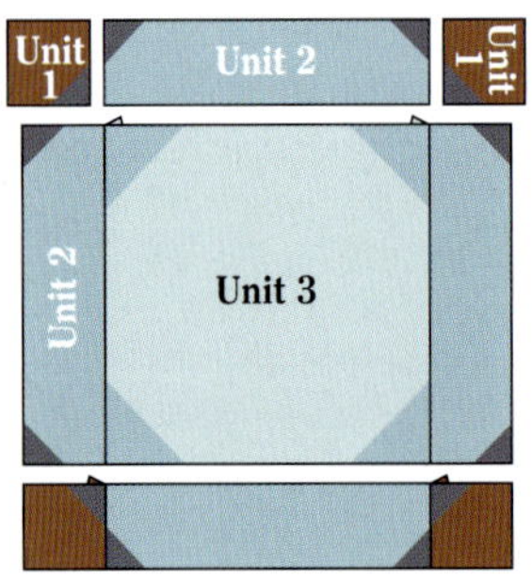

Block Assembly

Fold the block in half both ways and lightly crease the folds. Prepare patches E–G for turned-edge appliqué. Use the creases and appliqué placement diagram as guides to arrange the patches on the block. Use matching thread and a blanket stitch to appliqué the patches in place.

Applique Placement

block no. 394

Facet-nating

by June Dudley • Editor-in-Chief, *Quiltmaker*
quiltmaker.com

Fabric: Studio 8 Fantasia and Kensington Studio's Contempo Dots, both from Quilting Treasures, quiltingtreasures.com.

Section
Make 4

See page 177 on the PDF for pattern

Small Black Dot
section patch 1

Bright Green Print
section patches 2 and 3
4 rectangles (B) 1½" x 6½"

Large Black Dot
section patch 4

Large Scale Black Print
1 square (A) 7½" x 7½"

Small White Dot
4 rectangles (C) 1½" x 3½"
4 rectangles (D) 1½" x 4½"

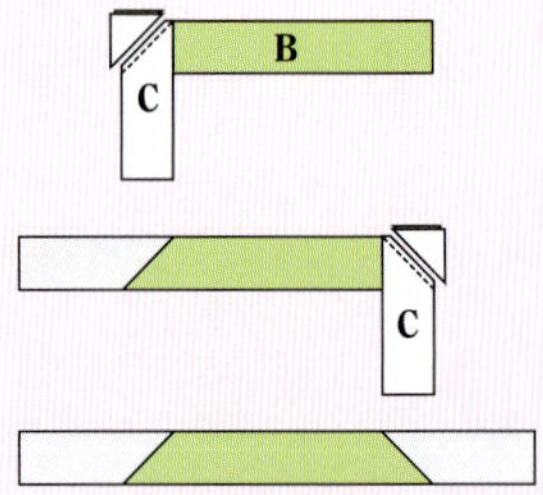

Unit 1 Stitch & Flip Make 2

Make 4 paper copies of the foundation section. Foundation piece the sections in numerical order, pressing and trimming after each patch addition.

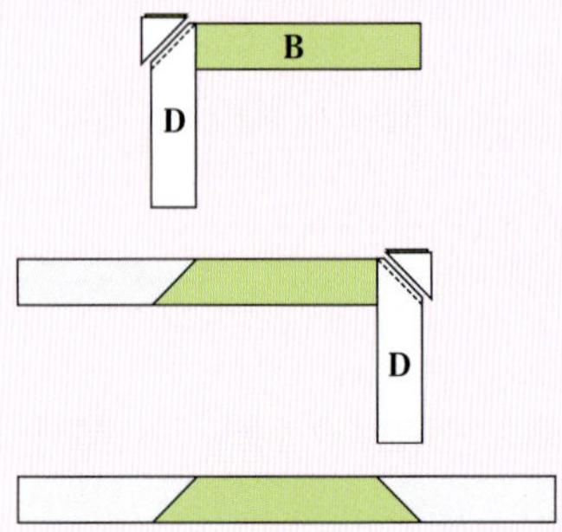

Unit 2 Stitch & Flip Make 2

Refer to "Stitch-and-Flip" in the Techniques file on the PDF. Join the C's and D's to the B's as shown to make the unit 1's and 2's.

Join the A, sections and units as shown to complete the block.

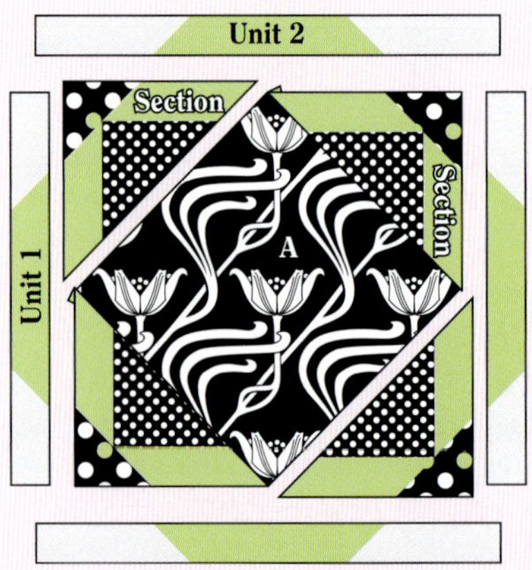

Block Assembly

block no. 395

Polka Party

by Jennifer Schifano Eutsler • Curlicue Creations
curlicuecreations.com

See page 169 on the PDF for pattern

Green Multiprint
1 square (A) 2½"x 2½"
Aqua Solid
4 squares (A) 2½"x 2½"
Black Solid
2 rectangles (B) 1½"x 2½"
2 rectangles (C) 1½"x 4½"
2 rectangles (E) 1"x 8½"
2 rectangles (F) 1"x 9½"
2 Lime Green Tone-on-Tones
from *each*
2 rectangles (D) 2½"x 4½"
Dark Brown Tone-on-Tone
2 rectangles (G) 2"x 9½"
2 rectangles (H) 2"x 12½"
Yellow Print
12 pattern I
1 pattern J
Orange Tone-on-Tone
1 pattern K
Fusible web

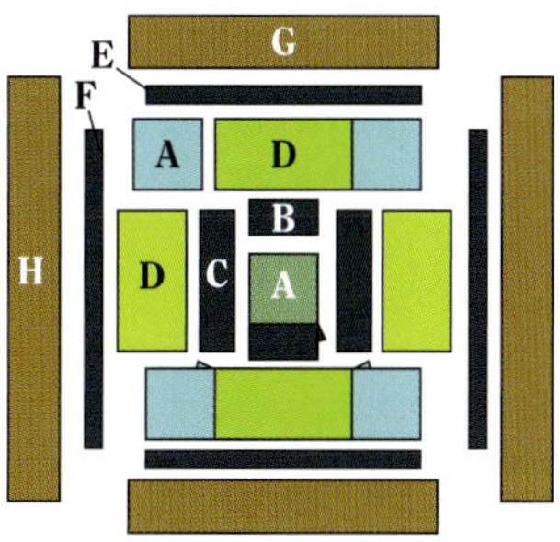

Block Piecing

Join the patches as shown to make the block background. Note that matching green D's are on opposite sides of the center.

Fold the block in half both ways and lightly crease the folds. Prepare patches I–K for fusible appliqué. Use the creases and appliqué placement diagram as guides to arrange the patches. Use matching thread and a machine zigzag stitch to sew around the patches.

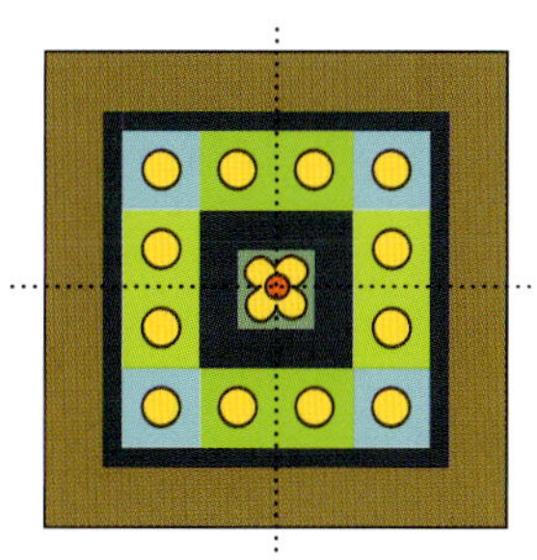

Applique Placement

block no. 396

Butterfly Dance

by Beth Ferrier • Applewood Farm
applewoodfarmquilts.com

Beth Ferrier is the author of *More! Hand Appliqué by Machine* for Applewood Farm Publications, applewoodfarmquilts.com.

See page 190 on the PDF for pattern

⊠ = cut in half twice diagonally

White with Green Print and White with Blue Print
from *each*
1 square 13¼"x 13¼" ⊠ (A) (there will be 2 extra from each fabric)
Black Print #1
4 *each* patterns B and E
Orange Tone-on-Tone
4 *each* patterns C, Cr, D and Dr
Red Tone-on-Tone
4 *each* patterns F, Fr, G and Gr
Black Print #2
4 pattern H
Fusible web
Black embroidery floss

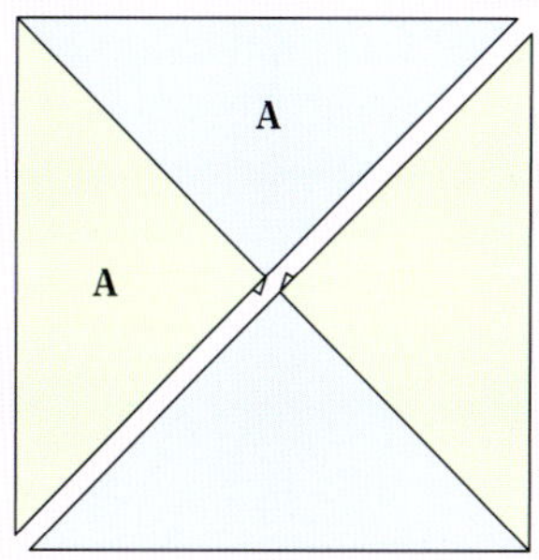

Block Piecing

Join the A's as shown to make the block background.

Fold the block in half both ways and lightly crease the folds. Prepare patches B–H for fusible appliqué. Use the creases and appliqué placement diagram as guides to arrange the patches on the block. Machine zigzag around the patches with monofilament thread. Add the antennae detail using a stem stitch and French knots to complete the block.

Applique Placement

block no. 397

Swimming Upstream

by Dianne Gardner

See page 183 on the PDF for pattern

Brown Print
- 2 squares (A) 3″ x 3″
- 3 pattern B
- 1 square (C) 5½″ x 5½″

Cream Dot
- 3 squares (A) 3″ x 3″
- 2 pattern B
- 1 pattern D

Blue Dot
- 2 rectangles (E) 2¾″ x 8″
- 2 rectangles (F) 2¾″ x 12½″

Button 1 at ¾″

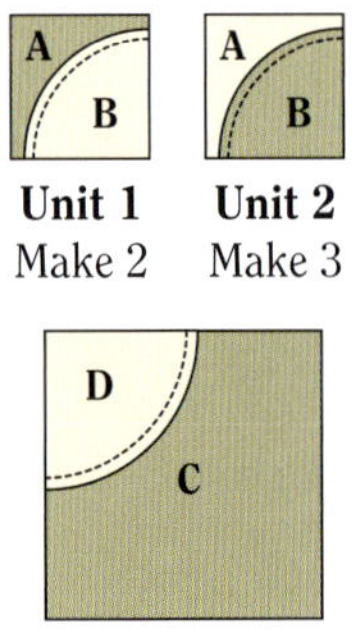

Unit 1 Make 2 · Unit 2 Make 3 · Unit 3 Make 1

Align a cream B in one corner of a brown A as shown. Using cream thread and a machine straight stitch, sew ¼" from the curved edge of B to make a unit 1. Repeat to make 2 unit 1's. Repeat with the cream A's and brown B's to make 3 unit 2's. Use the brown C and cream D to make a unit 3. The raw edges of the appliqué will fray.

Sew the units and patches together as shown. Sew the button in place to complete the block.

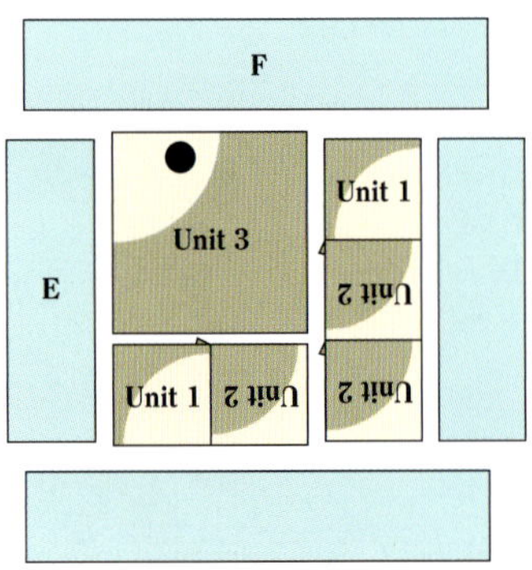

Block Assembly

block no. 398

A Little Peep

by Susan Geddes • Art Director, *Quilters Newsletter*
quiltersnewsletter.com

See page 161 on the PDF for pattern

Blue Batik
- 1 rectangle (A) 6½″ x 10½″

Green Tone-on-Tone
- 1 rectangle (B) 4½″ x 10½″

White Print
- 6 squares (C) 2½″ x 2½″

Multicolor Stripe and Yellow Plaid
from *each*
- 2 squares (C) 2½″ x 2½″

Yellow Print
- 1 square (C) 2½″ x 2½″

Yellow Batik
- 1 pattern D

Orange Batik
- 1 *each* pattern E and Er

Orange Solid
- 1 pattern F

Fusible web

Black Micron Pigma pen

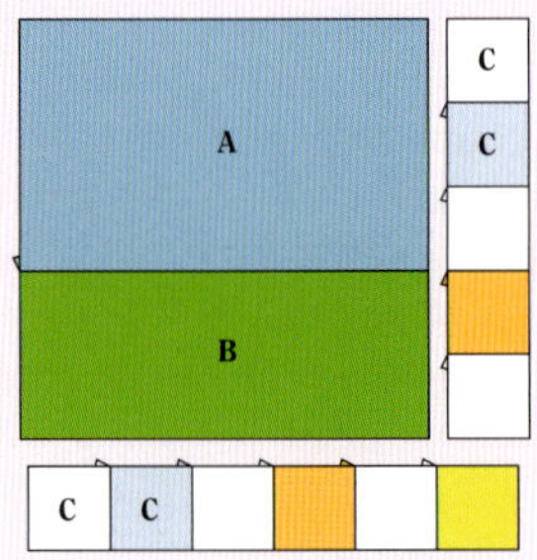

Block Piecing

Refer to the block piecing diagram and join the A, B and C's as shown to make the block.

Fold the block in half both ways and lightly crease the folds. Prepare patches D–F for fusible appliqué. Use the creases and the appliqué placement diagram as guides to arrange the patches on the block as shown; fuse in place.

Using matching thread and a straight stitch, sew close to the edges of each appliqué patch. Draw the chick's eyes with the black pen to complete the block.

Applique Placement

block no. 399

Trapped

by Bev Getschel • Bev Getschel Designs

Fabric: European Taupe designed by Kinkame for Clothworks, clothworkstextiles.com.

See page 173 on the PDF for pattern

Beige Print
- 5 squares (A) 2½" x 2½"
- 4 rectangles (D) 2½" x 3½"
- 2 rectangles (E) 1½" x 10½"
- 2 rectangles (F) 1½" x 12½"

Dark Brown Print
- 6 rectangles (B) 1½" x 2½"
- 8 rectangles (C) 1½" x 3½"
- 2 rectangles (E) 1½" x 10½"

Pink Tone-on-Tone
- 1 pattern G

Dark Red Tone-on-Tone
- 1 pattern H

Black Tone-on-Tone
- 1 pattern I

Fusible web

2 black seed beads

Embroidery floss

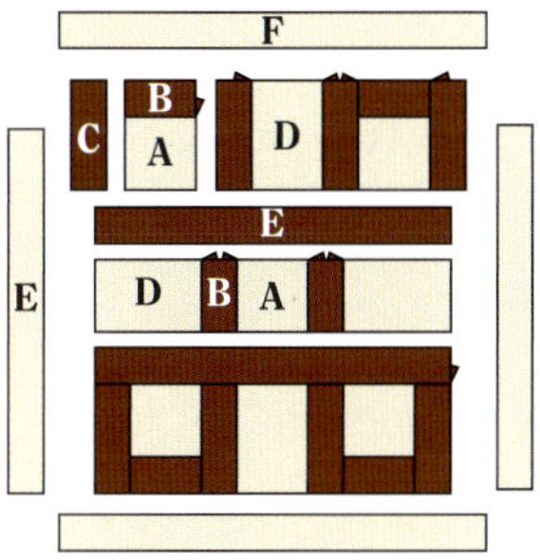

Block Piecing

Join patches A–F as shown to make the block background.

Fold the block in half both ways and lightly crease the folds. Prepare patches G–I for fusible appliqué. Use the creases and placement diagram as guides to arrange the patches on the block.

Use matching thread and a blanket stitch to sew around the patches. Sew the beads in place for the dragonfly's eyes. Use 6 strands of floss and a running stitch for the embroidery details to complete the block.

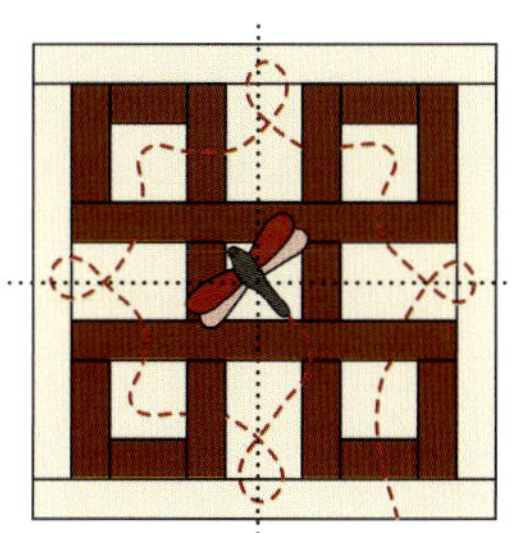

Applique and Embroidery Placement

block no. 400

Robox

by Julie Herman • Jaybird Quilts
jaybirdquilts.com

Fabric: Robot Factory designed by Caleb Gray for Robert Kaufman, robertkaufman.com.

See page 173 on the PDF for pattern

Cream Multiprint
- section patch 1

Dark Brown Print
- section patches 2–5

Light Blue Print
- section patches 6–9

Red Print
- 2 rectangles (A) 2½" x 8½"
- 2 rectangles (B) 2½" x 12½"

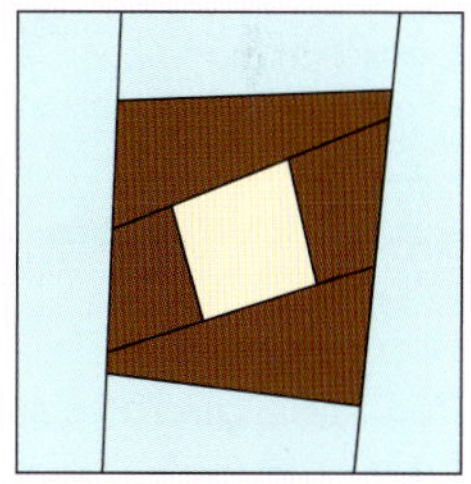

Section
Make 1

Julie fussy cut the center of her block.

Make 1 paper copy of the foundation section. Foundation piece the section in numerical order, pressing and trimming after each patch addition.

Sew the section and patches together as shown to complete the block.

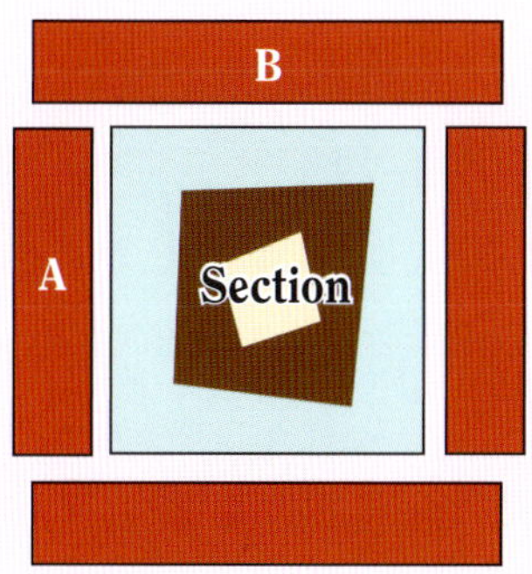

Block Assembly

block no. 401

Spring Has Sprung

by Amanda Herring • The Quilted Fish
thequiltedfishpatterns.com

Fabric: Delighted! by The Quilted Fish for Riley Blake Designs, rileyblakedesigns.com.

See page 174 on the PDF for pattern

Tan Print
1 square (A) 13½"x 13½" (trim to 12½"x 12½" after appliqué)
Aqua Tone-on-Tone and Aqua Stripe
from *each*
4 template B
Red Tone-on-Tone and Red Print
from *each*
4 template D
Yellow Print and Green Print
from *each*
4 template F
Cream Print
1 pattern C
Pink Tone-on-Tone
1 pattern E
Red Stripe
1 pattern G
Green Tone-on-Tone
1 *each* patterns H and I
2 pattern J
Embroidery floss
Aqua rickrack 11" long
Red rickrack 22" long
Yellow rickrack 16" long

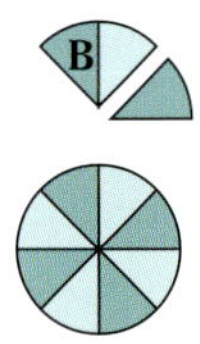

Flower Piecing

Applique Placement

Sew the B's together to make a flower as shown. Repeat with the D's and F's. Prepare each pieced design and the remaining patches for turned-edge appliqué. Baste the rickrack in place behind each flower. Fold A in half both ways and lightly crease the folds. Use the creases and appliqué placement diagram as guides to position the designs on A.

Use matching thread and a straight stitch to sew around the patches. Blanket stitch around the flower centers and leaves. Use 2 strands of embroidery floss and a chain stitch to add the vines. Add the small leaves with a satin stitch. Center the appliqué and trim to 12½"× 12½" to complete the block.

block no. 402

My Summer Sandal

by Barbara Jones • b.j. designs and patterns
bjdesignsandpatterns.com

See page 170 on the PDF for pattern

2 Light Pink Tone-on-Tones and 2 Light Green Tone-on-Tones
from *each*
1 square (A) 4½"x 4½"
Dark Green Tone-on-Tone
2 rectangles (B) 1"x 8½"
2 rectangles (C) 1"x 9½"
Dark Pink Dot
2 rectangles (D) 2"x 9½"
2 rectangles (E) 2"x 12½"
Lime Green Tone-on-Tone
1 pattern F
Orange Tone-on-Tone
1 pattern G
Purple Solid
1 pattern H
Dark Pink Solid
1 pattern I
Dark Orange Solid
1 *each* patterns J and K
1 circle 4½" diameter for yo-yo
Red Multiprint
1 pattern L
Light Brown Tone-on-Tone
1 pattern M
Fusible web
Button 1 at ¾"

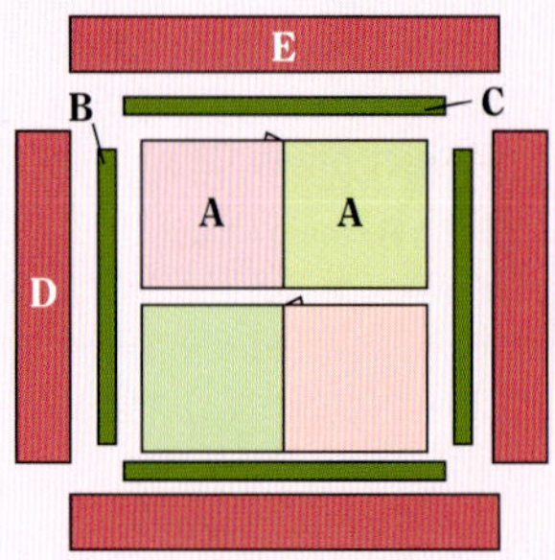

Block Piecing

Applique Placement

Join patches A–E as shown to make the block. Prepare patches F–M for fusible appliqué. Fold the block in half diagonally both ways and lightly crease the folds. Use the creases and appliqué placement diagram as guides to arrange the patches. Use dark thread and a machine zigzag stitch to sew around the patches.

Make a yo-yo from the orange circle. Tack in place. Add the button to complete the block.

block no. 403

Round and Round

by Nancy Mahoney
nancymahoney.com

Nancy Mahoney is the author of *Kaleido-scope Paper Piecing* and other books, all for Martingale & Co., martingale-pub.com.

See page 191 on the PDF for pattern

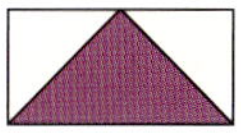

Flying Geese
Make 4

Medium Purple Tone-on-Tone #1
1 square (A) 5¼″x 5¼″
Cream Tone-on-Tone
4 squares (B) 2⅞″x 2⅞″
1 square (C) 4½″x 4½″
4 rectangles (E) 2½″x 8½″
Dark Purple Tone-on-Tone
1 pattern D
4 pattern F
Medium Purple Tone-on-Tone #2
8 squares (G) 2½″x 2½″

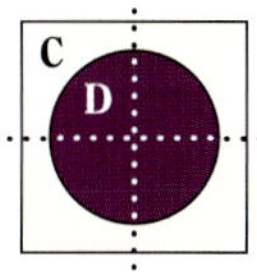

Unit 1
Make 1

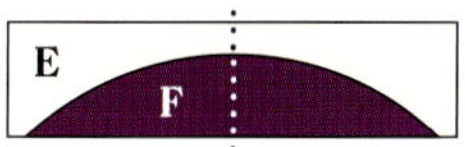

Unit 2
Make 4

Refer to "Fast Flying Geese" in the Techniques file on the PDF. Make 4 Flying Geese using the purple #1 A and cream B's.

Fold C in half both ways and lightly crease the folds. Prepare D for turned-edge appliqué. Use the creases and appliqué placement diagram as guides to arrange D on C. Use monofilament thread and a machine blanket stitch to appliqué around the patch to make unit 1.

Fold the E's in half; prepare the curved edges of the F's for turned-edge appliqué. Aligning raw edges, position the F's on the E's; appliqué the curved edges of the F's to make 4 unit 2's. Sew the units and patches together as shown to complete the block.

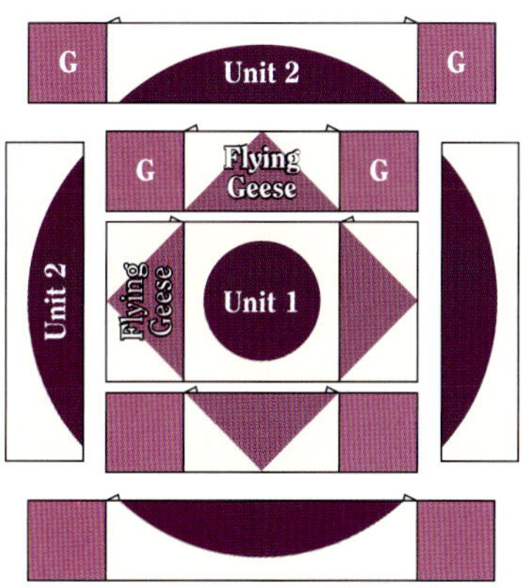

Block Assembly

block no. 404

Thor the Dragon

by Sue Marsh • Whistlepig Creek Productions
wpcreek.com

Fabric: Handspray plus various fabrics designed by Sue Marsh for RJR Fabrics, rjrfabrics.com.

See page 184 on the PDF for pattern

Purple Print
1 square (A) 11½″x 11½″ (trim to 10½″x 10½″ after appliqué)
Dark Blue Tone-on-Tone
1 *each* patterns B and I
Light Pink Tone-on-Tone
1 *each* patterns C, E and F
White Solid
2 *each* patterns D and M
Black Solid
1 pattern D
2 *each* patterns N and O
Green Tone-on-Tone
1 *each* patterns G and H
1 rectangle (P) 1″x 10½″
1 rectangle (Q) 1″x 11″
1 rectangle (R) 2″x 11″
1 rectangle (S) 2″x 12½″
Dark Pink Tone-on-Tone
1 pattern J
Yellow Tone-on-Tone
1 *each* patterns K and L
Fusible web

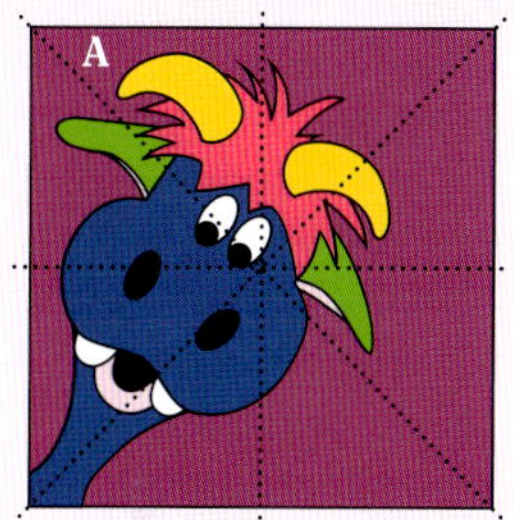

Applique Placement

Block Assembly

Fold A in half both ways and lightly crease the folds. Prepare patches B–O for fusible appliqué. Use the creases and appliqué placement diagram as guides to arrange the patches on A. Use black thread and a machine satin stitch to sew around the patches and to add cheeks and the nose. Center the appliqué and trim A to 10½"× 10½".

Sew the patches together as shown to complete the block.

block no. 405

Precious Moment

by Arlene Neely • Rabbit's Haven Quilt & Stitchery Designs • rabbitshaven.com

Fabric: Always Believe designed by Arlene Neely for Red Rooster Fabrics, redroosterfabrics.com.

See page 164 on the PDF for pattern

White Tone-on-Tone
1 rectangle (A) 9¾" x 10½"
Pale Green Print
2 rectangles (B) 1½" x 9¾"
1 rectangle (C) 1½" x 12½"
1 rectangle (D) 2¼" x 12½"
Assorted Solids and Tone-on-Tones
1 *each* patterns E–J
2 *each* patterns K–N
Acrylic paint for cheeks
Embroidery floss

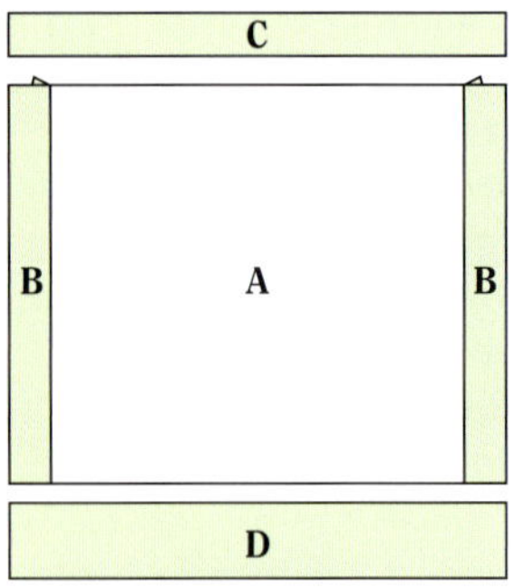

Block Piecing

Sew the patches together as shown to make the block.

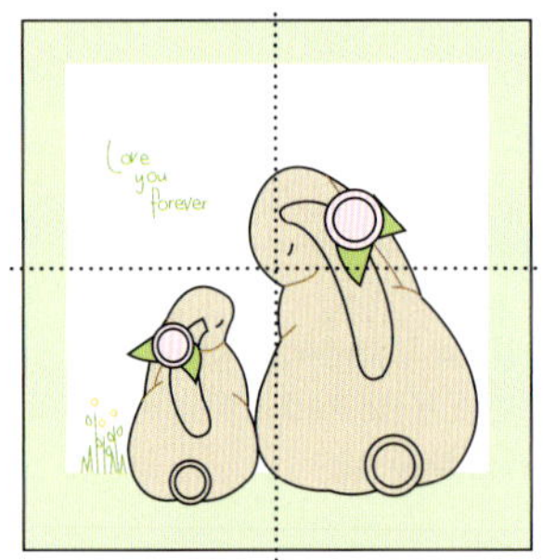
Applique and Embroidery Placement

Fold the block in half both ways and lightly crease the folds. Prepare patches E–J for turned-edge appliqué. Use the creases and appliqué placement diagram as guides to arrange the patches on the block. Use matching thread and a blind stitch to appliqué patches E–J in place. Pin K–N in place. Using matching thread and a straight stitch, sew patches K–N in place, allowing the edges of the patches to fray a little.

Use the acrylic paint and a dry brush to add color to the cheeks. Using 2 strands of floss, backstitch the letters, flowers and rabbit details to complete the block.

block no. 406

Button Sampler

by Jane Quinn • Quilting in the Country
quiltinginthecountry.com

Fabric: Heidi designed by Laura Ashley for Quilting Treasures, quiltingtreasures.com.

See page 194 on the PDF for pattern

Cream Print
5 squares (A) 4½" x 4½"
4 pattern B
Yellow Print
4 squares (A) 4½" x 4½"
5 pattern B
Fusible web
Buttons 5 at ¾"–⅞"

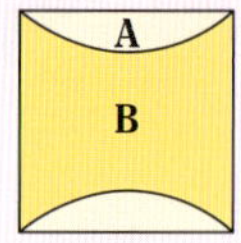

Unit 1
Make 5

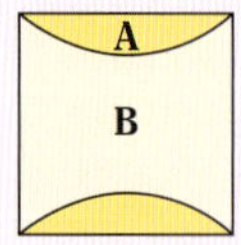

Unit 2
Make 4

Prepare the B's for fusible appliqué. Position a yellow B on a cream A as shown. Fuse in place to make a unit 1. Make 5 unit 1's. Repeat with the cream B's and yellow A's to make 4 unit 2's.

Sew the units together as shown to make the block.

Use contrasting thread and a large machine blanket stitch to sew along the curved edges of the B's and the vertical seam lines.

Sew the buttons to the centers of the yellow B's to complete the block.

Block Assembly

block no. 407
Pinwheel 9-Patch

by Peg Spradlin
handicraftsbypeg.com

Fabric: Nature's Chorus designed by April Cornell for Moda Fabrics, unitednotions.com.

See page 181 on the PDF for pattern

Green Tone-on-Tone, Green Solid and 2 Green Prints
from *each*
section, patch 1

Pink Tone-on-Tone, Pink Solid and 2 Pink Prints
from *each*
section reversed, patch 1

Cream Solid
section and section reversed, patch 2

Dark Green Tone-on-Tone
4 squares (A) 2½″ x 2½″

Make 16 copies *each* of the foundation section and foundation section reversed. Foundation piece the sections in numerical order, pressing and trimming after each patch addition.

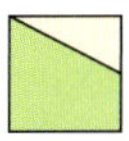

Section
Make 16

Sew 4 sections, 4 sections reversed and a green A together as shown to make each quadrant. Join the quadrants to complete the block.

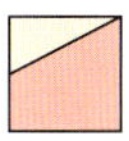

Section Reversed
Make 16

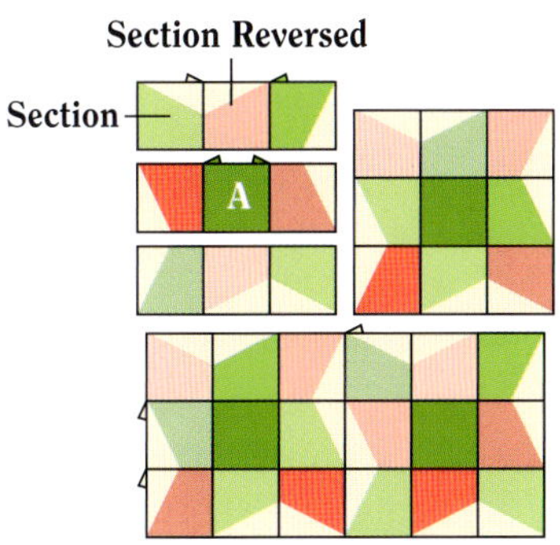

Block Assembly

block no. 408
Some-Bunny

by Paula Stoddard • Associate Editor, *Quiltmaker*
quiltmaker.com

Fabric: Woolies Flannel for Maywood Studio, maywoodstudio.com.

See page 165 on the PDF for pattern

Light Yellow Check Flannel
1 square (A) 9½″ x 9½″

Gray Wool
1 *each* patterns B, Br and D

Pink Wool
1 *each* patterns C and Cr

Black Wool
2 pattern E
1 pattern F

Blue Check Flannel and Orange Check Flannel
from *each*
1 rectangle (G) 2″ x 9½″

Red Check Flannel and Green Check Flannel
from *each*
1 rectangle (H) 2″ x 12½″

Fusible web

Gray, pink and black wool thread

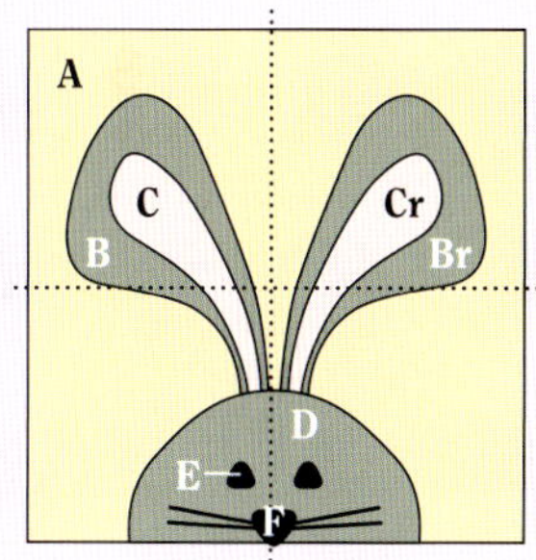

Applique Placement

Block Assembly

Fold A in half both ways and lightly crease the folds. Prepare patches B–F for fusible appliqué. Use the creases and appliqué placement diagram as guides to arrange the patches on A. Place the bunny's nose (F) close to the bottom edge of A so that it will be sewn into the seam allowance.

Use matching thread and a blanket stitch to sew around the patches. Use black thread and an outline stitch to embroider the whiskers.

Sew the G and H patches to A as shown to complete the block.

block no. 409

Flower Patch

by Ann Weber • Gingham Girls LLC
ginghamgirls.biz

See page 179 on the PDF for pattern

White Tone-on-Tone
4 squares (A) 6¼″x 6¼″
Pale Green Check
2 rectangles (B) 1″x 6¼″
1 rectangle (C) 1″x 12½″
Pink Print
1 pattern D
Yellow Tone-on-Tone
1 pattern E
Dark Brown Tone-on-Tone
1 pattern F
4 Green Prints
from *each*
1 pattern G

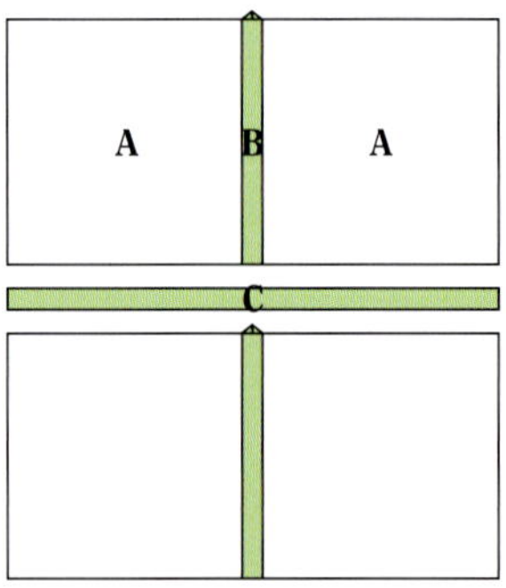

Block Piecing

Sew patches A–C together as shown to make the block.

Prepare patches D–G for turned-edge appliqué. Fold the block in half diagonally both ways and lightly crease the folds. Use the creases and appliqué placement diagram as guides to arrange the patches on the block. Use matching thread and a blind stitch to appliqué the patches in place to complete the block.

Applique Placement

block no. 410

Reason to Celebrate

by Sandra Workman • Pine Mountain Designs
pinemtndesigns.com

See page 171 on the PDF for pattern

White with Blue Dot
1 square (A) 6½″x 6½″
Red Check
1 pattern B
Red Stripe
1 pattern C
Light Blue Tone-on-Tone
1 pattern D
Green Tone-on-Tone
1 rectangle (E) 2″x 6½″
Light Blue Dot and Pink Tone-on-Tone
from *each*
1 rectangle (F) 2″x 8″
Red Print
1 rectangle (G) 2″x 9½″
White Solid
2 rectangles (G) 2″x 9½″
2 rectangles (H) 2″x 12½″
Assorted Prints
7 pattern I
Fusible web

Applique Placement

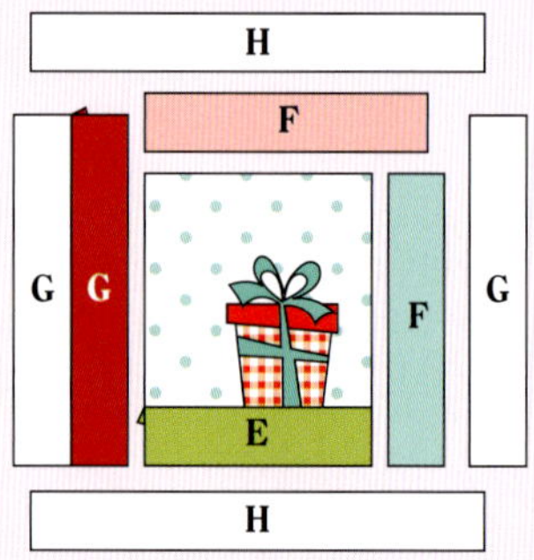

Block Piecing

Fold A in half both ways and lightly crease the folds. Prepare patches B–D and I for fusible appliqué. Use the creases and appliqué placement diagram as guides to arrange B–D on A. Fuse the patches in alphabetical order. Sew A and E–H together as shown. Arrange the I's on the block; fuse in place.

Applique Placement

Use matching thread and a straight stitch to sew around the patches. Straight stitch the pennant line twice with brown thread to complete the block.

block no. 411

Fan Fare

by Lisa Bassett • Relatively Creative
relativelycreativepatterns.com

Section 1
Make 2

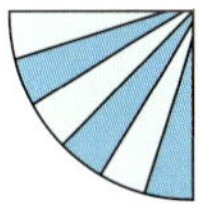

Section 2
Make 2

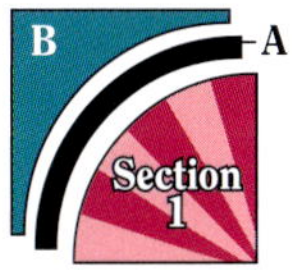

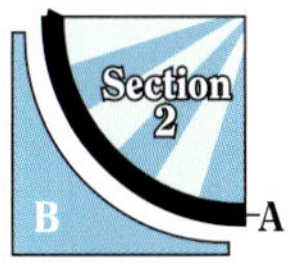

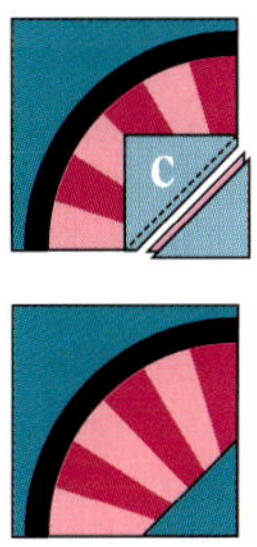

Unit 1
Stitch & Flip
Make 2

See page 228 on the PDF for pattern

Medium Pink Tone-on-Tone
section 1, patches 1, 3 and 5
Dark Pink Tone-on-Tone
section 1, patches 2, 4 and 6
4 squares (C) 3″ x 3″
Medium Turquoise Tone-on-Tone
section 2, patches 1, 3 and 5
Light Turquoise Tone-on-Tone
section 2, patches 2, 4 and 6
2 template B
Black Tone-on-Tone
4 template A
Dark Turquoise Tone-on-Tone
2 template B
2 squares (C) 3″ x 3″

Unit 2
Stitch & Flip
Make 2

For all techniques, refer to the Techniques file on the PDF. Make 2 paper copies of *each* foundation section. The colors for section 2 are shown in parentheses. Foundation piece the sections in numerical order, pressing and trimming after each patch addition. Carefully remove the foundation papers.

Sew the black A's to the foundation sections as shown. Add dark turquoise B's to the section 1's and medium turquoise B's to the section 2's as shown.

Add the C's as shown to make 2 unit 1's and 2 unit 2's. Sew the units together as shown to complete the block.

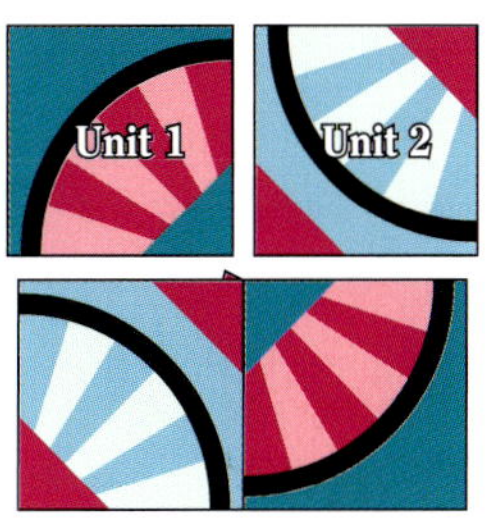

Block Assembly

block no. 412

Roly Poly Owl

by Mary Lane Brown
tulip-patch.blogspot.com

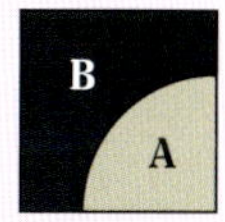

Unit 1
Make 2

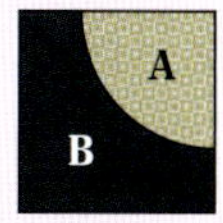

Unit 2
Make 1

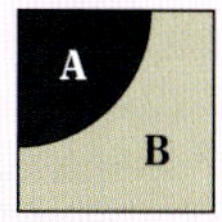

Partial Unit
Make 1

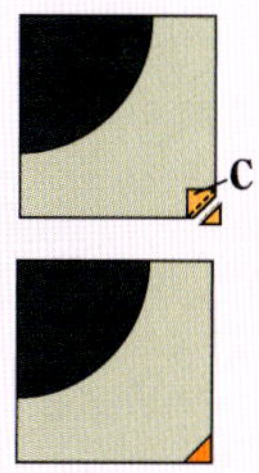

Unit 3
Stitch & Flip
Make 1

See page 222 on the PDF for pattern

⧄ = cut in half diagonally

Light Taupe Tone-on-Tone
2 template A
1 template B
Light Taupe Print
1 template A
Black Print
1 template A
3 template B
Orange Print
1 square (C) 1″ x 1″
Green Print
2 rectangles (D) 1¼″ x 7½″
2 rectangles (E) 1¼″ x 9″
Orange Check
2 squares 6⅞″ x 6⅞″ ⧄ (F)
Cream Solid
2 pattern G
Buttons 2 at ⅝″

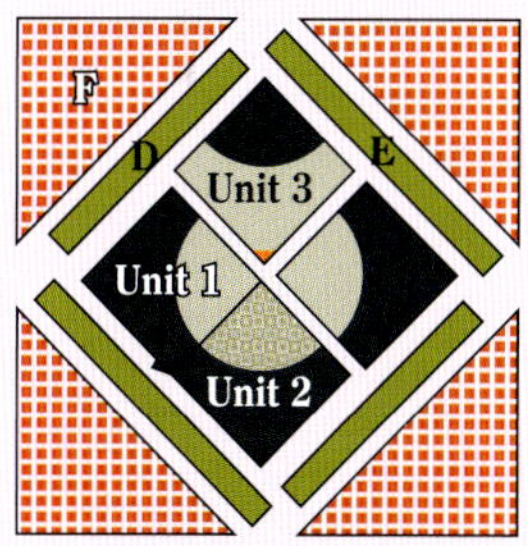

Block Assembly

For all techniques, refer to the Techniques file on the PDF. Sew the taupe tone-on-tone A's and the taupe print A to black B's as shown to make 2 unit 1's and 1 unit 2. Join the black A with the taupe tone-on-tone B to make a partial unit. Add the orange C to the partial unit as shown to make unit 3. Sew the units and patches together as shown to make the block.

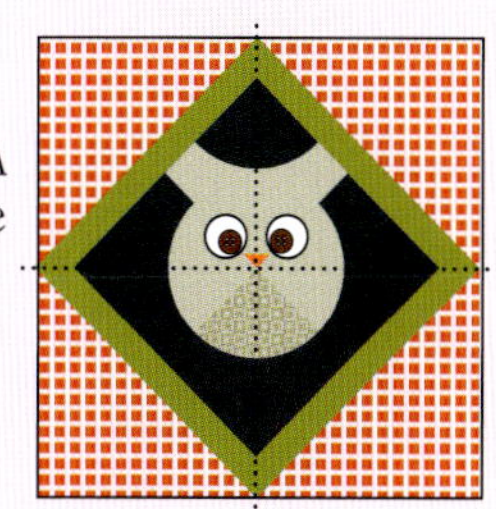

Applique Placement

Fold the block in half both ways and lightly crease the folds. Prepare the G's for turned-edge appliqué. Use the creases and appliqué placement diagram as guides to arrange the G's on the block. Use matching thread and a blind stitch to appliqué the G's in place. Tack the buttons in place to complete the block.

block no. 413

Holiday Doily

by Kari Carr • New Leaf Stitches
newleafstitches.com

Kari Carr is the author of *Just Around the Corner: Quilts with Easy Mitered Borders* for Martingale & Co., shopmartingale.com.

See page 229 on the PDF for pattern

⊠ = cut in half twice diagonally

2 Cream Tone-on-Tones
from *each*
- 2 rectangles (A) 3½" x 6½"
- 1 square 7¼" x 7¼" ⊠ (E) (there will be 2 extra)

Red Tone-on-Tone
- 4 *each* patterns B and C
- 4 pattern G
- 1 pattern H

Green Tone-on-Tone
- 4 squares (D) 3½" x 3½"
- 4 pattern F

Fusible web

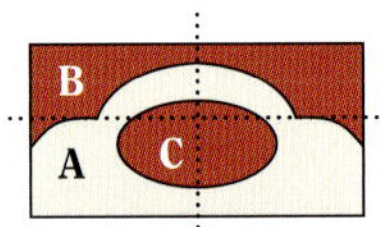

Unit 1
Make 2

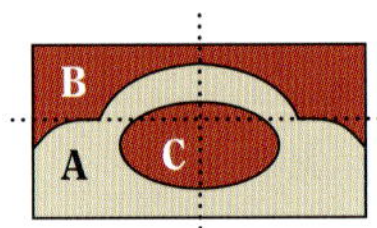

Unit 2
Make 2

Fold the A's in half both ways and lightly crease the folds. Prepare patches B, C and F–H for fusible appliqué. Use the creases and unit diagrams as guides to arrange the B's and C's on the A's. Fuse in place. Use monofilament thread and a machine blind stitch to sew around the patches. Make 2 unit 1's and 2 unit 2's as shown.

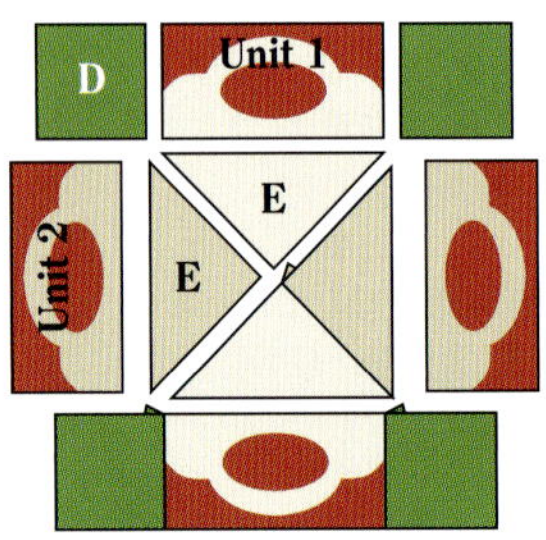

Block Assembly

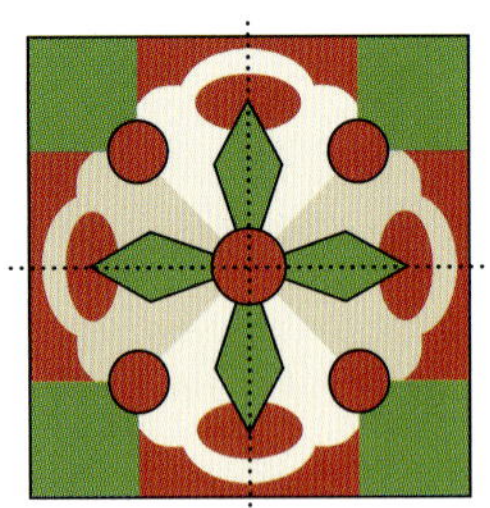

Applique Placement

Sew the units and patches together as shown to make the block. Fold the block in half both ways and lightly crease the folds. Use the creases and appliqué placement diagram as guides to arrange patches F–H on the block. Fuse in place. Use monofilament thread and a machine blind stitch to sew around the patches to complete the block.

block no. 414

Window Garden

by Sandi Colwell • Quilt Cabana Patterns
quiltcabanapatterns.com

Sandi Colwell is the author of *Little Quilts for Big Occasions* for Leisure Arts, Inc., leisurearts.com.

See page 242 on the PDF for pattern

Pink Tone-on-Tone
- 4 squares (A) 2" x 2"

Gray Tone-on-Tone
- 4 rectangles (B) 2" x 9½"

Light Blue Tone-on-Tone
- 1 square (C) 9½" x 9½"

Assorted Pink, Yellow, Purple and Orange Tone-on-Tones
- 1 pattern D
- 3 *each* patterns E and G
- 5 *each* patterns F and I
- 6 pattern H

Green Tone-on-Tone
- 6 pattern I

Green rickrack 10"

Fusible web

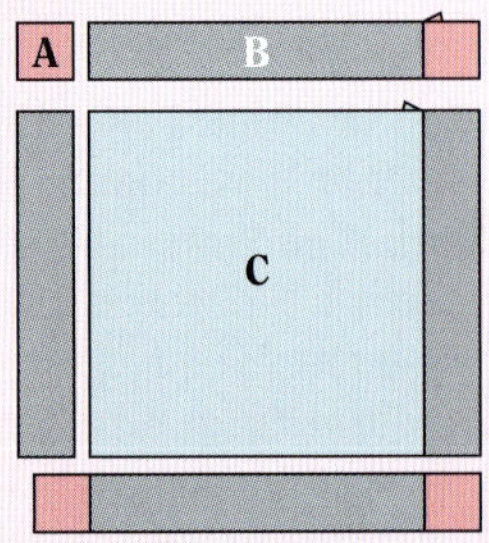

Block Piecing

Applique Placement

Sew patches A–C together as shown. Fold the block in half both ways and lightly crease the folds. Prepare patches D–I for fusible appliqué. Use the creases and appliqué placement diagram as guides to arrange the patches on the block. Cut the rickrack into 5 equal lengths; tuck rickrack stems under the green I's and lower flowers. Fuse the patches in place.

Use contrasting thread and a machine blanket stitch to sew around the patches. Use a matching thread and a straight stitch to tack down the rickrack.

Sandi embellished the flowers and bee with decorative stitches and used a straight stitch for the bee's path.

Add a French knot for the bee's eye to complete the block.

block no. 415

Shabby Spin

by Melissa Corry • Happy Quilting
happyquiltingmelissa.blogspot.com

Black Print
1 square (A) 10″ x 10″
Pink Print
2 rectangles (B) 2″ x 10″
2 rectangles (C) 2″ x 13″
1 circle (D) 5″ diameter
White Print
1 circle (E) 3″ diameter
Fusible web

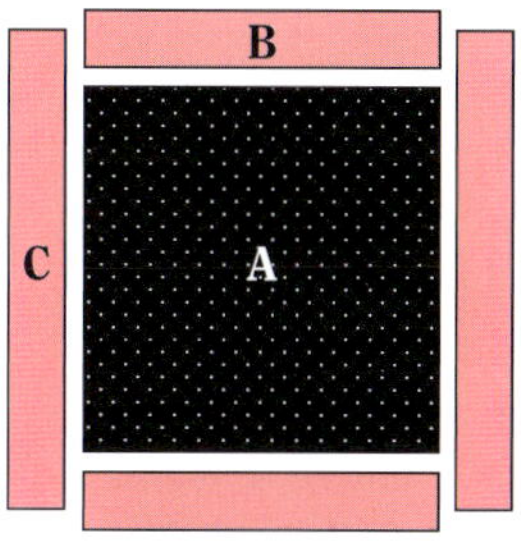

Block Piecing

Sew patches A–C together as shown. The block should measure 13″ × 13″.

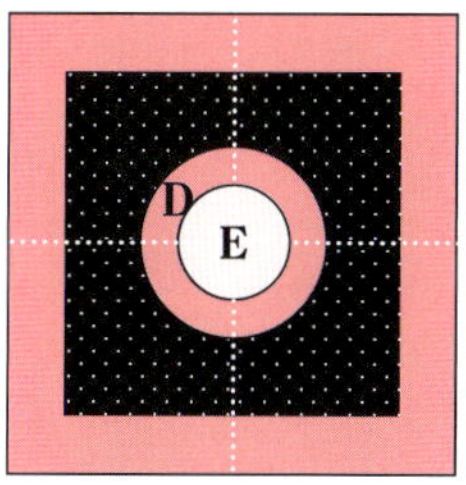

Applique Placement

Fold the block in half both ways and lightly crease the folds. Prepare patches D and E for fusible appliqué. Use the creases and appliqué placement diagram as guides to arrange the patches; fuse in place. Use matching thread and a straight stitch to sew close to the edges of the patches.

Refer to the trimming diagram to trim the block into four 6½″ × 6½″ quadrants. Rotate 2 of the quadrants as shown. Sew the quadrants together to complete the block.

Trimming Diagram

Block Assembly

block no. 416

Birds Holding a Quilt

by Erin Cox • Why Not Sew? Quilts
whynotsew.blogspot.com

Fabric: Ruby designed by Bonnie and Camille for Moda Fabrics, unitednotions.com.

Assorted Light and Medium Prints and Tone-on-Tones
16 squares (A) 1⅜″ x 1⅜″
8 squares (D) 4½″ x 4½″
1 *each* patterns E and Er
Red Dot
2 rectangles (B) ¾″ x 4″
2 rectangles (C) ¾″ x 4½″
Fusible web

Template for Birds Holding a Quilt block on page 33 of the PDF Templates file.

Sew the patches together as shown to make the block.

Fold the block in half diagonally both ways and lightly crease the folds. Prepare patches E and Er for fusible appliqué. Use the creases and appliqué placement diagram as guides to arrange the patches on the block; fuse the patches in place.

Use black thread and a machine straight stitch to sew close to the edge of the birds 3 times. Use a straight stitch to add the bird and branch detail to complete the block.

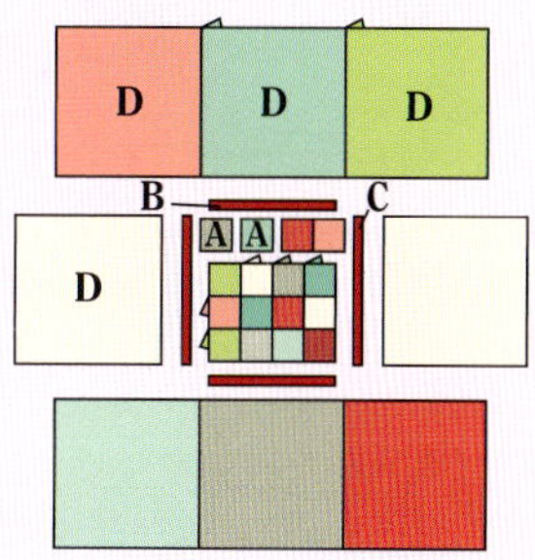

Block Piecing

Applique and Embroidery Placement

block no. 417
Bring on Winter

by Jana Davidson • Turnberry Lane
turnberrylanepatterns.com

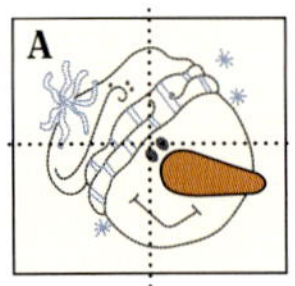

Embroidery Placement

Trimming Diagram

See page 203 on the PDF for pattern

Cream Solid
 1 rectangle (A) 7"x 7¾"
Orange Tone-on-Tone
 1 pattern B
Medium Blue Tone-on-Tone
 4 rectangles (C) 1½"x 14"
4 Assorted Blue Tone-on-Tones
from *each*
 1 rectangle (D) 3½"x 14"
Black Pigma Micron pen (.01 tip)
Embroidery floss

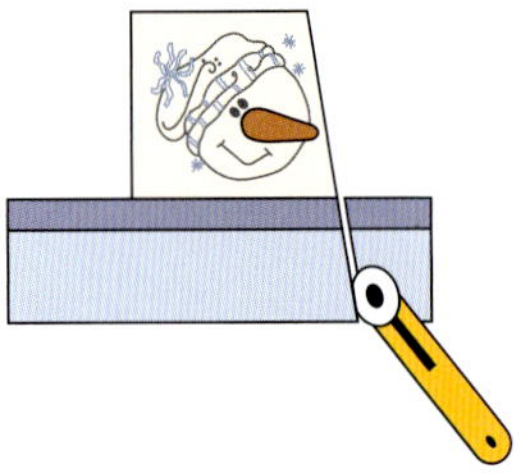

Fold A in half both ways and lightly crease the folds. Using the creases and placement diagram as guides, trace the embroidery design onto A with the pen. Use 2 strands of floss and an outline stitch to embroider the design. Use a satin stitch for the eyes, French knots for the hat detail, and a star stitch for the snowflakes. Prepare patch B for turned-edge appliqué. Use matching thread and a blind stitch to appliqué around the patch. Trim A to 6"× 6¾".

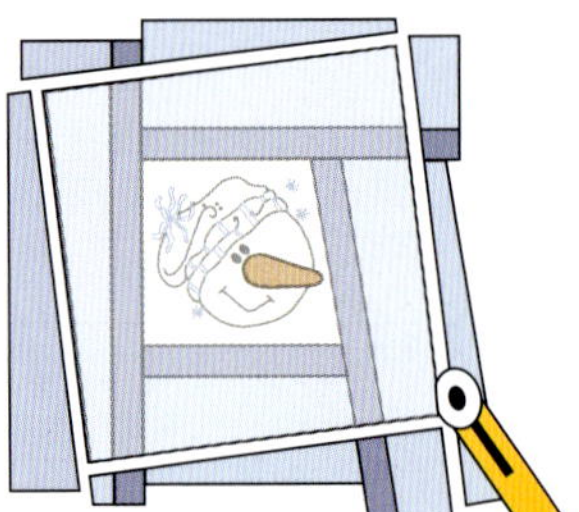

Trimming Diagram

Join each C with a D. Referring to the trimming diagram and the trimming line on the pattern sheet, trim the right side of A at an angle as shown. Sew a C/D to the bottom of A; trim the right side of the C/D even with the trimmed edge as shown. In the same way, add a C/D to the right side, top and left side, each time trimming the C/D even with the edge of the A. Place a 12½" square ruler on the block; skew the ruler slightly and trim to 12½"× 12½". Add the detail to the C's using a long running stitch to complete the block.

block no. 418
Scrollwork

by Monique Dillard • Open Gate Quilts
opengatequilts.com

Fabric: Papillon designed by 3 Sisters for Moda Fabrics, unitednotions.com.

Monique Dillard is the author of *Traditional Fat Quarter Quilts* for C&T Publishing, ctpub.com.

See page 212 on the PDF for pattern

Cream Tone-on-Tone
 1 square (A) 5¼"x 5¼"
 1 square (E) 8½"x 8½"
Pink Print #1
 4 squares (B) 2⅞"x 2⅞"
 4 rectangles (C) 2½"x 4½"
 4 squares (D) 2½"x 2½"
Pink Tone-on-Tone
 1 pattern F
Red Tone-on-Tone
 1 pattern G
 8 pattern J
Pink Print #2
 1 pattern H
Brown Print
 4 pattern I
Fusible web

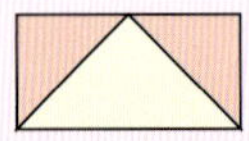

Flying Geese
Make 4

Applique Placement

Refer to "Fast Flying Geese" in the Techniques file on the PDF. Make 4 Flying Geese using the cream A and pink #1 B's. Sew the Flying Geese and patches together as shown to make the block.

Fold the block in half diagonally both ways and lightly crease the folds. Prepare patches F–J for fusible appliqué. Use the creases and appliqué placement diagram as guides to arrange the patches. Fuse the patches in alphabetical order.

Sew around the patches using matching thread and a machine zigzag stitch to complete the block.

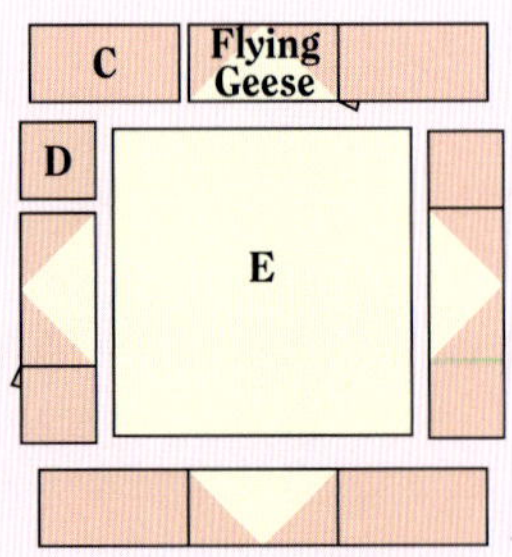

Block Assembly

block no. 419

Acorns Away!

by Sandy Fitzpatrick • Hissyfitz Designs
hissyfitzdesigns.com

See page 219 on the PDF for pattern

Black Solid
- 1 square (A) 11½" x 11½" (trim to 10½" x 10½" after appliqué)
- 2 rectangles (H) 1½" x 10½"
- 2 rectangles (I) 1½" x 12½"

Gold Print
- 1 pattern B

Green Batik
- 1 each patterns C and D

Brown Print
- 1 pattern E

Multicolor Print
- 1 pattern F

Black-and-White Stripe
- 4 rectangles (G) 1" x 10½"

Fusible web

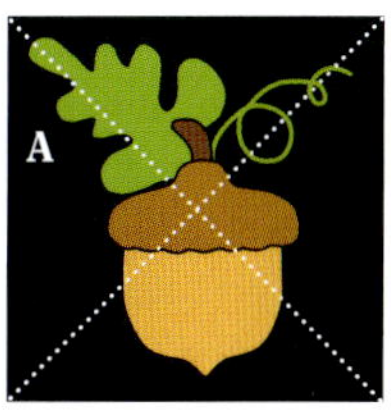

Applique Placement

Fold A in half diagonally both ways and lightly crease the folds. Prepare patches B–F for fusible appliqué. Use the creases and appliqué placement diagram as guides to arrange the patches on A. Fuse the patches to A in alphabetical order.

Use matching thread and a machine blanket stitch to sew around the patches. Center the appliqué and trim to 10½" × 10½".

Fold each G in half lengthwise with wrong sides together and press. Align the raw edges of each folded G with a side of A as shown and baste in place. Add the black H's and I's to complete the block.

Block Assembly

block no. 420

Year 'round Hibiscus

by Cynthia Foster • Carter Creek Quilts
etsy.com/shop/cartercreekquilts

See pages 233–234 on the PDF for pattern

Orange Batik
- sections 1–4, patches 1, 3, 5, 7, 9 and 11

Purple Batik
- sections 1–4, patches 2, 4, 6, 8 and 10

Green Batik
- 1 *each* templates A, C, E and G

Burgundy Batik
- 1 each templates B, D, F and H

7 silver bugle beads

7 clear seed beads

Make 1 paper copy of *each* foundation section. Foundation piece the sections in numerical order, pressing and trimming after each patch addition.

Refer to "Curved Piecing" in the Techniques file on the PDF. Join the patches and sections as shown. Tack the beads in place to complete the block.

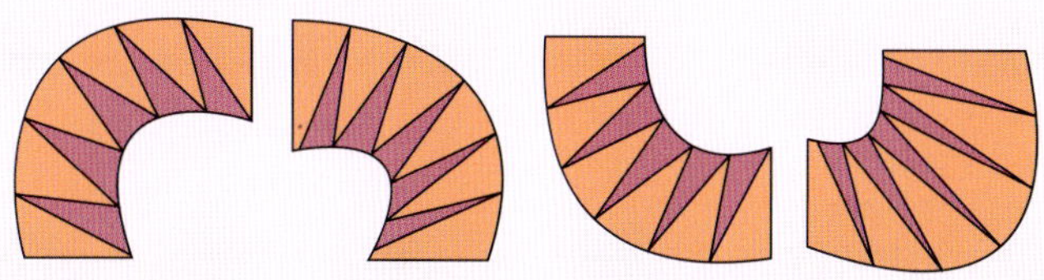

Section 1 Make 1 | Section 2 Make 1 | Section 3 Make 1 | Section 4 Make 1

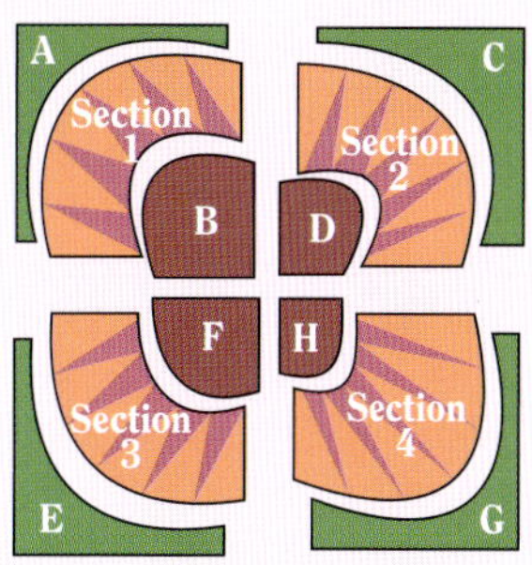

Block Assembly

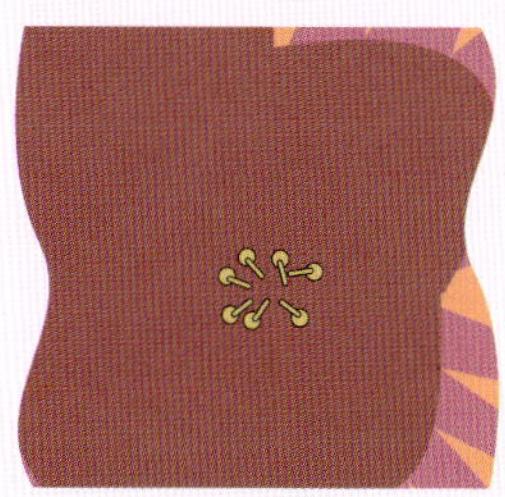

Bead Placement

block no. 421
Liberty Stamp

by Debra Gabel • Zebra Patterns
zebrapatterns.com

Fabric: Bali Handpaints by Hoffman California Fabrics, hoffmanfabrics.com.

Debra Gabel is the author of *Quilt Blocks Across America* for C&T Publishing, ctpub.com.

See page 222 on the PDF for pattern

Orange Batik
1 square (A) 9½″ x 9½″ (trim to 8½″ x 8½″ after appliqué)
Dark Blue Batik
1 pattern B
Dark Purple Batik
1 pattern C
Medium Blue Batik
1 pattern D
Gold Batik
1 pattern E
Black Solid
1 pattern F
16 pattern N
4 pattern O
Gray Batik
1 *each* patterns G, H and I
Black and White Stripe
2 rectangles (J) ⅞″ x 8½″
2 rectangles (K) ⅞″ x 9¼″
White Solid
2 rectangles (L) 2⅛″ x 9¼″
2 rectangles (M) 2⅛″ x 12½″
Fusible web
Embroidery floss
Fabric paint

Applique Placement

Block Piecing

Fold A in half both ways and lightly crease the folds.Prepare patches B–I and N–O for fusible appliqué. Use the creases and appliqué placement diagram as guides to arrange B–I on A. Fuse the patches in alphabetical order. Center the appliqué and trim to 8½″ × 8½″.

Sew the patches together as shown. Refer to the block photograph for placement of patches N and O; fuse in place. Referring to the appliqué placement diagram for placement, trace "FOREVER" on the block. Use matching thread and a small satin stitch to sew around the patches. Use white thread to hand satin stitch "FOREVER." Add windows to the buildings with fabric paint to complete the block.

block no. 422
Cat Nip

by Dianne Gardner

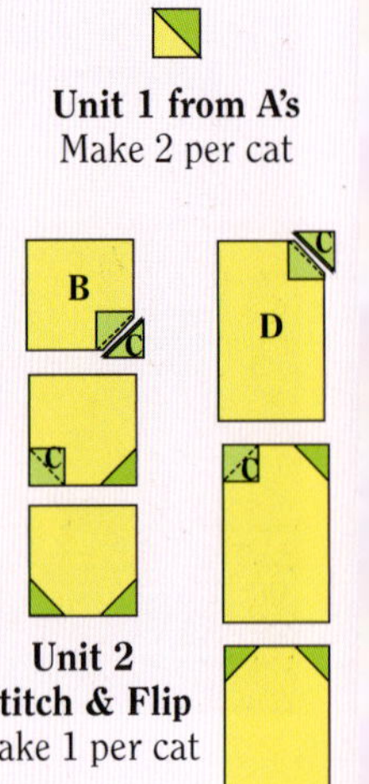

Unit 1 from A's
Make 2 per cat

Unit 2
Stitch & Flip
Make 1 per cat

Unit 3
Stitch & Fli
Make 1 per c

See page 240 on the PDF for pattern

Yellow Print
1 square (A) 1⅞″ x 1⅞″
1 square (B) 3½″ x 3½″
1 rectangle (D) 3½″ x 5½″
1 pattern F
Multicolor Stripe
1 square (A) 1⅞″ x 1⅞″
1 square (B) 3½″ x 3½″
1 rectangle (D) 3½″ x 5½″
1 pattern G
Green Solid
2 squares (A) 1⅞″ x 1⅞″
10 squares (C) 1½″ x 1½″
2 rectangles (E) 2½″ x 9½″
1 rectangle (H) 1¼″ x 9½″
2 rectangles (I) 1⅛″ x 9½″
2 rectangles (J) 2″ x 12½″
Buttons 4 at 5/8″ diameter
Black ribbon 12″ at ¼″ wide

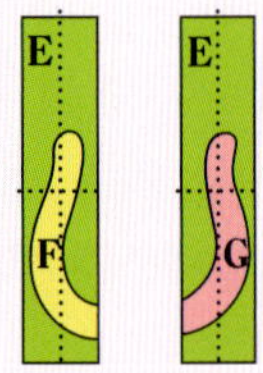

Applique Placement

For all techniques, refer to the Techniques file on the PDF. Pair the yellow A and the stripe A with green A's to make 4 unit 1's. Make 2 unit 2's using the yellow B and stripe B with green C's. Make 2 unit 3's using the yellow D and stripe D with green C's.

Fold the E's in half both ways and lightly crease the folds. Prepare patches F and G for turned-edge appliqué. Use the creases and appliqué placement diagram as guides to arrange the patches. Use matching thread and a blind stitch to appliqué the tails in place.

Sew the units and patches together as shown. Tack the buttons for eyes and ribbon bows to complete the block.

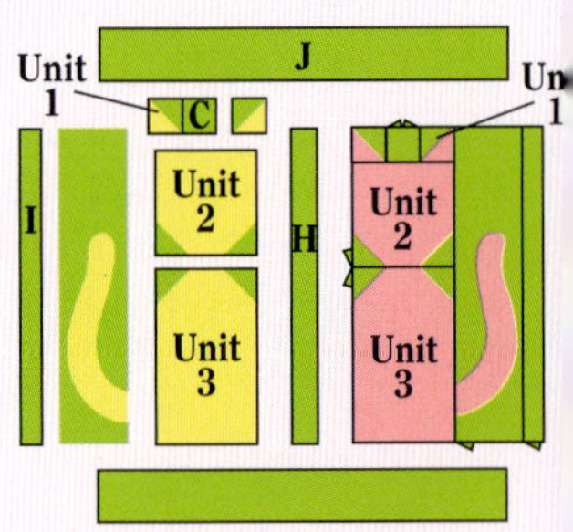

Block Assembly

block no. 423
Chicken Surprise

by Susan Geddes • Art Director, *Quilters Newsletter*
quiltersnewsletter.com

See page 204 on the PDF for pattern

⊠ = cut in half twice diagonally

Purple Batik
1 rectangle (A) 6½″ x 12½″
Yellow Batik
1 pattern B
Orange Tone-on-Tone
1 pattern C
Light Orange Batik
1 *each* patterns D and Dr
4 Assorted Prints and Batiks
from *each*
1 pattern E
Multicolor Print
4 squares (F) 2⅝″ x 2⅝″
Dark Gold Tone-on-Tone
2 squares (F) 2⅝″ x 2⅝″
2 squares 4¼″ x 4¼″ ⊠ (G)
(there will be 2 extra)
Purple Tone-on-Tone
1 *each* templates H and Hr
Fusible web
Black Micron Pigma pen

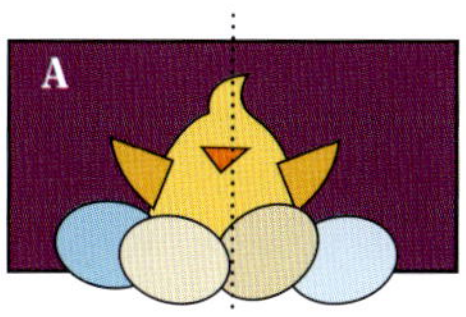

Applique Placement

Block Piecing

Fold A in half and lightly crease the fold. Prepare patches B–E for fusible appliqué. Use the crease and appliqué placement diagram as guides to arrange the patches on A. Fuse the patches in alphabetical order. Use matching thread and a straight stitch to sew close to the edges of each appliqué patch. Add the chick's eyes with the black pen. Trim the bottom of the E's along the bottom edge of A.

Sew patches F–Hr together as shown to make the bottom half of the block. Join the halves to complete the block.

Block Assembly

block no. 424
Remembering

by Bev Getschel • Bev Getschel Designs

Fabric: European Taupe designed by Kinkame for Clothworks, clothworks.com.

See page 211 on the PDF for pattern

⧄ = cut in half diagonally

Beige Tone-on-Tone
1 square (A) 7½″ x 7½″
(trim to 6½″ x 6½″ after embroidery)
2 squares 6⅞″ x 6⅞″ ⧄ (C)
Tan Tone-on-Tone
2 squares 5⅛″ x 5⅛″ ⧄ (B)
3 Assorted Green Tone-on-Tones
from *1*
2 bias strips 1″ x 14″
3 pattern D
from *1*
3 pattern D
from *1*
4 pattern D
Brown Pigma Micron pen (.01 tip) or pencil
Embroidery floss

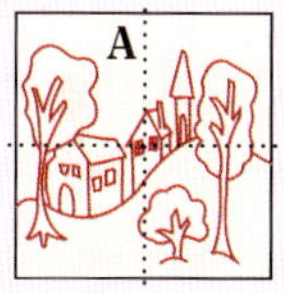

Embroidery Placement

Applique Placement

Fold A in half both ways and lightly crease the folds. Using the creases and placement diagram as guides, trace the embroidery design on the A with the pen or pencil. Use 2 strands of floss and an outline stitch to embroider the design. Center the design and trim A to 6½" × 6½".

Sew patches A–C together as shown. Refer to "Bias Strips" in the Techniques file on the PDF to make the stems. Prepare the leaves (D) for turned-edge appliqué. Fold the block in half diagonally both ways and lightly crease the folds. Use the creases and the appliqué placement diagram to arrange the stems and leaves. Use matching thread and a blind stitch to appliqué the patches in place to complete the block.

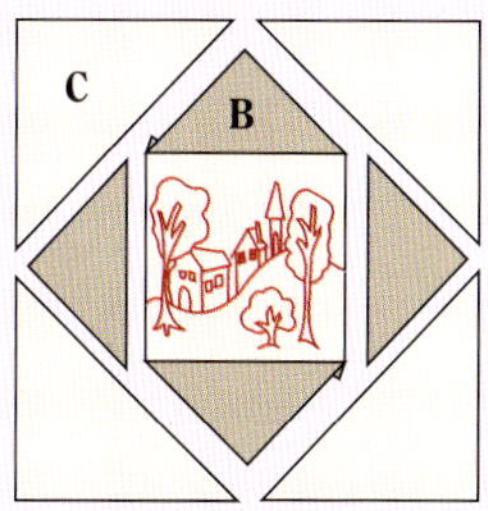

Block Piecing

block no. 425
Swirling Plovers

by Sue Hunt
suquilt.etsy.com

Sue Hunt is the author of *House Party - Coordinated Quilts and Pillows* for Martingale & Co., shopmartingale.com.

See page 216 on the PDF for pattern

Light Tan Tone-on-Tone
section patches 1, 4, 5, 8, 9, 12, 13, 16, 17 and 19
Navy Tone-on-Tone
section patches 2, 3, 6, 7, 10, 11, 14, 15 and 18
3 Red Tone-on-Tones
from *2*
1 pattern A
from *1*
1 pattern Ar
Embroidery floss

Section
Make 4

Make 4 paper copies of the foundation section. Foundation piece each section in numerical order, pressing and trimming after each patch addition. Sew the sections together as shown to make the block.

Fold the block in half diagonally both ways and lightly crease the folds. Prepare the birds for turned-edge appliqué. Use the creases and appliqué placement diagram as guides to arrange the patches on the block.

Use matching thread and a blind stitch to appliqué the patches in place. Outline stitch the bird detail with 2 strands of floss. Add French knots for the eyes to complete the block.

Applique Placement

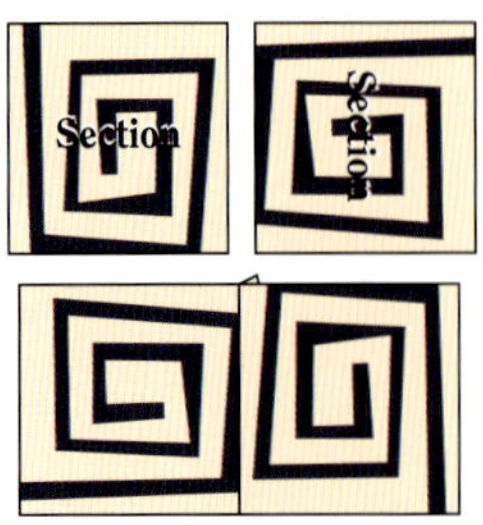

Block Piecing

block no. 426
Sleep Tight

by Kay Mackenzie • By Kay Mackenzie
kaymackenzie.com

Kay Mackenzie is the author of *Scrap-Appliqué Playground* for Martingale & Co., shopmartingale.com.

See page 226 on the PDF for pattern

Assorted Prints and Tone-on-Tones
33 squares (A) 1½″ x 1½″
1 *each* patterns H and K
5 pattern J
Light Brown Tone-on-Tone
1 rectangle (B) 1″ x 11½″
1 rectangle (E) 1″ x 4½″
1 rectangle (I) 1″ x 6½″
Assorted Blue Tone-on-Tones
2 rectangles (C) 1″ x 2″
4 rectangles (D) 1″ x 2½″
23 squares (F) 2½″ x 2½″
1 rectangle (G) 2″ x 2½″
Fusible web

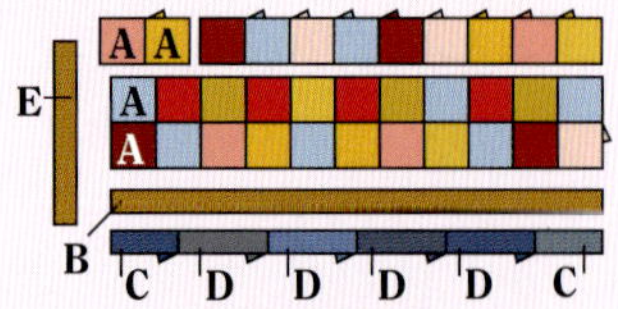

Section 1
Make 1

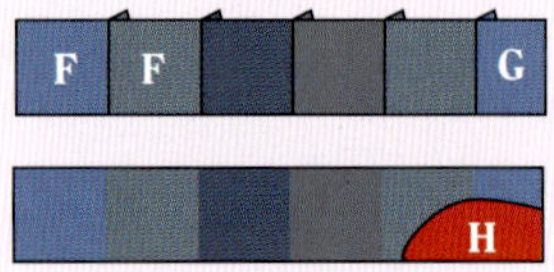

Section 2
Make 1

Sew patches A–E together as shown to make section 1. Sew 5 blue F's and the blue G together as shown to make section 2. Prepare patches H and J–K for fusible appliqué. Arrange the pillow (H) on section 2; fuse in place. Use matching thread and a machine blanket stitch to sew around the pillow.

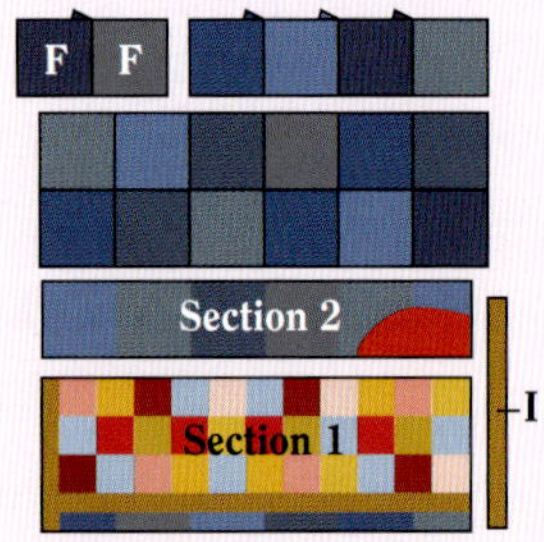

Block Assembly

Join sections 1 and 2 and the remaining patches to make the block background as shown. Fold the block in half diagonally both ways and lightly crease the folds. Use the creases and appliqué placement diagram as guides to arrange and fuse patches J–K to the block. Use matching thread and a machine blanket stitch to sew around the stars and moon to complete the block.

Applique Placement

block no. 427

Doodlebug

by Sue Marsh • Whistlepig Creek Productions
wpcreek.com

Fabric: Various fabrics designed by Sue Marsh for RJR Fabrics, rjrfabrics.com.

See page 237 on the PDF for pattern

Cream Solid
 1 square (A) 11½"x 11½" (trim to 10½"x 10½" after appliqué)
Assorted Prints and Tone-on-Tones
 1 set of appliqué patches
Teal Print
 2 rectangles (Y) 1½"x 10½"
 2 rectangles (Z) 1½"x 12½"
Fusible web
Black Micron Pigma pen

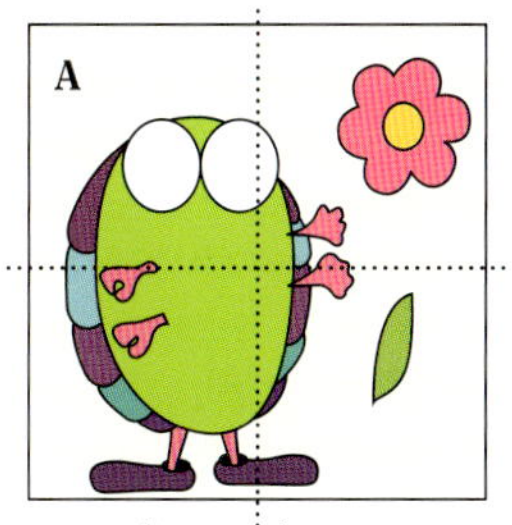

Applique Placement

Fold A in half both ways and lightly crease the folds. Prepare the appliqué patches for fusible appliqué. Use the creases andappliqué placement diagram as guides to arrange the patches on A. Fuse the patches in alphabetical order.

Use a machine satin stitch to sew around the patches. Center the design and trim A to 10½" × 10½". Join the Y's and Z's to A as shown. Use a machine satin stitch to add the stem and bug detail.

Color the pupils with the black pen to complete the block.

Stitching Diagram

Block Piecing

block no. 428

Baby Blocks

by Susan Marth • Suzn Quilts
suznquilts.com

See page 201 on the PDF for pattern

2 Dark Peach Prints and 2 Teal Prints
from *each*
 1 square (A) 6½"x 6½"
Black Solid
 1 set of appliqué patches
Fusible web

Sew the A's together as shown. Fold the block in half diagonally both ways and lightly crease the folds. Prepare the appliqué patches for fusible appliqué. Use the creases and appliqué placement diagram as guides to arrange the patches on the block.

Sew around the patches using tan thread and a machine blanket stitch to complete the block.

Susan used Sulky 12-wt. cotton thread for the machine blanket stitch.

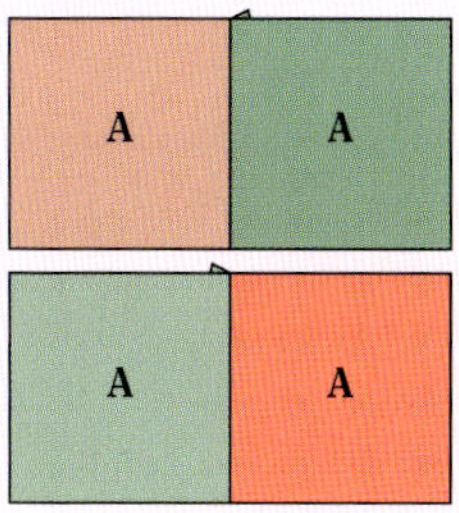

Block Piecing

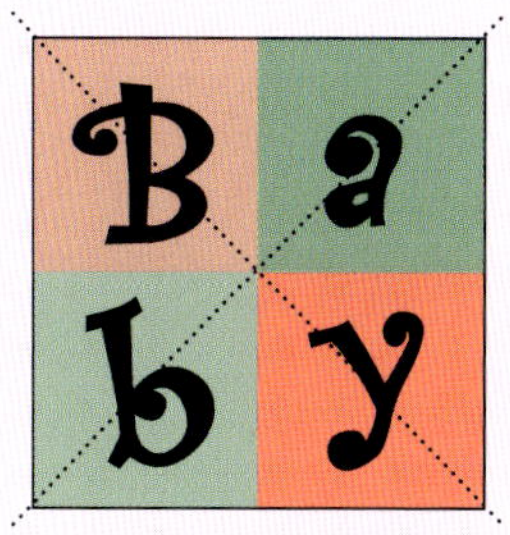

Applique Placement

block no. 429

Elephanté

by April Mazzoleni • April Mae Designs
april-makingendsmeet.blogspot.com

See page 221 on the PDF for pattern

Assorted Green Prints
81 squares (A) 1½" x 1½"
White Solid
1 square (B) 13½" x 13½" (trim to 12½" x 12½" after appliqué)
Gray Solid
1 pattern D
Pink Print
1 pattern E
Freezer paper
Fusible web
Embroidery floss

Block Piecing

Applique Placement

Sew the green A's together as shown. Trace a full-size C pattern on the paper side of the freezer paper; cut out the pattern. Pin the freezer paper pattern with the paper side on the wrong side of the green pieced section; cut out C. Carefully press the turn-under allowance on the curved edge to the shiny side of the freezer paper.

Prepare patches D and E for fusible appliqué. Fold B in half both ways and lightly crease the folds. Use the creases and appliqué placement diagram as guides to arrange the pieced C, D and E.

Use matching thread and a straight stitch to sew close to the turned edge of the hillside (C). Carefully cut away B behind the C and remove the freezer paper. Use black thread and a straight stitch to sew close to the edges of D and E 3 times. Backstitch the eyes, ear, tail and toenails using 2 strands of embroidery floss. Center the appliqué and trim to 12½" × 12½".

block no. 430

Winter's Jewel

by Amanda Murphy • Amanda Murphy Design
amandamurphydesign.com

Fabric: Brrr! designed by Laurie Wisbrun and Mixmasters by Patrick Lose, both for Robert Kaufman, robertkaufman.com.

See page 218 on the PDF for pattern

Aqua Tone-on-Tone
4 squares (A) 2⅞" x 2⅞"
1 square (B) 5¼" x 5¼"
1 square (D) 8½" x 8½"
Red Print
8 squares (A) 2⅞" x 2⅞"
1 pattern F
4 *each* patterns H and J
Multicolor Stripe
4 squares (C) 2½" x 2½"
White Tone-on-Tone
1 pattern E
Dark Aqua Print
4 *each* patterns G and I
Fusible web
Fusible stabilizer (optional)

Unit
Make 8

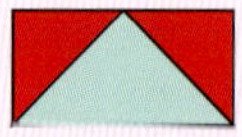

Flying Geese
Make 4

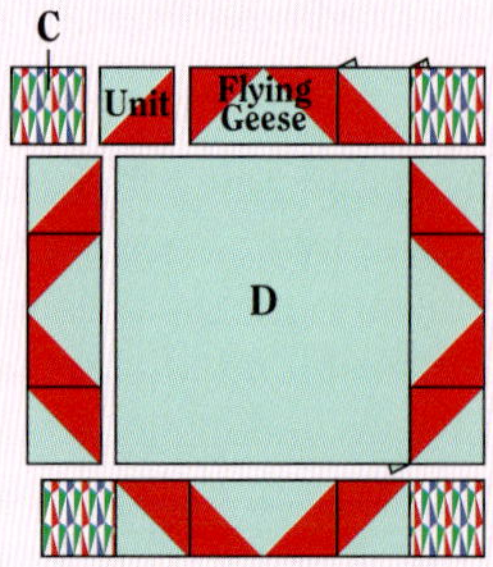

Block Assembly

For all techniques, refer to the Techniques file on the PDF. Pair the aqua A's with 4 red A's to make 8 units. Use the aqua B and 4 red A's to make 4 Flying Geese. Sew the units, Flying Geese and patches together as shown to make the block.

Applique Placement

Fold the block in half diagonally both ways and lightly crease the folds. Prepare patches E–J for fusible appliqué. Use the creases and appliqué placement diagram as guides to arrange the patches on the block. Sew around the patches using matching thread and a machine blanket stitch to complete the block.

Amanda fused her block to stabilizer before sewing around the appliqué patches.

block no. 431
Murtle the Turtle

by Allison Nicoll • Quilting Mumma
quiltingmumma.blogspot.com

See page 209 on the PDF for pattern

Cream Solid
1 square (A) 10½″ x 10½″ (trim to 9½″ x 9½″ after appliqué)
1 pattern D

Pale Yellow-Green Tone-on-Tone
1 pattern B

Red Print
1 pattern C
2 rectangles (I) 1½″ x 10½″
2 rectangles (J) 1½″ x 12½″

Black Solid
1 pattern E

Blue Dot
6 pattern F
2 rectangles (G) 1″ x 9½″
2 rectangles (H) 1″ x 10½″

Fusible web

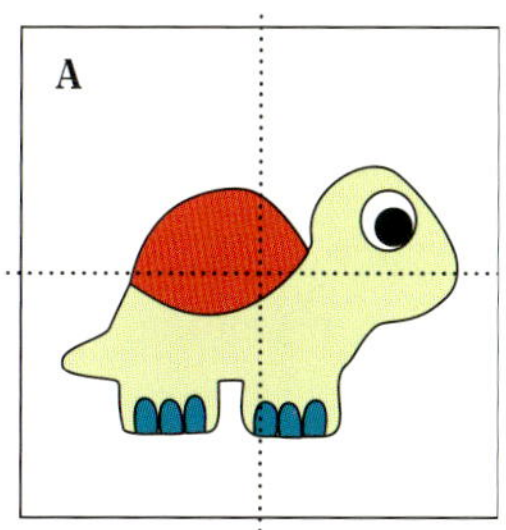

Applique Placement

Fold A in half both ways and lightly crease the folds. Prepare patches B–F for fusible appliqué. Use the creases and appliqué placement diagram as guides to arrange the patches on A. Fuse the patches to A in alphabetical order.

Use matching thread and a straight stitch to sew around the patches. Center the appliqué and trim to 9½" × 9½".

Sew the patches together as shown to complete the block.

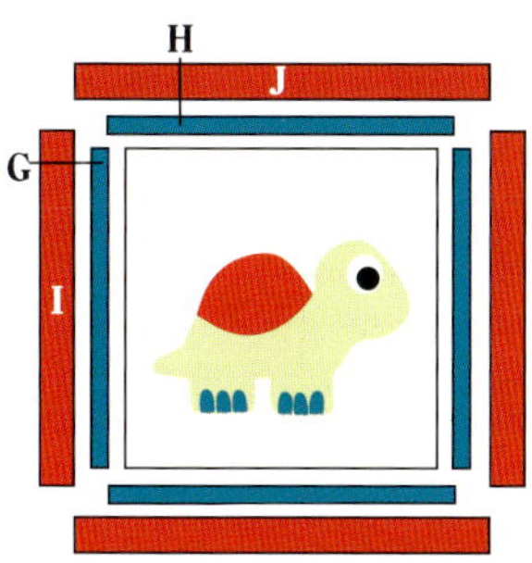

Block Assembly

block no. 432
Roving Ring

by Janelle Noack • Country Matters
janellenoack.blogspot.com.au

See page 212 on the PDF for pattern

⊠ = cut in half twice diagonally

4 Assorted Light Tan Prints and Tone-on-Tones
from *each*
1 square 7¼″ x 7¼″ ⊠ (A)

Assorted Red Prints and Tone-on-Tones
18 template B
1 pattern C

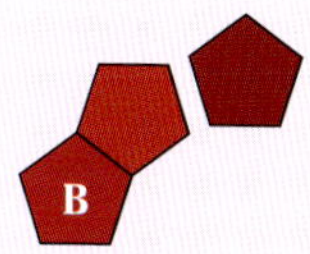

Block Piecing

Join the A's as shown to make a unit. Make 4 units.

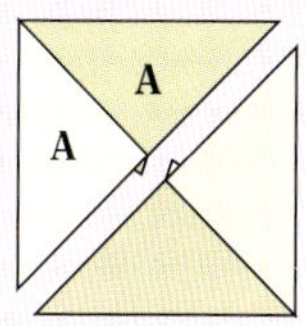

Unit
Make 4

The red pentagons (B) are hand sewn using English Paper Piecing. Follow the instructions for English Paper Piecing in the Techniques file on the PDF; baste the B's to the paper templates. Join 10 B's as shown in the block piecing diagram to form a circle. Join 2 B's for each of the block corners.

Prepare patch C for turned-edge appliqué. Fold the block in half diagonally both ways and lightly crease the folds. Use the creases and appliqué placement diagram as guides to position the pieced B's and the C. Use matching thread and a blind stitch to appliqué the pieced B's and the C on the block.

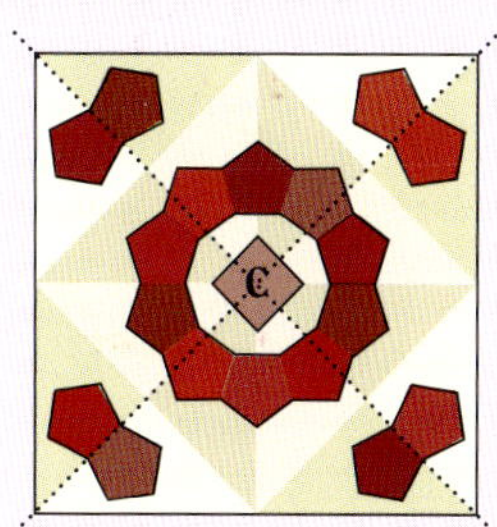

Applique Placement

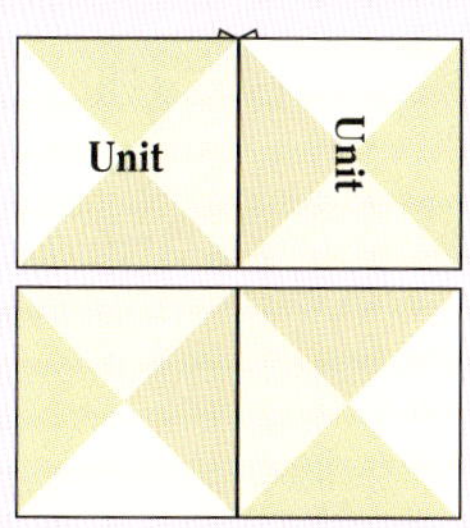

Block Assembly

block no. 433
Sunflower

by Benita Skinner • Victoriana Quilt Designs
victorianaquiltdesigns.com

See page 215 on the PDF for pattern

◸ = cut in half diagonally

Cream Tone-on-Tone
1 square (A) 10″ x 10″ (trim to 9″ x 9″ after appliqué)
Dark Green Tone-on-Tone
1 *each* patterns B and C
Dark Gold Tone-on-Tone
1 pattern D
Light Gold Tone-on-Tone
1 pattern E
Brown Tone-on-Tone
1 pattern F
Green Print
2 squares 6⅞″ x 6⅞″ ◸ (G)
Fusible web
Embroidery floss

Fold A in half both ways and lightly crease the folds. Prepare patches B–F for fusible appliqué. Use the creases and appliqué placement diagram as guides to arrange the patches on A. Fuse the patches to A in alphabetical order.

Applique Placement

Use 2 strands of matching embroidery floss and a hand blanket stitch to sew around the patches. Center the appliqué and trim to 9" × 9".

Sew the appliquéd A and green print G's together as shown to complete the block.

Block Assembly

block no. 434
Prairie Flowers

by Peg Spradlin
handicraftsbypeg.com

See page 210 on the PDF for pattern

White Tone-on-Tone
1 square (A) 13½″ x 13½″ (trim to 12½″ x 12½″ after appliqué)
Assorted Green Prints and Tone-on-Tones
4 *each* patterns B, G and F
8 squares (I) 2½″ x 2½″
Assorted Pink and Red Prints and Tone-on-Tones
4 *each* patterns C–E
1 pattern H
16 squares (I) 2½″ x 2½″
Fusible web

Fold A in half diagonally both ways and lightly crease the folds. Prepare patches B–H for fusible appliqué. Use the creases and appliqué placement diagram as guides to arrange the patches on A. Fuse the patches in alphabetical order.

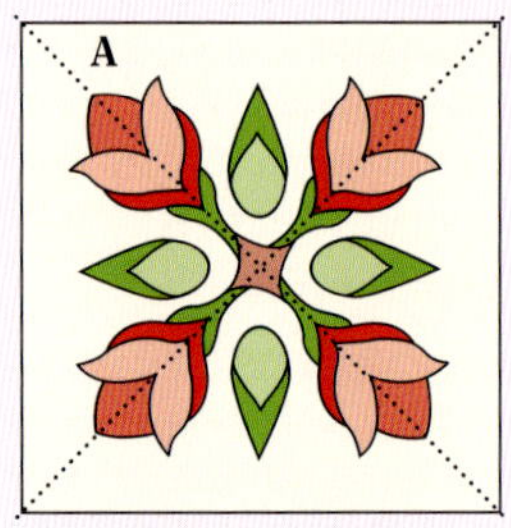

Applique Placement

Use monofilament thread and a machine zigzag stitch to sew around the patches. Center the appliqué and trim to 12½" × 12½".

Refer to "Prairie Points" in the Techniques file on the PDF. Prepare 24 Prairie Points using the assorted I's. Align 6 Prairie Points on each side of A and baste in place using a ⅛" seam allowance to complete the block.

Prairie Point Placement

block no. 435

So Tweet

by Paula Stoddard • Associate Editor, *Quiltmaker*
quiltmaker.com

Fabric: Robert Kaufman, robertkaufman.com.

See page 213 on the PDF for pattern

Light Blue Tone-on-Tone
1 rectangle (A) 10″ x 13″
1 rectangle (E) 2½″ x 12½″
Brown Tone-on-Tone
1 rectangle (B) 1 3/8″ x 6¾″
1 rectangle (C) 1 5/8″ x 11″
1 rectangle (D) 2″ x 12½″
2 Green Wools
5 pattern F
Orange Wool
1 pattern G
Red Wool #1
1 pattern H
Red Wool #2
1 pattern I
Fusible web
Embroidery floss
Button 1 at ¼″

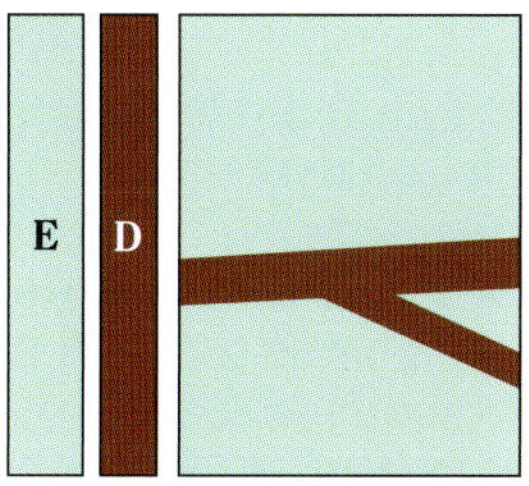

Block Assembly

Applique Placement

Make a random cut diagonally across A, starting approximately 4½" from the bottom left edge of A. Cut the bottom patch at a random angle starting approximately 2½" from the lower right corner as shown.

Sew the brown B between the 2 pieces of the bottom patch and trim as shown. Sew the brown C and top blue patch to the bottom as shown. Trim to 9" × 12½". Sew the brown D and blue E to the left side of the block as shown.

Fold the block in half both ways and lightly crease the folds. Prepare patches F–I for fusible appliqué. Use the creases and appliqué placement diagram as guides to arrange the patches; fuse in place. Use matching thread and a blanket stitch to sew around the patches.

Use 2 strands of floss and a backstitch to add the legs. Tack the button in place for the eye to complete the block.

block no. 436

Peppermint Petals

by Valerie Uland • Web Editor, *McCall's Quilting*
mccallsquilting.com

Fabric: Incense & Peppermints designed by Robyn Pandolph for RJR Fabrics, rjrfabrics.com.

Brown Print
2 rectangles (A) 3½″ x 12½″
2 Pink Prints
from *each*
1 pattern B
3 Cream Prints
from *2*
1 pattern B
from *1*
1 rectangle (C) 12″ x 18″
Pellon Fabric Magic

Template for Peppermint Petals block on page 32 of the PDF Templates file.

Prepare the B's for turned-edge appliqué. Refer to the appliqué placement diagram to arrange the B's on the A's. Use matching thread and a machine blanket stitch to appliqué the patches in place.

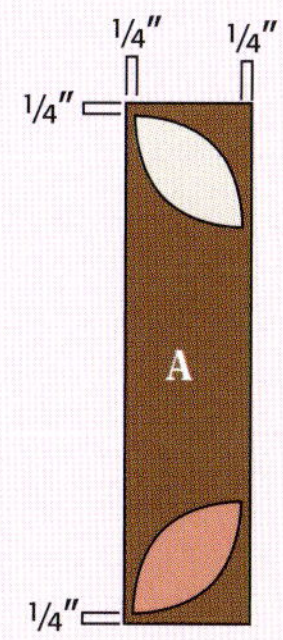

Applique Placement
Make 2

Valerie used Fabric Magic to add texture to her block. Following the manufacturer's instructions, place the Fabric Magic on the wrong side of the cream C. Use a straight stitch and matching thread to stitch across the short side of C at 1" intervals as shown (using a walking foot is helpful). Apply steam as directed to shrink C. Trim C to 6½" × 12½".

Sew the patches together as shown to complete the block.

Stitching Diagram

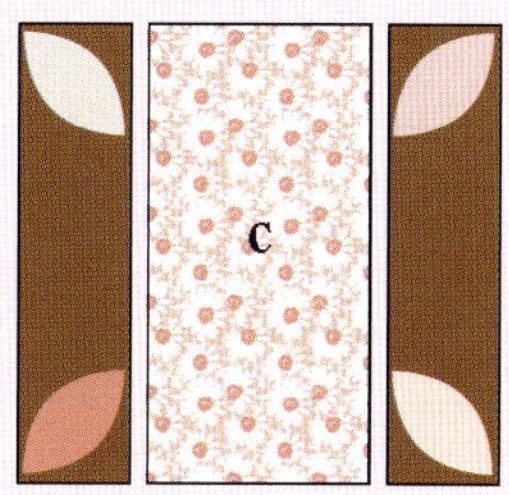

Block Assembly

block no. 437

Summer's in Bloom

by Cheryl Brown • QuilterChic
quilterchic.com

Cheryl Brown is the author of *Quilt Batik!* for Martingale & Co., shopmartingale.com.

See page 269 on the PDF for pattern

◩ = cut in half diagonally

Assorted Light Dots
12 squares (A) 3⅞" x 3⅞"
2 squares 6⅞" x 6⅞" ◩ (B)
(there will be 2 extra)

Green Batik
1 pattern C
1 *each* patterns D and Dr

Dark Pink Batik
1 pattern E

Yellow Batik
1 pattern F

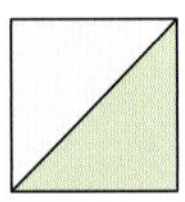

Unit
Make 12

Refer to "Triangle-Squares" in the Techniques file on the PDF. Pair the A's to make 12 units. Sew the units and patches together as shown to make the block.

Prepare patches C–F for turned-edge appliqué. Use the block seams as guides to arrange the patches.

Use matching thread and a blind stitch to appliqué the patches in place.

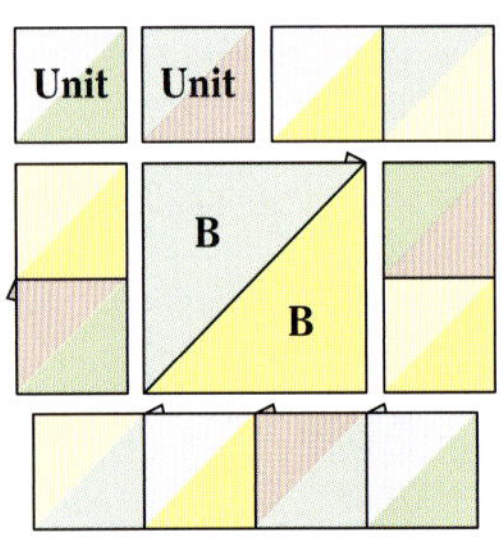

Block Assembly

Applique Placement

block no. 438

Professor Mousestache

by Sonja Callaghan • Artisania
artisania.ca

Fabric: Quilter's Linen and Kona Solids, both from Robert Kaufman, robertkaufman.com.

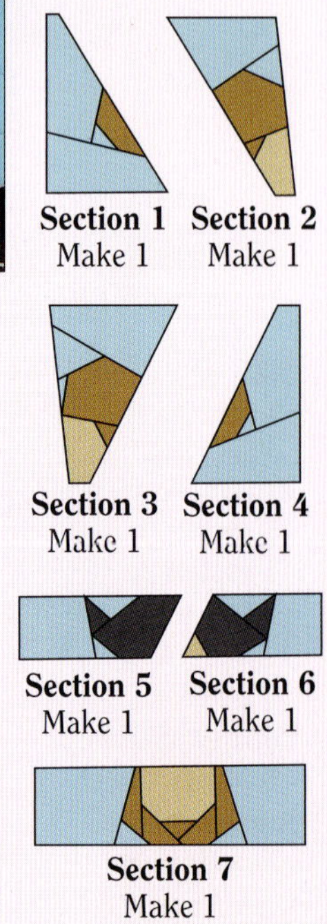

See page 264 on the PDF for pattern

Brown Tone-on-Tone
foundation patches

Blue Solid
1 rectangle (A) 2½" x 8½"
1 rectangle (B) 3½" x 8½"
1 rectangle (C) 1¾" x 3"
1 rectangle (E) 1¾" x 3½"
1 square (F) 1½" x 1½"
1 rectangle (I) 1½" x 2"
foundation patches

Tan Tone-on-Tone
foundation patches

Black Tone-on-Tone
foundation patches

Gold Print
1 rectangle (D) 1¾" x 7"

Red Solid
2 rectangles (G) 1½" x 3¼"

Cream Print
1 rectangle (H) 1½" x 4½"

Black Print
1 rectangle (J) 2¼" x 12½"

Embroidery floss

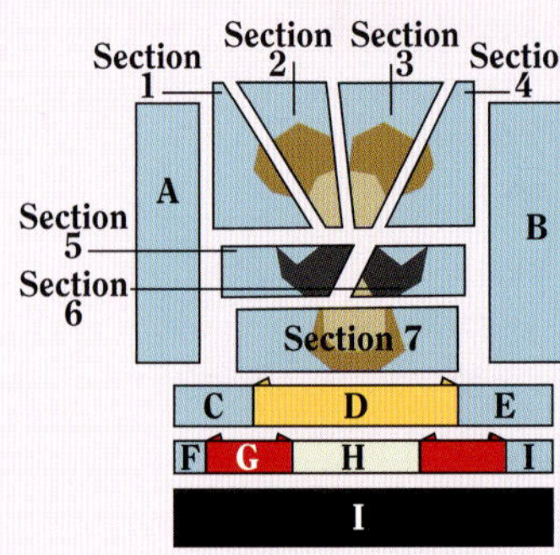

Block Assembly

Make 1 paper copy of each foundation section. Referring to the sections for color placement, foundation piece the sections in numerical order, pressing and trimming after each patch addition. Sew the sections and patches together as shown to make the block.

Use 4 strands of black floss and a stem stitch for the tail. Use 2 strands of black floss and a backstitch for the eyebrows and a satin stitch for the eyes. Use 2 strands of pink floss and a satin stitch for the nose to complete the block.

block no. 439

Bedtime Story

by Stacey Carey • Stacey Carey Designs
staceysplace.com

See page 283 on the PDF for pattern

Assorted Batiks
6 rectangles (A) 2¼" x 4"
9 squares (B) 4" x 4"
Cream Tone-on-Tone
1 square (A) 13½" x 13½" (trim to 12½" x 12½" after appliqué)
Peach Solid
1 pattern E
1 *each* patterns L, Lr, M, Mr, N, Nr, O and Or
Pale Green Print
1 pattern F
Brown Tone-on-Tone
1 pattern G
White Tone-on-Tone
1 *each* patterns H and I
Gray Tone-on-Tone
1 *each* patterns J and K
Template plastic
Fusible web

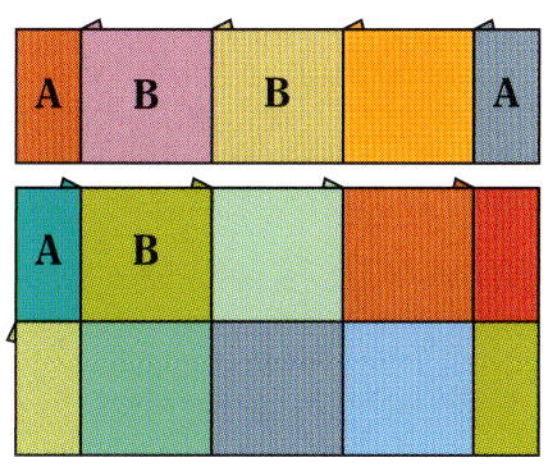

Block Piecing

Sew the assorted batik A's and B's together as shown. Make a plastic template of D. Trace and cut D from the pieced A/B's.

Fold C in half both ways and lightly crease the folds. Prepare patches D–Or for fusible appliqué. Use the creases and appliqué placement diagram as guides to arrange the patches on C. Fuse the patches to C in alphabetical order.

Use tan thread and a straight stitch to sew just inside the top edge of D. Use matching thread and a machine blanket stitch to sew around the rest of the appliqué patches. Center the appliqué and trim to 12½" × 12½".

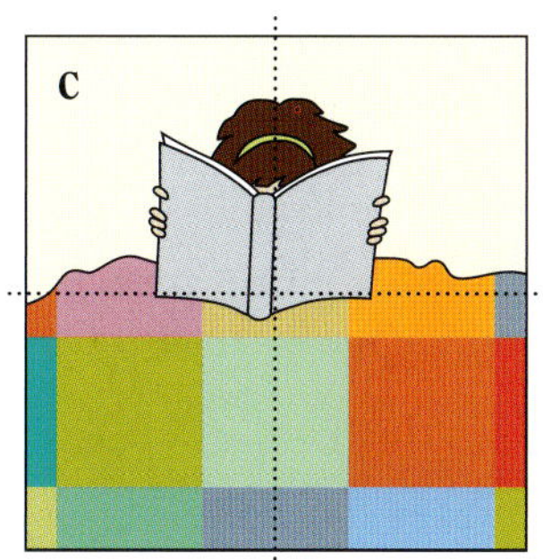

Applique Placement

block no. 440

Home Tweet Home

by Sandi Colwell • Quilt Cabana Patterns
quiltcabanapatterns.com

Sandi Colwell is the author of *Little Quilts for Big Occasions* for Leisure Arts leisurearts.com.

See page 253 on the PDF for pattern

Light Blue Tone-on-Tone
1 square (A) 10½" x 10½"
Orange Tone-on-Tone
2 rectangles (B) 1½" x 10½"
2 pattern I
Green Tone-on-Tone
2 rectangles (C) 1½" x 12½"
Brown Tone-on-Tone
1 *each* patterns D and E
Multicolor Print
1 pattern F
Purple Tone-on-Tone
1 pattern G
6 pattern I
Yellow Tone-on-Tone
1 *each* patterns H and Hr
4 pattern I
Pink Tone-on-Tone
7 pattern I
Fusible web
Black embroidery floss
Buttons 4 at ½"

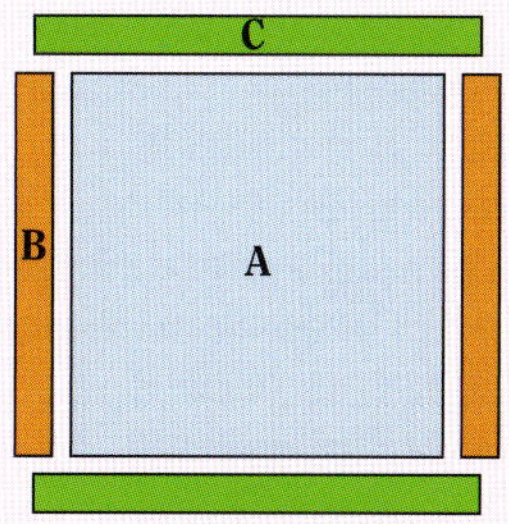

Block Piecing

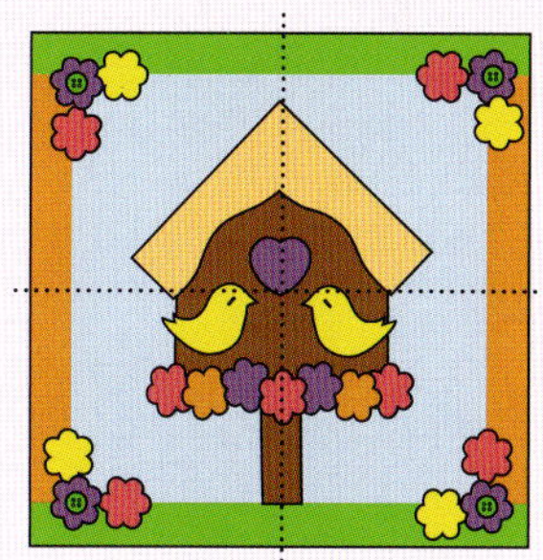

Applique Placement

Sew the patches together as shown to make the block.

Fold the block in half both ways and lightly crease the folds. Prepare patches D–I for fusible appliqué. Use the creases and appliqué placement diagram as guides to arrange the patches. Fuse the patches in alphabetical order.

Use matching thread and a machine blanket stitch to sew around the patches. Use 2 strands of floss and a stem stitch for the eyes. Tack the buttons in place to complete the block.

block no. 441
Anni's Flower Jug

by Anni Downs • Hatched and Patched
hatchedandpatched.com.au

Fabric: Love to Garden designed by Anni Downs for Henry Glass Fabrics, henryglassfabrics.com.

Anni Downs is the author of *Some Kind of Wonderful* for Kansas City Star Quilts, pickledish.com.

See page 247 on the PDF for pattern

Tan Stripe
1 square (A) 10″x 10″ (trim to 9″x 9″ after appliqué)

Dark Brown Print
bias strip 1″x 10½″

Assorted Prints and Tone-on-Tones
1 set of appliqué patches

Light Blue Print
4 rectangles (U) 1¼″x 9″

Olive Green Print
4 squares (V) 1¼″x 1¼″

Cream Print
4 rectangles (W) 1½″x 10½″

Pale Orange Print and Purple Print
from *each*
2 squares (X) 1½″x 1½″

Fold A in half both ways and lightly crease the folds. Refer to "Bias Strips" in the Techniques file on the PDF. Prepare patches B–T for turned-edge appliqué. Use the creases and appliqué placement diagram as guides to arrange the stems and patches on A.

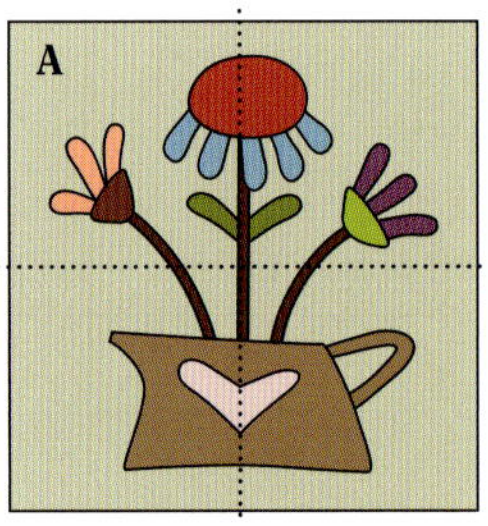

Applique Placement

Use matching thread and a blind stitch to appliqué the patches in place. Center the appliqué and trim A to 9"× 9".

Sew A and the patches together as shown to complete the block.

Block Assembly

block no. 442
Cuppity Cake

by Sandy Fitzpatrick • Hissyfitz Designs
hissyfitzdesigns.com

See page 252 on the PDF for pattern

Pale Green Tone-on-Tone
1 square (A) 11½″x 11½″ (trim to 10½″x 10½″ after appliqué)
2 rectangles (L) 1½″x 10½″
2 rectangles (M) 1½″x 12½″

Black Solid
1 pattern B

White Tone-on-Tone
1 *each* patterns C and E

White Stripe
1 pattern D

Gray Tone-on-Tone
5 pattern F

Pink Tone-on-Tone
1 pattern G

Brown Tone-on-Tone
1 pattern H

Medium Green Tone-on-Tone
1 pattern I

Red Tone-on-Tone
1 pattern J

Black Stripe
4 rectangles (K) 1″x 10½″

Fusible web

Applique Placement

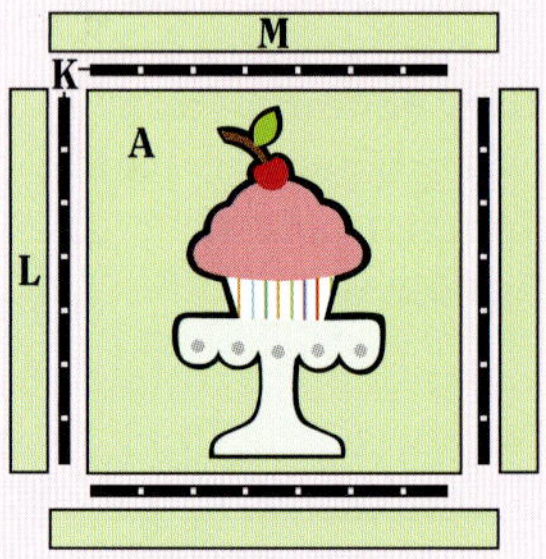

Block Assembly

Fold A in half both ways and lightly crease the folds. Prepare patches B–J for fusible appliqué. Use the creases and appliqué placement diagram as guides to arrange the patches. Fuse the patches in alphabetical order. Center the appliqué and trim to 10½"× 10½".

Use black thread and a machine blanket stitch to sew around the patches.

Fold the K's in half lengthwise with wrong sides together. Matching raw edges, baste a folded K to both sides of A; repeat to add K's to the top and bottom. Join the L's and M's to A to complete the block.

block no. 443

Melania

by Susan Geddes • Art Director, *Quilters Newsletter*
quiltersnewsletter.com

See page 261 on the PDF for pattern

White Print
8 squares (A) 2½″ x 2½″
6 Assorted Pink and Red Prints and Tone-on-Tones
from 2 medium reds
4 squares (A) 2½″ x 2½″
from 2 pinks
2 squares (A) 2½″ x 2½″
from 2 dark reds
2 *each* patterns C and D
4 Assorted Light Green Prints and Tone-on-Tones
from *each*
1 rectangle (B) 2½″ x 8½″
Medium Green Tone-on-Tone
4 pattern E
Dark Green Tone-on-Tone
4 pattern F
Fusible web

Applique Placement

Susan used the medium red A's for the checkerboard center and matching pink A's in opposite corners.

Sew the A's and B's together as shown to make the block.

Fold the block in half both ways and lightly crease the folds. Prepare patches C–F for fusible appliqué. Use the creases and appliqué placement diagram as guides to arrange the patches on the block. Fuse the patches in alphabetical order.

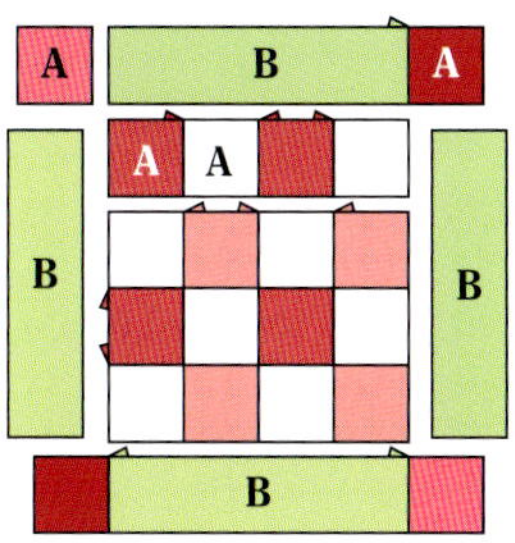

Block Piecing

Use matching thread and a straight stitch to sew close to the edges of each appliqué patch to complete the block.

block no. 444

Summertime Blues

by Becky Goldsmith • Piece O' Cake
pieceocake.com

Becky Goldsmith is the co-author of *Appliqué Outside the Lines* and *My Whimsical Quilt Garden* for C&T Publishing, ctpub.com.

See page 267 on the PDF for pattern

Gold Dot
1 square (A) 6½″ x 6½″
Gold Print
2 rectangles (B) 1″ x 6½″
2 rectangles (C) 1″ x 7½″
Gold Stripe
1 rectangle (D) 2½″ x 7½″
1 rectangle (E) 2½″ x 9½″
1 rectangle (F) 3½″ x 9½″
1 rectangle (G) 3½″ x 12½″
Light Turquoise Print
4 pattern H
4 Orange Tone-on-Tones
from *each*
1 pattern I
Dark Turquoise Print
bias strip 1″ x 9½″
4 pattern J
Green Solid
4 pattern K
Pink Print
1 pattern L

Applique Placement

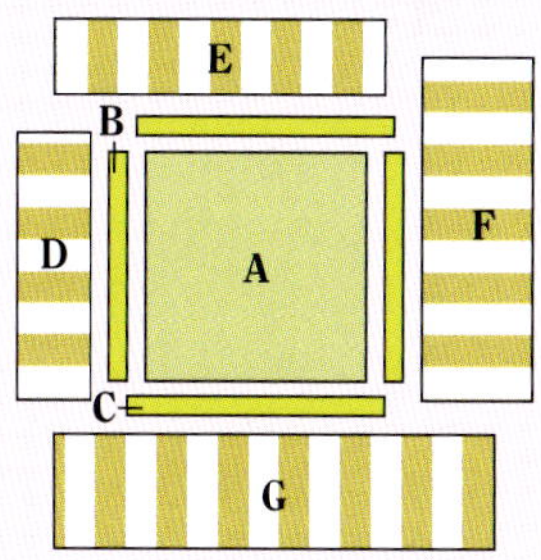

Block Piecing

Sew the patches together as shown to make the block.

Fold the block in half diagonally both ways and lightly crease the folds. Prepare patches H–L for turned-edge appliqué. Refer to "Bias Strips" in the Techniques file on the PDF to make the stems. Cut the strip into 4 lengths of 2¼". Use the creases and appliqué placement diagram as guides to arrange the patches on the block.

Use matching thread and a blind stitch to appliqué the patches in place to complete the block.

block no. 445

Groovy

by Susan Guzman • SuzGuz Designs
suzguzdesigns.com

Fabric: Alchemy designed by Amy Butler for Westminster Fibers, Inc., westminsterfibers.com.

See page 284 on the PDF for pattern

Assorted Prints
2″ to 2½″-wide strips up to 13″-long

Foundation paper
2 template A

Light Blue Print
1 pattern B

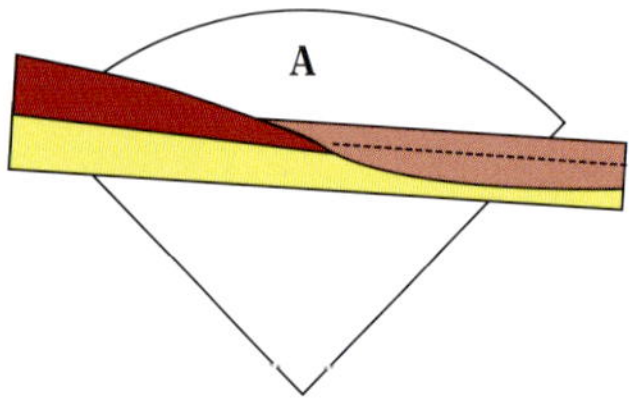

Notice that Susan cut some of her strips at a slight angle for interest.

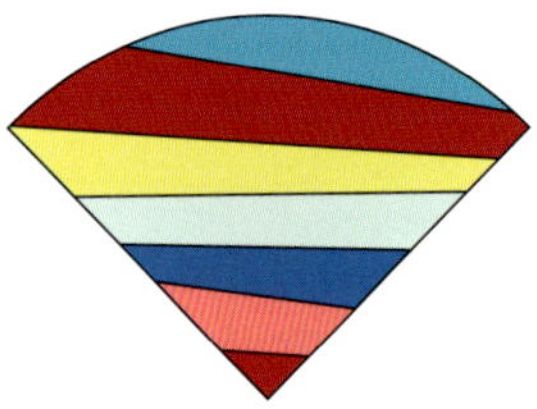

Unit
Make 2

Position a strip right side up on a foundation paper A. Lay another strip on top of the first with right sides together and aligning raw edges as shown. Join the strips by sewing through all layers ¼" from the raw edges. Flip the top strip open and press. Continue to add strips until the foundation is covered.

Trim the strips even with the edges of A. Repeat to make 2 units. Carefully remove the foundation papers.

Refer to "Curved Piecing" in the Techniques file on the PDF. Join the units and B as shown to complete the block.

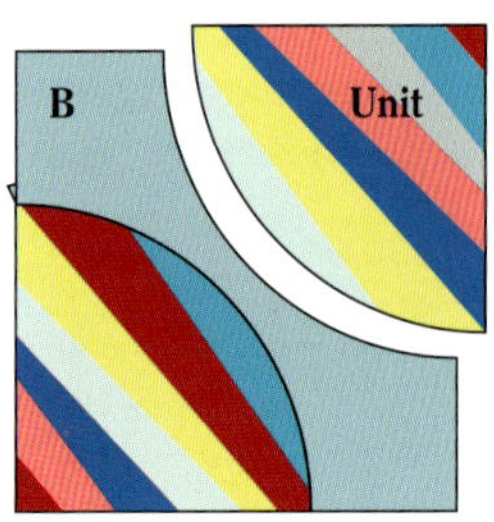

Block Assembly

block no. 446

Buzz Inn

by Melissa Harris and Arlene Stamper • The Quilt Co.
quiltcompany.com

See page 259 on the PDF for pattern

Assorted Gold Prints and Tone-on-Tones
1 rectangle (A) 1¾″x 3″
1 rectangle (C) 1¾″x 4″
1 rectangle (E) 1¾″x 5″
1 rectangle (F) 2″x 6″
1 rectangle (G) 2¼″x 7½″

Cream Tone-on-Tone
4 squares (B) 1¼″x 1¼″
6 squares (D) 1″x 1″
2 rectangles (L) 2¼″x 5¼″
2 rectangles (M) 2¼″x 4¾″
2 rectangles (N) 2¼″x 4¼″
2 rectangles (O) 2½″x 3¾″
2 rectangles (P) 2¼″x 3″
1 rectangle (Q) 3½″x 12½″

Black Print #1
1 rectangle (H) 1″x 3″
1 rectangle (I) 1″x 4″
1 rectangle (J) 1″x 5″
1 rectangle (K) 1″x 6″

Assorted Black Tone-on-Tones and Gold Tone-on-Tones
5 sets of bee patches
1 pattern R

Fusible web

Black embroidery floss

Unit 1
Stitch & Flip
Make 1

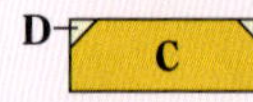

Unit 2
Stitch & Flip
Make 1

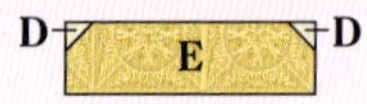

Unit 3
Stitch & Flip
Make 1

Unit 4
Stitch & Flip
Make 1

Unit 5
Stitch & Flip
Make 1

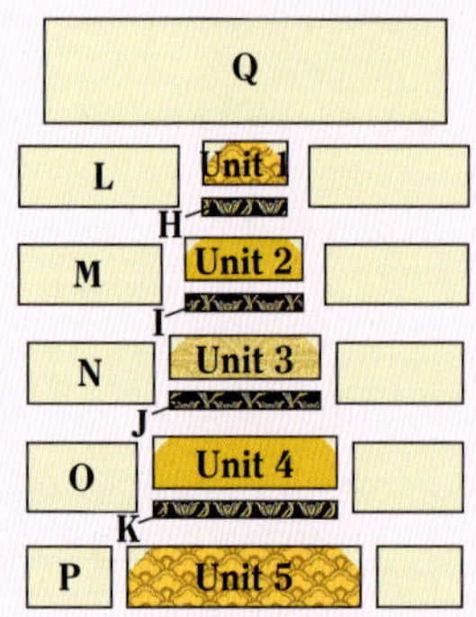

Block Assembly

Refer to "Stitch-and-Flip" in the Techniques file on the PDF. Make units 1–5 using the patches shown. Sew the units and patches together as shown.

Prepare R and the bee patches for fusible appliqué. Use the photographed block as guides to arrange the patches on the block; fuse in place.

Use gold and black thread and a machine blanket stitch to sew around the bee patches. Use 2 strands of floss and a long stitch and French knots to add the bee details to complete the block.

block no. 447

Clown Go Round

by Robin Koehler • Nestlings by Robin
nestlingsbyrobin.com

See page 276 on the PDF for pattern

Red Print
- section 1, patch 1
- sections 2 and 3, patch 2

Gold Dot
- section 1, patches 2 and 3
- section 3, patch 3
- 1 square (A) 4½″ x 4½″

Black Dot
- sections 2 and 3, patch 1
- 4 squares (A) 4½″ x 4½″

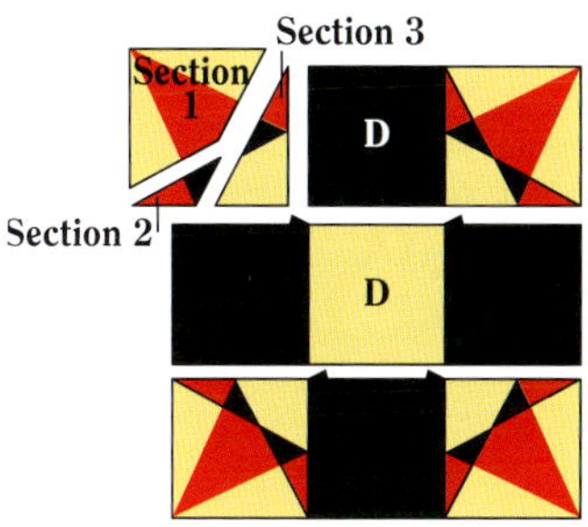

Block Assembly

Make 4 paper copies of *each* foundation section. Foundation piece the sections in numerical order, pressing and trimming after each patch addition.

Sew the sections and patches together as shown to complete the block.

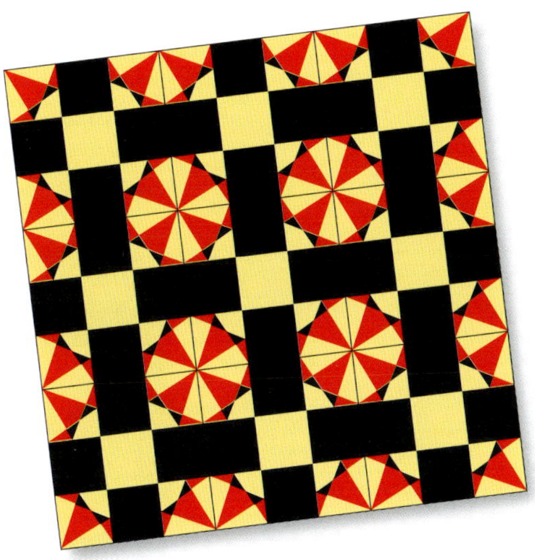

block no. 448

Meadow Glory

by Jo Moury

Fabric: Coquette designed by Chez Moi for Moda Fabrics, unitednotions.com.

See page 272 on the PDF for pattern

White Tone-on-Tone
- 1 square (A) 7½″ x 7½″
- 4 rectangles (B) 1¾″ x 7½″
- 4 squares (C) 1¾″ x 1¾″

Pale Green Tone-on-Tone
- 4 rectangles (B) 1¾″ x 7½″

Yellow Tone-on-Tone
- 4 squares (C) 1¾″ x 1¾″
- 4 rectangles (D) 1¾″ x 3″
- 4 *each* patterns E and G

Assorted Green Prints and Batiks
- 4 bias strips ⅜″ x 10½″
- 4 *each* patterns I, K and Kr

Pale Purple Print
- 4 pattern F
- 8 pattern J

Pink Print
- 1 pattern H

Pink Tone-on-Tone
- 4 pattern L

Green embroidery floss

Buttons
- 8 yellow at ½″
- 4 blue hearts at ⅜″
- 4 gold glass at ⅜″

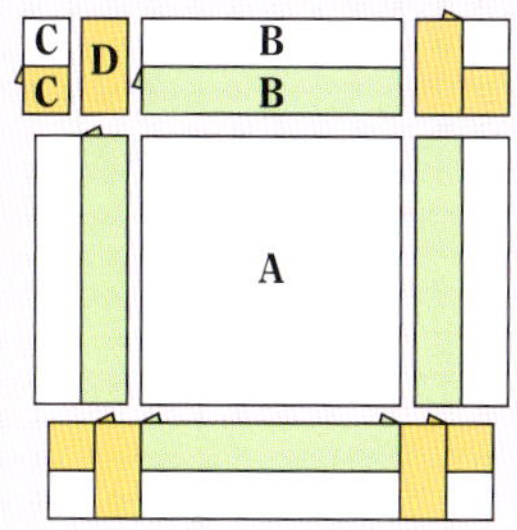

Block Piecing

Applique and Embroidery Placement

Join patches A–D as shown to make the block.

Refer to "Tiny Bias Stems" in the Techniques file on the PDF. Use the green bias strips to make the stems. Prepare patches E–L for turned-edge appliqué. Fold the block in half diagonally both ways and lightly crease the folds. Use the creases and appliqué placement diagram as guides to arrange the stems and patches.

Use matching thread and a blind stitch to appliqué the patches in place. Use 2 strands of floss and a fly stitch for embroidered leaves; use an outline stitch and backstitch to add the stem and leaf details. Tack the buttons in place as shown to complete the block.

block no. 449
Star Shine

by Arlene Neely • Rabbits Haven Quilt Designs
rabbitshaven.com

See page 277 on the PDF for pattern

Green Print
section patch 1
Cream Tone-on-Tone #1
section patches 2 and 3
Cream Tone-on-Tone #2
1 square (A) 7¼"x 7¼"
Red Print
4 squares (B) 3⅞"x 3⅞"
Brown Print
1 square (C) 6½"x 6½"
Red Stripe
4 squares (D) 3½"x 3½"

Section
Make 4

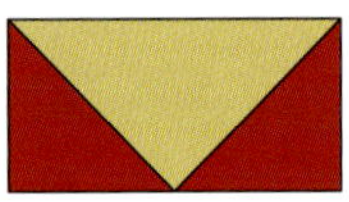

Flying Geese
Make 4

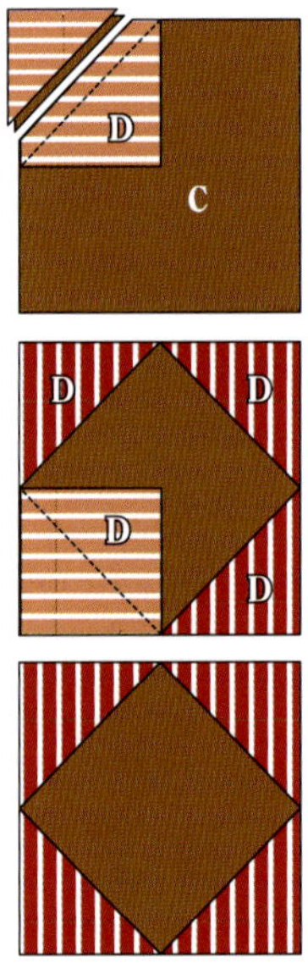

Unit
Stitch & Flip
Make 1

For all techniques, refer to the Techniques file on the PDF. Make 4 paper copies of the foundation section. Foundation piece each section in numerical order, pressing and trimming after each patch addition.

Use the cream #2 A and red print B's to make 4 Flying Geese.

Join the red stripe D's to the brown C as shown to make 1 Stitch-and-Flip unit.

Sew the sections, units and Flying Geese together as shown to complete the block.

Block Assembly

block no. 450
Flowers Around

by Gail Pan • Gail Pan Designs
gailpandesigns.typepad.com

Fabric: Panier de Fleurs designed by French General for Moda Fabrics, unitednotions.com.

See page 271 on the PDF for pattern

Cream Solid
1 square (A) 9½"x 9½" (trim to 8½"x 8½" after embroidery and appliqué)
Blue Print
1 pattern B
4 rectangles (C) 2½"x 8½"
Red Solid
4 squares (D) 2½"x 2½"
Brown Pigma Micron pen
(.01 tip) or pencil
Embroidery floss

Fold the cream A in half both ways and lightly crease the folds. Using the creases as a guide, trace the embroidery design onto A with a pencil or pen.

Prepare patch B for turned-edge appliqué. Center B on A. Use matching thread and a blind stitch to appliqué B in place. Use a backstitch and 2 strands of floss to embroider the flowers and stems. Use a satin stitch for the flower centers and a crossstitch for the bud centers. Add the small leaves with a lazy daisy stitch. Center the design and trim to 8½" × 8½".

Sew the embroidered A, blue C's and red D's together as shown to complete the block.

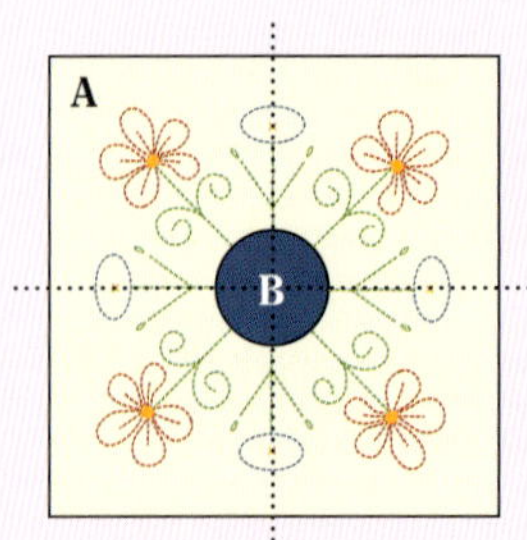

Applique and Embroidery Placement

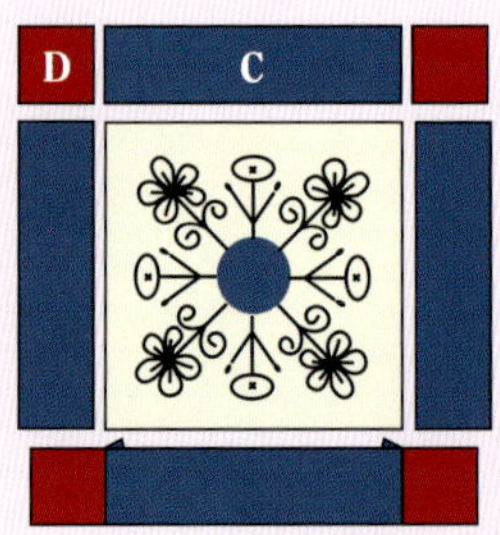

Block Assembly

block no. 451
Fancy Free

by Dodi Poulsen • Two Sisters at Squirrel Hollow
sashgals.com

Fabric: Gypsy Girl designed by Lily Ashbury for Moda Fabrics, unitednotions.com.

Dodi Poulsen is the author of *A Perfect Cut* for Two Sisters at Squirrel Hollow, sashgals.com.

See page 276 on the PDF for pattern

Cream Print #1
section, patch 1
section reversed, patch 3

Pink Tone-on-Tone
section and section reversed, patch 2

Blue Check
section, patch 3
section reversed, patch 1

Aqua Print
4 rectangles (A) 2½″x 5½″

Cream Print #2
1 square (B) 2½″x 2½″

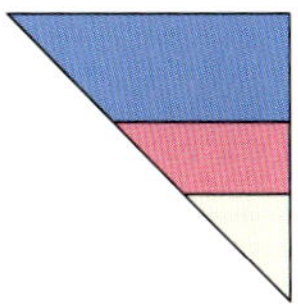

Section
Make 4

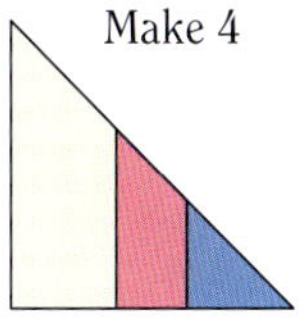

Section Reversed
Make 4

Make 4 paper copies *each* of the section and reversed section foundations. The colors for the reverse section are in parentheses on the foundation. Foundation piece the sections in numerical order, pressing and trimming after each patch addition.

Sew the sections and patches together as shown to complete the block.

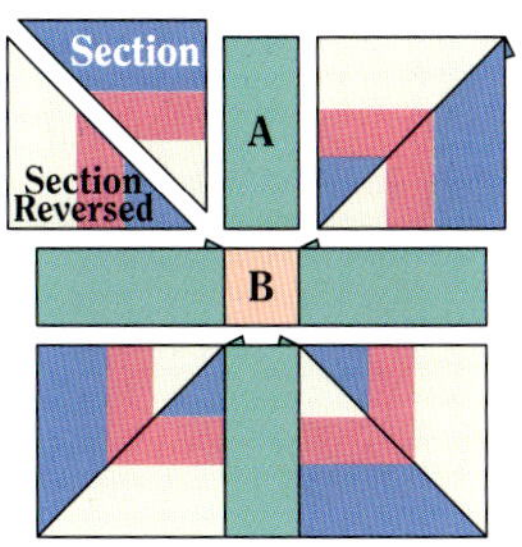

Block Assembly

block no. 452
Fairy Tale Castle

by Sarah Price • It's Sew Emma
itssewemma.com

Fabric: Princess and Fairy Frost, both by Michael Miller Fabrics, michaelmillerfabrics.com.

See page 271 on the PDF for pattern

Dark Purple Dot
1 rectangle (A) 3″x 10¾″
1 rectangle (C) 3″x 9¼″
6 rectangles (D) 1″x 1½″
2 rectangles (F) 3½″x 5½″

Pale Pink Tone-on-Tone
4 squares (B) 1¾″x 1¾″
6 rectangles (D) 1″x 1½″
2 rectangles (E) 3½″x 4¾″
1 rectangle (G) 2″x 3″
2 rectangles (I) 1″x 10¾″
1 rectangle (J) 1¼″x 12½″

Pale Purple Print
1 pattern H

Medium Purple Print
1 rectangle (K) 1½″x 12½″

Fusible web

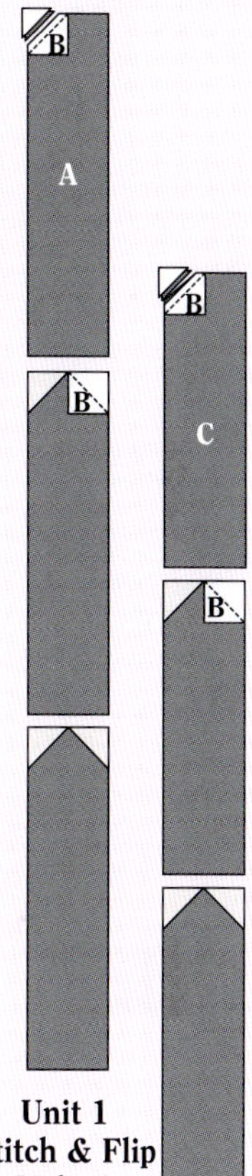

Unit 1
Stitch & Flip
Make 1

Unit 2
Stitch & Flip
Make 1

Refer to "Stitch-and-Flip" in the Techniques file on the PDF. Use the dark purple A and pink B's to make unit 1. Make unit 2 using the dark purple C and pink B's.

Sew the units and patches D–G together as shown.

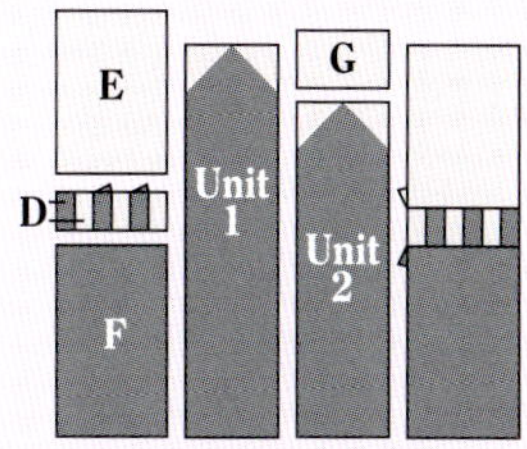

Block Assembly

Prepare the door (H) for fusible appliqué. Using the center seam as a guide, align H with the bottom of units 1 and 2. Fuse in place. Use matching thread and a machine blanket stitch to sew around H.

Join the remaining patches as shown to complete the block.

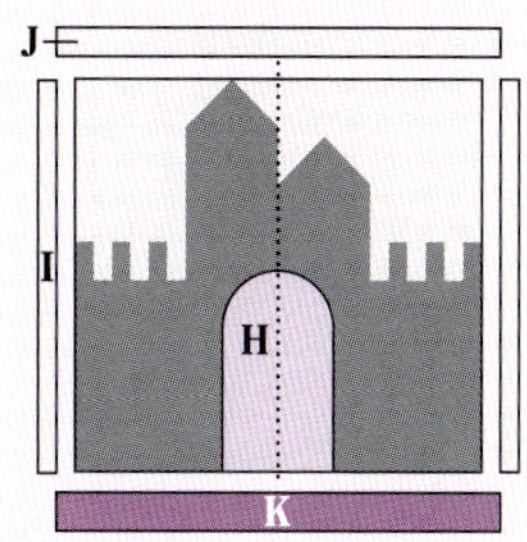

Applique Placement

block no. 453
Flowers for Kaylee

by Joanne Rowicki • Gingham Girls
ginghamgirls.biz

See page 271 on the PDF for pattern

White Print
- 2 rectangles (A) ¾″ x 3¼″
- 2 rectangles (C) 3½″ x 12½″
- 1 rectangle (D) 6″ x 12½″

Light Green Tone-on-Tone
- 2 rectangles (B) ¾″ x 9¾″
- 4 pattern F

Turquoise Tone-on-Tone
- 1 *each* patterns E and Er

Orange Check
- 2 pattern G

Fusible web

Applique Placement

Sew patches A–D together as shown to make the block.

Prepare patches E–F for fusible appliqué. Prepare the orange G's for turned-edge appliqué. Fold the block in half both ways diagonally and lightly crease the folds. Use the creases and appliqué placement diagram as guides to arrange and fuse the flower petals (E and Er) and leaves (F) to the block.

Use matching thread and a machine blanket stitch to sew around the flower petals and leaves. Use matching thread and a blind stitch to appliqué the circles (G) in place to complete the block.

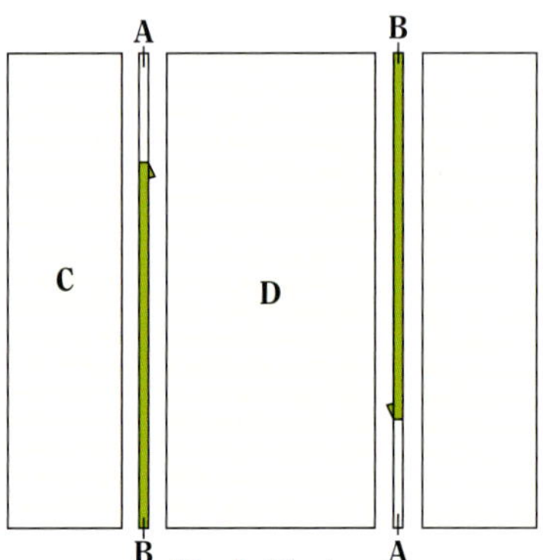

Block Piecing

block no. 454
Basket of Blooms

by Erin Russek • Assistant Editor
McCalls Quilting • mccallsquilting.com

Unit
Make 6

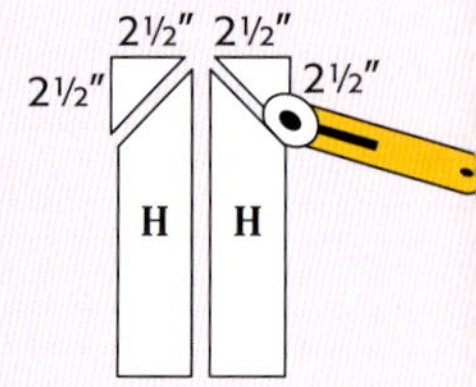

See page 248 on the PDF for pattern

⍁ = cut in half diagonally

White Solid
- 1 square (A) 13⅞″ x 13⅞″ (trim to 12⅞″ x 12⅞″ after appliqué)
- 2 rectangles (H) 2½″ x 8⅞″
- 1 square 4⅞″ x 4⅞″ ⍁ (I) (there will be 1 extra)

Medium Blue Tone-on-Tone
- bias strip 1½″ x 16½″
- 3 squares (F) 2⅞″ x 2⅞″
- 1 square 2⅞″ x 2⅞″ ⍁ (G)

2 Green Tone-on-Tones
from *each*
- 4 pattern B

Yellow Check
- 1 pattern C

Yellow Solid
- 3 pattern D

Light Blue Tone-on-Tone
- 3 pattern E

Light Blue Print
- 3 squares (F) 2⅞″ x 2⅞″
- 2 squares 2⅞″ x 2⅞″ ⍁ (G)

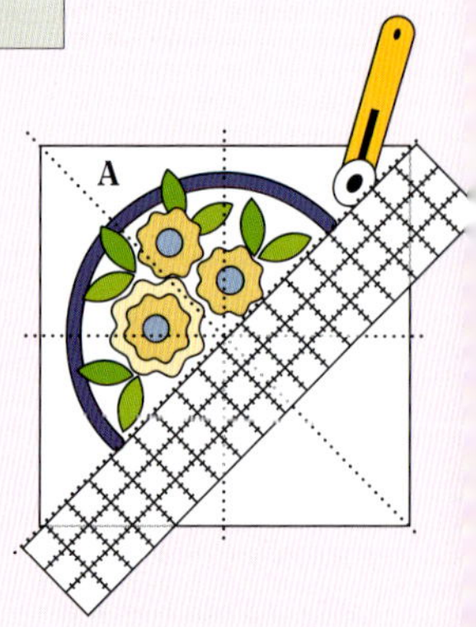

Applique Placement and Cutting Diagram

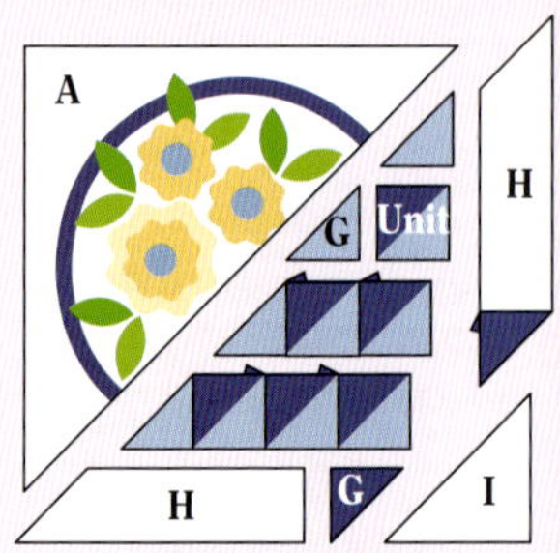

Block Assembly

For all techniques, refer to the Techniques file on the PDF. Fold A in half horizontally, vertically and diagonally and lightly crease the folds. Refer to "Bias Strips" to make the basket handle from the medium blue tone-on-tone. Prepare patches B–E for turned-edge appliqué. Use the creases and appliqué placement diagram as guides to arrange the handle and patches on A. Use matching thread and a blind stitch to appliqué the handle and patches in place. Center the design and trim A to 12⅞" × 12⅞"; cut in half diagonally as shown.

Pair the medium blue F's with the light blue print F's to make 6 Triangle-Square units. Trim the H's as shown. Sew the units and patches together as shown to complete the block.

block no. 455
Deep Blue Sea

by Mary Sanderson • Sea Quilts
seaquiltsshop.etsy.com

See page 260 on the PDF for pattern

Orange Dot
1 rectangle (A) 6½" x 12½"
Light Blue Print
1 rectangle (B) 1½" x 12½"
Medium Blue Tone-on-Tone
1 rectangle (C) 2½" x 12½"
Dark Blue Tone-on-Tone
1 rectangle (D) 3½" x 12½"
Dark Blue Solid
1 *each* patterns E–G
Orange Batik
1 pattern H
Fusible web

Sew patches A–D together as shown to make the block.

Fold the block in half both ways and lightly crease the folds. Prepare patches E–H for fusible appliqué. Use the creases and appliqué placement diagram as guides to arrange the patches on the block; fuse in place.

Sew around patches E–H using matching thread and a machine blanket stitch to complete the block.

Applique Placement

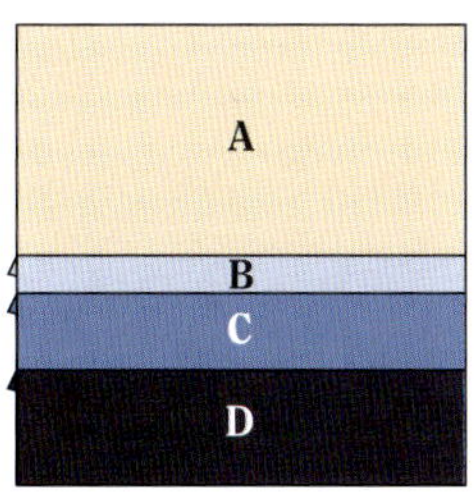

Block Piecing

block no. 456
Silhouettes

by Edyta Sitar • Laundry Basket Quilts
laundrybasketquilts.com

Fabric: Batiks by Edyta Sitar for Moda Fabrics, unitednotions.com.

Edyta Sitar is the author of *Scrappy Firework Quilts* for Landauer Publishing, landauerpub.com.

See page 257 on the PDF for pattern

Pale Gold Batik
1 square (A) 11½" x 11½" (trim to 10½" x 10½" after appliqué)
Assorted Prints and Batiks
1 complete set of appliqué patches
Gold Batik
6 squares (K) 2⅞" x 2⅞"
6 Assorted Medium and Dark Batiks
from *each*
1 square (K) 2⅞" x 2⅞"
Fusible web

Unit
Make 12

Applique Placement

Fold A in half both ways and lightly crease the folds. Prepare patches B–J for fusible appliqué. Use the creases and appliqué placement diagram as guides to arrange the patches on A. Fuse the patches to A in alphabetical order.

Use monofilament thread and a small zigzag stitch to sew around the patches. Center the appliqué and trim to 10½" × 10½".

Refer to "Triangle-Squares" in the Techniques file on the PDF. Pair the gold K's with the assorted batik K's to make 12 units (there will be 1 extra).

Sew the units and A together as shown to complete the block.

Block Assembly

block no. 457

Candy Stripe

by Jacquelynne Steves • The Noble Wife
thenoblewife.com

Fabric: Fruitful Hands designed by Jaquelynne Steves for Henry Glass Fabrics, henryglassfabrics.com.

Jacquelynne Steves is the author of *Fruitful Hands* for Kansas City Star Quilts, pickledish.com.

See page 260 on the PDF for pattern

Assorted Pink, Orange, Yellow and Green Tone-on-Tones

14–16 strips at 1″ to 1¾″-wide and 22″-long for band (see instructions below)

White Tone-on-Tone

2 squares (A) 6½″ x 6½″

2 template B

Template plastic

If available, use a 6½″ square ruler instead of making a template for A.

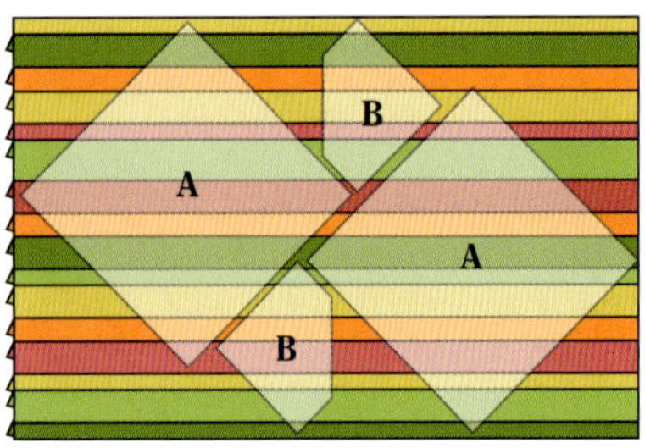

Band

Join the strips in a random order to make a band at least 12″ × 22″. Use the plastic to make templates of A and B. Position the templates on the band as shown and cut 2 *each* of A and B.

Align the B's in the corners of the A's as shown. Use matching thread and a short zigzag stitch to sew around the B's. Make 2 unit 1's and 2 unit 2's as shown.

Sew the units together as shown to complete the block.

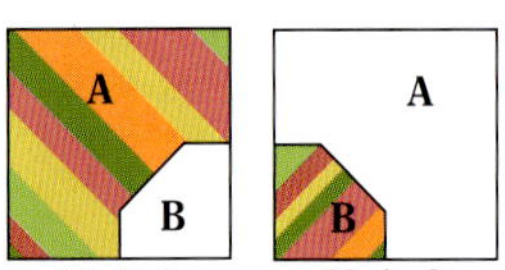

Unit 1 Make 2 | Unit 2 Make 2

Applique Placement

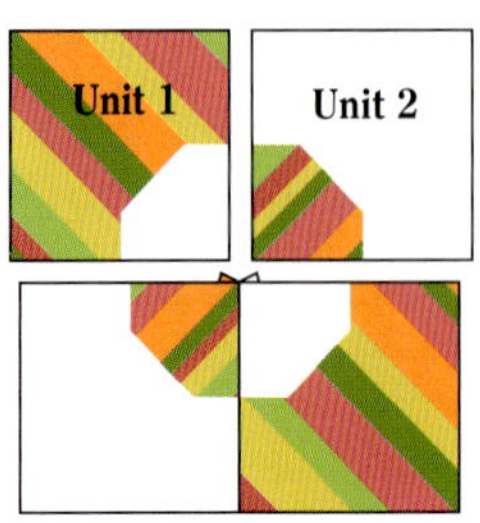

Block Assembly

block no. 458

Winter Village

by Paula Stoddard • Associate Editor, *Quiltmaker*
quiltmaker.com

Fabric: Aspen Frost designed by Basic Gray for Moda Fabrics, unitednotions.com.

See page 268 on the PDF for pattern

◸ = cut in half diagonally

☒ = cut in half twice diagonally

Red Print

1 square (A) 4¼″x 4¼″

White Tone-on-Tone

4 squares (B) 2⅜″x 2⅜″

2 squares 3⅞″x 3⅞″ ☒ (C)

8 rectangles (I) 2″x 3½″

Dark Brown Tone-on-Tone

4 rectangles (D) 1″x 2⅝″

4 Assorted Aqua Prints and Tone-on-Tones from *each*

1 square (E) 3½″x 3½″

1 square (H) 2″x 2″

Yellow Tone-on-Tone

4 pattern F

Red Tone-on-Tone

4 pattern G

Green Print

1 square (E) 3½″x 3½″

2 Green Tone-on-Tones from *each*

1 square 3⅞″x 3⅞″ ◸ (J)

Fusible web

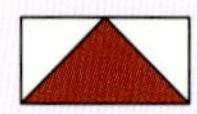

Flying Geese Make 4

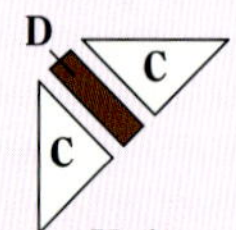

Unit Make 4

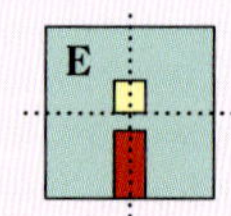

Applique Placement Make 4

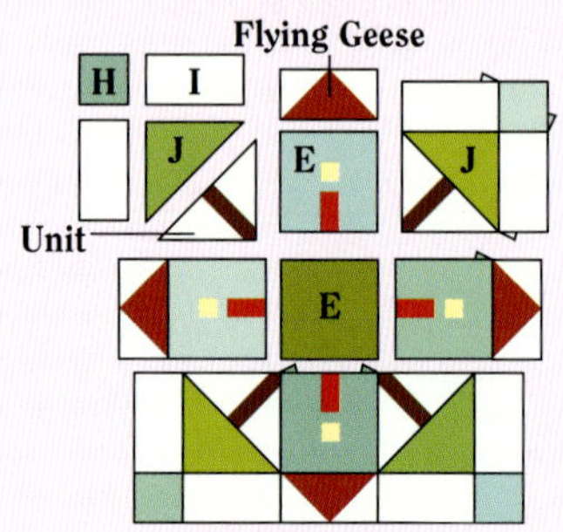

Block Assembly

Refer to "Fast Flying Geese" in the Techniques file on the PDF. Make 4 Flying Geese using the red print A and white B's.

Use the white C's and brown D's to make 4 units as shown.

Prepare patches F and G for fusible appliqué. Fold the aqua E's in half both ways and lightly crease the folds. Use the creases and appliqué placement diagram to arrange the patches on the aqua E's; fuse in place. Use matching thread and straight stitch to sew around the patches.

Sew the Flying Geese, units and patches together as shown to complete the block.

block no. 459
Sashed Circles

by Carol Ann Waugh
carolannwaugh.com

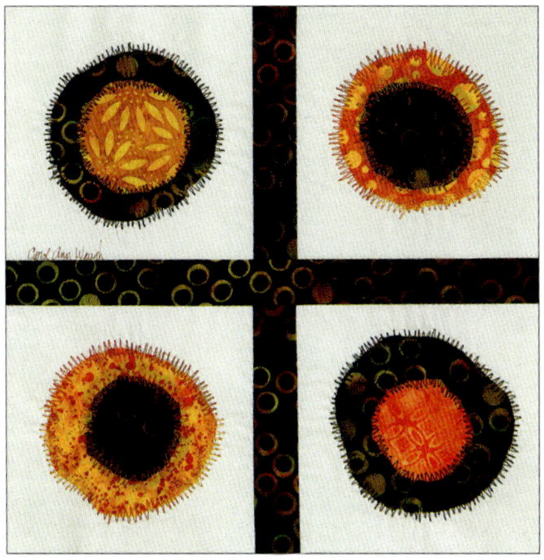

Carol Ann Waugh is the author of *Stupendous Stitching: How to Make Fun and Fabulous Fiber Art* for Xcellent Press.

White Tone-on-Tone
4 squares (A) 7″ x 7″ (trim to 6″ x 6″ after appliqué)
Black Batik
2 squares (B) 4¼″ x 4¼″
2 squares (C) 2½″ x 2½
2 rectangles (D) 1½″ x 6″
1 rectangle (E) 1½″ x 12½″
4 Assorted Orange Batiks
from *2*
2 squares (B) 4¼″ x 4¼″
from *2*
2 squares (C) 2½″ x 2½
Fabric glue

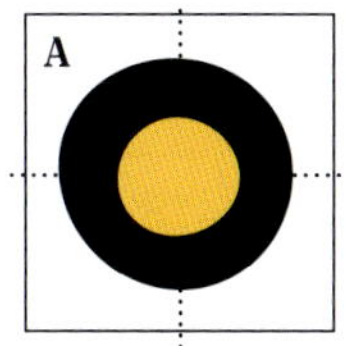

Applique Placement
Make 4

On the wrong side of the fabrics, draw 4" circles on the B's and 2¼" circles on the C's. Use scissors to cut out the circles. Irregular cutting lines will give the circles more interest.

Fold the A's in half both ways and lightly crease the folds. Use the creases and appliqué placement diagram as guides to arrange the circles on the A's as shown; lightly glue in place.

Use matching thread and a free-motion machine zigzag stitch to sew around the patches. Center the circles and trim the A's to 6" × 6".

Carol Ann lowers the feed dogs of her machine to achieve the free-motion zigzag stitch.

Sew the patches together as shown to complete the block.

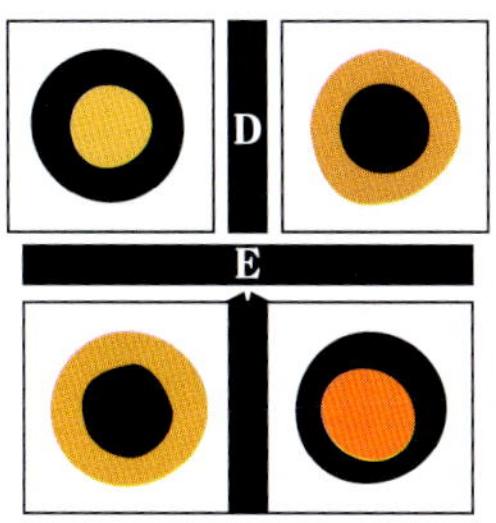

Block Assembly

block no. 460
Beanstalk

by Ann Weber • Gingham Girls
ginghamgirls.biz

Ann Weber is the author of *Season's Best* for Gingham Girls, ginghamgirls.biz.

See page 259 on the PDF for pattern

White Tone-on-Tone
1 rectangle (A) 7½″ x 13½″ (trim to 6½″ x 12½″ after appliqué)
Assorted Green Tone-on-Tones and Aqua Tone-on-Tones
8 pattern B
12 Assorted Prints and Tone-on-Tones
from *each*
1 rectangle (C) 2½″ x 3½″
Fusible web
Rickrack 13½″ long

Fold A in half both ways and lightly crease the folds. Position the rickrack on A as shown. Use matching thread and a straight stitch to tack down the rickrack.

Prepare the leaves (B's) for fusible appliqué. Use the creases and appliqué placement diagram as guides to arrange the patches on A. Fuse the patches to A. Use monofilament thread and a machine blanket stitch to sew around the patches.

Center the appliqué and trim A to 6½" × 12½". Sew the C's and A together as shown to complete the block.

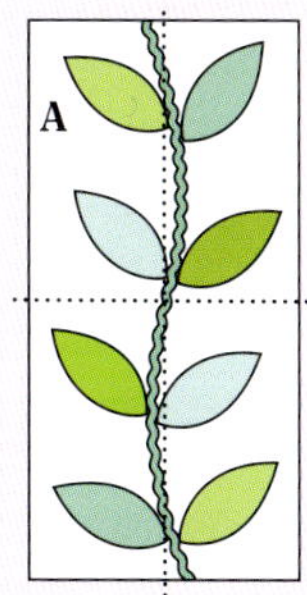

Applique Placement

Block Assembly

block no. 461

A Night Out

by Carolyn Beam • Creative Editor, *Quiltmaker*
quiltmaker.com

Fabric: Various lines from Northcott, northcott.com.

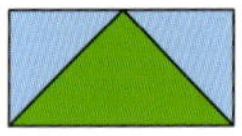

Flying Geese
Make 12

See page 330 on the PDF for pattern

3 Green Tone-on-Tones
from *each*
- 1 square (A) 5¼" x 5¼"

Medium Blue Tone-on-Tone
- 12 squares (B) 2⅞" x 2⅞"
- 2 rectangles (C) 1" x 4½"
- 4 rectangles (D) 1¾" x 2"
- 1 rectangle (G) 1¾" x 4½"

Dark Brown Tone-on-Tone
- 2 rectangles (E) 1½" x 1¾"

Tan Tone-on-Tone
- 2 rectangles (F) 2¾" x 4½"
- 1 rectangle (H) 3¼" x 4½"

Assorted Tone-on-Tones
- 1 set of appliqué patches

Assorted Pink and Purple Tone-on-Tones
- 5 sets of 4 matching circles (L) 1" in diameter for folded flowers

Fusible web

Buttons
- 5 pink at ⅜"
- 5 stars at ⅝"

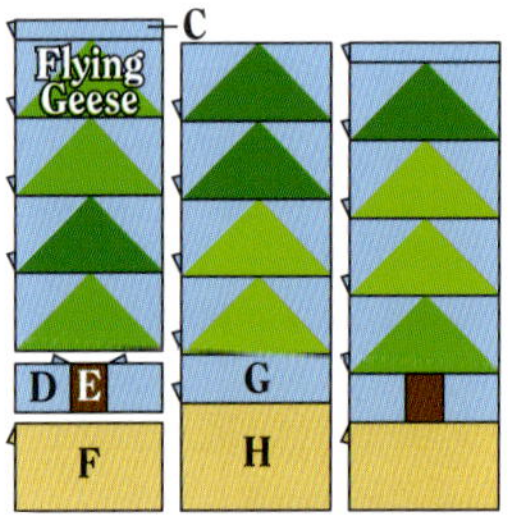

Block Piecing

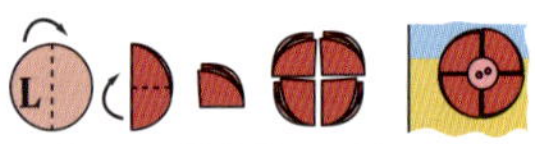

Flower Folding Diagram
Make 5 sets of 4 matching

Refer to "Fast Flying Geese" in the Techniques file on the PDF. Use the green A's and blue B's to make 12 Flying Geese. Sew the Flying Geese and patches together as shown to make the block.

Applique Placement

Prepare patches I–K for fusible appliqué. Refer to the appliqué placement diagram; use the diagram and the patchwork seams as guides to arrange the patches on the block. Fuse the patches in alphabetical order. Use matching thread and a machine blanket stitch to sew around the patches.

Fold each L circle in half twice as shown. Arrange folded quarter circles on the block in groups of 4 and tack down with a pink button at the center of each flower. Tack the star buttons in place as shown to complete the block.

block no. 462

It Snowed!

by Cheryl Brown • QuilterChic
quilterchic.com

Cheryl Brown is the author of *Quilt Batik!* for Martingale & Co., shopmartingale.com.

See page 331 on the PDF for pattern

Medium Blue Batik
- 1 square (A) 7½" x 7½" (trim to 6½" x 6½" after appliqué)
- 2 squares (F) 3⅞" x 3⅞"
- 1 square (G) 7¼" x 7¼"

White Tone-on-Tone
- 1 *each* patterns B and C

Black Tone-on-Tone
- 1 pattern D

Red Tone-on-Tone
- 1 pattern E

Light Blue Batik
- 6 squares (F) 3⅞" x 3⅞"

Embroidery floss

Applique and Embroidery Placement

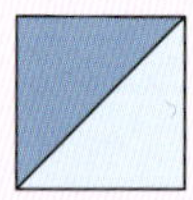

Unit
Make 4

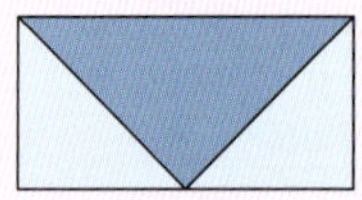

Flying Geese
Make 4

Block Assembly

Fold A in half both ways and lightly crease the folds. Prepare patches B–E for turned-edge appliqué. Use the creases and appliqué placement diagram as guides to arrange the patches on A.

Use matching thread and a blind stitch to appliqué the patches in place. Make French knots with black embroidery floss for the eyes and mouth. Use brown floss and a backstitch for the arms. Use orange floss and a backstitch to outline the carrot nose; satin stitch inside the carrot nose. Center the appliqué and trim A to 6½" × 6½".

For all techniques, refer to the Techniques file on the PDF. Pair the medium blue F's with light blue F's to make 4 Triangle-Square units. Use the medium blue G and light blue F's to make 4 Flying Geese.

Sew the units, Flying Geese and A together as shown to complete the block.

block no. 463

Vintage

by Kari Carr • New Leaf Stitches
newleafstitches.com

Fabric: Vintage Dry Goods by Daiwabo for Cara Collection, a division of E.E. Schenck eeschenck.com.

Kari Carr is the author of *Twice as Nice: Quilts with Scrap-Saving Bonus Projects* for Martingale & Co., shopmartingale.com.

See page 298 on the PDF for pattern

Tan Print
1 square (A) 9″x 9″ (trim to 8″x 8″ after appliqué)

Dark Brown Tone-on-Tone
1 pattern B
6 squares (D) 1½″x 1½″
3 squares (E) 2⅜″x 2⅜″
2 rectangles (G) 1¼″x 8″
2 rectangles (H) 1¼″x 9½″

Light Tan Tone-on-Tone
6 squares (C) 2″x 2″
3 squares (E) 2⅜″x 2⅜″
2 rectangles (F) 3½″x 6½″

Fusible web

Dark buttons
1 at ⅜″
2 at ½″
2 at ¾″
2 at 1″

Cream buttons 3 at ⅜″

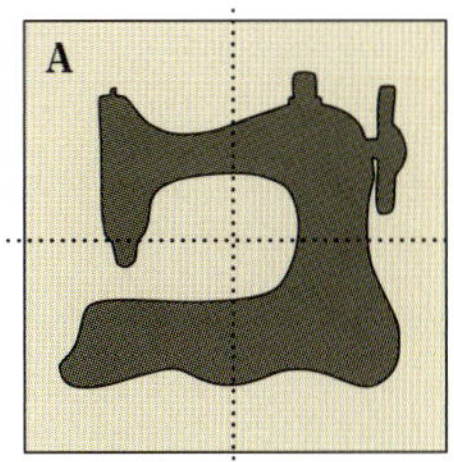

Applique Placement

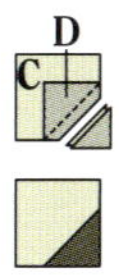

Unit 1
Stitch & Flip
Make 6

Unit 2
Make 6

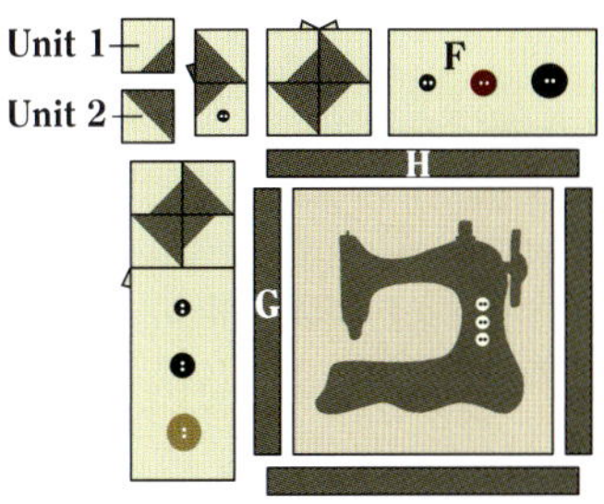

Block Assembly

Fold A in half both ways and lightly crease the folds. Prepare patch B for fusible appliqué. Use the creases and appliqué placement diagram as guides to arrange B on A; fuse in place. Use matching thread and a machine blanket stitch to sew around B. Center the appliqué and trim to 8"× 8".

For all techniques, refer to the Techniques file on the PDF. Use the light tan C's and brown D's to make 6 Stitch-and-Flip unit 1's. Pair the light tan E's with brown E's to make 6 Triangle-Square unit 2's.

Sew the units and patches together as shown. Tack the buttons in place to complete the block.

block no. 464

Delightful Doily

by Barbara H. Cline • Delightful Piecing
delightfulpiecing.com

Fabric: Kona solids by Robert Kaufman, robertkaufman.com.

Barbara Cline is the author of *Diamond Chain Quilts* for C&T Publishing, ctpub.com.

See page 289 on the PDF for pattern

Cream Solid
4 squares (A) 6½″x 6½″
8 pattern C

Orange, Gray, Blue and Green Solids
from *each*
1 pattern B

Black nylon netting, tulle or organza
4 rectangles 4″x 5½″ for overlay

Fusible web

Tear-away stabilizer (optional)

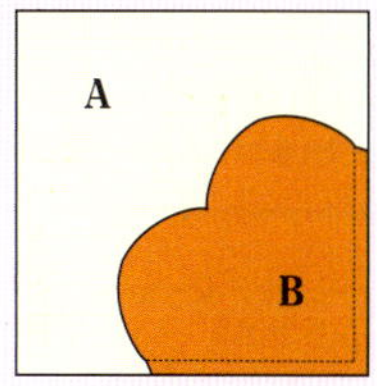

Applique Placement
Make 4

Netting

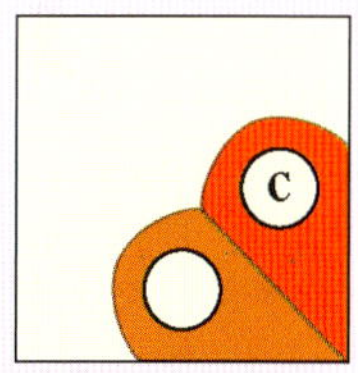

Unit
Make 4

Prepare patches B and C for fusible appliqué. Align a B on the corner of an A as shown and fuse in place. Lightly draw a line to bisect the B across the diagonal. Layer a netting rectangle over one half of B as shown; pin in place.

Barbara placed tear-away stabilizer on the back of her units before stitching around the appliqué.

Use gray thread and a narrow zigzag stitch to sew around the B and along the drawn diagonal line. Carefully trim the netting just outside the stitching lines. Position 2 C's as shown and fuse in place with a cool iron so the netting doesn't melt. Use cream thread and a zigzag stitch to sew around the C's. Repeat to make 4 units.

Sew the units together as shown. Echo B's curves using a light green thread and a straight stitch approximately ½" from appliqué edges as shown to complete the block.

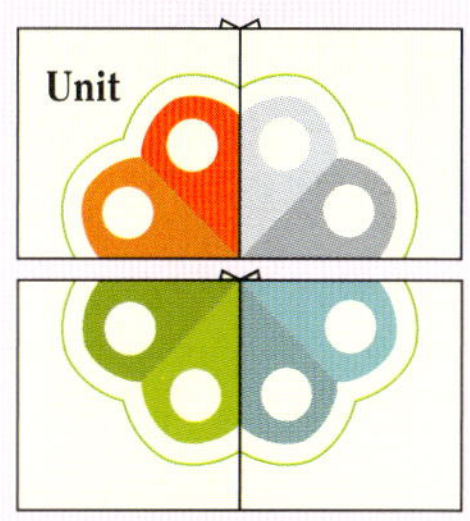

Block Assembly

block no. 465
Gelato Italiano

by Kristyne Czepuryk • Pretty by Hand
prettybyhand.com

Kristyne Czepuryk is the author of *S is for Stitch* for C&T Publishing, ctpub.com.

See page 291–292 on the PDF for pattern

Assorted Light Brown, Green, Pink and Purple Prints and Tone-on-Tones
from *1* green, *1* pink and *1* purple
  section patch 1
from *all*
  1 complete set of appliqué patches
White Dot
  section patches 2 and 3
  3 rectangles (A) 4½"x 4⅞"
Red Check
  1 rectangle (F) 2¾"x 12½"
Fusible web
Brown Pigma Micron pen (.01 tip)
Embroidery floss

Section 1
Make 1

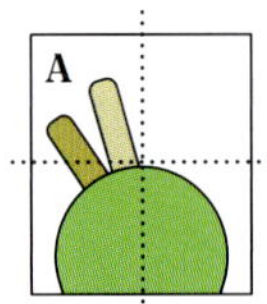

Unit 1
Make 1

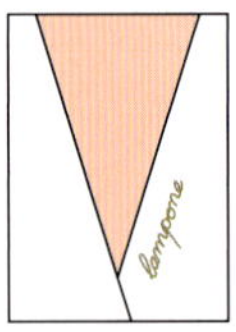

Section 2
Make 1

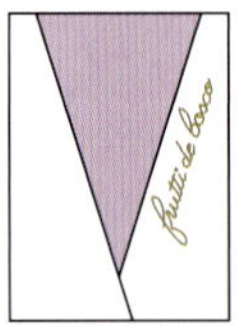

Section 3
Make 1

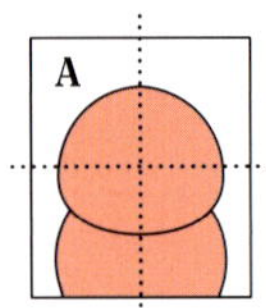

Unit 2
Make 1

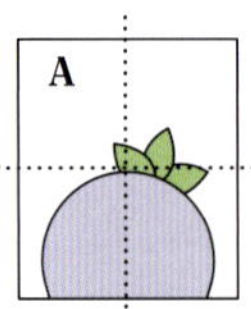

Unit 3
Make 1

Make 3 paper copies of the foundation section. Foundation piece the sections in numerical order, pressing and trimming after each patch addition.

Fold the A's in half both ways and lightly crease the folds. Prepare patches B–E for fusible appliqué. Use the creases, appliqué placement diagram and foundation sections as guides to arrange the patches on A. Fuse the patches to A in alphabetical order. Use matching thread and a straight stitch to sew just inside the edge of each patch.

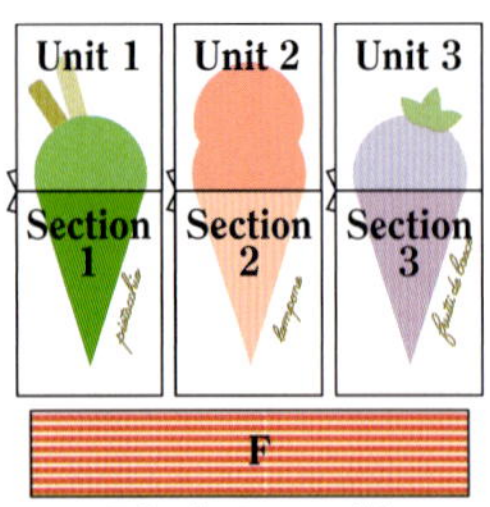

Block Assembly

Referring to the section diagrams as guides, lightly trace the gelato flavors onto the sections with the pen. Backstitch the gelato flavors with a single strand of floss.

Sew the units, sections and F together as shown to complete the block.

block no. 466
Yucatan Coast

by Ian Davis • Art Director, *Quiltmaker*
quiltmaker.com

Fabric: Scratch Texture, Suede Brights and Color Weave Soft Brights, all from P&B Textiles, pbtex.com.

See page 309 on the PDF for pattern

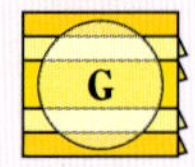

Sun Piecing

Light Blue Tone-on-Tone #1
  1 rectangle (A) 1½"x 12½"
  1 rectangle (C) 1"x 12½"
  1 rectangle (D) 2¾"x 12½"
Light Blue Tone-on-Tone #2
  2 rectangles (B) 2¼"x 12½"
  1 rectangle (E) 1¾"x 12½"
Dark Blue Tone-on-Tone
  1 rectangle (F) 4"x 12½"
3 Yellow Tone-on-Tones
from *1*
  1 rectangle 1¾"x 3¾"
from *2*
  2 rectangles 1⅛"x 3¾"
2 Green Tone-on-Tones
from *each*
  1 rectangle (E) 1¾"x 12½"
White Solid
  1 pattern H
Medium Blue Tone-on-Tone
  1 each patterns I and J
Fusible web

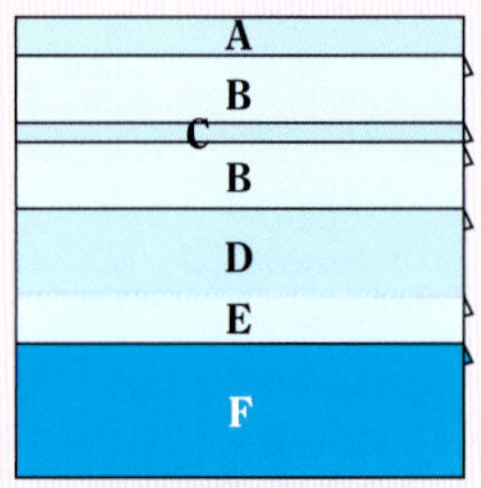

Block Piecing

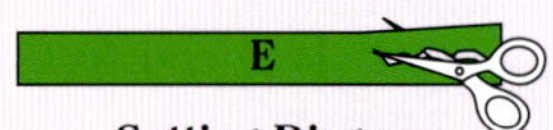

Cutting Diagram

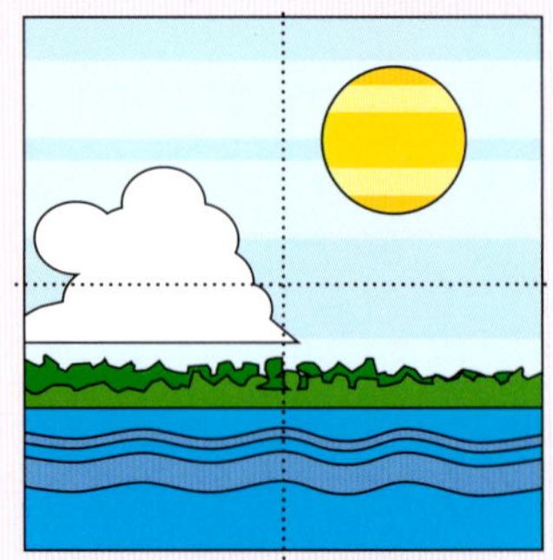

Applique Placement

Join patches A–F as shown. Referring to the sun piecing diagram, sew the yellow rectangles together as shown.

Fuse a piece of fusible web to the wrong side of each green E. Use scissors to make jagged cuts along one side of each E for the trees as shown. Prepare patches G–I for fusible appliqué, using the pieced yellow section for G. Fold the block in half both ways and lightly crease the folds. Use the creases and appliqué placement diagram as guides to arrange the patches on the block; fuse in alphabetical order.

Use matching thread and a machine blanket stitch to sew around the patches to complete the block.

block no. 467
Mod Posies

by Jenifer Dick • 42 Quilts
42quilts.com

Fabric: Kona Solids by Robert Kaufman, robertkaufman.com.

Jenifer Dick is the author of *Quilt Retro: 11 Designs to Make Your Own* for Kansas City Star Quilts, pickledish.com.

See page 293 on the PDF for pattern

Gold Solid and Orange Solid
from *each*
- 1 square (A) 7½″ x 7½″ (trim to 6½″ x 6½″ after appliqué)
- 1 pattern C
- 1 square (F) 2½″ x 2½″

Medium Gray Solid
- 2 pattern B
- 4 pattern E
- 8 squares (F) 2½″ x 2½″

Light Gray Solid
- 2 pattern D
- 8 squares (F) 2½″ x 2½″

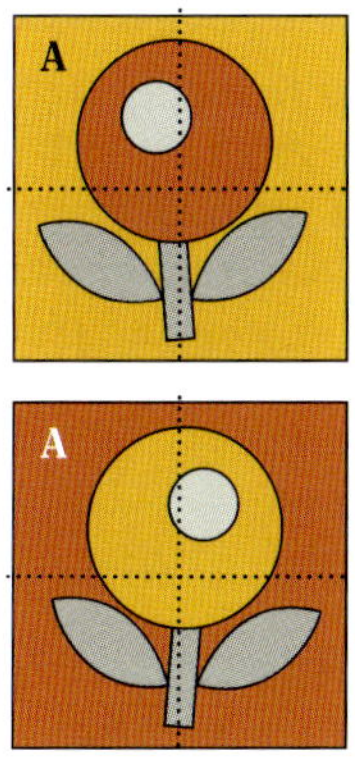

Applique Placement

Fold the A's in half both ways and lightly crease the folds. Prepare patches B–E for turned-edge appliqué. Use the creases and appliqué placement diagram as guides to arrange the patches on the A's.

Use monofilament thread and a zigzag stitch to appliqué the patches in place. Center the appliqué and trim the A's to 6½" × 6½".

Sew the F's and A's together as shown to complete the block.

Block Assembly

block no. 468
Shine a Little Light

by Sandy Fitzpatrick • Hissyfitz Designs
hissyfitzdesigns.com

See page 328 on the PDF for pattern

Blue Tone-on-Tone
- 1 square (A) 11½″ x 11½″ (trim to 10½″ x 10½″ after appliqué)

Black Solid
- 1 pattern B

2 White Tone-on-Tones
from *1*
- 3 pattern C

from *1*
- 3 pattern D

Gray Tone-on-Tone
- 1 *each* patterns E, Er and F

Assorted Tone-on-Tones
- 1 *each* patterns G–L

⅛″ **Metallic Gold Piping**
- 4 lengths at 10½″

Blue Print
- 2 rectangles (M) 1½″ x 10½″
- 2 rectangles (N) 1½″ x 12½″

Fusible web

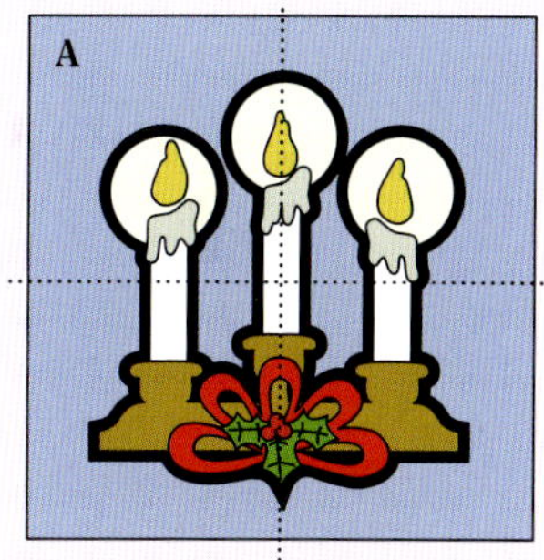

Applique Placement

Fold A in half both ways and lightly crease the folds. Prepare patches B–L for fusible appliqué. Use the creases and appliqué placement diagram as guides to arrange the patches on A. Fuse the patches to A in alphabetical order.

Use matching thread and a machine blanket stitch to sew around the patches. Use a straight stitch to add veins to the holly leaves. Center the appliqué and trim to 10½" × 10½".

Align the raw edges of each piping strip with a side of A and baste in place. Join the blue M's and N's to the sides as shown to complete the block.

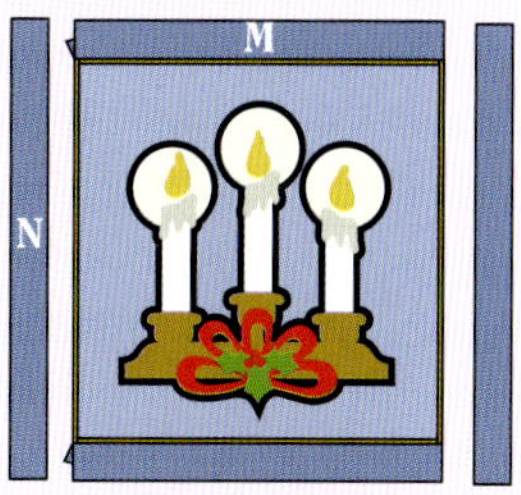

Block Assembly

block no. 469

Sunshine Sunflower

by Joan Ford • Hummingbird Highway
hummingbird-highway.com

Joan Ford is the author of *ScrapTherapy® Scraps Plus One!*: for Taunton Press, taunton.com.

See page 296 on the PDF for pattern

Assorted Green and Brown Prints and Tone-on-Tones
16 squares (A) 2″ x 2″
White Tone-on-Tone
1 square (A) 13½″ x 13½″ (trim to 12½″ x 12½″ after appliqué)
Gold Tone-on-Tone
8 pattern C
Fusible web
Template plastic

Sew the green and brown A's together with a scant ¼" as shown.

Fold B in half both ways and diagonally and lightly crease the folds. Prepare the C's for fusible appliqué. Apply fusible web to the back of the pieced A's. Use the plastic to make a template of D. Center the template over the pieced A's; trace and cut 1 D.

Use the creases and appliqué placement diagram as guides to arrange the C's and D on B; fuse the patches in place.

Use cream thread and a machine blanket stitch to sew around the patches. Center the appliqué and trim to 12½" × 12½".

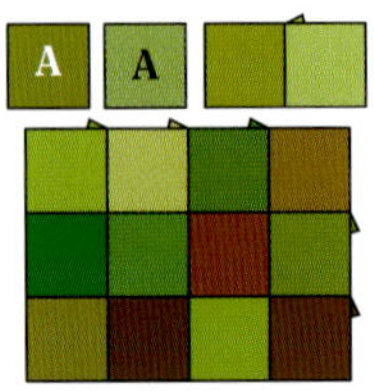

Block Piecing

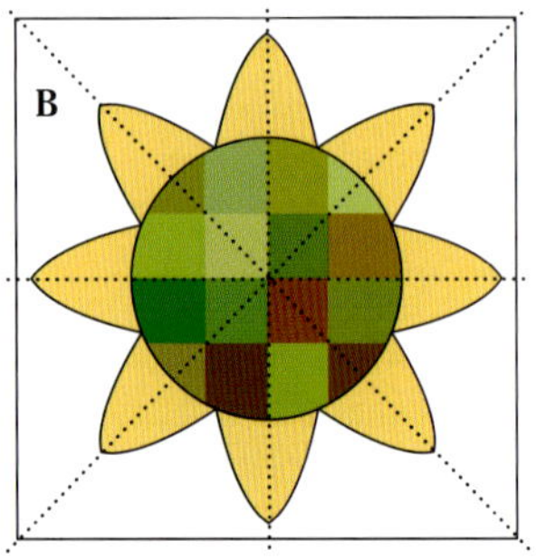

Applique Placement

block no. 470

Walk About

by Chris Hoover • Whirligig Designs
whirligigdesigns.com

See page 326 on the PDF for pattern

8 Assorted Batiks
section and section reversed, patch 1
Cream Batik
section and section reversed, patch 2
4 *each* templates A, Ar, B and Br

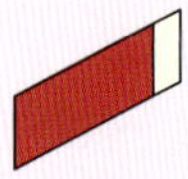

Section
Make 6

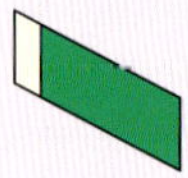

Section Reversed
Make 6

Make 6 paper copies *each* of the foundation section and the section reversed.

Note that 4 of the assorted batiks make both a section and a section reversed and 4 different assorted batiks make either 1 section or 1 section reversed.

Foundation piece the sections in numerical order, pressing and trimming after each patch addition.

Referring to the photo and assembly diagram for color placement, sew the patches and sections together as shown to complete the block.

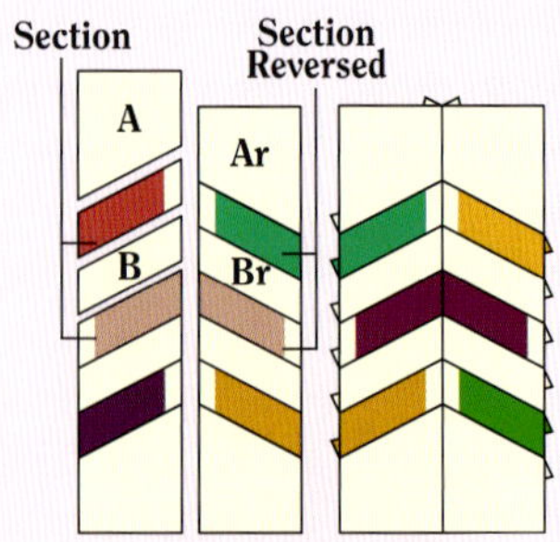

Block Assembly

block no. 471
Posies

by Lynda Howell • The Stitch Connection
stitchconnection.com

See page 313 on the PDF for pattern

Pale Blue Batik
1 square (A) 12″x 12″ (trim to 10½″x 10½″ after quilting)
Lightweight Batting
1 square (A) 12″x 12″ (trim to 10½″x 10½″ after quilting)
Medium Green Batik
3 pattern B
1 *each* patterns C and D
2 Pink Batiks
from *each*
1 *each* patterns E and F
Yellow Batik
1 pattern G
Dark Green Batik
2 rectangles (H) 1½″x 10½″
2 rectangles (I) 1½″x 12½″
Fusible web
Buttons 2 at ⅝″, 1 at 1″
Embroidery floss

Decorative Stitching

Applique Placement and Block Piecing

Layer the blue A right side up on the batting. Refer to the decorative stitching diagram. Quilt a grid of diagonal lines 1" apart. Add 2 lines of decorative stitching in opposite corners approximately 2" and 2½" away from the raw edges as shown. Center and trim A to 10½"× 10½".

Fold A in half both ways and lightly crease the folds. Prepare patches B–G for fusible appliqué. Use the creases and appliqué placement diagram as guides to arrange the patches; fuse in alphabetical order. Use matching thread and a machine blanket stitch to sew around the patches. Use embroidery floss and couching to embellish the edges of the H's and add veins to the leaves.

To complete the block, add the dark green H's and I's as shown. Stack a ⅝" button atop the 1" button and center on the left flower and center a ⅝" button on the right flower; tack in place with floss and fray the ends.

block no. 472
Spring Squared

by Deborah Johnson • In the Doghouse Designs
inthedoghousedesigns.com

See page 306 on the PDF for pattern

Cream Tone-on-Tone
4 rectangles (A) 4″x 9″
Green Tone-on-tone
4 *each* patterns B and C
4 Assorted Tone-on-Tones
from *each*
1 pattern D
1 square (E) 3″x 3″
Fusible web

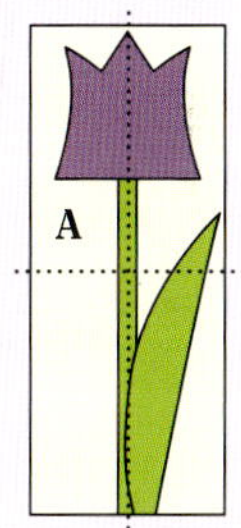

Unit
Make 4

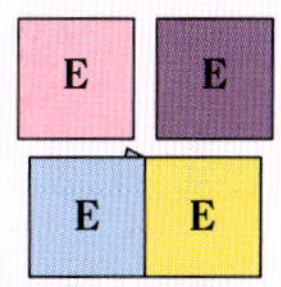

Center Piecing

Fold the A's in half both ways and lightly crease the folds. Prepare patches B–D for fusible appliqué. Use the creases and appliqué placement diagram as guides to arrange the patches on the A's. Fuse the patches in alphabetical order. Make 4 units. Use matching thread and a zigzag stitch to sew around the patches.

Join the E's as shown to make the block center. Noting the color placement relative to the center, sew a unit to the left of the center with a partial seam as shown. Sew a unit to the top, right and bottom of the center as shown. Complete the partial seam to complete the block.

• = Partial Seam

Block Assembly

block no. 473

Lone Star Twist

by Sara Khammash

Fabric: King of the Ranch designed by Sara Khammash for Moda Fabrics, unitednotions.com.

See page 318 on the PDF for pattern

Cream Tone-on-Tone
1 template A
1 pattern F
Tan Tone-on-Tone
2 rectangles (B) 2¼″x 6½″
2 *each* templates C and Cr
Blue Tone-on-Tone
1 pattern D
Red Tone-on-Tone
1 pattern E
Fusible web

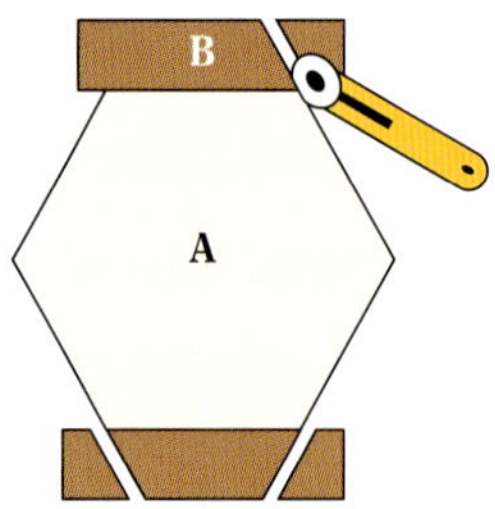

Trimming Diagram

Refer to the trimming diagram. Matching centers, join the B's to the A; trim the B's even with A as shown.

Add a C and Cr to the lower left and lower right of A as shown; trim even with A. Add a Cr and C to the upper left and upper right of A to complete the block background.

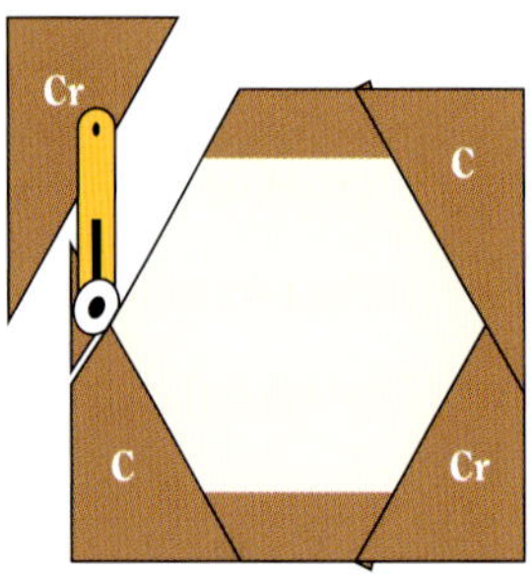

Block Piecing

Fold the block in half both ways and lightly crease the folds. Prepare patches D–F for fusible appliqué. Use the creases and appliqué placement diagram as guides to arrange the patches. Fuse the patches to the block in alphabetical order.

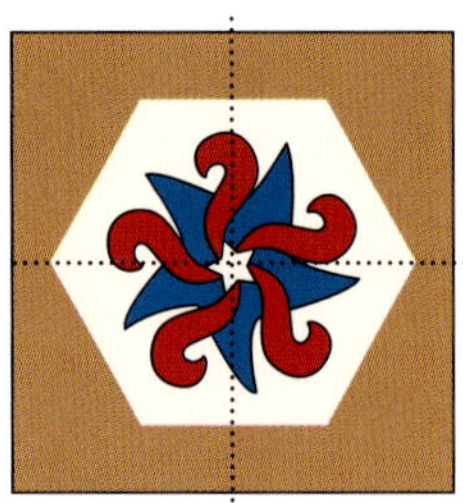

Applique Placement

Sew around the patches using matching thread and a machine blanket stitch to complete the block.

block no. 474

Lost Mittens

by Susan Marth • Suzn Quilts
suznquilts.com

Susan Marth is the author of several books including *A Christmas Sampler* and *Name that Quilt!* for Suzn Quilts, suznquilts.com.

See page 305 on the PDF for pattern

Cream Print #1
2 squares (A) 6½″x 6½″
Black Dot
1 *each* patterns B and Br
Cream Print #2
36 squares (C) 1½″x 1½″
Black Print and Green Tone-on-Tone
from *each*
8 squares (C) 1½″x 1½″
Red Print
20 squares (C) 1½″x 1½″
Fusible web

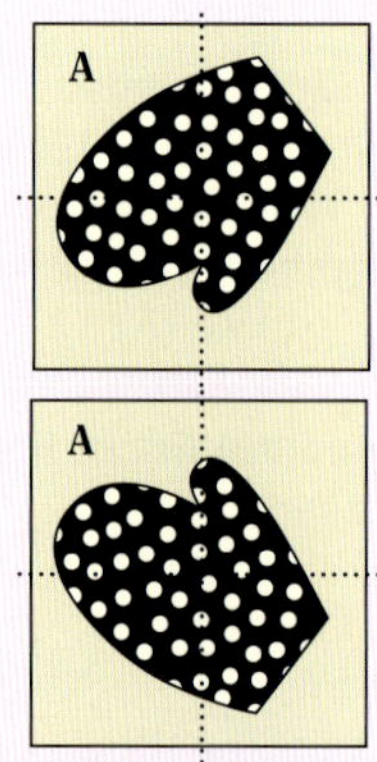

Applique Placement

Fold the A's in half both ways and lightly crease the folds. Prepare the B and Br for fusible appliqué. Use the creases and appliqué placement diagram as guides to arrange the patches on the A's; fuse in place.

Use cream thread and a machine blanket stitch to sew around the patches.

Sew the A's and C's together as shown to complete the block.

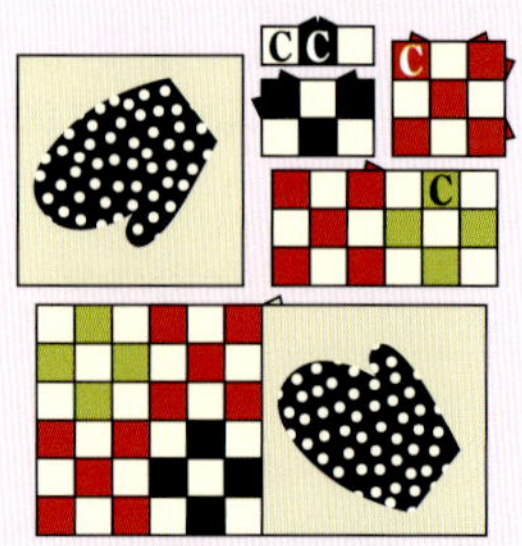

Block Assembly

block no. 475

Dutch Basket

by Jo Morton • Jo Morton Quilts
jomortonquilts.com

Fabric: Various lines designed by Jo Morton for Andover Fabrics, andoverfabrics.com.

Jo Morton is the author of many self-published books including *Prairie Flowers Encore and For All Seasons.*

See page 289 on the PDF for pattern

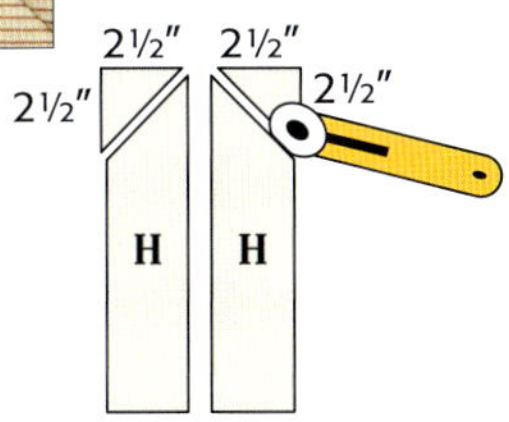

⧄ = cut in half diagonally

Tan Stripe
- 1 square (A) 13⅞" x 13⅞" (trim to 12⅞" x 12⅞" after appliqué)
- 3 squares 2⅞" x 2⅞" ⧄ (F) (there will be 1 extra)
- 1 square (G) 2½" x 2½"
- 2 rectangles (H) 2½" x 8⅞" (trimmed as shown)
- 1 square 4⅞" x 4⅞" ⧄ (I) (there will be 1 extra)

Assorted Green Tone-on-Tones
- 1 strip ⅝" x 5½" for stem
- 2 strips ⅝" x 4" for stems
- 2 pattern D
- 1 *each* patterns E and Er

Assorted Red Prints
- 3 pattern B
- 2 pattern C

Brown Print
- 6 squares 2⅞" x 2⅞" ⧄ (F) (there will be 1 extra)

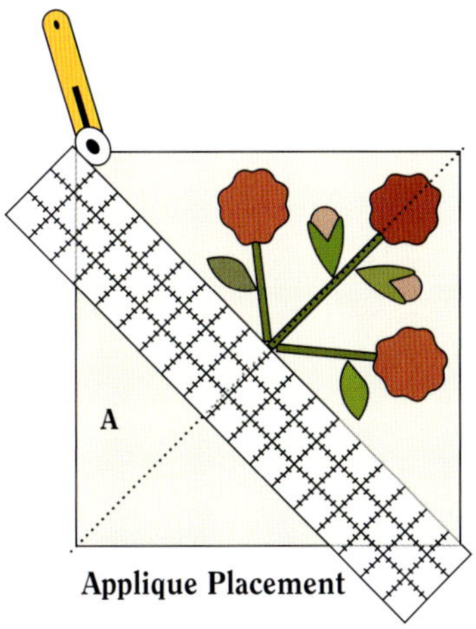

Applique Placement

Fold A in half diagonally both ways and lightly crease the folds. Prepare the stems and patches B–E for turned-edge appliqué. Use the creases and appliqué placement diagram as guides to arrange the patches on A.

Use matching thread and a blind stitch to appliqué the stems and patches in place. Center the appliqué and trim A to 12⅞" × 12⅞"; cut in half diagonally as shown.

Block Assembly

Sew the patches together as shown to complete the block.

block no. 476

Whimsical Bouquet

by Arlene Neely • Rabbits Haven Quilt & Stitchery
rabbitshaven.com

Fabric: Various lines designed by Arlene Neely for Red Rooster Fabrics, redroosterfabrics.com.

See page 299 on the PDF for pattern

Assorted White Tone-on-Tones
- 4 squares (A) 6½" x 6½"

Assorted Prints and Tone-on-Tones
- 4 sets of appliqué patches

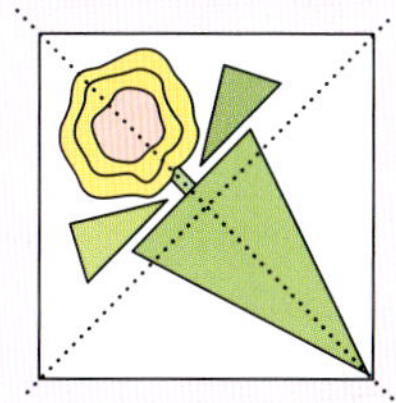

Applique Placement
Make 4

Fold the A's in half diagonally both ways and lightly crease the folds. Allowing for a ¼" seam allowance around all sides of A, use the creases and appliqué placement diagram as guides to arrange the patches in alphabetical order on each A; pin the patches in place.

Use matching thread and a straight stitch to sew inside the edges of each patch, allowing the edges of the patches to fray a little. Sew the A's together as shown to complete the block.

Block Assembly

block no. 477

Pretty Little Posy

by Kari Ramsay • Fresh Cut Quilts
freshcutquilts.com

Fabric: Folk Heart designed by Rosalie Quinlan for Lecien, lecienusa.com.

Quick Yo-Yo Maker (extra large) can be found at clover-usa.com.

See page 332 on the PDF for pattern

Aqua Tone-on-Tone
12 squares (A) 3½″ x 3½″
Red Print and Pink Print
from *each*
2 squares (A) 3½″ x 3½″
6 pattern B
Yellow Check
1 circle 5″ diameter for yo-yo (see below)
Extra Large Clover Yo-yo Maker (optional)

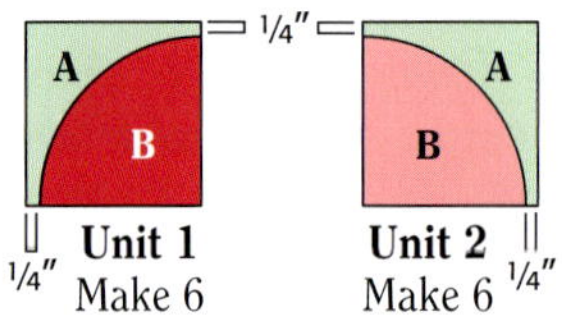

Unit 1 Make 6

Unit 2 Make 6

Prepare the curved edges of the B patches for turned-edge appliqué. Align the B's on the A's. Use monofilament thread and a machine blanket stitch to sew around the patches. Make 6 unit 1's and 6 unit 2's as shown. Sew the units and patches together as shown.

Kari made her yo-yo using the Clover extra-large yo-yo maker. Alternatively, follow the directions in the Techniques file on the PDF.

Follow the manufacturer's instructions to make a yo-yo with the yellow check. Tack the yo-yo in place to complete the block.

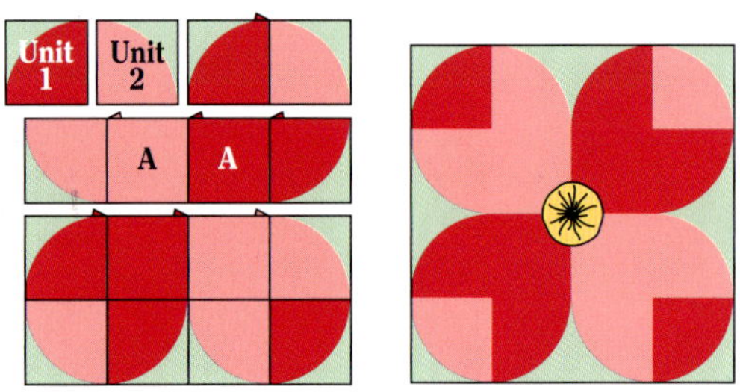

Block Assembly

block no. 478

Solar Flare

by Bethany Reynolds • BSR Designs
bethanyreynolds.com

Fabric: Barcelona designed by Bethany Reynolds for Troy Riverwoods Collection, troy-corp.com.

Bethany Reynolds is the author of *Stack-n-Whackier Quilts* for American Quilter's Society, americanquilter.com.

See page 315 on the PDF for pattern

Yellow Tone-on-Tone
1 square (A) 6½″ x 6½″
Yellow Print
1 pattern B
Medium Blue Tone-on-Tone and Multicolor Print
from *each*
4 squares (C) 3⅞″ x 3⅞″
2 squares (D) 3½″ x 3½″

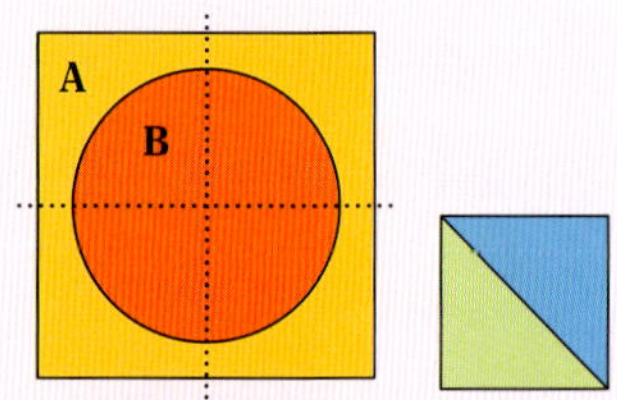

Unit 1 Make 1

Unit 2 Make 8

Fold A in half both ways and lightly crease the folds. Prepare patch B for turned-edge appliqué. Use the creases to center B on A. Pin B in place. Make unit 1 using matching thread and a machine blanket stitch to sew around B.

Refer to "Triangle-Squares" in the Techniques file on the PDF. Pair the blue C's with the multicolor C's to make 8 unit 2's. Sew the units and patches together as shown to complete the block.

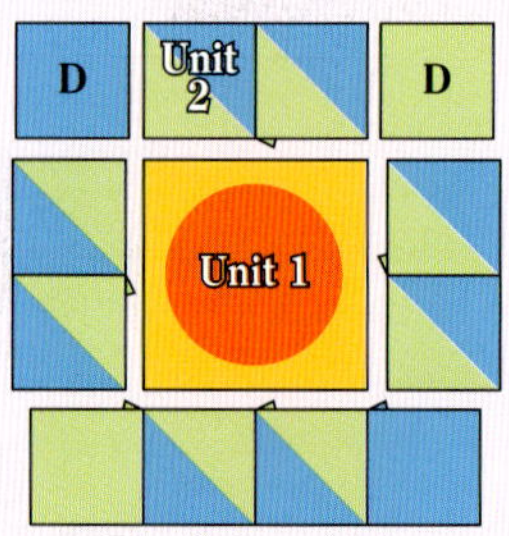

Block Assembly

block no. 479
Snowflake Snowman

by Joanne Rowicki • Gingham Girls
ginghamgirls.biz

Fabric: Sew Stitchy designed by Aneela Hoey for Moda Fabrics, unitednotions.com.

See page 332 on the PDF for pattern

Aqua Stripe
1 rectangle (A) 11½″ x 13½″ (trim to 10½″ x 12½″ after appliqué)
Brown Check
1 *each* patterns B and Br
White Tone-on-Tone
1 *each* patterns C–E
12 squares (H) 1½″ x 1½″
Pink Dot
1 pattern F
Orange Tone-on-Tone
1 pattern G
Aqua Tone-on-Tone
12 squares (H) 1½″ x 1½″
Fusible web
Black embroidery floss
Buttons 2 at ¼″

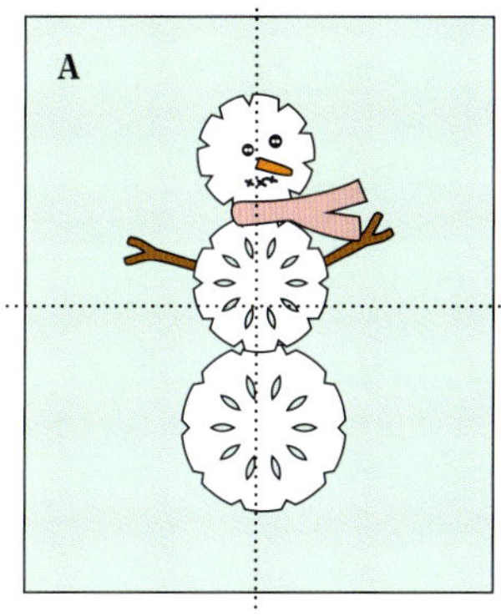

Applique Placement

Fold A in half both ways and lightly crease the folds. Prepare patches B–G for fusible appliqué. Use the creases and appliqué placement diagram as guides to arrange the patches on A. Fuse the patches to A in alphabetical order.

Use matching thread and a machine blanket stitch to sew around the patches. Use 2 strands of embroidery floss and a crossstitch for the mouth. Center the appliqué and trim to 10½" × 12½".

Sew the H's and A together as shown. Tack the snowman eye buttons in place to complete the block.

Block Assembly

block no. 480
Anchors Aweigh

by Mary Sanderson • Sea Quilts
seaquiltsshop.etsy.com

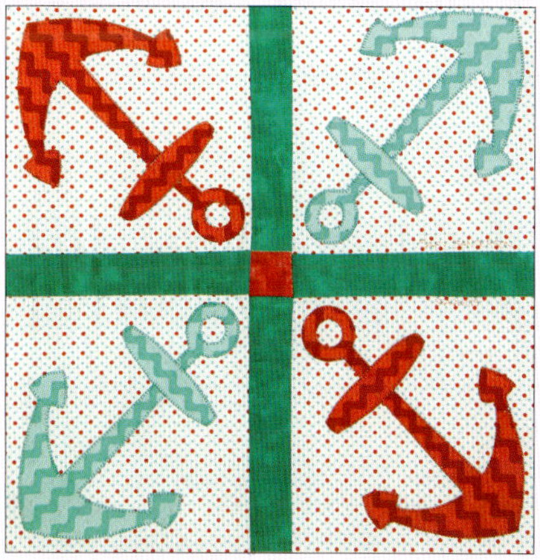

See page 332 on the PDF for pattern

White Print
4 squares (A) 7″ x 7″ (trim to 6″ x 6″ after appliqué)
Red Tone-on-Tone #1 and Teal Tone-on-Tone #1
from *each*
2 *each* patterns B and C
Teal Tone-on-Tone #2
4 rectangles (D) 1½″ x 6″
Red Tone-on-Tone #2
1 square (E) 1½″ x 1½″
Fusible web

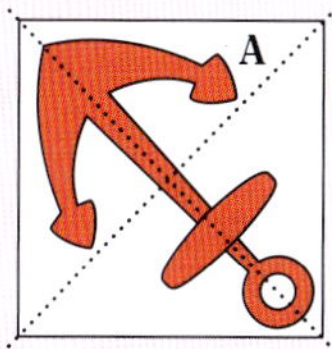

Unit 1
Make 2

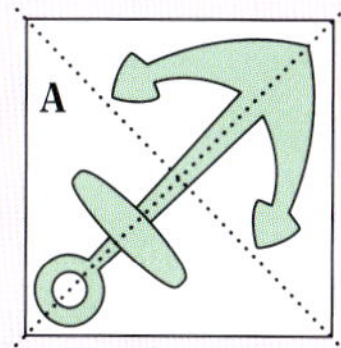

Unit 2
Make 2

Fold the A's in half diagonally both ways and lightly crease the folds. Prepare patches B–C for fusible appliqué. Use the creases and unit diagrams as guides to arrange the patches on the A's. Fuse the patches in alphabetical order.

Use matching thread and a machine blanket stitch to sew around the patches. Make 2 unit 1's and 2 unit 2's as shown. Center the appliqué and trim the A's to 6" × 6".

Sew the units and patches together as shown to complete the block.

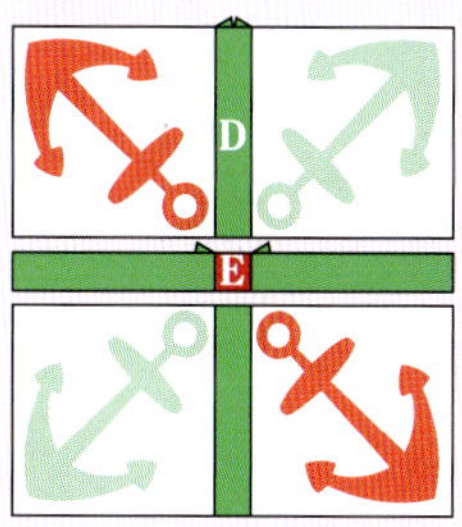

Block Assembly

block no. 481

Citrus Rainbow

by Dawn Stewart • Spring Water Designs
springwaterdesigns.com

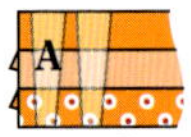

Band A

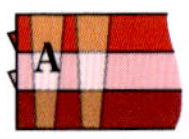

Band B

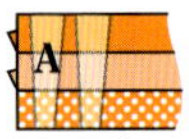

Band C

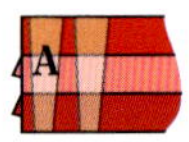

Band D

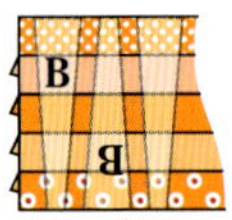

Band E

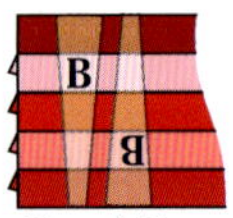

Band F

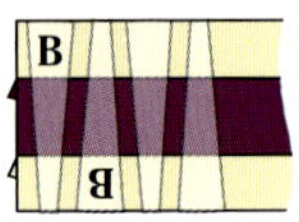

Band G

See page 305 on the PDF for pattern

Orange Tone-on-Tone #1 and Red Tone-on-Tone #1
from *each*
3 rectangles 1½" x 7"
Orange Prints and Tone-on-Tones #'s 2–5 and Red Prints and Tone-on-Tones #'s 2–5
from *each*
2 rectangles 1½" x 7"
Pale Yellow Solid
2 rectangles 2" x 8"
1 square (C) 12½" x 12½"
Purple Tone-on-Tone
1 rectangle 2½" x 8"
1 pattern D

Sew the various rectangles together *in the following order* to make bands A–F: band A—orange #1, #2 and #3; band B—red #1, #2 and #3; band C—orange #1, #4 and #5; band D—red #1, #4 and #5; band E—orange #5, #4, #1, #2 and #3; band F—red #3, #2, #1, #4 and #5. For band G, sew a purple rectangle between 2 yellow rectangles. Referring to the diagrams and noting orientation of the templates, cut A's and B's. Beginning and ending with orange and alternating orange and red, sew the A's together as shown to make section 1. Make section 2 using the B's.

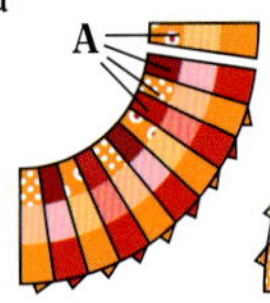

Section 1
Make 1

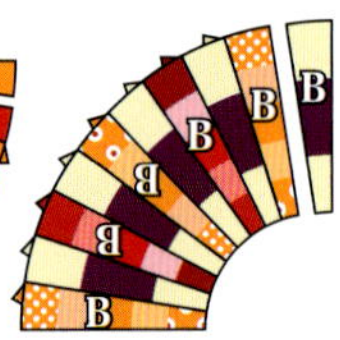

Section 2
Make 1

Prepare sections 1 and 2 and patch D for turned-edge appliqué. Align the patches on A as shown. Appliqué the sections and D in place using matching thread and a straight stitch to complete the block.

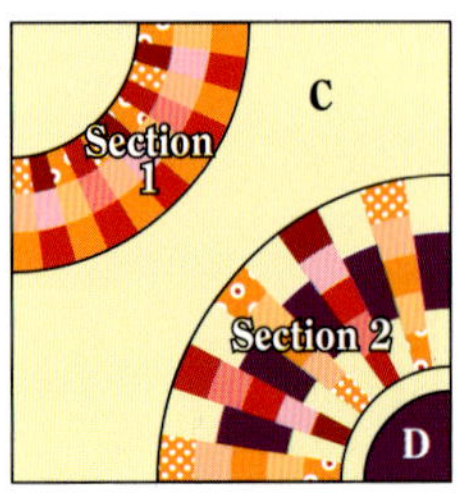

Applique Placement

block no. 482

Winter World

by Paula Stoddard • Associate Editor, *Quiltmaker*
quiltmaker.com

Fabric: Timeless Treasures, ttfabrics.com.

See page 308 on the PDF for pattern

2 Aqua Tone-on-Tones
from *each*
1 square (A) 7½" x 7½" (trim to 6½" x 6½" after appliqué)
White Tone-on-Tone
2 squares (A) 7½" x 7½" (trim to 6½" x 6½" after appliqué)
2 pattern B
2 Green Tone-on-Tones
from *each*
1 pattern B
Assorted Wool
1 complete set of appliqué patches
Embroidery floss
Fusible web

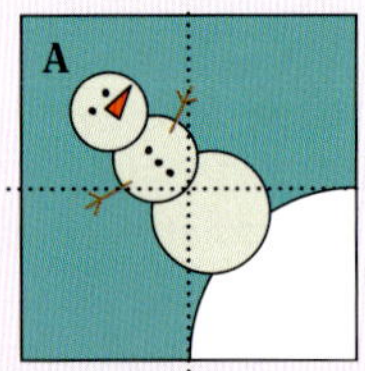

Unit 1
Make 2

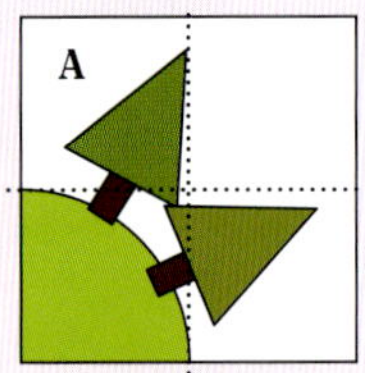

Unit 2
Make 1

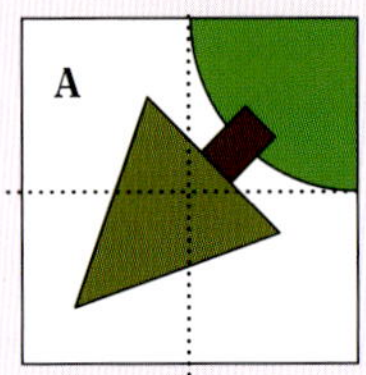

Unit 3
Make 1

Fold the A's in half both ways and lightly crease the folds. Prepare patches B–J for fusible appliqué. Use the creases and appliqué placement diagram as guides to arrange the patches on A. Fuse the patches in alphabetical order.

Using 2 strands of floss, outline stitch the arms and make French knots for the buttons and eyes. Sew around the appliqué patches with a blanket stitch. Center the appliqué and trim the A's to 6½" × 6½".

Sew the units together as shown to complete the block.

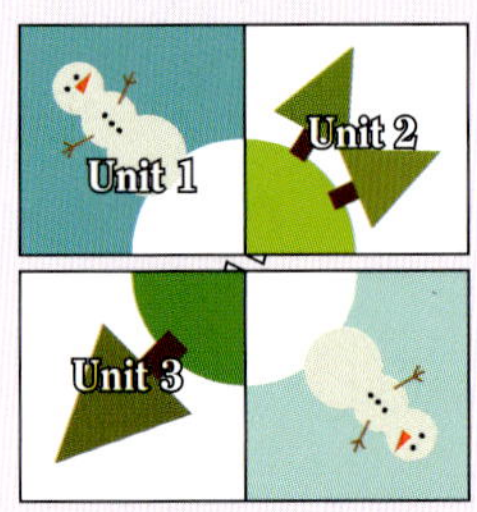

Block Assembly

block no. 483

Fairy Floss

by Helen Stubbings • Hugs 'n Kisses
hugsnkisses.net

Fabric: Nice People Nice Things designed by Helen Stubbings for Red Rooster Fabrics, redroosterfabrics.com.

Helen Stubbings is the author of *Faux Appliqué* for American Quilter's Society, americanquilter.com.

See page 329 on the PDF for pattern

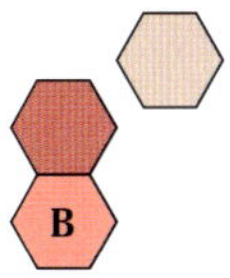

Block Piecing

Cream Solid and Lightweight Batting
from *each*
1 square (A) 12½" x 12½" (trim to 11½" x 11½" after appliqué and embroidery)

3 Assorted Pink Prints and Tone-on-Tones
from *each*
2 pattern B
from *1*
4 squares (E) 5" x 5"

Light Gray Print
2 rectangles (C) 1" x 11½"
2 rectangles (D) 1" x 12½"

Pigma Micron pen (.01 tip) or pencil

Embroidery floss

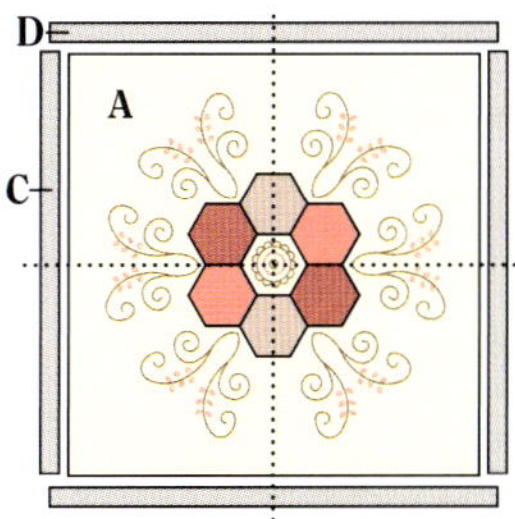

Applique/Embroidery Placement
Block Assembly

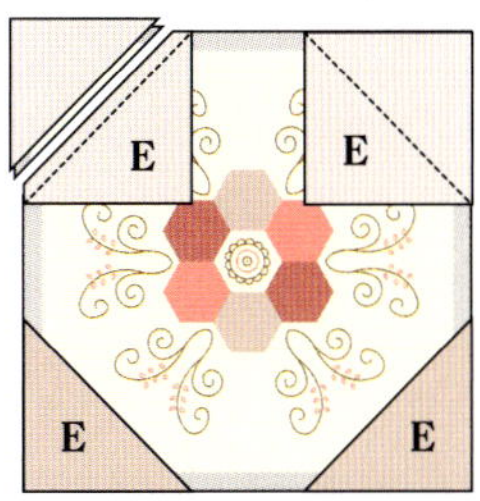

Stitch & Flip

Fold A in half both ways and lightly crease the folds.

Hand sew the pink hexagons (B's) following the instructions for "English Paper Piecing" in the Techniques file on the PDF. Baste the B's to the paper templates; join them as shown in the block piecing diagram to form a ring. Position the ring on A as shown. Using the creases and appliqué placement diagram as guides, trace the embroidery design onto A with the pen. Use matching thread and a blind stitch to appliqué the pieced B's in place.

Layer the cream A right side up on the batting and baste them together. Use 1 strand of floss for the stitches. Refer to pattern on page 329 of the PDF for stitches and floss colors. Center the design and trim to 11½" × 11½".

Join the gray C's and D's to A as shown. Sew the pink E's to the corners to complete the block.

block no. 484

Celebrate

by Margie Ullery • Ribbon Candy Quilt Co.
ribboncandyquilts.blogspot.com

Fabric: Reindeer Games designed by Sandy Gervais for Moda Fabrics, unitednotions.com.

See page 307 on the PDF for pattern

White Dot
1 rectangle (A) 9½" x 13½" (trim to 8½" x 12½" after appliqué)

Assorted Green Tone-on-Tones
7 pattern B
3 pattern E

Blue Tone-on-Tone
2 pattern C

Yellow Tone-on-Tone
2 pattern D
1 pattern G

Red Batik
1 pattern F
2 rectangles (H) 2½" x 12½"

Fusible web

Applique Placement

Fold A in half both ways and lightly crease the folds. Prepare patches B–G for fusible appliqué. Use the creases and appliqué placement diagram as guides to arrange the patches on A. Fuse the patches to A in alphabetical order.

Use matching thread and a machine blanket stitch to sew around the leaves and flower petals. Use a straight stitch to sew just inside the edges of the flower centers. Center the appliqué and trim to 8½" × 12½".

Sew the patches together as shown to complete the block.

Block Assembly

block no. 485

Martha's Basket

by Martha Walker • Wagons West Designs
wagonswestdesigns.com

Martha Walker is the author of *Annie's Scrapbag* for Wagons West Designs, wagonswestdesigns.com.

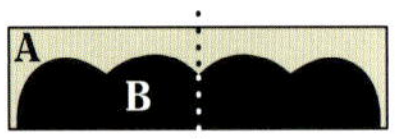

Unit 1
Make 2

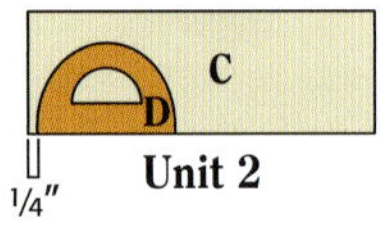

Unit 2

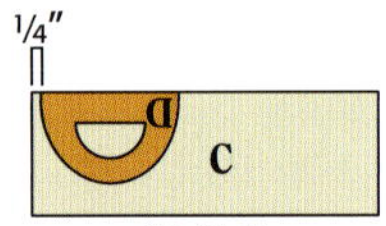

Unit 3

Unit 4
Make 4

Unit 5
Make 2

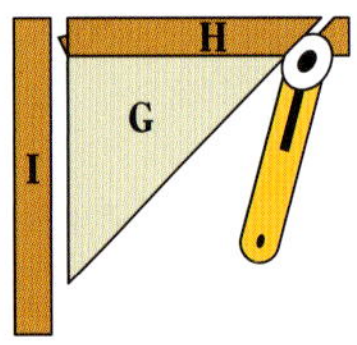

Trimming Diagram

See page 290 on the PDF for pattern

◸ = cut in half diagonally

Tan Print
- 2 rectangles (A) 2½" x 8½"
- 2 rectangles (C) 2½" x 6½"
- 1 square 6⅞" x 6⅞" ◸ (G) (there will be 1 extra)
- 3 squares (J) 2½" x 2½"
- 1 square 4⅞" x 4⅞" ◸ (K) (there will be 1 extra)

Black Tone-on-Tone
- 2 pattern B
- 3 squares (E) 2⅞" x 2⅞"
- 2 squares 2⅞" x 2⅞" ◸ (F)

Orange Tone-on-Tone #1
- 2 pattern D
- 2 squares (E) 2⅞" x 2⅞"
- 1 square 2⅞" x 2⅞" ◸ (F)
- 1 rectangle (H) 1½" x 8½"
- 1 rectangle (I) 1½" x 9½"

Orange Tone-on-Tone #2
- 1 square (E) 2⅞" x 2⅞"

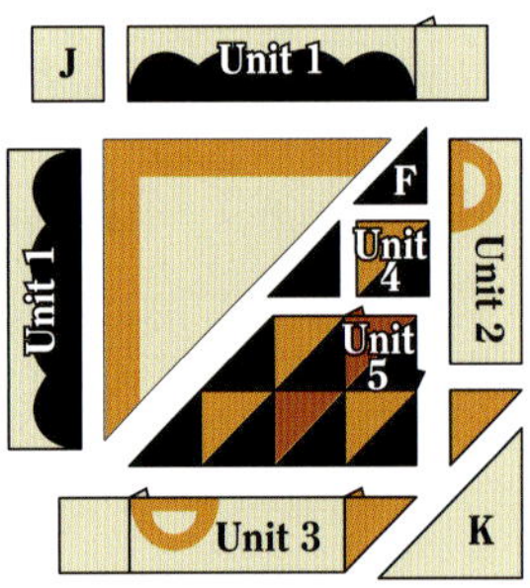

Block Assembly

Prepare the B's and D's for turned-edge appliqué. Fold the A's in half and lightly crease the folds. Use the creases and unit 1 diagram as guides to arrange the B's on the A's. Use matching thread and a blind stitch to appliqué the patches in place to make the unit 1's. Position orange D's on tan C's as shown; appliqué in the same way to make units 2–3.

Refer to "Triangle-Squares" in the Techniques file on the PDF. Pair the black E's with orange #1 E's to make 4 unit 4's. Make 2 unit 5's with black E's and orange #2 E's. Join the tan G, orange H and orange I as shown, trimming H and I even with G. Sew the units and patches together as shown to complete the block.

block no. 486

Dancing Daisy

by Ann Weber • Gingham Girls
ginghamgirls.biz

Fabric: Various lines designed by Lori Whitlock for Riley Blake Designs, rileyblakedesigns.com.

Ann Weber is the author of *Season's Best—Celebrate the Seasons with Quilts* for Gingham Girls, ginghamgirls.biz.

See page 288 on the PDF for pattern

Beige Tone-on-Tone
- 1 rectangle (A) 10½" x 13½" (trim to 9½" x 12½" after appliqué)

Assorted Green Tone-on-Tones
- bias strip 1¼" x 13"
- 5 pattern D

2 Red Tone-on-Tones
from *each*
- 3 pattern B

Orange Check
- 1 pattern C

Yellow Dot
- 1 rectangle (E) 1½" x 12½"

Red Print
- 1 rectangle (F) 2½" x 12½"

Fusible web

Applique Placement

Refer to "Bias Strips" in the Techniques file on the PDF to make the stem. Fold A in half both ways and lightly crease the folds. Prepare patches B–D for fusible appliqué. Use the creases and appliqué placement diagram as guides to arrange the patches on A. Pin the stem in place and fuse the patches to A in alphabetical order.

Use matching thread and a machine blanket stitch to sew around the patches and stem. Center the appliqué and trim to 9½" × 12½".

Sew A, E and F together as shown to complete the block.

Block Assembly

block no. 487
Bailey's Cross

by Anne Wiens • Sweetgrass Creative Designs
sweetgrassdesigns.com

Anne Wiens is the author of *The Thrifty Quilter—Make (Nearly) Free Quilts from Left-over Fabric* for Quilt-woman, quiltwoman.com.

See page 329 on the PDF for pattern

Green Tone-on-Tone
section patch 1

Cream Tone-on-Tone
section patches 2 and 3
8 squares (A) 2⅞″ x 2⅞″
8 squares (C) 2½″ x 2½″

Black Print
2 squares (A) 2⅞″ x 2⅞″
1 square (D) 4½″ x 4½″

Brown Tone-on-Tone
2 squares (A) 2⅞″ x 2⅞″
1 square (B) 5¼″ x 5¼″

Section
Make 8

Unit 1
Make 4

Unit 2
Make 4

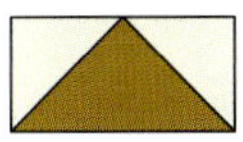

Flying Geese
Make 4

Make 8 paper copies of the foundation section. Foundation piece the sections in numerical order, pressing and trimming after each patch addition.

Pair the black A's with 2 cream A's to make Triangle-Square 4 unit 1's. Pair the brown A's with 2 cream A's to make 4 unit 2's.

Use the brown B and cream A's to make 4 Flying Geese.

Sew the units, Flying Geese, sections and patches together as shown to complete the block.

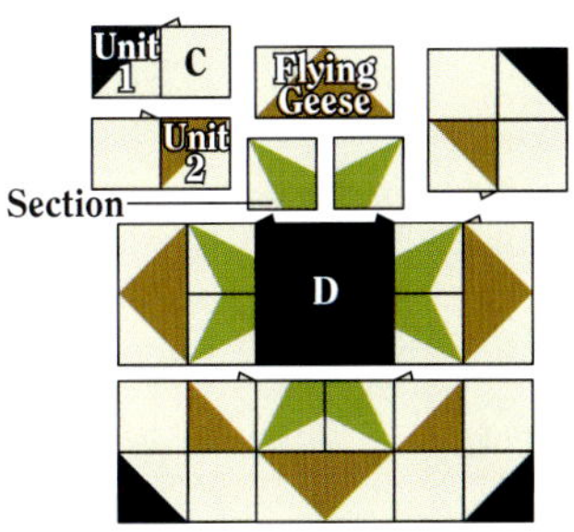

Block Assembly

block no. 488
Ring Around the Posy

by Cindy Wiens
liveacolorfullife.net

Fabric: Riley Blenders by Riley Blake Designs, rileyblakedesigns.com and Kona solid by Robert Kaufman, robertkaufman.com.

See page 319 on the PDF for pattern

⧄ = cut in half diagonally

White Solid
4 squares (A) 3½″ x 3½″
4 rectangles (B) 3½″ x 6½″
2 squares 3⅞″ x 3⅞″ ⧄ (C)

Assorted Tone-on-Tones
12 pattern D
4 squares 3⅞″ x 3⅞″ ⧄ (C)
(there will be 4 extra)

Fusible web

Sew patches A–C together as shown.

Prepare the D's for fusible appliqué. Use the seam lines to arrange the D's on the block; fuse in place. Use white thread and a machine blanket stitch to sew around the patches to complete the block.

Applique Placement

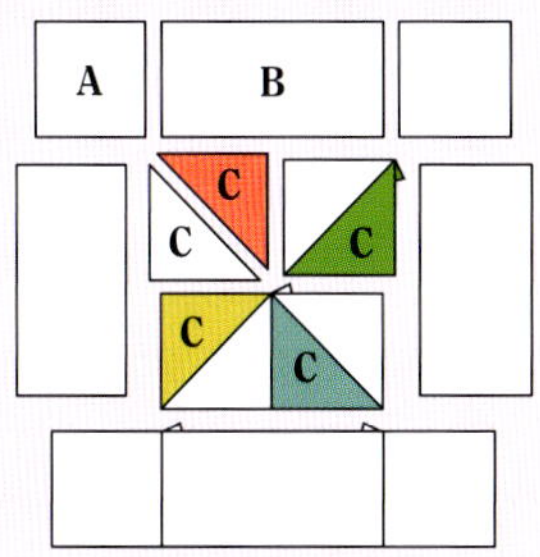

Block Piecing

block no. 489

Formation

by Shayla Wolf • Sassafras Lane Designs
sassafras-lane.com

See page 310 on the PDF for pattern

Orange Solid
section patches 1, 17 and 18
4 rectangles (A) 2½″ x 3¼″
4 rectangles (B) 2″ x 2½″
2 rectangles (C) 2½″ x 4½″
Dark Orange Tone-on-Tone
section patches 2–4
Pink Tone-on-Tone
section patches 5–7
Dark Pink Tone-on-Tone
section patches 8–10
Medium Purple Tone-on-Tone
section patches 11–13
Purple Solid
section patches 14–16

Section
Make 6

Make 6 paper copies of the foundation section. Foundation piece the sections in numerical order, pressing and trimming after each patch addition.

Join the sections and patches into rows as shown. Matching section seams, sew the vertical rows together. Trim to 12½" × 12½" as shown to complete the block.

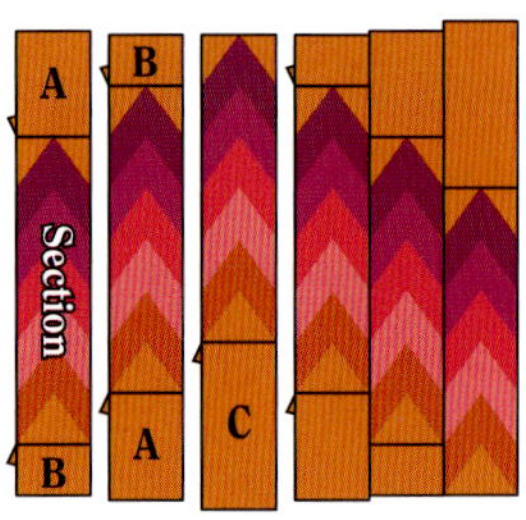

Block Assembly

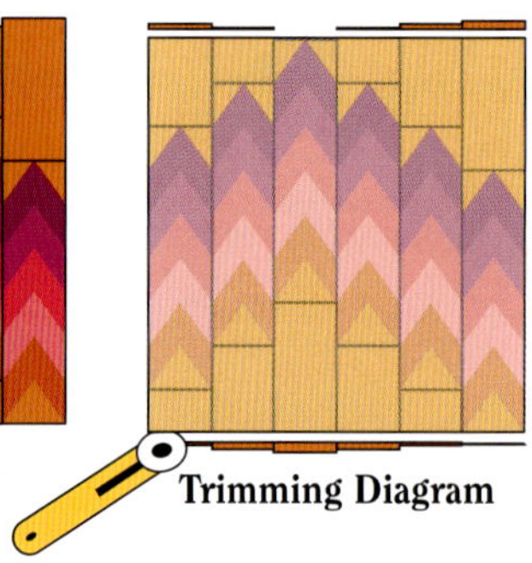

Trimming Diagram

block no. 490

Master Liu

by Cyrille Zellweger • Bubblestitch
bubblestitchquilts.blogspot.com

See page 319 on the PDF for pattern

Black Solid
foundation patches
4 squares (A) 2¾″ x 2¾″
White Solid
foundation patches
4 rectangles (B) 2¾″ x 8″
Rust Tone-on-Tone
foundation patches

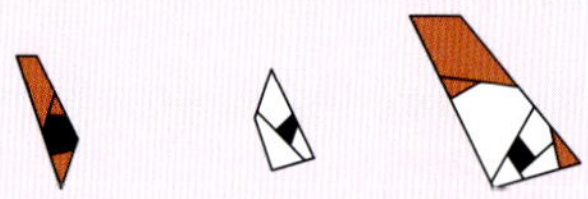

Section 1 Make 1 | Section 2 Make 1 | Section 3 Make 1

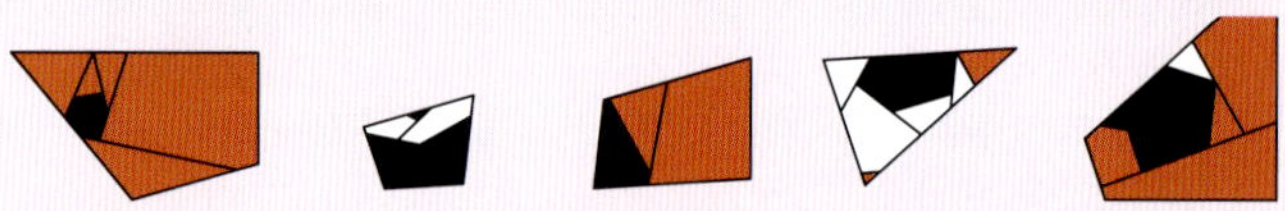

Section 4 Make 1 | Section 5 Make 1 | Section 6 Make 1 | Section 7 Make 1 | Section 8 Make 1

Make 1 paper copy of *each* foundation section. Using the colors listed above, refer to the foundations for color placement. Foundation piece the sections in numerical order, pressing and trimming after each patch addition.

Sew the sections and patches together in order as shown to complete the block.

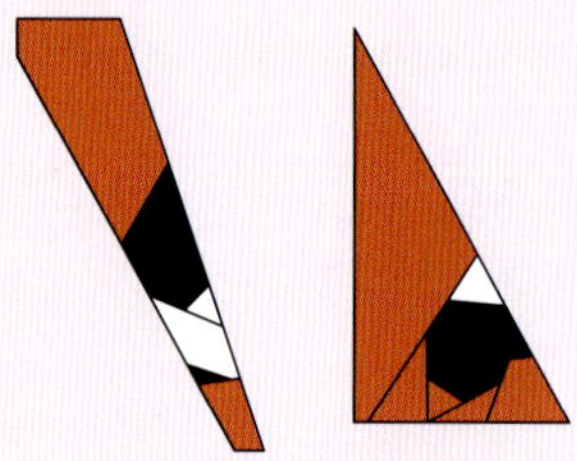

Section 9 Make 1 | Section 10 Make 1

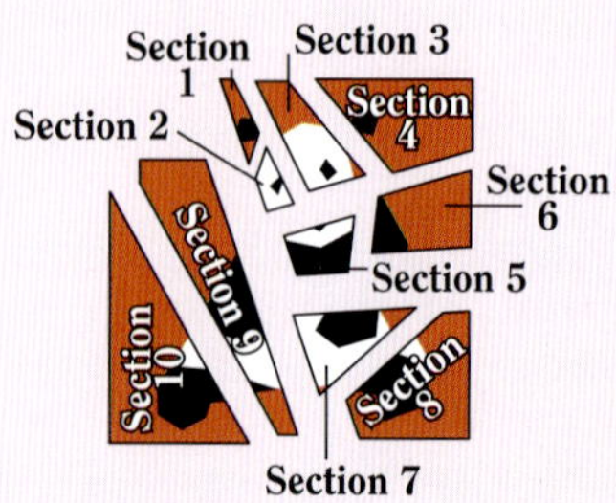

Block Assembly

block no. 491

Exploding Stars

by Carolyn Beam • Creative Editor, *Quiltmaker*
quiltmaker.com

Fabric: Bali Batiks from Hoffman California Fabrics, hoffmanfabrics.com.

Section 1
Make 1

Section 2
Make 1

See page 361 on the PDF for pattern

White Batik
2 squares (A) 3⅞″ x 3⅞″
2 squares (B) 2⅞″ x 2⅞″
2 squares (D) 1½″ x 1½″
2 rectangles (E) 1½″ x 2½″
2 squares (F) 3½″ x 3½″
6 squares (G) 2½″ x 2½″
foundation patches

Green Batik and Red Batik
from *each*
1 square (B) 2⅞″ x 2⅞″
1 rectangle (C) 1½″ x 3½″
1 square (D) 1½″ x 1½″
1 rectangle (E) 1½″ x 2½″
foundation patches

Orange Batik and Blue Batik
from *each*
1 square (A) 3⅞″ x 3⅞″
1 square (F) 3½″ x 3½″
foundation patches

Unit 1 from A's
Make 2

Unit 2 from A's
Make 2

Unit 3 from B's
Make 2

Unit 4 from B's
Make 2

Unit 5
Stitch & Flip
Make 1

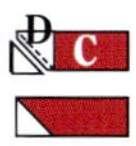

Unit 6
Stitch & Flip
Make 1

Unit 7
Stitch & Flip
Make 1

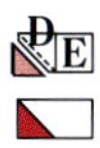

Unit 8
Stitch & Flip
Make 1

Make 1 paper copy of *each* foundation section. Referring to the foundations for color placement, foundation piece each section in numerical order, pressing and trimming after each patch addition.

For all techniques, refer to the Techniques file on the PDF. Pair the colors and patches shown to make 2 Triangle-Squares *each* of units 1–4.

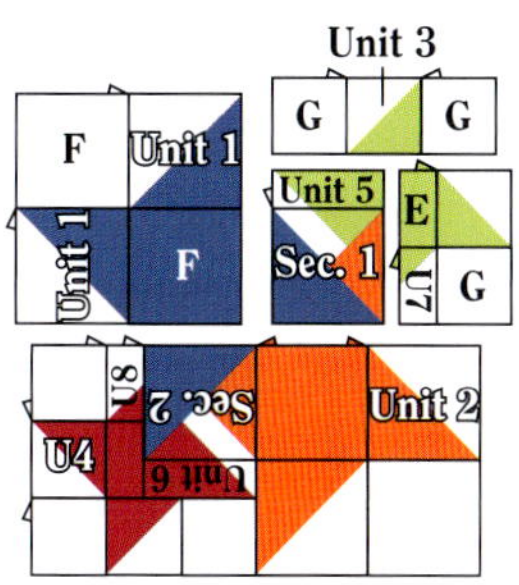

Block Assembly

Use the colors and patches as shown to make 1 Stitch-and-Flip *each* of units 5–8.

Sew the sections, units and patches together as shown to complete the block.

block no. 492

Fruit Juicy

by Cheryl Brown • QuilterChic
quilterchic.com

Cheryl Brown is the author of *Quilt Batik!* for Martingale & Co., shopmartingale.com.

See page 362 on the PDF for pattern

Cream Tone-on-Tone
1 square (A) 9½″ x 9½″ (trim to 8½″ x 8½″ after appliqué)

2 Gold Solids
from *each*
1 rectangle 3″ x 7½″
from *1*
4 squares (G) 2½″ x 2½″

2 Green Solids
from *each*
1 rectangle 1″ x 2″

Brown Solid
1 pattern B

White Solid
1 pattern D

Black Dot
4 rectangles (F) 2½″ x 8½″

Template Plastic

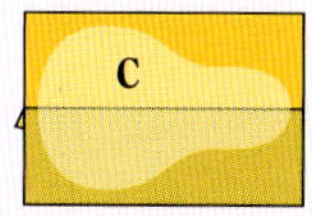

Cut 1

Cut 1

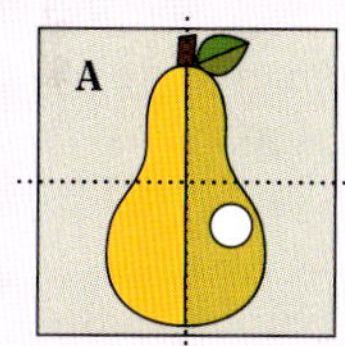

Applique Placement

Use the plastic to make templates of C and E (including seam allowances); mark the dotted lines on the templates. Join the 2 gold rectangles as shown. Align the dotted line on template C with the seam and cut 1 pattern C. Join the 2 green rectangles as shown; cut E in the same way as C.

Fold A in half both ways and lightly crease the folds. Prepare patches B–E for turned-edge appliqué. Use the creases and appliqué placement diagram as guides to arrange the patches on A. Use matching thread and a blind stitch to appliqué the patches in place. Center the appliqué and trim to 8½" × 8½".

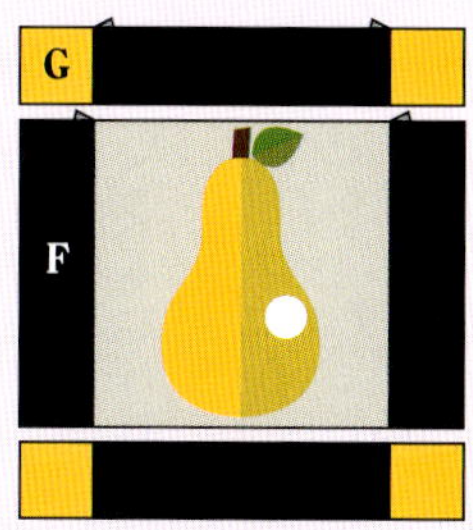

Block Assembly

Sew the patches together as shown to complete theblock.

block no. 493

Petal Pusher

by Kari Carr • New Leaf Stitches
newleafstitches.com

Fabric: Mimi designed by Chez Moi for Moda Fabrics, unitednotions.com.

Kari Carr is the author of *Twice as Nice: Quilts with Scrap-Saving Bonus Projects* for Martingale & Co., shopmartingale.com.

See page 351 on the PDF for pattern

Cream Solid
1 square (A) 7½″ x 7½″ (trim to 6½″ x 6½″ after appliqué)
1 pattern E
4 rectangles (G) 2¼″ x 6½″
Teal Tone-on-Tone
1 pattern B
Multicolor Print
4 pattern C
2 squares (F) 3⅞″ x 3⅞″
4 rectangles (H) 3½″ x 6½″
Orange Tone-on-Tone
1 pattern D
2 squares (F) 3⅞″ x 3⅞″
4 rectangles (G) 2¼″ x 6½″
Fusible web
Embroidery floss

Unit 1
Make 4

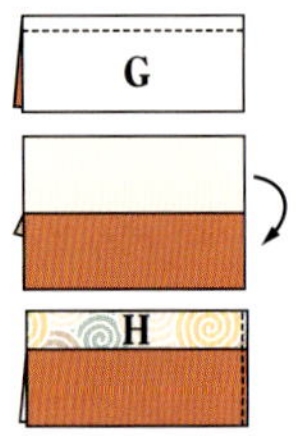

Unit 2
Make 4

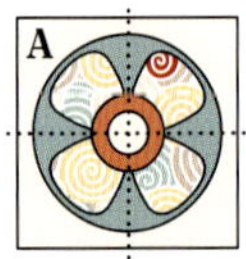

Applique Placement

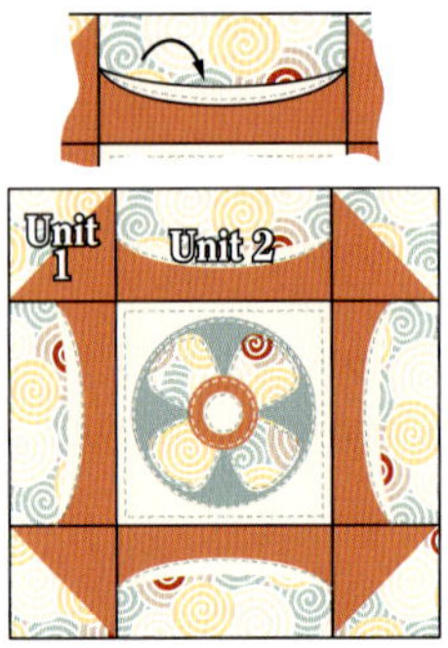

Block Assembly

Fold A in half both ways and lightly crease the folds. Prepare patches B–E for fusible appliqué. Using the creases and appliqué placement diagram as guides, arrange the patches in alphabetical order; fuse in place. Use the floss and a running stitch to sew ⅛" inside the edges of the appliqué patches. Center the appliqué and trim A to 6½" × 6½".

Pair the multicolor F's and orange F's to make 4 Triangle-Square unit 1's.

Refer to the unit 2 diagram. With right sides together, sew the cream G's and orange G's together as shown. Open each and press. Refold with wrong sides together and press. With orange side out, layer each G/G on a multicolor H; pin or baste in place to make 4 unit 2's. Sew the units and A together as shown to make the block.

Turn back the folded G/G seams to form a gentle curve. Using the floss and a running stitch, sew down the folded edges and ¼" inside the edge of A to complete the block.

block no. 494

Checker-a-Peel

by Keiko Clark • K Cotton Studio
kcottonstudio.com

Fabric: Rose Collection from Quilt Gate, quilt-gate.com.

See page 359 on the PDF for pattern

Medium Pink Print and Cream Print #1
from *each*
2 strips 2″ x 40″ for band
Light Green Print and Cream Print #2
from *each*
2 squares (B) 6½″ x 6½″
Template plastic

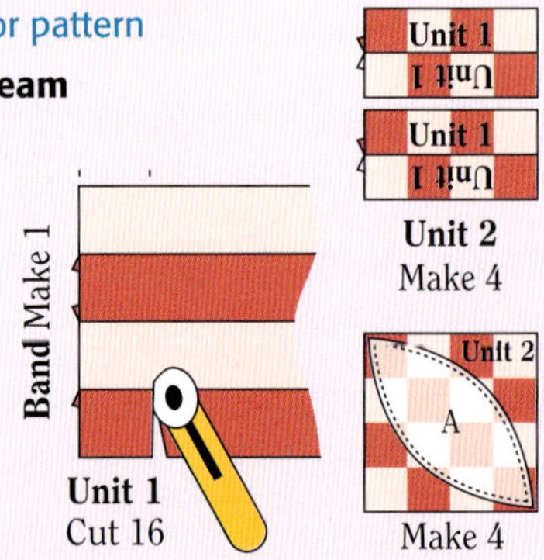

Unit 1
Cut 16

Unit 2
Make 4

Make 4

Sew the strips together as shown to make the band. Cut the band in 2" increments to make 16 unit 1's. Sew 4 unit 1's together as shown to make a unit 2. Make 4 unit 2's.

Use the plastic to make a template of A (including the seam allowance). Position the template A on each unit 2 as shown and cut 4 A's. Prepare the A's for turned-edge appliqué.

Sew the B's together as shown to make the block. Refer to the appliqué placement diagram and use the block seams as a guide to arrange the A's on the block.

Use matching thread and a blind stitch to appliqué the A's in place to complete the block.

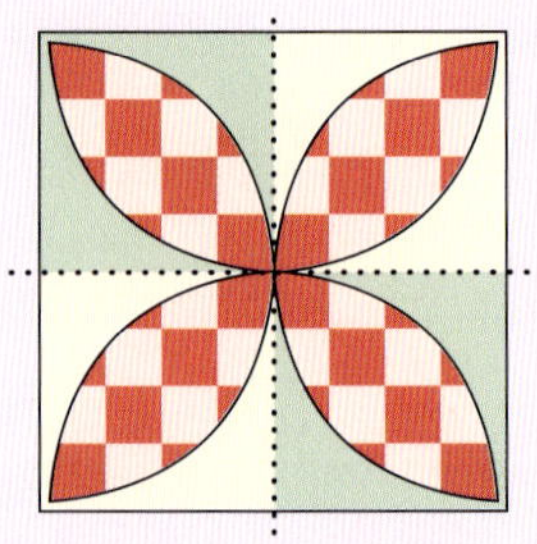

Applique Placement

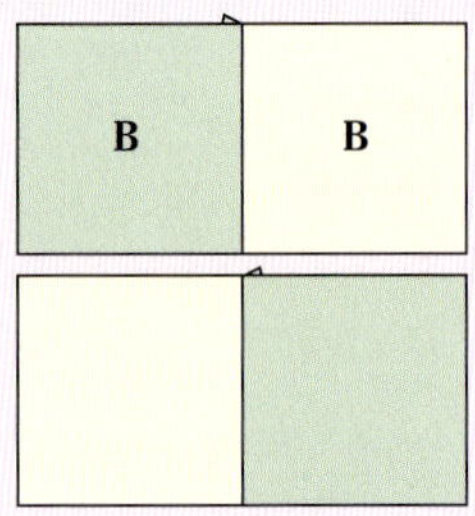

Block Piecing

block no. 495

Rose Arbor

by June Dudley • Editor-in-Chief, *Quiltmaker*
quiltmaker.com

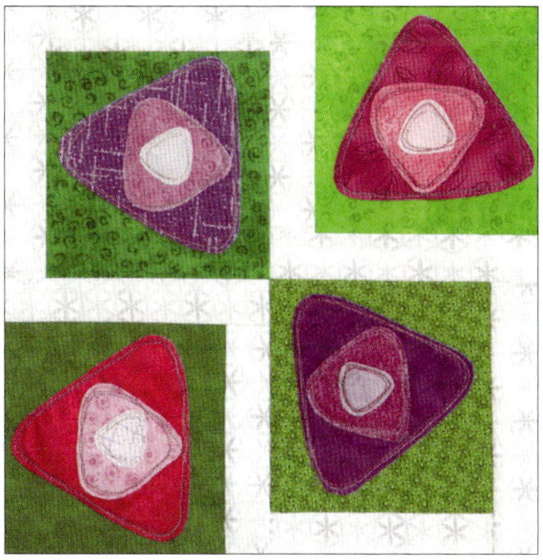

Fabric: Twilight designed by Kate Knight, Lola by Studio 8 and basics, all from Quilting Treasures, quiltingtreasures.com.

See page 369 on the PDF for pattern

Assorted Green Tone-on-Tones
4 squares (A) 6½″ x 6½″ (trim to 5½″ x 5½″ after appliqué)

Assorted Dark Purple and Dark Pink Tone-on-Tones
4 pattern B

Assorted Medium Purple and Medium Pink Tone-on-Tones
4 pattern C

Assorted Light Purple and Light Pink Tone-on-Tones
4 pattern D

White Print
4 rectangles (E) 1½″ x 5½″
4 rectangles (F) 1½″ x 6½″

Basting spray

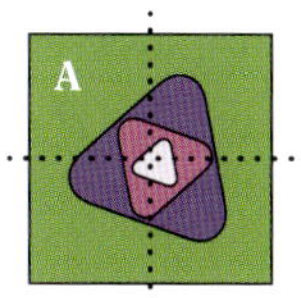

Unit
Applique Placement
Make 4

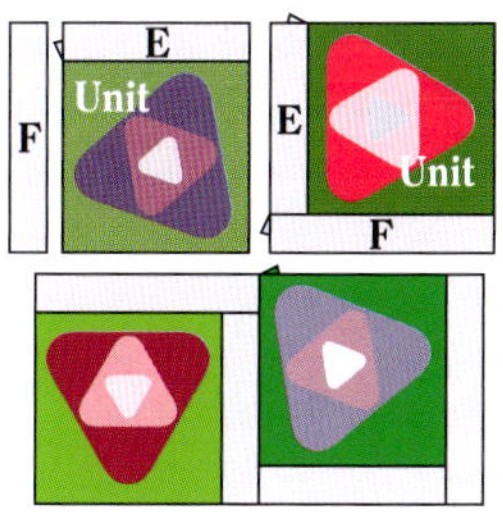

Block Assembly

Fold an A in half both ways and lightly crease the folds. Use a light coat of basting spray on the wrong side of patches B–D. Use the creases and unit appliqué placement diagram as guides to center and arrange 1 B, 1 C and 1 D in alphabetical order on A as shown, changing orientations of the appliqué patches for variety.

Drop or cover the feed dogs on your sewing machine. Using a darning or free-motion foot and a variegated thread, sew once around the appliqué patches close to the edges. Stitch around the patches 2 more times making slight swerves on either side of the first line of stitching. Center the appliqué and trim to 5½"× 5½". Repeat to make 4 units.

Join the patches and units as shown to complete the block.

block no. 496

Vintage Prom Dress

by Cynthia Frenette • Green Couch Designs
greencouchdesigns.com

Fabric: Blythe by Rebecca Bischoff and London Calling 3, both from Robert Kaufman, robertkaufman.com.

See page 344 on the PDF for pattern

Tan Solid
1 square (A) 12¼″ x 12¼″ (trim to 11¼″ x 11¼″ after appliqué)

Black Solid
1 pattern B
4 pattern J

Multiprint #1
1 *each* patterns C, Cr, E and F

Multiprint #2
1 *each* patterns D and G

White Solid
2 rectangles (H) 1⅛″ x 11¼″
2 rectangles (I) 1⅛″ x 12½″

Fusible web

Gold thread

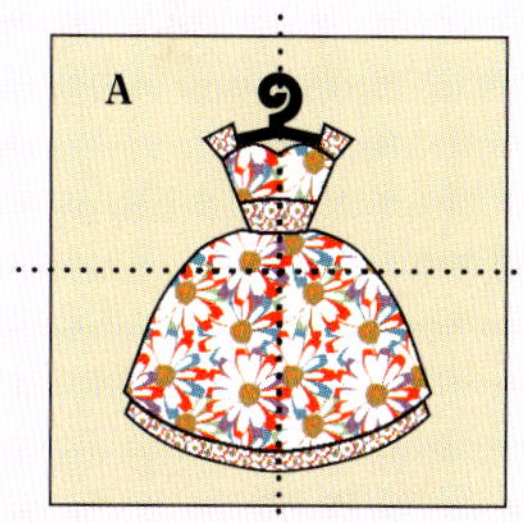

Applique Placement

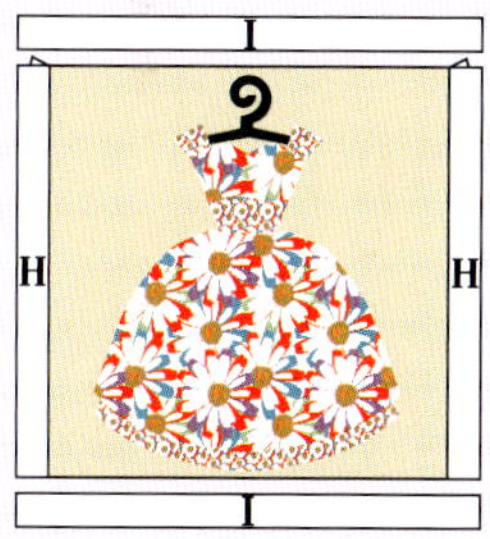

Block Assembly

Fold A in half both ways and lightly crease the folds. Prepare the B and J's for fusible appliqué. Prepare the dress patches C–G for turned-edge appliqué. Use the creases and appliqué placement diagram to arrange patches B–G in alphabetical order on A. Fuse B in place.

Use matching thread and a blind stitch to appliqué C–G in place. Center the appliqué and trim A to 11¼"× 11¼".

Applique & Stitching Placement

Sew the patches together as shown to make the block. Position a J on each corner of the block and fuse in place. Use gold thread and a straight stitch to add detail to the dress, hanger and J's to complete the block.

block no. 497

Hummingbird

by Regina Grewe • Textile Landscapes
reginagrewe.de

Regina Grewe has designed patterns for My EQ Boutique, myeqboutique.com.

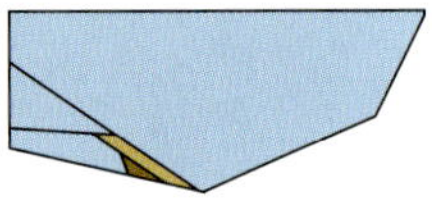

Section 1
Make 1

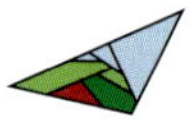

Section 2
Make 1

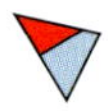

Section 3
Make 1

See page 375 on the PDF for pattern

Assorted Batiks, Tone-on-Tones and Solids
sections 1–8 foundation patches
Teal Batik
4 rectangles (A) 2″ x 9½″
section 8 foundation patches
Black Solid
1 pattern B
Fusible web
Embroidery floss

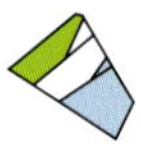

Section 4
Make 1

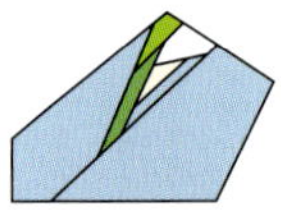

Section 5
Make 1

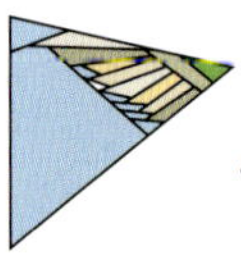

Section 6
Make 1

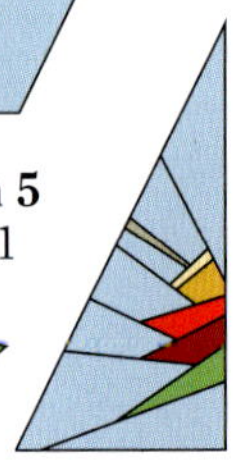

Section 7
Make 1

Make 1 paper copy *each* of foundation sections 1–7 and 4 copies of section 8. Referring to the foundations for color placement, foundation piece the sections in numerical order, pressing and trimming after each patch addition. Sew the sections and A's together as shown. Carefully remove the foundation papers.

Section 8
Make 1 of each color

Prepare the eye (B) for fusible appliqué. Refer to the pattern sheet for placement of the eye on the hummingbird; fuse in place. Use matching thread and a tiny straight stitch to sew the eye in place.

Refer to the pattern page for embroidery placement. Use 2 strands of embroidery floss and an outline stitch around the eye, for the feet and for the flower stamens. Add French knots to the ends of the stamens to complete the block.

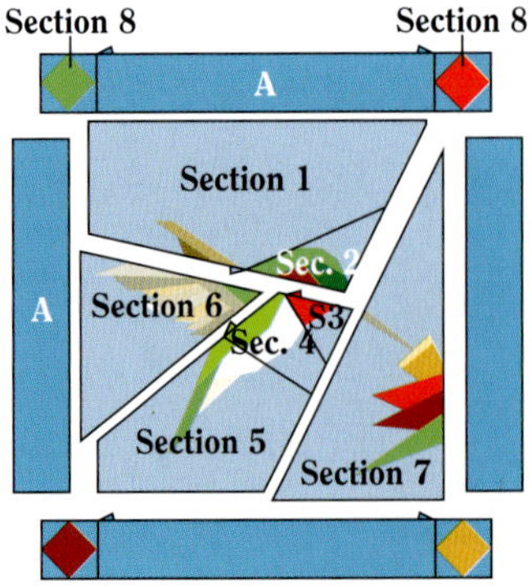

Block Assembly

block no. 498

The Queen

by Desiree Habicht • Desiree's Designs
desireesdesigns.com

Fabric: Gumdrops & Lollipops designed by Desiree Habicht for Quilting Treasures, quiltingtreasures.com, and Horsing Around by Desiree Habicht for Red Rooster Fabrics, redroosterfabrics.com.

See page 342 on the PDF for pattern

Red Print
1 square (A) 8½″ x 8½″
Black and White Stripe
2 rectangles (B) 1″ x 8½″
2 rectangles (C) 1″ x 9½″
White Print
2 rectangles (D) 2″ x 9½″
2 rectangles (E) 2″ x 12½″
Assorted Prints and Tone-on-Tones
1 complete set of appliqué patches
Fusible web
Star buttons 2 at ¾″
Heart button 1 at ¾″
Round jewels 1 blue at ½″, 2 green at ½″ and 4 clear at ¼″
Oval jewel 1 clear at ¾″ long

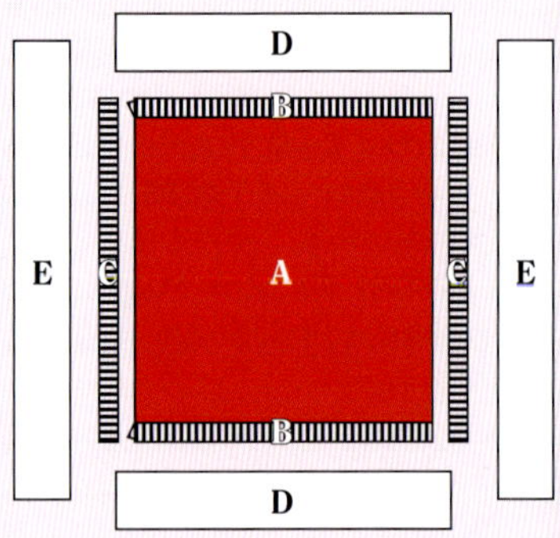

Block Piecing

Sew patches A–E together as shown.

Fold the block in half both ways and lightly crease the folds. Prepare patches F–R for fusible appliqué. Using the creases and appliqué placement diagram as guides, arrange and fuse the patches in alphabetical order.

Refer to the pattern sheet for stitch placement. Use black thread and a machine satin stitch to sew around the appliqué patches and to outline cat details. Use a straight stitch for the whiskers and add French knots next to the whiskers. Add the buttons and jewels to complete the block.

Applique, Stitching & Embellishment Placement

block no. 499

Sweet 'n Corny

by Melissa Harris and Arlene Stamper
The Quilt Company • quiltcompany.com

Fabric: Tomorrow's Promise designed by Marti Michell for Maywood Studio, maywoodstudio.com.

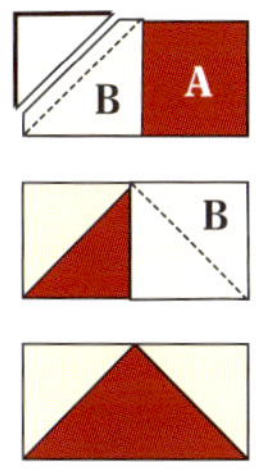

Unit 1
Stitch & Flip
Make 1

See page 373 on the PDF for pattern

Red Dot
- 1 rectangle (A) 4½" x 8½"
- 1 rectangle (C) 4" x 4½"
- 1 rectangle (F) 1" x 5"
- 2 rectangles (G) 2¼" x 6"

Cream Tone-on-Tone
- 2 squares (B) 4½" x 4½"
- 1 rectangle (H) 3¼" x 10"
- 1 rectangle (I) 1¾" x 10"
- 1 rectangle (J) 3" x 12½"

Cream Print
- 2 rectangles (D) ⅜" x 5¾"
- 2 rectangles (E) 1" x 4½"
- 2 rectangles (F) 1" x 5"

Black Tone-on-Tone, White Check, Yellow Tone-on-Tone, Medium Green Tone-on-Tone and Dark Green Tone-on-Tone
- 1 complete set of appliqué patches

Fusible web

Heart button 1 at 1"

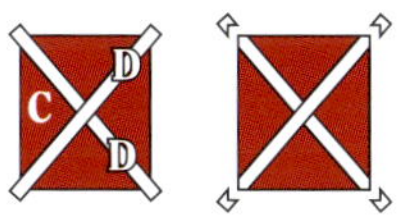

Unit 2
Make 1

Appliqué & Button Placement Diagram

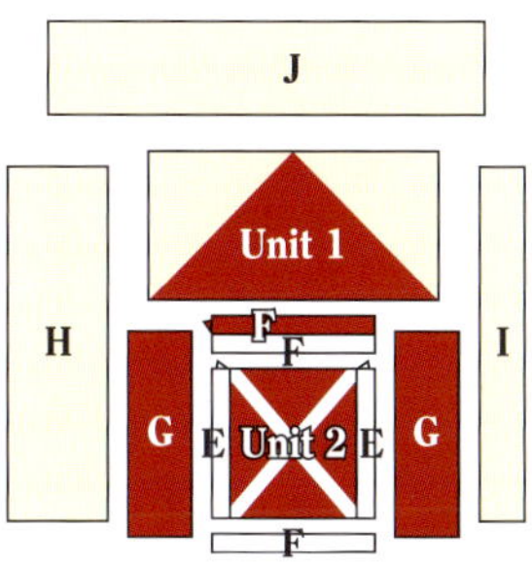

Block Assembly

Refer to "Stitch-and-Flip" in the Techniques file on the PDF. Use the red A and cream B's to make unit 1. Prepare patches D and K–Q for fusible appliqué. To make unit 2, position the D's on C as shown; fuse in place. Use matching thread and a machine blanket stitch to sew the long edges of the D's. Trim the D's as shown.

Sew the units and patches together as shown. Arrange patches K–Q on the block in alphabetical order; fuse in place. Use matching thread and a machine blanket stitch to sew around the patches. Add the heart button to complete the block.

block no. 500

American Crossroads

by Jo Kramer and Kelli Kramer • Jo's Country Junction
joscountryjunction.com

See page 346 on the PDF for pattern

⊠ = cut in half twice diagonally

Red Solid
- section patch 1
- 2 squares (A) 2¼" x 2¼"
- 3 squares 3¼" x 3¼" ⊠ (B)
- 1 square (E) 1¾" x 1¾"

Assorted Dark Blue Prints and Tone-on-Tones
- section patches 2–4
- 6 squares 3¼" x 3¼" ⊠ (B)
- 4 squares (D) 1¾" x 1⅞"

Cream Print
- section patch 5
- 2 squares (A) 2¼" x 2¼"
- 3 squares 3¼" x 3¼" ⊠ (B)
- 1 square 5¼" x 5¼" ⊠ (C)

Section 1
Make 4

Unit
Make 4

Make 4 paper copies of the foundation section. Foundation piece the sections in numerical order, pressing and trimming after each patch addition.

Pair the red A's with cream A's to make 4 Triangle-Square units.

Block Assembly

Note that the units are joined to the long sides of the D's and the E is joined to the short sides of the D's. Sew the sections, units and patches together as shown to complete the block.

block no. 501

Get in Gear

by Carol Le Maitre

See page 349 on the PDF for pattern

Cream Print
1 square (A) 13½″ x 13½″ (trim to 12½″ x 12½″ after appliqué)
Gold Tone-on-Tone
1 template B
Burgundy Print
6 pattern C
Green Print
6 template B
Brown Tone-on-Tone
6 template D

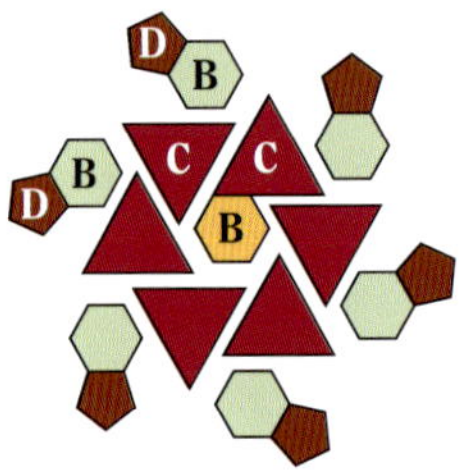

Block Piecing

Refer to “English Paper Piecing” in the Techniques file on the PDF. Baste the B’s–D’s to the paper templates.

Using a small whipstitch, first join the burgundy C’s to the gold B as shown in the block piecing diagram. Join the green B’s and brown D’s as shown; join these to the burgundy C’s to complete the block center.

Fold A in half both ways and lightly crease the folds. Using the creases and appliqué placement diagram as guides, position the B’s/C’s/D’s on A as shown. Use matching thread and a blind stitch to appliqué the block center in place.

Center the design and trim A to 12½" × 12½" to complete the block.

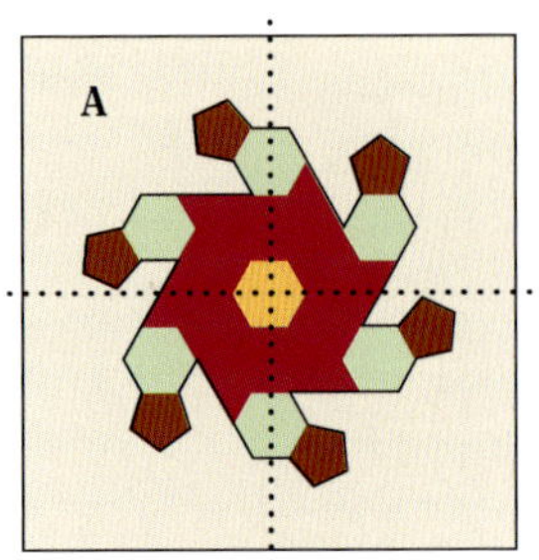

Applique Placement

block no. 502

Got Wheels?

by Cheryl Lynch • OyVey! Quilt Designs
cheryllynchquilts.com

Cheryl Lynch is the author of *iQuilt Fiesta!* and *Sew Embellished!* for Martingale & Co., shopmartingale.com.

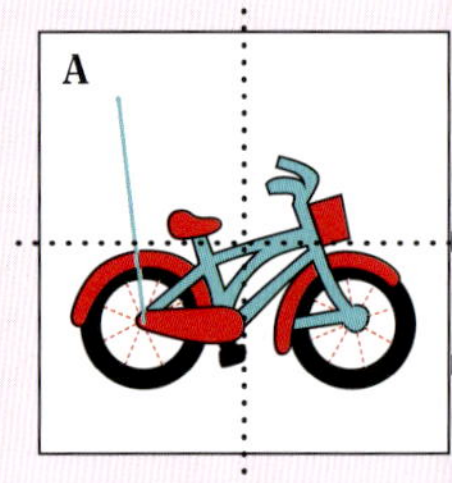

Applique & Embroidery Placement

See page 370 on the PDF for pattern

Light Gray Tone-on-Tone
1 square (A) 11″ x 11″ (trim to 10″ x 10″ after appliqué)
Black Tone-on-Tone
2 pattern B
1 pattern G
Red Print
1 *each* patterns C, D, E, H, I and J
4 squares (M) 3″ x 3″
Teal Print
1 pattern F
2 rectangles (K) 1¾″ x 10″
2 rectangles (L) 1¾″ x 12½″
Fusible web
Red and teal embroidery floss

Block Piecing

Stitch & Flip

Applique & Tassel Placement

Fold A in half both ways and lightly crease the folds. Prepare patches B–J for fusible appliqué. Use the creases and appliqué placement diagram as guides to arrange patches B–I on A in alphabetical order; fuse in place.

Use matching thread and a machine blanket stitch to sew around the patches. Use teal floss and an outline stitch to embroider the flag pole. Sew a French knot to the end of the flag pole. Use red floss and a running stitch to embroider the tire spokes. Center the appliqué and trim A to 10" × 10".

Sew the K’s and L’s to A as shown. Refer to the “Stitch-and-Flip” technique in the Techniques file on the PDFand add the red M’s to the block corners.

Fuse the flag (J) to the end of the flag pole; use matching thread and a machine blanket stitch to sew around the flag. To make the tassels on the handlebars, thread a needle with 12 strands of red floss. Take a stitch at the end of each handle, tie a knot and trim tails to 1".

block no. 503

Half Log Cabin Tulips

by Kay Mackenzie • By Kay Mackenzie
kaymackenzie.com

Kay Mackenzie is the author of *Scrap-Appliqué Playground* for Martingale & Co., shopmartingale.com.

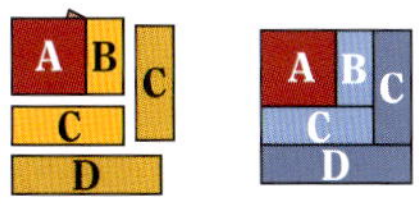

Unit 1
Make 1

Unit 2
Make 2

Unit 3
Make 1

See page 362 on the PDF for pattern

Red Print
3 squares (A) 2½″ x 2½″

Medium Gold Tone-on-Tone
1 rectangle (B) 1½″ x 2½″
1 rectangle (C) 1½″ x 3½″

Dark Gold Print
1 rectangle (C) 1½″ x 3½″
1 rectangle (D) 1½″ x 4½″

Medium Blue Print
2 rectangles (B) 1½″ x 2½″
2 rectangles (C) 1½″ x 3½″

Dark Blue Tone-on-Tone
2 rectangles (C) 1½″ x 3½″
2 rectangles (D) 1½″ x 4½″

Light Green Tone-on-Tone
1 rectangle (E) 1½″ x 11″

Medium Green Tone-on-Tone
1 rectangle (E) 1½″ x 11″
1 *each* patterns G, H and Hr

White Tone-on-Tone and Light Blue Print
from *each*
8 squares (F) 3½″ x 3½″

Fusible web

Template plastic

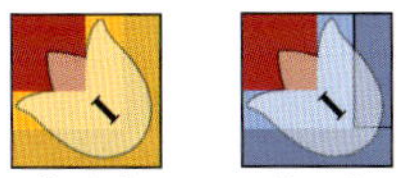

Cut 1 Cut 2

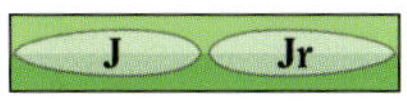

Cut 1 *each*

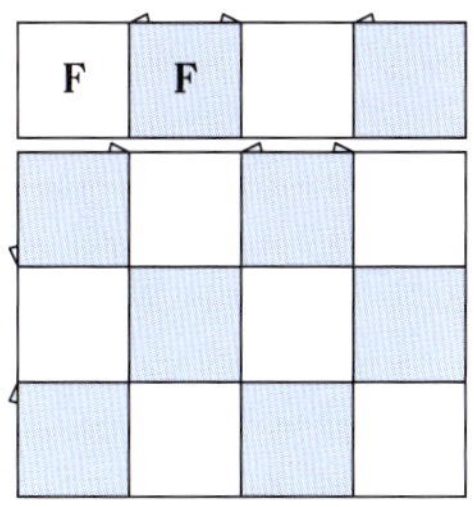

Block Piecing

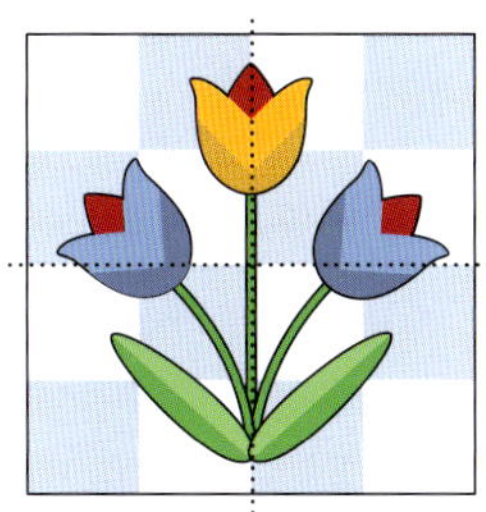

Applique Placement

Sew patches A–D together as shown to make 1 unit 1 and 2 unit 2's. Join the E's to make 1 unit 3. Apply fusible web to the back of the units; prepare patches G, H and Hr for fusible appliqué. Use the plastic to make templates of I and J; trace and cut I's, J and Jr from the units as shown.

Sew the blue F's and white F's together to make the block background as shown. Using the seam lines and appliqué placement diagram as guides, arrange and fuse the patches in alphabetical order. Sew around the patches using matching thread and a machine blanket stitch to complete the block.

block no. 504

Branching Out

by Diane Merritt

Unit
Make 27

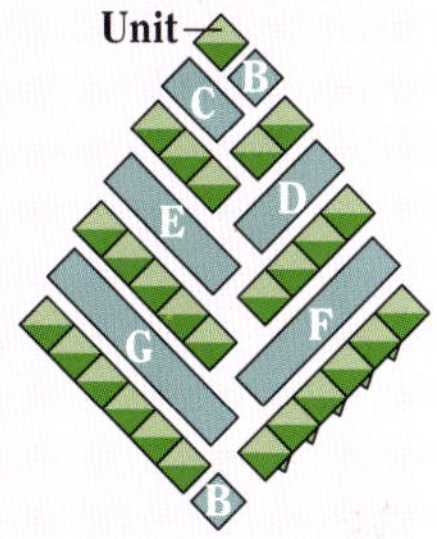

Tree Piecing

See page 357 on the PDF for pattern

◸ = cut in half diagonally

Light Green Batik and Dark Green Batik
from *each*
14 squares (A) 1⅞″ x 1⅞″

Teal Batik
2 squares (B) 1½″ x 1½″
1 rectangle (C) 1½″ x 2½″
1 rectangle (D) 1½″ x 3½″
1 rectangle (E) 1½″ x 4½″
1 rectangle (F) 1½″ x 5½″
1 rectangle (G) 1½″ x 6½″

Cream Batik
2 squares 11″ x 11″ ◸ (H)

Dark Brown Batik
1 pattern I

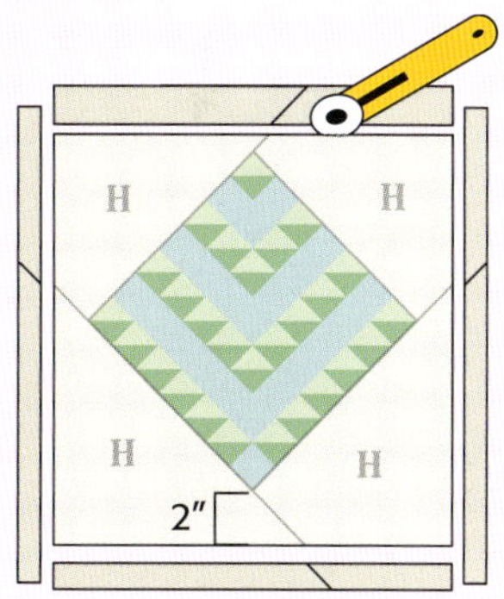

Block Trimming

Pair the light green A's with the dark green A's to make 28 Triangle-Square units (use 27). Sew the units and patches together as shown to make the tree.

Applique Placement

Matching centers, sew a cream H to each top corner of the tree as shown, pressing after each patch is added. Notice that the H's extend beyond the edges of the tree. Repeat on the bottom corners. Trim the excess from the H's on the back of the block. Refer to the trimming diagram to trim the block to 12½" × 12½" as shown, leaving 2" of back-ground at the bottom.

Prepare the trunk (I) for turned-edge appliqué. Use the appliqué placement diagram to arrange the trunk on the block. Appliqué the trunk in place using matching thread and a blind stitch to complete the block.

block no. 505

Hawaiian Morning

by Jo Moury

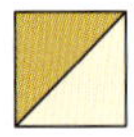

Unit
Make 11

See page 371 on the PDF for pattern

Cream Batik
1 square (A) 11½" x 11½" (trim to 10½" x 10½" after appliqué and embroidery)
6 squares (H) 2⅞" x 2⅞"
Assorted Wools
1 complete set of appliqué patches
6 Assorted Batiks
from *each*
1 square (H) 2⅞" x 2⅞"
Fusible web
Embroidery floss
Buttons 5 red at ½"
Beads 5 red at ¼", 5 green at ¼", 25 seed beads

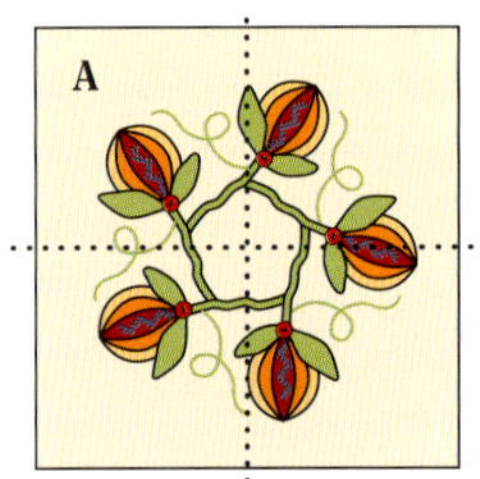

Applique & Embroidery Placement

Block Assembly

Fold A in half both ways and lightly crease the folds. Prepare patches B–G for fusible appliqué. Use the creases and appliqué placement diagram as guides to arrange the patches in alphabetical order on A; fuse in place.

Use 2 strands of matching floss and a blanket stitch to appliqué the patches in place. Refer to the pattern sheet for embroidery placement. Use 2 strands of floss and an outline stitch for the vines; use a zigzag feather stitch for the pomegranate details. Center the appliqué and trim to 10½" × 10½".

Pair the cream H's with the assorted batik H's to make 12 Triangle-Square units (use 11).

Sew the units and A together as shown. Sew the buttons and beads in place to complete the block.

block no. 506

Plant Perfect

by Amanda Murphy • Amanda Murphy Design
amandamurphydesign.com

Fabric: Topiary and Bonjour Mon Ami, both designed by Amanda Murphy for Blend Fabrics, blendfabrics.com.

Amanda Murphy is the author of *Color Essentials* and *Modern Holiday* for Stash Books, ctpub.com.

See page 354 on the PDF for pattern

Pale Yellow Print #1
1 rectangle (A) 7½" x 12½"
2 Light Blue Prints
from *each*
1 rectangle (B) 3" x 12½"
5 Assorted Pink Prints
from *each of 4*
1 square (C) 4¾" x 4¾"
from *1*
1 pattern F
Medium Blue Print
1 pattern D
Pale Yellow Print #2
1 pattern E
Green Print
1 *each* patterns G and H
Fusible web

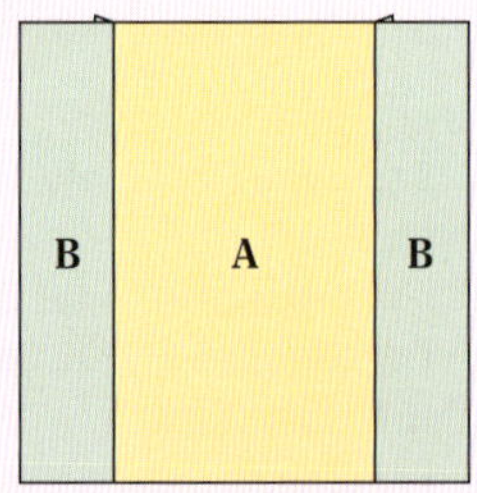

Block Piecing

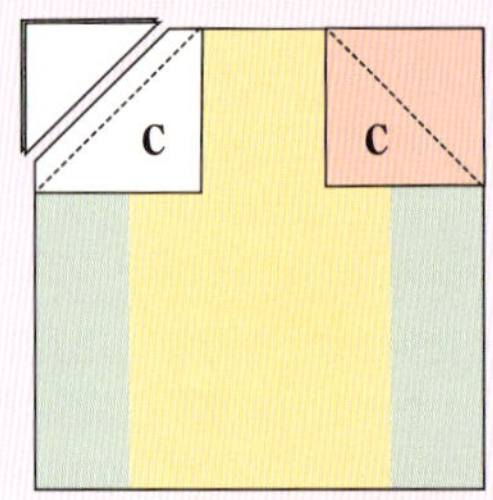

Block Stitch & Flip

Sew the A and B patches together as shown. Refer to "Stitch-and Flip" in the Techniques file on the PDF. Add the pink C's as shown to make the block.

Prepare patches D–H for fusible appliqué. Fold the block in half both ways and lightly crease the folds. Use the creases and appliqué placement diagram as guides to arrange the patches in alphabetical order; fuse in place.

Sew around patches D–H using matching thread and a machine blanket stitch to complete the block.

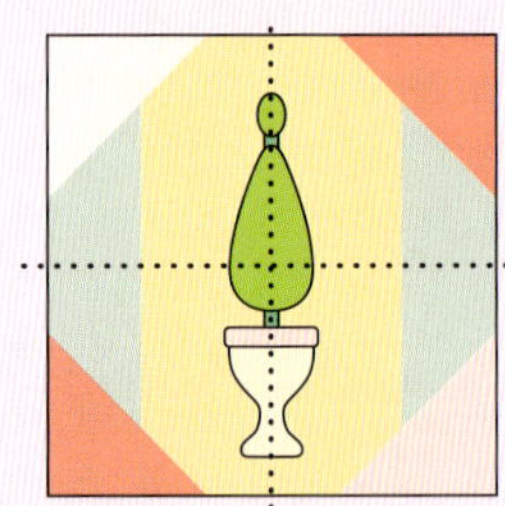

Applique Placement

block no. 507

Tweet-ness

by Heidi Pridemore • The Whimsical Workshop
thewhimsicalworkshop.com

Fabric: Stitched Garden by Heather Rosas for Camelot Fabrics, camelotfabrics.com.

Unit 1
Stitch & Flip
Make 1

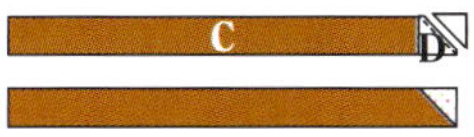

Unit 2
Stitch & Flip
Make 1

See page 343 on the PDF for pattern

Cream Dot
- 1 square (A) 3⅞" x 3⅞"
- 1 square (B) 2⅜" x 2⅜"
- 1 square (D) 1½" x 1½"
- 1 rectangle (E) 6½" x 12½"
- 1 rectangle (F) 3½" x 7½"
- 1 rectangle (G) 2½" x 3½"
- 1 rectangle (H) 2½" x 12½"

Brown Tone-on-Tone
- 1 square (A) 3⅞" x 3⅞"
- 1 rectangle (C) 1½" x 12½"

Assorted Prints and Solids
- 1 complete set of appliqué patches

Fusible web

Embroidery floss

Applique & Stitching Placement

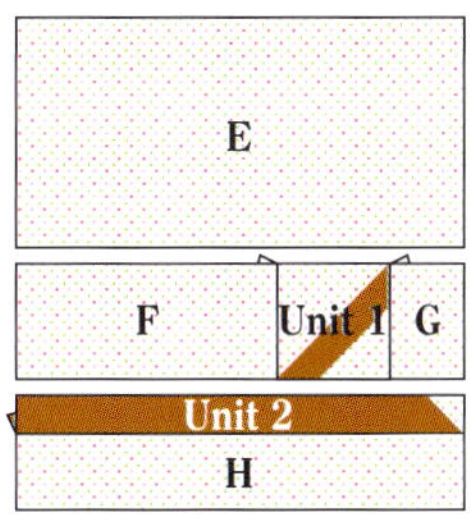

Block Assembly

Pair cream and brown A's to make 2 partial Triangle-Square unit 1's (use 1). Refer to "Stitch-and-Flip" in the Techniques file on the PDF to add a cream B to the brown triangle to complete unit 1. Use stitch-and-flip to add a cream D to the brown C to make unit 2.

Sew the units and patches together as shown to make the block.

Prepare patches I–P for fusible appliqué. Fold the block in half both ways and lightly crease the folds. Use the creases and appliqué placement diagram as guides to arrange the patches on the block; fuse in place. Use white and black thread and a machine blanket stitch to sew around the eye; use pink thread to sew around the remaining patches. Use 2 strands of embroidery floss and a backstitch to embroider the legs/feet to complete the block.

block no. 508

Chicken Hearted

by Sindy Rodenmayer • Fat Cat Patterns
fatcatpatterns.com

See page 359 on the PDF for pattern

White Print
- 1 square (A) 9½" x 9½"

Tan Print
- 4 rectangles (B) 2" x 9½"

Black Tone-on-Tone
- 4 squares (C) 2" x 2"

Assorted Prints and Tone-on-Tones
- 1 complete set of appliqué patches

Fusible web

Sindy fussy-cut a circle print for the eye (N).

Sew the A, B's and C's together as shown to make the block.

Fold the block in half both ways and lightly crease the folds. Prepare patches D–N for fusible appliqué. Using the creases and appliqué placement diagram as guides, arrange and fuse the patches in alphabetical order.

Use black thread and a machine blanket stitch to sew around the patches to complete the block.

Applique Placement

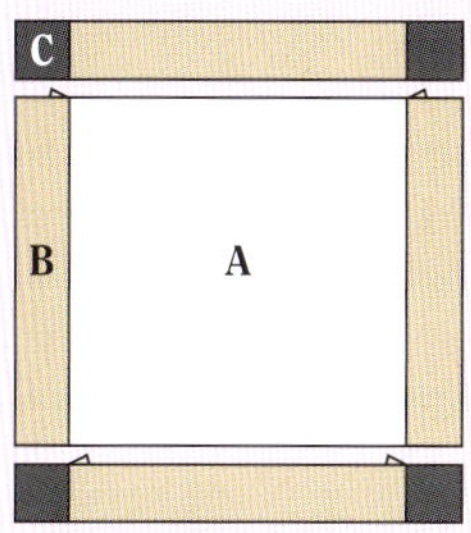

Block Piecing

block no. 509

Should'a Flown South

by Denise Russart
justquiltin.wordpress.com

Fabric: Various holiday lines from Hoffman California Fabrics, hoffmanfabrics.com.

See page 354 on the PDF for pattern

◪ = cut in half diagonally

Red Print
- 1 square 5⅞" x 5⅞" ◪ (A) (there will be 1 extra)

Gold Tone-on-Tone
- 1 rectangle (B) 1½" x 7¼"
- 1 rectangle (C) 1½" x 8¼"
- 1 square (I) 1½" x 1½"
- 1 rectangle (M) 1¾" x 12¼"

Cream Print
- 1 square 7⅞" x 7⅞" ◪ (D) (there will be 1 extra)
- 1 square (G) 2¾" x 2¾"
- 1 rectangle (H) 1¾" x 7½"
- 1 rectangle (J) 1¾" x 11"
- 1 rectangle (K) 2" x 8¾"
- 1 rectangle (L) 3" x 12½"

Black Print
- 1 square (E) 2½" x 2½"
- 1 rectangle (F) 2¾" x 7½"
- 2 pattern Q

Green and Red Plaid
- 1 pattern N
- 2 pattern R

Green Batik
- 1 *each* patterns O and P
- 2 pattern S

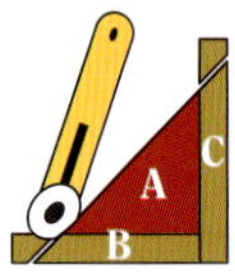

Unit 2
Stitch & Flip
Make 1

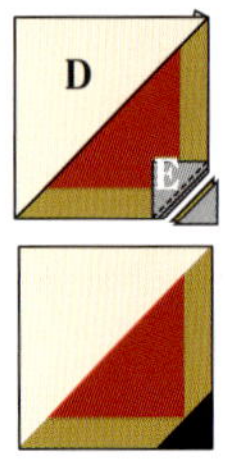

Unit 1
Stitch & Flip
Make 1

Unit 3
Stitch & Flip
Make 1

Sew the gold B and C to the red A and trim as shown. Add the cream D. Refer to "Stitch-and-Flip" in the Techniques file on the PDF; add the black E as shown to make unit 1. Use the black F and cream G as shown to make unit 2 and the cream H and gold I as shown to make unit 3. Sew the units and patches together as shown to make the top and bottom sections.

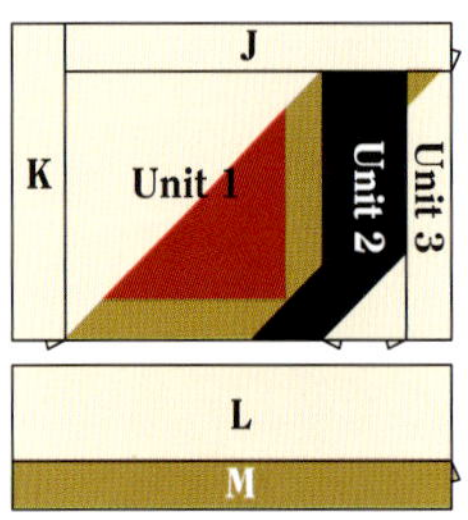

Section Piecing

Prepare patches N–S for turned-edge appliqué. Use the appliqué placement diagram as a guide to arrange the patches on the sections. Use matching thread and a blind stitch to appliqué the patches in place. Sew the sections together as shown to complete the block.

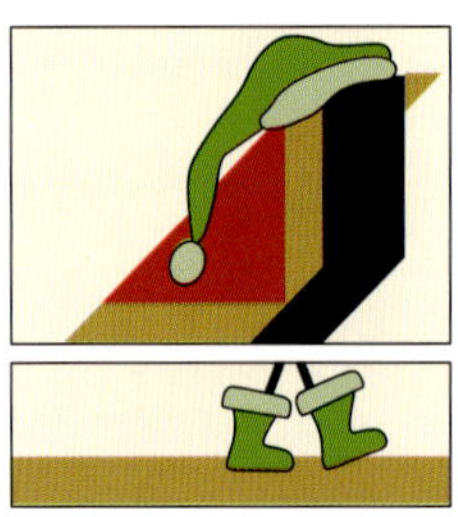

Appliqué Placement & Block Assembly

block no. 510

Blue Star Bloom

by Kathy Schmitz • Kathy Schmitz LLC
kathyschmitz.com

Fabric: Piecemakers designed by Kathy Schmitz for Moda Fabrics, unitednotions.com.

Kathy Schmitz is the author of *Simply Red* and *Gather the Passing Seasons* for Kathy Schmitz LLC, kathyschmitz.com.

See page 357 on the PDF for pattern

Cream Print #1
- 4 squares (A) 2⅞" x 2⅞"
- 1 square (B) 5¼" x 5¼"

Medium Blue Print
- 4 squares (A) 2⅞" x 2⅞"

Dark Blue Tone-on-Tone
- 4 squares (A) 2⅞" x 2⅞"
- 4 squares (C) 2½" x 2½"
- 1 pattern F
- 12 pattern H

Dark Blue Print
- 1 square (B) 5¼" x 5¼"

Cream Print #2
- 4 squares (A) 2⅞" x 2⅞"

Cream Tone-on-Tone
- 4 squares (C) 2½" x 2½"
- 1 square (D) 4½" x 4½"
- 1 pattern G

Medium Blue Tone-on-Tone
- 4 pattern E

Fusible web

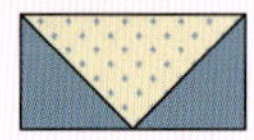

Flying Geese 1
Make 4

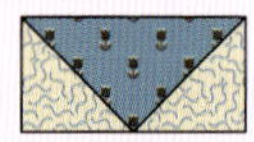

Flying Geese 2
Make 4

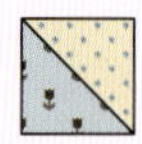

Unit
Make 8

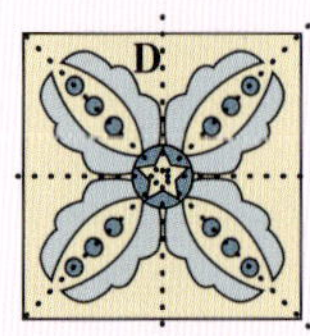

Applique Placement

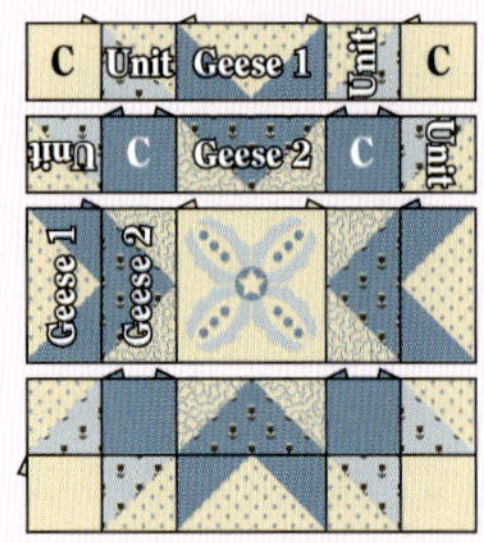

Block Assembly

Pair the cream #1 A's with the medium blue A's to make 8 Triangle-Square units.

Use the cream #1 B and dark blue tone-on-tone A's to make 4 Flying Geese 1's. Use the dark blue print B and cream #2 A's to make 4 Flying Geese 2's.

Fold D in half both ways and lightly crease the folds. Prepare patches E–H for fusible appliqué. Using the creases and appliqué placement diagram as guides, arrange and fuse the patches on D. Use matching thread and a straight stitch to sew around the patches.

Sew the units, Flying Geese, C's and D together as shown to complete the block.

block no. 511

Tribal Crossing

by Anita Grossman Solomon • Make It Simpler
makeitsimpler.com

Anita Grossman Solomon is the author of *Rotary Cutting Revolution* for C&T Publishing, ctpub.com.

See page 373 on the PDF for pattern

Pink Print
foundation patches
Black Solid
16 pattern A
foundation patches
Fusible web

Section
Make 8

Make 8 paper copies of the foundation section. Foundation piece the sections in numerical order, pressing and trimming after each patch addition.

Sew the sections together as shown. To reduce bulk, press the seams open. Carefully remove the foundation papers.

Prepare the A's for fusible appliqué. Use the seams and appliqué placement diagram as guides to arrange the A's as shown, allowing for a $\frac{1}{4}''$ seam allowance along the block's outside edges. Fuse the A's in place.

Sew around the A's using matching thread and a zigzag stitch to complete the block.

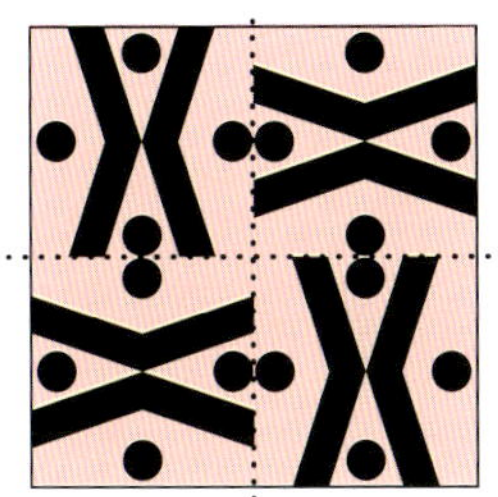

Applique Placement

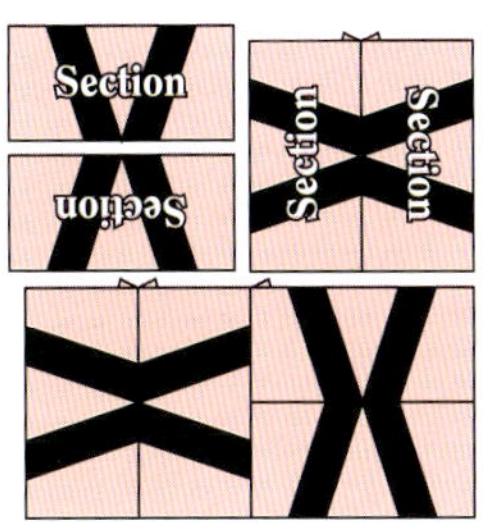

Block Assembly

block no. 512

A Whale of a Block

by Debbie Taylor • Fat Quarter Shop
fatquartershop.com

Fabric: Happy Go Lucky by Bonnie & Camille for Moda Fabrics, unitednotions.com, and Spot On Basics from Robert Kaufman, robertkaufman.com.

Debbie Taylor is a contributor to *Simply Fat Quarters* for Fat Quarter Shop, fatquartershop.com.

See page 358 on the PDF for pattern

White Solid and Aqua Dot
from *each*
18 squares (A) $2\frac{7}{8}''$ x $2\frac{7}{8}''$
Dark Blue Dot
1 *each* patterns B and C
Button 1 at $\frac{1}{4}''$
Fusible web

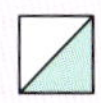

Unit
Make 36

Pair the white A's and aqua A's to make 36 Triangle-Square units. Join 4 rows of 6 units as shown to make the top of the block.

Prepare patches B and C for fusible appliqué. Use the seam lines and appliqué placement diagram as guides to arrange the patches on the top portion of the block; fuse the patches in place. Use matching thread and a straight stitch to sew just inside the edges of the whale patches.

Sew the top of the block and remaining units together as shown. Tack the button in place for the whale's eye to complete the block.

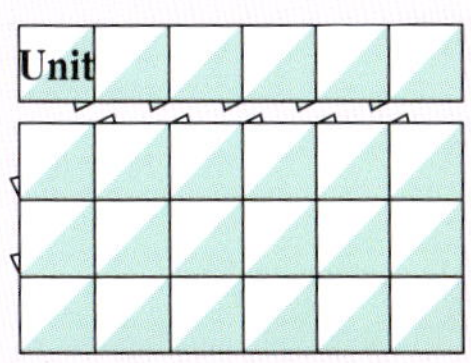

Block Piecing

Applique Placement

Block Assembly

block no. 513

Flower Child

by Jocelyn Ueng • It's Sew Emma
itssewemma.com

Fabric: Color Me Retro designed by Jeni Baker for Art Gallery Fabrics, artgalleryfabrics.com and Garden Pindot from Michael Miller Fabrics, michaelmillerfabrics.com.

See page 348 on the PDF for pattern

◸ = cut in half diagonally

Aqua Stripe
section 1, patch 1

Orange Dot
sections 1 and 2, patch 2

Pink Dot
sections 1 and 2, patch 3

Dark Blue Stripe
section 2, patch 1

Dark Blue Print and Aqua Print #1
from *each*
2 squares $4\frac{7}{8}$" x $4\frac{7}{8}$" ◸ (A)

Aqua Print #2 and Green Print
from *each*
2 squares $2\frac{7}{8}$" x $2\frac{7}{8}$" ◸ (B)

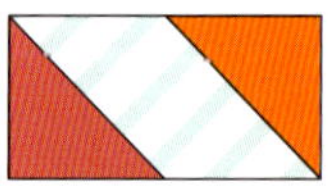

Section 1
Make 2

Section 2
Make 2

Make 4 paper copies of the foundation section. Fabrics for section 2's are shown on the foundations in parentheses. Foundation piece the sections in numerical order, pressing and trimming after each patch addition.

Sew the sections and patches together as shown to complete the block.

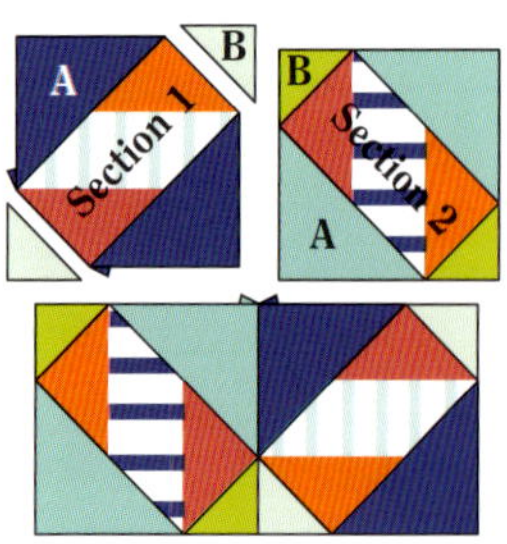

Block Assembly

block no. 514

Star Gazing

by Corey Yoder
littlemissshabby.com

Corey Yoder is the author of *Playful Petals* for Stash Books, ctpub.com.

See page 351 on the PDF for pattern

Section 1
Make 4

Section 2
Make 4

White Solid
sections 1 and 2, patch 1
4 squares (A) $4\frac{1}{2}$" x $4\frac{1}{2}$"
4 squares (B) $2\frac{1}{2}$" x $2\frac{1}{2}$"

Dark Blue Solid
section 1, patches 2–5
16 squares (B) $2\frac{1}{2}$" x $2\frac{1}{2}$"

Dark Pink Solid
section 2, patches 2–5
8 squares (B) $2\frac{1}{2}$" x $2\frac{1}{2}$"

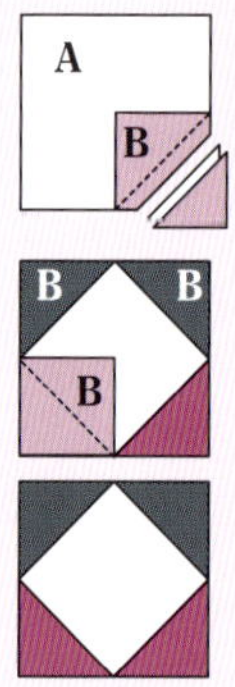

Unit
Stitch & Flip
Make 4

Make 4 paper copies *each* of foundation sections 1 and 2. Fabrics for section 2's are shown on the foundations in parentheses. Foundation piece the sections in numerical order, pressing and trimming after each patch addition.

Refer to "Stitch-and-Flip" in the Techniques file on the PDF. Use white A's, dark blue B's and dark pink B's as shown to make 4 units as shown.

Sew the sections, units and patches together as shown to complete the block.

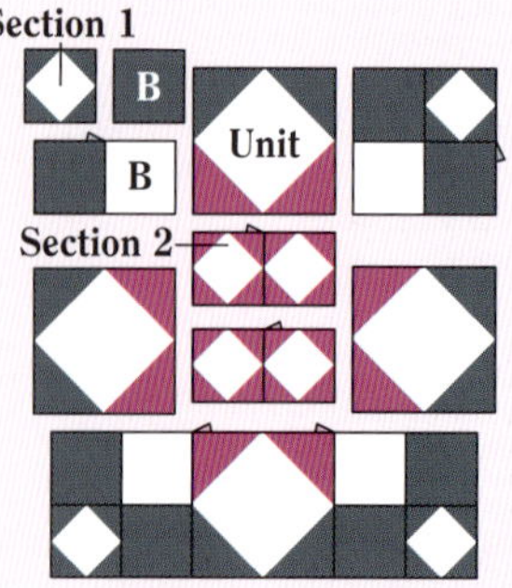

Block Assembly

block no. 515

Periwinkle

by Maaike Bakker and Françoise Maarse • Quilterij quilterij.nl

Fabric: Basics from Stof, stof-dk.com.

Maaike Bakker and Françoise Maarse are co-authors of *A Paper-Pieced Garden* for Martingale, shopmartingale.com.

See page 410 on the PDF for pattern

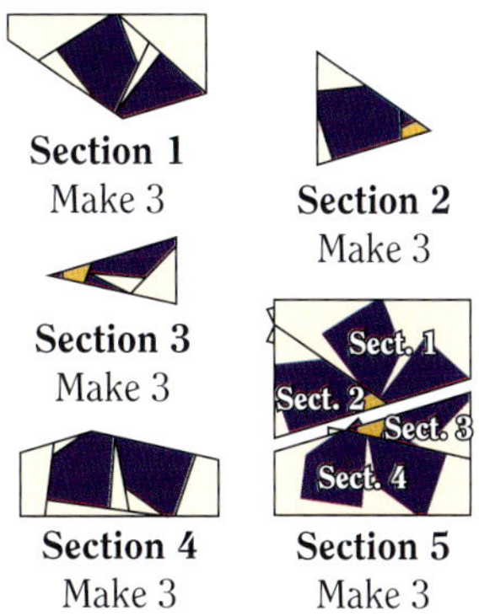

Dark Purple, Medium Purple and Gold Tone-on-Tones
- foundation patches

Cream Tone-on-Tone
- 2 rectangles (A) 1½″ x 4½″
- 2 rectangles (B) 1½″ x 5½″
- 2 rectangles (C) 2½″ x 4½″
- 1 rectangle (D) 2½″ x 7½″
- 1 rectangle (E) 2½″ x 6½″
- 1 square (F) 6½″ x 6½″
- foundation patches

Green Tone-on-Tone
- 1 *each* patterns G–L
- 8 *each* patterns M and N
- 2 pattern O

Fusible web

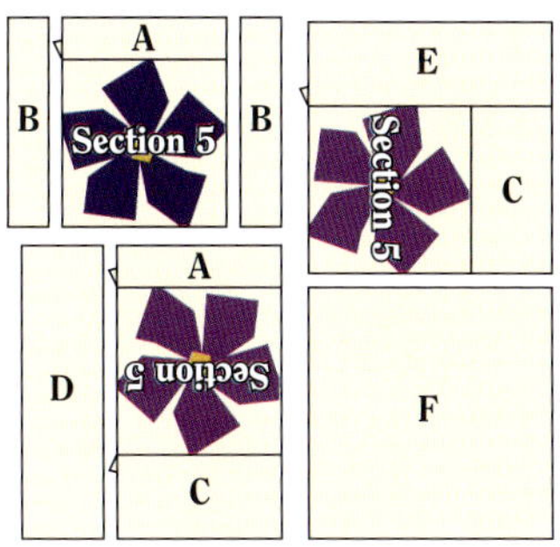

Block Assembly

Make 3 paper copies *each* of foundation sections 1–4. Refer to the foundations for color placement, using the dark purple on 1 set and the medium purple on 2 sets. Foundation piece the sections in numerical order, pressing and trimming after each patch addition. Sew the sections together as shown to make 3 section 5's.

Applique Placement

Sew cream patches and sections together as shown to make the block. Fold the block in half diagonally both ways and lightly crease the folds. Prepare patches G–O for fusible appliqué. Using the creases and appliqué placement diagram as guides, arrange and fuse the patches in alphabetical order.

Use matching thread and a machine blanket stitch to sew around the patches to complete the block.

block no. 516

Starry Heart

by Elizabeth Balderrama & Kate Colleran• Seams Like a Dream Quilt Designs • seamslikeadream.com

See page 406 on the PDF for pattern

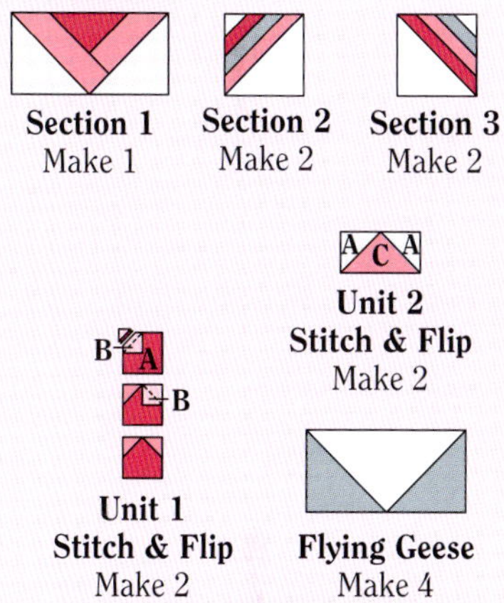

Dark Pink Tone-on-Tone
- 2 squares (A) 2″ x 2″
- section 1, patch 1
- section 2, patch 4
- section 3, patch 2

Pink Dot
- 2 squares (A) 2″ x 2″
- 4 squares (B) 1¼″ x 1¼″
- 2 rectangles (C) 2″ x 3½″
- section 1, patches 2 and 3
- section 2, patch 2
- section 3, patch 3

Pale Gray Tone-on-Tone
- 4 squares (A) 2″ x 2″
- section 1, patches 4 and 5
- section 2, patch 5

White Tone-on-Tone
- 1 square (D) 7¼″ x 7¼″
- sections 2 and 3, patch 1
- section 3, patch 5

Gray Dot
- 4 squares (E) 3⅞″ x 3⅞″
- section 2, patch 3
- section 3, patch 4

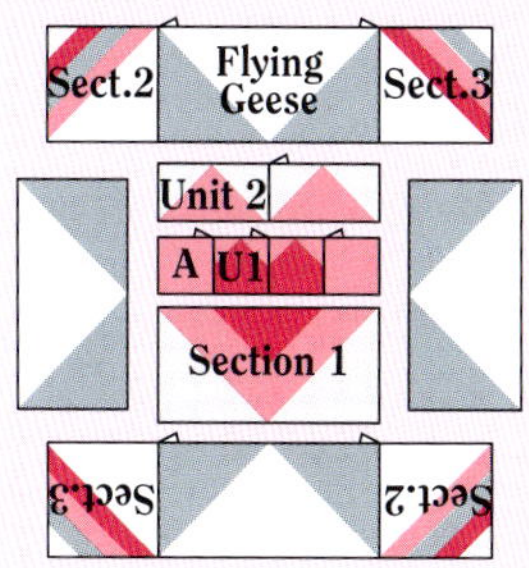

Block Assembly

Make 1 paper copy of foundation section 1 and 2 paper copies *each* of sections 2 and 3. Refer to the foundations for color placement; the colors for section 3 are shown in parentheses. Foundation piece the sections in numerical order, pressing and trimming after each patch addition.

Make 2 Stitch-and-Flip unit 1's using dark pink A's and pink dot B's. Make 2 Stitch-and-Flip unit 2's using pink dot C's and pale gray A's.

Use the white D and gray dot E's to make 4 Flying Geese.

Sew the sections, Flying Geese, units and patches together as shown to complete the block.

block no. 517

Christmas in My Soul

by Cheryl Brown • Quilter Chic
quilterchic.com

Cheryl Brown is the author of *Quilt Batik!* for Martingale, shopmartingale.com.

See page 383 on the PDF for pattern

White Tone-on-Tone
- 5 strips 1½" x 20"
- 1 rectangle (B) 8½" x 10½"
- 1 *each* patterns F, J and K

Red Tone-on-Tone
- 5 strips 1½" x 20"
- 2 squares (A) 2½" x 2½"
- 1 *each* patterns E–Gr and J
- 2 pattern H
- 3 pattern I
- 5 pattern K

Dark Green Tone-on-Tone
- 3 squares (A) 2½" x 2½"
- 1 *each* patterns C and D

Embroidery floss

For all techniques, refer to the Techniques file on the PDF. Sew the white strips and red strips together to make a band as shown. Cut the band at a 45° angle in 1½" increments to make 4 units.

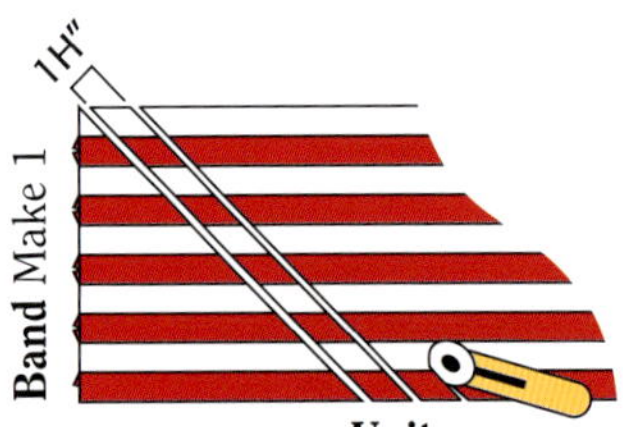

Unit
Cut 4

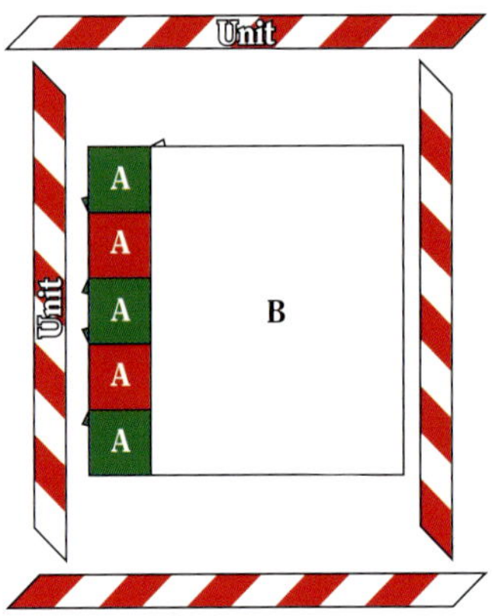

Block Piecing

Refer to the block piecing diagram. Sew the A's and B together as shown. Sew the units to the block center.

Prepare patches C–K for turned-edge appliqué. Use the appliqué placement diagram as a guide to arrange the patches on the block.

Applique and Embroidery Placement

Use matching thread and a blind stitch to appliqué the patches in place. Refer to the pattern on page 383 of the PDF for stitch placement. Use 2 strands of floss and a backstitch to add veins to C and D and the ornament detail to complete the block.

block no. 518

Nobility

by Kari Carr • New Leaf Stitches
newleafstitches.com

Fabric: Hand-dyed fabrics from Cherrywood, cherrywoodfabrics.com.

Kari Carr is the designer of the Kites Plus template from Creative Grids, creativegrids.com. She is the author of *Twice as Nice* and *Just Around the Corner* for Martingale, shopmartingale.com.

See page 389 on the PDF for pattern

⧄ = cut in half diagonally
⊠ = cut in half twice diagonally

Dark Purple Solid
- 1 square (A) 4½" x 4½"
- 1 square 7¼" x 7¼" ⊠ (C)
- 4 squares (H) 3½" x 3½"

Green Solid
- 4 squares (B) 2½" x 2½"
- 4 pattern D
- 5 pattern I

Gold Solid
- 4 squares 3⅞" x 3⅞" ⧄ (E)
- 2 rectangles (F) 1½" x 4½"
- 2 rectangles (G) 1½" x 6½"

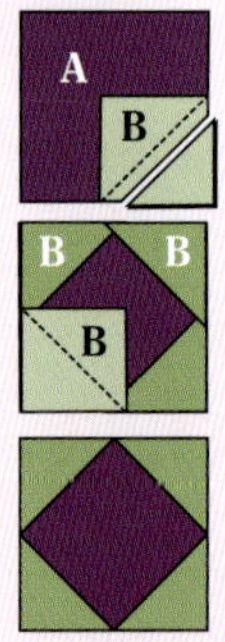

Unit 1
Stitch & Flip
Make 1

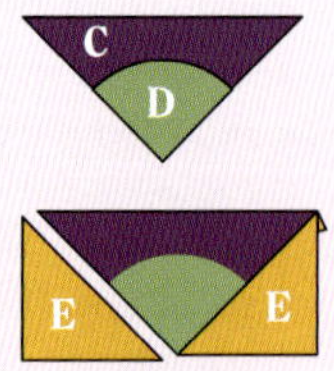

Unit 2
Make 4

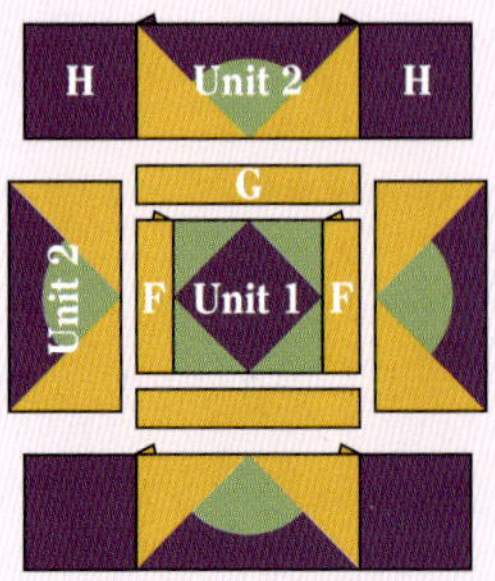

Block Assembly

Use the purple A and green B's to make a Stitch-and-Flip unit 1 as shown.

Prepare the curved edge of each D and the I's for turned-edge appliqué. Arrange a D on each C as shown; pin in place. Use matching thread and a machine blind stitch to appliqué the patches in place. Join 2 gold E's to each C/D as shown to make 4 unit 2's.

Sew the patches and units together as shown in the assembly diagram to make the block.

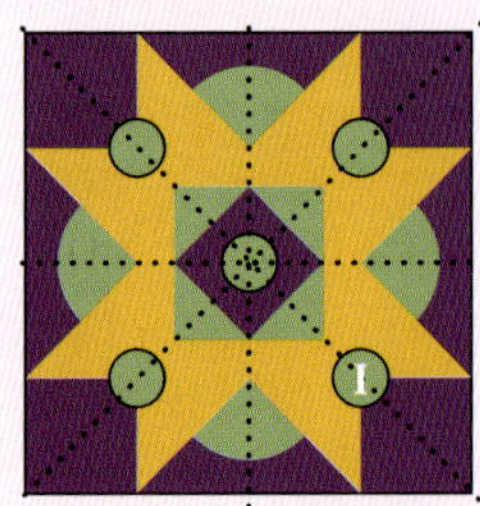

Applique Placement

Fold the block in half both ways and diagonally and lightly crease the folds. Using the creases and appliqué placement diagram as guides, arrange the I's on the block. Using matching thread and a machine blind stitch, appliqué the I's to complete the block.

block no. 519

Corkscrew

by Melissa Corry • Happy Quilting
happyquiltingmelissa.blogspot.com

Fabric: True Colors by Jenean Morrison from FreeSpirit Fabrics, freespiritfabrics.com.

See page 400 on the PDF for pattern

Teal Tone-on-Tone
4 squares (B) 2⅞″ x 2⅞″
section patches 1 and 4

White Tone-on-Tone
6 squares (B) 2⅞″ x 2⅞″
section patches 2 and 3

Purple Tone-on-Tone
2 squares (A) 5¼″ x 5¼″
2 squares (B) 2⅞″ x 2⅞″
section patches 5 and 6

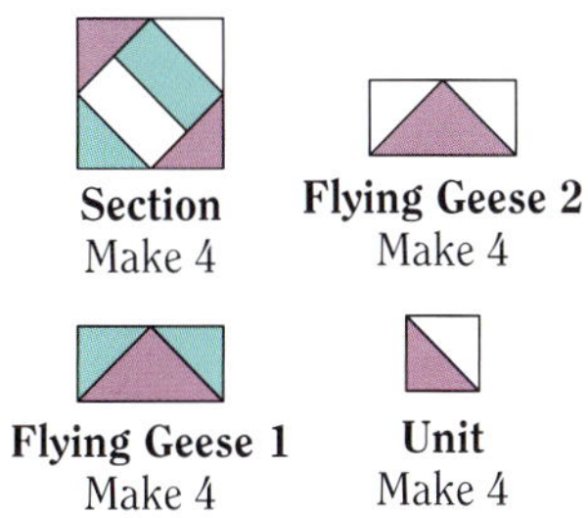

Make 4 paper copies of the foundation section. Foundation piece the sections in numerical order, pressing and trimming after each patch addition.

Make 4 Flying Geese 1's using a purple A and teal B's. Make 4 Flying Geese 2's using a purple A and white B's.

Pair white B's with purple B's to make 4 Triangle-Square units.

Sew the sections, Flying Geese and units together as shown to complete the block.

Block Assembly

block no. 520

Crossing the Circles

by Jenifer Dick • 42 Quilts
42quilts.com

Jenifer Dick is the author of *The Modern Appliqué Workbook* for Stash Books, ctpub.com.

See page 400 on the PDF for pattern

Assorted Solids
4 squares (A) 6½″ x 6½″
4 pattern B

Medium Gray Solid
4 rectangles (C) 1″ x 6½″

Dark Gray Solid
4 rectangles (C) 1″ x 6½″

Prepare the B patches for turned-edge appliqué. Roughly center a B on each A; pin in place. Use monofilament thread and a machine zigzag stitch to appliqué the B's in place.

Refer to the section diagrams. Cut the A/B unit 2¾" from the left edge; join a medium gray C to the 2 cut pieces as shown. Cut the A/B/C unit 2¾" from the top edge; join a medium gray C to the 2 cut pieces as shown to complete the section. Make 2 sections using medium gray C's and 2 sections using dark gray C's.

Noting the orientations, join the sections as shown to complete the block.

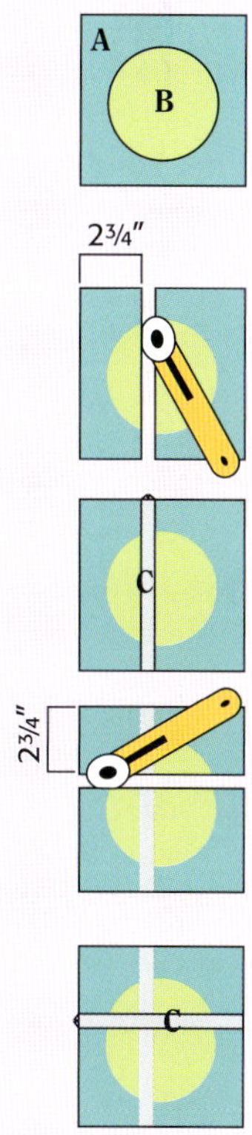

Section
Make 4

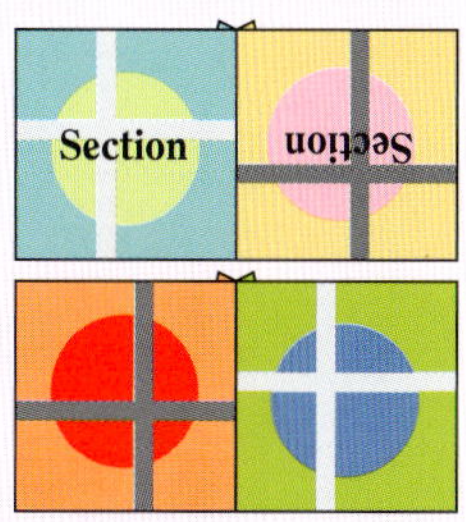

Block Assembly

block no. 521

Tulip Time

by Candace Door

Candace used the AccuQuilt GO! Fabric Cutter to make her block.

See page 393 on the PDF for pattern

◸ = cut in half diagonally
⊠ = cut in half twice diagonally

Teal Solid and Light Teal Solid
from *each*
 1 square 7¼" x 7¼" ⊠ (A)
Black Tone-on-Tone and White Tone-on-Tone
from *each*
 1 square 6⅞" x 6⅞" ◸ (B)
Light Green Solid
 2 pattern C
 4 pattern F
Medium Green Solid
 2 pattern C
 4 pattern Fr
Pink Solid and Orange Solid
from *each*
 2 *each* patterns D, E and Er
Fusible web

Applique Placement

Sew the A's and B's together as shown to make the block.

Fold the block in half diagonally both ways and lightly crease the folds. Prepare patches C–Fr for fusible appliqué. Using the creases and appliqué placement diagram as guides, arrange and fuse the patches in alphabetical order.

Candace used a variegated thread to sew around the flower patches.

Sew around the patches with matching thread and a machine blanket stitch to complete the block.

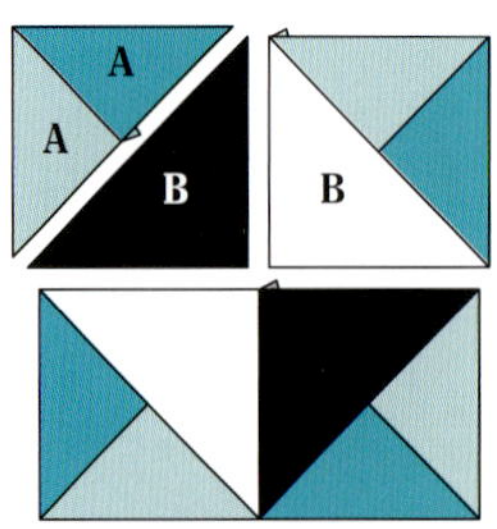

Block Piecing

block no. 522

Rainbow Houndstooth

by Theresa Eisinger • former *QM* Graphic Designer

Fabric: Tonga Batiks from Timeless Treasures, ttfabrics.com.

See page 407 on the PDF for pattern

Light Yellow, Light Gold, Light Orange and Light Pink Batiks (see note below)
 9 squares (A) 2½" x 2½"
 section, patches 2 and 3
Dark Teal, Blue, Violet and Purple Batiks (see note below)
 9 squares (A) 2½" x 2½"
 section, patches 1 and 4

Section
Make 18

Refer to the assembly diagram to cut the appropriate number of A's from each color. Notice how the light colors change from the upper right corner toward the lower left corner; the dark colors change from the upper left corner toward the lower right corner.

Make 18 paper copies of the foundation section.

To help with color placement, refer to the assembly diagram and mark the colors on each foundation.

Refer to the foundation sections for color/value placements. Foundation piece the sections in numerical order, pressing and trimming after each patch addition.

Paying careful attention to the color placements and section orientations, sew the patches and sections together to complete the block.

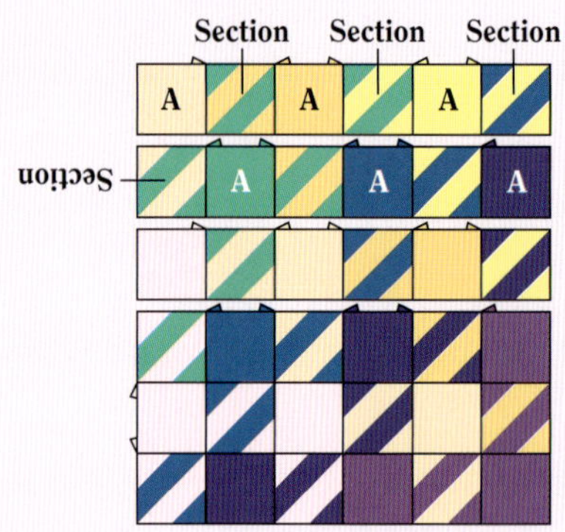

Block Assembly

block no. 523

Barn Quilt

by Camelia Elliott • Camelia's Unique Creations
cameliaelliott.com

Camelia used woodgrain prints for her barn patches.

See page 399 on the PDF for pattern

Blue Tone-on-Tone
1 rectangle (A) 9″ x 12½″

Dark Green Tone-on-Tone
1 rectangle (B) 4″ x 12½″

Multicolor Print
1 pattern C

4 Assorted Brown Prints
from 2
1 square (D) 4¼″ x 4¼″
from 2
1 *each* patterns M and N

Red Print
1 square (E) 1⅛″ x 1⅛″

Yellow Solid
1 rectangle (F) ⅞″ x 1⅛″
1 rectangle (G) ⅞″ x 1⅛″

Teal Solid
1 rectangle (G) ⅞″ x 1½″
1 rectangle (H) ⅞″ x 1⅞″

Blue Solid
1 rectangle (I) ¾″ x 1⅞″
1 rectangle (J) ¾″ x 2⅛″

Green Solid
1 rectangle (J) ¾″ x 2⅛″
1 rectangle (K) ¾″ x 2⅜″

2 Red Tone-on-Tones
1 *each* patterns L and O

Assorted Gold Tone-on-Tones
1 *each* patterns P–T

Fusible web

Nonstick pressing sheet

Join patches A and B, the 2 brown D's and E–K (the small log cabin) as shown. Prepare patches C and L–T for fusible appliqué. Apply fusible web to the wrong side of the D/D and the small Log Cabin.

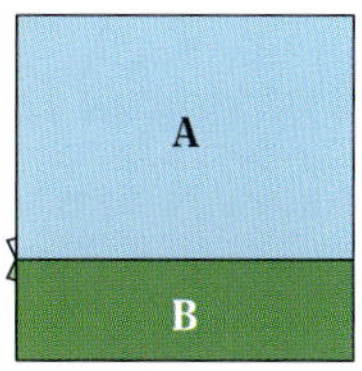

Block Piecing

Refer to "Fusible Appliqué" in the Techniques file on the PDF use the non-stick pressing sheet to arrange the barn patches.

Barn

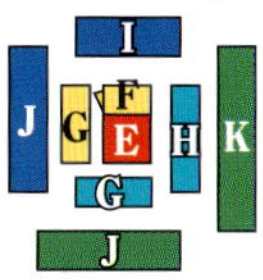

Log Cabin

Fold the block in half both ways and lightly crease the folds. Using the creases and appliqué placement diagram as guides, arrange C, the barn and sun; fuse in place.

Use black thread and a machine blanket stitch to sew around the barn and field patches and gold thread for the sun. Straight stitch the X on the barn door to complete the block.

Applique Placement

block no. 524

Diamonds in My Eyes

by Cynthia Foster • Carter Creek Quilts
etsy.com/shop/cartercreekquilts

See page 400 on the PDF for pattern

Dark Blue Tone-on-Tone
12 squares (A) 1½″ x 1½″
foundation patches

Light Blue Tone-on-Tone
foundation patches

White Tone-on-Tone
4 squares (A) 1½″ x 1½″
4 rectangles (B) 1½″ x 2½″
4 rectangles (C) 1½″ x 3½″
4 rectangles (D) 1½″ x 4½″
4 rectangles (E) 1½″ x 5½″
2 template F
foundation patches

Section 1
Make 2

Section 2
Make 2

Section 3
Make 2

Make 2 paper copies of *each* foundation section. Referring to the sections for color placement, foundation piece the sections in numerical order, pressing and trimming after each patch addition.

Carefully remove the foundation papers. Refer to "Curved Piecing" in the Techniques file on the PDF to join the sections and F's together as shown.

Sew the joined sections and patches together as shown to complete the block.

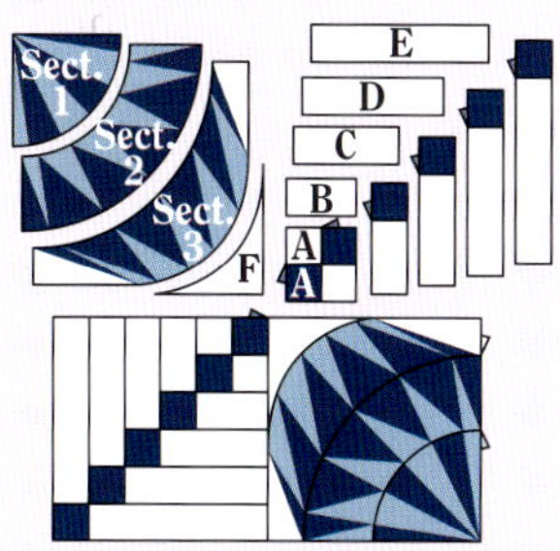

Block Assembly

block no. 525

Coneflower Playground

by Regina Grewe • Textile Landscapes
reginagrewe.de

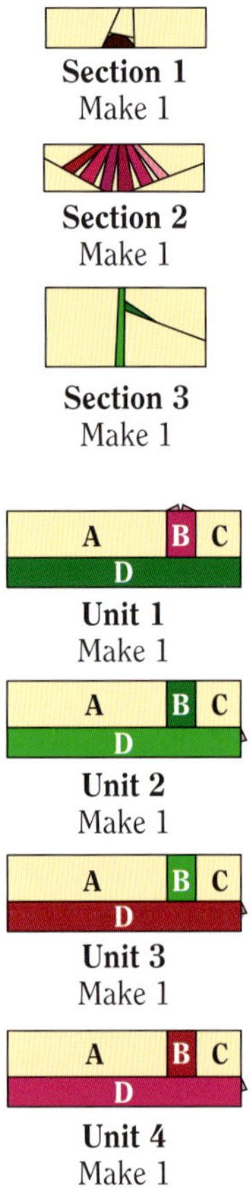

See page 382 on the PDF for pattern

Brown Tone-on-Tone
section 1, patch 1

Yellow Dot
4 rectangles (A) 2¼″ x 6¾″
4 squares (C) 2¼″ x 2¼″
section 1, patches 2–6
section 2, patches 1, 3, 5, 7, 9, 11 and 13–15
section 3, patches 1, 3 and 5

Assorted Pink Tone-on-Tones
from *each of 2*
1 rectangle (B) 1⅝″ x 2¼″
1 rectangle (D) 1⅝″ x 9⅝″
from *assorted*
section 2, patches 2, 4, 6, 8, 10 and 12

Dark Green Tone-on-Tone
1 rectangle (B) 1⅝″ x 2¼″
1 rectangle (D) 1⅝″ x 9⅝″
section 3, patch 2

Medium Green Tone-on-Tone
1 rectangle (B) 1⅝″ x 2¼″
1 rectangle (D) 1⅝″ x 9⅝″
section 3, patch 4

• = Partial Seam

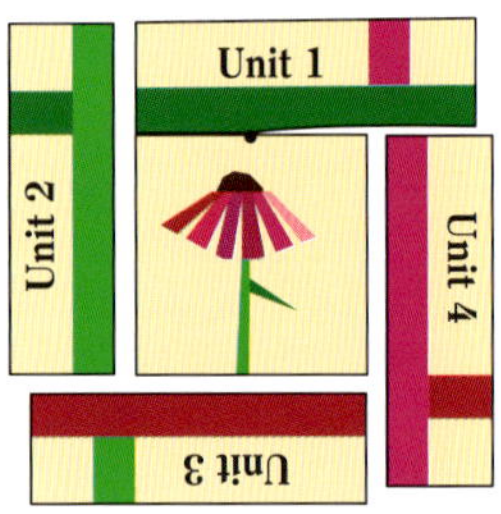

Block Assembly

Make 1 paper copy of *each* foundation section. Foundation piece the sections in numerical order, pressing and trimming after each patch addition. Sew the sections together to make the block center.

Use a yellow A, pink B, yellow C and dark green D to make unit 1 as shown. Using the appropriate colors, repeat to make 1 *each* of units 2–4.

Sew a unit 1 to the top of the foundation section with a partial seam as shown. Noting the orientation, sew unit 2 to the left of the foundation section, unit 3 to the bottom, and unit 4 to the right as shown. Complete the partial seam to finish the block.

block no. 526

Throw the Bones

by Diane Harris • Interactive Editor, *Quiltmaker*
quiltmaker.com

Fabric: Love More designed by Susan Black for P&B Textiles, pbtex.com.

See page 412 on the PDF for pattern

Cream Print
section, patch 1

Dark Gray Tone-on-Tone
4 squares (A) 3½″ x 3½″
1 square (B) 6½″ x 6½″
section, patches 2 and 3

Section
Make 4

Make 4 paper copies of the foundation section. Foundation piece the sections in numerical order, pressing and trimming after each patch addition.

Sew the patches and sections together as shown to complete the block.

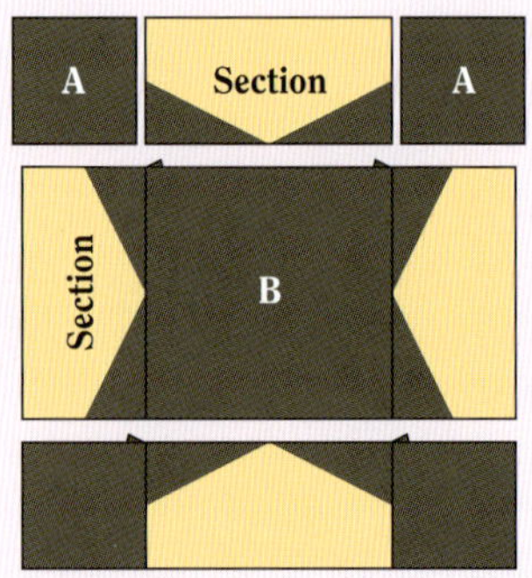

Block Assembly

block no. 527

Penguin Party

by Melissa Harris and Arlene Stamper
The Quilt Company • quiltcompany.com

Fabric: Christmas Classics from Maywood Studio, maywoodstudio.com.

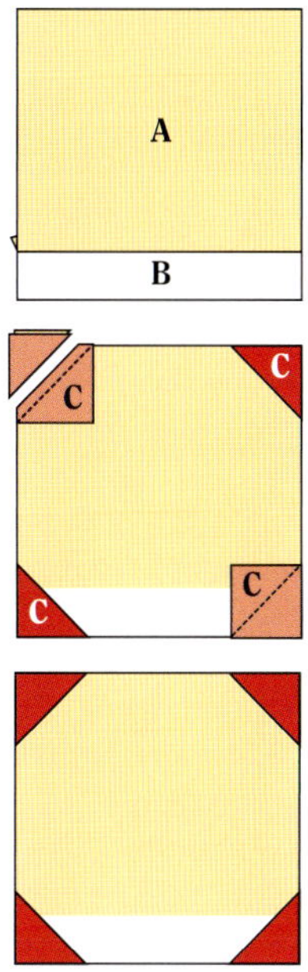

Block Piecing
Stitch & Flip
Make 1

See page 403 on the PDF for pattern

Cream Dot
1 rectangle (A) 10½" x 12½"
White Dot
1 rectangle (B) 2½" x 12½"
1 *each* patterns D and I
Red Print
4 squares (C) 3½" x 3½"
Green Tone-on-Tone
2 pattern E
Black Dot
1 *each* patterns F and J
Pink Dot
1 pattern G
Green Check
1 pattern H
Fusible web
Embroidery floss
2 giant paper clips
Button 1 at ¼"

Applique & Embroidery Placement

Sew the cream A and white B together as shown. Refer to "Stitch-and-Flip" in the Techniques file on the PDF. Add red C's to each corner to make the block.

Fold the block in half both ways and lightly crease the folds. Prepare patches D–J for fusible appliqué. Using the creases and appliqué placement diagram as guides, arrange and fuse the patches in alphabetical order.

Use matching thread and a machine blanket stitch to sew around the patches. With 2 strands of floss, add the snowflakes using a long stitch and French knots.

Tack the skates (paper clips) and button in place as shown to complete the block.

block no. 528

4 Corners of Happy

by Belinda Karis-Nace • Blue Ribbon Designs
blueribbondesigns.com

Belinda used the AccuQuilt GO! Fabric Cutter to make her block.

See page 398 on the PDF for pattern

White Tone-on-Tone
1 square (A) 7½" x 7½" (trim to 6½" x 6½" after appliqué)
1 square (G) 7¼" x 7¼"
Pink Tone-on-Tone
1 pattern B
4 squares (F) 2⅜" x 2⅜"
Orange Tone-on-Tone
1 pattern C
4 squares (F) 2⅜" x 2⅜"
Yellow Tone-on-Tone
1 pattern D
4 squares (I) 2" x 2"
Light Green Print
4 pattern E
Green Tone-on-Tone
4 squares (H) 3⅞" x 3⅞"
Blue Tone-on-Tone
4 squares (I) 2" x 2"
Fusible web

Applique Placement

Unit
Make 8

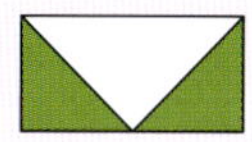

Flying Geese
Make 4

Block Assembly

Fold A in half diagonally both ways and lightly crease the folds. Prepare patches B–E for fusible appliqué. Using the creases and appliqué placement diagram as guides, arrange and fuse the patches in alphabetical order. Use matching thread and a machine blanket stitch to sew around the patches. Center the appliqué and trim A to 6½" × 6½".

Pair the orange F's with pink F's to make 8 Triangle-Square units.

Use the white G and green H's to make 4 Flying Geese.

Sew the units, Flying Geese and patches together as shown to complete the block.

block no 529

Dreaming of Spring

by Mary Elizabeth Kinch
maryelizabethkinch.com

Mary Elizabeth Kinch is the author of *Small Pieces, Spectacular Quilts—Patterns Inspired by Antique Quilts* for Martingale & Co., shopmartingale.com.

See page 398 on the PDF for pattern

◸ = cut in half diagonally

Assorted Pink and Orange Prints and Tone-on-Tones
- 11 squares (A) 1⅞″ x 1⅞″
- 1 square 5⅞″ x 5⅞″ ◸ (F)

White Solid
- 22 squares (A) 1⅞″ x 1⅞″
- 1 square (B) 5⅞″ x 5⅞″
- 3 squares 1⅞″ x 1⅞″ ◸ (E) (there will be 1 extra)
- 1 square (C) 6½″ x 6½″

Assorted Green Prints and Tone-on-Tones
- 11 squares (A) 1⅞″ x 1⅞″
- 2 pattern D

Green Solid
- 1 square (B) 5⅞″ x 5⅞″
- bias strip 1¼″ x 9½″

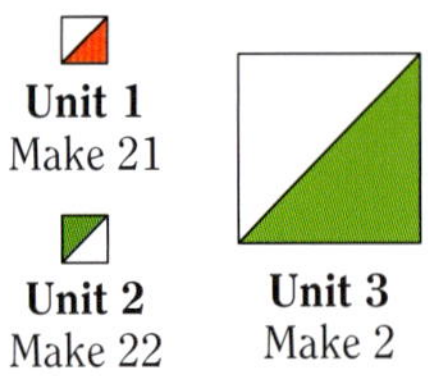

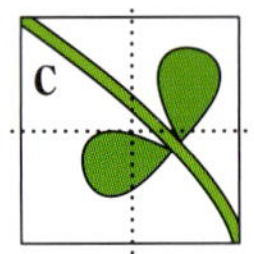

Applique Placement

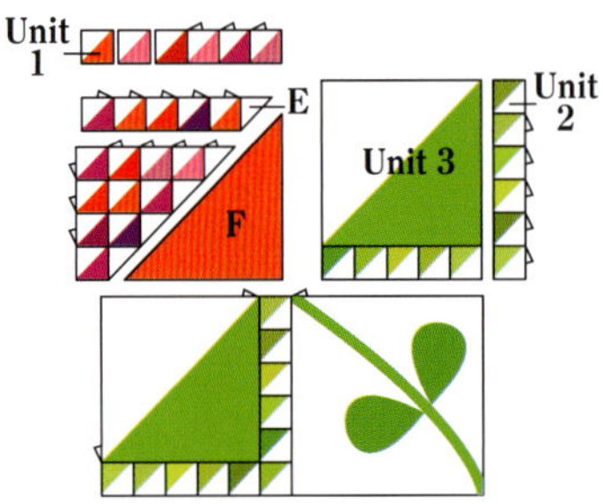

Block Assembly

Pair the assorted pink and orange A's with white A's to make 22 Triangle-Square unit 1's (use 21). Make 22 unit 2's using the assorted green A's and white A's. Pair the white B and green solid B to make 2 unit 3's.

Fold C in half both ways and lightly crease the folds. Refer to "Bias Strips" in the Techniques file on the PDF to make the stem from the green solid strip. Prepare the leaves (D) for turned-edge appliqué. Using the creases and appliqué placement diagram as guides, arrange the stem and leaves on C. Use matching thread and a blind stitch to appliqué the leaves in place.

Sew the units and patches together as shown to complete the block.

block no. 530

Pines and Spools

by Heather Kojan
heatherkojan.blogspot.com

See page 413 on the PDF for pattern

Assorted Green Tone-on-Tones
- section patches 1–6

White Solid
- 2 rectangles (C) 2″ x 9½″
- 2 rectangles (D) 2½″ x 5½″
- 1 rectangle (F) 1½″ x 12½″
- section patches 7 and 8

Light Brown Solid
- 2 rectangles (A) 1″ x 2½″

Red Tone-on-Tone
- 4 squares (B) 1″ x 1″
- 1 rectangle (E) 1½″ x 2½″

Yellow Tone-on-Tone
- 1 circle 2¾″ diameter for yo-yo

Section
Make 1

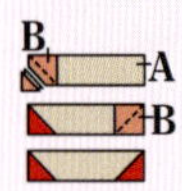

Unit
Make 2

Make 1 paper copy of the foundation section. Foundation piece the section in numerical order, pressing and trimming after each patch addition.

Refer to "Stitch-and-Flip" in the Techniques file on the PDF. Use the light brown A's and red B's to make 2 units as shown.

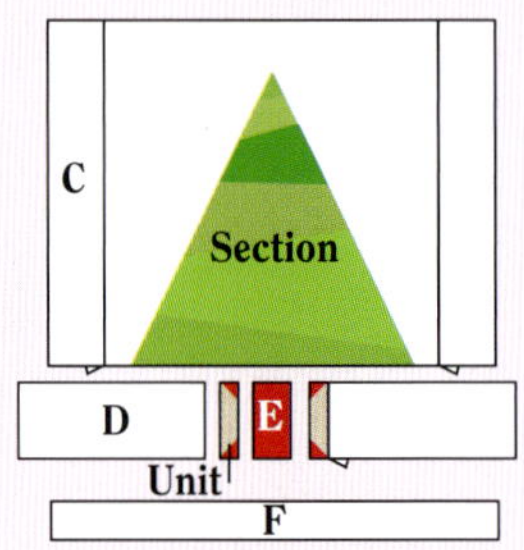

Block Assembly

Sew the patches, section and units together as shown.

Make a yo-yo from the yellow circle. Tack the yo-yo in place as shown to complete the block.

block no. 531

Nine-Patch Posies

by Kay Mackenzie • By Kay Mackenzie
kaymackenzie.com

Kay Mackenzie is the author of *Scrap-Appliqué Playground* for Martingale & Co., shopmartingale.com.

See page 415 on the PDF for pattern

Dark Teal Tone-on-Tone
 4 squares (A) 2″ x 2″
 1 pattern F

Medium Teal Tone-on-Tone and Pink Tone-on-Tone
from *each*
 4 squares (A) 2″ x 2″

Red Tone-on-Tone
 4 squares (A) 2″ x 2″
 1 pattern E

Gold Tone-on-Tone
 2 squares (A) 2″ x 2″

Cream Tone-on-Tone
 1 square (B) 13½″ x 13½″ (trim to 12½″ x 12½″ after appliqué)

Green Tone-on-Tone
 1 *each* patterns C and D
 2 pattern G

Fusible web

Template plastic

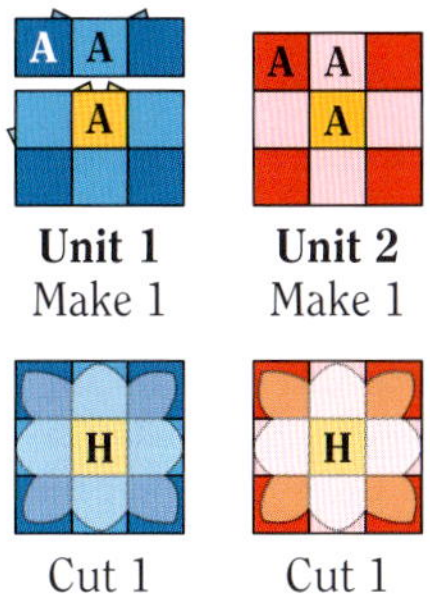

Sew the A's together as shown to make 1 unit 1 and 1 unit 2. Apply fusible web to the back of the units. Prepare patches C–G for fusible appliqué. Use the plastic to make a template of H; trace and cut the H's from the units as shown.

Applique Placement

Fold B in half both ways and lightly crease the folds. Using the creases and appliqué placement diagram as guides, arrange and fuse the patches in alphabetical order.

Use matching thread and a machine blanket stitch to sew around the patches. Center the appliqué and trim the block to 12½"× 12½".

block no. 532

Rainbow Star

by Nancy Mahoney
nancymahoney.com

Nancy Mahoney is the author of *Simple Circles and Quick Curves* for Martingale & Co., shopmartingale.com.

See page 404 on the PDF for pattern

⊠ = cut in half diagonally

White Tone-on-Tone
 4 squares (B) 2″ x 2″
 2 squares 3⅞″ x 3⅞″ ⊠ (C)
 sections 1–4, patch 1

Assorted Black Prints
 1 square (A) 3½″ x 3½″
 4 squares (B) 2″ x 2″
 sections 1–4, patch 2

Assorted Green, Blue, Yellow and Red Tone-on-Tones
from *each* color group
 1 square 3⅞″ x 3⅞″ ⊠ (C)
 (there will be 1 extra from each color group)
 foundation patches

White with Black Print
 8 squares (B) 2″ x 2″
 sections 2–5, patch 4

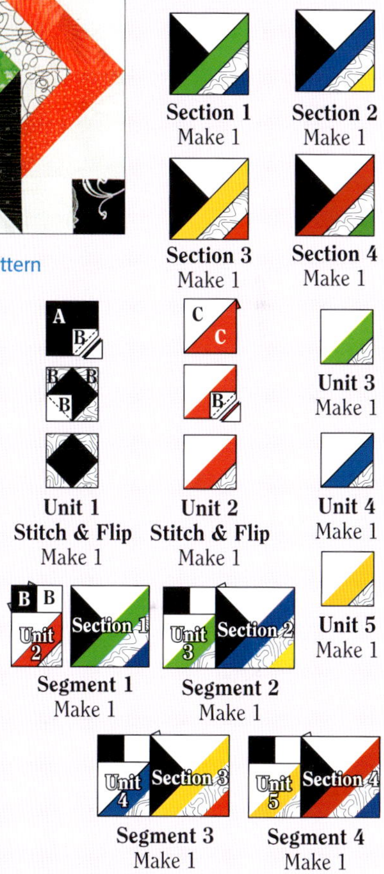

Make 1 paper copy of *each* foundation section. Refer to the foundations and diagrams for color placement. Foundation piece the sections in numerical order, pressing and trimming after each patch addition.

Refer to "Stitch-and-Flip" in the Techniques file on the PDF. Use the black A and white with black print B's to make unit 1. Sew a white C to a red C as shown. Using stitch-and-flip, add a white with black print B to one corner as shown to make unit 2. Refer to the diagrams and make units 3–5 in the same way.

Referring to the assembly diagram for color placement, join the patches, units and sections into 4 segments. Sew segment 1 to the bottom of unit 1 with a partial seam as shown. Sew a segment to the left, top and right side of unit 1 as shown. Complete the partial seam to finish the block.

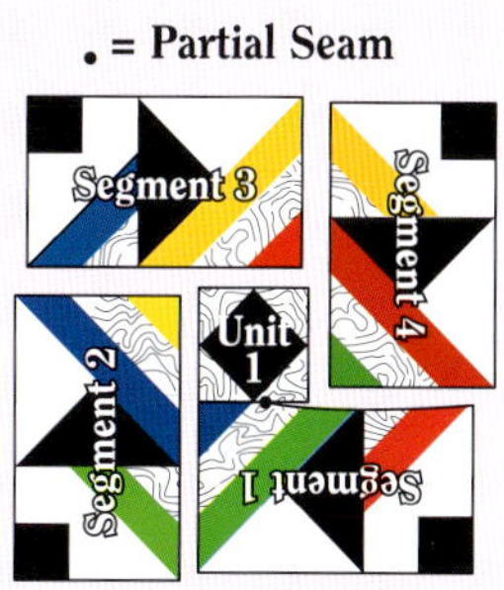

Block Assembly

block no. 533

Best Friends Forever

by Mary McGuire • Mary McGuire Design
marymcguiredesign.com

Fabric: Grace designed by Mary McGuire for RJR Fabrics, rjrfabrics.com.

See page 420 on the PDF for pattern

Assorted Solids and Prints
foundation patches

6 Assorted Medium and Dark Prints
from *each*
1 square (A) 2⅞" x 2⅞"

Cream Solid
6 squares (A) 2⅞" x 2⅞"

Fabric paint or fabric markers
(pink, brown and black)

Section 1
Make 3

Section 2
Make 3

Section 3
Make 3

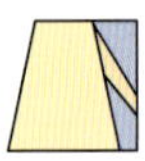

Section 4
Make 3

Section 5
Make 3

Section 6
Make 3

Unit
Make 12

Make 3 paper copies *each* of the foundation sections. Refer to the foundations for color placement. Foundation piece the sections in numerical order, pressing and trimming after each patch addition. Sew the sections together as shown to make 3 "friends."

Pair the assorted medium and dark A's with the cream A's to make 12 Triangle-Square units.

Sew the friends and units together as shown. Refer to the pattern sheet for face detail placement. Use fabric paint or markers to add the face details to complete the block.

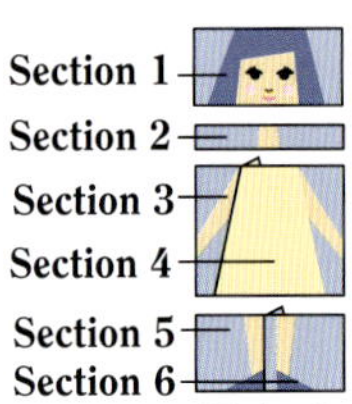

Make 3

Block Assembly

block no. 534

Garden Trellis

by Jo Moury

Flying Geese 1
Make 4

Flying Geese 2
Make 4

See page 388 on the PDF for pattern

Dark Brown Batik
1 square (A) 5¼" x 5¼"
4 squares (B) 2⅞" x 2⅞"

Cream Batik
1 square (A) 5¼" x 5¼"
4 squares (B) 2⅞" x 2⅞"
4 squares (C) 2½" x 2½"
1 square (E) 4½" x 4½"

Green Batik
4 squares (C) 2½" x 2½"
4 rectangles (D) 2½" x 4½"

Red Batik, Orange Batik and Purple Batik
1 set of appliqué patches

Fusible web

Green embroidery floss

21 beads assorted sizes

Button 1 at ½"

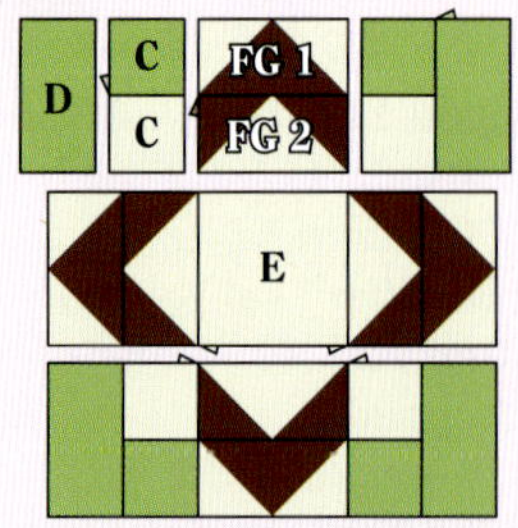

Block Assembly

Applique and Embroidery Placement

Use the brown A and cream B's to make 4 Flying Geese 1's. Make 4 Flying Geese 2's using the cream A and brown B's. Sew the Flying Geese and patches together as shown to make the block.

Fold the block in half both ways and lightly crease the folds. Prepare patches F–H for fusible appliqué. Using the creases and appliqué placement diagram as guides, arrange and fuse the patches in alphabetical order.

Use matching thread and a machine blanket stitch to sew around the patches. Refer to the pattern sheet for embroidery placement. Use 2 strands of floss and an outline stitch to add the swirls at the bottom and right of the flower. Use 3 strands of floss and an outline stitch for the tendrils at the top of the flower. Add French knots on the outer petals as shown. Sew the button and beads in place to complete the block.

block no. 535

American Pride

by Doris Rice • The Quilting Queen Online
quiltingqueenonline.com

Unit 1
Make 8

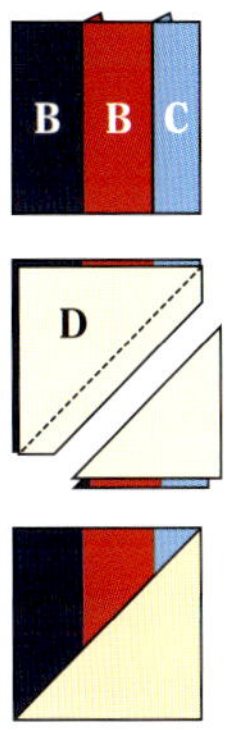

Unit 2
Stitch & Flip
Make 4

See page 398 on the PDF for pattern

Dark Blue Print
- 4 squares (A) 1⅞″ x 1⅞″
- 4 rectangles (B) 2″ x 4½″
- 1 pattern "U"

Red Tone-on-Tone
- 4 squares (A) 1⅞″ x 1⅞″
- 4 rectangles (B) 2″ x 4½″
- 2 squares (F) 2½″ x 2½″
- 1 pattern "A"

Medium Blue Print
- 4 rectangles (C) 1½″ x 4½″
- 4 rectangles (E) 1½″ x 8½″
- 1 pattern "S"

Cream Print
- 4 squares (D) 4½″ x 4½″
- 4 rectangles (E) 1½″ x 8½″

Fusible web

Tear-away stabilizer

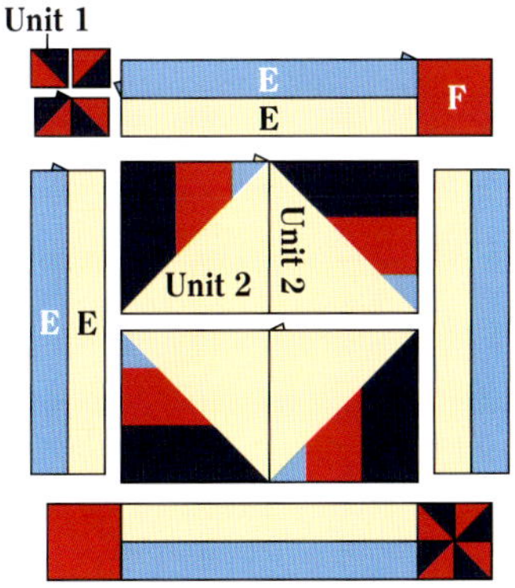

Block Assembly

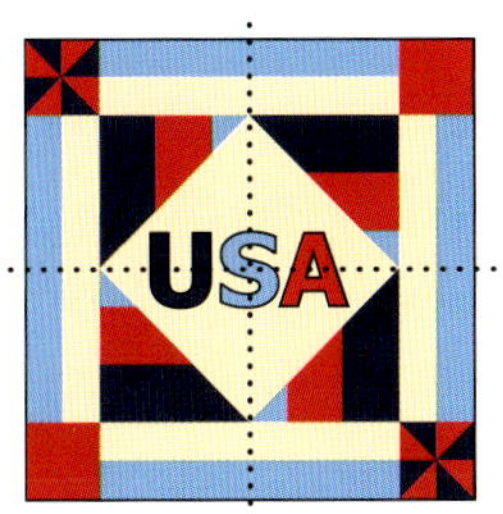

Applique Placement

Pair the dark blue A's with the red A's to make 8 Triangle-Square unit 1's.

Sew a dark blue B, a red B and a medium blue C together as shown. Refer to "Stitch-and-Flip" in the Techniques file on the PDF. Add the cream D as shown to complete unit 2. Make 4 unit 2's.

Sew the units and patches together as shown in the block assembly diagram.

Prepare the letters for fusible appliqué. Use the seam lines and appliqué placement diagram as guides to arrange the patches on the block; fuse the patches in place. Layer tear-away stabilizer on the back. Use contrasting thread and a satin stitch to sew around the letters to complete the block.

block no. 536

Grandma's Favorite

by Jacquelynne Steves
jacquelynnesteves.com

Fabric: Cottage Charm designed by Jacquelynne Steves for Henry Glass Fabrics, henryglassfabrics.com.

Jacquelynne Steves is the author of *Fruitful Hands* for Kansas City Star Quilts, pickledish.com.

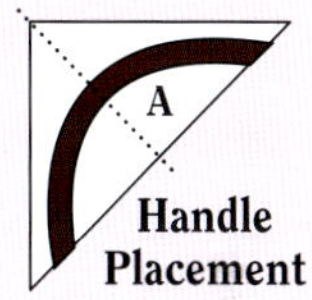

Handle Placement

See page 408 on the PDF for pattern

⧄ = cut in half diagonally

White Tone-on-Tone
- 1 square 7⅞″ x 7⅞″ ⧄ (A) (there will be 1 extra)
- 4 squares (C) 2⅝″ x 2⅝″
- 2 rectangles (E) 2¼″ x 5¾″
- 1 square 4⅜″ x 4⅜″ ⧄ (F)
- 2 rectangles (G) 2⅛″ x 9¼″
- 2 rectangles (H) 2⅛″ x 12½″

Brown Print
- 1 pattern B
- 1 square (C) 2⅝″ x 2⅝″
- 1 square 2⅝″ x 2⅝″ ⧄ (D)

Yellow Check
- 2 squares (C) 2⅝″ x 2⅝″

Light Green Print
- 1 square (C) 2⅝″ x 2⅝″

Blue Print
- 2 squares 2⅝″ x 2⅝″ ⧄ (D)

Assorted Prints
- 1 complete set of flower patches

Fusible web

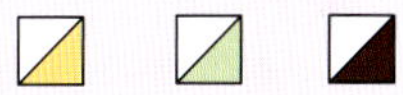

Unit 1 Make 3 **Unit 2** Make 2 **Unit 3** Make 1

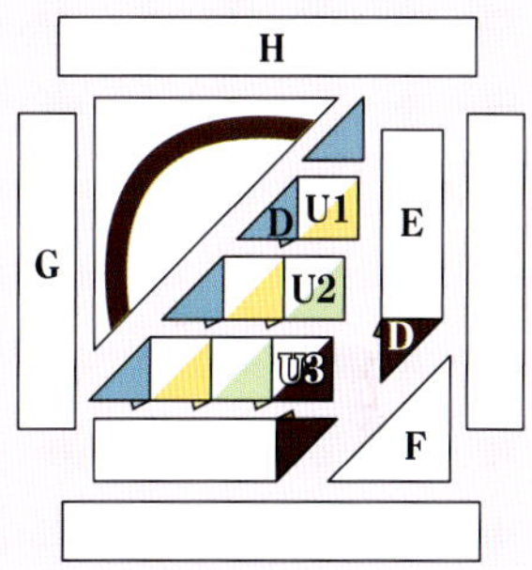

Block Assembly

Applique Placement

Fold A in half; lightly crease the fold. Prepare patches B and I–M for fusible appliqué. Use the crease and appliqué placement diagram as guides to arrange the handle (B) on A. Fuse in place. With matching thread, zigzag around the handle.

Refer to "Triangle-Squares" in the Techniques file on the PDF. Pair yellow C's with white C's to make 4 unit 1's (use 3). Pair the green C with a white C to make 2 unit 2's. Make 2 unit 3's (use 1) with a white C and brown C.

Sew the units and patches together as shown to make the block. Arrange the flower patches and fuse in place. Zigzag around the patches with matching thread to complete the block.

block no. 537

Spring

by Deonn Stott • Quiltscapes
quiltscapesquilting.com

Fabric: Basics from Riley Blake Designs, rileyblakedesigns.com.

Deonn used the AccuQuilt GO! Fabric Cutter to make her block.

The 3-dimensional flowers, leaves, sheep's ears and top of the head are made by fusing 2 layers of fabric together.

See page 392 in the PDF for pattern

Light Blue Tone-on-Tone
1 rectangle (A) 10"x 12½"
Green Stripe
1 rectangle (B) 3"x 12½"
Assorted Prints and Tone-on-Tones for flowers
from 7
2 squares 1¾"x 1¾" (C)
from 7
2 squares 1¼"x 1¼" (D)
Green Tone-on-Tone
12 squares 1"x 1½" for leaves (E)
White Dot
4 squares 1¼"x 1¼" for sheep's head
1 *each* patterns D and G
Black Solid
4 squares 1"x 1½" for ears (E)
3 pattern F
Gray Solid
1 pattern H
Fusible web
Template plastic

Use the assorted 1¾" squares for the flowers and the 1¼" squares for the flower centers. With wrong sides together, fuse matching squares together. Use the template plastic to trace the flower shapes on the fused patches; cut out the shapes. In the same way, make the leaves with green squares, the sheep's head with white squares and ears with black squares. Sew A and B together as shown. Fold the block in half both ways and lightly crease the folds. Prepare the sheep (white D and G, black F's and gray H) for fusible appliqué. Using the creases and appliqué placement diagram as guides, arrange and fuse the patches in alphabetical order.

Applique Placement

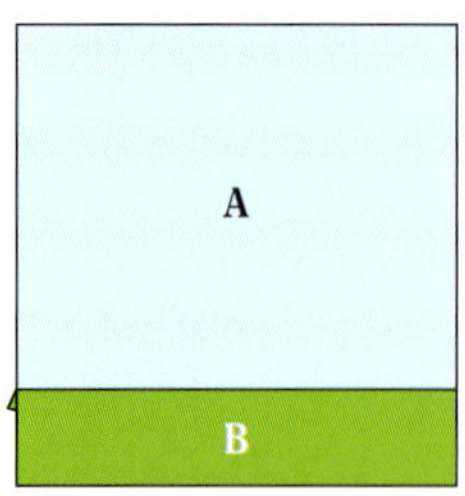

Block Piecing

Use matching thread and a machine blanket stitch to appliqué the fused patches. Satin stitch the flower stems. Use a straight stitch to add the sheep's face and path. Layer the dimensional leaves, head, ears and flowers on the block. Attach the leaves and ears by sewing a straight stitch down the center of the patches. Use the double crossstitch to tack on the head and flowers to complete the block.

block no. 538

Persuasion

by Jennifer Schifano Thomas • Curlicue Creations
curlicuecreations.com

Fabric: Table for Two designed by Sandy Gervais for Moda Fabrics, unitednotions.com.

See page 422 in the PDF for pattern

Black Print and Cream Solid
from *each*
2 squares (A) 6½"x 6½"
Lime Green Tone-on-Tone
1 *each* patterns B, D and E
Red Tone-on-Tone
1 pattern C
Fusible web

Sew the A's together as shown. Prepare patches B–E for fusible appliqué. Using the seam lines and appliqué placement diagram as guides, arrange and fuse the patches in alphabetical order.

Zigzag around the patches with matching thread to complete the block.

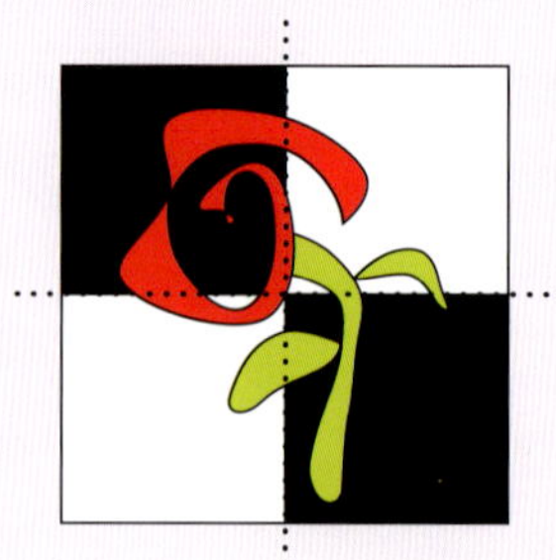

Applique Placement

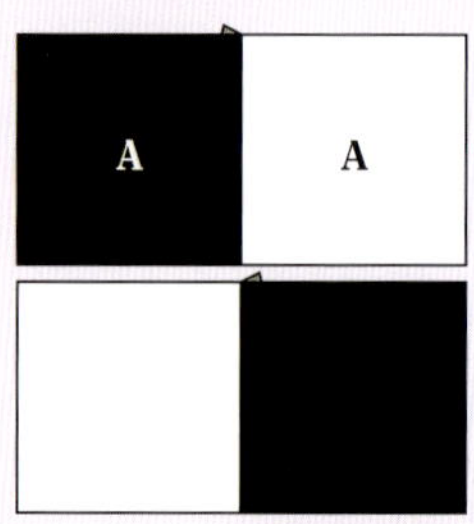

Block Piecing

block no. 539

Carnaby

by Stephanie Carter • Lily Ashbury
lilyashbury.com

Fabric: High Street designed by Lily Ashbury for Moda Fabrics, unitednotions.com.

See page 381 on the PDF for pattern

Orange Print and Cream Solid
from *each*
4 squares (A) 2⅞″ x 2⅞″
Pink Tone-on-Tone
2 squares (A) 2⅞″ x 2⅞″
Yellow Print
2 squares (A) 2⅞″ x 2⅞″
4 squares (B) 2½″ x 2½″
Gray Print #1
4 squares (B) 2½″ x 2½″
Gray Print #2
4 *each* templates C and Cr
Orange Tone-on-Tone
4 template D

Unit 1
Make 8

Unit 2
Make 4

Pair the orange print A's with the cream A's to make 8 Triangle-Square unit 1's. Pair the yellow A's with the pink A's to make 4 unit 2's.

Sew the units and patches together as shown to complete the block.

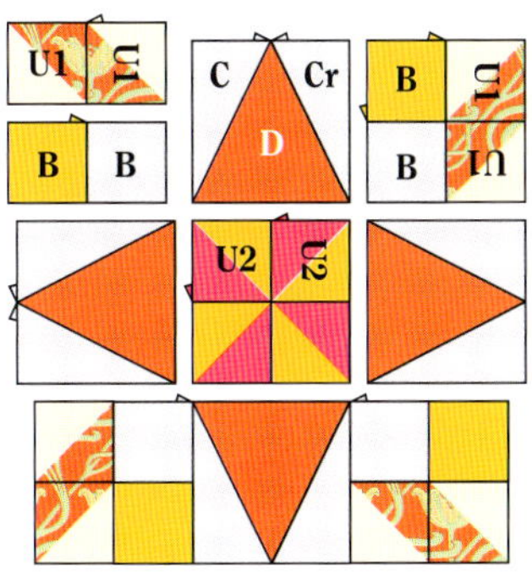

Block Assembly

block no. 540

Midnight Sky

by Keiko Clark • K Cotton Studio
kcottonstudio.com

Fabric: Chambray Rose designed by Rachel Ashwell for Treasures by Shabby Chic shabbychic.com.

Blue Tone-on-Tone
1 strip 1½″ x 40″
6 rectangles (A) 2½″ x 4½″
6 squares (B) 2½″ x 2½″
1 square (C) 2⅞″ x 2⅞″
2 squares (D) 4½″ x 4½″
White Print
1 strip 1½″ x 40″
12 squares (B) 2½″ x 2½″
1 square (C) 2⅞″ x 2⅞″

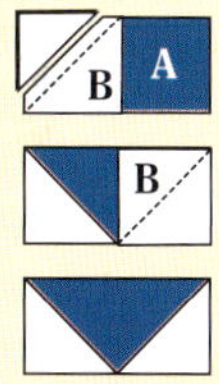

Unit 1
Stitch & Flip
Make 6

Unit 3
Make 2

Refer to "Stitch-and-Flip" in the Techniques file on the PDF. Use the blue A's and white B's to make 6 unit 1's as shown.

Sew the blue strip and white strip together to make a band. Cut the band in increments of 1½" to make 16 unit 2's.

Pair the blue C and white C to make 2 Triangle-Square unit 3's.

Sew the patches and units together as shown to complete the block.

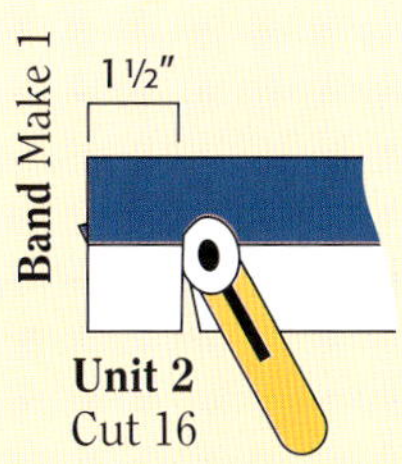

Unit 2
Cut 16

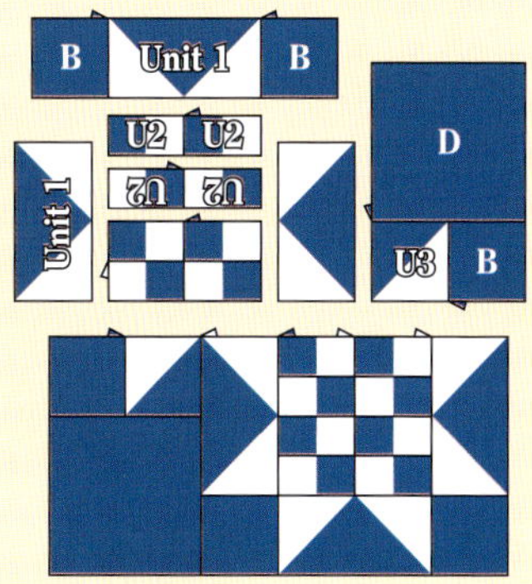

Block Assembly

block no. 541
Sweet Tweets

by Angie Hodapp

Fabric: Frippery designed by Kathy Hall for Andover Fabrics, andoverfabrics.com; Frosted Memories by Holly Taylor for Moda Fabrics, unitednotions.com.

See page 10 on the PDF for pattern

Gold Dot
4 template A
Green Print
4 template B
Beige Print
4 template A
Light Green Print
4 template B
Black Print
1 square (C) 4½" x 4½"

Using 1 gold dot A, 1 green B, 1 beige A and 1 light green B, assemble a section as shown. Make 4 sections.

Note the orientation of the sections. Sew a section to the bottom of the C with a partial seam as shown. Sew a section to the right, to the top and to the left of C. Complete the partial seam to finish the block.

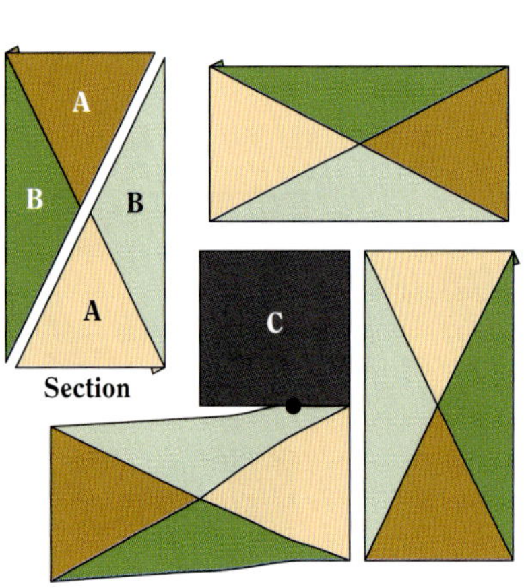

Block Piecing
● = Partial Seam

block no. 542
Posy Power

by Beth Hayes • Editor-in-Chief, *McCall's Quilting*
mccallsquilting.com

Fabric: FreeSpirit, freespiritfabric.com and Westminster Fibers, Inc., westminsterfibers.com.

Assorted Floral Prints
9 squares (A) 4½" x 4½"
Light Green Solid
18 squares (B) 1¾" x 1¾"
Dark Green Solid
18 squares (B) 1¾" x 1¾"

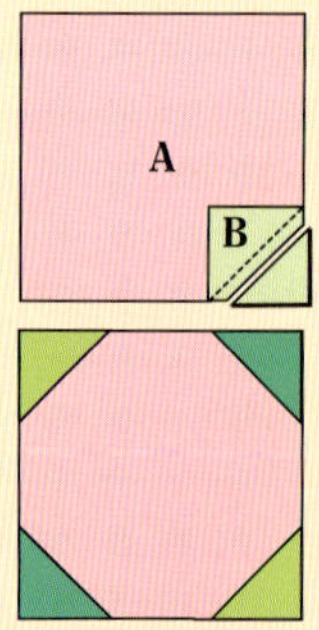

Unit
Stitch & Flip
Make 9

Notice that some of Beth's patches were cut to make the best use of the floral prints. Using the "Stitch & Flip" technique in the Techniques file on the PDF, add light green B's to the bottom right and top left corners of every A patch. Trim and press open. In the same way, add dark green B's to the remaining corners of each A patch to complete the units.

Placing the light and dark greens as shown in the assembly diagram, join the units to make the block.

Block Piecing

block no. 543
Wishing Star

by Bonnie Mitchell

Fabric: Sweet Rose by Skipping Stones Studio for Clothworks, clothworkstextiles.com.

⊠ = cut in half twice diagonally

Cream Print #1
- 8 rectangles (A) 2″ x 3½″
- 4 squares (H) 3½″ x 3½″
- 1 square 4¼″ x 4¼″ ⊠ (J)

Red Tone-on-Tone
- 8 squares (B) 2″ x 2″
- 2 squares 4¼″ x 4¼″ ⊠ (J)

Red Print
- 1 square (C) 4⅝″ x 4⅝″

Cream Print #2
- 2 rectangles (D) ⅞″ x 4⅝″
- 2 rectangles (E) ⅞″ x 5⅜″

Pink Print
- 2 rectangles (F) 1¼″ x 5⅞″
- 2 rectangles (G) 1¼″ x 6⅞″

Green Print
- 1 square 3⅜″ x 3⅜″ ⊠ (I)

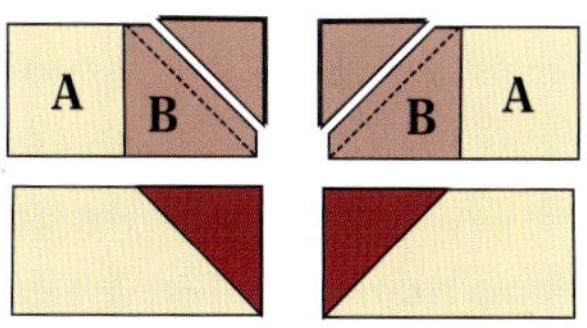

Unit 1 Stitch & Flip Make 4 — Unit 2 Stitch & Flip Make 4

Refer to "Stitch & Flip" in the Techniques file on the PDF. Use the cream A's and red B's to make 4 unit 1's and 4 unit 2's as shown.

Sew the units and patches together as shown to complete the block.

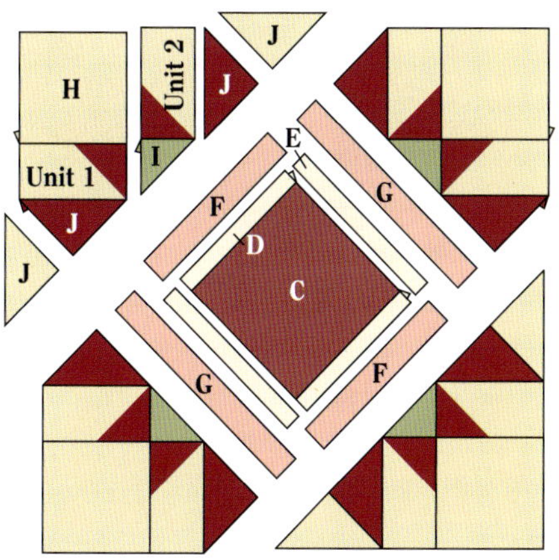

Block Piecing

block no. 544
Little Boxes

by Brenda Groelz • Director of Marketing and Education, Handi Quilter, Inc. • handiquilter.com

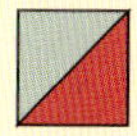

Unit 1
Make 2

Unit 2
Make 2

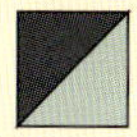

Unit 3
Make 2

Gray Batik
- 2 squares (A) 2⅞″ x 2⅞″
- 2 squares (D) 6½″ x 6½″

Red Batik
- 2 squares (A) 2⅞″ x 2⅞″
- 2 squares (B) 2½″ x 2½″

Black Batik
- 2 squares (A) 2⅞″ x 2⅞″
- 2 squares (B) 2½″ x 2½″

Pink Batik
- 2 squares (C) 4½″ x 4½″

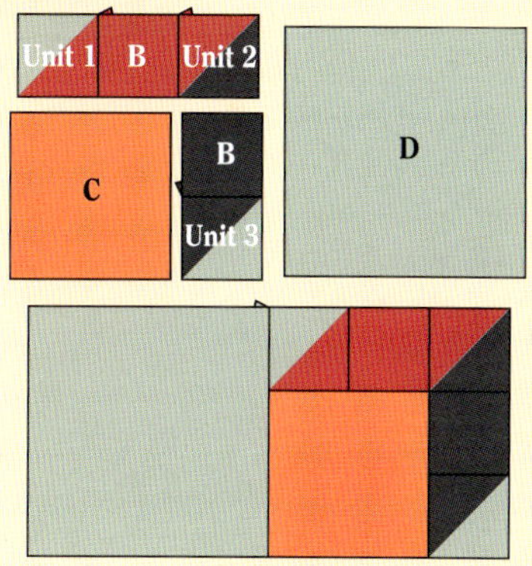

Block Piecing

Choosing a light, a medium and a dark fabric for the boxes creates the illusion of depth.

Refer to "Triangle-Squares" in the Techniques file on the PDF to make the unit 1's–3's as follows: Pair a gray A with a red A to make 2 unit 1's. Pair a red A and a black A to make 2 unit 2's. Pair a black A and a gray A to make 2 unit 3's.

Assemble the units and patches B–D as shown to complete the block.

See how fun these blocks are in a 3× 3 setting.

block no. 545

Ups & Downs

by Camille Roskelley • Thimble Blossoms
thimbleblossoms.com, camilleroskelley.com

Fabric: Simple Abundance by Bonnie Olaveson and Camille Roskelley for Moda Fabrics, unitednotions.com.

Natural Muslin
8 squares (A) 3⅞″ x 3⅞″
4 Red Prints
from *each*
1 square (A) 3⅞″ x 3⅞″
4 Blue Prints
from *each*
1 square (A) 3⅞″ x 3⅞″

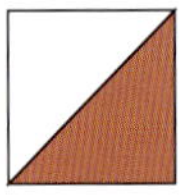

Unit
Make 16

Refer to "Triangle-Squares" in the Techniques file on the PDF and pair the muslin A's with the red and blue A's to make 16 units.

Noting unit placement, sew the units together to make the block.

Block Piecing

block no. 546

Criss Crossroads

by Carol Newby

Green and Blue Tone-on-Tones
from *each*
24 squares (A) 1½″ x 1½″
White Print
32 squares (A) 1½″ x 1½″
16 squares (B) 1⅞″ x 1⅞″
Light Orange and Dark Orange Tone-on-Tones
from *each*
16 squares (A) 1½″ x 1½″
8 squares (B) 1⅞″ x 1⅞″

Unit 1
Make 16

Unit 2
Make 16

Pair the white and dark orange B's to make 16 Triangle-Square unit 1's. Pair the white and light orange B's to make 16 unit 2's.

Join the patches and units as shown to make 4 sections. Sew the sections together to complete the block.

Block Piecing

pieced

block no. 547
Daughter's Delight

by Caroline Reardon and Maria Reardon Capp

White Print
32 squares (A) 2⅜" x 2⅜"
Purple, Green, Pink and Blue Prints
from *each*
8 squares (A) 2⅜" x 2⅜"

Unit
Make 64

Pair the white and colored A's to make 64 Triangle-Square units.

Join the units as shown to make 4 sections. Sew the sections together to complete the block.

Block Piecing

block no. 548
Roundabout

by Carolyn Beam • Creative Editor, *Quiltmaker*
quiltmaker.com

Fabric: Mama's Cottons 2 by Connecting Threads, connectingthreads.com.

Assorted Prints
72 squares (A) 1½" x 1½"
White Dot
4 rectangles (B) 1½" x 2½"
8 rectangles (C) 1½" x 4½"
2 squares (D) 2½" x 2½"
4 rectangles (E) 1½" x 6½"

Join the patches as shown to make 4 sections. Sew the sections together to complete the block.

Block Piecing

pieced

block no. 549

Ahoy

by Carolyn Goins • CPG Designs
cpgdesigns.com

Fabrics: Bali Hand-dyed Watercolors (style # 1895) from Hoffman California Fabrics, hoffmanfabrics.com; Island Batik, Inc., islandbatik.com.

⧄ = cut in half diagonally

Brown Batik
 2 squares (A) 2½″ x 2½″

Assorted Batiks
 8 rectangles (B) 2½″ x 4½″
 2 squares 6⅞″ x 6⅞″ ⧄ (C) (there will be 2 extra patches)

Light Gray Batik
 1 square 6⅞″ x 6⅞″ ⧄ (C)

Sew a B to the bottom edge of an A with a partial seam as shown. Sew another B to the right, to the top and to the left of A. Complete the partial seam. Repeat using the remaining A and B's.

Join an assorted batik C to each of the light gray C's.

Complete the block as shown.

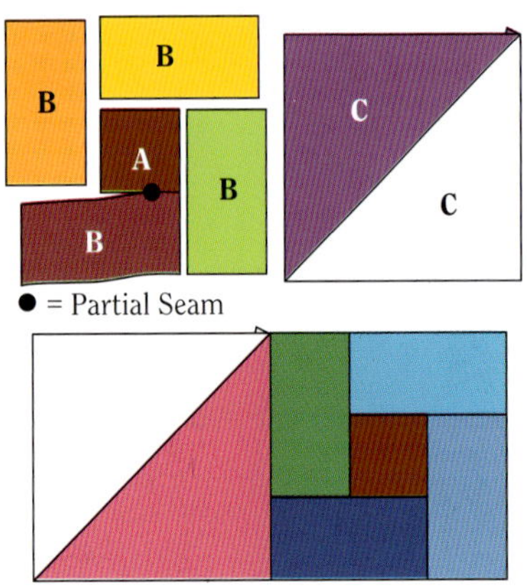

Block Piecing

block no. 550

Twist and Shout

by Chris Hoover • Whirligig Designs
whirligigdesigns.com

Fabric: Frosted Memories designed by Holly Taylor for Moda Fabrics, unitednotions.com.

⧄ = cut in half diagonally

Green Print and Red Print
from *each*
 1 square (A) 3⅜″ x 3⅜″
 1 square 3¾″ x 3¾″ ⧄ (C)
 (there will be 1 extra patch from each fabric)
 1 rectangle (D) 3⅜″ x 12″

Cream Print
 1 square (A) 3⅜″ x 3⅜″

Cream Tone-on-Tone
 2 pattern B
 2 pattern Br

Template for Twist and Shout block on page 49 of the Templates file on the PDF

Chris fussy cut the cream A patch to center the mistletoe motif. Sew the A's together as shown.

Using a partial seam, sew a Br to the green A as shown. In a counter-clockwise direction, join the red D, the Br and the green D to the A's. Complete the partial seam.

Join the B's and C's and complete the block as shown.

Trim the corners from the D's as shown.

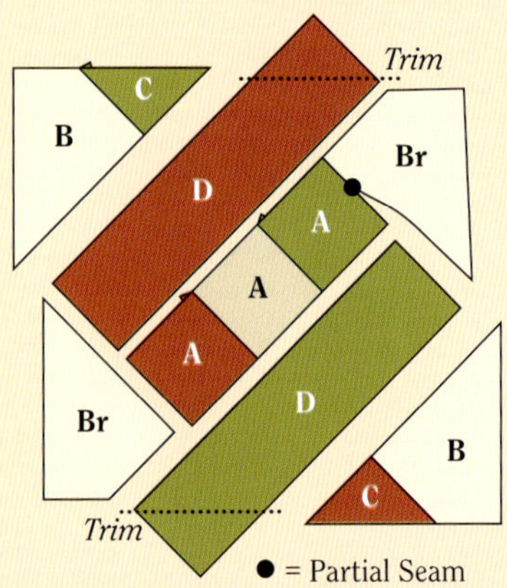

Block Piecing

block no. 551

Four Corners

by Celine Perkins • Perkins Dry Goods
perkinsdrygoods.com

Fabric: Frosted Memories by Holly Taylor for Moda Fabrics, unitednotions.com.

Assorted Green Prints and Tone-on-Tones
- 6 squares (A) 2½″ x 2½″
- 2 squares (B) 2⅞″ x 2⅞″

Assorted Beige Prints and Tone-on-Tones
- 10 squares (A) 2½″ x 2½″
- 6 squares (B) 2⅞″ x 2⅞″
- 4 rectangles (C) 2½″ x 4½″

Assorted Red Prints and Tone-on-Tones
- 8 squares (A) 2½″ x 2½″
- 4 squares (B) 2⅞″ x 2⅞″
- 4 rectangles (C) 2½″ x 4½″

Pair the green B's and 2 beige B's to make 4 Triangle-Square unit 1's. Pair the red B's and 4 beige B's to make 8 unit 2's.

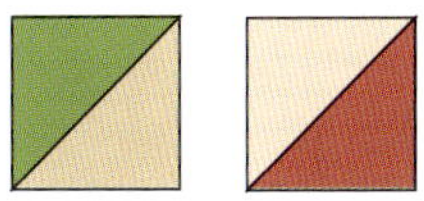

Unit 1 Make 4 **Unit 2** Make 8

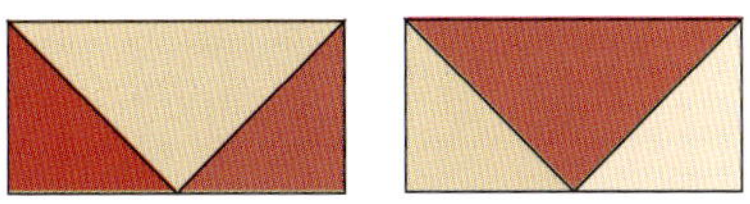

Unit 3 Make 4 **Unit 4** Make 4

Refer to "Stitch & Flip" in the Techniques file on the PDF. Use the red A's and the beige C's to make 4 unit 3's. Use the beige A's and the red C's to make 4 unit 4's.

Sew the patches and units together as shown to make the block.

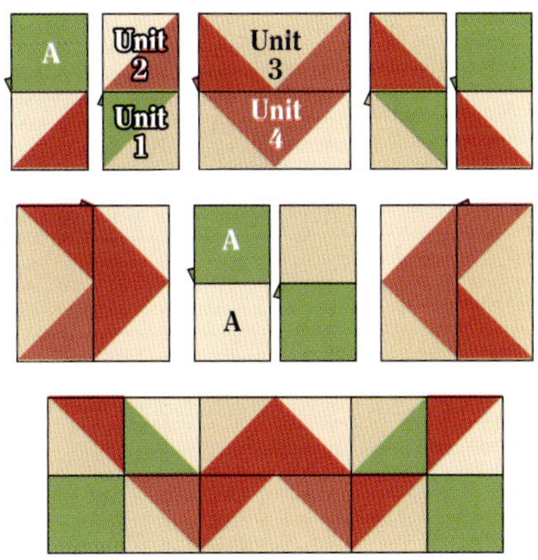

Block Piecing

block no. 552

Blazing Star

by Deanne Eisenman • Snuggles Quilts
snugglesquilts.com

Deanne is the author of Country Fresh Quilts for Martingale & Company, shopmartingale.com.

Black Print
- 12 squares (A) 2⅜″ x 2⅜″
- 4 squares (C) 2″ x 2″

Beige with Green Print
- 3 squares (B) 4¼″ x 4¼″

Beige with Red Print
- 2 squares (A) 2⅜″ x 2⅜″
- 2 squares (B) 4¼″ x 4¼″
- 4 squares (C) 2″ x 2″
- 4 rectangles (D) 2″ x 3½″

Green Print
- 6 squares (A) 2⅜″ x 2⅜″

Red Print
- 4 squares (A) 2⅜″ x 2⅜″
- 1 square (E) 3½″ x 3½″

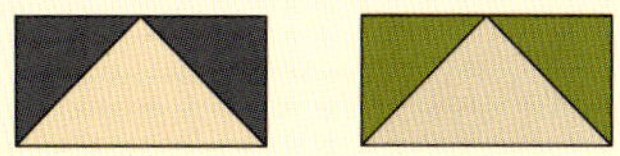

Unit 1 Make 12 **Unit 2** Make 4

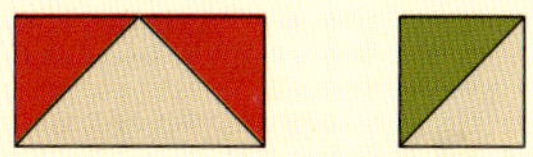

Unit 3 Make 4 **Unit 4** Make 4

Use the black A's and the beige with green B's to make 12 unit 1's. Use the green A's and the beige with red B's to make 4 unit 2's. Use the red A's and beige with red B's to make 4 unit 3's.

Refer to "Triangle-Squares" in the Techniques file on the PDF and use the green A's and the beige with red A's to make 4 unit 4's.

Sew the patches and units together as shown to complete the block.

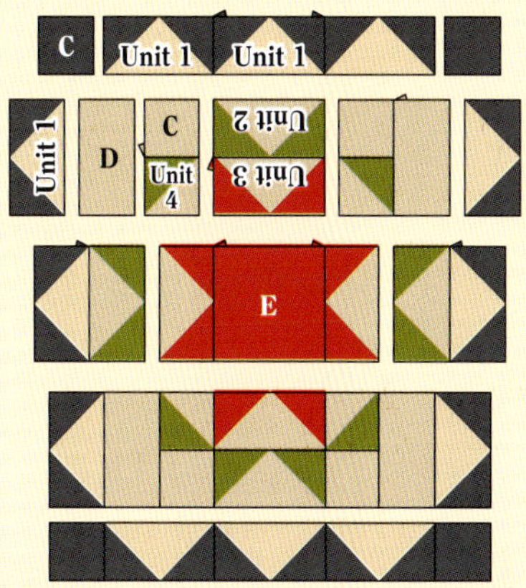

Block Piecing

block no. 553

Chameleon

by Deborah C. Vollbracht • Creative Folk Quilting
creativefolkquilting.blogspot.com

Fabric: Sketchbook designed by Yolanda V. Fundora for Blank Quilting, blankquilting.com.

See page 3 on the PDF for pattern

Red and Tan Stripe
2 *each* templates A and Ar
Brown Floral
4 *each* templates A and Ar
Black Print
2 *each* templates A and Ar

Join the patches as shown to make the block.

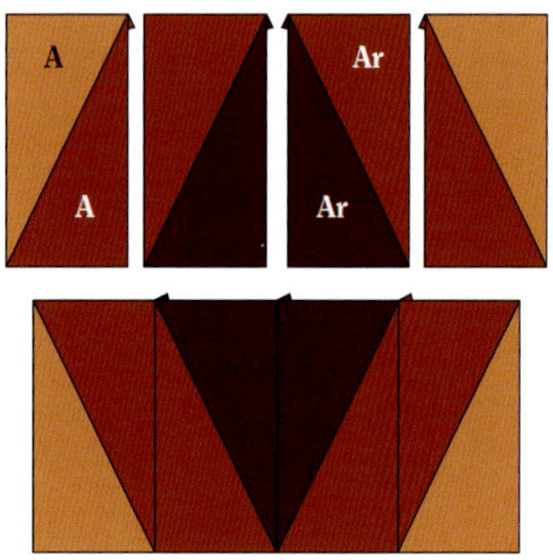

Block Piecing

block no. 554

Bar None

by Diane Harris • Interactive Editor, *Quiltmaker*
quiltmaker.com

2 White-on-Black Prints
from *each*
2 rectangles (A) 1½" x 4½"
2 rectangles (B) 1" x 4½"
2 rectangles (C) 1½" x 6½"
4 Assorted Blue Prints
from *each*
3 rectangles (A) 1½" x 4½"
2 Black-on-White Prints
from *each*
2 rectangles (A) 1½" x 4½"
2 rectangles (B) 1" x 4½"
2 rectangles (C) 1½" x 6½"

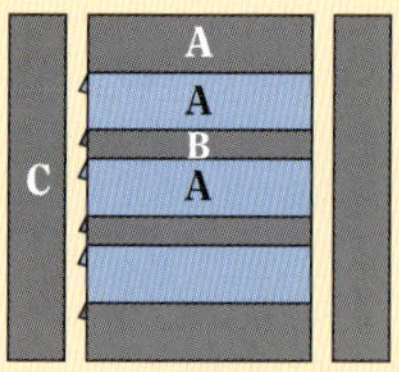

Unit
Make 4

Join the patches as shown to make a unit. Make 4 units. Join the units as shown to complete the block.

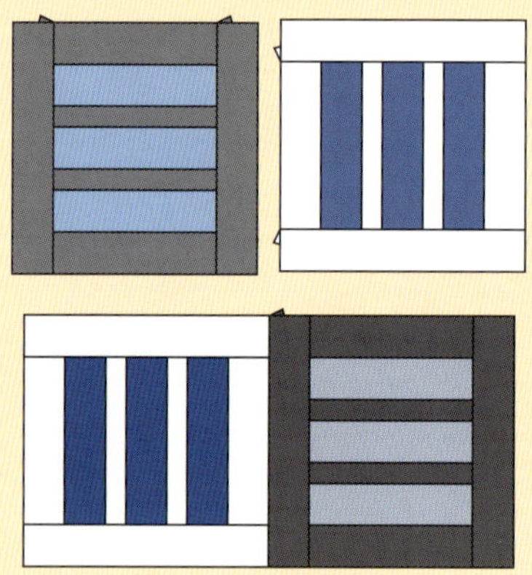

Block Piecing

block no. 555

Star Crossover

by Diane Nagle • Peddlecar Quilts
peddlecarquilts.blogspot.com

Fabric: Sophie from P&B Textiles, pbtex.com.

⧄ = cut in half diagonally

White Tone-on-Tone
- 6 squares (A) 2⅞″ x 2⅞″
- 4 squares (B) 1½″ x 1½″
- 4 rectangles (C) 1½″ x 2½″
- 4 squares (D) 1⅞″ x 1⅞″
- 4 squares 2⅞″ x 2⅞″ ⧄ (E)

Blue Print
- 4 squares (A) 2⅞″ x 2⅞″
- 4 squares 2⅞″ x 2⅞″ ⧄ (E)
- 1 square (G) 4½″ x 4½″

Pink Print
- 2 squares (A) 2⅞″ x 2⅞″
- 4 squares (D) 1⅞″ x 1⅞″
- 4 rectangles (F) 1⅞″ x 3¼″

Yellow Print
- 4 squares (B) 1½″ x 1½″

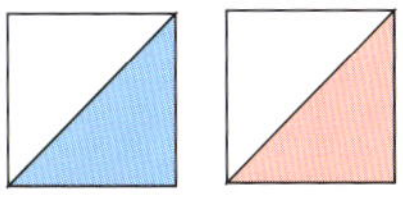

Unit 1 Make 8 **Unit 2** Make 4

Use the blue and the white A's to make 8 Triangle-Squae unit 1's. Use the pink and the white A's to make 4 unit 2's.

Sew the patches and units together as shown to complete the block.

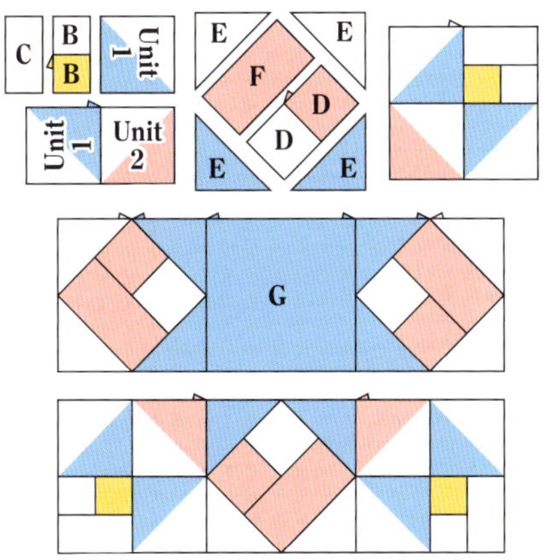

Block Piecing

block no. 556

Heartfelt

by Edyta Sitar • Laundry Basket Quilts
laundrybasketquilts.com

Fabric: Hoffman California Fabrics, hoffmanfabrics.com; Close to My Heart designed by Laundry Basket Quilts for Moda Fabrics, unitednotions.com.

Edyta is the author of Hop To It! for Landauer Publishing, landauercorp.com.

⧄ = cut in half diagonally
⊠ = cut in half twice diagonally

Tan Batik
- 1 square (A) 5¼″ x 5¼″
- 6 squares 2⅞″ x 2⅞″ ⧄ (D)

Green Batik
- 4 squares (B) 2⅞″ x 2⅞″
- 1 square 5¼″ x 5¼″ ⊠ (C)

Medium Purple Batik
- 1 square (E) 3⅞″ x 3⅜″

Purple Multiprint Batik
- 4 rectangles (F) 3⅞″ x 6⅛″

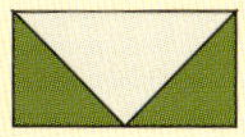

Flying Geese
Make 4

Use the tan A and green B's to make 4 Flying Geese.

Sew the patches and Flying Geese together as shown to complete the block.

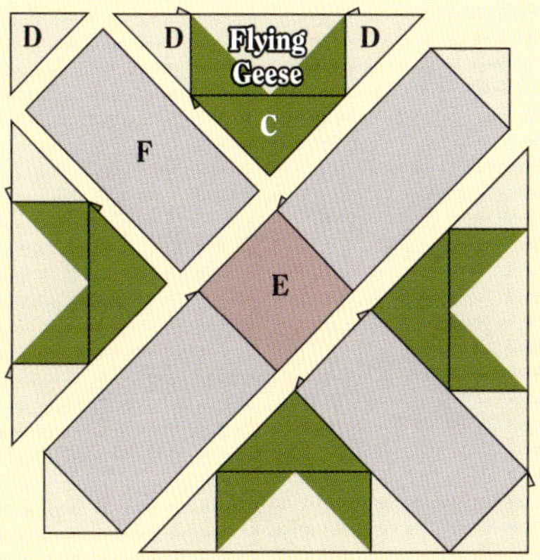

Block Piecing

block no. 557
Navajo Nights

by Eileen Fowler • Associate Editor, *Quiltmaker*
quiltmaker.com

Fabric: Tonga Batiks Ice for Timeless Treasures, ttfabrics.com.

Dark Blue Batik
- 4 rectangles (A) 2½" x 6½"
- 4 rectangles (B) 2½" x 4½"
- 4 squares (E) 2½" x 2½"

Medium Purple Batik #1
- 2 rectangles (B) 2½" x 4½"

Medium Purple Batik #2
- 2 rectangles (C) 2½" x 8½"

Gray Batik
- 2 rectangles (D) 2½" x 12½"

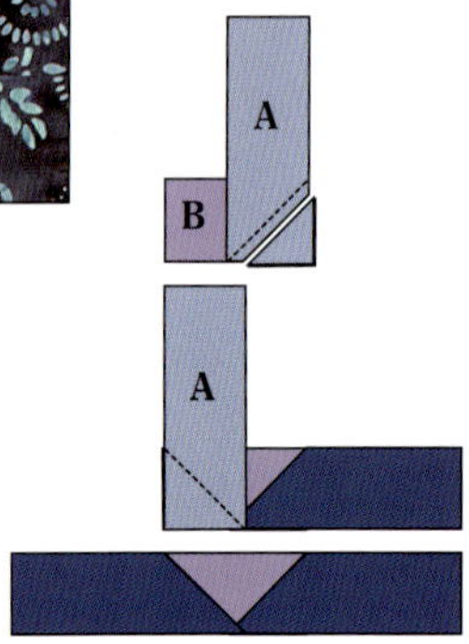

Unit 1
Stitch & Flip
Make 2

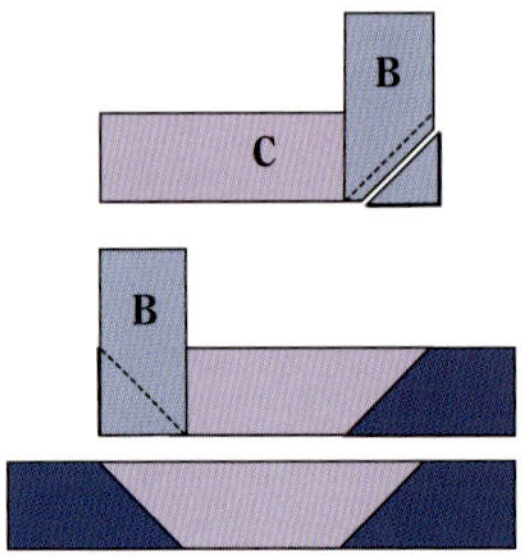

Unit 2
Stitch & Flip
Make 2

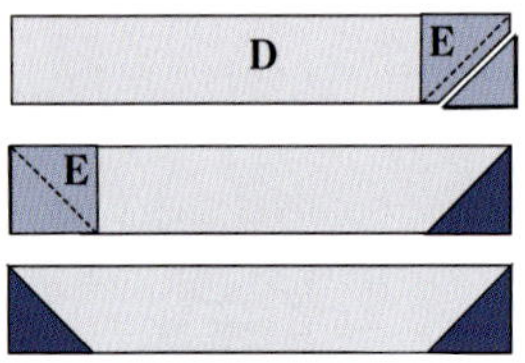

Unit 3
Stitch & Flip
Make 2

Refer to "Stitch & Flip" in the Techniques file on the PDF and the diagrams to make the unit 1's–3's as follows: Use the dark blue A's and the medium purple #1 B's to make 2 unit 1's. Use the dark blue B's and the medium purple #2 C's to make 2 unit 2's. Use the dark blue E's and the gray D's to make 2 unit 3's.

Join the units as shown to complete the block. ■

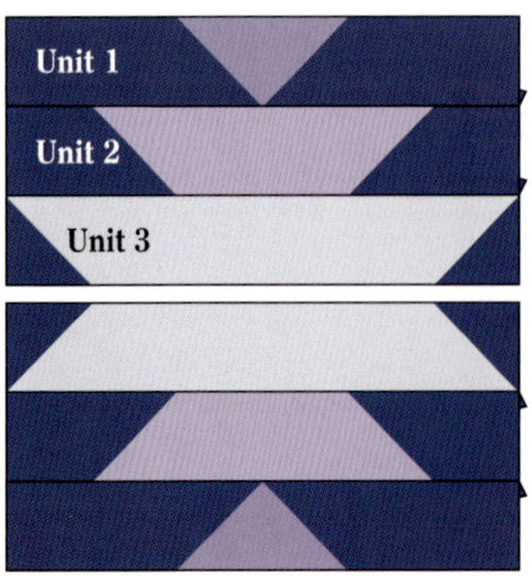

Block Piecing

block no. 558
Merry Go-Round

by Eleanor Burns • Quilt in a Day
quiltinaday.com

Eleanor Burns is the author of the well-known **Quilt in a Day** series of books and patterns. She has contributed significantly to the quilting community for more than 30 years in a variety of ways. For details, visit quiltinaday.com.

◩ = cut in half diagonally
⊠ = cut in half twice diagonally

White Tone-on-Tone
- 1 square 7¼" x 7¼" ⊠ (A)
- 4 rectangles 2" x 6⅞" (see diagram below to cut C's)

Yellow Print
- 1 square 7¼" x 7¼" ⊠ (A)

Green Print
- 2 squares 5⅜" x 5⅜" ◩ (B)

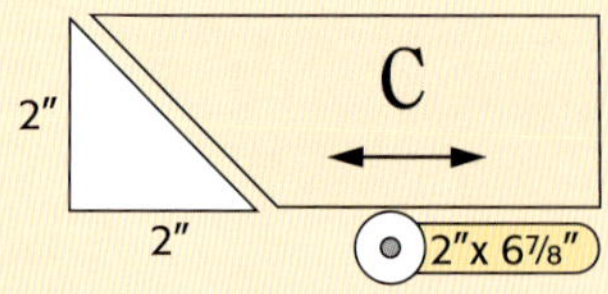

Join the patches as shown to make the block. ■

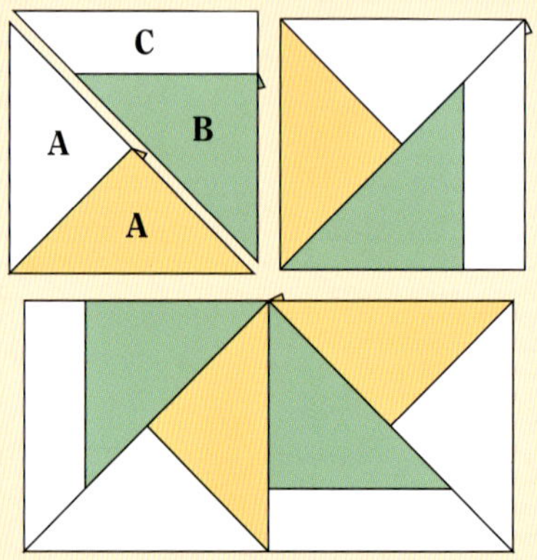

Block Piecing

block no. 559

Follow Me Home

by Elisa Wilson • Elisa's Backporch Design
backporchdesign.com

Fabric: Eva designed by Basic Gray for Moda Fabrics, unitednotions.com.

Cream Print
- 18 squares (A) 2⅜″ x 2⅜″
- 16 squares (B) 2″ x 2″

Dark Purple Print
- 12 squares (A) 2⅜″ x 2⅜″

Green Solid
- 6 squares (A) 2⅜″ x 2⅜″

Pink Print
- 12 squares (B) 2″ x 2″

Use the cream and the purple A's to make 24 Triangle-Square unit 1's. Use the cream and the green A's to make 12 unit 2's.

Sew the patches and units together as shown to complete the block.

Unit 1 Make 24 **Unit 2** Make 12

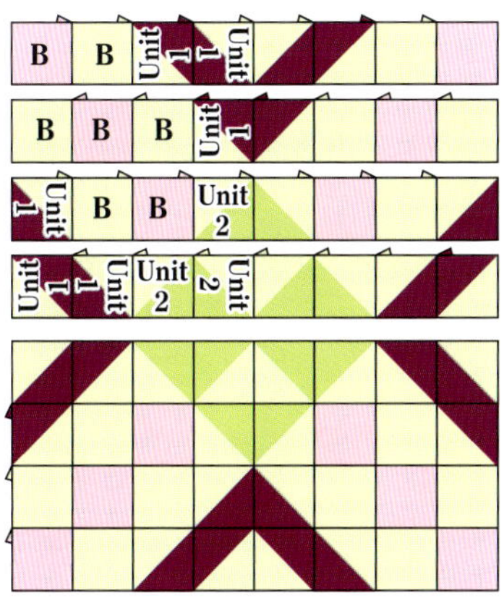

Block Piecing

block no. 560

Chain Link

by Emily Herrick • Crazy Old Ladies
crazyoldladiesquilts.blogspot.com.

Fabric: Authentic designed by Sweetwater for Moda Fabrics, unitednotions.com.

Black Print
- 4 rectangles (A) 1½″ x 3½″
- 4 rectangles (B) 2½″ x 5½″
- 1 square (C) 2½″ x 2½″

Green Print
- 4 rectangles (A) 1½″ x 3½″
- 4 rectangles (B) 2½″ x 5½″

Cream Print
- 4 rectangles (B) 2½″ x 5½″

Refer to "Stitch & Flip" in the Techniques file on the PDF and use the black and the green A's to make the unit 1's and 2's.

Sew the patches and units together as shown to complete the block.

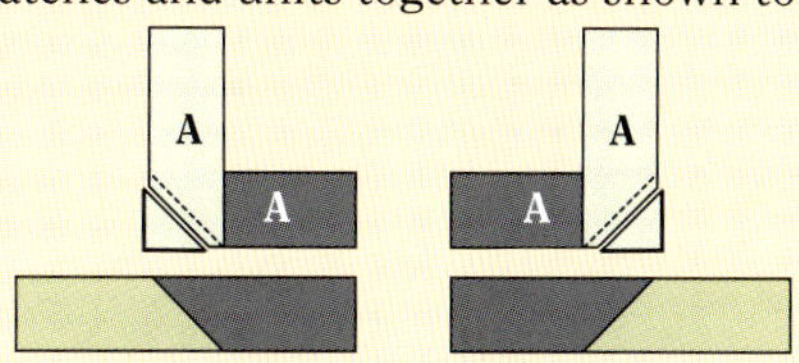

Unit 1 Stitch & Flip Make 2 **Unit 2** Stitch & Flip Make 2

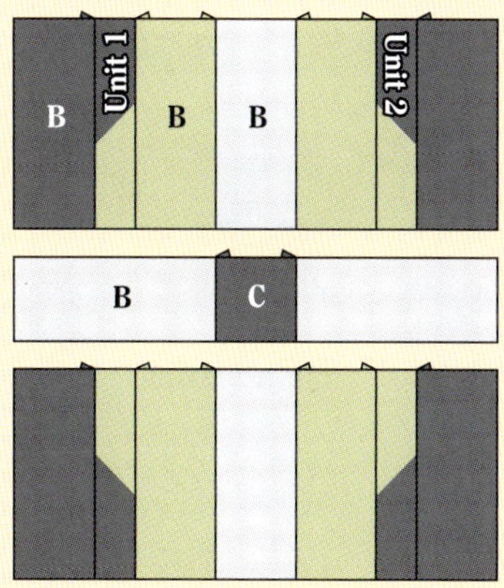

Block Piecing

block no. 561

A Country Mile

by Evonne M. Cook • Clothesline Quilts
clotheslinequilts.com

Fabric: Fairfax County by Jo Morton for Andover Fabrics, andoverfabrics.com.

Cream Print
- 4 squares (A) 2″ x 2″
- 4 rectangles (B) 2″ x 3½″
- 8 rectangles (C) 1½″ x 5″

Gold Print
- 12 squares (A) 2″ x 2″

Tan Print
- 8 squares (A) 2″ x 2″

Red Print
- 4 squares (A) 2″ x 2″

Black Print
- 4 rectangles (C) 1½″ x 5″

Dark Gray Print
- 9 squares (D) 1½″ x 1½″

Join the patches as shown to make the block.

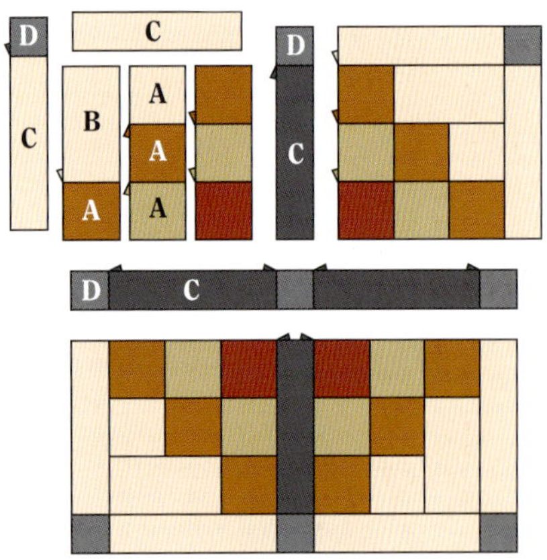

Block Piecing

block no. 562

Northern Flair

by Gudrun Erla • GE Designs
gequiltdesigns.com, gudrun.typepad.com

Fabric: Glow designed by Gudrun Erla for Red Rooster Fabrics, redroosterfabrics.com.

Gudrun is the author of Fast and Furious for GE Designs, gequiltdesigns.com.

◪ = cut in half diagonally
⊠ = cut in half twice diagonally

Rust Tone-on-Tone
- 8 rectangles (A) 1½″ x 2½″
- 4 rectangles (C) 1½″ x 3½″

Cream Tone-on-Tone
- 8 rectangles (A) 1½″ x 2½″
- 32 squares (B) 1½″ x 1½″
- 4 squares 2⅞″ x 2⅞″ ◪ (D)

Green Print
- 4 rectangles (A) 1½″ x 2½″
- 8 rectangles (C) 1½″ x 3½″

Gold Print
- 8 squares (B) 1½″ x 1½″

Brown Print
- 1 square 7¼″ x 7¼″ ⊠ (E)

Teal Print
- 1 square (F) 2½″ x 2½″

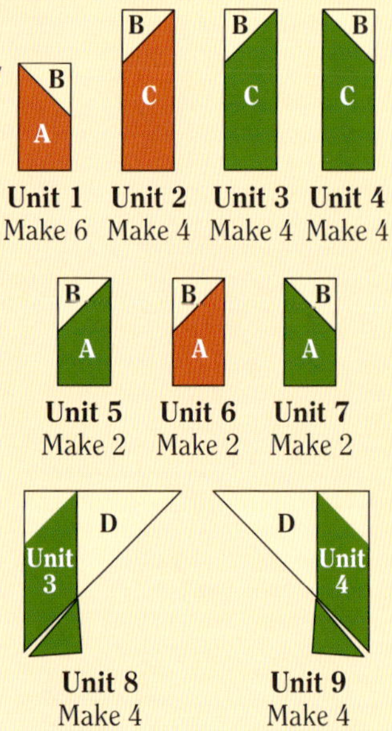

Refer to "Stitch & Flip" in the Techniques file on the PDF. Use the rust and the green A's and C's and the cream B's to make the unit 1's–7's as shown.

Join a unit 3 and cream D and trim as shown to make a unit 8. Make 4 unit 8's. Join a unit 4 and cream D and trim as shown to make a unit 9. Make 4 unit 9's.

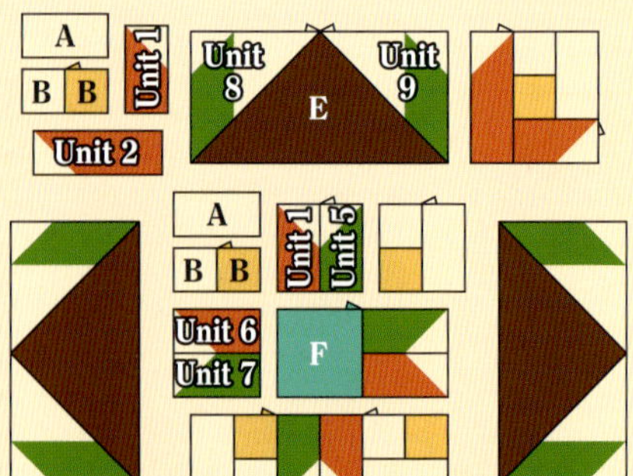

Join the patches and units as shown to complete the block.

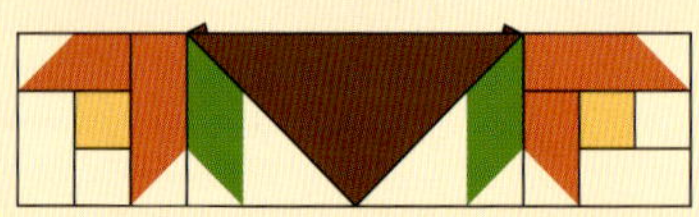

Block Piecing

block no. 563

Butterfly Cabin

by Jackie Robinson • Animas Quilts
animasquilts.com

Fabric: Poinsettia II designed by Jackie Robinson for Maywood Studio, maywoodstudio.com.

Jackie Robinson self-publishes books and patterns through her company, Animas Quilts, and teaches DVD workshops with Nine Patch Media, ninepatchmedia.com.

⍁ = cut in half diagonally

Cream Print
- 1 square 3⅞" x 3⅞" ⍁ (A)
- 4 squares (B) 2" x 2"

Red Print
- 1 square 3⅞" x 3⅞" ⍁ (A)

Gold Print
- 8 squares (B) 2" x 2"

Medium Green Print #1 and Dark Green Print #1
from *each*
- 1 rectangle (C) 2" x 6½"
- 1 rectangles (D) 2" x 8"

Medium Green Print #2 and Dark Green Print #2
from *each*
- 1 rectangle (E) 2" x 9½"
- 1 rectangle (F) 2" x 11"

Join the patches as shown to make the block.

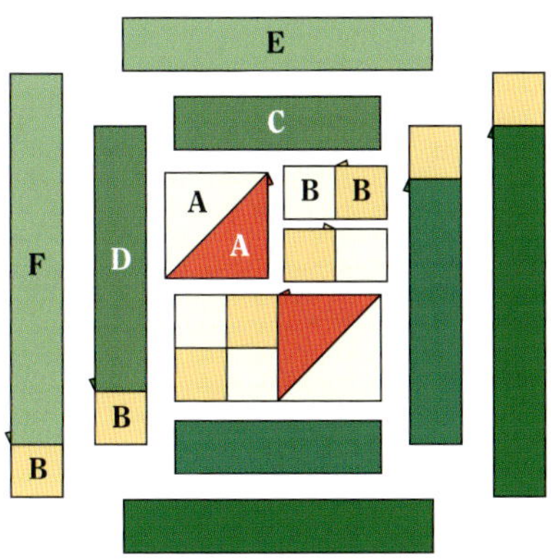

Block Piecing

block no. 564

Summer Star

by Joanna Figueroa • Fig Tree & Co.
figtreeandco.com

Fabric: Mill House Inn designed by Joanna Figueroa for Moda Fabrics, unitednotions.com.

Red Print
- 4 squares (A) 2⅜" x 2⅜"
- 9 squares (B) 2" x 2"

Cream Dot Print
- 8 squares (A) 2⅜" x 2⅜"
- 20 squares (B) 2" x 2"

Green Print
- 4 squares (A) 2⅜" x 2⅜"
- 4 squares (B) 2" x 2"

Gold Dot Print
- 2 rectangles (C) 1¼" x 11"
- 2 rectangles (D) 1¼" x 12½"

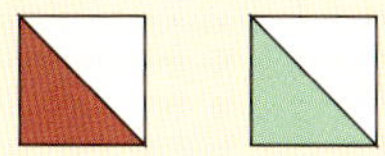

Unit 1
Make 8

Unit 2
Make 8

Pair the red A's with the cream dot A's to make 8 Triangle-Square unit 1's. Pair the green A's with the cream dot A's to make 8 unit 2's.

Sew the units and B's together as shown to make the block center.

Matching centers and ends, sew the C's to the block sides. Add the D's to the top and bottom in the same way to complete the block.

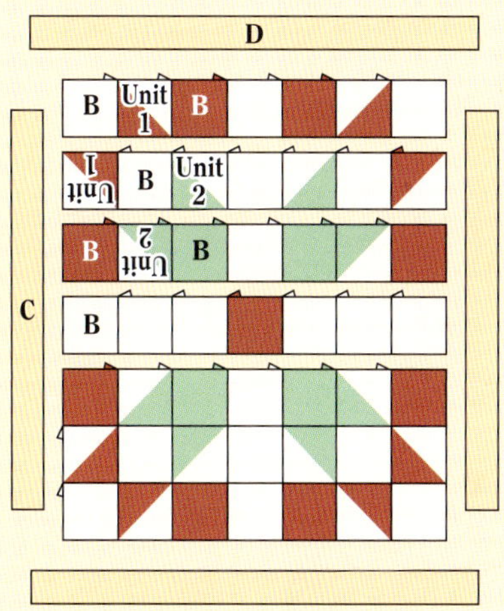

Block Piecing

pieced

block no. 565
Pinwheel Splash

by Joli Sayasane

Fabric: Danielle from P&B Textiles, pbtex.com.

⧄ = cut in half diagonally

Brown Print and Medium Blue Tone-on-Tone
from *each*
- 4 rectangles $1\frac{7}{8}$" x $6\frac{7}{8}$" (see diagram below to cut A's)

Rust Tone-on-Tone and Light Blue Tone-on-Tone
from *each*
- 4 squares $2\frac{7}{8}$" x $2\frac{7}{8}$" ⧄ (B)

Blue Print
- 4 squares $4\frac{7}{8}$" x $4\frac{7}{8}$" ⧄ (C)

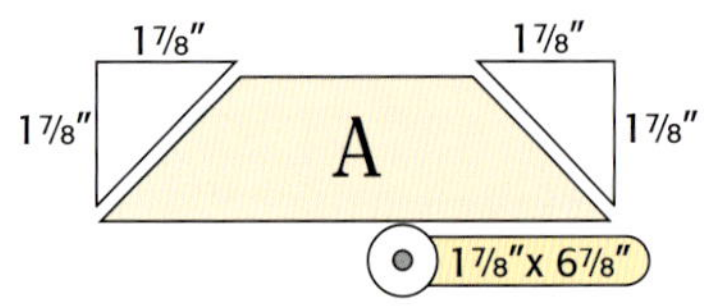

Join the patches as shown to make the block.

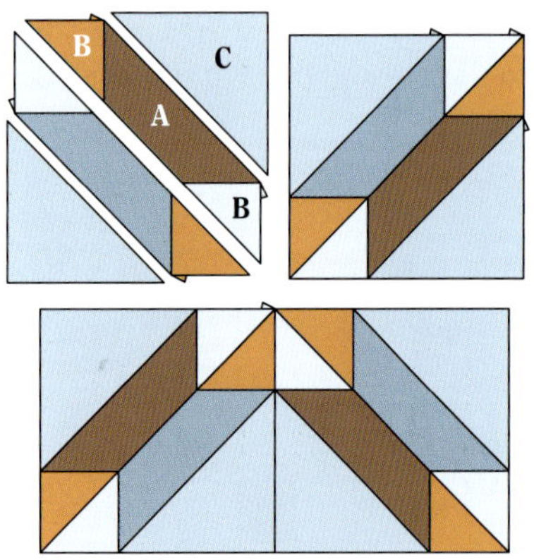

Block Piecing

block no. 566
Rolling River

by Joyce Robinson
joycerobinson.com

Purple Batik
- 6 strips 1" x 13" for band
- 1 rectangle (A) $3\frac{1}{2}$" x $12\frac{1}{2}$"

Light Gold Tone-on-Tone Batik
- 3 strips 2" x 13" for band

Gold Batik
- 3 strips 2" x 13" for band

Sew the purple, light gold and gold strips together as shown to make the band. Cut the band at 2" intervals to make 6 units.

Sew the units and A together as shown to complete the block.

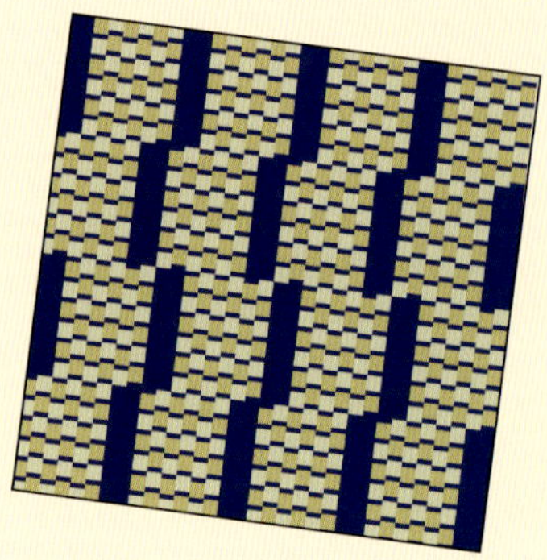

An interesting effect is created when 16 blocks are sewn together as shown.

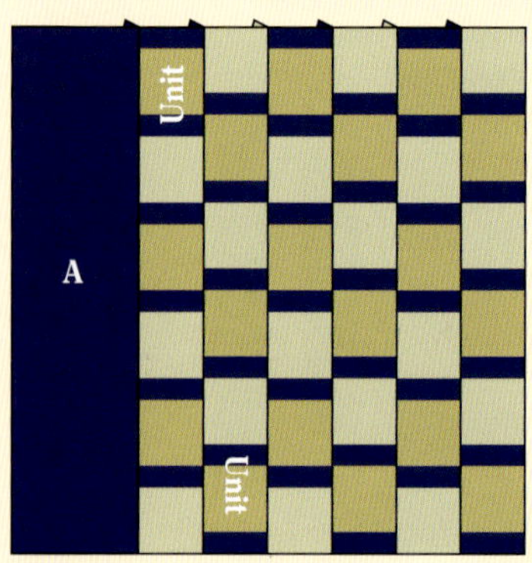

Block Piecing

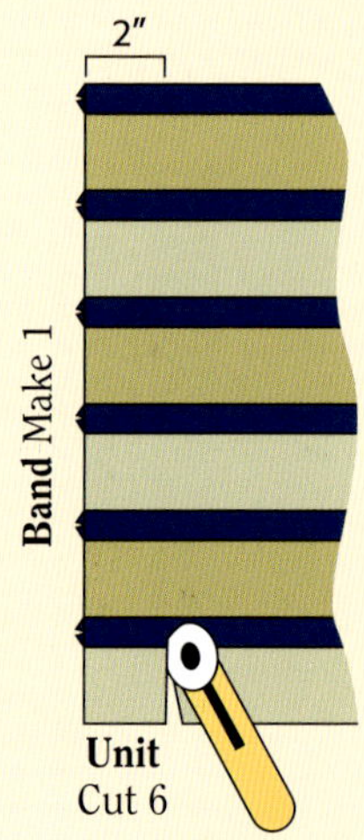

block no. 567

Jungle Boogie

by June Dudley • Editor-in-Chief, *Quiltmaker*
quiltmaker.com

Fabric: Brazilia and Bali Handpaints from Hoffman California Fabrics, hoffmanfabrics.com.

Medium Blue Print
1 square (A) 4⅞" x 4⅞"
Dark Blue Print
1 square (A) 4⅞" x 4⅞"
Light Green Print
1 square (B) 6⅞" x 6⅞"
Medium Green Print
1 square (B) 6⅞" x 6⅞"
Rust Stripe
1 rectangle (C) 2½" x 4½"
1 rectangle (E) 2½" x 6½"
1 rectangle (F) 2½" x 12½"
Multiprint
1 rectangle (D) 4½" x 6½"
Blue Batik
1 rectangle (D) 4½" x 6½"

Unit 1
Make 1

Unit 2
Make 1

Use the medium blue A and the dark blue A to make a Triangle-Square unit 1. (There will be 1 extra unit 1.) Use the light green B and the medium green B to make a unit 2. (There will be 1 extra unit 2.)

Sew the units and patches together as shown to complete the block.

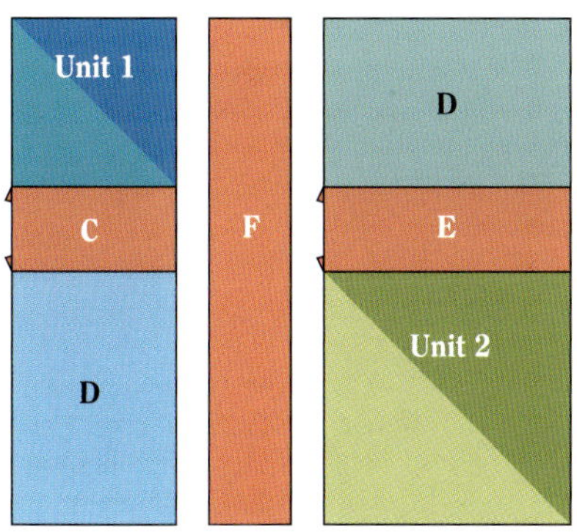

Block Piecing

block no. 568

Square and Diamond

by Karen Combs • Karen Combs Studio
karencombs.com

Fabric: Belle Fleur designed by Karen Combs for Avlyn, Inc., avlyn.com.

Karen is the author of Celtic Pieced Illusions for American Quilter's Society, americanquilter.com.

◸ = cut in half diagonally
☒ = cut in half twice diagonally

Black and Lime Green Print
1 square (A) 5⅛" x 5⅛"
Black Tone-on-Tone
2 squares 4⅛" x 4⅛" ◸ (B)
Black-on-White Print
4 rectangles (C) 1½" x 7"
Lime Green Tone-on-Tone
4 squares (D) 1½" x 1½"
4 squares (E) 2¼" x 2¼"
White-on-Black Print
12 squares (E) 2¼" x 2¼" (see note below)
White Print
4 squares 3⅝" x 3⅝" ☒ (F)
2 squares 2⅛" x 2⅛" ◸ (G)

Karen fussy cut the white-on-black E patches to center the flower motifs.

Join the patches as shown to complete the block.

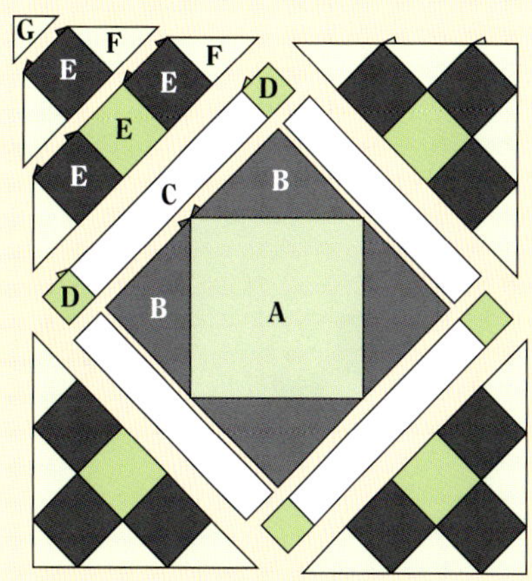

Block Piecing

block no. 569

Candlestick

by Karen Griska
selvageblog.blogspot.com

Fabric: Moda Fabrics, unitednotions.com.

Karen is the author of Quilts from the Selvage Edge for American Quilter's Society, americanquilter.com.

4 Assorted Cream Prints
from *1*
- 1 square (A) 3⅞″ x 3⅞″
- 4 squares (B) 2″ x 2″
- 2 squares (C) 3½″ x 3½″

from *1*
- 2 squares (A) 3⅞″ x 3⅞″

from *1*
- 4 squares (C) 3½″ x 3½″

from *1*
- 2 squares (C) 3½″ x 3½″

Dark Brown Print
- 1 square (A) 3⅞″ x 3⅞″
- 4 squares (B) 2″ x 2″

Medium Brown Print
- 2 squares (A) 3⅞″ x 3⅞″

Unit 1
Make 2

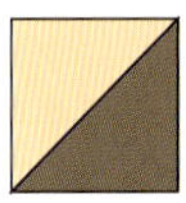

Unit 2
Make 4

Pair the first cream A with the dark brown A to make 2 Triangle-Square unit 1's. Pair the remaining cream A's with the medium brown A's to make 4 unit 2's.

Refer to the photographed block for placement of the cream C patches.

Sew the patches and units together as shown to complete the block.

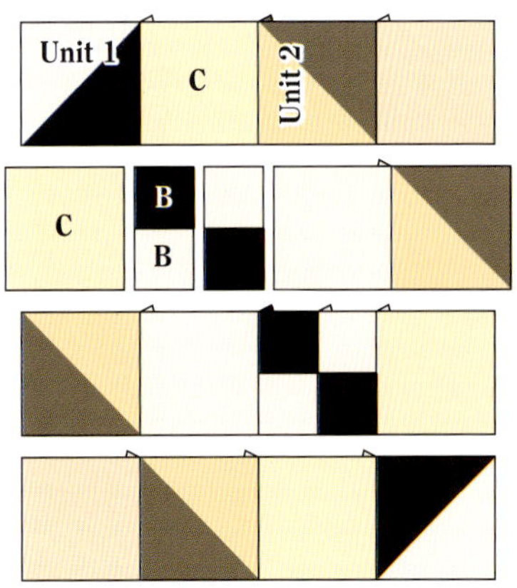

Block Piecing

block no. 570

Double Star

by Kim Brackett
magnoliabayquilts.blogspot.com

Fabric: Frosted Memories designed by Holly Taylor for Moda Fabrics, unitednotions.com.

Kim is the author of Scrap-Basket Surprises for Martingale & Company, shopmartingale.com.

Cream Print
- 4 rectangles (A) 2½″ x 6½″
- 8 squares (B) 2½″ x 2½″

Red Tone-on-Tone
- 6 squares (B) 2½″ x 2½″

Green Tone-on-Tone
- 4 rectangles (A) 2½″ x 6½″

Green Stripe
- 4 rectangles (C) 2½″ x 4½″

Light Green Print
- 2 squares (B) 2½″ x 2½″

Follow the diagrams and use the "Stitch & Flip" technique in the Techniques file on the PDF to make 4 of each of the units 1–3.

Sew the patches and units together as shown to complete the block.

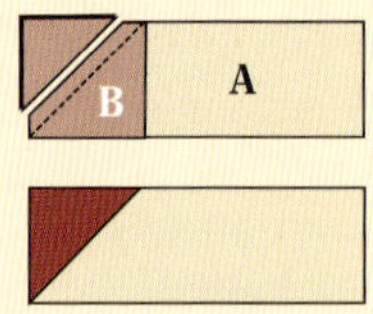

Unit 1
Stitch & Flip
Make 4

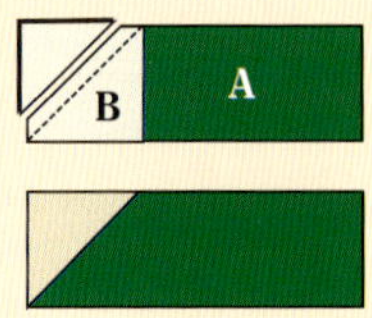

Unit 2
Stitch & Flip
Make 4

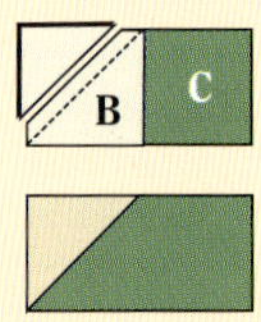

Unit 3
Stitch & Flip
Make 4

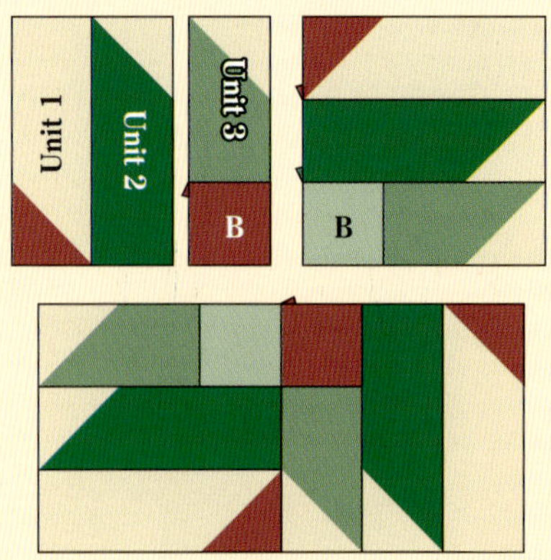

Block Piecing

pieced

block no. 571
Delicato

by Susan Knapp & Mary Jane Mattingly,
The Quilt Branch • quiltbranch.com

Fabric: Santorini designed by Lila Tueller for Moda Fabrics, unitednotions.com.

Susan and Mary Jane are the authors of Six Halves Make a Whole Lot More for The Quilt Branch, quiltbranch.com.

Green Tone-on-Tone
4 squares (A) 3⅞" x 3⅞"
Pink Print #1
8 squares (B) 2" x 2"
4 squares (D) 2¾" x 2¾"
Gold Tone-on-Tone
4 squares (A) 3⅞" x 3⅞"
4 squares (C) 3½" x 3½"
Pink Print #2
4 squares (C) 3½" x 3½"
Pink Stripe
4 squares (D) 2¾" x 2¾"

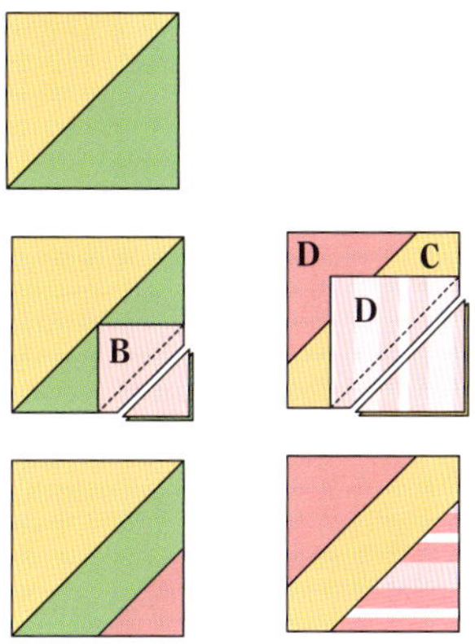

Unit 1
Stitch & Flip
Make 8

Unit 2
Stitch & Flip
Make 4

Pair the green A's with the gold A's to make 8 Triangle-Squares. To complete the unit 1's, use the "Stitch & Flip" technique in the Techniques file on the PDF; sew a pink B on the green corner of each Triangle-Square as shown. Make 8 unit 1's.

Refer to the diagram and use the stitch-and-flip technique to make the unit 2's. Sew a pink #1 D and a pink stripe D on opposite corners of each gold C as shown, keeping the stripe oriented the same way on each one. Make 4 unit 2's.

Noting the orientation of the units, join the units and patches as shown to complete the block.

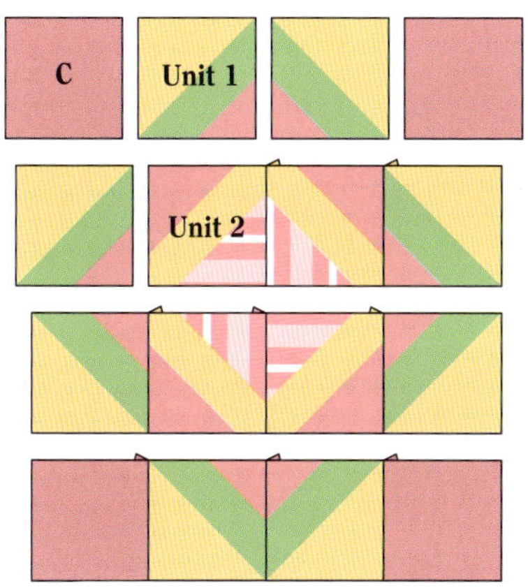

Block Piecing

block no. 572
Moss Rose

by Laura Roberts • Former Assistant Editor,
McCalls Quilting • mccallsquilting.com

10 Assorted Batiks
from *each*
1 strip 1¼" x 32" (see instructions below for fabric selection and to cut the A's)
Green Batik
4 rectangles (B) 2½" x 5½"
Red Batik
8 squares (C) 1½" x 1½"
Yellow Batik
1 square (D) 2½" x 2½"

Laura used batik strips starting with yellow and then a range of pinks from light to very dark. Make a plastic template 5½" × 5½". Sew the strips together as shown with yellow at one end and the darkest pink at the other end to make a band. Position the plastic template on the band and cut 4 A's as shown.

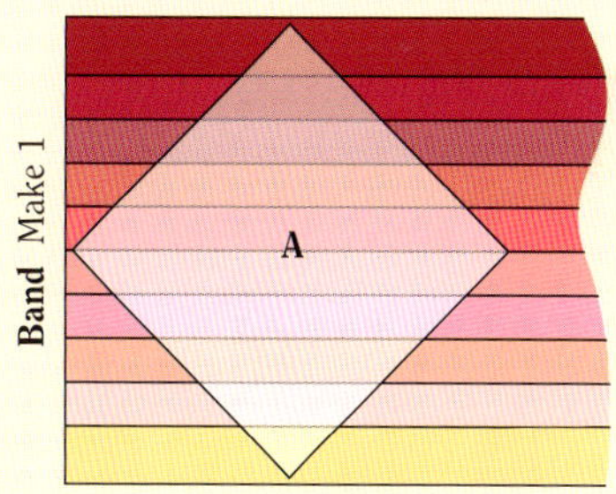

Unit
Make 4

Refer to "Stitch & Flip" in Techniques file on the PDF and use the green B's and red C's to make 4 units.

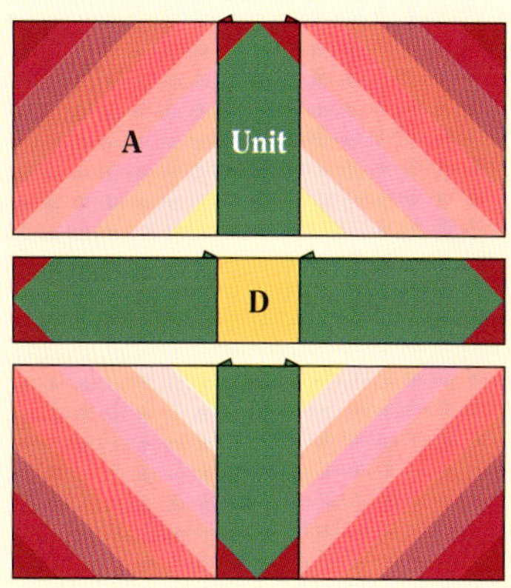

Block Piecing

Sew the units and patches together as shown to complete the block.

block no. 573

Texas Circle Around

by Lynn Roddy Brown
lynnroddybrown.com

Lynn Roddy Brown is the author of Simple Strategies for Scrap Quilts and Simple Strategies for Block-Swap Quilts for Martingale & Company, shopmartingale.com.

◪ = cut in half diagonally

Assorted Dark Prints

- 4 squares 4⅞" x 4⅞" ◪ (B)
  (you'll have 4 extras for another block)
- 8 rectangles (C) 1⅞" x 4½"

Assorted Light Prints

- 1 square (A) 4½" x 4½"
- 4 squares 4⅞" x 4⅞" ◪ (B)
  (you'll have 4 extras for another block)
- 4 rectangles (D) 1¾" x 4½"

Join the patches as shown to make the block.

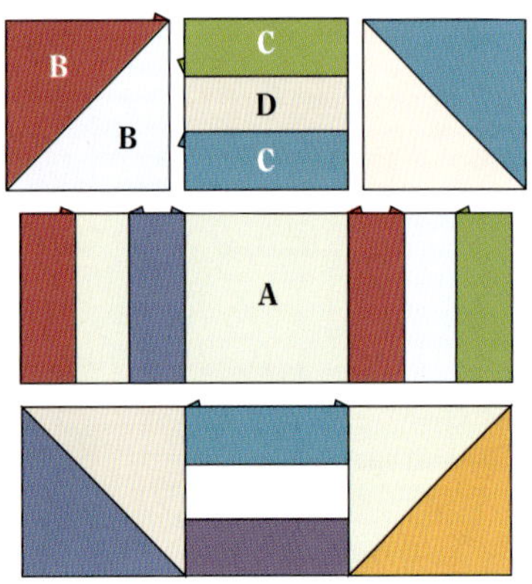

Block Piecing

block no. 574

Spring Blossom

by Peg Spradlin
handicraftsbypeg.com

Cream Dot

- 1 square (A) 2½" x 2½"
- 4 template C

Peach Tone-on-Tone

- 4 squares (B) 1½" x 1½"
- 4 *each* templates D and Dr

Blue Dot and Light Green Solid

from *each*

- 2 squares (E) 3⅜" x 3⅜"

Green Dot

- 4 squares (E) 3⅜" x 3⅜"

Light Blue Solid

- 4 *each* templates D and Dr
- 4 squares (E) 3⅜" x 3⅜"

Blue Tone-on-Tone

- 4 squares (F) 3" x 3"

Template for Spring Blossom block on page 50 of the Templates file on the PDF

Refer to "Stitch & Flip" in the Techniques file on the PDF and use the cream A and the peach B's to make the block center.

Use the blue dot and the green solid E's to make 4 Triangle-Square unit 1's. Use the green dot and the blue solid E's to make 8 unit 2's. Sew the patches and units together as shown.

Find a foundation for the C/D/Dr unit on our website at **quiltmaker.com**.

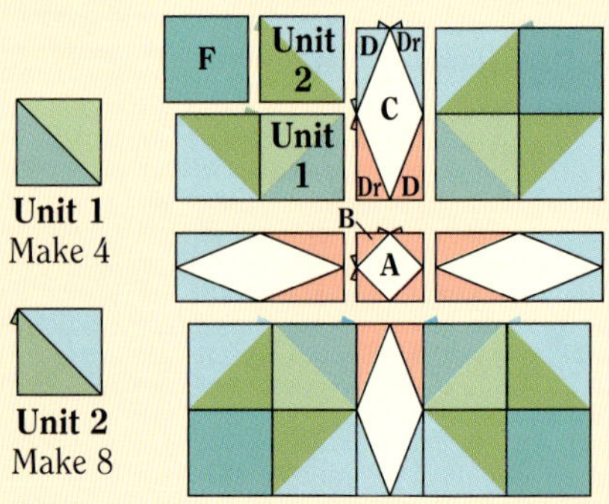

Block Piecing

pieced

block no. 575

Old Glory

by Maria Peagler
quiltsandcreativity.com

Maria is the author of Color Mastery: 10 Principles for Creating Stunning Quilts for Willow Ridge Press, colormastery.com.

⧄ = cut in half diagonally
⊠ = cut in half twice diagonally

Cream Print #1
- 1 square 3¼" x 3¼" ⊠ (A)
- 2 squares 2⅞" x 2⅞" ⧄ (B)

Navy Stripe
- 1 square 3¼" x 3¼" ⊠ (A)

Navy Print
- 2 squares 3¾" x 3¾" ⧄ (C)

2 Red Prints
from *each*
- 1 rectangle (D) 2⅜" x 6⅞"
- 1 rectangle (E) 2⅛" x 12½"

Cream Print #2
- 1 rectangle (D) 2⅜" x 6⅞"
- 2 rectangles (E) 2⅛" x 12½"

Join patches A–C to make the Pinwheel. Join the D and E patches into sections as shown. Join the Pinwheel and the sections to complete the block. Trim the block to 12½" × 12½".

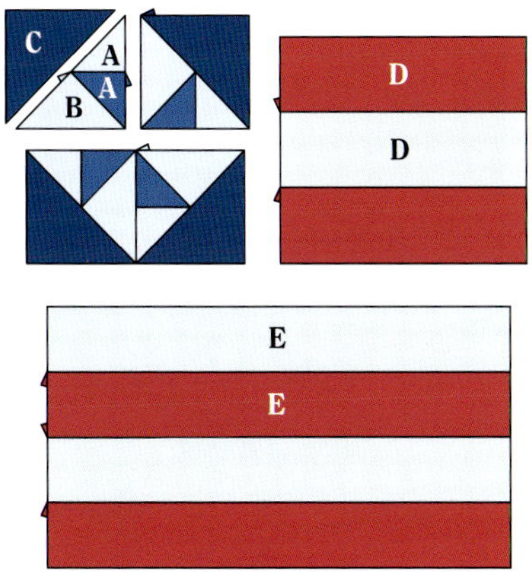

Block Piecing

block no. 576

Easy 3-D

by Maria Umhey • Cheerful Quilts

Fabric: Gathered Over Time II by Julie Hendrickson for Windham Fabrics, windhamfabrics.com.

Assorted Light Prints
- 3 squares (A) 2½" x 2½"
- 9 squares (B) 2⅞" x 2⅞"

Assorted Dark Blue Prints
- 3 squares (A) 2½" x 2½"
- 9 squares (B) 2⅞" x 2⅞"

Assorted Medium Blue Prints
- 12 squares (A) 2½" x 2½"

Unit
Make 18

Randomly join light and dark B's to make 18 Triangle-Square units.

Noting value placement, join the patches and units to make the block.

An interesting 3-D effect is created when blocks are sewn together. Nine blocks give the effect shown here.

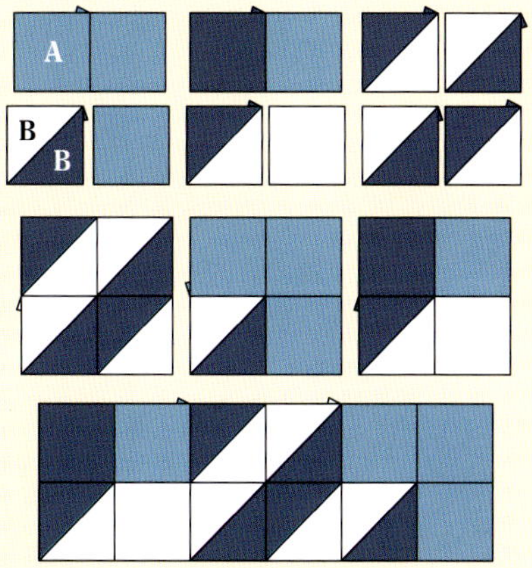

Block Piecing

block no. 577
Around the Rosie

by Monica Solorio-Snow • Happy Zombie
thehappyzombie.com

Fabric: Sweet designed by Urban Chiks for Moda Fabrics, unitednotions.com.

Cream Print
1 square (A) 5¼" x 5¼"
Green Print #1
4 squares (B) 2⅞" x 2⅞"
Cream Solid
2 squares (C) 4⅞" x 4⅞"
4 rectangles (D) 2½" x 4½"
Green Print #2
2 squares (C) 4⅞" x 4⅞"
Large-Scale Floral Print
1 square (E) 4½" x 4½"

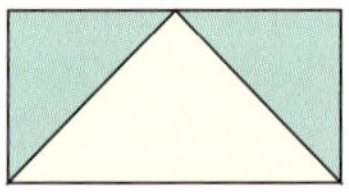

Flying Geese
Make 4

Unit
Make 4

Use the cream A and the green B's to make 4 Flying Geese. Pair the cream C's with the green C's to make 4 Triangle-Square units.

Sew the Flying Geese, units and patches together as shown to complete the block. ■

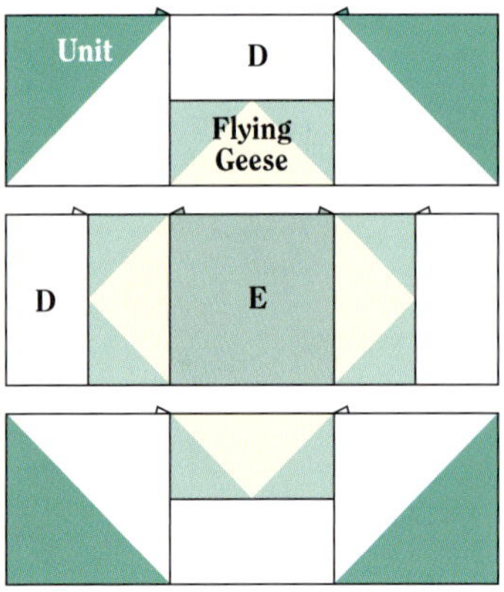

Block Piecing

block no. 578
Courtyard Square

by Pam Vieira-McGinnis
pamkittymorning.blogspot.com

Fabric: Sweet designed by Urban Chiks for Moda Fabrics, unitednotions.com.

Red Print
1 square (A) 5¼" x 5¼"
Cream Solid
4 squares (B) 2⅞" x 2⅞"
4 rectangles (D) 2½" x 4½"
4 squares (F) 2½" x 2½"
Cream Print
1 square (C) 4½" x 4½"
Pink Stripe
2 rectangles (D) 2½" x 4½"
2 rectangles (E) 2½" x 8½"

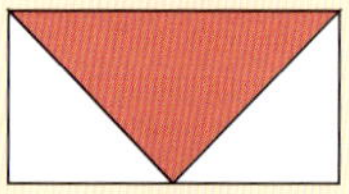

Flying Geese
Make 4

Use the red A and the cream B's to make 4 Flying Geese.

Sew the Flying Geese and patches together as shown to complete the block. ■

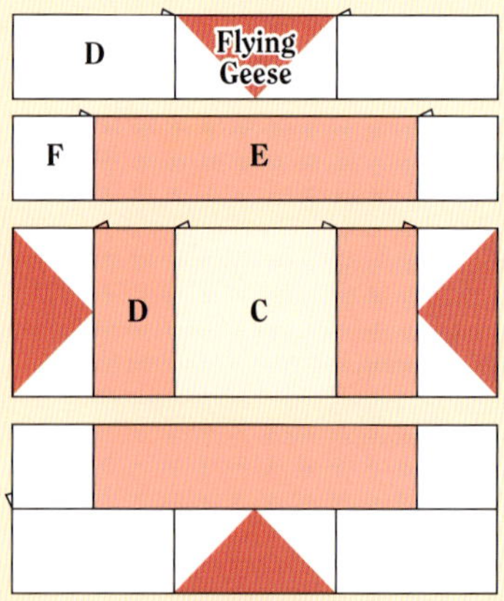

Block Piecing

block no. 579
Late Bloomer

by Pam Buda • Heartspun Quilts
heartspunquilts.com

Fabric: Blessings by Brannock and Patek for Moda Fabrics, unitednotions.com.

⧄ = cut in half diagonally

Tan Print
- 8 rectangles (A) 2″ x 4½″
- 4 squares (C) 2½″ x 2½″

Blue Print
- 4 rectangles (B) 1½″ x 4½″
- 2 squares 4⅞″ x 4⅞″ ⧄ (E)
- 4 rectangles (G) 1½″ x 2″

Red Print
- 8 squares (C) 2½″ x 2½″
- 4 squares (F) 2″ x 2″
- 1 square (H) 1½″ x 1½″

Green Print
- 4 squares 2⅞″ x 2⅞″ ⧄ (D)

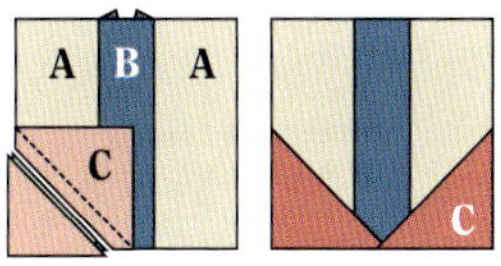

Unit
Stitch & Flip
Make 4

Sew 2 A's to a B as shown. Refer to "Stitch & Flip" in the Techniques file on the PDF, and add C's to 2 adjacent corners to make a unit as shown. Make 4 units.

Follow the block piecing diagram to combine the units with the remaining patches to complete the block.

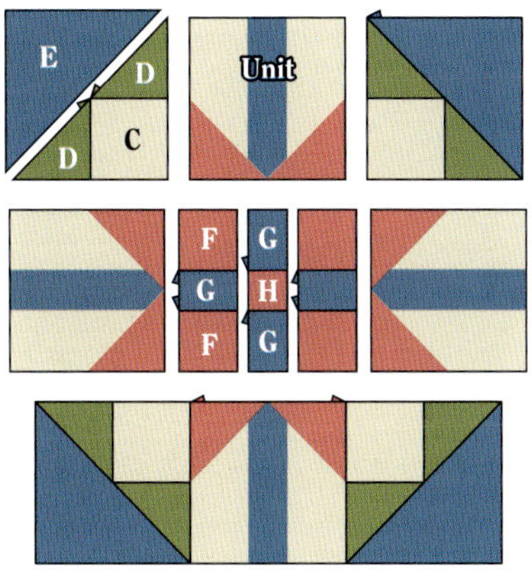

Block Piecing

block no. 580
Red Rover

by Monique Dillard • Open Gate
opengatequilts.com

Fabric: Sturbridge Village Scarlet designed by Judie Rothermel for Marcus Fabrics, marcusfabrics.com; Hemming House designed by Brannock and Patek for Moda Fabrics, unitednotions.com.

⧄ = cut in half diagonally

Cream Print
- 2 squares 5⅜″ x 5⅜″ ⧄ (A)
- 16 squares (B) 2⅜″ x 2⅜″

4 Red Prints
from *each*
- 1 square 5⅜″ x 5⅜″ ⧄ (A) (there will be 4 extra A's)
- 4 squares (B) 2⅜″ x 2⅜″

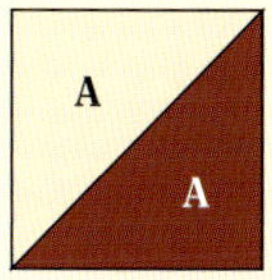

Unit 1
Make 4

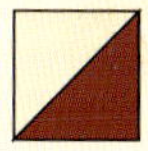

Unit 2
Make 28

Join each cream A with a different red print A to make the unit 1's.

From the cream B's and red B's, make the Triangle-Square unit 2's.

Using just one of the red prints in each of the block quadrants, join the units as shown to complete the block. (You will have 1 leftover unit 2 from each red fabric.)

Block Piecing

block no. 581

America the Beautiful

by Paula Barnes • Red Crinoline Quilts
redcrinolinequilts.com

Fabric: Bonnie Blue's America by Paula Barnes for Marcus Fabrics, marcusfabrics.com.

Tan Print
- 4 squares (A) 2⅜″ x 2⅜″
- 16 squares (B) 2″ x 2″
- 8 rectangles (C) 2″ x 3½″

Navy Print
- 4 squares (A) 2⅜″ x 2⅜″
- 8 squares (B) 2″ x 2″

Red Print
- 8 rectangles (C) 2″ x 3½″

Novelty Print
- 1 square (D) 6½″ x 6½″

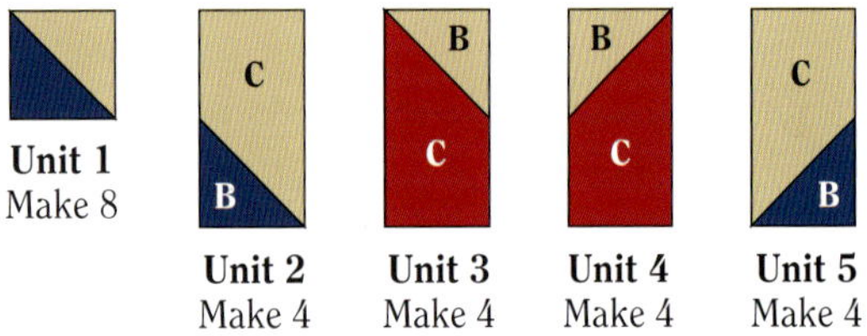

Paula fussy cut the D patch from the novelty print to center the eagle motif.

Use the tan and the navy A's to make 8 Triangle-Square unit 1's. Refer to "Stitch & Flip" in the Techniques file on the PDF. Use the navy and the tan B's and the tan and the red C's to make the unit 2's–5's as shown.

Join the units and patches as shown to complete the block. ▪

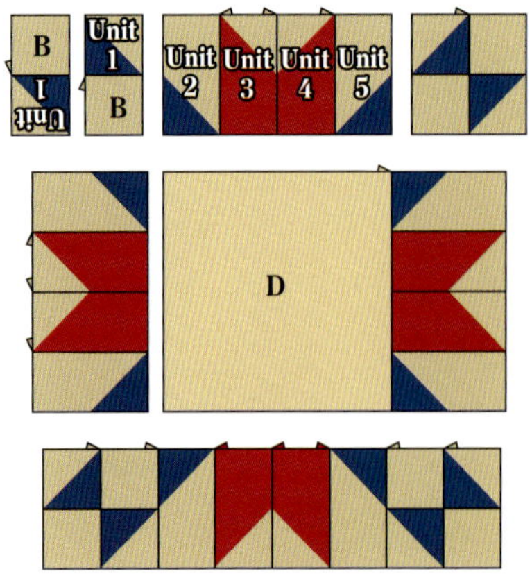

Block Piecing

block no. 582

Four Patch Star

by Lynn Schiefelbein • Oak Street Quilts
oakstreetquilts.com

⧄ = cut in half diagonally
☒ = cut in half twice diagonally

4 Assorted Prints
from *each*
- 1 square (A) 2″ x 2″
- 1 square 2⅞″ x 2⅞″ ⧄ (B)
- 1 square 5¼″ x 5¼″ ☒ (C)
- 1 square (D) 4⅞″ x 4⅞″ ⧄ (D)

Cream Tone-on-Tone
- 1 square 5¼″ x 5¼″ ☒ (C)
- 4 squares (E) 4½″ x 4½″

If you make just one block, you will have extra B, C and D patches. Noticing the placement of the various prints, join the patches as shown in the diagram to make the block. ▪

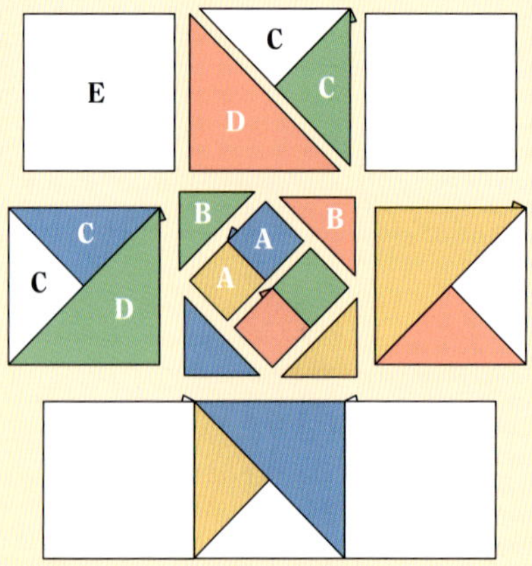

Block Piecing

pieced

block no. 583

Star-Crossed Love

by Scott Hansen • Blue Nickel Studios
bluenickelstudios.com

Fabric: Flower Sugar from Lecien, lecien.co.jp/en/hobby/.

Blue Dot Print
- 1 square (A) 5¼″ x 5¼″
- 1 square (C) 2½″ x 2½″

White and Blue Plaid
- 1 square (A) 5¼″ x 5¼″
- 8 squares (B) 2⅞″ x 2⅞″

Red Print
- 4 squares (B) 2⅞″ x 2⅞″
- 2 rectangles (D) 1½″ x 2½″
- 2 rectangles (E) 1½″ x 4½″

Blue Print
- 4 squares (B) 2⅞″ x 2⅞″
- 4 squares (C) 2½″ x 2½″

White Print
- 4 squares (C) 2½″ x 2½″

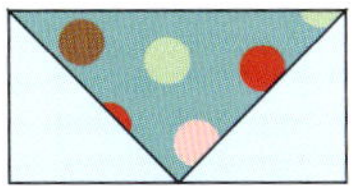

Unit 1
Make 4

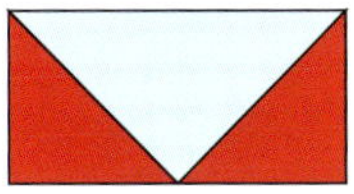

Unit 2
Make 4

Unit 3
Make 8

Use the blue dot A with the white and blue plaid B's to make 4 unit 1's. Use the white and blue plaid A with the red B's to make 4 unit 2's.

Pair the white and blue plaid B's with the blue print B's to make the 8 Triangle-Square unit 3's.

Sew the patches and units together as shown to complete the block.

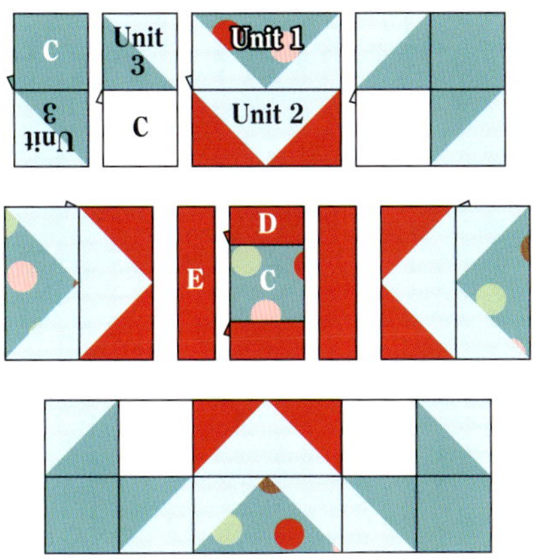

Block Piecing

block no. 584

A-Maze-Ment

by Sue Beevers

Fabric: Ribbons & Swirls designed by Sue Beevers for RJR Fabrics, rjrfabrics.com.

Sue Beevers is the author of Off-the-Shelf Fabric Painting and Dancing Dragonfly Quilts, both for C&T Publishing, ctpub.com.

⧄ = cut in half diagonally

Beige Print
- 10 squares (A) 1½″ x 1½″
- 4 rectangles (B) 1½″ x 2½″
- 2 rectangles (C) 1½″ x 3½″
- 2 rectangles (F) 1¼″ x 1½″
- 4 rectangles (G) 1½″ x 4½″
- 1 square 2⅝″ x 2⅝″ ⧄ (I)
- 2 squares 4⅝″ x 4⅝″ ⧄ (J)

Light Green Print and Blue Print
from each
- 3 squares (A) 1½″ x 1½″
- 1 rectangle (B) 1½″ x 2½″
- 2 rectangles (C) 1½″ x 3½″
- 1 rectangle (H) 1½″ x 5¼″

Dark Green Print
- 2 rectangles (C) 1½″ x 3½″
- 2 rectangles (H) 1½″ x 5¼″

Red Print
- 2 rectangles (D) 1¼″ x 3½″
- 4 rectangles (E) 1¼″ x 4¼″
- 6 rectangles (F) 1¼″ x 1½″

Gold Print
- 1 rectangle (C) 1½″ x 3½″
- 2 rectangles (K) 1½″ x 6¾″

Join the patches as shown.

Use contrasting thread and decorative machine stitches to embellish the green, gold and red patches as shown. You can preserve the block's woven effect by ending the stitching whenever one color appears to weave under another color.

Center and trim the block to 12½″ × 12½″.

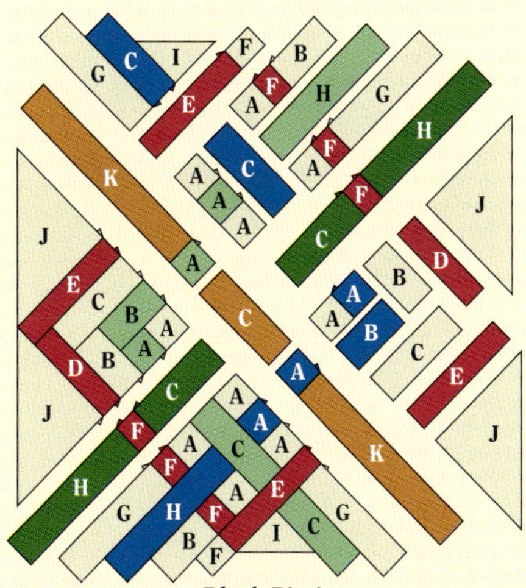

Block Piecing

block no. 585

Wild Blue Yonder

by Scott Murkin • Patchwork Possibilities
patchworkpossibilities.com

⧄ = cut in half diagonally
⊠ = cut in half twice diagonally

Light Blue Tone-on-Tone
- 4 rectangles (A) 2⅝″ x 4¾″
- 2 squares 3⅞″ x 3⅞″ ⧄ (B)
- 2 squares 4¼″ x 4¼″ ⊠ (C)

Dark Blue Stripe
- 4 rectangles (A) 2⅝″ x 4¾″

Dark Blue Tone-on-Tone
- 2 squares 3⅞″ x 3⅞″ ⧄ (B)
- 2 squares 4¼″ x 4¼″ ⊠ (C)

Join the patches as shown to complete the block.

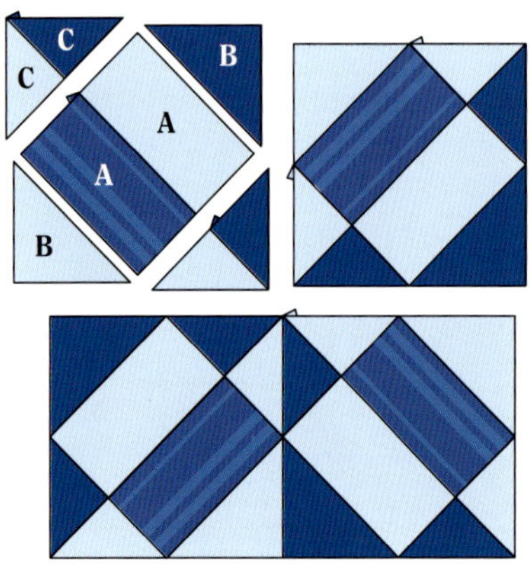

Block Piecing

block no. 586

Star Checks

by Sue Garman
suegarman.blogspot.com

Fabric: Judie Rothermel for Marcus Fabrics, marcusfabrics.com; Rambling Favorites, P&B Textiles, pbtex.com.

Assorted Red Prints
- 6 squares (A) 3⅞″ x 3⅞″
- 20 squares (B) 1½″ x 1½″

Cream Print
- 6 squares (A) 3⅞″ x 3⅞″
- 8 squares (B) 1½″ x 1½″
- 4 rectangles (C) 1½″ x 2½″

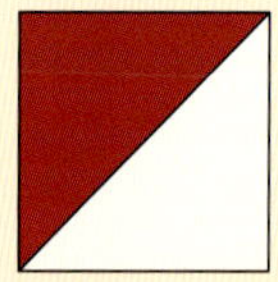

Unit
Make 12

Use the red and the cream A's to make 12 Triangle-Square units.

Assemble the center section in rows as shown in the diagram. Join the units with the center section to complete the block as shown.

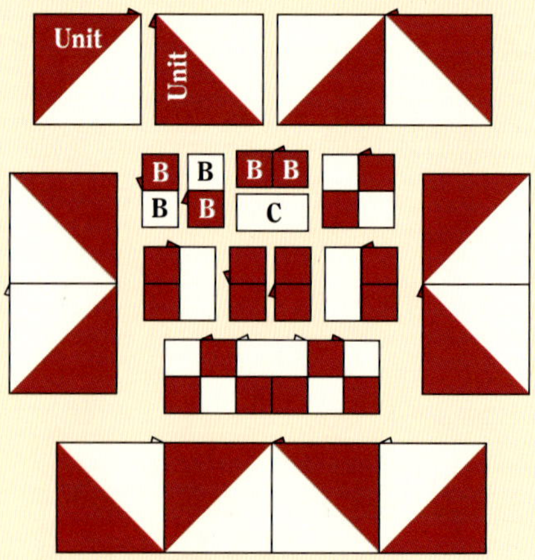

Block Piecing

pieced

block no. 587
Snow Shoo

by Theresa Eisinger • former Graphic Designer, *Quiltmaker*
quiltmaker.com

Fabric: Snow Days designed by MaryJo Tuttle for Connecting Threads, connectingthreads.com.

Teal Print
2 squares (A) 4 7/8" x 4 7/8"

White Print
2 squares (A) 4 7/8" x 4 7/8"
1 square (F) 4 1/2" x 4 1/2"

Blue Print
4 squares (B) 3 1/4" x 3 1/4"
16 squares (D) 1 1/2" x 1 1/2"

Light Teal Print
16 squares (C) 1 7/8" x 1 7/8"

Novelty Print
4 squares (E) 2 1/2" x 2 1/2"

Unit 1
Make 4

Flying Geese
Make 16

Use the teal and white A's to make 4 Triangle-Square unit 1's. Use the blue B's and light teal C's to make 16 Flying Geese.

Sew the patches, unit 1's and Flying Geese together as shown to complete the block.

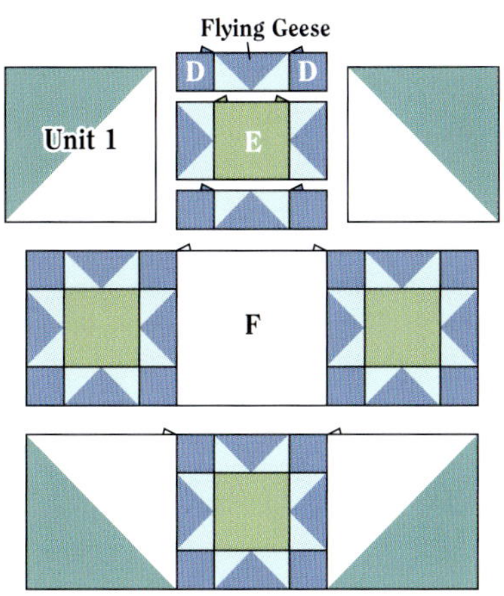

Block Piecing

block no. 588
Jewel in the Pond

by Wendy Slotboom

Fabric: Lily Pond designed by Wendy Slotboom for In the Beginning Fabrics, inthebeginningfabrics.com.

Dark Pink Print
2 squares (A) 6 1/2" x 6 1/2"

2 Brown Dot Prints
from *each*
2 squares (B) 3 1/2" x 3 1/2"

2 Cream and Pink Prints
from *each*
1 square (A) 6 1/2" x 6 1/2"

Green Print
circle 5 1/2" diameter

Pink rickrack
4 pieces, *each* 5" long

Button 1 at 7/8" wide

Fold a B in half diagonally. Pin the B to a corner of an A, matching raw edges. Tuck a strip of the rickrack under the B fold and pin in place. Sew close to B's folded edge through all layers as shown. Repeat to make a total of 4 A/B sections.

Join the A/B sections as shown.

Make a yo-yo from the green print. Sew the yo-yo to the center of the block. Sew the button to the center of the yo-yo.

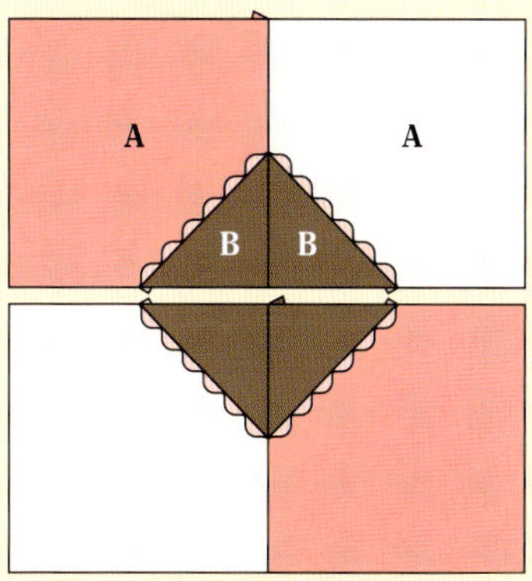

Block Piecing

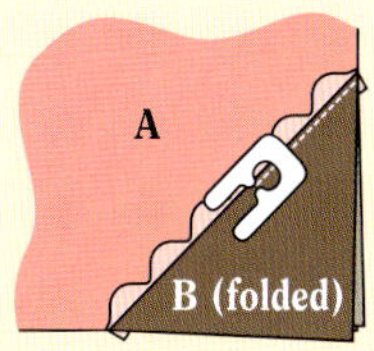

block no. 589
Spectrum Square

by Linda Ambrosini

Fabric: Bali Batiks from Hoffman California Fabrics, hoffmanfabrics.com.

◩ = cut in half diagonally

Assorted Batiks
6 rectangles (A) 2½″ x 12½″

Multicolor Batik
2 squares 6⅞″ x 6⅞″ ◩ (B)

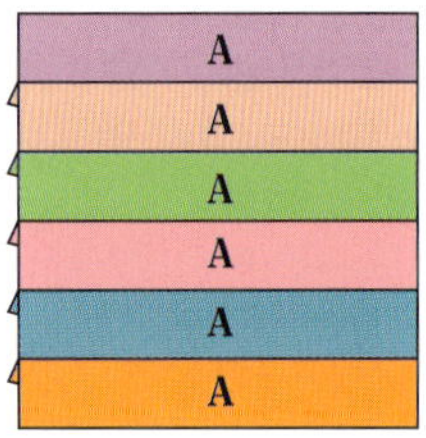

Section Assembly

Matching centers and ends, sew the A's together as shown. The section made from the joined A's should measure 12½″ × 12½″

Fold the section made from the A's in half both ways and lightly crease the folds; using the folds as guides, trim as shown.

Add the B's as shown to complete the block.

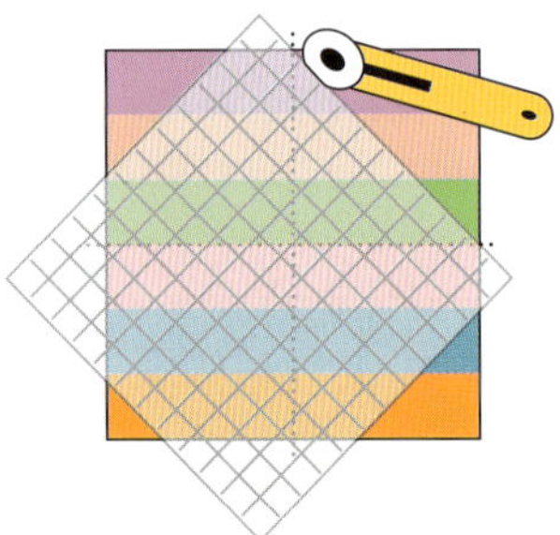

Block Piecing

block no. 590
May Flowers

by Carolyn Beam • Creative Editor, *Quiltmaker*
quiltmaker.com

Fabric: Rainy Days and Mondays designed by Melimba & Beccabury for Riley Blake Designs, rileyblakedesigns.com.

White Tone-on-Tone
4 rectangles (A) 2½″ x 5½″
12 squares (C) 1½″ x 1½″

Green Print
4 squares (B) 2½″ x 2½″

2 Pink Prints
from *each*
4 rectangles (A) 2½″ x 5½″
4 rectangles (D) 1½″ x 2½″

Red Tone-on-Tone
4 squares (C) 1½″ x 1½″

Green Tone-on-Tone
4 squares (C) 1½″ x 1½″
1 square (B) 2½″ x 2½″

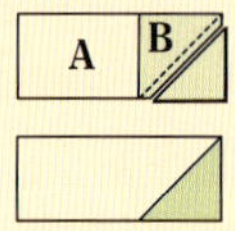

Unit 1
Stitch & Flip
Make 4

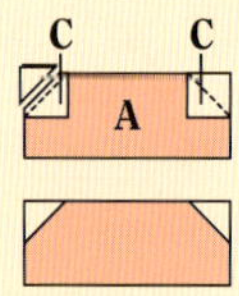

Unit 2
Stitch & Flip
Make 4

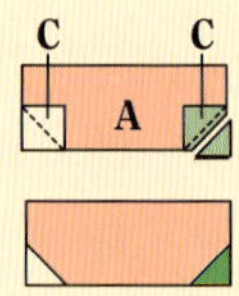

Unit 3
Stitch & Flip
Make 4

Refer to "Stitch-and-Flip" in the Techniques file on the PDF. Use the white A's and green print B's to make 4 unit 1's. Add white C's to the top corners of 2 pink A's from *each* of the pink prints to make 4 unit 2's. Add a white C to the bottom left corner and a green tone-on-tone C to bottom right corner of 2 pink A's from *each* of the pink prints to make 4 unit 3's.

Join a C and 2 D's with a matching unit 2 and unit 3, and then add unit 1 to make a section. Make 4 sections. Noting the orientation, sew a section to the right side of B with a partial seam as shown. Sew a section to the bottom, to the left and to the top of B as shown. Complete the partial seam to finish the block.

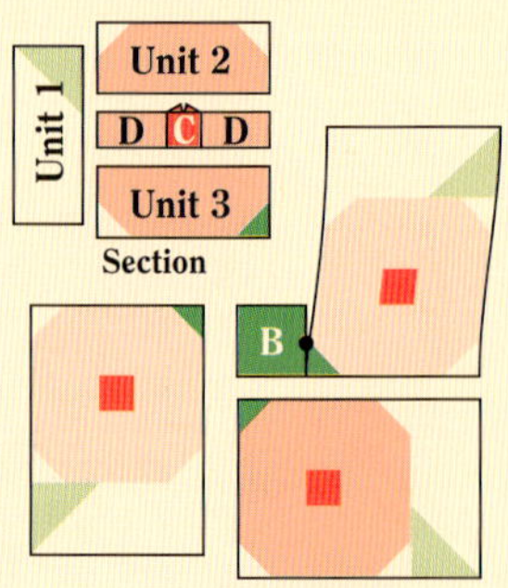

Block Assembly
• = Partial Seam

pieced

block no. 591

Star Across

by Laura Blanchard • Plum Tree Quilts
plumtreequilts.com

Aqua Batik
4 squares (A) 5" x 5"
Dark Blue Batik
8 squares (B) 3½" x 3½"
Light Purple Batik
4 squares (B) 3½" x 3½"
Light Blue Batik
1 square (B) 3½" x 3½"
8 squares (C) 2" x 2"
Dark Purple Batik
4 rectangles (D) 2" x 3½"

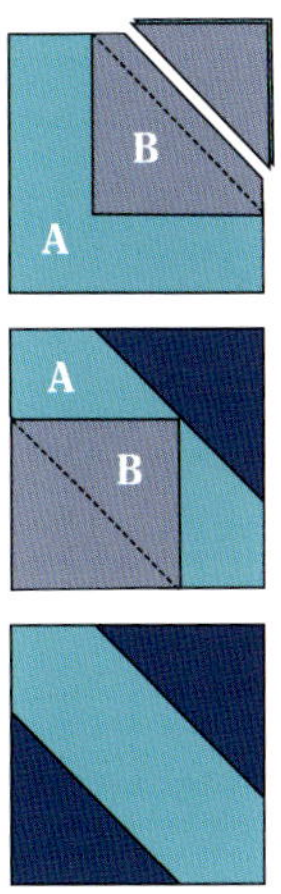

Unit 1
Stitch & Flip
Make 4

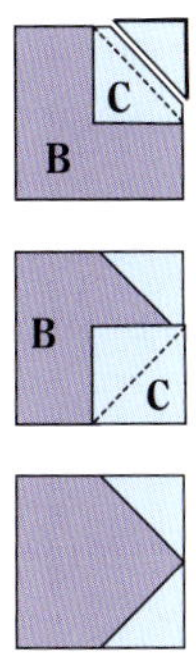

Unit 2
Stitch & Flip
Make 4

Refer to "Stitch-and-Flip" in the Techniques file on the PDF. Use an aqua A and 2 dark blue B's to make a unit 1 as shown. Make 4 unit 1's. Use a light purple B and 2 light blue C's to make a unit 2 as shown. Make 4 unit 2's.

Join the units and patches as shown to complete the block.

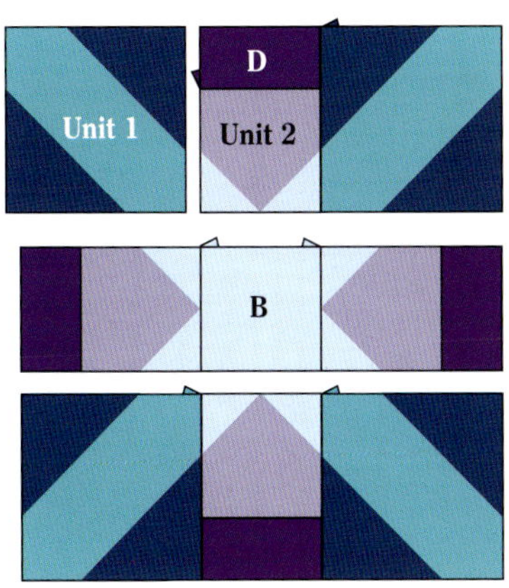

Block Piecing

block no. 592

Antique Aster

by Deborah Borsos • Painted Pony 'n Quilts
ppnq.com

Fabric: More Pink Chocolate 1860–1885 designed by Nancy Gere for Windham Fabrics, windhamfabrics.com.

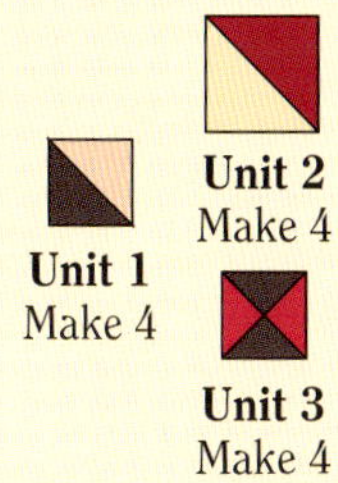

◸ = cut in half diagonally
⊠ = cut in half twice diagonally

Pink Print
2 squares (A) 1⅞" x 1⅞"
4 rectangles (H) 1½" x 10½"
Large Scale Brown Print
2 squares (A) 1⅞" x 1⅞"
2 squares 4⅞" x 4⅞" ◸ (F)
2 squares (I) 2¼" x 2¼"
Cream Print
2 squares (B) 2⅞" x 2⅞"
2 squares 2⅞" x 2⅞" ◸ (C)
1 square 3¼" x 3¼" ⊠ (D)
4 squares (G) 2½" x 2½"
Burgundy Print #1
2 squares (B) 2⅞" x 2⅞"
Burgundy Print #2
1 square 3¼" x 3¼" ⊠ (D)
2 squares (I) 2¼" x 2¼"
Small Scale Brown Print
1 square 5¼" x 5¼" ⊠ (E)

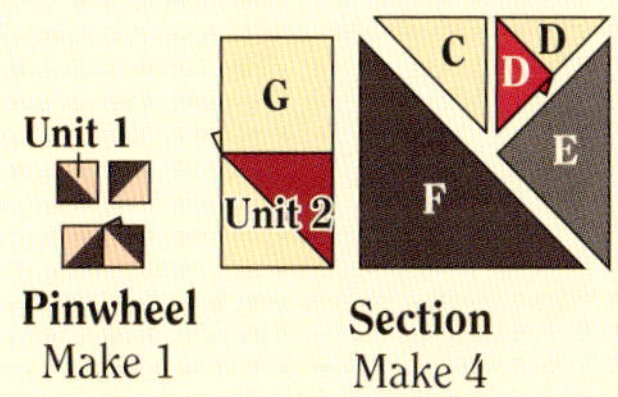

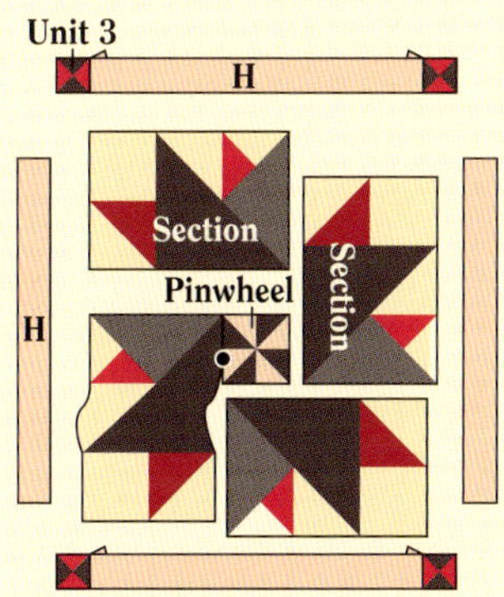

Block Assembly
● = Partial Seam

Pair the pink and brown A's to make 4 Triangle-Square unit 1's. Pair the cream and burgundy B's to make 4 unit 2's. Use the brown and burgundy I's to make 4 Quarter-Square Triangle unit 3's.

Sew 4 unit 1's together as shown to make a Pinwheel. Sew a unit 2 and patches C–G together as shown to make a section. Make 4 sections. Sew a section to the left side of the Pinwheel with a partial seam as shown. Sew a section to the top, to the right and to the bottom of the Pinwheel. Complete the partial seam.

Sew an H to each side of the block. Add unit 3's to each end of the 2 remaining H's as shown; sew these strips to the top and bottom to complete the block.

block no. 593
Star Flight

by Kathy Brown • The Teacher's Pet
the-teachers-pet.com

Fabric: Moda Fabrics, unitednotions.com.

Kathy Brown is the author of *Take 5: Quilts from Just 5 Fabrics* for Martingale & Co., martingale-pub.com.

Red Print
- 1 square (A) 4½" x 4½"
- 4 squares (B) 2½" x 2½"
- 1 square (C) 5¼" x 5¼"

Tan Solid
- 8 squares (B) 2½" x 2½"
- 4 rectangles (E) 2½" x 4½"

Brown Print
- 8 squares (B) 2½" x 2½"
- 4 squares (D) 2⅞" x 2⅞"

Unit 1
Stitch & Flip
Make 1

Unit 2
Make 4

Refer to "Stitch-and-Flip" in the Techniques file on the PDF and use the red A and 4 tan B's as shown to make the unit 1.

Use the red C and brown D's to make 4 Flying Geese unit 2's.

Sew the units and patches together as shown to complete the block.

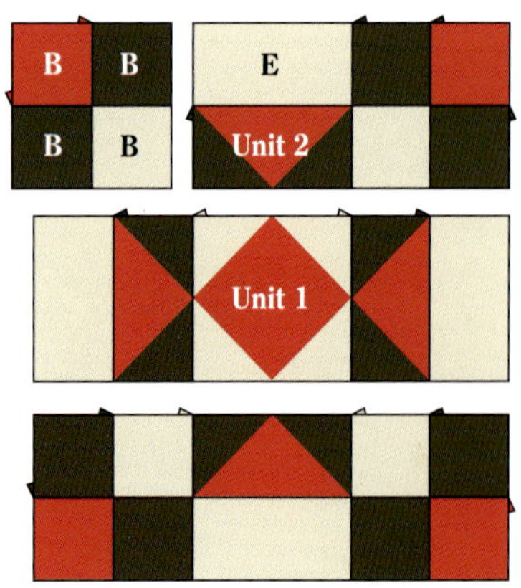

Block Piecing

block no. 594
Kraut Cutter

by Mickey Charleston

Fabric: Born to be Wild, Hoffman California Fabrics, hoffmanfabrics.com.

See page 54 on the PDF for pattern

Assorted Pink, Orange and Brown Prints and Tone-on-Tones
- 4 squares (A) 6½" x 6½"
- 12 template B (see instructions below)

Save time by first cutting 1½"-wide strips. Cut the B patches from these strips using the B template.

Join 2 A patches and trim at an angle to make a section as shown. Repeat for the remaining A patches.

Join the sections and B's to complete the block.

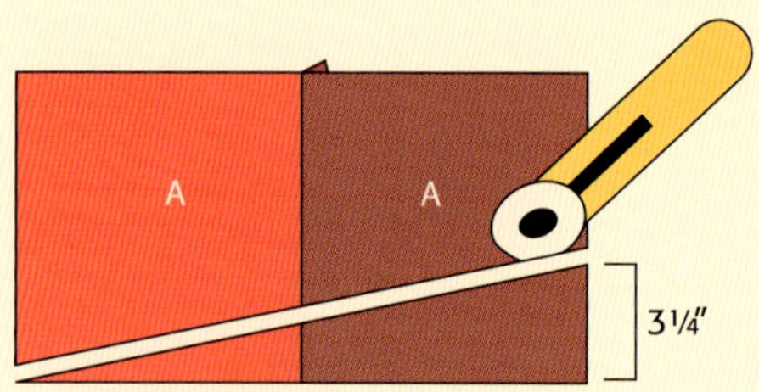

Section
Make 2

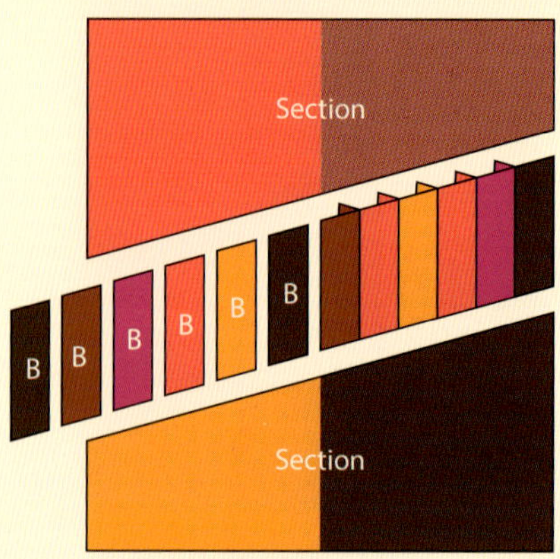

Block Piecing

block no. 595

Mini Pod

by Emily Cier • Carolina Patchworks
carolinapatchworks.com

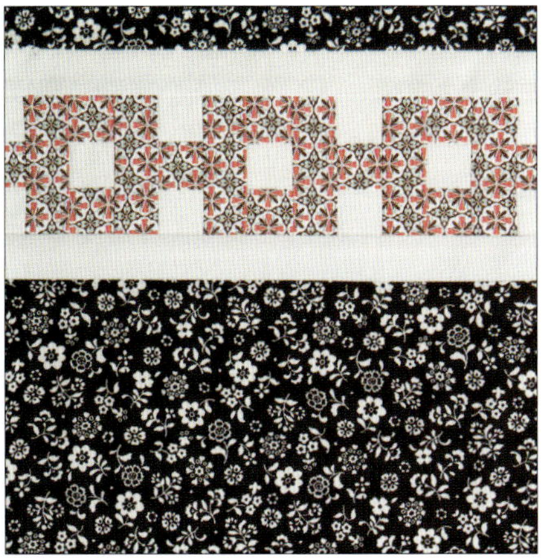

Pink and Black Print
- 8 squares (A) 1½″x 1½″
- 6 rectangles (B) 1½″x 3½″
- 2 rectangles (C) 1″x 1½″

Cream Solid
- 7 squares (A) 1½″x 1½″
- 4 rectangles (C) 1″x 1½″
- 2 rectangles (D) 1½″x 12½″

Black Print
- 1 rectangle (D) 1½″x 12½″
- 1 rectangle (E) 6½″x 12½″

Sew the patches together as shown to complete the block.

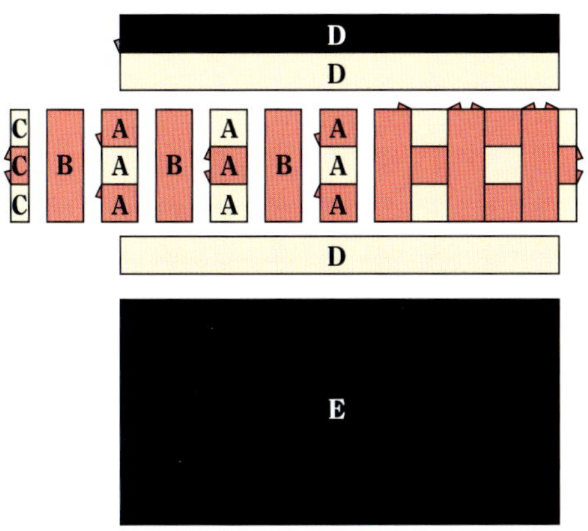

Block Piecing

block no. 596

Colorful Star Tricks

by Barbara Cline • Delightful Piecing
delightfulpiecing.com

Fabric: Bear Essentials from P&B Textiles, pbtex.com.

Barbara Cline is the author of *Star Struck Quilts* for C&T Publishing, ctpub.com.

See page 39 on the PDF for pattern

◸ = cut in half diagonally
⊠ = cut in half twice diagonally

Light Pink, Light Teal, Light Green and Light Yellow Tone-on-Tones
from *each*
- 4 template A

Medium Pink, Medium Teal, Medium Green and Medium Yellow Tone-on-Tones
from *each*
- 6 template A

Medium Brown and Dark Brown Tone-on-Tones
from *each*
- 4 squares 3¼″x 3¼″ ⊠ (B)

Cream Print
- 6 squares 3¼″x 3¼″ ⊠ (B)
- 2 squares 4⅜″x 4⅜″ ◸ (C)

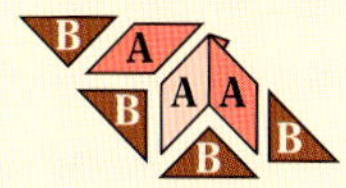

Section 1
Make 8

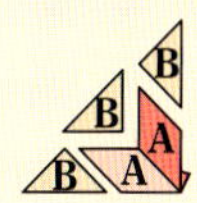

Section 2
Make 8

Refer to "Set-in Seams" in the Techniques section on the PDF. Paying close attention to color placement, use the A's and B's to sew 8 section 1's and 8 section 2's.

Join the sections and patches as shown to complete the block.

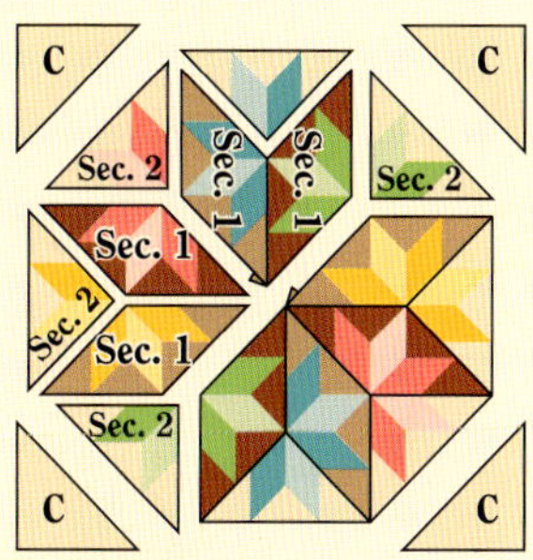

Block Piecing

block no. 597

Odd Fellow's Chain

by Karen Combs • Karen Combs' Studio
karencombs.com

Fabric: Batik Colorwheel designed by Karen Combs for Avlyn, Inc., avlyn.com.

Karen Combs is the author of *Celtic Pieced Illusions* for American Quilters Society, americanquilter.com.

⧄ = cut in half diagonally
⊠ = cut in half twice diagonally

Lime Batik
- 4 squares (A) 2⅜″ x 2⅜″
- 1 square (B) 4¼″ x 4¼″
- 4 squares (C) 2″ x 2″
- 4 squares 2⅜″ x 2⅜″ ⧄ (D)

Medium Green Batik
- 8 squares (A) 2⅜″ x 2⅜″

Dark Green Batik
- 4 squares (C) 2″ x 2″
- 1 square 4¼″ x 4¼″ ⊠ (E)

Medium Blue Batik
- 4 squares 3⅞″ x 3⅞″ ⧄ (F)

Dark Blue Batik
- 1 square (B) 4¼″ x 4¼″
- 4 squares (C) 2″ x 2″

Purple Batik
- 4 squares (A) 2⅜″ x 2⅜″

Pink Batik
- 1 square (G) 3½″ x 3½″

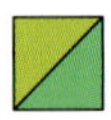

Unit
Make 8

Flying Geese 1
Make 4

Flying Geese 2
Make 4

Pair the lime green A's and medium green A's to make 8 Triangle-Square units.

Use the medium green A's and the lime B to make 4 of Flying Geese 1. Use the purple A's and dark blue B to make 4 of Flying Geese 2.

Join the patches and units as shown to make the block.

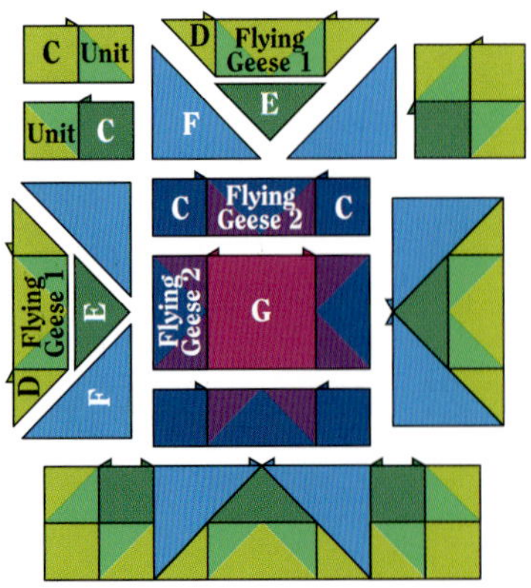

Block Piecing

block no. 598

Payton's Star

by Sharyn Craig
sharyncraig.com

Sharyn Craig is a quilt instructor and the designer of the *Cutting Corners Ruler*. She has authored numerous quilting titles including *Layer 'em Up #'s 1, 2 and 3* for Cozy Quilt Designs, cozyquilt.com.

Blue Batik
- 1 square (A) 5¼″ x 5¼″
- 4 squares (D) 2½″ x 2½″

Cream Print
- 1 square (A) 5¼″ x 5¼″
- 4 squares (B) 2⅞″ x 2⅞″
- 2 squares (C) 4⅞″ x 4⅞″

Light Green Print
- 4 squares (B) 2⅞″ x 2⅞″

Tan Batik
- 2 squares (C) 4⅞″ x 4⅞″

Green Batik
- 1 square (E) 4½″ x 4½″

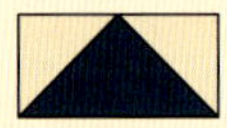

Flying Geese 1
Make 4

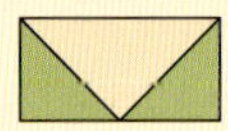

Flying Geese 2
Make 4

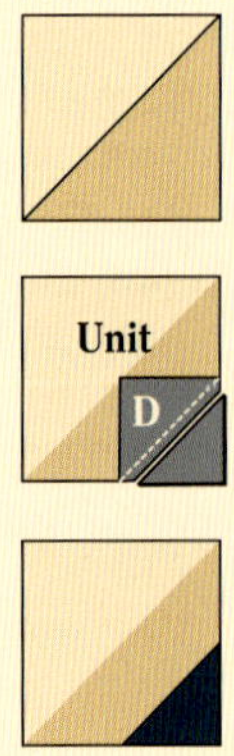

Unit
Stitch & Flip
Make 4

Use the blue A and cream B's to make 4 of Flying Geese 1. Use the cream A and green B's to make 4 of Flying Geese 2.

Use the cream and tan C's to make 4 Ttriangle-Squares. Refer to "Stitch-and-Flip" in the Techniques section on the PDF; sew a blue D on the tan corner of a triangle-square as shown to make a unit. Make 4 units.

Noting the orientation of the units, join the units, Flying Geese and E as shown to complete the block.

Block Assembly

pieced

block no. 599

Jessie's Flag

by Tina Curran and Jessica Lane
tinacurran.com

⍁ = cut in half diagonally

Assorted Cream Prints and Tone-on-Tones

14 squares 2⅞" x 2⅞" ⍁ (A) (there will be 1 extra patch)

Assorted Red Prints and Tone-on-Tones

14 squares 2⅞" x 2⅞" ⍁ (A) (there will be 1 extra patch)

Dark Blue Print

5 squares (B) 2½" x 2½"

Medium Blue Print

4 squares (B) 2½" x 2½"

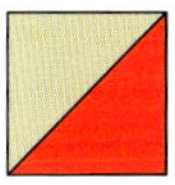

Unit
Make 27

Pair a cream A and a red A to make a unit. Make 27 units.

Join the B's and units into rows as shown. Sew the rows together to complete the block.

Block Assembly

block no. 600

Tile Works

by Monique Dillard • Open Gate
opengatequilts.com

Fabric: Olde World Style designed by Monique Dillard for Maywood Studio, maywoodstudio.com.

Monique has also designed a line of rulers, including Fit to Be Geese, which can be used to make the unit 2's and unit 3's in her block.

Black Print

4 squares (A) 2⅞" x 2⅞"
1 square (B) 5¼" x 5¼"
4 squares (C) 2½" x 2½"

Beige Tone-on-Tone

8 squares (A) 2⅞" x 2⅞"
4 squares (C) 2½" x 2½"
1 square (D) 4½" x 4½"

Red Tone-on-Tone

4 squares (A) 2⅞" x 2⅞"
1 square (B) 5¼" x 5¼"

Unit 1
Make 8

Unit 2
Make 4

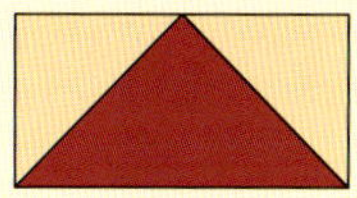

Unit 3
Make 4

Pair the black A's and beige A's to make 8 Trianlge-Square unit 1's.

Use the black B and red A's to make 4 Flying Geese unit 2's. Use the red B and beige A's to make 4 Flying Geese unit 3's.

Join the units and patches as shown to complete the block.

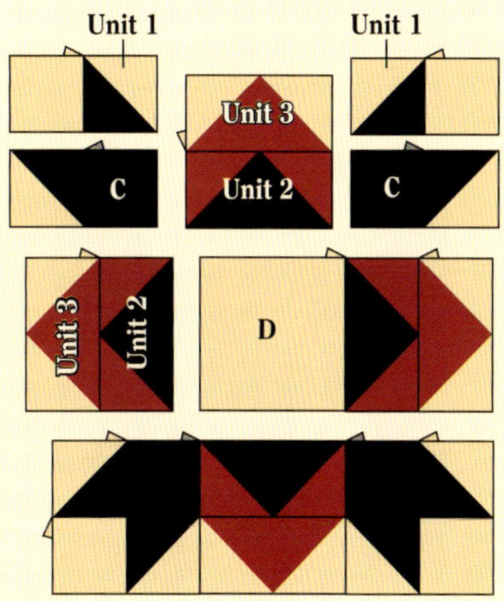

Block Piecing

block no. 601
What's the Point?

by Sherri Driver • Associate Editor, *McCall's Quilting*
mccallsquilting.com

Fabric: Textile Creations, textilecreations.com and Kaffe Fassett for Westminster Fibers, Inc., westminsterfibers.com.

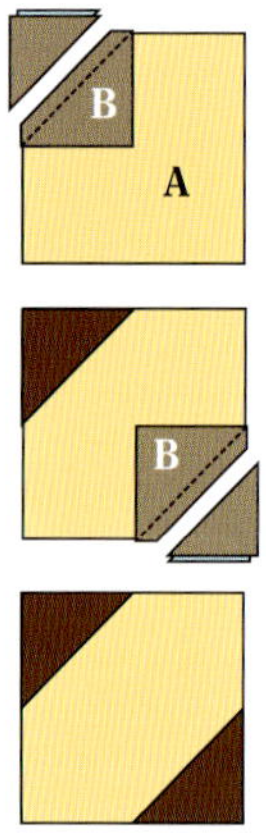

Unit 1
Stitch & Flip
Make 4

Yellow Print
4 squares (A) 4½″ x 4½″

Brown Print
16 squares (B) 2½″ x 2½″

Green Stripe (see note below)
8 rectangles (C) 2½″ x 4½″ (cut 4 with stripe running diagonally in 1 direction and 4 with stripe running diagonally in opposite direction)

Green Print
1 square (A) 4½″ x 4½″

Make a transparent plastic template of the C patch. Refer to the diagram above; mark the stripes' placement on the template as a guide to cutting mirror-image C patches as shown.

Refer to "Stitch-and-Flip" in the Techniques file on the PDF. Use the yellow A's and brown B's to make 4 unit 1's. Noting the direction of the stripe in the C's, use the brown B's and stripe C's to make 4 unit 2's and 4 unit 3's.

Join the units with A as shown to complete the block.

Unit 2
Stitch & Flip
Make 4

Unit 3
Stitch & Flip
Make 4

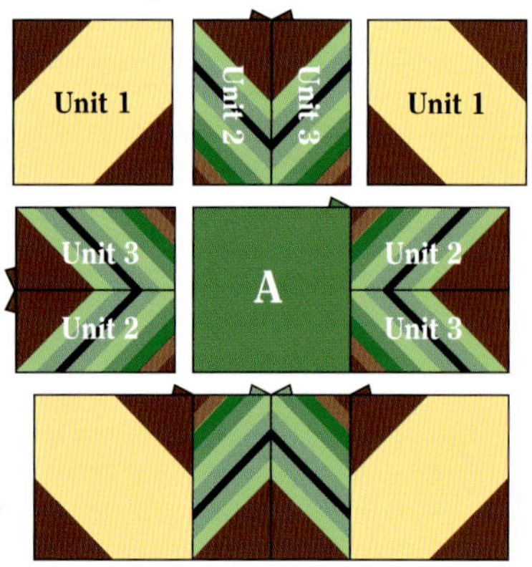

Block Assembly

block no. 602
Infinity

by Vickie Eapen • Spun Sugar Quilts
spunsugarquilt.com

Fabric: Freebird designed by MoMo for Moda Fabrics, unitednotions.com.

Cream Multiprint
4 squares (A) 2″ x 2″
4 squares (C) 3½″ x 3½″
1 square (E) 3⅞″ x 3⅞″

Red Print
4 squares (A) 2″ x 2″
1 square (E) 3⅞″ x 3⅞″

Brown Tone-on-Tone
4 squares (A) 2″ x 2″
2 rectangles (B) 2″ x 3½″
2 squares (C) 3½″ x 3½″
2 rectangles (D) 3½″ x 6½″

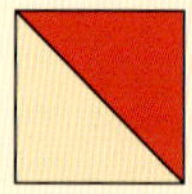

Unit
Make 2

Use the cream multiprint E and the red print E to make 2 Triangle-Square units. Join the units and patches as shown to complete the block.

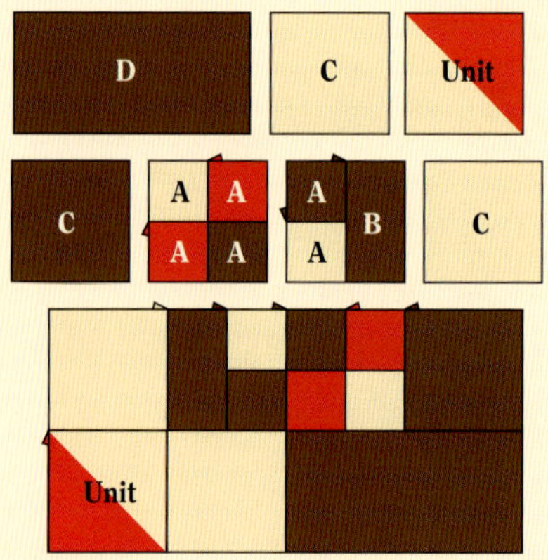

Block Piecing

block no. 603

Tulip Twist

by Deanne Eisenman • Snuggles Quilts
snugglesquilts.com

Deanne Eisenman is the author of *Country-Fresh Quilts* for Martingale & Company, martingale-pub.com.

Light Blue Tone-on-Tone
- 4 squares (A) 2⅜" x 2⅜"
- 8 squares (C) 1½" x 1½"
- 4 rectangles (F) 2" x 2½"
- 4 rectangles (G) 2" x 4"

Purple Multiprint
- 4 squares (A) 2⅜" x 2⅜"
- 4 rectangles (F) 2" x 2½"

Green Tone-on-Tone
- 4 rectangles (B) 1½" x 6½"
- 4 rectangles (D) 1½" x 5½"

Purple Tone-on-Tone
- 4 squares (C) 1½" x 1½"

Dark Blue Tone-on-Tone
- 4 squares (E) 2½" x 2½"

Aqua Multiprint
- 4 rectangles (G) 2" x 4"

Unit 1
Make 8

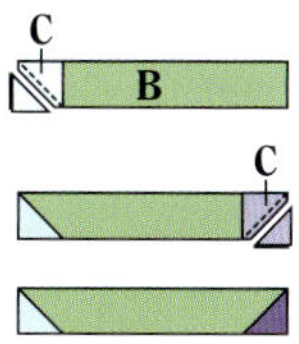

Unit 2
Stitch & Flip
Make 4

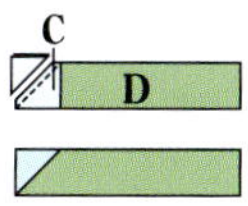

Unit 3
Stitch & Flip
Make 4

Join the A's as shown to make 8 Triangle-Square unit 1's. Refer to "Stitch-and-Flip" in the Techniques file on the PDF. Noticing the placement of each color of C patch, use B's and C's to make 4 unit 2's. Use the C's and D's as shown to make 4 unit 3's. Join the patches with the units as shown to make each section. Sew the sections together to complete the block.

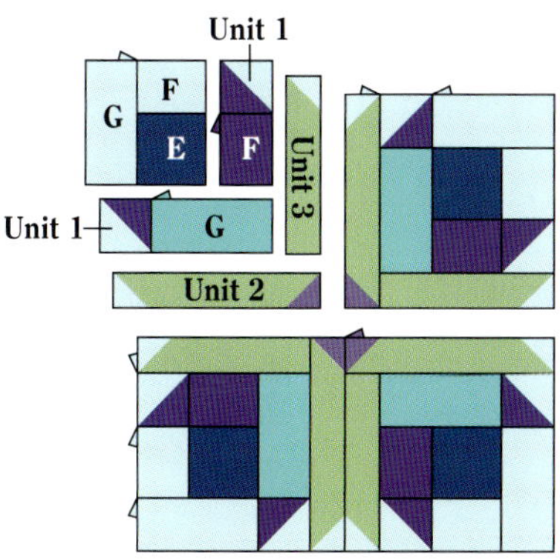

Block Assembly

block no. 604

Halfsies

by Theresa Eisinger • Past QM Graphic Designer

Fabric: Bali Fabrics by Hoffman California Fabrics, hoffmanfabrics.com.

Teal Batik
- 4 squares (A) 2½" x 2½"

Assorted Medium Green Batiks
- 4 squares (B) 2⅞" x 2⅞"

Assorted Cream Batiks
- 4 squares (B) 2⅞" x 2⅞"

Assorted Peach Batiks
- 4 squares (A) 2½" x 2½"

Assorted Light Green Batiks
- 8 squares (B) 2⅞" x 2⅞"

4 Assorted Orange Batiks
from *each*
- 2 squares (B) 2⅞" x 2⅞"

Blue Batik
- 4 squares (A) 2½" x 2½"

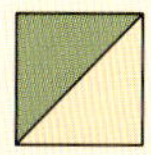

Unit
Make 24

Pair 4 medium green B's with 4 cream B's to make 8 Triangle-Square units. Pair the light green B's with the assorted orange B's to make 16 units (4 sets of 4 matching units).

Arrange the A's and units as shown in the assembly diagram, with each matching set of 4 units forming a star. Join the A's and units into rows. Sew the rows together to complete the block.

Block Assembly

block no. 605

Geese 'Round the Rosie

by Gudrun Erla • GE Designs
gequiltdesigns.com, gudrun.typepad.com

Fabric: Halo designed by Gudrun Erla for Red Rooster Fabrics, redroosterfabrics.com.

Gudrun Erla is the author of *Fast & Furious* and *Strip On* for GE Designs, gequiltdesigns.com.

Burgundy Print
4 rectangles (A) 2½"x 4½"

Cream Tone-on-Tone
16 squares (B) 2½"x 2½"
4 rectangles (F) 2½"x 8½"

4 Assorted Prints
from *each*
1 rectangle (A) 2½"x 4½"

Multiprint
1 square (C) 3½"x 3½"

Green Print
2 rectangles (D) 1"x 3½"
2 rectangles (E) 1"x 4½"

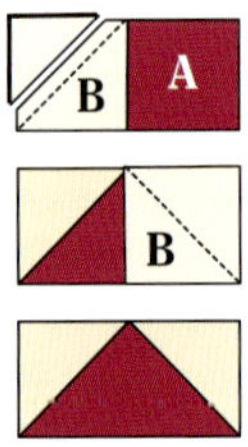

Unit
Stitch & Flip
Make 8
(4 matching and 4 different)

Refer to "Stitch-and-Flip" in the Techniques file on the PDF. Use the burgundy A's and cream B's to make 4 units. Use the assorted print A's and cream B's to make 4 additional units.

Join a burgundy unit and an assorted print unit with an F as shown to make a section. Make 4 sections.

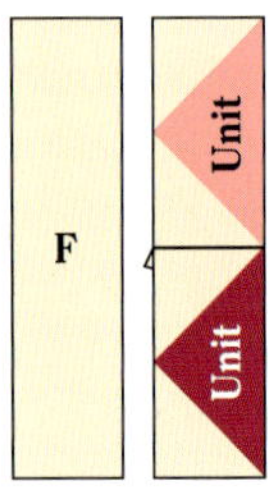

Section
Make 4

Sew the C–E patches together for the block center. Sew a section to the right of the block center with a partial seam as shown. Sew a section to the top, to the left and to the bottom of the block center.

Complete the partial seam to finish the block.

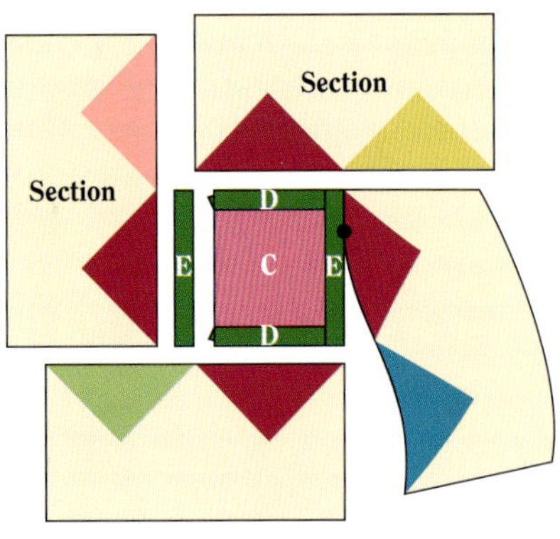

Block Assembly
● = Partial Seam

block no. 606

Upcycle

by Karen Griska • Online Quilt Museum.com
onlinequiltmuseum.com

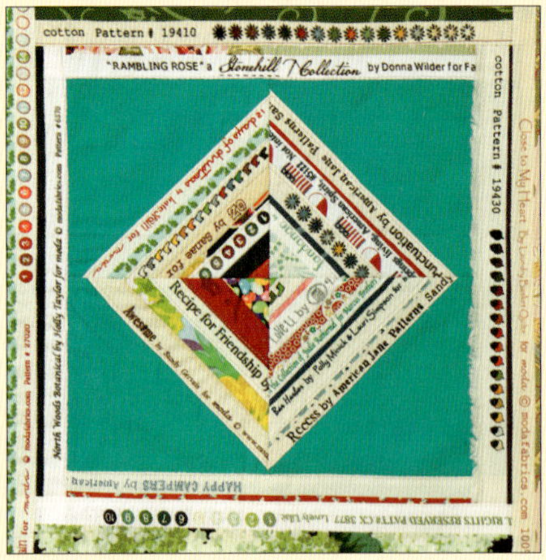

Karen Griska is the author of *Quilts from the Selvage Edge* for American Quilter's Society, americanquilter.com.

Teal Solid
4 squares (A) 5¼"x 5¼"

Selvages
1⅛"-wide strips to total about 100"
(see instructions below)
2 strips (B) 1⅛"x 10"
4 strips (C) 1⅛"x 11¼"
2 strips (D) 1⅛"x 12½"

Cut the selvage strips about 1½" wide and with extra length. This will give you more room to position the words and color windows wherever you like.

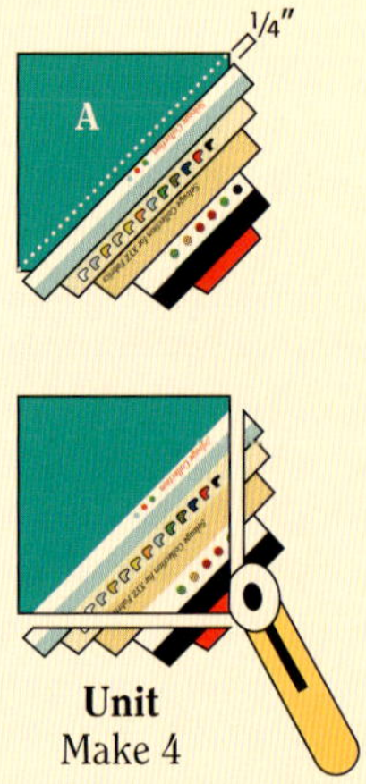

Unit
Make 4

Fold an A in half diagonally and gently crease the fold. With the right side up, lay the first selvage strip ¼" from the fold as shown. Sew along the bound edge of the strip (not the raw edge). Lay the next strip right side up along the first strip, covering the raw edge of the first strip with the bound edge of the second strip; sew along the bound edge. Keep adding and sewing strips to cover half of A as shown. Trim the strips even with the edges of A to complete the unit. Make 4 units.

Join the 4 units as shown. On one side of the joined units, lay the bound edge of a B over the ¼" seam allowance, matching the centers and ends. Sew along B's bound edge. Repeat to add the second B to the opposite side. Add the C's and D's in the same way. Center and trim the block to 12½"× 12½".

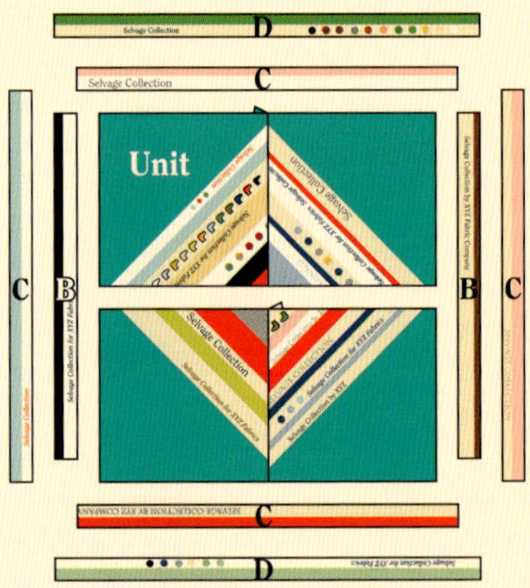

Block Piecing

block no. 607
Summer Fun

by Barbara Groves and Mary Jacobson • Me and My Sister Designs • meandmysisterdesigns.com

Fabric: Spring Fever designed by Barbara Groves and Mary Jacobson for Moda Fabrics, unitednotions.com.

Barbara and Mary are the authors of several books including *Still Crazy for Baby* for Leisure Arts, Inc., leisurearts.com.

White Dot
2 squares (A) 5¼" x 5¼"
Green Plaid
2 squares (A) 5¼" x 5¼"
4 squares (B) 2½" x 2½"
Pink Tone-on-Tone
4 squares (B) 2½" x 2½"
4 rectangles (C) 2½" x 4½"
Blue Print
1 square (D) 4½" x 4½"

Unit
Make 4

Pair the white A's and green A's to make 4 Quarter-Square Triangle units.

Join the patches and units as shown to make the block.

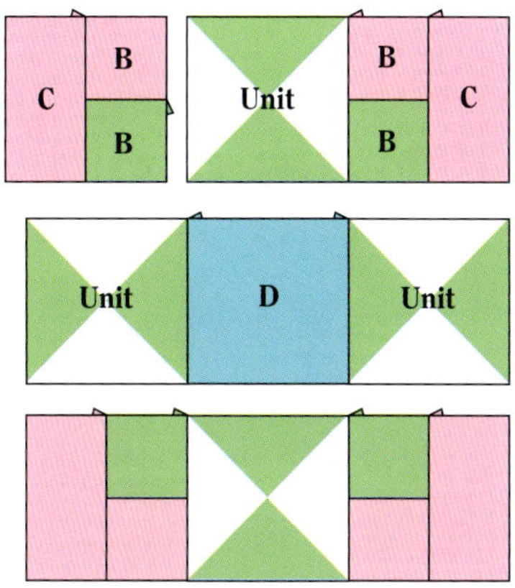

Block Piecing

block no. 608
Potted Posies

by Lynne Hagmeier • Kansas Troubles Quilters ktquilts.com

Fabric: Kansas Troubles Quilters designed by Lynne Hagmeier and other fabrics all from Moda Fabrics, unitednotions.com.

= cut in half diagonally
Tan Print
2 squares 3⅞" x 3⅞" (A)
4 squares (B) 3½" x 3½"
4 rectangles (C) 3½" x 6½"
4 Dark Red Prints
from *each*
1 square 3⅞" x 3⅞" (A)
(you'll have 4 extra triangles)
4 Dark Green Prints
from *each*
1 square (B) 3½" x 3½"
Dark Green Plaid
4 rectangles (D) ⅜" x 4"
4 Gold Prints
from *each*
1 square (E) 1⅛" x 1⅛"

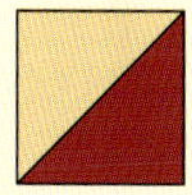

Unit 1
Make 4

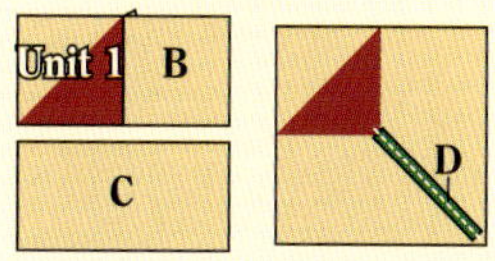

Unit 2 Partial Assembly

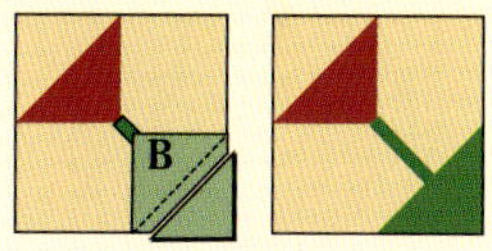

Unit 2 Stitch & Flip
Make 4

Pair an A from *each* of the dark red prints with a tan A to make 4 unit 1's as shown.

To make a unit 2, join a unit 1 to a tan B and C patch as shown. Position a D patch as shown; use matching thread and stitch down the center of the D. Refer to the diagram and the "Stitch-and-Flip" technique in the Techniques file on the PDF and add a dark green B as shown.

Refer to the block piecing diagram and position an E on a unit 2 as shown; use matching thread and stitch ⅛" from the raw edges. Repeat to make 4 unit 2's. Each unit 2 should measure 6½" × 6½".

Join the unit 2's as shown to complete the block.

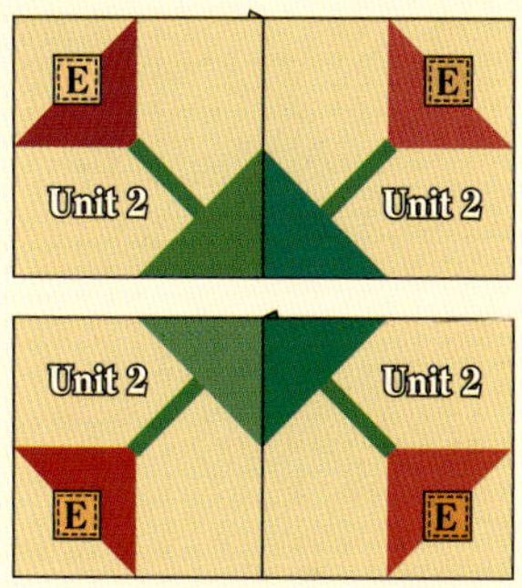

Block Piecing

block no. 609

Boxed In

by Julie Herman • Jaybird Quilts
jaybirdquilts.com

Fabric: Hunky Dory designed by Chez Moi for Moda Fabrics, unitednotions.com.

Assorted Prints
20 squares (A) 2½" x 2½"
Tan Tone-on-Tone
2 rectangles (B) 1½" x 4½"
2 rectangles (C) 1½" x 6½"
2 rectangles (D) 1½" x 10½"
2 rectangles (E) 1½" x 12½"

Join the patches as shown to complete the block.

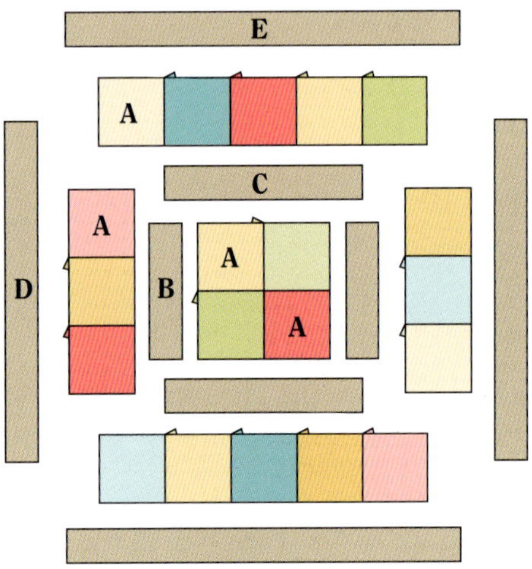

Block Piecing

block no. 610

Soldier's Star

by Carol Hopkins • Carol Hopkins Designs
carolhopkinsdesigns.com

Fabric: Civil War Tribute and Butter Churn and Cheddar, both designed by Judie Rothermel for Marcus Fabrics, marcusbrothers.com.

Rust Print
8 squares (A) 2⅞" x 2⅞"
4 squares (B) 4½" x 4½"
Brown Print
4 squares (A) 2⅞" x 2⅞"
1 square (B) 4½" x 4½"
8 squares (C) 2½" x 2½"
Cream Print
4 squares (A) 2⅞" x 2⅞"

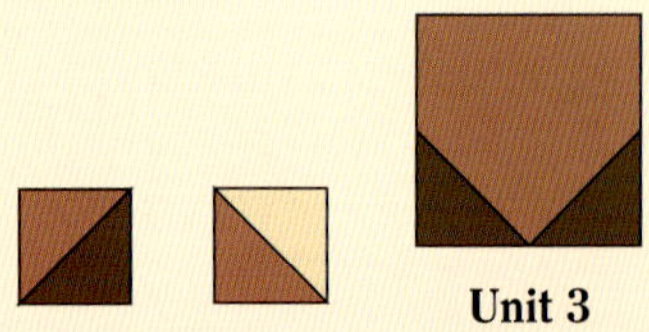

Unit 1 Make 8 | Unit 2 Make 8 | Unit 3 Stitch & Flip Make 4

Pair the dark brown A's and 4 rust A's to make 8 Triangle-Square unit 1's. Pair the cream A's with 4 rust A's to make 8 unit 2's.

Refer to "Stitch-and-Flip" in the Techniques file on the PDF and use the rust B's and the brown C's to make 4 unit 3's.

Sew the units and patches together as shown to complete the block.

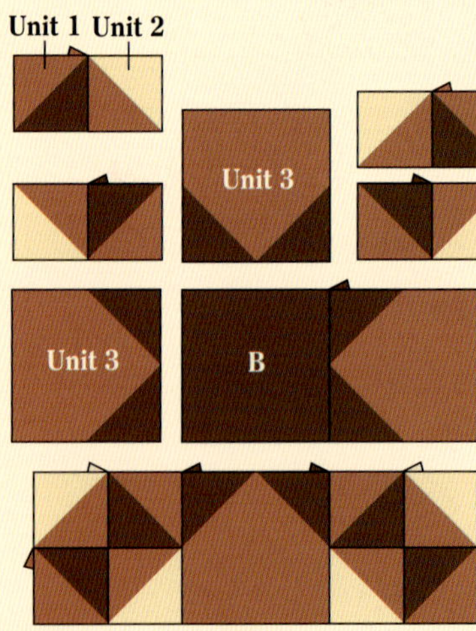

Block Piecing

block no. 611
Fusion

by Maria Hrabovsky • Maria Michaels Designs
mariamichaelsdesigns.com, quiltsforsale.ca

See page 42 on the PDF for pattern

Dark Blue, Red, Green and Purple Tone-on-Tones
from *each*
1 *each* templates A, Ar, C and D
Light Blue Tone-on-Tone
4 *each* templates B and Br

Matching the black dots on A and Ar to the black dots on C, join patches A–D in the appropriate colors to make each section.

It may be helpful to mark the sewing lines and the points where the seams intersect; place a pin through the marks at each intersection.

Join the sections as shown to complete the block.

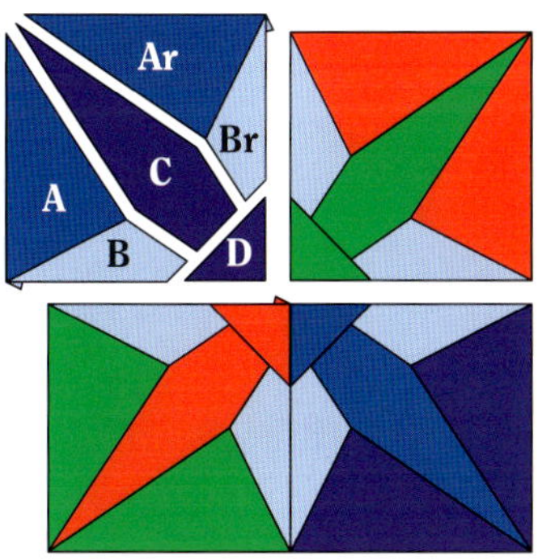

Block Piecing

block no. 612
Birthday Girl

by Bonnie Hunter
quiltville.com

Bonnie Hunter writes the "Addicted to Scraps" column for *Quiltmaker*. She is the author of *Scraps & Shirttails: Reuse, Re-purpose and Recycle* and *Adventures with Leaders & Enders* for Kansas City Star Quilts, pickledish.com.

⧄ = cut in half diagonally
Assorted Yellow Prints
16 squares (A) 2½″ x 2½″
2 squares 2⅞″ x 2⅞″ ⧄ (C)
Assorted Purple Prints
8 rectangles (B) 2½″ x 4½″
2 squares 4⅞″ x 4⅞″ ⧄ (D)
Assorted Red Prints
4 squares 2⅞″ x 2⅞″ ⧄ (C)
Assorted Cream Prints
6 squares 2⅞″ x 2⅞″ ⧄ (C)

Refer to "Stitch-and-Flip" in the Techniques file on the PDF. Use the yellow A's and the purple B's to make 4 unit 1's and 4 unit 2's as shown. Pair a yellow C and a red C to make a unit 3. Make 4 unit 3's.

Sew 4 red C's and 4 cream C's together as shown to make a Pinwheel.

Join the units, the patches and the Pinwheel as shown to complete the block.

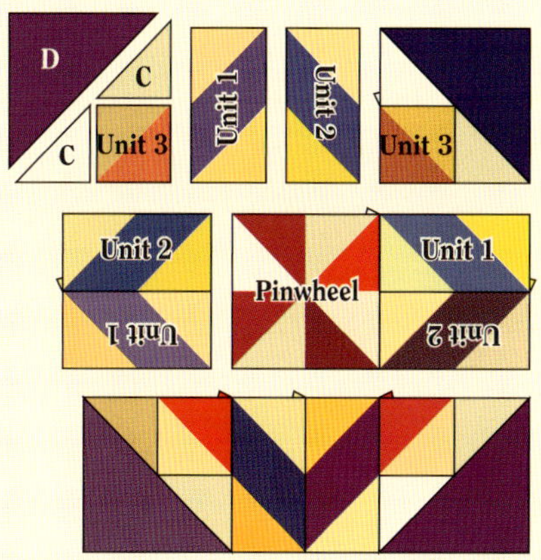

Block Piecing

block no. 613

Vanishing Squares

by Sandi Irish • The Irish Chain
irishchain.com

Fabric: Tonga Batiks by Timeless Treasures, ttfabrics.com.

◸ = cut in half diagonally

Reddish-Orange Batiks *and* Green Batiks

from *each* color group

- 1 square 2⅞" x 2⅞" ◸ (A) (there will be an extra triangle from each color group)
- 1 rectangle (B) 1½" x 2½"
- 1 rectangle (D) 2½" x 3½"
- 1 rectangle (F) 3½" x 5½"
- 1 rectangle (H) 4½" x 8½"

Black Batik

- 1 square (C) 1½" x 1½"
- 2 squares (E) 2½" x 2½"
- 1 square (G) 3½" x 3½"
- 1 rectangle (I) 2½" x 4½"

Blue Batik

- 1 square (E) 2½" x 2½"

Sew the patches together as shown to complete the block.

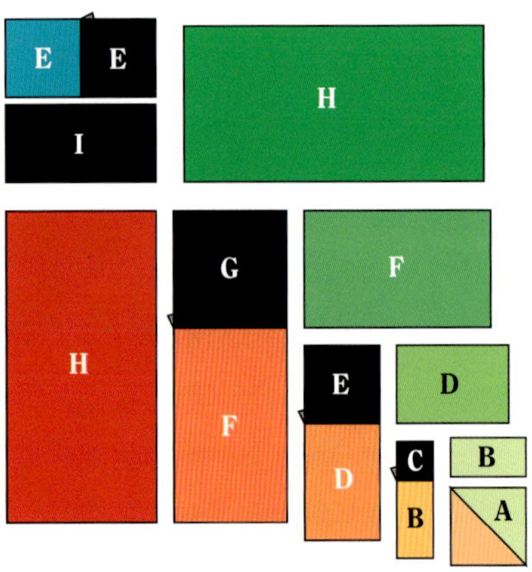

Block Piecing

block no. 614

Scarlet Days

by Kimberly Jolly • Fat Quarter Shop
fatquartershop.com

Fabric: Rural Jardin designed by French General for Moda Fabrics, unitednotions.com.

Red Print

- 1 square (A) 2½" x 2½"
- 6 squares (B) 1⅞" x 1⅞"
- 2 squares (D) 5¼" x 5¼"
- 6 squares (E) 2⅞" x 2⅞"

Tan Solid

- 4 squares (A) 2½" x 2½"
- 2 squares (B) 1⅞" x 1⅞"
- 1 square (C) 3¼" x 3¼"
- 14 squares (E) 2⅞" x 2⅞"

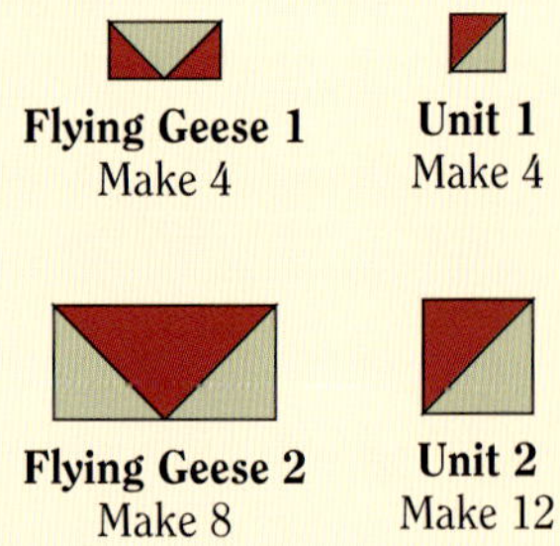

Use 4 red B's and the tan C to make 4 Flying Geese 1. Use the red D's and 8 tan E's to make 8 Flying Geese 2.

Pair 2 red and 2 tan B's to make 4 Triangle-Square unit 1's. Pair 6 red and 6 tan E's to make 12 unit 2's.

Sew the units and patches together as shown to complete the block.

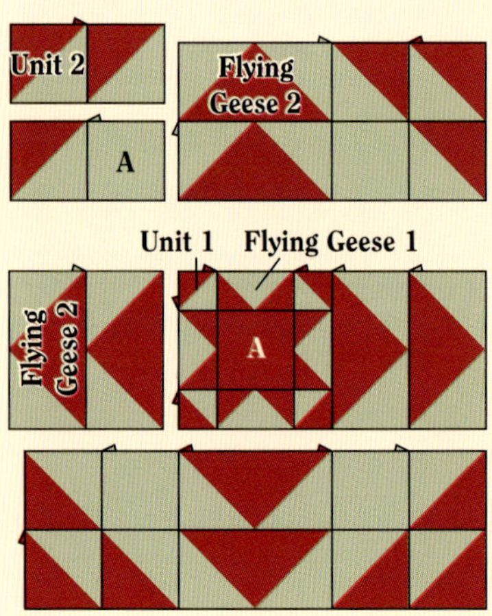

Block Piecing

pieced

block no. 615

Bar Code

by Bill Kerr and Weeks Ringle • FunQuilts
funquilts.com

Fabric: Cotton Supreme Solids from RJR Fabrics, rjrfabrics.com.

Weeks Ringle and Bill Kerr are co-authors of *Quiltmaker's Color Workshop*, *Modern Quilt Workshop* and the new *Quilts Made Modern* for C&T Publishing, ctpub.com.

Assorted Blue, Green and Purple Solids
about 45 strips, 7″ long, ¾″ to 1½″ wide

Pale Green Solid
2 strips (A) ¾″ x 6⅜″
1 strip (B) ¾″ x 12½″

Join strips randomly to make a section about 7″ × 7″. Trim the section to 6⅜″ × 6⅜″. Repeat to make a total of 4 sections. Join the sections with patches A and B as shown to complete the block.

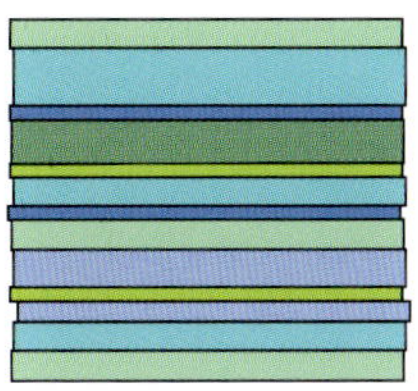

Section Piecing
Make 4

Trim to 6⅜″ x 6⅜″

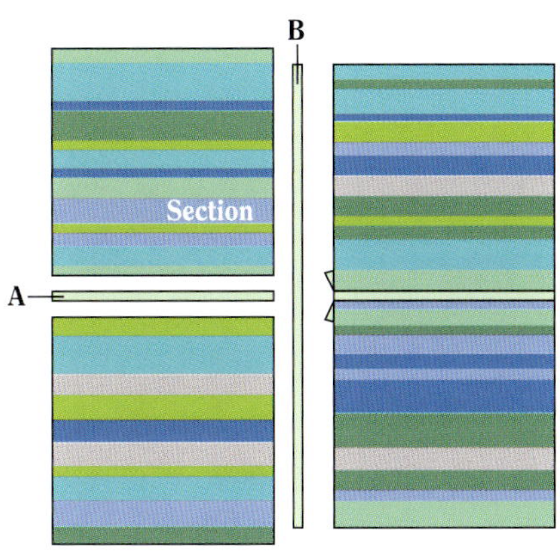

Block Piecing

block no. 616

Garden Star

by Perle Louise Krush • Perle Louise Designs
thimblecottagevillage.com

Fabric: Petal Pushers designed by Perle Louise Krush for Troy Riverwoods Collection, troy-corp.com.

Red Print
1 square (A) 4½″ x 4½″
4 squares (C) 2⅞″ x 2⅞″

Pale Green Dot
1 square (B) 5¼″ x 5¼″

Pale Yellow Print
1 square (B) 5¼″ x 5¼″
4 squares (C) 2⅞″ x 2⅞″

Blue Tone-on-Tone
2 squares (D) 4⅞″ x 4⅞″

Green Tone-on-Tone
2 squares (D) 4⅞″ x 4⅞″

Unit
Make 4

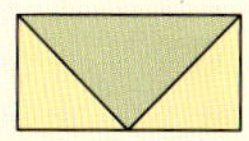

Flying Geese 1
Make 4

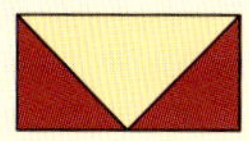

Flying Geese 2
Make 4

Pair the blue and green D's to make 4 Triangle-Square units.

Use the green dot B and yellow C's to make 4 Flying Geese 1. Use the yellow B and red C's to make 4 Flying Geese 2.

Join the units, Flying Geese and A as shown to complete the block.

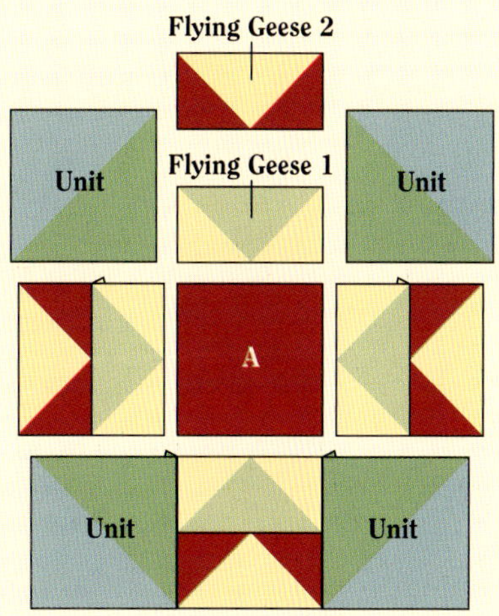

Block Piecing

block no. 617

Sunset Fiesta

by Judy Laquidara • Patchwork Times
patchworktimes.com

Fabric: Dimples designed by Gail Kessler for Andover Fabrics, andoverfabrics.com.

Judy Laquidara is the author of *Nine Patch Extravaganza* and *Weekend Quilts* for AQS, americanquilter.com.

Black Tone-on-Tone
- 2 squares (A) 4⅞" x 4⅞"
- 4 squares (B) 2½" x 2½"
- 2 rectangles (C) 1" x 4½"
- 2 rectangles (F) 1" x 2¼"

Teal Tone-on-Tone
- 2 squares (A) 4⅞" x 4⅞"
- 4 rectangles (D) 2¼" x 4½"
- 1 square (G) 1" x 1"

Yellow Tone-on-Tone
- 4 squares (B) 2½" x 2½"
- 2 rectangles (C) 1" x 4½"
- 4 rectangles (D) 2¼" x 4½"
- 2 rectangles (F) 1" x 2¼"

Pink Tone-on-Tone
- 4 squares (B) 2½" x 2½"
- 4 squares (E) 2¼" x 2¼"

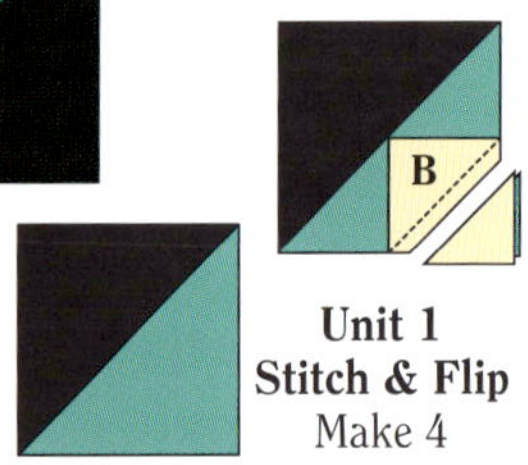

Unit 1
Stitch & Flip
Make 4

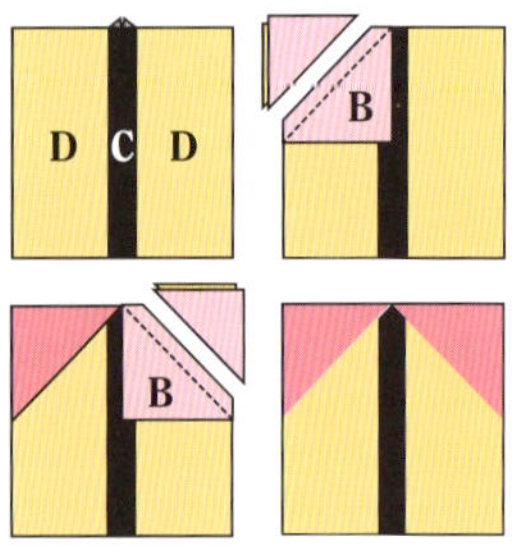

Unit 2
Stitch & Flip
Make 2

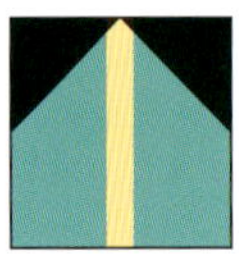

Unit 3
Stitch & Flip
Make 2

Pair the black A's and teal A's to make 4 Triangle-Square unit 1's. Refer to "Stitch-and-Flip" in the Techniques file on the PDF. Add yellow B's to the teal patches as shown to complete the unit 1's.

Sew a black C between 2 yellow D's. Use the Stitch-and-Flip technique to add pink B's to the corners as shown to make a unit 2. Make 2 unit 2's. In the same way, use the yellow C, teal D's and black B's to make 2 unit 3's.

Join units and patches as shown to complete the block.

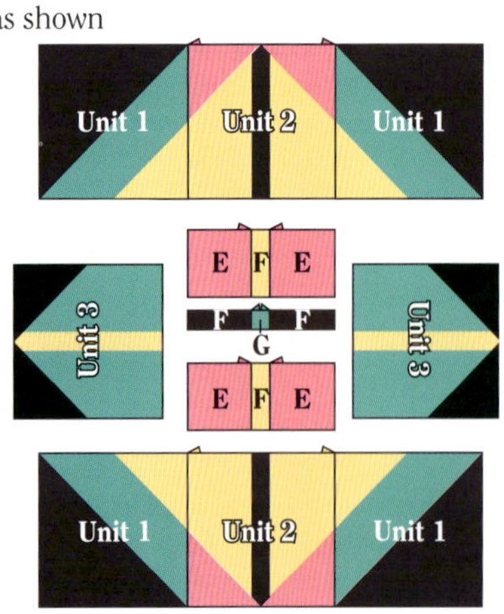

Block Assembly

block no. 618

Focal Point

by Doug Leko • Antler Quilt Design
antlerquiltdesign.com

Fabric: Bon Voyage Batiks designed by Laundry Basket Quilts for Moda Fabrics, unitednotions.com.

Cream Batik
- 10 squares (A) 2⅞" x 2⅞"
- 1 square (C) 4½" x 4½"
- 4 squares (D) 2½" x 2½"
- 8 rectangles (E) 1½" x 4½"

Red Batik
- 4 squares (A) 2⅞" x 2⅞"
- 4 squares (D) 2½" x 2½"

Black Print
- 2 squares (A) 2⅞" x 2⅞"
- 1 square (B) 5¼" x 5¼"

Unit 1
Make 8

Unit 2
Make 4

Unit 3
Make 4

Unit 4
Stitch & Flip
Make 1

Pair the cream A's and red A's to make 8 Triangle-Square unit 1's. Pair the cream A's and black A's to make 4 unit 2's.

Use the black B and cream A's to make 4 Flying Geese unit 3's.

Refer to "Stitch-and-Flip" in the Techniques file on the PDF. Use the cream C and red D's to make 1 unit 4.

Join the units and patches as shown to complete the block.

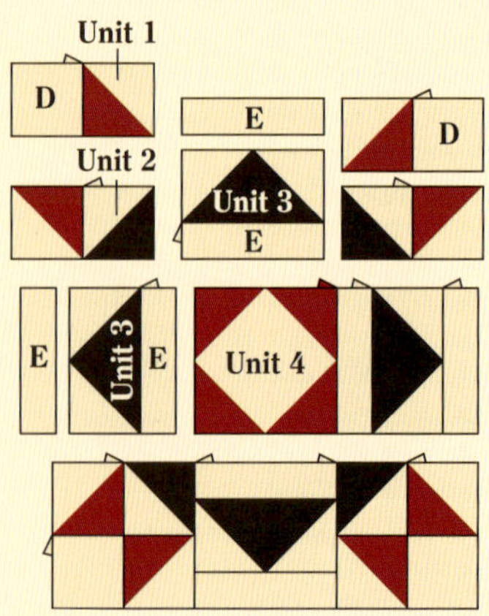

Block Assembly

block no. 619

Nouveau Riche

by Toby Lischko • Gateway Quilts & Stuff
gatewayquiltsnstuff.com

Toby Lischko is the author of *St. Louis Stars* for Kansas City Star Quilts, pickledish.com.

Acrylic templates for *Nouveau Riche* are available from gatewayquiltsnstuff.com.

See pages 44–45 on the PDF for pattern

Assorted Gold Batiks
4 template A
4 template D

Assorted Black Batiks
2 template B
2 template C

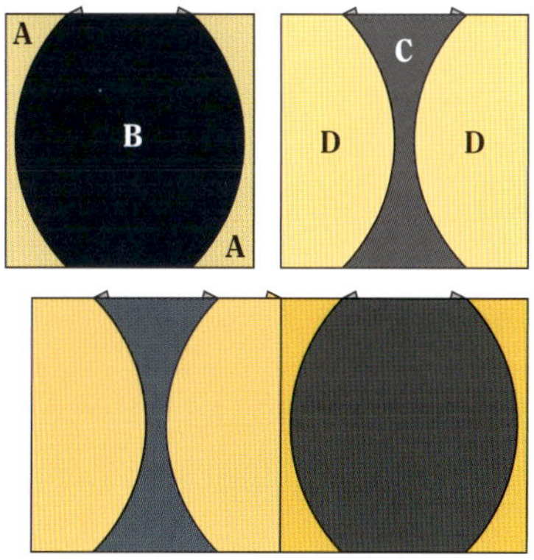

Block Piecing

Find tips for curved piecing on Toby's blog (gatewayquiltsnstuff .blogspot.com).

Join patches A–D as shown in the block piecing diagram.

block no. 620

Tapestry

by Rebecca LoGiudice • Willow Hill Quilts
willowhillquilts.net

Fabric: Borders 2008, Porcelana and Hermitage, all by Jinny Beyer for RJR Fabrics, rjrfabrics.com.

Dark Red Tone-on-Tone
1 square (A) 4½" x 4½"

Red Print
2 rectangles (B) 1½" x 2½"
4 rectangles (D) 2½" x 4½"
8 squares (F) 2½" x 2½"

Medium Red Tone-on-Tone
2 rectangles (B) 1½" x 2½"

Gold Print
4 rectangles (C) 2" x 2½"
4 rectangles (D) 2½" x 4½"
12 squares (F) 2½" x 2½"
4 rectangles (G) 2½" x 4"

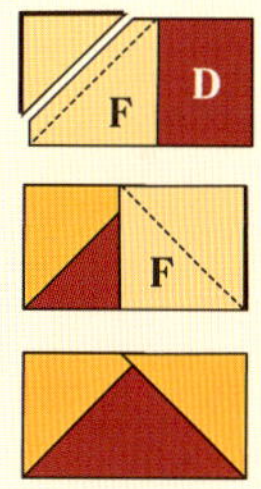

Unit 1
Stitch & Flip
Make 4

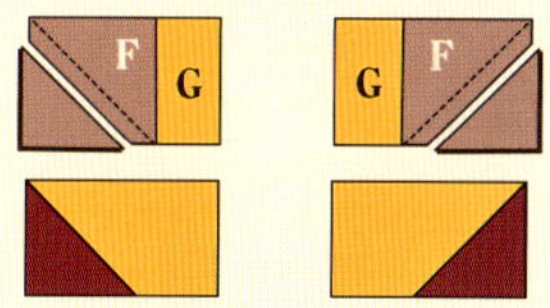

Unit 2
Stitch & Flip
Make 2

Unit 3
Stitch & Flip
Make 2

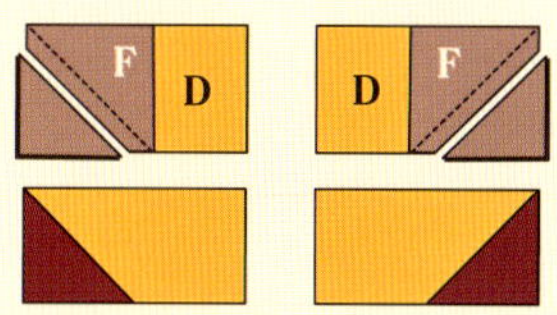

Unit 4
Stitch & Flip
Make 2

Unit 5
Stitch & Flip
Make 2

Becca fussy cut the red print patches. She suggests auditioning fabric by cutting a "window" in freezer paper the size of the finished patch.

Refer to "Stitch-and-Flip" in the Techniques file on the PDF. Use the gold print F's and red print D's to make 4 unit 1's as shown. Use red print F's and gold G's to make 2 unit 2's and 2 unit 3's as shown. Use red print F's and gold D's to make 2 unit 4's and 2 unit 5's.

Positioning matching red B's opposite each other, join the patches and units as shown in the block piecing diagram to complete the block.

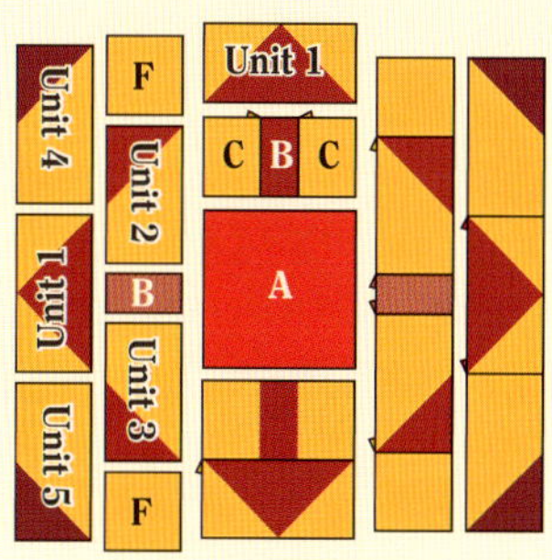

Block Piecing

block no. 621
Sunburst

by Nancy Mahoney
nancymahoney.com

Nancy Mahoney designs fabric for P&B Textiles, pbtex.com, and is the author of *Treasures From the 30s* for Martingale & Co., martingale-pub.com.

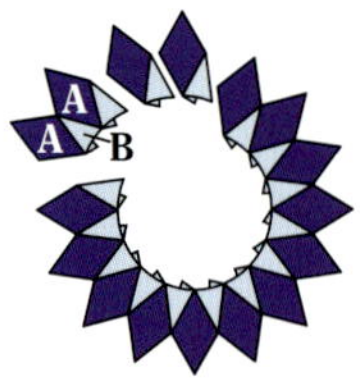

See page 50 on the PDF for pattern

Purple Batik
16 template A
Light Blue Batik
16 template B
Beige Batik
16 template C
1 square (E) 12½" x 12½"
Blue and Purple Batik
1 circle (D) 5⅜" diameter
Transparent plastic
Heavy metallic thread

Center Unit

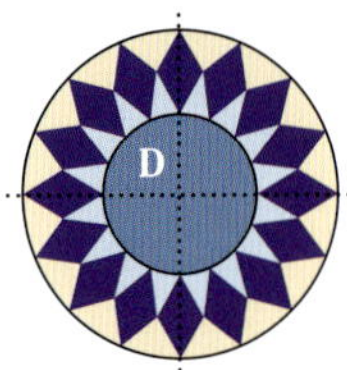

Applique Placement

Refer to "Set-in Seams" in the Techniques file on the PDF. Sew the A's and B's together as shown. Add the C's to A/B to make the center unit. Prepare D for turned-edge appliqué. Use a machine zigzag stitch to appliqué D to the center unit as shown in the appliqué placement diagram. The center unit should measure 10½". Fold the center unit in half both ways and lightly crease the folds.

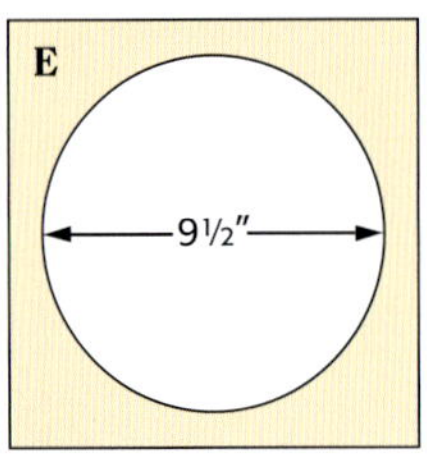

Frame

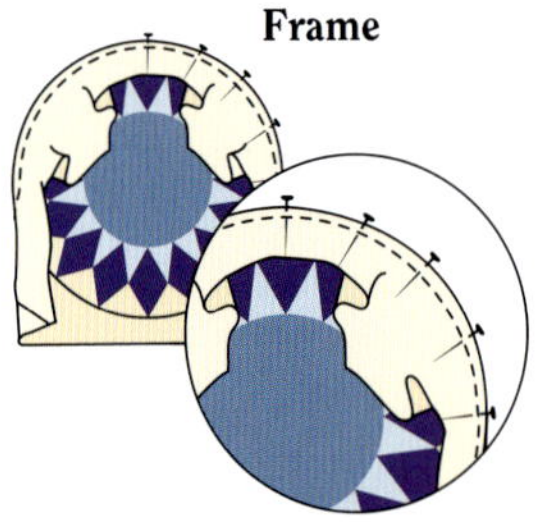

Fold E in half both ways and lightly crease the folds. Trace a 9½" circle on the transparent plastic. Use this template to cut a circle from the center of E to make the frame. To set the center unit in the frame, align the creases and pin. Add a few more pins between the creases as shown. With the center unit next to the feed dogs, join to complete the block. Couch metallic thread around the D with a machine zigzag stitch.

Block

block no. 622
Homestead Album

by Sarah Maxwell and Dolores Smith • Homestead Hearth • homesteadhearth.com

Fabric: Family Album designed by Homestead Hearth for Marcus Fabrics, marcusbrothers.com.

⧄ = cut in half diagonally
⊠ = cut in half twice diagonally

Cream Print
2 squares (A) 2⅜" x 2⅜"
4 rectangles (C) 2" x 6½"
1 square 4¼" x 4¼" ⊠ (D)
Medium Blue Print
2 squares (A) 2⅜" x 2⅜"
Brown Print and Rust Print #1
from *each*
2 squares (A) 2⅜" x 2⅜"
4 rectangles (B) 1¼" x 3½"
Dark Blue Print
4 rectangles (C) 2" x 6½"
Rust Print #2
1 square 4¼" x 4¼" ⊠ (D)
Green Print
2 squares 3⅞" x 3⅞" ⧄ (E)

Unit 1
Make 4

Unit 2
Make 4

Pair the cream A's and medium blue A's to make 4 Triangle-Square unit 1's. Pair the brown A's and rust A's to make 4 unit 2's.

Sew the units and patches together as shown to make the block.

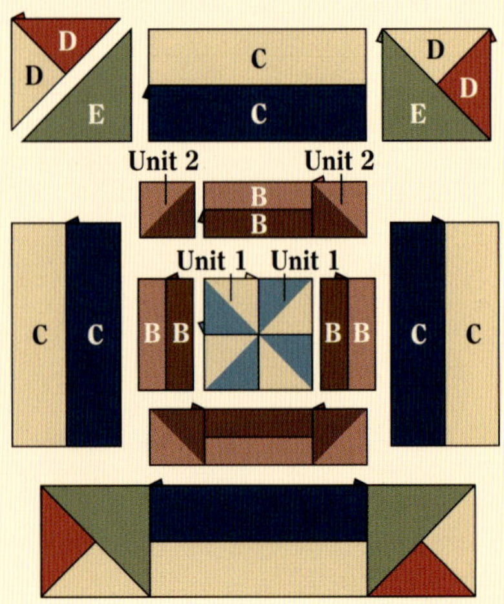

Block Piecing

block no. 623

Joyful Noise

by Margaret Miller • Miller Quilts, Inc.
millerquilts.com

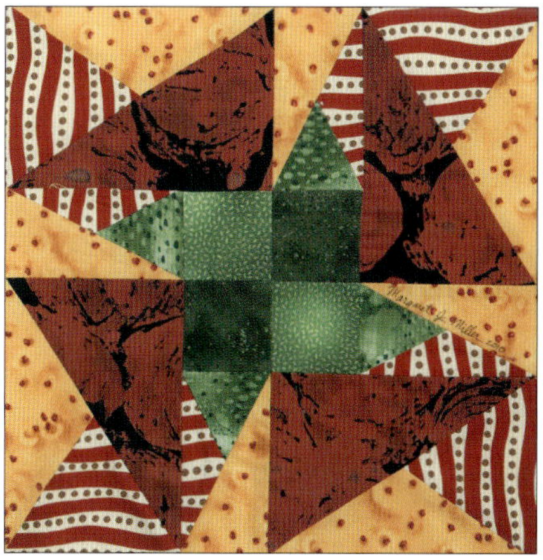

Margaret Miller is the author of *AnglePlay Blocks* and other titles for C&T Publishing, ctpub.com.

Margaret has also designed a line of AnglePlay Templates to simplify the cutting for these and other similar patches.

See page 70 on the PDF for pattern

⧄ = cut in half diagonally

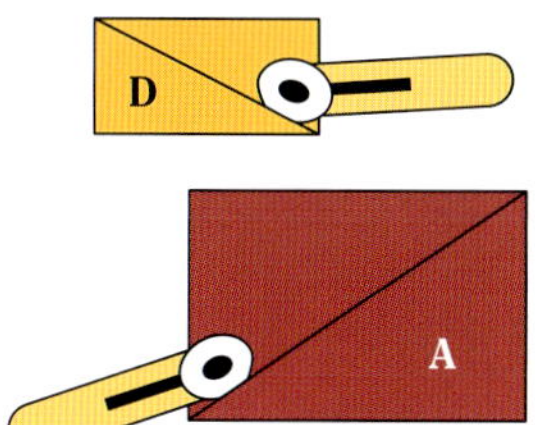

Cutting

Red Print
4 rectangles...

Red Print

2 rectangles 4¾″ x 7″ ⧄ (A)

Red and Cream Stripe

4 *each* templates B and F

Gold Print

4 template C

2 rectangles 2⅝″ x 5⅜″ ⧄ (D)

Medium Green Tone-on-Tone #1

4 template E

Medium Green Tone-on-Tone #2 and Dark Green Tone-on-Tone

from *each*

4 squares (G) 2½″ x 2½″

If you stack your fabrics before cutting, have all of the right sides facing up.

Sew patches A–C together as shown to make a unit 1. Make 4 unit 1's. Sew patches D–F together as shown to make a unit 2. Make 4 unit 2's.

Join the units and G's as shown to complete the block.

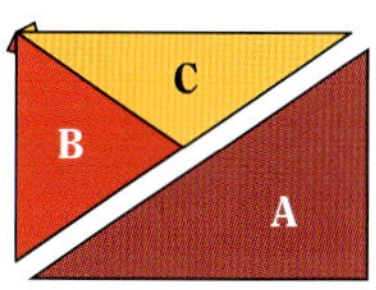

Unit 1
Make 4

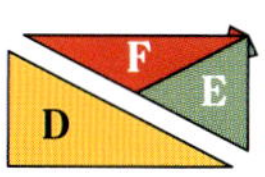

Unit 2
Make 4

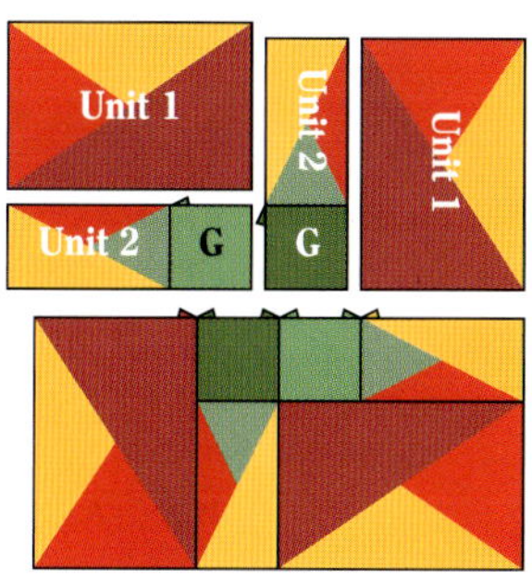

Block Piecing

block no. 624

Shifting Star

by Scott Murkin • Patchwork Possibilities
patchworkpossibilities.com

Rust Print

4 rectangles (A) 3½″ x 6½″

Cream Tone-on-Tone

4 squares (B) 3½″ x 3½″

Light Brown Print #1

4 squares (B) 3½″ x 3½″

Light Brown Print #2

4 rectangles (C) 2½″ x 6½″

Dark Brown Stripe

4 rectangles (D) 1½″ x 6½″

Refer to "Stitch-and-Flip" in the Techniques file on the PDF. Noticing the difference in color placement, use the A and B patches as shown to make the unit 1's and unit 2's.

Join the units with C and D patches as shown to make each section. Join the sections to complete the block.

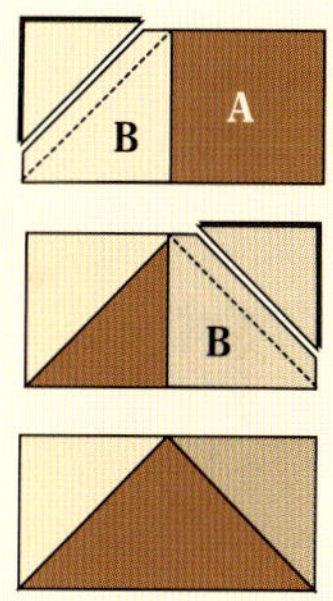

Unit 1
Stitch & Flip
Make 2

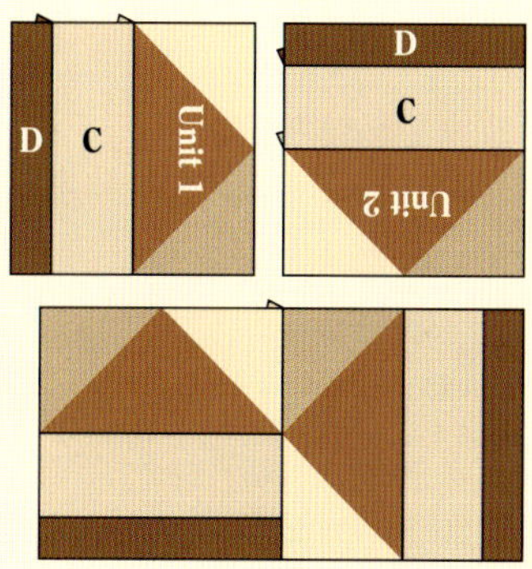

Block Piecing

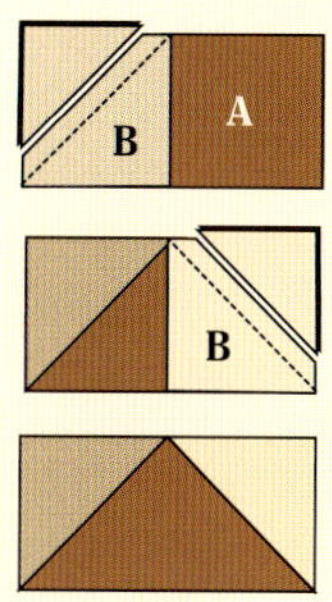

Unit 2
Stitch & Flip
Make 2

pieced

block no. 625

Chunky Monkey

by Carrie Nelson • Miss Rosie's Quilt Co.
missrosiesquiltco.com

Fabric: Simple Abundance from Cotton Blossoms for Moda Fabrics, unitednotions.com.

Carrie Nelson is the author of numerous quilting titles including *Schnibbles Times Two* for Martingale & Company, martingale-pub.com.

Cream Dot
- 8 squares (A) 2⅜″ x 2⅜″
- 16 rectangles (B) 1¼″ x 3″

12 Assorted Prints

from *4*
- 2 squares (A) 2⅜″ x 2⅜″

from *4*
- 4 rectangles (B) 1¼″ x 3″

from *4*
- 1 square (C) 3″ x 3″

Blue Print
- 4 rectangles (D) 1½″ x 6″

Red Print
- 1 square (E) 1½″ x 1½″

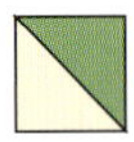

Unit
Make 16

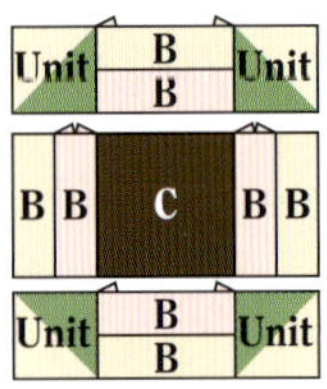

Section
Make 4

Pair the cream dot A's with the print A's to make 16 Triangle-Square units.

Refer to the diagram; join units and patches as shown to make 4 sections. Each section will measure 6" × 6".

Join the sections and patches as shown to complete the block.

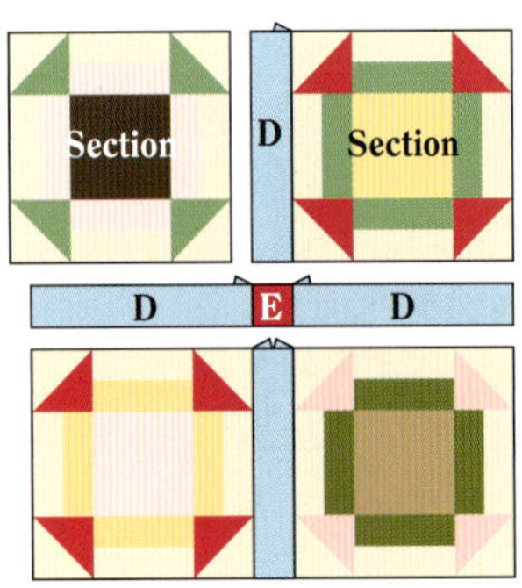

Block Piecing

block no. 626

Star Dance

by Celine Perkins • Perkins Dry Goods
perkinsdrygoods.com

Fabric: Assorted fabrics by Jo Morton for Andover Fabrics, andoverfabrics.com.

◸ = cut in half diagonally
☒ = cut in half twice diagonally

Brown Print
- 1 square (A) 4½″ x 4½″
- 4 squares (B) 2½″ x 2½″
- 2 squares (E) 2⅞″ x 2⅞″

Tan Print
- 12 squares (B) 2½″ x 2½″
- 2 squares (E) 2⅞″ x 2⅞″
- 1 square 5¼″ x 5¼″ ☒ (D)

Dark Blue Print
- 2 squares 4⅞″ x 4⅞″ ◸ (C)

Medium Blue Print
- 1 square 5¼″ x 5¼″ ☒ (D)

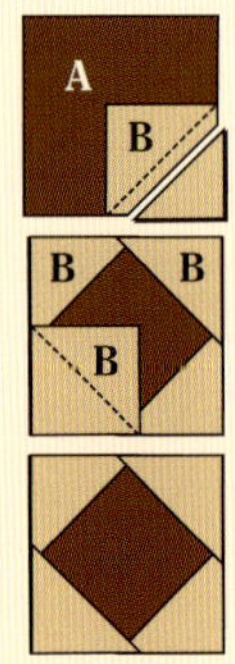

Unit 1
Stitch & Flip
Make 1

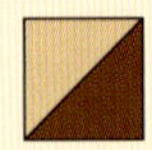

Unit 2
Make 4

Refer to "Stitch-and-Flip" in the Techniques file on the PDF and use the brown A and 4 tan B's to make unit 1 as shown.

Pair the brown E's with the tan E's to make 4 Triangle-Square unit 2's.

Sew the units and patches together as shown to complete the block.

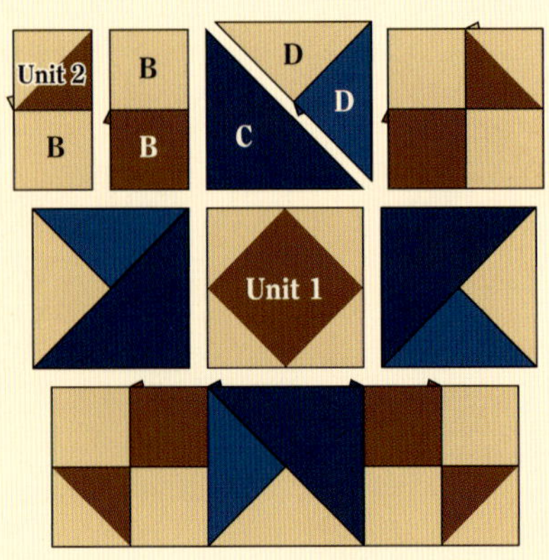

Block Piecing

block no. 627

Diamond Blade

by Leslee Price • Painted Pony 'n Quilts
ppnq.com

White Tone-on-Tone
6 squares (A) 2⅞″ x 2⅞″
12 squares (B) 2½″ x 2½″
24 squares (C) 1½″ x 1½″
Blue Print
6 squares (A) 2⅞″ x 2⅞″
Pink Print
24 squares (C) 1½″ x 1½″

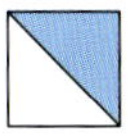

Unit 1
Make 12

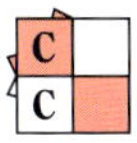

Unit 2
Make 12

Pair the white A's and the blue A's to make 12 Triangle-Square unit 1's.

Join the C patches as shown to make the unit 2's.

Join the unit 1's and 2's with the B patches to make the 4 sections as shown. Sew the sections together to complete the block.

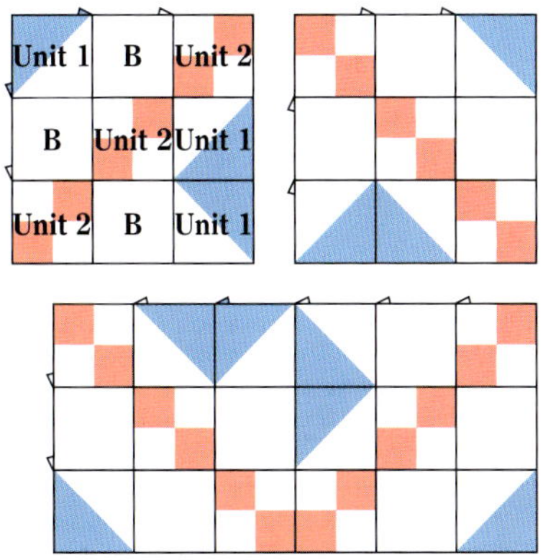

Block Piecing

block no. 628

Night Owl

by Marjorie Rhine • Quilt Design NW
quiltdesignnw.com

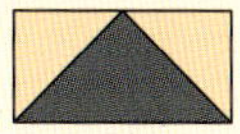

Unit
Stitch and Flip
Make 2

◩ = cut in half diagonally

Tan Tone-on-Tone
1 rectangle (A) 6½″ x 9½″
4 squares (B) 1¼″ x 1¼″
2 rectangles (C) 1¼″ x 2″
Gray Print
2 rectangles (C) 1¼″ x 2″
1 pattern G
Brown Plaid
2 squares (B) 1¼″ x 1¼″
1 square 2⅜″ x 2⅜″ ◩ (D)
Assorted Dark Prints
8 squares 2⅜″ x 2⅜″ ◩ (D)
Black Tone-on-Tone
2 rectangles (C) 1¼″ x 2″
3 squares 2⅜″ x 2⅜″ ◩ (D)
2 rectangles (E) 2″ x 10¼″
1 rectangle (F) 2¾″ x 12½″

Template for Night Owl block on page 46 of the PDF Templates file.

White Tone-on-Tone
2 pattern H
Gold Tone-on-Tone
2 pattern I
Black Solid
2 pattern J
Fusible web

Refer to "Stitch-and-Flip" in the Techniques file on the PDF. Use the gray C's and tan B's to make 2 units. Add plaid B's to the top 2 corners of A as shown.

Fold A in half vertically. Prepare patches G–J for fusible appliqué. Use the crease and the block assembly diagram to arrange the patches on A. Fuse the patches to A. Use matching thread and a zigzag stitch to sew around the appliqué patches.

Join the units and patches to complete the block.

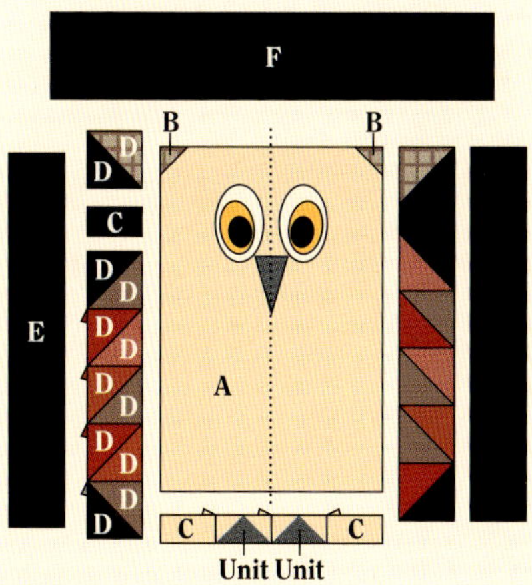

Block Assembly

block no. 629
Ripples

by Laura Stone Roberts • Assistant Editor, *McCall's Quilting* • mccallsquilting.com

Brown Tone-on-Tone
- 14 squares (A) 1½″ x 1½″
- 14 rectangles (B) 1½″ x 2½″
- 4 rectangles (C) 1½″ x 3½″

Pink Tone-on-Tone
- 16 squares (A) 1½″ x 1½″
- 10 rectangles (B) 1½″ x 2½″
- 8 rectangles (C) 1½″ x 3½″

Pale Blue Tone-on-Tone
- 30 squares (A) 1½″ x 1½″

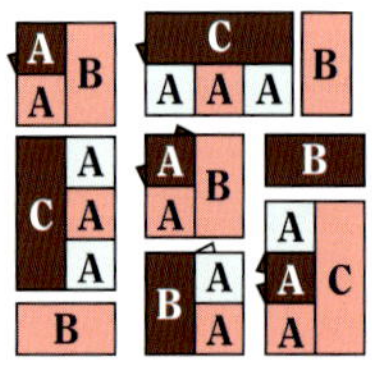

Section 1
Make 2

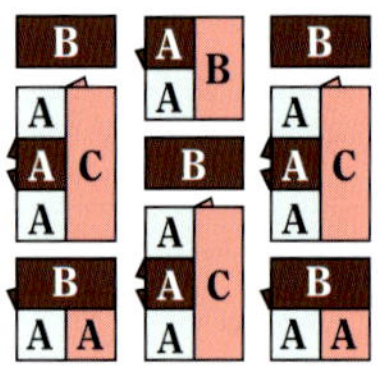

Section 2
Make 1

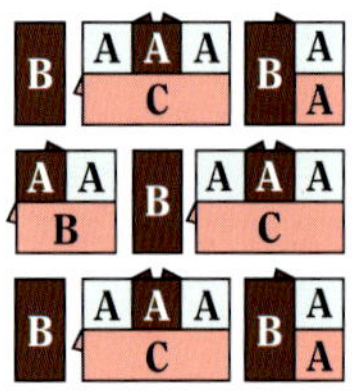

Section 3
Make 1

Referring to the diagrams, sew the patches for each section together as shown. Each section will measure 6½" × 6½".

Note the orientation of the sections in the block assembly diagram; join the sections to finish the block as shown.

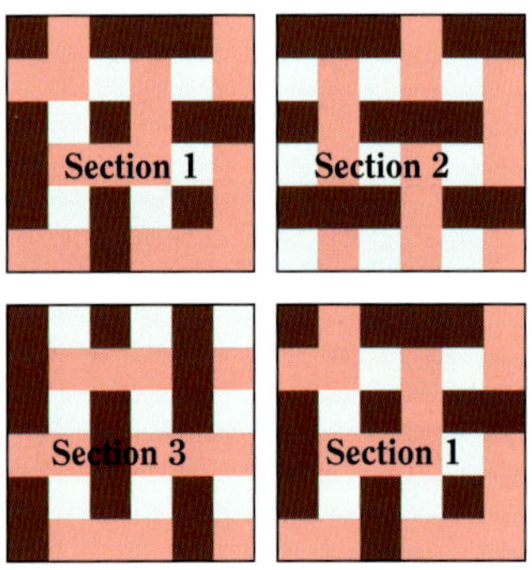

Block Assembly

block no. 630
Carousel

by Gerri Robinson • Planted Seed Designs
plantedseeddesigns.com

Fabric: Sugar designed by Patricia Bravo for Art Gallery Fabrics, artgalleryfabrics.com.

White Solid
- 18 squares (A) 1⅞″ x 1⅞″

Assorted Prints
- 18 squares (A) 1⅞″ x 1⅞″ (9 sets of 2 matching A's)
- 8 rectangles (B) 1½″ x 2½″
- 8 rectangles (C) 1½″ x 6½″

Red Print
- 2 rectangles (D) 1½″ x 10½″
- 2 rectangles (E) 1½″ x 12½″

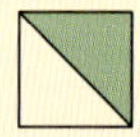

Unit
Make 9 sets of 4 matching units.

Pinwheel
Make 9

Pair 2 white A's with 2 matching assorted A's to make 4 Triangle-Square units. Repeat to make 9 sets of 4 matching units.

Sew together 4 matching units to make a Pinwheel.

Join the Pinwheels and patches as shown to complete the block.

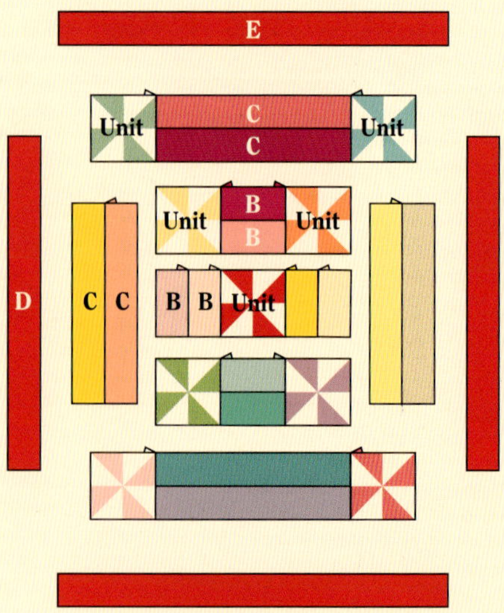

Block Piecing

block no. 631

Dragonfly

by Cindy Simms • Kats Designs
cindysimms.net

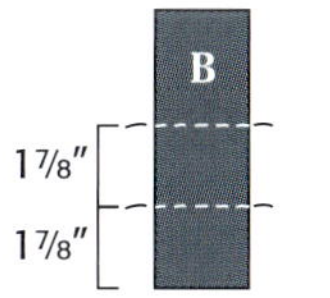

Tail Basting

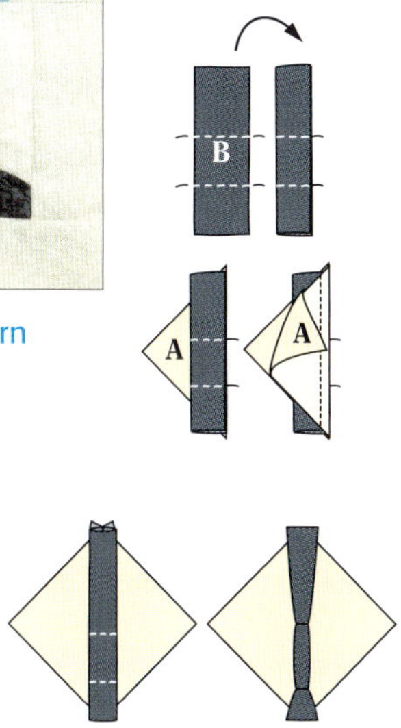

Unit

See page 63 on the PDF for pattern

⧄ = cut in half diagonally

Cream Print

- 1 square 5⅜" x 5⅜" ⧄ (A)
- 2 rectangles (E) 2¼" x 2¾"
- 1 square (F) 2¾" x 2¾"
- 1 square 4½" x 4½" ⧄ (G)
- 1 rectangle (H) 2" x 5"
- 1 rectangle (I) 2" x 6½"
- 1 *each* templates M and Mr
- 1 square 3¾" x 3¾" ⧄ (N)

Assorted Black Prints

- 1 rectangle (B) 2½" x 7¼"
- 1 square (C) 2¼" x 2¼"
- 2 rectangles (D) 2½" x 4¼" for eyes
- 1 template J

Green Batik

- 1 *each* templates K and Kr

Blue Batik

- 1 *each* templates L and Lr

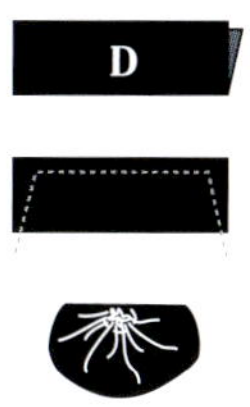

Eye Basting

Refer to the tail basting diagram. Prepare the B by basting across in 2 places as shown. With wrong sides together, fold in half lengthwise. Matching raw edges, layer the B between 2 A's as shown. Sew through all the layers to create the unit. From the back, pull on the basting threads to gather the tail into sections as shown. Tie knots in the basting threads to secure. Press the seam open.

Refer to the eye basting diagram. Fold a D in half lengthwise, wrong sides together. Baste through both layers as shown. Pull the basting threads to gather the edges. Repeat for the other D. Sandwich the D's into the seams on adjoining sides of C as shown; be sure raw edges are well within the seam allowance. Join the patches and unit to make the block as shown.

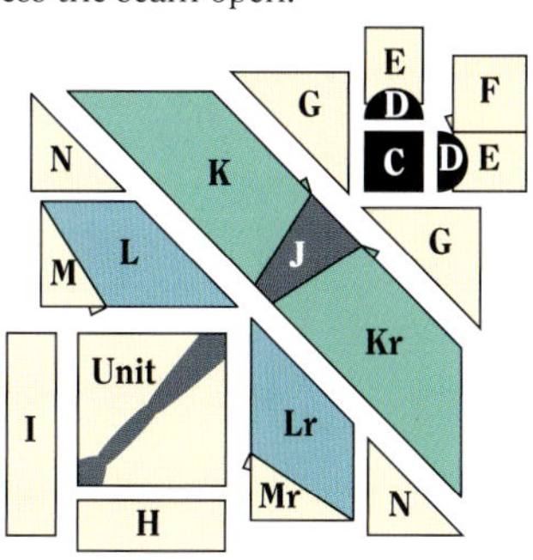

Block Piecing

block no. 632

Tumbler Star

by Benita Skinner • Victoriana Quilt Designs
victorianaquiltdesigns.com

⧄ = cut in half diagonally
⊠ = cut in half twice diagonally

White Tone-on-Tone

- 1 square 5¼" x 5¼" ⊠ (A)
- 4 squares (C) 4½" x 4½"

Medium Purple Tone-on-Tone

- 1 square 5¼" x 5¼" ⊠ (A)
- 1 square 4⅞" x 4⅞" ⧄ (B)

Dark Purple Tone-on-Tone

- 1 square 5¼" x 5¼" ⊠ (A)
- 1 square 4⅞" x 4⅞" ⧄ (B)

Join the patches as shown to make the block.

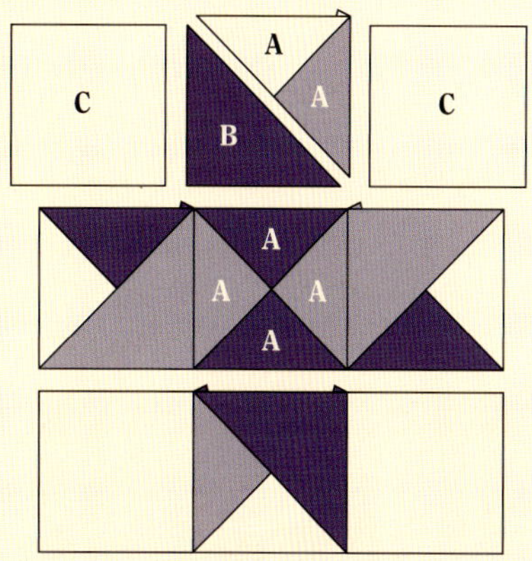

Block Piecing

block no. 633

Mount Vernon Steps

by Maria Umhey • Cheerful Quilts

Fabric: Washington's Legacy designed by Nancy Gere for Windham Fabrics, windhamfabrics.com.

⊠ = cut in half twice diagonally

Cream Print

1 square 5¼" x 5¼" ⊠ (A) (there will be 2 extra)

Dark Red Floral

1 square 5¼" x 5¼" ⊠ (A) (there will be 2 extra)

Assorted Light Prints

2 rectangles (B) 1½" x 4½"
2 rectangles (C) 1½" x 6½"
2 rectangles (D) 1½" x 8½"
2 rectangles (E) 1½" x 10½"

Assorted Dark Prints

2 rectangles (C) 1½" x 6½"
2 rectangles (D) 1½" x 8½"
2 rectangles (E) 1½" x 10½"
2 rectangles (F) 1½" x 12½"

Join the A's to make the block center. Add 2 light logs followed by 2 dark logs. Continue adding logs in this manner to complete the block.

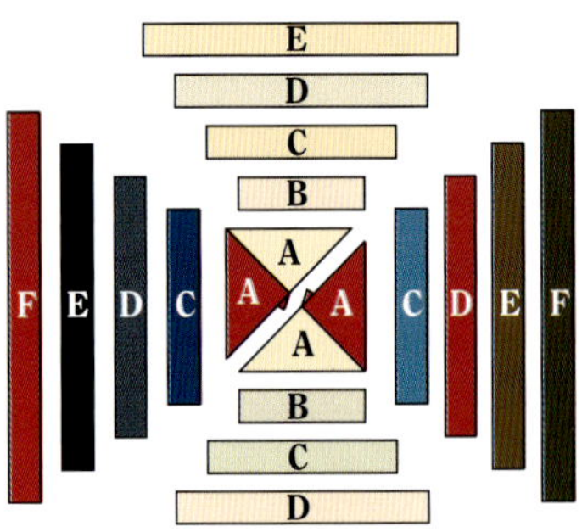

Block Piecing

block no. 634

Summer Picnic

by Pam Vieira-McGinnis • PamKittyMorning
pamkittymorning.blogspot.com

Fabric: Flower Sugar and Color Basic from Lecien, lecien.co.jp.

Cream Print

6 squares (A) 2⅞" x 2⅞"
12 squares (C) 2½" x 2½"

Red Check

6 squares (A) 2⅞" x 2⅞"
4 squares (C) 2½" x 2½"

Blue Print

8 rectangles (B) 2½" x 4½"
1 square (D) 4½" x 4½"

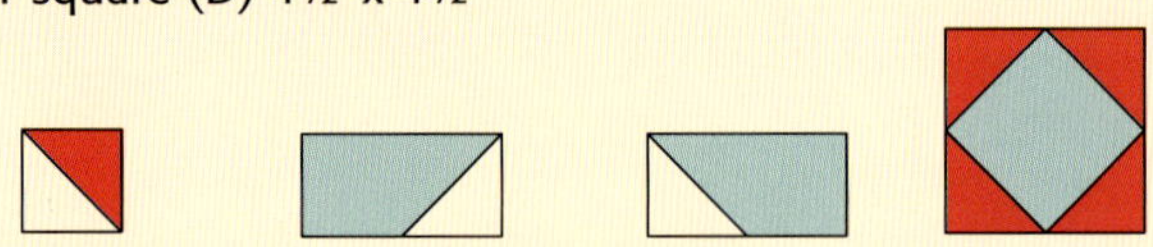

Unit 1 Make 12 | **Unit 2 Stitch & Flip** Make 4 | **Unit 3 Stitch & Flip** Make 4 | **Unit 4 Stitch & Flip** Make 1

Pair the red A's with the cream A's to make 12 Triangle-Square unit 1's. Refer to "Stitch-and-Flip" in the Techniques file on the PDF. With blue B's and cream C's make 4 unit 2's and 4 unit 3's. Make 1 unit 4 from the red C's and D.

Join the remaining cream C patches with the various units as shown in the block piecing diagram to complete the block.

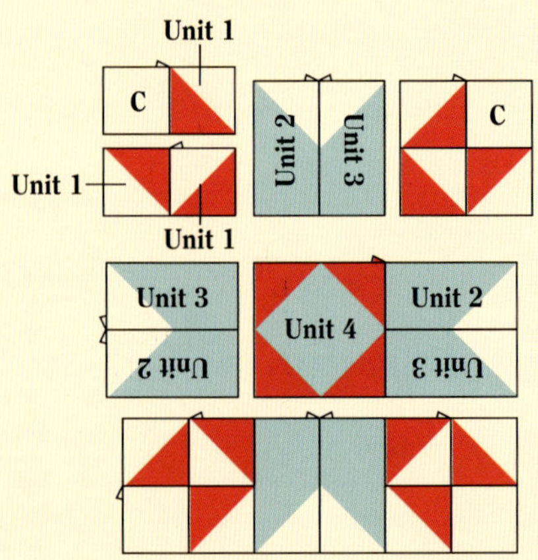

Block Piecing

pieced

block no. 635

Porch Swing

by Cyndi Walker • Stitch Studios
stitchstudios.com

Yellow Check
- 2 squares (A) 2⅞" x 2⅞"
- 4 rectangles (B) 2½" x 4½"

Cream Solid
- 4 squares (A) 2⅞" x 2⅞"
- 4 rectangles (B) 2½" x 4½"

Pink Solid and Red Print
from *each*
- 3 squares (A) 2⅞" x 2⅞"

Blue Tone-on-Tone and Green Print
from *each*
- 4 squares (A) 2⅞" x 2⅞"

Blue Plaid and Blue Print
from *each*
- 4 squares (C) 2½" x 2½"

Unit 1 Make 2 **Unit 2** Make 8 **Unit 3** Make 2

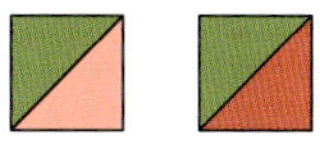

Unit 4 Make 4 **Unit 5** Make 4

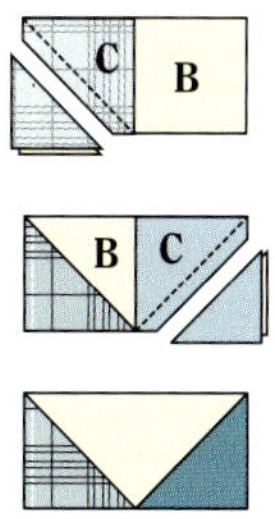

Stitch & Flip
Unit 6
Make 4

Pair A's in the appropriate fabrics to make the Triangle-Square unit 1's–5's as shown in the diagrams.

Refer to "Stitch-and-Flip" in the Techniques file on the PDF. Noting the placement of each blue fabric, use the blue plaid C's, the blue print C's and the cream B's to make 4 unit 6's.

Join the patches and units as shown in the assembly diagram to complete the block.

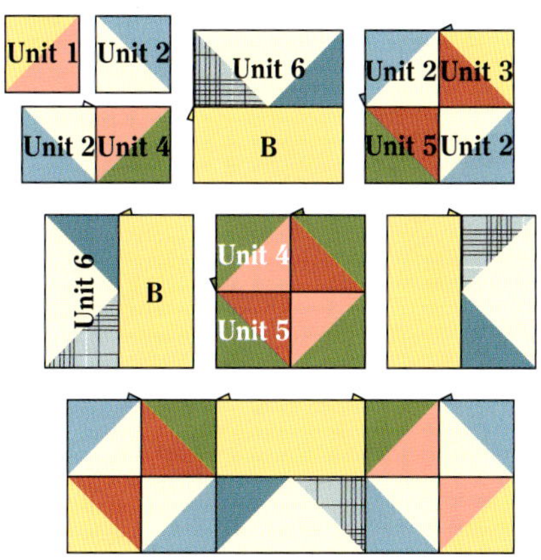

Block Assembly

block no. 636

Rose Twirls

by Elisa Wilson • Elisa's Backporch Design
backporchdesign.com

Fabric: Artisan Batiks: Painterly Palette designed by Lunn Studios for Robert Kaufman, robertkaufman.com.

Elisa Wilson is the author of *Crazy Curves Continues* for Elisa's Backporch Design, backporchdesign.com.

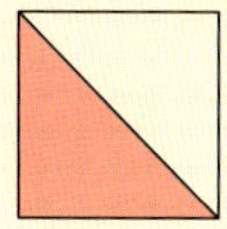

Unit
Make 8

See page 72 on the PDF for pattern

Dark Pink Batik and White Batik
from *each*
- 4 squares (A) 6⅞" x 6⅞"

Blue Batik
- 4 squares (D) 4½" x 4½"

Light Pink Batik and Orange Batik
from *each*
- 4 squares (E) 1¾" x 1¾"

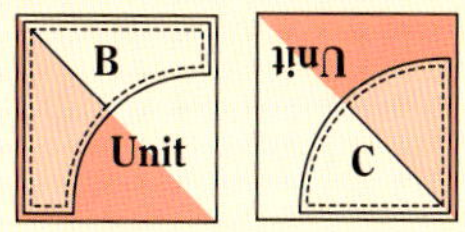

Cut 4 Cut 4

Pair the dark pink and white A's to make 8 Triangle-Square units.

Noting the color orientation of the units, cut 4 B's and 4 C's as shown. Refer to "Curved Piecing" in the Techniques file on the PDF to sew each C to a B.

Refer to the diagrams below. Align D on the corner of B/C right sides together as shown. Mark a line on the wrong side of D starting 1" down one side to the opposite corner and sew on the marked line. Trim the seam allowance to ¼". Flip D open and trim as shown. Use the "Stitch-and-Flip" technique to add light pink and orange E's to the corners as shown to complete a section. Make 4 sections.

Join the sections as shown to complete the block.

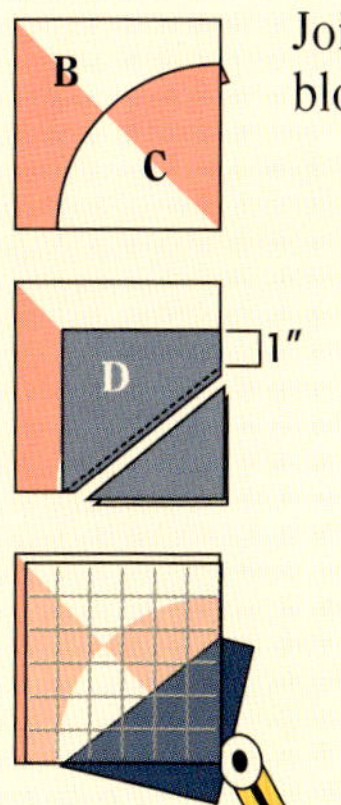

Section
Make 4

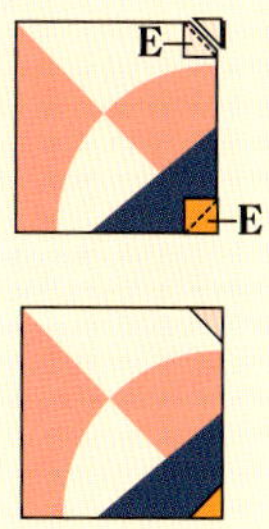

Section
Stitch & Flip
Make 4

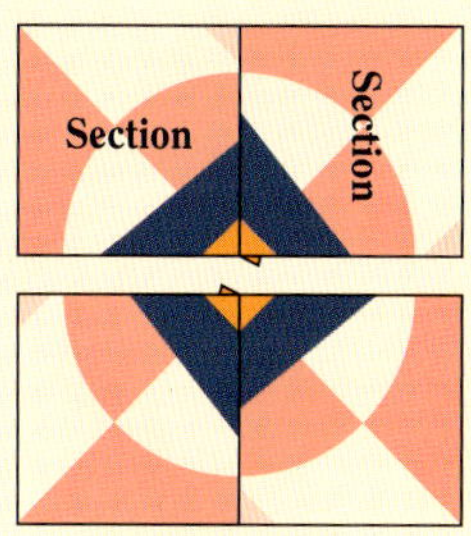

Block Assembly

block no. 637
Flutter
by Patty Young • MODKID, LLC
modkidboutique.com

Fabric: Flora & Fauna designed by Patty Young for Michael Miller Fabrics, michaelmillerfabrics.com.

Patty Young owns MODKID, for which she designs boutique children's sewing patterns.

Large-Scale Aqua Print
1 square (A) 7¾" x 7¾"
Red Print
2 rectangles (B) 2¼" x 7¾"
2 rectangles (C) 2¼" x 11½"
Dark Teal Print
4 rectangles (B) 2¼" x 7¾"
Red and Aqua Print
4 rectangles (D) 2⅜" x 4"

Patty personalized her block by adding a selvage strip to the side of A.

Mark the center of each patch by folding it in half and pressing lightly. Matching centers, sew each D to a dark teal B. Refer to the block assembly diagram. Matching centers, join the patches as shown. Center the A patch and trim the block to 12½" × 12½".

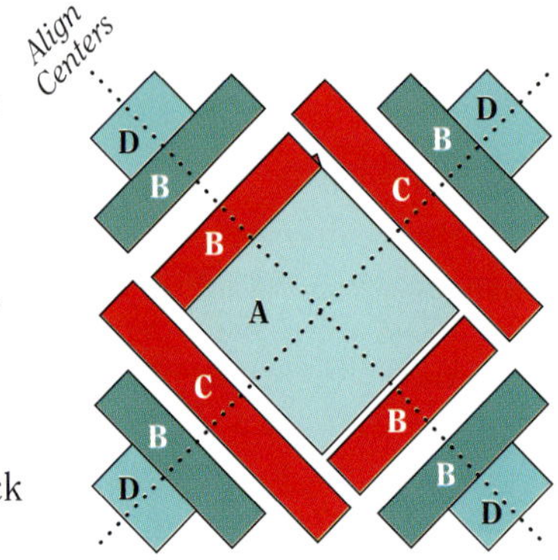

Block Piecing

Block

Trim to 12½" x 12½" after piecing.

block no. 638
Sew-Easy Butterflies
by Darlene Zimmerman • Needlings, Inc.
feedsacklady.com

Fabric: Paper Dolls designed by Darlene Zimmerman for Robert Kaufman, robertkaufman.com.

Darlene Zimmerman is the author of *Quilting: The Complete Guide* for Krause Publications, krausebooks.com.

4 Assorted Prints
from *each*
3 rectangles (A) 2½" x 6½"
White Print
16 squares (B) 2½" x 2½"

Refer to "Stitch-and-Flip" in the Techniques file on the PDF. Use the white print B's and 2 A's from each of the assorted prints to make 8 units.

Sew the units and patches together as shown to complete the block.

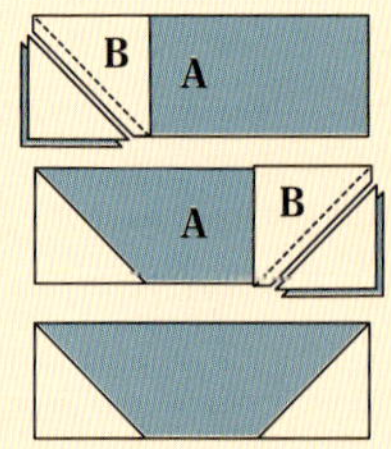

Unit
Stitch & Flip
Make 8

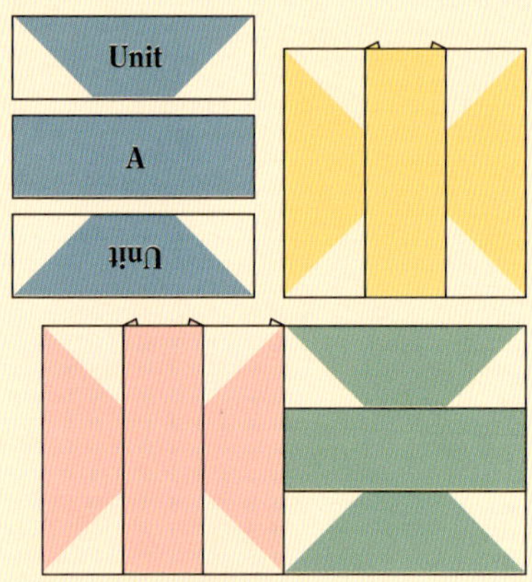

Block Assembly

block no. 639

Happy

by Barbara Groves and Mary Jacobson • Me and My Sister Designs • meandmysisterdesigns.com

Fabric: Happy designed by Me and My Sister Designs for Moda Fabrics, unitednotions.com.

White Dot

1 square (A) 4½" x 4½"

Black Stripe

2 rectangles (B) 2½" x 4½"
2 rectangles (C) 2½" x 8½"

Assorted Prints

4 rectangles (B) 2½" x 4½"
4 rectangles (D) 2½" x 6½"

Join the patches as shown to complete the block.

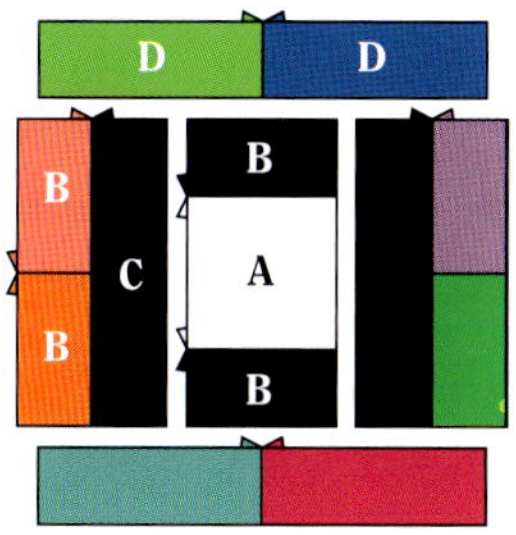

Block Piecing

block no. 640

Starstruck

by Scott Hansen • Blue Nickel Studios
bluenickelstudios.com

Fabric: Country Lane by Bari J. Ackerman for Windham Fabrics, windhamfabrics.com.

⧄ = cut in half diagonally

Light Blue Print

1 square 2⅞" x 2⅞" ⧄ (A)
2 rectangles (D) 2½" x 8½"
1 square 5⅞" x 5⅞" ⧄ (E) (there will be 1 extra patch)
2 rectangles (F) 3½" x 5½"

Red Print

1 square 2⅞" x 2⅞" ⧄ (A) (there will be 1 extra patch)
1 rectangle (B) 2½" x 6½"
1 square (C) 2½" x 2½"
1 square (G) 3½" x 3½"

White Print

2 squares (C) 2½" x 2½"

Dark Blue Print #1

1 square 2⅞" x 2⅞" ⧄ (A) (there will be 1 extra patch)
1 rectangle (B) 2½" x 6½"
1 square (C) 2½" x 2½"

Dark Blue Print #2

1 square 5⅞" x 5⅞" ⧄ (E) (there will be 1 extra patch)

Sew the patches together as shown to complete the block.

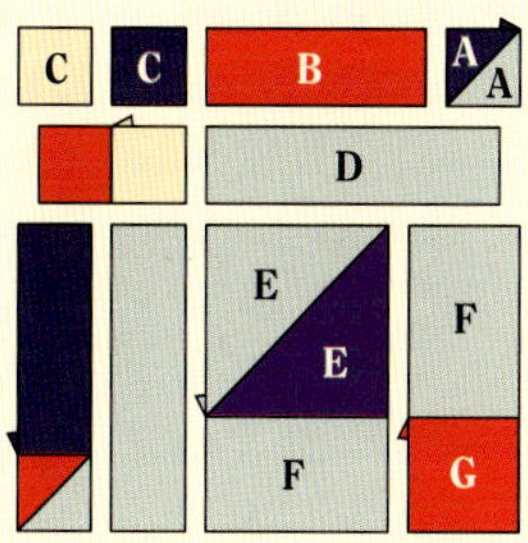

Block Piecing

block no. 641

Writer's Block

by Diane Harris • Interactive Editor, *Quiltmaker*
quiltmaker.com

Fabric: Gerta and Third in Line designed by Marcia Derse for the Riverwoods Collection by Troy Corporation, troy-corp.com.

Dark Brown Print
1 square (A) $4\frac{7}{8}$" x $4\frac{7}{8}$"
Light Teal Tone-on-Tone
1 square (A) $4\frac{7}{8}$" x $4\frac{7}{8}$"
Dark Gold Print
4 rectangles (B) $1\frac{1}{2}$" x $4\frac{1}{2}$"
4 rectangles (C) $1\frac{1}{2}$" x $6\frac{1}{2}$"
Gold Tone-on-Tone
2 squares (D) $2\frac{1}{2}$" x $2\frac{1}{2}$"
Dark Teal Tone-on-Tone
4 squares (D) $2\frac{1}{2}$" x $2\frac{1}{2}$"
4 rectangles (E) $2\frac{1}{2}$" x $6\frac{1}{2}$"

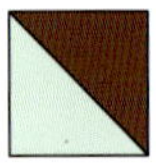

Unit
Make 2

Pair the brown and light teal A's to make 2 Triangle-Square units.

Sew the patches and units together as shown to complete the block.

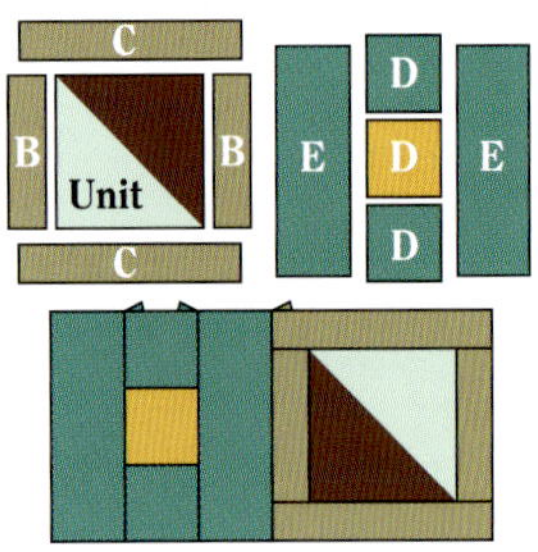

Block Assembly

pieced

block no. 642

Chained Star

by Sandy Harris • Sundrop Designs
sundropdesigns.com

Beige Tone-on-Tone and Blue Print
from *each*
2 squares (A) $3\frac{7}{8}$" x $3\frac{7}{8}$"
4 squares (B) $2\frac{7}{8}$" x $2\frac{7}{8}$"
Green Print
8 rectangles (C) $1\frac{1}{2}$" x $2\frac{1}{2}$"
4 rectangles (D) $2\frac{1}{2}$" x $3\frac{1}{2}$"
Beige Floral Print
1 square (E) $6\frac{1}{2}$" x $6\frac{1}{2}$"

Unit 1
Make 4

Unit 2
Make 8

Pair the beige and blue A's to make 4 Triangle-Square unit 1's. Pair the beige and blue B's to make 8 unit 2's.

Sew the units and patches together as shown to complete the block.

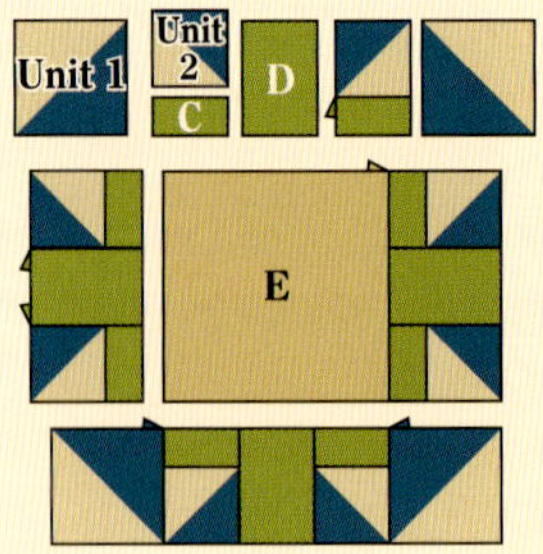

Block Assembly

block no. 643

Spike Ball

by Denniele Bohannon • Louanna Mary Quilt Design

Fabric: Kona Cotton Solids from Robert Kaufman, robertkaufman.com.

Denniele Bohannon is the co-designer of *Where Poppies Grow: Quilts & Other Projects* for Kansas City Star Quilts, pickledish.com.

Gray Solid
- 4 squares (A) 4½" x 4½"
- 4 squares (C) 2¾" x 2¾"
- 8 squares (E) 1¾" x 1¾"
- 6 rectangles (F) 1¾" x 2"
- 4 rectangles (H) 2" x 2¾"
- 2 rectangles (J) 1¾" x 4½"

Red Solid
- 4 squares (B) 3¼" x 3¼"
- 4 rectangles (G) 1" x 2"

Black Solid
- 8 rectangles (D) 1¾" x 4½"
- 1 square (I) 2" x 2"

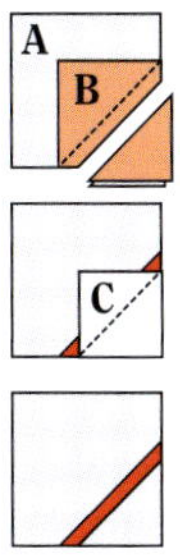

Unit 1
Stitch & Flip
Make 4

Unit 2 **Stitch & Flip** Make 4

Unit 3 **Stitch & Flip** Make 4

Refer to "Stitch-and-Flip" in the Techniques file on the PDF. Use the gray A's and red B's to make 4 partial units as shown. Add a gray C to the red corner as shown to make 4 unit 1's.

Use stitch and flip with the black D's and gray E's to make 4 unit 2's and 4 unit 3's.

Sew the unit and patches together as shown to complete the block.

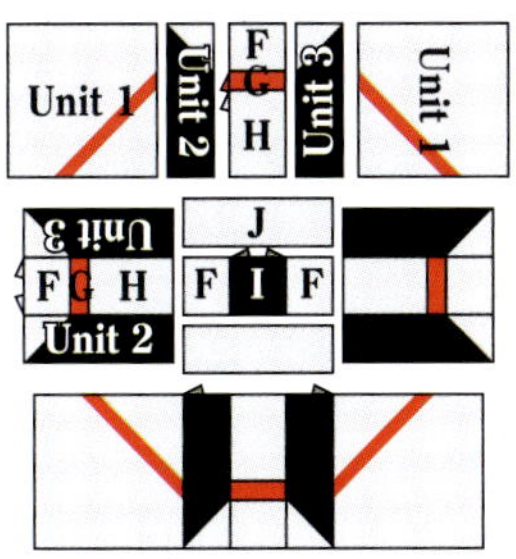

Block Assembly

block no. 644

Sewing Triangles

by Cheryl Brickey • Meadow Mist Designs
meadowmistdesigns.blogspot.com

Fabric: Various fabric lines from Moda Fabrics, unitednotions.com; Windham Fabrics, windhamfabrics.net; Riley Blake, rileyblakedesigns.com; Robert Kaufman, robertkaufman.com.

Black Tone-on-Tone
- 8 squares (A) 2⅞" x 2⅞"

Assorted White Prints and Tone-on-Tones
- 8 squares (A) 2⅞" x 2⅞"
- 20 squares (B) 2½" x 2½"

Unit
Make 16

Use the black A's and assorted white A's to make 16 Triangle-Square units.

Sew the units and patches together as shown to complete the block.

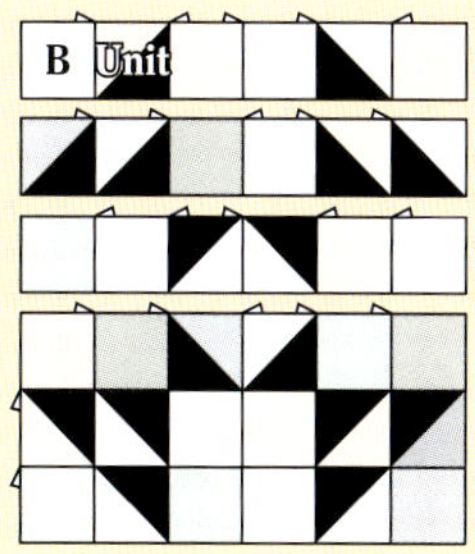

Block Assembly

block no. 645

Snack Time

by Pat Harrison • Ocean Waves Quilting Co.
oceanwavesqc.com

Fabric: House Mouse by Ellen Jareckie for Quilting Treasures, quiltingtreasures.com.

⊠ = cut in half twice diagonally

Multicolor Stripe
- 4 squares 2½″ x 2½″ ⊠ (A) (there will be 8 extra triangles)
- 2 rectangles (E) 1¾″ x 8¾″
- 2 rectangles (I) 1¾″ x 6¼″

Pink Tone-on-Tone
- 1 square 2½″ x 2½″ ⊠ (A)
- 4 squares (C) 1½″ x 1½″
- 2 rectangles (D) 1⅛″ x 8¾″
- 2 rectangles (J) 1⅛″ x 6¼″

Teal Tone-on-Tone
- 1 square 2½″ x 2½″ ⊠ (A)
- 4 squares (C) 1½″ x 1½″
- 2 rectangles (D) 1⅛″ x 8¾″
- 4 rectangles (G) ¾″ x 2½″
- 4 rectangles (H) ¾″ x 3″
- 2 rectangles (J) 1⅛″ x 6¼″

Purple Tone-on-Tone
- 2 squares (B) 2½″ x 2½″

Multiprint (Pat fussy cut these squares from a pre-printed panel)
- 2 squares (F) 2½″ x 2½″
- 1 square (K) 7½″ x 7½″

Unit 1
Make 2

Unit 2
Make 2

Flying Geese 1
Make 4

Flying Geese 2
Make 4

Noting the orientation of the stripe, pair stripe A's with the pink A's to make 2 unit 1's. Make 2 unit 2's with stripe A's and the teal A's.

Use a purple B and the teal C's to make 4 Flying Geese 1. Use a purple B and the pink C's to make 4 Flying Geese 2. Sew the patches, units and Flying Geese together to complete the block.

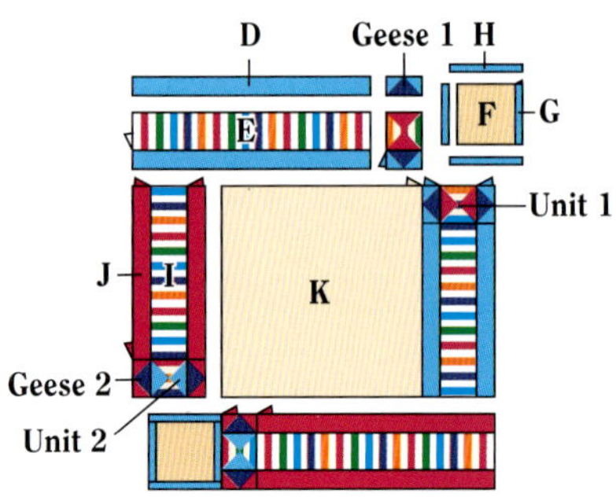

Block Assembly

block no. 646

Illusion

by Julie Herman • Jaybird Quilts
jaybirdquilts.com

Fabric: Kona Solids by Robert Kaufman, robertkaufman.com.

Yellow Solid
- 2 squares (A) 2½″ x 2½″

Orange Solid and Red Solid
from *each*
- 2 rectangles (B) 1½″ x 2½″
- 4 rectangles (C) 1½″ x 4½″
- 2 rectangles (D) 1½″ x 6½″

Purple Solid
- 2 squares (E) 3½″ x 3½″

Cream Solid
- 2 squares (E) 3½″ x 3½″
- 2 rectangles (F) 3½″ x 6½″

Join the patches as shown to complete the block.

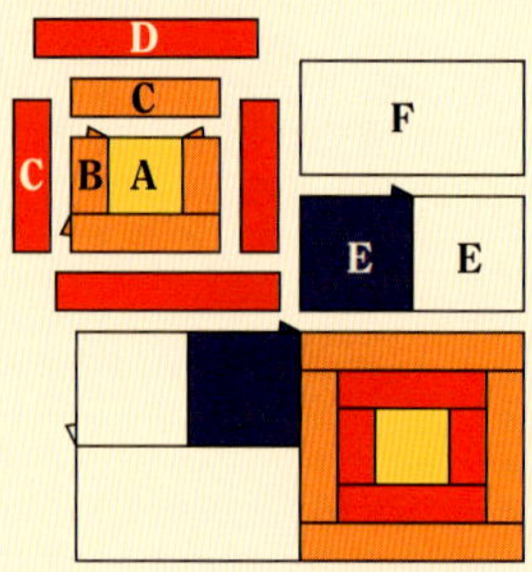

Block Piecing

block no. 647
Winston Ways

by Bonnie Hunter
quiltville.com

Bonnie Hunter writes the "Addicted to Scraps" column for Quiltmaker*. She is the author of* Scraps & Shirttails II: Continuing the Art of Quilting Green *and* Adventures with Leaders and Enders *for Kansas City Star Quilts, pickledish.com.*

Gold Tone-on-Tone and Black Print
from each
6 squares (A) 2⅞″ x 2⅞″
Blue Tone-on-Tone and White Stripe
from each
4 squares (A) 2⅞″ x 2⅞″
Assorted Red Prints and Assorted Light Prints
from each
32 squares (B) 1½″ x 1½″

Unit 1 Make 12 **Unit 2** Make 8

Pair the gold A's with the black A's to make 12 Triangle-Square unit 1's. Pair the blue A's with the white stripe A's to make 8 unit 2's.

Join the units and B's as shown to complete the block.

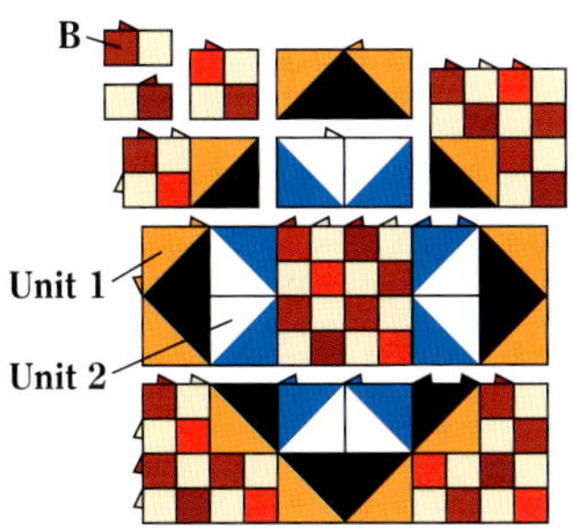

Block Assembly

block no. 648
Kansas Fortune

by Deborah Johnson • In the Doghouse Designs
inthedoghousedesigns.com

White Tone-on-Tone
2 rectangles (A) 2″ x 5″
2 rectangles (B) 2″ x 6½″
2 rectangles (E) 2½″ x 5½″
2 rectangles (F) 2½″ x 7½″
Gold Tone-on-Tone
2 rectangles (B) 2″ x 6½″
2 rectangles (C) 2″ x 8″
Multiprint
2 squares (D) 3″ x 3″
2 squares (G) 2½″ x 2½″
Brown Tone-on-Tone
2 squares (D) 3″ x 3″

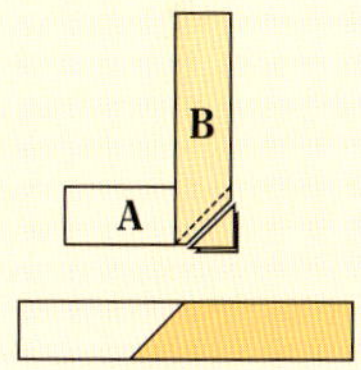

Unit 1
Make 2

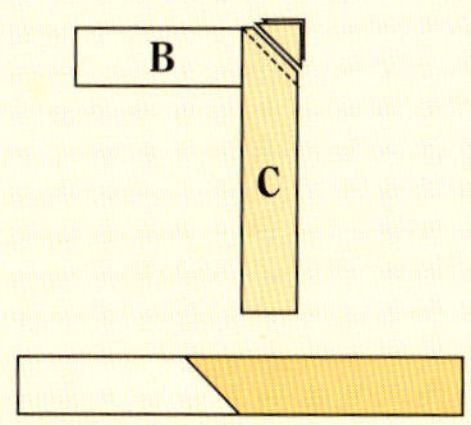

Unit 2
Make 2

Refer to "Stitch-and-Flip" in the Techniques file on the PDF. Pair the white A's with the gold B's to make 2 unit 1's. Pair the white B's with the gold C's to make 2 unit 2's.

Join the patches and units as shown to complete the block.

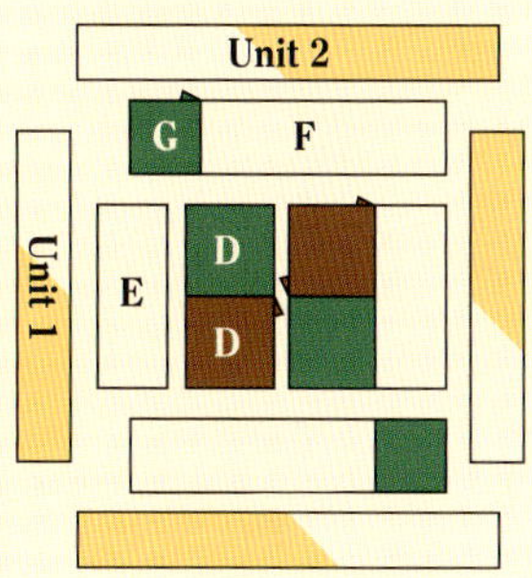

Block Assembly

block no. 649

Vintage Spools

by Kimberly Jolly • Owner, Fat Quarter Shop
fatquartershop.com

Fabric: Aunt Grace Circle of Friends designed by Judie Rothermel for Marcus Fabrics, marcusbrothers.com.

Purple, Green, Blue and Pink Prints
from *each*
- 2 rectangles (A) 2″ x 6½″
- 1 square (C) 3½″ x 3½″

Cream Solid
- 16 squares (B) 2″ x 2″
- 8 rectangles (D) 2″ x 3½″

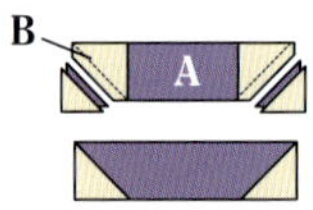

Unit
Stitch & Flip
Make 8

Refer to "Stitch-and-Flip" in the Techniques file on the PDF. Use the purple, green, blue and pink A's and cream B's to make 8 units.

Join the units and patches as shown to complete the block.

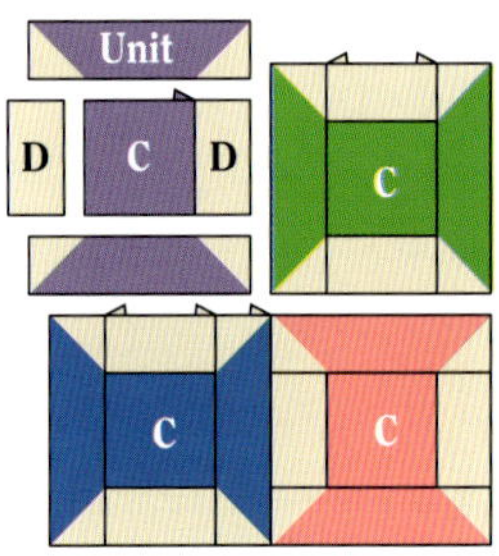

Block Assembly

block no. 650

Whirligig

by Susan Knapp & Mary Jane Mattingly
The Quilt Branch • quiltbranch.com

Susan Knapp and Mary Jane Mattingly are the authors of *Six Halves Make a Whole* for The Quilt Branch, quiltbranch.com.

See page 88 on the PDF for pattern

⊠ = cut in half diagonally twice

Blue Tone-on-Tone
- 2 strips 3½″ x 40″ for band A

Red Tone-on-Tone
- 4 strips 2″ x 40″ for band A

Yellow Tone-on-Tone
- 1 strip 5″ x 18″ for band B

Multicolor Stripe
- 1 strip 3″ x 18″ for band B
- 2 squares 7¼″ x 7¼″ ⊠ (C) (there will be four extra)

Band A Make 2

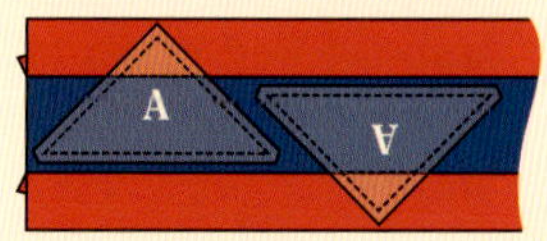

Unit 1 Cut 8

Band B Make 1

Unit 2 Cut 4

Sew 2 band A's using the blue and red strips as shown. Make a plastic template of A; use a permanent marker to draw the dotted lines on the template. Align the template's line with the seam line on band A as shown. Trace and cut 8 unit 1's as shown. Sew 1 band B using the yellow and stripe strips. Make a template of B as described above. Trace and cut 4 unit 2's from the band B as shown.

Noting the orientation of the stripes (C), join 2 unit 1's, 1 unit 2 and 1 C as shown to make each block quadrant. Join the quadrants as shown to complete the block.

Block Assembly

pieced

block no. 651
Rain Dance

by Judy Laquidara • Sunshine Quilts
patchworktimes.com

Judy Laquidara is the author of *Nine Patch Extravaganza* and *Weekend Quilts* for AQS, americanquilter.com.

⧄ = cut in half diagonally

Light Purple and Dark Purple Prints
from *each*
- 2 squares (A) 2⅜″ x 2⅜″
- 2 squares (B) 3⅛″ x 3⅛″

Light Orange and Dark Orange Prints
from *each*
- 1 square 3⅛″ x 3⅛″ ⧄ (C)
- 1 square 4″ x 4″ ⧄ (E)
- 4 rectangles (F) 2″ x 5″

Cream Batik
- 2 squares 3⅛″ x 3⅛″ ⧄ (C)
- 1 square 5⅜″ x 5⅜″ ⧄ (D)

Unit 1
Make 4

Unit 2
Make 4

Pair the light purple and dark purple A's to make 4 Triangle-Square unit 1's. Pair the light purple and dark purple B's to make 4 unit 2's.

Join the units and patches as shown to complete the block.

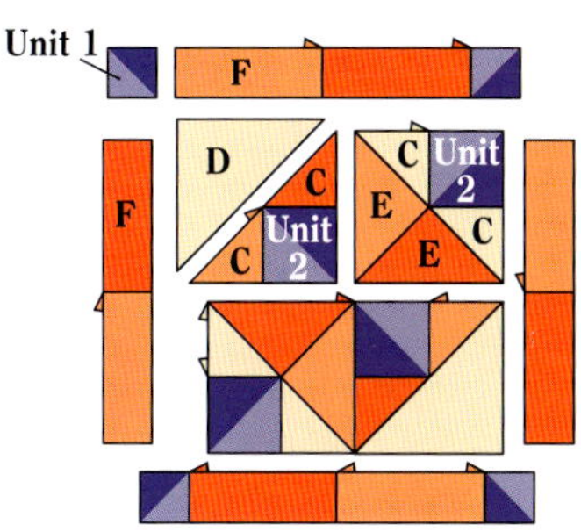

Block Assembly

block no. 652
Skewed Star

by Toby Lischko • Gateway Quilts & Stuff
gatewayquiltsnstuff.com

Toby Lischko is the author of *St. Louis Stars for* Kansas City Star Quilts, pickledish.com.

Assorted Dark Prints
- 2 squares (A) 3⅜″ x 3⅜″
- 2 squares (B) 4⅜″ x 4⅜″
- 16 rectangles (C) 1¾″ x 4″

Assorted Light Prints
- 2 squares (A) 3⅜″ x 3⅜″
- 2 squares (B) 4⅜″ x 4⅜″

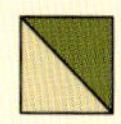

Unit 1
Make 4

Unit 2
Make 4

Pair the dark and light A's to make 4 Triangle-Square unit 1's. Pair the dark and light B's to make 4 unit 2's.

Join the patches and units as shown to complete the block.

Block Assembly

block no. 653
Magic Squares

by Konda Luckau • Moose on the Porch Quilts
moosequilts.com

Fabric: Modern Meadow by Joel Dewberry for Westminster Fibers Inc., westminsterfibers.com, and Kona cotton solids, robertkaufman.com.

Konda Luckau is the author of *Simply Charming Kids* for Moose on the Porch Quilts, moosequilts.com.

Assorted Prints
9 squares (A) 2″ x 2″
Light Gray Solid
12 rectangles (B) 1¼″ x 2″
4 rectangles (D) 1½″ x 6½″
8 rectangles (G) 1½″ x 2½″
Dark Brown Solid
4 squares (C) 1¼″ x 1¼″
4 squares (E) 1½″ x 1½″
4 rectangles (F) 2½″ x 6½″
4 squares (H) 2½″ x 2½″

Join the patches as shown to complete the block.

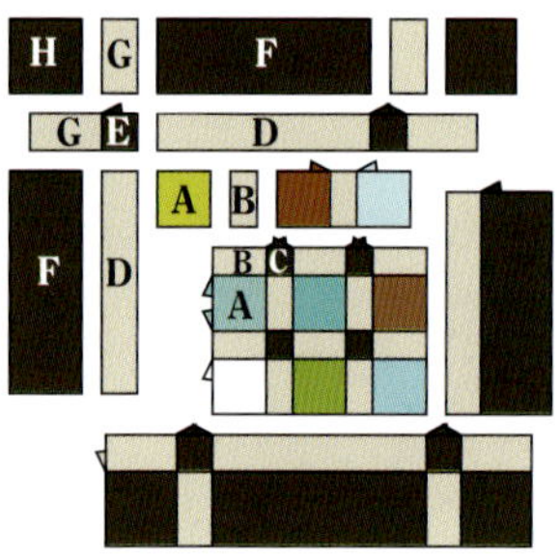

Block Piecing

block no. 654
Twister

by Christina McCourt • C McCourt Quilt Designs

Fabric: Adelaide by Faye Burgos for Marcus Fabrics, marcusbrothers.com.

Christina McCourt designs patterns for Quiltwoman, quiltwoman.com.

⊠ = cut in half twice diagonally

Assorted Light Prints
8 squares 5½″ x 5½″ ⊠ (A)
8 rectangles (B) 2″ x 5¼″
Assorted Dark Prints and Tone-on-Tones
8 squares 5½″ x 5½″ ⊠ (A)
8 rectangles (B) 2″ x 5¼″

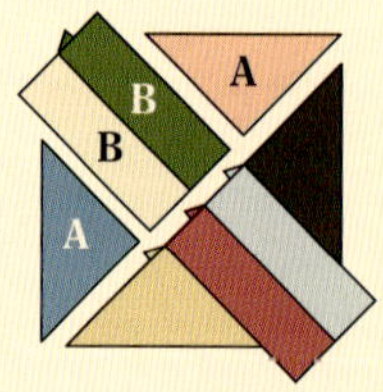

There will be 3 extra A's from each print that can be used to make additional blocks.

This block is made from 4 sections. Noticing the placement of the dark and light fabrics, join 4 A's and 4 B's as shown. Center and trim the section to 6½" × 6½" as shown. Make 4 sections.

Trim to 6½″ x 6½″

Join the sections as shown to complete the block.

Section
Make 4

Block Assembly

pieced

block no. 655

Diamond Jubilee

by Pam McMahon • Pam's Piece by Piece
piecebypiecequiltdesigns.com

Fabric: Hope from Collections for a Cause for Moda Fabrics, unitednotions.com.

Tan Print
2 squares (A) 2⅞" x 2⅞"
1 square (B) 5¼" x 5¼"
Blue Print
2 squares (A) 2⅞" x 2⅞"
2 squares (C) 2½" x 2½"
Cream Print
8 squares (A) 2⅞" x 2⅞"
Dark Brown Solid
4 squares (A) 2⅞" x 2⅞"
Red Print
4 squares (A) 2⅞" x 2⅞"
1 square (B) 5¼" x 5¼"
Medium Brown Tone-on-Tone
4 squares (C) 2½" x 2½"
Dark Brown Print
2 squares (C) 2½" x 2½"

Unit 1
Make 4

Unit 2
Make 8

Flying Geese 1
Make 4

Flying Geese 2
Make 4

Pair the tan and blue A's to make 4 Triangle-Square unit 1's. Pair the dark brown A's with cream A's to make 8 Triangle-Square unit 2's.

Pair the tan B with red A's to make 4 Flying Geese 1's. Use the red B and 4 cream A's to make 4 Flying Geese 2's.

Join the Flying Geese, units and patches as shown to complete the block.

Block Assembly

block no. 656

Juliet's Garden Star

by Paige Stanley Miller • Paige Stanley Miller, Inc.
paigestanleymiller.com

Fabric: Juliet Collection by Paige Stanley Miller for Windham Fabrics, windhamfabrics.com.

Cream Print #1
1 square (A) 6½" x 6½"
2 squares (B) 3½" x 3½"
1 square (C) 3⅞" x 3⅞"
2 rectangles (D) 3½" x 6½"
Cream Print #2, Light Pink Tone-on-Tone and Medium Pink Tone-on-Tone
from *each*
2 squares (B) 3½" x 3½"
1 square (C) 3⅞" x 3⅞"
Light Green Tone-on-Tone
4 squares (B) 3½" x 3½"
Lavender Tone-on-Tone
2 rectangles (D) 3½" x 6½"

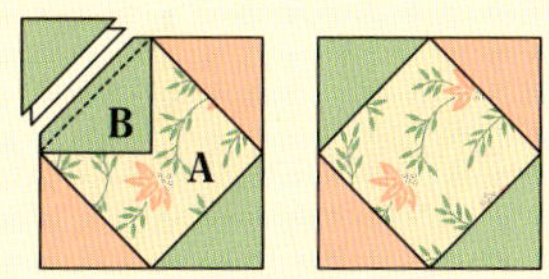

Unit 1
Stitch & Flip
Make 1

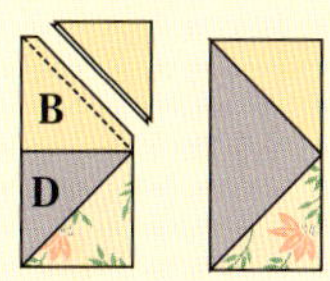

Unit 2
Stitch & Flip
Make 2

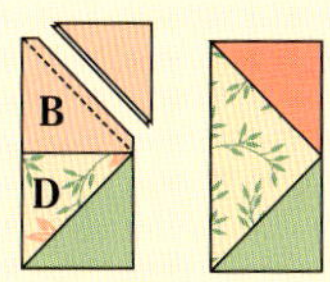

Unit 3
Stitch & Flip
Make 2

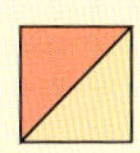

Unit 4
Make 2

Unit 5
Make 2

Refer to "Stitch-and-Flip" in the Techniques file on the PDF. Sew 2 light pink B's and 2 green B's to the cream print #1 A to make unit 1 as shown. Sew the cream print #2 B and cream print #1 B to the purple D as shown to make a unit 2. Make 2 unit 2's. Sew the medium pink B and green B to the cream print #1 D as shown to make a unit 3. Make 2 unit 3's.

Pair the medium pink C with the cream print #2 C to make 2 Triangle-Square unit 4's. Pair the light pink C with the cream print #1 C to make 2 Triangle-Square unit 5's. Join the units as shown to complete the block.

Block Assembly

block no. 657

Filmstrip

by Scott Murkin • Patchwork Possibilities
patchworkpossibilities.com

Red Floral
1 square (A) 4½″ x 4½″

Light Blue Tone-on-Tone
2 rectangles (B) 1½″ x 4½″
2 rectangles (C) 1½″ x 6½″
8 squares (D) 2½″ x 2½″
2 rectangles (E) 1½″ x 10½″
2 rectangles (F) 1½″ x 12½″

Red Stripe
4 squares (D) 2½″ x 2½″

Teal Print
4 squares (D) 2½″ x 2½″

Join the patches as shown to complete the block.

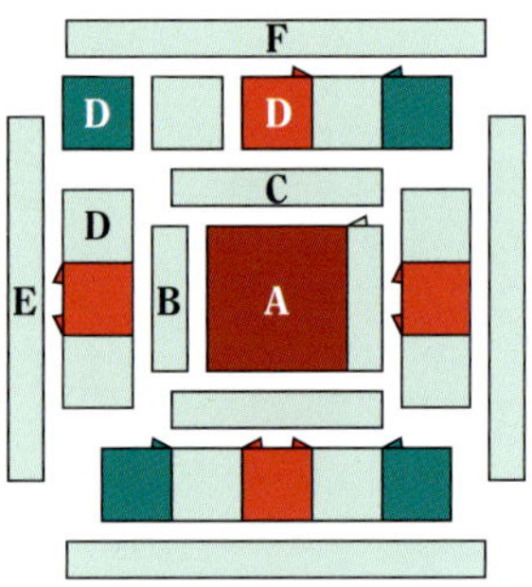

Block Piecing

block no. 658

Hidden Star

by Karen Neary • Sew Karen-ly Created…
www3.ns.sympatico.ca/sewkaren

Fabric: Fossil Fern designed by Pat Campbell for Benartex, benartex.com.

See page 79 on the PDF for pattern

◪ = cut in half diagonally

Light Purple Tone-on-Tone and Medium Purple Tone-on-Tone
from *each*
1 square 10⅞″ x 10⅞″ ◪ (A) (there will be 1 extra)

Medium Blue Tone-on-Tone and Dark Blue Tone-on-Tone
from *each*
2 rectangles (B) 1½″ x 9″

Yellow Tone-on-Tone and Orange Tone-on-Tone
from *each*
2 *each* templates C and Cr

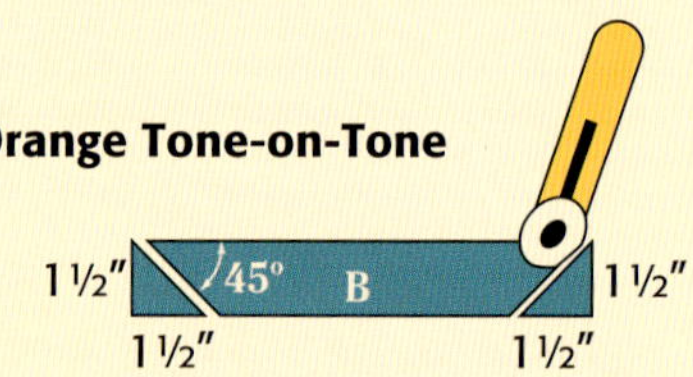

Trim the medium blue and dark blue B's as shown. Join the C's, Cr's and B's as shown to make 2 unit 1's and 2 unit 2's.

Unit 1
Make 2

Unit 2
Make 2

Paying careful attention to color placement, sew a unit 1 to one side of the light purple A as shown, stopping and back-stitching ¼" from each end. Sew a unit 2 to the adjacent side of the light purple A, stopping and back-stitching ¼" from each end. Fold A in half and stitch the diagonal seam as shown below to complete the mitered corner. Repeat with the medium purple A.

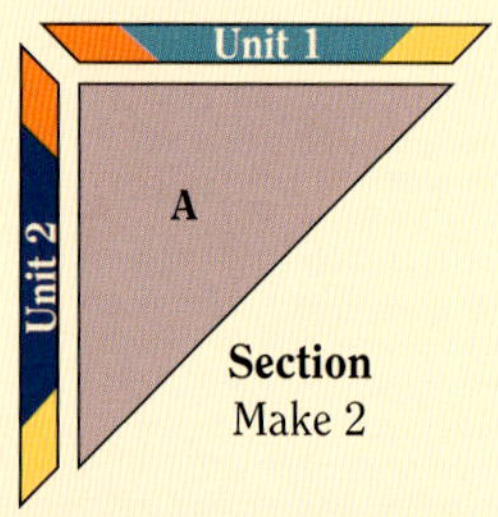

Section
Make 2

Join the two sections to complete the block.

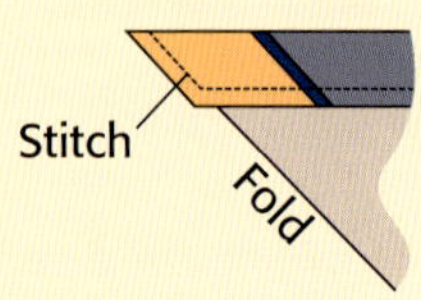

Block Assembly

block no. 659

Get the Point?

by Carrie Nelson • Miss Rosie's Quilt Co.
missrosiesquiltco.com

Fabric: Paradise by Patricia Bravo for Art Gallery Fabrics, artgalleryfabrics.com.

Carrie Nelson is the author of numerous quilting titles including *Schnibbles Times Two* for Martingale & Co., martingale-pub.com.

◪ = cut in half diagonally

White Solid

- 4 rectangles (A) 2½″ x 6½″
- 8 squares (B) 2½″ x 2½″
- 2 squares 2⅞″ x 2⅞″ ◪ (C)

4 Assorted Prints

from *each*

- 1 rectangle (A) 2½″ x 6½″
- 2 squares (B) 2½″ x 2½″
- 1 square 2⅞″ x 2⅞″ ◪ (C) (there will be 1 extra)

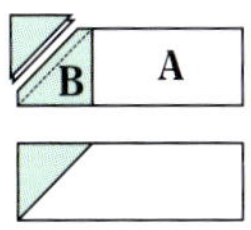

Unit 1
Stitch & Flip
Make 4

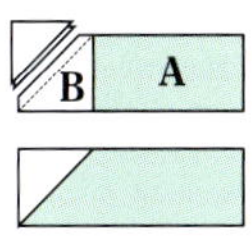

Unit 2
Stitch & Flip
Make 4

Refer to "Stitch-and-Flip" in the Techniques file on the PDF. Use the white A's with the print B's to make 4 unit 1's. Use the print A's with the white B's to make 4 unit 2's.

Join the units and patches as shown to complete the block.

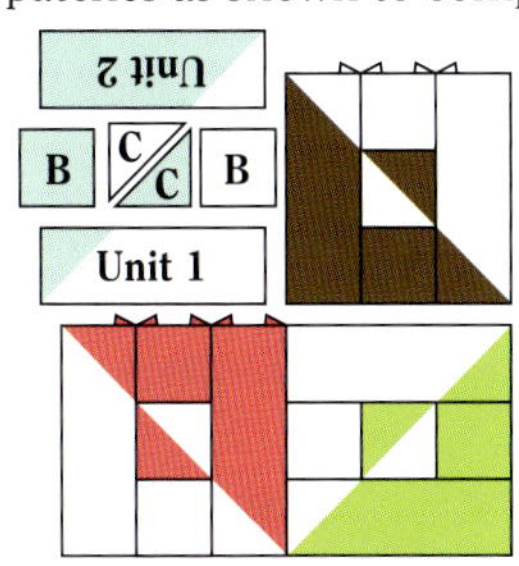

Block Assembly

block no. 660

Rubber Band Ball

by Lorraine Olsen • Lorraine Olsen Quilts
lorraineolsenquilts.com

Fabric: Laurel Burch Basics and Celestial Dreams by Laurel Burch for Clothworks, clothworks.com.

Lorraine Olsen is the author of *Little Lone Star Quilts* for C&T Publishing, ctpub.com.

See page 107 on the PDF for pattern

Assorted Prints

- 1–1½″-wide strips to total about 100″

Foundation paper

- 4 template A

Blue Print

- 4 template B

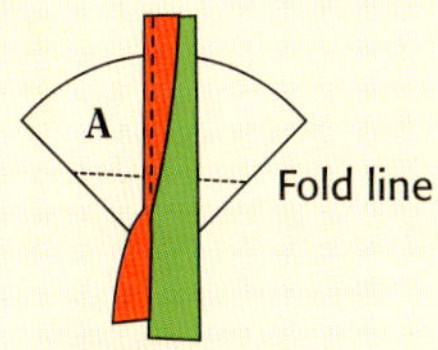

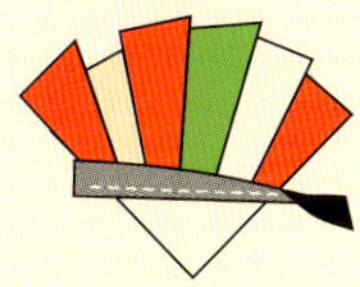

Randomly fold each template A foundation into 2 sections. Position a strip right side up and perpendicular to the fold. Aligning raw edges, lay another strip on top of the first with right sides together. Join the strips by sewing through all the layers ¼" from the raw edges. Flip the top strip open and press. Continue adding strips until that section of the foundation is covered. Turn the foundation back on the fold and trim the strips ¼" beyond the folded edge.

Unit
Make 4

Position a strip right side down on the pieced unit so that the raw edge of the strip aligns with the trimmed strip ends. Sew through all layers on the fold line. Continue to add strips parallel to the fold until the entire foundation is covered. Trim the strips even with the edges of the A. Repeat to make 4 units. Carefully remove the foundation papers.

Refer to "Curved Piecing" in the Technqiues file on the PDF. Join the units and patches as shown to complete the block.

Block Assembly

block no. 661

In and Out

by Celine Perkins • Perkins Dry Goods
perkinsdrygoods.com

Fabric: Halo designed by Gudrun Erla for Red Rooster Fabrics, redroosterfabrics.com.

⧄ = cut in half diagonally

Pink Print
8 squares (A) 2½" x 2½"

Cream Tone-on-Tone
4 squares 2⅞" x 2⅞" ⧄ (B)

Cream and Pink Print
2 squares 4⅞" x 4⅞" ⧄ (C)

Green Print
8 rectangles (D) 2½" x 4½"

Join the patches as shown to make the block.

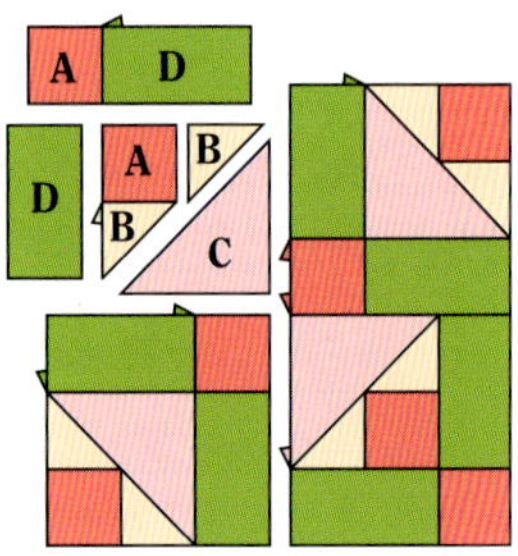

Block Piecing

block no. 662

Rose Garden

by Laura Stone Roberts • Assistant Editor, *McCall's Quilting* • mccallsquilting.com

See page 84 on the PDF for pattern

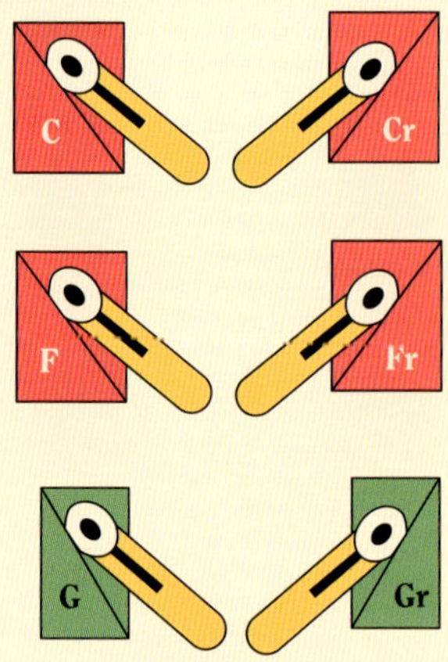

⧄ = cut in half diagonally

Floral Print
1 square (A) 4½" x 4½"

Green Batik
4 *each* templates B and E
2 rectangles 2¼" x 3⅝" ⧄ (G)
2 rectangles 2¼" x 3⅝" ⧄ (Gr)
4 squares (H) 3" x 3"

Pink Batik
2 rectangles 2¼" x 3" ⧄ (C)
2 rectangles 2¼" x 3" ⧄ (Cr)
2 rectangles 2⅞" x 3½" ⧄ (F)
2 rectangles 2⅞" x 3½" ⧄ (Fr)
2 rectangles 2¼" x 3⅝" ⧄ (G)
2 rectangles 2¼" x 3⅝" ⧄ (Gr)

Yellow Batik
20 squares (D) 1" x 1"

Dark Green Batik
16 squares (D) 1" x 1"

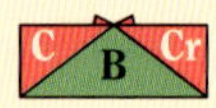

Unit 1
Make 4

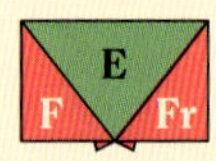

Unit 2
Make 4

Referring to the diagrams for orientation, carefully cut patches C, Cr, F, Fr, G and Gr as shown.

Join the pink C's and Cr's to green B's to make 4 unit 1's as shown. Join pink F's and Fr's to green E's to make 4 unit 2's as shown.

Join the units and patches as shown to complete the block.

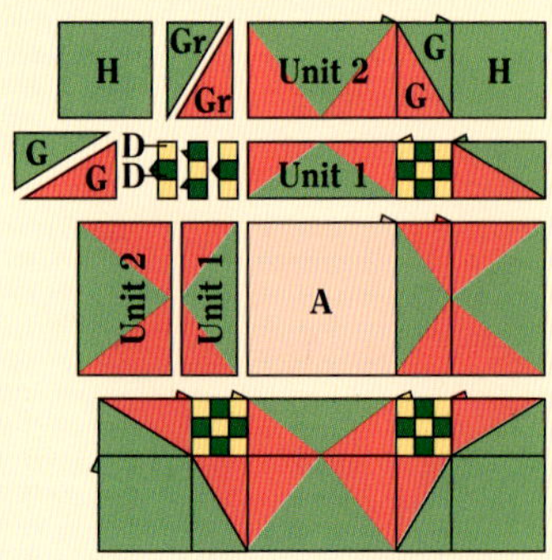

Block Assembly

pieced

block no. 663

Starburst

by Gerri Robinson • Planted Seed Designs
plantedseeddesigns.com

Fabric: Sunkissed designed by Sweetwater for Moda Fabrics, unitednotions.com.

Cream Tone-on-Tone
8 rectangles (A) 2½" x 4½"
12 squares (B) 2½" x 2½"
2 squares (C) 2⅞" x 2⅞"
Pink Plaid
4 rectangles (A) 2½" x 4½"
2 squares (C) 2⅞" x 2⅞"
Yellow Print and Gold Solid
from each
4 squares (B) 2½" x 2½"
2 squares (C) 2⅞" x 2⅞"

Unit 1
Make 4

Unit 2
Make 4

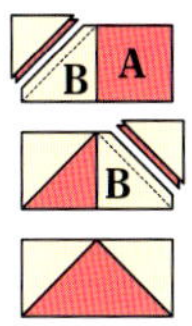

Unit 3
Stitch & Flip
Make 4

Unit 4
Stitch & Flip
Make 4

Note: The pink plaid Gerri used is a diagonal plaid. A straight of grain plaid will yield a different effect.

Use the pink C's and the cream C's to make 4 Triangle-Square unit 1's. Use the yellow C's and the gold C's to make 4 Triangle-Square unit 2's.

Refer to "Stitch-and-Flip" in the Techniques file on the PDF. Use the pink A's and the cream B's to make 4 unit 3's. Use the cream A's and the yellow and gold B's to make 4 unit 4's.

Join the units and patches as shown to complete the block.

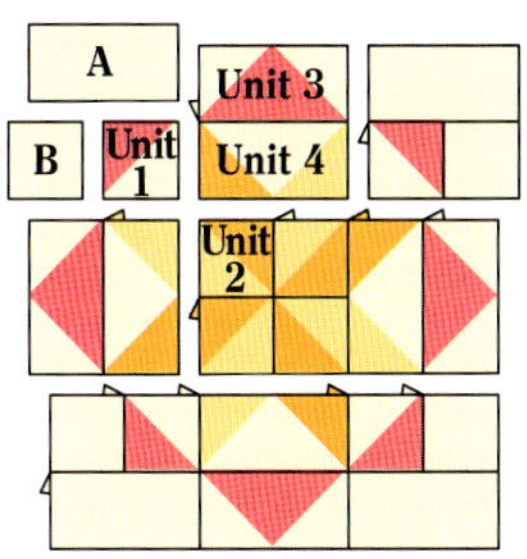

Block Assembly

block no. 664

Around the Square

by Cindy Simms • Kats Designs
cindysimms.net

◸ = cut in half diagonally

Pink Print
4 rectangles (A) 2½" x 7¼"
Blue Tone-on-Tone
4 squares 3⅞" x 3⅞" ◸ (B)
Tan Tone-on-Tone
4 squares 4⅞" x 4⅞" ◸ (C)
Pink Tone-on-Tone
1 square (D) 4½" x 4½"

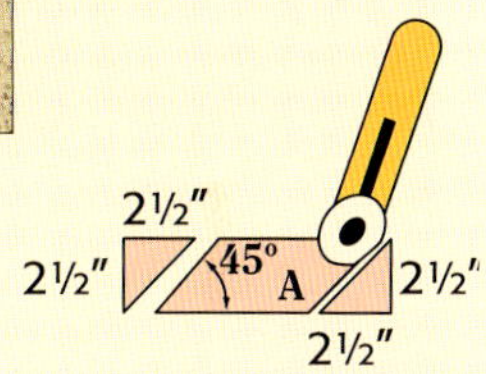

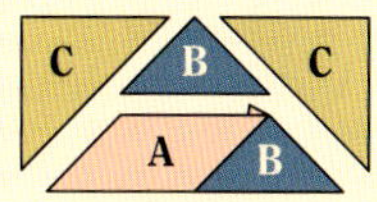

Section
Make 4

Refer to the diagram to trim the A's.

Make 4 sections using the pink A's, blue B's and tan C's as shown. It can be helpful to use spray starch or sizing on the patches to stabilize them for sewing.

Sew a section to the bottom of D with a partial seam as shown. Sew a section to the right, top and left sides of D. Complete the partial seam to finish the block.

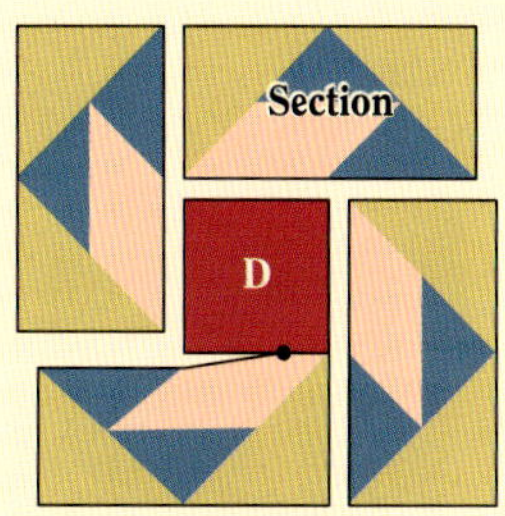

Block Assembly
• = Partial Seam

block no. 665
Four Square

by Kelly Smith • Senior Editor, *Quilters Newsletter*
quiltersnewsletter.com

See page 89 on the PDF for pattern

Purple Solid
- 1 square (A) 4½″ x 4½″
- 4 squares (B) 2½″ x 2½″
- 4 template C
- 4 rectangles (E) 2½″ x 4½″

Green Batik
- 4 squares (B) 2½″ x 2½″

4 Gold Tone-on-Tones
from *each*
- 1 square (B) 2½″ x 2½″
- 1 *each* templates D and Dr

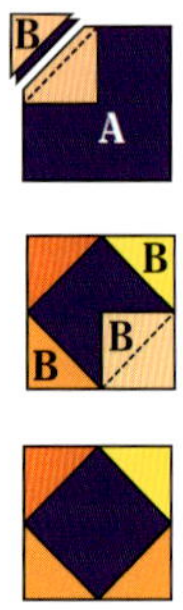

Unit
Stitch & Flip
Make 1

Refer to "Stitch-and-Flip" in the Techniques file on the PDF. Use the A and gold B's to make a unit.

Join the unit and patches as shown to complete the block.

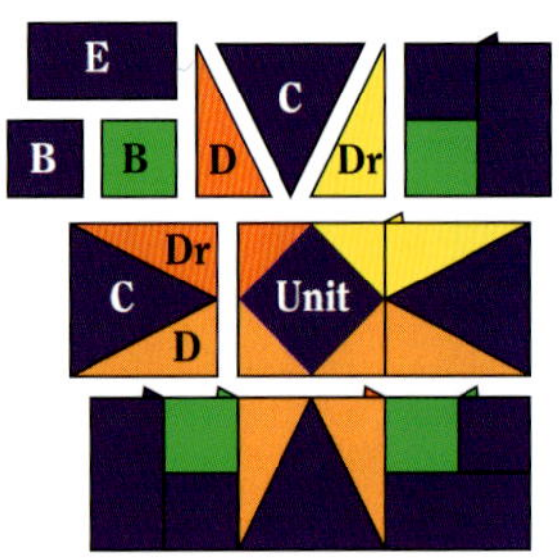

Block Assembly

block no. 666
Game Board

by Pam Vieira-McGinnis
pamkittymorning.blogspot.com

Fabric: Red Rose Farm designed by Elizabeth Scott for P&B Fabrics, pbtex.com, and background fabric by Holly Holderman for Lake House Dry Goods, lakehousedrygoods.com.

Blue Print
- 4 squares (A) 4½″ x 4½″

White Tone-on-Tone
- 20 squares (B) 2½″ x 2½″
- 4 squares (D) 2⅞″ x 2⅞″
- 8 rectangles (E) 1¾″ x 2½″

Pink Dot
- 1 square (A) 4½″ x 4½″
- 1 square (C) 5¼″ x 5¼″
- 4 rectangles (F) 2″ x 2½″

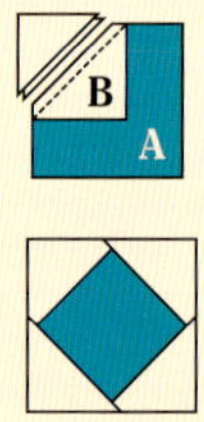

Unit 1
Stitch & Flip
Make 4

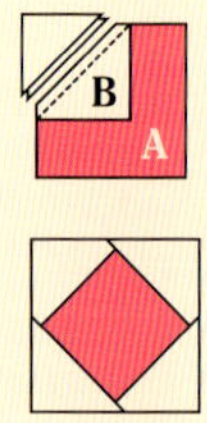

Unit 2
Stitch & Flip
Make 1

Refer to "Stitch-and-Flip" in the Techniques file on the PDF. Use the blue print A's and white B's to make 4 unit 1's. Use the pink A and white B's to make 1 unit 2.

Flying Geese
Make 4

Use the pink C and white D's to make 4 Flying Geese.

Join the units and patches as shown to complete the block.

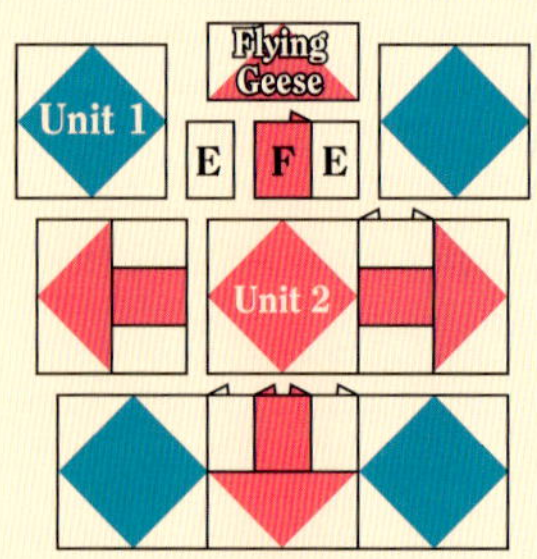

Block Assembly

pieced

block no. 667

Khanam's Surprise

by Cinzia White • Cinzia White Designs
cinziawhite.com

See page 105 in the PDF for pattern

Tan Tone-on-Tone
1 square (A) $3\frac{1}{4}$" x $3\frac{1}{4}$"
8 template C
4 *each* templates F, Fr and G
Dark Brown Tone-on-Tone
4 *each* templates B, D, E, Er, H and Hr

Section 1
Make 4

Refer to "Set-in Seams" in the Techniques file on the PDF. Join a D, F and Fr as shown in the section 1 diagram. Sew a B, C and E to D/F/Fr as shown to complete section 1. Make 4 section 1's.

Section 2
Make 4

Sew together C, Er, G, H and Hr to make a section 2 as shown. Make 4 section 2's.

Join the A patch and sections as shown to complete the block.

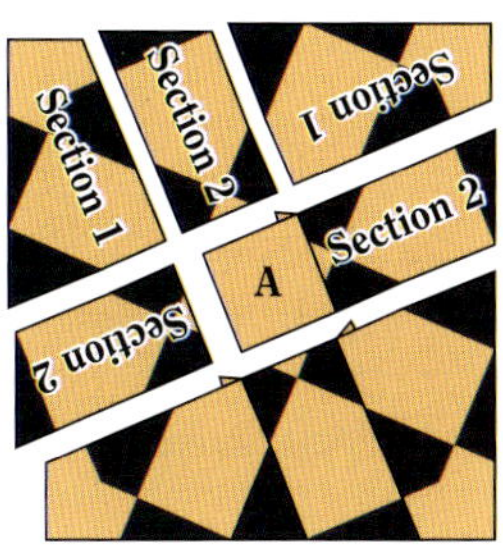

Block Assembly

block no. 668

Patched Geese

by Karrie Winters
freckledwhimsy.com

Fabric: Sanctuary by Patty Young for Michael Miller Fabrics, michaelmillerfabrics.com and Kona Cotton by Robert Kaufman, robertkaufman.com.

Brown Print
1 square (A) $7\frac{1}{4}$" x $7\frac{1}{4}$"
White Solid
4 squares (B) $3\frac{7}{8}$ x $3\frac{7}{8}$"
Assorted Prints
12 rectangles (C) $2\frac{1}{2}$" x $3\frac{1}{2}$"

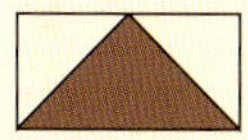
Flying Geese
Make 4

Pair the brown A with the white B's to make 4 Flying Geese.

Join the Flying Geese and patches as shown to complete the block.

Block Assembly

block no. 669

Crosstrack

by Joan Bassett • Jay Bee Designs
quiltersfun.com

Joan Bassett is the author of *One Unit Mystery* for Quiltwoman, quiltwoman.com.

Cream Print
8 rectangles (A) 1½″ x 4½″
8 rectangles (C) 1½″ x 5½″
Purple Print
24 squares (B) 1½″ x 1½″
4 squares (D) 4½″ x 4½″

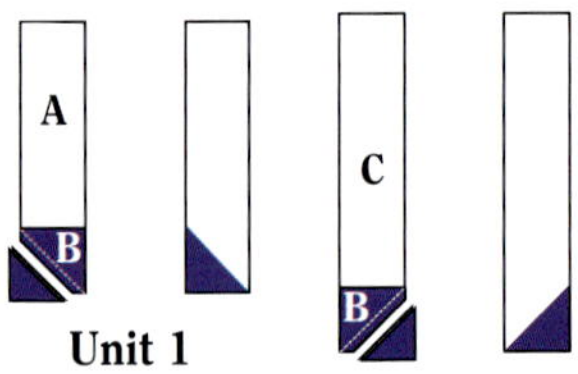

Unit 1
Stitch & Flip
Make 8

Unit 2
Stitch & Flip
Make 8

Refer to "Stitch-and-Flip" in the Techniques file on the PDF and use the cream A's and purple B's to make 8 unit 1's. Use the cream C's and purple B's to make 8 unit 2's.

Sew the units and patches together as shown to complete the block.

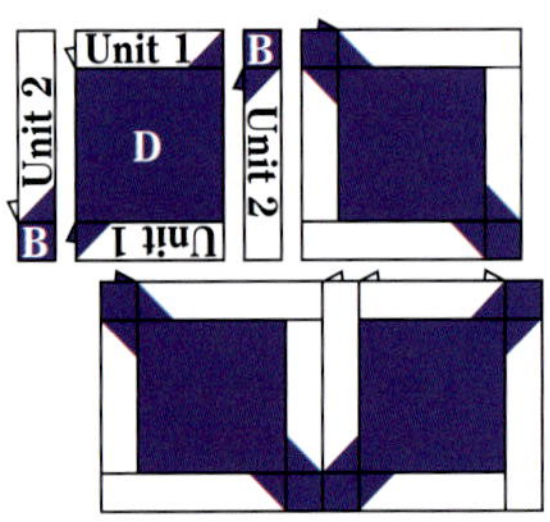

Block Assembly

block no. 670

Tweet Street

by Carolyn Beam • Creative Editor, *Quiltmaker*
quiltmaker.com

Fabric: Spring Street by Carolyn Gavin and Little Bear Counts by Linda Hohag, both by P&B Textiles, pbtex.com.

White Print
5 squares (A) 3⅞″ x 3⅞″
6 squares (B) 3½″ x 3½″
Teal Tone-on-Tone
1 square (A) 3⅞″ x 3⅞″
Green Dot and Orange Dot
from *each*
2 squares (A) 3⅞″ x 3⅞″

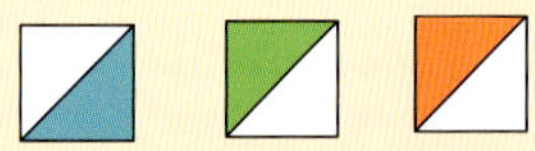

Unit 1
Make 2

Unit 2
Make 4

Unit 3
Make 4

Pair 1 white A with the teal A to make 2 Triangle-Square unit 1's. Pair 2 white A's with the green A's to make 4 unit 2's. Pair 2 white A's with the orange A's to make 4 unit 3's.

Sew the units and patches together as shown to complete the block.

Block Assembly

block no. 671
Pinwheel Surprise

by Donna Benham • DB Designs

Fabric: Gobble Gobble by Sandy Gervais for Moda Fabrics, unitednotions.com.

Cream Print
- 2 squares (A) 5¼" x 5¼"

Brown Print
- 1 square (A) 5¼" x 5¼"
- 2 squares (B) 2⅞" x 2⅞"
- 4 rectangles (C) 2½" x 4½"

Rust Print
- 1 square (A) 5¼" x 5¼"
- 2 squares (B) 2⅞" x 2⅞"
- 4 rectangles (C) 2½" x 4½"

Unit 1
Make 4

Unit 2
Make 4

Refer to "Quarter-Square Triangles" and "Triangle-Squares" in the Techniques file on the PDF. Pair the cream A's with the rust and brown A's to make 4 Quarter-Square Triangle unit 1's as shown. Use the rust and brown B's to make 4 Triangle-Square unit 2's.

Sew the units and patches together as shown to complete the block.

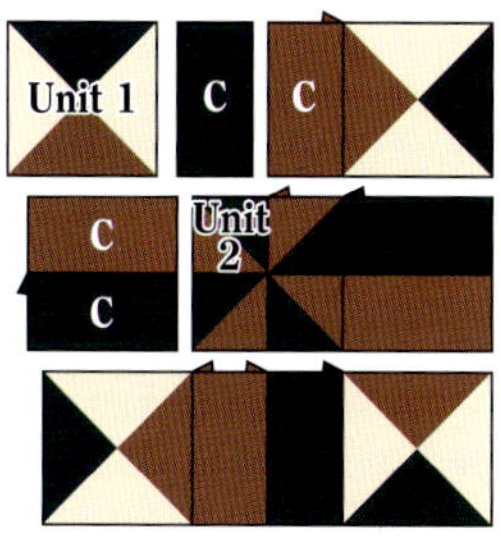

Block Assembly

block no. 672
Amish #8

by Sandi Blackwell • Stitched Buy
stitchedbuy.com

⧄ = cut in half diagonally

Blue Tone-on-Tone and Brown Tone-on-Tone
from *each*
- 2 squares (A) 3⅞" x 3⅞"
- 1 square 3⅞" x 3⅞" ⧄ (B) (there will be one extra)
- 1 square (C) 3½" x 3½"
- 1 square 6⅞" x 6⅞" ⧄ (E) (there will be one extra)

Cream Print
- 1 square 3⅞" x 3⅞" ⧄ (B)
- 2 rectangles (D) 3½" x 6½"

Unit
Make 4

Pair the blue and brown A's to make 4 Triangle-Square units.

Sew the units and patches together as shown to complete the block.

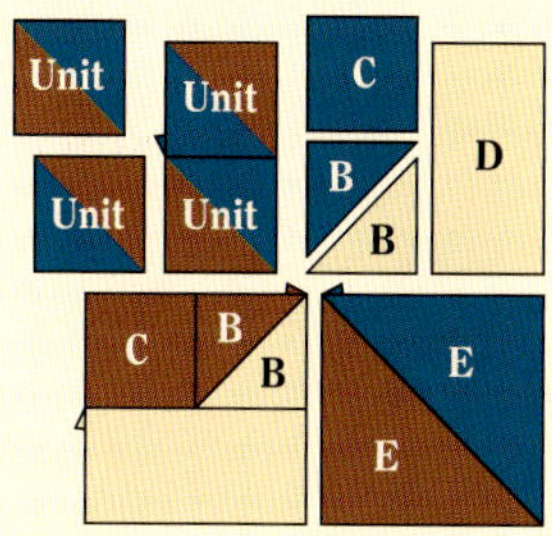

Block Assembly

block no. 673
Spinning Star

by Lynn Roddy Brown
LynnRoddyBrown.com

Lynn Roddy Brown authored *Simple Strategies for Scrap Quilts* and *Simple Strategies for Block-Swap Quilts* for Martingale & Co., martingale-pub.com.

= cut in half diagonally
= cut in half diagonally twice

Cream Print and Red Print
from *each*
4 squares 3⅞" x 3⅞" (A)
Light Blue Print and Dark Blue Print
from *each*
4 squares 4¼" x 4¼" (B)

Sew the patches together as shown to complete the block.

Block Piecing

block no. 674
Good Time Charlie

by Pam Buda • Heartspun Quilts
heartspunquilts.com

Fabric: Little Pink Stars by Margo Krager for Blue Hill Fabrics, bluehillfabrics.net.

See page 82 on the PDF for pattern

Pink Print
1 square (A) 4½" x 4½"
8 squares (B) 2½" x 2½"
4 squares (E) 2⅞" x 2⅞"
Dark Blue Print #1
4 squares (B) 2½" x 2½"
4 squares (F) 1½" x 1½"
Cream Print
4 squares (B) 2½" x 2½"
4 *each* templates D and Dr
4 squares (E) 2⅞" x 2⅞"
4 squares (F) 1½" x 1½"
4 rectangles (G) 1½" x 2½"
Dark Blue Print #2
4 template C

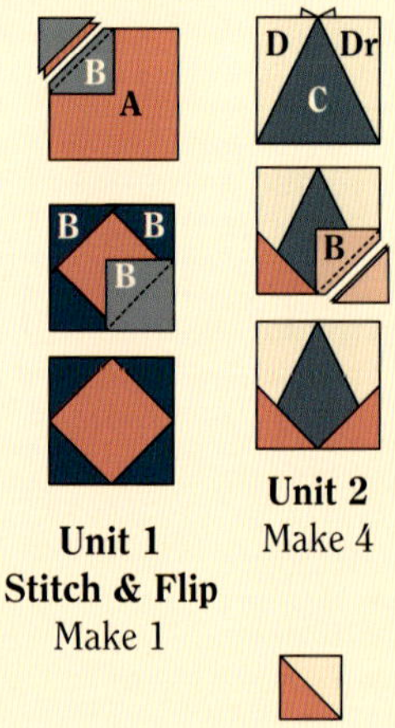

Unit 1
Stitch & Flip
Make 1

Unit 2
Make 4

Unit 3
Make 8

For all techniques, refer to the Techniques file on the PDF. Pair the pink A with the dark blue print #1 B's to make Stitch-and-Flip unit 1. Sew together the C's, D's and Dr's. Use the Stitch-and-Flip technique to add pink B's to the corners as shown to make 4 unit 2's.

Pair the pink E's and cream E's to make 8 Trianlge-Square unit 3's. Sew the patches and units together as shown to complete the block.

Block Assembly

pieced

block no. 675

Happy-Go-Lucky

by Debbie Caffrey • Debbie's Creative Moments, Inc.
debbiescreativemoments.com

Fabric: Happy designed by Me and My Sister for Moda Fabrics, unitednotions.com.

Debbie Caffrey is the author of several books, including *Open a Can of Worms* for Debbie's Creative Moments, debbiescreative moments.com.

See pages 48 and 103 on the PDF for patterns

Templates for Happy-Go-Lucky block on pages 48 and 103 of the Templates file on the PDF

White Print
section, patch 1

Aqua Tone-on-Tone #1
section, patches 2, 3, 5 and 7

Pink Print
section, patches 4 and 6

Light Green Print
4 template A
8 squares (D) 1½" x 1½"

Aqua Tone-on-Tone #2
4 *each* templates B and Br
1 square (C) 2½" x 2½"

Green Print
8 squares (D) 1½" x 1½"

Multiprint
2 rectangles (E) 1¾" x 6½"
2 rectangles (F) 1¾" x 9"

Make 4 paper copies of the foundation section. Foundation piece the sections in numerical order, pressing and trimming after each patch addition. Join each A with a B and Br to make 4 units.

Sew the patches, units and sections together as shown to complete the block.

Section
Make 4

Unit
Make 4

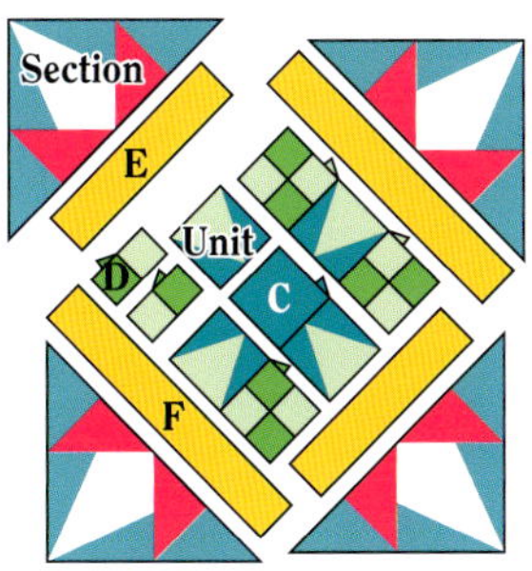

Block Assembly

block no. 676

High Tea

by Patti Carey • Northcott
northcott.net

Fabric: High Tea 10th Anniversary designed by Ro Gregg for Northcott, northcott.net.

⧄ = cut in half diagonally
⊠ = cut in half twice diagonally

Black Print
1 square (A) 4¾" x 4¾"

Light Pink Tone-on-Tone
2 squares 3⅞" x 3⅞" ⧄ (B)

Pink Print
4 squares 3⅞" x 3⅞" ⧄ (B)

Dark Pink Tone-on-Tone
4 squares (C) 2⅝" x 2⅝"

Black Tone-on-Tone
2 squares 4¼" x 4¼" ⊠ (D)
4 squares (E) 3½" x 3½"

Sew the patches together as shown to complete the block.

Block Piecing

block no. 677

Commencement

by Jennifer Chiaverini
elmcreek.net

Fabric: Elm Creek Quilts: Anneke's Collection by Jennifer Chiaverini for Red Rooster Fabrics, redroosterfabrics.com.

Bestselling novelist Jennifer Chiaverini has written several books, including *Elm Creek Quilts: Quilt Projects Inspired by the Elm Creek Quilt Novels* for C&T Publishing, ctpub.com.

See page 89 on the PDF for pattern

⧄ = cut in half diagonally

Red Print
- 1 square (A) 3½" x 3½"
- 4 squares 2⅜" x 2⅜" ⧄ (C)
- 4 *each* templates H and Hr

Cream Print #1
- 4 squares (B) 2⅝" x 2⅝"
- 4 squares (D) 2" x 2"
- 2 squares 3⅞" x 3⅞" ⧄ (I)

Brown Print
- 4 *each* templates E and Er

Cream Print #2
- 2 squares 3" x 3" ⧄ (F)
- 2 squares 3⅞" x 3⅞" ⧄ (G)

Join the cream #1 B's with the red C's, then add the cream #1 D's as shown.

Refer to "Set-in Seams" in the Techniques file on the PDF. Sew a brown E and Er to each B as shown, paying close attention to the patch orientation.

Sew the remaining patches together as shown to complete the block.

Block Piecing

block no. 678

Knot: My Block

by Tina Curran
tinacurran.com

White Dot
- 5 squares (A) 2½" x 2½"
- 4 rectangles (B) 2½" x 3½"
- 2 rectangles (D) 1½" x 10½"
- 2 rectangles (E) 1½" x 12½"

Assorted Red, Orange, Yellow, Green, Dark Blue, Light Blue, Purple and Pink Prints
from *each* of the 8 color groups
- 7 squares (C) 1½" x 1½"

Sew the patches together as shown to make the block.

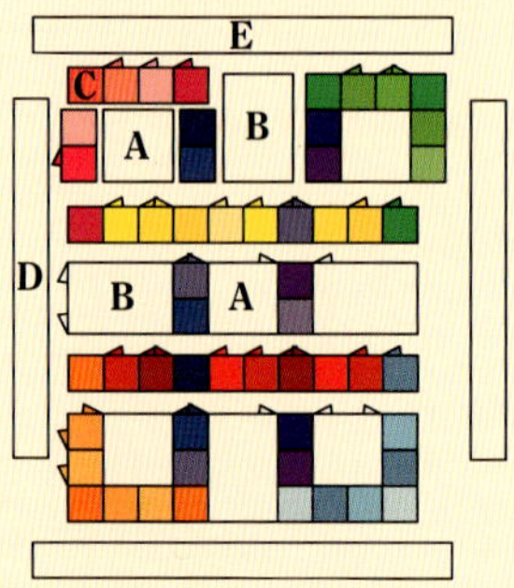

Block Piecing

block no. 679

Black Pearl

by Monique Dillard • Open Gate
opengatequilts.com

Fabric: Olde World Style by Monique Dillard for Maywood Studio, maywoodstudio.com.

⧄ = cut in half diagonally
⊠ = cut in half diagonally twice

Cream Print
- 1 square 4¼" x 4¼" ⊠ (A) (there will be 2 extra patches)
- 4 rectangles (B) 2" x 3½"
- 8 squares 2⅜" x 2⅜" ⧄ (C)

Black Print
- 1 square 4¼" x 4¼" ⊠ (A) (there will be 2 extra patches)
- 4 squares 3⅞" x 3⅞" ⧄ (D)

Black Solid
- 4 rectangles (B) 2" x 3½"
- 4 squares (E) 2" x 2"
- 4 rectangles (F) 2" x 6½"

Sew the patches together as shown to complete the block.

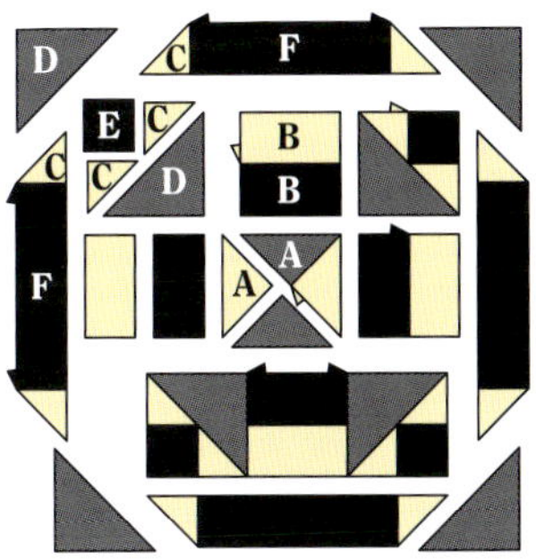

Block Piecing

block no. 680

Garden Spot

by Sherri Driver • Associate Editor, *McCall's Quilting*
mccallsquilting.com

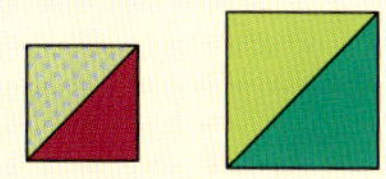

Unit 1
Make 12

Unit 2
Make 4

⧄ = cut in half diagonally

Floral Print
- 1 square (A) 6" x 6"

Teal Stripe
- 4 rectangles (B) 1" x 4"
- 8 squares (C) 1" x 1"

Dark Teal Tone-on-Tone
- 4 squares (C) 1" x 1"

Lime Green Dot
- 4 rectangles (D) 2" x 3"
- 6 squares (E) 2⅜" x 2⅜"

Purple Tone-on-Tone
- 6 squares (E) 2⅜" x 2⅜"

Teal Tone-on-Tone
- 2 squares (F) 3⅞" x 3⅞"

Lime Print
- 2 squares (F) 3⅞" x 3⅞"
- 4 squares 3⅞" x 3⅞" ⧄ (G)

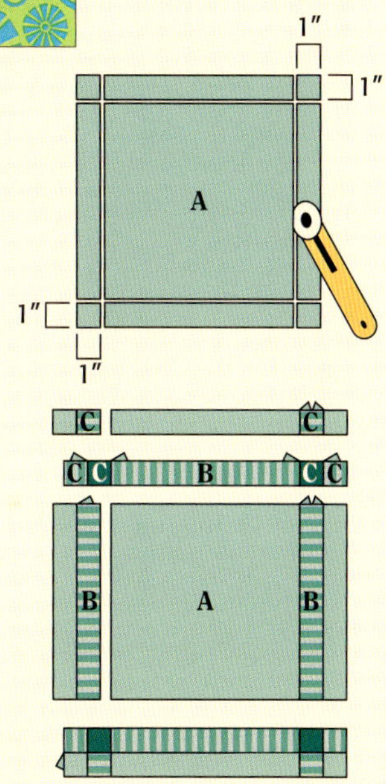

Section
Make 1

Carefully trim 1" from each edge of A as shown, keeping the patches in the same orientation. To make the section, insert and join the teal stripe B's and C's and the dark teal C's as shown.

Pair the purple E's and lime dot E's to make 12 Triangle-Square unit 1's. Pair the lime F's with the teal F's to make 4 unit 2's. Sew the section, units and patches together as shown to complete the block.

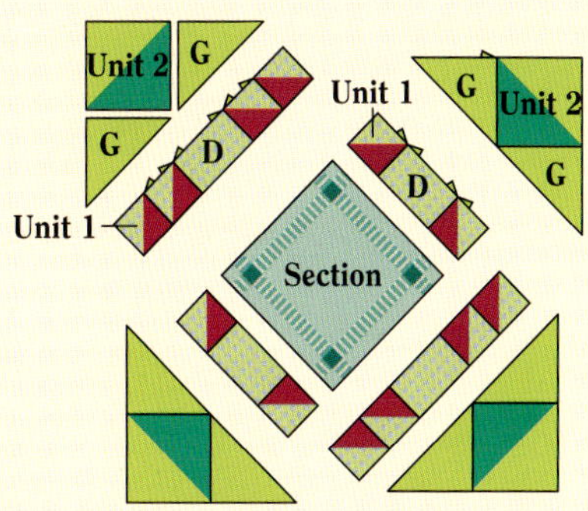

Block Assembly

block no. 681

Around the Park

by Vickie Eapen • Spun Sugar Quilts
spunsugarquilt.com

Fabric: Central Park by Kate Spain for Moda Fabrics, unitednotions.com.

White Print and Yellow Tone-on-Tone
from *each*
- 2 squares (A) 4⅞″ x 4⅞″
- 4 rectangles (B) 2½″ x 4½″

Multiprint
- 1 square (C) 4½″ x 4½″

Unit
Make 4

Refer to "Triangle-Squares" in the Techniques file on hte PDF. Make 4 units using the white and yellow A's.

Join the units and patches as shown to complete the block.

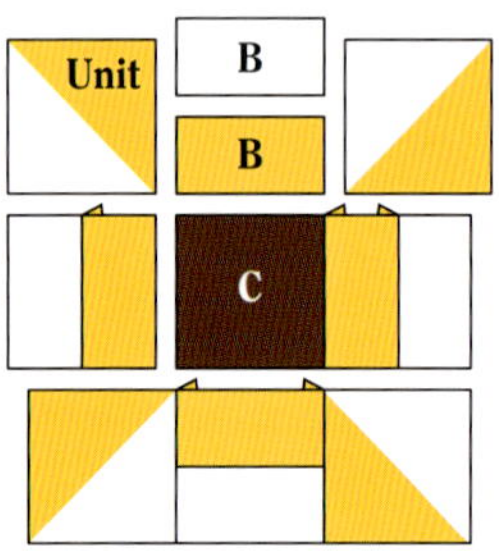

Block Assembly

block no. 682

Crossroads

by Deanne Eisenman • Snuggles Quilts
snugglesquilts.com

Deanne Eisenman is the author of *Country Fresh Quilts* for Martingale & Co., martingalepub.com.

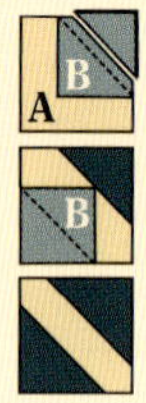

Unit 1
Stitch & Flip
Make 2

Cream Print #1
- 4 squares (A) 3½″ x 3½″
- 4 squares (E) 2″ x 2″

Blue Print and Pink Print
from *each*
- 4 squares (B) 2¾″ x 2¾″
- 2 rectangles (C) 2″ x 3½″
- 2 rectangles (D) 2″ x 5″
- 4 squares (E) 2″ x 2″

Cream Print #2
- 4 rectangles (D) 2″ x 5″
- 4 rectangles (F) 2″ x 6½″

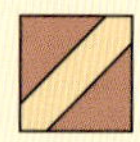

Unit 2
Stitch & Flip
Make 2

Unit 3
Stitch & Flip
Make 2

Unit 4
Stitch & Flip
Make 2

Unit 5
Stitch & Flip
Make 2

Unit 6
Stitch & Flip
Make 2

Unit 7
Stitch & Flip

Unit 8
Stitch & Flip

Refer to "Stitch-and-Flip" in the Techniques file on the PDF. Use the cream #1 A's and the blue and pink B's to make 2 unit 1's and 2 unit 2's as shown.

Using the same technique, pair the blue and pink D's with cream #1 E's to make 2 unit 3's and 2 unit 4's. Make 2 unit 5's and 2 unit 6's with the cream #2 D's and the blue and pink E's.

Make 2 unit 7's using cream #2 F's and pink E's, and 2 unit 8's with cream #2 F's and blue E's.

Join the patches and units as shown to complete the block.

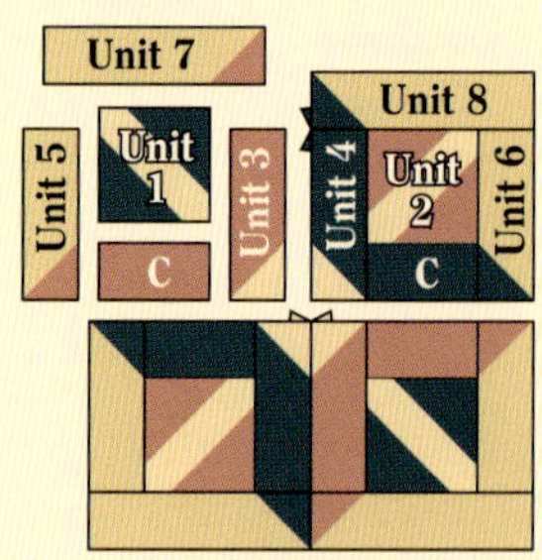

Block Assembly

block no. 683

Royal Star

by Robin Gallagher • Robin Quilts, etc.
robinquiltsetc.com

Dark Purple Batik
1 square (A) 4½" x 4½"
8 squares (C) 2⅞" x 2⅞"
4 rectangles (D) 2½" x 4½"
Light Pink Batik
12 squares (B) 2½" x 2½"
4 squares (C) 2⅞" x 2⅞"
1 square (E) 5¼" x 5¼"

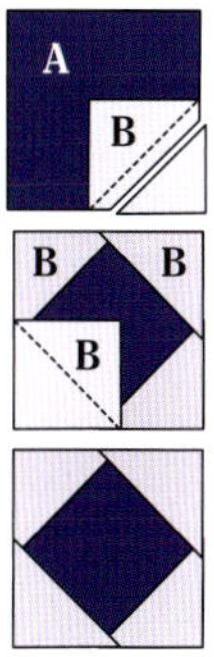

Unit 1
Stitch & Flip
Make 1

Unit 2
Make 8

Flying Geese
Make 4

Refer to "Stitch-and-Flip" in the Techniques file on the PDF. Use the dark purple A and 4 light pink B's to make unit 1.

Pair the light pink C's with 4 dark purple C's to make 8 Triangle-Square unit 2's.

Use the light pink E and 4 dark purple C's to make 4 Flying Geese.

Join the units, Flying Geese, and patches as shown to complete the block.

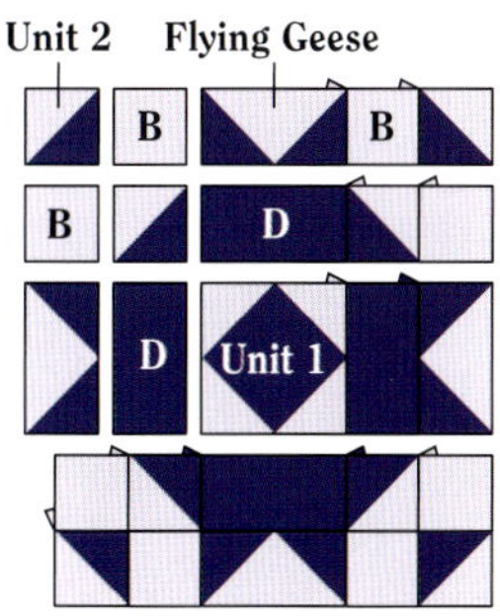

Block Assembly

block no. 684

Half and Half

by Kay Gentry • Noble Needle Quilting and Sewing
nobleneedle.com

Dark Blue Tone-on-Tone and Medium Blue Tone-on-Tone from *each*
4 squares (A) 2⅞" x 2⅞"
6 squares (B) 2½" x 2½"
Dark Purple, Medium Purple, Dark Red, Medium Red, Dark Gold, Medium Gold, Dark Green and Medium Green Tone-on-Tones from *each*
2 squares (A) 2⅞" x 2⅞"

Unit
Make 24

Pair the A's in the dark and medium values of each color to make 24 Triangle-Square unit 1's.

Join the units and patches as shown to complete the block.

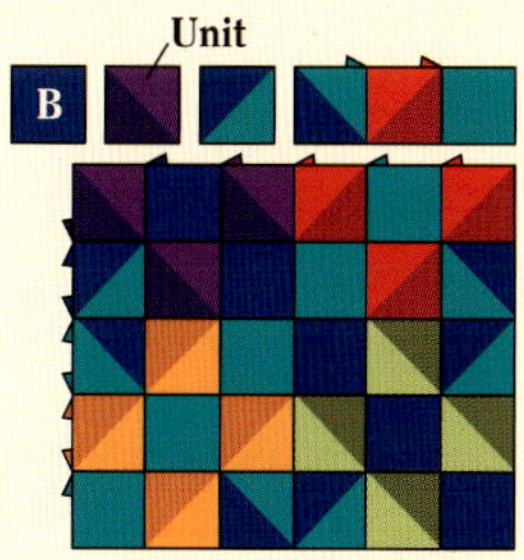

Block Assembly

block no. 685
Spiked Punch

by John Adams
quiltdad.com

Fabric: Olympus Collection I by Olympus of Japan for Clothworks, clothworks.com.

4 Assorted Light Prints
from each
1 rectangle (A) $2\frac{1}{2}$" x $7\frac{1}{2}$"
6 Assorted Dark Prints
from each
1 rectangle (A) $2\frac{1}{2}$" x $7\frac{1}{2}$"
Red Print
2 rectangles (A) $2\frac{1}{2}$" x $7\frac{1}{2}$"

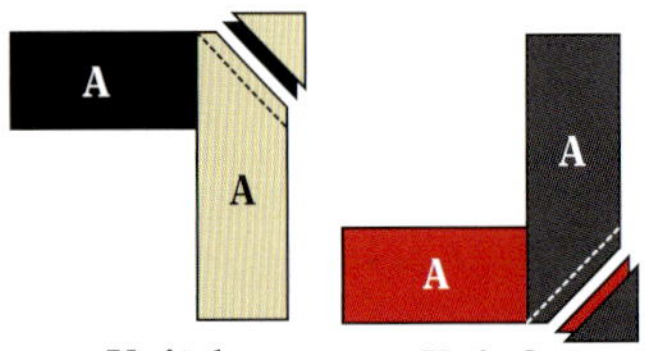

Unit 1 **Stitch & Flip** Make 2
Unit 2 **Stitch & Flip** Make 1

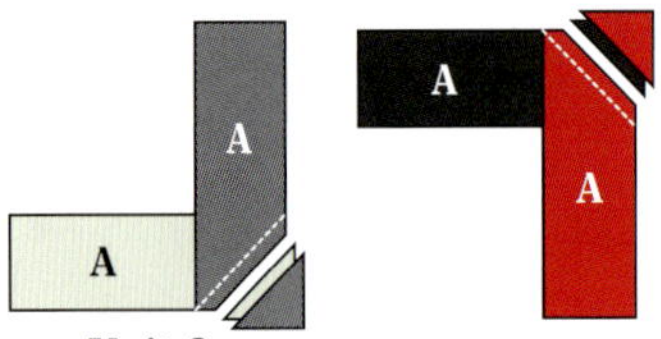

Unit 3 **Stitch & Flip** Make 2
Unit 4 **Stitch & Flip** Make 1

Refer to "Stitch-and-Flip" in the Techniques file on the PDF. Pair light A's with dark A's to make 2 unit 1's. Make 1 unit 2 with a red A and a dark A. Make 2 unit 3's with light A's and dark A's. Make 1 unit 4 with a dark A and a red A.

Sew the units together as shown to complete the block.

Block Assembly

block no. 686
Whirly Jig

by Janice Averill • Iris Quilts & Dyed Fabrics

Fabric: Kew Gardens designed by Laura Ashley for Quilting Treasures, quiltingtreasures.com.

Black with Cream Print and Cream with Black Print
from each
2 strips $2\frac{11}{16}$" x 15" for bands A and B
1 strip $2\frac{1}{2}$" x 15" for bands A and B

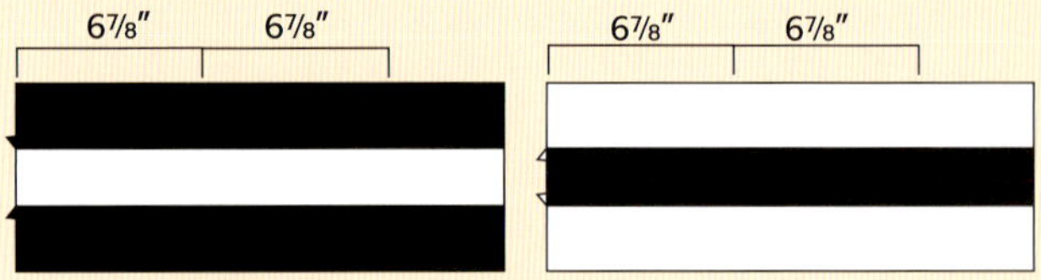

Band A **Band B**

Unit 1 Make 4
Section Make 4
Unit 2 Make 4

Sewing the $2\frac{1}{2}$" strips in the middle, sew the strips together to make band A and band B as shown. Cut band A into 2 squares $6\frac{7}{8}$" × $6\frac{7}{8}$". Noting the orientation of the strips, cut each band A square in half diagonally to make 4 unit 1's. Repeat with band B to make 4 unit 2's.

Join units 1 and 2 to make 4 identical sections. Sew the sections together as shown to complete the block.

Block Assembly

block no. 687

Wind-Surfing

by Nan Baker • Purrfect Spots
purrfectspots.com

Light Blue Batik
- 9 squares (A) 2⅞″ x 2⅞″
- 9 squares (B) 2½″ x 2½″

6 Assorted Tone-on-Tones

from 3
- 2 squares (A) 2⅞″ x 2⅞″
- 2 squares (B) 2½″ x 2½″

from 3
- 1 square (A) 2⅞″ x 2⅞″
- 1 square (B) 2½″ x 2½″

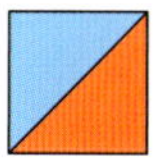

Unit
Make 18

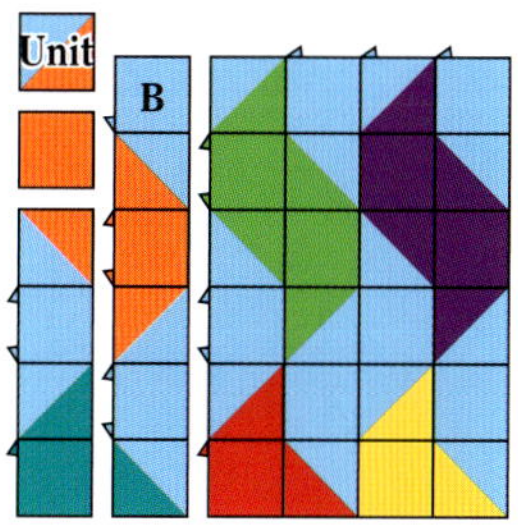

Block Assembly

Refer to "Triangle-Squares" in the Techniques file on the PDF. Pair each light blue batik A with an assorted tone-on-tone A to make a total of 18 units.

Sew the patches and units together as shown to complete the block.

Design note: Preplan color placement for adjoining blocks for a continuous design.

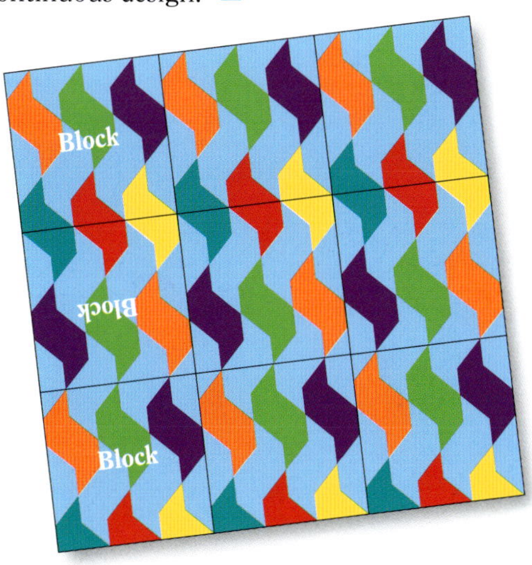

block no. 688

Guiding Light

by Carolyn Beam • Creative Editor, *Quiltmaker*
quiltmaker.com

Unit 1 from A's
Make 4

Unit 2 from B's
Make 6

Unit 3 from B's
Make 2

Unit 4 from B's
Make 2

Unit 5 from B's
Make 16

Light Blue Tone-on-Tone
- 2 squares (A) 1⅞″ x 1⅞″
- 4 squares (B) 2⅜″ x 2⅜″
- 5 squares (D) 1½″ x 1½″
- 2 squares (F) 2″ x 2″
- 1 rectangle (G) 3½″ x 6″
- 1 rectangle (H) 1″ x 1½″
- 1 rectangle (J) 1½″ x 2½″
- 1 rectangle (K) 2″ x 3½″
- 1 rectangle (L) 2″ x 5″
- 1 rectangle (M) 3″ x 5″
- 1 rectangle (O) 1″ x 4½″

Yellow Tone-on-Tone
- 2 squares (A) 1⅞″ x 1⅞″
- 1 square (D) 1½″ x 1½″
- 1 rectangle (I) 2½″ x 3″

Dark Blue Print
- 8 squares (B) 2⅜″ x 2⅜″

Medium Blue Print
- 10 squares (B) 2⅜″ x 2⅜″
- 1 square (F) 2″ x 2″

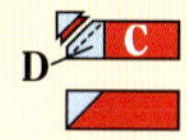

Unit 6
Stitch & Flip
Make 1

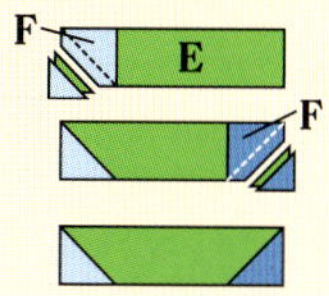

Unit 7
Stitch & Flip
Make 1

White Solid
- 4 squares (B) 2⅜″ x 2⅜″
- 1 rectangle (N) 2½″ x 3½″

Red Solid
- 1 rectangle (C) 1½″ x 3½″
- 1 rectangle (N) 2½″ x 3½″
- 1 rectangle (P) 1″ x 4″

Green Tone-on-Tone
- 1 rectangle (E) 2″ x 6½″

Pair the light blue A's and yellow A's to make 4 Triangle-Square unit 1's. Pair the light blue, white, medium blue and dark blue B's to make the appropriate number of unit 2's, 3's, 4's and 5's as shown.

Refer to "Stitch-and-Flip" in the Techniques file on the PDF. Use the red C and a light blue D to make unit 6. Use the green E with a light blue F and medium blue F to make unit 7. Sew the units and patches together as shown to complete the block.

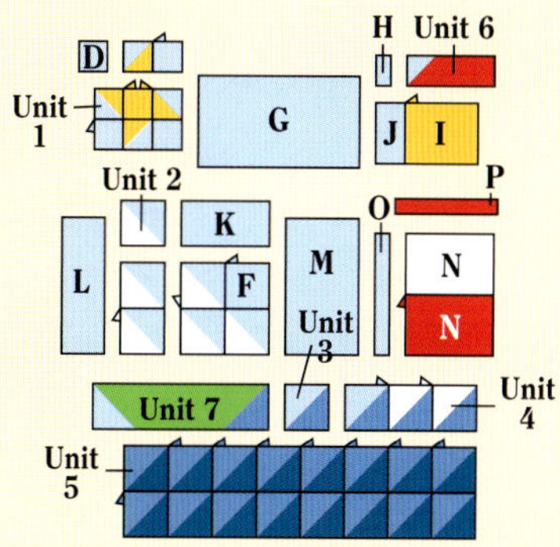

Block Assembly

block no. 689

Oblique

by Debbie Bowles • Maple Island Quilts
mapleislandquilts.com

Debbie Bowles is the author of *Cutting Curves from Straight Pieces* and *Dancing Quilts from Straight Pieces* for American Quilter's Society, americanquilter.com.

Olive Green Print
- 2 squares (A) 4″ x 4″

Dark Blue Batik
- 4 rectangles (B) 2″ x 4″
- 4 rectangles (C) 2″ x 5½″
- 4 rectangles (D) 2″ x 7″
- 4 rectangles (E) 2″ x 8½″

Light Blue Batik
- 2 squares (A) 4″ x 4″
- 4 rectangles (C) 2″ x 5½″
- 4 rectangles (D) 2″ x 7″

6½″ square ruler or template plastic (see instructions below)

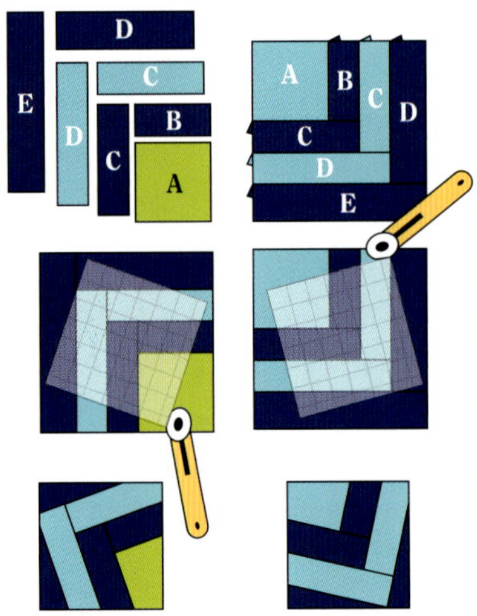

Section 1 Make 2 **Section 2** Make 2

Sew the patches together as shown to make 2 each of sections 1 and 2.

If you don't have a 6½″ square ruler, make a 6½″ square from the template plastic.

Place the 6½″ square ruler on a section 1; turn the ruler slightly clockwise and trim as shown. Repeat to trim the remaining section 1.

For each section 2, turn the ruler slightly counterclockwise and trim as shown.

Sew the sections together as shown to complete the block.

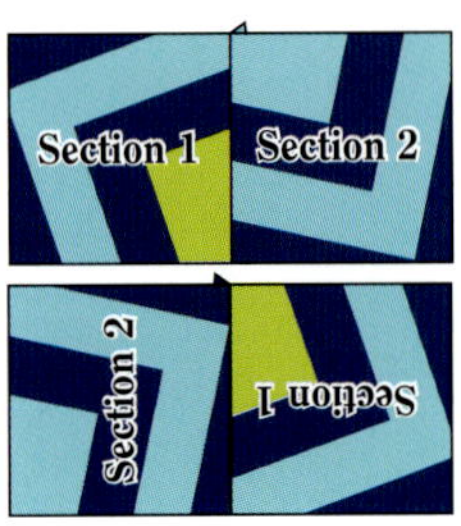

Block Assembly

block no. 690

Radiant Star

by Eleanor Burns • Quilt In a Day
quiltinaday.com

Fabric: Fresh Flowers designed by Deb Strain for Moda Fabrics, unitednotions.com, and background from RJR Fabrics, rjrfabrics.com

Eleanor Burns has authored numerous titles, including *Radiant Star Quilts* for Quilt In a Day, quiltinaday.com.

See page 137 on the PDF for pattern

◸ = cut in half diagonally

Blue Print and Red Print
from *each*
- 8 template A

Yellow Tone-on-Tone
- 16 template A

White Tone-on-Tone
- 4 *each* templates B and Br
- 4 squares 4¾″ x 4¾″ ◸ (C)

Section Make 8

Make 8 sections using the red, blue and yellow A's.

Sew the patches and sections together as shown to complete the block.

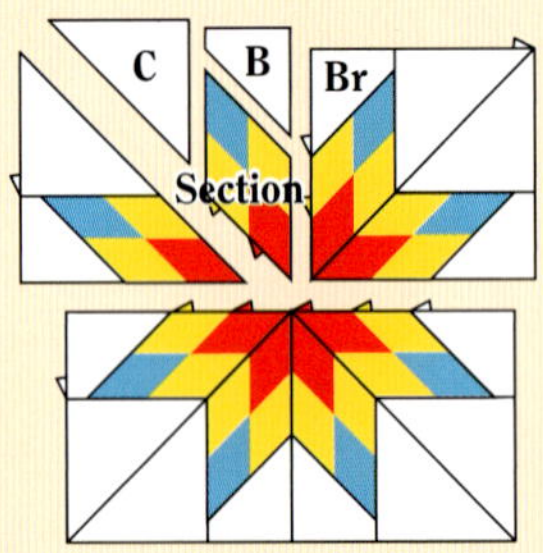

Block Assembly

block no. 691
Gettysburg

by Jennifer Chiaverini
elmcreek.net

Fabric: Elm Creek Quilts: Anneke's Collection by Jennifer Chiaverini for Red Rooster Fabrics, redroosterfabrics.com.

Best-selling novelist Jennifer Chiaverini has written several books, including *Traditions from Elm Creek Quilts* for C&T Publishing, ctpub.com.

⧄ = cut in half diagonally

Dark Green Print
- 5 squares (A) 4½″ x 4½″
- 4 squares (B) 2½″ x 2½″

Red Print
- 4 squares (B) 2½″ x 2½″
- 2 squares 4⅞″ x 4⅞″ ⧄ (D)

Cream Print
- 8 squares (B) 2½″ x 2½″

Cream Tone-on-Tone
- 8 squares (B) 2½″ x 2½″
- 4 squares 2⅞″ x 2⅞″ ⧄ (C)

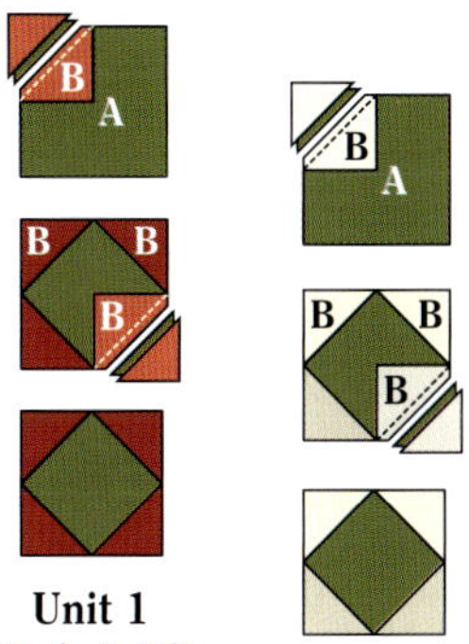

Unit 1
Stitch & Flip
Make 1

Unit 2
Stitch & Flip
Make 4

Refer to "Stitch-and-Flip" in the Techniques file on the PDF. Use a green A and the red B's to make unit 1. Use a green A, 2 cream print B's and 2 cream tone-on-tone B's to make a unit 2. Repeat to make 4 unit 2's.

Sew the units and patches together as shown to complete the block.

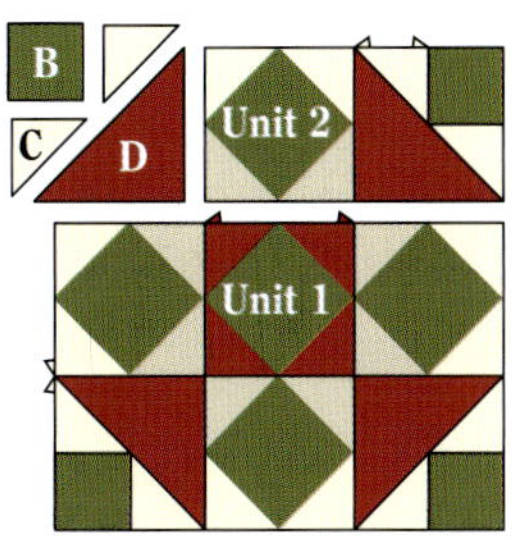

Block Assembly

block no. 692
Blue Ribbon

by Tina Curran
tinacurran.com

Unit 1
Make 12

⧄ = cut in half diagonally

Yellow Tone-on-Tone
- 6 squares (A) 1⅞″ x 1⅞″
- 4 rectangles (B) 1½″ x 2½″
- 1 rectangle (D) 3½″ x 4½″
- 3 squares (E) 2½″ x 2½″
- 3 squares 2⅞″ x 2⅞″ ⧄ (G)
- 3 rectangles (H) 2½″ x 3½″
- 2 rectangles (I) 1½″ x 10½″
- 2 rectangles (J) 1½″ x 12½″

Assorted Blue Prints and Tone-on-Tones
- 6 squares (A) 1⅞″ x 1⅞″
- 26 squares (C) 1½″ x 1½″
- 1 square (E) 2½″ x 2½″
- 6 squares 1⅞″ x 1⅞″ ⧄ (F)

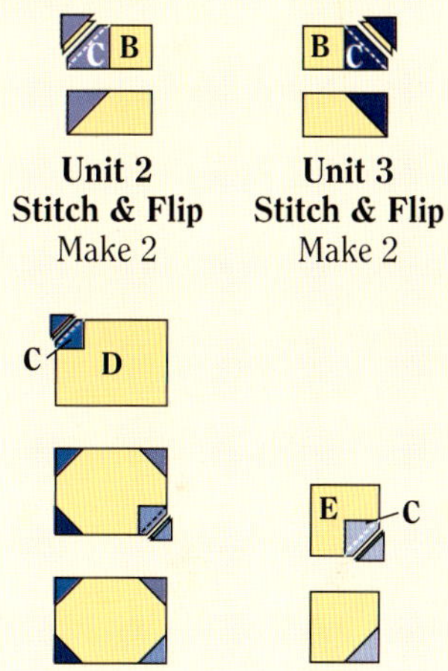

Unit 2
Stitch & Flip
Make 2

Unit 3
Stitch & Flip
Make 2

Unit 4
Stitch & Flip
Make 1

Unit 5
Stitch & Flip
Make 2

Pair the yellow A's and blue A's to make 12 Triangle-Square unit 1's.

Refer to "Stitch-and-Flip" in the Techniques file on the PDF. Use the yellow B's and blue C's to make 2 unit 2's and 2 unit 3's as shown. Make 1 unit 4 with the yellow D and 4 blue C's. Use the yellow E's and blue C's to make 2 unit 5's.

Sew the patches and units together as shown to complete the block.

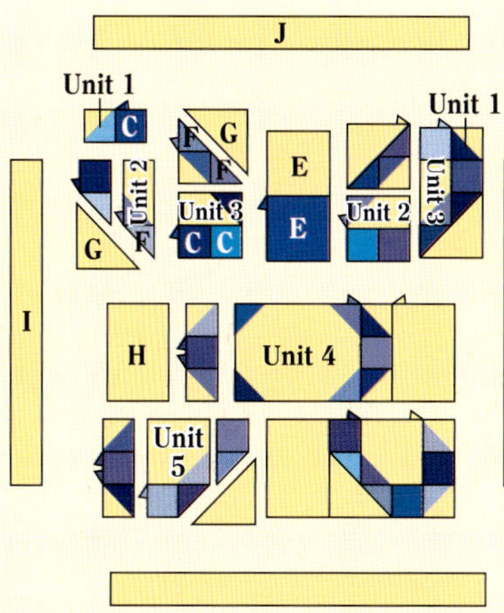

Block Assembly

block no. 693

Tumbling Down

by Kim Diehl
kimdiehl.com

Fabric: Various collections by Kim Diehl for Henry Glass & Co., henryglassfabrics.com.

Kim Diehl has authored numerous titles including *Simple Comforts* for Martingale & Co., martingale-pub.com.

Black Print
6 squares (A) 2½" x 2½"
Assorted Medium and Dark Prints
15 squares (A) 2½" x 2½"
Assorted Cream Prints and Tone-on-Tones
1 square (A) 2½" x 2½"
1 rectangle (B) 2½" x 4½"
1 rectangle (C) 2½" x 6½"
1 rectangle (D) 2½" x 8½"
1 rectangle (E) 2½" x 10½"

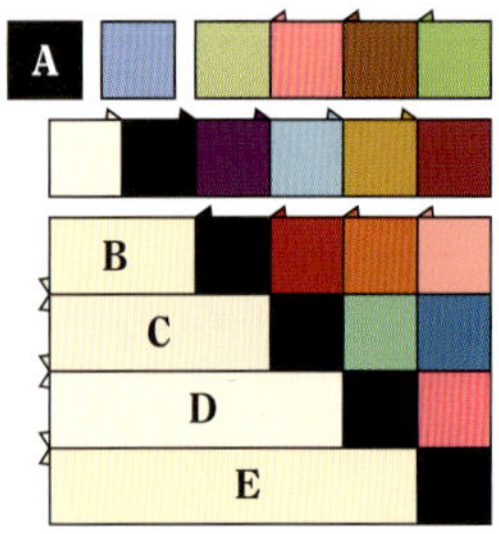

Block Piecing

Sew the patches together as shown to complete the block.

block no. 694

Pinwheel Pizzazz

by June Dudley • Editor-in-Chief, *Quiltmaker*
quiltmaker.com

Fabric: Kona Solids, Flower Shop and New Traditions all from Robert Kaufman, robertkaufman.com.

Red Solid and White Solid
from each
2 squares (A) 1⅝" x 1⅝"
2 squares (B) 2⅛" x 2⅛"
2 squares (C) 2⅝" x 2⅝"
2 squares (D) 3⅛" x 3⅛"
Black Print #1
2 rectangles (E) 2" x 3"
Black and Red Stripe
2 rectangles (F) 4" x 4½"
Black Print #2
2 rectangles (G) 5" x 8"

Unit 1 from A's
Make 4

Unit 2 from B's
Make 4

Unit 3 from C's
Make 4

Unit 4 from D's
Make 4

Pair the red and the white A's to make 4 Triangle-Square unit 1's, the red and the white B's to make 4 unit 2's, the red and the white C's to make 4 unit 3's, and the red and the white D's to make 4 unit 4's. Sew each set of 4 matching units together as shown to make 4 Pinwheels.

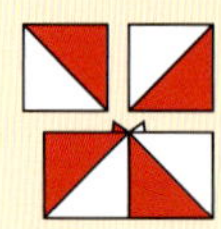
Pinwheel
Make 1 pinwheel from each set of units

Sew the Pinwheels and patches together as shown to complete the block.

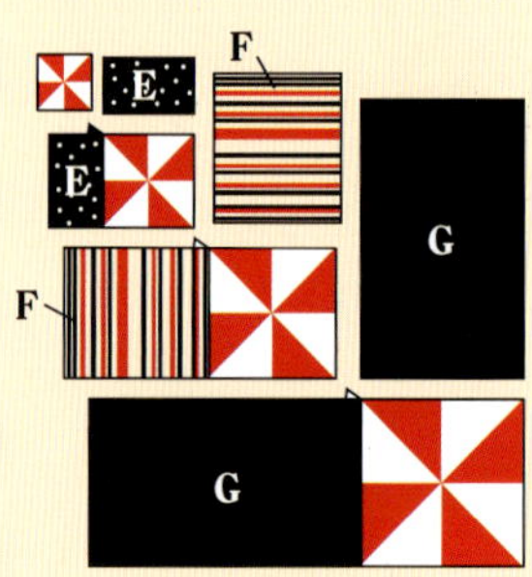

Block Assembly

pieced

block no. 695

County Crossroads

by Heidi Foltz • Handmade by Heidi
handmadebyheidi.com

Fabric: Neptune designed by Tula Pink for Moda Fabrics, unitednotions.com.

Aqua Print
2 squares (A) 4⅞″ x 4⅞″

White Solid
2 squares (A) 4⅞″ x 4⅞″
4 squares (C) 2″ x 2″
8 rectangles (D) 2″ x 4½″

Green Print
1 square (B) 4½″ x 4½″
4 rectangles (E) 1½″ x 4½″

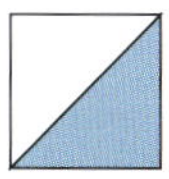

Unit 1
Make 4

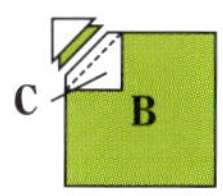

Unit 2
Stitch & Flip

In order to have the pattern in the aqua print facing the same direction, mark the diagonal lines for the unit 1's in opposite directions.

Pair the aqua A's with the white A's to make 4 Triangle-Square unit 1's. Refer to "Stitch-and-Flip" in the Techniques file on the PDF. Use the green B and white C's to make the unit 2.

Sew the units and patches together as shown to complete the block.

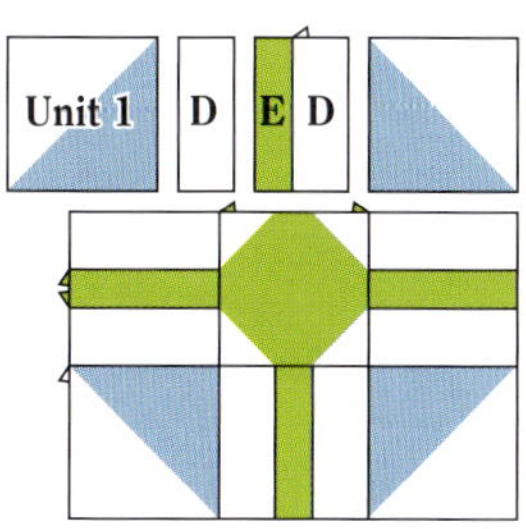

Block Assembly

block no. 696

Holiday Splendor

by Marilyn Foreman • Quilt Moments
quiltmoments.com

Marilyn Foreman is the author of *Kaleidoscope Symphony* for Quilt Moments, quiltmoments.com.

⊠ = cut in half twice diagonally

White Tone-on-Tone
2 squares (A) 3⅞″ x 3⅞″

Dark Red Tone-on-Tone
2 squares (A) 3⅞″ x 3⅞″
2 squares 4¼″ x 4¼″ ⊠ (C)

Black Print
4 squares (B) 2″ x 2″
2 squares 4¼″ x 4¼″ ⊠ (C)

Bright Red Tone-on-Tone
2 squares 4¼″ x 4¼″ ⊠ (C)

Green Tone-on-Tone
2 squares 4¼″ x 4¼″ ⊠ (C)

Multiprint
4 squares (D) 3½″ x 3½″ (see note below)

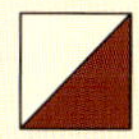

Partial Unit
Make 4

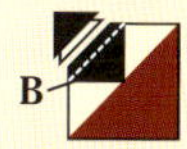

Unit
Stitch & Flip
Make 4

Marilyn fussy cut the 4 multiprint D patches to create the design in the center of the block.

Refer to "Triangle-Squares" in the Techniques file on the PDF. Make 4 partial units using the white A's and dark red A's. Refer to "Stitch-and-Flip" in the Techniques file on the PDF. Sew a black B on the white corner to complete each unit as shown.

Sew the units and patches together as shown to complete the block.

Block Assembly

pieced

block no. 697

Kaleidoscope

by Kay Gentry • Noble Needle Quilting and Sewing
nobleneedle.com

Pink Tone-on-Tone
10 squares (A) 2⅜″ x 2⅜″
Blue Print
9 squares (A) 2⅜″ x 2⅜″
Green Tone-on-Tone
7 squares (A) 2⅜″ x 2⅜″
Orange Tone-on-Tone
6 squares (A) 2⅜″ x 2⅜″
White Tone-on-Tone
16 squares (B) 2″ x 2″
4 squares (C) 3½″ x 3½″

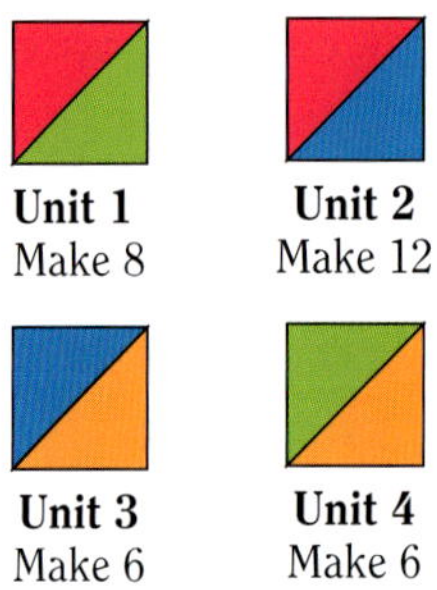

Make 8 Triangle-Square unit 1's using the green and pink A's. Use the pink and blue A's to make 12 unit 2's. Make 6 unit 3's with the blue print and orange A's. Use the green and orange A's to make 6 unit 4's.

Sew the patches and units together as shown to complete the block.

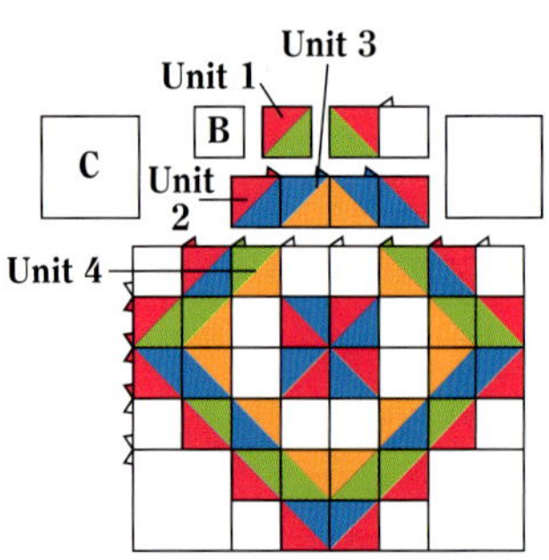

Block Assembly

block no. 698

Starry Eyed

by Allison Harris • Cluck Cluck Sew
cluckclucksew.com

Fabric: Various collections from Moda Fabrics, unitednotions.com.

White Solid
1 square (A) 7¼″ x 7¼″
4 squares (C) 3½″ x 3½″
Aqua Print
4 squares (B) 3⅞″ x 3⅞″
1 rectangle (G) 1″ x 2½″
2 rectangles (H) 1″ x 3″
1 rectangle (I) 1″ x 3½″
Gold Print
1 square (D) 1½″ x 1½″
Red Solid
1 rectangle (E) 1″ x 1½″
2 rectangles (F) 1″ x 2″
1 rectangle (G) 1″ x 2½″
1 rectangle (M) 1⅛″ x 5¼″
2 rectangles (N) 1⅛″ x 5⅞″
1 rectangle (O) 1⅛″ x 6½″
Gray Print
1 rectangle (I) 1″ x 3½″
1 rectangle (J) 1″ x 4″
1 rectangle (K) 1¾″ x 4″
1 rectangle (L) 1¾″ x 5¼″

Flying Geese
Make 4

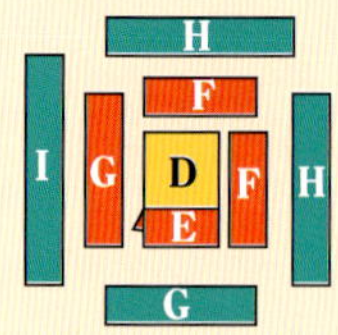

Section
Make 1

Use the white A and aqua B's to make 4 Flying Geese.

Sew D–I together as shown to make the section.

Sew the section, patches and Flying Geese together as shown to complete the block.

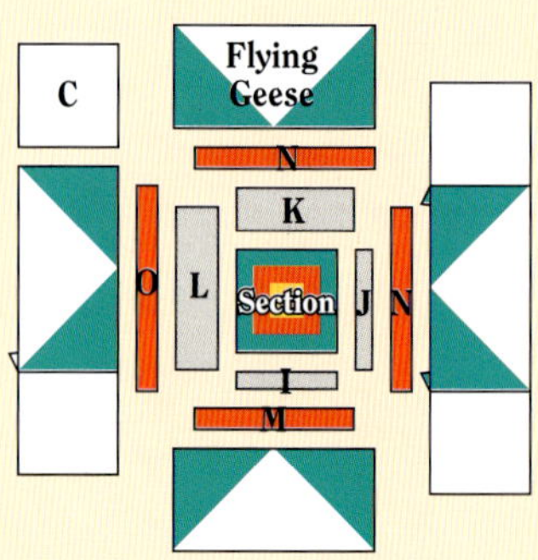

Block Assembly

block no. 699

Block Positive

by Diane Harris • Interactive Editor, *Quiltmaker*
quiltmaker.com

Fabric: Melrose designed by Anna Fishkin and Monika Zhu and basics for Red Rooster Fabrics, redroosterfabrics.com.

Medium Purple Print
1 square (A) 4½" x 4½"
4 rectangles (C) 2½" x 4½"

Dark Purple Print
4 squares (B) 1½" x 1½"
8 rectangles (D) 1½" x 4½"

Gold Tone-on-Tone
4 squares (A) 4½" x 4½"

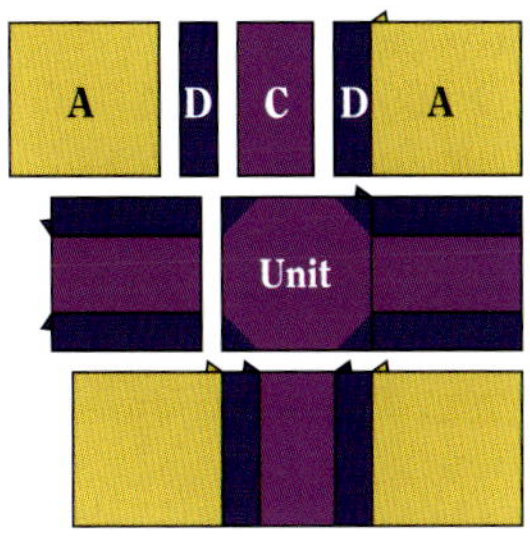

Block Assembly

Refer to "Stitch-and-Flip" in the Techniques file on the PDF. Make the unit using the medium purple A and the dark purple B's.

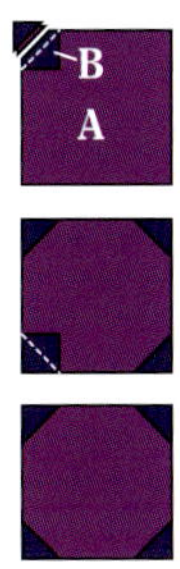

Unit
Stitch & Flip
Make 1

Sew the unit and patches together as shown to complete the block.

block no. 700

Perfect Petals

by Emily Herrick • Crazy Old Ladies
crazyoldladiesquilts.blogspot.com

Assorted Red Tone-on-Tones
4 squares (A) 3½" x 3½"
4 rectangles (C) 2½" x 4½"
2 rectangles (G) 1½" x 10½"
2 rectangles (H) 1½" x 12½"

White Solid
16 squares (B) 1½" x 1½"
4 rectangles (D) 1½" x 3½"
4 rectangles (E) 1½" x 4½"

Gold Tone-on-Tone
8 squares (B) 1½" x 1½"
1 square (F) 2½" x 2½"

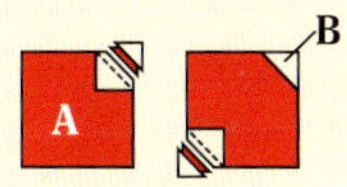

Unit 1
Stitch & Flip
Make 4

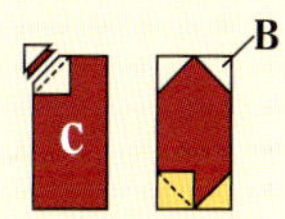

Unit 2
Stitch & Flip
Make 4

Refer to "Stitch-and-Flip" in the Techniques file on the PDF. Make 4 unit 1's using the red A's and white B's. Use the red C's with the gold B's and white B's to make 4 unit 2's as shown.

Sew the units and patches together as shown to complete the block.

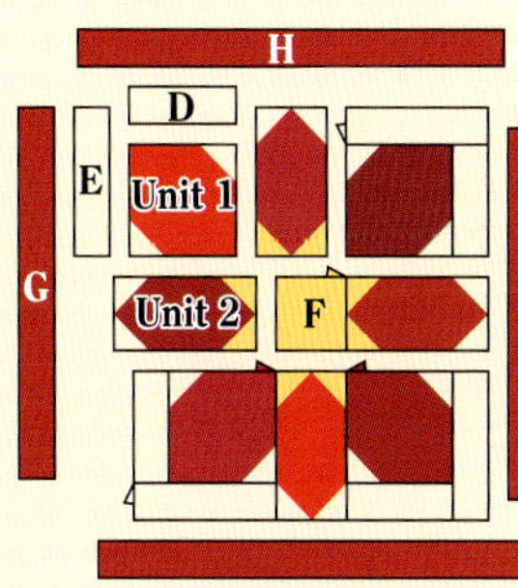

Block Assembly

block no. 701
Midnight Flight

by Bonnie Hunter • Quiltville
quiltville.com

Bonnie Hunter writes the "Addicted to Scraps" column for *Quiltmaker.* She is the author of *Scraps & Shirttails II: Continuing the Art of Quilting Green* and *Adventures with Leaders and Enders* for Kansas City Start Quilts, pickledish.com.

8 Assorted Blue Prints
from *each*
1 rectangle (A) 2½" x 4½"
Assorted Cream Prints
16 squares (B) 2½" x 2½"
4 squares (C) 2⅞" x 2⅞"
24 squares (D) 1½" x 1½"
4 Assorted Black Prints
from *each*
1 square (C) 2⅞" x 2⅞"
Red Solid and Gold Solid
from *each*
12 squares (D) 1½" x 1½"

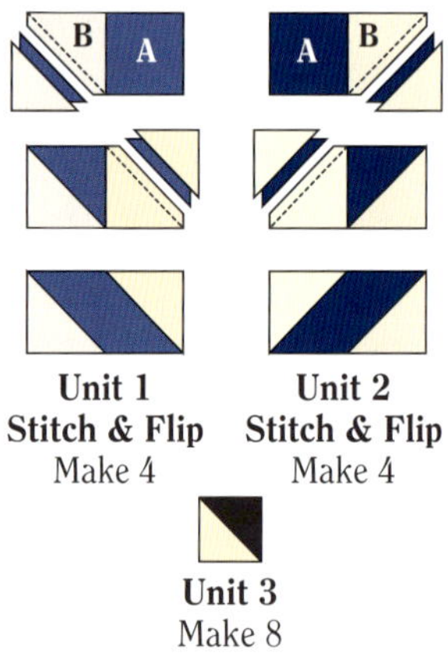

Refer to "Stitch-and-Flip" in the Techniques file on the PDF. Use the blue A's and cream B's to make 4 unit 1's and 4 unit 2's as shown.

Bonnie makes "bonus" units as she creates the units above: after sewing the first diagonal lines, sew a second seam ⅜" away. Cut between the seams. The bonus triangle-squares should be 2" x 2"; trim if necessary. If the triangle-squares are smaller than 2", you may need to adjust the seam allowance.

Make 8 Triangle-Square unit 3's with the black C's and cream C's.

Sew the patches and units together as shown to complete the block.

Block Assembly

block no. 702
Hometown Star

by Kimberly Jolly • Fat Quarter Shop
fatquartershop.com

Fabric: Kansas Troubles Favorites by Kansas Troubles for Moda Fabrics, unitednotions.com.

Red Print
1 square (A) 4¼" x 4¼"
12 squares (C) 2" x 2"
Tan Print #1
4 squares (B) 2⅜" x 2⅜"
8 rectangles (D) 2" x 3½
Navy Print and Green Print
from *each*
1 square (A) 4¼" x 4¼"
Tan Print #2
4 squares (B) 2⅜" x 2⅜"
8 squares (C) 2" x 2"
Tan Print #3
4 squares (B) 2⅜" x 2⅜"
1 square (E) 3½" x 3½"

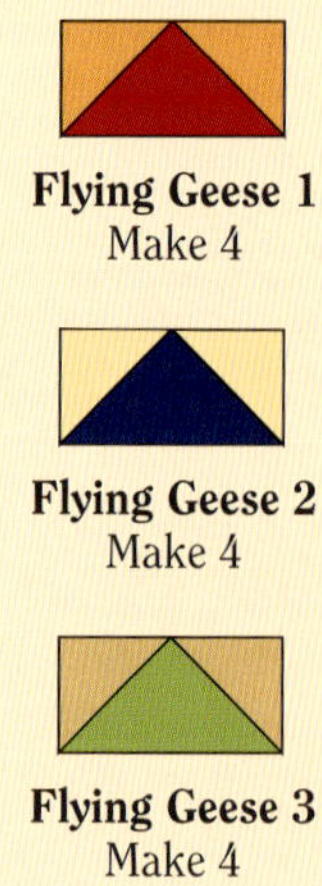

Use the red A and tan print #1 B's to make 4 Flying Geese 1. Use the navy A and tan print #2 B's to make 4 Flying Geese 2. Make 4 Flying Geese 3 with the green A and tan print #3 B's.

Sew the Flying Geese and patches together as shown to complete the block.

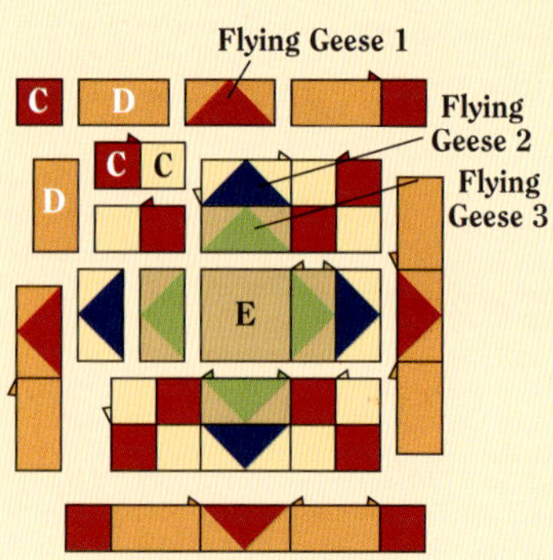

Block Assembly

block no. 703

B Squared

by Jessie Kurtz • Harding Hill Designs
hardinghilldesigns.com

Fabric: Celia designed by Jennifer Young for Benartex, benartex.com.

Red Print
- 4 squares (A) 2″ x 2″
- 1 square (F) 3″ x 3″
- 4 squares (G) 1¼″ x 1¼″

Blue Print
- 8 rectangles (B) 1¾″ x 2″
- 8 rectangles (C) 1¾″ x 4½″
- 4 rectangles (E) 1½″ x 3″

Cream Print
- 8 rectangles (D) 2″ x 3″
- 4 rectangles (H) 1¼″ x 11″

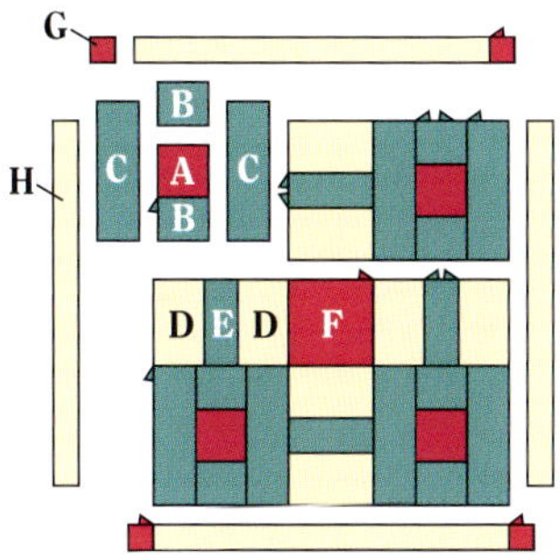

Block Piecing

Sew the patches together as shown to complete the block.

block no. 704

Ozark Cactus

by Judy Laquidara • Patchwork Times
patchworktimes.com

Judy Laquidara is the author of *Nine Patch Extravaganza* and *Weekend Quilts* for American Quilter's Society, americanquilter.com.

⊠ = cut in half twice diagonally

Gold Tone-on-Tone
- 4 squares (A) 2″ x 2″
- 4 rectangles (B) 2″ x 3½″
- 2 squares 4¼″ x 4¼″ ⊠ (C)
- 4 squares (F) 1½″ x 1½″

Red Print and **Green Tone-on-Tone** from *each*
- 2 squares (A) 2″ x 2″
- 1 square 4¼″ x 4¼″ ⊠ (C)
- 1 square 5½″ x 5½″ ⊠ (D) (there will be two extra)
- 2 rectangles (E) 1½″ x 4¾″

White Tone-on-Tone
- 2 rectangles (G) 1⅝″ x 6¾″
- 2 rectangles (H) 1⅝″ x 9″

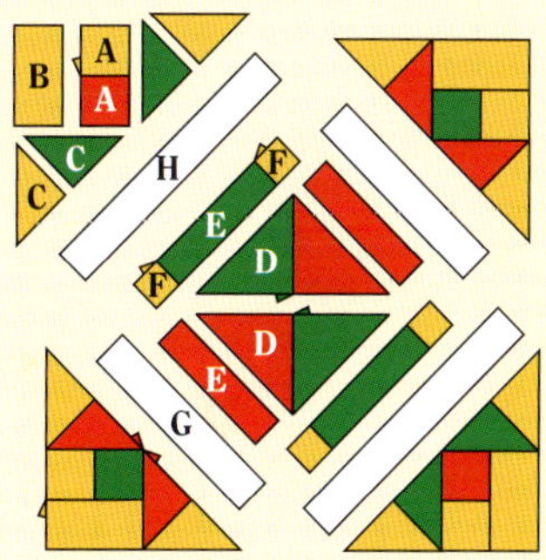

Block Piecing

Sew the patches together as shown to complete the block.

block no. 705

Point Me Home

by Doug Leko • Antler Quilt Design
antlerquiltdesign.com

Fabric: Northern Cardinal by Holly Taylor for Moda Fabrics, unitednotions.com.

⧄ = cut in half diagonally
⊠ = cut in half twice diagonally

Cream Print
- 4 rectangles (A) 2½″ x 4½″
- 1 square 3¼″ x 3¼″ ⊠ (C)
- 1 square 5¼″ x 5¼″ ⊠ (E)
- 4 rectangles (F) 2½″ x 6½″

Dark Brown Print
- 4 squares (B) 2½″ x 2½″
- 1 square 3¼″ x 3¼″ ⊠ (C)
- 1 square 5¼″ x 5¼″ ⊠ (E)

Light Brown Tone-on-Tone
- 6 squares 2⅞″ x 2⅞″ ⧄ (D)

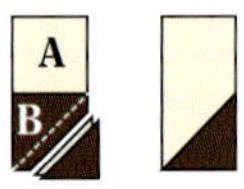

Unit
Stitch & Flip
Make 4

Refer to "Stitch-and-Flip" in the Techniques file on the PDF. Make 4 units using the cream A's and dark brown B's.

Sew the patches and units together as shown to complete the block.

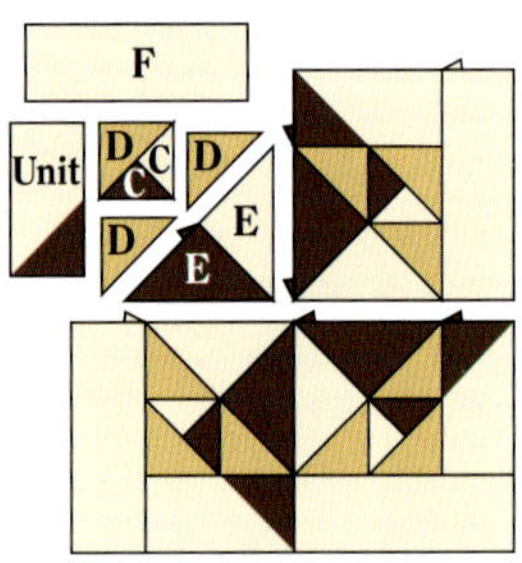

Block Assembly

block no. 706

Stained Glass Star

by Toby Lischko • Gateway Quilts & Stuff
gatewayquiltsnstuff.com

Fabric: Tonga Treats from Timeless Treasures, ttfabrics.com.

Toby Lischko is the author of *St. Louis Stars* for Kansas City Star Quilts, pickledish.com.

⧄ = cut in half diagonally

Cream Batik
- 4 squares 2⅞″ x 2⅞″ ⧄ (A)
- 4 squares 3⅞″ x 3⅞″ ⧄ (D)

Assorted Bright Batiks
- 8 squares 2⅞″ x 2⅞″ ⧄ (A) (there will be 8 extra for additional blocks)
- 8 rectangles (B) 1½″ x 2½″
- 8 rectangles (C) 1½″ x 3½″
- 8 squares 3⅞″ x 3⅞″ ⧄ (D) (there will be 8 extra for additional blocks)

Block Piecing

Sew the patches together as shown to complete the block.

pieced

block no. 707

Picture This!

by Sue Marsh • Whistlepig Creek Productions
wpcreek.com

Fabric: Pound Hounds designed by Sue Marsh for RJR Fabrics, rjrfabrics.com.

Unit 1
Stitch & Flip
Make 2

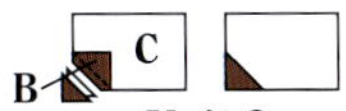

Unit 2
Stitch & Flip
Make 2

Dark Brown Print
- 2 rectangles (A) 1½″ x 2½″
- 2 squares (B) 1½″ x 1½″
- 2 rectangles (D) 1½″ x 11½″
- 2 rectangles (J) 1½″ x 6½″

Black Solid
- 4 squares (B) 1½″ x 1½″

Cream Print
- 2 rectangles (A) 1½″ x 2½″
- 4 squares (B) 1½″ x 1½″
- 2 rectangles (C) 2½″ x 3½″
- 2 squares (H) 2½″ x 2½″
- 4 rectangles (I) 2½″ x 6½″

Multiprint
- 1 square (E) 5½″ x 5½″

White Solid
- 2 rectangles (F) 1″ x 5½″
- 2 rectangles (G) 1″ x 6½″

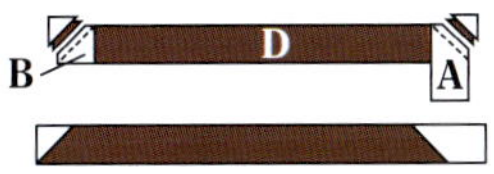

Unit 3
Stitch & Flip
Make 1

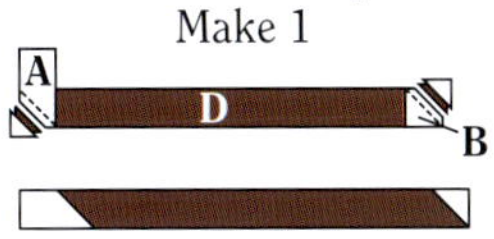

Unit 4
Stitch & Flip
Make 1

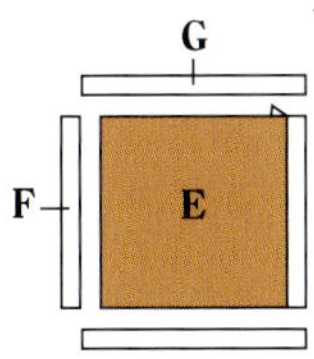

Unit Piecing

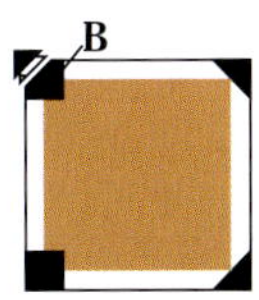

Unit 5
Stitch & Flip
Make 1

Sue fussy cut E from a large-scale novelty print.

Refer to "Stitch-and-Flip" in the Techniques file on the PDF. Make 2 unit 1's using the brown A's and cream print B's. Use the cream print C's and brown B's to make 2 unit 2's. Make units 3 and 4 using the brown D's with the cream print A's and B's as shown.

Sew the white F's and G's to the multiprint E. Use the stitch-an-flip method to add black B's as shown to complete unit 5.

Sew the patches and units together as shown to complete the block.

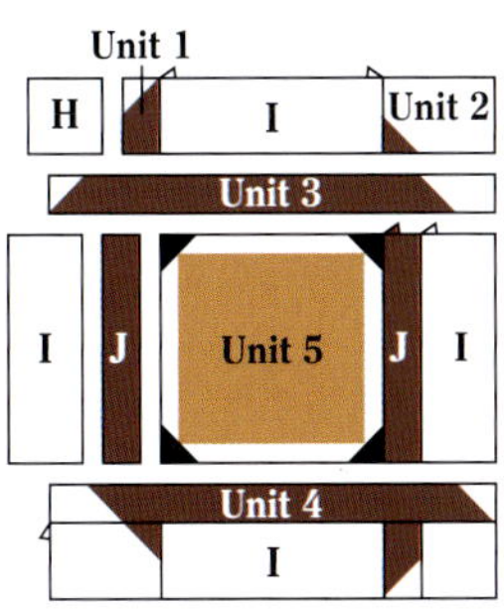

Block Assembly

block no. 708

Pinwheel Crossroads

by Christina McCourt • C McCourt Quilt Designs

Fabric: Cocheco Mills Collection for Marcus Fabrics, marcusbrothers.com.

⊠ = cut in half twice diagonally

Cream Print
- 16 squares (A) 1⅞″ x 1⅞″
- 2 squares 3¼″ x 3¼″ ⊠ (B)

Assorted Red Prints
- 8 squares (A) 1⅞″ x 1⅞″
- 4 squares 3¼″ x 3¼″ ⊠ (B) (you will have 12 extras for additional blocks)
- 4 squares 5⅛″ x 5⅛″ ⊠ (C) (you will have 12 extras for additional blocks)

Assorted Dark Green Prints
- 8 squares (A) 1⅞″ x 1⅞″
- 4 squares 3¼″ x 3¼″ ⊠ (B) (you will have 12 extras for additional blocks)
- 4 squares 5⅛″ x 5⅛″ ⊠ (C) (you will have 12 extras for additional blocks)

2 Black Prints
from *each*
- 1 square 5⅛″ x 5⅛″ ⊠ (C)

By cutting the B's and C's as instructed, the outside edges of the block are stabilized by the straight grain of the fabric patches.

Sew the patches together as shown to complete the block.

Block Piecing

block no. 709

Window Box

by Felicity Miller • Felicity
felicitymiller.com

Fabric: Gypsy designed by Felicity Miller for FreeSpirit, freespiritfabric.com.

Pink Multiprint
2 rectangles (A) 3½" x 12½"
Gray Print
2 rectangles (B) ⅞" x 12½"
Green Multiprint
2 rectangles (C) 3¾" x 5¾"
Pink Tone-on-Tone
1 rectangle (D) 5¾" x 6"

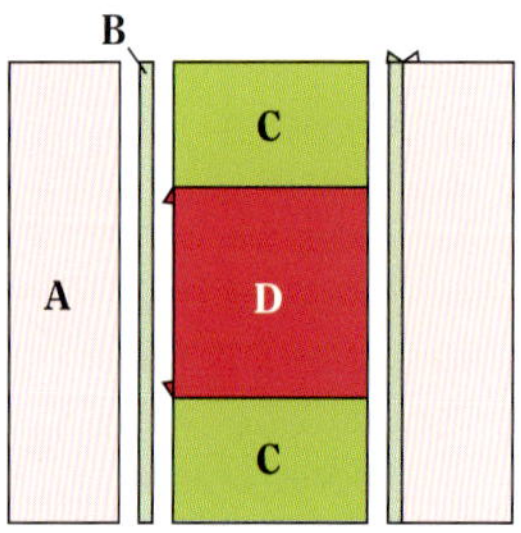

Block Piecing

Sew the patches together as shown to complete the block.

block no. 710

Times Nine

by Jo Morton • Jo Morton Quilts
jomortonquilts.com

Fabric: Various lines designed by Jo Morton for Andover Fabrics, andoverfabrics.com.

Jo Morton is the author of many self-published books including *Vintage Journey*, *Remembrances* and her newest title *Banner Day*.

Assorted Light Prints, Medium Prints and Dark Prints (see note below)
36 squares (A) 2⅜" x 2⅜"
72 rectangles (B) 1¼" x 1½"
9 squares (C) 1½" x 1½"

Unit
Make 9 sets of 4 matching

For each section, you'll need 2 A's from each of 2 different prints, 4 B's from each of 2 different prints and 1 C.

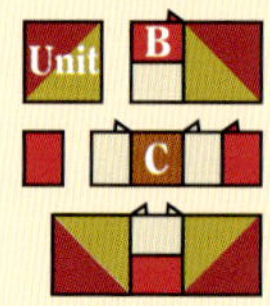

Section
Make 9

Refer to "Triangle-Squares" in the Techniques file on the PDF. Use 2 A's from each of 2 different prints to make 4 matching units. Make 9 sets of 4 matching units.

Join 4 matching units and patches as shown to make a section. Make 9 sections.

Sew the sections together as shown to complete the block.

Block Assembly

block no. 711

Miss Ruby

by Camille Roskelley • Thimble Blossoms
thimbleblossoms.com

Fabric: Ruby designed by Bonnie & Camille for Moda Fabrics, unitednotions.com.

Camille Roskelley is the author of *Simplify with Camille Roskelley* for C&T Publishing, ctpub.com.

Light Blue Print
5 squares (A) 4½″ x 4½″
Red Tone-on-Tone
4 squares (A) 4½″ x 4½″
4 squares (B) 2½″ x 2½″

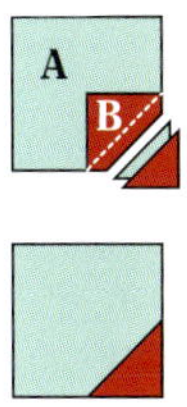

Unit
Make 4

Refer to "Stitch-and-Flip" in the Techniques file on the PDF. Make 4 units using the blue A's and red B's.

Sew the patches and units together as shown to complete the block.

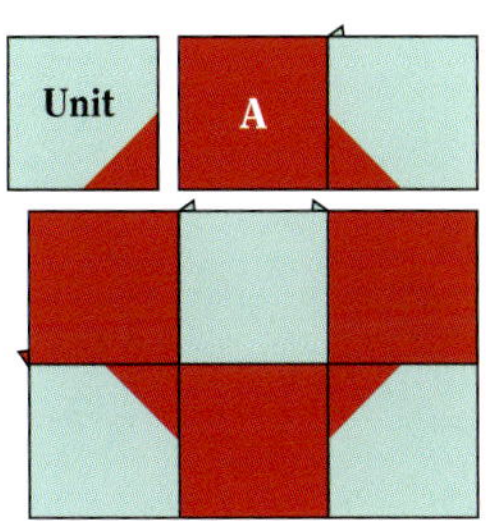

Block Assembly

block no. 712

Downstream

by Amy Rullkoetter • Freelance Editor, *Quiltmaker*
quiltmaker.com

Dark Blue Batik and Pale Green Batik
from *each*
4 squares (A) 2⅜″ x 2⅜″
Medium Blue Batik and Dark Green Batik
from *each*
4 squares (A) 2⅜″ x 2⅜″
2 squares (B) 3½″ x 3½″
1 square (C) 6½″ x 6½″

Unit 1
Make 4

Unit 2
Make 4

Unit 3
Make 4

Unit 4
Make 4

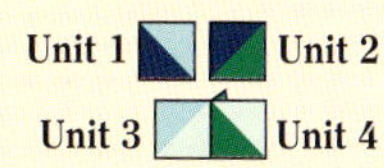

Pinwheel
Make 4

Refer to "Triangle-Squares" in the Techniques file on the PDF. Make 4 unit 1's using medium blue A's and dark blue A's. Use dark blue and dark green A's to make 4 unit 2's. Make 4 unit 3's with medium blue and pale green A's. Use pale green and dark green A's to make 4 unit 4's.

For each Pinwheel, join 1 each of units 1–4 as shown. Make 4 Pinwheels. Sew the Pinwheels and patches together as shown to complete the block.

Block Assembly

block no. 713

Blooming

by Kathy Schmitz • Kathy Schmitz LLC
kathyschmitz.com

Fabric: Towne Square Quilts designed by Kathy Schmitz for Moda Fabrics, unitednotions.com.

See page 134 on the PDF for pattern

⧄ = cut in half diagonally

Tan Print
- 1 square (A) 13⅞" x 13⅞" (trim to 12⅞" x 12⅞" after embroidery)
- 1 square 4⅞" x 4⅞" ⧄ (B) (there will be 1 extra triangle)
- 2 rectangles (C) 2½" x 10⅞" (trimmed as shown)

Blue Print
- 2 squares 4⅞" x 4⅞" ⧄ (B) (there will be 1 extra triangle)
- 1 square (D) 2½" x 2½"

Black embroidery floss

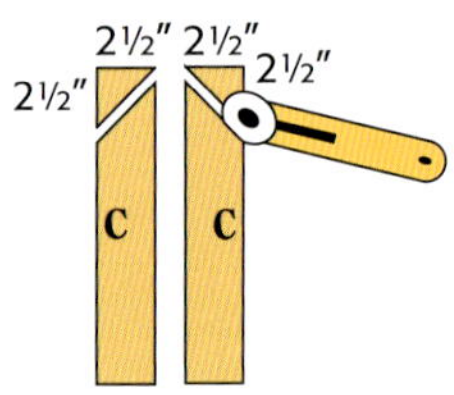

Fold A in half diagonally both ways and lightly crease the folds. Using the folds as a guide, trace the embroidery design onto A. Reverse the smaller flower to trace on the right side. Embroider the design using 3 strands of floss and a combination of stem, lazy daisy, French knots, running and blanket stitches.

Kathy used an "inverted" blanket stitch to add the small circles.

Center the design and trim A to 12⅞" × 12⅞"; cut in half diagonally as shown. Sew the patches together as shown. Use 3 strands of floss and a running stitch to add stitching approximately ⅛" inside the seam lines of the B's as shown in the photographed block.

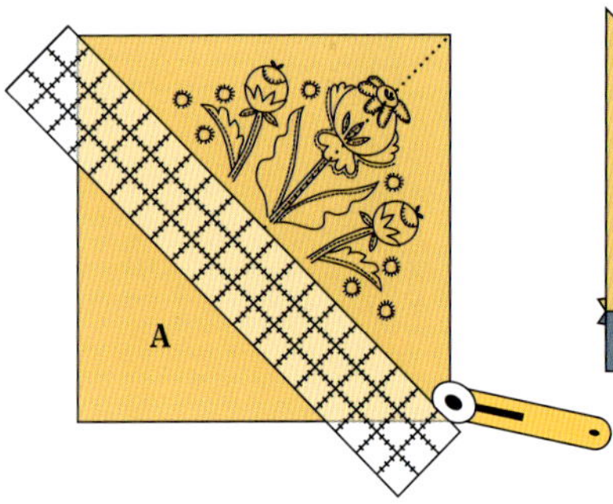

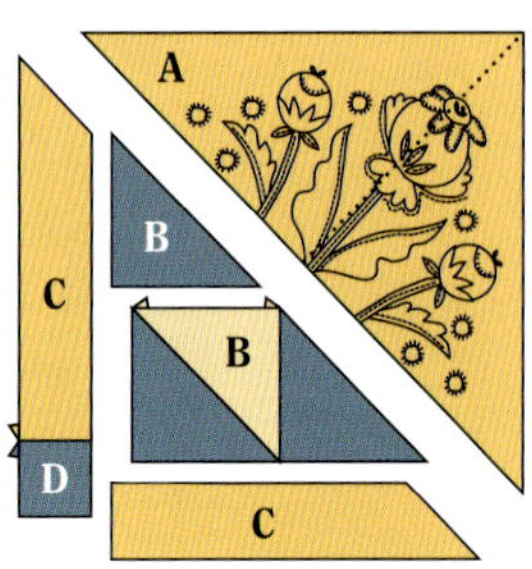

Block Piecing

block no. 714

X-Blox

by Charles Scott & Ryan Walsh • Patchwork Squared
patchworksquared.com

Fabric: Kona Solids by Robert Kaufman, robertkaufman.com.

⊠ = cut in half twice diagonally

Gold Solid
- 1 square 7¼" x 7¼" ⊠ (A)

Blue Solid
- 4 rectangles (B) 1½" x 6"
- 4 rectangles (C) 1½" x 7¼"

Black Solid
- 4 rectangles (D) 2¾" x 8¼"

White Solid
- 1 square (E) 2¾" x 2¾"

Sew the patches together as shown. Center the E patch and trim the block to 12½" × 12½".

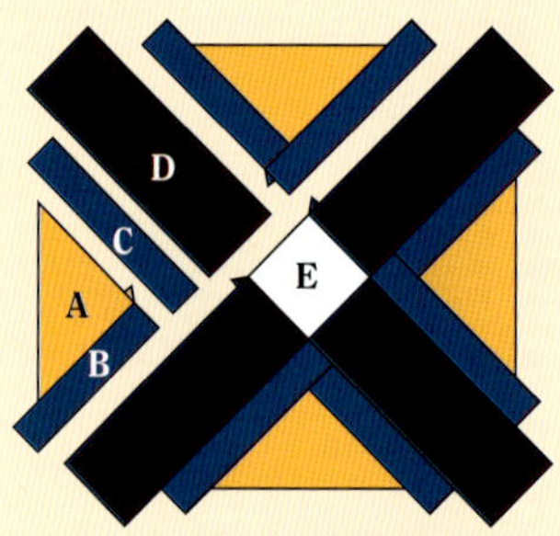

Block Piecing

block no. 715

Neapolitan

by Jacquelynne Steves • The Noble Wife
thenoblewife.com

Jacquelynne Steves is the author of *Fruitful Hands* for Kansas City Star Quilts, pickledish.com.

See page 159 on the PDF for pattern

Assorted Pink and Brown Prints and Tone-on-Tones
9–13 strips at 1¼" to 1¾"-wide and 22"-long for band (see instructions below)
Cream Tone-on-Tone
4 template B
Template plastic

Join the strips in a random order to make a band at least 9" wide.

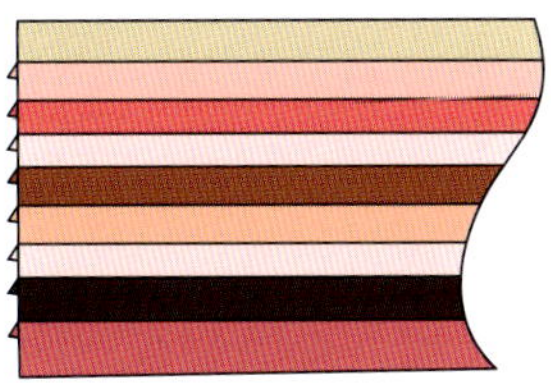

Band

Use the plastic to make a template of A. Position A on the band as shown and cut 4 units.

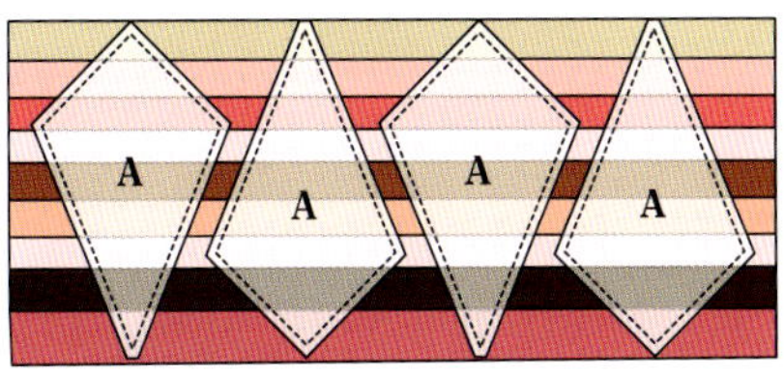

Unit Cut 4

Join the units and B's as shown to complete the block.

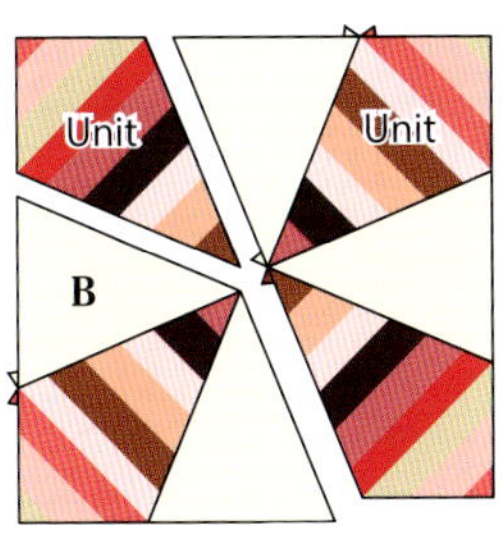

Block Assembly

block no. 716

Best Friends

by Paula Stoddard • Associate Editor, *Quiltmaker*
quiltmaker.com

Fabric: Sugar and Spice designed by The Quilted Fish for Riley Blake Designs, rileyblakedesigns.com.

Paula Stoddard is the author of several books, including *3 Color Crazy* for Pacific Patchwork, pacificpatchwork.com.

Green Print
2 squares (A) 3⅞" x 3⅞"
1 square (C) 3½" x 3½"
White Solid
2 squares (A) 3⅞" x 3⅞"
4 squares (B) 2⅜" x 2⅜"
2 squares (C) 3½" x 3½"
2 rectangles (D) 2" x 6½"
2 rectangles (E) 2" x 8"
8 squares (F) 2" x 2"
Turquoise Tone-on-Tone and Red Tone-on-Tone
from *each*
2 squares (B) 2⅜" x 2⅜"
1 square (F) 2" x 2"

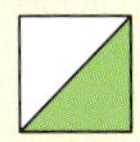

Unit 1 from A's
Make 4

Unit 2 from B's
Make 4

Unit 3 from B's
Make 4

Make 4 Triangle-Square unit 1's using the green print and white A's. Make 4 unit 2's with the turquoise and white B's. Use the red and white B's to make 4 unit 3's.

Sew the units and patches together as shown to complete the block.

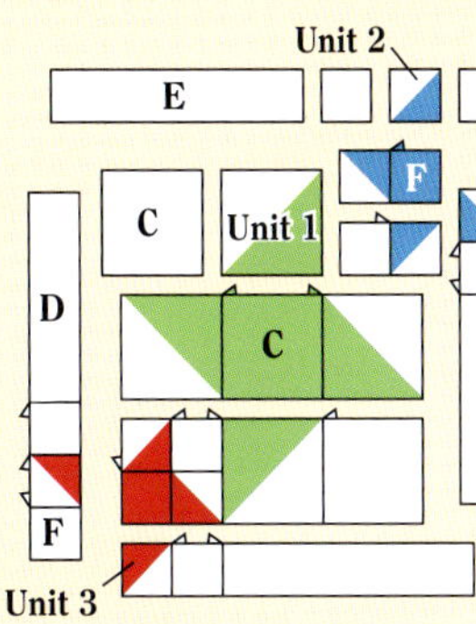

Block Assembly

block no. 717

Just Chillin'

by Margie Ullery • Ribbon Candy Quilt Company
ribboncandyquilts.blogspot.com

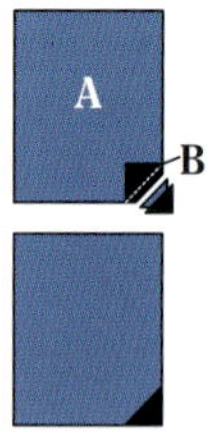

Unit 1
Stitch & Flip
Make 1

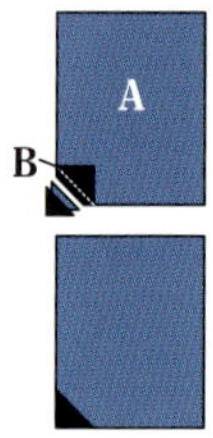

Unit 2
Stitch & Flip
Make 1

Blue Tone-on-Tone
2 rectangles (A) 4½" x 5½"
6 squares (B) 1½" x 1½"
1 rectangle (C) 1½" x 4½"
2 rectangles (E) 2½" x 7½"
2 rectangles (H) 1½" x 2½"
1 rectangle (I) 1¾" x 8½"
Black Print
8 squares (B) 1½" x 1½"
3 rectangles (C) 1½" x 4½"
2 squares (D) 1⅞" x 1⅞"
2 rectangles (G) 2½" x 5¼"
Gold Tone-on-Tone
2 squares (B) 1½" x 1½"
2 squares (D) 1⅞" x 1⅞"
Black Tone-on-Tone
2 rectangles (F) 1½" x 5¼"
White Tone-on-Tone
1 rectangle (G) 2½" x 5¼"
1 rectangle (H) 1½" x 2½"
Buttons 2 at ⅜"

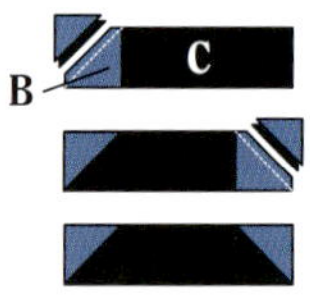

Unit 3
Stitch & Flip
Make 1

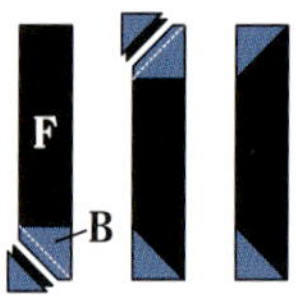

Unit 4
Stitch & Flip
Make 2

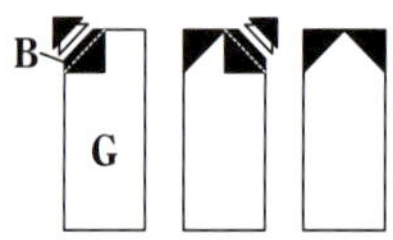

Unit 5
Stitch & Flip
Make 1

Refer to "Stitch-and-Flip" in the Techniques file on the PDF. Use the appropriate patches and colors to make units 1–8.

Make 4 Triangle-Square unit 9's using the gold and black print D's. Sew the units and patches together as shown. Attach 2 buttons for eyes to complete the block.

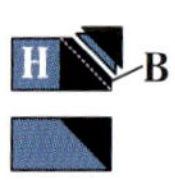

Unit 6
Stitch & Flip
Make 1

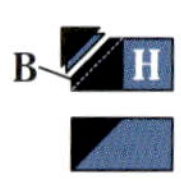

Unit 7
Stitch & Flip
Make 1

Unit 8
Stitch & Flip
Make 1

Unit 9 from D's
Make 4

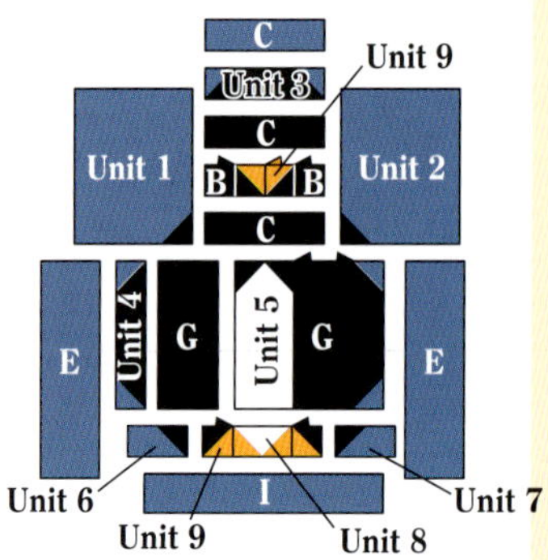

Block Assembly

block no. 718

Round Rosie

by Pam Vieira-McGinnis
pamkittymorning.blogspot.com

Fabric: Color Basic by Lecien, lecien.co.jp/en/hobby.

Cream Dot
8 squares (A) 2⅞" x 2⅞"
16 squares (B) 2½" x 2½"
4 Pink Prints
from *each*
1 square (A) 2⅞" x 2⅞"
1 square (B) 2½" x 2½"
4 Green Prints
from *each*
1 square (A) 2⅞" x 2⅞"

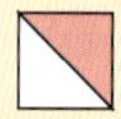

Unit 1
Make 8

Unit 2
Make 8

Pair the pink A's with cream A's to make 8 Triangle-Square unit 1's. Pair the green A's with cream A's to make 8 unit 2's.

Sew the patches and units together as shown to complete the block.

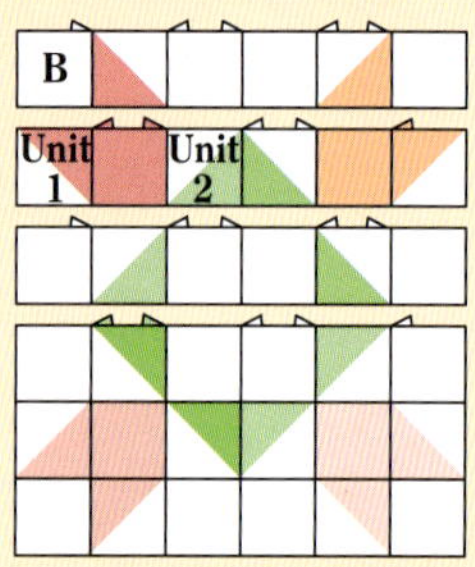

Block Assembly

block no. 719

Corner Paths

by Elisa Wilson • Elisa's Backporch Design
backporchdesign.com

Fabric: Tonga Batiks by Timeless Treasures, ttfabrics.com.

Elisa Wilson is the author of *Crazy Curves Continues* for Elisa's Backporch Design, backporchdesign.com.

See page 160 on the PDF for pattern

Cream Batik
- 4 pattern A
- 1 square (G) 1½" x 1½"

Dark Blue Batik
- 4 pattern B
- 4 rectangles (D) 1½" x 4½"
- 4 squares (E) 2" x 2"

Medium Blue Batik
- 8 rectangles (C) 2" x 4½"
- 4 rectangles (F) 1½" x 2"

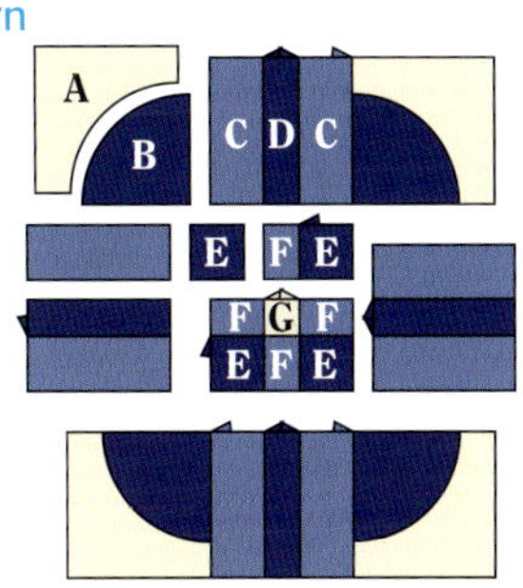

Block Piecing

Refer to "Curved Piecing" in the Techniques file on the PDF. Sew the patches together as shown to complete the block.

block no. 720

Square Intentions

by Karrie Winters
freckledwhimsy.com

Fabric: Pick a Bunch designed by Nancy Mims for Robert Kaufman, robertkaufman.com.

⧄ = cut in half diagonally

White Solid
- 2 squares 2⅞" x 2⅞" ⧄ (A)
- 4 squares (C) 2⅞" x 2⅞"
- 4 rectangles (E) 2½" x 4½"

4 Assorted Prints

from *each*
- 1 square 2⅞" x 2⅞" ⧄ (A) (there will be 4 extra for additional blocks)

Green Print
- 1 square (B) 5¼" x 5¼"
- 1 square (F) 4½" x 4½"

Dark Pink Print
- 4 squares (D) 2½" x 2½"
- 4 rectangles (E) 2½" x 4½"

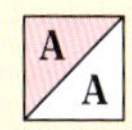

Unit
Make 4

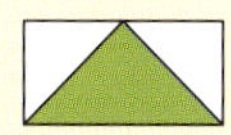

Flying Geese
Make 4

Make 4 units using the white A's and assorted print A's.

Use the green B and white C's to make 4 Flying Geese.

Sew the units, Flying Geese and patches together as shown to complete the block.

Block Assembly

block no. 721
Road Block

by Judi Madsen • Green Fairy Quilts
greenfairyquilts.com

Fabric: Reunion designed by Sweetwater for Moda Fabrics, unitednotions.com.

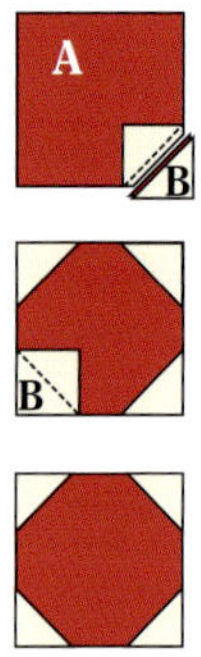

Unit 1
Stitch & Flip
Make 4

4 Red Prints
from each
1 square (A) 3½" x 3½"
from 1
2 squares (E) 2½" x 2½"
White Solid
64 squares (B) 1½" x 1½"
2 squares (D) 3⅞" x 3⅞"
4 Green Prints
from each
1 rectangle (C) 2½" x 3½"
4 Dark Blue Prints
from each
1 rectangle (C) 2½" x 3½"
from 1
2 squares (D) 3⅞" x 3⅞"
4 Gold Prints
from each
1 rectangle (C) 2½" x 3½"
from 1
2 squares (E) 2½" x 2½"

Unit 2
Stitch & Flip
Make 12

Unit 3
Stitch & Flip
Make 2

Unit 4
Stitch & Flip
Make 2

Refer to "Stitch-and-Flip" in Techniques file on the PDF. Use the red A's and white B's to make 4 unit 1's. Use the blue, green and gold C's and the white B's to make 12 unit 2's as shown.

Pair the white D's and blue D's to make 4 Triangle-Squares; use stitch-and-flip to add a gold or red E to the blue corners as shown to make 2 unit 3's and 2 unit 4's.

Sew the units and patches together as shown to complete the block.

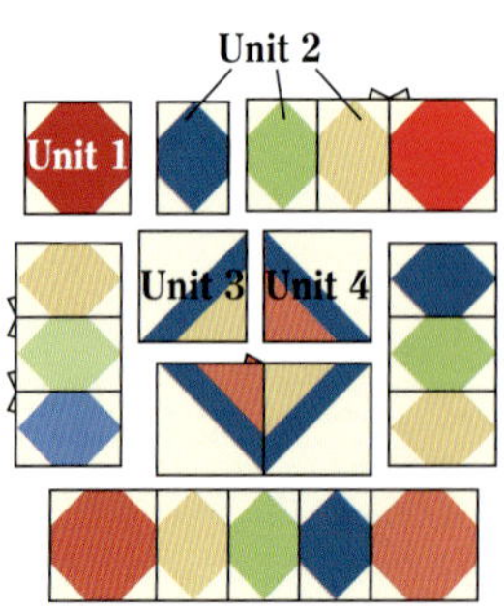

Block Assembly

block no. 722
Linked In

by Marian Mapes

Fabric: Bali Batiks and Handpaints from Hoffman California Fabrics, hoffmanfabrics.com.

◸ = cut in half diagonally
⊠ = cut in half twice diagonally

Lime Green Batik
5 squares 3⅞" x 3⅞" ◸ (A) (there will be 1 extra)
1 square 4¼" x 4¼" ⊠ (B) (there will be 2 extra)
Light Green Batik
4 squares 3⅞" x 3⅞" ◸ (A)
Blue Batik
5 squares 3⅞" x 3⅞" ◸ (A) (there will be 1 extra)
1 square 4¼" x 4¼" ⊠ (B) (there will be 2 extra)
Turquoise Batik
2 squares 3⅞" x 3⅞" ◸ (A)

Sew the patches together as shown to complete the block.

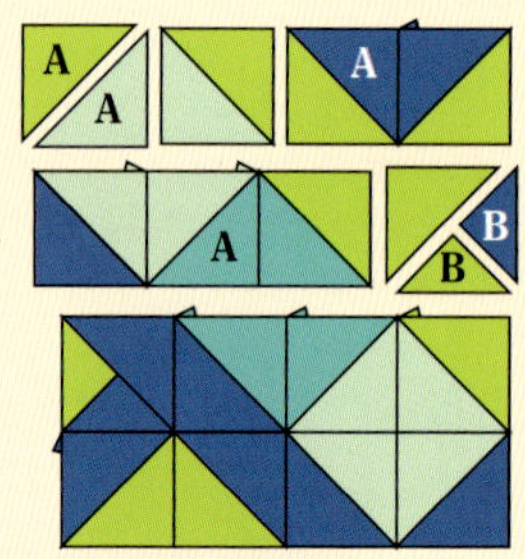

Block Piecing

block no. 723

Mia Bella

by Judy Martin • Judy Martin Books
judymartin.com

Judy Martin is the author of more than 20 books, including *Patchwork Among Friends* for Judy Martin Books, judymartin.com.

⧄ = cut in half diagonally
⊠ = cut in half twice diagonally

Multicolor Plaid
4 squares (A) 3½″ x 3½″
2 squares 4¼″ x 4¼″ ⊠ (B)

Dark Pink Tone-on-Tone
1 square (A) 3½″ x 3½″
2 squares 3⅞″ x 3⅞″ ⧄ (F)

Dark Purple Tone-on-Tone
2 squares 4¼″ x 4¼″ ⊠ (B)
4 squares 2⅜″ x 2⅜″ ⧄ (E)

Medium Pink Tone-on-Tone
4 rectangles (C) 2″ x 3½″

Medium Purple Tone-on-Tone
4 squares (D) 2⅝″ x 2⅝″

Sew the patches together as shown to complete the block.

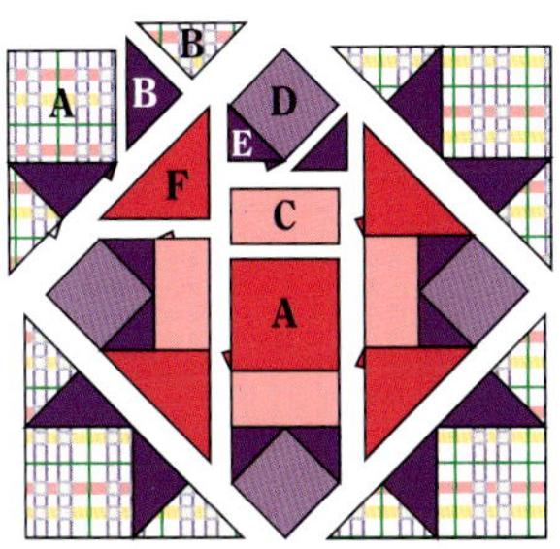

Block Piecing

block no. 724

Summer Garden Dream

by Sherri McConnell
aquiltinglife.com

Fabric: Terrain designed by Kate Spain for Moda Fabrics, unitednotions.com.

White Solid
2 squares (A) 3¼″ x 3¼″
2 squares (C) 2⅞″ x 2⅞″
1 square (D) 2½″ x 2½″
2 rectangles (F) 1½″ x 8½″
2 rectangles (G) 1½″ x 10½″

Light Blue Tone-on-Tone
8 squares (B) 1⅞″ x 1⅞″
2 squares (C) 2⅞″ x 2⅞″

Green Multiprint
2 rectangles (E) 1½″ x 6½″
2 rectangles (F) 1½″ x 8½″

Green Tone-on-Tone
2 rectangles (G) 1½″ x 10½″
2 rectangles (H) 1½″ x 12½″

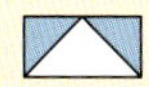

Flying Geese
Make 8

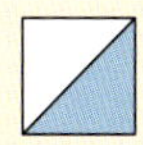

Unit
Make 4

Use the white A's and light blue B's to make 8 Flying Geese. Pair the white and light blue C's to make 4 Triangle-Square units.

Sew the Flying Geese, units and patches together as shown to complete the block.

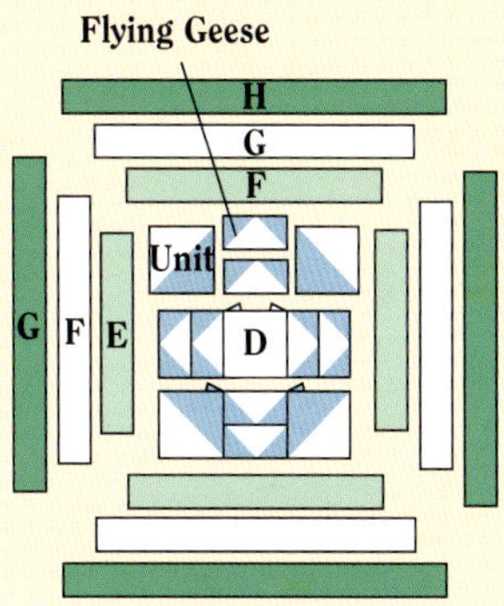

Block Assembly

block no. 725
Spice it Up!

by Pam McMahon • Pam's Piece by Piece
piecebypiecequiltdesigns.com

Fabric: various collections designed by Jo Morton for Andover Fabrics, andoverfabrics.com.

⧄ = cut in half diagonally
⊠ = cut in half twice diagonally

Red Print #1
2 squares (A) 2⅞″ x 2⅞″

Cream Print
8 squares (A) 2⅞″ x 2⅞″

Black Print
4 squares (A) 2⅞″ x 2⅞″
1 square (D) 4½″ x 4½″

Gold Print
2 squares (A) 2⅞″ x 2⅞″
1 square 5¼″ x 5¼″ ⊠ (B)

Red Print #2
1 square 5¼″ x 5¼″ ⊠ (B)

Dark Brown Stripe
2 squares 4⅞″ x 4⅞″ ⧄ (C) (see note below)

Unit 1
Make 4

Unit 2
Make 8

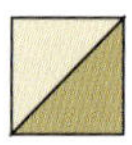

Unit 3
Make 4

In order to have the stripe in the dark brown C's facing the same direction, cut the 2 squares in opposite directions.

Pair 2 cream A's with the red #1 A's to make 4 Triangle-Square unit 1's. Make 8 unit 2's using 4 cream A's and the black A's. Use 2 cream A's and the gold A's to make 4 unit 3's.

Sew the units and patches together as shown to complete the block.

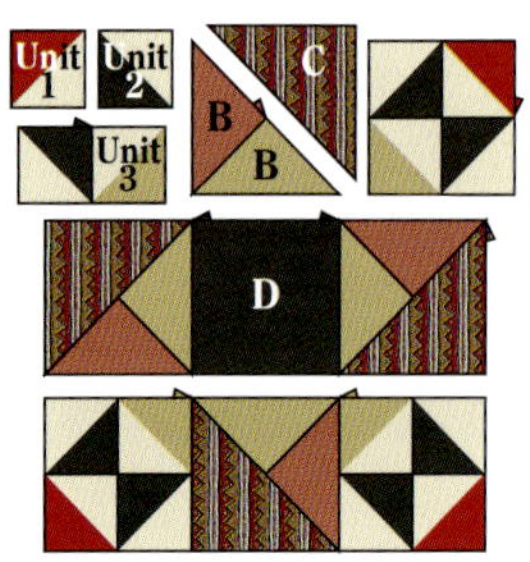

Block Assembly

block no. 726
All Framed Up

by Nancy McNally
nancysonestitchatatime.blogspot.com

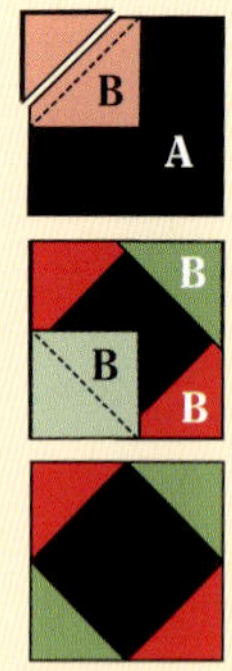

Unit 1
Stitch & Flip
Make 1

See page 186 on the PDF for pattern

Black Print
1 square (A) 3¼″ x 3¼″
4 squares (C) 2¾″ x 2¾″
4 rectangles (D) 2¾″ x 7¼″

Red Tone-on-Tone and Green Print
from *each*
2 squares (B) 1⅞″ x 1⅞″
2 *each* templates F and Fr

Medium Orange Print #1
2 squares (C) 2¾″ x 2¾″

Light Orange Solid
4 squares (B) 1⅞″ x 1⅞″
4 template E
4 rectangles (G) 1⅞″ x 3¼″

Pink Tone-on-Tone and Medium Orange Print #2
from *each*
2 squares (B) 1⅞″ x 1⅞″

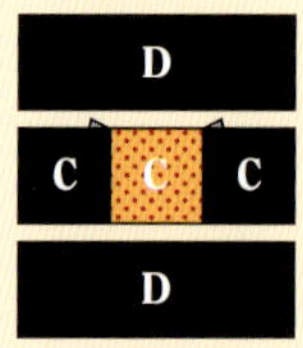

Unit 2
Make 2

Trimming Diagram

Refer to "Stitch-and-Flip" in the Techniques file on the PDF. Use the black A with the red B's and green B's to make unit 1.

Use the black C's and D's and the orange print #1 C's to make 2 unit 2's. Refer to the trimming diagram and cut each unit in half as shown.

Sew the units and patches together as shown. Center the design and trim to 12½″× 12½″.

Block Assembly

block no. 727

Star Light, Star Bright

by Scott Murkin • Patchwork Possibilities
patchworkpossibilities.com

See page 182 on the PDF for pattern

Dark Red Print
- 1 strip 2½" x 38" for band
- 2 template A

Orange Print
- 2 template A
- 4 template B

Gold Tone-on-Tone
- 1 strip 2½" x 38" for band

Dark Green Print
- 2 rectangles 3¾" x 6½" (see note in blue below)
- 2 rectangles (D) 1½" x 13"

Template plastic

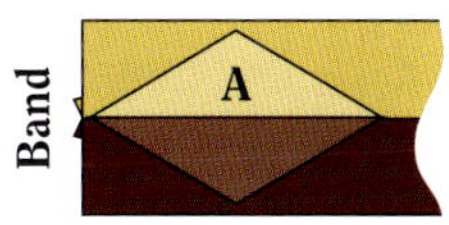

Unit
Cut 6

Cutting

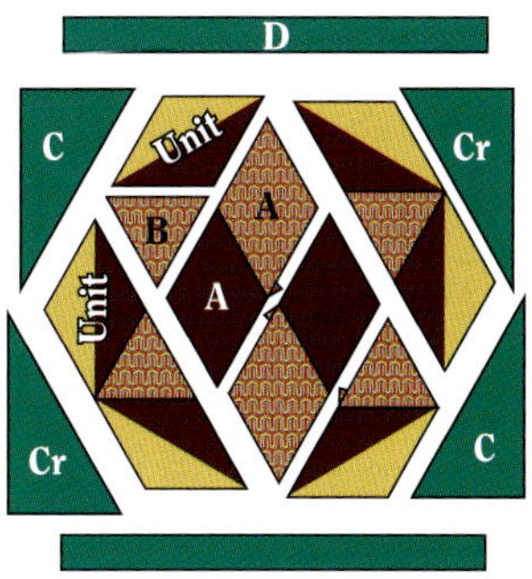

Block Assembly

Layer the dark green 3¾" x 6½" rectangles with wrong sides together before cutting in half diagonally to make 2 C's and 2 Cr's.

Sew the strips together to make the band. Use the plastic to make a template of A. Position A on the band as shown and cut 6 units.

Join the units and patches as shown. Center the block and trim to 12½" x 12½".

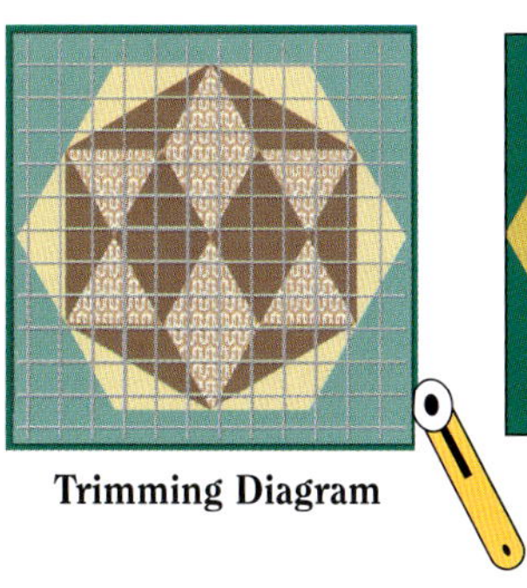

Trimming Diagram

block no. 728

All Buttoned Up!

by Amanda Murphy • Amanda Murphy Design
amandamurphydesign.com

Fabric: Veranda designed by Amanda Murphy for Robert Kaufman, robertkaufman.com.

Light Green Dot, Light Green Print and Dark Pink Print from *each*
- 6 squares (A) 2⅞" x 2⅞"

Orange Print
- 6 squares (A) 2⅞" x 2⅞"
- 2 rectangles (B) 1½" x 12½"

Light Pink Tone-on-Tone
- 1 rectangle (C) 2½" x 12½"

Dark Pink Solid
- 5 circles 2¾" diameter for yo-yos

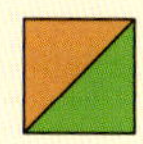

Unit 1
Make 12

Unit 2
Make 12

Pair the orange A's with the light green dot A's to make 12 Triangle-Square unit 1's. Pair the light green print A's and dark pink print A's to make 12 unit 2's. Sew the units and patches together as shown.

Make yo-yos from the dark pink circles. Arrange the yo-yos on the C as shown and tack in place to complete the block.

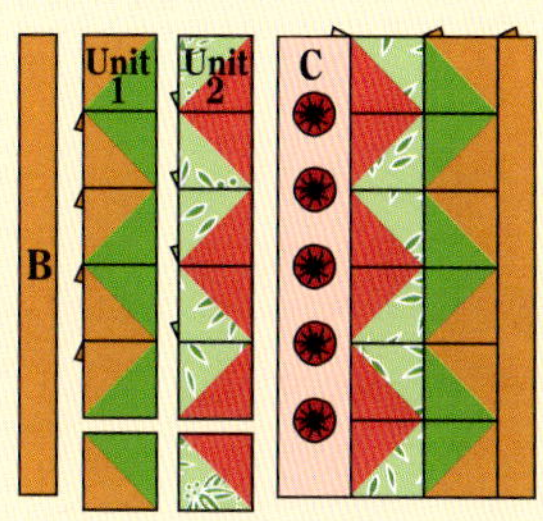

Block Assembly

block no. 729

Desert Dash

by Janelle Noack • Country Matters

Fabric: Crossroads to Texas designed by Betsy Chutchian for Blue Hill Fabrics, bluehillfabric.net.

Cream Tone-on-Tone #1
- 2 squares (A) 2⅞" x 2⅞"
- 16 squares (B) 1½" x 1½"
- 4 rectangles (D) 1½" x 2½"

Brown Print
- 2 squares (A) 2⅞" x 2⅞"
- 8 squares (B) 1½" x 1½"
- 4 rectangles (D) 1½" x 2½"

Cream Tone-on-Tone #2
- 8 squares (B) 1½" x 1½"
- 4 rectangles (C) 1½" x 6½"

Cream Tone-on-Tone #3
- 4 rectangles (C) 1½" x 6½"
- 1 square (E) 2½" x 2½"

Orange Print
- 4 squares (B) 1½" x 1½"
- 4 rectangles (C) 1½" x 6½"

Unit from A's
Make 4

Pair the cream #1 A's with the brown A's to make 4 Triangle-Square units.

Sew the units and patches together as shown to complete the block.

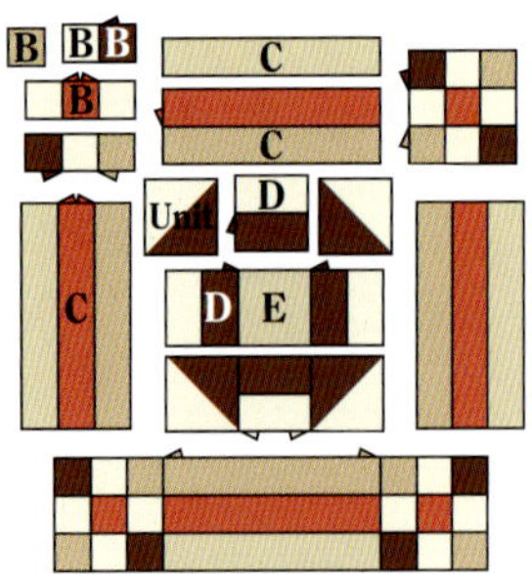

Block Assembly

block no. 730

String Twist

by Lorraine Olsen • Lorraine Olsen Quilts
lorraineolsenquilts.com

Lorraine Olsen is the author of *Lone Star Quilts* for C&T Publishing, ctpub.com.

Section
Make 4

Assorted Prints
- strips 1"–2" wide and 4½" long

Pink Solid and Red Solid
from *each*
- 4 rectangles (A) 1¾" x 6½"

Foundation paper
- 4 rectangles 4" x 6½"

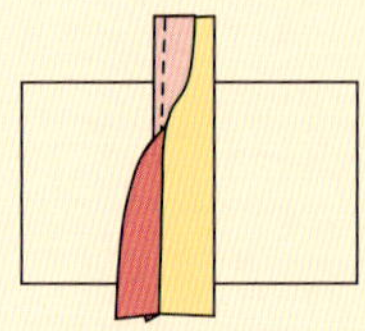

Section Piecing

Position a strip, right side up, across the center of the foundation rectangle as shown. Aligning raw edges, lay a strip right side down on the center strip as shown. Join the strips by sewing through all the layers ¼" from the raw edges. Flip the top strip open and press. Continue adding strips from the center outward in both directions until the entire foundation has been covered. Trim the fabric even with the paper. Repeat to make 4 sections.

If your machine's feed dogs have trouble feeding the paper, an alternative is a muslin foundation.

Sew a pink A and red A to each section as shown. Sew the sections together as shown to complete the block. Carefully remove the foundation papers.

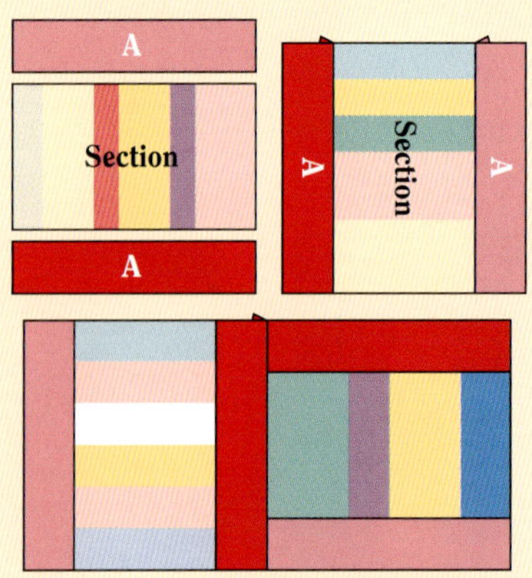

Block Assembly

pieced

block no. 731
Home Again

by Celine Perkins • Perkins Dry Goods
perkinsdrygoods.com

Fabric: Northern Cardinals designed by Holly Taylor for Moda Fabrics, unitednotions.com.

◪ = cut in half diagonally

Dark Red Print
- 1 square (A) 5¼″ x 5¼″
- 4 squares (C) 2½″ x 2½″
- 1 square (I) 1½″ x 1½″

Beige Print
- 4 squares (B) 2⅞″ x 2⅞″
- 4 squares 2⅞″ x 2⅞″ ◪ (D)
- 4 rectangles (F) 2½″ x 4½″
- 4 rectangles (H) 1½″ x 2″

Dark Green Print
- 2 squares 4⅞″ x 4⅞″ ◪ (E)
- 4 squares (G) 2″ x 2″

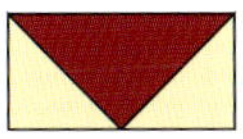

Flying Geese
Make 4

Use the red A and beige B's to make 4 Flying Geese.

Sew the Flying Geese and patches together as shown to complete the block.

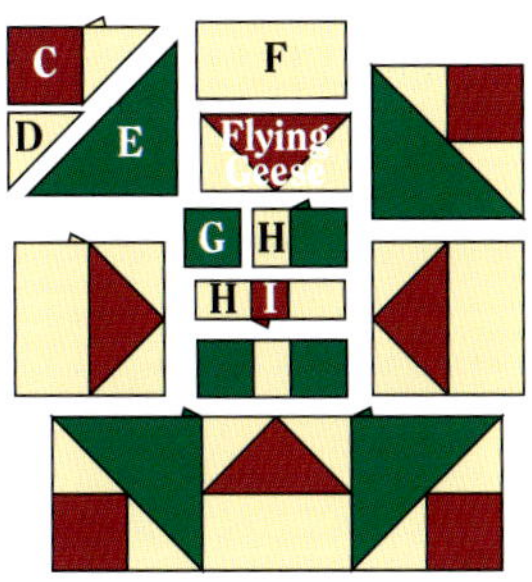

Block Assembly

block no. 732
Mermaid Blossoms

by Angela Pingel • Cut to Pieces
cuttopieces.blogspot.com

See page 199 on the PDF for pattern

Orange Tone-on-Tone and Gray Print
from *each*
- 2 strips 1⅞″ x 25″ for band

Cream Print
- 2 strips 2⅞″ x 25″ for band

Template plastic

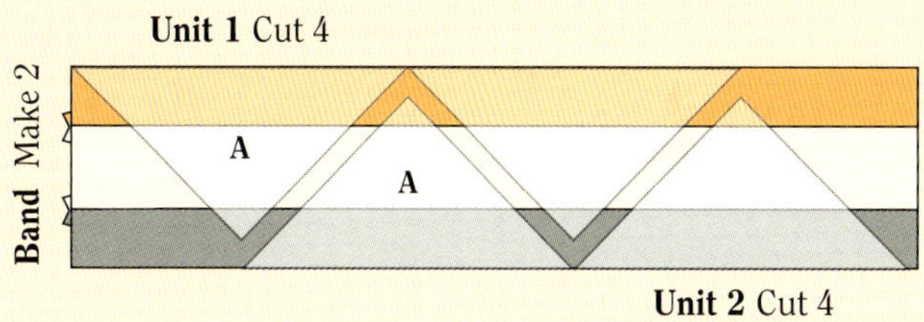

Sew the strips together as shown to make 2 bands. Use the plastic to make a template of A. Position A on the bands as shown and cut 4 unit 1's and 4 unit 2's.

Join the units as shown to complete the block.

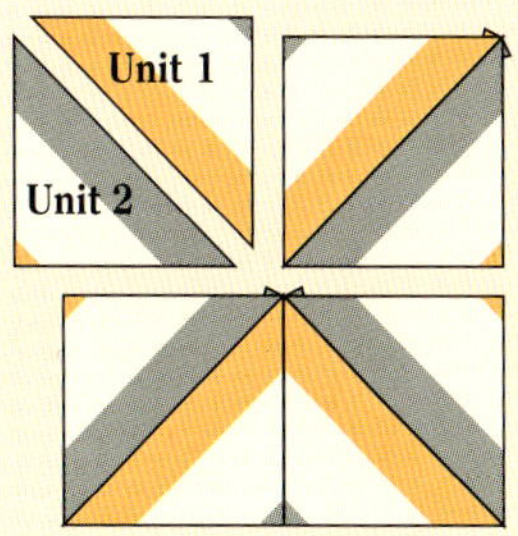

Block Assembly

block no. 733

Five of Diamonds

by Jina Barney • Jina Barney Designz
jinabarneydesignz.com

Fabric: Riley Blake Designs Solids by Riley Blake Designs, rileyblakedesigns.com.

◻ = cut in half diagonally

Cream Solid
- 4 squares (A) 1½" x 1½"
- 2 squares 3" x 3" ◻ (B)
- 2 rectangles (D) 1⅜" x 6¾"
- 2 rectangles (E) 1⅜" x 8½"
- 2 rectangles (G) 1⅝" x 10¼"
- 2 rectangles (H) 1⅝" x 12½"

Pink Solid
- 9 squares (A) 1½" x 1½"
- 4 rectangles (E) 1⅜" x 8½"

Medium Brown Solid
- 4 rectangles (C) 1½" x 4¾"
- 4 squares (F) 1⅜" x 1⅜"

Sew the patches together as shown to complete the block.

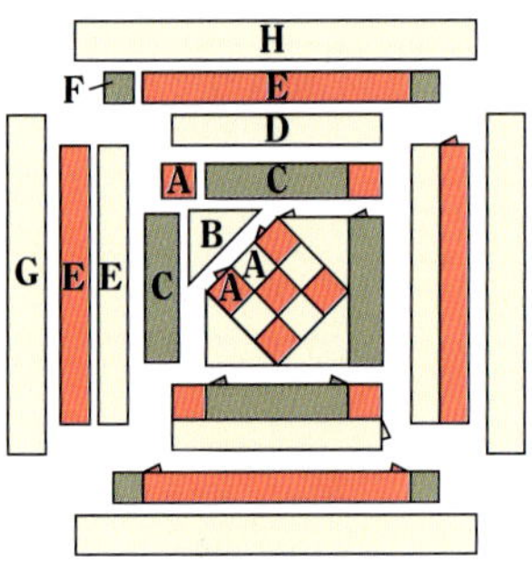

Block Piecing

block no. 734

Star Glow

by Carolyn Beam • Creative Editor, *Quiltmaker*
quiltmaker.com

Fabric: Midnight Blue designed by Karen Combs for Troy, Troy-corp.com.

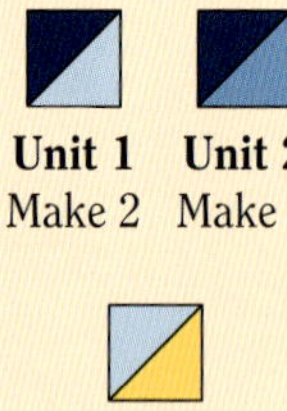

Unit 1 Make 2 **Unit 2** Make 2

Unit 3 Make 2

◻ = cut in half diagonally
⊠ = cut in half twice diagonally

Dark Blue Tone-on-Tone
- 2 squares (A) 1⅞" x 1⅞"
- 1 square (C) 2½" x 2½"
- 2 squares 1⅞" x 1⅞" ◻ (J)

Light Blue Tone-on-Tone
- 2 squares (A) 1⅞" x 1⅞"
- 1 square (B) 2⅞" x 2⅞"
- 2 squares (C) 2½" x 2½"
- 3 squares (D) 1½" x 1½"
- 2 rectangles (G) 3½" x 6½"
- 3 squares (H) 3½" x 3½"
- 1 square 2¼" x 2¼" ⊠ (I) (there will be 2 extra)

Medium Blue Tone-on-Tone
- 1 square (A) 1⅞" x 1⅞"
- 5 squares (C) 2½" x 2½"
- 1 square (D) 1½" x 1½"
- 1 rectangle (E) 2½" x 4½"
- 1 square 2¼" x 2¼" ⊠ (I)
- 1 square 2⅞" x 2⅞"" ◻ (K)

Yellow Tone-on-Tone
- 2 squares (A) 1⅞" x 1⅞"
- 2 squares (D) 1½" x 1½"
- 2 rectangles (E) 2½" x 4½"
- 2 rectangles (F) 1½" x 6½"
- 5 squares (H) 3½" x 3½"
- 1 square 2¼" x 2¼" ⊠ (I) (there will be 2 extra)

Pair a dark blue A and a light blue A to make 2 Triangle-Square unit 1's. Pair a dark blue A and the medium blue A to make 2 unit 2's. Pair one light blue A and one yellow A to make 2 unit 3's.

Refer to "Stitch-and-Flip" in the Techniques file on the PDF. Sew a light blue B and yellow A as shown; cut in half diagonally to make 2 unit 4's. Use the appropriate patches and colors to make units 5–9 as shown.

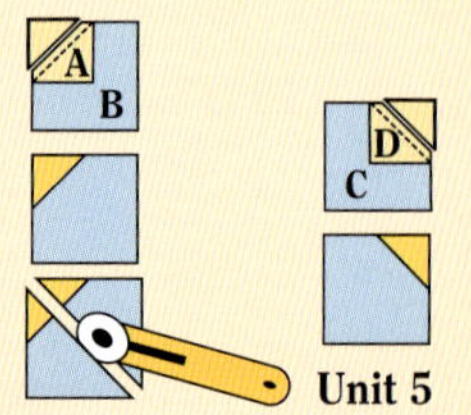

Unit 4 Stitch & Flip Make 2 **Unit 5** Stitch & Flip Make 2

Join units and patches as shown to complete the block.

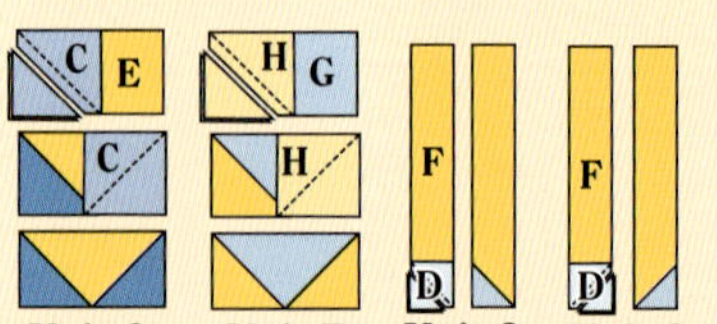

Unit 6 Stitch & Flip Make 2 **Unit 7** Stitch & Flip Make 2 **Unit 8** Stitch & Flip Make 1 **Unit 9** Stitch & Flip Make 1

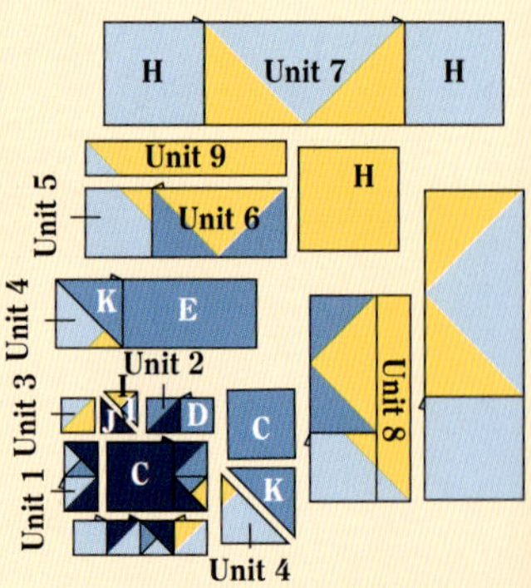

Block Assembly

block no. 735

Country Pride

by Donna Benham • DB Designs

Dark Blue Print #1
- 2 squares (A) 4¼″ x 4¼″

White Print
- 2 squares (A) 4¼″ x 4¼″
- 8 squares (B) 1⅞″ x 1⅞″
- 4 squares (C) 1½″ x 1½″

Dark Blue Print #2
- 8 squares (B) 1⅞″ x 1⅞″
- 16 squares (C) 1½″ x 1½″

Multiprint
- 4 squares (D) 3½″ x 3½″

Red Print
- 1 square (D) 3½″ x 3½″
- 6 rectangles (E) 1½″ x 3½″

Multicolor Stripe
- 3 rectangles (E) 1½″ x 3½″

Unit 1
Make 4

Unit 2
Make 16 from B's

Refer to "Quarter-Square Triangles" in the Techniques file on the PDF. Pair the dark blue A's and white A's to make 4 unit 1's.

Make 16 Triangle-Square unit 2's using the dark blue B's and white B's.

Sew the units and patches together as shown to complete the block.

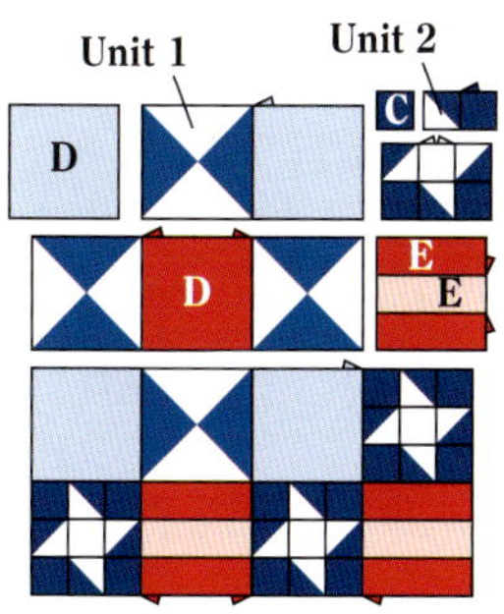

Block Assembly

block no. 736

Old Town Star

by Katie Blakesley • Swim, Bike, Quilt
swimbikequilt.com

Black Solid
- 4 squares (A) 2⅞″ x 2⅞″
- 4 squares (B) 2½″ x 2½″
- 4 rectangles (C) 2½″ x 4½″

Cream Print
- 4 squares (A) 2⅞″ x 2⅞″
- 4 squares (B) 2½″ x 2½″
- 1 square (D) 4½″ x 4½″

Teal Print
- 4 rectangles (C) 2½″ x 4½″

Unit
Make 8

Pair the black A's with the cream A's to make 8 Triangle-Square units.

Sew the units and patches together as shown to complete the block.

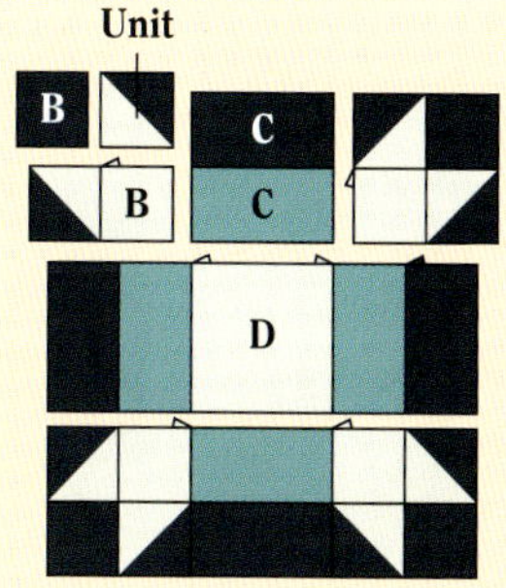

Block Assembly

block no. 737

Virginia Crossroads

by Laura Blanchard • Plum Tree Quilts
plumtreequilts.com

Fabric: Tokyo designed by Red Rooster Studio for Red Rooster Fabrics, redroosterfabrics.com.

⊠ = cut in half twice diagonally

Light Brown Tone-on-Tone
5 squares (A) 1⅞" x 1⅞"

Tan Tone-on-Tone
8 squares (A) 1⅞" x 1⅞"

Green Tone-on-Tone
12 squares (A) 1⅞" x 1⅞"

Light Green Tone-on-Tone
16 squares (A) 1⅞" x 1⅞"

Dark Purple Tone-on-Tone
5 squares 4¼" x 4¼" ⊠ (B)

Cream Tone-on-Tone
4 rectangles (C) 1⅞" x 8¾"

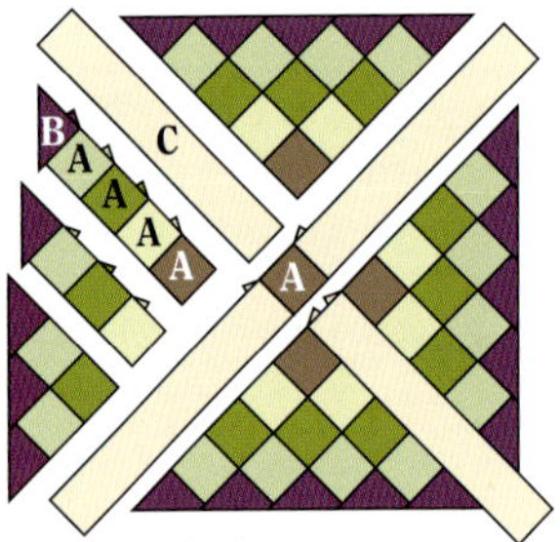

Block Piecing

Sew the patches together as shown. Center and trim the block to 12½" × 12½".

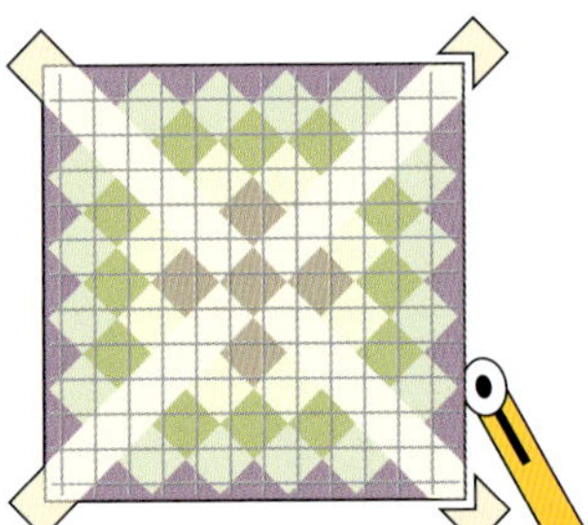

Trimming Diagram

block no. 738

Heartwarming

by Pam Buda • Heartspun Quilts
heartspunquilts.com

Fabric: Warm Memories designed by Lynne Hagmeier for Moda Fabrics, unitednotions.com.

◪ = cut in half diagonally
⊠ = cut in half twice diagonally

Tan Print
8 rectangles (A) 2" x 3½"
7 squares (C) 2⅜" x 2⅜"
2 squares 3⅞" x 3⅞" ◪ (F)
1 square 4¼" x 4¼" ⊠ (G)

Dark Red Print
12 squares (B) 2" x 2"
3 squares (C) 2⅜" x 2⅜"
2 squares 3⅞" x 3⅞" ◪ (F)
1 square 4¼" x 4¼" ⊠ (G)

Green Print
2 squares (C) 2⅜" x 2⅜"
1 square (D) 4¼" x 4¼"
4 squares 2⅜" x 2⅜" ◪ (E)

Unit 1 Stitch & Flip
Make 4

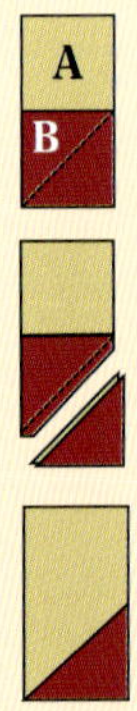

Unit 2 Stitch & Flip
Make 4

Refer to "Stitch-and-Flip" in the Techniques file on the PDF. Use the tan A's and red B's to make 4 unit 1's and 4 unit 2's as shown.

Unit 3 from C's
Make 4

Unit 4 from C's
Make 2

Pair 2 tan C's with 2 red C's to make 4 Triangle-Square unit 3's. Pair a green C and a red C to make 2 unit 4's. Pair a green B and a tan B to make 2 unit 5's.

Unit 5 from C's
Make 2

Flying Geese
Make 4

Use the green D and tan C's to make 4 Flying Geese.

Sew the units, Flying Geese, and patches together as shown to complete the block.

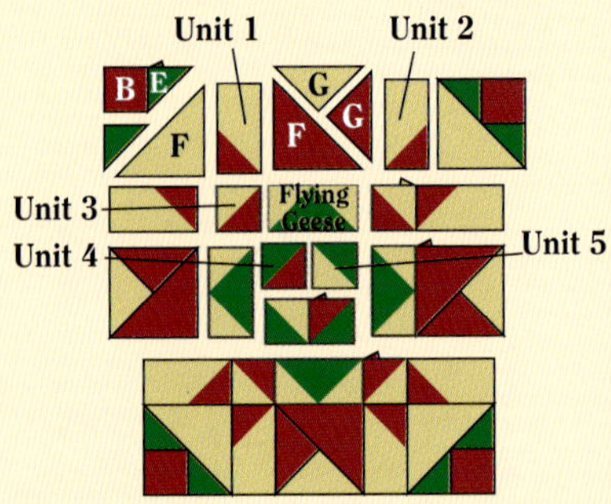

Block Assembly

pieced

block no. 739

Check It Out!

by Debbie Caffrey • Debbie's Creative Moments, Inc.
debbiescreativemoments.com

Debbie Caffrey is the author of several books, including *Open a Can of Worms* for Debbies Creative Moments, debbiescreative moments.com.

◪ = cut in half diagonally
⊠ = cut in half twice diagonally

White with Black Print and Black Solid from *each*
- 1 strip 1¼″ x 40″ for units

Red Print
- 4 rectangles (A) 1½″ x 6½″

Black Print #1
- 1 square 5⅛″ x 5⅛″ ◪ (B)

Black Print #2
- 2 squares 5⅛″ x 5⅛″ ◪ (B)
- 1 square 4¾″ x 4¾″ ⊠ (C)

Blue Stripe
- 2 squares (D) 2⅝″ x 2⅝″

White Tone-on-Tone
- 2 squares 3″ x 3″ ◪ (E)

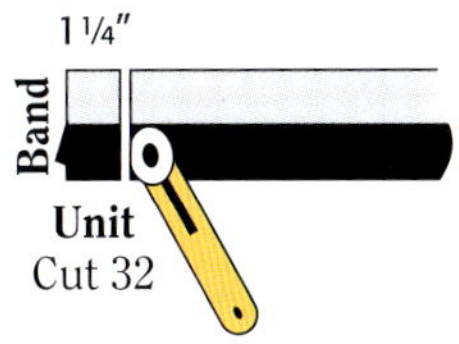

Join the white with black print strip and the black solid strip to make a band. Cut the band at 1¼" increments as shown to make 32 units.

Sew the patches and units together as shown to complete the block.

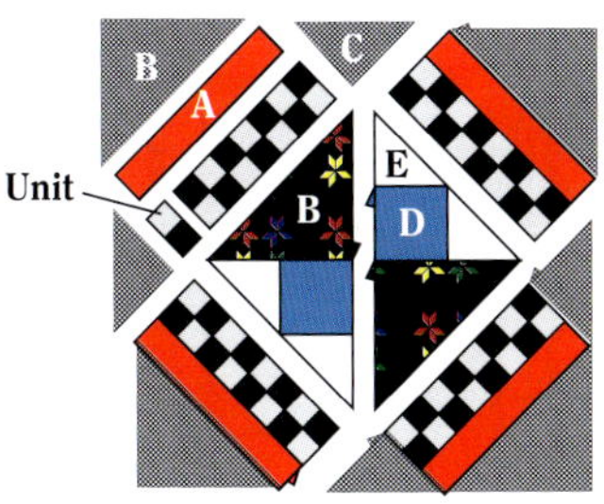

Block Assembly

block no. 740

Pinwheel Paws

by Stacey Carey • Stacey's Place
staceysplace.com

Fabric: Terrain by Kate Spain for Moda Fabrics, unitednotions.com.

White Print, Medium Purple Tone-on-Tone, Teal Tone-on-Tone and Dark Pink Print from *each*
- 3 squares (A) 2⅞″ x 2⅞″

White Solid
- 4 squares (A) 2⅞″ x 2⅞″
- 10 squares (B) 2½″ x 2½″

Medium Pink Tone-on-Tone
- 10 squares (B) 2½″ x 2½″

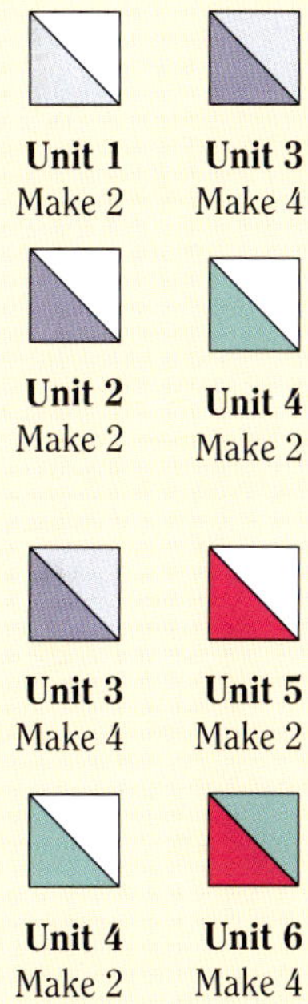

Pair a white print A with a white A to make 2 Trianlge-Square unit 1's. Pair a medium purple A and white A to make 2 unit 2's. Pair medium purple A's and white print A's to make 4 unit 3's.

Pair a teal A with a white A to make 2 unit 4's. Pair a dark pink A and white A to make 2 unit 5's. Pair teal A's and dark pink A's to make 4 unit 6's.

Sew the units and patches together as shown to complete the block.

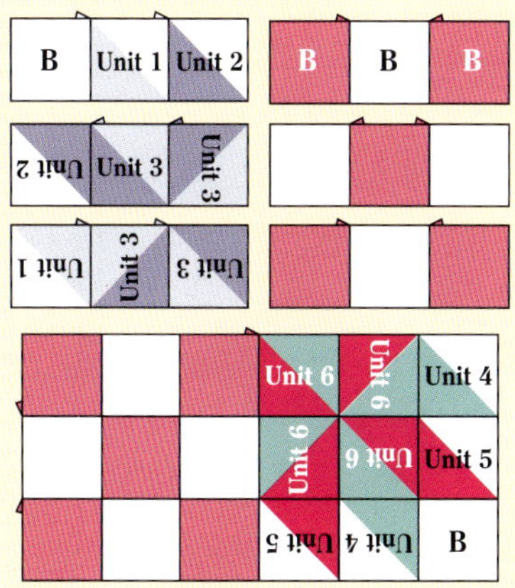

Block Assembly

block no. 741
Loyal Daughter

by Jennifer Chiaverini
elmcreek.net

Fabric: Elm Creek Quilts: The Winding Ways Collection designed by Jennifer Chiaverini for Red Rooster Fabrics, redroosterfabrics.com.

Best-selling novelist Jennifer Chiaverini has written several books, including *Traditions from Elm Creek Quilts* for C&T Publishing, ctpub.com.

See page 169 on the PDF for pattern

⊠ = cut in half twice diagonally

Green Tone-on-Tone
24 template A

Tan Tone-on-Tone
8 squares (B) 2¼″ x 2¼″
4 rectangles (D) 2¼″ x 3″
2 squares 3¾″ x 3¾″ ⊠ (C)

Pink Tone-on-Tone
8 squares (B) 2¼″ x 2¼″
1 square 3¾″ x 3¾″ ⊠ (C)
1 square (E) 3″ x 3″

Refer to "Set-in Seams" in the Techniques file on the PDF. Sew the patches together as shown to complete the block.

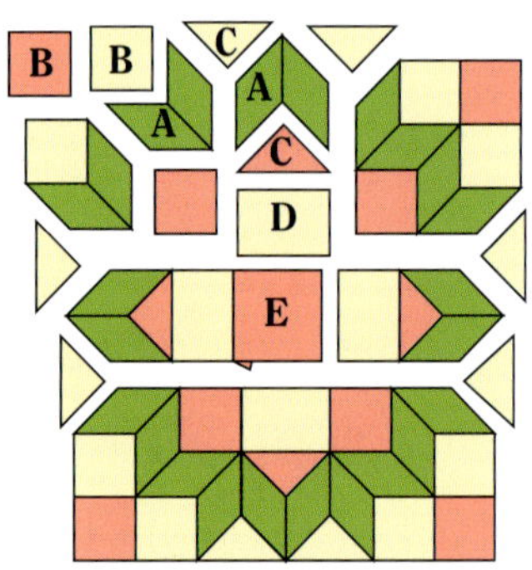

Block Piecing

block no. 742
Framework

by Emily Cier • Carolina Patchworks
carolinapatchworks.com

Fabric: Tilly designed by Jan DiCintio for Daisy Janie, daisyjanie.com.

Emily Cier is the author of *Scrap Republic* and *Quilt Remix* both for C&T Publishing, ctpubcom.

Gold Print
1 rectangle (A) 2½″ x 3″

Dark Brown Tone-on-Tone
6 rectangles (B) ¾″ x 3″
4 rectangles (E) ¾″ x 7½″
4 rectangles (H) ¾″ x 7¼″
4 rectangles (K) ¾″ x 12½″

Beige Solid
2 rectangles (B) ¾″ x 3″
2 rectangles (E) ¾″ x 7½″
2 rectangles (H) ¾″ x 7¼″
2 rectangles (K) ¾″ x 12½″

Orange Print
1 rectangle (C) 2¼″ x 3″
1 rectangle (D) 1¾″ x 3″
1 rectangle (F) 2¼″ x 7½″
1 rectangle (G) 1½″ x 7½″

Medium Brown Print
1 rectangle (I) 1¾″ x 7¼″
1 rectangle (J) 2¾″ x 7¼″
1 rectangle (L) 1¾″ x 12½″
1 rectangle (M) 3″ x 12½″

Sew the patches together as shown to complete the block.

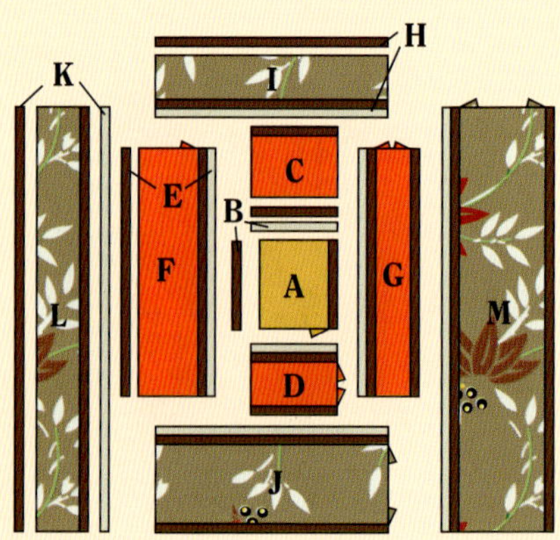

Block Piecing

pieced

block no. 743

Compass Points

by Karen Combs • Karen Combs' Studio
karencombs.com

Fabric: Serendipity designed by Karen Combs for Troy Riverwoods Collection, troy-corp.com.

Karen Combs is the author of *Celtic Pieced Illusions* for American Quilter's Society, americanquilter.com.

See page 191 on the PDF for pattern

⧄ = cut in half diagonally

Dark Purple and Dark Blue Tone-on-Tones from *each*
 3 squares (A) 2⅞″ x 2⅞″

Medium Orange and Medium Green Tone-on-Tones from *each*
 2 squares (A) 2⅞″ x 2⅞″

Dark Orange and Dark Green Tone-on-Tones from *each*
 1 square (A) 2⅞″ x 2⅞″

Light Orange and Light Green Tone-on-Tones from *each*
 2 squares 2⅞″ x 2⅞″ ⧄ (B)

Medium Purple and Medium Blue Tone-on-Tones from *each*
 1 square 2⅞″ x 2⅞″ ⧄ (B)
 2 template C

Light Purple and Light Blue Tone-on-Tones from *each*
 2 *each* templates D and Dr

Unit 1
Make 4 from A's

Unit 2
Make 4 from A's

Unit 3
Make 2 from A's

Unit 4
Make 2 from A's

Serendipity is a gradated fabric line. Karen cut each color's light, medium and dark patches from one fabric.

Pair 2 dark purple A's with the medium orange A's to make 4 Triangle-Square unit 1's. Pair 2 dark blue A's with medium green A's to make 4 unit 2's. Pair the dark orange A with a dark purple A to make 2 unit 3's. Pair the dark green A with a dark blue A to make 2 unit 4's.

Sew the units and patches together as shown to complete the block.

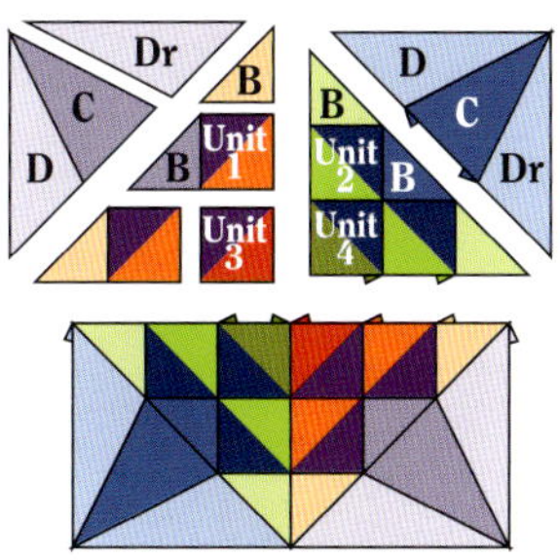

Block Assembly

block no. 744

Gear Works

by Melissa Corry

Fabric: Dimples from Andover Fabrics, andoverfabrics.com.

White Solid
 4 rectangles (A) 1″ x 12½″
 8 rectangles (D) 1½″ x 2½″
 8 rectangles (E) 1½″ x 3″

Blue Tone-on-Tone and Green Tone-on-Tone from *each*
 2 rectangles (B) 1½″ x 12½″
 4 rectangles (C) 2″ x 2½″

Yellow Tone-on-Tone
 1 rectangle (B) 1½″ x 12½″

Sew the patches together as shown to complete the block.

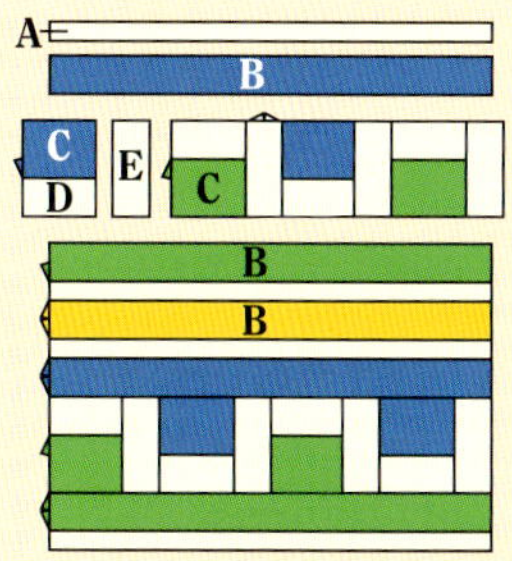

Block Piecing

block no. 745
Beautiful Math

by Elizabeth Dackson
dontcallmebetsy.com

Fabric: Good Folks designed by Anna Maria Horner for FreeSpirit Fabrics, freespiritfabric.com.

Cream Print
- 4 squares (A) 3″ x 3″
- 4 rectangles (C) 3″ x 4½″
- 1 square (F) 4½″ x 4½″

Pink Print and Dark Pink Tone-on-Tone
from *each*
- 2 rectangles (B) 2″ x 3″
- 2 rectangles (D) 2″ x 6½″
- 2 rectangles (E) 2″ x 2½″

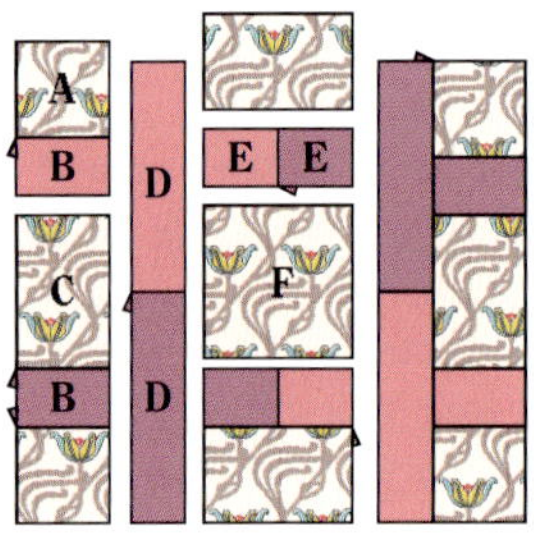

Block Piecing

Sew the patches together as shown to complete the block.

block no. 746
Window Panes

by Jenifer Dick • 42 Quilts
42quilts.blogspot.com

Fabric: Kona cotton solids by Robert Kaufman, robertkaufman.com, and Bella Solids by Moda Fabrics, unitednotions.com.

Jenifer Dick is the author of *Quilt Retro: 11 Designs to Make Your Own* for Kansas City Star Quilts, pickledish.com.

Dark Gray Solid
- 4 squares (A) 2½″ x 2½″
- 1 square (G) 6½″ x 6½″

Orange Solid
- 4 rectangles (B) 1″ x 2½″
- 4 rectangles (C) 1″ x 3″
- 2 rectangles (E) 1½″ x 5½″
- 2 rectangles (F) 1½″ x 6½″

Light Gray Solid
- 2 squares (D) 3″ x 3″

Aqua Solid
- 1 square (D) 3″ x 3″

White Solid
- 1 square (D) 3″ x 3″
- 1 square (G) 6½″ x 6½″

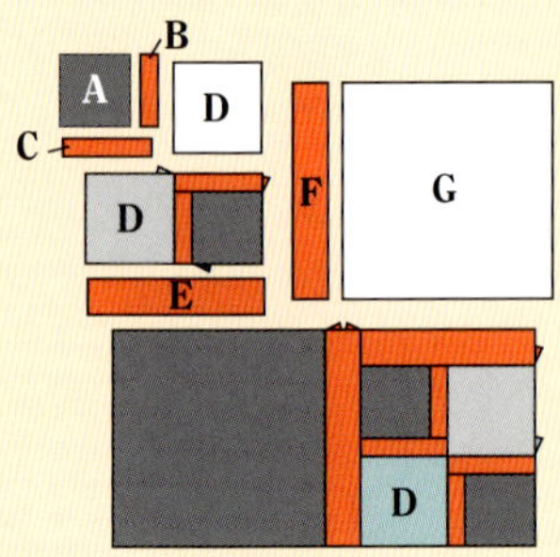

Block Piecing

Sew the patches together as shown to complete the block.

block no. 747

Diamond Eyes

by Monique Dillard • Open Gate
opengatequilts.com

Fabric: Memories of Provence designed by Monique Dillard for Maywood Studio, maywoodstudio.com.

Monique Dillard is the author of *Fat Quarter Winners* for C&T Publishing, ctpub.com.

Blue Tone-on-Tone
5 squares (A) 3½″ x 3½″
Cream Print
20 squares (B) 2″ x 2″
2 squares (C) 2⅜″ x 2⅜″
1 square (D) 4¼″ x 4¼″
8 rectangles (E) 1½″ x 6½″
Green Print
6 squares (C) 2⅜″ x 2⅜″
4 rectangles (E) 1½″ x 6½″

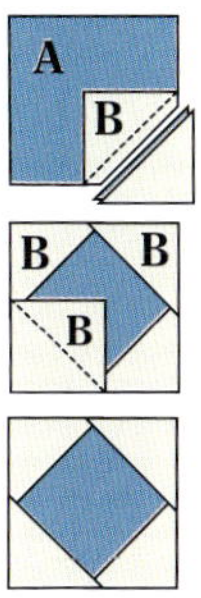

Unit 1
Stitch & Flip
Make 5

Unit 2
Make 4

Flying Geese
Make 4

Refer to "Stitch-and-Flip" in the Techniques file on the PDF. Make 5 unit 1's using the blue A's and cream B's.

Pair the cream C's with 2 green C's to make 4 Triangle-Square unit 2's.

Use the cream D and 4 green C's to make 4 Flying Geese.

Sew the units, Flying Geese, and patches together as shown to complete the block.

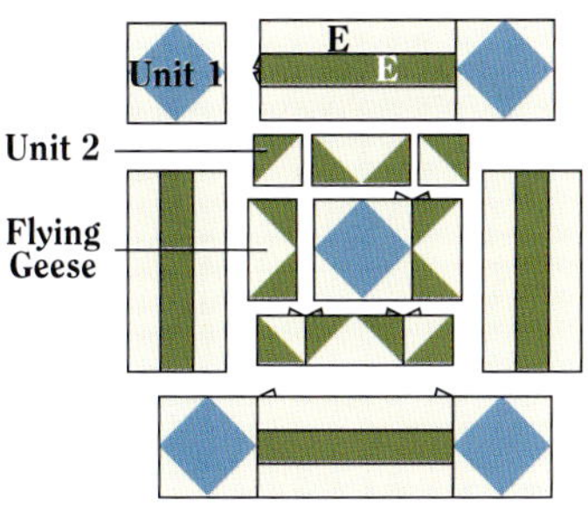

Block Assembly

block no. 748

Magazine Beads

by Victoria Eapen • Spun Sugar Quilts
spunsugarquilt.com

Fabric: Sophie designed by Chez Mois for Moda Fabrics, unitednotions.com.

Cream Solid
2 rectangles (A) 2″ x 12½″
4 rectangles (B) 1½″ x 5½″
4 rectangles (D) 1½″ x 4½″
4 rectangles (E) 1½″ x 3½″
4 squares (F) 1½″ x 1½″
Assorted Prints
2 rectangles (B) 1½″ x 5½″
9 rectangles (C) 1½″ x 2½″
3 rectangles (D) 1½″ x 4½″
3 rectangles (E) 1½″ x 3½″
4 squares (F) 1½″ x 1½″
2 rectangles (G) 1½″ x 2″

Sew the patches together as shown to complete the block.

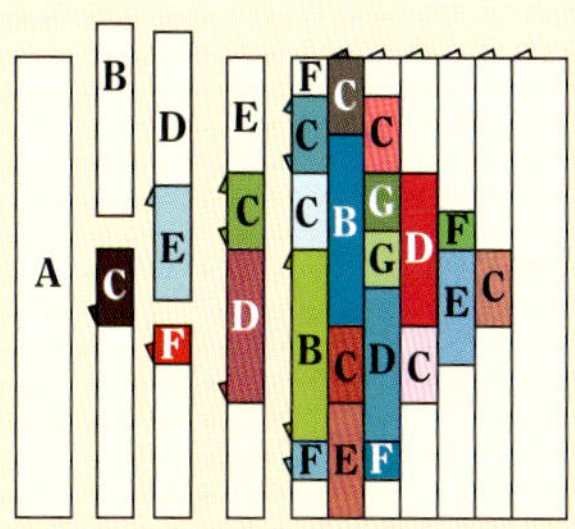

Block Piecing

block no. 749

Shooting Star

by Deanne Eisenman • Snuggles Quilts
snugglesquilts.com

Deanne Eisenman is the author of *Scrap Quilts Go Country* for Martingale & Co., martingale-pub.com.

Black Print
4 squares (A) 3½" x 3½"
5 squares (F) 2½" x 2½"
Tan Print
16 squares (B) 2" x 2"
44 squares (D) 1½" x 1½"
3 squares (G) 3¼" x 3¼"
8 rectangles (I) 1½" x 2½"
Purple Print #1
4 rectangles (C) 1½" x 4½"
Blue Print #1
4 rectangles (E) 1½" x 6½"
Purple Print #2
2 squares (G) 3¼" x 3¼"
Blue Print #2
4 squares (H) 1⅞" x 1⅞"

Unit 1
Stitch & Flip
Make 4

Unit 4
Stitch & Flip
Make 5

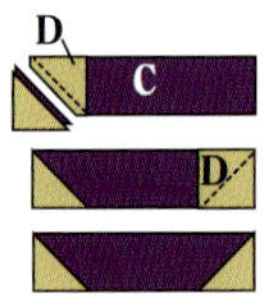

Unit 2
Stitch & Flip
Make 4

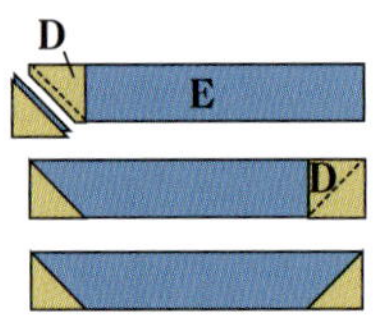

Unit 3
Stitch & Flip
Make 4

Refer to "Stitch-and-Flip" in the Techniques file on the PDF. Use the black A's and tan B's to make 4 unit 1's. Use the purple #1 C's and tan D's to make 4 unit 2's. Use the blue #1 E's and tan D's to make 4 unit 3's. Use the black F's and tan D's to make 5 unit 4's.

Flying Geese
Make 4

Unit 5
Make 4

Use 1 tan G and blue #2 H's to make 4 Flying Geese.

Refer to "Quarter-Square Triangles" in the Techniques file on the PDF. Pair 2 tan G's with the purple #2 G's to make 4 unit 5's.

Sew the units, Flying Geese, and patches together as shown to complete the block.

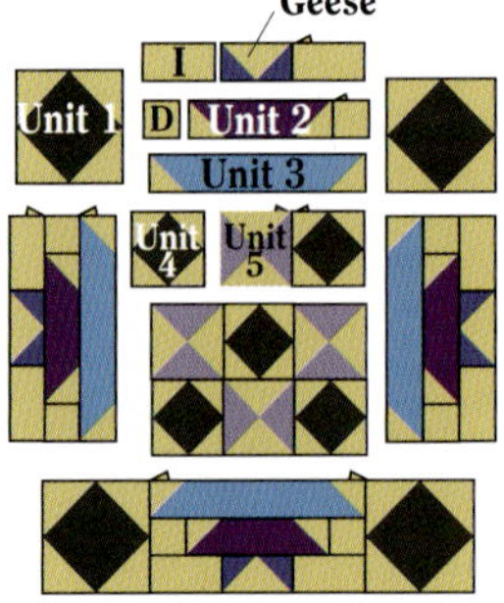

Block Assembly

block no. 750

Star-Crossed

by Theresa Eisinger • former *QM* Graphic Designer
quiltmaker.com

Fabric: Tied Up designed by Dawn Spencer for Northcott, northcott.com.

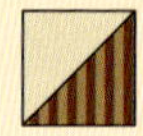

Unit 1 from A's
Make 4

Cream Tone-on-Tone
2 squares (A) 2⅞" x 2⅞"
Brown Stripe
2 squares (A) 2⅞" x 2⅞"
1 square (F) 3¼" x 3¼"
Black Print
8 rectangles (B) 2½" x 4½"
Brown Print #1
1 square (D) 4½" x 4½"
Gray Tone-on-Tone
8 squares (C) 2½" x 2½"
4 squares (E) 1½" x 1½"
8 rectangles (G) 1½" x 2½"
Black Dot
2 squares (F) 3¼" x 3¼"
Cream Print
1 square (F) 3¼" x 3¼"
Brown Print #2
4 squares (C) 2½" x 2½"

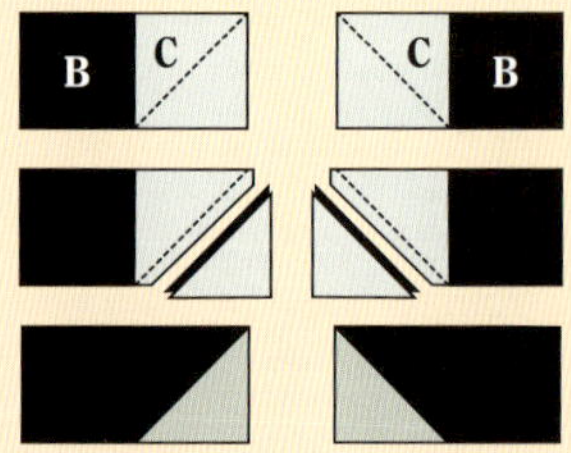

Unit 2
Stitch & Flip
Make 4

Unit 3
Stitch & Flip
Make 4

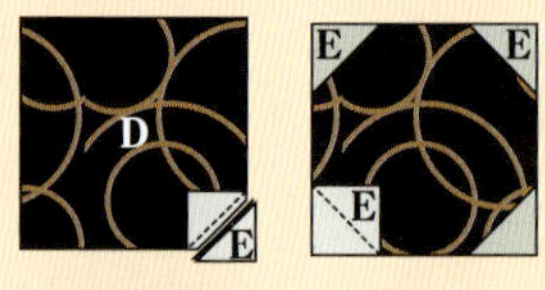

Unit 4
Stitch & Flip
Make 1

Unit 5
Make 4

Pair the cream tone-on-tone A's with the brown stripe A's to make 4 Triangle-Square unit 1's.

Refer to "Stitch-and-Flip" in the Techniques file on the PDF. Use the black print B's and gray C's to make 4 unit 2's and 4 unit 3's as shown. Use the brown print #1 D and gray E's to make unit 4.

Refer to "Quarter-Square Triangles" in the Techniques file on the PDF. Use the brown stripe F's, the black dot F's and the cream print F's to make 4 unit 5's as shown.

Sew the units and patches together as shown to complete the block.

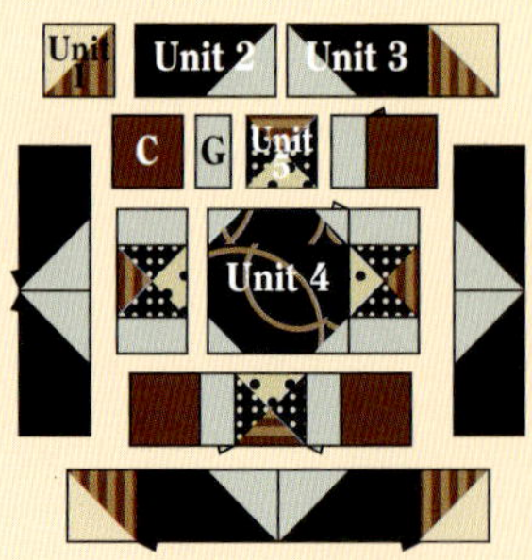

Block Assembly

pieced

block no. 751

Split Chain

by Cindy Erickson • Cindy Erickson Designs
cindyerickson.com

⧄ = cut in half diagonally

Beige Batik
- 1 square (A) 2⅞″ x 2⅞″
- 1 square 3½″ x 3½″ ⧄ (B)
- 4 squares 2⅞″ x 2⅞″ ⧄ (D)
- 4 squares (F) 2½″ x 2½″

Blue Batik
- 1 square (A) 2⅞″ x 2⅞″
- 1 square 4⅞″ x 4⅞″ ⧄ (E)
- 2 squares (F) 2½″ x 2½″

Medium Green Batik
- 2 rectangles (C) 1¼″ x 6⅞″

Dark Brown Batik
- 8 squares (F) 2½″ x 2½″

Dark Green Batik
- 2 squares (G) 4½″ x 4½″

Unit 1 from A's Make 2 **Unit 2** Make 2

Pair the beige and blue A's to make 2 Triangle-Square unit 1's.

Sew each beige B to a medium green C. Trim as shown to make 2 unit 2's.

Sew the units and patches together as shown to complete the block.

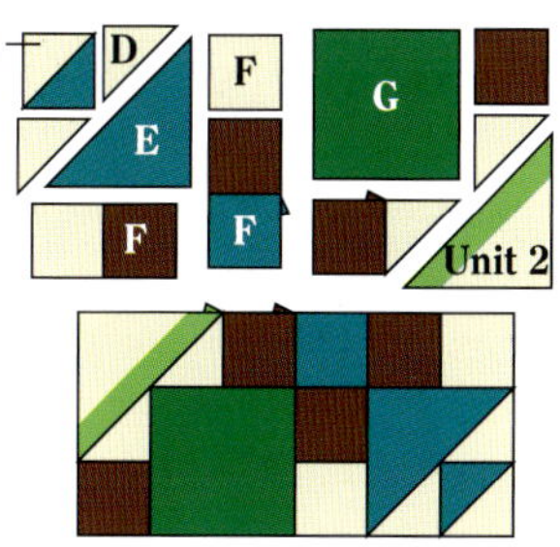

Block Assembly

block no. 752

Christmas Cards

by Heidi Foltz • Handmade by Heidi
handmadebyheidi.com

Fabric: Jovial designed by Basic Gray for Moda Fabrics, unitednotions.com.

⧄ = cut in half diagonally
⊠ = cut in half twice diagonally

Black Print, Red Tone-on-Tone, Green Tone-on-Tone, and Green Print
from *each*
- 1 square 3⅞″ x 3⅞″ ⧄ (A) (there will be 1 extra)
- 1 square 4⅞″ x 4⅞″ ⧄ (C)
- 1 square 5¼″ x 5¼″ ⊠ (D) (there will be 2 extra)

Cream Tone-on-Tone
- 4 rectangles (B) 1¼″ x 7″
- 1 square 5¼″ x 5¼″ ⊠ (D)

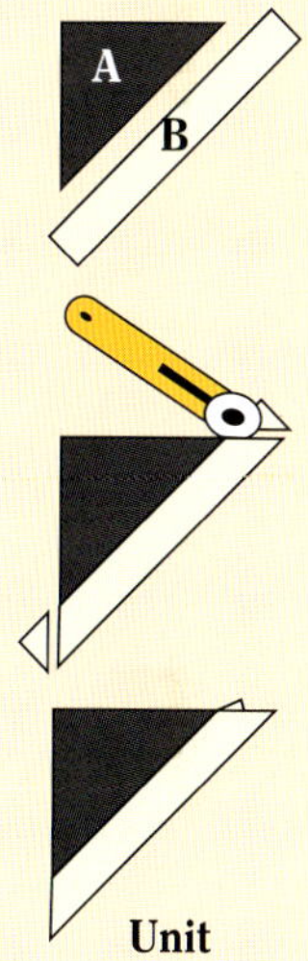

Unit Make 4

Sew a cream B to one black A; trim as shown to make a unit. In the same way, sew a cream B to a red A, a green A, and a green print A; trim to make 3 more units.

Sew the units and patches together as shown to complete the block.

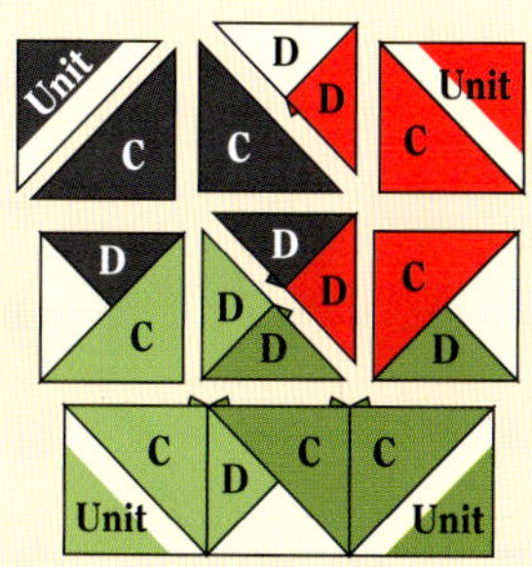

Block Assembly

block no. 753

Starfire

by Kay Gentry • Noble Needle Quilting and Sewing
nobleneedle.com

⧄ = cut in half diagonally
⊠ = cut in half twice diagonally

Black Solid
2 squares (A) 2 7/8″ x 2 7/8″
4 squares (B) 2 1/2″ x 2 1/2″

Light Gray Tone-on-Tone
2 squares (A) 2 7/8″ x 2 7/8″
8 squares (B) 2 1/2″ x 2 1/2″
2 squares 3 1/4″ x 3 1/4″ ⊠ (D)

Red Tone-on-Tone
4 squares (B) 2 1/2″ x 2 1/2″
4 squares (C) 1 7/8″ x 1 7/8″

Dark Gray Tone-on-Tone
4 squares 2 7/8″ x 2 7/8″ ⧄ (E)
4 rectangles (F) 2 1/2″ x 4 1/2″

Unit
Make 4

pieced

Pair the black A's with the light gray A's to make 4 Triangle-Square units.

Sew the units and patches together as shown to complete the block.

Block Assembly

block no. 754

Crossroads in Life

by Carolyn Goins • CPG Designs
cpgdesigns.com

Fabric: Baltimore Album from Windham Fabrics, windhamfabrics.com.

⧄ = cut in half diagonally
⊠ = cut in half twice diagonally

Gold Tone-on-Tone
2 squares (A) 5 1/8″ x 5 1/8″

Red Print
1 square (A) 5 1/8″ x 5 1/8″
1 square 4 1/8″ x 4 1/8″ ⊠ (B)

Blue Print
1 square (A) 5 1/8″ x 5 1/8″
2 squares 2 7/8″ x 2 7/8″ ⧄ (D)

Green Print
1 square 4 1/8″ x 4 1/8″ ⊠ (B)
2 squares 3 3/4″ x 3 3/4″ ⧄ (C)

Cream Tone-on-Tone
2 squares 5 1/4″ x 5 1/4″ ⊠ (E)

Unit 1 from A's
Make 2

Unit 2 from A's
Make 2

Pair a gold A with a red A to make 2 unit 1's. Pair a gold A and blue A to make 2 Triangle-Square unit 2's.

Sew the units and patches together as shown to complete the block.

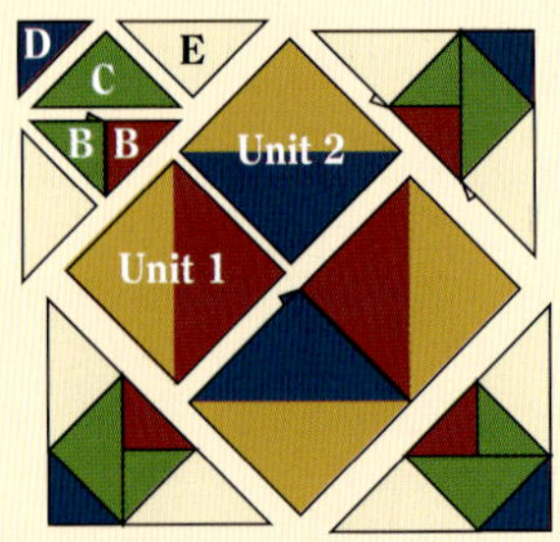

Block Assembly

block no. 755

Scrappy Summer

by Allison Harris • Cluck Cluck Sew
clucksew.com

⧄ = cut in half diagonally

White Solid
4 squares 3⅞" x 3⅞" ⧄ (A)

4 Assorted Red Prints
from *each*
1 square 3⅞" x 3⅞" ⧄ (A) (there will be 4 extra)

Assorted Blue Prints
4 squares 3⅞" x 3⅞" ⧄ (A) (there will be 4 extra)
16 rectangles (B) 2" x 3½"

Sew the patches together as shown to complete the block.

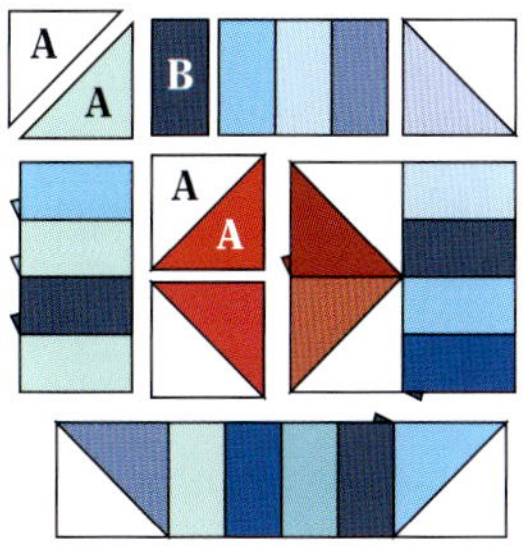

Block Piecing

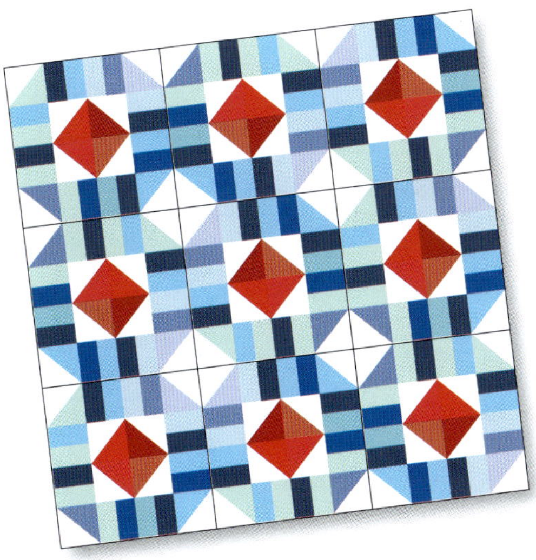

block no. 756

Starsteps

by Diane Harris • Interactive Editor, *Quiltmaker*
quiltmaker.com

Assorted Cream Prints
4 rectangles (A) 2½" x 4½"
8 squares (C) 1½" x 1½"
8 rectangles (D) 1½" x 3½"
8 rectangles (E) 1½" x 2½"

Dark Gold Stripe and Medium Blue Tone-on-Tone
from *each*
2 rectangles (A) 2½" x 4½"
4 squares (B) 2½" x 2½"
2 rectangles (E) 1½" x 2½"

Assorted Red Prints and Tone-on-Tones
12 squares (C) 1½" x 1½"

Yellow Print
1 square (B) 2½" x 2½"
4 squares (C) 1½" x 1½"

Dark Blue Tone-on-Tone
4 squares (C) 1½" x 1½"

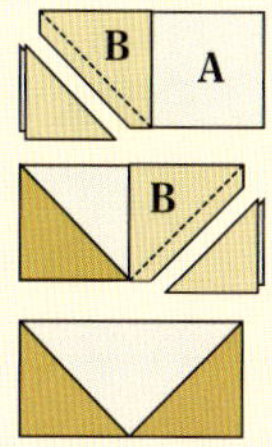

Unit 1
Stitch & Flip
Make 2

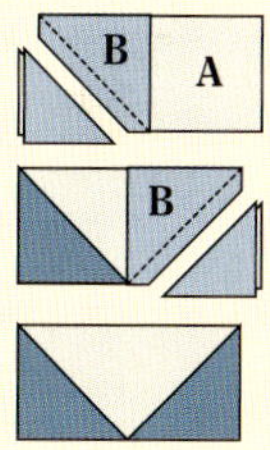

Unit 2
Stitch & Flip
Make 2

Refer to "Stitch-and-Flip" in the Techniques file on the PDF. Make 2 unit 1's using 2 cream A's and 4 dark gold B's. Make 2 unit 2's using 2 cream A's and 4 medium blue B's.

Sew the patches and units together as shown to complete the block.

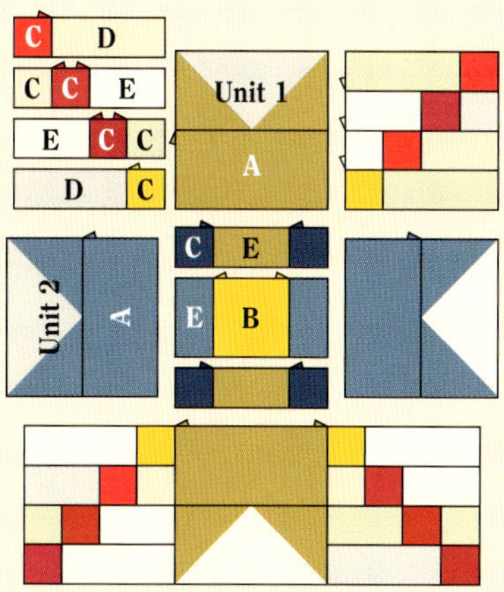

Block Assembly

block no. 757

Cathedral Square

by Lee Heinrich
freshlypieced.blogspot.com

Fabric: Taza designed by Dena Designs for FreeSpirit Fabrics, freespiritfabrics.com, and Kona cotton solids, robertkaufman.com.

Light Pink Print
- 1 square (A) 4¼″ x 4¼″
- 4 squares (B) 2⅜″ x 2⅜″

Gray Solid
- 1 square (A) 4¼″ x 4¼″
- 4 squares (B) 2⅜″ x 2⅜″
- 4 squares (C) 3½″ x 3½″
- 8 squares (D) 2″ x 2″

2 Aqua Prints and 2 Yellow Prints
from *each*
- 1 square (C) 3½″ x 3½″

Pink and Orange Print
- 8 squares (D) 2″ x 2″

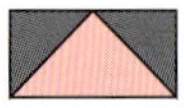

Flying Geese 1
Make 4

Flying Geese 2
Make 4

Pair the light pink A with 4 gray B's to make 4 Flying Geese 1. Make 4 Flying Geese 2 using the gray A and 4 light pink B's.

Sew the Flying Geese and patches together as shown to complete the block.

pieced

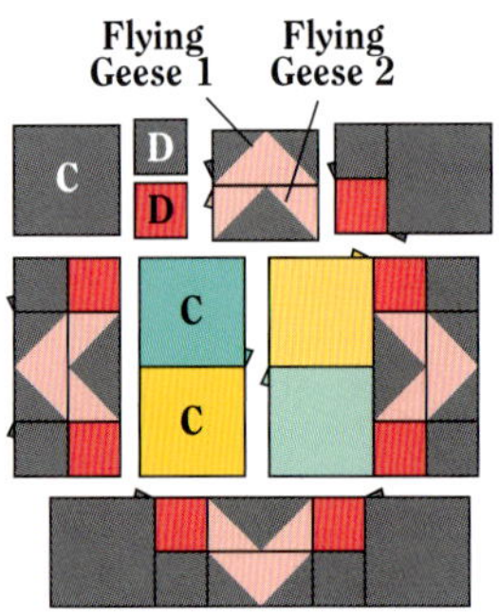

Block Assembly

block no. 758

Macy's Ladies

by Chris Hoover • Whirligig Designs
whirligigdesigns.com

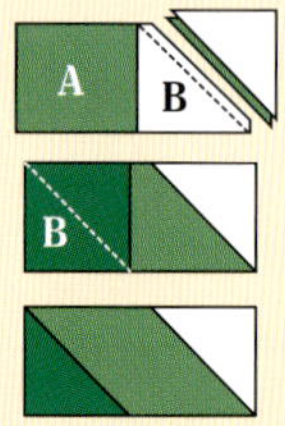

Unit 1
Stitch & Flip
Make 1

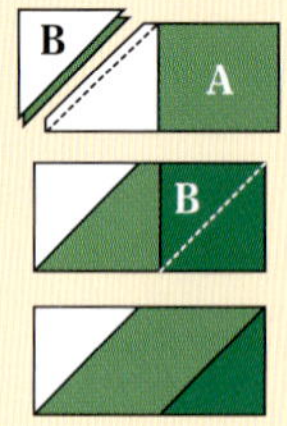

Unit 2
Stitch & Flip
Make 1

Dark Green Tone-on-Tone #1
- 2 rectangles (A) 3″ x 6″
- 2 squares (B) 3″ x 3″
- 1 square (F) 1⅞″ x 1⅞″
- 2 rectangles (H) 2″ x 2½″

Medium Green Tone-on-Tone
- 2 rectangles (A) 3″ x 6″
- 2 squares (E) 1½″ x 1½″
- 4 squares (G) 2½″ x 2½″

White Print
- 4 squares (B) 3″ x 3″
- 2 rectangles (J) 5½″ x 6″

Red Print
- 2 rectangles (C) 1½″ x 2½″
- 2 squares (D) 1″ x 1″
- 1 square (F) 1⅞″ x 1⅞″
- 2 rectangles (I) 1″ x 1½″

Black Solid
- 4 squares (D) 1″ x 1″

Dark Green Tone-on-Tone #2
- 1 rectangle (K) 1½″ x 12½″

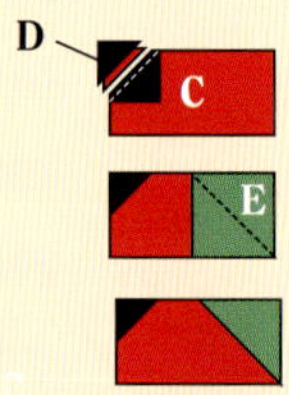

Unit 3
Stitch & Flip
Make 1

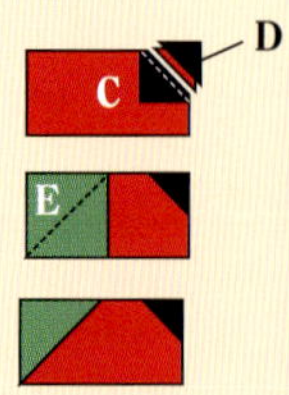

Unit 4
Stitch & Flip
Make 1

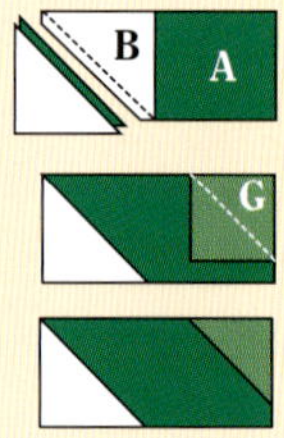

Unit 5
Stitch & Flip
Make 1

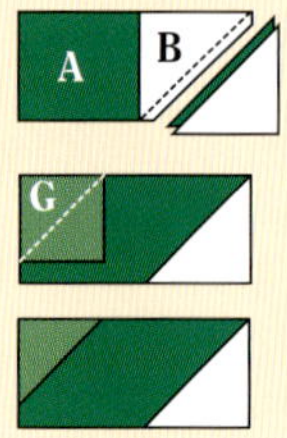

Unit 6
Stitch & Flip
Make 1

Refer to "Stitch-and-Flip" in the Techniques file on the PDF. Use the medium green A's with the dark green #1 B's and white B's to make units 1 and 2 as shown. Use the red C's, black D's and green E's to make units 3 and 4. Make units 5 and 6 using the dark green #1 A's with white B's and green G's as shown.

Pair the red F with the dark green F to make 2 Triangle-Square unit 7's. Sew the units and patches together as shown to complete the block.

Unit 7
Make 2

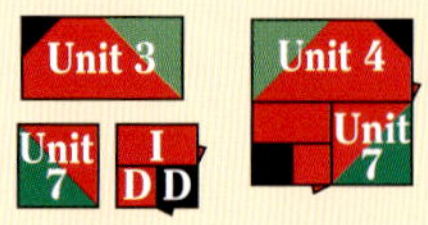

Section 1
Make 1

Section 2
Make 1

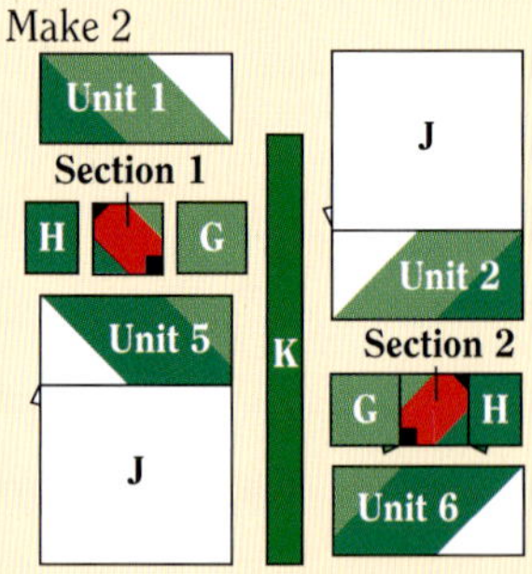

Block Assembly

block no. 759

Talkin' Turkey!

by Bonnie Hunter • Quiltville
quiltville.com

Bonnie Hunter writes the "Addicted to Scraps" column for *Quiltmaker*. She is the author of *Scraps & Shirttails II: Continuing the Art of Quilting Green* and *Adventures with Leaders and Enders* for Kansas City Star Quilts, pickledish.com.

Assorted Cream Prints and Tone-on-Tones
- 12 rectangles (A) 2″ x 3½″
- 4 squares (B) 2″ x 2″
- 4 squares (C) 2⅝″ x 2⅝″

Assorted Red Prints and Tone-on-Tones
- 16 squares (B) 2″ x 2″
- 5 squares (C) 2⅝″ x 2⅝″
- 1″ to 1¾″-wide strips to total 125″

Foundation paper
- 2 squares 5⅜″ x 5⅜″

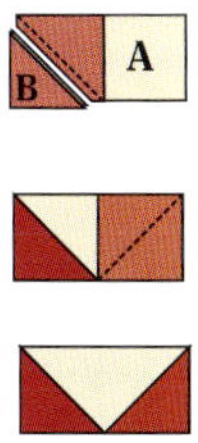

Unit
Stitch & Flip
Make 8

Refer to "Stitch-and-Flip" in the Techniques file on the PDF. Use 8 cream A's and the red B's to make 8 units.

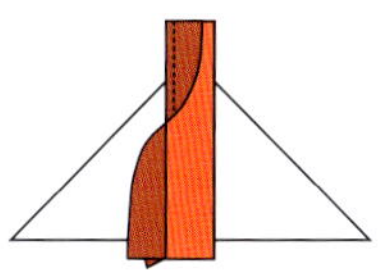

Section Piecing

Cut each paper square in half diagonally. Fold the paper triangles in half, then draw a line on the fold. Center a red strip right side up on one of the foundation triangles. Aligning raw edges, lay another strip right side down on the center strip as shown. Join the strips by sewing through all the layers ¼" from the raw edges. Flip the top strip open and press. Continue adding strips from the center outward in both directions until the entire foundation has been covered. Trim the fabric even withthe paper. Repeat to make4 sections.

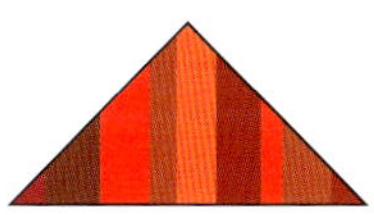

Section
Make 4

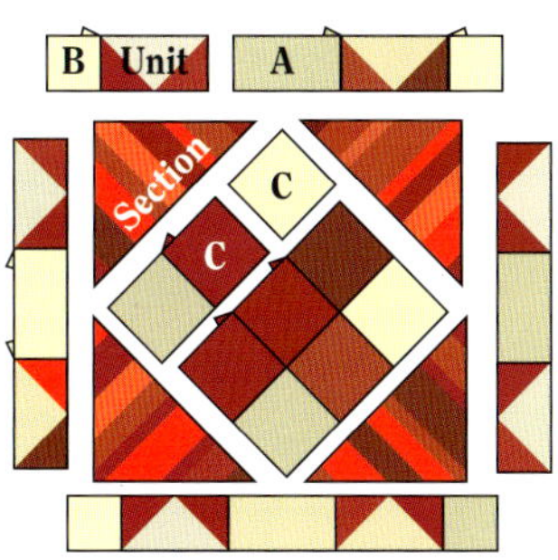

Block Assembly

Sew the units, sections and patches together as shown to complete the block. Carefully remove the papers.

block no. 760

Galaxy X

by Deborah Johnson • In the Doghouse Designs
inthedoghousedesigns.com

Green Batik
- 4 squares (A) 4″ x 4″
- 1 square (G) 2½″ x 2½″

Cream Tone-on-Tone
- 8 squares (B) 2″ x 2″
- 4 rectangles (C) 2″ x 6½″
- 4 rectangles (F) 2½″ x 4″

Red Batik
- 4 rectangles (D) 2″ x 3½″
- 4 rectangles (E) 2″ x 5″

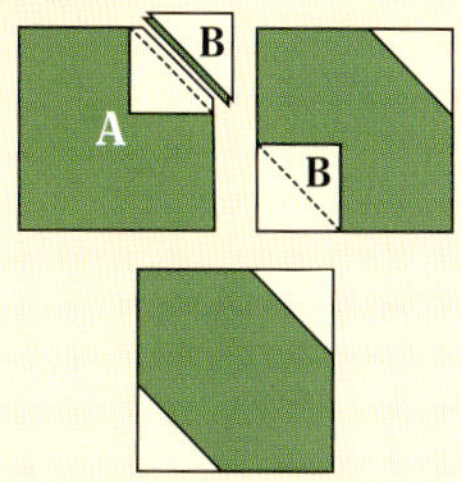

Unit 1
Stitch & Flip
Make 4

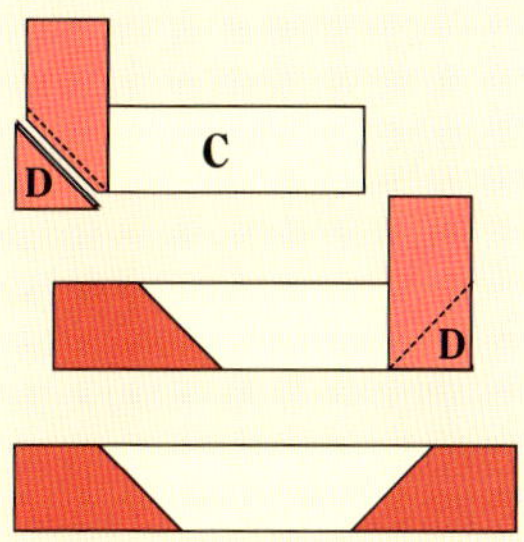

Unit 2
Stitch & Flip
Make 2

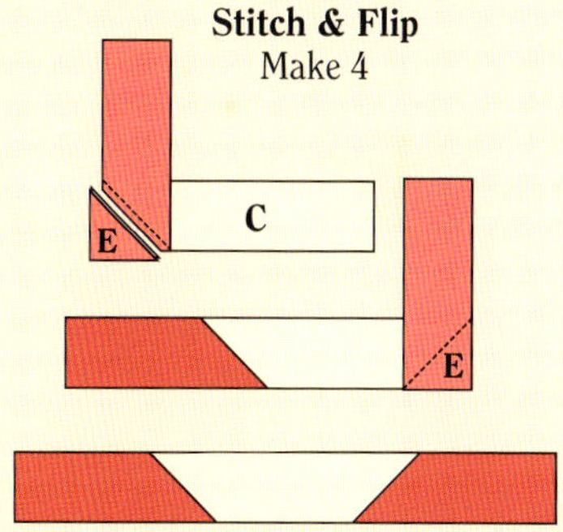

Unit 3
Stitch & Flip
Make 2

Refer to "Stitch-and-Flip" in the Techniques file on the PDF. Use the green A's and cream B's to make 4 unit 1's as shown. Use the cream C's and the red D's to make 2 unit 2's. Make 2 unit 3's using the cream C's and red E's.

Sew the units and patches together as shown to complete the block.

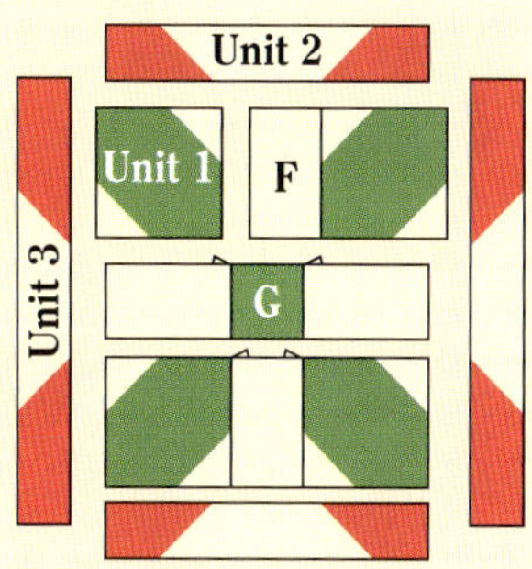

Block Assembly

block no. 761
House on a Hill

by Kimberly Jolly • Fat Quarter Shop
fatquartershop.com

Fabric: Warm Memories by Kansas Troubles Quilters and Little Gatherings by Primitive Gatherings, both from Moda Fabrics, unitednotions.com.

◸ = cut in half diagonally

Medium Cream Tone-on-Tone
3 rectangles (A) 1½" x 3½"

Dark Cream Tone-on-Tone
2 rectangles (A) 1½" x 3½"
1 rectangle (C) 1½" x 4½"
1 square 3⅞" x 3⅞" ◸ (D)

Red Print #1
2 rectangles (A) 1½" x 3½"
1 rectangle (C) 1½" x 4½"
1 rectangle (I) 1" x 2½"

Black Print
3 rectangles (A) 1½" x 3½"
1 rectangle (L) 2½" x 3½"

Dark Brown Print
3 squares (B) 1½" x 1½"
2 rectangles (C) 1½" x 4½"
1 rectangle (E) 3½" x 7¼" (see diagram for further cutting)
2 squares (J) 2½" x 2½"
1 rectangle (K) 1½" x 6½"

Tan Print
2 squares (B) 1½" x 1½"
1 rectangle (G) 1½" x 12½"
1 rectangle (K) 1½" x 6½"

Light Cream Tone-on-Tone
3 squares (B) 1½" x 1½"
1 rectangle (H) 2" x 2½"

Red Print #2
1 rectangle (F) 3½" x 10¼" (see diagram for further cutting)

Dark Green Print
1 rectangle (G) 1½" x 12½"

Sew the patches together as shown to complete the block.

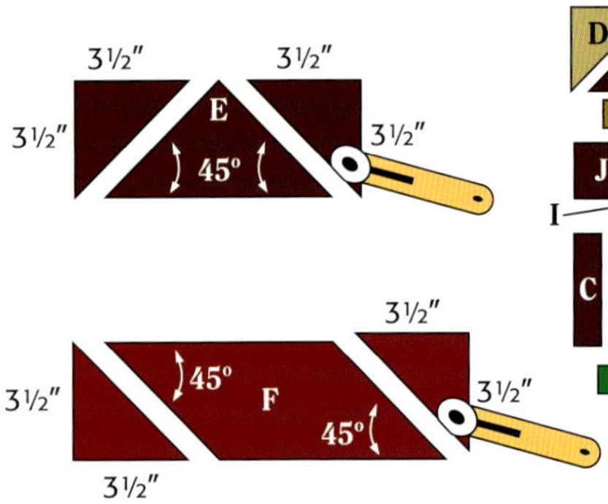

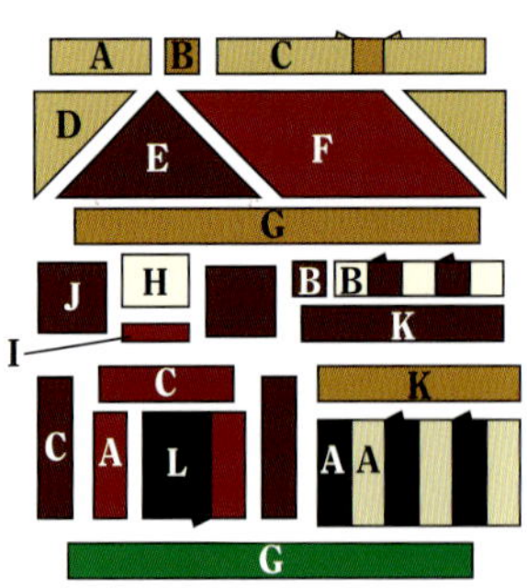

Block Piecing

block no. 762
Diamond Mine

by Faith Jones • Fresh Lemons Quilts
freshlemonsquilts.com

Fabric: Designer Solids from FreeSpirit Fabrics, freespiritfabrics.com and Kona cotton solids from Robert Kaufman, robert-kaufman.com.

◸ = cut in half diagonally
⊠ = cut in half twice diagonally

Light Orange Solid and Dark Orange Solid
from *each*
1 square (A) 3" x 3"

White Solid
2 squares (B) 2⅝" x 2⅝"
1 square 7¼" x 7¼" ⊠ (E)

Light Green Solid and Yellow Solid
from *each*
2 squares 3" x 3" ◸ (C)

Turquoise Solid and Pink Solid
from *each*
2 squares 3⅞" x 3⅞" ◸ (D)

Gray Solid
1 square 7¼" x 7¼" ⊠ (E)

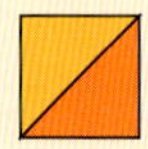

Unit from A's
Make 2

Pair the light orange A with the dark orange A to make 2 Triangle-Square units.

Sew the units and patches together as shown to complete the block.

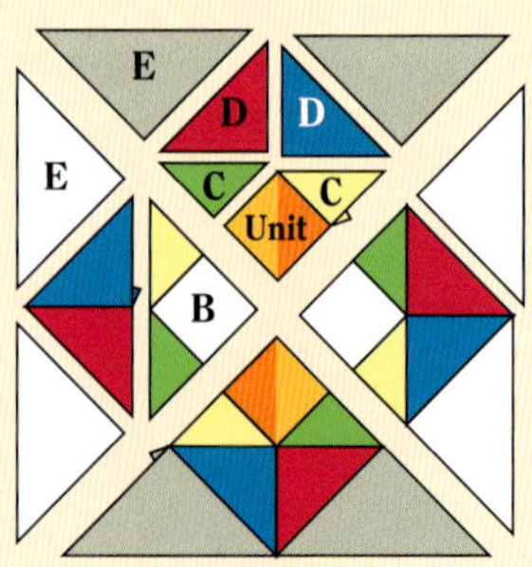

Block Assembly

pieced

block no. 763

Four Gables

by Susan Knapp & Mary Jane Mattingly
The Quilt Branch • quiltbranch.com

Fabric: Circa 1934 designed by Cosmo Cricket for Moda Fabrics, unitednotions.com.

Susan Knapp and Mary Jane Mattingly are the authors of *Cottage Creations* and *Six Halves Make a Whole Starburst* for The Quilt Branch, quiltbranch.com.

Green Dot
4 rectangles (A) 3½″ x 4½″
Cream Solid
8 squares (B) 2½″ x 2½″
4 rectangles (D) 1½″ x 2½″
4 rectangles (E) 1½″ x 3½″
8 squares (F) 1½″ x 1½″
Gold Print
4 squares (B) 2½″ x 2½″
Red Solid
4 rectangles (C) 1½″ x 4½″
Black Print
4 rectangles (D) 1½″ x 2½″
4 rectangles (E) 1½″ x 3½″
Green Print
1 square (G) 4½″ x 4½″ (Susan and Mary Jane fussy cut this square from a large print)

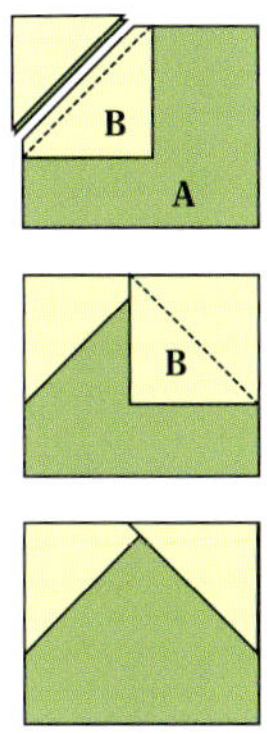

Unit Stitch & Flip
Make 4

Refer to "Stitch-and-Flip" in the Techniques file on the PDF. Make 4 units using the green dot A's and cream B's.

Sew the units and patches together as shown to complete the block.

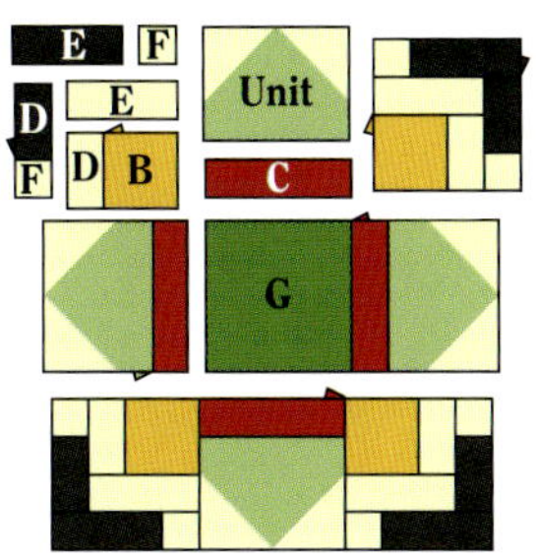

Block Assembly

block no. 764

Flower Burst

by Debby Kratovil • Quilter by Design
quilterbydesign.com

Fabric: Arianna designed by Jennifer Young for Benartex, benartex.com.

Debby Kratovil is the author of *Supersize 'Em* for Martingale & Co., martingale-pub.com.

See page 178 on the PDF for pattern

Green Print
4 template A
Pink Tone-on-Tone and Light Green Print
from *each*
2 template B
Multiprint
1 pattern C
Template plastic (optional)

Refer to "Curved Piecing" in the Techniques file on the PDF. Join the A's and B's as shown to make the block background.

To fussy cut the center circle from a large-scale print, make a plastic template for C.

Fold the block in half diagonally both ways. Prepare C for turned-edge appliqué. Use the creases and appliqué placement diagram as guides to center C on the block. Use monofilament thread and a blind stitch to appliqué the circle in place to complete the block.

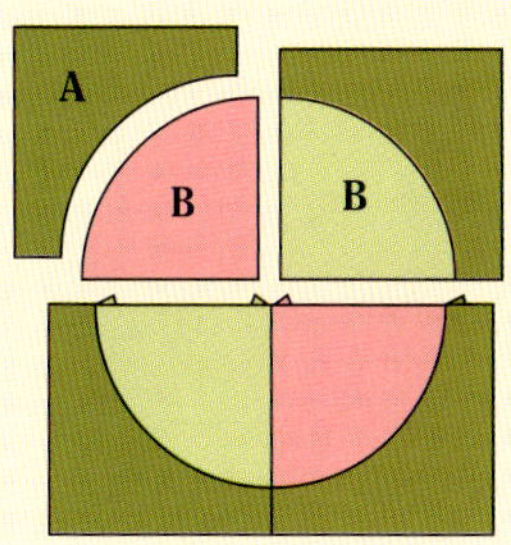

Block Piecing

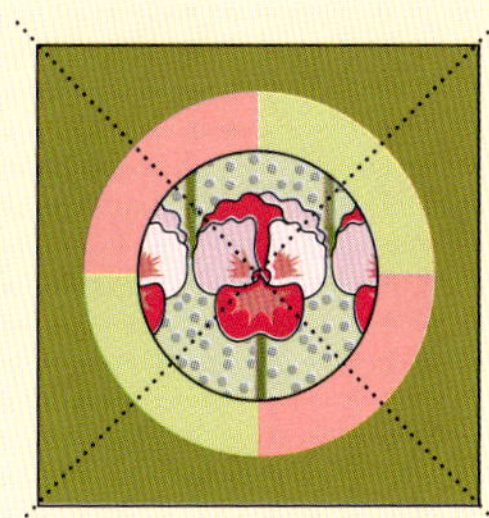

Applique Placement

block no 765

Bingo

by Jessie Kurtz • Harding Hill Designs
hardinghilldesigns.com

Fabric: Treasures and Tidbits designed by Piece O'Cake Designs for Robert Kaufman, robertkaufman.com.

White Solid
 6 squares (A) 2½"x 2½"
Turquoise Print and Red Print
from each
 1 rectangle (B) 2½"x 10½"
Orange Print and Green Print
from each
 1 square (A) 2½"x 2½"
 1 rectangle (C) 2½"x 8½"
Blue Print and Yellow Print
from each
 1 rectangle (D) 2½"x 4½"
 1 rectangle (E) 2½"x 6½"

Sew the patches together as shown to complete the block.

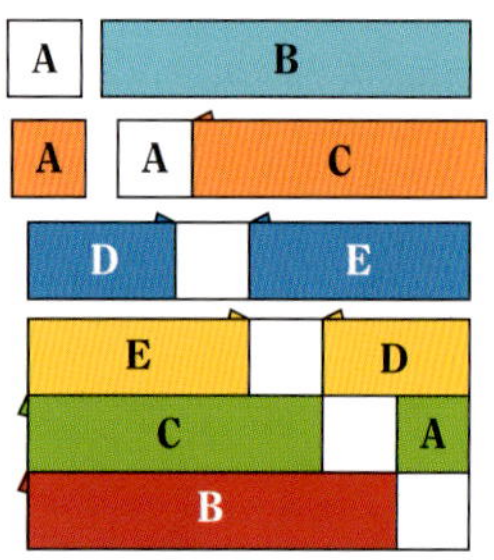

Block Piecing

pieced

block no. 766

One Way Home

by Judy Laquidara • Patchwork Times
patchworktimes.com

Judy Laquidara is the author of *60 Pieced Quilt Borders: Mix & Match* for American Quilter's Society, americanquilter.com.

⧄ = cut in half diagonally
⊠ = cut in half twice diagonally

Purple Tone-on-Tone
 4 rectangles (A) 2"x 3½"
 4 rectangles (D) 1½"x 3" (see diagram for further cutting)
 2 squares 1⅞"x 1⅞" ⧄ (F)
 4 squares (G) 3½"x 3½"
Gold Dot
 8 rectangles (A) 2"x 3½"
 4 squares (B) 2"x 2"
 1 square 4¼"x 4¼" ⊠ (C)
Green Dot
 4 rectangles (A) 2"x 3½"
 4 squares (B) 2"x 2"
 2 squares 3⅞"x 3⅞" ⧄ (E) (see diagram and instructions for further cutting)
 2 squares 1⅞"x 1⅞" ⧄ (F)

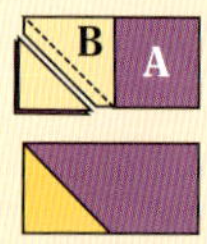

Unit 1
Stitch & Flip
Make 4

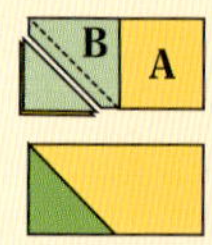

Unit 2
Stitch & Flip
Make 4

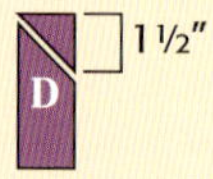

Trimming Diagram

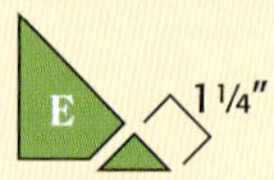

Trimming Diagram

Refer to "Stitch-and-Flip" in the Techniques file on the PDF. Use the purple A's and the yellow B's to make 4 unit 1's. Use the yellow A's and green B's to make 4 unit 2's.

Refer to the diagrams to trim the purple D's and green E's. To trim the E's, align your ruler perpendicular to the longest side and cut 1¼" from the corner as shown.

Sew the units and patches together as shown to complete the block.

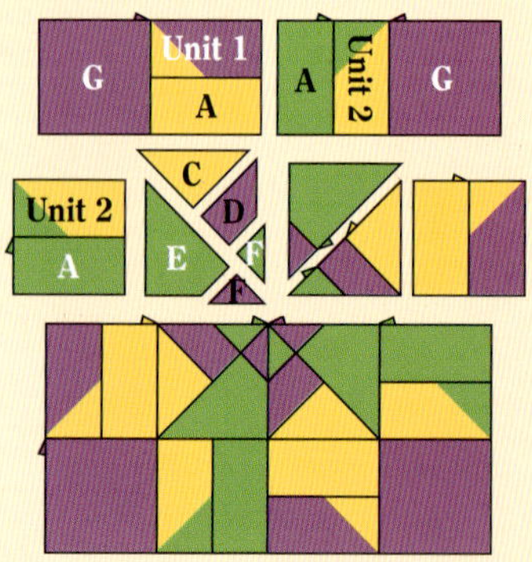

Block Assembly

block no. 767

North Country

by Doug Leko • Antler Quilt Design
antlerquiltdesign.com

Fabric: Dragonfly Summer designed by Holly Taylor for Moda Fabrics, unitednotions.com.

Cream Print
- 2 squares (A) 2⅞″ x 2⅞″
- 4 rectangles (B) 2½″ x 4½″
- 12 squares (C) 2½″ x 2½″

Red Tone-on-Tone
- 2 squares (A) 2⅞″ x 2⅞″
- 12 squares (C) 2½″ x 2½″

Tan Print
- 4 squares (A) 2⅞″ x 2⅞″
- 8 rectangles (B) 2½″ x 4½″
- 4 squares (C) 2½″ x 2½″

Unit 1
Make 4

Unit 2
Make 4

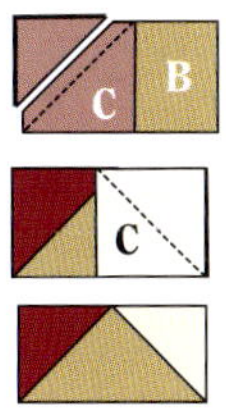

Unit 3
Stitch & Flip
Make 4

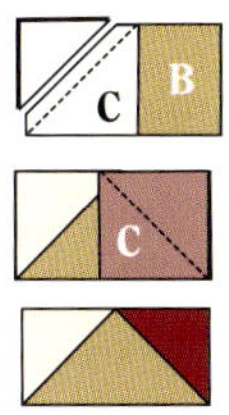

Unit 4
Stitch & Flip
Make 4

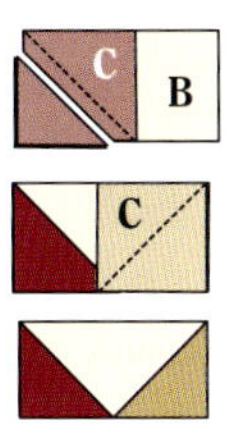

Unit 5
Stitch & Flip
Make 4

Pair the cream A's with 2 tan A's to make 4 Triangle-Square unit 1's. Make 4 unit 2's using the red A's and 2 tan A's.

Refer to "Stitch-and-Flip" in the Techniques file on the PDF. Use the tan B's with red C's and cream C's to make 4 unit 3's and 4 unit 4's as shown. Make 4 unit 5's using the cream B's with red C's and tan C's.

Sew the units and patches together as shown to complete the block.

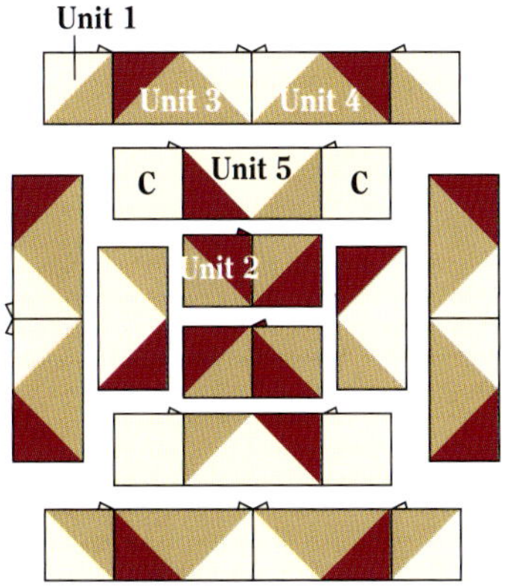

Block Assembly

block no. 768

On the Path

by Konda Luckau • Moose on the Porch Quilts
moosequilts.com

Fabric: Hope Valley designed by Denyse Schmidt for FreeSpirit Fabrics, freespiritfabrics.com, and Kona cotton solids, robertkaufman.com.

Konda Luckau is the author of *Simply Charming Modern* for Moose on the Porch Quilts, moosequilts.com.

Turquoise Solid
- 4 squares (A) 2″ x 2″
- 2 rectangles (B) 2″ x 3½″
- 6 rectangles (C) 1¼″ x 2″
- 2 rectangles (D) 2″ x 5¾″
- 2 rectangles (E) 1¾″ x 12½″
- 4 rectangles (F) 1″ x 12½″
- 2 rectangles (G) 2″ x 4¼″

Assorted Pink, Orange and Brown Prints
- 5 squares (A) 2″ x 2″
- 6 rectangles (B) 2″ x 3½″

Sew the patches together as shown to complete the block.

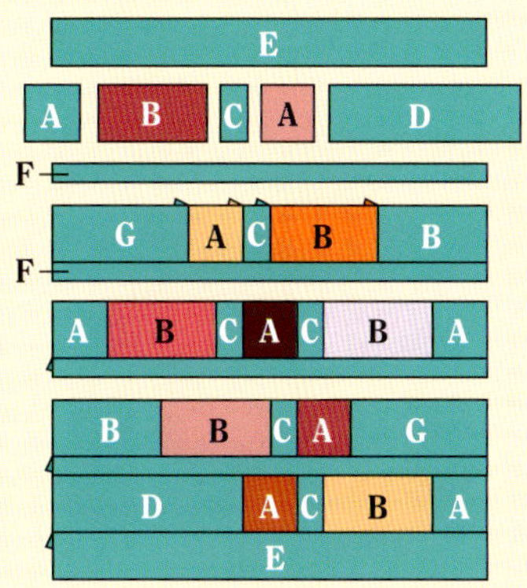

Block Piecing

block no. 769

Watercolor Dreams

by Dodi Lee Poulsen • Two Sisters at Squirrel Hollow
twosashquilts.com

Fabric: Modernology designed by Patricia Bravo for Art Gallery, artgalleryfabrics.com.

Dodi Lee Poulsen is the author of *Fresh from the Garden: 15 Quick and Easy Quilting Projects for Home Decor* for Landauer Corporation, landauercorp.com.

⧄ = cut in half diagonally

Pink Tone-on-Tone
12 squares (A) 2" x 2"

Light Teal Tone-on-Tone
8 squares (A) 2" x 2"
4 squares 2 3/8" x 2 3/8" ⧄ (B)
4 rectangles (D) 2" x 3 1/2"

Dark Blue Print
2 squares 3 7/8" x 3 7/8" ⧄ (C)
4 rectangles (D) 2" x 3 1/2"

Large Scale Floral
1 square (E) 6 1/2" x 6 1/2"

Sew the patches together as shown to complete the block.

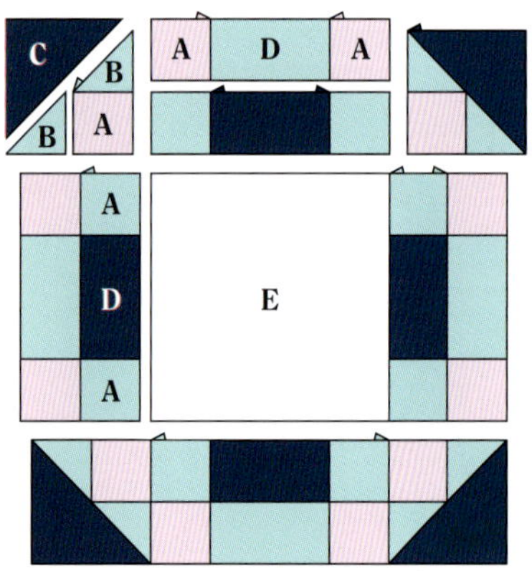

Block Piecing

block no. 770

Convergence

by Amy Rullkoetter • Freelance Editor, *Quiltmaker*
quiltmaker.com

⧄ = cut in half diagonally
⊠ = cut in half twice diagonally

Blue Print
4 squares (A) 1 7/8" x 1 7/8"

Beige Tone-on-Tone
16 squares (A) 1 7/8" x 1 7/8"
2 squares 3" x 3" ⧄ (B)

Blue Tone-on-Tone
8 rectangles (C) 1 7/8" x 3 1/4"

Green Print
2 squares 5 1/4" x 5 1/4" ⊠ (D)

Beige Multiprint
1 square (E) 6 1/2" x 6 1/2"

Dark Brown Stripe
2 squares 5 1/8" x 5 1/8" ⧄ (F)

Unit 1
Make 4

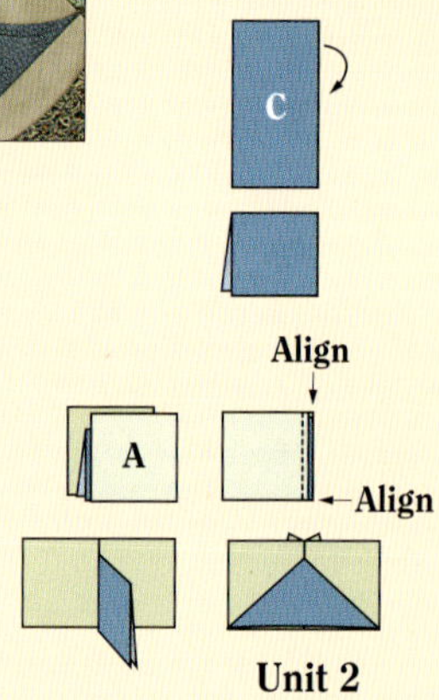

Unit 2
Make 8

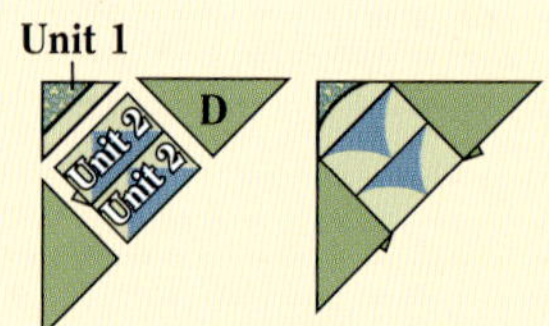

Section
Make 4

Fold each blue A in half diagonally, wrong sides together. Align the raw edges of the folded A's with the B's as shown. Baste 1/8" from the raw edges to make 4 unit 1's.

Fold a blue C rectangle in half with wrong sides together. With right sides together, layer the folded C between 2 beige A's, aligning the bottom and side raw edges (the fold will be at the top). Sew 1/4" from the side as shown. Open the seam and position the center fold of C over the seam, creating a triangle. Press in place. Repeat to make 8 unit 2's. Join the unit 1's, unit 2's and green D's to make 4 sections as shown.

Folded Edge
Make 4

Turn back the folded edges of the blue print A's and blue C's to form a gentle curve. Use matching thread and a straight stitch to sew down the folded edges. Sew the sections and patches E–F together as shown to complete the block.

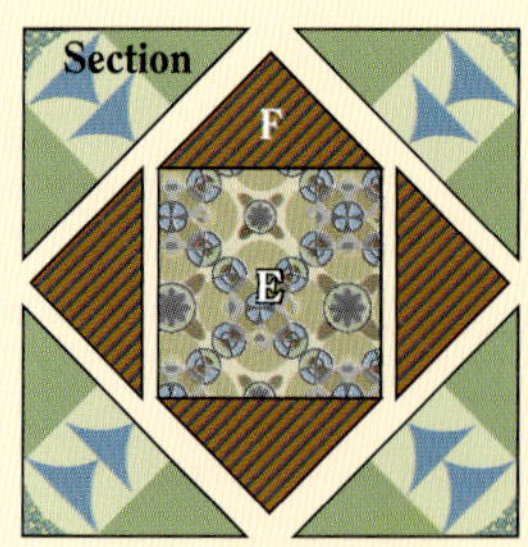

Block Assembly

pieced

block no. 771

Pinwheel Posey

by Denise Russart
justquiltin.wordpress.com

Fabric: Jakarta and Bliss Blenders, both from Hoffman California Fabrics, hoffmanfabrics.com.

⧄ = cut in half diagonally
⊠ = cut in half twice diagonally

Blue Print
- 4 rectangles (A) 3½″ x 6½″
- 4 rectangles (D) 2″ x 5¾″ (see diagram for further cutting)

Blue Tone-on-Tone
- 4 squares (B) 3½″ x 3½″
- 4 rectangles (C) 2″ x 6½″
- 2 squares 2⅜″ x 2⅜″ ⧄ (E)

Red Tone-on-Tone
- 4 squares (B) 3½″ x 3½″
- 1 square 4¼″ x 4¼″ ⊠ (F)

Gold Tone-on-Tone
- 2 squares 2⅜″ x 2⅜″ ⧄ (E)

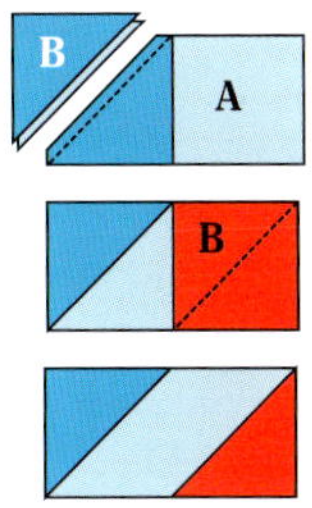

Unit
Stitch & Flip
Make 4

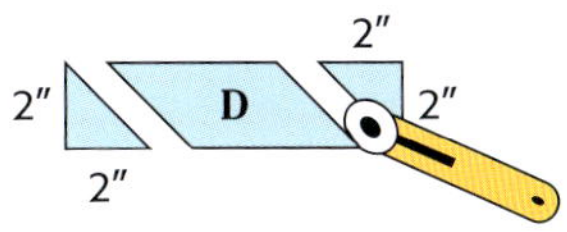

Refer to "Stitch-and-Flip" in the Techniques file on the PDF. Use the blue print A's with the blue tone-on-tone B's and red B's to make 4 units.

Sew the units and patches together as shown to complete the block.

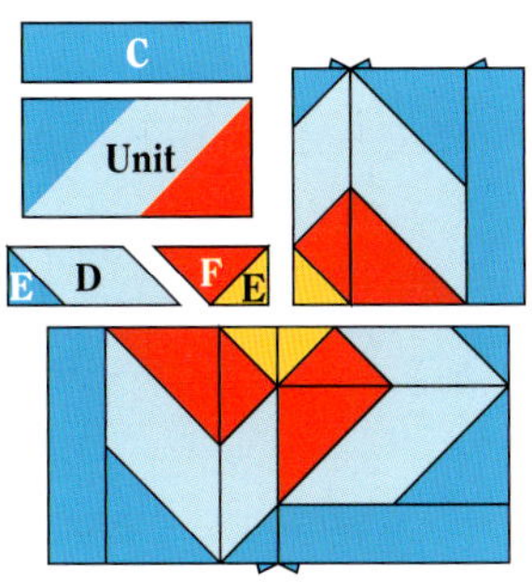

Block Assembly

block no. 772

Ginger and Fred

by Anita Grossman Solomon • Make It Simpler
makeitsimpler.com

Anita Grossman Solomon is the author of *Rotary Cutting Revolution and Make It Simpler Paper Piecing*, both for C&T Publishing, ctpub.com.

⧄ = cut in half diagonally

Red Print
- 4 rectangles (A) 3⅜″ x 6⅛″

Light Green Print
- 4 squares 2⅞″ x 2⅞″ ⧄ (B)
- 4 squares 4⅞″ x 4⅞″ ⧄ (C)

Anita used Electric Quilt Company software to design her block.

Sew the patches together as shown to complete the block.

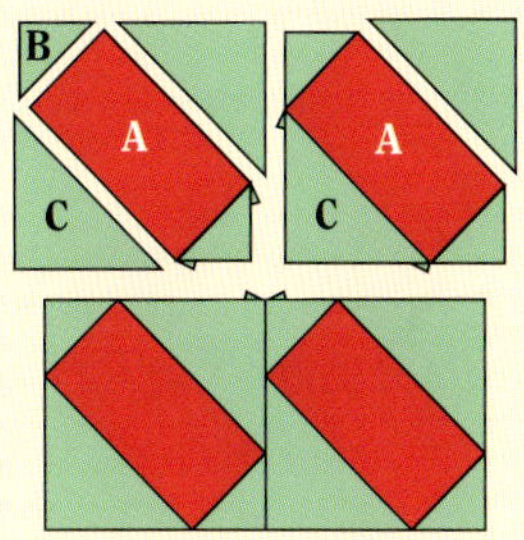

Block Piecing

block no. 773

Triangle Tracks

by Denise Starck • Graphic Designer, *Quiltmaker*
quiltmaker.com

Fabric: Central Park designed by Deborah Edwards for Northcott, northcott.net.

Light Green Tone-on-Tone
9 squares (A) 2⅜" x 2⅜"
8 rectangles (B) 2" x 3½"
2 squares (C) 2" x 2"
3 squares (D) 3½" x 3½"

Teal Tone-on-Tone
1 square (A) 2⅜" x 2⅜"
14 squares (C) 2" x 2"

Dark Brown Tone-on-Tone
8 squares (A) 2⅜" x 2⅜"

Brown Print
16 squares (C) 2" x 2"

Unit 1
Make 2

Unit 2
Make 16

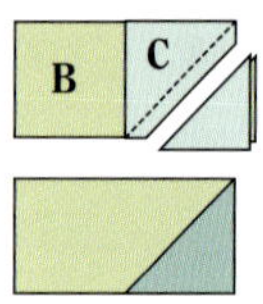

Unit 3
Stitch & Flip
Make 6

Pair a green A with the teal A to make 2 Triangle-Square unit 1's. Make 16 unit 2's using green A's and the dark brown A's.

Refer to "Stitch-and-Flip" in the Techniques file on the PDF. Use the green B's and teal C's to make 6 unit 3's and 2 unit 4's as shown. Make 3 unit 5's using the green D's and teal C's.

Sew the units and patches together as shown to complete the block.

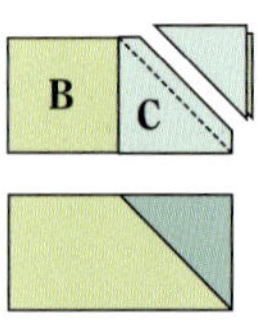

Unit 4
Stitch & Flip
Make 2

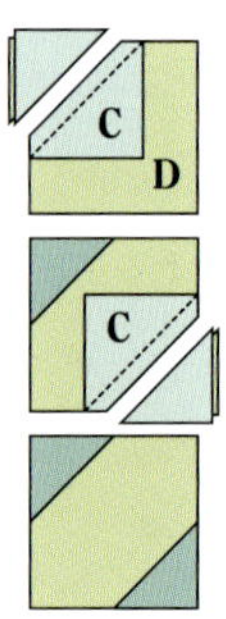

Unit 5
Stitch & Flip
Make 3

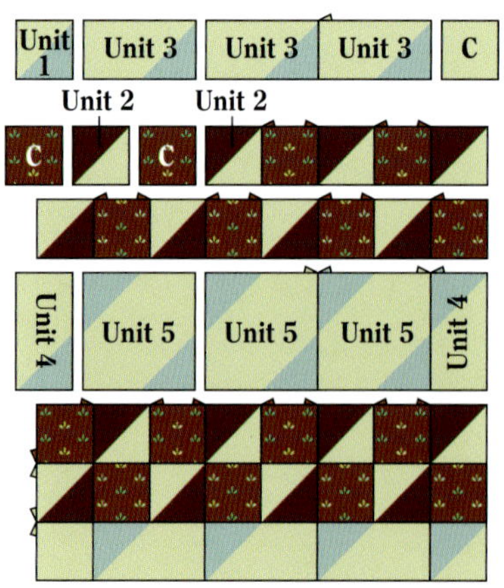

Block Assembly

pieced

block no. 774

Mirrored Ribbon Star

by Donna Lynn Thomas • Pre-furred Quilts
donnalynnthomas.com

Donna Lynn Thomas is the author of numerous books including *Flip Your Way to Fabulous Quilts* for Martingale & Co., martingale-pub.com.

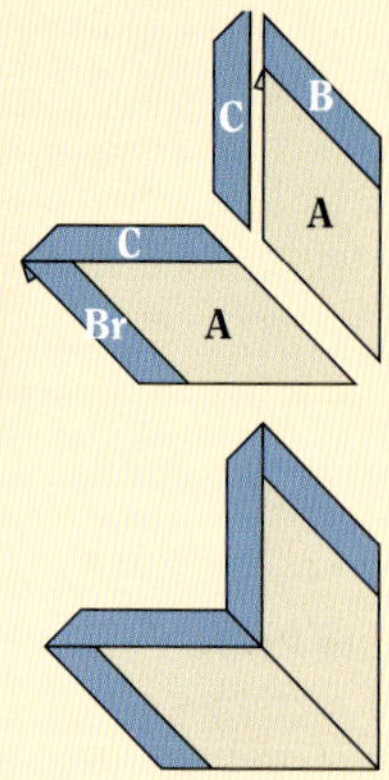

Section
Make 4

See page 181 on the PDF for pattern

◸ = cut in half diagonally
☒ = cut in half twice diagonally

Cream Print
8 template A

Medium Blue Tone-on-Tone
4 *each* templates B and Br
8 template C

Pale Green Print
2 squares 3½" x 3½" ◸ (D)
1 square 5½" x 5½" ☒ (E)
2 squares 4¾" x 4¾" ◸ (F)

Dark Blue Print
4 squares (G) 3" x 3"

To achieve a kaleidosopic affect, Donna fussy cut identical A's from the cream print.

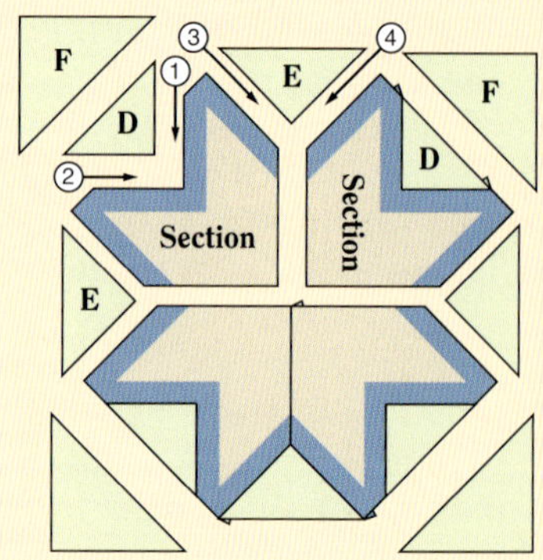

Block Assembly

Refer to "Set-in Seams" in the Techniques file on the PDF. Paying close attention to patch orientation, join 1 beige A with a blue B and a blue C. Repeat with an A, a Br and a C as shown. Sew each A/B/C to an A/Br/C to make a section. Repeat to make 4 sections.

Sew the sections and patches D–F together as shown, pressing the seams open to reduce bulk.

Refer to "Stitch-and-Flip" in the Techniques file on the PDF. Add a dark blue G to each corner as shown to complete the block.

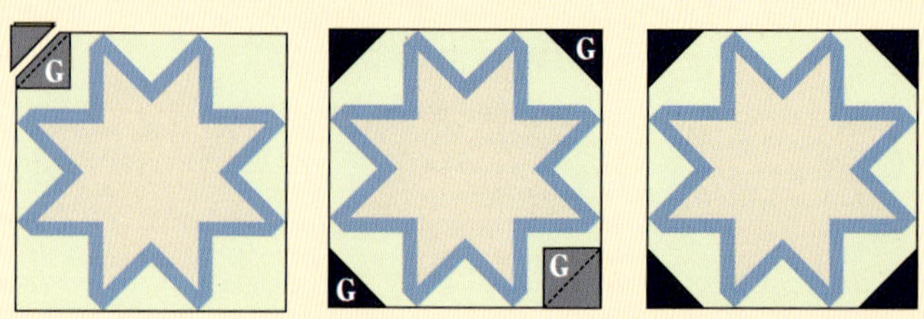

Stitch & Flip

block no. 775

Summer Breeze

by Pam Vieira-McGinnis
pamkittymorning.blogspot.com

Fabric: Doll Dresses and Annie's Farmstand, both designed by Holly Holderman for Lakehouse Dry Goods, lakehousedrygoods.com.

Blue Tone-on-Tone
3 squares (A) 4¼″x 4¼″

White Tone-on-Tone
14 squares (B) 2⅜″x 2⅜″
12 squares (C) 2″x 2″
4 rectangles (D) 2″x 6½″

Yellow Print
2 squares (B) 2⅜″x 2⅜″
8 squares (C) 2″x 2″

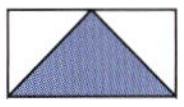

Flying Geese
Make 12

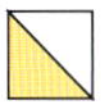

Unit from B's
Make 4

Make 12 Flying Geese using the blue A's and 12 of the white B's.

Pair the yellow B's with 2 white B's to make 4 Triangle-Square units. Sew the Flying Geese, units and patches together as shown to complete the block.

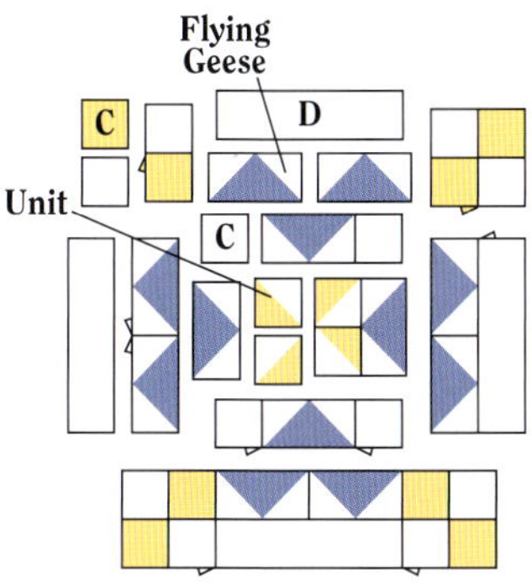

Block Assembly

block no. 776

Feng Shui

by Deborah C. Vollbracht • Creative Folk Quilting
creativefolkquilting.com

Black Solid
4 rectangles (A) 1¾″x 11¼″
4 rectangles (E) 1¾″x 2½″

Light Gray Solid
2 rectangles (B) 1¾″x 9¼″
2 rectangles (D) 1¾″x 4¾″

Medium Gray Solid
4 rectangles (C) 1¾″x 7″

Dark Gray Solid
2 rectangles (B) 1¾″x 9¼″
2 rectangles (D) 1¾″x 4¾″

Orange Batik
1 square (F) 5½″x 5½″

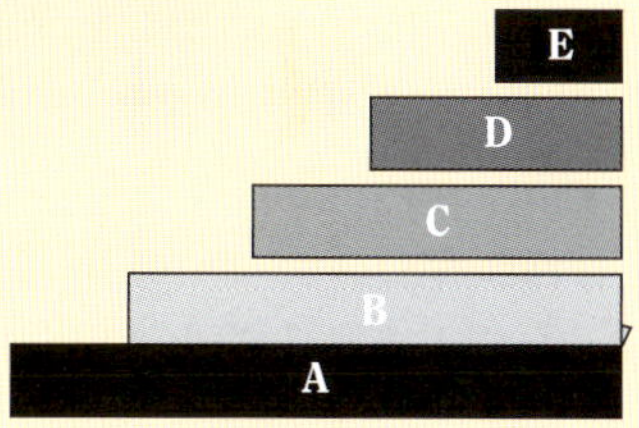

Section 1
Make 2

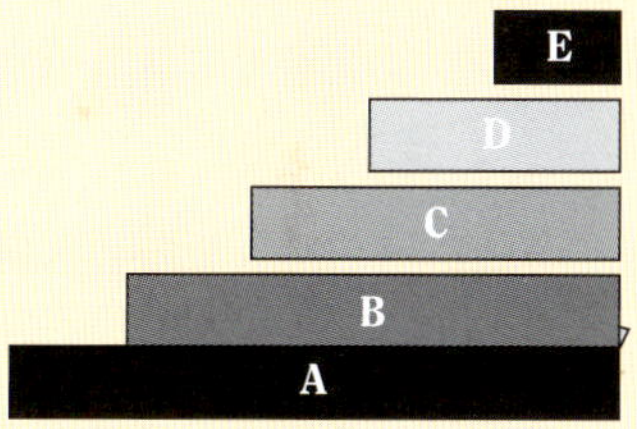

Section 2
Make 2

Sew patches A–E together as shown to make 2 section 1's and 2 section 2's. Sew a section 1 to the top of F with a partial seam as shown. Sew a section 1 to the right as shown. Sew the section 2's to the bottom and left as shown. Complete the partial seam.

Center the design and trim to 12½″ × 12½″.

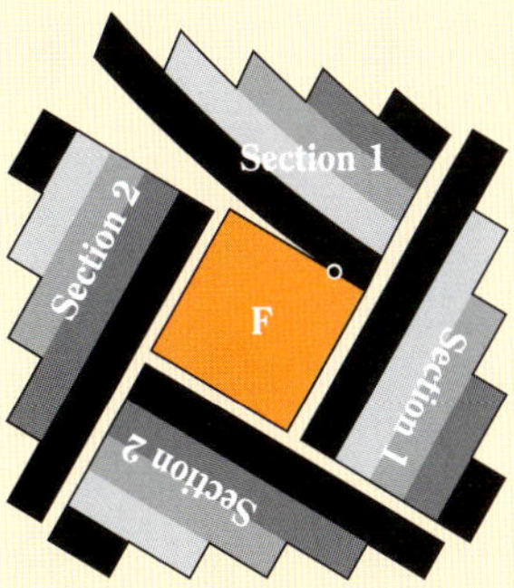

Block Assembly
• = Partial Seam

Trimming Diagram

block no. 777

Reflecting Cityscape

by Pippa Eccles Armbrester • Pippa Patchwork
pippapatchwork.com

Dark Purple Solid, Orange Solid, Yellow Solid and Green Solid
from *each*
- 1 strip 1¼″x 15″
- 3 rectangles (A) 1″x 5″

Red Solid, Turquoise Solid, Dark Blue Solid and Medium Purple Solid
from *each*
- 1 strip 1¼″x 10″
- 3 rectangles (B) 1″x 3½″

Black Solid
- 4 rectangles (C) 2″x 3½″
- 4 squares (D) 3½″x 3½″

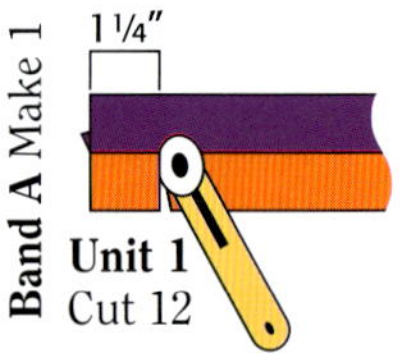

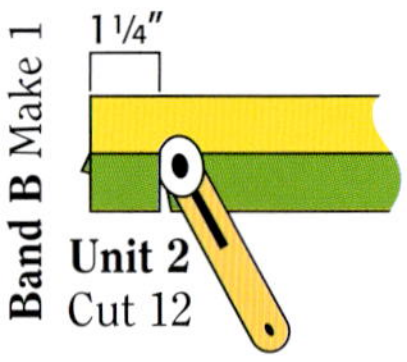

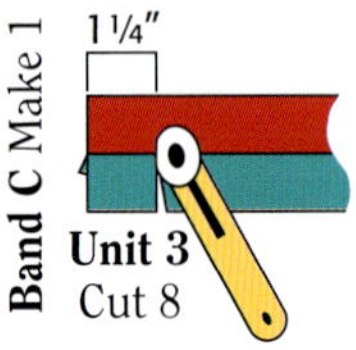

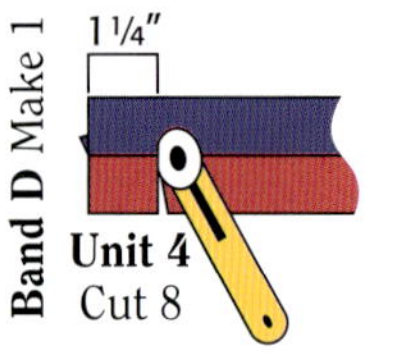

Join the dark purple strip with the orange strip and the yellow strip with the green strip as shown to make 1 band A and 1 band B. Cut the bands at 1¼" increments to make 12 unit 1's and 12 unit 2's.

Join the red and turquoise strips and the dark blue and medium purple strips as shown to make bands C and D. Cut the C and D bands at 1¼" increments to make 8 unit 3's and 8 unit 4's.

Sew the units and patches together as shown to complete the block.

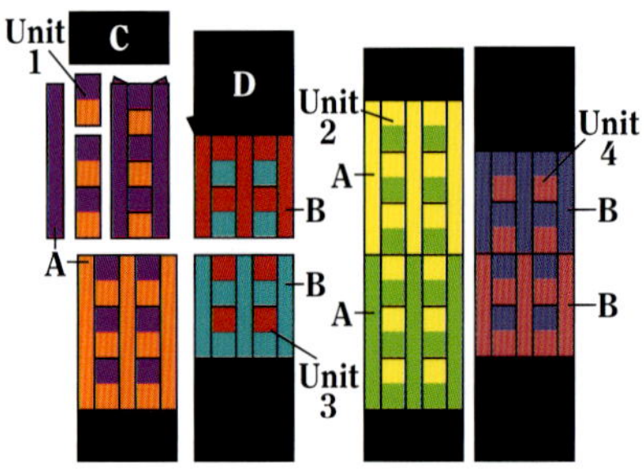

Block Assembly

block no. 778

Pecking Order

by Laurie Baker

Laurie Baker is the co-author of *Homestyle Quilts: Simple Patterns and Savory Recipes* for Martingale & Co., shopmartingale.com.

⊠ = cut in half twice diagonally

Assorted Cream Tone-on-Tones
- 6 squares 4¼″x 4¼″ ⊠ (A)

12 Assorted Medium Prints and Tone-on-Tones from *8*
- 1 square 4¼″x 4¼″ ⊠ (A) (you will have 24 extras for additional blocks)

from *4*
- 1 square 7¼″x 7¼″ ⊠ (B) (you will have 12 extras for additional blocks)

2 Red Prints
from *each*
- 1 square 7¼″x 7¼″ ⊠ (B) (you will have 4 extras for additional blocks)

Block Piecing

By cutting the A's and B's as instructed, the outside edges of the block are stabilized by the straight grain of the fabric patches.

Sew the patches together as shown to complete the block.

block no. 779

Don't Feed the Animals

by Lori Baker • Creative Editor, *Quilters Newsletter*
quiltersnewsletter.com

Fabric: Baby Safari designed by Carina Gardner for Northcott, northcott.net.

Light Aqua Print and Light Purple Tone-on-Tone
from *each*
8 squares (A) $2\frac{3}{8}$" x $2\frac{3}{8}$"

White Tone-on-Tone
16 squares (B) 2" x 2"

Dark Brown Print #1
4 squares (B) 2" x 2"

Aqua Tone-on-Tone
4 rectangles (C) $3\frac{1}{2}$" x 5"

Dark Brown Print #2
1 square (D) $3\frac{1}{2}$" x $3\frac{1}{2}$"

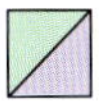

Unit
Make 16

Pair the light aqua A's with the light purple A's to make 16 Triangle-Square units.

Sew the units and patches together as shown to complete the block.

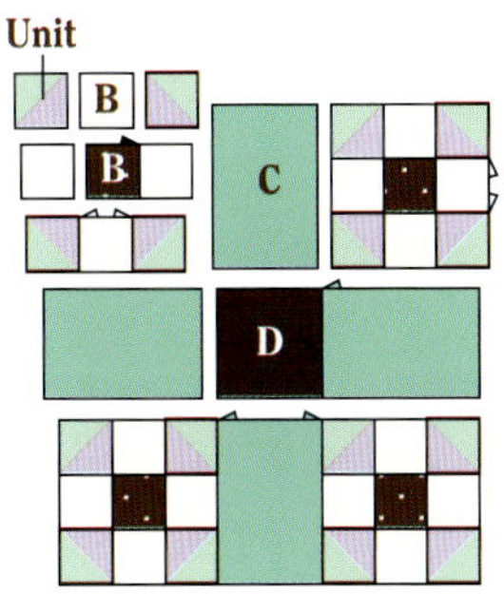

Block Assembly

block no. 780

Shady

by Jina Barney • Jina Barney Designz
jinabarneydesignz.com

Fabric: Shades from Riley Blake Designs, rileyblakedesigns.com

⧄ = cut in half diagonally
⊠ = cut in half twice diagonally

Cream Tone-on-Tone
6 squares (A) 3" x 3"
1 square $4\frac{1}{4}$" x $4\frac{1}{4}$" ⊠ (B) (you will have 2 extras)
1 square $9\frac{7}{8}$" x $9\frac{7}{8}$" ⧄ (C)

Pink Tone-on-Tone
2 squares (A) 3" x 3"
1 square $4\frac{1}{4}$" x $4\frac{1}{4}$" ⊠ (B) (you will have 2 extras)

Gray Tone-on-Tone and Light Green Tone-on-Tone
from *each*
2 squares (A) 3" x 3"

Unit 1
Make 4

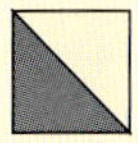

Unit 2
Make 4

Unit 3
Make 4

Pair 2 cream A's with the pink A's to make 4 Triangle-Square unit 1's. Make 4 unit 2's using 2 cream A's and the gray A's. Use 2 cream A's and the light green A's to make 4 unit 3's.

Sew the units and patches together as shown to complete the block.

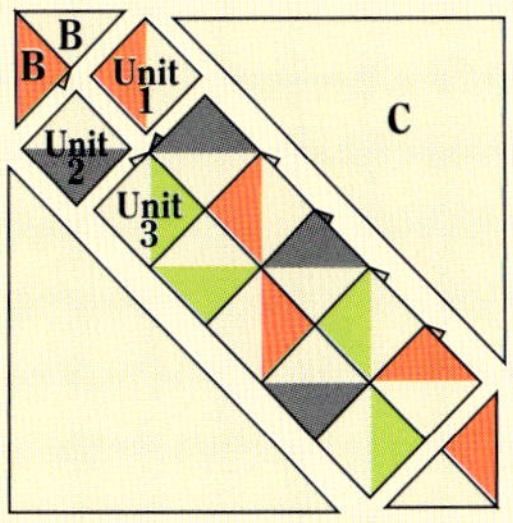

Block Assembly

block no. 781

Disappearing Act

by Carolyn Beam • Creative Editor, *Quiltmaker*
quiltmaker.com

Fabric: Planes, Trains & Automobiles from Timeless Treasures, ttfabrics.net.

Black Solid
- 2 squares (A) 1½" x 1½"
- 2 rectangles (B) 1½" x 2½"

Cream Solid
- 12 squares (A) 1½" x 1½"
- 4 rectangles (B) 1½" x 2½"
- 6 rectangles (C) 1½" x 3½"
- 4 squares (D) 3½" x 3½"
- 2 rectangles (F) 1½" x 4½"

Gold Check
- 10 squares (A) 1½" x 1½"
- 4 rectangles (B) 1½" x 2½"

Gold Solid
- 2 squares (A) 1½" x 1½"
- 4 rectangles (C) 1½" x 3½"

Black Print #1
- 2 squares (E) 2½" x 2½"

Black Print #2
- 1 square (G) 4½" x 4½"

Sew the patches together as shown to complete the block.

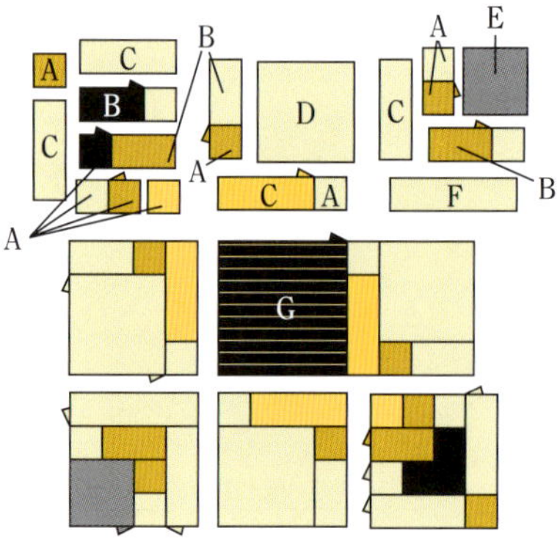

Block Piecing

block no. 782

Traveling Eddie

by Sarah Bisel
milkandhoneydesigns.blogspot.com

Sarah Bisel is the author of *Fast, Flirty, and Fun—Easy Quilts from Fabulous Fabrics* for Martingale & Co., shopmartingale.com.

White Solid
- 6 squares (A) 2⅞" x 2⅞"
- 1 square (B) 5¼" x 5¼"
- 4 rectangles (D) 2½" x 4½"

Gray Solid
- 2 squares (A) 2⅞" x 2⅞"

Orange Print #1
- 4 squares (A) 2⅞" x 2⅞"

Dark Teal Print
- 4 squares (A) 2⅞" x 2⅞"
- 4 squares (C) 2½" x 2½"

Orange Print #2 and Light Teal Print from *each*
- 2 squares (C) 2½" x 2½"

Unit 1
Make 4

Unit 2
Make 8

Flying Geese
Make 4

Pair 2 white A's with the gray A's to make 4 Triangle-Square unit 1's. Make 8 unit 2's using 4 white A's and the orange print #1 A's.

Use the white B and dark teal A's to make 4 Flying Geese.

Sew the units and patches together as shown to complete the block.

Block Assembly

block no. 783

Split Decision

by Laura Blanchard • Plum Tree Quilts
plumtreequilts.com

⊠ = cut in half twice diagonally

Dark Brown Batik and Medium Brown Batik
from *each*
- 1 square (A) 3″ x 3″
- 4 rectangles (B) 2⅝″ x 7¼″
- 4 squares (C) 2⅝″ x 2⅝″

Cream Batik
- 2 squares (A) 3″ x 3″
- 1 square 7¾″ x 7¾″ ⊠ (D)

Unit 1
Make 2 from A's

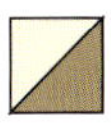

Unit 2
Make 2 from A's

Unit 3
Stitch & Flip
Make 4

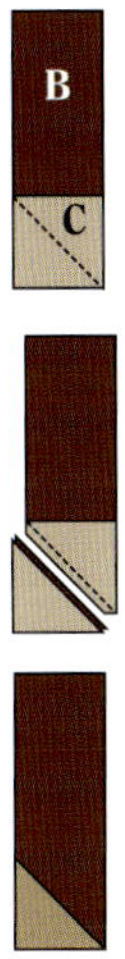

Unit 4
Stitch & Flip
Make 4

Pair the dark brown A with a cream A to make 2 Triangle-Square unit 1's. Make 2 unit 2's using the medium brown A and a cream A.

Refer to "Stitch-and-Flip" in the Techniques file on the PDF. Use the medium brown B's and dark brown C's to make 4 unit 3's. Make 4 unit 4's using the dark brown B's and medium brown C's.

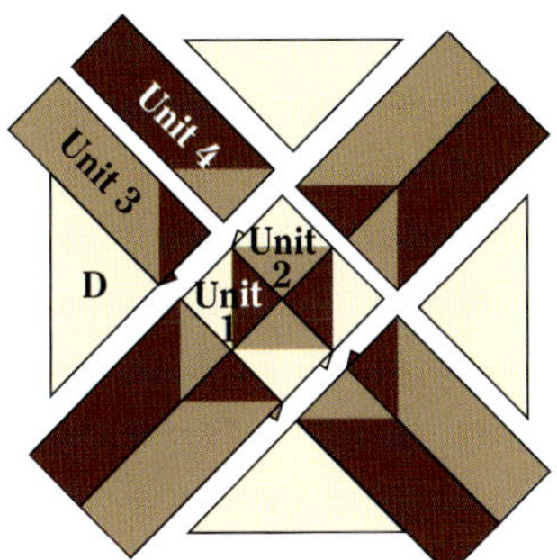

Block Assembly

Sew the units and patches together as shown. Center the design and trim to 12½" × 12½" to finish the block.

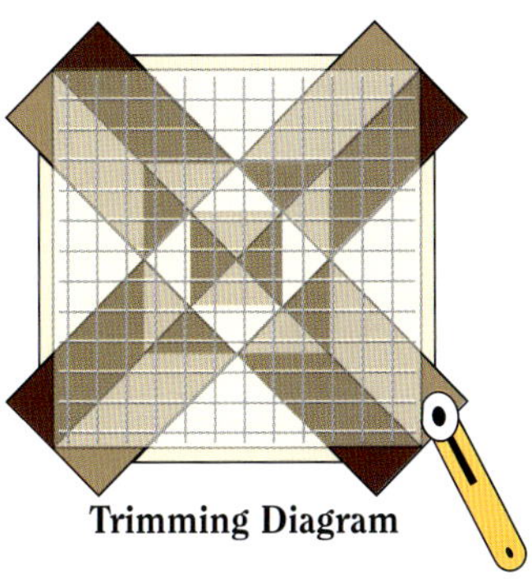

Trimming Diagram

block no. 784

3-D Split Rail Fence

by Kathy Brown • The Teacher's Pet
the-teachers-pet.com

Fabric: Sassy designed by Sandy Gervais for Moda Fabrics, unitednotions.com.

Kathy Brown is the author of *More Take 5 Quilts—16 New Quick and Easy Projects* for Martingale & Co., shopmartingale.com.

Teal Print #1, Teal Print #2 and Orange Print
from *each*
- 4 rectangles (A) 2½″ x 6½″

Cream Solid
- 12 rectangles (A) 2½″ x 6½″

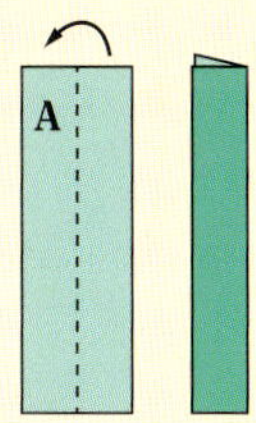

Folding Diagram

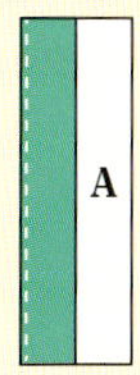

Unit
Make 12

The teal and orange patches are folded to add dimension to this block.

Fold a print rectangle in half lengthwise with wrong sides together and press. Align the raw edges of the print rectangle with the left raw edge of a cream rectangle; baste ⅛" from the raw edge on the long side of the rectangles as shown to make a unit. Repeat with the remaining rectangles to make 12 units.

Sew the units together as shown to complete the block.

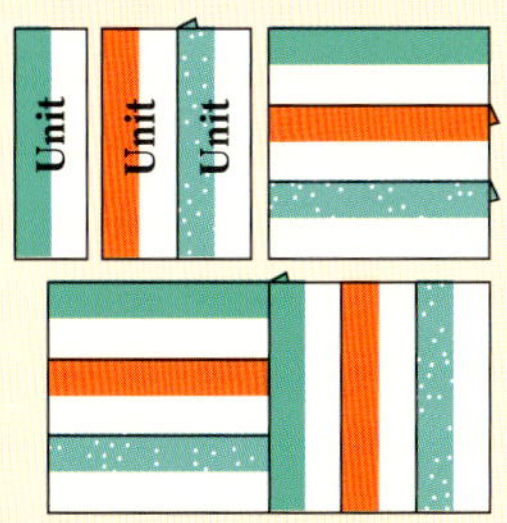

Block Assembly

block no. 785
Coffee Mill

by Jennifer Chiaverini • Elm Creek Quilts
elmcreek.net

Fabric: Elm Creek Quilts: Rosa's Collection designed by Jennifer Chiaverini for Red Rooster Fabrics, redroosterfabrics.com.

Best-selling author Jennifer Chiaverini has written several books including *Traditions from Elm Creek Quilts* for C&T Publishing, ctpub.com.

⧄ = cut in half diagonally
⊠ = cut in half twice diagonally

Dark Purple Tone-on-Tone
2 squares (A) 2 7/8" x 2 7/8"
2 squares 4 7/8" x 4 7/8" ⧄ (C)

Cream Tone-on-Tone
2 squares (A) 2 7/8" x 2 7/8"
2 squares 4 7/8" x 4 7/8" ⧄ (C)
1 square 5 1/4" x 5 1/4" ⊠ (D)

Gold Tone-on-Tone
4 squares 2 7/8" x 2 7/8" ⧄ (B)

Medium Purple Tone-on-Tone
1 square 5 1/4" x 5 1/4" ⊠ (D)
1 square (E) 4 1/2" x 4 1/2"

Unit
Make 4

Pair the dark purple A's with the cream A's to make 4 Triangle-Square units.

Sew the units and patches together as shown to complete the block.

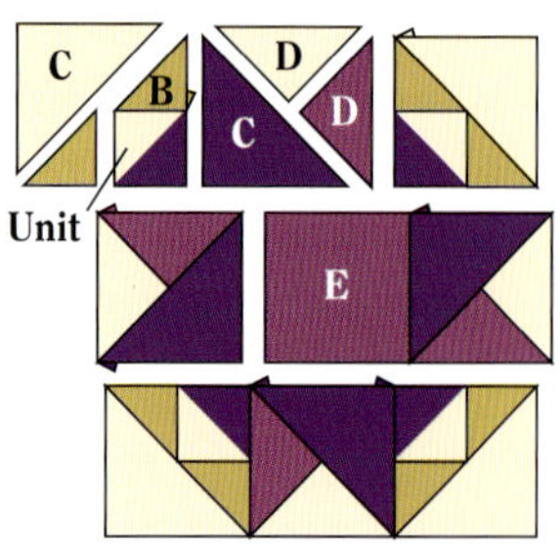

Block Assembly

pieced

block no. 786
Smoky Mountains

by Karen Combs • Karen Combs Studio
karencombs.com

Fabric: Serendipity designed by Karen Combs for Troy Riverwoods Collection, troy-corp.com.

Karen Combs is the author of *Celtic Pieced Illusions* for American Quilter's Society, americanquilter.com.

⧄ = cut in half diagonally

Medium Purple Batik, Medium Gray Batik, Medium Blue Batik and Medium Brown Batik
from *each*
2 squares (A) 2 7/8" x 2 7/8"

Dark Purple Batik, Light Gray Batik, Dark Blue Batik and Light Brown Batik
from *each*
1 square (A) 2 7/8" x 2 7/8"

Light Purple Batik and Light Blue Batik
from *each*
3 squares 2 7/8" x 2 7/8" ⧄ (B)

Dark Gray Batik and Dark Brown Batik
from *each*
1 square 6 7/8" x 6 7/8" ⧄ (C)

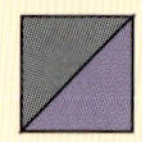

Unit 1
Make 4

Unit 2
Make 2

Unit 3
Make 4

Unit 4
Make 2

Serendipity is a gradated fabric line. Karen cut each color's light, medium and dark patches from one fabric.

Pair the medium purple A's with medium gray A's to make 4 Triangle-Square unit 1's. Make 2 unit 2's using the dark purple A and light gray A.

Pair the medium blue A's with medium brown A's to make 4 unit 3's. Make 2 unit 4's using the dark blue A and light brown A.

Sew the units and patches together as shown to complete the block.

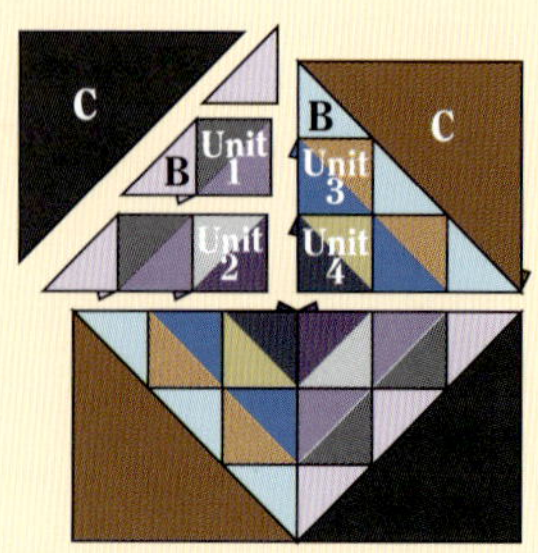

Block Assembly

block no. 787

LOVE Squared

by Julie Comstock • Cosmo Cricket
cosmocricket.com

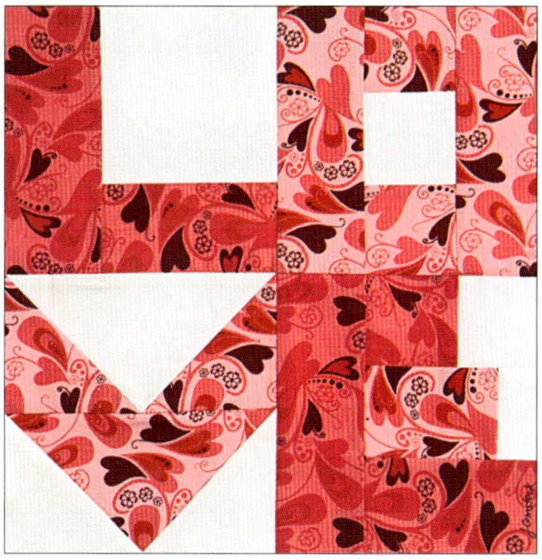

Fabric: Chemistry designed by Julie Comstock for Moda Fabrics, unitednotions.com.

White Solid
- 1 rectangle (A) 3½" x 6½"
- 2 squares (B) 3½" x 3½"
- 1 square (C) 4½" x 4½"
- 2 squares (F) 2½" x 2½"
- 1 rectangle (H) 1½" x 2½"

Medium Pink Print
- 1 rectangle (A) 3½" x 6½"
- 2 squares (B) 3½" x 3½"
- 2 rectangles (E) 2½" x 6½"
- 2 squares (F) 2½" x 2½"
- 1 rectangle (G) 2½" x 3½"

Dark Pink Print
- 2 rectangles (D) 2½" x 4½"
- 2 rectangles (E) 2½" x 6½"
- 1 square (F) 2½" x 2½"

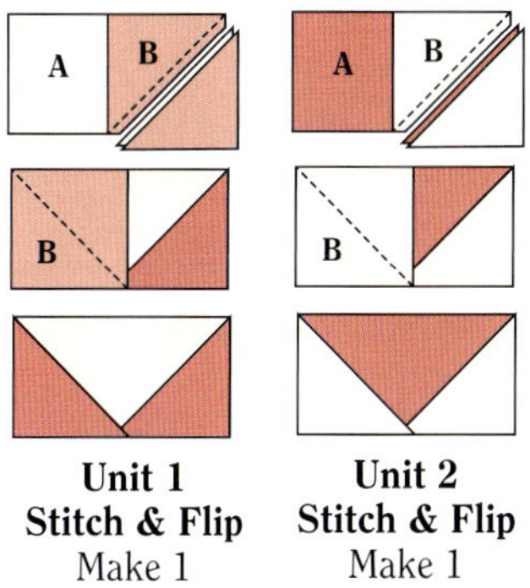

Refer to "Stitch-and-Flip" in the Techniques file on the PDF. Use the white A and medium pink B's to make unit 1. Use the medium pink A and white B's to make unit 2.

Sew the units and patches together as shown to complete the block.

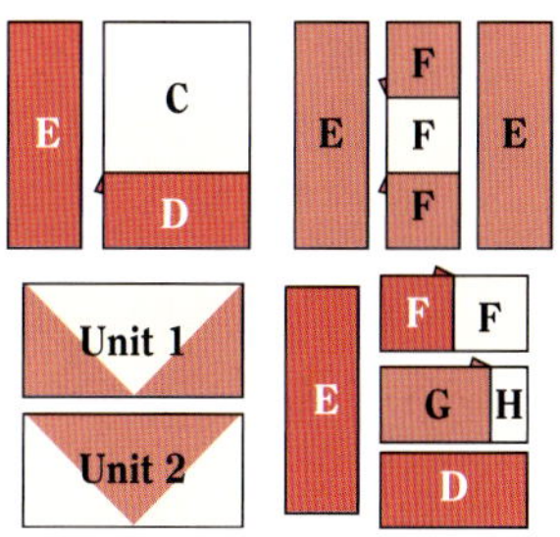

Block Assembly

block no. 788

Checkerboard Star

by Evonne Cook • Clothesline Quilts
clotheslinequilts.com

Fabric: Assorted collections designed by Jo Morton for Andover Fabrics, andoverfabrics.com.

Red Tone-on-Tone and Dark Blue Tone-on-Tone
from *each*
- 4 squares (A) 2⅞" x 2⅞"

Tan Tone-on-Tone #1
- 8 squares (A) 2⅞" x 2⅞"
- 4 squares (C) 2½" x 2½"

Dark Blue Print
- 1 square (B) 5¼" x 5¼"

Red Print
- 4 rectangles (D) 1½" x 4½"

Tan Tone-on-Tone #2
- 4 rectangles (D) 1½" x 4½"
- 8 squares (E) 1½" x 1½"

Gold Print
- 8 squares (E) 1½" x 1½"

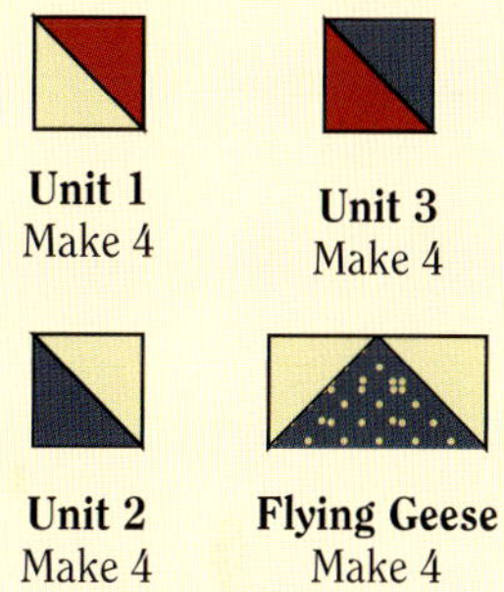

Pair 2 red tone-on-tone A's with tan #1 A's to make 4 Triangle-Square unit 1's. Make 4 unit 2's using blue tone-on-tone A's and tan #1 A's. Use red tone-on-tone A's and blue tone-on-tone A's to make 4 unit 3's.

Use the blue print B and tan #1 A's to make 4 Flying Geese. Sew the Flying Geese, units and patches together as shown to complete the block.

Block Assembly

block no. 789

Square City

by Elizabeth Dackson
dontcallmebetsy.com

5 Aqua Tone-on-Tones
from *4*
 16 squares (A) 2″ x 2″ (see below)
from *1*
 4 squares (B) 3½″ x 3½″
5 Gray Tone-on-Tones
from *4*
 16 squares (A) 2″ x 2″ (see below)
from *1*
 4 squares (B) 3½″ x 3½″

Note that each Four Patch within the block uses 2 matching aqua A's and 2 matching gray A's. Sew the patches together as shown to complete the block.

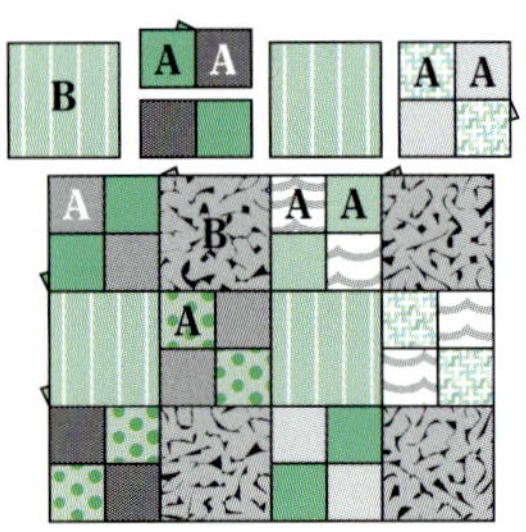

Block Piecing

block no. 790

Shortcut

by June Dudley • Editor-in-Chief, *Quiltmaker*
quiltmaker.com

Fabric: Artisan Batiks from Lunn Studios for Robert Kaufman, robertkaufman.com.

Tan Batik and Dark Purple Batik
from *each*
 2 squares (A) 3⅞″ x 3⅞″
Light Purple Batik and Dark Teal Batik
from *each*
 2 squares (B) 3½″ x 3½″
Medium Purple Batik #1 and Light Teal Batik
from *each*
 1 square (B) 3½″ x 3½″
Medium Purple Batik #2 and Medium Teal Batik from *each*
 1 square (B) 3½″ x 3½″
 1 rectangle (C) 3½″ x 6½″

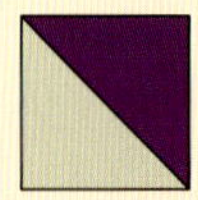

Unit
Make 4

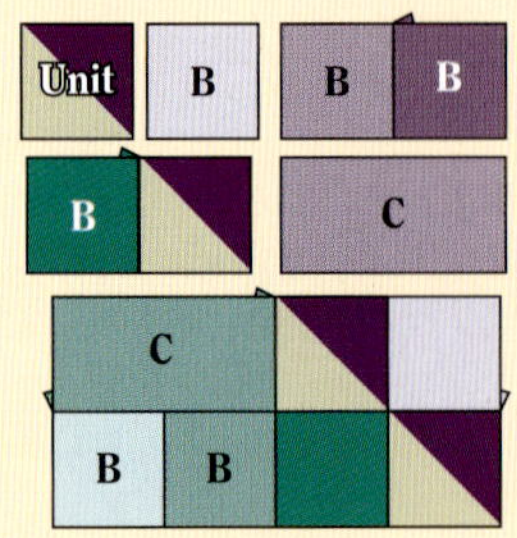

Block Assembly

Pair the tan A's with the dark purple A's to make 4 Triangle-Square units.

Sew the units and patches together as shown to complete the block.

pieced

block no. 791

X-act

by Victoria Eapen • Spun Sugar Quilts
spunsugarquilt.com

Fabric: Ruby and Bliss, both designed by Bonnie and Camille for Moda Fabrics, unitednotions.com.

= cut in half diagonally

White Tone-on-Tone
2 squares (A) 3⅞" x 3⅞"
2 squares 3⅞" x 3⅞" (B)

Red Dot
2 squares (A) 3⅞" x 3⅞"
2 squares 3⅞" x 3⅞" (B)
2 rectangles (C) 3½" x 6½"

Aqua Print, Pink Tone-on-Tone, Pink Print and Aqua Tone-on-Tone
from *each*
1 square 3⅞" x 3⅞" (B)

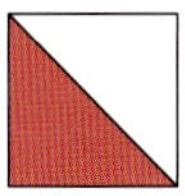

Unit
Make 4

Pair the white A's with the red A's to make 4 Triangle-Square units. Sew the units and patches together as shown to complete the block.

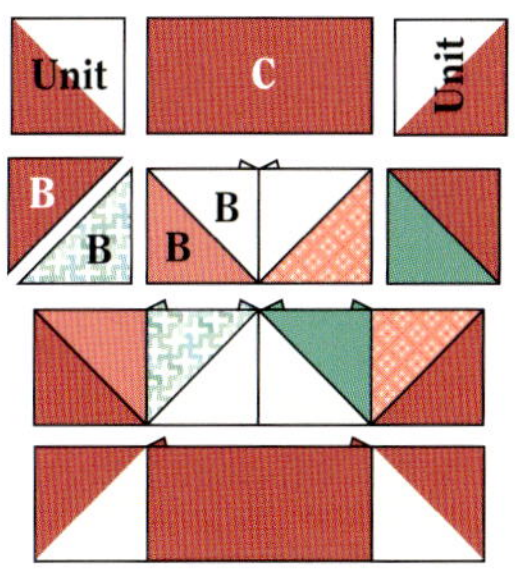

Block Assembly

block no. 792

Fire Burst

by Gudrun Erla • GE Designs
gequiltdesigns.com

Fabric: Reflections designed by Gudrun Erla for Red Rooster Fabrics, redroosterfabrics.com.

Gudrun Erla is the author of *Big Blocks—Big Style* and others, all for GE Designs, gequiltdesigns.com.

= cut in half diagonally

Medium Gray Print
2 rectangles (A) 3½" x 6½"

Red Tone-on-Tone
3 squares (B) 3½" x 3½"
1 square 3⅞" x 3⅞" (D)
(there will be 1 extra)

Light Gray Tone-on-Tone
1 rectangle (A) 3½" x 6½"
5 squares (B) 3½" x 3½"

Dark Gray Tone-on-Tone
2 rectangles (C) 3½" x 9½"

Yellow Print
1 square (B) 3½" x 3½"

White Print
1 square 3⅞" x 3⅞" (D)
(there will be 1 extra)

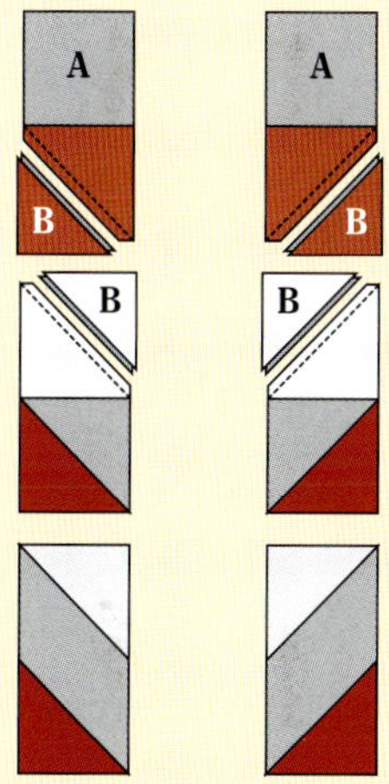

Unit 1
Stitch & Flip
Make 1

Unit 2
Stitch & Flip
Make 1

Refer to "Stitch-and-Flip" in the Techniques file on the PDF. Use the medium gray A's, the red B's and 2 light gray B's to make the unit 1 and unit 2 as shown. Use the dark gray C's and light gray B's to make the unit 3 and unit 4.

Sew the units and patches together as shown to complete the block.

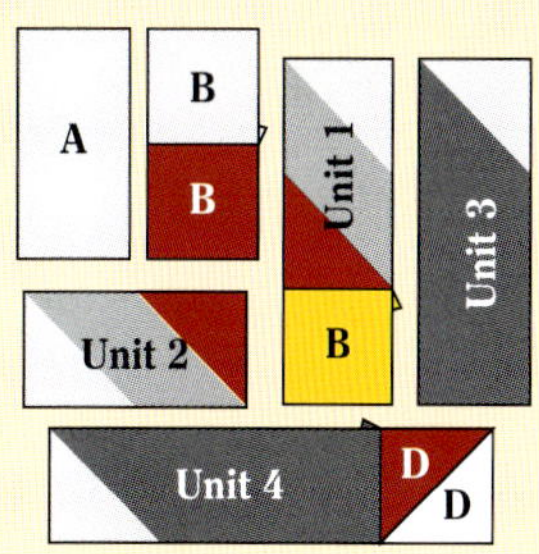

Block Assembly

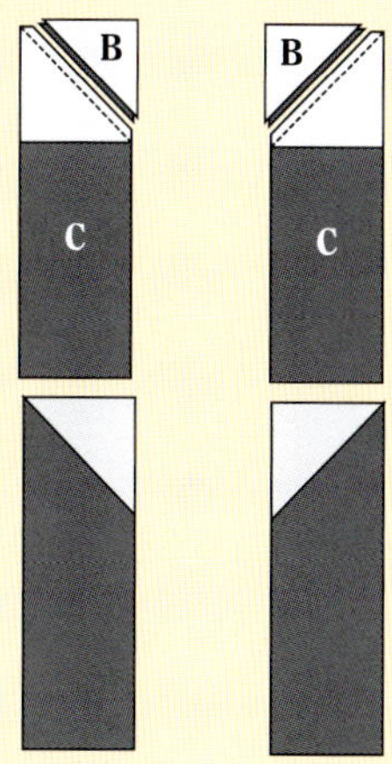

Unit 3
Stitch & Flip
Make 1

Unit 4
Stitch & Flip
Make 1

block no. 793

Cross Keys

by Gina Gempesaw • Gem Hill Quilts
gemhillquilts.blogspot.com

Light Blue Batik
8 squares (A) 2⅞″ x 2⅞″

Medium Blue Dot and Dark Blue Tone-on-Tone
from each
5 squares (A) 2⅞″ x 2⅞″

Green Tone-on-Tone
2 squares (A) 2⅞″ x 2⅞″
8 squares (B) 2½″ x 2½″

White Tone-on-Tone
8 squares (B) 2½″ x 2½″

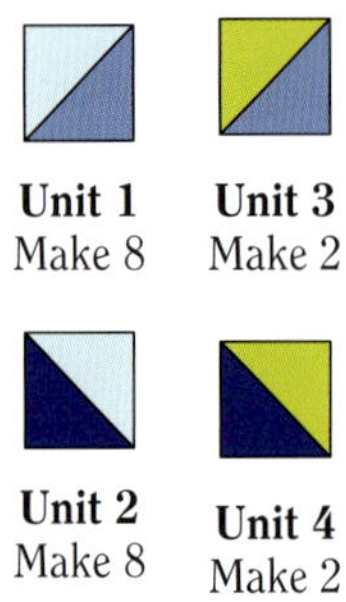

Pair 4 light blue A's with 4 medium blue dot A's to make 8 Triangle-Square unit 1's. Make 8 unit 2's using 4 light blue A's and 4 dark blue A's. Use a medium blue dot A and a green A to make 2 unit 3's. Make 2 unit 4's using a dark blue A and green A.

Sew the units and patches together as shown to complete the block.

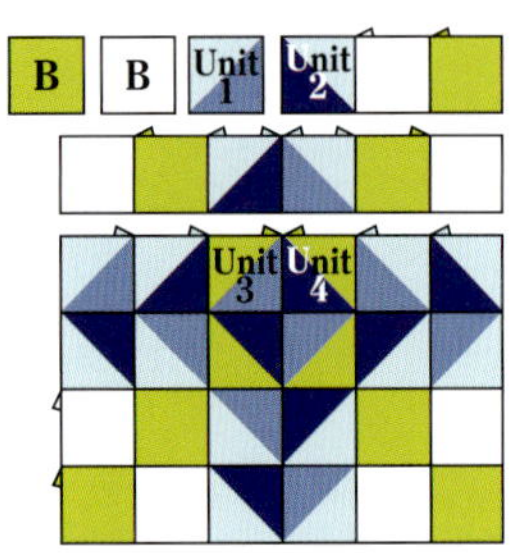

Block Assembly

block no. 794

Sawtooth Log Cabin

by Kay Gentry • Noble Needle Quilting and Sewing
nobleneedle.com

Dark Brown Tone-on-Tone and Tan Print
from each
9 squares (A) 2⅜″ x 2⅜″

Green Tone-on-Tone and Rust Tone-on-Tone
from each
5 squares (A) 2⅜″ x 2⅜″
1 rectangle (B) 2″ x 3½″
1 rectangle (C) 2″ x 5″
1 rectangle (D) 2″ x 9½″
1 rectangle (E) 2″ x 11″

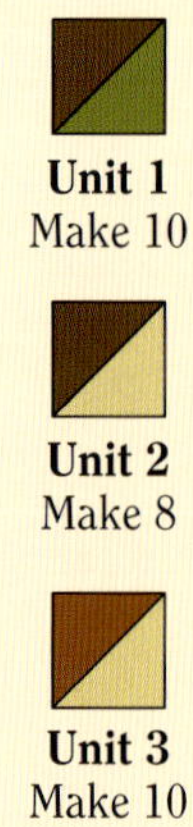

Pair 5 dark brown A's with the green A's to make 10 Triangle-Square unit 1's. Make 8 unit 2's using 4 dark brown A's and 4 tan A's. Pair 5 tan A's with the rust A's to make 10 unit 3's.

Sew the units and patches together as shown to complete the block.

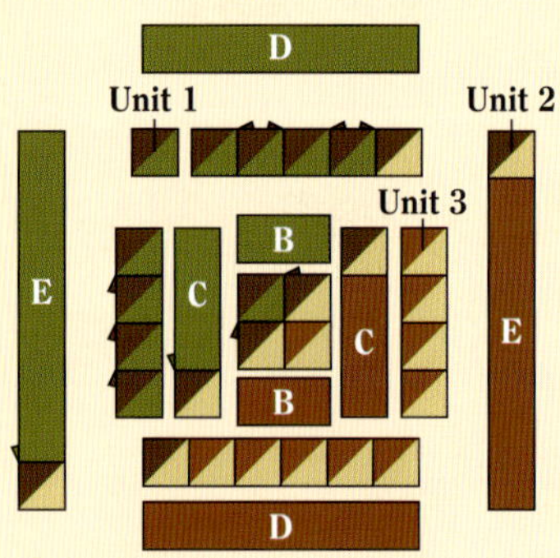

Block Assembly

block no. 795
Tic Tac Toe

by Diane Harris • Interactive Editor, *Quiltmaker*
quiltmaker.com

Fabric: Chicopee by Denyse Schmidt for FreeSpirit. freespiritfabric.com.

Dark Gray Tone-on-Tone
8 squares (A) 2½" x 2½"
2 rectangles (C) 1½" x 10½"
2 rectangles (D) 1½" x 12½"
Lime Green Print
6 squares (A) 2½" x 2½"
2 rectangles (B) 2½" x 10½"
Light Turquoise Tone-on-Tone
1 square (A) 2½" x 2½"

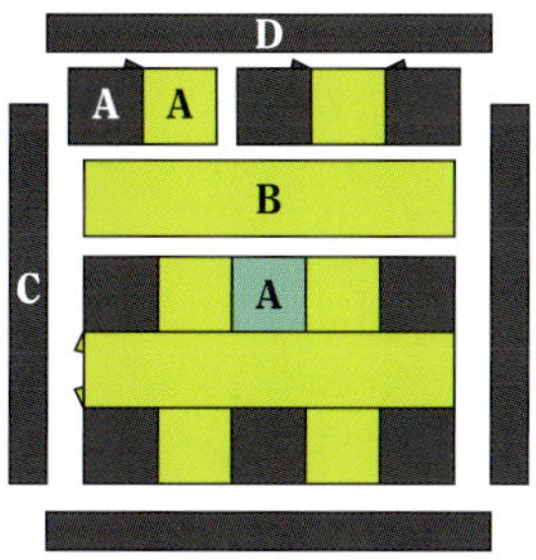

Block Piecing

Sew the patches together as shown to complete the block.

block no. 796
Poinsettia Plaid

by Pat Harrison • Ocean Waves Quilting Co.
oceanwavesqc.com

Fabric: Holiday Dazzle from Studio 8 for Quilting Treasures, quiltingtreasures.com.

Cream Print #1
1 square (A) 6½" x 6½" (Pat fussy cut this square from a large print)
Black Print #1
4 squares (B) 2" x 2"
4 squares (H) 3½" x 3½"
Cream Tone-on-Tone
4 rectangles (C) 1¼" x 3½"
16 rectangles (G) 1" x 3½"
Black Print #2
8 squares (D) 1¼" x 1¼"
8 rectangles (F) 1¼" x 2¾"
Cream Print #2
4 rectangles (E) 2" x 2¾"
Red Plaid
8 rectangles (G) 1" x 3½"

Unit 1
Stitch & Flip
Make 1

Refer to "Stitch-and-Flip" in the Techniques file on the PDF. Make unit 1 using the A and 4 black print #1 B's. Use the cream tone-on-tone C's and black print #2 D's to make 4 unit 2's.

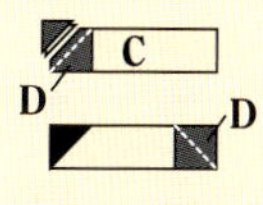

Unit 2
Stitch & Flip
Make 4

Sew the units and patches together as shown to complete the block.

Block Assembly

block no. 797

Facets

by Chris Hoover • Whirligig Designs
whirligigdesigns.com

⧄ = cut in half diagonally

Dark Blue Batik
20 squares (A) 1½″ x 1½″

Light Blue Batik
10 squares 1⅞″ x 1⅞″ ⧄ (B)
4 squares (D) 4½″ x 4½″

Dark Green Batik
20 squares (A) 1½″ x 1½″
5 squares 2⅞″ x 2⅞″ ⧄ (C)

Medium Blue Batik
20 squares (A) 1½″ x 1½″

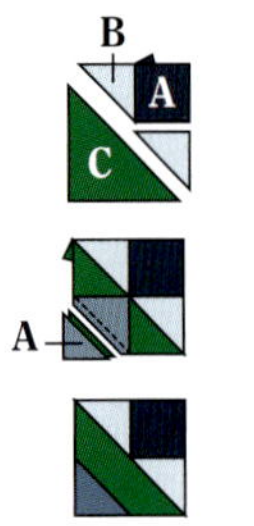

Unit
Stitch & Flip
Make 10

Sew the dark blue A's, light blue B's and dark green C's together as shown. Refer to "Stitch-and-Flip" in the Techniques file on the PDF. Add a medium blue A to the corner of each A/B/C to make 10 units.

Sew the units and patches together as shown to complete the block.

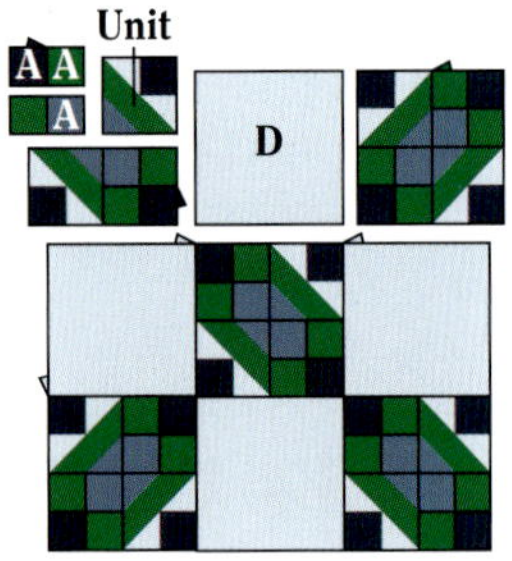

Block Assembly

block no. 798

Big Bang!

by Bonnie Hunter • Quiltville
quiltville.com

Bonnie Hunter writes the "Addicted to Scraps" column for *Quiltmaker*. She is the author of several books, including her newest book *String Fling*, for Kansas City Star Quilts, pickledish.com.

4 Assorted Black Prints
from *each*
1 square (A) 2⅞″ x 2⅞″
from *2*
1 square (C) 2½″ x 2½″

Red Solid
4 squares (A) 2⅞″ x 2⅞″
12 squares (C) 2½″ x 2½″

Assorted Purple Prints and Tone-on-Tones
8 rectangles (B) 2½″ x 4½″

Gold Solid
12 squares (C) 2½″ x 2½″

2 White Prints
from *each*
1 square (C) 2½″ x 2½″

Unit 1
Make 8

Unit 2
Stitch & Flip
Make 8

Pair the black A's with red A's to make 8 Triangle-Square unit 1's.

Refer to "Stitch-and-Flip" in the Techniques file on the PDF. Use the purple B's, gold C's and red C's to make 8 unit 2's.

Sew the units and patches together as shown to complete the block.

Block Assembly

pieced

block no. 799

Spring Favorite

by Kimberly Jolly • Fat Quarter Shop
fatquartershop.com

Fabric: Aunt Grace Keepsakes designed by Judie Rothermel for Marcus Fabrics, marcusfabrics.com.

Cream Solid
- 3 rectangles (A) 3½″ x 6½″
- 2 squares (B) 3½″ x 3½″
- 2 rectangles (C) 1½″ x 3″
- 1 square (E) 3⅞″ x 3⅞″
- 2 squares (F) 3⅜″ x 3⅜″

Red Print
- 1 rectangle (A) 3½″ x 6½″
- 2 squares (B) 3½″ x 3½″
- 1 square (E) 3⅞″ x 3⅞″

Pink Print
- 2 squares (B) 3½″ x 3½″
- 1 square (F) 3⅜″ x 3⅜″

Green Print
- 2 squares (D) 1½″ x 1½″
- 1 square (F) 3⅜″ x 3⅜″
- 1 rectangle (G) 1½″ x 6½″

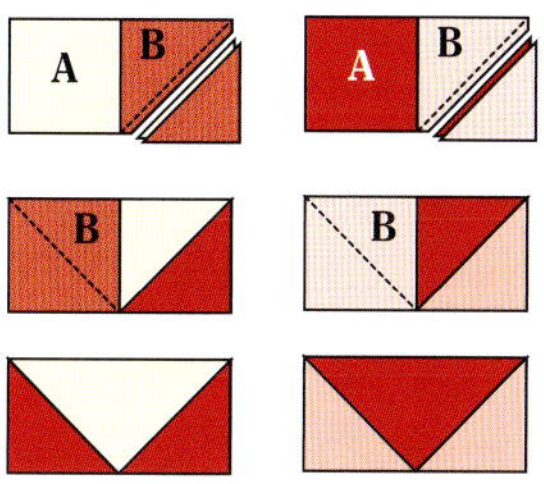

Unit 1
Stitch & Flip
Make 1

Unit 2
Stitch & Flip
Make 1

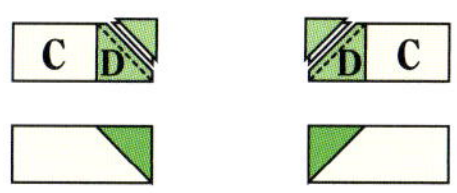

Unit 3
Stitch & Flip
Make 1

Unit 4
Stitch & Flip
Make 1

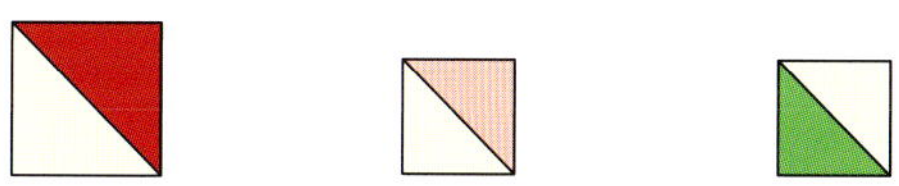

Unit 5
Make 2 from E's

Unit 6
Make 2 from F's

Unit 7
Make 2 from F's

Refer to "Stitch-and-Flip" in the Techniques file on the PDF. Use a cream A and the red B's to make unit 1. Use the red A and pink B's to make unit 2. Make 1 unit 3 and 1 unit 4 as shown using cream C's and green D's.

Pair the cream E and red E to make 2 Triangle-Square unit 5's. Make 2 unit 6's using a cream F and the pink F. Use a cream F and the green F to make 2 unit 7's.

Sew the patches and units together as shown to complete the block.

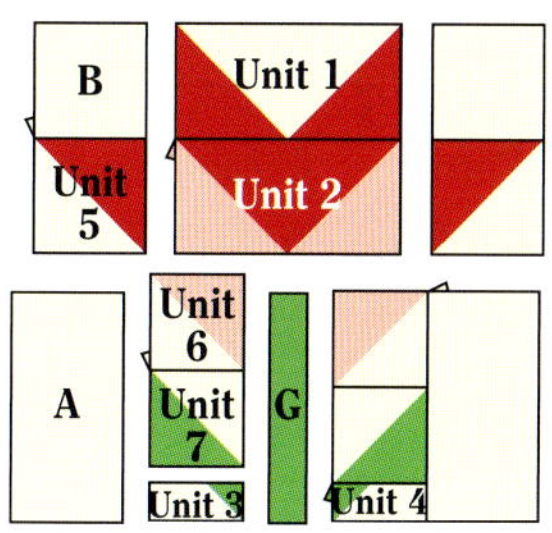

Block Assembly

block no. 800

Cozy Caps

by Susan Knapp and Mary Jane Mattingly
The Quilt Branch • quiltbranch.com

Fabric: Let it Snow designed by Deb Strain for Moda Fabrics, unitednotions.com.

Susan Knapp and Mary Jane Mattingly are the authors of *Cottage Creations* and the *Six Halves Make a Whole* series for The Quilt Branch, quiltbranch.com.

2 Dark Blue Prints
from *each*
- 2 rectangles (A) 3½″ x 4½″

White Tone-on-Tone
- 2 rectangles (A) 3½″ x 4½″
- 8 squares (B) 2½″ x 2½″
- 2 rectangles (D) 4½″ x 5½″
- 2 rectangles (E) 2½″ x 4½″

Dark Blue Tone-on-Tone
- 4 rectangles (C) 1½″ x 4½″

Red Tone-on-Tone
- 4 circles 2½″ diameter for yo-yos

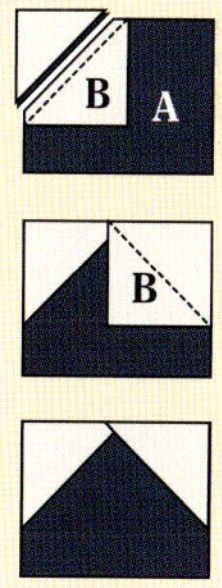

Unit
Stitch & Flip
Make 4

Refer to "Stitch-and-Flip" in the Techniques file on the PDF. Use the blue print A's and white B's to make 4 units. Sew the patches together as shown to make the block.

Make 4 yo-yos from the red circles. Tack them to the caps as shown to complete the block.

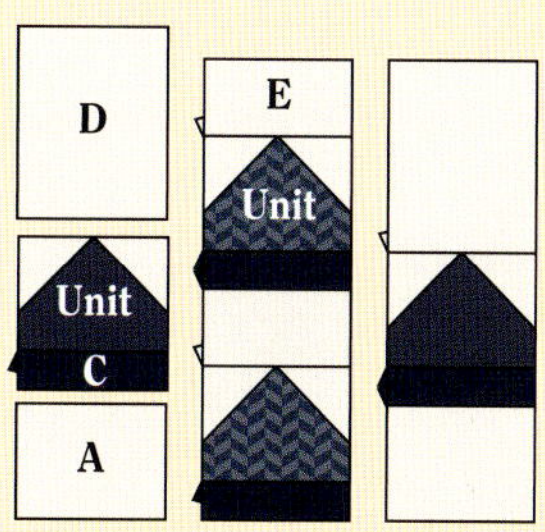

Block Assembly

block no. 801
Flighting

by Thomas Knauer • Thomas Knauer
thomasknauersews.com

Fabric: Flock designed by Thomas Knauer for Andover Fabrics, andoverfabrics.com.

Orange Print
3 squares (A) 1½" x 1½"
Yellow Print and Teal Print
from *each*
4 squares (A) 1½" x 1½"
Cream Solid
2 squares (A) 1½" x 1½"
2 rectangles (B) 1½" x 3½"
2 rectangles (D) 1½" x 5½"
2 rectangles (E) 1½" x 7½"
1 rectangle (G) 1½" x 9½"
1 rectangle (H) 1½" x 10½"
2 rectangles (J) 1" x 11½"
2 rectangles (K) 1" x 12½"
Beige Solid
4 squares (A) 1½" x 1½"
4 rectangles (B) 1½" x 3½"
4 rectangles (C) 1½" x 2½"
1 rectangle (D) 1½" x 5½"
6 rectangles (F) 1½" x 4½"
1 rectangle (I) 1½" x 6½"
Perle cotton

Join the patches as shown.

Use perle cotton and a running stitch to embroider squares as shown to complete the block.

Embroidery Placement

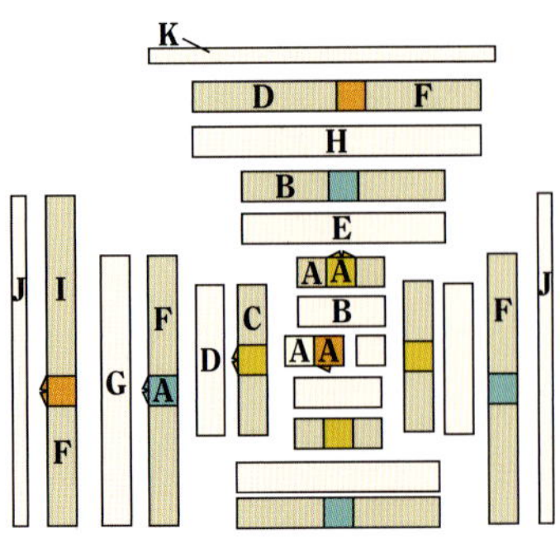

Block Piecing

block no. 802
Indian Cabins

by Wayne Kollinger • Tuxedo Park Design
tuxedoparkdesign.com

Wayne Kollinger is the author of *Designing Quilts is Easy!* for C&T Publishing, ctpub.com.

Dark Brown Tone-on-Tone
2 squares (A) 4⅞" x 4⅞"
Light Tan Tone-on-Tone
2 squares (A) 4⅞" x 4⅞"
4 rectangles (C) 2½" x 4½"
4 rectangles (D) 2½" x 6½"
Black Tone-on-Tone
8 squares (B) 2½" x 2½"
Tan Tone-on-Tone
4 squares (B) 2½" x 2½"

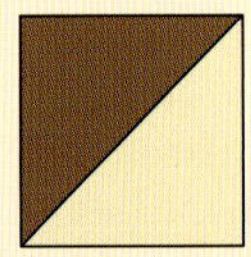

Partial Unit
Make 4 from A's

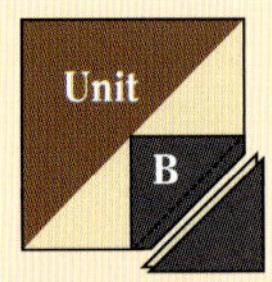

Unit 1
Stitch & Flip
Make 4

Refer to "Triangle-Squares" in the Techniques file on the PDF. Pair the dark brown A's with the light tan A's to make 4 partial units. Refer to "Stitch-and-Flip" in the Techniques file on the PDF. Sew a black B on the light tan corner of each unit as shown to make 4 unit 1's.

Use the black B's and tan B's with the light tan C's to make 4 unit 2's.

Sew the units and patches together as shown to complete the block.

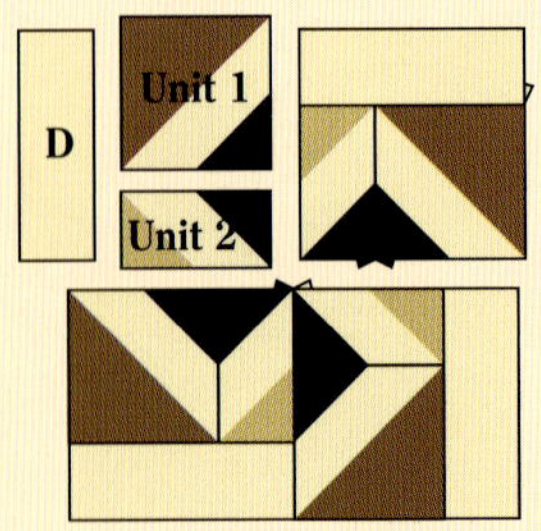

Block Assembly

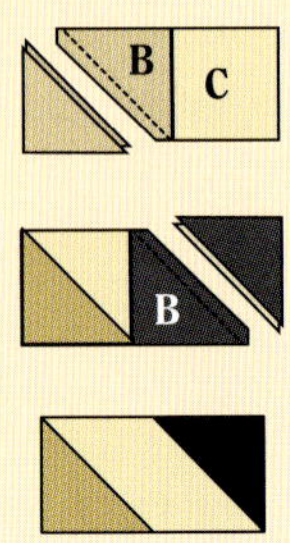

Unit 2
Stitch & Flip
Make 4

block no. 803
Lattice

by Cindy Lammon • Hyacinth Quilt Designs
hyacinthquiltdesigns.com

Fabric: Lark designed by Amy Butler for Westminster Fibers, Inc., westminsterfibers.com.

Cindy Lammon is the author of *Flowers All Around: Garden-Inspired Quilts* for Martingale & Co., shopmartingale.com.

White Solid
- 4 rectangles (A) 1½″ x 2″
- 4 rectangles (D) 1½″ x 3″
- 4 rectangles (G) 1½″ x 4″
- 4 rectangles (H) 1½″ x 5″

Blue Print
- 8 squares (B) 1½″ x 1½″
- 2 rectangles (I) 1½″ x 10½″
- 2 rectangles (J) 1½″ x 12½″

Multicolor Print
- 1 square (C) 4½″ x 4½″

White with Black Print
- 2 rectangles (E) 1½″ x 6½″
- 2 rectangles (F) 1½″ x 8½″

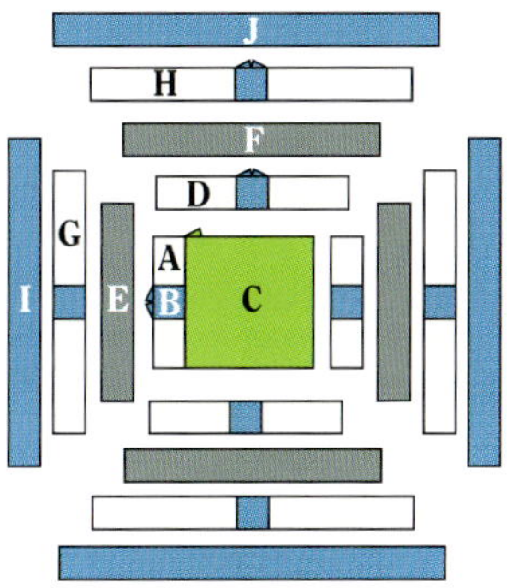

Block Piecing

Sew the patches together as shown to complete the block.

block no. 804
Rainbow Dreams

by Judy Laquidara • Patchwork Times
patchworktimes.com

Fabric: Modern Textures designed by Marcia Derse for Troy Riverwoods Collection, troy-corp.com.

Judy Laquidara is the author of *60 Pieced Quilt Borders: Mix & Match* for American Quilter's Society, americanquilter.com.

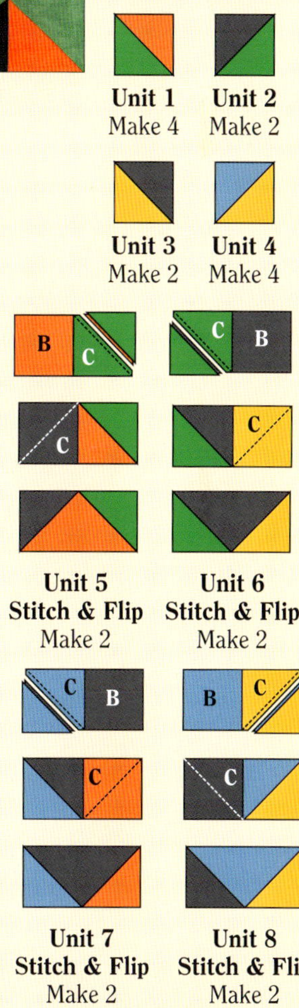

Green Solid and Yellow Solid
from *each*
- 3 squares (A) 2⅞″ x 2⅞″
- 4 squares (C) 2½″ x 2½″
- 4 rectangles (D) 1½″ x 2½″

Orange Solid and Blue Solid
- 2 squares (A) 2⅞″ x 2⅞″
- 2 rectangles (B) 2½″ x 4½″
- 2 squares (C) 2½″ x 2½″
- 4 rectangles (D) 1½″ x 2½″

Black Solid
- 2 squares (A) 2⅞″ x 2⅞″
- 4 rectangles (B) 2½″ x 4½″
- 4 squares (C) 2½″ x 2½″

Pair 2 green A's with 2 orange A's to make 4 Triangle-Square unit 1's. Pair 1 green A and 1 black A to make 2 unit 2's. Pair 1 yellow A and 1 black A to make 2 unit 3's. Pair 2 blue A's with 2 yellow A's to make 4 unit 4's.

Refer to "Stitch-and-Flip" in the Techniques file on the PDF. Use green C's and the black C's with orange B's to make 2 unit 5's. Make 2 unit 6's using green C's, yellow C's and black B's. Use blue C's and orange C's with black B's to make 2 unit 7's. Use yellow C's and black C's with blue B's to make 2 unit 8's.

Sew the units and patches together as shown to complete the block.

Block Assembly

block no. 805

Freedom Star

by Doug Leko • Antler Quilt Design
antlerquiltdesign.com

Fabric: Prairie Paisley II designed by Minick and Simpson for Moda Fabrics, unitednotions.com.

See page 221 on the PDF for pattern

Cream Print
3 squares (A) 4¼"x 4¼"
8 *each* templates D and Dr
4 squares (E) 2"x 2"

Red Print
4 squares (B) 2⅜"x 2⅜"
1 square (F) 3½"x 3½"

Medium Blue Print
2 squares (A) 4¼"x 4¼"

Dark Blue Tone-on-Tone
8 template C

Flying Geese
Make 4

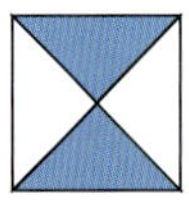

Unit 1
Make 4

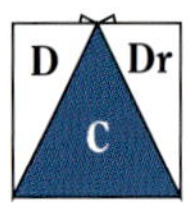

Unit 2
Make 8

Use one cream A and the red B's to make 4 Flying Geese.

Refer to "Quarter-Square Triangles" in the Techniques file on the PDF. Make 4 unit 1's using 2 cream A's and the medium blue A's.

Join each dark blue C with a cream D and Dr to make 8 unit 2's.

Sew the units, patches and Flying Geese together as shown to complete the block.

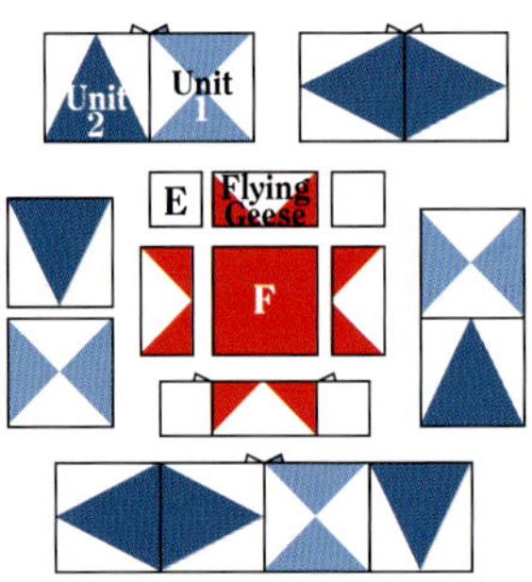

Block Assembly

pieced

block no. 806

Ladder Up

by Toby Lischko • Gateway Quilts & Stuff
gatewayquiltsnstuff.com

Fabric: Civil War Ladies designed by Pat L. Nickols for RJR Fabrics, rjrfabrics.com.

Toby Lischko is the author of *St. Louis Stars* for Kansas City Star Quilts, pickledish.com.

Purple Tone-on-Tone
2 squares (A) 2⅞"x 2⅞"

Cream Print #1
7 squares (A) 2⅞"x 2⅞"

Dark Brown Print
2 squares (A) 2⅞"x 2⅞"
6 squares (B) 2½"x 2½"

Rust Tone-on-Tone
4 squares (A) 2⅞"x 2⅞"

Cream Print #2
1 square (A) 2⅞"x 2⅞"
4 squares (B) 2½"x 2½"

Tan Print #1
6 squares (B) 2½"x 2½"

Tan Print #2
4 squares (B) 2½"x 2½"

Unit 1
Make 2

Unit 2
Make 4

Unit 3
Make 8

Unit 4
Make 2

Pair 1 purple A with 1 cream #1 A to make 2 Triangle-Square unit 1's. Use 2 cream #1 A's and the dark brown A's to make 4 unit 2's. Make 8 unit 3's using the rust A's and cream #1 A's. Pair a purple A with the cream #2 A to make 2 unit 4's.

Sew the units and patches together as shown to complete the block.

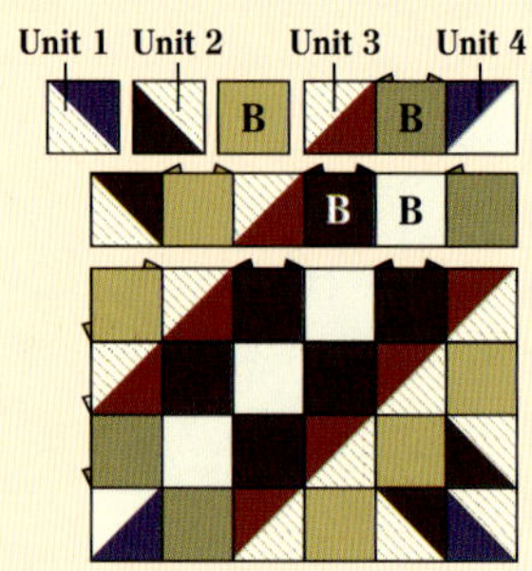

Block Assembly

block no. 807
Chain Mail

by Debbie Maddy • Calico Carriage Quilt Designs
calicocarriage.com

Fabric: Tonga Gumdrop batiks from Timeless Treasures, ttfabrics.com.

Cream Batik
- 3 squares (A) 1½″ x 1½″
- 6 rectangles (B) 1½″ x 2½″
- 4 rectangles (C) 1½″ x 3½″
- 1 rectangle (D) 1½″ x 4½″
- 3 rectangles (E) 1½″ x 5½″
- 5 squares (F) 2½″ x 2½″

Red Batik and Teal Batik
from *each*
- 2 squares (A) 1½″ x 1½″
- 4 rectangles (B) 1½″ x 2½″
- 1 rectangle (D) 1½″ x 4½″

Orange Batik and Green Batik
from *each*
- 1 square (A) 1½″ x 1½″
- 1 rectangle (B) 1½″ x 2½″
- 1 rectangle (C) 1½″ x 3½″
- 1 rectangle (D) 1½″ x 4½″
- 1 rectangle (E) 1½″ x 5½″

Magenta Batik
- 2 squares (A) 1½″ x 1½″
- 2 rectangles (C) 1½″ x 3½″

Blue Batik
- 2 rectangles (B) 1½″ x 2½″
- 2 rectangles (D) 1½″ x 4½″

Sew the patches together as shown to complete the block.

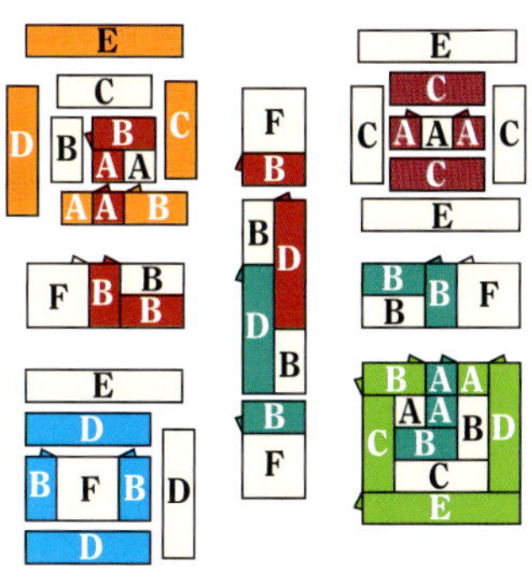

Block Piecing

block no. 808
Petit Fours

by Marian Mapes

Fabric: Bali Batiks and Handpaints from Hoffman California Fabrics, hoffmanfabrics.com.

⊠ = cut in half twice diagonally

Medium Green Batik, Light Green Batik, Medium Blue Batik and Light Blue Batik
from *each*
- 4 rectangles (A) 2¼″ x 7¼″

Light Pink Batik and Light Orange Batik
from *each*
- 1 square 4¾″ x 4¾″ ⊠ (B)

Trim the A's as shown. Refer to "Set-in Seams" in the Techniques file on the PDF. Paying close attention to patch orientation, join 2 A's to each B as shown.

Sew the A/A/B sections together as shown to complete the block.

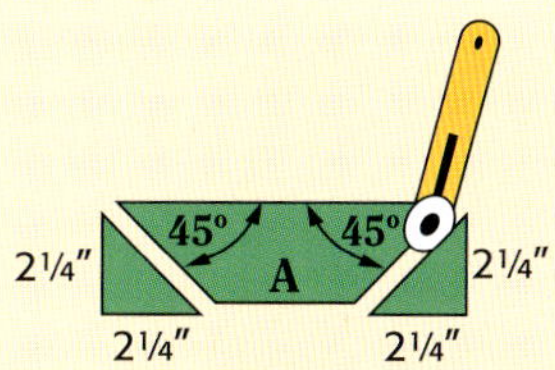

Trimming Diagram

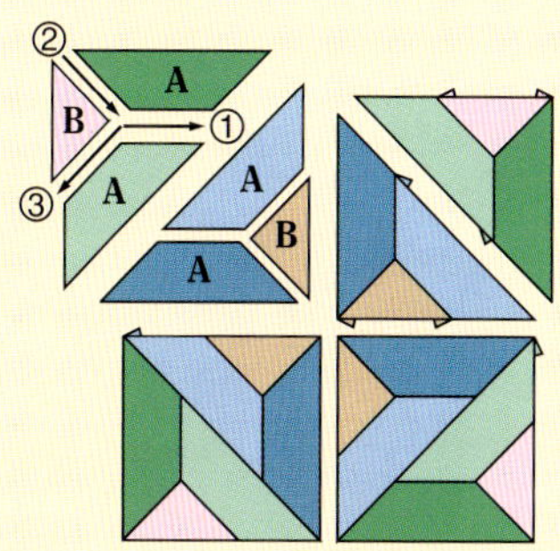

Block Piecing

block no. 809

Codex

by Scott Murkin • Patchwork Possibilities
patchworkpossibilities.com

Light Brown Tone-on-Tone
1 square (A) 2½″ x 2½″
Cream Tone-on-Tone
2 rectangles (B) 1½″ x 2½″
2 rectangles (C) 1½″ x 4½″
8 rectangles (D) 1½″ x 2″
2 rectangles (G) 1½″ x 7½″
2 rectangles (H) 1½″ x 9½″
Medium Brown Print
4 squares (E) 2″ x 2″
4 rectangles (F) 2″ x 3½″
Dark Brown Tone-on-Tone
4 rectangles (I) 2″ x 4½″
4 rectangles (J) 2″ x 6″

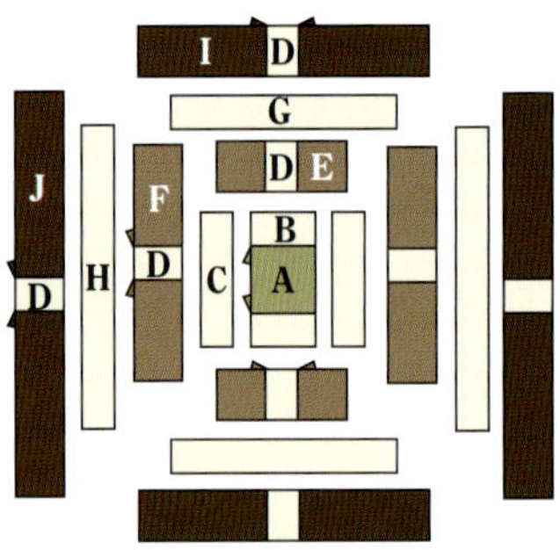

Block Piecing

Sew the patches together as shown to complete the block.

block no. 810

Little Rescued Scraps

by Arlene Neely • Rabbits Haven Quilt Designs
rabbitshaven.com

Fabric: Dancing with Sparkle designed by Arlene Neely for Red Rooster Fabrics, redroosterfabrics.com.

Assorted Pastel Prints and Tone-on-Tones
36 squares (A) 1½″ x 1½″
28 squares (D) 2″ x 2″
Aqua Tone-on-Tone
2 rectangles (B) 2″ x 6½″
2 rectangles (C) 2″ x 9½″

Using a scant ¼″ seam allowance is particularly important when piecing lots of small patches together.

Sew the patches together as shown to complete the block.

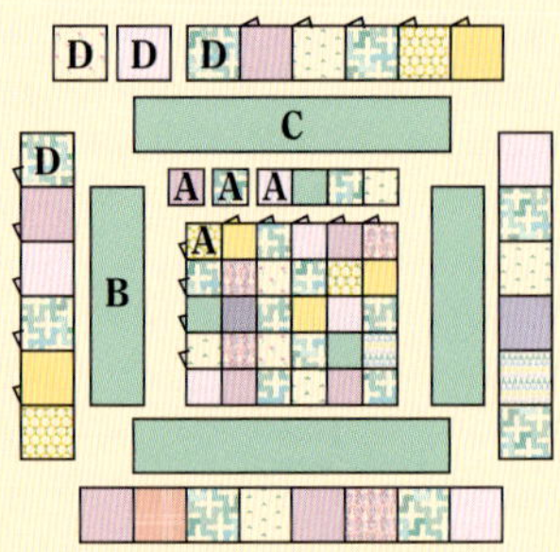

Block Piecing

block no. 811
Reel Time

by Carrie Nelson • Miss Rosie's Quilt Co.
missrosiesquiltco.com

Fabric: Punctuation designed by American Jane for Moda Fabrics, unitednotions.com.

Carrie Nelson is the author of *Another Bite of Schnibbles: 24 Quilts from 5" or 10" Squares* and others for Martingale & Co., shopmartingale.com.

4 Black Prints
from *each*
- 2 rectangles (A) 1¼"x 5½"

Cream Print
- 16 squares (B) 1¼"x 1¼"
- 8 rectangles (D) 1¼"x 5"
- 4 rectangles (E) 1½"x 6½"

12 Assorted Medium Prints
from *each*
- 1 rectangle (C) 2"x 4"

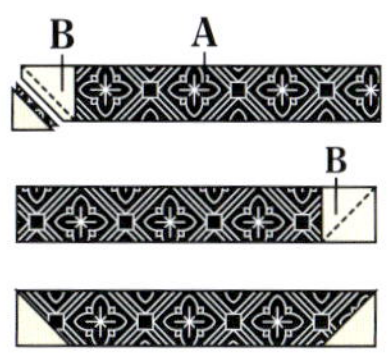

Unit
Stitch & Flip
Make 8

Refer to "Stitch-and-Flip" in the Techniques file on the PDF. Use the black A's and cream B's to make 8 units.

Sew the units and patches together as shown to complete the block.

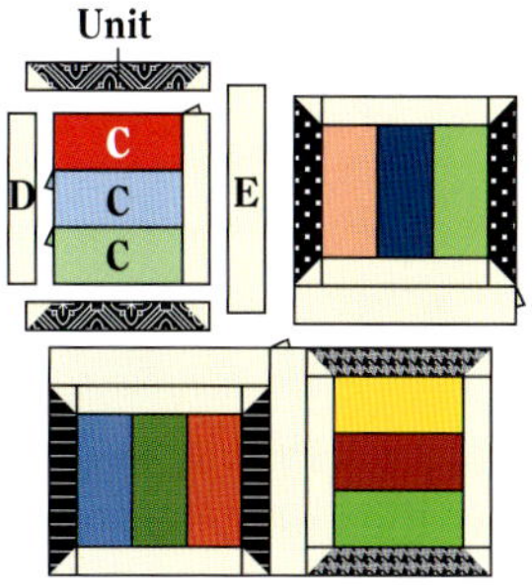

Block Assembly

block no. 812
Zen Garden

by Laura Nownes • From Me to You
lauranownes.com

Laura Nownes is the author of several books including *Q is for Quilt* for C&T Publishing, ctpub.com.

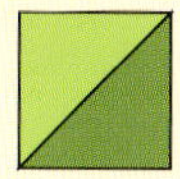

Unit
Make 2

Light Green Tone-on-Tone and Green Print from *each*
- 1 square (A) 4⅛"x 4⅛"

White Tone-on-Tone
- 4 rectangles (B) 3¾"x 4"

Red Print
- 2 squares (C) 3¾"x 3¾"

Black Tone-on-Tone
- 2 rectangles (D) 1"x 3¾"
- 2 rectangles (E) 1"x 7¾"
- 2 rectangles (G) 1"x 3½"

Red Multicolor Print
- 1 square (F) 3½"x 3½"

Green Stripe
- 2 rectangles (H) 1¼"x 11"
- 2 rectangles (I) 1¼"x 12½"

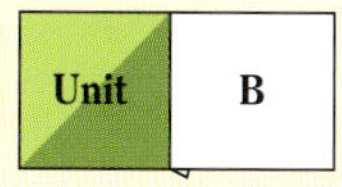

Section 1
Make 2

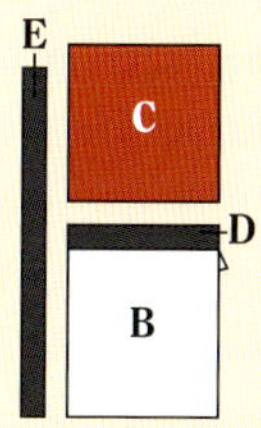

Section 2
Make 2

Section 3
Make 1

Laura fussy cut one A from a large-scale floral print.

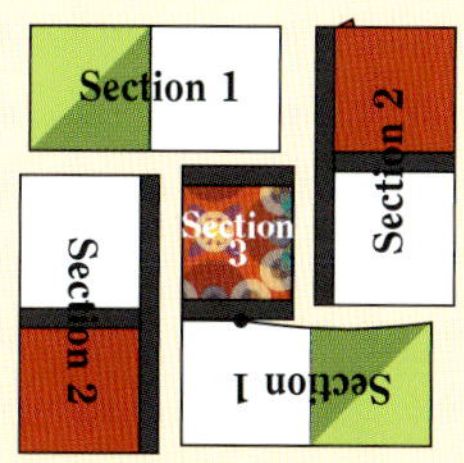

• = Partial Seam

Block Assembly

Pair the light green A and green print A to make 2 Triangle-Square units. Sew the units and 2 white B's together as shown to make 2 section 1's. Join the red print C's, black D's and E's and white B's as shown to make 2 section 2's. Sew the black G's to the red F to make section 3.

Sew a section 1 to the bottom of section 3 with a partial seam as shown. Sew a section 2 to the left, a section 1 to the top, and a section 2 to the right as shown. Complete the partial seam. Add the remaining patches to complete the block.

block no. 813

California Dreaming

by Celine Perkins • Perkins Dry Goods
perkinsdrygoods.com

Fabric: California Girl designed by Fig Tree & Co. for Moda Fabrics, unitednotions.com.

⧄ = cut in half diagonally
⊠ = cut in half twice diagonally

Light Yellow Print
8 squares (A) 2 7/8" x 2 7/8"
2 squares 4 7/8" x 4 7/8" ⧄ (D)
Light Green Print
2 squares (A) 2 7/8" x 2 7/8"
2 squares 5 1/4" x 5 1/4" ⊠ (C)
Light Red Tone-on-Tone
2 squares (A) 2 7/8" x 2 7/8"
1 square (B) 5 1/4" x 5 1/4"
1 square 5 1/4" x 5 1/4" ⊠ (C)

Unit 1 Make 4 **Unit 2** Make 4

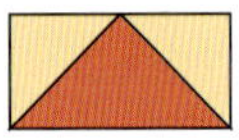

Flying Geese
Make 4

Pair 2 yellow A's with the green A's to make 4 Triangle-Square unit 1's. Make 4 unit 2's using 2 yellow A's and the red A's.

Use the red B and 4 yellow A's to make 4 Flying Geese.

Sew the units, Flying Geese and patches together as shown to complete the block.

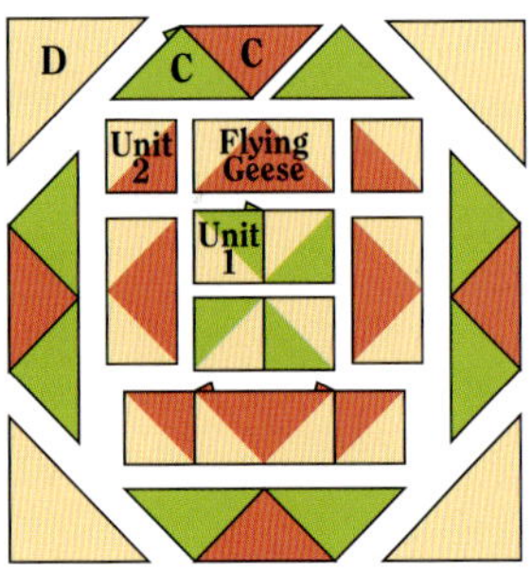

Block Assembly

pieced

block no. 814

Tunnel Vision

by Amy Rullkoetter • Freelance Editor, *Quiltmaker*
quiltmaker.com

Unit 1
Stitch & Flip
Make 4

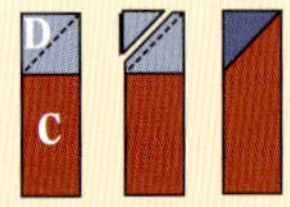

Unit 2
Stitch & Flip
Make 4

Green Batik, Red Batik, Blue Batik and Gold Batik
from *each*
1 rectangle (A) 1" x 2"
1 square (B) 1" x 1"
1 rectangle (C) 1 1/2" x 3 1/2"
1 square (D) 1 1/2" x 1 1/2"
1 rectangle (E) 2 1/2" x 6 1/2"
2 squares (F) 2 1/2" x 2 1/2"
Black Batik
1 square (D) 1 1/2" x 1 1/2"
4 squares (F) 2 1/2" x 2 1/2"
4 rectangles (G) 2 1/2" x 10 1/2"

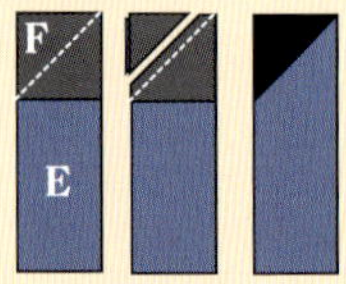

Unit 3
Stitch & Flip
Make 4

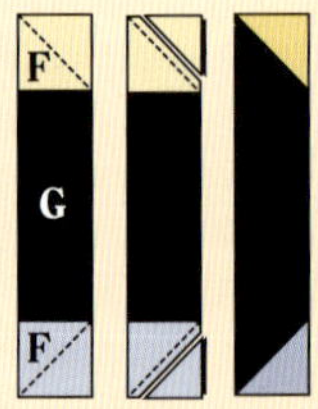

Unit 4
Stitch & Flip
Make 4

Amy used batiks with value gradation to create depth in the center.

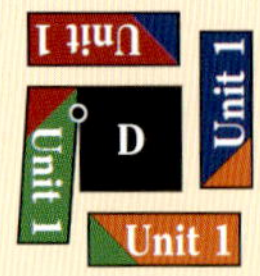

• = Partial Seam

Refer to Stitch-and-Flip" in the Techniques file on the PDF. Make 4 unit 1's pairing the green A with the red B, the red A with the blue B, the blue A with the gold B and the gold A with the green B. Make 4 unit 2's pairing the red C with the blue D, the blue C with the gold D, the gold C with the green D and the green C with the red D.

Pair the blue, gold, green and red E's with black F's to make 4 unit 3's. Refer to the block assembly diagram and make 4 unit 4's using a black G with a gold F and blue F, a black G with a green F and gold F, a black G with a red F and green F and a black G with a blue F and red F.

Paying close attention to color placement; sew the green/red unit 1 to one side of the black D with a partial seam as shown. Sew the red/blue unit 1 to the top, the blue/gold unit 1 to the right and the gold/green unit 1 to the bottom of the black D. Complete the partial seam. Repeat with the unit 2's, 3's and 4's to complete the block.

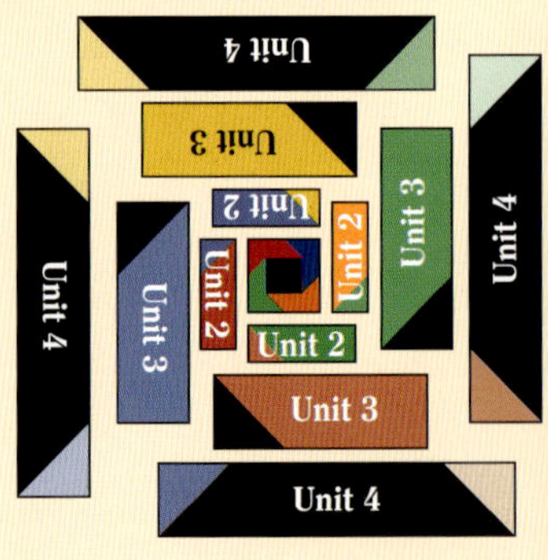

Block Assembly

block no. 815

Night Blooms

by Joli Sayasane

Fabric: Floral Whimsy by Deborah Edwards for Northcott, northcott.com

Multicolor Stripe and Green Tone-on-Tone
from *each*
 8 rectangles (A) 2″ x 3½″
White Dot and Yellow Tone-on-Tone
from *each*
 4 rectangles (A) 2″ x 3½″
Black Print
 1 square (B) 6½″ x 6½″

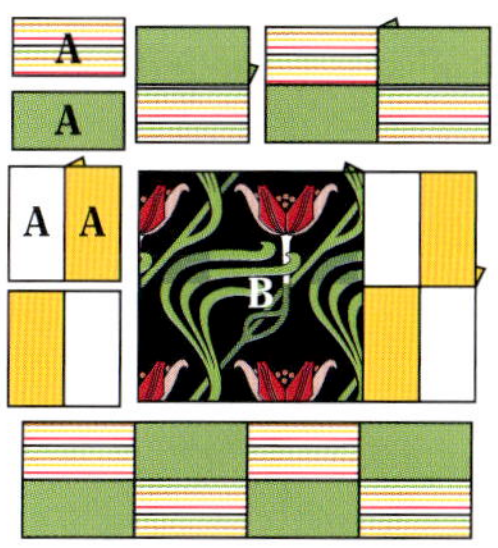

Block Piecing

Sew the patches together as shown to complete the block.

block no. 816

Carson City

by Pat Speth • Pat Speth Quilts
patspeth.com

Pat Speth is the author of *Nickel Quilts & Borders* for Pat Speth Quilts, patspeth.com.

⧄ = cut in half diagonally

Blue Print and Green Tone-on-Tone
from *each*
 4 rectangles (A) 2½″ x 4½″
Cream Print
 12 squares (B) 2½″ x 2½″
 4 squares 2⅞″ x 2⅞″ ⧄ (C)
Pink Tone-on-Tone
 4 squares (B) 2½″ x 2½″
Dark Brown Multiprint
 2 squares 4⅞″ x 4⅞″ ⧄ (D)
Maroon Print
 1 square (E) 4½″ x 4½″

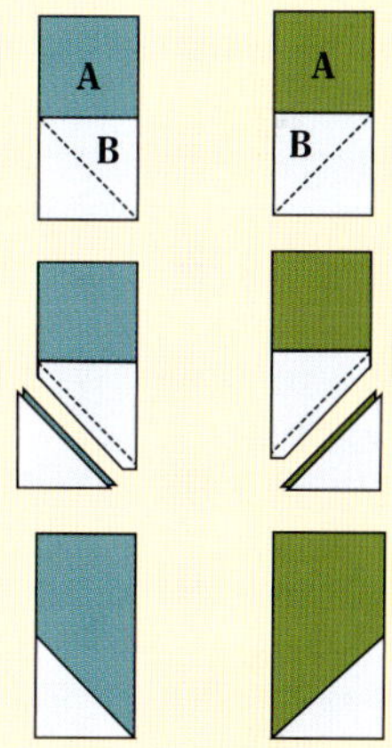

Unit 1
Stitch & Flip
Make 4

Unit 2
Stitch & Flip
Make 4

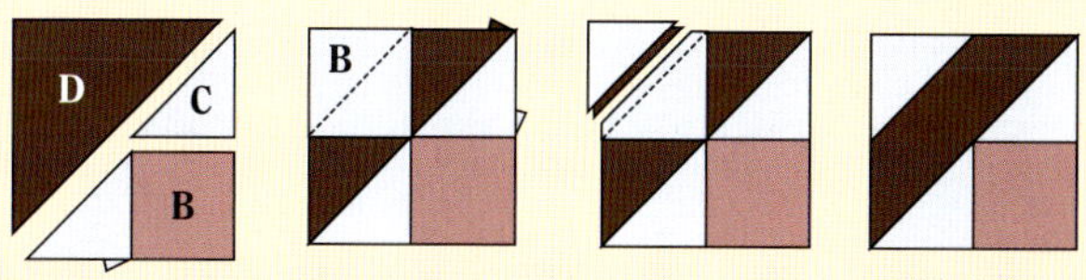

Unit 3
Stitch & Flip
Make 4

Refer to "Stitch-and-Flip" in the Techniques file on the PDF. Use the blue A's and green A's with the cream B's to make 4 unit 1's and 4 unit 2's as shown.

Sew the pink B's, cream C's and brown D's together as shown; use stitch-and-flip to add a cream B to each to make 4 unit 3's.

Sew the units and patches together as shown to complete the block.

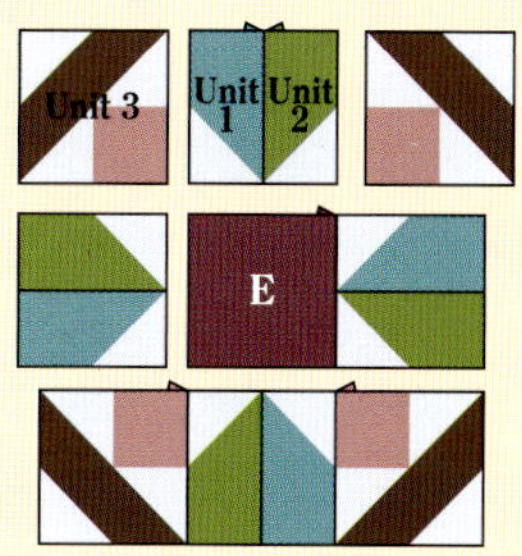

Block Assembly

block no. 817

Rescue No. 1

by Denise Starck • Graphic Designer, *Quiltmaker*
quiltmaker.com

See page 203 on the PDF for pattern

White
- 1 rectangle (A) 2⅛"x 2½"
- 2 squares (E) 1¾"x 1¾"
- 6 rectangles (K) 1"x 1⅜"
- 2 rectangles (L) ⅞"x 7"

Light Blue
- 1 square (B) 1¼"x 1¼"
- 1 square (D) 1½"x 1½"
- 1 square (F) 1"x 1"
- 1 square (H) 2½"x 2½"
- 1 rectangle (I) ⅞"x 2½"
- 1 rectangle (J) 2⅜"x 4½"
- 7 rectangles (K) 1"x 1⅜"
- 1 rectangle (M) 2"x 2⅛"
- 1 rectangle (N) 2¾"x 8½"
- 1 rectangle (Q) 1½"x 3¼"
- 3 rectangles (R) 1"x 2"
- 1 rectangle (S) 1"x 3¾"
- 2 rectangles (T) 1"x 1½"
- 1 rectangle (U) ⅞"x 6"
- 1 rectangle (Y) 1"x 5⅛"
- 1 rectangle (AA) 1"x 3¼"

Red
- 1 rectangle (C) 1½"x 4½"
- 1 square (F) 1"x 1"
- 1 rectangle (G) 2"x 5"
- 3 rectangles (O) 1"x 1¾"
- 1 rectangle (P) 1"x 4½"
- 3 rectangles (R) 1"x 2"
- 1 rectangle (W) 1½"x 6½"
- 1 rectangle (X) 2⅝"x 6½"

Light Gray
- 1 square (D) 1½"x 1½"
- 4 squares (F) 1"x 1"
- 1 rectangle (Q) 1½"x 3¼"
- 1 rectangle (S) 1"x 3¾"
- 1 rectangle (Z) 1½"x 3¾"

Dark Gray
- 4 squares (F) 1"x 1"
- 1 rectangle (R) 1"x 2"
- 2 rectangles (S) 1"x 3¾"
- 1 rectangle (BB) 2"x 12½"

Black
- 2 squares (H) 2½"x 2½"

Dark Red
- 2 rectangles (V) 2"x 2¾"

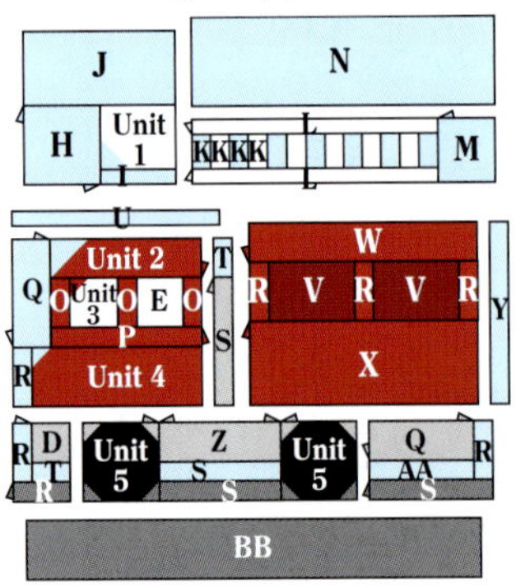

Block Assembly

Refer to "Stitch-and-Flip" in the Techniques file on the PDF. Pair the white A with the blue B to make 1 unit 1. Make 1 unit 2 with the red C and blue D. Make 1 unit 3 with 1 white E and the red F. Make 1 unit 4 using the red G and blue F. Use the black H's with the light gray F's and dark gray F's to make 2 unit 5's. Sew the units and patches together as shown to complete the block.

block no. 818

Sunrise

by Dawn Stewart • Spring Water Designs
springwaterdesigns.com

Fabric: Kate's Garden designed by Kate Knight for Quilting Treasures, quiltingtreasures.com.

Black Print
- 4 rectangles (A) 2½"x 4½"
- 1 square (C) 4½"x 4½"

Yellow Tone-on-Tone and Pink Tone-on-Tone
from *each*
- 4 rectangles (A) 2½"x 4½"
- 8 squares (B) 2½"x 2½"

Orange Multiprint
- 4 rectangles (A) 2½"x 4½"
- 4 squares (B) 2½"x 2½"

Red Tone-on-Tone
- 4 squares (B) 2½"x 2½"

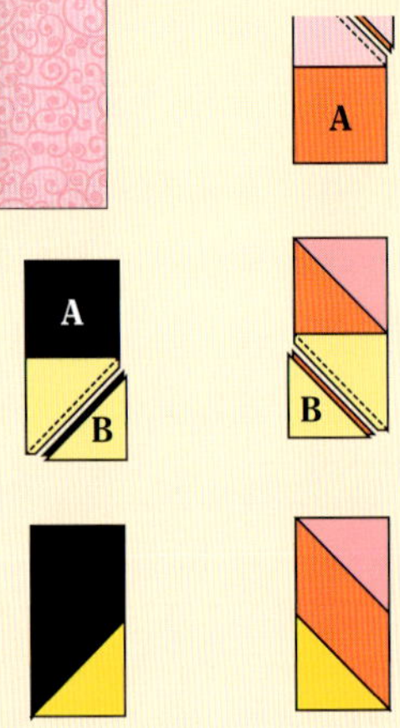

Unit 1
Stitch & Flip
Make 4

Unit 2
Stitch & Flip
Make 4

Refer to "Stitch-and-Flip" in the Techniques file on the PDF. Use the black A's with yellow B's to make 4 unit 1's. Make 4 unit 2's using the orange A's, pink B's and yellow B's. Use the yellow A's with pink B's and orange B's to make 4 unit 3's.

Use the black C and red B's to make unit 4. Sew the units and patches together as shown to complete the block.

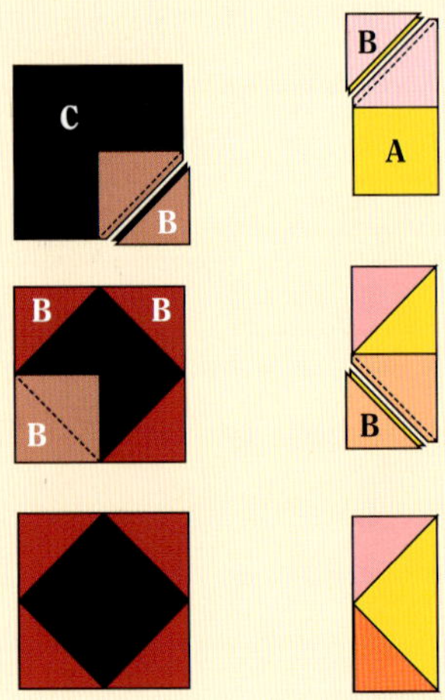

Block Assembly

Unit 4
Stitch & Flip
Make 1

Unit 3
Stitch & Flip
Make 4

block no. 819

Hit the Slopes

by Jocelyn Ueng • It's Sew Emma
itssewemma.com

Fabric: Joy designed by Kate Spain for Moda Fabrics, unitednotions.com.

Green Print and White with Red Print
from *each*
- 1 rectangle (A) 2½″ x 5½″

Cream Tone-on-Tone
- 1 rectangle (B) 4½″ x 7½″
- 1 rectangle (E) 3½″ x 6½″
- 1 rectangle (H) 5½″ x 8½″

Red Tone-on-Tone
- 1 rectangle (C) 4½″ x 8½″
- 1 rectangle (F) 3½″ x 7½″
- 1 rectangle (I) 5½″ x 7½″

Aqua Print #1
- 1 rectangle (D) 3½″ x 5½″

Aqua Print #2
- 1 rectangle (F) 3½″ x 7½″

Red Print
- 1 rectangle (G) 2½″ x 7½″

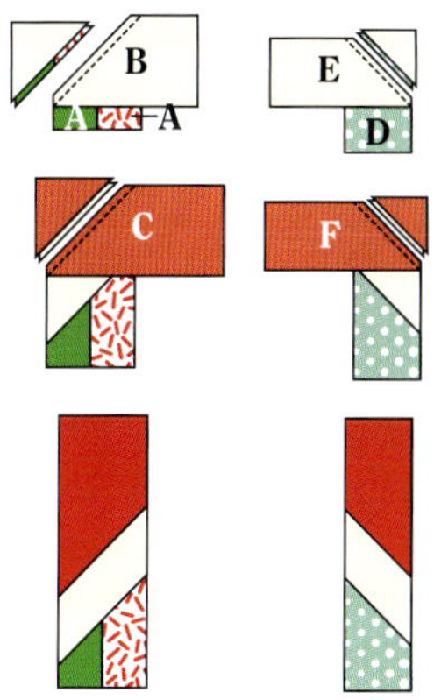

Unit 1
Stitch & Flip
Make 1

Unit 2
Stitch & Flip
Make 1

Sew the green A to the white with red A. Refer to "Stitch-and-Flip" in the Techniques file on the PDF. Make unit 1 using the A/A, the cream B and the red C as shown. Use the aqua #1 D, the cream E and the red F to make unit 2. Sew the red print G to the aqua #2 F. Make unit 3 using the G/F, the cream H and the red I.

Sew the units together as shown to complete the block.

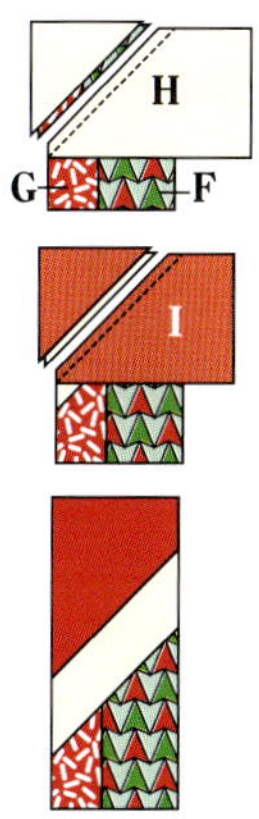

Unit 3
Stitch & Flip
Make 1

Block Assembly

block no. 820

Springtime Spools

by Pam Vieira-McGinnis
pamkittymorning.blogspot.com

Fabric: Pam Kitty Morning designed by Pam Vieira-McGinnis for Lakehouse Dry Goods, lakehousedrygoods.com.

⧄ = cut in half diagonally

Yellow Print #1 and Yellow Print #2
from *each*
- 2 squares (A) 2⅜″ x 2⅜″

Red Print
- 8 squares (A) 2⅜″ x 2⅜″

Light Blue Print
- 4 squares (A) 2⅜″ x 2⅜″
- 4 squares 3⅞″ x 3⅞″ ⧄ (C)

Medium Blue Print
- 4 squares (A) 2⅜″ x 2⅜″

White Dot
- 4 squares (A) 2⅜″ x 2⅜″
- 8 squares (B) 2″ x 2″
- 8 squares 2⅜″ x 2⅜″ ⧄ (D)
- 4 rectangles (E) 2″ x 3½″

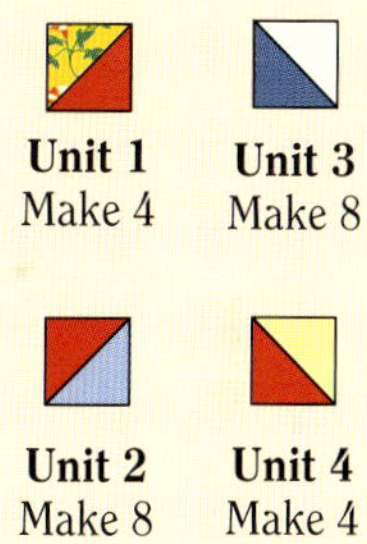

Pair the yellow print #1 A's with 2 red A's to make 4 Triangle-Square unit 1's. Make 8 unit 2's using 4 red A's and the light blue A's. Use the medium blue A's and white A's to make 8 unit 3's. Pair the yellow print #2 A's with 2 red A's to make 4 unit 4's.

Sew the units and patches together as shown to complete the block.

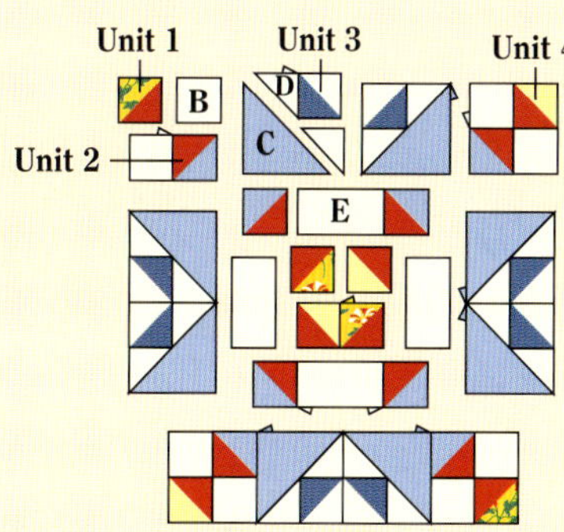

Block Assembly

block no. 821

Rainbow Brick Road

by Pippa Armbrester • Pippa Patchwork
pippapatchwork.com

Fabric: Kona Solids from Robert Kaufman, robertkaufman.com.

Pippa Armbrester is the author of *Solids, Stripes, Circles, and Squares—16 Modern Patchwork Quilt Patterns* for Martingale & Co., shopmartingale.com.

Black Solid
4 rectangles (A) 2½" x 3½"
4 rectangles (C) 2" x 2½"
4 rectangles (D) 2½" x 2¾"
White Solid
18 rectangles (B) 1" x 2½"
12 Assorted Solids
from *each*
1 rectangle (A) 2½" x 3½"

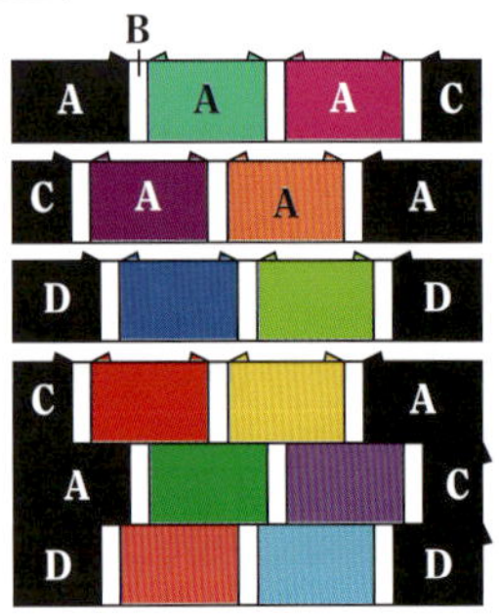

Block Piecing

Sew the patches together as shown to complete the block.

pieced

block no. 822

Engine Ready

by Carolyn Beam • Creative Editor, *Quiltmaker*
quiltmaker.com

Fabric: Soho Solids and others, all from Timeless Treasures, ttfabrics.com.

Dark Gray Solid
2 rectangles (A) 2½" x 3"
White with Black Print
1 rectangle (A) 2½" x 3"
White Solid
1 rectangle (B) 1" x 2½"
2 rectangles (C) ¾" x 2½"
2 rectangles (D) ¾" x 6½"
2 rectangles (F) 1½" x 1¾"
Yellow Tone-on-Tone
2 rectangles (E) 1" x 1½"
1 rectangle (M) 1" x 3½"
Red Solid
2 rectangles (G) 1¼" x 2¼"
2 rectangles (H) 1½" x 2¼"
1 rectangle (I) ¾" x 3"
1 rectangle (J) 1" x 3"
2 rectangles (L) 1" x 1¾"
Light Gray Solid
2 rectangles (K) 1½" x 5¾"
2 rectangles (L) 1" x 1¾"
1 rectangle (N) 1¾" x 8½"
2 squares (O) 1¼" x 1¼"
2 rectangles (Q) 1½" x 2"
1 rectangle (S) 1½" x 3½"
Medium Gray Solid
1 rectangle (P) 1¼" x 7"
Black Tone-on-Tone
2 squares (R) 1½" x 1½"
Beige Batik #1
8 squares (R) 1½" x 1½"
2 rectangles (T) 1¼" x 1½"
1 rectangle (U) 2¾" x 10½"
Beige Batik #2
8 squares (R) 1½" x 1½"
Brown Batik
2 rectangles (V) 1½" x 11½"
1 rectangle (W) 1½" x 12½"

Sew the patches together as shown to complete the block.

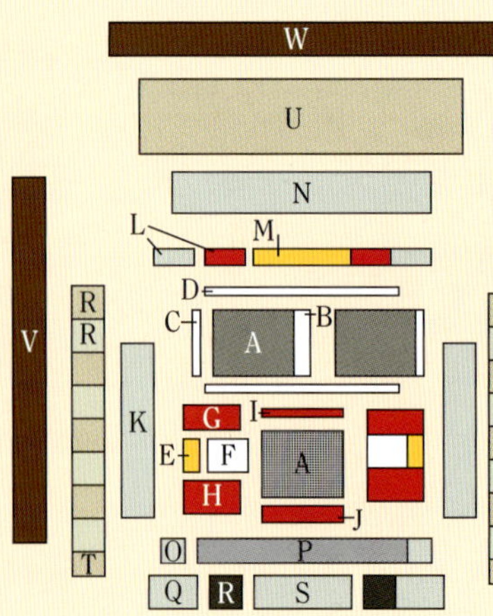

Block Piecing

block no. 823

Towne Square

by Pam Buda • Heartspun Quilts
heartspunquilts.com

Fabric: Heart of the Prairie designed by Pam Buda for Marcus Fabrics, marcusbrothers.com.

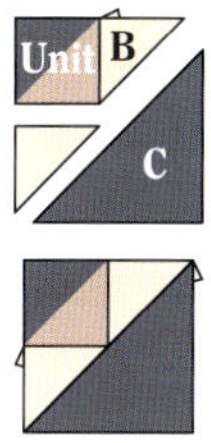

Partial Section 1
Make 4

⧄ = cut in half diagonally
⊠ = cut in half twice diagonally

Blue Print
- 6 squares (A) 2⅜″ x 2⅜″
- 8 squares 2⅜″ x 2⅜″ ⧄ (B)
- 2 squares 3⅞″ x 3⅞″ ⧄ (C)
- 1 square (G) 1⅞″ x 1⅞″

Pink Tone-on-Tone
- 6 squares (A) 2⅜″ x 2⅜″
- 4 squares (D) 2″ x 2″
- 4 rectangles (F) 1⅞″ x 5″

Cream Print
- 4 squares 2⅜″ x 2⅜″ ⧄ (B)
- 4 squares 3⅞″ x 3⅞″ ⧄ (C)
- 1 square 5¾″ x 5¾″ ⊠ (E)

Unit
Make 12

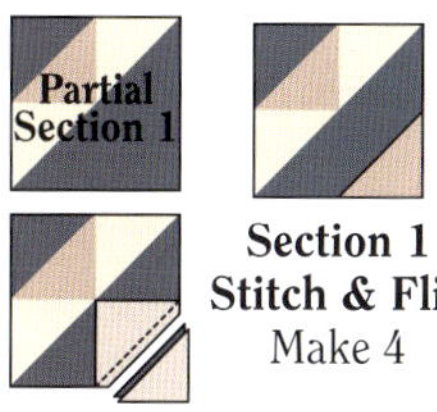

Section 1 Stitch & Flip
Make 4

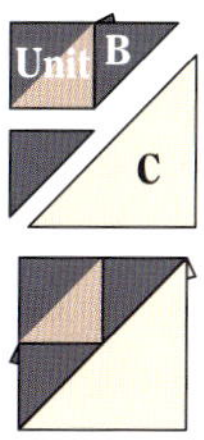

Section 2
Make 8

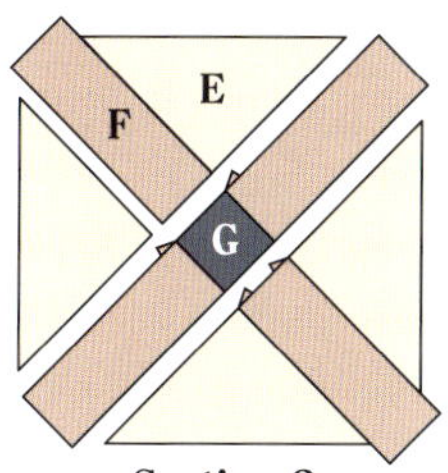

Section 3
Make 1

Pair the blue A's with the pink A's to make 12 Triangle-Square units.

Make 4 partial section 1's using units, cream B's and blue C's as shown. Refer to "Stitch-and-Flip" in the Techniques file on the PDF. Add a pink D to the corner of each partial section 1 as shown to make 4 section 1's.

Use units, blue B's and cream C's to make 8 section 2's as shown.

Join the cream E's, pink F's and blue G to make section 3 as shown. Center and trim to 6½" × 6½". Sew the sections together as shown to complete the block.

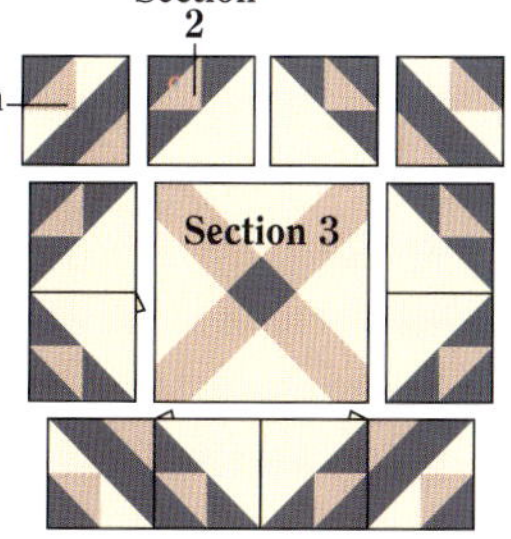

Block Assembly

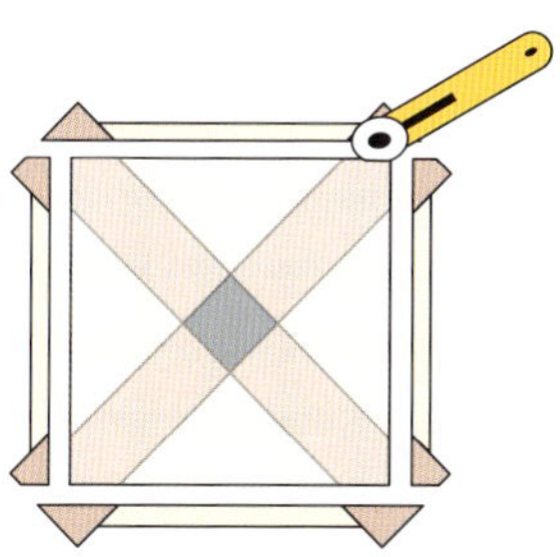

Trimming Diagram

block no. 824

Red is a Neutral

by Emily Carr • Creative Chicks
creativechicksatplay.blogspot.com

Red Stripe
- 4 squares (A) 2½″ x 2½″

Red Print
- 8 squares (A) 2½″ x 2½″

Red Check
- 8 squares (A) 2½″ x 2½″

Red Dot #1
- 4 squares (A) 2½″ x 2½″

Red Dot #2
- 1 square (A) 2½″ x 2½″

White Solid
- 2 rectangles (B) ¾″ x 10½″
- 2 rectangles (C) ¾″ x 11″

Red Dot #3
- 2 rectangles (D) 1¼″ x 11″
- 2 rectangles (E) 1¼″ x 12½″

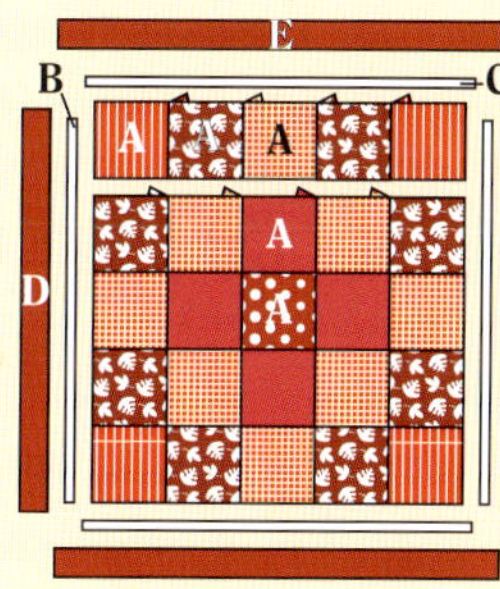

Block Piecing

Refer to the photographed block for placement of the various red A prints. Sew the patches together as shown to complete the block.

block no. 825

Star Search

by Kari Carr • New Leaf Stitches
newleafstitches.com

Fabric: Reflections designed by Gudrun Erla for Red Rooster Fabrics, redroosterfabrics.com.

Kari Carr is the author of *Twice as Nice* for Martingale & Co, shopmartingale.com.

◪ = cut in half diagonally
⊠ = cut in half twice diagonally

Light Gray Tone-on-Tone
- 4 squares (A) 2½" x 2½"
- 4 squares 2⅞" x 2⅞" ◪ (H)

Dark Gray Tone-on-Tone
- 12 squares (A) 2½" x 2½"
- 32 squares (B) 1½" x 1½"
- 4 squares (E) 2⅞" x 2⅞"
- 4 squares (F) 2" x 2"

Red Tone-on-Tone
- 4 squares (A) 2½" x 2½"
- 2 squares 3¼" x 3¼" ⊠ (G)

Yellow Print
- 1 square (C) 4½" x 4½"
- 1 square (D) 5¼" x 5¼"

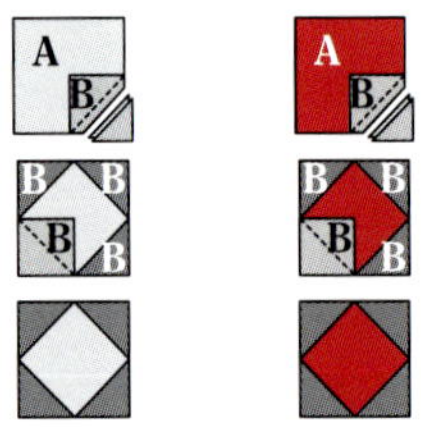

Unit 1
Stitch & Flip
Make 4

Unit 2
Stitch & Flip
Make 4

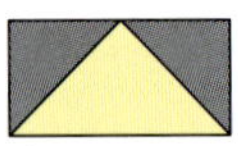

Flying Geese
Make 4

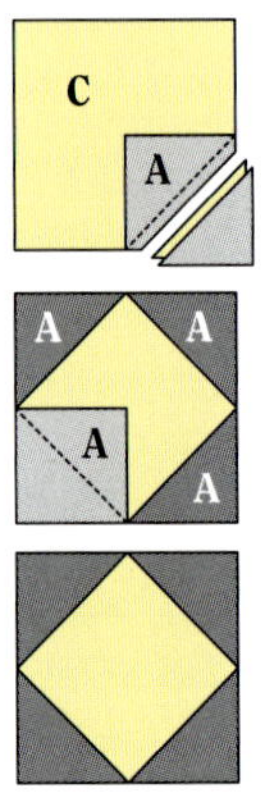

Unit 3
Stitch & Flip
Make 1

Refer to "Stitch-and-Flip" in the Techniques file on the PDF. Make 4 unit 1's using the light gray A's and dark gray B's. Use red A's and dark gray B's to make 4 unit 2's. Make unit 3 using the yellow C and 4 dark gray A's.

Use the yellow D and dark gray E's to make 4 Flying Geese.

Sew the units, Flying Geese and patches together as shown to complete the block.

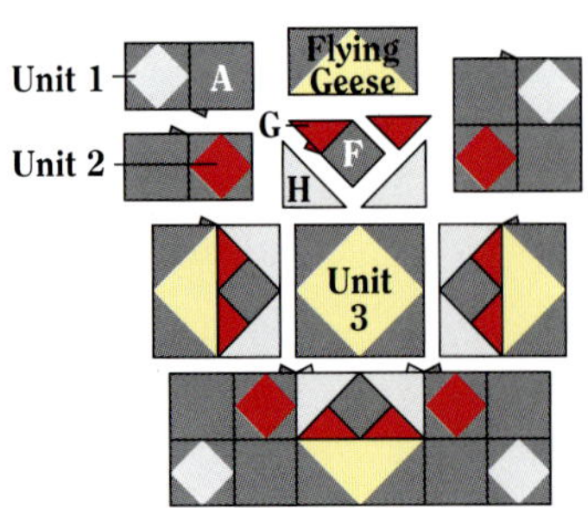

Block Assembly

pieced

block no. 826

Double Crossed

by AnneMarie Chany • Gen X Quilters
genxquilters.com

Fabric: Terrain designed by Kate Spain and Strawberry Fields by Fig Tree Quilts, both for Moda Fabrics, unitednotions.com.

◪ = cut in half diagonally
⊠ = cut in half twice diagonally

White Solid
- 4 squares (A) 4½" x 4½"
- 4 squares (C) 1½" x 1½"
- 4 squares 1⅞" x 1⅞" ◪ (D)
- 1 square 3¼" x 3¼" ⊠ (E)
- 4 rectangles (G) 2½" x 4½"

Orange Print
- 4 squares (B) 3" x 3"
- 4 squares 2⅞" x 2⅞" ◪ (F)

Pale Yellow Print and Gold Dot
from *each*
- 6 squares (C) 1½" x 1½"
- 2 rectangles (H) 1½" x 2½"

Unit
Stitch & Flip
Make 4

Refer to "Stitch-and-Flip" in the Techniques file on the PDF. Make 4 units using the white A's and orange B's.

Sew the units and patches together as shown to complete the block.

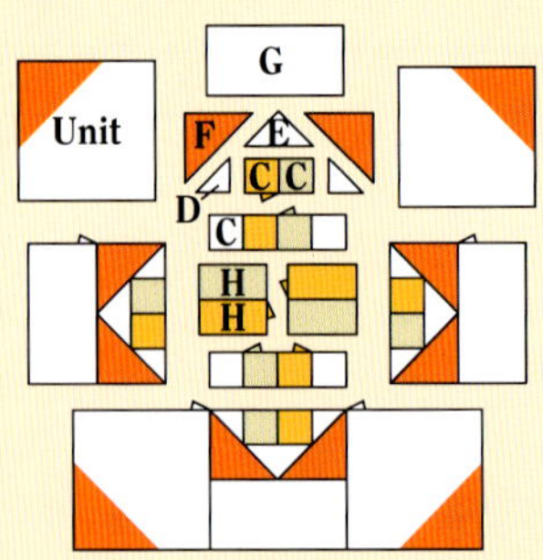

Block Assembly

block no. 827
Diamond Chain

by Barbara Cline • Delightful Piecing

Barbara Cline is the author of *Simply Triangles* for C&T Publishing, ctpub.com.

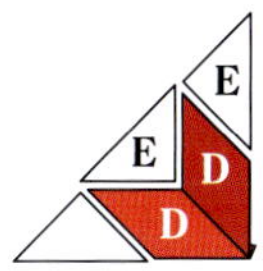

Unit 2
Make 1

See page 265 on the PDF for pattern

◪ = cut in half diagonally

Red Solid
- 5 template A
- 1 template D

White Solid
- 8 template B
- 2 each templates C and Cr
- 2 squares 3⅝"x 3⅝" ◪ (E) (there will be 1 extra)

Red Print
- 1 template D

7 Assorted Medium and Dark Blue Tone-on-Tones
- 1 rectangle (F) 2"x 13¾"
- 1 rectangle (G) 2"x 16¾"
- 1 rectangle (H) 2¼"x 9¼"
- 2 rectangles (I) 2¼"x 7¾"
- 2 rectangles (J) 2¼"x 6¼"
- 2 rectangles (K) 2¼"x 4½"
- 1 square 3"x 3" ◪ (L)

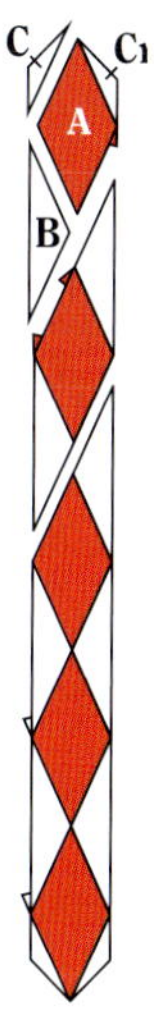

Unit 1
Make 1

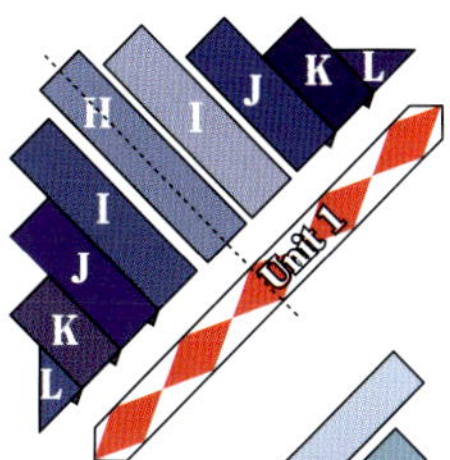

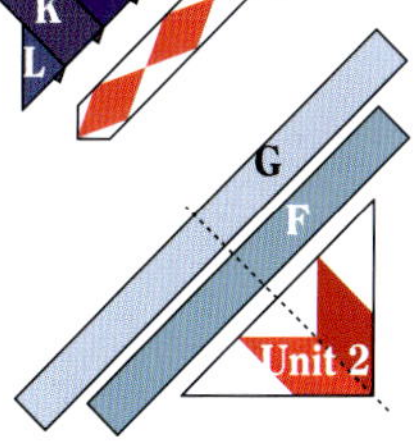

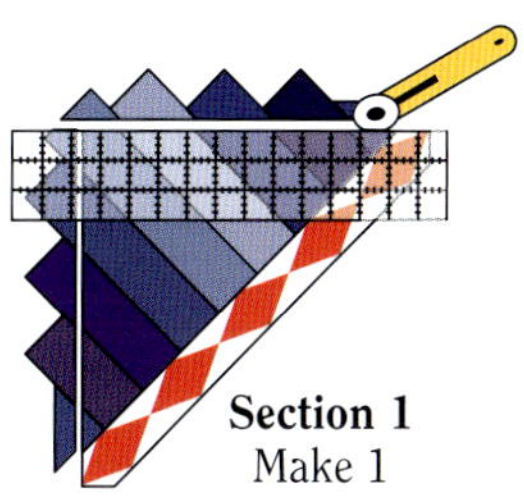

Section 1
Make 1

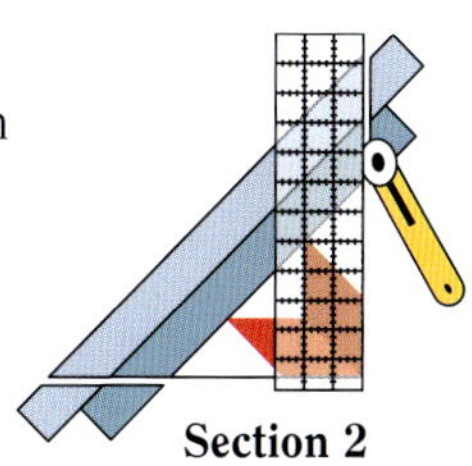

Section 2
Make 1

Sew the A's, B's and C's together as shown to make unit 1. Refer to "Set-in Seams" in the Techniques file on the PDF. Sew the D's together as shown; add the E's to make a unit 2.

Align and join H–L as shown; matching centers, sew to the unit 1. Trim the H–L patches even with the edges of unit 1 as shown to make section 1.

Matching the centers, sew F to G; join to unit 2 as shown. Trim the edges of F and G even with unit 2 as shown to make section 2. Join sections 1 and 2 to complete the block.

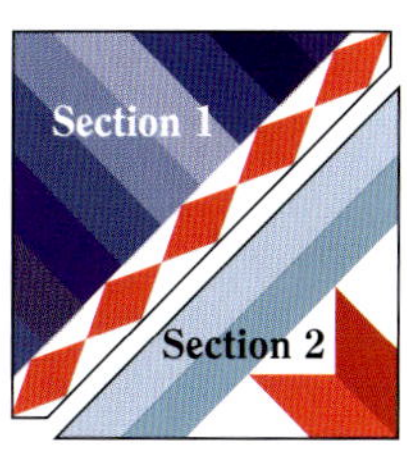

Block Assembly

block no. 828
Serendipitiy

by Karen Combs • Karen Combs Studio
karencombs.com

Fabric: Serendipity designed by Karen Combs for Troy Riverwoods Collection, troy-corp.com.

Karen Combs is the author of *Celtic Pieced Illusions* for American Quilter's Society, americanquilter.com.

◪ = cut in half diagonally

Medium Teal Tone-on-Tone
- 1 square (A) 5¼"x 5¼"

Medium Olive Green Tone-on-Tone
- 4 squares (B) 2⅞"x 2⅞"

Light Olive Green Tone-on-Tone
- 2 squares (B) 2⅞"x 2⅞"

Light Teal Tone-on-Tone
- 2 squares (B) 2⅞"x 2⅞"
- 4 squares (C) 2½"x 2½"
- 2 squares 4⅞"x 4⅞" ◪ (E)

Dark Olive Green Tone-on-Tone
- 4 squares 2⅞"x 2⅞" ◪ (D)

Dark Teal Tone-on-Tone
- 4 rectangles (F) 2½"x 4½"

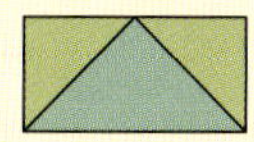

Flying Geese
Make 4

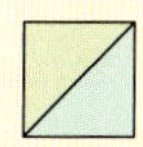

Unit
Make 4

Use the medium teal A and medium green B's to make 4 Flying Geese.

Pair the light teal B's with the light green B's to make 4 Triangle-Square units.

Sew the Flying Geese, units and patches together as shown to complete the block.

Block Assembly

block no. 829

Plaid Squared

by Melissa Corry • Happy Quilting
happyquiltingmelissa.blogspot.com

Cream Solid
16 squares (A) 1½″ x 1½″
8 rectangles (D) 1½″ x 5½″
1 square (F) 5½″ x 5½″
Blue Solid
8 rectangles (B) 1″ x 1½″
4 rectangles (C) 1″ x 3″
4 rectangles (E) 1″ x 5½″
Gray Solid
4 rectangles (C) 1″ x 3″
2 rectangles (E) 1″ x 5½″
4 rectangles (G) 1″ x 11½″
2 rectangles (H) 1″ x 12½″

Sew the patches together as shown to complete the block.

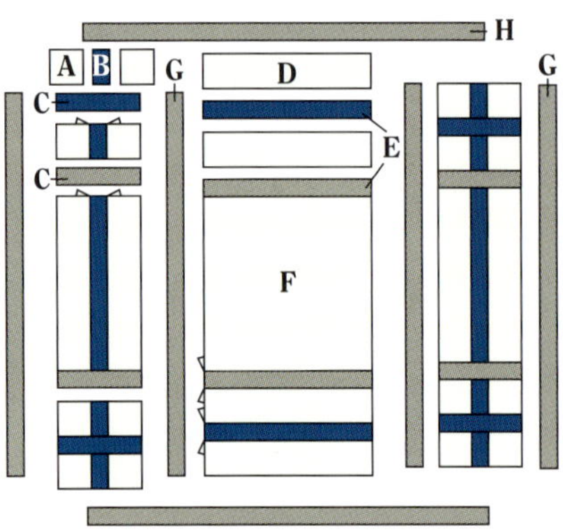

Block Piecing

block no. 830

A Divided Flock

by Elizabeth Dackson
dontcallmebetsy.com

Light Green Print, Dark Blue Print and Pink Tone-on-Tone
from *each*
3 rectangles (A) 2½″ x 4½″
1 rectangle (D) 1½″ x 12½″
Medium Green Tone-on-Tone
3 rectangles (A) 2½″ x 4½″
Black Solid
24 squares (B) 2½″ x 2½″
2 rectangles (C) 1″ x 12½″

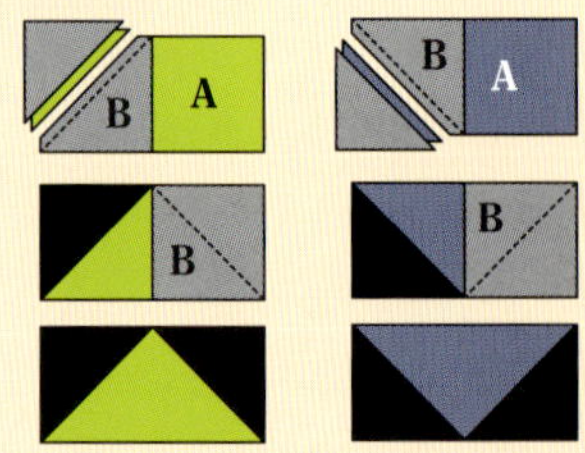

Unit 1
Stitch & Flip
Make 3

Unit 2
Stitch & Flip
Make 3

Refer to "Stitch-and-Flip" in the Techniques file on the PDF. Use the light green A's and 6 black B's to make 3 unit 1's. Make 3 unit 2's using the blue A's and 6 black B's. Use the pink A's and 6 black B's to make 3 unit 3's. Make 3 unit 4's using the medium green A's and 6 black B's.

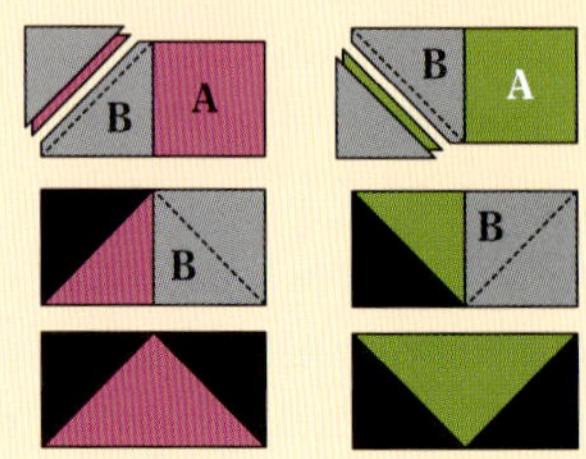

Unit 3
Stitch & Flip
Make 3

Unit 4
Stitch & Flip
Make 3

Sew the units and patches together as shown to complete the block.

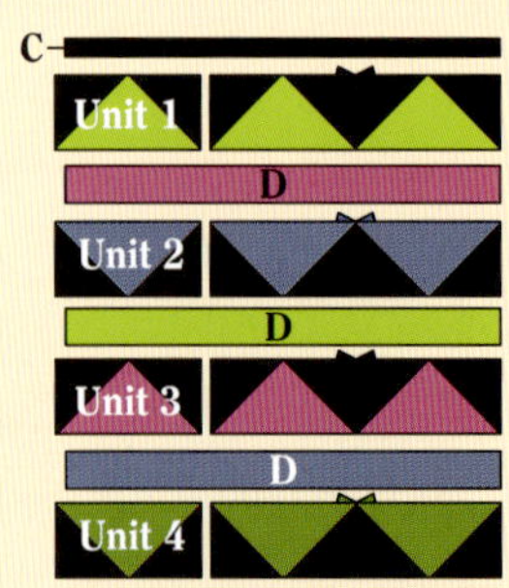

Block Assembly

block no. 831

Tiara

by Monique Dillard • Open Gate
opengatequilts.com

Fabric: Royal Gardens designed by Monique Dillard for Maywood Studio, maywoodstudio.com.

Monique Dillard is the author of *Traditional Fat Quarter Quilts* for C&T Publishing, ctpub.com.

Purple Print #1
- 1 square (A) 6½" x 6½"

Green Solid
- 2 rectangles (B) 2" x 6½"
- 2 rectangles (C) 2" x 9½"

Purple Print #2
- 4 squares (D) 3½" x 3½"
- 8 squares (E) 2⅜" x 2⅜"
- 4 squares (G) 2" x 2"

Tan Dot
- 8 squares (E) 2⅜" x 2⅜"
- 4 rectangles (F) 2" x 3½"

Unit 2
Make 16

Sew the purple print #1 A and green B's and C's together as shown. Refer to "Stitch-and-Flip"in the Techniques file on the PDF. Add the purple print #2 D's to make unit 1.

Pair the purple print #2 E's with the tan E's to make 16 Triangle-Square unit 2's. Sew the units and patches together as shown to complete the block.

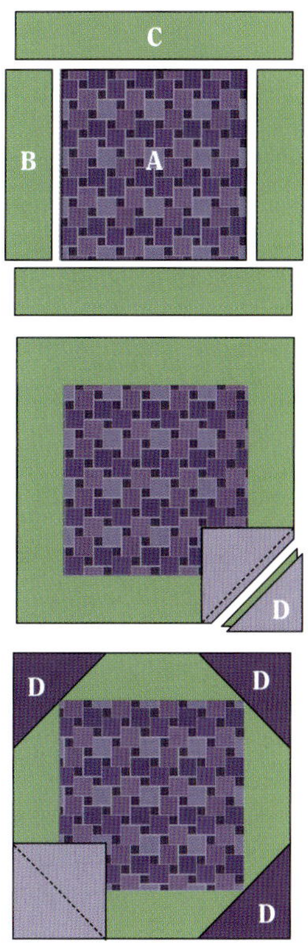

Unit 1
Stitch & Flip
Make 1

Block Assembly

block no. 832

Apple Tree

by June Dudley • Editor-in-Chief, *Quiltmaker*
quiltmaker.com

Fabric: P&B Textiles, pbtex.com.

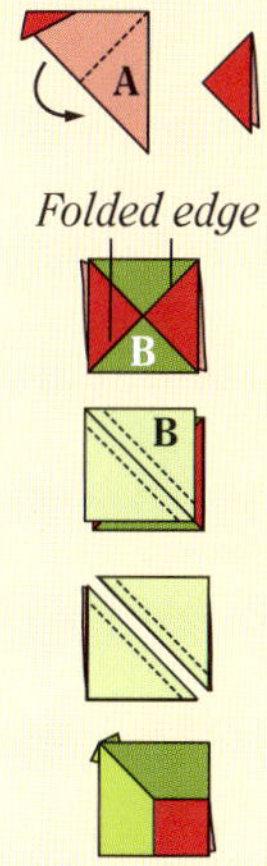

Unit 1
Make 20

◸ = cut in half diagonally

Red Tone-on-Tone
- 10 squares 2⅞" x 2⅞" ◸ (A)

Green Plaid and Green Dot
from *each*
- 10 squares (B) 2⅞" x 2⅞"

Light Blue Tone-on-Tone
- 6 squares (C) 2½" x 2½"
- 4 squares (D) 1½" x 1½"
- 1 square (E) 1⅞" x 1⅞"
- 2 rectangles (F) 2½" x 9½"

Brown Tone-on-Tone
- 1 square (C) 2½" x 2½"
- 2 squares (D) 1½" x 1½"
- 1 square (E) 1⅞" x 1⅞"

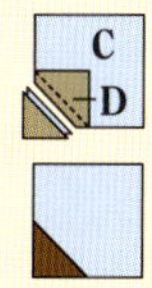

Unit 2
Stitch & Flip
Make 2

Unit 4
Make 2

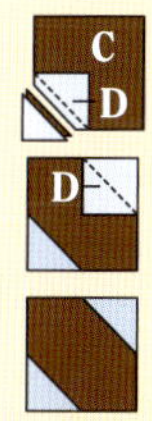

Unit 3
Stitch & Flip
Make 1

Fold the red A's in half as shown. Draw a diagonal line on the wrong side of the green dot B's. Noting the placement of the folds, arrange 2 folded red A's on opposite sides of a green plaid B as shown; pin in place. Layer a green dot B on top of the green plaid B with right sides together as shown. Sew ¼" on either side of the drawn line; cut on the drawn line. Open the green B's. Open out the red A, matching the point to the corner seam to form the small red square; press to make a unit 1. Make 20 unit 1's; there will be 1 extra.

Refer to "Stitch-and-Flip" in the Techniques file on the PDF. Use the blue C's and brown D's to make 2 unit 2's. Use the brown C and blue D's to make 1 unit 3.

Pair the blue E with the brown E to make 2 Triangle-Square unit 4's. Sew the units and patches together as shown to complete the block.

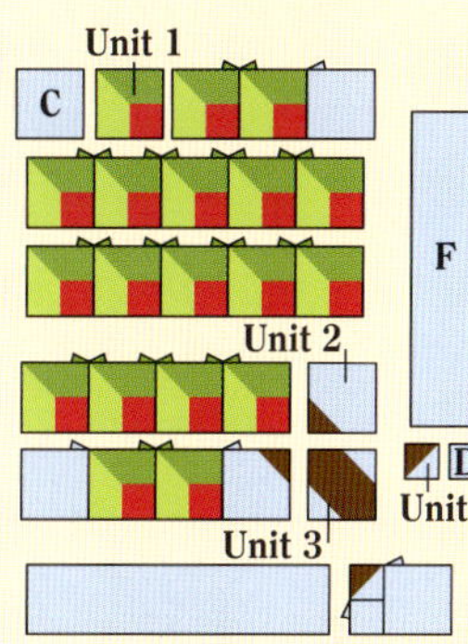

Block Assembly

block no. 833

Prairie Sunburst

by Deanne Eisenman • Snuggles Quilts
snugglesquilts.com

Deanne Eisenman is the author of *Scrap Quilts Go Country* for Martingale & Co., shopmartingale.com.

Dark Tan Print
4 squares (A) 3⅞"x 3⅞"
Cream Print
4 squares (A) 3⅞"x 3⅞"
16 squares (B) 2⅜"x 2⅜"
Red Print
16 squares (B) 2⅜"x 2⅜"

Pair the dark tan A's with the cream A's to make 8 Triangle-Square unit 1's. Pair the red B's with the cream B's to make 32 unit 2's.

Sew the units together as shown to complete the block.

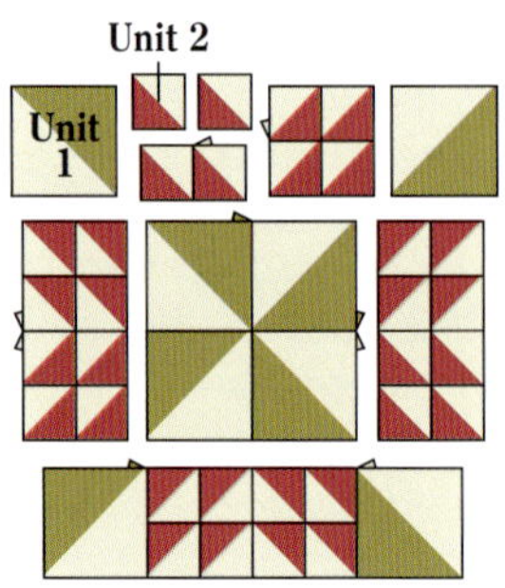

Block Assembly

block no. 834

Enchanted

by Amy Ellis • Amy's Creative Side
amyscreativeside.com

Fabric: Frippery designed by Thomas Knauer for Andover Fabrics, andoverfabrics.com and Kona cotton solids by Robert Kaufman, robertkaufman.com.

Amy Ellis is the author of *Modern Basics* and *Modern Basics II* for Martingale & Co., shopmartingale.com.

⊠ = cut in half twice diagonally

4 Assorted Prints
from *each*
1 square (A) 6⅛"x 6⅛"
Teal Solid and White Solid
from *each*
1 square 5¼"x 5¼" ⊠ (B)

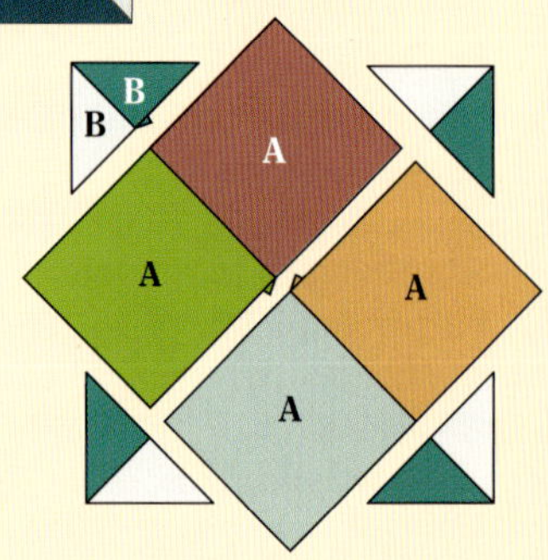

Block Piecing

Trimming Diagram

Sew the patches together as shown. Trim as shown to 12½"× 12½" to complete the block.

block no. 835

Whirly Zig

by Heidi Foltz • Handmade by Heidi
handmadebyheidi.com

Fabric: Old Glory Gatherings designed by Primitive Gatherings for Moda Fabrics, unitednotions.com.

Red Print
2 squares (A) 3⅞″ x 3⅞″
Cream Solid
4 squares (A) 3⅞″ x 3⅞″
20 squares (B) 1¾″ x 1¾″
16 squares (D) 2″ x 2″
Assorted Dark Blue Prints
from *2*
1 square (A) 3⅞″ x 3⅞″
from *8*
2 rectangles (C) 2″ x 3½″

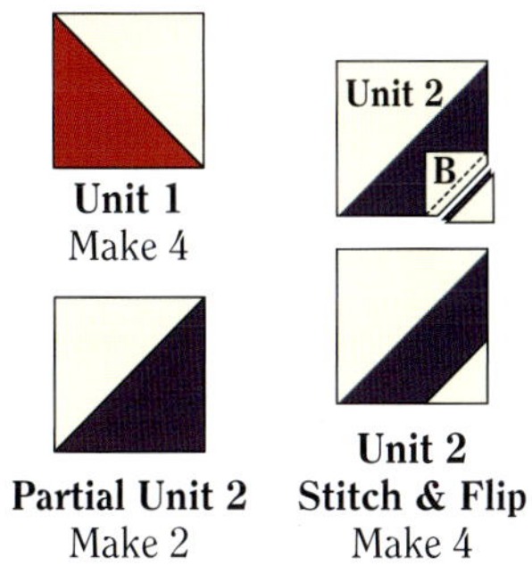

Pair the red A's with cream A's to make 4 Triangle-Square unit 1's. Pair the blue A's with cream A's to make 4 partial unit 2's.

Refer to "Stitch-and-Flip" in the Techniques file on the PDF. Add cream B's to the partial units as shown to make 4 unit 2's. Make 1 unit 3 and 1 unit 4 from each pair of matching dark blue C's and the cream B's and cream D's.

Sew the units together as shown to complete the block.

Block Assembly

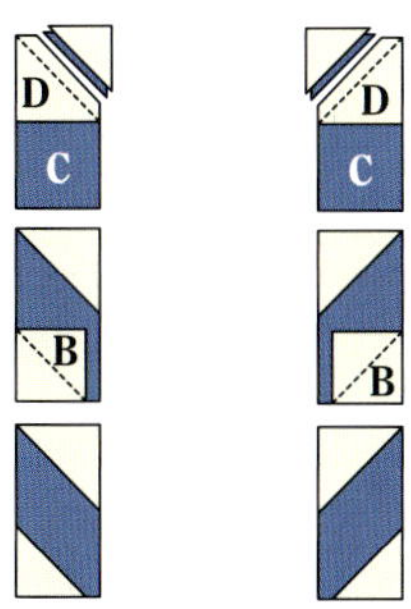

Unit 3 Stitch & Flip Make 8

Unit 4 Stitch & Flip Make 8

block no. 836

Kaleidoscope Star

by Marilyn Foreman • Quilt Moments
quiltmoments.com

Fabric: Love Flows designed by Jan Douglas for Maywood Studio, maywoodstudio.com.

Marilyn Foreman is the author of *Kaleidoscope Symphony* for Quilt Moments, quiltmoments.com.

Dark Green Tone-on-Tone
8 rectangles (A) 2″ x 3½″
Dark Pink Tone-on-Tone
12 squares (B) 2″ x 2″
8 squares (D) 2⅜″ x 2⅜″
Light Green Tone-on-Tone
8 squares (B) 2″ x 2″
1 square (C) 4¼″ x 4¼″
Cream Tone-on-Tone
1 square (C) 4¼″ x 4¼″
4 squares (E) 3½″ x 3½″
Multicolor Print
4 squares (E) 3½″ x 3½″

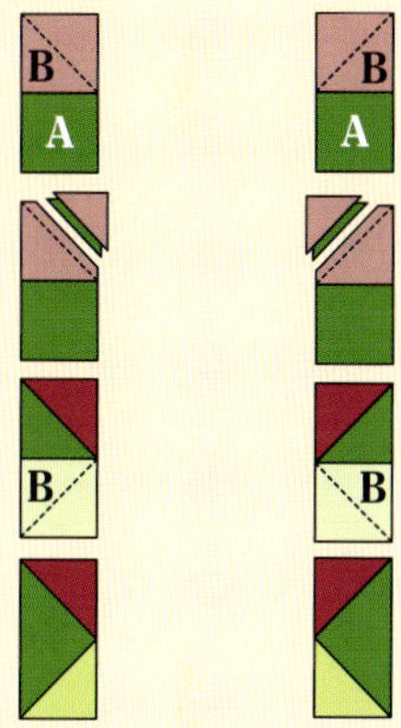

Unit 1 Stitch & Flip Make 4

Unit 2 Stitch & Flip Make 4

Marilyn fussy cut 4 identical multicolor print E's for the kaleidoscope look.

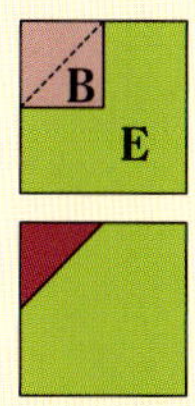

Unit 3 Stitch & Flip Make 4

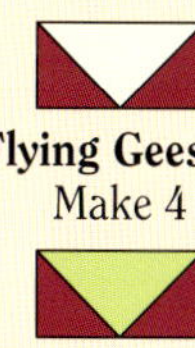
Flying Geese 1 Make 4

Flying Geese 2 Make 4

Refer to "Stitch-and-Flip" in the Techniques file on the PDF. Use the dark green A's, dark pink B's and light green B's to make 4 unit 1's and 4 unit 2's.

Noting the orientation of the E's, use the multicolor print E's and 4 dark pink B's to make 4 unit 3's.

Use the cream C and 4 dark pink D's to make 4 Flying Geese 1's. Use the light green C and 4 dark pink D's to make 4 Flying Geese 2's.

Sew the units, Flying Geese and patches together as shown to complete the block.

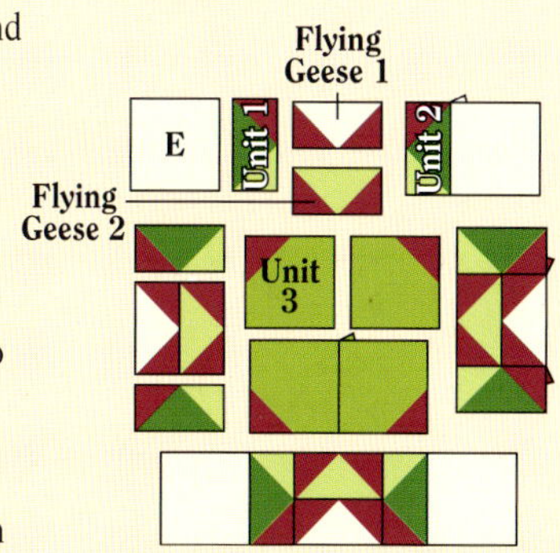

Block Assembly

block no. 837

Fizzy Pop

by Kay Gentry • Noble Needle Quilting and Sewing
nobleneedle.com

Fabric: Mixmasters Fizz designed by Patrick Lose for Robert Kaufman, robertkaufman.com.

Yellow Tone-on-Tone
1 square (A) 4¼"x 4¼"
2 squares (C) 3⅞"x 3⅞"
1 square (D) 3½"x 3½"

Dark Pink Tone-on-Tone
4 squares (B) 2⅜"x 2⅜"
2 squares (C) 3⅞"x 3⅞"

Green Tone-on-Tone and Blue Tone-on-Tone
from *each*
8 squares (E) 2"x 2"

Orange Tone-on-Tone
8 squares (E) 2"x 2"
8 rectangles (F) 2"x 3½"

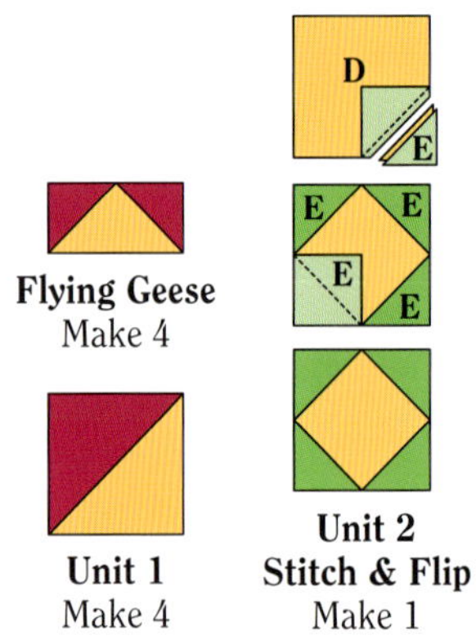

Use the yellow A and the pink B's to make 4 Flying Geese.

Pair the yellow C's with the pink C's to make 4 Triangle-Square unit 1's.

Refer to "Stitch-and-Flip" in the Techniques file on the PDF. Make unit 2 using the yellow D and 4 green E's.

Sew the Flying Geese, units and patches together as shown to complete the block.

Block Assembly

block no. 838

Counter Spin

by Carolyn Goins • CPG Designs
cpgdesigns.com

Fabric: Spin designed by Whistler Studios for Windham Fabrics, windhamfabrics.com.

Yellow Tone-on-Tone
4 squares (A) 6½"x 6½"

White Tone-on-Tone
16 squares (B) 3½"x 3½"

Purple Tone-on-Tone
4 rectangles (C) 3½"x 7"

Buttons 4 at ¼"

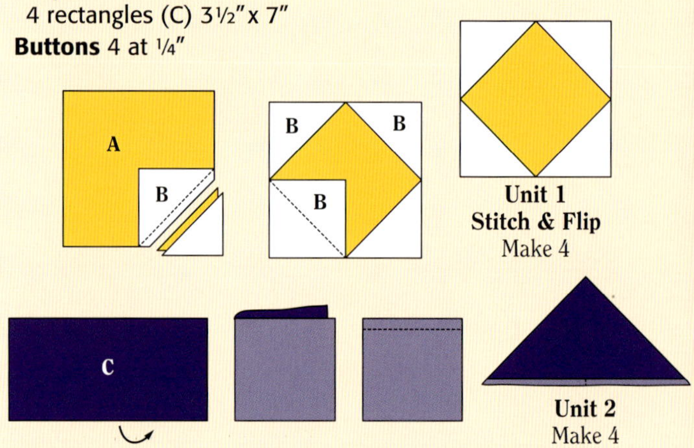

Refer to "Stitch-and-Flip" in the Techniques file on the PDF. Use the yellow A's and white B's to make 4 unit 1's.

Button Placement

Fold a purple C in half crosswise with right sides together. Stitch ¼" from the top edge as shown, securing the stitches at the ends. Turn right side out and press the triangle open. Repeat with the other purple C's to make 4 unit 2's.

Baste a unit 2 to each unit 1, stitching ⅛" from the raw edge. Sew the units together as shown.

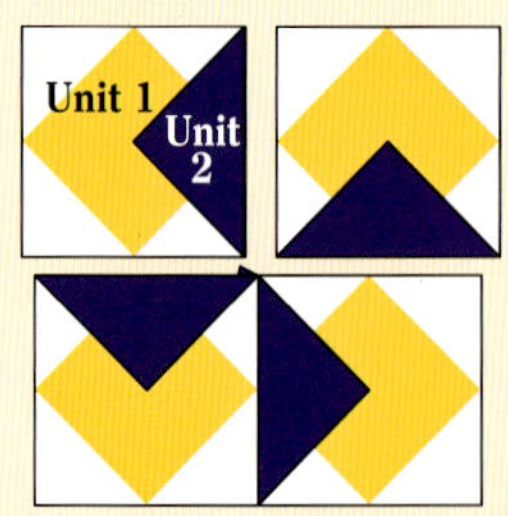

Block Assembly

Tack a button to the tip of each purple triangle as shown to complete the block.

block no. 839

Sky on Fire

by Diane Harris • Interactive Editor, *Quiltmaker*
quiltmaker.com

Fabric: Batiks designed by Karen Combs for Troy Riverwoods Collection, troy-corp.com.

See page 281 on the PDF for pattern

Pale Gray Batik
section patch 1
2 squares (A) 2 7/8" x 2 7/8"

Dark Green Batik
section patch 2

8 Assorted Orange Batiks
from *each*
2 squares (A) 2 7/8" x 2 7/8"

Blue Batik
2 squares (A) 2 7/8" x 2 7/8"

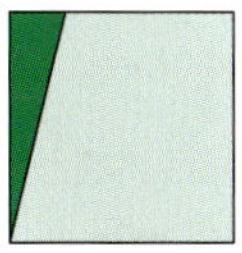

Section
Make 4

Unit 2
Make 4

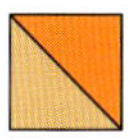

Unit 1
Make 4 sets of 4 matching

Pinwheel 1
Make 4

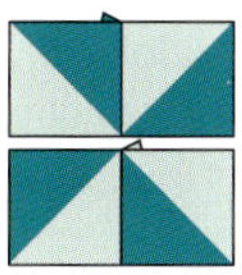

Pinwheel 2
Make 1

Make 4 paper copies of the foundation section. Foundation piece the sections in numerical order, pressing and trimming after each patch addition.

Pair the orange A's to make 4 sets of 4 matching Triangle-Square unit 1's. Use the pale gray A's and blue A's to make 4 unit 2's.

Join the matching unit 1's together as shown to make 4 Pinwheel 1's. Repeat with the unit 2's to make 1 Pinwheel 2.

Sew the sections and Pinwheels together as shown to complete the block.

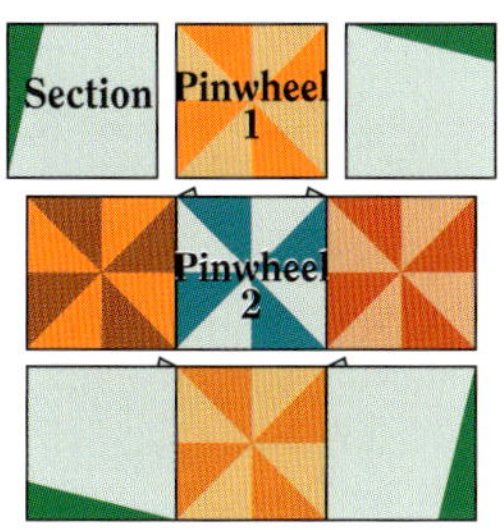

Block Assembly

block no. 840

Patch Charming

by Sandy Harris • Sundrop Designs
sundropdesigns.com

Black Tone-on-Tone
4 squares (A) 1 3/4" x 1 3/4"
4 rectangles (E) 1 1/2" x 5"

Orange Tone-on-Tone, Pink Tone-on-Tone, Yellow Print and Pale Purple Tone-on-Tone
from *each*
2 rectangles (B) 1 3/4" x 3"
1 square (C) 3" x 3"

Teal Tone-on-Tone
4 rectangles (D) 2 1/4" x 5"

Light Green Tone-on-Tone
4 rectangles (E) 1 1/2" x 5"

Multicolor Print
1 square (F) 5" x 5"

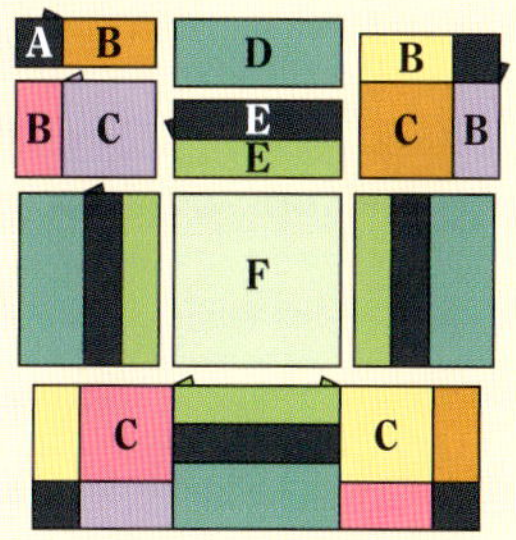

Block Piecing

Sew the patches together as shown to complete the block.

block no. 841

Tilt-a-Whirl

by Chris Hoover • Whirligig Designs
whirligigdesigns.com

Fabric: Fragrance Blush designed by Deborah Edwards for Northcott, northcott.net.

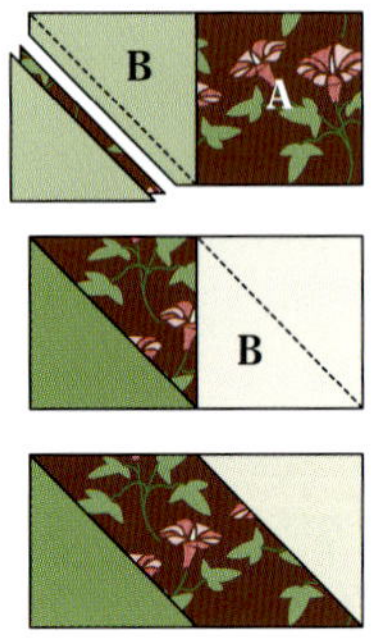

Unit 1
Stich & Flip
Make 4

See page 259 on the PDF for pattern

Dark Brown Print and Pink Print
from each
4 rectangles (A) 3½″ x 6½″
Green Tone-on-Tone and Dark Brown Tone-on-Tone
from each
4 squares (B) 3½″ x 3½″
Cream Tone-on-Tone
8 squares (B) 3½″ x 3½″
Multicolor Stripe
4 template C
Transparent template plastic

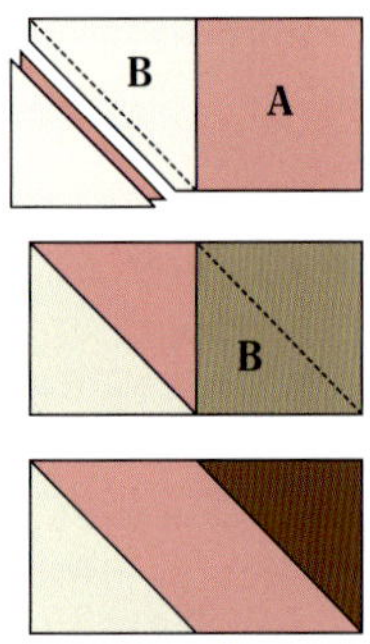

Partial Unit 2
Stich & Flip
Make 4

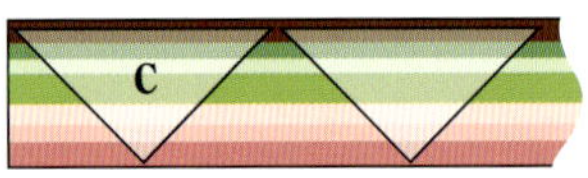

Cut 4

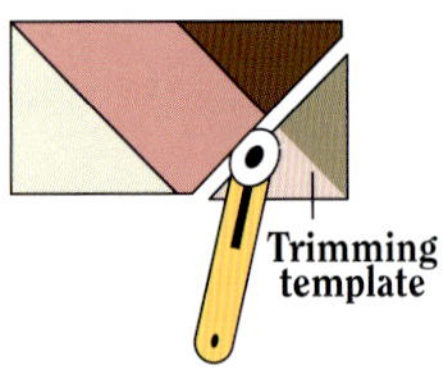

Partial Unit 2
Trimming Diagram

Refer to “Stitch-and-Flip” in the Techniques file on the PDF. Make 4 unit 1’s using the dark brown print A’s, green B’s and 4 cream B’s. Make 4 partial unit 2’s using pink A’s, cream B’s and dark brown B’s.

Use the plastic to make a template of C and the trimming template.

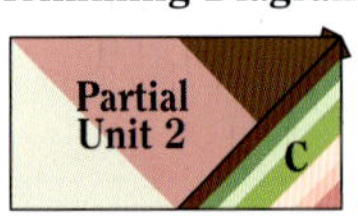

Unit 2
Make 4

Position the plastic template of C on the multicolor stripe as shown and cut 4 C’s.

Refer to the trimming diagram. Align the trimming template on the corner of each partial unit 2 and trim as shown. Sew a stripe C to each partial unit 2 to make 4 unit 2’s.

Sew the units together as shown to complete the block.

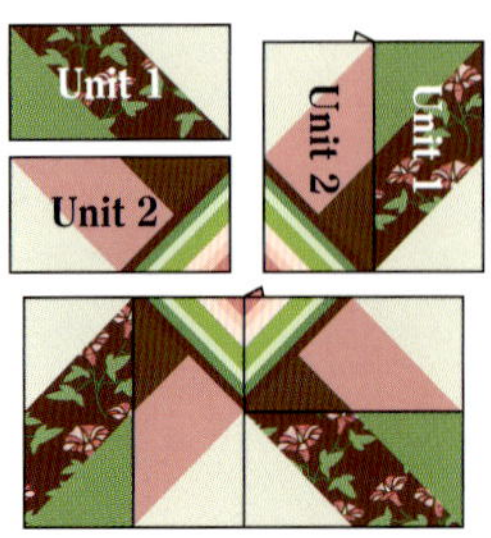

Block Assembly

block no. 842

Jelly Bean Blast

by Bonnie Hunter • Quiltville
quiltville.com

Bonnie Hunter writes the “Addicted to Scraps” column for *Quiltmaker*. She is the author of *Scraps & Shirttails II: Continuing the Art of Quilting Green* and *Adventures with Leaders and Enders* for Kansas City Star Quilts, pickledish.com.

Pink, Purple, Green and Yellow Tone-on-Tones
from each
2 squares (A) 2⅞″ x 2⅞″
2 squares (C) 2½″ x 2½″
6 White Prints
from 4
2 squares (A) 2⅞″ x 2⅞″
from 1
1 square (D) 5¼″ x 5¼″
from 1
1 square (E) 3¼″ x 3¼″
4 squares (G) 1½″ x 1½″
Black Dot
4 rectangles (B) 2½″ x 4½″
Orange Tone-on-Tone
4 squares (A) 2⅞″ x 2⅞″
Teal Tone-on-Tone
4 squares (F) 1⅞″ x 1⅞″
Dark Purple Tone-on-Tone
1 square (C) 2½″ x 2½″

Unit 1 Make 4 · **Unit 2** Make 4 · **Unit 3** Make 4 · **Unit 4** Make 4

Unit 5 **Stitch & Flip** Make 1 · **Unit 6** **Stitch & Flip** Make 1

Unit 7 **Stitch & Flip** Make 1 · **Unit 8** **Stitch & Flip** Make 1

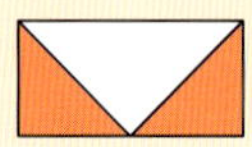

Flying Geese 1
Make 4

Flying Geese 2
Make 4

Pair each color (pink, purple, green or yellow) A with a different white print A to make sets of 4 matching Triangle-Square unit 1’s–4’s.

Refer to “Stitch-and-Flip” in the Techniques file on the PDF. Use the black B’s with pink, purple, green and yellow C’s to make units 5–8 as shown.

Using the white D and orange A’s, make 4 Flying Geese 1. Make 4 Flying Geese 2 using the white E and teal F’s. Sew the units, Flying Geese and patches together as shown to complete the block.

Block Assembly

block no. 843

Marmalade Flower

by Kimberly Jolly • Fat Quarter Shop
fatquartershop.com

Fabric: Marmalade designed by Bonnie and Camille for Moda Fabrics, unitednotions.com.

Pink Print
4 squares (A) 3½″ x 3½″
Cream Solid
16 squares (B) 1¼″ x 1¼″
8 squares (D) 2″ x 2″
8 rectangles (E) 2″ x 3½″
Turquoise Stripe
1 square (A) 3½″ x 3½″
Yellow Print
4 rectangles (C) 3½″ x 5″
Turquoise Print
4 squares (D) 2″ x 2″

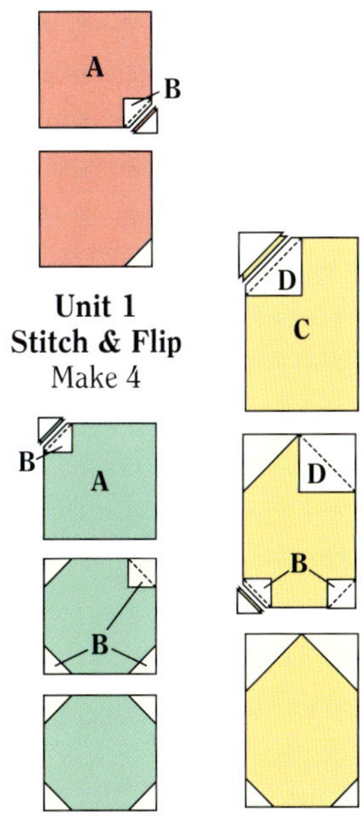

Unit 1
Stitch & Flip
Make 4

Unit 2
Stitch & Flip
Make 1

Unit 3
Stitch & Flip
Make 4

Refer to "Stitch-and-Flip" in the Techniques file on the PDF. Make 4 unit 1's using the pink A's and 4 cream B's. Use the turquoise stripe A and 4 cream B's to make unit 2. Use the yellow C's, cream D's, and 8 cream B's to make 4 unit 3's.

Sew the units and patches together as shown to complete the block.

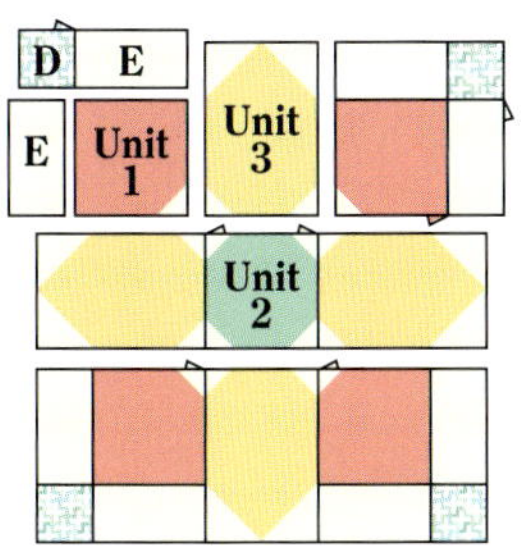

Block Assembly

block no. 844

Twin Star

by Susan Knapp and Mary Jane Mattingly
The Quilt Branch • quiltbranch.com

Fabric: Various batiks from Hoffman California Fabrics, hoffmanfabrics.com.

Susan Knapp and Mary Jane Mattingly are the authors of *I've Been Framed* and the *Six Halves Make a Whole* series for The Quilt Branch, quiltbranch.com.

⊠ = cut in half twice diagonally

Gray Batik
4 squares (A) 3½″ x 3½″
4 squares (C) 2″ x 2″
1 square 7¼″ x 7¼″ ⊠ (E)
Cream Batik
8 rectangles 2″ x 3⅞″
(see diagram to cut 4 B's and 4 Br's)
Dark Brown Batik
2 squares 4¼″ x 4¼″ ⊠ (D)
Cream and Brown Batik
1 square (F) 4¾″ x 4¾″

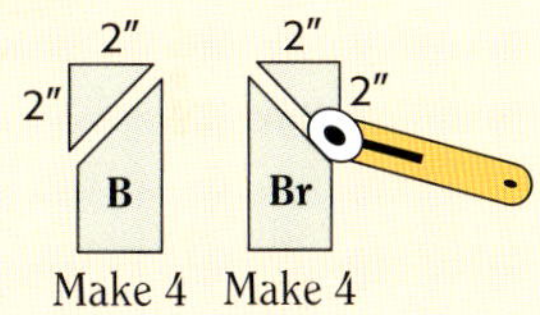

Trimming Diagram

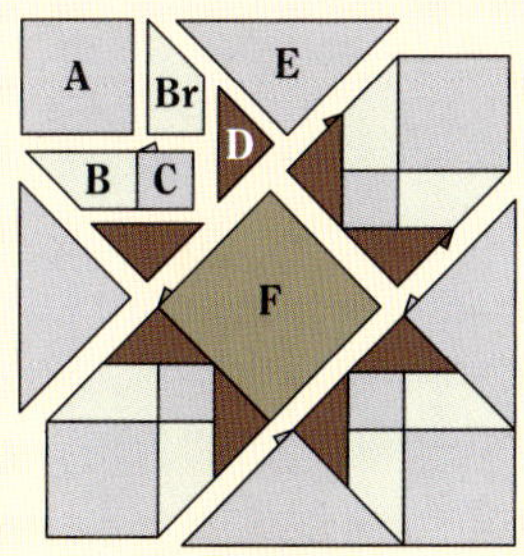

Block Piecing

Sew the patches together as shown to complete the block.

block no. 845

Criss Cross

by Jo & Kelli Kramer • Jo's Country Junction
joscountryjunction.com

⧄ = cut in half diagonally

Red Tone-on-Tone
12 squares 2⅜"x 2⅜" ⧄ (A)

Assorted Tan Prints and Tone-on-Tones
8 squares 2⅜"x 2⅜" ⧄ (A) (there will be 8 extra)
4 squares 3⅞" x 3⅞" ⧄ (B)
4 squares (C) 3½" x 3½"
4 squares (D) 2½" x 2½"

Blue Print
5 squares (D) 2½" x 2½"

Using 8 different tan A's contributes to the scrappy look of this block.

Sew the patches together as shown to complete the block.

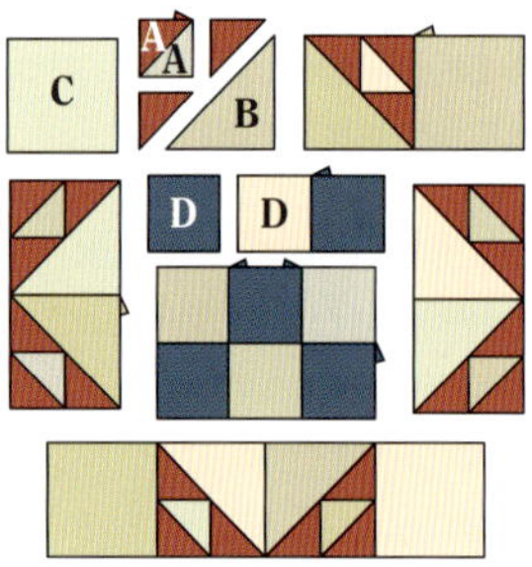

Block Piecing

block no. 846

Paris Square

by Jessie Kurtz • Harding Hill Designs
hardinghilldesigns.com

Fabric: Various lines from Art Gallery Fabrics, artgalleryfabrics.com.

Gray Solid
2 rectangles (A) 2½" x 12½"
2 rectangles (C) 2½" x 8½"

Assorted Light, Medium and Dark Prints
20 squares (B) 2½" x 2½"

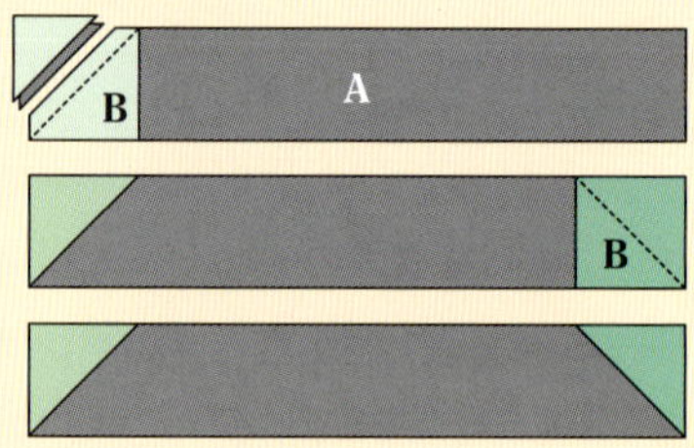

Unit
Stitch & Flip
Make 2

Refer to "Stitch-and-Flip" in the Techniques file on the PDF. Use the gray A's and 4 different B's to make 2 units.

Sew the units and patches together as shown to complete the block.

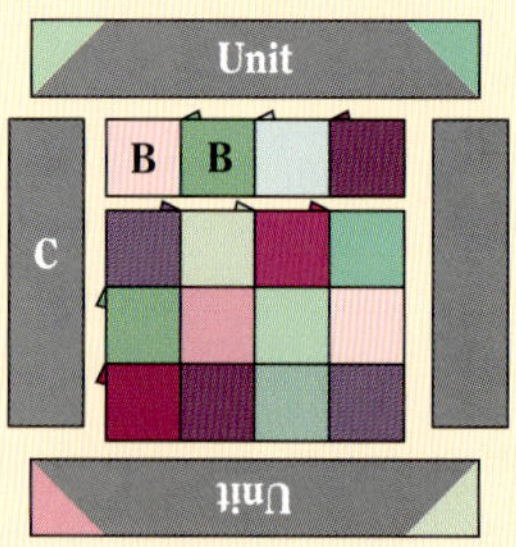

Block Assembly

block no. 847

Spinwheel

by Cindy Lammon • Hyacinth Quilt Designs
hyacinthquiltdesigns.blogspot.com

Fabric: Mama Said Sew designed by Sweetwater for Moda Fabrics, unitednotions.com.

Cindy Lammon is the author of *Flowers All Around—Garden-Inspired Quilts* for Martingale & Co., shopmartingale.com.

⧄ = cut in half diagonally

Assorted Gray, Red and Black Prints
24 squares $2\frac{7}{8}$" x $2\frac{7}{8}$" ⧄ (A) (there will be 24 extra)

Cream Solid
6 squares $2\frac{7}{8}$" x $2\frac{7}{8}$" ⧄ (A)
2 squares $6\frac{7}{8}$" x $6\frac{7}{8}$" ⧄ (B)

Cutting the assorted prints as indicated enhances the scrappy look of this block.

Sew the patches together as shown to complete the block.

Block Piecing

block no. 848

Sailing Pinwheel

by Judy Laquidara • Patchwork Times
patchworktimes.com

Fabric: Dimples designed by Gail Kessler for Andover Fabrics, andoverfabrics.com.

Judy Laquidara is the author of *60 Pieced Quilt Borders: Mix & Match* for American Quilter's Society, americanquilter.com.

Gold Tone-on-Tone and Orange Tone-on-Tone
from *each*
2 squares (A) $4\frac{7}{8}$" x $4\frac{7}{8}$"
6 squares (B) $2\frac{1}{2}$" x $2\frac{1}{2}$"

Dark Blue Tone-on-Tone
12 squares (B) $2\frac{1}{2}$" x $2\frac{1}{2}$"
2 squares (D) $2\frac{7}{8}$" x $2\frac{7}{8}$"

Cream Tone-on-Tone
4 rectangles (C) $2\frac{1}{2}$" x $4\frac{1}{2}$"
2 squares (D) $2\frac{7}{8}$" x $2\frac{7}{8}$"

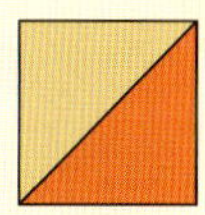

Partial Unit
Make 4

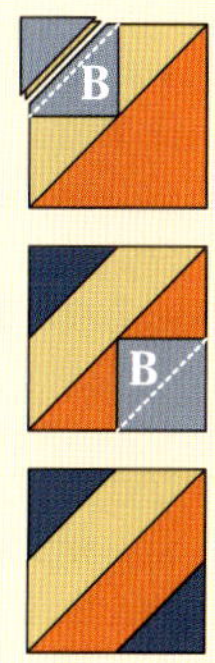

Unit 1
Stitch & Flip
Make 4

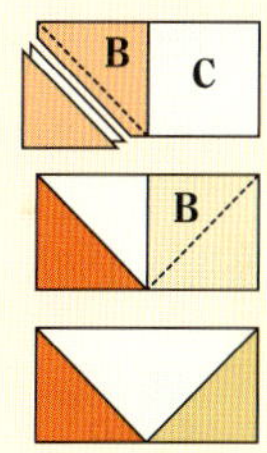

Unit 2
Stitch & Flip
Make 2

Unit 4
Make 4

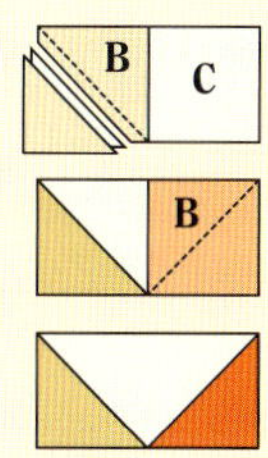

Unit 3
Stitch & Flip
Make 2

Refer to "Triangle-Squares" in the Techniques file on the PDF. Pair the gold A's with the orange A's to make 4 partial units. Refer to "Stitch-and-Flip" in the Techniques file on the PDF. Sew dark blue B's to the corners of the partial units as shown to make 4 unit 1's.

Use the cream C's, orange B's and gold B's to make 2 unit 2's and 2 unit 3's as shown. Pair the cream D's with the dark blue D's to make 4 unit 4's.

Noting the orientation of the unit 1's, sew the units and patches together as shown to complete the block.

Block Assembly

block no. 849

Bows and Arrows

by Doug Leko • Antler Quilt Design
antlerquiltdesign.com

Dark Teal Batik
- 4 rectangles (A) 2½"x 4½"
- 4 squares (E) 1½"x 1½"

Dark Blue Batik
- 6 squares (B) 2½"x 2½"
- 1 square (C) 2⅞"x 2⅞"

Pale Gray Batik
- 8 squares (B) 2½"x 2½"
- 3 squares (C) 2⅞"x 2⅞"
- 8 rectangles (D) 1½"x 2½"
- 4 squares (F) 3½"x 3½"

Green Batik
- 2 squares (C) 2⅞"x 2⅞"
- 2 squares (B) 2½"x 2½"

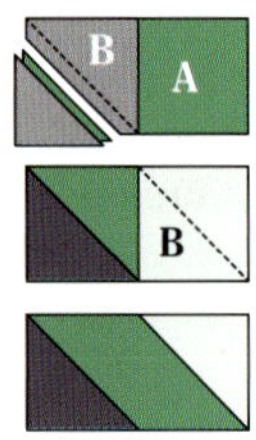

Unit 1
Stitch & Flip
Make 2

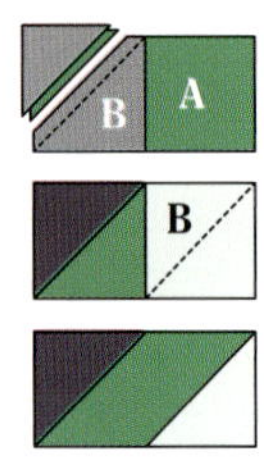

Unit 2
Stitch & Flip
Make 2

Refer to "Stitch-and-Flip" in the Techniques file on the PDF. Use the teal A's, blue B's and gray B's to make 2 unit 1's and 2 unit 2's as shown.

Pair the green C's with the gray C's to make 4 Triangle-Square unit 3's. Pair a gray C and a blue C to make 2 unit 2's.

Unit 3 Make 4

Unit 4 Make 2

Sew the units and patches together as shown to complete the block.

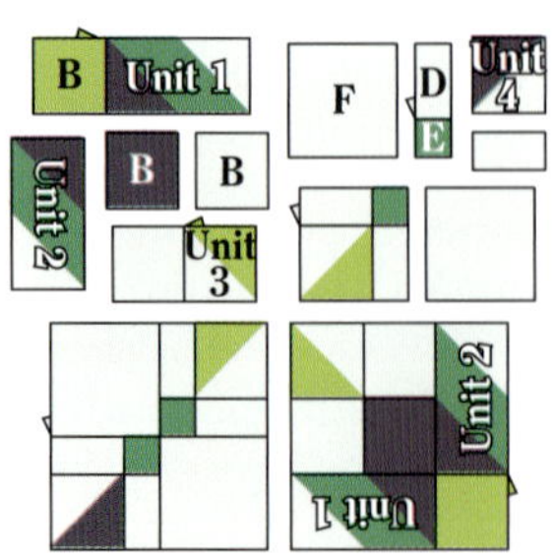

Block Assembly

block no. 850

Beach Cabanas

by Cheryl Lynch • Oy Vey! Quilt Designs
cheryllynchquilts.com

Cheryl Lynch is the author of *iQuilt Fiesta!* for Martingale & Co., shopmartingale.com.

See page 270 on the PDF for pattern

Medium Blue Dot
- 2 template A
- 1 rectangle (F) 2"x 2¾"

White Dot
- 3 *each* templates B and Br
- 1 rectangle (C) 1¾"x 12½"

Multicolor Stripe
- 1 template A
- 2 rectangles (D) 4"x 4½"
- 4 rectangles (E) 1¾"x 2¾"

Green Dot
- 1 rectangle (D) 4"x 4½"
- 2 rectangles (E) 1¾"x 2¾"
- 2 rectangles (F) 2"x 2¾"

White rickrack 12½"

Buttons
- 3 at ¾"
- 16 at ¼"

White cording 36"

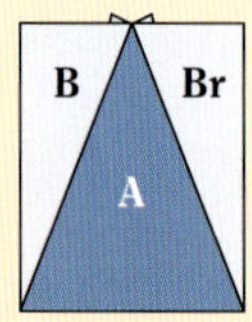

Unit 1
Make 2

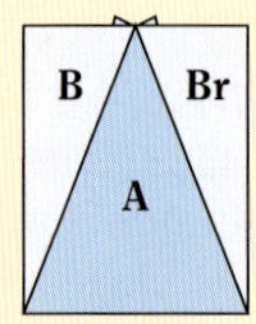

Unit 2
Make 1

Tie and Button Placement

Sew the A's, B's and Br's together as shown to make 2 unit 1's and 1 unit 2. Sew the units and the white C together as shown.

Sew the D's, E's and F's together. Baste the rickrack along the top of the D's. Join the top and bottom halves of the block as shown.

Refer to the tie placement diagram. Cut the white cording into 12 lengths of 3" and gather into 3 sets of 4 lengths. Thread one set through each large button to tack in place and tie a knot to secure, leaving a tail at both ends.

Cheryl recommends Fray-Check to keep the cording knots tied.

Tack the ¼" buttons along the rickrack as shown to complete the block.

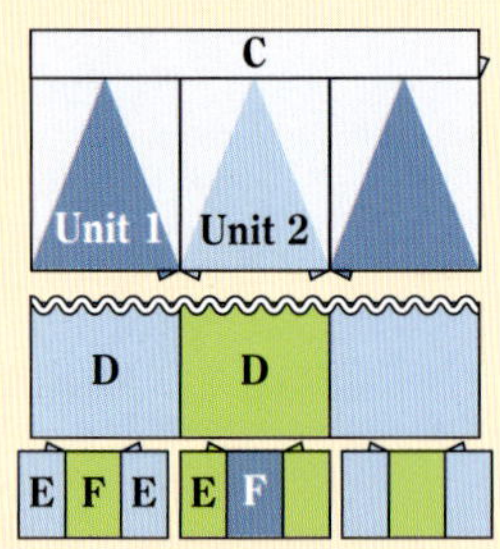

Block Assembly

pieced

block no. 851

Rick Rack Row

by Marian Mapes

Fabric: Bali Batiks from Hoffman California Fabrics, hoffmanfabrics.com.

◩ = cut in half diagonally
⊠ = cut in half twice diagonally

Light Green Batik
4 squares 3⅞"x 3⅞" ◩ (A)

Medium Green Batik and Red Batik
from *each*
3 squares 3⅞"x 3⅞" ◩ (A)
(there will be 1 extra from each)
1 square 4¼"x 4¼" ⊠ (B)
(there will be 1 extra from each)

Orange Batik
2 squares 4¼"x 4¼" ⊠ (B)

Blue Batik
3 squares 3⅞"x 3⅞" ◩ (A)
1 square 4¼"x 4¼" ⊠ (B)
(there will be 2 extra)

Sew the patches together as shown to complete the block.

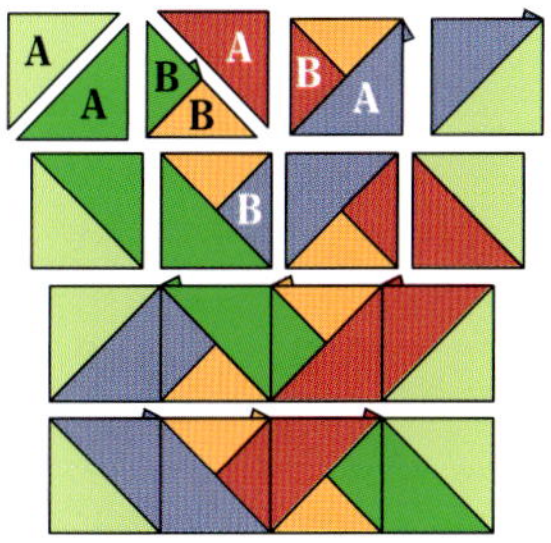

Block Piecing

block no. 852

Stepping Stone Stars

by Marsha McCloskey • Feathered Star Productions
marshamccloskey.com

Marsha McCloskey is the author of *Feathered Star Quilt Blocks II* and other titles for Feathered Star Productions, Inc., marshamccloskey.com.

Cream Tone-on-Tone #1
1 square (A) 7¼"x 7¼"
4 squares (F) 1⅝"x 1⅝"
24 squares (G) 1¼"x 1¼"
9 squares (H) 2"x 2"

Brown Print
4 squares (B) 3⅞"x 3⅞"

Cream Tone-on-Tone #2
1 square (C) 4¼"x 4¼"

Red Print
4 squares (D) 2⅜"x 2⅜"

Dark Brown Tone-on-Tone
1 square (E) 2¾"x 2¾"
28 squares (G) 1¼"x 1¼"

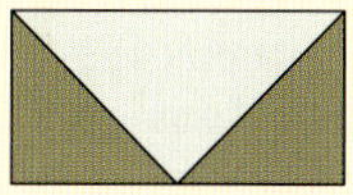

Flying Geese 1
Make 4

Flying Geese 2
Make 4

Flying Geese 3
Make 4

Use the cream #1 A and brown print B's to make 4 Flying Geese 1's.

Use the cream #2 C and red D's to make 4 Flying Geese 2's.

Use the dark brown E and cream #1 F's to make 4 Flying Geese 3's.

Sew the Flying Geese and patches together as shown to complete the block.

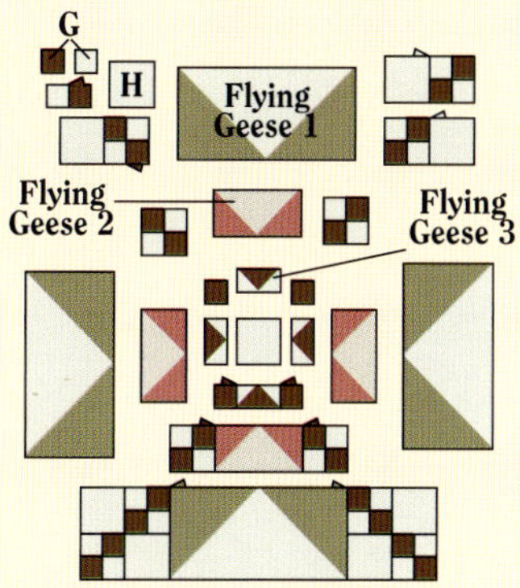

Block Assembly

block no. 853

Entwined Squares

by Moira McSpadden • The Quilted Snail
thequiltedsnail.com

Green Tone-on-Tone
- 1 square (A) 3⅞" x 3⅞"

White Tone-on-Tone
- 1 square (A) 3⅞" x 3⅞"
- 2 rectangles (B) 2" x 8"
- 2 squares (C) 2" x 2"
- 2 squares (E) 3½" x 3½"
- 2 rectangles (G) 2" x 9½"

Purple Tone-on-Tone and Purple Print
from *each*
- 1 square (C) 2" x 2"
- 1 rectangle (D) 2" x 11"
- 1 rectangle (F) 2" x 6½"

Unit 1
Make 2

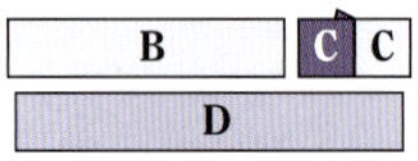

Unit 2
Make 1

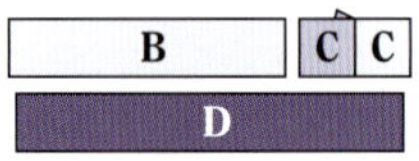

Unit 3
Make 1

Pair the green A with the white A to make 2 Triangle-Square unit 1's.

Sew a white B, purple print C, white C and purple tone-on-tone D together as shown to make unit 2. Use a white B, purple tone-on-tone C, a white C and a purple print D to make unit 3. Refer to the center piecing diagram to sew the unit 1's, white E's and purple F's together.

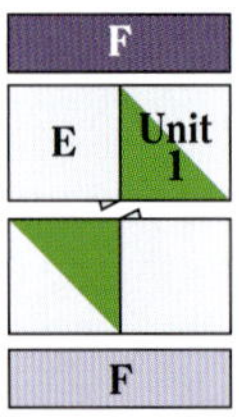

Center Piecing

Sew a white G to the top of the center with a partial seam as shown. Noting the orientation, sew unit 2 to the left of the center. Sew a white G to the bottom and unit 3 to the right as shown. Complete the partial seam to finish the block.

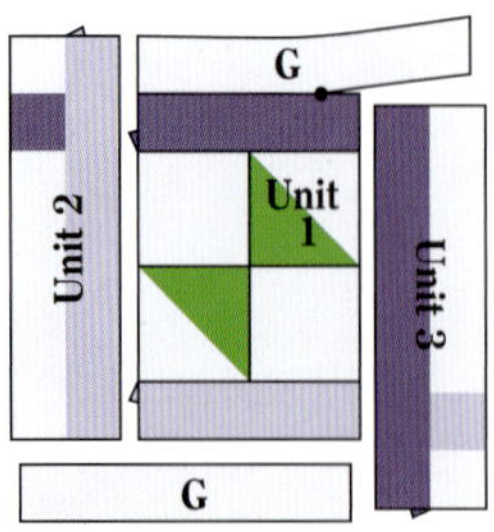

Block Assembly

block no. 854

Stairway to Heaven

by Scott Murkin • Patchwork Possibilities

Red Print
- 8 rectangles (A) 2" x 4½"
- 2 squares (C) 2" x 2"
- 2 rectangles (F) 2" x 3"

Yellow Print
- 3 rectangles (B) 1½" x 4½"
- 2 rectangles (D) 1½" x 2"
- 2 rectangles (E) 1½" x 3"

Black Tone-on-Tone and White Print
from *each*
- 8 rectangles (B) 1½" x 4½"

Sew the patches together as shown to complete the block.

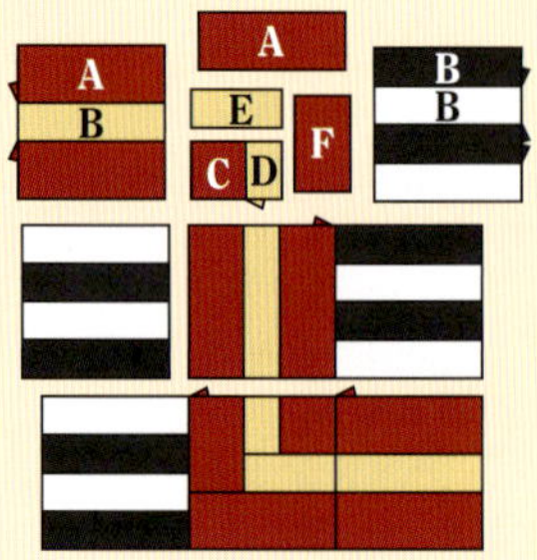

Block Piecing

block no. 855

Lollipop Lollipop

by Amanda Murphy • Amanda Murphy Design
amandamurphydesign.com

Fabric: Bella designed by Amanda Murphy for Blend Fabrics, blendfabrics.com.

4 Assorted Pink and Orange Prints
from *each*
 1 square (A) 5½″ x 5½″
Pale Yellow Tone-on-Tone
 12 squares (B) 2″ x 2″
 8 rectangles (C) 2″ x 2½″
Teal Tone-on-Tone
 4 squares (B) 2″ x 2″
 1 square (D) 2½″ x 2½″
Green Print
 4 squares (D) 2½″ x 2½″

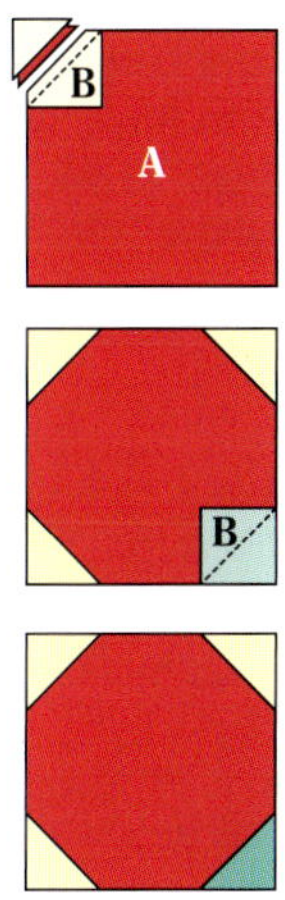

Partial Unit
Stitch & Flip
Make 4

Refer to "Stitch-and-Flip" in the Techniques file on the PDF. Use the 4 assorted print A's, pale yellow B's and teal B's to make 4 partial units. Join 2 yellow C's and a green D to each partial unit as shown to make 4 units.

Noting the orientation, sew a unit to the top of the teal D with a partial seam as shown. Sew a unit to the right, to the bottom, and to the left of the teal D as shown. Complete the partial seam to finish the block.

Unit
Make 4

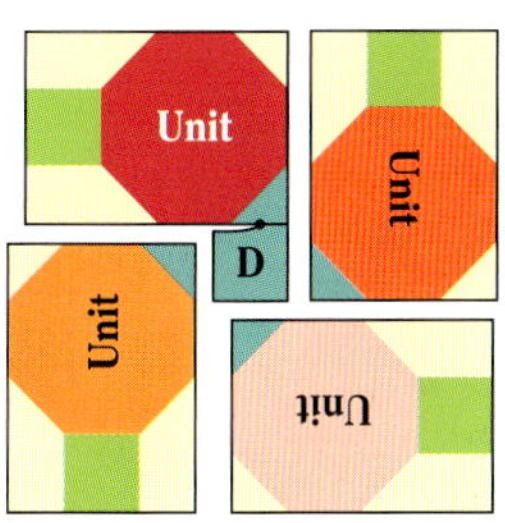

Block Assembly

block no. 856

Sarah's Twirl

by Jennifer Oden • Quilt Specially by Jennifer
quiltspeciallybyjen.blogspot.com

⧄ = cut in half diagonally

Multicolor Print
 4 rectangles (A) 4¾″ x 8″
Green Print #1
 8 rectangles (B) ¾″ x 8″
Green Print #2
 2 squares 5⅛″ x 5⅛″ ⧄ (C)
Orange Print
 1 square (D) 3½″ x 3½″

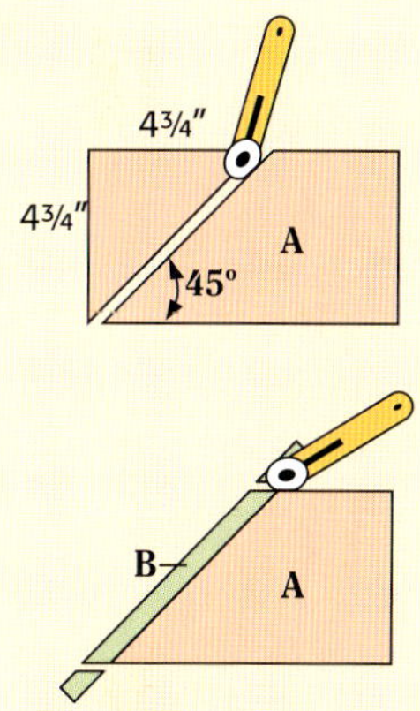

Refer to the diagram to trim the multicolor A's as shown.

Join a green #1 B to an A; trim as shown. Join a green #2 C and green #1 B to complete the unit. Repeat to make 4 units.

Sew a unit to the right side of the orange D with a partial seam as shown. Sew a unit to the top, left and bottom as shown. Complete the partial seam to finish the block.

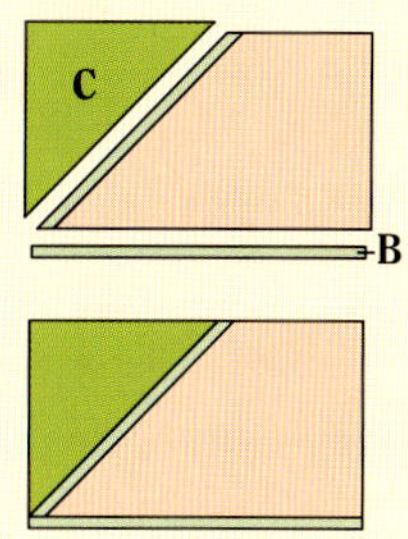

Unit
Make 4

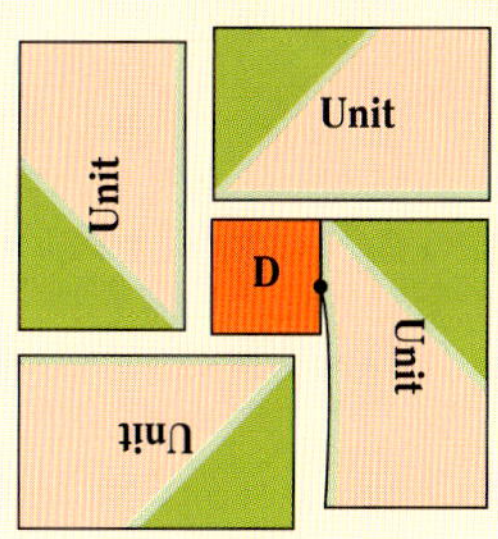

Block Assembly

block no. 857

Between the Lines

by Melissa Peda • 100 Billion Stars
100billionstars.com

Fabric: Early Birds designed by Jane Sassaman and Flower Power by Jennifer Paganelli both for FreeSpirit Fabrics, freespiritfabrics.com.

◸ = cut in half diagonally

White Solid
1 square (A) 3⅞"x 3⅞"
2 rectangles (C) 1¾"x 2¼"
2 rectangles (D) 1¾"x 3½"

Red Dot
1 square (A) 3⅞"x 3⅞"
4 rectangles (E) 1¾"x 6½"

Black Print
2 squares (B) 2¼"x 2¼"
4 squares (F) 1¾"x 1¾"

Green Tone-on-Tone
2 squares 6⅞"x 6⅞" ◸ (G)

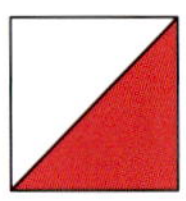

Unit
Make 2

Pair the white A with the red A to make 2 Triangle-Square units.

Sew the units and patches together as shown to complete the block.

Block Assembly

block no. 858

Spring Julep

by Renelda Peldunas-Harter
quiltedcora.blogspot.com

Dark Green, Dark Pink, Yellow, Medium Orange, Dark Orange, Medium Pink, Medium Green and Dark Brown Batiks
from *each*
1 rectangle (A) 2"x 18"

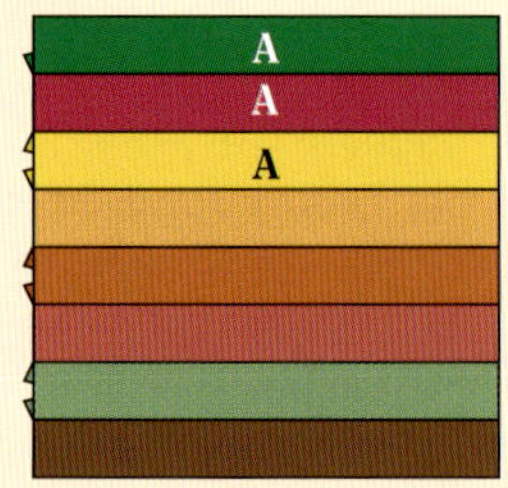

Band

Sew the strips together as shown to make a band. Join the dark brown strip to the dark green strip as shown to make a tube.

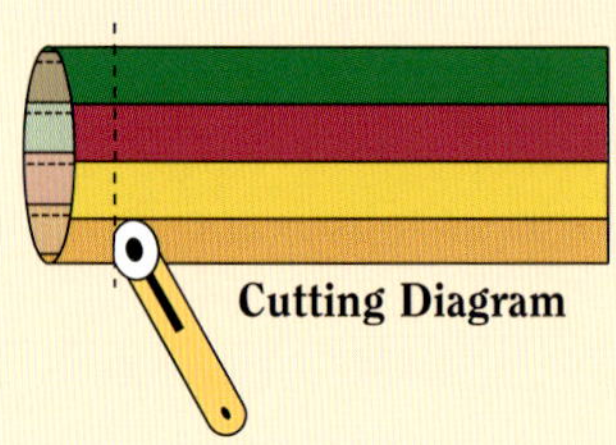

Cutting Diagram

Cut the following segments from the tube: 3 at 2¼", 2 at 1½", 1 at 1¼", 1 at 3" and 1 at 2".

Referring to the diagram, remove the stitches at the seam between colors as indicated for each cut segment. Sew the segments together as shown to complete the block.

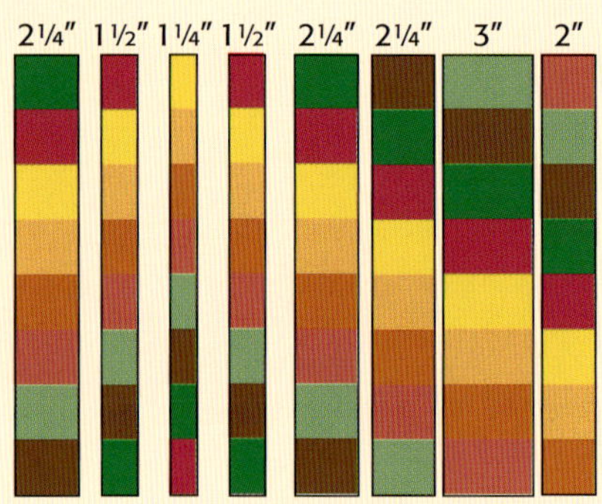

Block Piecing

pieced

block no. 859

Apron Strings

by Celine Perkins • Perkins Dry Goods
perkinsdrygoods.com

Fabric: Various lines designed by Darlene Zimmerman for Robert Kaufman, robertkaufman.com.

◸ = cut in half diagonally

Yellow Print
1 square (A) $3\frac{7}{8}$" x $3\frac{7}{8}$"

Blue Print
2 squares (A) $3\frac{7}{8}$" x $3\frac{7}{8}$"
4 squares (C) 2" x 2"

Red Print
1 square (A) $3\frac{7}{8}$" x $3\frac{7}{8}$"
8 squares (C) 2" x 2"

White Dot
2 squares $5\frac{5}{8}$" x $5\frac{5}{8}$" ◸ (B)
4 rectangles (D) 2" x $6\frac{1}{2}$"

Unit 1
Make 2

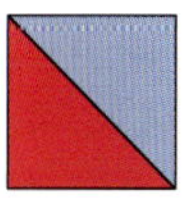

Unit 2
Make 2

Pair the yellow A with a blue A to make 2 Triangle-Square unit 1's. Use the red A with a blue A to make 2 unit 2's.

Sew the units and patches together as shown to complete the block.

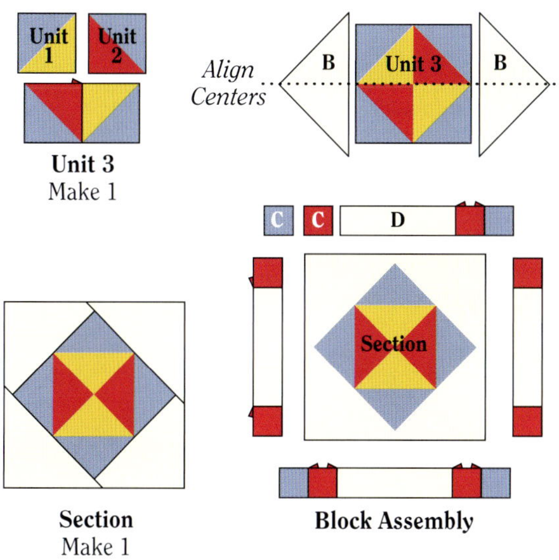

Block Assembly

block no. 860

Hearts Around

by Marjorie Rhine • Quilt Design NW
quiltdesignnw.com

Marjorie Rhine is the author of *Painless Paper Piecing* for Quiltwoman, quiltwoman.com.

◸ = cut in half diagonally
☒ = cut in half twice diagonally

Cream Tone-on-Tone
8 rectangles (A) $2\frac{1}{2}$" x $4\frac{1}{2}$"
2 squares $4\frac{7}{8}$" x $4\frac{7}{8}$" ◸ (D)

Pink Tone-on-Tone, Green Print, Yellow Print and Blue Tone-on-Tone
from *each*
4 squares (B) $2\frac{1}{2}$" x $2\frac{1}{2}$"
1 square $5\frac{1}{4}$" x $5\frac{1}{4}$" ☒ (C)
(there will be 1 extra)

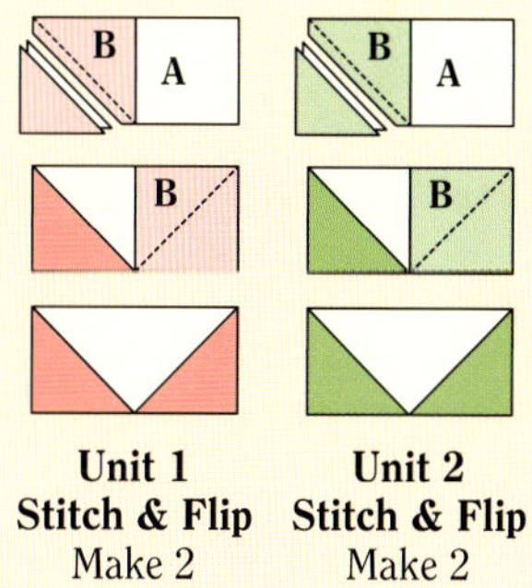

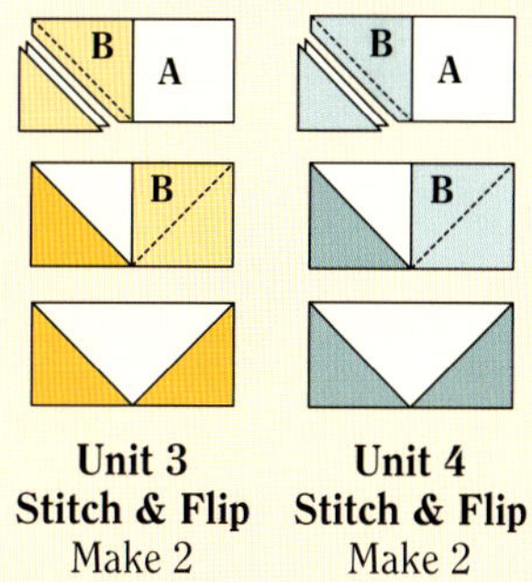

Refer to "Stitch-and-Flip" in the Techniques file on the PDF. Use a cream A and the pink B's to make 2 unit 1's as shown. Make 2 unit 2's using a cream A and the green B's. Use a cream A and the yellow B's to make 2 unit 3's. Make 2 unit 4's using a cream A and the blue B's.

Sew the units and patches together as shown to complete the block.

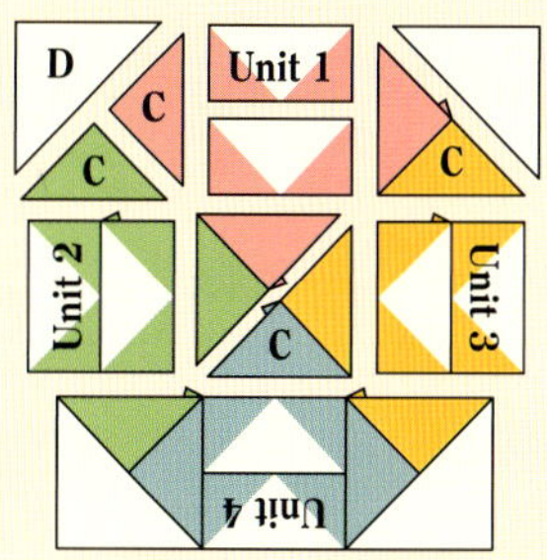

Block Assembly

block no. 861

Square Crossing

by Lindsey Rhodes • LRstitched
LRstitched.com

Teal Tone-on-Tone, Orange Print, Green Print and Purple Tone-on-Tone
from *each*
 1 square (A) 2½″x 2½″

Teal Print, Orange Tone-on-Tone, Green Dot and Purple Print
from *each*
 2 rectangles (B) 2″x 2½″
 2 rectangles (C) 2″x 5½″

Light Blue Print
 2 squares (A) 2½″x 2½″
 1 rectangle (E) 2½″x 6½″

4 Assorted Prints and Tone-on-Tones from *each*
 1 rectangle (D) 2½″x 3½″

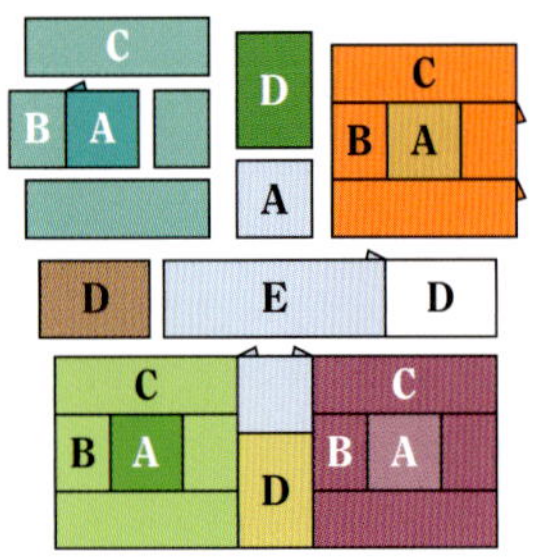

Block Piecing

Sew the patches together as shown to complete the block.

block no. 862

Peaceful Pagoda

by Andra Ridout • Simply Quilted by Andra
simplyquiltedbyandra.com

Gold Print
 1 rectangle (A) 2″x 3½″
 1 rectangle (C) 2″x 8½″
 1 rectangle (D) 2″x 10″
 1 rectangle (E) 2″x 11½″

Dark Blue Print
 2 rectangles (A) 2″x 3½″
 8 squares (B) 2″x 2″
 1 rectangle (F) ⅞″x 12½″
 2 rectangles (G) 2″x 5″
 2 rectangles (H) 2″x 5½″
 2 rectangles (I) 2″x 2½″
 2 rectangles (K) 1¾″x 2″
 2 rectangles (L) 2″x 3″
 2 rectangles (N) 1″x 2″
 2 rectangles (O) 1⅝″x 2½″

Red Tone-on-Tone
 1 rectangle (I) 2″x 2½″
 1 rectangle (J) 2″x 6½″
 1 rectangle (M) 2″x 7½″
 1 rectangle (P) 1⅝″x 8½″

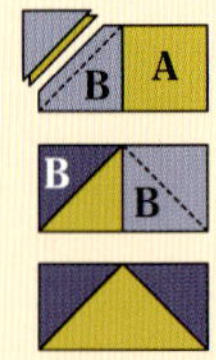

Unit 1
Stitch & Flip
Make 1

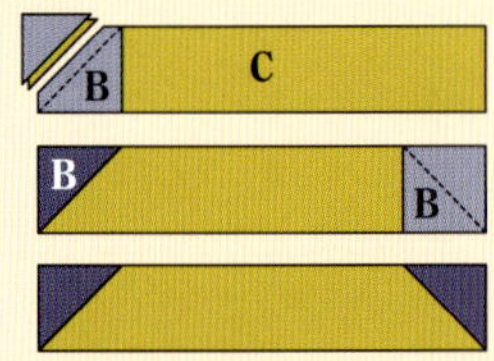

Unit 2
Stitch & Flip
Make 1

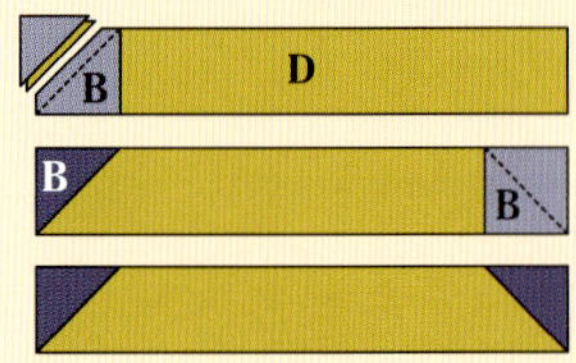

Unit 3
Stitch & Flip
Make 1

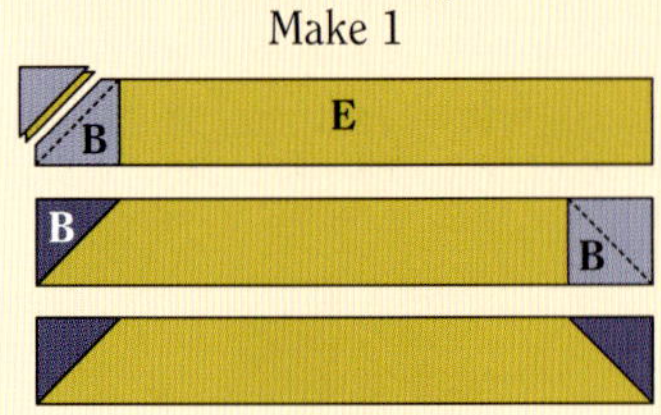

Unit 4
Stitch & Flip
Make 1

Refer to "Stitch-and-Flip" in the Techniques file on the PDF. Make unit 1 using the gold A and blue B's. Make unit 2 using the gold C and blue B's. Use the gold D and blue B's to make unit 3. Make unit 4 using the gold E and blue B's.

Sew the units and patches together as shown to complete the block.

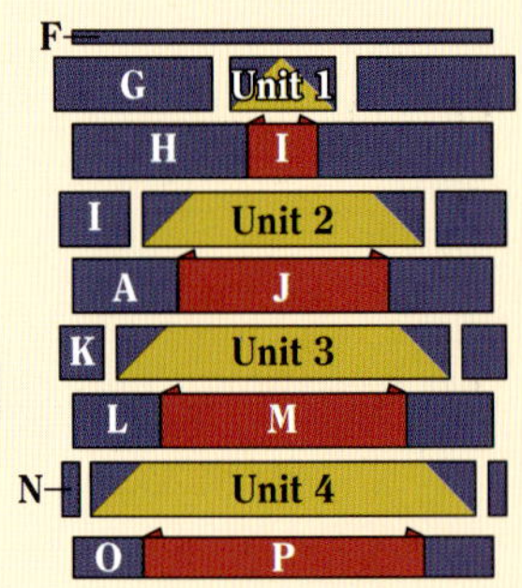

Block Assembly

pieced

block no. 863

Tulip Garden

by Jackie Robinson • Animas Quilts
animasquilts.com

Fabric: Tulip Festival designed by Jackie Robinson for Benartex, benartex.com.

⧄ = cut in half diagonally

Purple Print
1 square (A) 4¼″x 4¼″
1 square (C) 3½″x 3½″

Cream Tone-on-Tone
12 squares (B) 2⅜″x 2⅜″
2 squares (C) 3½″x 3½″
12 squares (D) 2″x 2″
2 rectangles (E) 2″x 3½″
1 square 3⅞″x 3⅞″ ⧄ (F)

Dark Green Tone-on-Tone #1
2 squares (A) 4¼″x 4¼″

Light Green Tone-on-Tone and Dark Green Tone-on-Tone #2
from *each*
3 squares (D) 2″x 2″

Dark Purple Tone-on-Tone #1
2 squares (D) 2″x 2″

Dark Purple Tone-on-Tone #2 and Medium Purple Tone-on-Tone
from *each*
1 square 3⅞″x 3⅞″ ⧄ (F) (there will be two extra)

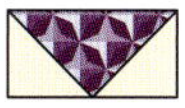

Flying Geese 1
Make 4

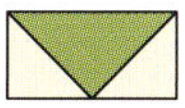

Flying Geese 2
Make 8

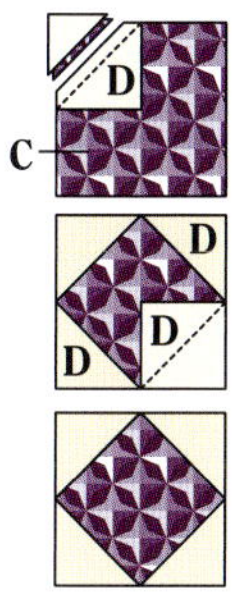

Unit
Stitch & Flip
Make 1

Make 4 Flying Geese 1 with the purple print A and cream B's. Use the dark green #1 A's and cream B's to make 8 Flying Geese 2.

Refer to "Stitch-and-Flip" in the Techniques file on the PDF. Use the purple print C and cream D's to make 1 unit.

Sew the Flying Geese, units and patches together as shown to complete the block.

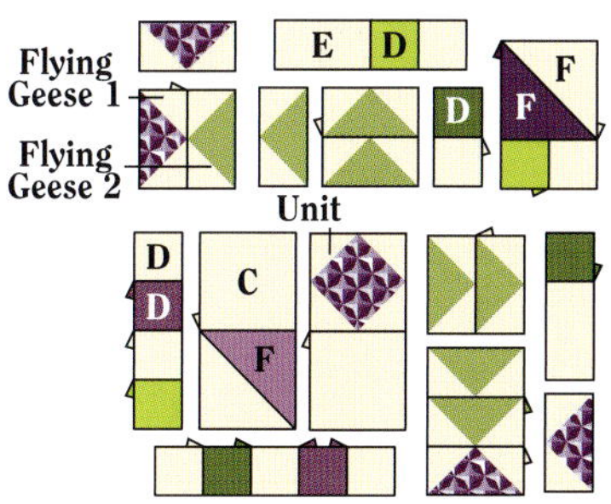

Block Assembly

block no. 864

Love Blooms

by Amy Rullkoetter • Freelance Editor, *Quiltmaker*
quiltmaker.com

Fabric: Dominique designed by Denise Urban for Quilting Treasures, quiltingtreasures.com.

Teal Print
4 squares (A) 2¾″x 2¾″
1 square (D) 8″x 8″
1 square (F) 5¾″x 5¾″

Orange Check and Orange Tone-on-Tone
from *each*
8 squares (B) 1⅝″x 1⅝″

Brown Print
8 rectangles (C) 2″x 2¾″
8 squares (E) 3⅛″x 3⅛″

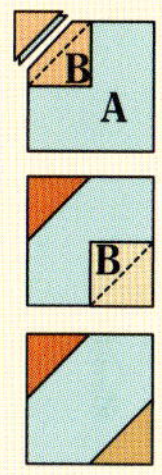

Unit 1
Stitch & Flip
Make 4

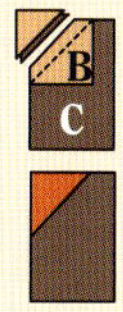

Unit 2
Stitch & Flip
Make 2

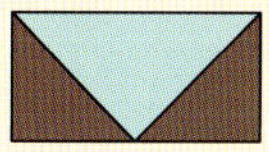

Flying Geese
Make 4

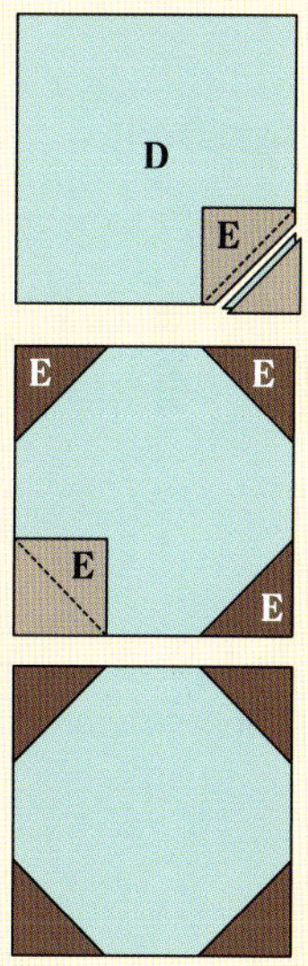

Unit 6
Stitch & Flip
Make 1

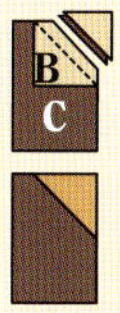

Unit 3
Stitch & Flip
Make 2

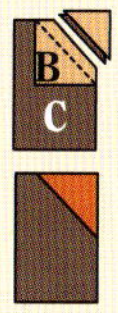

Unit 4
Stitch & Flip
Make 2

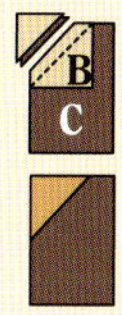

Unit 5
Stitch & Flip
Make 2

Refer to "Stitch-and-Flip" in the Techniques file on the PDF. Use the teal A's, orange check B's and orange tone-on-tone B's to make 4 unit 1's. Use the brown C's, orange check B's and orange tone-on-tone B's to make 2 unit 2's, 2 unit 3's, 2 unit 4's and 2 unit 5's as shown. Make unit 6 using the teal D and 4 brown E's.

Use the teal F and 4 brown E's to make 4 Flying Geese.

Sew the units and Flying Geese together as shown to complete the block.

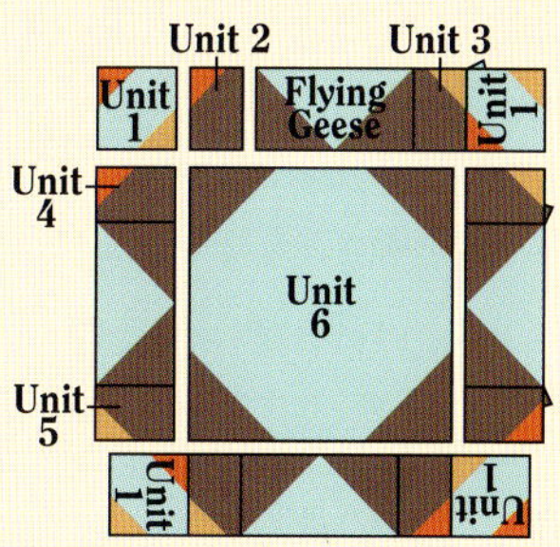

Block Assembly

block no. 865

All Roads Lead Home

by Amy Smart
diaryofaquilter.com

Fabric: Millie's Closet designed by Lori Holt for Riley Blake Designs, rileyblakedesigns.com and Kona cotton solids by Robert Kaufman, robertkaufman.com.

⧄ = cut in half diagonally
⊠ = cut in half twice diagonally

Tan Dot
1 square (A) 5½" x 5½"

Yellow Solid
2 rectangles (B) 1½" x 5½"
2 rectangles (D) 1½" x 8¼"
4 rectangles (E) 2" x 5½"

Gray Solid
2 squares 4⅜" x 4⅜" ⧄ (C)

White Solid
2 squares 6¼" x 6¼" ⊠ (F)

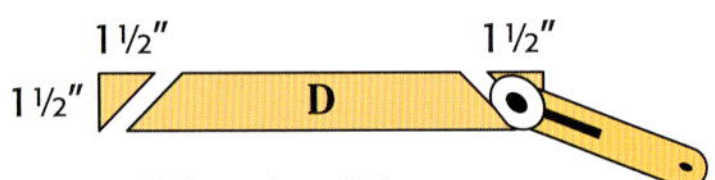

Trimming Diagram

Refer to the trimming diagram to trim the 2 yellow D's.

Sew the patches together as shown. Center the design and trim to 12½" × 12½" to complete the block.

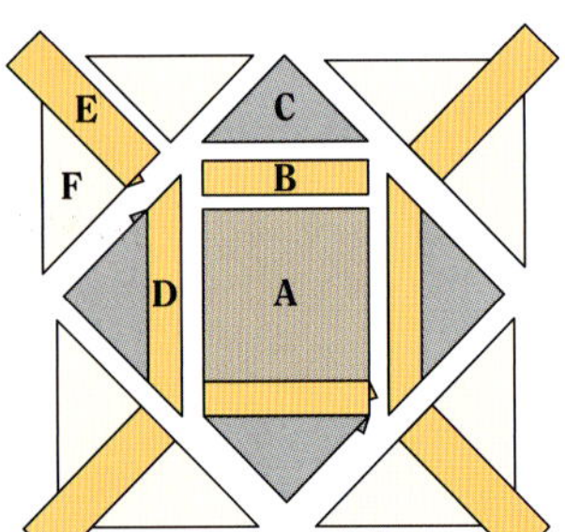

Block Piecing

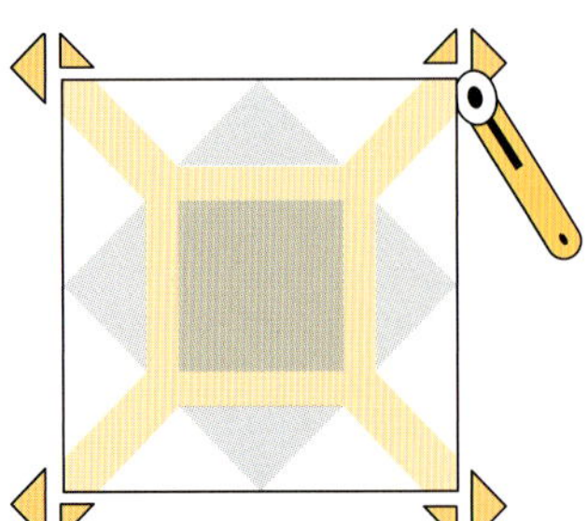
Block Trimming

pieced

block no. 866

Quadrangle

by Anita Grossman Solomon • Make It Simpler
makeitsimpler.com

Anita Grossman Solomon is the author of *Rotary Cutting Revolution* for C&T Publishing, ctpub.com.

See page 265 on the PDF for pattern

Brown Batik
4 template A
5 squares (C) 4½" x 4½"

Cream Solid
4 *each* templates B and Br

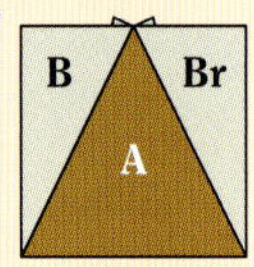

Unit
Make 4

Make 4 units using the brown A's, cream B's and cream Br's.

Sew the units and patches together as shown to complete the block.

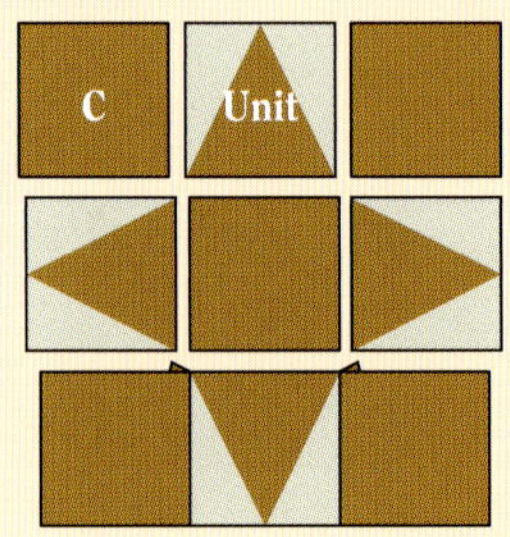

Block Assembly

block no. 867

Pay Day

by Peg Spradlin • Handicrafts by Peg
handicraftsbypeg.com

Fabric: Kaleidoscope designed by Deborah Edwards and Picadilly Circle, both from Northcott, northcott.net.

Dark Pink Tone-on-Tone
- 17 squares (A) 1½″ x 1½″
- 12 squares (E) 1″ x 1″

White Print
- 12 squares (A) 1½″ x 1½″
- 8 rectangles (B) 1½″ x 2½″
- 4 squares (D) 3½″ x 3½″

Green Tone-on-Tone
- 12 rectangles (C) 1″ x 3½″

Brown Tone-on-Tone
- 24 rectangles (C) 1″ x 3½″
- 8 squares (E) 1″ x 1″
- 8 rectangles (F) 1″ x 1½″

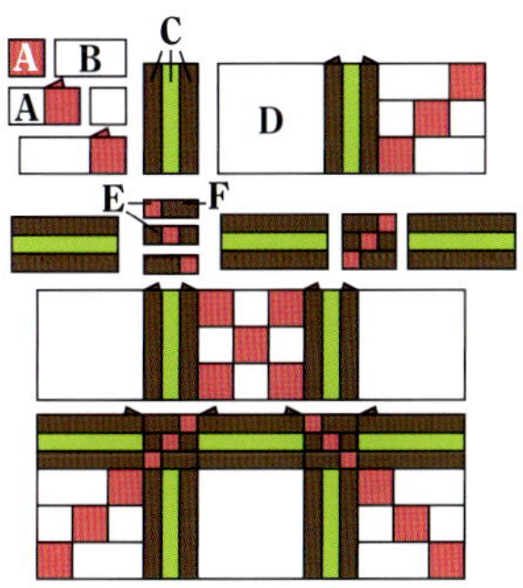

Block Piecing

Sew the patches together as shown to complete the block.

block no. 868

Bus Stop

by Denise Starck • Graphic Designer, *Quiltmaker*
quiltmaker.com

Unit 1
Stitch & Flip
Make 1

Unit 3
Stitch & Flip
Make 1

See page 259 on the PDF for pattern

Yellow Tone-on-Tone
- 1 rectangle (A) 1¼″ x 10¾″
- 1 square (B) 1¼″ x 1¼″
- 2 rectangles (D) 1¼″ x 11½″
- 4 squares (F) 1″ x 1″
- 2 rectangles (G) 1⅛″ x 2¼″
- 3 rectangles (H) 1″ x 2¼″
- 1 rectangle (K) ⅞″ x 11½″
- 2 squares (O) 1½″ x 1½″
- 1 rectangle (Q) 1½″ x 5½″
- 2 rectangles (N) 1″ x 1½″
- 2 rectangles (P) 1″ x 2″
- 1 rectangle (R) 1″ x 5½″

Light Blue Tone-on-Tone
- 3 squares (B) 1¼″ x 1¼″
- 1 rectangle (I) 1¾″ x 3″
- 1 rectangle (J) 3⅞″ x 12½″
- 1 rectangle (L) 1″ x 3⅛″
- 1 rectangle (M) 1″ x 5⅝″

Light Gray Tone-on-Tone
- 5 rectangles (C) 2″ x 2¼″

Black Solid
- 2 squares (E) 2½″ x 2½″
- 2 rectangles (K) ⅞″ x 11½″

Dark Gray Tone-on-Tone
- 4 squares (F) 1″ x 1″
- 2 rectangles (P) 1″ x 2″
- 1 rectangle (R) 1″ x 5½″
- 1 rectangle (S) 2″ x 12½″

Red Tone-on-Tone
- 1 pattern T

Fusible web

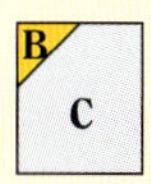

Unit 2
Stitch & Flip
Make 1

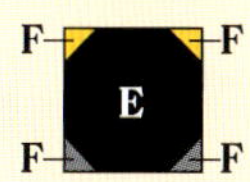

Unit 4
Stitch & Flip
Make 2

Applique Placement

Refer to "Stitch-and-Flip" in the Techniques file on the PDF. Use the colors shown to make units 1–4. Sew the units and patches together as shown.

Prepare the red T for fusible appliqué. Use the appliqué placement diagram as a guide to position T; fuse in place. Use matching thread and a machine blanket stitch to sew around T to complete the block.

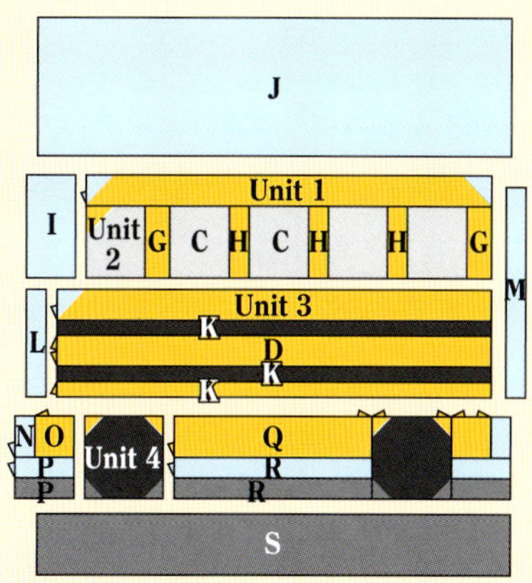

Block Assembly

block no. 869
Trendster

by Jocelyn Ueng • It's Sew Emma
itssewemma.com

Fabric: Simply Color designed by V & Co. for Moda Fabrics, unitednotions.com.

Aqua Solid and Green Solid
from *each*
3 squares (A) 2⅞" x 2⅞"
White Solid
10 squares (A) 2⅞" x 2⅞"
12 squares (D) 2½" x 2½"
Dark Blue Print
1 square (B) 5¼" x 5¼"
Aqua Tone-on-Tone and Purple Tone-on-Tone
from *each*
2 squares (C) 4½" x 4½"

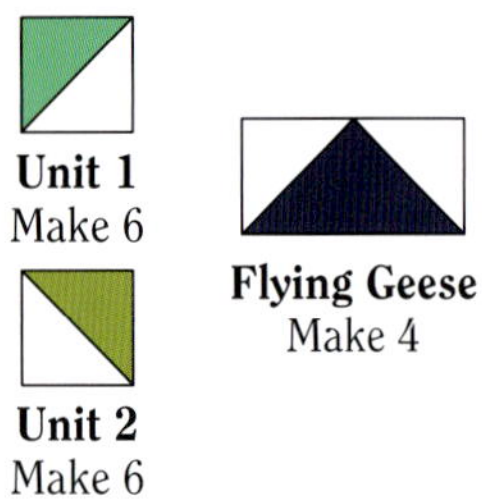

Pair the aqua A's with white A's to make 6 Triangle-Square unit 1's. Make 6 unit 2's pairing the green solid A's with white A's.

Use the dark blue B and 4 white A's to make 4 Flying Geese.

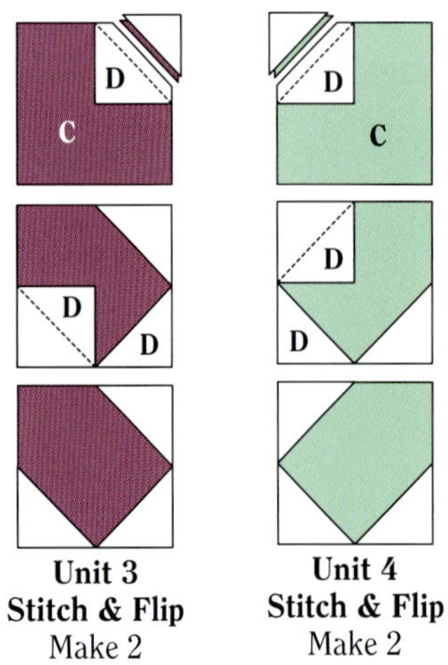

Refer to "Stitch-and-Flip" in the Techniques file on the PDF. Make 2 unit 3's using the purple C's and white D's. Use the aqua tone-on-tone C's and white D's to make 2 unit 4's.

Sew the units and Flying Geese together as shown to complete the block.

Block Assembly

block no. 870
Sweet Peas

by Margie Ullery • Ribbon Candy Quilt Co.
ribboncandyquilts.blogspot.com

White Tone-on-Tone
6 rectangles (A) 1½" x 2½"
16 squares (B) 1½" x 1½"
2 rectangles (D) 1½" x 4½"
8 squares (E) 2½" x 2½"
Pink Print
6 rectangles (A) 1½" x 2½"
12 squares (B) 1½" x 1½"
2 rectangles (D) 1½" x 4½"
4 rectangles (F) 1½" x 3½"
Pink Dot
4 rectangles (C) 2½" x 3½"
Green Tone-on-Tone
4 rectangles (A) 1½" x 2½"
4 squares (B) 1½" x 1½"
Blue Tone-on-Tone
8 squares (B) 1½" x 1½"
Yellow Tone-on-Tone
1 square (E) 2½" x 2½"

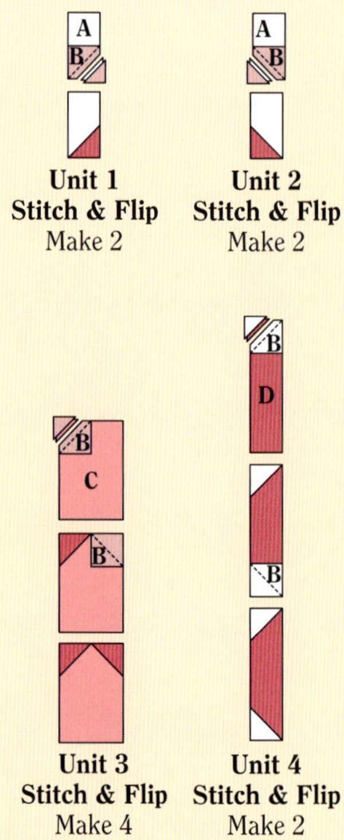

Refer to "Stitch-and-Flip" in the Techniques file on the PDF. Use white A's and pink print B's to make 2 unit 1's and 2 unit 2's as shown.

Make 4 unit 3's using the pink dot C's and pink print B's.

Use the pink print D's and white B's to make 2 unit 4's.

Sew the units and patches together as shown to complete the block.

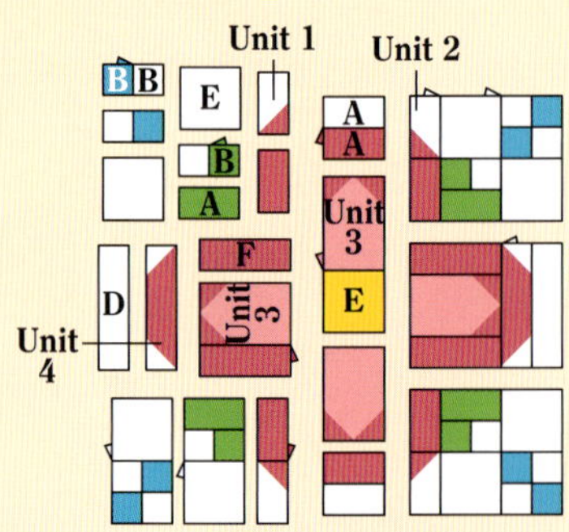

Block Assembly

block no. 871

Crossed Spools

by Pam Vieira-McGinnis
pamkittymorning.blogspot.com

Fabric: Pam Kitty Morning designed by Pam Vieira-McGinnis for Lakehouse Dry Goods, lakehousedrygoods.com.

Blue Print
- 1 square (A) 2 7/8" x 2 7/8"
- 2 squares (C) 2 1/2" x 2 1/2"

Red Check
- 1 square (A) 2 7/8" x 2 7/8"
- 4 squares (C) 2 1/2" x 2 1/2"

Green Dot
- 2 squares (B) 4 7/8" x 4 7/8"

Cream Dot
- 2 squares (B) 4 7/8" x 4 7/8"
- 4 squares (D) 4 1/2" x 4 1/2"

Red Print and Blue Check
from *each*
- 4 squares (C) 2 1/2" x 2 1/2"

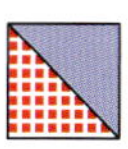

Unit 1
Make 2 from A's

Partial Unit
Make 4 from B's

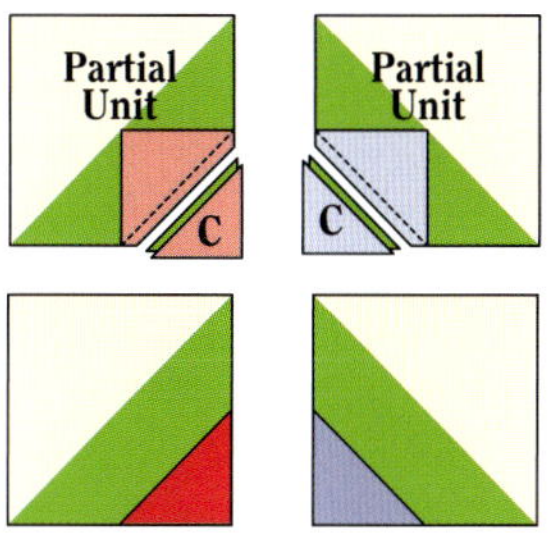

Unit 2
Stitch & Flip
Make 2

Unit 3
Stitch & Flip
Make 2

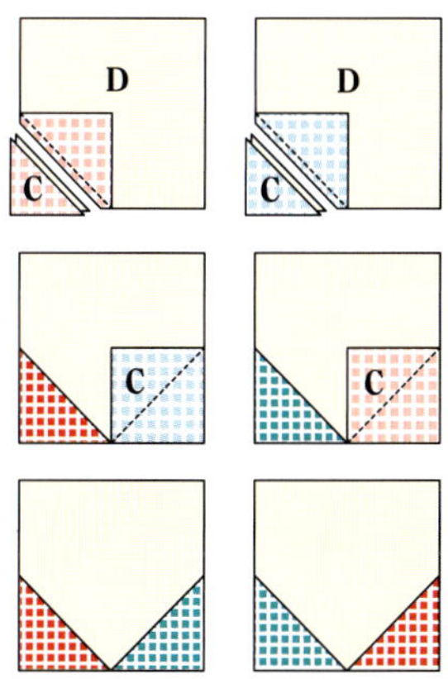

Unit 4
Stitch & Flip
Make 2

Unit 5
Stitch & Flip
Make 2

Pair the red check A with the blue print A to make 2 Triangle-Square unit 1's. Pair the green B's with the cream B's to make 4 partial units.

Refer to "Stitch-and-Flip" in the Techniques file on the PDF. Add red print C's to the corners of 2 partial units as shown to make 2 unit 2's. Add blue print C's to 2 partial units to make 2 unit 3's. Use the cream D's with the red check C's and blue check C's to make 2 unit 4's and 2 unit 5's as shown.

Sew the units and patches together as shown to complete the block.

Block Assembly

block no. 872

Framed

by Corey Yoder
littlemissshabby.com

◪ = cut in half diagonally

9 Assorted Solids
- 9 squares (A) 2 1/2" x 2 1/2"
- 8 rectangles (C) 2 1/2" x 5 1/4"

Cream Solid
- 2 squares 5 1/8" x 5 1/8" ◪ (B)
- 2 squares 4 1/4" x 4 1/4" ◪ (D)

Sew the patches together as shown.

Center and trim to 12½" × 12½" as shown to complete the block.

Block Trimming

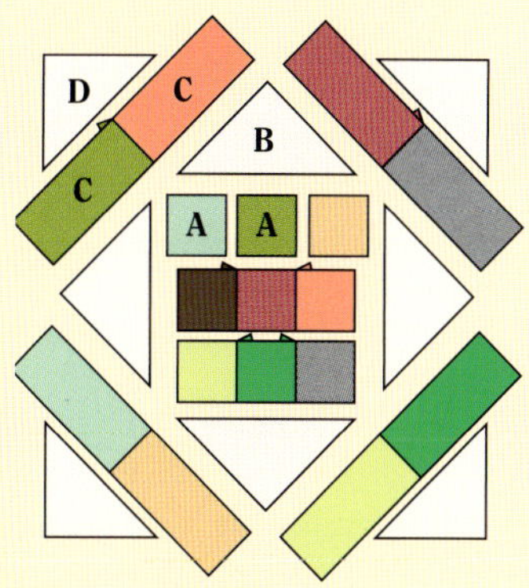

Block Piecing

block no. 873

Deseret

by Nancy Allen
bountifulheirlooms.blogspot.com

Fabric: Moda Fabrics, unitednotions.com. Nancy Allen is the author of *Triple-Play Scrap Quilting* for Martingale & Co., shopmartingale.com.

Black Print
1 rectangle (A) 1¾"x 3½"
Tan Tone-on-Tone
18 squares (B) 1¼"x 1¼"
2 rectangles (H) 1¾"x 12½"
2 rectangles (I) 1¾"x 5"
2 rectangles (J) 2¼"x 4"
2 rectangles (K) 2⅝"x 3⅛"
2 rectangles (L) 2¼"x 2½"
2 rectangles (M) 1⅜"x 2⅞"
Gold Print #1
1 rectangle (C) 2¼"x 5½"
Dark Green Tone-on-Tone
1 rectangle (D) 2⅝"x 7¼"
Gold Print #2
1 rectangle (E) 2½"x 9"
Dark Red Print
2 rectangles (F) 2⅞"x 4½"
2 squares (B) 1¼"x 1¼"
Black Tone-on-Tone
1 rectangle (G) 2¾"x 2⅞"

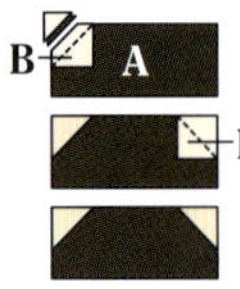

Unit 1
Stitch & Flip
Make 1

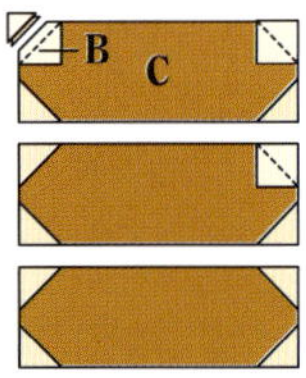

Unit 2
Stitch & Flip
Make 1

Unit 3
Stitch & Flip
Make 1

Unit 4
Stitch & Flip
Make 1

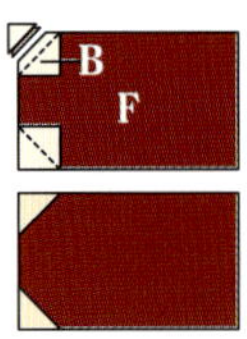

Unit 5
Stitch & Flip
Make 2

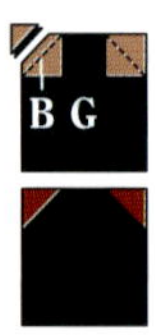

Unit 6
Stitch & Flip
Make 1

Refer to "Stitch-and-Flip" in the Techniques file on the PDF. Make 1 unit 1 using the black print A and 2 tan B's. Use the gold #1 C and 4 tan B's to make 1 unit 2.

In the same way, use the dark green D and tan B's to make 1 unit 3 and the gold #2 E and tan B's to make 1 unit 4. Make 2 unit 5's using the dark red F's and tan B's. Use the black G and dark red B's to make 1 unit 6.

Sew the units and patches together as shown to complete the block.

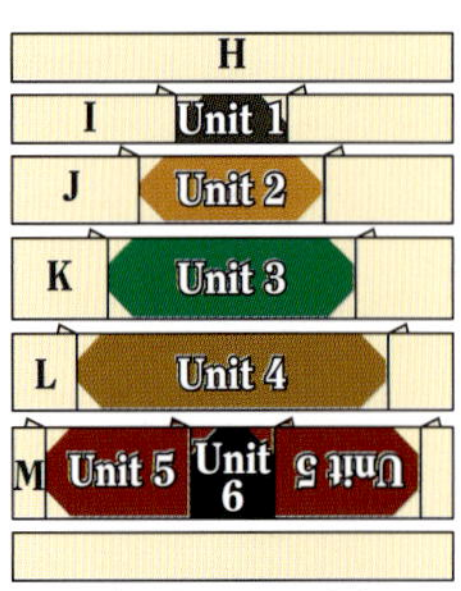

Block Assembly

block no. 874

Shrinking Squares

by Pippa Eccles Armbrester • Pippa Patchwork
pippapatchwork.com

Fabric: Kona Solids from Robert Kaufman, robertkaufman.com.

Pippa Armbrester is the author of *Solids, Stripes, Circles, and Squares—16 Modern Patchwork Quilt Patterns* for Martingale & Co., shopmartingale.com.

Light Gray Solid
16 rectangles (A) 1"x 1¾"
16 rectangles (C) 1¾"x 3½"
8 squares (D) 2½"x 2½"
8 Assorted Solids
from *each*
1 square (B) 1"x 1"
2 rectangles (E) 1"x 2½"
2 rectangles (F) 1"x 3½"

Sew the patches together as shown to complete the block.

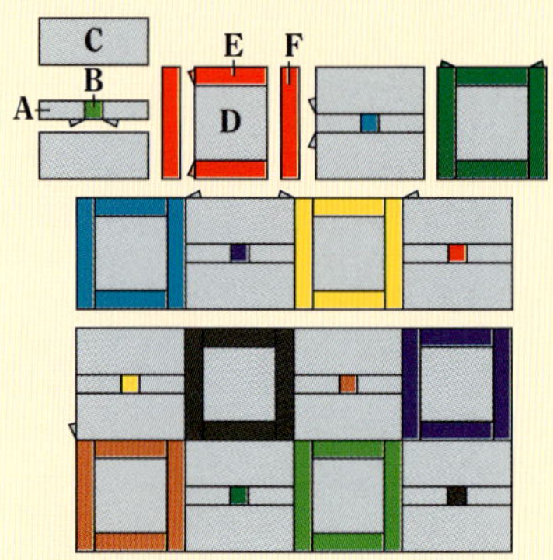

Block Piecing

block no. 875

Summer Heat

by Elizabeth Balderrama & Kate Colleran • Seams Like a Dream Quilt Designs • seamslikeadream.com

See page 296 on the PDF for pattern

Medium Teal Tone-on-Tone and Dark Teal Tone-on-Tone
from *each*
6 squares (A) 2⅞" x 2⅞"

Pale Aqua Solid and Blue Tone-on-Tone
from *each*
4 squares (A) 2⅞" x 2⅞"

Pink Tone-on-Tone
4 *each* templates B and Br

Yellow Tone-on-Tone
4 template C

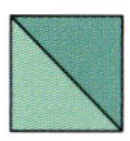

Unit 1
Make 12

Unit 2
Make 8

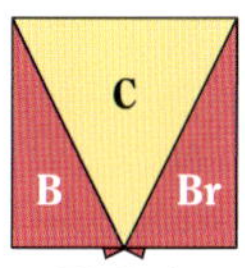

Unit 3
Make 4

Pair the medium teal A's with the dark teal A's to make 12 Triangle-Square unit 1's. Pair the pale aqua A's with the blue A's to make 8 unit 2's.

Join the pink B's and Br's to the yellow C's as shown to make 4 unit 3's.

Sew the units together as shown to complete the block.

Block Assembly

block no. 876

Autumn Ways

by Donna Benham • DB Designs

Fabric: Late Bloomers designed by Sandy Gervais for Moda Fabrics, unitednotions.com.

See page 317 on the PDF for pattern

Gold Print
sections 1 and 2, patch 1
1 square (A) 3¾" x 3¾"
2 squares (C) 4⅜" x 4⅜"
4 squares (D) 1¾" x 1¾"

Brown Print
section 1, patches 2 and 3
section 2, patches 2–5
4 squares (B) 2⅛" x 2⅛"
2 squares (C) 4⅜" x 4⅜"
1 square (E) 3" x 3"

Section 1
Make 8

Flying Geese
Make 4

Section 2
Make 4

Unit
Make 4

Make 8 paper copies of the foundation section 1 and 4 paper copies of the foundation section 2. Foundation piece the sections in numerical order, pressing and trimming after each patch addition.

Use the gold A and brown B's to make 4 Flying Geese.

Pair the gold C's and brown C's to make 4 Triangle-Square units.

Sew the sections, Flying Geese, units and patches together as shown to complete the block.

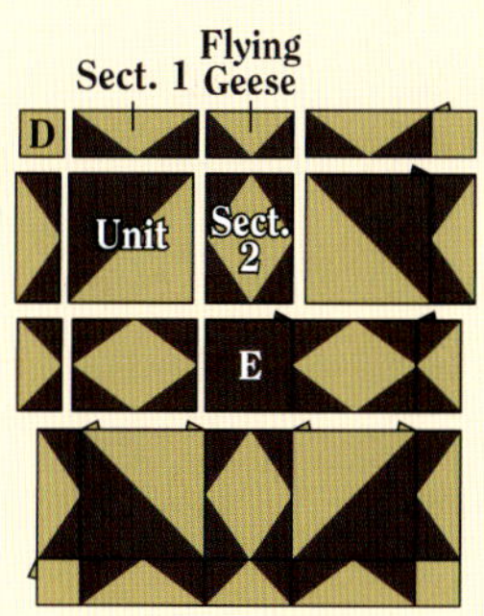

Block Assembly

block no. 877
The Weaver Block

by Sandi Blackwell • Stitched Buy
stitchedbuy.com

Sandi Blackwell is the author of *Simple Sensational Square-agonals Quilts* for Landauer Publishing, landauerpub.com.

⊠ = cut in half twice diagonally

Blue Tone-on-Tone
1 strip 2½" x 34"
Light Blue/Green Batik
2 strips 2¼" x 34"
Teal Tone-on-Tone
1 square 5½" x 5½" ⊠ (A)

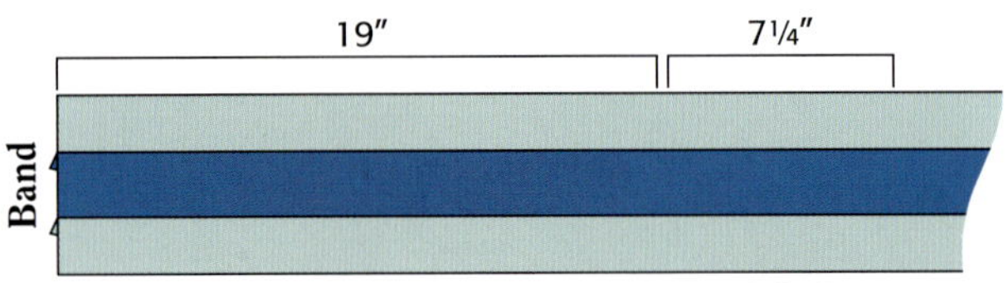

Unit 1 Cut 1 **Unit 2** Cut 2

Join the blue strip with the blue/green batik strips to make 1 band as shown. Cut 1 section 19" long (unit 1) and 2 sections 7¼" long (unit 2's).

Sew the units and patches together as shown. Center and trim to 12½" × 12½" to complete the block.

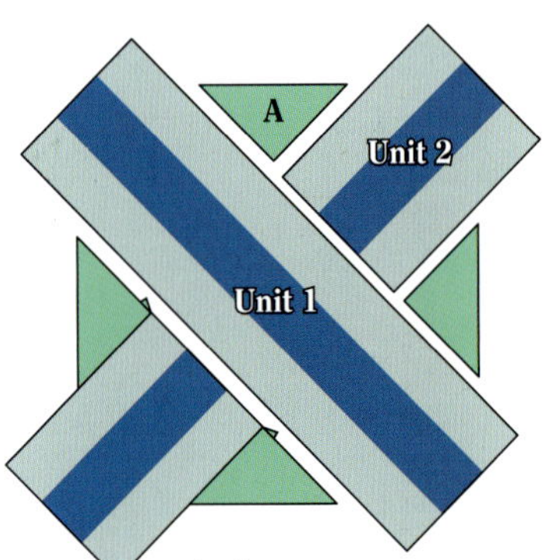

Block Piecing

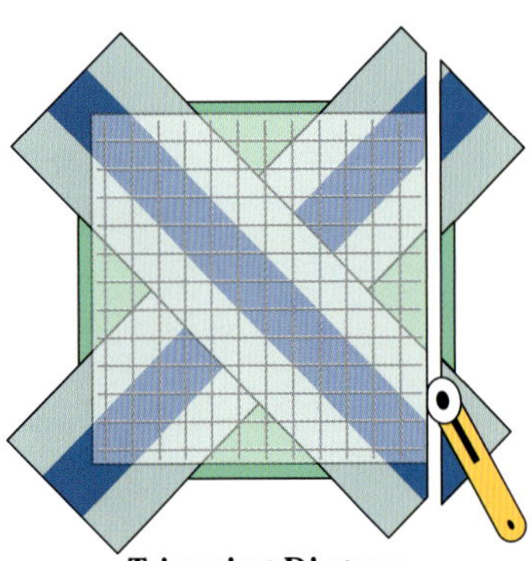
Trimming Diagram

pieced

block no. 878
Diamonds in the Sky

by Alyce Blyth • Blossom Heart Quilts
blossomheartquilts.com

Fabric: Cuzco by Kate Spain for Moda Fabrics, unitednotions.com and Painter's Canvas by Laura Gunn for Michael Miller Fabrics, michaelmillerfabrics.com.

Aqua Tone-on-Tone
4 squares (A) 2⅞" x 2⅞"
White Solid
4 squares (A) 2⅞" x 2⅞"
1 square (B) 5¼" x 5¼"
8 squares (C) 2½" x 2½"
1 square (D) 4½" x 4½"
Gold Tone-on-Tone and Purple Print from *each*
4 squares (A) 2⅞" x 2⅞"
Orange Tone-on-Tone
1 square (B) 5¼" x 5¼"

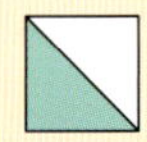
Unit Make 8

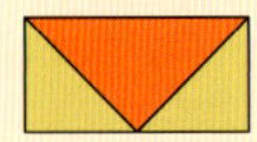
Flying Geese 1 Make 4

Flying Geese 2 Make 4

Pair the aqua A's and white A's to make 8 Triangle-Square units.

Use the gold A's and orange B to make 4 Flying Geese 1's. Make 4 Flying Geese 2's using the purple A's and white B.

Sew the units, Flying Geese and patches together as shown to complete the block.

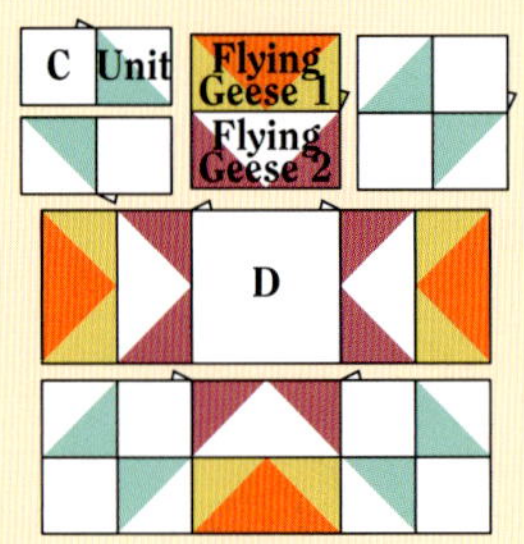

Block Assembly

block no. 879

Five Star General

by Lisa Bongean • Primitive Gatherings
primitivegatherings.us

Fabric: Various lines designed by Primitive Gatherings for Moda Fabrics, unitednotions.com.

5 Dark Blue Tone-on-Tones
from *each*
- 1 square (A) 3¼″ x 3¼″
- 4 squares (C) 1½″ x 1½″

Assorted Beige Tone-on-Tones
from *5*
- 4 squares (B) 1⅞″ x 1⅞″
- 1 square (D) 2½″ x 2½″

from *4*
- 4 squares (C) 1½″ x 1½″
- 1 square (D) 2½″ x 2½″

4 Red Tone-on-Tones
from *each*
- 4 rectangles (E) 1½″ x 2½″

Flying Geese
Make 5 sets of 4 matching

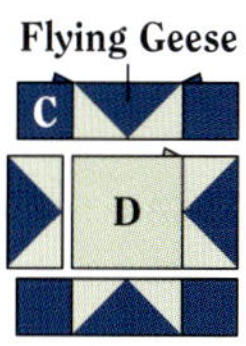

Star
Make 5

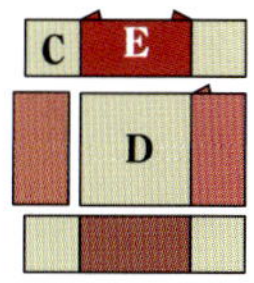

Nine Patch
Make 4

Lisa used matching dark blue A's, C's and beige B's in each star. She used matching beige C's and D's in each Nine Patch.

Use the dark blue A's and beige B's to make 5 sets of 4 matching Flying Geese.

Join matching Flying Geese, blue C's and a beige D to make a star as shown. Make 5 stars. Join 4 beige C's, a beige D and 4 red E's as shown to make a Nine Patch. Make 4 Nine Patches.

Sew the stars and Nine Patches together as shown to complete the block.

Block Assembly

block no. 880

Squared

by Kelly Bowser
kelbysews.blogspot.com

Sewn on a Symphony by Babylock.

15 Assorted Solids
from *9*
- 1 square (A) 2½″ x 2½″

from *1*
- 2 squares (A) 2½″ x 2½″
- 2 rectangles (B) 2½″ x 6½″

from *2*
- 2 rectangles (C) 1½″ x 2½″
- 2 rectangles (D) 1½″ x 4½″

from *1*
- 2 rectangles (D) 1½″ x 4½″
- 2 rectangles (E) 1½″ x 6½″

from *2*
- 1 square (F) 4½″ x 4½″

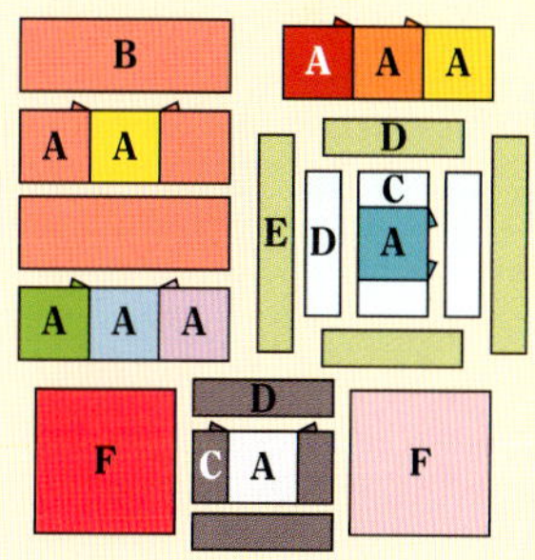

Block Piecing

Sew the patches together as shown to complete the block.

block no. 881

Stepping Stones

by Lynn Roddy Brown
lynnroddybrown.com

Lynn Roddy Brown is the author of *Patchwork-Play Quilts—Make the Most of Scraps, Spare Parts, and Leftovers* for Martingale & Co., shopmartingale.com.

◸ = cut in half diagonally

12 Assorted Dark Prints and Tone-on-Tones
12 squares 3⅞" x 3⅞" ◸ (A) (there will be 12 extra)

16 Assorted Light Prints and Tone-on-Tones
12 squares 3⅞" x 3⅞" ◸ (A) (there will be 12 extra)
4 squares (B) 3½" x 3½"

Cutting the A's as indicated enhances the scrappy look of this block. The extra patches can be used for additional blocks.

Sew the patches together as shown to complete the block.

Block Piecing

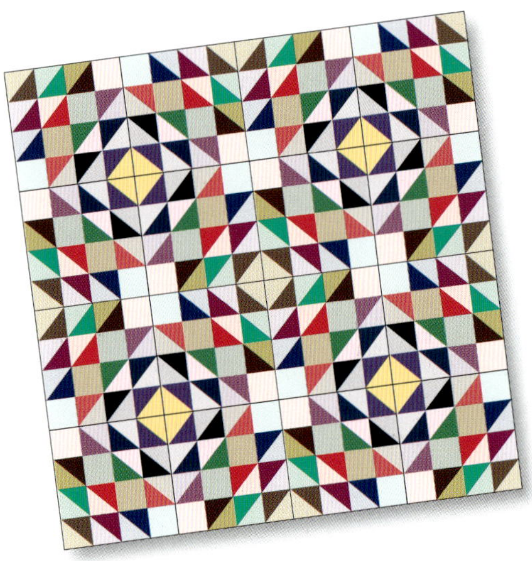

block no. 882

Lovely Garden

by Debbie Caffrey • Debbie's Creative Moments, Inc.
debbiescreativemoments.com

Fabric: Lovely designed by Sandy Gervais for Moda Fabrics, unitednotions.com.

Debbie Caffrey is the author of numerous self-published books including *Surprise Yourself: Simple Steps to Making Fabulous Quilts,* debbiescreativemoments.com.

Aqua Print
2 rectangles (A) 3¾" x 9¾"

Green Tone-on-Tone
4 rectangles (B) 1¾" x 9¾"

Cream Print
4 rectangles (C) 2¼" x 9¾"

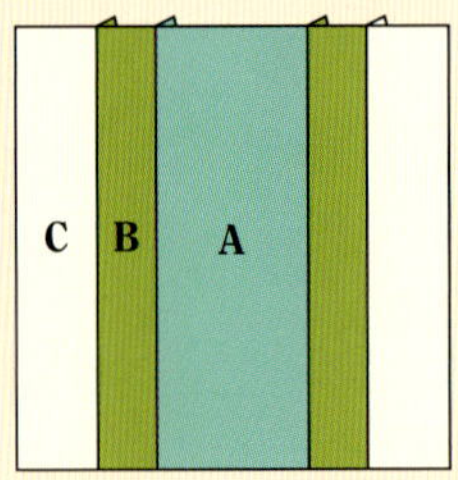

Partial Unit Piecing
Make 2

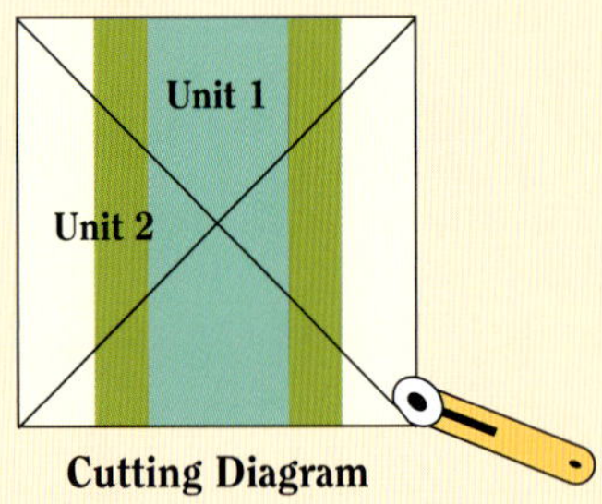

Cutting Diagram

Sew the A's, B's and C's together as shown to make 2 partial units.

Refer to the cutting diagram. Cut each partial unit in half twice diagonally as shown to make 2 unit 1's and 2 unit 2's.

Join a unit 1 to a unit 2 as shown to make a section. Make 4 sections, pressing 2 toward the unit 1's and 2 toward the unit 2's. Sew the sections together as shown to complete the block.

Section
Make 4

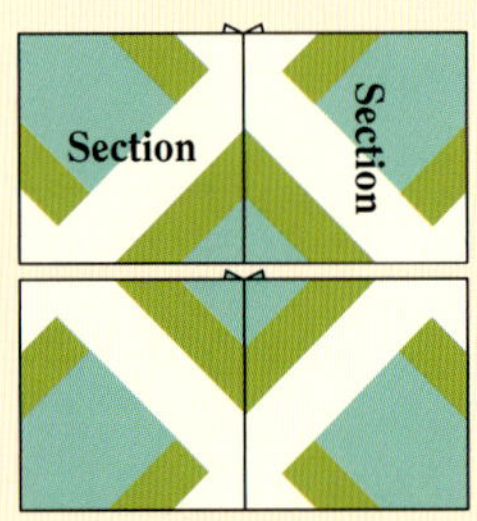

Block Assembly

block no. 883

Waffle

by AnneMarie Chany • Gen X Quilters
genxquilters.com

Gray Print
- 5 squares (A) 4¼"x 4¼"
- 2 squares (B) 2⅜"x 2⅜"

White Solid
- 22 squares (B) 2⅜"x 2⅜"

Turquoise Tone-on-Tone
- 8 squares (C) 2"x 2"
- 1 square (E) 3½"x 3½"

Green Print
- 4 rectangles (D) 2"x 3½"

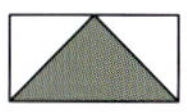

Flying Geese
Make 20

Unit
Make 4

Use the gray A's and 20 white B's to make 20 Flying Geese.

Pair the gray B's with 2 white B's to make 4 Triangle-Square units.

Sew the Flying Geese, units and patches together as shown to complete the block.

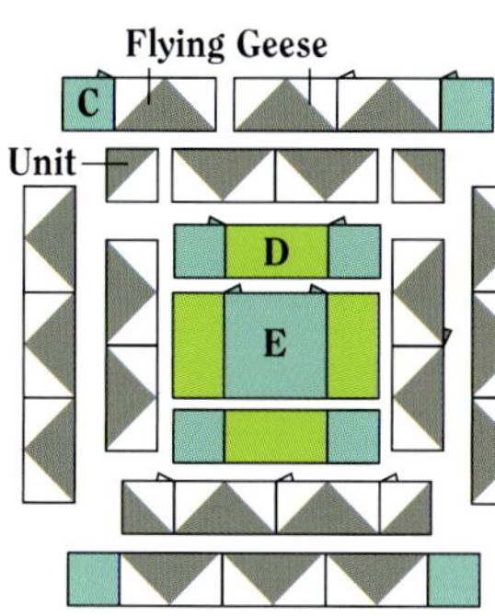

Block Assembly

block no. 884

A Study in Quilting

by Melissa Corry • Happy Quilting
happyquiltingmelissa.blogspot.com

Fabric: Mama Said Sew designed by Sweetwater for Moda Fabrics, unitednotions.com.

⊘ = cut in half diagonally

5 Assorted Red Tone-on-Tones
- 2 rectangles (A) 3½"x 6½"
- 1 square 3⅞"x 3⅞" ⊘ (C) (there will be 1 extra)
- 2 squares (B) 3½"x 3½"

5 Assorted Black Tone-on-Tones
- 2 rectangles (A) 3½"x 6½"
- 1 square 3⅞"x 3⅞" ⊘ (C) (there will be 1 extra)
- 2 squares (B) 3½"x 3½"

White Solid
- 10 squares (B) 3½"x 3½"
- 1 square 3⅞"x 3⅞" ⊘ (C)

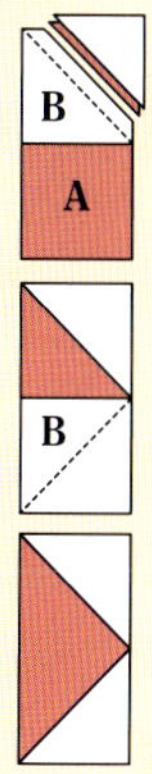

Unit 1
Stitch & Flip
Make 2

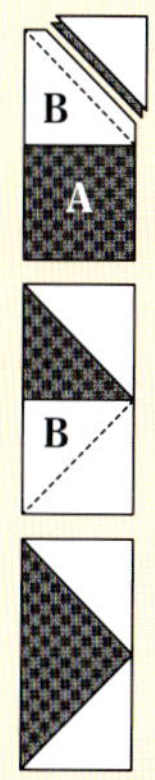

Unit 2
Stitch & Flip
Make 2

Refer to "Stitch-and-Flip" in the Techniques file on the PDF. Use the red A's and white B's to make 2 unit 1's as shown. Repeat with the black A's and white B's to make 2 unit 2's.

Sew the units and patches together as shown to complete the block.

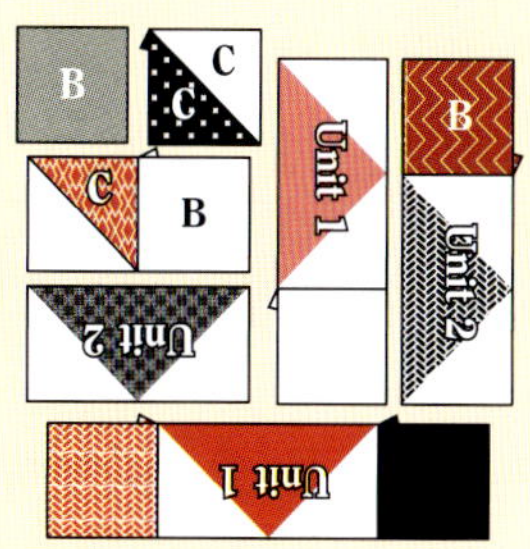

Block Assembly

block no. 885

Celtic Cross

by Monique Dillard • Open Gate
opengatequilts.com

Fabric: Royal Gardens designed by Monique Dillard for Maywood Studio, maywoodstudio.com.

Monique Dillard is the author of *Diamond Traditions* and *Fat Quarter Winners,* both for C&T Publishing, ctpub.com.

Tan Print
- 4 squares (A) 3½" x 3½"
- 4 rectangles (C) 2" x 3½"
- 4 rectangles (D) 2" x 5"
- 4 squares (F) 2⅜" x 2⅜"

Black Print
- 4 squares (A) 3½" x 3½"
- 12 squares (B) 2" x 2"
- 2 squares (E) 4¼" x 4¼"
- 4 squares (F) 2⅜" x 2⅜"

Green Dot
- 1 square (A) 3½" x 3½"
- 1 square (E) 4¼" x 4¼"
- 4 squares (F) 2⅜" x 2⅜"

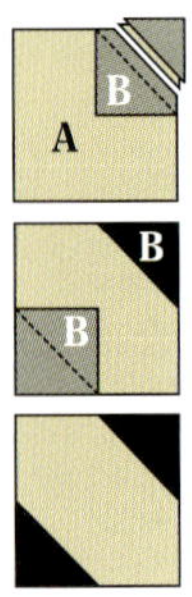

Partial Unit
Stitch & Flip
Make 4

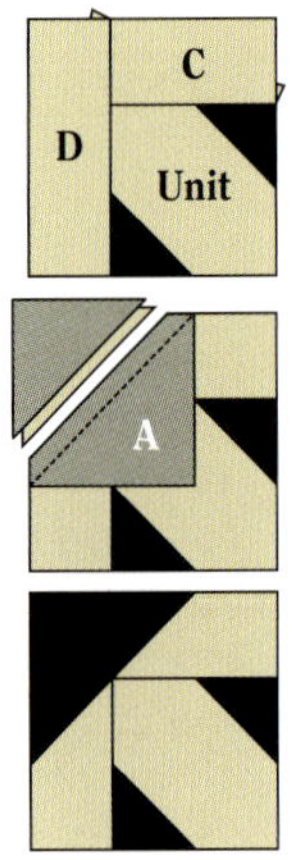

Unit 1
Stitch & Flip
Make 4

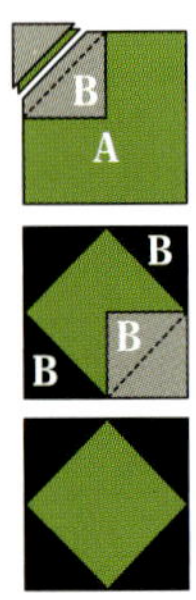

Unit 2
Stitch & Flip
Make 1

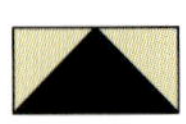

Flying Geese 1
Make 4

Flying Geese 2
Make 4

Flying Geese 3
Make 4

Refer to "Stitch-and-Flip" in the Techniques file on the PDF. Use the tan A's and black B's to make 4 partial units. Join the tan C's and D's to the partial units as shown. Add a black A to the corner of each partial unit as shown to make 4 unit 1's. Make unit 2 using the green A and 4 black B's.

Make 4 Flying Geese 1's, 4 Flying Geese 2's and 4 Flying Geese 3's using E's and F's of the colors indicated in the diagrams.

Sew the units and Flying Geese together as shown to complete the block.

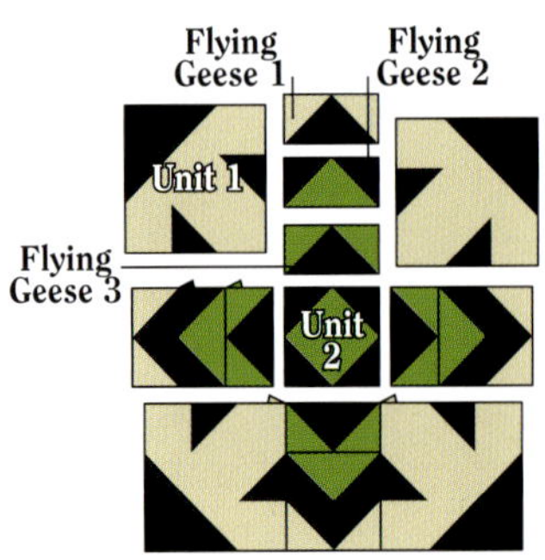

Block Assembly

block no. 886

Sawtooth Pinwheel

by Deanne Eisenman • Snuggles Quilts
snugglesquilts.com

Deanne Eisenman is the author of *Scrap Quilts Go Country* for Martingale & Co., shop-martingale.com.

⧄ = cut in half diagonally

Light Green Tone-on-Tone
- 12 squares (A) 2⅞" x 2⅞"

Tan Tone-on-Tone
- 12 squares (A) 2⅞" x 2⅞"
- 4 squares 2⅞" x 2⅞" ⧄ (B)

Purple Tone-on-Tone
- 2 squares 4⅞" x 4⅞" ⧄ (C)

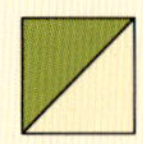

Unit
Make 24

Pair the green A's with the tan A's to make 24 Triangle-Square units.

Sew the units and patches together as shown to complete the block.

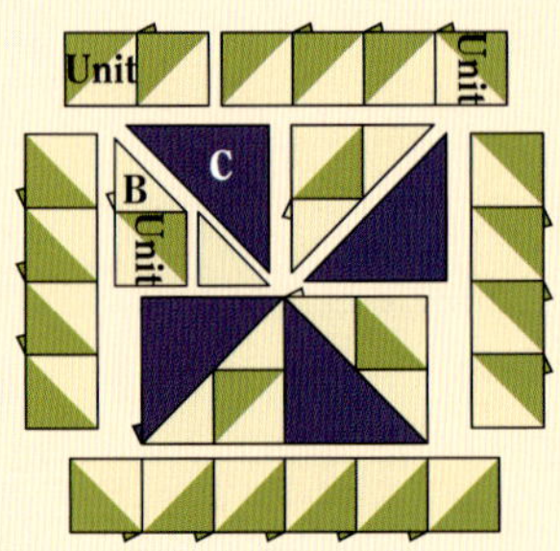

Block Assembly

pieced

block no. 887

Nordic Garden

by Gudrun Erla • GE Designs
gequiltdesigns.com

Fabric: Nordic Visions designed by Gudrun Erla for Red Rooster Fabrics, redroosterfabrics.com.

Gudrun Erla is the author of *Big Blocks—Big Style* for GE Designs, gedesigns.com.

Gudrun choreographed the *Quiltmaker* Shuffle available at quiltmaker.com/shuffle.

Multicolor Print
 1 square (A) 4½"x 4½"

Black Print
 2 rectangles (B) 1½"x 4½"
 2 rectangles (C) 1½"x 6½"

Green Tone-on-Tone and Red Tone-on-Tone
from *each*
 4 squares (D) 2"x 2"
 4 rectangles (E) 2"x 3½"

Cream Tone-on-Tone
 4 rectangles (E) 2"x 3½"
 4 rectangles (F) 2"x 6½"

Sew the patches together as shown to complete the block.

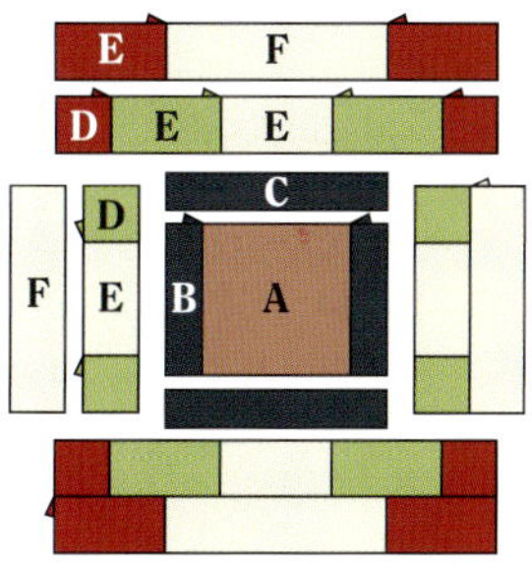

Block Piecing

block no. 888

Winter for the Birds

by Connie Ewbank • Butterfly Stitches
butterflystitches.net

Connie Ewbank is the author of *Quick & Easy Quilts for Kids* for Annie's Publishing, annies-publishing.com.

Buttons can be found at justanotherbutton company.com.

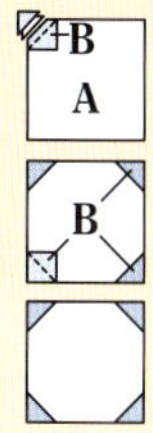

Unit 1
Stitch & Flip
Make 1

White Tone-on-Tone
 1 square (A) 2½"x 2½"
 1 rectangle (C) 4"x 4½"
 1 rectangle (E) 5"x 6½"

Light Blue Batik
 4 squares (B) 1"x 1"
 4 squares (D) 1½"x 1½"
 4 squares (F) 2"x 2"
 2 rectangles (G) 2½"x 4½"
 2 rectangles (H) 3½"x 4"
 2 rectangles (I) 2½"x 5"

Dark Blue Tone-on-Tone
 2 rectangles (J) 1½"x 10½"
 2 rectangles (K) 1½"x 12½"

Black embroidery floss

Buttons
 2 at ¼", 3 at ⅜"
 1 carrot, 2 birds

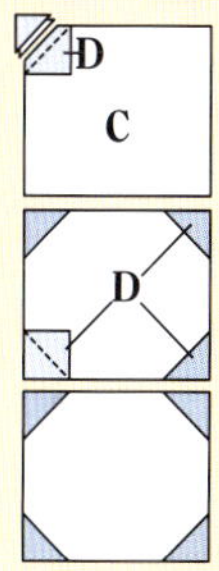

Unit 2
Stitch & Flip
Make 1

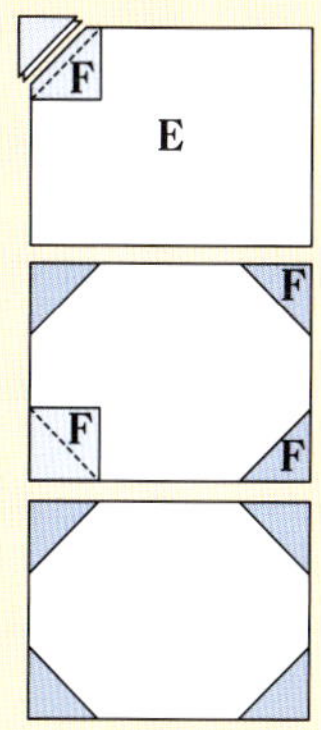

Unit 3
Stitch & Flip
Make 1

Refer to "Stitch-and-Flip" in the Techniques file on the PDF. Use the white A and light blue B's to make unit 1. Use the white C and light blue D's to make unit 2. Use the white E and light blue F's to make unit 3. Sew the units and patches together as shown.

Use 3 strands of floss and a stem stitch for the arms. Tack the buttons in place as shown to complete the block.

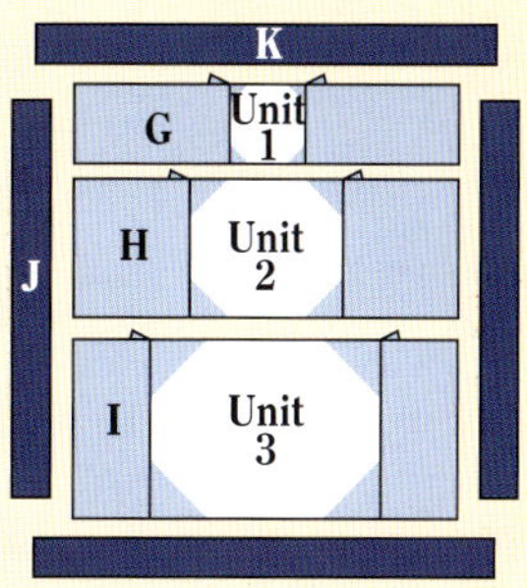

Block Assembly

Embroidery Placement

block no. 889

New Directions

by Kay Gentry • Noble Needle Quilting and Sewing
nobleneedle.com

⧄ = cut in half diagonally

Assorted Black Tone-on-Tones
20 squares (A) 1⅞″ x 1⅞″
16 Assorted Tone-on-Tones
from *each*
1 square (A) 1⅞″ x 1⅞″
1 square 3⅞″ x 3⅞″ ⧄ (B)
(there will be 1 extra from each fabric)

Block Piecing

Sew the patches together as shown to complete the block.

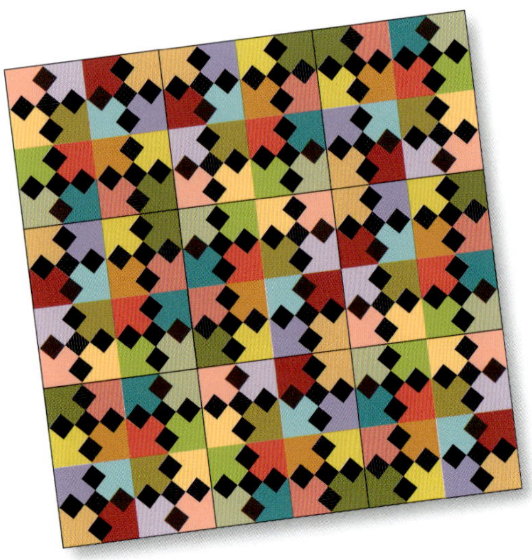

block no. 890

Red Rosy

by Melissa Harris and Arlene Stamper
The Quilt Company • quiltcompany.com

Fabric: My Secret Garden designed by Marti Michell for Maywood Studio, maywoodstudio.com.

⧄ = cut in half diagonally

Red Tone-on-Tone
4 squares (A) 3¼″ x 3¼″
Dark Green Print
8 squares (B) 1½″ x 1½″
8 rectangles (D) 1½″ x 2¼″
4 squares (G) 2⅜″ x 2⅜″
Cream Tone-on-Tone
16 squares (B) 1½″ x 1½″
4 squares (C) 2″ x 2″
1 square (F) 4¼″ x 4¼″
4 squares 2⅝″ x 2⅝″ ⧄ (H)
Red Print
5 squares (E) 3½″ x 3½″
Green Tone-on-Tone
2 squares 4⅜″ x 4⅜″ ⧄ (I)

Refer to "Stitch-and-Flip" in the Techniques file on the PDF. Use the red tone-on-tone A's, dark green B's and cream C's to make 4 unit 1's. Make 4 unit 2's and 4 unit 3's using the dark green D's and cream B's. Use the red print E's and cream B's to make 4 unit 4's.

Make 4 Flying Geese using the cream F and dark green G's.

Sew the units, Flying Geese and patches together as shown to complete the block.

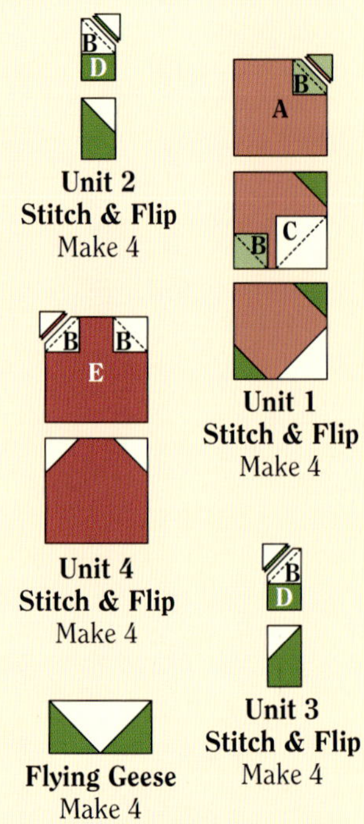

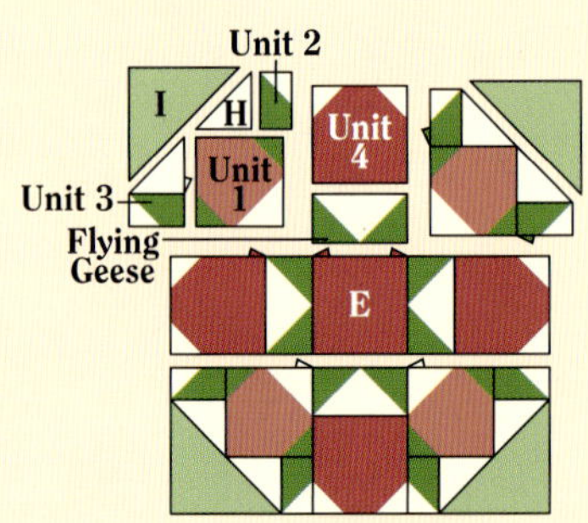

Block Assembly

pieced

block no. 891

Hidden Garden

by Beth Helfter • EvaPaige Quilt Designs
evapaigequiltdesigns.com

Fabric: Paradise designed by Pat Bravo for Art Gallery Fabrics, artgalleryfabrics.com.

Assorted Pink and Green Prints

- 8 squares (A) 2½" x 2½"
- 8 rectangles (B) 1½" x 4½"
- 4 rectangles (D) 1½" x 3½"

Green Solid

- 4 rectangles (B) 1½" x 4½"
- 4 rectangles (C) 1½" x 2½"
- 2 rectangles (E) 1½" x 10½"
- 2 rectangles (F) 1½" x 12½"

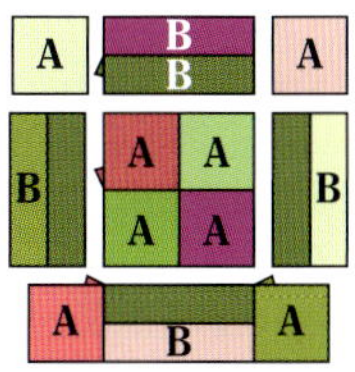

Center Piecing

Sew the print A's, 4 green solid B's and 4 print B's together as shown to make the block center.

Refer to the block piecing diagram; join 1 print B, 1 green solid C and 1 print D as shown to make a B/C/D strip. Make 4 B/C/D strips. Sew 1 B/C/D to the left side of the center with a partial seam as shown. Sew a B/C/D to the top, to the right and to the bottom of the center as shown. Complete the partial seam.

Add the green solid E's and F's as shown to complete the block.

• = Partial Seam

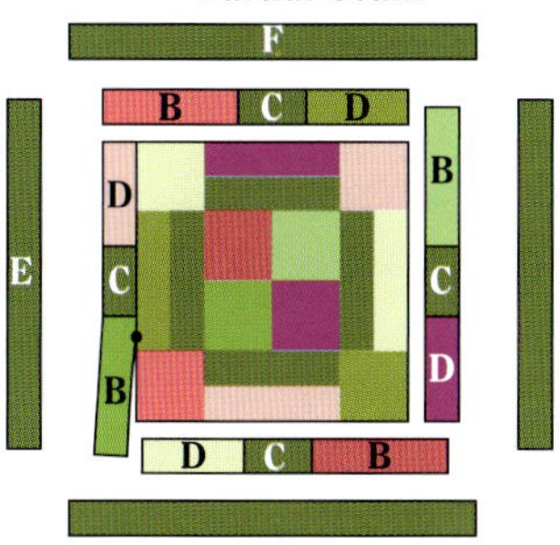

Block Piecing

block no. 892

Fall in Line

by Julie Herman • Jaybird Quilts
jaybirdquilts.com

Fabric: Architextures designed by Carolyn Friedlander and Kona Solids, both for Robert Kaufman, robertkaufman.com.

Julie Herman is the author of *Skip the Borders: Easy Patterns for Modern Quilts* for Martingale & Co., shopmartingale.com.

Dark Blue Solid, Medium Blue Solid and Light Teal Solid

from *each*

- 2 rectangles (A) 1½" x 12½"

Assorted Light Prints

- 18 squares (B) 2½" x 2½"

Sew the patches together as shown to complete the block.

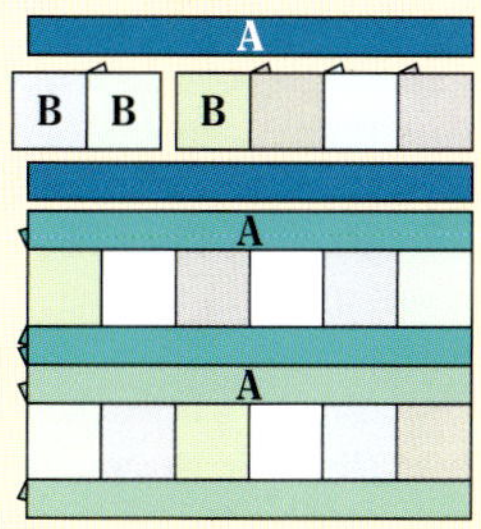

Block Piecing

block no. 893

Home Sweet Home

by Lori Holt • Bee in My Bonnet Co.
beeinmybonnetco.blogspot.com

Fabric: Various lines designed by Lori Holt for Riley Blake Designs, rileyblakedesigns.com.

Gray Solid

1 square (A) 3⅞" x 3⅞"
2 squares (C) 3½" x 3½"
1 rectangle (D) 1½" x 4½"

Aqua Print

1 square (A) 3⅞" x 3⅞"
2 rectangles (D) 1½" x 4½"
1 rectangle (F) 1½" x 2½"
2 rectangles (M) 1½" x 7½"

White Print

8 squares (B) 1½" x 1½"
2 rectangles (D) 1½" x 4½"
2 rectangles (G) 2" x 2½"
2 squares (H) 2½" x 2½"
1 rectangle (I) 1½" x 10½"
4 rectangles (J) 1½" x 3½"

Green Check

2 rectangles (E) 1½" x 5½"

Yellow Tone-on-Tone

3 rectangles (F) 1½" x 2½"

Yellow Print

2 rectangles (K) 2½" x 3½"

Red Print

1 rectangle (L) 2½" x 4½"

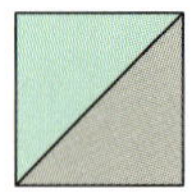

Partial Unit
Make 2 from A's

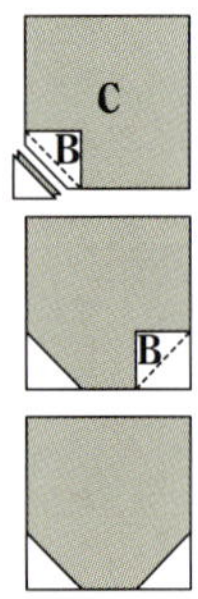

Unit 2
Stitch & Flip
Make 2

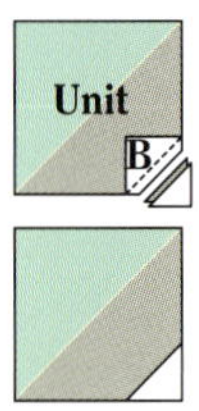

Unit 1
Stitch & Flip
Make 2

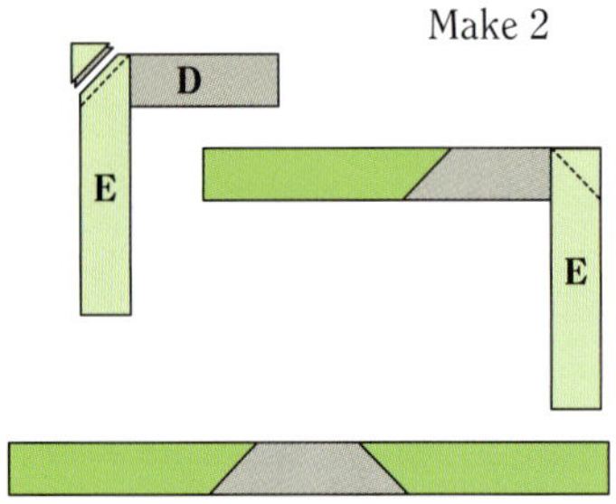

Unit 3
Stitch & Flip
Make 1

Refer to "Triangle-Squares" in the Techniques file on the PDF. Pair the gray A with the aqua A to make 2 partial units.

Refer to "Stitch-and-Flip" in the Techniques file on the PDF. Sew a white B on the corner of each partial unit as shown to make 2 unit 1's.

Use the gray C's and white B's to make 2 unit 2's. Use the gray D and green E's to make unit 3.

Sew the units and patches together as shown to complete the block.

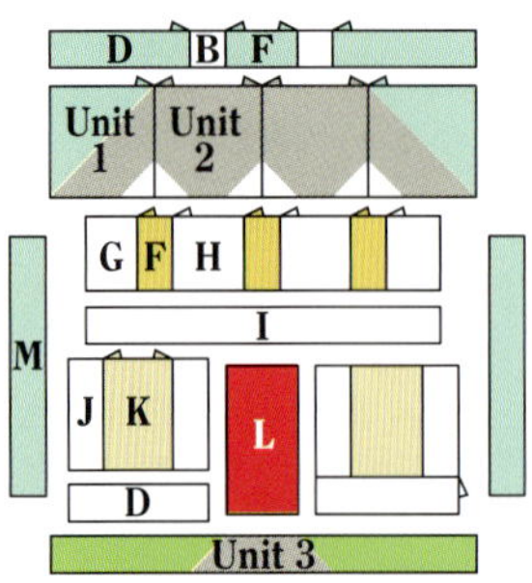

Block Assembly

block no. 894

Scrap Crystals

by Bonnie Hunter • Quiltville
quiltville.com

Bonnie Hunter writes the "Addicted to Scraps" column for *Quiltmaker.* She is the author of several books, including *Ring Around the Hexies—A Collaboration Celebration* with Mickey Depre for Kansas City Star Quilts, pickledish.com.

Assorted Light Prints and Tone-on-Tones

16 squares (A) 2⅜" x 2⅜"
16 squares (B) 2" x 2"

Assorted Medium to Dark Blue Prints and Tone-on-Tones

16 squares (A) 2⅜" x 2⅜"

Assorted Medium to Dark Green Prints and Tone-on-Tones

16 squares (B) 2" x 2"

Unit
Make 32

Pair the light A's with the blue A's to make 32 Triangle-Square units.

Noting the placement of the light B's and green B's, sew the units and patches together as shown to complete the block.

Block Assembly

pieced

block no. 895
Rush Hour

by Kimberly Jolly • Fat Quarter Shop
fatquartershop.com

Fabric: Cruiser Boulevard designed by Sheri McCulley for Riley Blake Designs, rileyblakedesigns.com.

Green Print and Aqua Print
from *each*
2 rectangles (A) 3½"x 10½"
White Solid
8 squares (B) 3½"x 3½"
Red Tone-on-Tone
2 rectangles (C) 1½"x 12½"

Refer to "Stitch-and-Flip" in the Techniques file on the PDF. Use the green A's and aqua A's with white B's to make 2 unit 1's and 2 unit 2's as shown.

Sew the units and patches together as shown to complete the block.

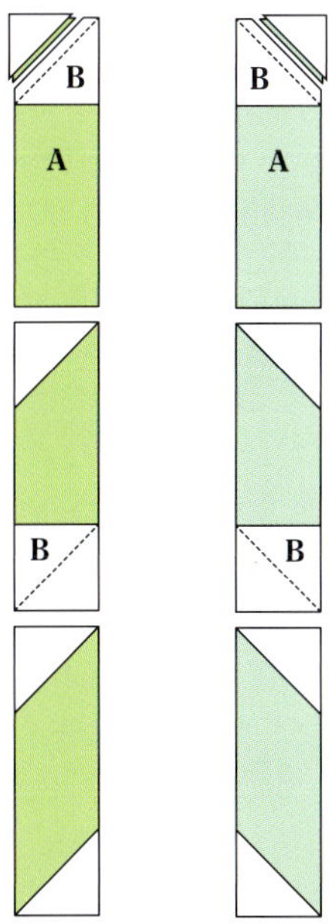

Unit 1
Stitch & Flip
Make 2

Unit 2
Stitch & Flip
Make 2

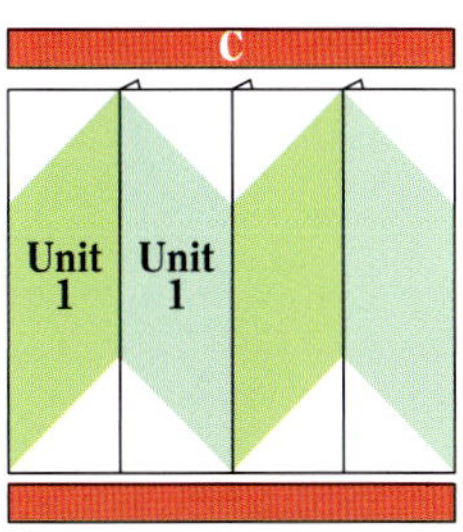

Block Assembly

block no. 896
Aloha

by Susan Knapp & Mary Jane Mattingly
The Quilt Branch • quiltbranch.com

Mary Jane Mattingly and Susan Knapp are the authors of the *Six Halves Make a Whole* series for The Quilt Branch, quiltbranch.com.

◪ = cut in half diagonally

Red Print
4 squares 2⅞"x 2⅞" ◪ (A)
1 square (E) 4½"x 4½"
Blue Tone-on-Tone
4 squares (B) 2½"x 2½"
8 rectangles (D) 2½"x 4½"
Yellow Tone-on-Tone
8 squares (B) 2½"x 2½"
2 squares 4⅞"x 4⅞" ◪ (C)
Light Green Tone-on-Tone
12 squares (B) 2½"x 2½"

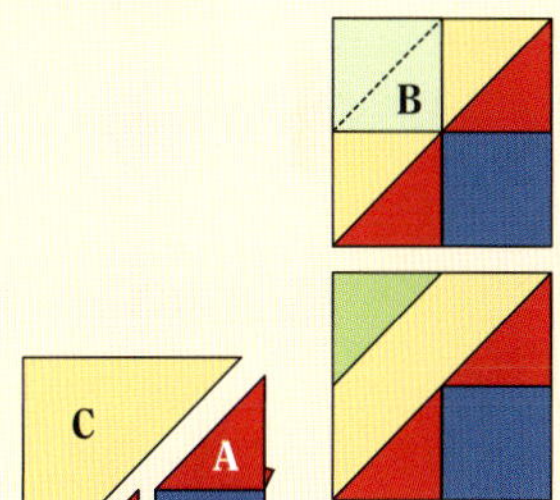

Partial Unit

Unit 1
Stitch & Flip
Make 4

Join 2 red A's, 1 blue B and 1 yellow C as shown to make a partial unit; make 4 partial units. Refer to "Stitch-and-Flip" in the Techniques file on the PDF. Add a light green B to the corner of each partial unit as shown to make 4 unit 1's.

Use the blue D's, green B's and yellow B's to make 4 unit 2's and 4 unit 3's as shown.

Sew the units and red E together as shown to complete the block.

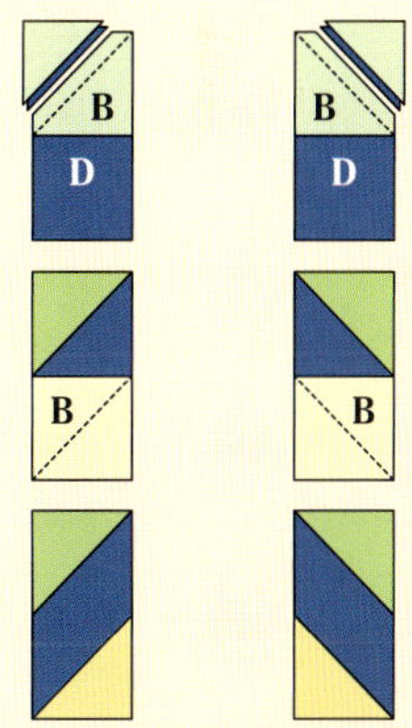

Unit 2
Stitch & Flip
Make 4

Unit 3
Stitch & Flip
Make 4

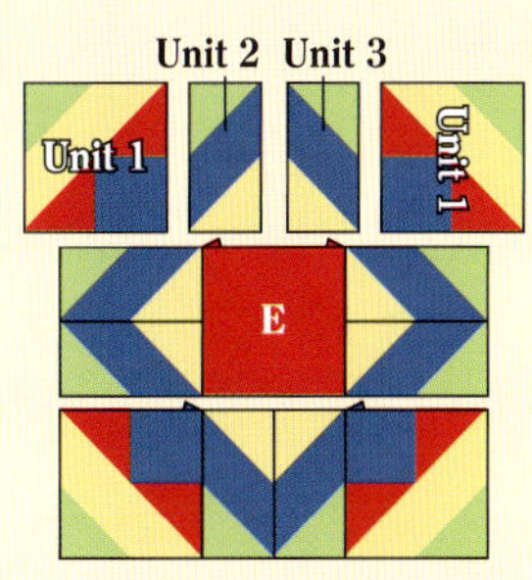

Block Assembly

block no. 897
Always

by Thomas Knauer
thomasknauersews.com

Fabric: Kona Solids by Robert Kaufman, robertkaufman.com.

Assorted Solids
16 squares (A) 2½" x 2½"
10 rectangles (B) 2½" x 4½"

Sew the patches together as shown to complete the block.

Block Assembly

block no. 898
Sailor's Delight

by Jo Kramer & Kelli Kramer • Jo's Country Junction
joscountryjunction.com

⧄ = cut in half diagonally

Assorted Tan Prints and Tone-on-Tones
4 squares (A) 4½" x 4½"
8 squares 2⅞" x 2⅞" ⧄ (C)

Assorted Red Prints and Tone-on-Tones
1 square (A) 4½" x 4½"
8 squares (B) 2½" x 2½"

Assorted Dark Blue Prints and Tone-on-Tones
8 squares (B) 2½" x 2½"
4 squares 2⅞" x 2⅞" ⧄ (C)

Red Solid
4 squares 2⅞" x 2⅞" ⧄ (C)

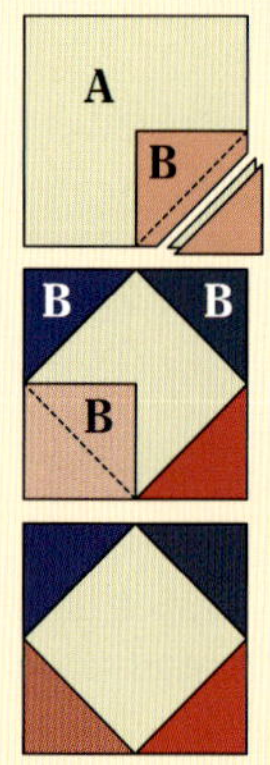

Unit
Stitch & Flip
Make 4

Jo and Kelli gave their block a scrappier look by cutting more tan and blue squares to make the C's. The leftover triangles can be used to make additional blocks.

Refer to "Stitch-and-Flip" in the Techniques file on the PDF. Use the tan A's and assorted red B's and blue B's to make 4 units as shown.

Sew the units and patches together as shown to complete the block.

Block Assembly

pieced

block no. 899
All Square

by Jessie Kurtz • Harding Hill Designs
hardinghilldesigns.typepad.com

Fabric: Mama Said Sew designed by Sweetwater for Moda Fabrics, unitednotions.com.

Black and White Check
8 squares (A) 2⅞" x 2⅞"
Black Stripe
10 squares (A) 2⅞" x 2⅞"
8 squares (B) 2½" x 2½"
White Stripe
4 squares (A) 2⅞" x 2⅞"
Red Print
6 squares (A) 2⅞" x 2⅞"

Unit 1
Make 16

Unit 2
Make 8

Unit 3
Make 4

Note: The black-and-white check Jessie used is a diagonal check. A straight of grain check will yield a different effect.

Pair the black-and-white check A's with black stripe A's to make 16 Triangle-Square unit 1's. Make 8 unit 2's using the white A's and red A's. Use 2 red A's and 2 black A's to make 4 unit 3's.

Sew the units and patches together as shown to complete the block.

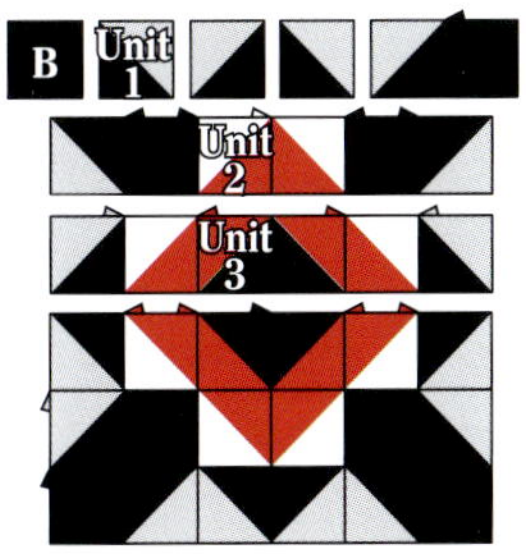

Block Assembly

block no. 900
Watermark

by Cindy Lammon • Hyacinth Quilt Designs
hyacinthquiltdesigns.blogspot.com

Fabric: Comma designed by Zen Chic for Moda Fabrics, unitednotions.com.

Cindy Lammon is the author of *Simply Modern Christmas* for Martingale & Co., shopmartingale.com.

Gray Tone-on-Tone #1 and Gray Tone-on-Tone #2
from *each*
2 rectangles (A) 2½" x 4½"
White Solid
8 squares (B) 2½" x 2½"
4 rectangles (C) 1½" x 4½"
2 Orange Tone-on-Tones and 2 Green Tone-on-Tones
from *each*
1 rectangle (D) 3½" x 4½"
1 rectangle (E) 1½" x 3½"
Gray Dot
4 squares (F) 1½" x 1½"
Yellow Tone-on-Tone
4 rectangles (C) 1½" x 4½"
Cream with Yellow Print
1 square (G) 4½" x 4½"

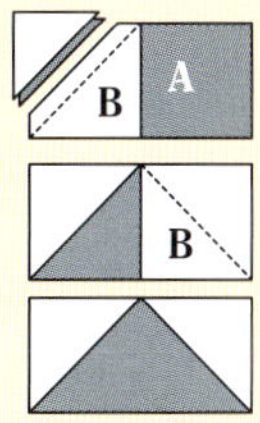

Unit 1
Stitch & Flip
Make 2

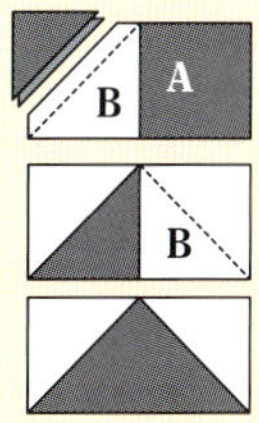

Unit 2
Stitch & Flip
Make 2

Refer to "Stitch-and-Flip" in the Techniques file on the PDF. Use the gray tone-on-tone A's and white B's to make 2 unit 1's and 2 unit 2's as shown.

Sew the units and patches together as shown to complete the block.

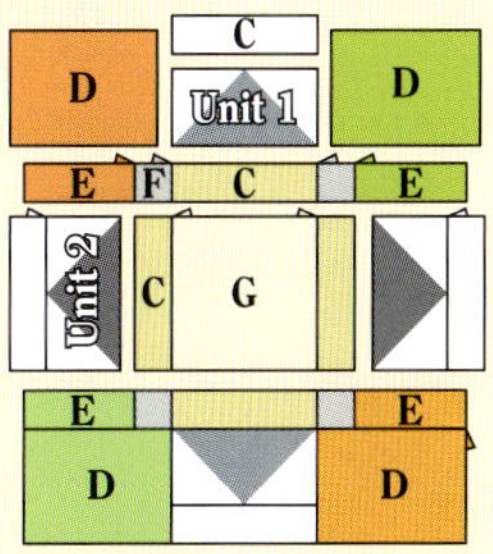

Block Assembly

block no. 901

Pieces of My Heart

by Melva Nolan
melvalovesscraps.blogspot.com

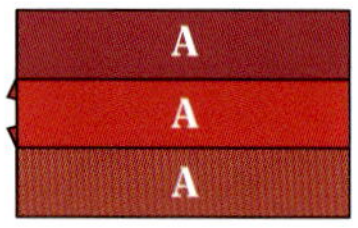

Partial Unit 1
Make 1

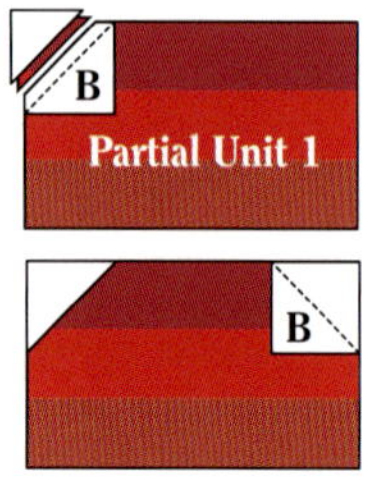

Unit 1
Stitch & Flip
Make 1

Assorted Red Tone-on-Tones
- 4 rectangles (A) 2″ x 8″
- 1 rectangle (D) 2″ x 5″
- 1 rectangle (E) 2″ x 6½″
- 1 rectangle (F) 2″ x 3½″
- 1 square (H) 2″ x 2″

White Tone-on-Tone
- 4 squares (B) 2½″ x 2½″
- 1 square (C) 5″ x 5″

Assorted Pink Tone-on-Tones
- 1 rectangle (A) 2″ x 8″
- 1 rectangle (D) 2″ x 5″
- 1 rectangle (E) 2″ x 6½″
- 1 rectangle (G) 2″ x 9½″
- 1 rectangle (I) 2″ x 11″

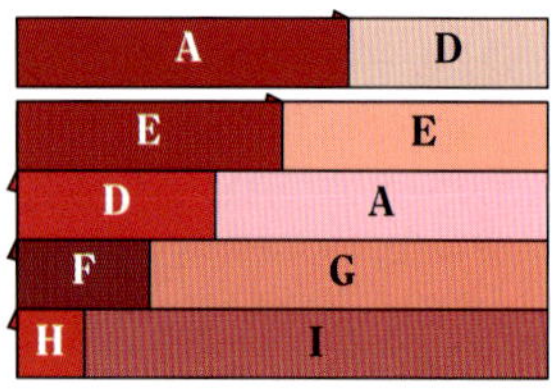

Partial Unit 2
Make 1

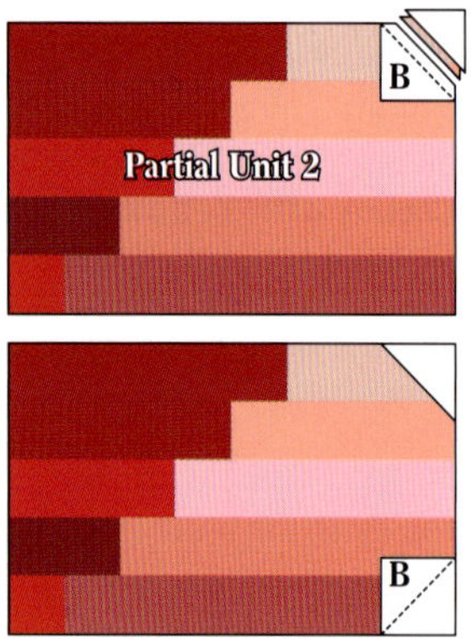

Unit 2
Stitch & Flip
Make 1

Join 3 red A's to make a partial unit 1. Refer to "Stitch-and-Flip" in the Techniques file on the PDF. Add white B's as shown to make unit 1.

Join the red and pink patches to make a partial unit 2. Add white B's as shown to make unit 2.

Sew the units and C together as shown to complete the block.

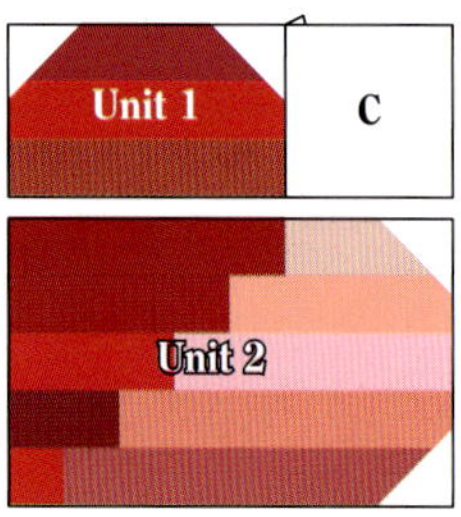

Block Assembly

block no. 902

Ruffled Feathers

by Jennifer Oden
quiltspeciallybyjen.blogspot.com

⊠ = cut in half twice diagonally

4 Orange Batiks
from *each*
- 2 squares (A) 2⅞″ x 2⅞″
- 1 square 7¼″ x 7¼″ ⊠ (B)
  (there will be 3 extra from each fabric)

Pale Orange Batik
- 8 squares (A) 2⅞″ x 2⅞″
- 2 rectangles (C) 1½″ x 10½″
- 2 rectangles (D) 1½″ x 12½″

Unit 1
Make 4

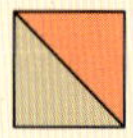

Unit 2
Make 4

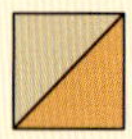

Unit 3
Make 4

Unit 4
Make 4

Pair the 4 sets of orange A's with pale orange A's to make 4 Triangle-Square unit 1's, 4 unit 2's, 4 unit 3's and 4 unit 4's as shown.

Sew the units and patches together as shown to complete the block.

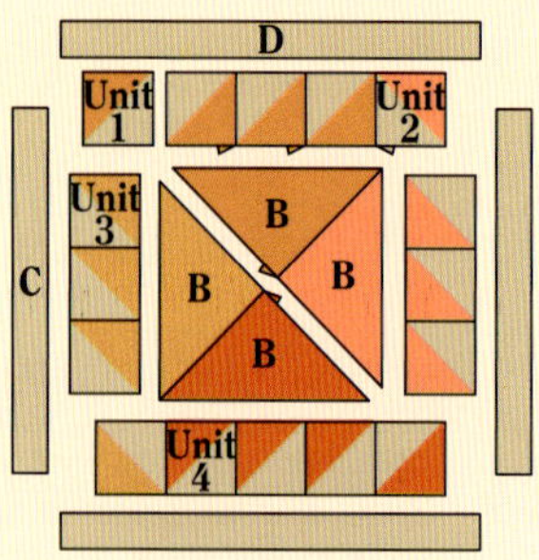

Block Assembly

pieced

block no. 903

Garden Cottage

by Gail Pan • Gail Pan Designs
gailpandesigns.typepad.com

Fabric: Independence Trail designed by Minnick & Simpson for Moda Fabrics, unitednotions.com.

Gail Pan is the author of *Simply Christmas 2013* for Gail Pan Designs, gailpandesigns.typepad.com.

See page 327 on the PDF for pattern

Beige Dot
1 square (A) 8½″ x 8½″ (trim to 7½″ x 7½″ after embroidery)
Muslin
1 square (A) 8½″ x 8½″ (trim to 7½″ x 7½″ after embroidery)
Red Print
2 rectangles (B) 1½″ x 7½″
2 rectangles (C) 1½″ x 9½″
Beige Print
2 rectangles (D) 2″ x 9½″
2 rectangles (E) 2″ x 12½″
Brown Pigma Micron pen (.01 tip) **or pencil**
Red Perle cotton

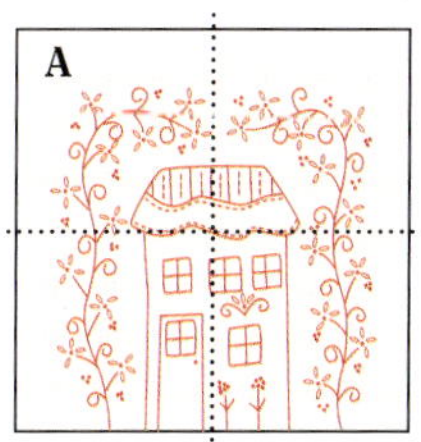

Embroidery Placement

Fold the beige dot A in half both ways and lightly crease the folds. Using the creases and placement diagram as guides, lightly trace the embroidery design onto A with a pencil or pen. Layer the traced A right side up on top of the muslin A and baste them together.

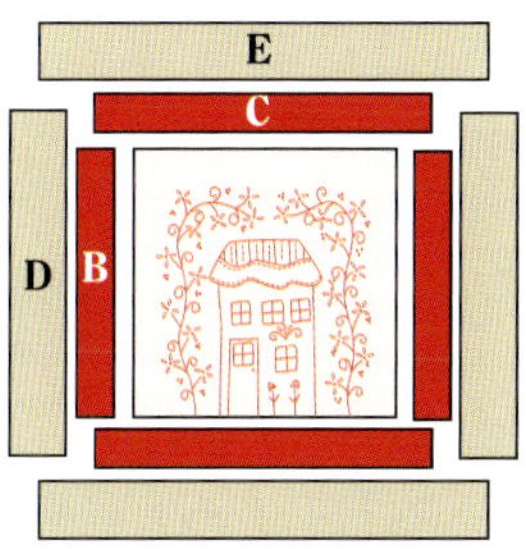

Block Assembly

Use a backstitch to embroider the house, house details and stems. Use a lazy daisy stitch and French knots to create the flowers and buds. Center the design and trim to 7½″ × 7½″.

Sew the embroidered A, red B's and C's and beige print D's and E's together as shown to complete the block.

block no. 904

Orion

by Celine Perkins • Perkins Dry Goods
perkinsdrygoods.com

See page 293 on the PDF for pattern

White Dot
4 *each* templates A and Ar
8 rectangles (D) 1½″ x 2½″
8 rectangles (E) 1½″ x 4½″
Red Dot
4 template A
2 squares (B) 2⅞″ x 2⅞″
Black Print
4 template Ar
2 squares (B) 2⅞″ x 2⅞″
4 squares (C) 2½″ x 2½″

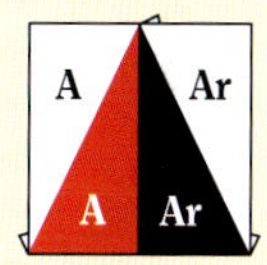

Unit 1
Make 4

Unit 2
Make 4

Join 1 white A, 1 white Ar, a red A and black Ar as shown to make a unit 1. Make 4 unit 1's.

Pair the red B's with black B's to make 4 Triangle-Square unit 2's.

Sew the units and patches together as shown to complete the block.

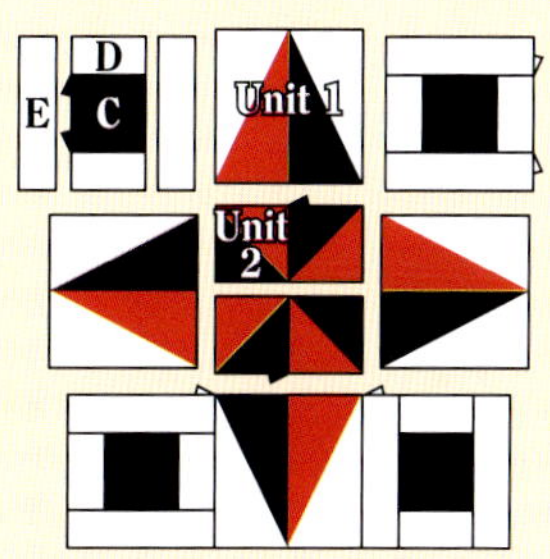

Block Assembly

block no. 905
Heart's Desire

by Doris Rice • The Quilting Queen
thequiltingqueenonline.blogspot.com

Fabric: Always and Forever designed by Deb Strain for Moda Fabrics, unitednotions.com.

Red Tone-on-Tone
2 squares (A) 3½″ x 3½″
1 square (F) 3⅞″ x 3⅞″
White Solid
8 squares (B) 2″ x 2″
2 squares (E) 3½″ x 3½″
1 square (F) 3⅞″ x 3⅞″
White with Pink Print
2 rectangles (C) 2″ x 3½″
1 rectangle (D) 3½″ x 6½″
1 rectangle (G) 2″ x 6½″
Black Print
4 rectangles (D) 3½″ x 6½″

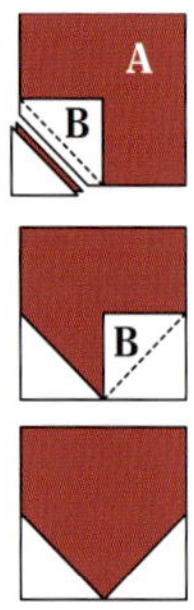

Unit 1
Stitch & Flip
Make 2

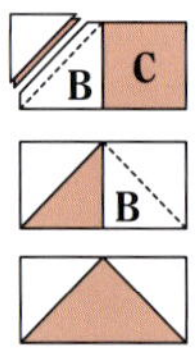

Unit 2
Stitch & Flip
Make 2

Refer to "Stitch-and-Flip" in the Techniques file on the PDF. Use the red A's and white B's to make 2 unit 1's. Make 2 unit 2's as shown using the white with pink print C's and white B's. Use the white with pink print D and white E's to make unit 3.

Pair the red F's with the white F's to make 2 Triangle-Square unit 4's.

Sew the units and patches together as shown to complete the block.

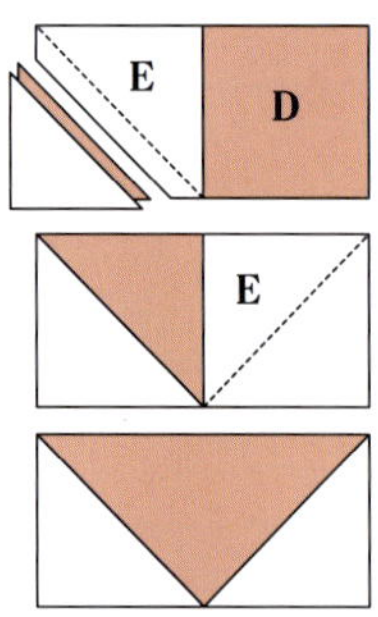

Unit 3
Stitch & Flip
Make 1

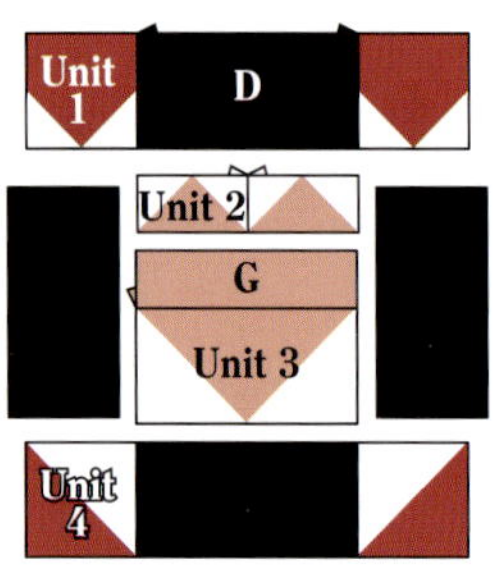

Block Assembly

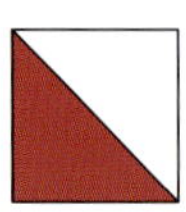

Unit 4
Make 2

block no. 906
Too Many Pinwheels?

by Peg Spradlin
handicraftsbypeg.com

Fabric: Spa designed by Deb Strain and Bella Solids for Moda Fabrics, unitednotions.com.

◸ = cut in half diagonally
⊠ = cut in half twice diagonally

White with Blue Print
2 squares (A) 3⅞″ x 3⅞″
4 squares 2⅜″ x 2⅜″ ◸ (B)
2 squares 4¼″ x 4¼″ ⊠ (C)
Assorted Medium Blue Tone-on-Tones
2 squares (A) 3⅞″ x 3⅞″
4 squares 3⅞″ x 3⅞″ ◸ (D)
Assorted Light Blue Tone-on-Tones
4 squares 2⅜″ x 2⅜″ ◸ (B)
Gold Solid
4 squares 3⅞″ x 3⅞″ ◸ (D)

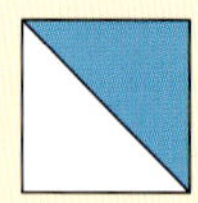

Unit
Make 4

Pair the white A's with the medium blue A's to make 4 Triangle-Square units.

Sew the units and patches together as shown to complete the block.

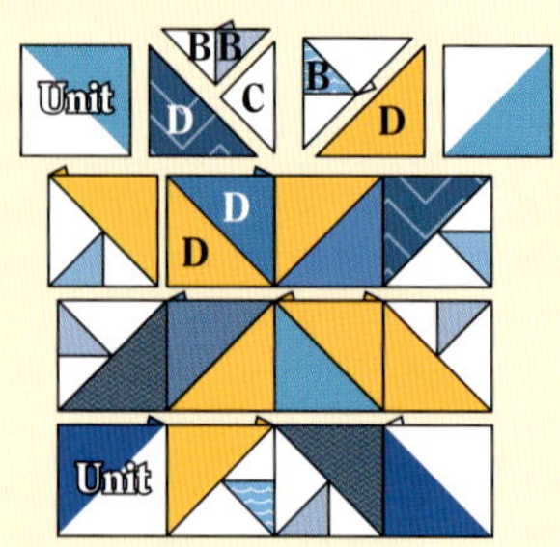

Block Assembly

block no. 907

Mixmaster

by Denise Starck • Graphic Designer, *Quiltmaker*
quiltmaker.com

Fabric: Quilting Treasures, quiltingtreasures.com.

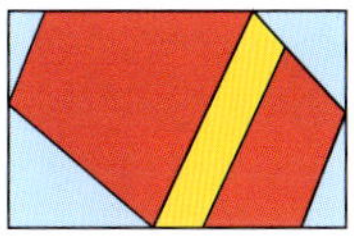

Section
Make 1

See page 320 on the PDF for pattern

Yellow Tone-on-Tone
section patch 1

Red Tone-on-Tone
section patches 2 and 3

Light Blue Tone-on-Tone
section patches 4–7
1 square (B) 1″x 1″
1 square (D) 1¼″x 1¼″
1 rectangle (H) 2″x 2⅛″
1 rectangle (I) 2½″x 4¾″
1 rectangle (J) 1⅜″x 2¾″
1 rectangle (M) 1″x 4″
2 rectangles (O) 1″x 1¾″
2 rectangles (Q) 1″x 2¼″
1 rectangle (R) 2½″x 12½″

Dark Blue Tone-on-Tone
2 rectangles (A) 1⅜″x 2″
1 rectangle (C) 2¾″x 3⅞″
1 rectangle (F) 1⅛″x 1⅜″
1 rectangle (K) 1⅜″x 8¼″

Black Tone-on-Tone
3 squares (E) 2½″x 2½″

Light Gray Tone-on-Tone
6 squares (B) 1″x 1″
1 square (G) 1⅜″x 1⅜″
1 rectangle (L) 1½″x 4″
1 rectangle (N) 1¼″x 10″
2 rectangles (P) 1¼″x 2¼″

Dark Gray Tone-on-Tone
6 squares (B) 1″x 1″
1 rectangle (M) 1″x 4″
2 rectangles (O) 1″x 1¾″
1 rectangle (S) 2″x 12½″

Unit 1
Stitch & Flip
Make 1

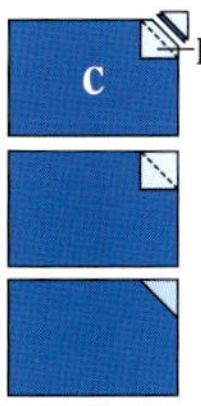

Unit 2
Stitch & Flip
Make 1

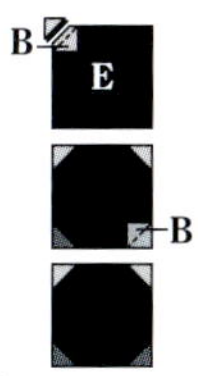

Unit 3
Stitch & Flip
Make 3

Make 1 paper copy of the foundation section. Foundation piece the section in numerical order, pressing and trimming after each patch addition.

Refer to "Stitch-and-Flip" in the Techniques file on the PDF. Use the dark blue A and light blue B to make unit 1. Make unit 2 using the dark blue C and light blue D. Make 3 unit 3's using black E's, light gray B's and dark gray B's.

Sew the section, units and patches together as shown to complete the block.

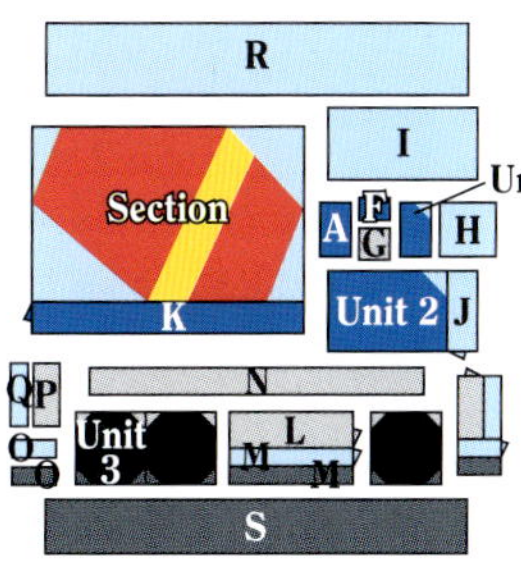

Block Assembly

block no. 908

Aspen Retreat

by Debbie Taylor • Fat Quarter Shop
fatquartershop.com

Fabric: Aspen Frost designed by Basic Gray for Moda Fabrics, unitednotions.com.

Assorted White Tone-on-Tones
2 squares (A) 1⅞″x 1⅞″
4 squares (B) 1½″x 1½″
1 rectangle (C) 1½″x 3½″
1 rectangle (D) 1½″x 4½″

Assorted Red Prints and Tone-on-Tones
2 squares (A) 1⅞″x 1⅞″
1 square (B) 1½″x 1½″
1 rectangle (E) 1½″x 5½″
1 rectangle (F) 1½″x 6½″
1 rectangle (G) 1½″x 7½″
1 rectangle (H) 1½″x 8½″
1 rectangle (I) 1½″x 9½″
2 rectangles (J) 1½″x 10½″
1 rectangle (K) 1½″x 12½″
from *one*
4 squares (L) 2½″x 2½″

Assorted Aqua Prints and Tone-on-Tones
1 rectangle (D) 1½″x 4½″
1 rectangle (E) 1½″x 5½″
1 rectangle (F) 1½″x 6½″
1 rectangle (G) 1½″x 7½″
1 rectangle (H) 1½″x 8½″
1 rectangle (I) 1½″x 9½″
1 rectangle (J) 1½″x 10½″
1 rectangle (K) 1½″x 12½″

Unit
Make 4

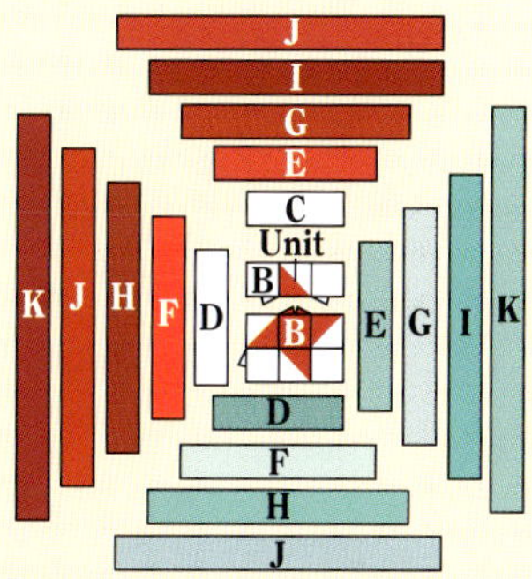

Block Piecing

Pair the white A's with red A's to make 4 Triangle-Square units. Sew the units and patches B–K together as shown.

Refer to "Stitch-and-Flip" in the Techniques file on the PDF. Add a red L to each corner as shown to complete the block.

Stitch & Flip

block no. 909

Which Way

by Kathryn Wilson Tucker • Next Step Quilt Designs
nextstepquiltdesigns.com

⊠ = cut in half twice diagonally

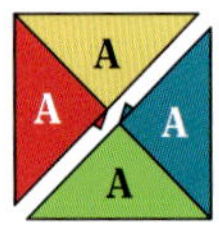

Yellow, Red, Green and Blue Tone-on-Tones
from *each*
- 1 square 5¼″x 5¼″ ⊠ (A) (there will be 3 extra from each fabric)
- 1 rectangle (B) 1½″x 5½″
- 1 rectangle (C) 1½″x 7½″
- 1 rectangle (D) 1½″x 9½″
- 1 rectangle (E) 1½″x 11½″

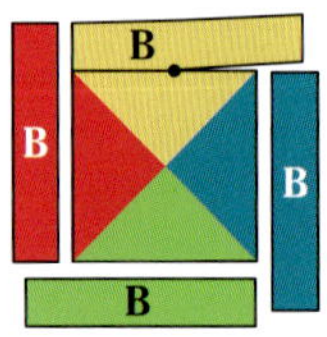

• = Partial Seam

Join the A's as shown to make the block center. Sew the yellow B to the top of the center with a partial seam as shown. Sew the red B to the left, the green B to the bottom, and the blue B to the right of the center as shown. Complete the partial seam. Continue using partial seams with the C's, D's and E's as shown to complete the block.

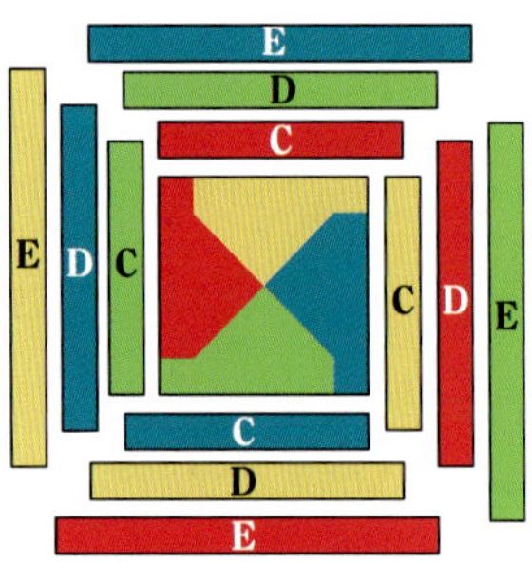

Block Assembly

block no. 910

On the Grid

by Jocelyn Ueng • It's Sew Emma
itssewemma.com

Fabric: Happy Go Lucky designed by Bonnie & Camille for Moda Fabrics, unitednotions.com.

Aqua Print and Aqua Stripe
from *each*
- 1 square (A) 2⅞″x 2⅞″
- 4 squares (C) 2″x 2″

White Tone-on-Tone
- 2 squares (A) 2⅞″x 2⅞″
- 4 rectangles (G) 1½″x 5″
- 2 rectangles (H) 1½″x 12½″

Red Print and Dark Blue Print
from *each*
- 2 rectangles (B) 2″x 3½″
- 2 rectangles (D) 2″x 5″

Light Green Dot and Orange Dot
from *each*
- 2 rectangles (E) 1½″x 2½″
- 2 rectangles (F) 1½″x 3½″

Aqua Check
- 2 rectangles (G) 1½″x 5″
- 1 rectangle (H) 1½″x 12½″

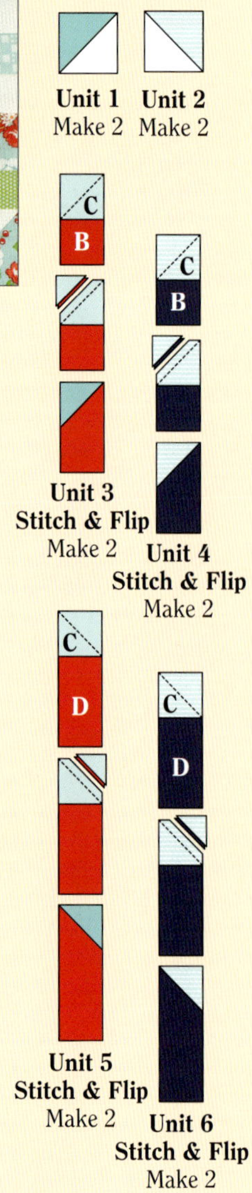

Pair the aqua print and aqua stripe A's with white A's to make 2 Triangle-Square unit 1's and 2 unit 2's as shown.

Refer to "Stitch-and-Flip" in the Techniques file on the PDF. Using red B's and D's and the aqua print C's, make 2 unit 3's and 2 unit 5's as shown. Make 2 unit 4's and 2 unit 6's using dark blue B's and D's and the aqua stripe C's.

Sew the units and patches together as shown to complete the block.

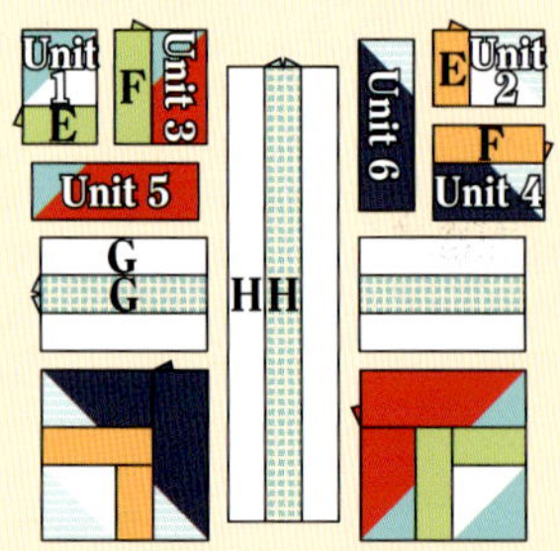

Block Assembly

block no. 911

Twin Baskets

by Andee Andriole and Candee Ferris • Sisters' Quilting Trunk, sisterssquiltingtrunk.com

Fabric: Timeless Treasures, ttfabrics.com and Michael Miller Fabrics, michaelmillerfabrics.com.

◩ = cut in half diagonally

Black Print and Black Dot
from *each*
- 3 squares (A) 1⅞" x 1⅞"
- 1 square (B) 3⅞" x 3⅞"
- 1 square 1⅞" x 1⅞" ◩ (C)
- 1 square 6⅞" x 6⅞" ◩ (F) (there will be 1 extra from each fabric)

White Solid
- 6 squares (A) 1⅞" x 1⅞"
- 2 squares 1⅞" x 1⅞" ◩ (C)
- 1 square 4⅞" x 4⅞" ◩ (D)
- 1 square 2⅞" x 2⅞" ◩ (E)
- 2 squares (G) 3½" x 3½"
- 2 rectangles (H) 3½" x 6½"

Unit 1 from A's
Make 6

Unit 2 from A's
Make 6

Unit 3 from B's
Make 2

Pair the black print A's with 3 white A's to make 6 Triangle-Square unit 1's and the black dot A's with 3 white A's to make 6 unit 2's. Pair the black print B with the black dot B to make 2 unit 3's.

Sew the units and patches together as shown to complete the block.

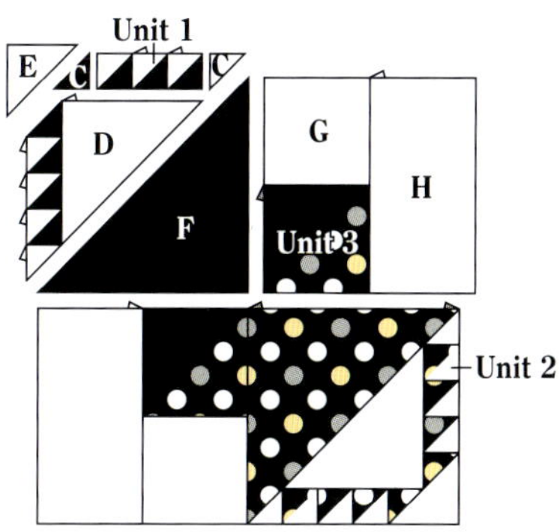

Block Assembly

block no. 912

Christmas Cactus

by Donna Benham • DB Designs

See page 359 on the PDF for pattern

Cream Tone-on-Tone
- 1 square (A) 4¼" x 4¼"
- 4 squares (B) 2⅜" x 2⅜"
- 4 template C
- 4 *each* templates D and Dr
- 4 squares (E) 2" x 2"

Green Tone-on-Tone
- 4 squares (B) 2⅜" x 2⅜"
- 8 *each* templates D and Dr

Red Tone-on-Tone
- 4 squares (B) 2⅜" x 2⅜"
- 8 squares (E) 2" x 2"
- 1 square (F) 3½" x 3½"

Flying Geese
Make 4

Unit 1
Make 8

Unit 2
Make 4

Use the cream A and green B's to make 4 Flying Geese.

Pair the cream B's with red B's to make 8 Triangle-Square unit 1's.

Join the cream C's to the green D's and Dr's as shown to make 4 unit 2's.

Sew the units and patches together as shown to complete the block.

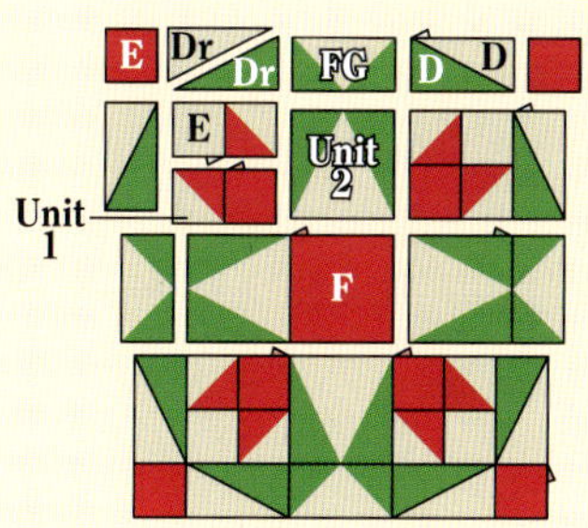

Block Assembly

block no. 913

Desert Mirage

by Debbie Caffrey • Debbie's Creative Moments, Inc.
debbiescreativemoments.com

Debbie Caffrey is the author of numerous self-published books including *Surprise Yourself: Simple Steps to Making Fabulous Quilts*, debbiescreativemoments.com.

Dark Green Batik
2 squares (A) 3⅞″ x 3⅞″
16 squares (C) 2″ x 2″
Light Gold Batik
2 squares (A) 3⅞″ x 3⅞″
8 rectangles (B) 2″ x 3½″
Teal Batik
16 squares (C) 2″ x 2″
4 squares (D) 3½″ x 3½″
Dark Gold Batik
4 squares (D) 3½″ x 3½″
1 square (E) 6½″ x 6½″

Unit 1
Make 4

Unit 2
Stitch & Flip
Make 4

Unit 3
Stitch & Flip
Make 4

Pair the dark green A's with the light gold A's to make 4 Triangle-Square unit 1's.

Refer to "Stitch-and-Flip" in the Techniques file on the PDF. Use the light gold B's, dark green C's and teal C's to make 4 unit 2's and 4 unit 3's as shown. Make 4 unit 4's using the dark gold D's, dark green C's and teal C's. Make unit 5 using the dark gold E and teal D's.

Sew the units and patches together as shown to complete the block.

pieced

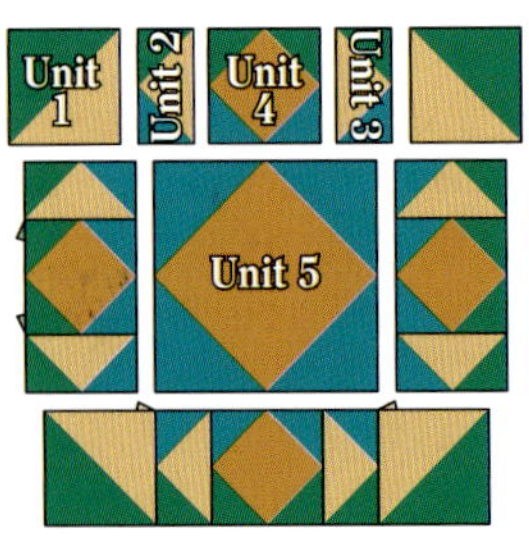

Block Assembly

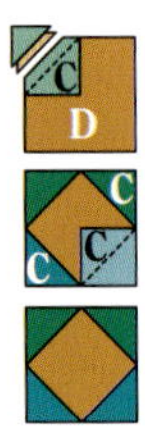

Unit 4
Stitch & Flip
Make 4

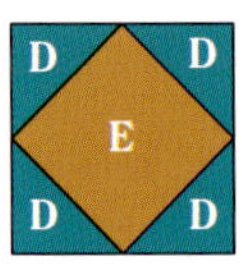

Unit 5
Stitch & Flip
Make 1

block no. 914

Lavender Lattice

by Patti Carey
pattispatchwork.com

Fabric: Lavender Market designed by Deborah Edwards for Northcott, northcott.com.

◸ = cut in half diagonally
⊠ = cut in half twice diagonally

Green Tone-on-Tone
8 squares (A) 2½″ x 2½″
White Solid
8 squares (A) 2½″ x 2½″
1 square 5¼″ x 5¼″ ⊠ (B)
4 Assorted Purple and Green Prints
from *each*
1 square 5¼″x 5¼″ ⊠ (B)
(there will be 2 extra from each)
1 square 4⅞″ x 4⅞″ ◸ (C)
(there will be 1 extra from each)

The extra B's and C's can be used for additional blocks.

Sew the patches together as shown to complete the block.

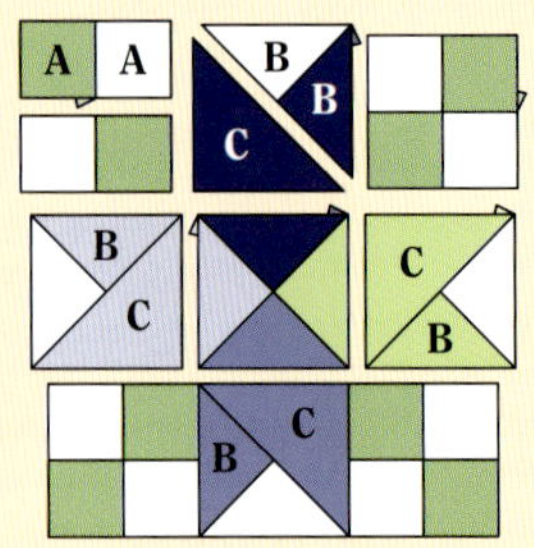

Block Piecing

block no. 915

Piccadilly

by Stephanie Carter • Lily Ashbury
lilyashbury.com

Fabric: High Street designed by Lily Ashbury for Moda Fabrics, unitednotions.com.

◸ = cut in half diagonally
⊠ = cut in half twice diagonally

Cream Solid
- 2 squares (A) 1⅞" x 1⅞"
- 6 squares (B) 2⅞" x 2⅞"
- 4 squares (D) 2½" x 2½"
- 4 squares (F) 1½" x 1½"
- 4 rectangles (G) 1½" x 2½"
- 1 square 3¼" x 3¼" ⊠ (H)

Pink Tone-on-Tone #1
- 2 squares (A) 1⅞" x 1⅞"
- 1 square (E) 5¼" x 5¼"

Gray Print
- 2 squares (B) 2⅞" x 2⅞"
- 4 rectangles (C) 2½" x 4½"

Pink Tone-on-Tone #2
- 2 squares (B) 2⅞" x 2⅞"

Orange Tone-on-Tone
- 2 squares (B) 2⅞" x 2⅞"
- 4 squares (D) 2½" x 2½"
- 1 square 3¼" x 3¼" ⊠ (H)

Gray Tone-on-Tone
- 4 squares (B) 2⅞" x 2⅞"

Yellow Tone-on-Tone
- 2 squares 2⅞" x 2⅞" ◸ (I)

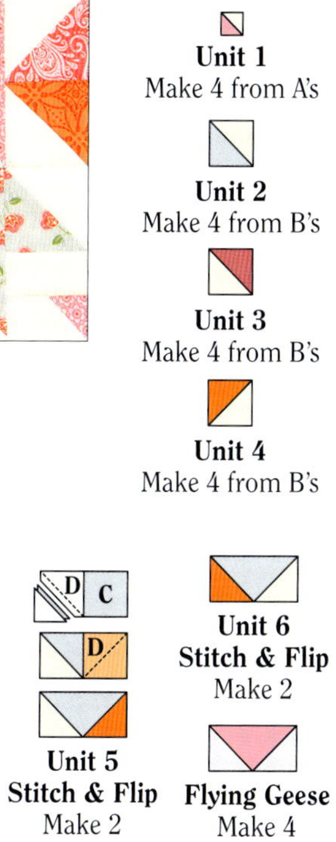

Block Assembly

Pair the cream A's with pink #1 A's to make 4 Triangle-Square unit 1's. Make 4 *each* of units 2–4 pairing cream B's with gray print B's, pink #2 B's and orange B's as shown.

Refer to "Stitch-and-Flip" in the Techniques file on the PDF. Use the gray print C's, cream D's and orange D's to make 2 unit 5's and 2 unit 6's as shown.

Make 4 Flying Geese using the pink #1 E and gray tone-on-tone B's.

Sew the units, Flying Geese and patches together as shown to complete the block.

block no. 916

Climbing Squares

by Caroline Critchfield • SewCanShe
sewcanshe.com

Aqua Tone-on-Tone and Orange Tone-on-Tone
from *each*
- 2 rectangles (A) 2½" x 6½"
- 4 squares (B) 2½" x 2½"
- 1 rectangle (D) 2½" x 4½"

Multicolor Print
- 3 squares (C) 4½" x 4½"

Caroline fussy cut the C's from her multicolor print.

Sew the patches together as shown to complete the block.

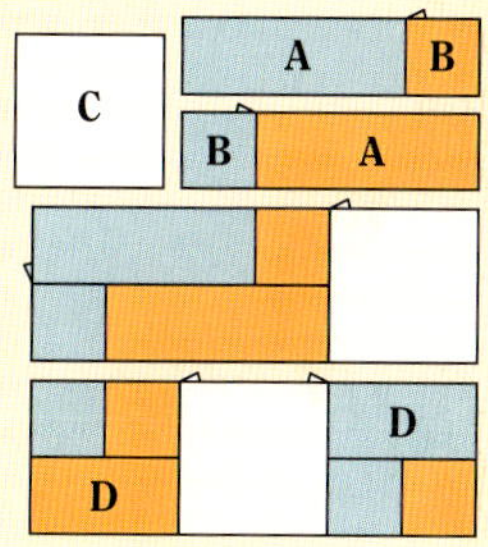

Block Piecing

block no. 917

Sixty Scrap Dash

by Mickey Depre
mdquilts.com

Mickey Depre is the author of *Pieced Hexies: A New Tradition in English Paper Piecing* and *Pieced Hexies Deux* for Kansas City Star Quilts, pickledish.com.

⊠ = cut in half diagonally

Assorted Blue Prints and Tone-on-Tones and Assorted Green Prints and Tone-on-Tones
from *each* color group
- 8 squares 2⅞" x 2⅞" ⊠ (A) (there will be 8 extra)
- 8 squares (B) 2½" x 2½"
- 2 rectangles (D) 1" x 2½"

Assorted Cream, Tan and Light Gold Prints and Tone-on-Tones
- 16 squares 2⅞" x 2⅞" ⊠ (A) (there will be 16 extra)
- 8 rectangles (C) 1¼" x 2½"

Cutting the A's as indicated enhances the scrappy look of this block. The extra patches can be used for additional blocks.

Sew the patches together as shown to complete the block.

Block Piecing

block no. 918

Scandinavian Sun

by Jenifer Dick • 42 Quilts
42quilts.com

Fabric: Kona Cotton by Robert Kaufman, robertkaufman.com.

Jenifer Dick is the author of *Quilt Retro: 11 Designs to Make Your Own* for Kansas City Star Quilts, pickledish.com.

Light Gray Solid
- 4 squares (A) 2" x 2"

Gold Solid
- 4 rectangles (B) 2" x 2½"
- 4 rectangles (C) 2½" x 4"
- 4 rectangles (F) 1½" x 4½"
- 4 rectangles (G) 1½" x 5½"
- 1 square (I) 2½" x 2½"

Dark Gray Solid
- 4 rectangles (D) 1" x 4"
- 4 rectangles (E) 1" x 4½"

Medium Gray Solid
- 4 rectangles (H) 2½" x 5½"

Sew the patches together as shown to complete the block.

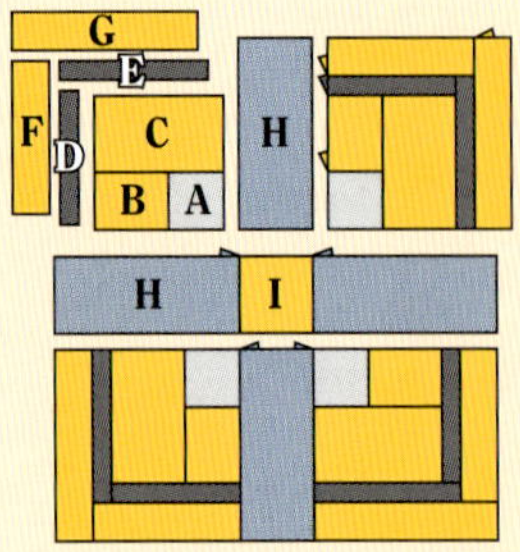

Block Piecing

block no. 919

To the Point

by Monique Dillard • Open Gate
opengatequilts.com

Fabric: Northgate Manor designed by Monique Dillard for Maywood Studio, maywoodstudio.com.

Monique Dillard is the author of *Diamond Traditions* and *Fat Quarter Winners*, both for C&T Publishing, ctpub.com.

⍁ = cut in half diagonally

Red Tone-on-Tone
8 squares (A) 2½″ x 2½″

Cream Tone-on-Tone
8 squares (A) 2½″ x 2½″
4 squares 2⅞″ x 2⅞″ ⍁ (B)

Dark Blue Print
8 squares (A) 2½″ x 2½″
2 squares 4⅞″ x 4⅞″ ⍁ (C)

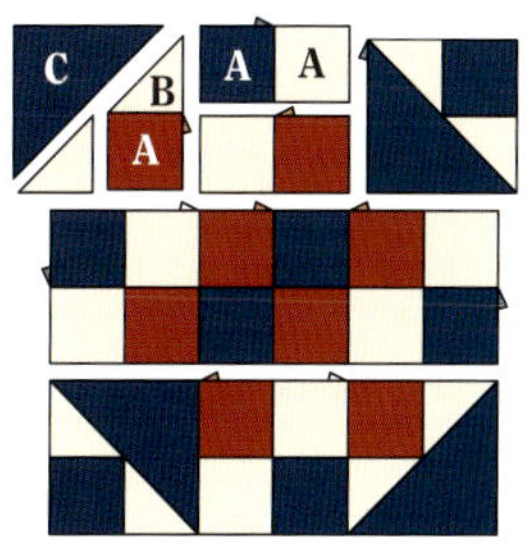

Block Piecing

Sew the patches together as shown to complete the block.

block no. 920

March to Spring

by Abigail Dolinger
abyquilts.wordpress.com

3 Assorted Black with White Prints
from *2*
2 rectangles (A) 1½″ x 4½″
from *1*
1 square (E) 2½″ x 2½″

2 Assorted White with Black Prints
from *each*
2 rectangles (D) 1½″ x 3½″

White Tone-on-Tone
6 squares (B) 1½″ x 1½″
4 squares (C) 4½″ x 4½″
4 rectangles (E) 2½″ x 3½″

Black Solid
2 squares (B) 1½″ x 1½″

Green Batik
4 squares (F) 2½″ x 2½″

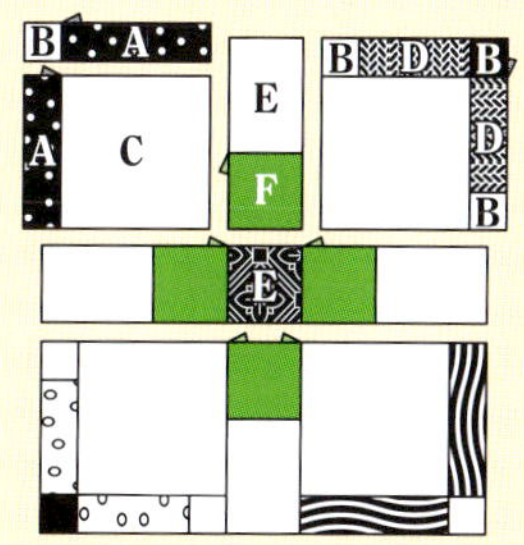

Block Piecing

Sew the patches together as shown to complete the block.

block no. 921

Puzzle Star

by Deanne Eisenman • Snuggles Quilts
snugglesquilts.com

Deanne Eisenman is the author of *Scrap Quilts Go Country* for Martingale & Co., shopmartingale.com.

⧄ = cut in half diagonally
⊠ = cut in half twice diagonally

Black Print and Cream Print
from *each*
2 squares (A) 3⅞″ x 3⅞″
3 squares 4¼″ x 4¼″ ⊠ (B)

Gold Tone-on-Tone
2 squares 3⅞″ x 3⅞″ ⧄ (C)

Green Stripe
4 squares 3⅞″ x 3⅞″ ⧄ (C)

Unit
Make 4

Block Assembly

Pair the black A's with the cream A's to make 4 Triangle-Square units.

Sew the units and patches together as shown to complete the block.

block no. 922

Camelia's Garden

by Camelia Elliott • Camelia's Unique Creations
cameliaelliott.com

Black Solid
2 strips 1½″ x 40″

White Solid
2 strips 1½″ x 40″

Red Tone-on-Tone
4 squares (A) 2½″ x 2½″
2 rectangles 2⅝″ x 5⅜″ for D and Dr
1 square (E) 4½″ x 4½″

Yellow Print
1 square (B) 1½″ x 1½″

Teal Tone-on-Tone
3 squares (A) 2½″ x 2½″
1 square (B) 1½″ x 1½″
1 rectangle (C) 1½″ x 2½″
2 rectangles 2⅝″ x 5⅜″ for D's and Dr's

Green Tone-on-Tone
2 rectangles 2⅝″ x 5⅜″ for D and Dr

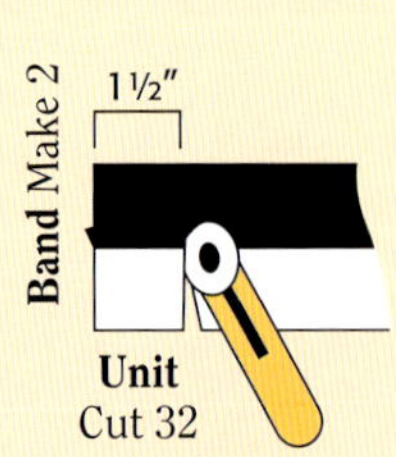

Unit
Cut 32

Cutting Diagram

Cutting Diagram

Join 1 black strip and 1 white strip as shown to make a band. Make 2 bands. Cut the bands in 1½" increments to make 32 units.

Refer to the cutting diagrams. Cut 1 red rectangle as shown to make 2 D's and 1 rectangle as shown to make 2 Dr's. (Use 1 red D and 1 red Dr.) In the same way, cut the teal rectangles and green rectangles, to make 2 D's and 2 Dr's from each color. (Use 1 green D and 1 green Dr.)

Sew the patches and units together as shown to complete the block.

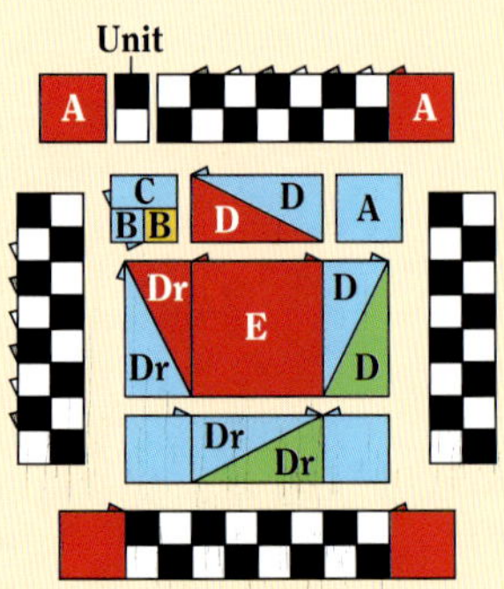

Block Assembly

block no. 923
Spin Cycle

by Gudrun Erla • GE Designs
gequiltdesigns.com

Fabric: Nordic Visions designed by Gudrun Erla and Tokyo, both by Red Rooster Fabrics, redroosterfabrics.com.

Gudrun Erla is the author of *Fast and Furious Home* for GE Designs, gequiltdesigns.com.

White Solid
8 rectangles (A) 2" x 6½"
8 squares (B) 2" x 2"
8 rectangles (C) 2" x 3½"

Gray Tone-on-Tone
8 squares (B) 2" x 2"

8 Assorted Tone-on-Tones
from *each*
1 square (D) 3½" x 3½"

Partial Unit
Make 4

Join the white A's, white B's, gray B's and white C's as shown to make 4 partial units.

Refer to "Stitch-and-Flip" in the Techniques file on the PDF. Add 2 different D's to opposite corners of a partial unit as shown to make 1 unit. Repeat to make 4 units.

Sew the units together as shown to complete the block.

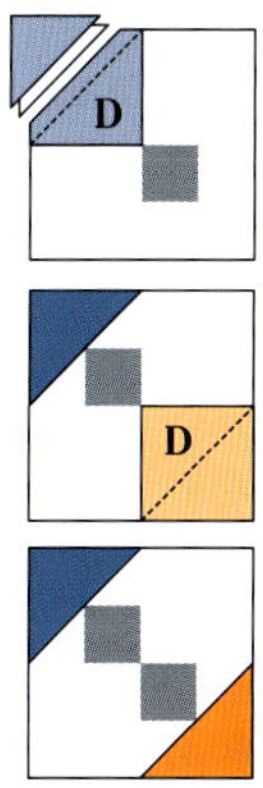

Unit
Stitch & Flip
Make 4

Block Assembly

block no. 924
Pinwheel Polka

by Marilyn Foreman • Quilt Moments
quiltmoments.com

Fabric: Nouveau Rouge by Alice Kennedy and Soho Solids, both from Timeless Treasures, ttfabrics.com.

Marilyn Foreman is the author of *Kaleidoscope Symphony* for Quilt Moments, quiltmoments.com.

Black Print
4 rectangles (A) 3½" x 6½"

Black Solid
4 rectangles (A) 3½" x 6½"
4 squares (B) 3½" x 3½"

Red Solid
4 squares (C) 5" x 5"

Black Dot
4 squares (B) 3½" x 3½"

Marilyn fussy cut 4 identical black print A's for the kaleidoscope look.

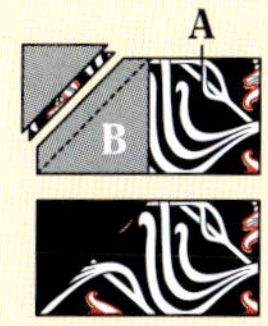

Partial Unit
Stitch & Flip
Make 4

Refer to "Stitch-and-Flip" in the Techniques file on the PDF. Use the black print A's and black solid B's to make 4 partial units as shown.

Partial Unit

Referring to the diagram, sew a black solid A to each partial unit.

Using the stitch-and-flip method, add a red solid C to the corner of each partial unit, then a black dot B as shown to make 4 units.

Sew the units together as shown to complete the block.

Unit
Stitch & Flip
Make 4

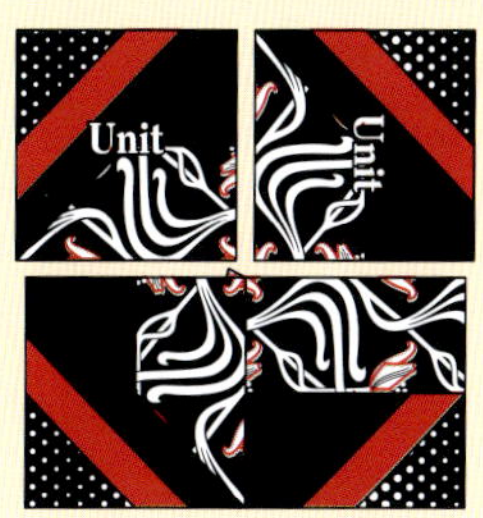

Block Assembly

block no. 925

Patriot Games

by Kay Gentry • Noble Needle Quilting and Sewing
nobleneedle.com

Dark Blue Tone-on-Tone
- 1 square (A) 2⅞" x 2⅞"
- 1 square (B) 3¼" x 3¼"
- 8 squares (D) 1½" x 1½"
- 1 square (E) 2½" x 2½"

Cream Print
- 2 squares (A) 2⅞" x 2⅞"
- 2 squares (B) 3¼" x 3¼"
- 16 squares (D) 1½" x 1½"
- 12 rectangles (C) 2½" x 3½"

Red Tone-on-Tone
- 1 square (A) 2⅞" x 2⅞"
- 1 square (B) 3¼" x 3¼"
- 12 squares (D) 1½" x 1½"

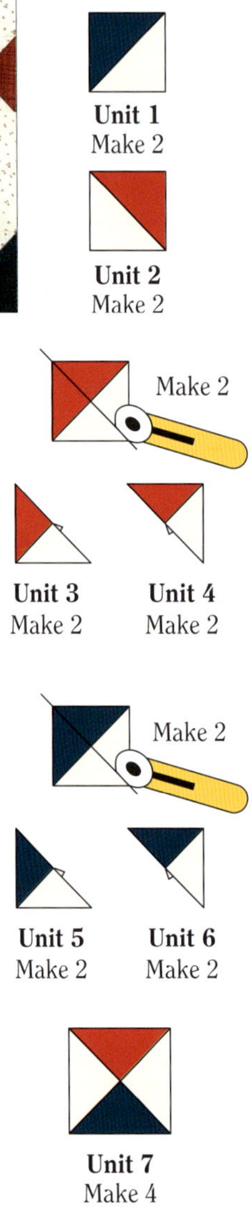

Pair the dark blue A with 1 cream A to make 2 Triangle-Square unit 1's. Make 2 unit 2's using 1 red A and 1 cream A.

Pair 1 cream B and 1 red B to make 2 triangle-squares. Cut each one diagonally as shown to make 2 unit 3's and 2 unit 4's.

Pair 1 cream B and 1 dark blue B to make 2 triangle-squares. Cut each one diagonally as shown to make 2 unit 5's and 2 unit 6's.

Join the unit 3's with the unit 5's and the unit 4's with the unit 6's to make a total of 4 unit 7's.

Sew the units and patches together as shown to complete the block.

Block Assembly

block no. 926

Season's Greetings

by Sara Hardwig • Blueberry Backroads
blueberrybackroads.com

Fabric: Holiday in the Pines by Holly Taylor for Moda Fabrics, unitednotions.com, plus others.

See Pattern Sheet 78

Tan Tone-on-Tone
- 1 square (A) 9½" x 9½" (trim to 8½" x 8½" after embroidery)

Red Solid
- 2 rectangles (B) 1" x 8½"
- 2 rectangles (C) 1" x 9½"

Assorted Red Prints and Tone-on-Tones
- 14 rectangles (D) 2" x 3½"

Brown Pigma Micron pen (.01 tip) **or pencil**

Embroidery floss

Fold the tan A in half both ways and lightly crease the folds. Using the creases as a guide, trace the embroidery design onto A with a pen or pencil.

Use 3 strands of floss to backstitch the letters and outlines, adding French knots where indicated. Fill in the heart on the mitten, the eyes and mouth with a satin stitch. Backstitch the smaller details with 1 strand of floss. Center the design and trim to 8½" × 8½".

Sew the patches together as shown. Use 3 strands of floss and a running stitch to embroider around the edge of A as shown to complete the block.

Embroidery Placement

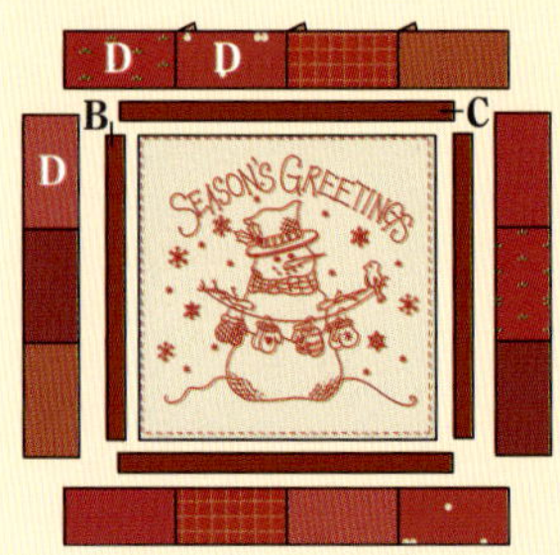

Block Assembly

block no. 927

Happy Valley

by Allison Harris • Cluck Cluck Sew
cluckclucksew.com

Allison Harris is the author of *Growing Up Modern* for Stash Books, ctpub.com.

Assorted Red Prints and Tone-on-Tones

8 squares (A) $3\frac{7}{8}$" x $3\frac{7}{8}$"

White Solid

8 squares (A) $3\frac{7}{8}$" x $3\frac{7}{8}$"

Unit
Make 16

Pair the red A's with the white A's to make 16 Triangle-Square units.

Sew the units together as shown to complete the block.

Block Assembly

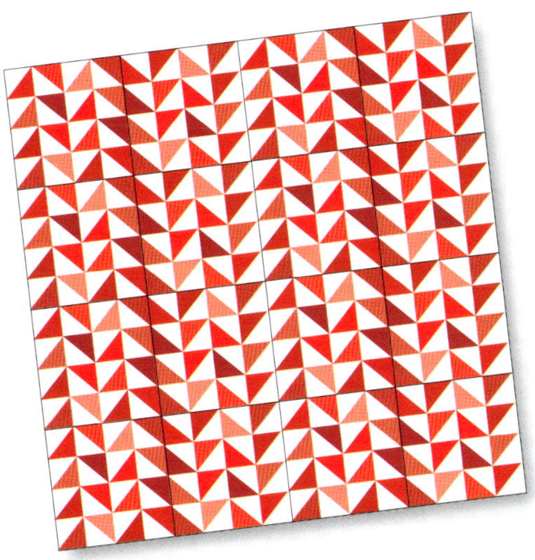

block no. 928

I'm Sew Happy

by Diane Harris • Interactive Editor, *Quiltmaker*
quiltmaker.com

Fabric: P&B Textiles, pbtex.com, plus scraps.

See page 350 on the PDF for pattern

Blue Tone-on-Tone

section 1, patch 1

Gray Print

sections 1 and 2, patches 2 and 3
8 squares (B) $1\frac{1}{2}$" x $1\frac{1}{2}$"
4 squares (D) 2" x 2"
6 rectangles (E) 1" x $5\frac{1}{2}$"
4 rectangles (F) $1\frac{1}{2}$" x $3\frac{1}{2}$"
1 rectangle (H) $1\frac{1}{2}$" x $6\frac{1}{2}$"
2 rectangles (I) 1" x $6\frac{1}{2}$"
4 squares (K) 1" x 1"
1 rectangle (M) 1" x $12\frac{1}{2}$"

Dark Blue Batik

section 2, patch 1

Tan Tone-on-Tone

4 rectangles (A) $1\frac{1}{2}$" x $5\frac{1}{2}$"

Pink Print

2 rectangles (C) $2\frac{1}{2}$" x $6\frac{1}{2}$"
1 rectangle (H) $1\frac{1}{2}$" x $6\frac{1}{2}$"
4 rectangles (J) 1" x $2\frac{1}{2}$"
2 rectangles (L) 1" x $1\frac{1}{2}$"

2 Striped Batiks

from *each*
1 square (G) $3\frac{1}{2}$" x $3\frac{1}{2}$"

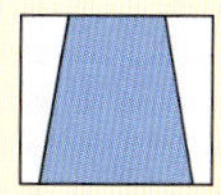

Section 1
Make 1

Section 2
Make 1

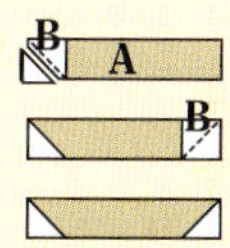

Unit 1
Stitch & Flip
Make 4

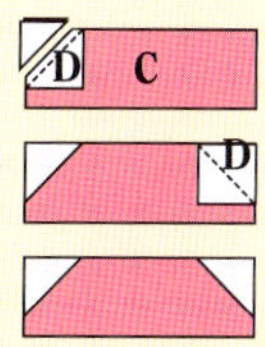

Unit 2
Stitch & Flip
Make 2

Make 1 paper copy *each* of foundation sections 1 and 2. Foundation piece the sections in numerical order, pressing and trimming after each patch addition.

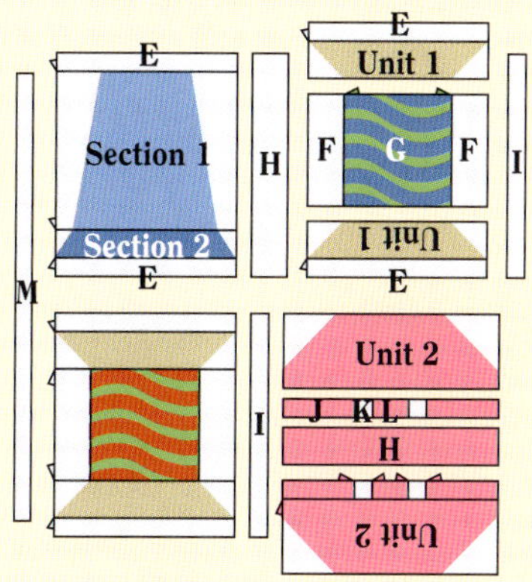

Block Assembly

Refer to "Stitch-and-Flip" in the Techniques file on the PDF Use the tan A's and gray B's to make 4 unit 1's. Use the pink C's and gray D's to make 2 unit 2's.

Sew the sections, units and patches together as shown to complete the block.

block no. 929

Stencil Star

by Lee Heinrich • Freshly Pieced
freshlypieced.com

Lee Heinrich is a co-author of *Vintage Quilt Revival: 22 Modern Designs from Classic Blocks* for Krause Craft, prh.com/krausecraft.

⧄ = cut in half diagonally

White Solid
- 4 rectangles (A) 3″ x 6″
- 4 squares (C) 3¼″ x 3¼″
- 2 squares 3⅜″ x 3⅜″ ⧄ (E)
- 4 rectangles (F) 1¼″ x 3″
- 2 rectangles (G) 1¼″ x 6″
- 2 rectangles (H) 1¼″ x 12½″

Dark Pink Print
- 8 squares (B) 3″ x 3″

4 Teal Tone-on-Tones and 4 Green Tone-on-Tones
from each
- 1 square (D) 2¾″ x 2¾″

from each of 2 teals and 2 greens
- 1 square 3⅜″ x 3⅜″ ⧄ (E)
  (there will be 1 extra from each)

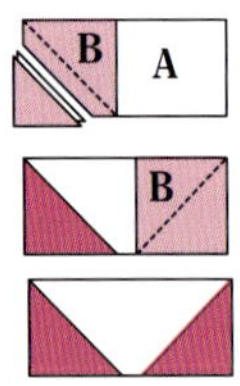

Unit 1
Stitch & Flip
Make 4

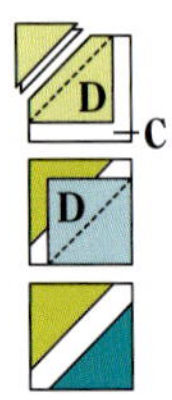

Unit 2
Stitch & Flip
Make 4

Refer to "Stitch-and-Flip" in the Techniques file on the PDF. Use the white A's and pink B's to make 4 unit 1's. Using the white C's, green D's and teal D's, make 4 units 2's as shown.

Sew the units and patches together as shown to complete the block.

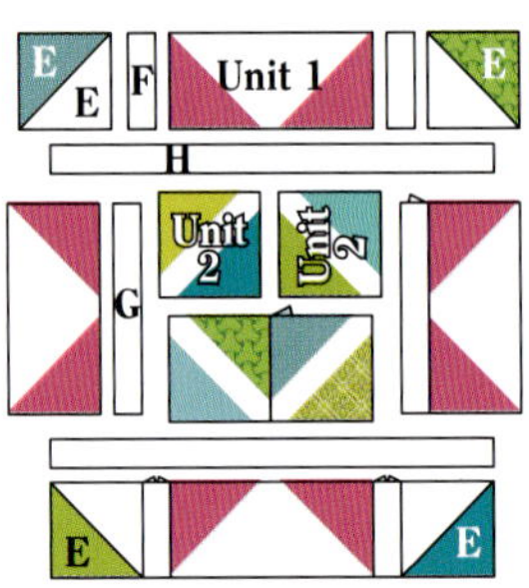

Block Assembly

block no. 930

Banner Day

by Chris Hoover • Whirligig Designs
whirligigdesigns.com

Fabric: Quilted in Honor designed by Kathy Engle for Island Batik, islandbatik.com.

Dark Blue Batik #1
- 2 rectangles (A) 2½″ x 4½″
- 1 square (B) 2½″ x 2½″
- 2 rectangles (C) 2½″ x 6½″

Gold Batik
- 8 squares (B) 2½″ x 2½″

Cream Batik and Red Batik #1
from *each*
- 2 rectangles (C) 2½″ x 6½″

Red Batik #2
- 1 square (D) 4½″ x 4½″

Dark Blue Batik #2
- 1 square (E) 6½″ x 6½″

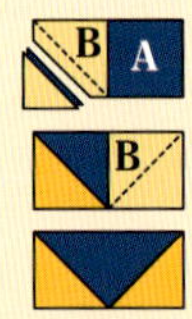

Unit 1
Stitch & Flip
Make 2

Refer to "Stitch-and-Flip" in the Techniques file on the PDF. Use the dark blue #1 A's and gold B's to make 2 unit 1's. Make units 2–5 as shown using gold B's with cream C's and red #1 C's.

Sew the units and patches together as shown to complete the block.

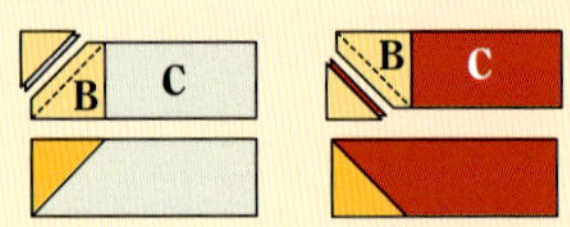

Unit 2
Stitch & Flip
Make 1

Unit 3
Stitch & Flip
Make 1

Unit 4
Stitch & Flip
Make 1

Unit 5
Stitch & Flip
Make 1

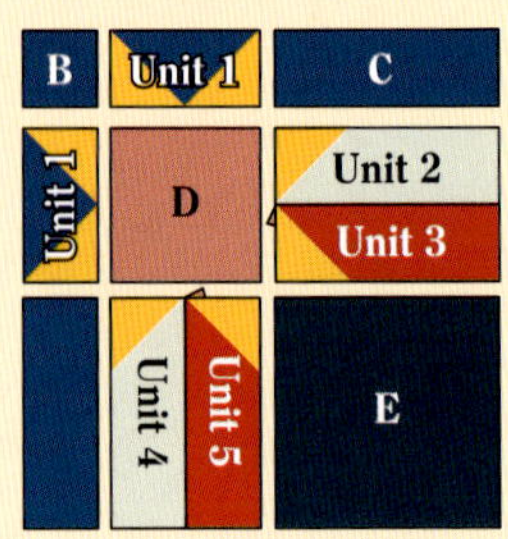

Block Assembly

pieced

block no. 931

Hovering Stars

by Bonnie Hunter • Quiltville
quiltville.com

Bonnie Hunter writes the "Addicted to Scraps" column for *Quiltmaker.* She is the author of several books, including *Ring Around the Hexies: A Collaboration Celebration* with Mickey Depre for Kansas City Star Quilts, pickledish.com.

Assorted Light Batiks, Prints and Tone-on-Tones
from 5
1 square (A) 3¼″x 3¼″
from 4
2 squares (C) 2⅞″x 2⅞″
from 5
4 squares (D) 1½″x 1½″
Assorted Medium and Dark Batiks
from 5
4 squares (B) 1⅞″x 1⅞″
from 4
2 squares (C) 2⅞″x 2⅞″
from 5
1 square (E) 2½″x 2½″

Flying Geese
Make 5 sets of 4 matching

Flying Geese

Star
Make 5

Unit
Make 4 sets of 4 matching

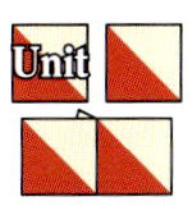

Section
Make 4

Use the light A's and medium/dark B's to make 5 sets of 4 matching Flying Geese. Sew 4 matching Flying Geese, 4 matching D's and an E together as shown to make a star. Make 5 stars.

Pair light C's with medium/dark C's to make 4 sets of 4 matching Triangle-Square units. Join 4 matching units to make each section as shown.

Sew the stars and sections together as shown to complete the block.

Block Assembly

block no. 932

Cherry Starburst

by Deborah Johnson • In the Doghouse Designs
inthedoghousedesigns.com

Fabric: Blank Quilting, blankquilting.com.

Red Batik
4 squares (A) 3½″x 3½″
8 squares (D) 4″x 4″
5 squares (F) 2½″x 2½″
White Tone-on-Tone
8 rectangles (B) 1½″x 3½″
8 rectangles (C) 1½″x 5½″
4 rectangles (E) 2½″x 5½″

Sew the red A's, white B's and white C's together as shown. Refer to "Stitch-and-Flip" in the Techniques file on the PDF. Referring to the diagrams, add the red D's to make 2 unit 1's and 2 unit 2's. Make 4 unit 3's using white E's and red F's.

Sew the units and F together as shown to complete the block.

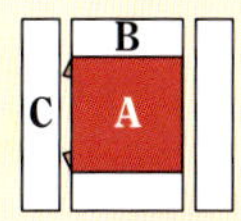

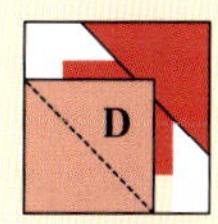

Unit 1
Stitch & Flip
Make 2

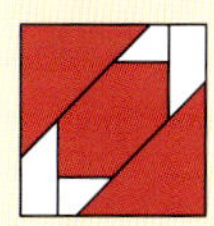

Unit 2
Stitch & Flip
Make 2

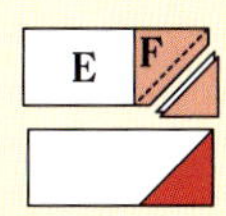

Unit 3
Stitch & Flip
Make 4

Block Assembly

block no. 933

Robo-Bop

by Kimberly Jolly • Fat Quarter Shop
fatquartershop.com

Fabric: Mixed Bag designed by Studio M for Moda Fabrics, unitednotions.com.

Kimberly Jolly is the co-author of *Simply Fat Quarters: Quilts with Comfort and Style* for Fat Quarter Shop, fatquartershop.com.

⧄ = cut in half diagonally
⊠ = cut in half twice diagonally

Dark Blue Solid
- 3 rectangles (A) 1½″ x 4½″
- 2 rectangles (D) 3½″ x 4½″
- 1 square 2¼″ x 2¼″ ⊠ (E) (there will be 2 extra)
- 2 rectangles (G) 1½″ x 2½″
- 5 squares (H) 1½″ x 1½″
- 1 rectangle (I) 1″ x 3½″
- 2 rectangles (J) 1½″ x 4″
- 2 rectangles (K) 3½″ x 4″
- 6 rectangles (L) 1″ x 1½″
- 2 rectangles (N) 1″ x 5½″
- 1 rectangle (P) 2″ x 3½″
- 2 rectangles (Q) 1″ x 12½″

Aqua Print
- 2 rectangles (B) 1½″ x 3″
- 2 rectangles (C) 1½″ x 2″
- 2 squares (H) 1½″ x 1½″
- 2 rectangles (L) 1″ x 1½″
- 1 rectangle (O) 4½″ x 5½″

Orange Tone-on-Tone
- 4 rectangles (C) 1½″ x 2″
- 1 square 2¼″ x 2¼″ ⊠ (E) (there will be 2 extra)
- 1 square 1⅞″ x 1⅞″ ⧄ (F)
- 2 squares (H) 1½″ x 1½″
- 1 rectangle (M) 2½″ x 3½″

Refer to "Stitch-and-Flip" in the Techniques file on the PDF. Use the dark blue A's and aqua print B's to make 1 unit 1 and 1 unit 2 as shown.

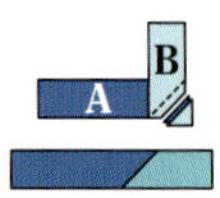

Unit 1
Stitch & Flip
Make 1

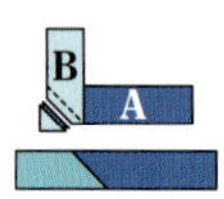

Unit 2
Stitch & Flip
Make 1

Sew the units and patches together as shown to complete the block.

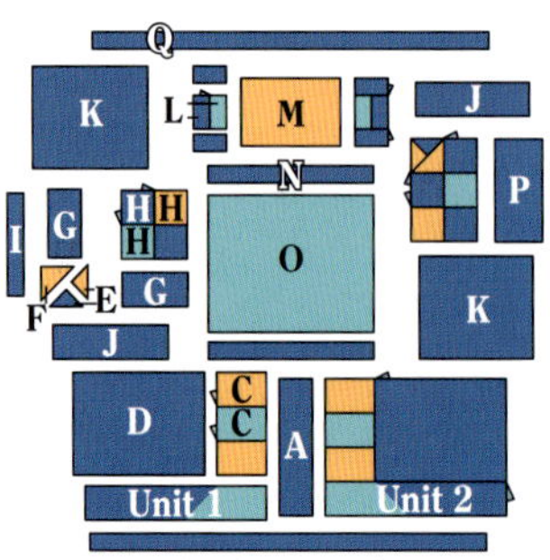

Block Assembly

block no. 934

Bits and Pieces

by Mary Elizabeth Kinch
maryelizabethkinch.com

Mary Elizabeth Kinch is the co-author of *Small Pieces, Spectacular Quilts* and *Small Blocks, Stunning Quilts* for Martingale & Co., shopmartingale.com.

⧄ = cut in half diagonally

Assorted Medium and Dark Prints and Tone-on-Tones
- 20 squares 1⅝″ x 1⅝″ ⧄ (A) (there will be 20 extra)
- 28 squares 1⅞″ x 1⅞″ ⧄ (B) (there will be 28 extra)
- 6 squares (C) 1½″ x 1½″
- 2 rectangles (D) 1″ x 2½″
- 2 rectangles (E) 1″ x 3½″
- 2 rectangles (F) 1¼″ x 5″
- 2 rectangles (G) 1¼″ x 6½″
- 2 rectangles (I) 1½″ x 10½″
- 2 rectangles (J) 1½″ x 12½″

Unit 1
Make 20 from A's

Unit 2
Make 28 from B's

Assorted White Prints
- 20 squares 1⅝″ x 1⅝″ ⧄ (A) (there will be 20 extra)
- 28 squares 1⅞″ x 1⅞″ ⧄ (B) (there will be 28 extra)
- 2 squares (C) 1½″ x 1½″
- 4 rectangles (H) 1½″ x 8½″

Cutting the A's and B's as instructed enhances the scrappy look of the block. Use the extra patches for additional blocks. A scant ¼″ seam allowance is particularly important when piecing lots of small patches together.

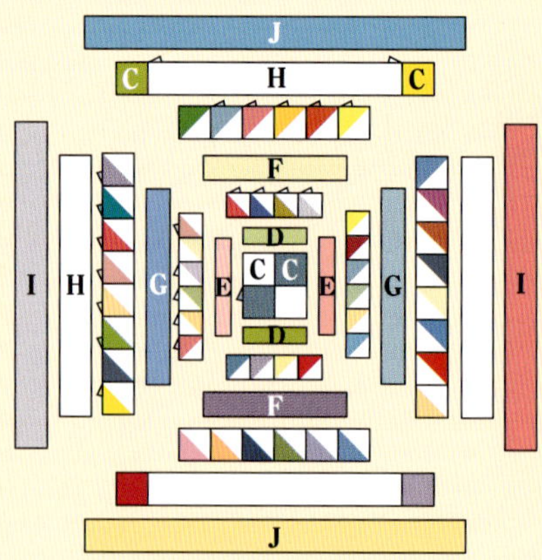

Block Assembly

Make 20 unit 1's using medium/dark A's and white A's.
Make 28 unit 2's using medium/dark B's and white B's.

Sew the units and patches together as shown to complete the block.

block no. 935

Diamond Dash

by Susan Knapp • The Quilt Branch
quiltbranch.com

Fabric: Daydream designed by Swirly Girls for Michael Miller Fabrics, michaelmillerfabrics.com.

Susan Knapp is the co-author of the *Six Halves Make a Whole* series for The Quilt Branch, quiltbranch.com.

Light Green Print and Dark Blue Print #1
from *each*
2 squares (A) 2⅞" x 2⅞"
4 squares (C) 2½" x 2½"
Purple Print
2 rectangles (B) 2½" x 4½"
Teal Tone-on-Tone
4 squares (C) 2½" x 2½"
2 rectangles (D) 2½" x 8½"
Dark Blue Print #2
1 rectangle (E) 4½" x 12½"
Multicolor Stripe
8 squares (C) 2½" x 2½"

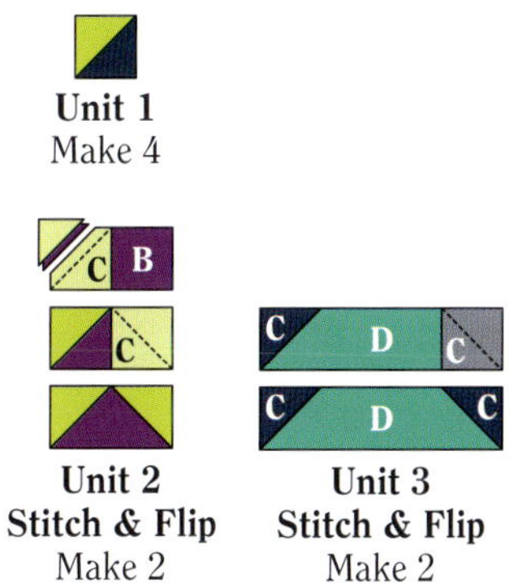

Pair the light green A's with the dark blue #1 A's to make 4 Triangle-Square unit 1's.

Refer to "Stitch-and-Flip" in the Techniques file on the PDF. Use the purple B's and light green C's to make 2 unit 2's as shown. Make 2 unit 3's using the teal D's and dark blue #1 C's. Use the dark blue #2 E and teal C's to make 1 unit 4.

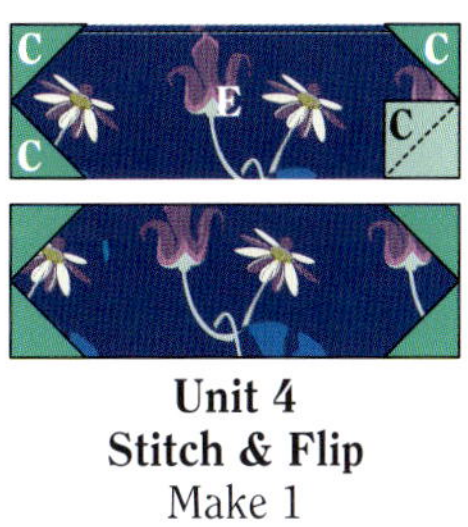

Sew the units and patches together as shown to complete the block.

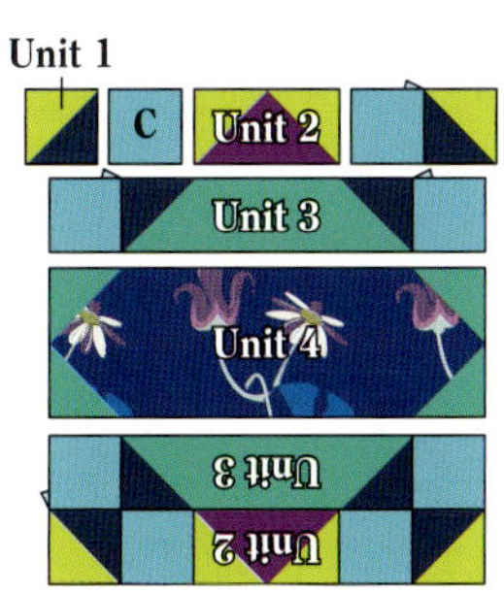

Block Assembly

block no. 936

Gretchen's Sunflowers

by Debby Kratovil • Quilter by Design
quilterbydesign.com

Fabric: Gazebo by Valerie Evers Wenk for Windham Fabrics, windhamfabrics.com.

Debby is the author of *Paper Piecing Perfect Points* for Martingale, shopmartingale.com.

⧄ = cut in half diagonally

Gold Tone-on-Tone, Red Print, Blue Print and Green Tone-on-Tone
from *each*
2 squares (A) 4⅞" x 4⅞"
2 squares 2⅞" x 2⅞" ⧄ (B)

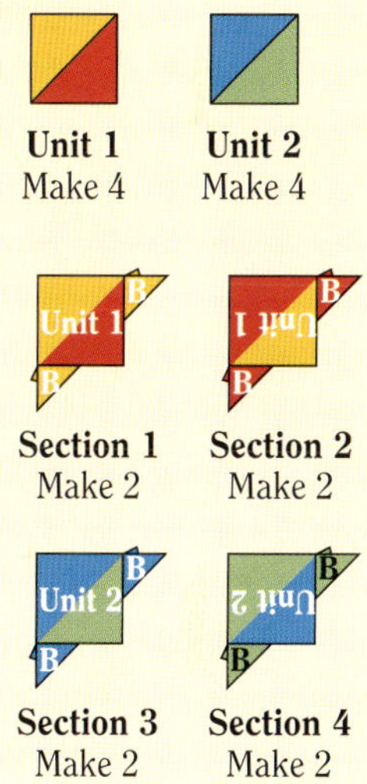

Pair gold and red A's to make 4 Triangle-Square unit 1's. Pair blue and green A's to make 4 unit 2's.

Sew gold B's to a unit 1 as shown to make a section 1. Make 2 section 1's. Repeat with the red B's to make 2 section 2's. In the same way, make 2 section 3's using unit 2's and blue B's and 2 section 4's using unit 2's and green B's.

Refer to the trimming diagram to trim the sections even with the B's as shown.

Trimming Diagram

Sew the sections together as shown to complete the block.

Block Assembly

block no. 937

Positive Outlook

by Jessie Kurtz • Harding Hill Designs
hardinghilldesigns.com

Fabric: Kona Cotton Solids from Robert Kaufman, robertkaufman.com.

White Solid
- 4 squares (A) 2½″ x 2½″

Dark Gray Solid
- 7 squares (A) 2½″ x 2½″
- 2 squares (B) 4½″ x 4½″
- 2 rectangles (C) 2½″ x 4½″

Teal Solid
- 3 squares (A) 2½″ x 2½″
- 1 rectangle (C) 2½″ x 4½″

Red Solid
- 6 squares (A) 2½″ x 2½″
- 1 rectangle (C) 2½″ x 4½″

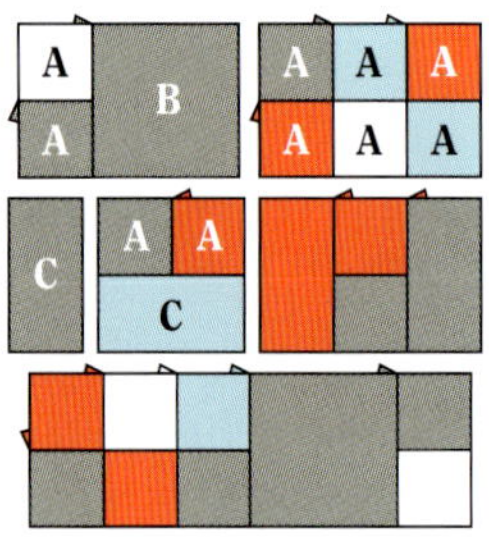

Block Piecing

Sew the patches together as shown to complete the block.

block no. 938

Read

by Cindy Lammon • Hyacinth Quilt Designs
hyacinthquiltdesigns.com

Fabric: Hello Pilgrim by Lizzy House for Andover, andoverfabrics.com, and Chicopee and Flea Market Fancy, both by Denyse Schmidt for FreeSpirit, freespiritfabric.com.

Cindy Lammon is the author of *Simply Modern Christmas* for Martingale & Co., shopmartingale.com.

White Solid
- 2 rectangles (A) 2″ x 9½″
- 1 rectangle (C) 1″ x 2½″
- 1 rectangle (D) 1½″ x 2½″
- 2 rectangles (F) 1½″ x 2″
- 1 rectangle (K) 2″ x 3″
- 1 rectangle (N) 2″ x 12½″

Dark Gray Tone-on-Tone
- 2 squares (B) 2″ x 2″
- 1 rectangle (N) 2″ x 12½″

Teal Tone-on-Tone
- 1 rectangle (D) 1½″ x 2½″
- 1 rectangle (E) 2½″ x 7″

Assorted Cream Prints
- 2 rectangles (D) 1½″ x 2½″
- 1 rectangle (F) 1½″ x 2″
- 1 square (H) 1½″ x 1½″
- 1 rectangle (L) 1½″ x 3″

Pink Tone-on-Tone
- 1 rectangle (F) 1½″ x 2″
- 1 rectangle (G) 2″ x 6½″

Light Gray Tone-on-Tone
- 1 square (H) 1½″ x 1½″
- 1 rectangle (I) 1½″ x 6″

Orange Tone-on-Tone
- 1 rectangle (D) 1½″ x 2½″
- 1 rectangle (J) 2½″ x 6½″

Green Print
- 1 rectangle (L) 1½″ x 3″
- 1 rectangle (M) 3″ x 6″

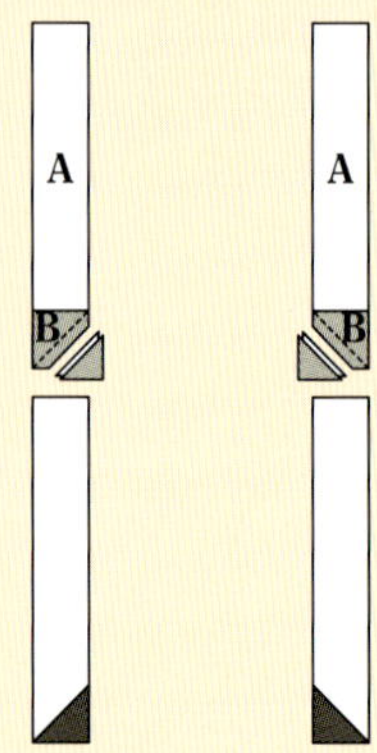

Unit 1
Stitch & Flip
Make 1

Unit 2
Stitch & Flip
Make 1

Refer to "Stitch-and-Flip" in the Techniques file on the PDF. Use the white A's and dark gray B's to make 1 unit 1 and 1 unit 2 as shown.

Sew the units and patches together as shown to complete the block.

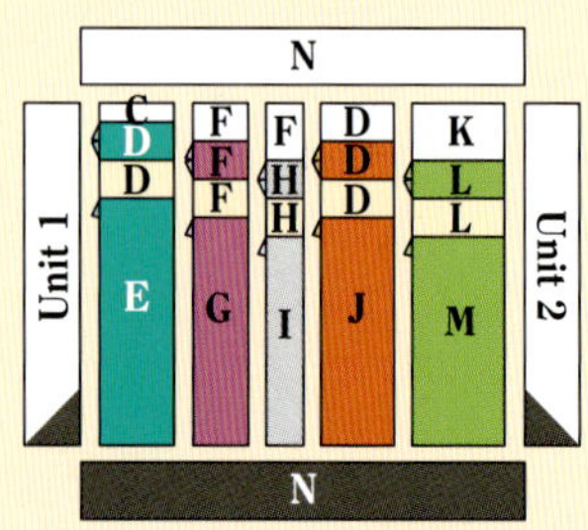

Block Assembly

block no. 939

Twinkle, Twinkle

by Judy Laquidara
patchworktimes.com

Judy Laquidara is the author of *60 Pieced Quilt Borders: Mix & Match* for American Quilter's Society, americanquilter.com.

Black Solid
8 rectangles (A) 2½″ x 4½″
4 squares (B) 2½″ x 2½″
2 rectangles (D) 1½″ x 2½″
2 rectangles (E) 1½″ x 4½″

Blue Batik, Pink Batik, Purple Batik and Green Batik from *each*
4 squares (B) 2½″ x 2½″
1 square (C) 1½″ x 1½″

Cream Batik
4 rectangles (A) 2½″ x 4½″
4 squares (B) 2½″ x 2½″

Refer to "Stitch-and-Flip" in the Techniques file on the PDF. Use a black A, blue B and pink B to make 1 unit 1 as shown. Make 1 unit 2 using a cream A, blue B and pink B. In the same way, make 1 *each* of units 3–8 as shown.

Sew the units and patches together as shown to complete the block.

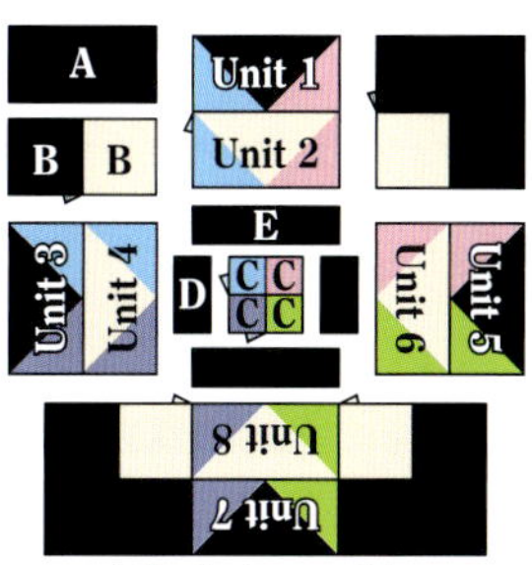

Block Assembly

block no. 940

Dart Board

by Doug Leko • Antler Quilt Design
antlerquiltdesign.com

⧄ = cut in half diagonally
⊠ = cut in half twice diagonally

Blue Print
2 squares (A) 2⅞″ x 2⅞″
4 squares (C) 3⅜″ x 3⅜″

Green Tone-on-Tone
6 squares (A) 2⅞″ x 2⅞″
1 square (C) 3⅜″ x 3⅜″

Cream Print
4 squares (A) 2⅞″ x 2⅞″
1 square (B) 5¼″ x 5¼″
2 squares 2⅞″ x 2⅞″ ⧄ (D)

Red Tone-on-Tone
4 squares (A) 2⅞″ x 2⅞″
1 square 5¼″ x 5¼″ ⊠ (E)

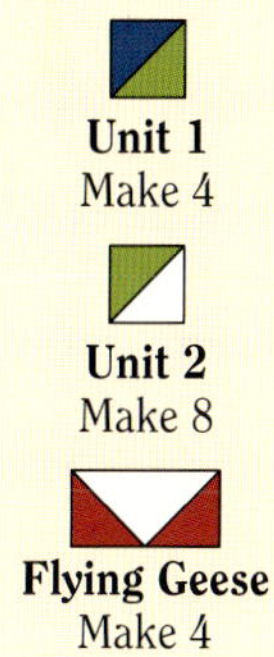

Pair the blue A's with green A's to make 4 Triangle-Square unit 1's. Make 8 unit 2's using the green A's and cream A's.

Use the cream B and red A's to make 4 Flying Geese.

Sew the units, Flying Geese and patches together as shown to complete the block.

Block Assembly

block no. 941
Dashing Geese

by Debbie Martin
shadowsoftheblueridge.blogspot.com

See page 341 on the PDF for pattern

Tan Tone-on-Tone
section patches 1, 4 and 7
Blue Tone-on-Tone
section patches 2, 3, 5, 6, 8 and 9
2 squares (A) 4⅞" x 4⅞"
Tan Print
2 squares (A) 4⅞" x 4⅞"
4 rectangles (B) 2½" x 4½"
1 square (C) 4½" x 4½"

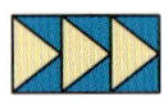

Section
Make 4

Unit
Make 4

Make 4 paper copies of the foundation section. Foundation piece the sections in numerical order, pressing and trimming after each patch addition.

Pair the blue A's with the tan print A's to make 4 Triangle-Square units.

Sew the sections, units and patches together as shown to complete the block.

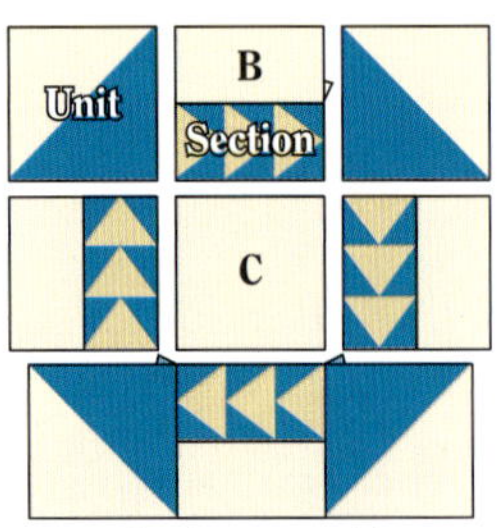

Block Assembly

block no. 942
Watch Your Step

by Mary McGuire • Mary McGuire Design
marymcguiredesign.com

Fabric: Cold Spring Dream designed by Mary McGuire for RJR Fabrics, rjrfabrics.com.

Cream Print
4 squares (A) 3½" x 3½"
Light Purple Solid
16 squares (B) 2" x 2"
Cream Solid
1 rectangle (C) 2" x 3½"
Multicolor Stripe
8 rectangles (D) 1" x 3½"
Dark Purple Solid
2 rectangles (E) 1" x 7"
2 rectangles (G) 1" x 5½"
2 rectangles (J) 1" x 4"
2 rectangles (M) 1" x 2½"
Floral Print
1 rectangle (F) 2½" x 7"
1 rectangle (H) 2½" x 5½"
1 rectangle (K) 2½" x 4"
1 square (N) 2½" x 2½"
Light Yellow Solid
1 square (A) 3½" x 3½"
Medium Yellow Solid
1 rectangle (I) 3½" x 5"
Light Orange Solid
1 rectangle (L) 3½" x 6½"

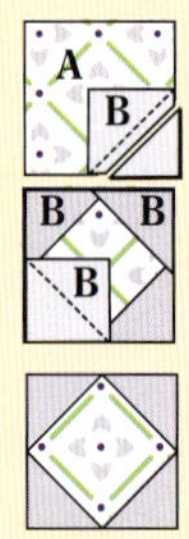

Unit
Stitch & Flip
Make 4

Mary fussy cut the cream print A's from a small scale print.

Refer to "Stitch-and-Flip" in the Techniques file on the PDF. Use the cream print A's and light purple B's to make 4 units.

Sew the units and patches together as shown to complete the block.

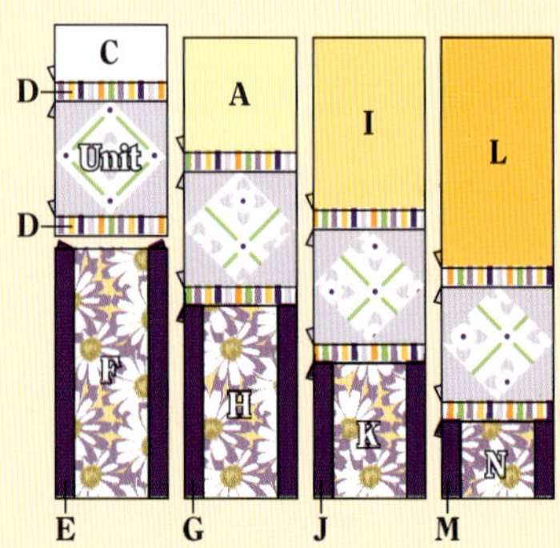

Block Assembly

block no. 943

Feeling Breezy

by Pam McMahon • Pam's Piece by Piece
piecebypiecequiltdesigns.com

Fabric: Snowman Gatherings designed by Primitive Gatherings for Moda Fabrics, unitednotions.com.

Pam McMahon is the author of *A Passion for Precuts* for Leisure Arts, leisurearts.com.

◪ = cut in half diagonally
⊠ = cut in half twice diagonally

White Print
- 4 squares (A) 2½″ x 2½″
- 1 square 3¼″ x 3¼″ ⊠ (D)

Medium Blue Tone-on-Tone
- 4 squares (A) 2½″ x 2½″
- 8 squares (B) 1½″ x 1½″
- 2 squares 2⅞″ x 2⅞″ ◪ (E)

Dark Blue Tone-on-Tone
- 2 squares (C) 5¼″ x 5¼″

Tan Tone-on-Tone
- 8 squares (A) 2½″ x 2½″
- 1 square (C) 5¼″ x 5¼″

Tan Print
- 1 square (C) 5¼″ x 5¼″
- 1 square 3¼″ x 3¼″ ⊠ (D)

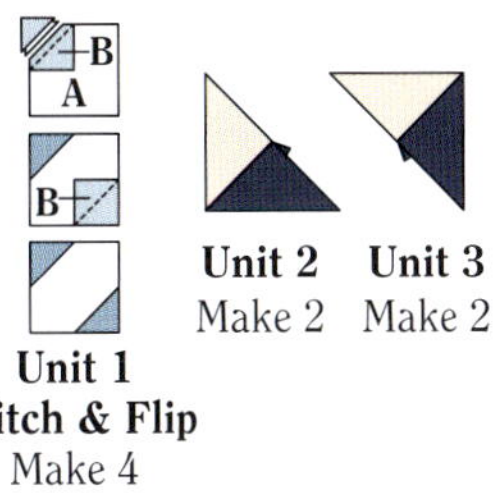

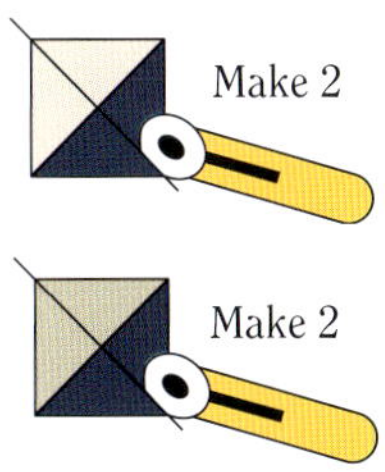

Refer to "Stitch-and-Flip" in the Techniques file on the PDF. Use the white A's and medium blue B's to make 4 unit 1's.

Use a dark blue C and tan tone-on-tone C to make 2 Triangle-Squares as shown. Cut each one diagonally to make 2 unit 2's and 2 unit 3's. Use a dark blue C and tan print C to make 2 Triangle-Squares as shown. Cut each one diagonally to make 2 unit 4's and 2 unit 5's. Join the unit 2's with the unit 4's and the unit 3's with the unit 5's to make a total of 4 unit 6's.

Sew the units and patches together as shown to complete the block. ▪

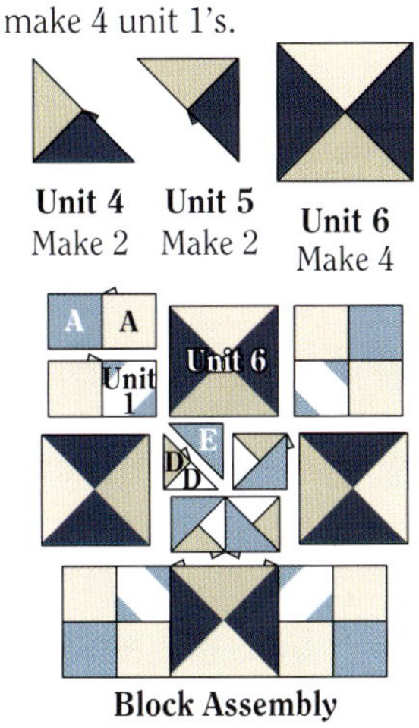

block no. 944

Floating Tiles

by Scott Murkin • Patchwork Possibilities
patchworkpossibilities.com

Green Batik
- 2 rectangles (A) 3½″ x 5″
- 1 rectangle (C) 3½″ x 12½″

White Tone-on-Tone
- 8 squares (B) 2″ x 2″
- 4 rectangles (E) 2″ x 3½″
- 4 rectangles (F) 2″ x 5″

Red Print
- 4 squares (D) 3½″ x 3½″

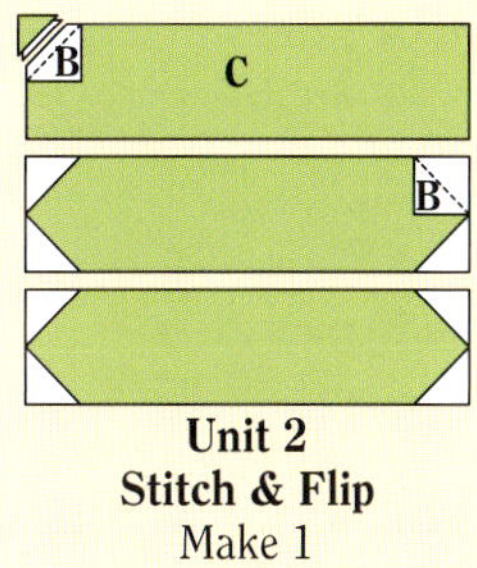

Refer to "Stitch-and-Flip" in the Techniques file on the PDF. Use the green A's and white B's to make 2 unit 1's. Make unit 2 using the green C and white B's.

Sew the units and patches together as shown to complete the block. ▪

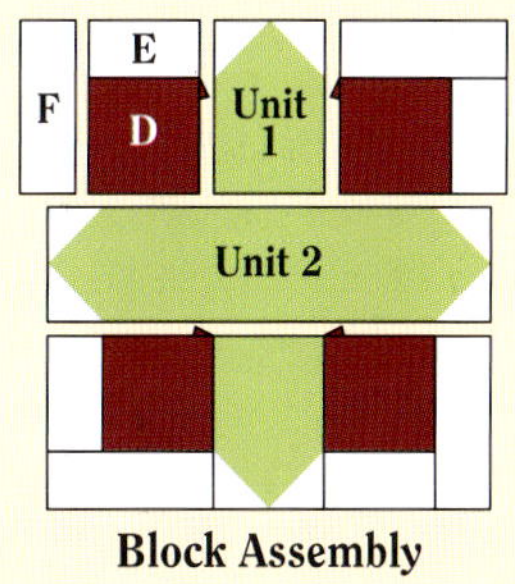

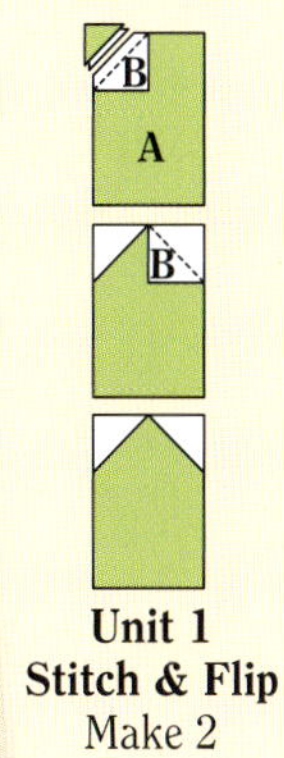

block no. 945

Starry Pinwheels

by Lerlene Nevaril
lerlenenevaril.com

Fabric: Fossil Fern by Benartex, benartex.com.

Lerlene Nevaril is the author of *Midnight Quilts* for C&T Publishing, ctpub.com.

Black Tone-on-Tone
- 1 square (A) $7\frac{1}{4}$"x $7\frac{1}{4}$"
- 8 squares (C) $2\frac{3}{8}$"x $2\frac{3}{8}$"
- 8 squares (D) 2"x 2"
- 4 rectangles (E) 2"x $3\frac{1}{2}$"

Multicolor Print
- 4 squares (B) $3\frac{7}{8}$"x $3\frac{7}{8}$"

Gold Tone-on-Tone
- 4 squares (C) $2\frac{3}{8}$"x $2\frac{3}{8}$"

Green Tone-on-Tone and Dark Pink Tone-on-Tone
from *each*
- 2 squares (C) $2\frac{3}{8}$"x $2\frac{3}{8}$"

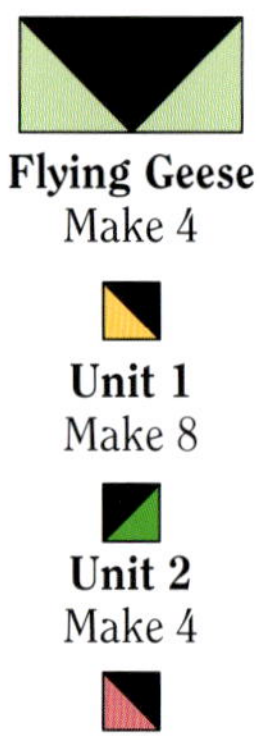

Use the black A and multi-color B's to make 4 Flying Geese.

Pair 4 black C's with the gold C's to make 8 Triangle-Square unit 1's. Pair 2 black C's with green C's to make 4 unit 2's. Make 4 unit 3's using black C's and dark pink C's.

Sew the Flying Geese, units and patches together as shown to complete the block.

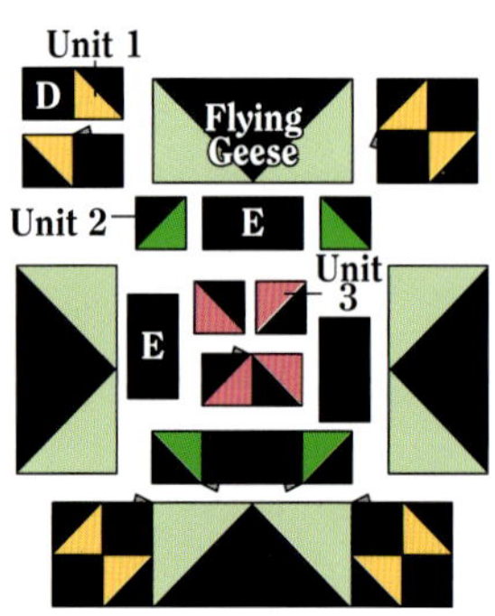

Block Assembly

block no. 946

Winter Path

by Jennifer Oden
quiltspeciallybyjen.blogspot.com

Fabric: Winter's Lane designed by Kate and Birdie Paper Co. for Moda Fabrics, unitednotions.com.

◩ = cut in half diagonally

Brown Print
- 4 rectangles (A) $4\frac{1}{4}$"x $8\frac{3}{4}$" (trim as shown)

Red Solid
- 8 rectangles (B) $\frac{3}{4}$"x 8"
- 2 rectangles (E) $\frac{3}{4}$"x $4\frac{1}{2}$"
- 2 rectangles (F) $\frac{3}{4}$"x 5"

Cream Print
- 4 squares $4\frac{5}{8}$"x $4\frac{5}{8}$" ◩ (C)

Multicolor Print
- 1 square (D) $4\frac{1}{2}$"x $4\frac{1}{2}$"

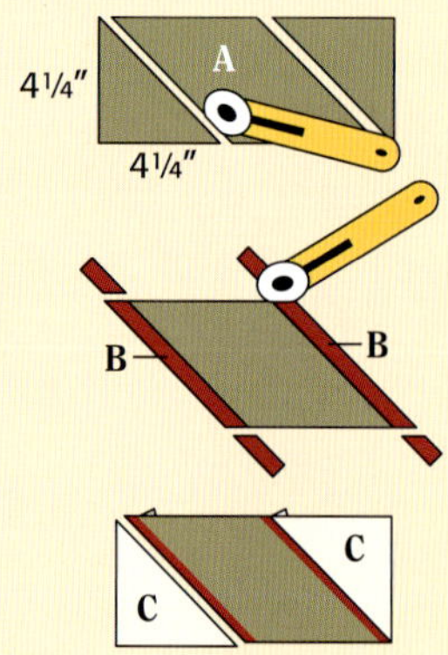

Unit
Make 4

Refer to the diagram to trim the brown print A's as shown. Join a red B to 2 sides of an A; trim as shown. Join a cream C to the sides as shown to complete the unit. Repeat to make 4 units.

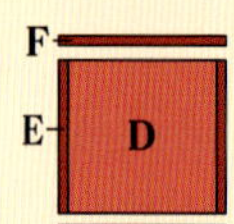

Center Piecing

Join the red E's and F's to the multicolor D as shown. Sew a unit to the right side of the block center with a partial seam as shown. Sew a unit to the bottom, left and top as shown. Complete the partial seam to finish the block.

• = Partial Seam

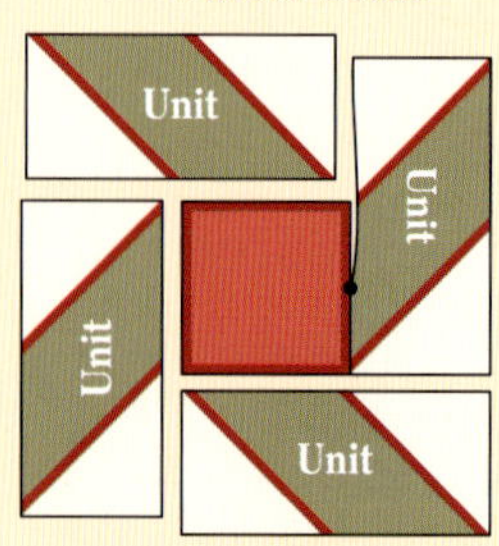

Block Assembly

pieced

block no. 947

Contained Chaos

by Melissa Peda • 100 Billion Stars
100billionstars.com

Fabric: Various Sis Boom lines designed by Jennifer Paganelli for Free Spirit, freespiritfabrics.com.

Assorted Pink Prints and Tone-on-Tones
16 rectangles (A) 1½" x 4½" from *1*
4 squares (C) 2½" x 2½"
White Solid
4 rectangles (B) 2½" x 8½"

Sew the patches together as shown to complete the block.

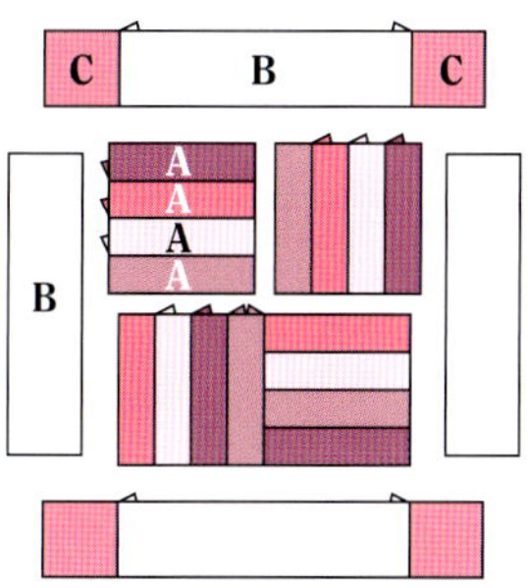

Block Piecing

block no. 948

Building Blocks

by Celine Perkins • Perkins Dry Goods
perkinsdrygoods.com

Fabric: Vintage Play designed by Susan Marth for Red Rooster Fabrics, redroosterfabrics.com.

Multicolor Print
1 square (A) 7¼" x 7¼"
Cream Tone-on-tone
4 squares (B) 3⅞" x 3⅞"
Red Print and Yellow Tone-on-Tone
from *each*
4 squares (C) 3½" x 3½"

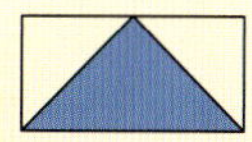
Flying Geese
Make 4

Use the multicolor A and cream B's to make 4 Flying Geese.

Sew the Flying Geese and patches together as shown to complete the block.

Block Assembly

block no. 949

Garden Party

by Susie M. Robbins • Peddlers of Danville

Fabric: Paradise designed by Susie M. Robbins for Quilting Treasures, quiltingtreasures.com.

Susie M. Robbins is the author of *Christmas Heart Lights* for Peddlers of Danville.

⍁ = cut in half diagonally
☒ = cut in half twice diagonally

Pale Green Tone-on-Tone
2 squares (A) 3¼" x 3¼"
4 squares (D) 1½" x 1½"
4 squares 1⅞" x 1⅞" ⍁ (E)

Green Print
8 squares (B) 1⅞" x 1⅞"
2 squares 2⅞" x 2⅞" ⍁ (F)

Dark Blue with Teal Print
1 square (A) 3¼" x 3¼"
4 squares (D) 1½" x 1½"

Light Teal Print
4 squares (B) 1⅞" x 1⅞"

Purple Stripe and Purple Plaid
from each
2 squares (C) 2⅞" x 2⅞"

Pale Purple Tone-on-Tone
4 squares 2⅞" x 2⅞" ⍁ (F)
1 square 5¼" x 5¼" ☒ (G)

Multicolor Print
2 squares 5¼" x 5¼" ☒ (G)
1 square (H) 2½" x 2½"

White Print
1 square 5¼" x 5¼" ☒ (G)

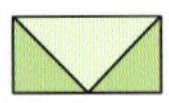

Flying Geese 1
Make 8

Flying Geese 2
Make 4

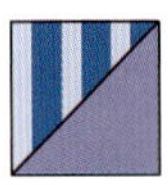

Unit
Make 4

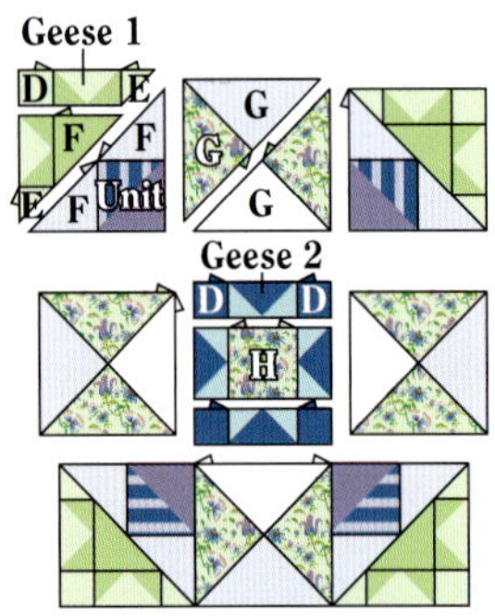

Block Assembly

Use pale green A's and green print B's to make 8 Flying Geese 1's. Use the dark blue/teal A and light teal B's to make 4 Flying Geese 2's.

Pair the purple stripe C's and purple plaid C's to make 4 Triangle-Square units.

Sew the Flying Geese, units and patches together as shown to complete the block.

block no. 950

Love Letters

by Amy Rullkoetter • Freelance Editor, *Quiltmaker*
quiltmaker.com

Fabric: Daphne designed by Skipping Stones Studio for Clothworks, clothworks.com.

Cream Print #1
2 squares (A) 3⅞" x 3⅞"

Pink Tone-on-Tone
6 squares (A) 3⅞" x 3⅞"
4 squares (D) 3½" x 3½"

Teal Tone-on-Tone
8 squares (B) 2½" x 2½"

Cream Print #2
1 square (C) 6½" x 6½"

Maroon Print
1 square (E) 7¼" x 7¼"

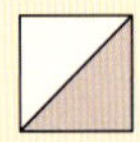

Partial Unit
Make 4 from A's

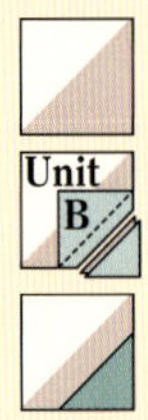

Unit 1
Stitch & Flip
Make 4

Unit 2
Stitch & Flip
Make 1

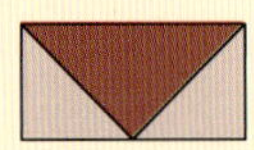

Flying Geese
Make 4

Refer to "Triangle-Squares" in the Techniques file on the PDF. Pair the cream #1 A's with the pink A's to make 4 partial units. Refer to "Stitch-and-Flip" in the Techniques file on the PDF. Sew a teal B on the corner of each partial unit as shown to make 4 unit 1's.

Using stitch-and-flip, sew a pink D to each corner of the cream #2 C as shown. Add a teal B to each corner to make 1 unit 2.

Use the maroon E and 4 pink A's to make 4 Flying Geese.

Sew the units and Flying Geese together as shown to complete the block.

Block Assembly

block no. 951

Starlet

by Rebecca Silbaugh • Ruby Blue Quilting Studio
rubybluequilts.blogspot.com

Rebecca Silbaugh is the author of Seemingly Scrappy: Get the Look You Love with Fat Quarters and Precuts for Martingale & Co., shopmartingale.com.

Brown Solid
2 strips 1½"x 30" for band
4 rectangles (D) 1½"x 2½"
8 squares (E) 1½"x 1½"

Red Tone-on-Tone
1 strip 1½"x 30" for band
5 squares (C) 2½"x 2½"
4 rectangles (D) 1½"x 2½"
12 squares (E) 1½"x 1½"

Cream Dot
4 rectangles (B) 3½"x 6½"
8 rectangles (D) 1½"x 2½"

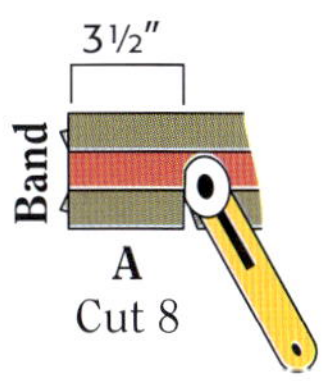

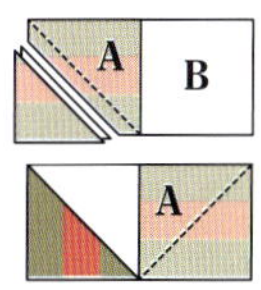

Unit
Stitch & Flip
Make 4

If you are making multiple blocks, consider strip piecing the center sections as well.

Sew the brown and red strips together as shown to make a band. Cut the band in increments of 3½" to make 8 A's.

Refer to "Stitch-and-Flip" in the Techniques file on the PDF. Noting the orientation of the A's, use the cream B's and pieced A's to make 4 units.

Sew the units and patches together as shown to complete the block.

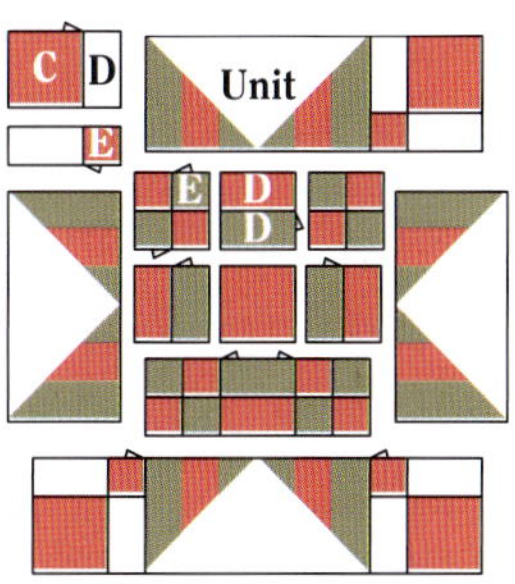

Block Assembly

block no. 952

Fade In

by Peg Spradlin
handicraftsbypeg.com

Fabric: Passion and Kaleidoscope, both designed by Deborah Edwards for Northcott, northcott.net.

Pale Purple Tone-on-Tone
2 squares (A) 3¼"x 3¼"
2 squares (B) 1⅞"x 1⅞"
1 square (E) 4½"x 4½"

Pale Green Tone-on-Tone
10 squares (B) 1⅞"x 1⅞"

Medium Purple Tone-on-Tone
2 squares (C) 4¼"x 4¼"
2 squares (D) 2⅜"x 2⅜"

Medium Green Tone-on-Tone
10 squares (D) 2⅜"x 2⅜"

Dark Green Tone-on-Tone
3 squares (C) 4¼"x 4¼"

Dark Purple Tone-on-Tone
12 squares (D) 2⅜"x 2⅜"
4 squares (F) 2"x 2"

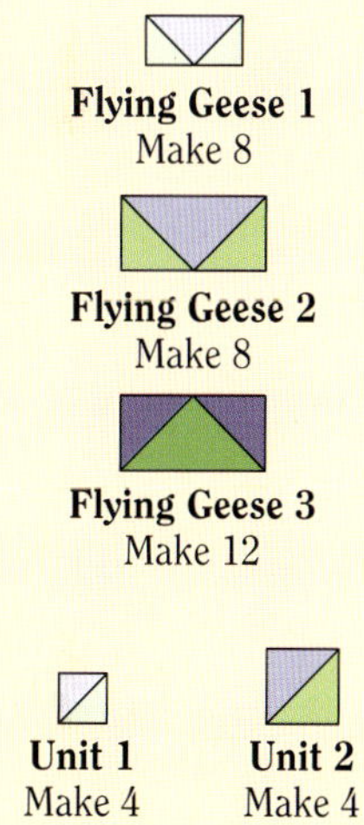

Use the pale purple A's and pale green B's to make 8 Flying Geese 1's. Make 8 Flying Geese 2's using the medium purple C's and medium green D's. Use the dark green C's and dark purple D's to make 12 Flying Geese 3's.

Pair the pale purple B's with pale green B's to make 4 Triangle-Square unit 1's. Make 4 unit 2's using the medium purple D's and medium green D's.

Sew the Flying Geese, units and patches together as shown to complete the block.

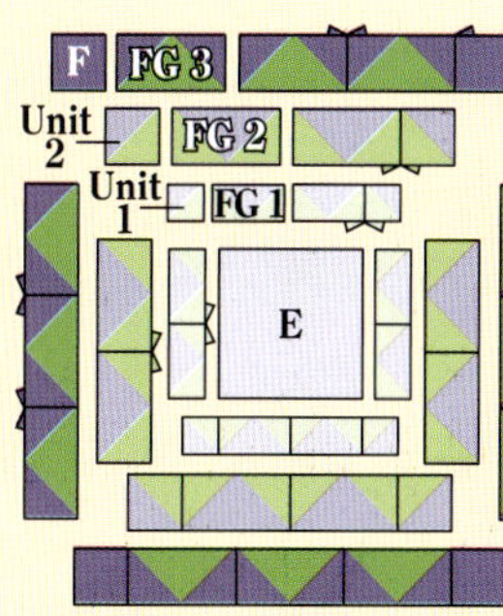

Block Assembly

block no. 953
Traffic Chopper

by Denise Starck • Graphic Designer, *Quiltmaker*
quiltmaker.com

Unit 5
Stitch & Flip
Make 1

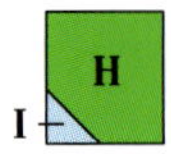

Unit 4
Stitch & Flip
Make 1

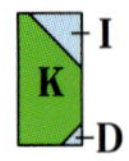

Unit 6
Stitch & Flip
Make 1

Red Solid
1 rectangle (A) 1″ x 6¼″

Light Blue Tone-on-Tone
3 rectangles (B) 1″ x 4″
1 rectangle (C) 1″ x 3¾″
3 squares (D) 1″ x 1″
1 rectangle (F) 2½″ x 4¼″
2 squares (I) 1¾″ x 1¾″
1 rectangle (J) 1½″ x 2½″
1 rectangle (K) 2″ x 3½″
1 rectangle (N) 2″ x 2½″
1 rectangle (O) 1⅛″ x 6¾″
1 rectangle (Q) 1⅛″ x 5¾″
3 rectangles (R) 1″ x 2″
1 rectangle (T) 1⅛″ x 6¼″
1 rectangle (U) 1⅛″ x 2½″
1 rectangle (V) 1⅛″ x 3¾″
2 rectangles (W) 2⅛″ x 12½″
2 squares (X) 1½″ x 1½″
1 rectangle (Y) 1½″ x 2″
1 rectangle (Z) 1¼″ x 2″

Dark Blue Tone-on-Tone
1 square (D) 1″ x 1″
1 rectangle (E) 1½″ x 4¼″
1 square (G) 1¼″ x 1¼″
1 rectangle (L) 1″ x 7½″
2 rectangles (P) 1″ x 1⅛″

Green Tone-on-Tone
1 square (D) 1″ x 1″
1 rectangle (H) 3¼″ x 3½″
1 rectangle (K) 2″ x 3½″
1 rectangle (M) 1″ x 2½″
1 rectangle (N) 2″ x 2½″

Gray Solid
1 rectangle (J) 1½″ x 2½″
1 rectangle (K) 2″ x 3½″
1 rectangle (P) 1″ x 1⅛″
1 rectangle (S) 1″ x 9½″
1 rectangle (Z) 1¼″ x 2″

Light Gray Tone-on-Tone
1 rectangle (H) 3¼″ x 3½″
1 rectangle (N) 2″ x 2½″

Medium Gray Tone-on-Tone
1 rectangle (J) 1½″ x 2½″
1 rectangle (K) 2″ x 3½″
1 rectangle (N) 2″ x 2½″

Unit 3
Stitch & Flip
Make 1

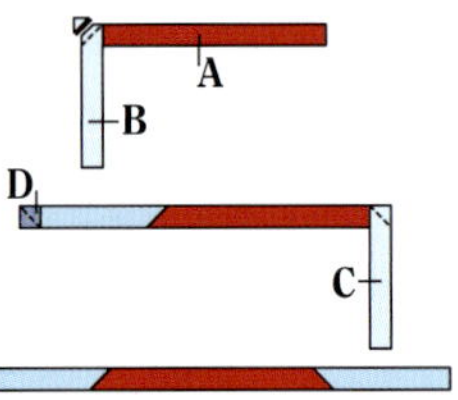

Unit 2
Stitch & Flip
Make 1

Unit 1
Stitch & Flip
Make 1

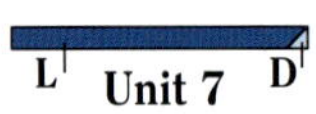

Unit 7
Stitch & Flip
Make 1

Refer to "Stitch-and-Flip" in the Techniques file on the PDF to make units 1–7. Use the red A, light blue B and C and dark blue D to make unit 1 as shown. Refer to the diagrams to make units 2–7.

Sew the units and patches together as shown to complete the block.

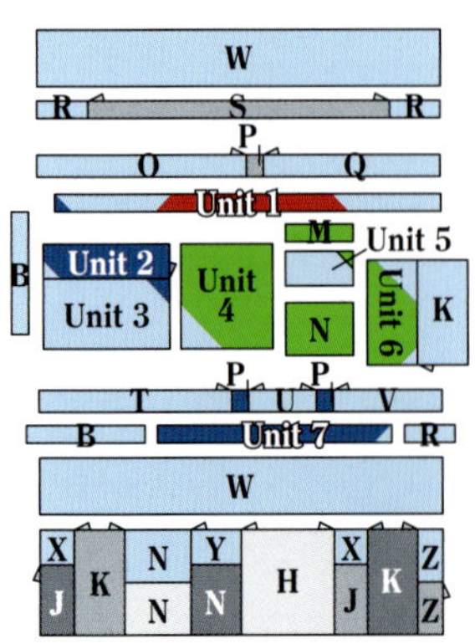

Block Assembly

block no. 954
Metro Mod

by Paula Stoddard • Associate Editor, *Quiltmaker*
quiltmaker.com

Fabric: Metro designed by Studio 8 for Quilting Treasures, quiltingtreasures.com.

Teal Print
8 rectangles (A) 2½″ x 4½″
8 squares (B) 2½″ x 2½″

White Print and Lime Green Tone-on-Tone from *each*
4 rectangles (A) 2½″ x 4½″
8 squares (B) 2½″ x 2½″

Brown Print
4 squares (B) 2½″ x 2½″

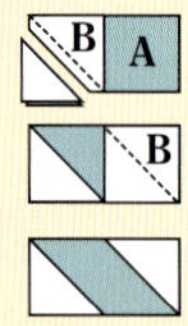

Unit 1
Stitch & Flip
Make 4

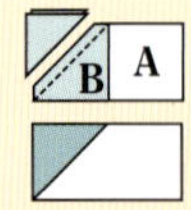

Unit 2
Stitch & Flip
Make 4

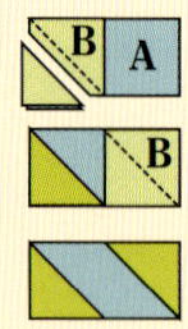

Unit 3
Stitch & Flip
Make 4

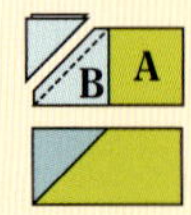

Unit 4
Stitch & Flip
Make 4

Refer to "Stitch-and-Flip" in the Techniques file on the PDF. Make 4 unit 1's using the teal A's and white B's. Use white A's and teal B's to make 4 unit 2's.

Make 4 unit 3's using teal A's and green B's. Use green A's and teal B's to make 4 unit 4's.

Sew a unit 2 to the top of a brown B with a partial seam as shown. Sew a unit 1 to the left, a unit 2 to the bottom and a unit 1 to the right as shown. Finish the partial seam to complete section 1. Make 2 section 1's.

Repeat with unit 3's and 4's and brown B's as shown to make 2 section 2's.

Sew the sections together as shown to complete the block.

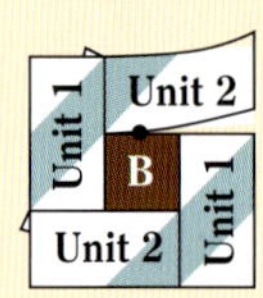

Section 1
Make 2
•=partial seam

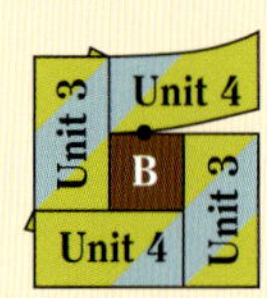

Section 2
Make 2
•=partial seam

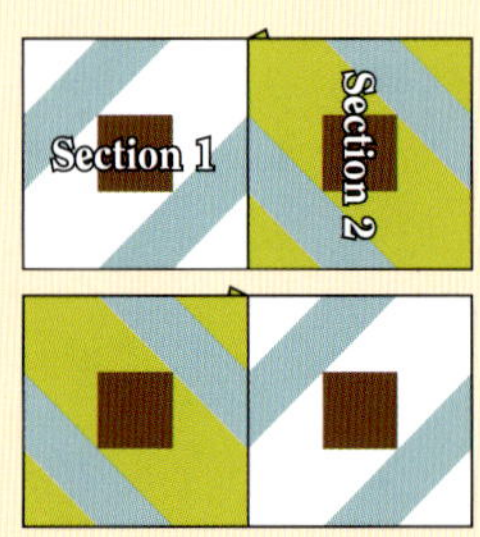

Block Assembly

pieced

block no. 955

Triangle-O-Rama

by Jennifer Schifano Thomas • Curlicue Creations
curlicuecreations.com

◸ = cut in half diagonally
☒ = cut in half twice diagonally

Tan Tone-on-Tone and Dark Brown Tone-on-Tone
from *each*
- 2 squares (A) 2⅜″x 2⅜″
- 1 square 4¼″x 4¼″ ☒ (C)
- 1 square 7¼″x 7¼″ ☒ (E)

Medium Brown Tone-on-Tone and Gold Batik
from *each*
- 2 squares 2⅜″x 2⅜″ ◸ (B)
- 2 squares 3⅞″x 3⅞″ ◸ (D)

Unit
Make 4

Pair the tan A's with the dark brown A's to make 4 Triangle-Square units.

Sew the units and patches together as shown to complete the block.

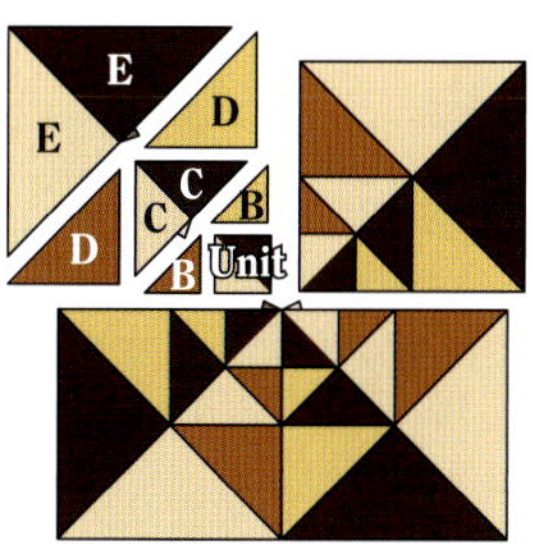

Block Assembly

block no. 956

Two Tulips

by Margie Ullery • Ribbon Candy Quilt Co.
ribboncandyquilts.blogspot.com

Fabric: Hoffman California Fabrics, hoffmanfabrics.com, and Timeless Treasures, ttfabrics.com.

Margie Ullery is the author of *Adorable Animal Appliqué* for Annie's, annies-publishing.com.

Aqua Batik
- 1 rectangle (A) 2½″x 3½″
- 1 rectangle (C) 2½″x 5½″

White Tone-on-Tone
- 1 rectangle (A) 2½″x 3½″
- 4 squares (B) 2½″x 2½″
- 1 rectangle (C) 2½″x 5½″
- 1 rectangle (D) 2½″x 6½″
- 9 squares (G) 1½″x 1½″
- 5 rectangles (L) 1½″x 2½″
- 1 rectangle (M) 3½″x 6½″

Teal Tone-on-Tone
- 1 rectangle (D) 2½″x 6½″
- 1 rectangle (E) 2½″x 8½″

Green Batik
- 1 rectangle (F) 1½″x 7½″
- 1 rectangle (H) 1½″x 8½″

Orange Tone-on-Tone
- 1 rectangle (I) 1½″x 3½″
- 1 rectangle (J) 1½″x 4½″

Green Tone-on-Tone
- 1 square (G) 1½″x 1½″
- 1 rectangle (J) 1½″x 4½″
- 1 rectangle (K) 1½″x 6½″

Yellow Tone-on-Tone #1
- 1 square (B) 2½″x 2½″

Yellow Tone-on-Tone #2
- 2 rectangles (L) 1½″x 2½″

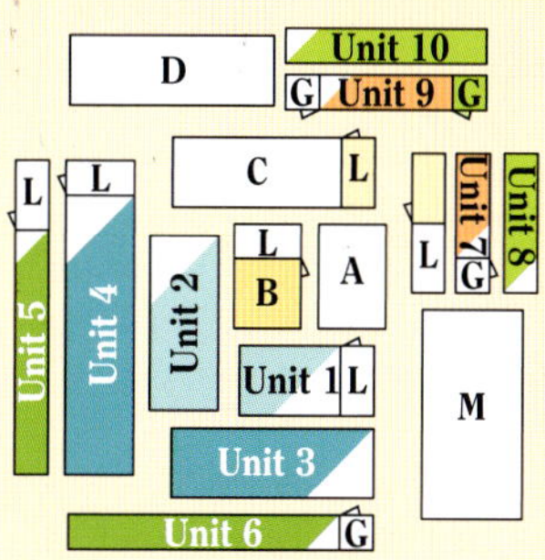

Block Assembly

Refer to "Stitch-and-Flip" in the Techniques file on the PDF. Use the aqua batik A and white B to make 1 unit 1 as shown. Refer to the diagrams and use stitch-and-flip to make 1 *each* of units 2–10 as shown.

Sew the units and patches together as shown to complete the block.

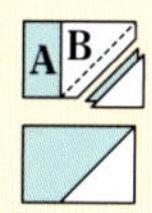

Unit 1
Stitch & Flip
Make 1

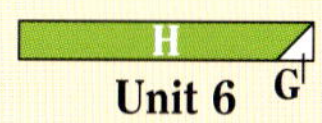

Unit 6
Stitch & Flip
Make 1

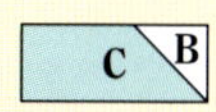

Unit 2
Stitch & Flip
Make 1

Unit 7
Stitch & Flip
Make 1

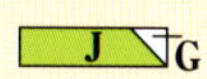

Unit 8
Stitch & Flip
Make 1

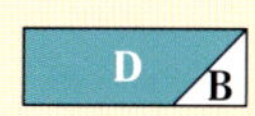

Unit 3
Stitch & Flip
Make 1

Unit 9
Stitch & Flip
Make 1

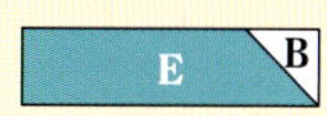

Unit 4
Stitch & Flip
Make 1

Unit 10
Stitch & Flip
Make 1

Unit 5
Stitch & Flip
Make 1

block no. 957

Picnic Table

by Joyce Weeks • Geoff's Mom Pattern Co.
geoffsmompatterns.com

Fabric: Somerset Shirtings by Windham Fabrics, windhamfabrics.com.

Joyce Weeks is the author of *For the Love of a Nine Patch* for Geoff's Mom Pattern Company, geoffsmompatterns.com.

Dark Blue Print
5 squares (A) 2½″ x 2½″
4 rectangles (E) 1½″ x 2½″

White Print #1
16 squares (B) 1½″ x 1½″
4 rectangles (E) 1½″ x 2½″

White Print #2
1 square (C) 7¼″ x 7¼″
4 squares (F) 3½″ x 3½″

Red Print
4 squares (D) 3⅞″ x 3⅞″

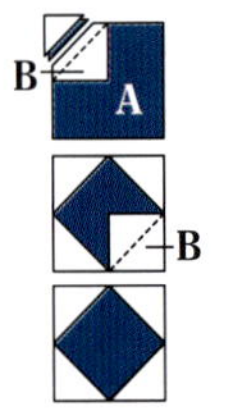

Unit
Stitch & Flip
Make 4

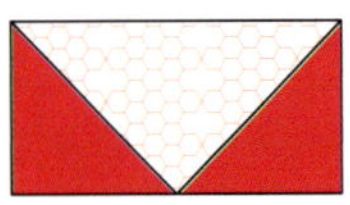

Flying Geese
Make 4

Refer to "Stitch-and-Flip" in the Techniques file on the PDF. Use the blue A's and white #1 B's to make 4 units.

Make 4 Flying Geese using the white #2 C and red D's.

Sew the Flying Geese, units and patches together as shown to complete the block.

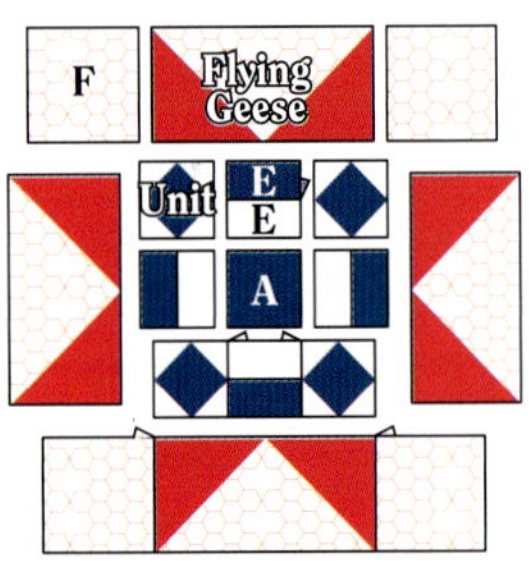

Block Assembly

block no. 958

Common Thread

by Anne Wiens • Sweetgrass Creative Designs
sweetgrassdesigns.com

Anne Wiens is the author of *The Thrifty Quilter: Make (Nearly) Free Quilts from Leftover Fabric* for Quiltwoman, quiltwoman.com.

⧄ = cut in half diagonally

Cream Print
4 rectangles (A) 2½″ x 8½″
2 squares 2⅞″ x 2⅞″ ⧄ (F)

4 Assorted Purple Prints,
4 Assorted Red Prints,
4 Assorted Green Prints and
4 Assorted Blue Prints
total from *each color group*
3 squares (B) 2½″ x 2½″
1 square 2⅞″ x 2⅞″ ⧄ (F)
(there will be 1 extra of each color)

Cream Solid
1 square (C) 4⅞″ x 4⅞″
2 squares (E) 4½″ x 4½″

Dark Brown Tone-on-Tone
1 square (C) 4⅞″ x 4⅞″

Gold Tone-on-Tone
4 squares (D) 3″ x 3″

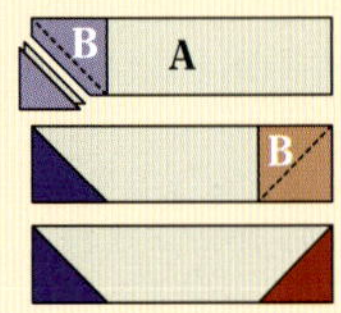

Unit 1
Stitch & Flip
Make 1

Unit 2
Stitch & Flip
Make 1

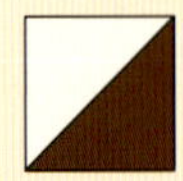

Partial Unit
Make 2 from C

Unit 5
Stitch & Flip
Make 1

Unit 7
Stitch & Flip
Make 1

Unit 6
Stitch & Flip
Make 1

Unit 8
Stitch & Flip
Make 1

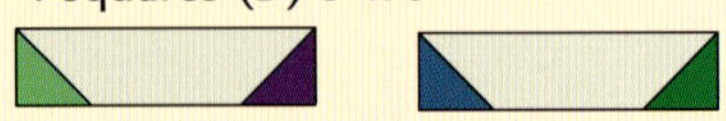

Unit 3
Stitch & Flip
Make 1

Unit 4
Stitch & Flip
Make 1

Refer to "Stitch-and-Flip" in the Techniques file on the PDF. Noting the color placement, use the cream print A's and assorted B's to make units 1–4.

Refer to "Triangle-Squares" in the Techniques file on the PDF. Pair the cream C and dark brown C to make 2 partial units. Using stitch-and-flip, join B's and D's to the partial units and cream E's as shown to make 1 *each* of units 5–8.

Sew the units and patches together as shown to complete the block.

Block Assembly

block no. 959

Village Square

by Mickey Depre
mdquilts.com

Mickey Depre is the author of Pieced Hexies Deux—10 New Designs to Rock Your Quilts *for Kansas City Star Quilts, pickledish.com.*

Black Batik
6 squares (A) 2⅞″ x 2⅞″
Pale Gold Tone-on-Tone
2 squares (A) 2⅞″ x 2⅞″
4 rectangles (C) 2½″ x 4½″
Teal Batik #1
4 squares (A) 2⅞″ x 2⅞″
Teal Batik #2
4 squares (B) 2½″ x 2½″
Gray Batik
4 rectangles (C) 2½″ x 4½″
Pale Green Batik
4 squares (B) 2½″ x 2½″

Unit 1
Make 4

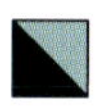

Unit 2
Make 8

Pair the black A's with pale gold A's to make 4 Triangle-Square unit 1's. Make 8 unit 2's using black A's and teal #1 A's.

Sew the units and patches together as shown to complete the block.

Block Assembly

block no. 960

Creamsicle

by Monique Dillard • Open Gate Quilts
opengatequilts.com

Fabric: Java Batiks by Fresh Water Designs for E.E. Schenck, eeschenck.com.

Monique Dillard is the author of *Diamond Traditions and* Fat Quarter Winners, both for C&T Publishing, ctpub.com.

◸ = cut in half diagonally

Assorted Pink, Yellow and Orange Batiks
44 squares (A) 2″ x 2″
10 squares 2⅜″ x 2⅜″ ◸ (B)
White Solid
2 squares 2⅜″x 2⅜″ ◸ (B)
4 squares 3⅞″ x 3⅞″ ◸ (C)

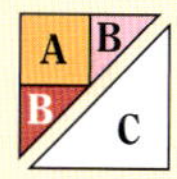

Partial Unit
Make 8

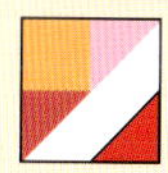

Unit
Stitch & Flip
Make 8

Randomly select 1 A and 2 B's from the assorted batiks; sew the A, B's and 1 white C together as shown to make a partial unit. Refer to "Stitch-and Flip" in the Techniques file on the PDF. Sew a batik A on the corner of the white C as shown to complete the unit. Make 8 units.

Sew the patches and units together as shown to complete the block.

Block Assembly

pieced

block no. 961

Intersections

by Abigail Dolinger
abyquilts.wordpress.com

Cream Print
8 squares (A) 3½″ x 3½″
Green Tone-on-Tone and Red Print from *each*
8 squares (B) 2″ x 2″
Orange Tone-on-Tone, Green Print #1 and Blue Print from *each*
4 squares (B) 2″ x 2″
Green Print #2
1 square (A) 3½″ x 3½″

Block Piecing

Sew the patches together as shown to complete the block.

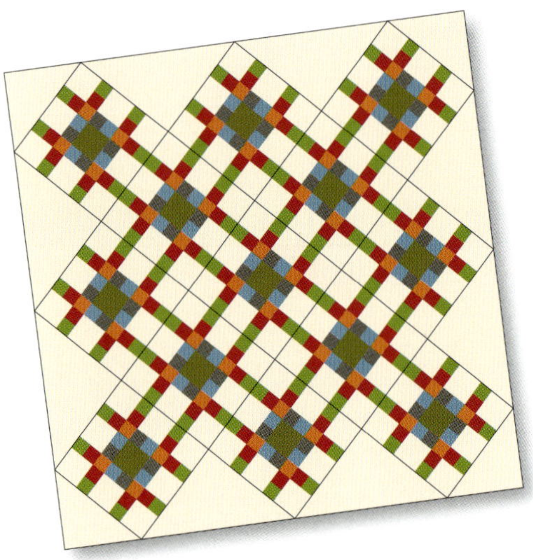

block no. 962

American Spirit

by Chery Ann Edholm • Sisters' Quilting Trunk
sistersquiltingtrunk.com

Fabric: Old Glory Gatherings designed by Primitive Gatherings for Moda Fabrics, unitednotions.com.

Dark Blue Solid
2 squares (A) 3⅞″ x 3⅞″
8 squares (B) 1½″ x 1½″
Red Solid
2 squares (A) 3⅞″ x 3⅞″
8 squares (B) 1½″ x 1½″
4 squares (C) 3½″ x 3½″
Cream Print
20 squares (B) 1½″ x 1½″
4 squares (C) 3½″ x 3½″

Unit
Make 4

Pair the blue A's with red A's to make 4 Triangle-Square units.

Sew the units and patches together as shown to complete the block.

Block Assembly

block no. 963

Fast Track

by Gudrun Erla • GE Designs
gequiltdesigns.com

Fabric: Victory designed by Gudrun Erla for Red Rooster Fabrics, redroosterfabrics.com.

Gudrun Erla is the author of *Fast & Furious Home* for GE Designs, gequiltdesigns.com.

White Tone-on-Tone and Black Tone-on-Tone
from *each*
- 2 squares (A) 2⅞" x 2⅞"

Gray Tone-on-Tone
- 8 rectangles (B) 1½" x 2½"
- 2 rectangles (C) 2½" x 4½"
- 2 rectangles (D) 2½" x 6½"
- 2 rectangles (E) 1½" x 4½"
- 2 squares (H) 2½" x 2½"

Red Tone-on-Tone and Teal Tone-on-Tone
from *each*
- 1 rectangle (C) 2½" x 4½"
- 1 rectangle (G) 2½" x 3½"

Yellow Tone-on-Tone and Green Tone-on-Tone
from *each*
- 1 rectangle (B) 1½" x 2½"
- 1 rectangle (F) 3½" x 4½"

Unit
Make 4

Pair the white A's with the black A's to make 4 Triangle-Square units.

Sew the units and patches together as shown to complete the block.

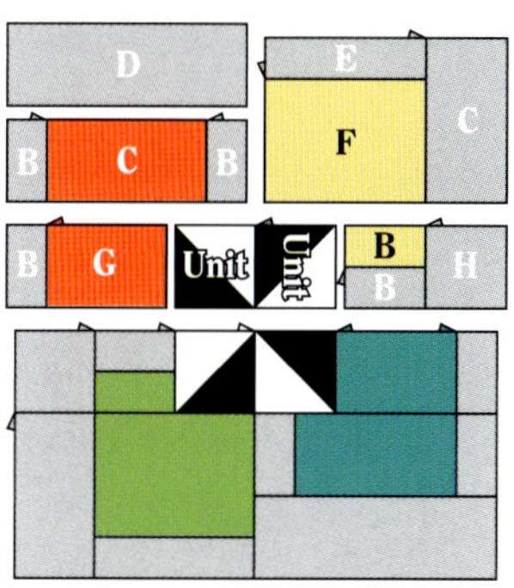

Block Assembly

block no. 964

...and so on...

by Kelli Fannin • Kelli Fannin Quilts
thatlookslikeitneedsstitches.blogspot.com

Fabric: Dancing Paisley designed by Brandon Mably for Rowan Fabrics, westminsterfibers.com.

◸ = cut in half diagonally
⊠ = cut in half twice diagonally

Purple Print
- 6 squares (A) 2⅞" x 2⅞"
- 5 squares (B) 2½" x 2½"
- 1 square 3¼" x 3¼" ⊠ (C)
- 2 squares 2⅞" x 2⅞" ◸ (D)

White Print
- 6 squares (A) 2⅞" x 2⅞"
- 2 squares (B) 2½" x 2½"
- 1 square 3¼" x 3¼" ⊠ (C)
- 1 rectangle (E) 4½" x 6½"
- 1 rectangle (F) 2½" x 4½"
- 1 rectangle (G) 2½" x 12½"

Unit
Make 11

Pair the print A's with white A's to make 12 Triangle-Square units (use 11).

Sew the units and patches together as shown to complete the block.

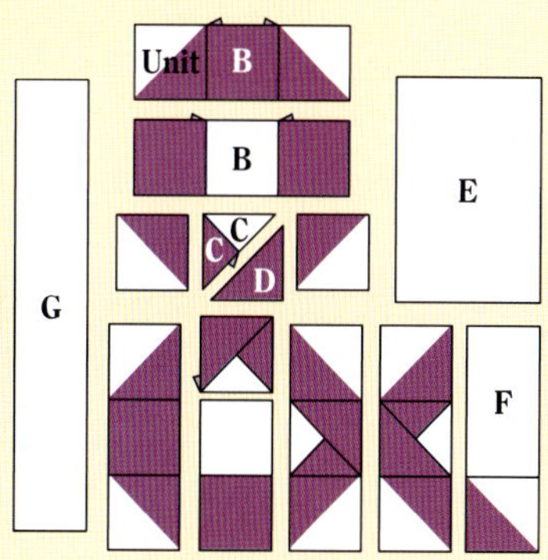

Block Assembly

block no. 965

Self-Sashed Medallion

by Kay Gentry • Noble Needle Quilting and Sewing
nobleneedle.com

Gold Tone-on-Tone
20 squares (A) 1⅞" x 1⅞"

Medium Green Tone-on-Tone
4 squares (A) 1⅞" x 1⅞"
4 squares (C) 1½" x 1½"

Purple Tone-on-Tone
1 square (B) 3¼" x 3¼"
2 squares (C) 1½" x 1½"

Dark Blue Tone-on-Tone
4 squares (A) 1⅞" x 1⅞"
4 squares (C) 1½" x 1½"
4 rectangles (G) 1½" x 10½"

Brown Tone-on-Tone
4 squares (B) 3¼" x 3¼"
2 rectangles (E) 1½" x 6½"
2 rectangles (F) 1½" x 8½"

Red Tone-on-Tone
2 squares (C) 1½" x 1½"
4 rectangles (D) 1½" x 4½"

Unit
Make 8

Flying Geese 1
Make 4

Flying Geese 2
Make 16

Pair the gold A's with green A's to make 8 Triangle-Square units as shown.

Use the purple B and dark blue A's to make 4 Flying Geese 1's. Make 16 Flying Geese 2's using brown B's and gold A's.

Sew the units, Flying Geese and patches together as shown to complete the block.

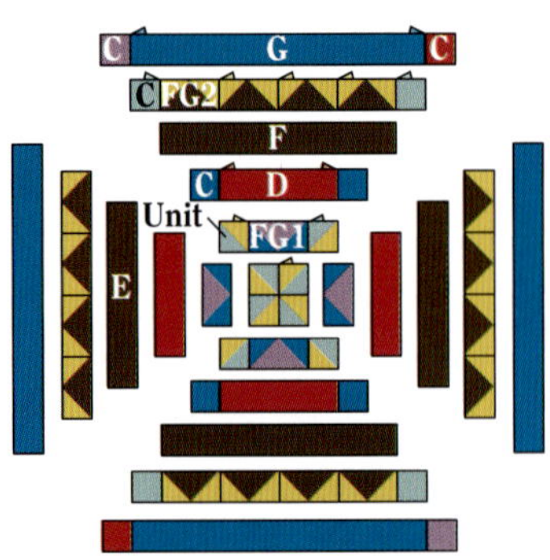

Block Assembly

block no. 966

Winter Red

by Sara Hardwig • Blueberry Backroads
blueberrybackroads.com

See page 397 on the PDF for pattern

Tan Tone-on-Tone and Muslin
from *each*
1 square (A) 10" x 10" (trim to 7" x 7" after embroidery)

Black Solid
2 rectangles (B) 1" x 7"
2 rectangles (C) 1" x 8"
2 rectangles (E) 1½" x 10½"
2 rectangles (F) 1½" x 12½"

Assorted Black Prints
12 rectangles (D) 1¾" x 3"

Red Print
2 rectangles (D) 1¾" x 3"

Brown Pigma Micron pen (.01 tip) **or water soluble fabric marker**
Embroidery floss (see instructions)

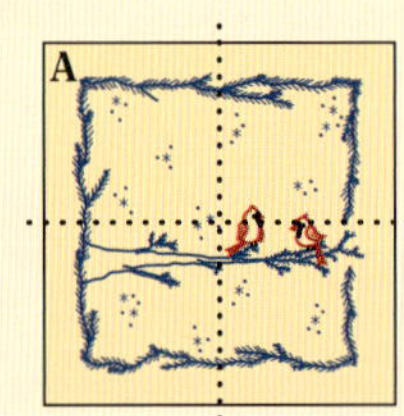

Embroidery Placement

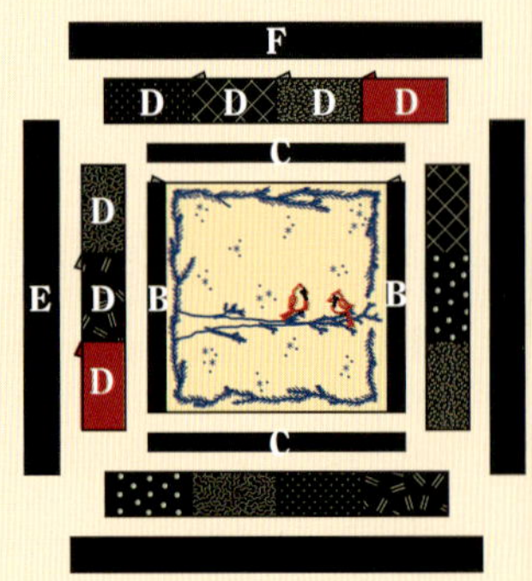

Block Piecing

Sara used the following DMC floss colors: DMC 53 for the branches, pine needles and snowflakes, DMC 221 for the cardinals and DMC 310 for the cardinal faces.

Fold the tan A in half both ways and lightly crease the folds. Using the creases as a guide, trace the embroidery design onto A with the pen or marker. Layer the tan A on top of the muslin and baste them together.

Refer to the pattern sheet for the embroidery details. With 3 strands of floss, stitch the branches with a stem stitch, details to the cardinal faces with a satin stitch and add French knots for the eyes. With 2 strands of floss, stitch the pine needles and snowflakes with a straight stitch, and add French knots in the sky. Backstitch the details on the cardinal wings and tails with 1 strand of floss. Center the design and trim to 7" × 7".

Sew the embroidered A and patches together as shown to complete the block.

block no. 967

Puddle Jumper

by Beth Helfter • Eva Paige Quilt Designs
evapaigequiltdesigns.com

2 Violet Batiks
from *each*
- 1 square (A) $3\frac{7}{8}$" x $3\frac{7}{8}$"
- 2 squares (C) $3\frac{1}{2}$" x $3\frac{1}{2}$"

Cream Tone-on-Tone
- 2 squares (A) $3\frac{7}{8}$" x $3\frac{7}{8}$"
- 2 rectangles (B) $3\frac{1}{2}$" x $6\frac{1}{2}$"

2 Teal Batiks
from *each*
- 2 rectangles (B) $3\frac{1}{2}$" x $6\frac{1}{2}$"

2 Purple Batiks
from *each*
- 4 squares (C) $3\frac{1}{2}$" x $3\frac{1}{2}$"

Unit 1
Make 2

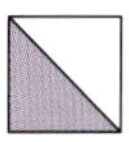

Unit 2
Make 2

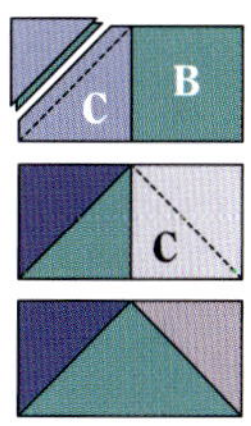

Unit 3
Stitch & Flip
Make 1

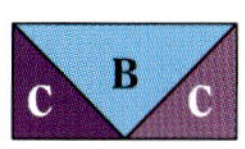

Unit 4
Stitch & Flip
Make 1

Pair a violet A with a cream A to make 2 Triangle-Square unit 1's. Make 2 unit 2's using the other violet A and a cream A.

Refer to "Stitch-and-Flip" in the Techniques file on the PDF. Use a teal B and a C from each of the 2 violets to make unit 3 as shown. In the same way, make the remaining units as shown in the diagrams.

Noting the color placements, sew the units and patches together as shown to complete the block.

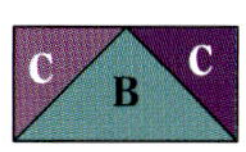

Unit 5
Stitch & Flip
Make 1

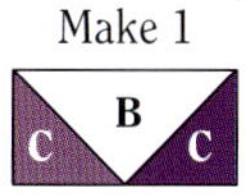

Unit 6
Stitch & Flip
Make 2

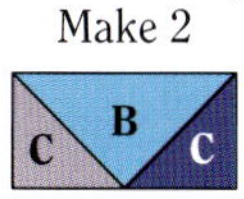

Unit 7
Stitch & Flip
Make 2

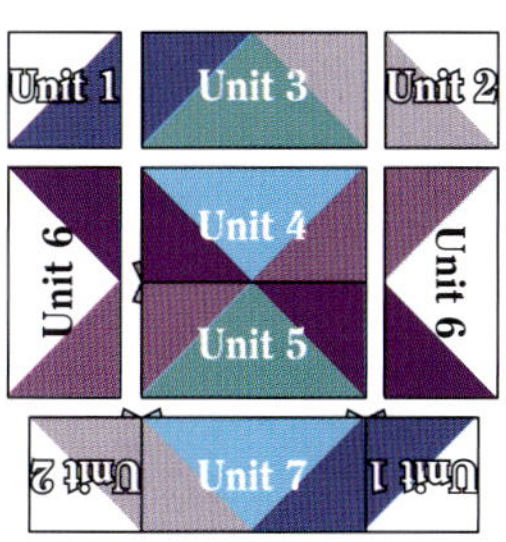

Block Assembly

block no. 968

Above and Beyond

by Chris Hoover • Whirligig Designs
whirligigdesigns.com

Fabric: Artisan Spirit Shimmer designed by Deborah Edwards for Northcott, northcott.com.

⊠ = cut in half twice diagonally

White Tone-on-Tone
- 4 squares (A) $2\frac{7}{8}$" x $2\frac{7}{8}$"
- 2 squares (B) $3\frac{3}{4}$" x $3\frac{3}{4}$"
- 16 squares (C) $1\frac{1}{2}$" x $1\frac{1}{2}$"
- 1 square $5\frac{1}{4}$" x $5\frac{1}{4}$" ⊠ (D)

Light Teal Tone-on-Tone
- 4 squares (A) $2\frac{7}{8}$" x $2\frac{7}{8}$"
- 1 square $5\frac{1}{4}$" x $5\frac{1}{4}$" ⊠ (D)

Medium Teal Print
- 2 squares (B) $3\frac{3}{4}$" x $3\frac{3}{4}$"

Yellow Tone-on-Tone
- 16 squares (C) $1\frac{1}{2}$" x $1\frac{1}{2}$"

Dark Blue Tone-on-Tone
- 1 square $5\frac{1}{4}$" x $5\frac{1}{4}$" ⊠ (D)

Unit 1
Make 8 from A's

Unit 2
Make 4 from B's

It's helpful to starch the fabric before cutting the D's to stabilize the bias edges.

Pair the white A's with the light teal A's to make 8 Triangle-Square unit 1's. Make 4 unit 2's using white B's and medium teal B's.

Sew the patches and units together as shown to complete the block.

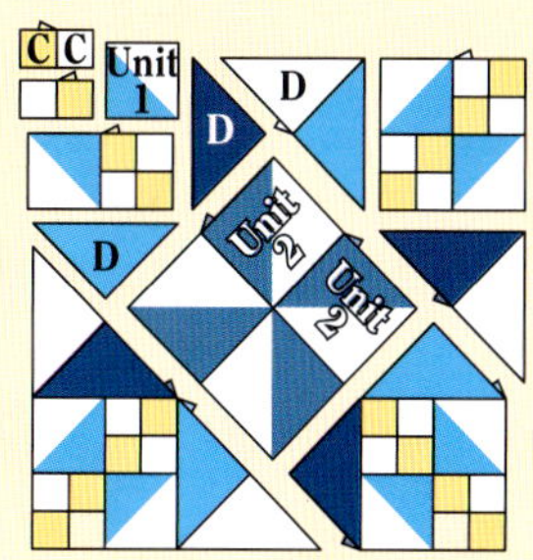

Block Assembly

block no. 969

Something Blue

by Bonnie Hunter • Quiltville
quiltville.com

Bonnie Hunter writes the "Addicted to Scraps" column for *Quiltmaker*. She is the author of several books, including her newest book, *More Adventures with Leaders and Enders* for Kansas City Star Quilts, pickledish.com.

⧄ = cut in half diagonally

Assorted Blue Prints and Tone-on-Tones
- 8 squares (A) 2"x 2"
- 32 squares 2³⁄₈"x 2³⁄₈" ⧄ (B) (there will be 32 extra)
- ³⁄₄" to 1³⁄₄"-wide strips to total 80"

Gold Tone-on-Tone
- 4 squares (A) 2"x 2"
- 8 squares 2³⁄₈"x 2³⁄₈" ⧄ (B)

Assorted Cream Prints and Tone-on-Tones
- 4 squares (A) 2"x 2"
- 16 squares 2³⁄₈"x 2³⁄₈" ⧄ (B) (there will be 16 extra)

Foundation paper
- 4 squares 3½"x 3½"

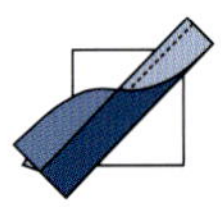

Section Piecing

Section
Make 4

Cutting the B's as instructed enhances the scrappy look of the block. Use the leftover patches for additional blocks.

Fold the paper squares in half diagonally, then draw a line on the fold. Place a blue strip right side up and parallel to the marked line on one of the foundation squares. Aligning raw edges, lay another strip right side down on the first strip as shown. Join the strips by sewing through all the layers ¼" from the raw edges. Flip the top strip open and press. Continue adding strips from the center outward in both directions until the entire foundation has been covered. Trim the fabric even with the paper. Repeat to make 4 sections.

Sew the sections and patches together as shown to complete the block. Carefully remove the papers.

Block Assembly

pieced

block no. 970

Starberry

by Kimberly Jolly • Fat Quarter Shop
fatquartershop.com

Fabric: April Showers designed by Bonnie & Camille for Moda Fabrics, unitednotions.com.

Kimberly Jolly is the co-author of *Simply Fat Quarters: Quilts with Comfort and Style* for Fat Quarter Shop, fatquartershop.com.

Cream Dot
- 4 rectangles (A) 2"x 3½"
- 8 squares (B) 2"x 2"
- 1 square (D) 6½"x 6½"
- 2 squares (E) 2³⁄₈"x 2³⁄₈"

Red Tone-on-Tone
- 8 squares (B) 2"x 2"
- 2 squares (E) 2³⁄₈"x 2³⁄₈"

Green Print
- 4 squares (C) 3½"x 3½"

Yellow Print
- 12 squares (B) 2"x 2"

Green Stripe
- 8 squares (A) 2"x 2"

Unit 4
Make 4

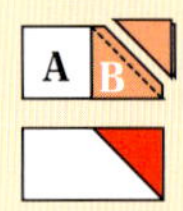

Unit 1
Stitch & Flip
Make 4

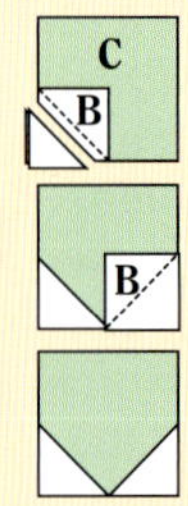

Unit 2
Stitch & Flip
Make 4

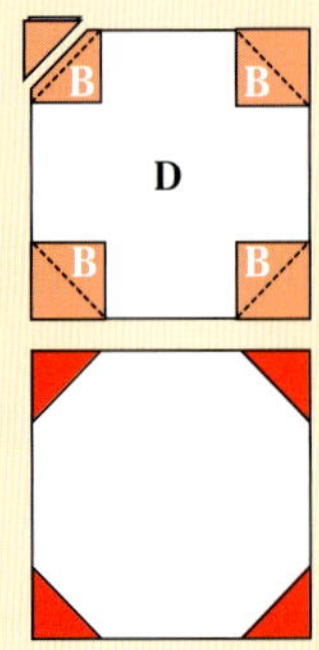

Unit 3
Stitch & Flip
Make 1

Refer to "Stitch-and-Flip" in the Techniques file on the PDF. Use the cream A's and red B's to make 4 unit 1's as shown. Use the green print C's and cream B's to make 4 unit 2's as shown. Use the cream D and red B's to make 1 unit 3.

Pair the cream E's with the red E's to make 4 Triangle-Square unit 4's.

Sew the units and patches together as shown to complete the block.

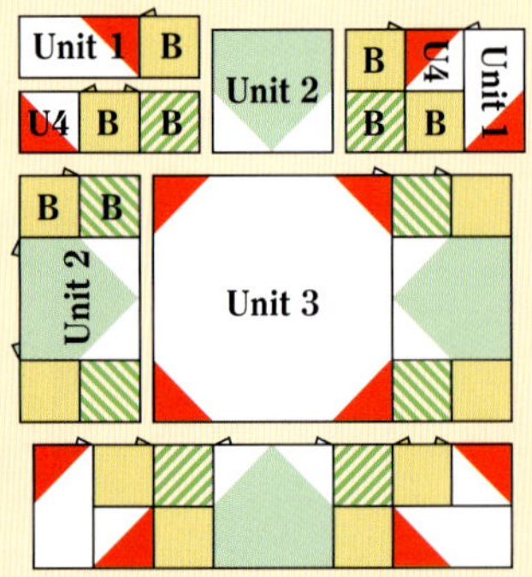

Block Assembly

block no. 971

Windmill

by Heather Jones • Heather Jones Studio
heatherjonesstudio.com

Fabric: American Made Brand Cotton Solids from Clothworks, clothworks.com.

Purple Solid
- 2 squares (A) 3⅞″ x 3⅞″
- 8 rectangles (B) 1½″ x 3½″

White Solid
- 2 squares (A) 3⅞″ x 3⅞″
- 4 rectangles (B) 1½″ x 3½″
- 8 squares (C) 3½″ x 3½″

Unit
Make 4

Pair purple A's with white A's to make 4 Triangle-Square units.

Sew the units and patches together as shown to complete the block.

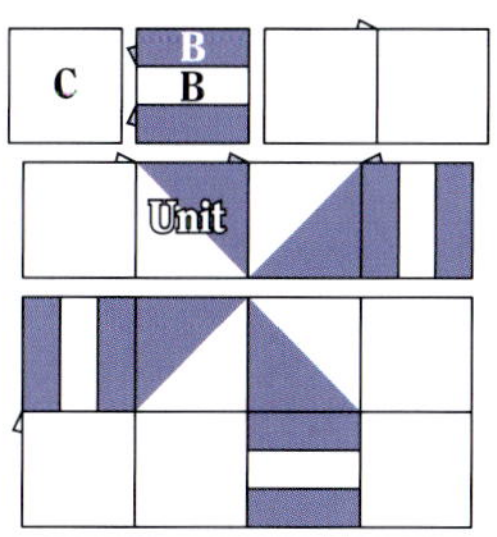

Block Assembly

block no. 972

Cottage Blooms

by Susan Knapp • The Quilt Branch
quiltbranch.com

Fabric: Weeds designed by Me & My Sister Designs for Moda Fabrics, unitednotions.com.

Susan Knapp is the co-author of the *Six Halves Make a Whole* series for The Quilt Branch, quiltbranch.com.

◪ = cut in half diagonally

Two Red Prints
from *each*
- 4 squares (A) 3½″ x 3½″

White Tone-on-Tone
- 4 squares (A) 3½″ x 3½″
- 8 squares (B) 2″ x 2″

White Print
- 1 square (C) 4¾″ x 4¾″

Black Stripe
- 2 squares 3⅞″ x 3⅞″ ◪ (D)

Black Tone-on-Tone
- 4 squares (E) 5″ x 5″

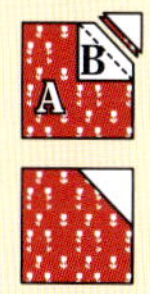

Unit 1
Stitch & Flip
Make 4

Unit 2
Stitch & Flip
Make 4

Refer to "Stitch-and-Flip" in the Techniques file on the PDF. Use one set of red A's with white B's to make 4 unit 1's. Make 4 unit 2's using the other red print A's with white B's.

Sew the units, A's, C and D's together as shown. Use the stitch-and-flip technique to add black E's at each corner to finish the block.

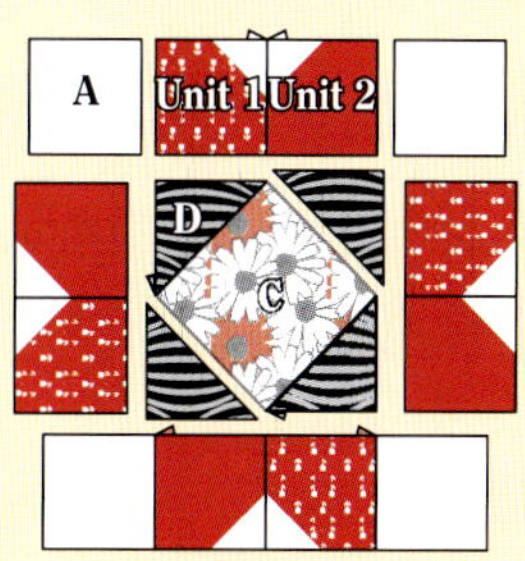

Block Piecing

Stitch & Flip

block no. 973

Railroad Crossing

by Jo and Kelli Kramer • Jo's Country Junction
joscountryjunction.com

⊠ = cut in half twice diagonally

Unit
Make 12

Black Tone-on-Tone
6 squares (A) 3″ x 3″

White Print
6 squares (A) 3″ x 3″
1 square 4¼″ x 4¼″ ⊠ (B)

Orange Tone-on-Tone and Green Print
from *each*
1 square 10¼″ x 10¼″ ⊠ (C)
(there will be 2 extra of each color)

Pair the black A's with white A's to make 12 Triangle-Square units.

Sew the units and patches together as shown to complete the block.

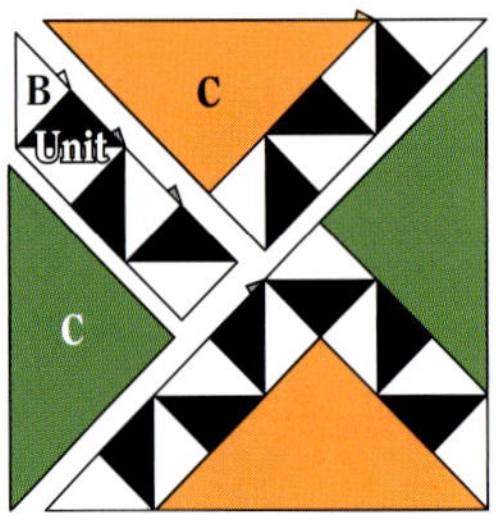

Block Assembly

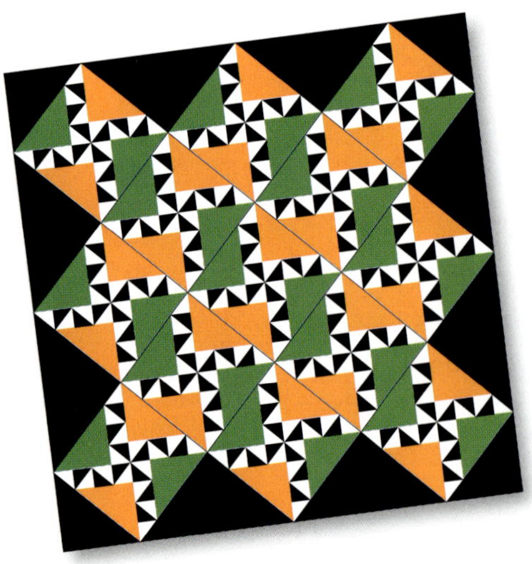

pieced

block no. 974

Nested Bear Paw

by Debbie Martin
shadowsoftheblueridge.blogspot.com

Black Tone-on-Tone
2 squares (A) 4⅞″ x 4⅞″
1 square (F) 4½″ x 4½″

Teal Tone-on-Tone
2 squares (A) 4⅞″ x 4⅞″
8 squares (B) 1⅞″ x 1⅞″
4 squares (C) 1½″ x 1½″
4 rectangles (E) 2½″ x 3½″

Orange Tone-on-Tone
8 squares (B) 1⅞″ x 1⅞″
5 squares (D) 2½″ x 2½″

Unit 1 from A's
Make 4

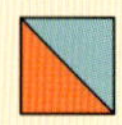

Unit 2 from B's
Make 16

Pair the black A's with the teal A's to make 4 Triangle-Square unit 1's. Pair the teal B's with the orange B's to make 16 unit 2's.

Sew the units and patches together as shown to complete the block.

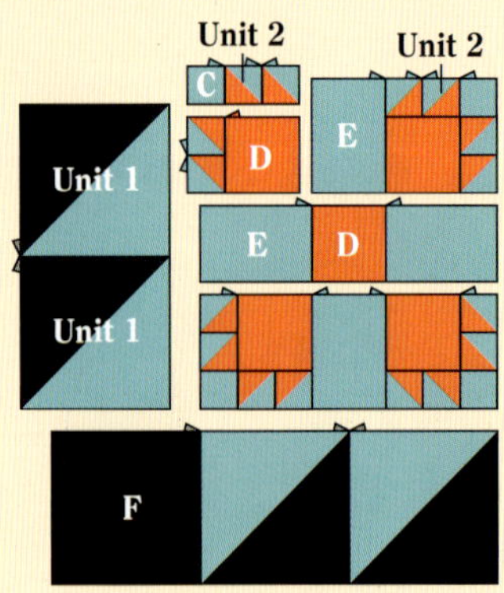

Block Assembly

block no. 975

Four O'Clock Blossom

by Bonnie Mitchell

Fabric: American Made Brand Cotton Solids from Clothworks, clothworks.com.

Dark Pink Solid
- 3 squares (A) 2⁷⁄₈" x 2⁷⁄₈"
- 4 rectangles (B) 2¹⁄₂" x 4¹⁄₂"

Light Gray Solid
- 7 squares (A) 2⁷⁄₈" x 2⁷⁄₈"
- 24 squares (C) 2¹⁄₂" x 2¹⁄₂"

Purple Solid and Medium Pink Solid
from *each*
- 2 squares (A) 2⁷⁄₈" x 2⁷⁄₈"
- 2 rectangles (B) 2¹⁄₂" x 4¹⁄₂"

Unit 1 Make 6 **Unit 2** Make 3 **Unit 3** Make 3

Pair dark pink A's with gray A's to make 6 Triangle-Square unit 1's. Make 4 unit 2's using purple A's and gray A's (use 3). Use the medium pink A's and gray A's to make 4 unit 3's (use 3).

Refer to "Stitch-and-Flip" in the Technique file on the PDF. Make 1 unit 4 using a purple B and 2 gray C's as shown. In the same way, make the indicated number of units 5–9 as shown.

Sew the units and patches together as shown to complete the block.

Block Assembly

block no. 976

Balancing Waltzer

by Lee Monroe • May Chappell
maychappell.com

Fabric: Botanics and Architextures both designed by Carolyn Friedlander for Robert Kaufman, robertkaufman.com; Henna Garden designed by Sandi Henderson for Michael Miller Fabrics, michaelmillerfabrics.com; Oval Elements designed by Pat Bravo for Art Gallery, artgalleryfabrics.com.

See page 379 on the PDF for pattern

Cream Print and Orange Print
from *each*
- 5 squares (A) 2⁷⁄₈" x 2⁷⁄₈"
- 4 template B
- 2 template Br

Magenta Print
- 2 squares (A) 2⁷⁄₈" x 2⁷⁄₈"
- 4 template B

Teal Print
- 4 template C

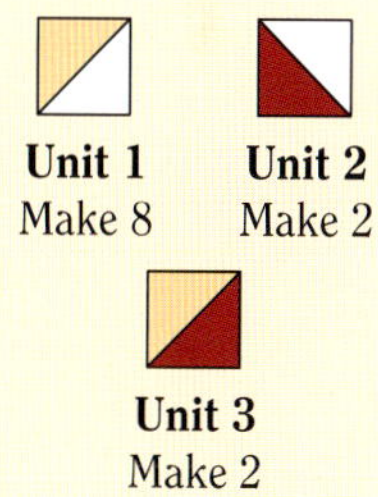

Pair 4 cream A's with 4 orange A's to make 8 Triangle-Squrae unit 1's. Pair a cream A with a magenta A to make 2 unit 2's. Pair an orange A with a magenta A to make 2 unit 3's.

Sew the units and patches together as shown to complete the block.

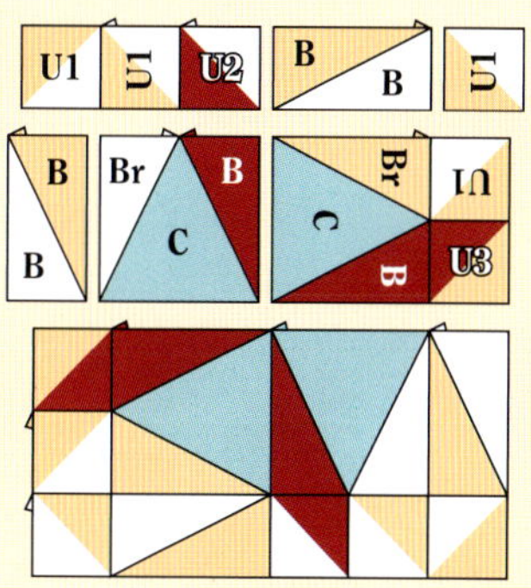

Block Assembly

block no. 977

Palazzo

by Scott Murkin • Patchwork Possibilities
patchworkpossibilities.com

Pale Purple Batik
- 2 squares (A) $3\frac{7}{8}$" x $3\frac{7}{8}$"
- 1 square (B) $4\frac{1}{4}$" x $4\frac{1}{4}$"
- 8 rectangles (E) 2" x $3\frac{1}{2}$"
- 1 square (F) $3\frac{1}{2}$" x $3\frac{1}{2}$"

Medium Purple Print
- 2 squares (A) $3\frac{7}{8}$" x $3\frac{7}{8}$"
- 4 squares (C) $2\frac{3}{8}$" x $2\frac{3}{8}$"
- 4 squares (D) 2" x 2"

Dark Purple Batik
- 4 squares (F) $3\frac{1}{2}$" x $3\frac{1}{2}$"

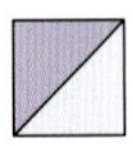

Unit
Make 4

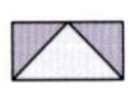

Flying Geese
Make 4

Pair the pale purple A's with medium purple A's to make 4 Triangle-Square units.

Use the pale purple B and medium purple C's to make 4 Flying Geese.

Sew the patches, units and Flying Geese together as shown to complete the block.

pieced

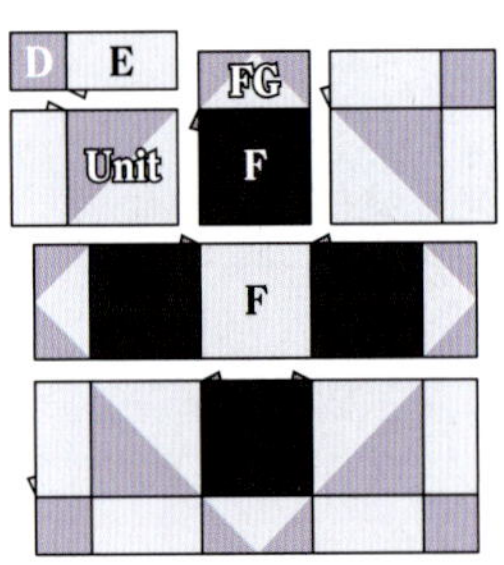

Block Assembly

block no. 978

Chevron Squares

by Amanda Murphy • Amanda Murphy Design
amandamurphydesign.com

Fabric: Topiary designed by Amanda Murphy for Blend Fabrics, blendfabrics.com.

Amanda Murphy is the author of *Color Essentials: Crisp and Vibrant Quilts* for Stash Books, ctpub.com.

⧄ = cut in half diagonally

White Tone-on-Tone
- 1 rectangle (A) $2\frac{1}{2}$" x $6\frac{1}{2}$"
- 1 rectangle (C) $2\frac{1}{2}$" x $9\frac{1}{2}$"
- 2 rectangles (D) $2\frac{1}{2}$" x $7\frac{1}{2}$"
- 2 rectangles (E) $2\frac{1}{2}$" x $3\frac{1}{2}$"

Assorted Aqua Prints
- 6 squares (B) $2\frac{1}{2}$" x $2\frac{1}{2}$"

Assorted Pink Prints
- 9 squares (B) $2\frac{1}{2}$" x $2\frac{1}{2}$"
- 3 rectangles (F) $1\frac{1}{2}$" x $2\frac{1}{2}$"
- 6 squares $2\frac{7}{8}$" x $2\frac{7}{8}$" ⧄ (G) (there will be 6 extra)

Assorted Light Green Prints
- 2 squares (B) $2\frac{1}{2}$" x $2\frac{1}{2}$"
- 2 rectangles (F) $1\frac{1}{2}$" x $2\frac{1}{2}$"
- 6 squares $2\frac{7}{8}$" x $2\frac{7}{8}$" ⧄ (G) (there will be 6 extra)

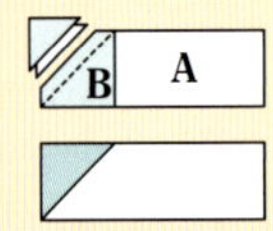

Unit 1
Stitch & Flip
Make 1

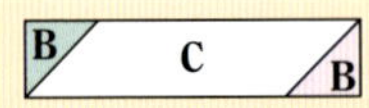

Unit 2
Stitch & Flip
Make 1

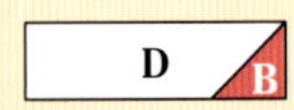

Unit 3
Stitch & Flip
Make 2

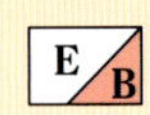

Unit 4
Stitch & Flip
Make 2

Cutting the G's as instructed enhances the scrappy look of the block. The extra patches can be used in additional blocks.

Refer to "Stitch-and-Flip" in the Techniques file on the PDF and the diagrams above to make unit 1–4's. Use the white A and an aqua B to make unit 1. Make a unit 2 using a white C, aqua B and pink B. Use a white D and pink B to make 2 unit 3's. Make 2 unit 4's using white E's and pink B's.

Sew the units and patches together as shown to complete the block.

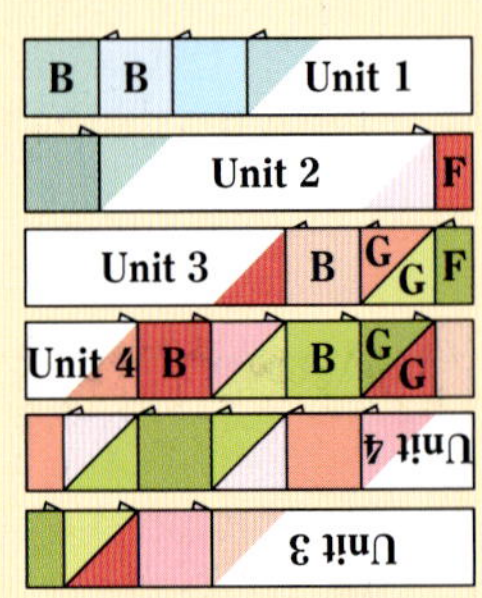

Block Assembly

block no. 979

Woven Ribbons

by Lerlene Nevaril
lerlenenevaril.com

Fabric: Fusions from Robert Kaufman, robertkaufman.com.

Lerlene Nevaril is the author of *Midnight Quilts* for C&T Publishing, ctpub.com.

Black Tone-on-Tone
8 rectangles (A) 2″ x 3½″
8 squares (B) 2″ x 2″
1 square (C) 4¼″ x 4¼″
Medium Teal Tone-on-Tone
16 squares (B) 2″ x 2″
Orange Tone-on-Tone
4 rectangles (A) 2″ x 3½″
4 squares (D) 2⅜″ x 2⅜″
Light Teal Tone-on-Tone
4 rectangles (A) 2″ x 3½″
4 squares (B) 2″ x 2″
Green Tone-on-Tone
1 square (E) 3½″ x 3½″

Unit 1
Stitch & Flip
Make 4

Unit 2
Stitch & Flip
Make 4

Flying Geese
Make 4

Refer to "Stitch-and-Flip" in the Techniques file on the PDF. Use 4 black A's and 4 medium teal B's to make 4 unit 1's as shown. Use 4 black A's and 4 medium teal B's to make 4 unit 2's as shown.

Use the black C and orange D's to make 4 Flying Geese.

Sew the patches and units together as shown to complete the block.

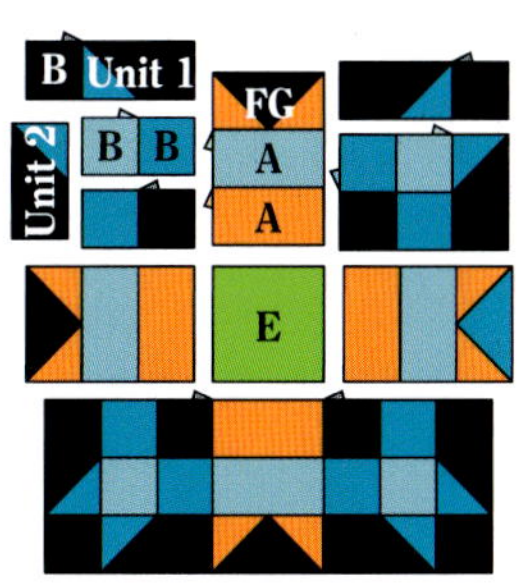

Block Assembly

block no. 980

Anna's Cross

by Jennifer Oden
quiltspeciallybyjen.blogspot.com

⊠ = cut in half twice diagonally

Teal Tone-on-Tone
2 squares (A) 4⅞″ x 4⅞″
Red Tone-on-Tone
2 squares (A) 4⅞″ x 4⅞″
4 rectangles (D) ¾″ x 3⅜″
2 rectangles (E) ¾″ x 4″
2 rectangles (F) ¾″ x 4½″
Teal Print
4 squares (B) 4″ x 4″
Yellow Print (see instructions)
2 squares 4⅜″ x 4⅜″ ⊠ (C) (there will be 4 extra)
4 squares (G) 4½″ x 4½″

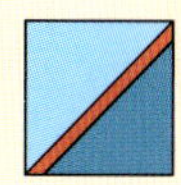

Unit 1
Make 4

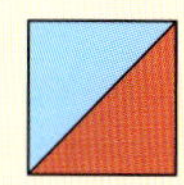

Partial Unit
Make 4

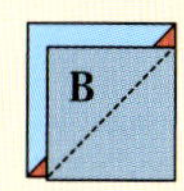

Stitch & Flip

Unit 2
Make 4

The yellow print Ellen used is directional. After cutting the C's, use the 4 triangles with the directional print running perpendicular to the longest side. If you choose not to use a directional print, only 1 square will be needed to cut the C's.

Refer to "Triangle-Squares" in the Techniques file on the PDF. Pair teal tone-on-tone A's with red A's to make 4 partial units. Refer to "Stitch-and-Flip" in the Techniques file on the PDF; join a teal print B to each partial unit as shown to make 4 unit 1's.

Refer to the diagram to join a red D to a yellow C and trim the D even with the edge of C as shown to make a unit 2. Make 4 unit 2's.

Noting the orientations, join the units and patches as shown to complete the block.

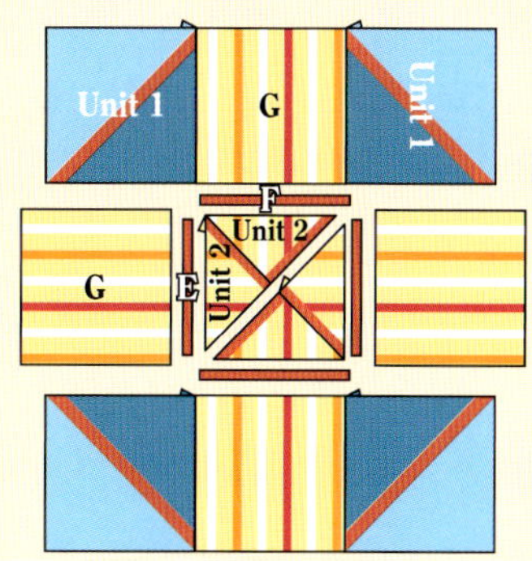

Block Assembly

block no. 981

French Twist

by Celine Perkins • Perkins Dry Goods
perkinsdrygoods.com

Fabric: Downton Abbey from Andover Fabrics, andoverfabrics.com.

Cream Print
2 squares (A) $4\frac{7}{8}$" x $4\frac{7}{8}$"
8 squares (B) $2\frac{1}{2}$" x $2\frac{1}{2}$"
Gray Print
2 squares (A) $4\frac{7}{8}$" x $4\frac{7}{8}$"
4 squares (B) $2\frac{1}{2}$" x $2\frac{1}{2}$"
Purple Tone-on-Tone
8 squares (B) $2\frac{1}{2}$" x $2\frac{1}{2}$"

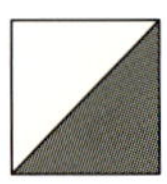

Unit
Make 4

Pair the cream A's with gray A's to make 4 Triangle-Square units.

Sew the units and patches together as shown to complete the block.

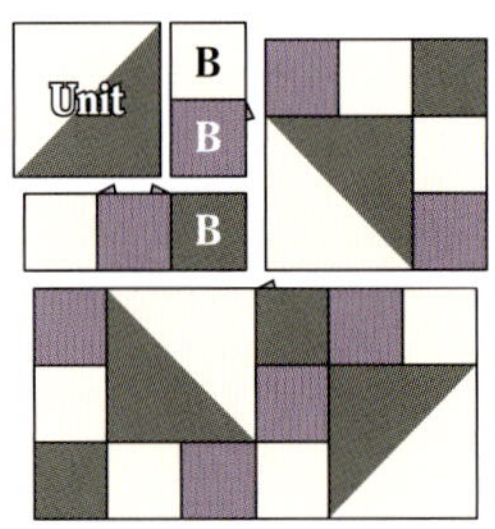

Block Assembly

block no. 982

Well-Suited

by Sarah Price • It's Sew Emma
itssewemma.com

Fabric: Botanics designed by Carolyn Friedlander and Kona Cotton Solids, both from Robert Kaufman, robertkaufman.com.

Green Print
1 square (A) $3\frac{1}{2}$" x $3\frac{1}{2}$"
1 rectangle (C) $3\frac{1}{2}$" x $9\frac{1}{2}$"
Light Gray Solid
6 squares (B) 2" x 2"
2 rectangles (D) 2" x $12\frac{1}{2}$"
4 rectangles (E) $1\frac{1}{2}$" x $12\frac{1}{2}$"
White Print
2 squares (A) $3\frac{1}{2}$" x $3\frac{1}{2}$"
Medium Gray Tone-on-Tone
2 rectangles (E) $1\frac{1}{2}$" x $12\frac{1}{2}$"

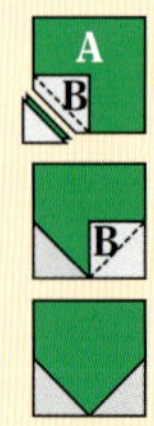

Unit 1
Stitch & Flip
Make 1

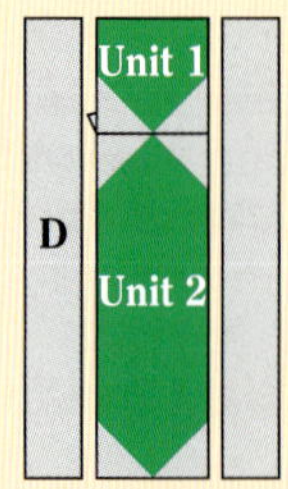

Partial Unit Piecing

Refer to "Stitch-and-Flip" in the Techniques file on the PDF. Use the green A and 2 light gray B's to make unit 1. Make unit 2 using the green C and 4 light gray B's.

Sew unit 1, unit 2 and 2 light gray D's together as shown to make a partial unit. Referring to the diagram, use stitch-and-flip to join white print A's to the top to complete unit 3.

Sew the unit 3 and patches together as shown to complete the block.

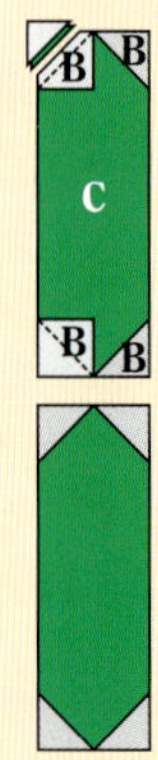

Unit 2
Stitch & Flip
Make 1

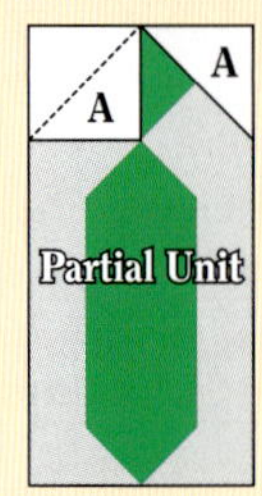

Unit 3
Stitch & Flip
Make 1

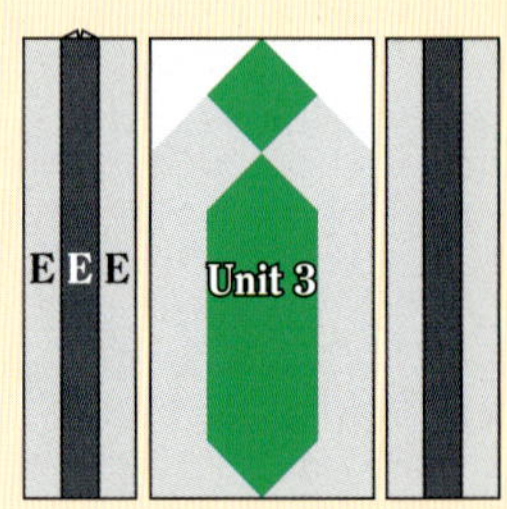

Block Assembly

block no. 983

Sea Glitz

by Rebecca Silbaugh • Ruby Blue Quilting Studio
rubybluequilts.blogspot.com

Rebecca Silbaugh is the author of *Seemingly Scrappy: Get the Look You Love with Fat Quarters and Precuts* for Martingale & Co., shopmartingale.com.

Medium Teal Batik
16 rectangles (A) 1½″ x 2½″
4 squares (B) 1½″ x 1½″

Cream Solid
8 rectangles (A) 1½″ x 2½″
16 squares (B) 1½″ x 1½″
4 rectangles (D) 2½″ x 3½″
4 rectangles (E) 1½″ x 4½″

Light Teal Batik
8 squares (B) 1½″ x 1½″
4 rectangles (C) 2½″ x 4½″

Dark Teal Solid
16 squares (B) 1½″ x 1½″
1 square (F) 2½″ x 2½″

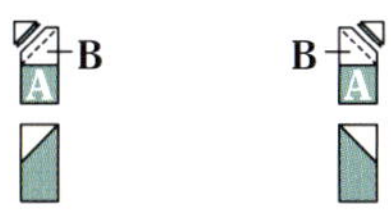

Unit 1
Stitch & Flip
Make 8

Unit 2
Stitch & Flip
Make 8

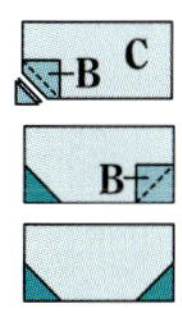

Unit 3
Stitch & Flip
Make 4

Refer to "Stitch-and-Flip" in the Techniques file on the PDF. Use the medium teal A's and cream B's to make 8 unit 1's and 8 unit 2's as shown. Make 4 unit 3's using the light teal C's and dark teal B's as shown.

Sew the units and patches together as shown to complete the block.

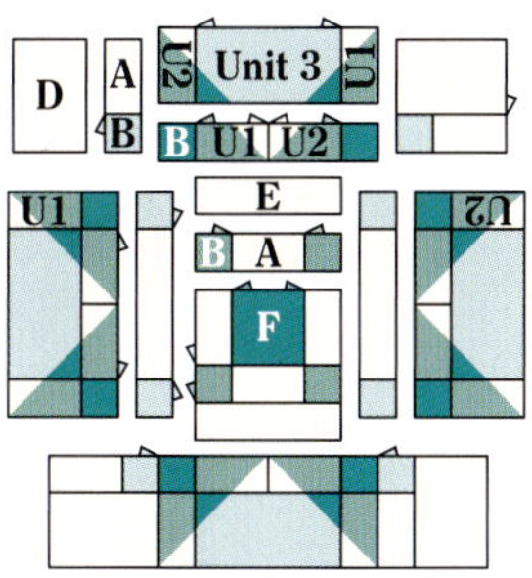

Block Assembly

block no. 984

Star Wash

by Peg Spradlin
handicraftsbypeg.com

Fabric: Tomorrow's Promise designed by Marti Michell for Maywood Studio, maywoodstudio.com.

Cream Tone-on-Tone
4 squares (A) 2⅞″ x 2⅞″
1 square (B) 3¼″ x 3¼″
4 squares (D) 2½″ x 2½″
8 rectangles (E) 1½″ x 2″
16 squares (F) 1½″ x 1½″
8 rectangles (G) 1″ x 1½″
4 rectangles (H) 1½″ x 2½″

Red Tone-on-Tone
4 squares (A) 2⅞″ x 2⅞″
4 squares (C) 1⅞″ x 1⅞″

Light Green Print
5 squares (D) 2½″ x 2½″

Assorted Prints and Tone-on-Tones
28 squares (F) 1½″ x 1½″

Unit
Make 8

Flying Geese
Make 4

Pair the cream A's with red A's to make 8 Triangle-Square unit 1's.

Use the cream B and red C's to make 4 Flying Geese.

Sew the units, Flying Geese and patches together as shown to complete the block.

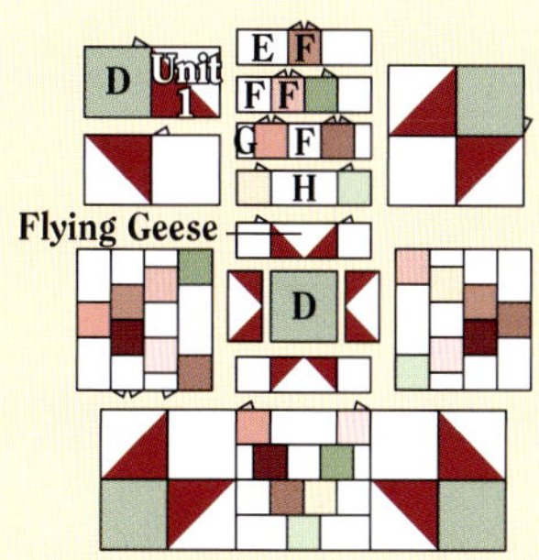

Block Assembly

block no. 985

Scream for Ice Cream

by Denise Starck • Graphic Designer, *Quiltmaker*
quiltmaker.com

Fabric: Various basics from Quilting Treasures, quiltingtreasures.com.

See page 391 on the PDF for patterns and diagrams

Dark Gray Tone-on-Tone
- 4 squares (D) 1" x 1"
- 1 rectangle (E) 2" x 2½"
- 2 rectangles (O) 1" x 1¾"
- 1 rectangle (P) 1" x 6"
- 1 rectangle (S) 2" x 12½"
- foundation patches

White Solid
- 1 rectangle (A) 3⅝" x 4"
- 1 rectangle (J) 5⅞" x 6½"
- foundation patches

Light Blue Tone-on-Tone
- 1 square (B) 1½" x 1½"
- 1 rectangle (F) 1" x 2½"
- 1 rectangle (I) 1" x 4"
- 1 rectangle (L) 1" x 7"
- 2 rectangles (M) 1" x 1½"
- 2 rectangles (O) 1" x 1¾"
- 1 rectangle (Q) 1½" x 6"
- 1 rectangle (R) 2½" x 12½"
- foundation patches

Black Tone-on-Tone
- 2 squares (C) 2½" x 2½"

Dark Blue Tone-on-Tone
- 4 squares (D) 1" x 1"
- 1 rectangle (K) 1" x 10"
- 2 rectangles (N) 1¼" x 1½"
- 1 rectangle (P) 1" x 6"

Light Gray Tone-on-Tone
- 2 rectangles (F) 1" x 2½"
- 1 rectangle (G) 1" x 3"
- 1 rectangle (H) 3" x 4"

Light Brown Tone-on-Tone
- 3 pattern T

Pink, Cream and Medium Brown Tone-on-Tones
from *each*
- 1 pattern U

Fusible web

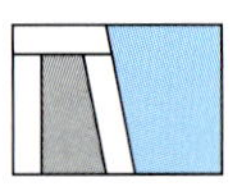

Section
Make 1

Make a paper copy of the foundation section. Refer to the foundation for color placement. Foundation piece the section in numerical order, pressing and trimming after each patch addition.

Refer to "Stitch-and-Flip" in the Techniques file on the PDF. Refer to the diagrams. Make unit 1 using the white A and blue B as shown. Make 2 unit 2's using the black C's, dark gray D's and dark blue D's as shown. Sew the patches, section and units together as shown.

Prepare patches T and U for fusible appliqué; arrange and fuse the patches in place as shown in the appliqué placement diagram. Use matching thread and a machine blanket stitch to sew around the patches to complete the block.

block no. 986

Zig and Zag

by Paula Stoddard • Creative Editor, *Quiltmaker*
quiltmaker.com

Fabric: Flying Sweetly designed by Kim Gann, Zenith and Fizz, all for P&B Textiles, pbtex.com.

◸ = cut in half diagonally
⊠ = cut in half twice diagonally

Dark Purple Tone-on-Tone and Medium Purple Tone-on-Tone
from *each*
- 2 squares 2¾" x 2¾" ⊠ (A)
- 4 squares 2⅜" x 2⅜" ◸ (B)

White Solid
- 4 squares 2¾" x 2¾" ⊠ (A)
- 2 squares 4¼" x 4¼" ⊠ (C)
- 2 rectangles (E) 2" x 12½"

Dark Blue Print and Medium Blue Tone-on-Tone
from *each*
- 1 square 4¼" x 4¼" ⊠ (C)
- 2 squares 3⅞" x 3⅞" ◸ (D)

Unit 1
Make 8

Unit 2
Make 8

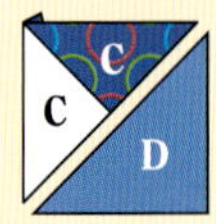

Unit 3
Make 4

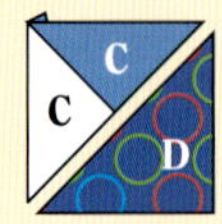

Unit 4
Make 4

Join a dark purple A to a white A as shown; add a medium purple B to make a unit 1. Make 8 unit 1's. Join a medium purple A to a white A as shown; add a dark purple B to make a unit 2. Make 8 unit 2's.

Join a white C to a dark blue C as shown; add a medium blue D to make a unit 3. Make 4 unit 3's. Join a white C to a medium blue C as shown; add a dark blue D to make a unit 4. Make 4 unit 4's.

Sew the units and patches together as shown to complete the block.

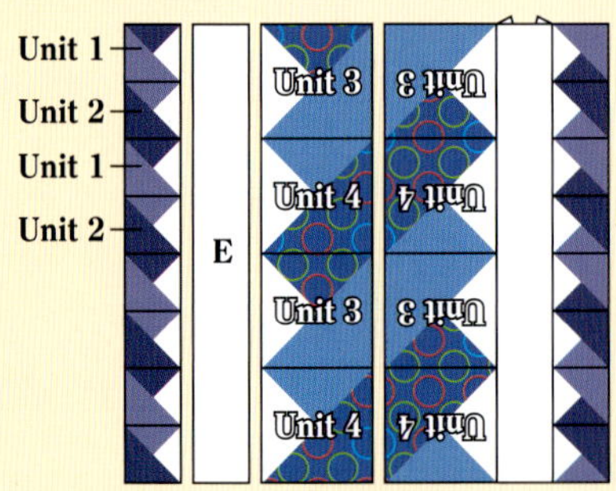

Block Assembly

pieced

block no. 987

Parasol

by Jocelyn Ueng • It's Sew Emma
itssewemma.com

Fabric: Glitz from Michael Miller Fabrics, michaelmillerfabrics.com.

Jocelyn Ueng is the co-author of *Simply Fat Quarters: Quilts with Comfort and Style* for Fat Quarter Shop, fatquartershop.com.

⊠ = cut in half twice diagonally

Aqua Print and Pale Pink Print
from *each*
- 2 rectangles (A) 2½″ x 9½″
- 2 rectangles (D) 2½″ x 8″

White Solid
- 4 squares (B) 2½″ x 2½″
- 1 square 8″ x 8″ ⊠ (C)

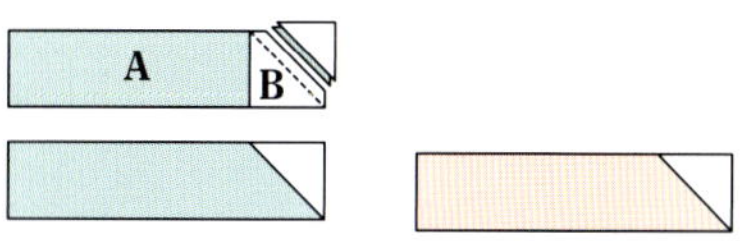

Unit 1
Stitch & Flip
Make 2

Unit 2
Stitch & Flip
Make 2

Refer to "Stitch-and-Flip" in the Techniques file on the PDF. Use the aqua A's and white B's to make 2 unit 1's as shown. Use the pink A's and white B's to make 2 unit 2's.

Sew the units and patches together as shown.

Refer to the trimming diagram; center and trim to 12½" × 12½" as shown to complete the block.

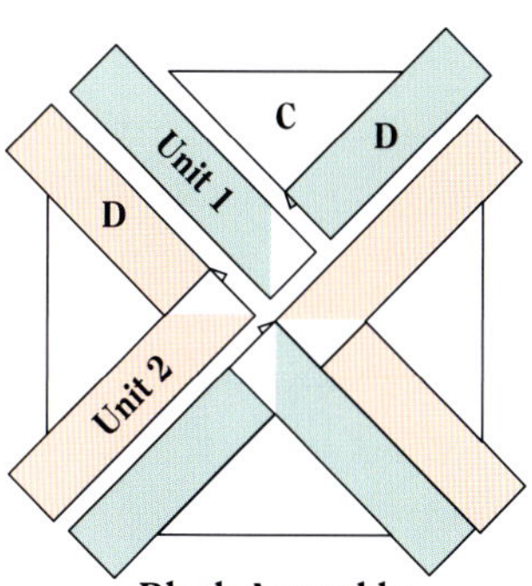

Block Assembly

Trimming Diagram

block no. 988

Chinese Lantern

by Margie Ullery • Ribbon Candy Quilt Co.
ribboncandyquiltcompany.com

Fabric: Botanica by Fresh Batiks for Cloth-works, clothworks.com.

Dark Orange Batik
- 2 rectangles (A) 1½″ x 4½″
- 2 rectangles (C) 1½″ x 2½″

White Solid
- 6 rectangles (A) 1½″ x 4½″
- 20 squares (B) 1½″ x 1½″
- 4 rectangles (C) 1½″ x 2½″
- 1 square (E) 2½″ x 2½″
- 2 rectangles (F) 1½″ x 6½″
- 2 rectangles (G) 1½″ x 8½″
- 2 rectangles (H) 1½″ x 10½″

Orange Batik
- 4 rectangles (C) 1½″ x 2½″
- 4 rectangles (D) 1½″ x 3½″

Yellow Batik
- 4 rectangles (A) 1½″ x 4½″
- 4 rectangles (D) 1½″ x 3½″

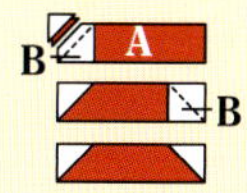

Unit 1
Stitch & Flip
Make 2

Unit 2
Stitch & Flip
Make 2

Unit 3
Stitch & Flip
Make 2

Unit 4
Stitch & Flip
Make 2

Unit 5
Stitch & Flip
Make 2

Unit 6
Stitch & Flip
Make 2

Unit 7
Stitch & Flip
Make 2

Unit 8
Stitch & Flip
Make 2

Unit 9
Stitch & Flip
Make 2

Refer to "Stitch-and-Flip" in the Techniques file on the PDF. Use the dark orange A's and white B's to make 2 unit 1's as shown. Refer to the diagrams and make unit 2's–9's in the same way, using the colors and patches shown.

Sew the units and patches together as shown to complete the block.

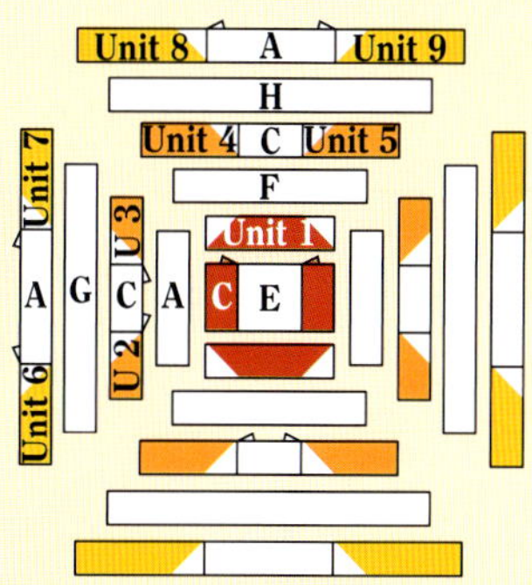

Block Assembly

block no. 989
Firelight

by Martha Walker • Wagons West Designs
wagonswestdesigns.com

Martha Walker is the author of *Be Merry: Quilts and Projects for Your Holiday Home* for Kansas City Star Quilts, pickledish.com.

◸ = cut in half diagonally

Assorted Red Prints and Tone-on-Tones
- 4 (matching) squares (A) 3½″ x 3½″
- 18 squares (B) 2″ x 2″ (cut 1 pair of matching B's for the block center)
- 8 squares 2⅜″ x 2⅜″ ◸ (D)

Assorted Tan Prints and Tone-on-Tones
- 8 squares (B) 2″ x 2″
- 12 rectangles (C) 2″ x 3½″
- 8 squares 2⅜″ x 2⅜″ ◸ (D)

Teal Tone-on-Tone
- 8 squares (B) 2″ x 2″

Teal Print
- 2 squares (B) 2″ x 2″

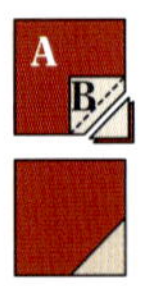

Unit 1
Stitch & Flip
Make 4

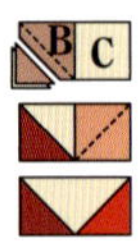

Unit 2
Stitch & Flip
Make 8

Unit 3
Stitch & Flip
Make 4

Refer to "Stitch-and-Flip" in the Techniques file on the PDF. Use the red A's and tan B's to make 4 unit 1's.

Using assorted red B's and tan C's, make 8 unit 2's as shown. Use the teal tone-on-tone B's with tan C's to make 4 unit 3's.

Sew the units and patches together as shown to complete the block.

Block Assembly

block no. 990
Glee

by Shayla Wolf • Sassafras Lane Designs
sassafras-lane.com

Fabric: Indian Summer designed by Sarah Watson for Art Gallery Fabrics, artgalleryfabrics.com.

Dark Blue Solid
- 1 square (A) 4½″ x 4½″
- 1 rectangle (J) 6½″ x 15½″

Pale Orange Tone-on-Tone
- 1 rectangle (B) 2″ x 9½″
- 1 rectangle (C) 2″ x 6¼″

Gray Print
- 1 rectangle (D) 2″ x 11″
- 1 rectangle (E) 2″ x 7¾″

Blue Print
- 1 rectangle (F) 2″ x 12½″
- 1 rectangle (G) 2″ x 9¼″

Orange Print
- 1 rectangle (H) 2″ x 14″
- 1 rectangle (I) 2″ x 10¾″

Light Blue Tone-on-Tone
- 1 rectangle (K) 2½″ x 7″
- 1 rectangle (L) 3½″ x 7½″

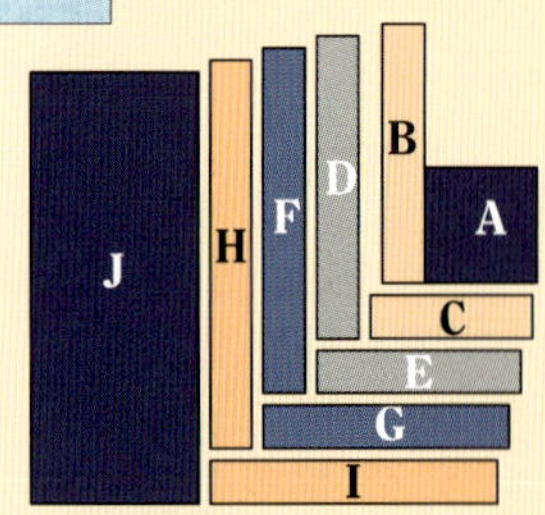

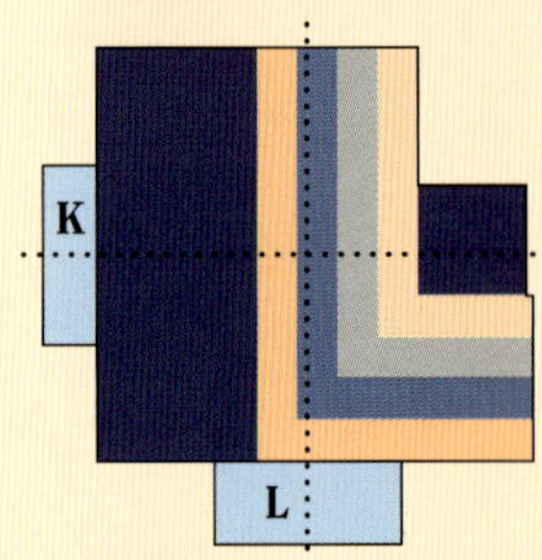

Block Piecing

Sew patches A–J together as shown. Fold the partial block in half both ways and fold patches K and L crosswise; lightly crease the folds. Matching the folds, join the K and L to the partial block as shown.

Aligning a 12½" square ruler as shown in the trimming diagram; trim to 12½" × 12½" to complete the block.

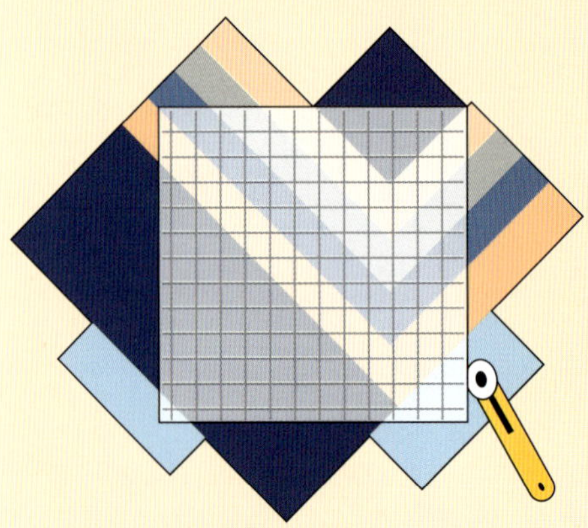
Trimming Diagram

block no. 991
Diamonds Are Forever

by Susan Work • Clothesline Quilts
clotheslinequilts.com

Fabric: Ameila and Dovetail Batiks II, both by Jo Morton for Andover Fabrics, andoverfabrics.com.

Black Print
- 2 squares (A) 3⅞"x 3⅞"
- 1 square (B) 5¼"x 5¼"
- 4 squares (C) 2⅞"x 2⅞"

Mauve Batik
- 2 squares (A) 3⅞"x 3⅞"
- 1 square (D) 4½"x 4½"

Cream Print
- 1 square (B) 5¼"x 5¼"
- 4 squares (C) 2⅞"x 2⅞"
- 4 squares (E) 2½"x 2½"
- 4 rectangles (F) 1½"x 3½"
- 4 rectangles (G) 1½"x 4½"

Unit 1
Make 4

Flying Geese 1
Make 4

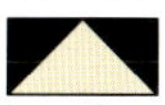

Flying Geese 2
Make 4

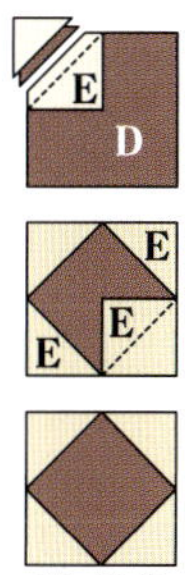

Unit 2
Make 1

Pair the black A's with mauve A's to make 4 Triangle-Square unit 1's.

Use the black B and cream C's to make 4 Flying Geese 1's. Use the cream B and black C's to make 4 Flying Geese 2's.

Refer to "Stitch-and-Flip" in the Techniques file on the PDF. Use the mauve D and cream E's to make unit 2.

Sew the units, Flying Geese and patches together as shown to complete the block.

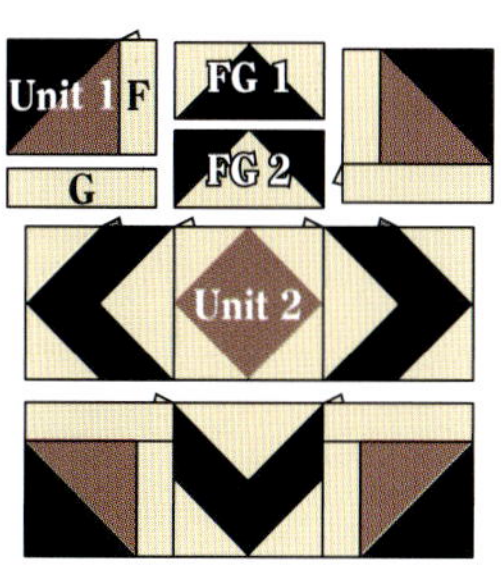

Block Assembly

block no. 992
Serendipity Stars

by Corey Yoder
littlemissshabby.com

Fabric: Various lines from Moda Fabrics, unitednotions.com.

Corey Yoder is the author of *Playful Petals* for Stash Books, ctpub.com.

Red Print
- 8 squares (A) 2⅜"x 2⅜"
- 1 square (B) 4¼"x 4¼"
- 4 squares (E) 2"x 2"

Cream Solid
- 12 squares (A) 2⅜"x 2⅜"
- 1 square (B) 4¼"x 4¼"
- 1 square (C) 2¾"x 2¾"
- 4 squares (E) 2"x 2"
- 4 squares (G) 1¼"x 1¼"

Aqua Print
- 8 squares (A) 2⅜"x 2⅜"
- 1 square (B) 4¼"x 4¼"
- 4 squares (E) 2"x 2"
- 4 rectangles (F) 2"x 3½"

Brown Tone-on-Tone
- 4 squares (D) 1⅝"x 1⅝"
- 1 square (E) 2"x 2"

Unit 1
Make 8

Unit 2
Make 8

Flying Geese 1
Make 4

Flying Geese 2
Make 4

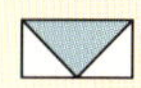

Flying Geese 3
Make 4

Flying Geese 4
Make 4

Pair 4 red A's with cream A's to make 8 Triangle-Square unit 1's. Use 4 aqua A's and cream A's to make 8 unit 2's.

Use a cream B with red A's to make 4 Flying Geese 1's. Use a red B with aqua A's to make 4 Flying Geese 2's. Use an aqua B with cream A's to make 4 Flying Geese 3's. To make 4 Flying Geese 4's, use a cream C with brown D's.

Sew the units, Flying Geese and patches together as shown to complete the block.

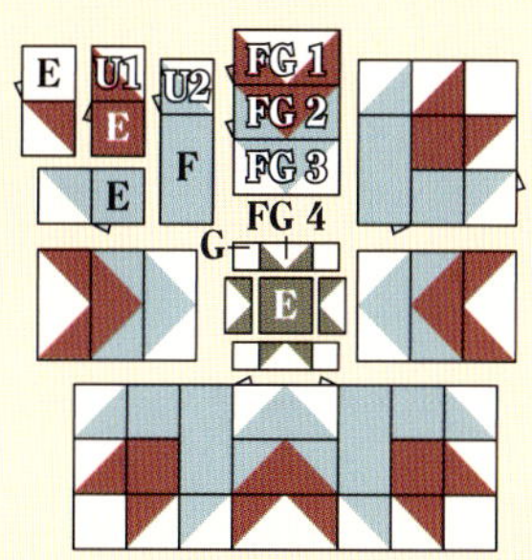

Block Assembly

block no. 993

Churned Star

by Nancy Allen
bountifulheirlooms.blogspot.com

Nancy Allen is the author of *Triple-Play Scrap Quilting–Planned, Coordinated, and Make-Do Styles* for Martingale & Co., shopmartingale.com.

⧄ = cut in half diagonally
⊠ = cut in half twice diagonally

Cream Print
- 4 squares 2 3/8″x 2 3/8″ ⧄ (A)
- 2 squares 4 1/4″x 4 1/4″ ⊠ (B)
- 1 square (D) 3 1/2″ x 3 1/2″

Black Print
- 4 squares 2 3/8″x 2 3/8″ ⧄ (A)
- 2 rectangles (E) 2″x 3 1/2″
- 2 rectangles (F) 2″x 6 1/2″

Rust Print
- 1 square 7 1/4″x 7 1/4″ ⊠ (C)
- 4 squares (D) 3 1/2″x 3 1/2″

Noting the orientation of the A's, sew the patches together as shown to complete the block.

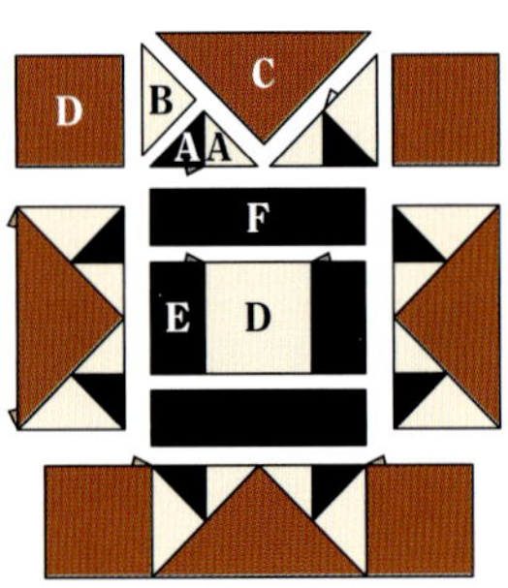

Block Piecing

pieced

block no. 994

Cabin Stars

by Andee Andriole • Sisters' Quilting Trunk
sistersquiltingtrunk.com

Fabric: Nature Elements from Art Gallery Fabrics, artgalleryfabrics.com.

⊠ = cut in half twice diagonally

Pale Aqua Print
- 2 squares (A) 1 7/8″x 1 7/8″
- 2 squares 5 1/4″x 5 1/4″ ⊠ (F)
- 1 square 3 1/4″x 3 1/4″ ⊠ (G) (there will be 2 extra)

Cream Print
- 2 squares (A) 1 7/8″x 1 7/8″
- 1 square 5 1/4″x 5 1/4″ ⊠ (F)
- 1 square 3 1/4″x 3 1/4″ ⊠ (G) (there will be 2 extra)

Light Teal Print
- 4 squares (B) 1 1/2″x 1 1/2″
- 4 rectangles (C) 1 1/2″x 2 1/2″

Medium Teal Print
- 4 rectangles (C) 1 1/2″x 2 1/2″
- 4 rectangles (D) 1 1/2″x 3 1/2″

Dark Teal Print
- 4 rectangles (D) 1 1/2″x 3 1/2″
- 4 rectangles (E) 1 1/2″x 4 1/2″

Light Gray Print
- 1 square 5 1/4″x 5 1/4″ ⊠ (F)

Medium Gray Print
- 2 rectangles (C) 1 1/2″x 2 1/2″
- 2 rectangles (E) 1 1/2″x 4 1/2″

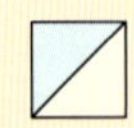

Unit
Make 4

Pair the pale aqua A's with the cream A's to make 4 Triangle-Square units.

Sew the units and patches together as shown to complete the block.

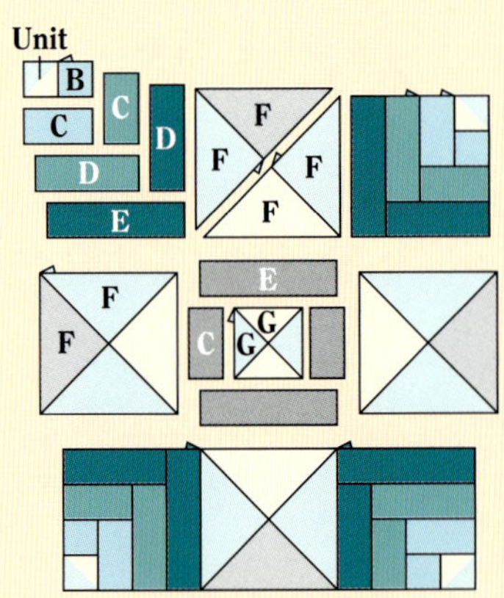

Block Assembly

block no. 995

Bunny-Go-Round

by Deborah Bahr-Johnson • In the Doghouse Designs
inthedoghousedesigns.com

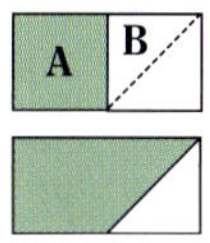

Unit 1
Stitch & Flip
Make 1 of each color

Green, Pink, Yellow and Blue Tone-on-Tones
from *each*
- 2 rectangles (A) 2½" x 4½"
- 1 square (C) 4½" x 4½"

Cream Tone-on-Tone
- 12 squares (B) 2½" x 2½"
- 4 squares (D) 1¾" x 1¾"

Buttons 8 black at ⅜"

Black embroidery floss

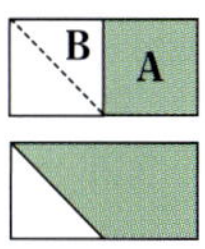

Unit 2
Stitch & Flip
Make 1 of each color

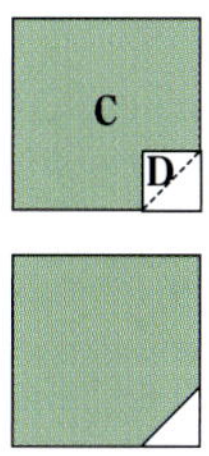

Unit 3
Stitch & Flip
Make 1 of each color

Refer to "Stitch-and-Flip" in the Techniques file on the PDF. Use the A's from each color and the cream B's to make 1 unit 1 from each color and 1 unit 2 from each color as shown. Use a C from each color and the cream D's to make 1 unit 3 from each color.

Sew the units and patches together as shown to make the block.

Refer to the embroidery and button placement diagram; use 3 strands of floss and an outline stitch as shown for the whiskers. Add the buttons for eyes to complete the block.

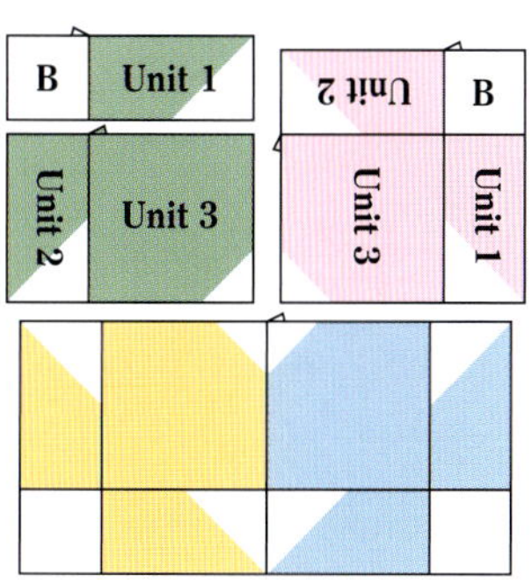

Block Assembly

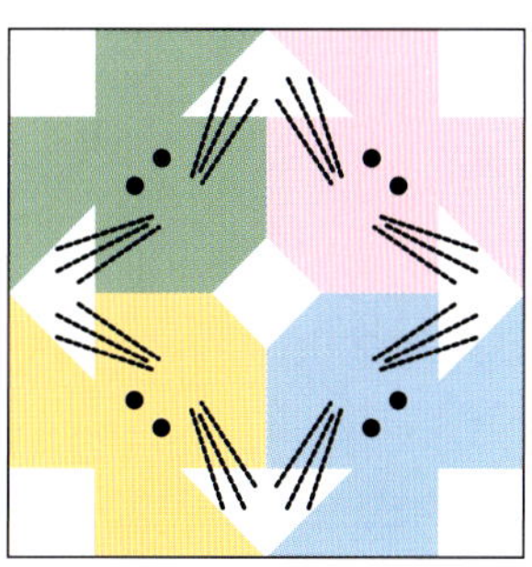

Embroidery & Button Placement

block no. 996

Butterfly

by Jennifer Ball
thequiltedcat.wordpress.com

Fabric: Tokyo from Red Rooster Fabrics, redroosterfabrics.com.

White Tone-on-Tone
- 2 rectangles (A) 2½" x 12½"
- 8 rectangles (B) 1½" x 3½"
- 8 squares (C) 1½" x 1½"
- 2 rectangles (D) 1½" x 4½"
- 14 rectangles (E) 1½" x 2½"

Assorted Blue Tone-on-Tones
- 28 squares (C) 1½" x 1½"

Metallic thread

Sew the patches together as shown.

Refer to the embroidery placement diagram. Use a straight stitch and metallic thread for the butterfly antennae to complete the block.

Block Piecing

Embroidery Placement

block no. 997

In the Middle

by Carolyn Beam • Content Director, *Quiltmaker*
quiltmaker.com

Fabric: Zuzu designed by Alice Kennedy and Rain Basic, both from Timeless Treasures, ttfabrics.com.

Black Tone-on-Tone
- 4 squares (A) 2½″ x 2½″

Cream Print
- 4 rectangles (B) 1″ x 2½″
- 4 rectangles (C) 1″ x 3″
- 8 rectangles (D) 1½″ x 2″
- 4 rectangles (G) 1″ x 4½″
- 4 rectangles (H) 1″ x 5″
- 8 rectangles (I) 2″ x 2½″

Red Tone-on-Tone
- 4 squares (E) 2″ x 2″
- 4 rectangles (F) 2″ x 3½″

Black and White Print
- 4 rectangles (J) 2″ x 3″
- 4 rectangles (K) 2″ x 4½″

Sew the patches together as shown to complete the block.

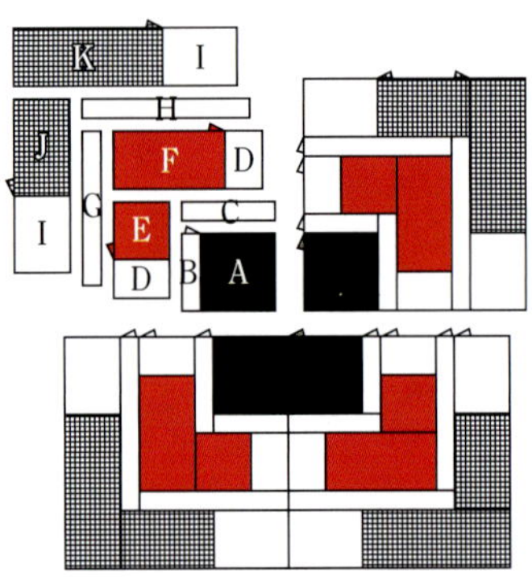

Block Piecing

block no. 998

Pivot Point

by Donna Benham • DB Designs

⧄ = cut in half diagonally

Teal Batik
- 2 squares (A) 5½″ x 5½″

Gold Batik
- 2 squares (A) 5½″ x 5½″
- 4 rectangles (B) 2⅝″ x 5″

Dark Blue Batik
- 1 square (C) 2⅝″ x 2⅝″
- 2 squares 5⅜″ x 5⅜″ ⧄ (D)

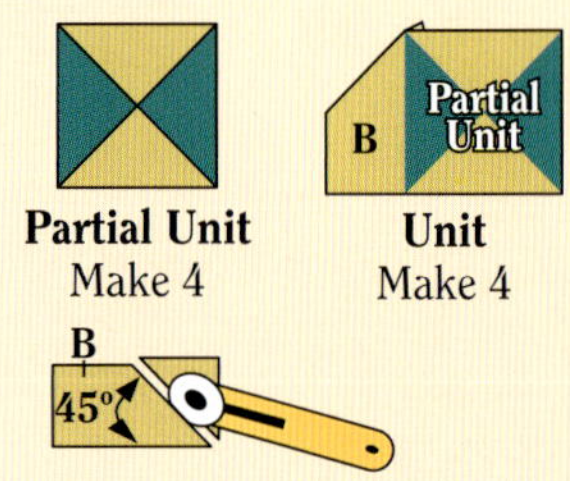

Refer to "Quarter-Square Triangles" in the Techniques file on the PDF. Pair the teal A's with gold A's to make 4 partial units. Trim the gold B's as shown. Referring to the diagram, sew a gold B to each partial unit. Make 4 units.

Sew a unit to the top of the dark blue C with a partial seam as shown. Sew a unit to the right, a unit to the bottom, and a unit to the left as shown. Finish the partial seam to make the block center.

Sew the dark blue D's to the block corners as shown to complete the block.

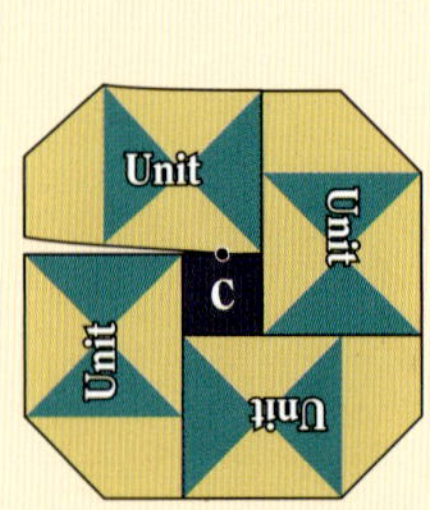

• = Partial Seam

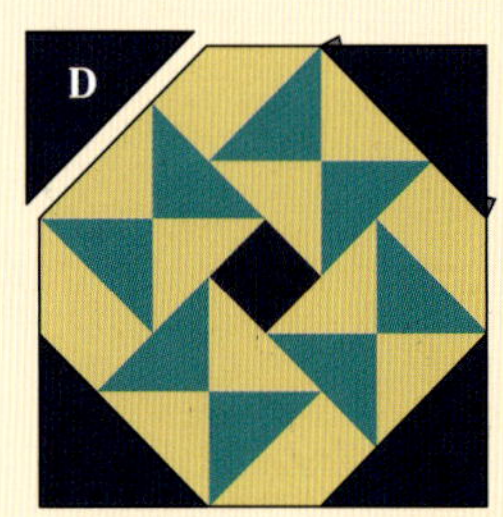

Block Assembly

pieced

block no. 999

Shimmer

by Karen Bialik • The Fabric Addict
fabricaddict.net

Fabric: Artisan Spirit Shimmer designed by Deborah Edwards for Northcott, Northcott.com.

See page 404 on the PDF for pattern

Light Orange and Yellow Tone-on-Tones
from *each*
 6 squares (A) 1⅞″ x 1⅞″

Light Blue Tone-on-Tone
 8 squares (A) 1⅞″ x 1⅞″
 4 template C

Medium Orange Tone-on-Tone
 4 *each* templates B and Br

Medium Blue Print
 2 rectangles (D) 1½″ x 8¾″
 2 rectangles (F) 1½″ x 10½″

Dark Blue Print and Dark Blue Tone-on-Tone
from *each*
 4 rectangles (D) 1½″ x 8¾″

Navy Blue Tone-on-Tone
 4 rectangles (E) 2½″ x 8¾″

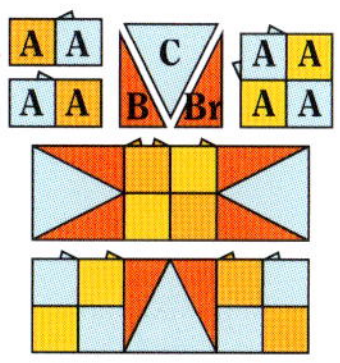

Center Piecing

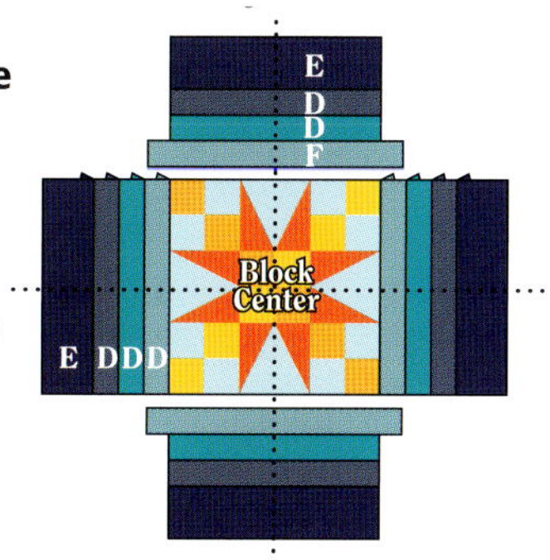

Block Assembly

Join patches A–C as shown in the center piecing diagram.

Refer to the block assembly diagram. Fold the block center in half both ways and strips D–F in half crosswise and lightly crease the folds. Matching centers, join the medium blue D's, dark blue print D's, dark blue tone-on-tone D's and the navy blue E's to the sides of the block center as shown. Join the medium blue F's, dark blue print D's, dark blue tone-on-tone D's and the navy blue E's to the top and bottom in the same way.

To finish the block, use a 12½" square ruler to center and trim the block as shown in the block trimming diagram.

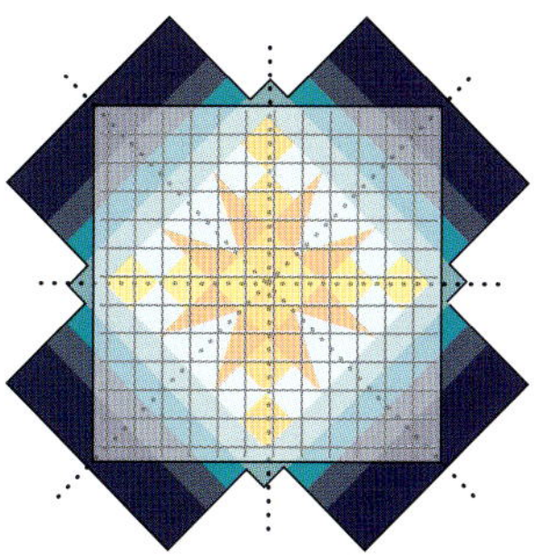

Block Trimming

block no. 1000

Forever

by Sandi Blackwell • Stitched Buy
stitchedbuy.com

Fabric: Quilted in Honor designed by Kathy Engle for Island Batik, islandbatik.com.

Sandi Blackwell is the author of *Simply Sensational Square-agonals Quilts* for Landauer Publishing, landauerpub.com.

Dark Blue Batik
 2 squares (A) 5″ x 5″
 4 squares (E) 1½″ x 1½″

Red Batik
 2 rectangles (B) 2″ x 5″
 6 rectangles (C) 2″ x 3½″
 2 rectangles (D) 2″ x 8″

White Tone-on-Tone
 2 rectangles (B) 2″ x 5″
 4 rectangles (C) 2″ x 3½″
 5 squares (E) 1½″ x 1½″

Sew the patches together as shown to complete the block.

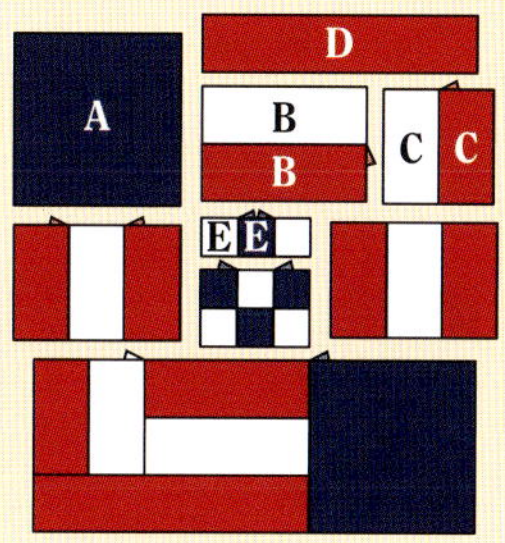

Block Piecing

SETTINGS & YARDAGES

Use these sample settings to join multiple 12" blocks.

Before cutting and sewing bed sizes, measure the length and width of your mattress top and determine how many inches you want your quilt to drop over each side. Adjust border widths as needed; additional yardage may be required.

Twin, 62" x 90"

Block Setting: 4 x 6

Sashes $1\frac{1}{8}$ yards
38 rectangles (A) $2\frac{1}{2}$" x $12\frac{1}{2}$"
Cornerstones $\frac{1}{8}$ yard
15 squares (B) $2\frac{1}{2}$" x $2\frac{1}{2}$"
Border/Binding $2\frac{1}{2}$ yards
2 strips $4\frac{1}{2}$" x 85" for sides
2 strips $4\frac{1}{2}$" x 65" for top/bottom
4 strips $2\frac{1}{4}$" x 81" for binding
Backing $5\frac{7}{8}$ yards
Batting 70" x 98"

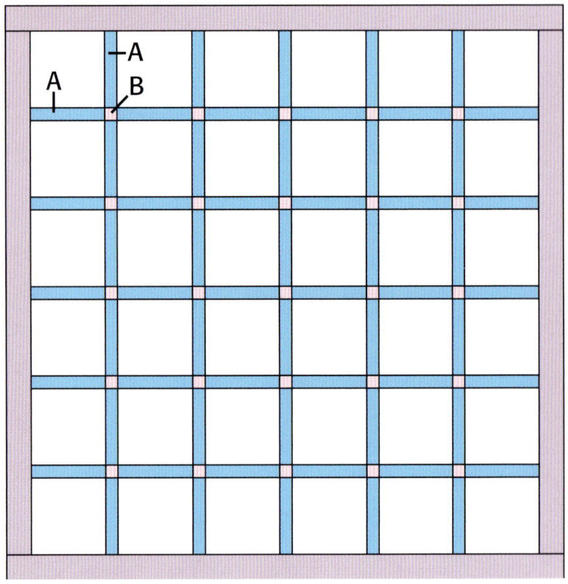

Queen, 90" x 90"

Block Setting: 6 x 6

Sashes $1\frac{5}{8}$ yards
60 rectangles (A) $2\frac{1}{2}$" x $12\frac{1}{2}$"
Cornerstones $\frac{1}{4}$ yard
25 squares (B) $2\frac{1}{2}$" x $2\frac{1}{2}$"
Border/Binding $2\frac{3}{4}$ yards
2 strips $4\frac{1}{2}$" x 85" for sides
2 strips $4\frac{1}{2}$" x 93" for top/bottom
5 strips $2\frac{1}{4}$" x 77" for binding
Backing $8\frac{3}{4}$ yards
Batting 98" x 98"

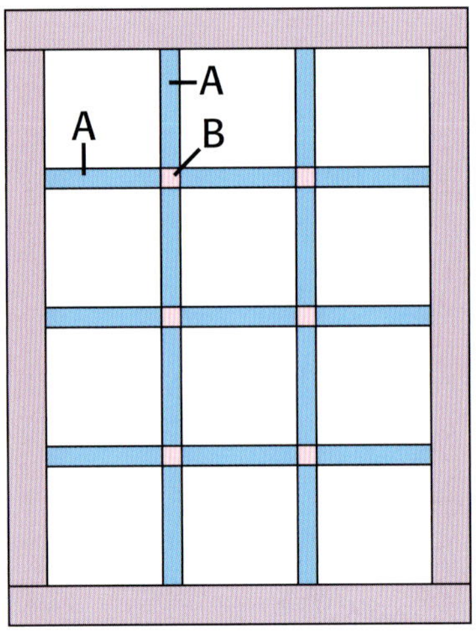

Throw, 50" x 64"

Block Setting: 3 x 4

Sashes $\frac{5}{8}$ yard
17 rectangles (A) $2\frac{1}{2}$" x $12\frac{1}{2}$"
Cornerstones $\frac{1}{8}$ yard
6 squares (B) $2\frac{1}{2}$" x $2\frac{1}{2}$"
Border/Binding $1\frac{3}{4}$ yards
2 strips $4\frac{1}{2}$" x 57" for sides
2 strips $4\frac{1}{2}$" x 51" for top/bottom
5 strips $2\frac{1}{4}$" x 51" for binding
Backing $3\frac{3}{4}$ yards
Batting 54" x 72"

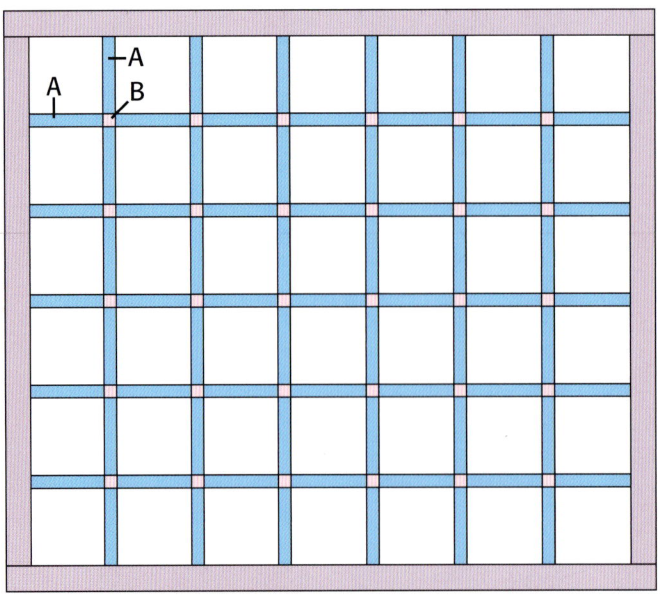

King, 104" x 90"

Block Setting: 7 x 6

Sashes $1\frac{7}{8}$ yard
71 rectangles (A) $2\frac{1}{2}$" x $12\frac{1}{2}$"
Cornerstones $\frac{1}{4}$ yard
30 squares (B) $2\frac{1}{2}$" x $2\frac{1}{2}$"
Border/Binding $3\frac{1}{8}$ yards
2 strips $4\frac{1}{2}$" x 85" for sides
2 strips $4\frac{1}{2}$" x 107" for top/bottom
4 strips $2\frac{1}{4}$" x 102" for binding
Backing $8\frac{3}{4}$ yards
Batting 112" x 98"

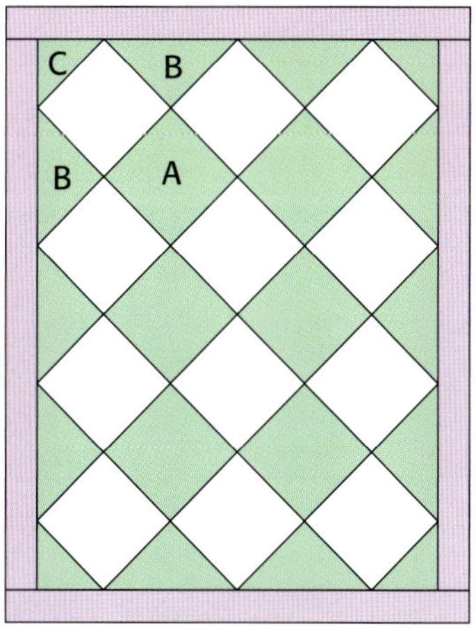

Throw, 59″ x 76″

Block Setting: 3 x 4

Setting Squares and Triangles 2 yards
- 6 squares (A) 12½″ x 12½″
- 3 squares 18¼″ x 18¼″ cut diagonally twice to yield 12 triangles (B) ⊠ (2 extra)
- 2 squares 9⅜″ x 9⅜″ cut diagonally to yield 4 triangles (C) ⧄

Border/Binding 2¼ yards
- 2 strips 4½″ x 71″ for sides
- 2 strips 4½″ x 62″ for top/bottom
- 5 strips 2¼″ x 59″ for binding

Backing 5 yards

Batting 67″ x 84″

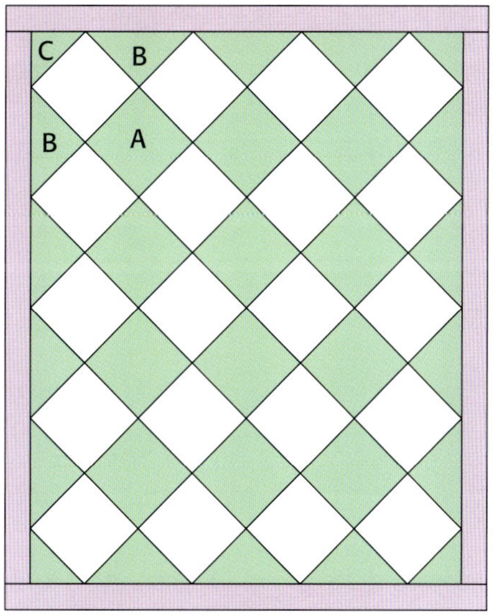

Twin, 76″ x 93″

Block Setting: 4 x 5

Setting Squares and Triangles 3 yards
- 12 squares (A) 12½″ x 12½″
- 4 squares 18¼″ x 18¼″ cut diagonally twice to yield 16 triangles (B) ⊠ (2 extra)
- 2 squares 9⅜″ x 9⅜″ cut diagonally to yield 4 triangles (C) ⧄

Border/Binding 2¾ yards
- 2 strips 4½″ x 88″ for sides
- 2 strips 4½″ x 79″ for top/bottom
- 5 strips 2¼″ x 73″ for binding

Backing 7½ yards

Batting 84″ x 101″

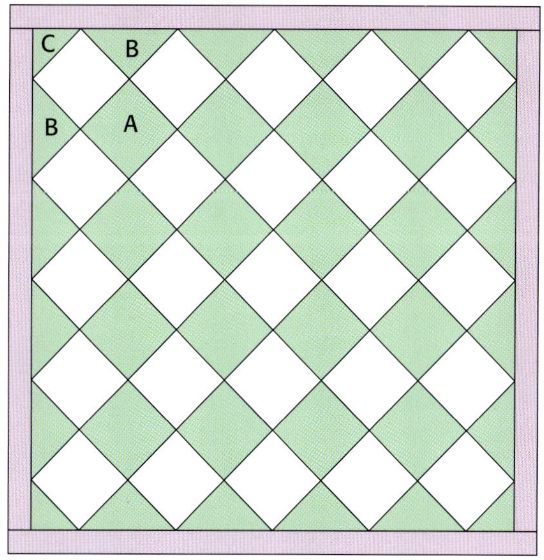

Queen, 93″ x 93″

Block Setting: 5 x 5

Setting Squares and Triangles 3⅜ yards
- 16 squares (A) 12½″ x 12½″
- 4 squares 18¼″ x 18¼″ cut diagonally twice to yield 16 triangles (B) ⊠
- 2 squares 9⅜″ x 9⅜″ cut diagonally to yield 4 triangles (C) ⧄

Border/Binding 3 yards
- 2 strips 4½″ x 88″ for sides
- 2 strips 4½″ x 96″ for top/bottom
- 5 strips 2¼″ x 79″ for binding

Backing 9 yards

Batting 101″ x 101″

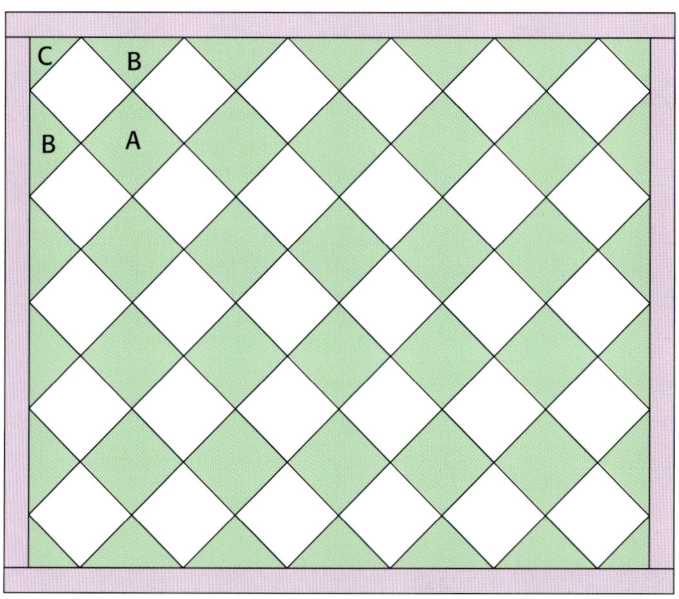

King, 110″ x 93″

Block Setting: 6 x 5

Setting Squares and Triangles 4¼ yards
- 20 squares (A) 12½″ x 12½″
- 5 squares 18¼″ x 18¼″ cut diagonally twice to yield 20 triangles (B) ⊠ (2 extra)
- 2 squares 9⅜″ x 9⅜″ cut diagonally to yield 4 triangles (C) ⧄

Border/Binding 3½ yards
- 2 strips 4½″ x 88″ for sides
- 2 strips 4½″ x 113″ for top/bottom
- 4 strips 2¼″ x 107″ for binding

Backing 9 yards

Batting 118″ x 101″

SETTINGS & YARDAGES

Use these sample settings to join multiple 12" blocks.

Before cutting and sewing bed sizes, measure the length, width and depth of your mattress top and determine how many inches you want your quilt to drop over each side. Adjust border widths as needed; additional yardage may be required. See more settings and yardages at quiltmaker.com.

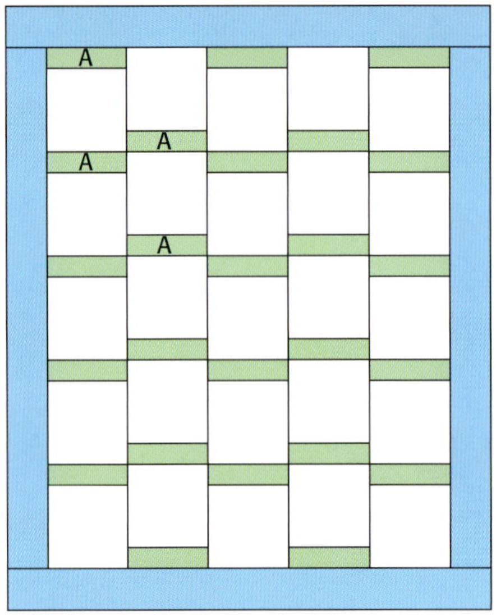

Twin, 72″ x 87″

Block Setting: 5 x 5

Sashes $1\frac{1}{8}$ yards
25 rectangles (A) $3\frac{1}{2}$″ x $12\frac{1}{2}$″

Border/Binding $2\frac{3}{8}$ yards
2 strips $6\frac{1}{2}$″ x 78″ for sides
2 strips $6\frac{1}{2}$″ x 75″ for top/bottom
5 strips $2\frac{1}{4}$″ x 69″ for binding

Backing $5\frac{3}{4}$ yards

Batting 80″ x 95″

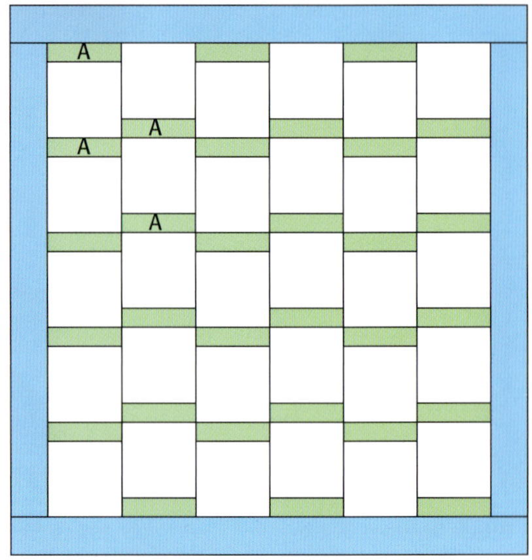

Double, 84″ x 87″

Block Setting: 6 x 5

Sashes $1\frac{1}{8}$ yards
30 rectangles (A) $3\frac{1}{2}$″ x $12\frac{1}{2}$″

Border/Binding $2\frac{5}{8}$ yards
2 strips $6\frac{1}{2}$″ x 78″ for sides
2 strips $6\frac{1}{2}$″ x 87″ for top/bottom
5 strips $2\frac{1}{4}$″ x 73″ for binding

Backing $8\frac{1}{4}$ yards

Batting 92″ x 95″

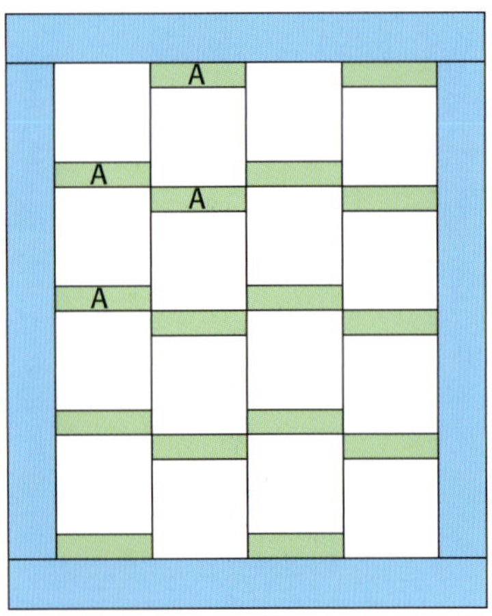

Throw, 60″ x 72″

Block Setting: 4 x 4

Sashes $\frac{3}{4}$ yard
16 rectangles (A) $3\frac{1}{2}$″ x $12\frac{1}{2}$″

Border/Binding $1\frac{7}{8}$ yards
2 strips $6\frac{1}{2}$″ x 63″ for sides
2 strips $6\frac{1}{2}$″ x 63″ for top/bottom
5 strips $2\frac{1}{4}$″ x 58″ for binding

Backing $4\frac{1}{8}$ yards

Batting 68″ x 80″

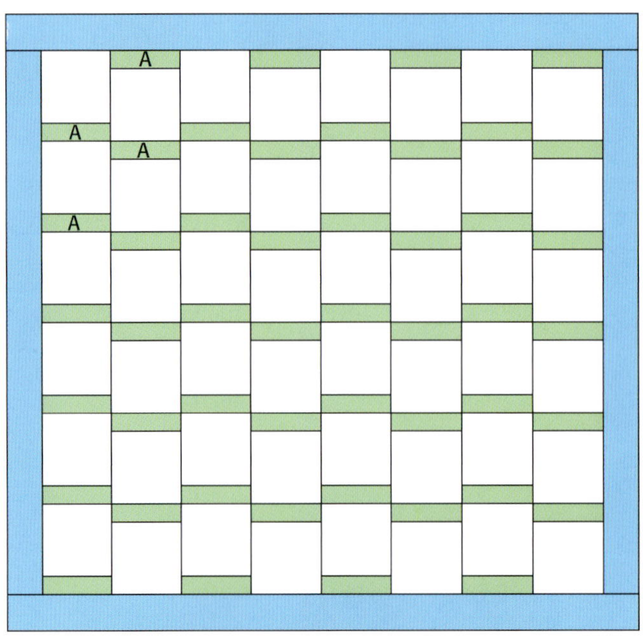

King, 108″ x 102″

Block Setting: 8 x 6

Sashes $1\frac{3}{4}$ yards
48 rectangles (A) $3\frac{1}{2}$″ x $12\frac{1}{2}$″

Border/Binding $3\frac{1}{4}$ yards
2 strips $6\frac{1}{2}$″ x 93″ for sides
2 strips $6\frac{1}{2}$″ x 111″ for top/bottom
4 strips $2\frac{1}{4}$″ x 89″ for binding

Backing $9\frac{3}{4}$ yards

Batting 116″ x 110″

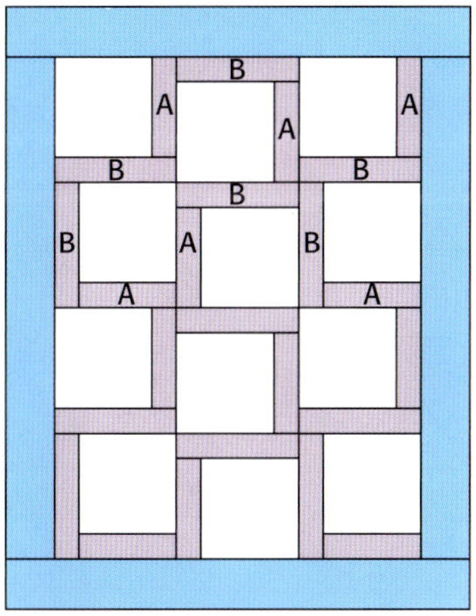

Throw, 57" x 72"

Block Setting: 3 x 4

Sashes 1⅛ yards
- 12 rectangles (A) 3½" x 12½"
- 12 rectangles (B) 3½" x 15½"

Border/Binding 1⅞ yards
- 2 strips 6½" x 63" for sides
- 2 strips 6½" x 60" for top/bottom
- 5 strips 2¼" x 57" for binding

Backing 4 yards

Batting 65" x 80"

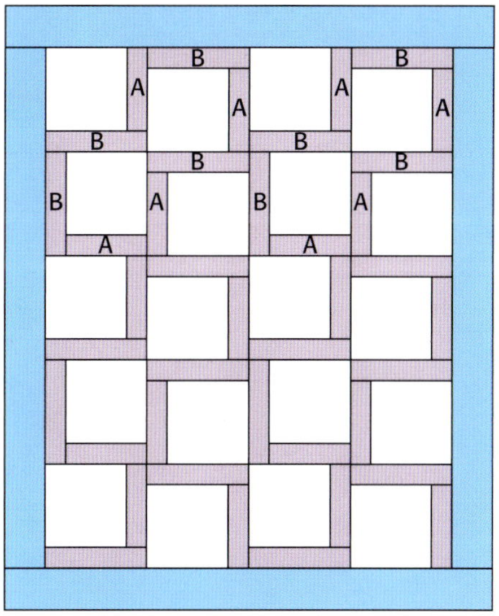

Twin, 72" x 87"

Block Setting: 4 x 5

Sashes 1⅞ yards
- 20 rectangles (A) 3½" x 12½"
- 20 rectangles (B) 3½" x 15½"

Border/Binding 2⅜ yards
- 2 strips 6½" x 78" for sides
- 2 strips 6½" x 75" for top/bottom
- 5 strips 2¼" x 69" for binding

Backing 5¾ yards

Batting 80" x 95"

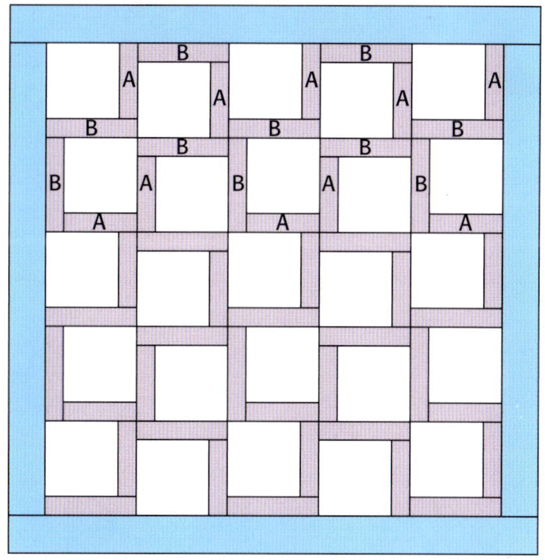

Double/Queen, 87" x 87"

Block Setting: 5 x 5

Sashes 2⅜ yards
- 25 rectangles (A) 3½" x 12½"
- 25 rectangles (B) 3½" x 15½"

Border/Binding 2⅝ yards
- 2 strips 6½" x 78" for sides
- 2 strips 6½" x 90" for top/bottom
- 5 strips 2¼" x 75" for binding

Backing 8½ yards

Batting 95" x 95"

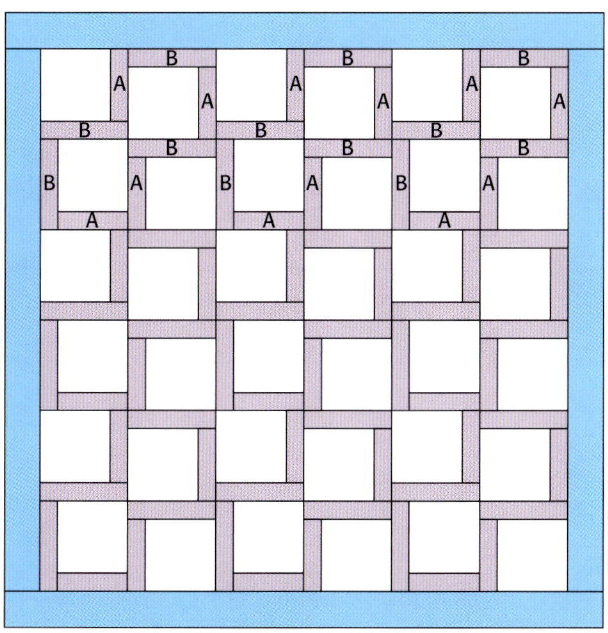

Queen/King, 102" x 102"

Block Setting: 6 x 6

Sashes 3¼ yards
- 36 rectangles (A) 3½" x 12½"
- 36 rectangles (B) 3½" x 15½"

Border/Binding 3⅛ yards
- 2 strips 6½" x 93" for sides
- 2 strips 6½" x 105" for top/bottom
- 5 strips 2¼" x 89" for binding

Backing 9¾ yards

Batting 110" x 110"

SETTINGS & YARDAGES

Use these sample settings to join multiple 12" blocks.

Before cutting and sewing bed sizes, measure the length, width and depth of your mattress top and determine how many inches you want your quilt to drop over each side. Adjust border widths as needed; additional yardage may be required. See more settings and yardages at quiltmaker.com.

Twin, 67" x 86"

Block Setting: 3 x 4

Sashes 1⅛ yards
48 rectangles (A) 2" x 12½"
Cornerstones ⅛ yard
17 squares (B) 2" x 2"
Setting Triangles 1⅛ yards
3 squares 16⅛" x 16⅛" cut diagonally twice to yield 12 triangles (C) ⊠ (there will be 2 extra)
2 squares 7¼" x 7¼" cut diagonally to yield 4 triangles (D) ⧄
Border/Binding 2¼ yards
2 strips 6½" x 77" for sides
2 strips 6½" x 70" for top/bottom
5 strips 2¼" x 66" for binding
Backing 5⅝ yards
Batting 75" x 94"

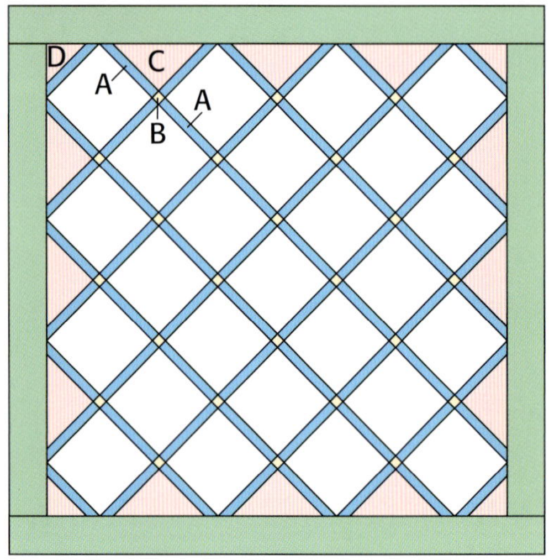

Double, 86" x 86"

Block Setting: 4 x 4

Sashes 1⅜ yards
64 rectangles (A) 2" x 12½"
Cornerstones ¼ yard
24 squares (B) 2" x 2"
Setting Triangles 1⅛ yards
3 squares 16⅛" x 16⅛" cut diagonally twice to yield 12 triangles (C) ⊠
2 squares 7¼" x 7¼" cut diagonally to yield 4 triangles (D) ⧄
Border/Binding 2⅝ yards
2 strips 6½" x 77" for sides
2 strips 6½" x 89" for top/bottom
5 strips 2¼" x 74" for binding
Backing 8⅜ yards
Batting 94" x 94"

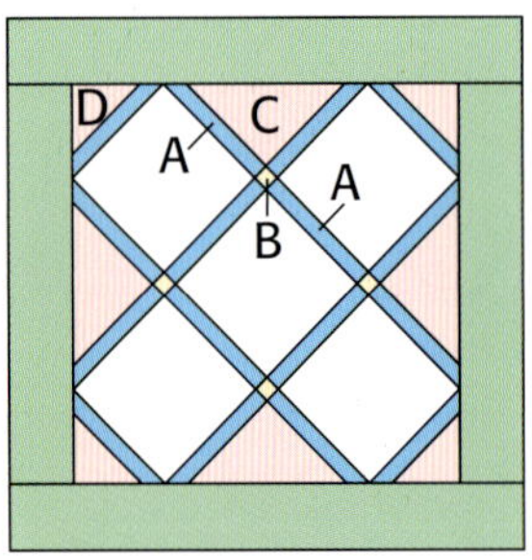

Wall/Crib, 48" x 48"

Block Setting: 2 x 2

Sashes ½ yard
16 rectangles (A) 2" x 12½"
Cornerstones scrap
4 squares (B) 2" x 2"
Setting Triangles ½ yard
1 square 16⅛" x 16⅛" cut diagonally twice to yield 4 triangles (C) ⊠
2 squares 7¼" x 7¼" cut diagonally to yield 4 triangles (D) ⧄
Border/Binding 1½ yards
2 strips 6½" x 39" for sides
2 strips 6½" x 51" for top/bottom
5 strips 2¼" x 43" for binding
Backing 3⅛ yards
Batting 52" x 52"

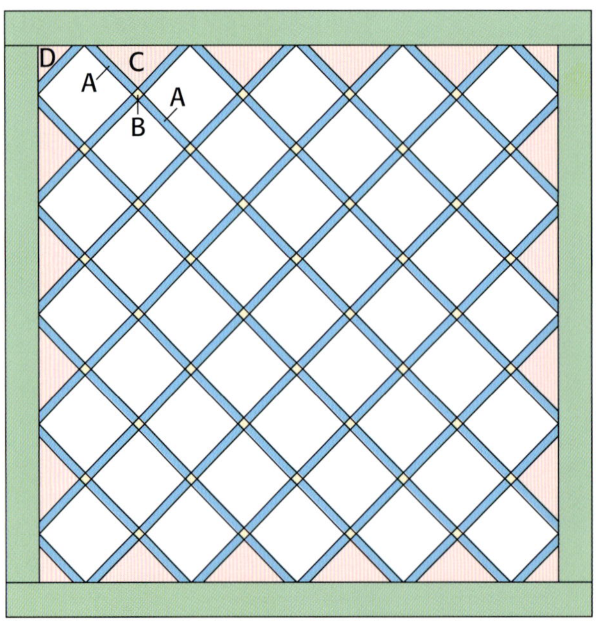

King, 105" x 105"

Block Setting: 5 x 5

Sashes 2⅛ yards
100 rectangles (A) 2" x 12½"
Cornerstones ¼ yard
40 squares (B) 2" x 2"
Setting Triangles 1⅛ yards
4 squares 16⅛" x 16⅛" cut diagonally twice to yield 16 triangles (C) ⊠
2 squares 7¼" x 7¼" cut diagonally to yield 4 triangles (D) ⧄
Border/Binding 3¼ yards
2 strips 6½" x 96" for sides
2 strips 6½" x 108" for top/bottom
5 strips 2¼" x 89" for binding
Backing 10 yards
Batting 113" x 113"

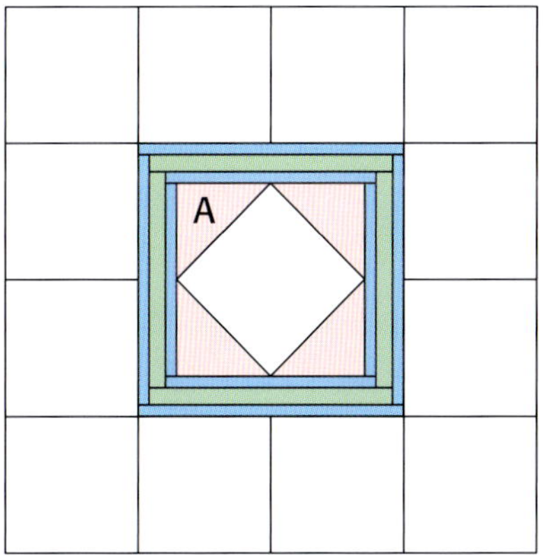

Crib, 48" x 48" (13–12" blocks)

Setting Triangles $\frac{3}{8}$ yard
2 squares $9\frac{3}{8}$" x $9\frac{3}{8}$" cut diagonally to yield 4 triangles (A)

Borders #1 and #3, $\frac{3}{8}$ yard
for border #1
2 strips $1\frac{1}{2}$" x $17\frac{1}{2}$" for sides
2 strips $1\frac{1}{2}$" x $19\frac{1}{2}$" for top/bottom
for border #3: Cut 3 strips $1\frac{1}{2}$" x 40". Sew together and cut:
2 strips $1\frac{1}{2}$" x $22\frac{1}{2}$" for sides
2 strips $1\frac{1}{2}$" x $24\frac{1}{2}$" for top/bottom

Border #2, $\frac{3}{8}$ yard
2 strips 2" x $19\frac{1}{2}$" for sides
2 strips 2" x $22\frac{1}{2}$" for top/bottom

Binding $\frac{1}{2}$ yard
6 strips $2\frac{1}{4}$" x 40" for binding

Backing $3\frac{1}{8}$ yards

Batting 52" x 52"

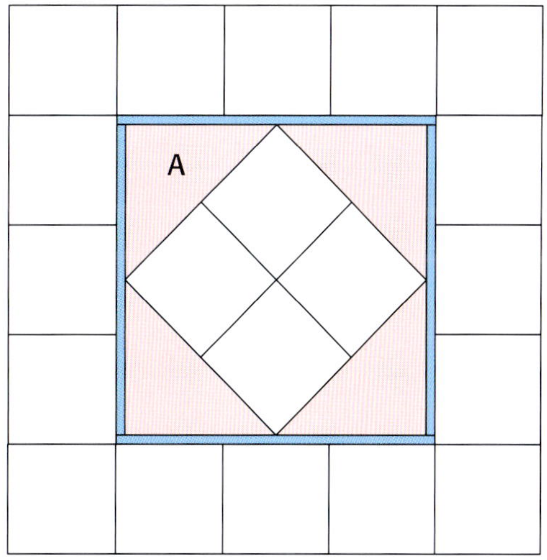

Wall/Throw, 60" x 60" (20–12" blocks)

Setting Triangles $\frac{5}{8}$ yard
2 squares $17\frac{7}{8}$" x $17\frac{7}{8}$" cut diagonally to yield 4 triangles (A)

Border #1, $\frac{3}{8}$ yard
2 strips $1\frac{1}{2}$" x $34\frac{1}{2}$" for sides
2 strips $1\frac{1}{2}$" x $36\frac{1}{2}$" for top/bottom

Binding $\frac{5}{8}$ yard
7 strips $2\frac{1}{4}$" x 40" for binding

Backing $4\frac{1}{8}$ yards

Batting 68" x 68"

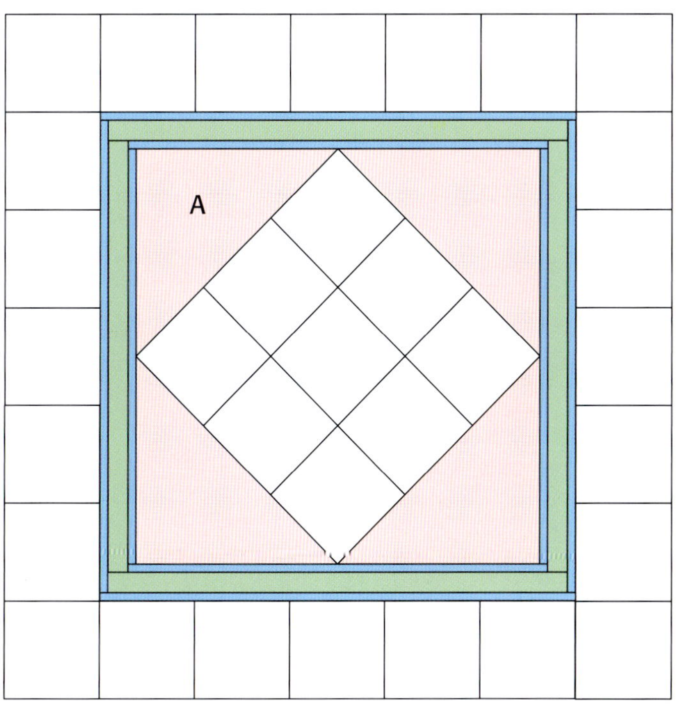

Double, 84" x 84" (33–12" blocks)

Setting Triangles $1\frac{3}{4}$ yards
2 squares $26\frac{3}{8}$" x $26\frac{3}{8}$" cut diagonally to yield 4 triangles (A)

Borders #1 and #3, $\frac{2}{3}$ yard
Cut 12 strips $1\frac{1}{2}$" x 40". Sew together and cut:
for border #1
2 strips $1\frac{1}{2}$" x $51\frac{1}{2}$" for sides
2 strips $1\frac{1}{2}$" x $53\frac{1}{2}$" for top/bottom
for border #3
2 strips $1\frac{1}{2}$" x $58\frac{1}{2}$" for sides
2 strips $1\frac{1}{2}$" x $60\frac{1}{2}$" for top/bottom

Border #2, $\frac{5}{8}$ yard
Cut 6 strips 3" x 40". Sew together and cut:
2 strips 3" x $53\frac{1}{2}$" for sides
2 strips 3" x $58\frac{1}{2}$" for top/bottom

Binding $\frac{3}{4}$ yard
10 strips $2\frac{1}{4}$" x 40" for binding

Backing $8\frac{1}{4}$ yards

Batting 92" x 92"

SETTINGS & YARDAGES

Use these sample settings to join multiple 12" blocks.

Before cutting and sewing bed sizes, measure the length, width and depth of your mattress top and determine how many inches you want your quilt to drop over each side. Adjust border widths as needed; additional yardage may be required. See more settings and yardages at quiltmaker.com.

Twin, 71″ x 86″

Block Setting: 4 x 5

Make 226

Color #1 (white) 1½ yards
113 squares (A) 3⅞″ x 3⅞″

Color #2 (blue) 1½ yards
113 squares (A) 3⅞″ x 3⅞″

Border/Binding 2⅜ yards
2 strips 4½″ x 81″ for sides
2 strips 4½″ x 74″ for top/bottom
5 strips 2¼″ x 68″ for binding

Backing 5⅝ yards

Batting 79″ x 94″

Queen, 86″ x 86″

Block Setting: 5 x 5

Make 276

Color #1 (white) 1¾ yards
138 squares (A) 3⅞″ x 3⅞″

Color #2 (blue) 1¾ yards
138 squares (A) 3⅞″ x 3⅞″

Border/Binding 2⅝ yards
2 strips 4½″ x 81″ for sides
2 strips 4½″ x 89″ for top/bottom
5 strips 2¼″ x 74″ for binding

Backing 8⅜ yards

Batting 94″ x 94″

Throw, 56″ x 71″

Block Setting: 3 x 4

Make 144

Color #1 (white) 1 yard
72 squares (A) 3⅞″ x 3⅞″

Color #2 (blue) 1 yard
72 squares (A) 3⅞″ x 3⅞″

Border/Binding 2 yards
2 strips 4½″ x 66″ for sides
2 strips 4½″ x 59″ for top/bottom
5 strips 2¼″ x 56″ for binding

Backing 3⅞ yards

Batting 64″ x 79″

King, 101″ x 101″

Block Setting: 6 x 6

Make 386 (use 385)

Color #1 (white) 2⅜ yards
193 squares (A) 3⅞″ x 3⅞″

Color #2 (blue) 2⅜ yards
193 squares (A) 3⅞″ x 3⅞″

Border/Binding 3⅛ yards
2 strips 4½″ x 96″ for sides
2 strips 4½″ x 104″ for top/bottom
5 strips 2¼″ x 86″ for binding

Backing 9⅝ yards

Batting 109″ x 109″

Refer to "Triangle-Squares" in the Techniques file on the PDF. Use the color #1 and color #2 A's to make the triangle-squares for each setting.

Throw, 62″ x 80″

Block Setting: 3 x 4

Make 48

Make 96

Color #1 (pink) $\frac{1}{2}$ yard
24 squares (A) $3\frac{7}{8}$″ x $3\frac{7}{8}$″

Color #2 (white) $1\frac{1}{2}$ yards
24 squares (A) $3\frac{7}{8}$″ x $3\frac{7}{8}$″
24 squares (B) $7\frac{1}{4}$″ x $7\frac{1}{4}$″

Color #3 (blue) $1\frac{1}{4}$ yards
96 squares (A) $3\frac{7}{8}$″ x $3\frac{7}{8}$″

Border/Binding $2\frac{1}{4}$ yards
2 strips $4\frac{1}{2}$″ x 75″ for sides
2 strips $4\frac{1}{2}$″ x 65″ for top/bottom
5 strips $2\frac{1}{4}$″ x 62″ for binding

Backing $5\frac{1}{4}$ yards

Batting 70″ x 88″

Long Twin, 80″ x 98″

Block Setting: 4 x 5

Make 80

Make 160

Color #1 (pink) $\frac{5}{8}$ yard
40 squares (A) $3\frac{7}{8}$″ x $3\frac{7}{8}$″

Color #2 (white) $2\frac{1}{4}$ yards
40 squares (A) $3\frac{7}{8}$″ x $3\frac{7}{8}$″
40 squares (B) $7\frac{1}{4}$″ x $7\frac{1}{4}$″

Color #3 (blue) 2 yards
160 squares (A) $3\frac{7}{8}$″ x $3\frac{7}{8}$″

Border/Binding $2\frac{3}{4}$ yards
2 strips $4\frac{1}{2}$″ x 93″ for sides
2 strips $4\frac{1}{2}$″ x 83″ for top/bottom
5 strips $2\frac{1}{4}$″ x 76″ for binding

Backing $7\frac{7}{8}$ yards

Batting 88″ x 106″

Queen, 98″ x 98″

Block Setting: 5 x 5

Make 100

Make 200

Color #1 (pink) $\frac{3}{4}$ yard
50 squares (A) $3\frac{7}{8}$″ x $3\frac{7}{8}$″

Color #2 (white) $2\frac{7}{8}$ yards
50 squares (A) $3\frac{7}{8}$″ x $3\frac{7}{8}$″
50 squares (B) $7\frac{1}{4}$″ x $7\frac{1}{4}$″

Color #3 (blue) $2\frac{3}{8}$ yards
200 squares (A) $3\frac{7}{8}$″ x $3\frac{7}{8}$″

Border/Binding 3 yards
2 strips $4\frac{1}{2}$″ x 93″ for sides
2 strips $4\frac{1}{2}$″ x 101″ for top/bottom
5 strips $2\frac{1}{4}$″ x 83″ for binding

Backing $9\frac{3}{8}$ yards

Batting 106″ x 106″

Refer to "Triangle-Squares" in the Technique file on the PDF. Use the color #1 and color #2 A's to make the triangle-squares for each setting.

Refer to "Fast Flying Geese" in the Techniques file on the PDF. Use the color #2 B's and color #3 A's to make the Flying Geese for each setting.

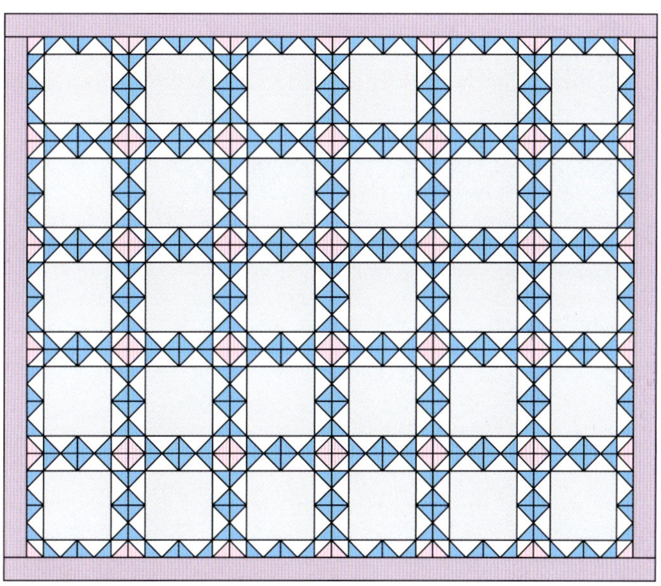

King, 116″ x 98″

Block Setting: 6 x 5

Make 120

Make 240

Color #1 (pink) $\frac{7}{8}$ yard
60 squares (A) $3\frac{7}{8}$″ x $3\frac{7}{8}$″

Color #2 (white) $3\frac{3}{8}$ yards
60 squares (A) $3\frac{7}{8}$″ x $3\frac{7}{8}$″
60 squares (B) $7\frac{1}{4}$″ x $7\frac{1}{4}$″

Color #3 (blue) $2\frac{7}{8}$ yards
240 squares (A) $3\frac{7}{8}$″ x $3\frac{7}{8}$″

Border/Binding $3\frac{1}{2}$ yards
2 strips $4\frac{1}{2}$″ x 93″ for sides
2 strips $4\frac{1}{2}$″ x 119″ for top/bottom
4 strips $2\frac{1}{4}$″ x 112″ for binding

Backing $9\frac{3}{8}$ yards

Batting 124″ x 106″

SETTINGS & YARDAGES

Framed Hourglass Setting. Use this sample setting, shown for different sizes, to join multiple 12" blocks (shown in gray) with Hourglass blocks. This layout will work well for 1–2 blocks repeated or for a sampler quilt with a variety of blocks. Play with two contrasting fabrics in the Hourglass blocks or match the Hourglass fabrics to two different block backgrounds. Lots of fun potential!

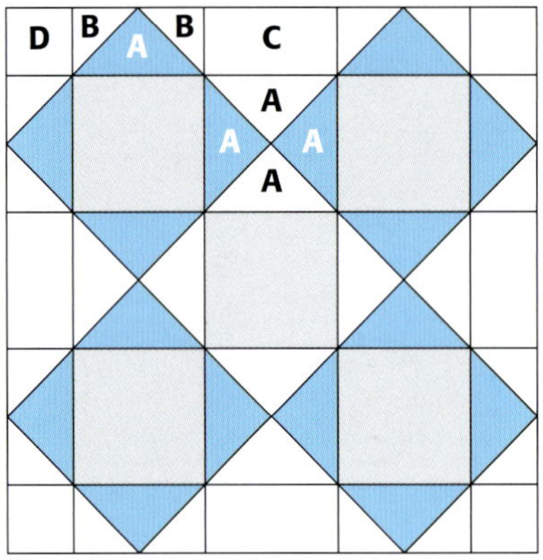

Crib, 48″ x 48″

Block Setting: 3 x 3

Color #1 (white) 1½ yards

2 squares 13¼″ x 13¼″ cut diagonally twice to yield 8 triangles ⊠ (A)

8 squares 6⅞″ x 6⅞″ cut diagonally to yield 16 triangles ◪ (B)

4 rectangles (C) 6½″ x 12½″

4 squares (D) 6½″ x 6½″

Color #2 (blue) M yard

4 squares 13¼″ x 13¼″ cut diagonally twice to yield 16 triangles ⊠ (A)

Binding ½ yard

6 strips 2¼″ x 40″ for binding

Backing 3⅛ yards

Batting 52″ x 52″

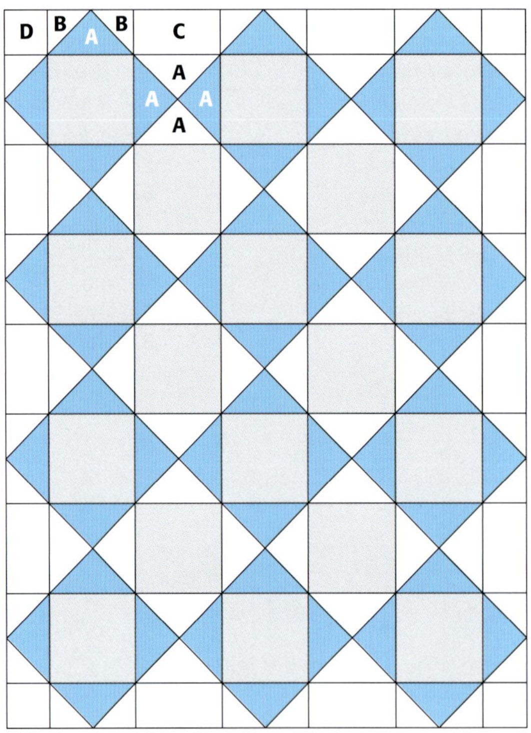

Twin, 72″ x 96″

Block Setting: 5 x 7

Color #1 (white) 2⅞ yards

9 squares 13¼″ x 13¼″ cut diagonally twice to yield 36 triangles ⊠ (A) (there will be 2 extra)

14 squares 6⅞″ x 6⅞″ cut diagonally to yield 28 triangles ◪ (B)

10 rectangles (C) 6½″ x 12½″

4 squares (D) 6½″ x 6½″

Color #2 (blue) 1¾ yards

12 squares 13¼″ x 13¼″ cut diagonally twice to yield 48 triangles ⊠ (A)

Binding ¾ yard

10 strips 2¼″ x 40″ for binding

Backing 6¼ yards

Batting 80″ x 104″

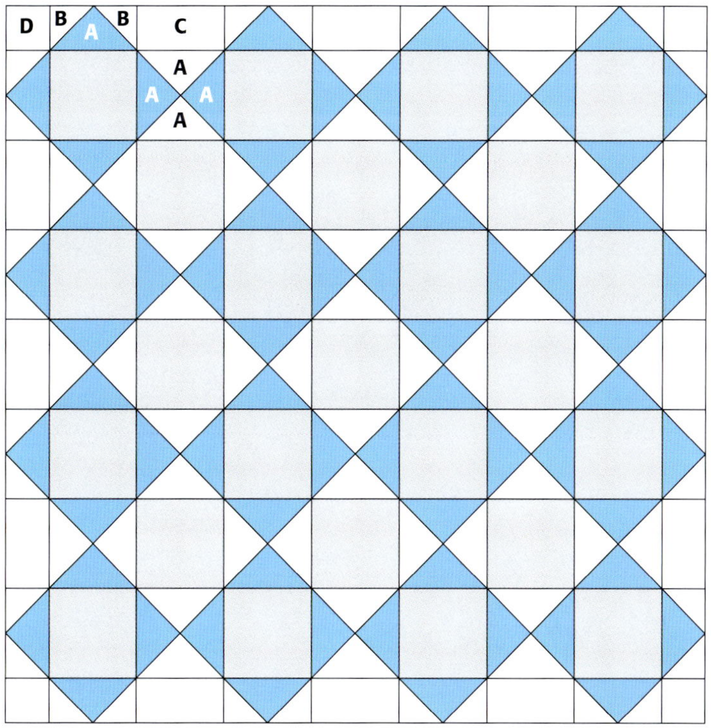

Queen, 96″ x 96″

Block Setting: 7 x 7

Color #1 (white) 3H yards

12 squares 13¼″x 13¼″ cut diagonally twice to yield 48 triangles ⊠ (A)

16 squares 6⅞″ x 6⅞″ cut diagonally to yield 32 triangles ⧄ (B)

12 rectangles (C) 6½″x 12½″

4 squares (D) 6½″x 6½″

Color #2 (blue) 2H yards

16 squares 13¼″x 13¼″ cut diagonally twice to yield 64 triangles ⊠ (A)

Binding ⅞ yard

11 strips 2¼″ x 40″ for binding

Backing 9¼ yards

Batting 104″ x 104″

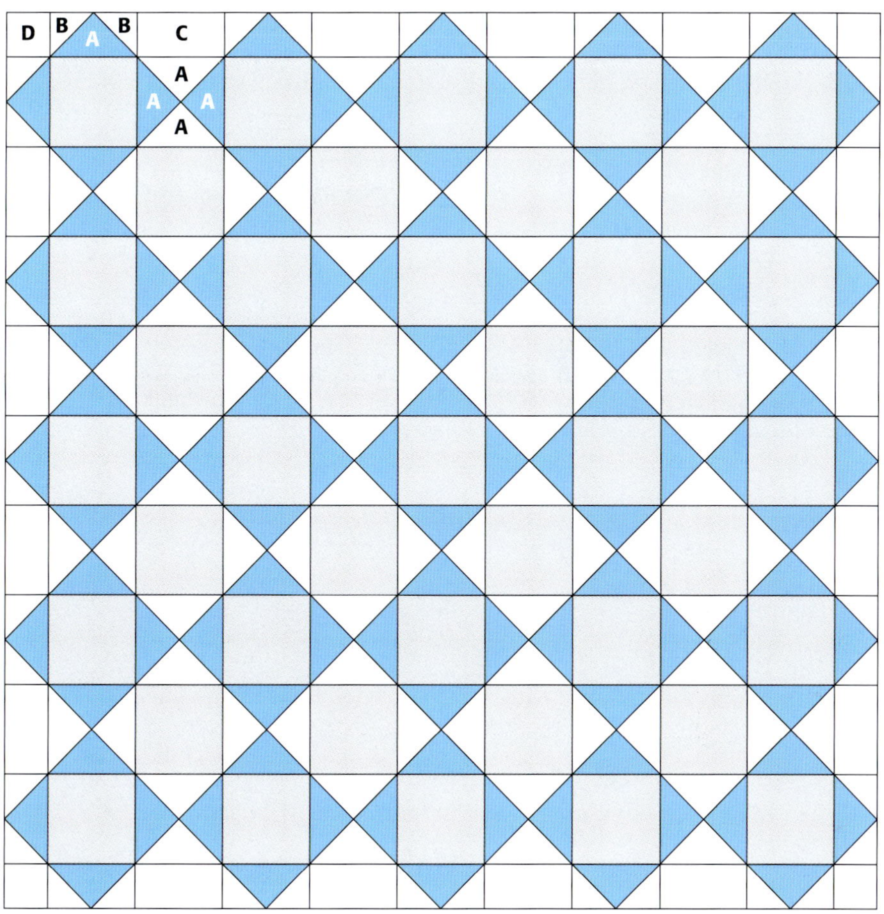

King, 120″ x 120″

Block Setting: 9 x 9

Color #1 (white) 5 yards

20 squares 13¼″x 13¼″ cut diagonally twice to yield 80 triangles ⊠ (A)

20 squares 6⅞″ x 6⅞″ cut diagonally to yield 40 triangles ⧄ (B)

16 rectangles (C) 6½″x 12½″

4 squares (D) 6½″x 6½″

Color #2 (blue) 3⅝ yards

25 squares 13¼″x 13¼″ cut diagonally twice to yield 100 triangles ⊠ (A)

Binding 1 yard

14 strips 2¼″ x 40″ for binding

Backing 11⅜ yards

Batting 128″ x 128″

SETTINGS & YARDAGES

Irish Chain Setting. Use this sample setting, shown for different sizes, to join multiple 12" blocks (shown in white) with Irish Chain blocks. This layout will work well for 1–2 blocks repeated or for a sampler quilt with a variety of blocks. The yardage is given for two contrasting fabrics in the Irish Chain blocks. You could also coordinate by using the same background as other 12" blocks for the Irish Chain background (yardage not given). Lots of fun potential!

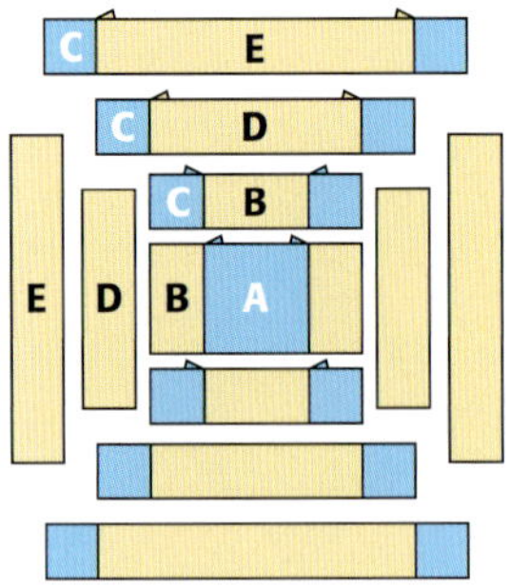

Block Y

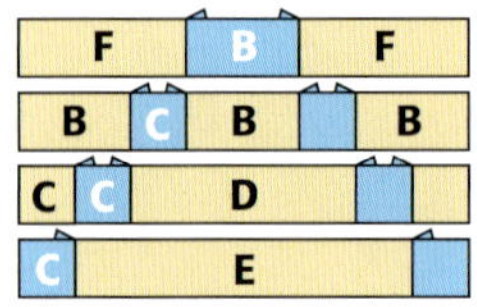

Block Z

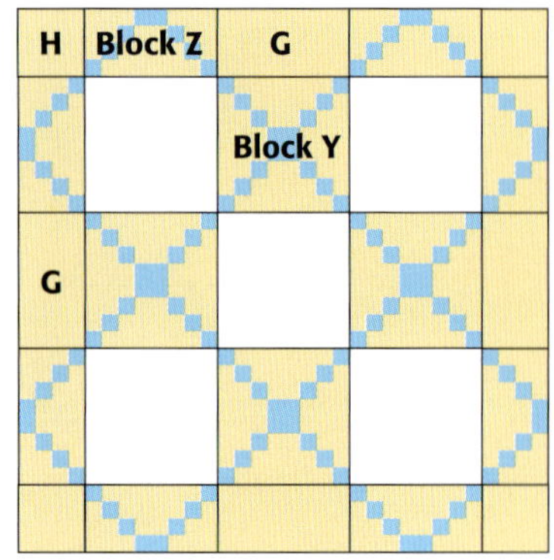

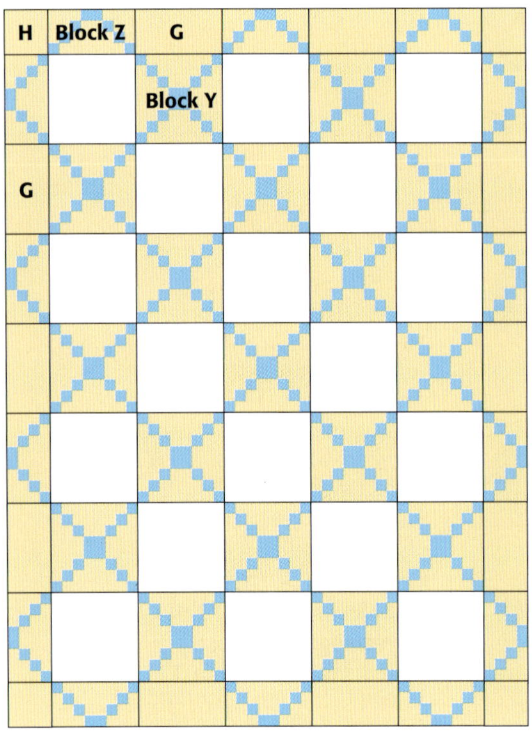

Twin, 72″ x 96″

Block Setting: 5 x 7
Make 17 Block Y
Make 14 Block Z

Color #1 (blue) 1¼ yards
- 17 squares (A) 3½″x 3½″
- 14 rectangles (B) 2″x 3½″
- 288 squares (C) 2″x 2″

Color #2 (yellow) 3⅞ yards
- 110 rectangles (B) 2″x 3½″
- 28 squares (C) 2″x 2″
- 82 rectangles (D) 2″x 6½″
- 82 rectangles (E) 2″x 9½″
- 28 rectangles (F) 2″x 5″
- 10 rectangles (G) 6½″x 12½″
- 4 squares (H) 6½″x 6½″

Binding ¾ yard
- 10 strips 2¼″x 40″ for binding

Backing 6¼ yards
Batting 80″x 104″

Crib, 48″ x 48″

Block Setting: 3 x 3
Make 4 Block Y
Make 8 Block Z

Color #1 (blue) ½ yard
- 4 squares (A) 3½″x 3½″
- 8 rectangles (B) 2″x 3½″
- 96 squares (C) 2″x 2″

Color #2 (yellow) 1½ yards
- 40 rectangles (B) 2″x 3½″
- 16 squares (C) 2″x 2″
- 24 rectangles (D) 2″x 6½″
- 24 rectangles (E) 2″x 9½″
- 16 rectangles (F) 2″x 5″
- 4 rectangles (G) 6½″x 12½″
- 4 squares (H) 6½″x 6½″

Binding ¾ yard
- 6 strips 2¼″x 40″ for binding

Backing 3⅛ yards
Batting 52″x 52″

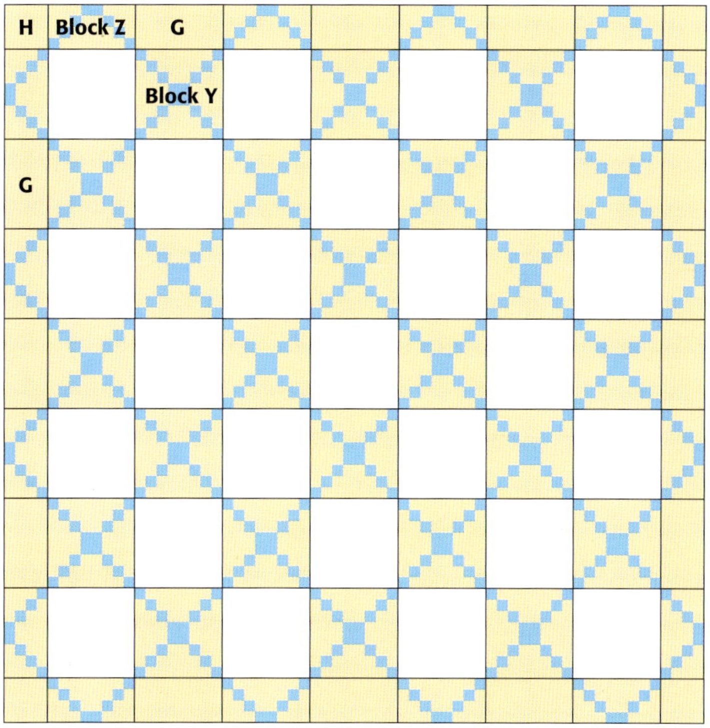

Queen, 96″ x 96″

Block Setting: 7 x 7
Make 24 Block Y
Make 16 Block Z

Color #1 (blue) 1⅝ yards
24 squares (A) 3½″ x 3½″
16 rectangles (B) 2″ x 3½″
384 squares (C) 2″ x 2″
Color #2 (yellow) 5 yards
144 rectangles (B) 2″ x 3½″
32 squares (C) 2″ x 2″
112 rectangles (D) 2″ x 6½″
112 rectangles (E) 2″ x 9½″
32 rectangles (F) 2″ x 5″
12 rectangles (G) 6½″ x 12½″
4 squares (H) 6½″ x 6½″
Binding ⅞ yard
11 strips 2¼″ x 40″ for binding
Backing 9¼ yards
Batting 104″ x 104″

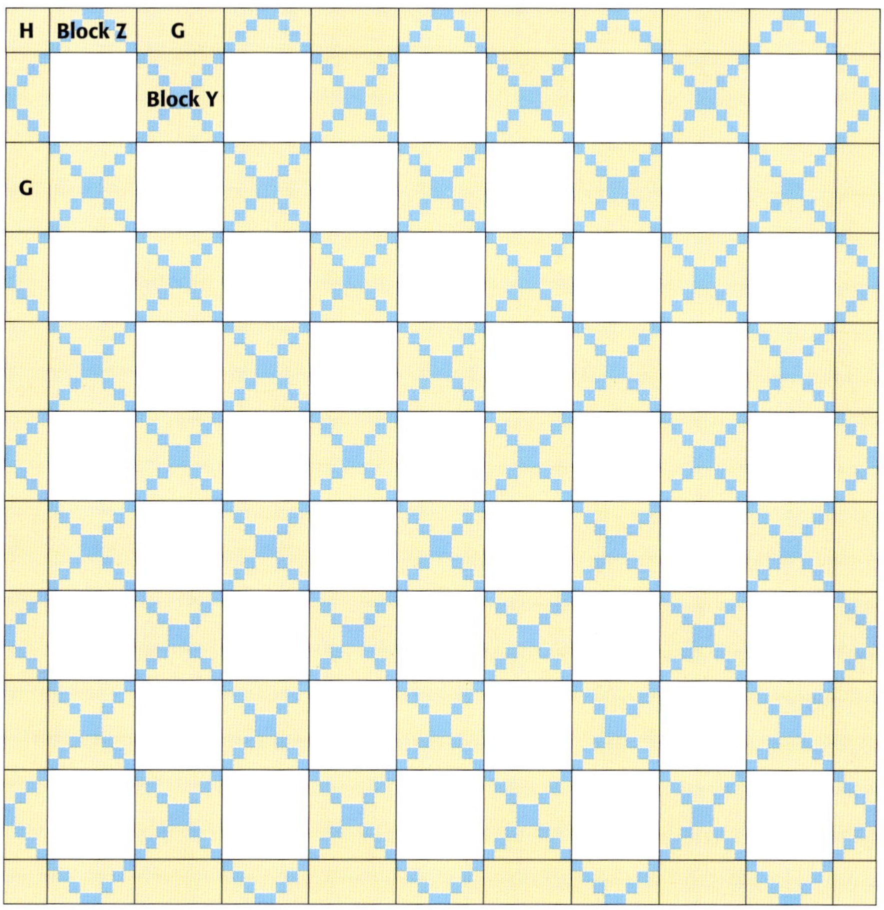

King, 120″ x 120″

Block Setting: 9 x 9
Make 40 Block Y
Make 20 Block Z

Color #1 (blue) 2⅜ yards
40 squares (A) 3½″ x 3½″
20 rectangles (B) 2″ x 3½″
600 squares (C) 2″ x 2″
Color #2 (yellow) 7⅜ yards
220 rectangles (B) 2″ x 3½″
40 squares (C) 2″ x 2″
180 rectangles (D) 2″ x 6½″
180 rectangles (E) 2″ x 9½″
40 rectangles (F) 2″ x 5″
16 rectangles (G) 6½″ x 12½″
4 squares (H) 6½″ x 6½″
Binding 1⅛ yards
14 strips 2¼″ x 40″ for binding
Backing 11⅜ yards
Batting 128″ x 128″

SETTINGS & YARDAGES

Zigzag Setting. Use this sample setting, shown for different sizes, to join multiple 12" blocks (shown in white) with setting triangles to create a zigzag effect. This layout will work well for 1–2 blocks repeated or for a sampler quilt with a variety of blocks.

The yardage is given for one fabric for the setting triangles (shown in green) and one fabric for the border and binding (shown in blue).

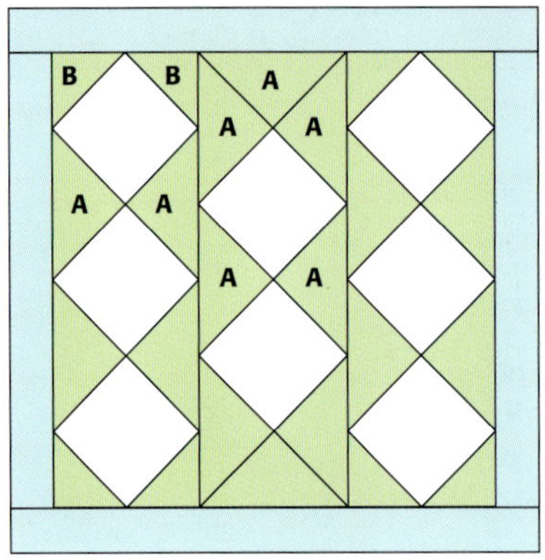

Wall, 61″ x 61″

Block Setting: 3 x 3

Setting Triangles 1½ yards
- 4 squares 18¼″ x 18¼″ cut diagonally twice to yield 16 triangles ⊠ (A)
- 4 squares 9⅜″ x 9⅜″ cut diagonally to yield 8 triangles ⧄ (B)

Border and Binding 1⅞ yards
- for border
  - 2 strips 5½″ x 54″ for sides
  - 2 strips 5½″ x 64″ for top/bottom
- 5 strips 2¼″ x 54″ for binding

Backing 4⅛ yards

Batting 69″ x 69″

Throw, 61″ x 78″

Block Setting: 3 x 4

Setting Triangles 2 yards
- 6 squares 18¼″ x 18¼″ cut diagonally twice to yield 24 triangles ⊠ (A) (there will be 2 extra)
- 4 squares 9⅜″ x 9⅜″ cut diagonally to yield 8 triangles ⧄ (B)

Border and Binding 2⅛ yards
- for border
  - 2 strips 5½″ x 71″ for sides
  - 2 strips 5½″ x 64″ for top/bottom
- 5 strips 2¼″ x 61″ for binding

Backing 5⅛ yards

Batting 69″ x 86″

Twin, 78″ x 95″

Block Setting: 4 x 5

Setting Triangles 3⅛ yards
- 10 squares 18¼″ x 18¼″ cut diagonally twice to yield 40 triangles ⊠ (A)
- 4 squares 9⅜″ x 9⅜″ cut diagonally to yield 8 triangles ⧄ (B)

Border and Binding 2⅝ yards
- for border
  - 2 strips 5½″ x 88″ for sides
  - 2 strips 5½″ x 81″ for top/bottom
- 5 strips 2¼″ x 74″ for binding

Backing 7⅝ yards

Batting 86″ x 103″

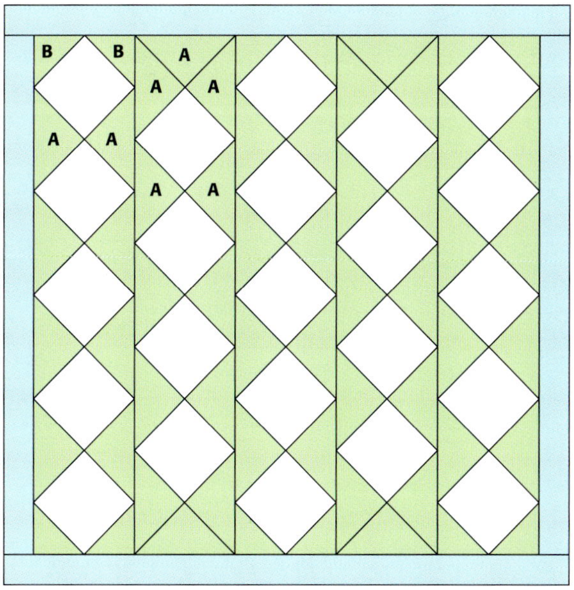

Queen, 95″ x 95″

Block Setting: 5 x 5

Setting Triangles 3⅞ yards
12 squares 18¼″ x 18¼″ cut diagonally twice to yield 48 triangles (A)
6 squares 9⅜″ x 9⅜″ cut diagonally to yield 12 triangles (B)

Border and Binding 2⅞ yards
for border
2 strips 5½″ x 88″ for sides
2 strips 5½″ x 98″ for top/bottom
5 strips 2¼″ x 81″ for binding

Backing 9⅛ yards

Batting 103″ x 103″

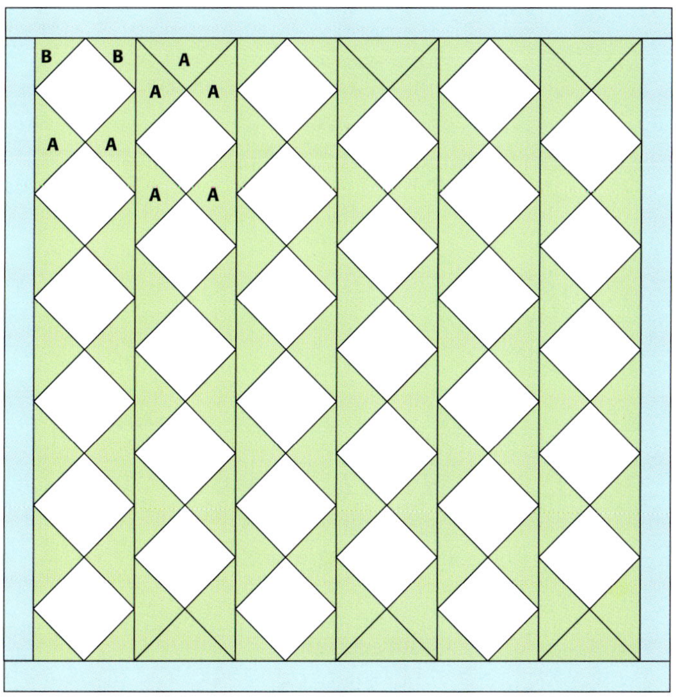

King, 112″ x 112″

Block Setting: 6 x 6

Setting Triangles 5½ yards
18 squares 18¼″ x 18¼″ cut diagonally twice to yield 72 triangles (A)
6 squares 9⅜″ x 9⅜″ cut diagonally to yield 12 triangles (B)

Border and Binding 3⅜ yards
for border
2 strips 5½″ x 105″ for sides
2 strips 5½″ x 115″ for top/bottom
5 strips 2¼″ x 95″ for binding

Backing 10⅝ yards

Batting 120″ x 120″

SETTINGS & YARDAGES

Diagonal Rows Setting. Use this sample setting, shown for different sizes, to join multiple 12" blocks (shown in gray) with triangle-squares to create diagonal rows. This layout will work well for 1–2 blocks repeated or for a sampler quilt with a variety of blocks.

The yardage is given for two fabrics for the triangle-squares (color #1: white and color #2: yellow) and a different fabric for the binding.

Crib, 48″ x 48″

Block Setting: 4 x 4
Make 8

Triangle-Squares ⅞ yard *each* from *each* color
4 squares (A) 12⅞″ x 12⅞″
Binding ½ yard
6 strips 2¼″ x 40″
Backing 3⅛ yards
Batting 52″ x 52″

Throw, 60″ x 60″

Block Setting: 5 x 5
Make 12

Triangle-Squares ⅞ yard *each* from *each* color
6 squares (A) 12⅞″ x 12⅞″
Binding ⅝ yard
7 strips 2¼″ x 40″
Backing 4⅛ yards
Batting 68″ x 68″

Twin, 72″ x 84″

Block Setting: 6 x 7
Make 22 (use 21)

Triangle-Squares 1⅝ yards *each* from *each* color
11 squares (A) 12⅞″ x 12⅞″ (there will be 1 extra triangle-square)
Binding ¾ yard
9 strips 2¼″ x 40″
Backing 5½ yards
Batting 80″ x 92″

Refer to "Triangle-Squares" in the Techniques file on the PDF. Use the color #1 and color #2 A's to make the triangle-squares for each setting.

Queen, 96″ x 96″

Block Setting: 8 x 8

Make 32

Triangle-Squares 2⅜ yards *each* from *each* color
16 squares (A) 12⅞″ x 12⅞″

Binding ⅞ yard
11 strips 2¼″ x 40″

Backing 9¼ yards

Batting 104″ x 104″

King, 108″ x 108″

Block Setting: 9 x 9

Make 40

Triangle-Squares 2¾ yards *each* from *each* color
20 squares (A) 12⅞″ x 12⅞″

Binding ⅞ yard
12 strips 2¼″ x 40″

Backing 10¼ yards

Batting 116″ x 116″

INDEX

INDEX

INDEX

Krause Craft
An imprint of Penguin Random House LLC
penguinrandomhouse.com

Previously published as *Quiltmaker's 1,000 Blocks*

Printed in China
10 9 8 7 6 5 4 3 2 1

ISBN 979-8-217-04658-4

Edited by Noel Rivera
Designed by Clare Finney and Ronson Slagle